SPINNEY FAMILY GENEALOGY

Genealogy of Thomas Spinney and Margery Randall

—REVISED EDITION—

Judy Phillips

HERITAGE BOOKS
2010

HERITAGE BOOKS

AN IMPRINT OF HERITAGE BOOKS, INC.

Books, CDs, and more—Worldwide

For our listing of thousands of titles see our website
at
www.HeritageBooks.com

Published 2010 by
HERITAGE BOOKS, INC.
Publishing Division
100 Railroad Ave. #104
Westminster, Maryland 21157

International Standard Book Numbers
Paperbound: 978-0-7884-5248-2
Clothbound: 978-0-7884-8473-5

Table of Contents

Descendants of Thomas Spinney

Generation No. 1

1. THOMAS[1] SPINNEY was born Nov 1630 in Devon England, and died 31 Aug 1701 in Kittery, ME. He married MARGERY RANDALL 30 Sep 1651 in Kittery, ME. She was born Abt. 1628, and died Abt. 1695.

Notes for THOMAS SPINNEY:
Noyes, Libby & Davis's Genealogical Dictionary of Maine and New Hampshire Page 653

" Thomas,weaver, Kittery, ag. ±67 in Nov. 1697, first seen when John Webster wit. ag. him and Margerie, late w. of Wm. Norman, in N. H. ct. 30 Sept. 1651. She was orig. Margery Randall and soon became his wife; see Norman(2). A tradition was pub. in 1863 to the effect that the first Spinney here was b. near Manchester, Eng., went to Wapping Stairs near London, shipped as a fisherman for the No. Am. coast and was carried thence to the Piscat. by a Capt. Fernald, abt 1650. Kittery constable 1656. A wit, in 1658 (Edw. Melcher and the Websters). Gr. of 200 a. on both sides of Great Cove, afterw. Spinney's Cove, in 1659. Gr.j. 1660, 1666 (did not appear), 1670, 1688, 1692-3, 1695, 1698-9; tr.j. 1669; ferry lic. 1668, 1671; selectman 1674. Lists 282, 283, 298, 25, 96. Margery was liv. 23 Mar. 1694, but not in will, 9 July–23 Sept. (d. 31 Aug.) 1701, naming ch. and 2 gr.ch.; wit. by Thomas and Mary Fernald. Ch: Hannah, m. Samuel Fernald(3). Samuel, b. ±1658. James, b. ±1662. Thomas, b. ±1665. John, fa.'s exec., b. ±1668."

(Rambles about Portsmouth CXXXIII Page 283)

1St School Master in Kittery

Will of Thomas Spinney

Source Page: Probate Office, I, 79.
     Name: Thomas Spinney
": I Thomas Spinney of Kittery in the County of Yorke in the Prouince of the Masachusets Bay in New England yeoman, being aged and uery weak and Infirm in body but by the mercy of God, of Perfect Mind Memory and calling to Mind the Mortallity of My body, not knowing how soon it may please god to remoue me hence Do make and ordain this my last Will and Testament hereby revoking all former and other Wills at any time by me made either by word or Writing. That is to Say. Principally and first of all.I recomend my soul to god my blessed Creator and my body to the Earth to be buried in such Decent and christian manner as to my Executor hereafter named shall Seem meet, not doubting but at the General resurection to receiue the same again by the mighty power of God/ and touching such worldly Estate wherewith it hath pleased god to bless me in this life I giue Devise and dispose of the same in the following manner and formeImprs I giue and bequeath unto my well beloued son Samuel Spinney one feather bed bolster two pillows two blankets one rug one bedsted standing now in the Chamber ouer the Hall and the sett of Curtains & vallts that now belongs to it; I also giue him all my wearing Clothes both Wollen and linnen, Except my best coat and hatt, with a confirmation of fifteen Acres of land formerly to him given as by Deed of Gift may appeartly I giue and bequeath unto my well beloued son James Spinney one Yoake of oxen, one Cow & four Ewe sheep.3dly I giue and bequeath unto my welbeloved son Thomas Spinney, my best Wearing Coat & best hatt, and fiue pounds in money.4dly I giue and bequeath unto my wellbeloved son John Spinney all the land which had in Exchange, of my Daughter Hannah Fernald and Nathaniel Fernald, also twenty acres of land on the back side of the Great Coue lying betwene the land of Samuel Spinney and the land of Nathaniel Fernald which was formerly purchased of Mr Richard Jose, I do also giue unto my said son John all my Houshold stuff and other my psonal Estate Except what I haue giuen to any other in this my Willfullly I giue unto my Daughter Hannah Fernald three pounds in money, one pair of Sheets and my largest Bible,6dly I giue and bequeath unto my Grand Children each of them one shilling in money.7ly I giue and bequeath unto my two grand Daughters namly Mercy and Margery, all my Pewter that belongs to the Shelues in my Hall, two brass Candlesticks, one cupboard, & one table which stands in the Chamber ouer Sd Hall to be Equally divided betwene them by my son John Spinney their Father when they ariue to ye age of Eighteen years or be marryed, and if it soe happen that either of them should die before they come to age or be marryed, Then

the whole to be the Survivrs.8ly I do make ordain and constitute my welbeloued son John Spinney aforesd, my onely and sole Executor of this my last Will and Testament and doe hereby Will and require him my sd Executor in all things faithfully to dispose of all and singular ye sum or sums of money goods or Chattels mentioned and by me given in this my Will, and also to pay all my Just Debts wherein I stand obleiged; In Witness whereof I the sd Thomas Spinney have hereunto set my hand and seal this Ninth day of July, In the Thirteenth year of the Reigne of our Soveraign Lord William the third King ouer England &c: and in the year of our Lord one Thousand Seaven Hundred and one.Signed & sealed and Published In presence of vsThomas FernaldMary X Fernald Her markeJos: Hamond Judg of Probate &c:Tho: Spinney"

    (His: Seal:)Recorded 23 Sept. 1701.

BIRTH REC:book"Genealogical & Family Hist.,State of Maine"#974.1/D2l,Pg.1511
DEATH REC:book" Stackpoles Old Kittery & Her Families"#974.195/K1/H2s,Pg.740
also in book"Piscataqua Pioneers 1623-1775"#974. C,Pg.195.
MARR.REC:book"Old Kittery...." # & Pg.same as above.

"North of Glanfield was a lot owned by Thomas Spinney. His grant of two hundred acres lay on both sides of the "Great Cove," later called "Spinney's Cove." Though the grant was made in 1659, it is
probable that he had been living here for some time.
Above Thomas Spinney, on the east side of Great Cove, was a lot of fifteen acres originally owned by Thomas Turner and mortgaged by him to George Walton of Portsmouth, 16 Aug. 1659. Probably the land was unimproved and therefore was regranted by the town to Richard Carle. He sold six acres of it to his son-in-law, Samuel Knight, in 1684. Knight sold this, and Carle sold all the rest of the original grant to Samuel Spinney in 1682 and 1693.
Then came Christian Remick's twenty acres, granted 17 July 1661, and laid out 22 Feb. 1665. He
deeded this and other grants east of it to his son Isaac, who sold the same to John Dennet, Jr., 2 May
1698, and moved to South Carolina. Dennet added to his farm by purchase of Richard King's seventeen acres in 1700 and by town grants. This farm has been in the possession of the Dennet family until now. The house, built about the year 1720, stands "on the east side of the Eliot road about a mile above Portsmouth Bridge." . . . "The Remick of whom the farm was purchased resided in a house on the bank of the Creek west of the road, and opposite the Dennet house.(1)
In 1697 there was a dispute between Thomas Spinney and Christian Remick about their boundary line, and in consequence the accompanying plot of lands appears in the records of the Superior Court at Boston with the following statement:

"Kittery, December 18th, 1697. At the motion and Request of Mr. Thomas Spinney layd out the Norther bounds of his old lot in the great Cove as also his addition at the head thereof containing fifteen acres, and in running out the aforesaid bounds as they were shewed to me by the sd ThomasSpinney and John Spinney I find the land in Controversie claimed by Mr Christian Remmick and Improved by Samll Spinney to fall within Mr Thomas Spinneys

(1)Historic Homes of Kittery, by Moses A. Safford, Esq., Me. Hist.
    Coll. Vol. V., 398.

bounds of his fifteen acre lot as is demonstrated in the figure by a pricked line, the other lots being but demonstrations of the Scituations of jacent places. "

           By me William Godsoe
           Surveighr for the Town
           of Kittery."

Notes for MARGERY RANDALL:
Genealogical Dictionary of Maine and New Hampshire by Noyes, Libby & Davis
    page 512
" William,Cape Porpus, fisherman, pretending that he had been divorced from his w. in England, contracted a bigamous mar. with Marjorie Randall(13). In Wells ct. 11 Mar. 1650-1 they were legally sep., their common prop. div. and he was banished from the Prov. if he could not present legal ev. of his alleged divorce within 18 months. As he failed to do this, she was gr. a 'divorce,' altho the ct. seemed doubtful if she had gone thru with a

mar. ceremony, and for good measure Norman got 25 lashes at the whipping-post. At the same ct. poer Marjorie was fined for lying and for abusing the government, and was obliged to make due apologies to the w. of Thomas Withers for making 'threatening speeches' to her. Also she was warned to avoid the attentions of one Thomas 'Spleny,' but six months later Marjorie, the late w. of William Norman, and Thomas Spinney were 'keeping company together at unseasonable times' (N. H. ct.), which led to marriage. By Norman she had a dau. Mary, who m. John Fernald(1). Norman went eastward and bot House Isl. in Casco Bay with three other fishermen, John Wallis, Nicholas White and Geo. Bartell (Bartlett 3), selling his ¼ to Geo. Munjoy 10 Nov. 1663. Sued by Thos. Mills for 'disappointing his voyage' in 1662. Abs. from Scarboro meet. in 1672. Called of Black Pt. in 1674 when Ralph Tristram was app. adm. of his est."

Children of THOMAS SPINNEY and MARGERY RANDALL are:

2.   i.   MARY NORMAN² SPINNEY, b. 1651, Kittery, ME; d. Abt. 1700.
3.   ii.   HANNAH SPINNEY, b. 1656, Kittery, ME.
4.   iii.   SAMUEL SPINNEY, b. 1658, Kittery, ME; d. Mar 1736/37, Kittery, ME.
5.   iv.   JAMES SPINNEY, b. 1662, Kittery, ME; d. Bef. 18 Feb 1723/24, Kittery, ME.
6.   v.   THOMAS SPINNEY, b. 1665, Kittery, ME; d. Aft. 1732.
7.   vi.   JOHN SPINNEY, b. 1668, Kittery, ME; d. Abt. 1705, Kittery, ME.

Generation No. 2

2. MARY NORMAN² SPINNEY *(THOMAS¹)* was born 1651 in Kittery, ME, and died Abt. 1700. She married JOHN FERNALD Bef. 1670, son of RENALD FERNALD and JOANNA WARBURTON. He was born Abt. 1642, and died 19 Apr 1687.

Children of MARY SPINNEY and JOHN FERNALD are:

8.   i.   JOHN³ FERNALD, b. Abt. 1672.
        ii.   JAMES FERNALD, b. Abt. 1675; m. MARY.
        iii.   THOMAS FERNALD, b. Abt. 1678; d. Aft. 1735; m. MARY THOMPSON.
9.   iv.   LYDIA FERNALD, b. Abt. 1681.
        v.   AMOS FERNALD, b. Abt. 1686; m. (1) MARY WOODMAN; m. (2) ELIZABETH CHADBOURNE.
        vi.   MARGERY FERNALD, b. 16 Apr 1686; m. JOHN MARSHALL.

3. HANNAH² SPINNEY *(THOMAS¹)* was born 1656 in Kittery, ME. She married SAMUEL NATHANIEL FERNALD, son of RENALD FERNALD and JOANNA WARBURTON. He was born Abt. 1644, and died 01 Dec 1698.

Children of HANNAH SPINNEY and SAMUEL FERNALD are:

10.   i.   NATHANIEL³ FERNALD, b. 28 May 1671.
        ii.   SAMUEL FERNALD, b. 09 Mar 1675/76.
        iii.   SARAH FERNALD, b. 17 Jun 1678.
        iv.   HANNAH FERNALD, b. 16 Oct 1684.
        v.   MARTHA FERNALD, b. 18 Feb 1691/92.

4. SAMUEL² SPINNEY *(THOMAS¹)* was born 1658 in Kittery, ME, and died Mar 1736/37 in Kittery, ME. He married (1) ELIZABETH KNIGHT 26 Sep 1687 in Kittery, ME, daughter of SAMUEL KNIGHT and AMY CARLE. She died 1708. He married (2) MARGARET SHEPHARD 27 Sep 1708 in Kittery, ME. She was born Abt. 1670, and died Bef. Jul 1731. He married (3) MARY RICE 15 Jul 1731. He married (4) JANE MCCLURE 26 Sep 1734 in Kittery, ME.

Children of SAMUEL SPINNEY and ELIZABETH KNIGHT are:

        i.   SAMUEL³ SPINNEY, b. 13 Oct 1688, Kittery, ME; d. Bef. 1716, Kittery, ME; m. ELIAZBETH.
        ii.   JAMES SPINNEY, b. 08 Mar 1689/90, Kittery, ME; d. 24 Sep 1690, Kittery, ME.
11.   iii.   JOHN SPINNEY, b. 17 Jul 1691, Kittery, ME; d. 04 Jul 1726, Kittery, ME.
12.   iv.   THOMAS SPINNEY, b. 20 Jul 1693, Kittery, ME.
13.   v.   JAMES SPINNEY, b. 01 Feb 1694/95, Kittery, ME.
14.   vi.   NATHAN SPINNEY, b. 27 Sep 1697, Kittery, ME; d. Abt. 1730, Kittery, ME.
15.   vii.   JEREMIAH SPINNEY, b. 19 Oct 1699, Kittery, ME; d. 1745, Georgetown, ME.
        viii.   ELIZABETH SPINNEY, b. 1703, Kittery, ME.
        ix.   DAVID SPINNEY, b. 12 Sep 1706, Kittery, ME; d. 1745; m. JESUAHA COLE, 16 Oct 1731; b. 23 Apr 1711; d. Feb 1744/45.
16.   x.   JONATHAN SPINNEY, b. 28 Jun 1708, Kittery, ME.

Children of SAMUEL SPINNEY and MARGARET SHEPHARD are:
17.   xi. LYDIA[3] SPINNEY, b. 17 Dec 1710, Kittery, ME; d. Kittery, ME.
18.   xii. PATIENCE SPINNEY, b. 03 Dec 1713, Kittery, ME.
        xiii. MARGARET SPINNEY, b. Abt. 1715, Kittery, ME.
19.   xiv. SAMUEL SPINNEY, b. 03 Jul 1717, Kittery, ME; d. 11 Jun 1784, Granville, NS.
20.   xv. SARAH SPINNEY, b. 1720, Kittery, ME.
        xvi. ELIZABETH SPINNEY, b. 16 Jul 1721, Kittery, ME.

5. JAMES[2] SPINNEY *(THOMAS[1])* was born 1662 in Kittery, ME, and died Bef. 18 Feb 1723/24 in Kittery, ME. He married GRACE DENNETT in Kittery, ME, daughter of ALEXANDER DENNETT. She was born 1667 in Kittery, ME.

Child of JAMES SPINNEY and GRACE DENNETT is:
        i. SARAH[3] SPINNEY, b. 19 Jul 1697, Kittery, ME; m. JOSEPH DOWNING, 21 Jun 1716.

6. THOMAS[2] SPINNEY *(THOMAS[1])* was born 1665 in Kittery, ME, and died Aft. 1732. He married CHRISTINA.

Children of THOMAS SPINNEY and CHRISTINA are:
        i. MARGERY[3] SPINNEY, m. CHRISTOPHER HAWKINS, 24 Jan 1727/28.
21.   ii. HANNAH SPINNEY, b. 16 Jan 1699/00.
22.   iii. THOMAS SPINNEY, b. Abt. 1703.
23.   iv. JOSEPH SPINNEY, b. 18 Aug 1703.

7. JOHN[2] SPINNEY *(THOMAS[1])* was born 1668 in Kittery, ME, and died Abt. 1705 in Kittery, ME. He married MARY DIAMOND 1689 in Kittery, ME, daughter of JOHN DIAMOND and DAUGHTER RAYNES. She was born Abt. 1678 in Kittery, ME, and died Abt. 1744.

Children of JOHN SPINNEY and MARY DIAMOND are:
24.   i. JOHN[3] SPINNEY, b. Abt. 1693, Kittery, ME; d. Aft. 1757.
25.   ii. MERCY SPINNEY, b. Abt. 1695.
        iii. MARGERY SPINNEY, b. Abt. 1697; m. SAMUEL TETHERLY, 12 May 1715.
26.   iv. MARY SPINNEY, b. Abt. 1699.
27.   v. ANDREW SPINNEY, b. 1701, Kittery, ME; d. Abt. 1755, Kittery, ME.
28.   vi. LYDIA SPINNEY, b. 1703; d. Bef. 1742.

Generation No. 3

8. JOHN[3] FERNALD *(MARY NORMAN[2] SPINNEY, THOMAS[1])* was born Abt. 1672. He married SARAH HINKS.

Children of JOHN FERNALD and SARAH HINKS are:
        i. MARY[4] FERNALD, b. 1699.
29.   ii. JAMES FERNALD, b. 1704.

9. LYDIA[3] FERNALD *(MARY NORMAN[2] SPINNEY, THOMAS[1])* was born Abt. 1681. She married (1) JOHN HARMON. She married (2) BENJAMIN MILLER.

Children of LYDIA FERNALD and BENJAMIN MILLER are:
        i. MARY[4] MILLER, b. 1706, Portsmouth, NH; m. JOHN LIBBY; b. 1702, Portsmouth, NH.
        ii. SARAH MILLER, b. 25 Dec 1712, Portsmouth, NH; m. EDWARD SKILLINGS.

10. NATHANIEL[3] FERNALD *(HANNAH[2] SPINNEY, THOMAS[1])* was born 28 May 1671. He married ANN ALLEN.

Children of NATHANIEL FERNALD and ANN ALLEN are:
        i. MARY[4] FERNALD.
        ii. TIMOTHY FERNALD.
        iii. RUTH FERNALD, m. KNIGHT.

	iv.	ELIZABETH FERNALD.
	v.	HANNAH FERNALD, m. BRYANT BRADDEN.
30.	vi.	NATHANIEL FERNALD, b. 1707; d. 1760.
31.	vii.	TOBIAS FERNALD.

11. JOHN[3] SPINNEY *(SAMUEL[2], THOMAS[1])* was born 17 Jul 1691 in Kittery, ME, and died 04 Jul 1726 in Kittery, ME. He married PATIENCE SHEPHERD 1714. She was born 1691 in Kittery, ME, USA, and died in York, ME, USA.

Children of JOHN SPINNEY and PATIENCE SHEPHERD are:

	i.	ELIZABETH[4] SPINNEY, b. 23 Oct 1714, Kittery, ME; d. died young.
32.	ii.	ANNE SPINNEY, b. 12 Apr 1719, Kittery, ME.
	iii.	ZEBULEN SPINNEY, b. 20 Oct 1720.
33.	iv.	JOHANNAH SPINNEY, b. 28 Nov 1723, Kittery, ME.
	v.	SHEEPHERD SPINNEY, b. 16 Jul 1725; d. died young.

12. THOMAS[3] SPINNEY *(SAMUEL[2], THOMAS[1])* was born 20 Jul 1693 in Kittery, ME.

Children of THOMAS SPINNEY are:

34.	i.	JOHN[4] SPINNEY, b. Abt. 1715, Kittery, ME; d. Marblehead, MA.
	ii.	THOMAS SPINNEY, b. Abt. 1720, Kittery, ME.

13. JAMES[3] SPINNEY *(SAMUEL[2], THOMAS[1])* was born 01 Feb 1694/95 in Kittery, ME. He married MARY COUCH 28 Dec 1718 in Kittery, ME, daughter of JOSEPH COUCH and ANNE ADAMS. She was born 03 Jan 1697/98.

Children of JAMES SPINNEY and MARY COUCH are:

35.	i.	NICHOLAS[4] SPINNEY, b. 05 Oct 1719.
36.	ii.	EUNICE SPINNEY, b. 29 Jan 1721/22, Kittery, ME.
	iii.	ELEANOR SPINNEY, b. 07 Mar 1726/27, Kittery, ME; m. JAMES ADAMS.

14. NATHAN[3] SPINNEY *(SAMUEL[2], THOMAS[1])* was born 27 Sep 1697 in Kittery, ME, and died Abt. 1730 in Kittery, ME. He married ELIZABETH POMEROY 01 Mar 1720/21 in Newington, NH, daughter of RICHARD POMEROY and DELIVERANCE BERRY. She was born Abt. 1700 in Portsmouth, NH.

Children of NATHAN SPINNEY and ELIZABETH POMEROY are:

37.	i.	MARY[4] SPINNEY, b. 1722, Kittery, ME.
	ii.	GEORGE SPINNEY, b. 1724.
38.	iii.	SUSANNAH SPINNEY, b. 1726.

15. JEREMIAH[3] SPINNEY *(SAMUEL[2], THOMAS[1])* was born 19 Oct 1699 in Kittery, ME, and died 1745 in Georgetown, ME. He married HANNAH PETTEGREW 1737, daughter of THOMAS PETTEGREW and MARY HUTCHINS.

Children of JEREMIAH SPINNEY and HANNAH PETTEGREW are:

	i.	JOHN[4] SPINNEY, b. 18 Sep 1737.
39.	ii.	RUTH SPINNEY, b. Abt. 1742; d. 16 Aug 1816, Georgetown, ME.
	iii.	RICHARD SPINNEY, b. Abt. 1742.
40.	iv.	JEREMIAH SPINNEY, b. 18 Apr 1742, Kittery, ME; d. 30 Oct 1812.
	v.	DORCAS SPINNEY, b. 29 Sep 1745, Kittery, ME.
	vi.	HENRY SPINNEY, b. 29 Sep 1745.

16. JONATHAN[3] SPINNEY *(SAMUEL[2], THOMAS[1])* was born 28 Jun 1708 in Kittery, ME. He married SARAH PARKER 23 Feb 1729/30 in Kittery, ME, daughter of NATHANIAL PARKER and HANNAH BLOOD. She was born in Kittery, ME.

Children of JONATHAN SPINNEY and SARAH PARKER are:

41.	i.	EBENEZER[4] SPINNEY, b. 14 Dec 1735, Kittery, ME; d. 1779, Lost At Sea.

	ii.	ELIZABETH SPINNEY, b. Abt. 1737.
42.	iii.	HANNAH (BETSY) SPINNEY, b. Abt. 1746, Kittery, ME.
	iv.	SARAH SPINNEY, b. Abt. 1747.
43.	v.	NATHANIEL SPINNEY, b. Abt. 1753, Kittery, ME; d. 1824, New Orleans.
	vi.	DAVID SPINNEY, b. 12 Aug 1753, Kittery, ME.

17. LYDIA[3] SPINNEY *(SAMUEL[2], THOMAS[1])* was born 17 Dec 1710 in Kittery, ME, and died in Kittery, ME. She married JOSEPH HANSCOM 18 Mar 1731/32 in Kittery, ME. He was born 13 Jul 1708, and died 1736.

Child of LYDIA SPINNEY and JOSEPH HANSCOM is:
  i.   JOSEPH[4] HANSCOM, b. 26 May 1733.

18. PATIENCE[3] SPINNEY *(SAMUEL[2], THOMAS[1])* was born 03 Dec 1713 in Kittery, ME. She married ABNER COLE 13 Oct 1731, son of THOMAS COLE and LYDIA REMICK. He was born 23 Jun 1706.

Children of PATIENCE SPINNEY and ABNER COLE are:
  i.   ELEANOR[4] COLE, m. JOHN COLE.
  ii.   ABNER COLE, b. 09 Nov 1734.
  iii. MARY COLE, b. 29 Dec 1736.
  iv.   SAMUEL COLE, b. 10 Apr 1739.
  v.   TIMOTHY COLE, b. 25 Apr 1742.
  vi.   JOSIAH COLE, b. 07 Nov 1744.
  vii. JOSEPH COLE, b. 12 Dec 1746.
  viii. OBADIAH COLE, b. 12 Jan 1748/49.
  ix.   SUSANNA COLE, b. 15 Mar 1750/51; m. JOHN REMICK; b. 1746.

19. SAMUEL[3] SPINNEY *(SAMUEL[2], THOMAS[1])* was born 03 Jul 1717 in Kittery, ME, and died 11 Jun 1784 in Granville, NS. He married (1) ELIZABETH AVERILLE 09 Jul 1761 in Kittery, ME, daughter of JOB AVERILLE and MARY PREBBLE. She was born 08 Feb 1714/15, and died 11 Feb 1766 in Granville, NS. He married (2) HANNAH SMITH 26 Nov 1766 in Granville NS, daughter of GAMELIEL SMITH and HANNAH HARDING. She was born 10 Jun 1750 in Port Hood, NS.

Children of SAMUEL SPINNEY and ELIZABETH AVERILLE are:
| 44. | i. | JOSEPH[4] SPINNEY, b. 13 Apr 1763, Granville, NS.; d. Nov 1844, Kings, NS. |
| | ii. | DAVID SPINNEY, b. 19 Feb 1764, Granville, NS; d. 09 Jun 1765, Granville NS. |

Children of SAMUEL SPINNEY and HANNAH SMITH are:
	iii.	HANNA[4] SPINNEY, b. Granville, NS.
	iv.	JOAN SPINNEY, b. Granville, NS.
	v.	JANE OR JOANNA ?? SPINNEY.
	vi.	ELEANOR SPINNEY, b. Granville, NS.
45.	vii.	DAVID SPINNEY, b. 23 Oct 1767, Granville, NS.
	viii.	ELIZABETH SPINNEY, b. 13 Nov 1769, Granville, NS.
46.	ix.	MARY SPINNEY, b. Abt. 1770, Cronwallis, NS..
47.	x.	SAMUEL MCCLURE SPINNEY, b. 11 Nov 1771, Granville, NS.; d. 24 Apr 1832, Aylesford NS..
48.	xi.	BENIAH SPINNEY, b. 1774, Granville, NS.; d. Greenwood, NS..

20. SARAH[3] SPINNEY *(SAMUEL[2], THOMAS[1])* was born 1720 in Kittery, ME. She married RICHARD POPE.

Child of SARAH SPINNEY and RICHARD POPE is:
  i.   ELIZABETH[4] POPE, b. 09 Apr 1729, Kittery, ME; d. 1780, Kittery, ME.

21. HANNAH[3] SPINNEY *(THOMAS[2], THOMAS[1])* was born 16 Jan 1699/00. She married (1) JOHN CANE Abt. 1723. She married (2) WILLIAM SMITH Abt. 1740.

Children of HANNAH SPINNEY and JOHN CANE are:
  i.   JOHN[4] CANE, b. 13 Apr 1723.

ii. MARY CANE, b. 14 Mar 1724/25.
iii. THOMAS CANE, b. 25 Aug 1727.
iv. LYDIA CANE, b. 19 May 1731.
v. HANNAH CANE, b. 11 Sep 1733.

Children of HANNAH SPINNEY and WILLIAM SMITH are:
vi. KEZIAH[4] SMITH, b. 27 Apr 1742.
vii. EUNICE SMITH, b. 16 Oct 1743.

22. THOMAS[3] SPINNEY *(THOMAS[2], THOMAS[1])* was born Abt. 1703. He married TAMSEN HAM 28 Dec 1731, daughter of JOSEPH HAM and TAMSEN MESERVE. She was born 19 Jul 1708 in Dover, NH, and died 1799.

Children of THOMAS SPINNEY and TAMSEN HAM are:
49. i. JOHN[4] SPINNEY, b. 1733, Kittery, ME; d. 1805, Londonderry, NH.
ii. ROBERT SPINNEY, b. 1736.

Notes for ROBERT SPINNEY:
Settled in Plymouth, England

iii. MERCY SPINNEY, b. 1738, Kittery, ME.

Notes for MERCY SPINNEY:
Mercy was unmarried in 1769

iv. CHRISTIAN SPINNEY, b. 1740, Kittery, ME; m. (1) STROUT; m. (2) JEFFERS.
v. THOMAS SPINNEY, b. Abt. 1743; m. SARAH HENDLEY, 15 Jul 1790, Marblehead, MA.
vi. ELEANOR SPINNEY, b. 1747; m. JAMES REED, 15 Feb 1780.
50. vii. DOROTHY SPINNEY, b. 1751.

23. JOSEPH[3] SPINNEY *(THOMAS[2], THOMAS[1])* was born 18 Aug 1703. He married JANE MCCLURE. She was born 18 Nov 1707.

Children of JOSEPH SPINNEY and JANE MCCLURE are:
i. SAMUEL[4] SPINNEY, b. 14 Aug 1726, Newbury, MA.
ii. JANE SPINNEY, b. 05 Jul 1729.
iii. ANNE SPINNEY, b. 19 Jul 1735, Kittery, ME.

24. JOHN[3] SPINNEY *(JOHN[2], THOMAS[1])* was born Abt. 1693 in Kittery, ME, and died Aft. 1757. He married MARY WATERHOUSE 10 Jul 1728 in Portsmouth, NH, daughter of TIMOTHY WATERHOUSE and RUTH MOSES. She was born 25 Jan 1706/07.

Children of JOHN SPINNEY and MARY WATERHOUSE are:
i. MARY[4] SPINNEY, b. Abt. 1731; d. Abt. 1731.
51. ii. JOHN SPINNEY, b. 1733, Kittery, York, Maine, USA; d. 08 Apr 1793, Argle, Yarmouth, Nova Scotia, Canada.
52. iii. TIMOTHY SPINNEY, b. Abt. 1736; d. 1810.
iv. DIAMOND SPINNEY, b. Aug 1736, Kittery, ME; d. died young.
v. GEORGE SPINNEY, b. Abt. 1743, Kittery, ME; d. in infancy.

25. MERCY[3] SPINNEY *(JOHN[2], THOMAS[1])* was born Abt. 1695. She married WILLIAM TETHERLY 13 Jun 1710 in Kittery, ME. He was born 03 Nov 1685 in Kittery, ME, and died 1748 in Kittery, ME.

Children of MERCY SPINNEY and WILLIAM TETHERLY are:
53. i. MARY[4] TETHERLY, b. 1712.
ii. MERCY TETHERLY, b. 1714.
iii. RUTH TETHERLY, b. 1717.
iv. ELIZABETH TETHERLY, b. 1721.
54. v. SUSANNA TETHERLY, b. 1725.
vi. ELENNOR TETHERLY, b. 1727.

55.   vii. WILLIAM TETHERLY, b. 28 Dec 1729.

55.   vii. WILLIAM TETHERLY, b. 28 Dec 1729.
        viii. ANNE TETHERLY, b. 1731.
         ix. JOHN TETHERLY, b. 1734.
         x. CATHERINE TETHERLY, b. 1736.

26. MARY[3] SPINNEY *(JOHN[2], THOMAS[1])* was born Abt. 1699. She married SAMUEL TOBEY 29 Dec 1720. He was born 1692.

Children of MARY SPINNEY and SAMUEL TOBEY are:
      i. ABIGAIL[4] TOBEY, m. WILLIAM FERNALD, 10 Apr 1752.
     ii. WILLIAM TOBEY, b. Abt. 1730; m. HANNAH REMICK.
    iii. MARY TOBEY, b. 1733.
56.   iv. SAMUEL TOBEY, b. Aug 1734; d. 05 Mar 1807.

27. ANDREW[3] SPINNEY *(JOHN[2], THOMAS[1])* was born 1701 in Kittery, ME, and died Abt. 1755 in Kittery, ME. He married ABIGAIL WINGATE 25 Jun 1726 in Kittery, ME, daughter of JOHN WINGATE and ANN HODSDON. She was born 02 Mar 1703/04 in Dover, NH.

Children of ANDREW SPINNEY and ABIGAIL WINGATE are:
      i. REUBEN[4] SPINNEY, b. 07 Feb 1727/28.

        Notes for REUBEN SPINNEY:
        Died young

57.   ii. WILLIAM SPINNEY, b. 25 Mar 1729.
58. iii. ABIGAIL SPINNEY, b. 13 Mar 1730/31, Kittery, ME.
59. iv. EDMUND SPINNEY, b. 18 Apr 1733, Kittery, ME; d. 05 Jul 1811, Kittery, ME.
60.   v. JOHN SPINNEY, b. 10 Sep 1737, Kittery, ME; d. 1776, Long Island, ME.
61. vi. ANNE SPINNEY, b. Abt. 1740, Kittery, ME; d. 16 Mar 1818.
     vii. MARY SPINNEY, b. 1743; m. ISAAC MOORE, 02 Jun 1768.
    viii. REUBEN SPINNEY, b. 06 Aug 1750.

        Notes for REUBEN SPINNEY:
        Soldier in the Revolution

28. LYDIA[3] SPINNEY *(JOHN[2], THOMAS[1])* was born 1703, and died Bef. 1742. She married GEORGE HAMMOND. He was born 20 Feb 1702/03.

Notes for GEORGE HAMMOND:
IV) GEORGE HAMMOND, (Joseph3) b. Eliot, Me., Feb. 11, 1704; d. Eliot, Me., m. Nov. 10, 1730, Hannah Coburn, of York, Me., dau. of Ebenezer Coburn, b. (???) --, 1710; d. Jan. 22, 1805. She left six children, thirteen grandchildren and twenty great grandchildren. By his father's will, dated August 1, 1751, he inherited a part of his father's lands, (Maine Wills 1640-1760, pp. 691-6,) on which he lived his entire life. This farm descended from him to his grandson, John, who in turn left it to his son, George A. Hammond, who died there recently. The house which he first built on this farm was burned in 1799.

Hannah, his wife, inherited from her father, Ebenezer Coburn, some personal property and   household furniture. Will dated Dec. 26, 1749. (Maine Wills 1640-1760, p. 620.) He was the father of a natural daughter, Dorcas Hammond, b. Jan. 12, 1723, by Lydia Spinney. She m. Michael Kennard, and was the mother of five children. He was in the First Company of Kittery Militia in the French War March15, 1757, under command of Capt. John Frost. He was ensign of the Company. (Mass. Arch.
    Muster Rolls, Vol. 95, p. 375.)

    Children:

1. SARAH, b. August 27, 1731; d. Sept. 18, 1731.
2. GEORGE, b. Jan. 31, 1733; d. Dec. 25, 1752.
3. EBENEZER, b. Sept. 16, 1734. He was a soldier in the French War in the First Company, Kittery Militia, commanded by Capt. John Frost. (Mass. Arch. Muster Rolls, Vol. 95, p. 374.) He was also a Revolutionary

soldier in Capt. Samuel Leighton's Company, Col. James Scammon's Regiment, from August 1, 1775, to Oct. 1775, and in Capt. Samuel Grant's Company,

Child of LYDIA SPINNEY and GEORGE HAMMOND is:
62.   i.   DORCAS[4] HAMMOND, b. 12 Jan 1722/23; d. 1807.

Generation No. 4

29. JAMES[4] FERNALD *(JOHN[3], MARY NORMAN[2] SPINNEY, THOMAS[1])* was born 1704. He married HANNAH ROGERS.

Children of JAMES FERNALD and HANNAH ROGERS are:
            i.   KEZIAH[5] FERNALD.
            ii.   JOHN FERNALD, b. 1737; m. SARAH WENTWORTH.

30. NATHANIEL[4] FERNALD *(NATHANIEL[3], HANNAH[2] SPINNEY, THOMAS[1])* was born 1707, and died 1760. He married MARY WEEKS.

Children of NATHANIEL FERNALD and MARY WEEKS are:
63.   i.   ANN[5] FERNALD, b. 1759.
64.   ii.   TIMOTHY FERNALD, b. 18 Sep 1738.

31. TOBIAS[4] FERNALD *(NATHANIEL[3], HANNAH[2] SPINNEY, THOMAS[1])* He married ABIGAIL SMITH.

Child of TOBIAS FERNALD and ABIGAIL SMITH is:
            i.   GEORGE[5] FERNALD.

32. ANNE[4] SPINNEY *(JOHN[3], SAMUEL[2], THOMAS[1])* was born 12 Apr 1719 in Kittery, ME. She married THOMAS WORCESTER 20 Jan 1738/39 in Gouldsboro, ME, son of THOMAS WORCESTER and SARAH GOWELL. He was born 26 Jan 1715/16.

Children of ANNE SPINNEY and THOMAS WORCESTER are:
            i.   RICHARD[5] WORCESTER, b. 1741.
65.   ii.   MOSES WORCESTER, b. 10 Nov 1743; d. 02 Jul 1836.

33. JOHANNAH[4] SPINNEY *(JOHN[3], SAMUEL[2], THOMAS[1])* was born 28 Nov 1723 in Kittery, ME. She married NATHANIEL INGERSOLL 16 Feb 1743/44.

Children of JOHANNAH SPINNEY and NATHANIEL INGERSOLL are:
            i.   DORCAS[5] INGERSOLL, b. 02 Oct 1748, North Yarmouth, ME.
            ii.   JOANNA INGERSOLL, b. 02 Oct 1748, North Yarmouth, ME.
            iii. MATHA INGERSOLL, b. 1750, Falmouth, ME.
            iv.   OLIVE INGERSOLL, b. 1752.
            v.   WILLIAM INGERSOLL, b. 1755.

34. JOHN[4] SPINNEY *(THOMAS[3], SAMUEL[2], THOMAS[1])* was born Abt. 1715 in Kittery, ME, and died in Marblehead, MA. He married (1) MARY Abt. 1740 in Marblehead, Essex Co., MA. She was born Abt. 1715. He married (2) GRACE BOWDEN 05 Jan 1764 in Marblehead, MA.

Children of JOHN SPINNEY and MARY are:
            i.   ELIZABETH[5] SPINNEY, b. 24 Nov 1741.
            ii.   ROBERT SPINNEY, b. 23 Sep 1744, Marblehead, MA; m. ALICE GIRDLER, 03 Jul 1767, Marblehead, MA.

                  Notes for ROBERT SPINNEY:
                  Died Young

66. iii. REBECCA SPINNEY, b. 03 Aug 1746, Marblehead, MA; d. 25 Nov 1834, Maugerville, NB..
     iv. ELIZABETH SPINNEY, b. 25 Sep 1748, Marblehead, MA.

          Notes for ELIZABETH SPINNEY:
          Died Young

     v.   MARY ANN SPINNEY, b. 22 Sep 1751.

Children of JOHN SPINNEY and GRACE BOWDEN are:
     vi.   GRACE[5] SPINNEY, b. 14 Oct 1764, Marblehead, MA; d. Marblehead Mass; m. THOMAS DENNIS, 26 Feb
           1789, Marblehead, MA.
67. vii. JOHN S SPINNEY, b. 19 Oct 1766, Marblehead, MA.
68. viii. ROBERT SPINNEY, b. 23 Oct 1768, Marblehead, MA; d. 1811, Lynnfield, MA.
69. ix.   BENJAMIN SPINNEY, b. 15 Sep 1771, Marblehead, MA; d. 06 Dec 1842, Taunton, MA.
     x.   MOLLY SPINNEY, b. 22 Jan 1775, Marblehead, MA.
70. xi.   THOMAS SPINNEY, b. 02 Oct 1778, Marblehead, MA; d. 22 May 1860.
71. xii. SAMUEL SPINNEY, b. 02 Oct 1785, Marblehead, MA.
72. xiii. FRANCIS SPINNEY, b. 02 Oct 1785, Marblehead, MA.

35. NICHOLAS[4] SPINNEY *(JAMES[3], SAMUEL[2], THOMAS[1])* was born 05 Oct 1719. He married ALICE GODSOE Oct
1742, daughter of WILLIAM GODSOE and ELIZABETH ROBERTS. She was born 02 Apr 1716.

Children of NICHOLAS SPINNEY and ALICE GODSOE are:
     i.   MARY[5] SPINNEY, b. 18 May 1744, Kittery, ME; m. JAMES.
73. ii. NICHOLAS SPINNEY, b. 30 Jan 1745/46.
     iii. JOSIAH SPINNEY, b. 13 Jun 1748; m. SALLY JAMES, 29 Jun 1799; b. Abt. 1750.
74. iv. EUNICE SPINNEY, b. 26 Dec 1750, Kittery, ME.
     v.   ALICE SPINNEY, b. 27 Mar 1753, Kittery, ME; m. ROBERT TATE, 22 Aug 1776, Kittery, ME; b. Portsmouth,
          NH.
75. vi. CALEB SPINNEY, b. 30 Apr 1755, Kittery, ME; d. Aft. 1834, Kittery, ME.
76. vii. JOHN SPINNEY, b. 07 Oct 1757.

36. EUNICE[4] SPINNEY *(JAMES[3], SAMUEL[2], THOMAS[1])* was born 29 Jan 1721/22 in Kittery, ME. She married JOHN
DEARING 01 Feb 1743/44 in Kittery, ME, son of JOHN DEARING and MARY CARPENTER. He was born 13 Oct
1722, and died 22 Sep 1792.

Children of EUNICE SPINNEY and JOHN DEARING are:
77. i.   JOHN JAMES[5] DEARING.
     ii. THOMAS JOSEPH DEARING.
     iii. JAMES DEARING, m. RUTH.
78. iv. MARY GUILFORD DEARING.
     v.   EUNICE DEARING, m. ELIAKIM TARBOX.
79. vi. JOSEPH JOHN DEARING, b. 06 Oct 1753; d. 25 Sep 1834, Saco, ME.
     vii. LUCRETIA DEARING, m. THOMAS EDGECOMB.

37. MARY[4] SPINNEY *(NATHAN[3], SAMUEL[2], THOMAS[1])* was born 1722 in Kittery, ME. She married JOHN
CHADBOURNE 1741.

Children of MARY SPINNEY and JOHN CHADBOURNE are:
     i.   SUSANNAH[5] CHADBOURNE, b. 1742, Kittery, ME.
     ii. SUSANNAH CHADBOURNE, b. 1743, Kittery, ME.
     iii. ELEAZER CHADBOURNE, b. 1750, Kittery, ME; m. ANNA HARMON.
     iv. JOHN CHADBOURNE, b. 24 Mar 1750/51, Sanford, ME.
     v.   JAMES H CHADBOURNE, b. 04 Feb 1757; m. (1) SARAH CHADBOURNE; b. 1766, Sandford, ME; m. (2)
          DEBROAH HARMON; b. 08 May 1760.
     vi. POLLY CHADBOURNE, b. 1760; m. GRANT.

38. SUSANNAH[4] SPINNEY *(NATHAN[3], SAMUEL[2], THOMAS[1])* was born 1726. She married JOSHUA CHADBOURNE 27
Dec 1750, son of JAMES CHADBOURNE and SARAH HATCH. He was born 25 Jun 1729 in Kittery, ME, and died in

York, ME.

Children of SUSANNAH SPINNEY and JOSHUA CHADBOURNE are:
- i. BETSY[5] CHADBOURNE, b. 26 Oct 1755.
- ii. LUCY CHADBOURNE, b. 11 Mar 1756, Wells, ME.
- iii. WILLIAM CHADBOURNE, b. 1760, Sanford, ME; m. ELEANOR WILSON.
- iv. JOSEPH CHADBOURNE, b. 1763, Sanford, ME.
- v. SARAH CHADBOURNE, b. 1766, Sandford, ME; m. JAMES H CHADBOURNE; b. 04 Feb 1757.
- vi. GEORGE CHADBOURNE, b. 1768, Sanford, ME.
- vii. JOSHUA CHADBOURNE, b. 1770, Sandford, ME.
- viii. JERUSHA CHADBOURNE, b. 1773, Sandford, ME.
- ix. SUSAN CHADBOURNE, b. 1787, Sandford, ME.
- x. PATTY CHADBOURNE, b. 1789, Sanford, ME.

39. RUTH[4] SPINNEY *(JEREMIAH[3], SAMUEL[2], THOMAS[1])* was born Abt. 1742, and died 16 Aug 1816 in Georgetown, ME. She married WILLIAM MARR, son of JOHN MARR and CATHERINE. He was born 04 Aug 1728.

Children of RUTH SPINNEY and WILLIAM MARR are:
- 80.   i. JOHN[5] MARR, b. 1760; d. 1829, Georgetown, ME.
- 81.   ii. OLIVE MARR, b. 1751.

40. JEREMIAH[4] SPINNEY *(JEREMIAH[3], SAMUEL[2], THOMAS[1])* was born 18 Apr 1742 in Kittery, ME, and died 30 Oct 1812. He married MEHITABLE HINCKLEY 08 Nov 1757 in Georgetown, ME. She was born 26 Oct 1735 in Berwick, ME, and died 16 Aug 1827.

Children of JEREMIAH SPINNEY and MEHITABLE HINCKLEY are:
- i. HENRY[5] SPINNEY, b. 10 Oct 1758.
- 82.   ii. SARAH SPINNEY, b. 22 Feb 1760, Georgetown, ME; d. 1838.
- 83.   iii. MARY SPINNEY, b. 19 Jan 1762; d. 07 Sep 1832, Phippsburg Maine.
- 84.   iv. ANNA SPINNEY, b. 14 Jan 1765; d. 1814.
- v. RUTH SPINNEY, b. 29 Jul 1770, Georgetown, ME; d. 18 Nov 1840; m. THOMAS MC FADDEN, 20 Dec 1807; b. 28 Oct 1740; d. 18 Nov 1840.

41. EBENEZER[4] SPINNEY *(JONATHAN[3], SAMUEL[2], THOMAS[1])* was born 14 Dec 1735 in Kittery, ME, and died 1779 in Lost At Sea. He married PHEBE COLE 1764 in Kittery, York, Maine, USA, daughter of ROBERT COLE and PHOEBE SHEPARD. She was born 1751, and died in Suicide By hanging.

Notes for EBENEZER SPINNEY:
Notes from Melinda McDonald

Ebenezer was probably a fisherman and at sea most of the time for there are a very few printed records of him. With the exception of the church records and his mention in the will of his uncle David Spinney, whose estate he was to have by "entail" I can find but one other, taken from the "Acts and Resolves of the Province of Mass. Bay 1769-1780 Vol. 5 where his name appears with others to "prevent seining of shad, alewives and other small fish in Spruce Creek" 25 Feb 1772 and the names of John Spinney ye 3rd and John Spinay, with others appear on a counter petition of remonstrance to the above.

He evidently did not get the estate mentioned in his uncle David's will, according to all tradition, and probably had little property as he left no will or an adminstration of an estate.
Ebenezer and his father Jonathan were on the 3rd Parish Tax List in Kittery in 1763.

We find in the WILL OF DAVID SPINNEY who was brother to Jonathan, that Ebenezzer was the son of Jonathan. In this will he gives all his household goods and personal estate, -and the use and improvement of all his lands buildings and appurtenances to his wife Jerusha during her lifetime.
Jerusha was sister to Robert Cole whose daughter Phoebe married Ebenezer Spinney; she had no children by David so he left his property in "Entail" in the following manner: "after the decease of my said wife Jerusha Spinney, I give and bequeath all my lands and buildings, with all and singular of the appurtences to the same belonging, to my brother Samuel Spinney, and the Eldest son lawfully begotten of his body, forever, and if my said brother Samuel should decease without having a son or male heir, I give all my said lands and buildings to

my Brother Jonathan Spinney, and to his son Ebenezer Spinney, forever, and if Ebenezer should decease before his said father, then I give said land and Premises, to the next son in age to Eberezer, and if the said Jonathan Spinney should decease and his sons before my said wife, ythen I give my said lands and buildings to my Brother Nathan Spinney and his eldest surviving son forever, it being understood that the entail is to run to the eldest son of each mentioned herein and so on in the same tenor forever."

He appointed his wife Executrix, and the will was dated 20 Feb 1744/5, probated 14 Jan 1745/6
INVENTORY RETURNED -27 Jan 1745/6 at 769 lbs.9:4

Children of EBENEZER SPINNEY and PHEBE COLE are:
85.   i.   ABIGAIL COLE[5] SPINNEY, b. 1765; d. 1834.
86.   ii.   HANNAH SPINNEY, b. 05 Apr 1767; d. 13 Jan 1835.
87.   iii. DAVID SPINNEY, b. 14 Sep 1768, Kittery, ME; d. 19 Jul 1848, Wakefield, NH.
        iv.   SARAH SPINNEY, b. 1772; m. (1) PARKER FOSTER; m. (2) SIMON FOSTER, 22 Nov 1792.
88.   v.   CHARLES SPINNEY, b. 1773; d. 07 Apr 1862, Milton NH.
89.   vi.   PARKER SPINNEY, b. Abt. 1775; d. Bet. 1800 - 1810.
90.   vii. MARY GOWELL SPINNEY, b. 19 Apr 1775; d. 01 Mar 1867.
91.   viii. JOSIAH SPINNEY, b. Abt. 1776.
92.   ix.   EBENEZER SPINNEY, b. 22 Dec 1779; d. 12 Feb 1832.

42. HANNAH (BETSY)[4] SPINNEY *(JONATHAN[3], SAMUEL[2], THOMAS[1])* was born Abt. 1746 in Kittery, ME. She married BENJAMIN FERNALD 08 Dec 1764 in Columbia, ME, son of THOMAS FERNALD and MARY SCRIGGINS. He was born 1743.

Child of HANNAH SPINNEY and BENJAMIN FERNALD is:
93.   i.   SALLY[5] FERNALD, b. 1777, Columbia, Maine.

43. NATHANIEL[4] SPINNEY *(JONATHAN[3], SAMUEL[2], THOMAS[1])* was born Abt. 1753 in Kittery, ME, and died 1824 in New Orleans. He married LOIS WEBBER 06 Dec 1773 in Wells, ME, daughter of STEPHEN WEBBER and SARAH DURRELL. She was born Abt. 1753 in Wells, ME.

Notes for NATHANIEL SPINNEY:
I have not found any positive proof to confirm that Nathaniel and Lois are the Parent of these children, Death records of Jonathan's Children state he was born in Kennebunk which is part Wells and Nathaniel is the only Spinney in the area in 1790. The 1790 Census shows Nathaniel and Lois with 4 males and 3 female children

Phillip Durrell bought 4 arces of saltmarsh from Nathaniel Spinney on the 28th of March 1786 18 dollars (York Deeds 51:39)

Children of NATHANIEL SPINNEY and LOIS WEBBER are:
94.   i.   JONATHAN[5] SPINNEY, b. 1777, Kennebunk, ME; d. 26 Feb 1867, St. Stevens NB..
95.   ii.   HANNAH SPINNEY, b. 1780; d. Bef. 1881.
        iii. SON SPINNEY, b. Bet. 1785 - 1794.
96.   iv.   LOUISA SPINNEY, b. Abt. 1787; d. 02 Dec 1846, Portsmouth, NH.
97.   v.   EBENEZER SPINNEY, b. Abt. 1788, Portsmouth, NH; d. 05 Oct 1865, St George, NB..
        vi.   DAUGHTER SPINNEY, b. Bet. 1795 - 1800.
        vii. SON SPINNEY, b. Bet. 1795 - 1800.

44. JOSEPH[4] SPINNEY *(SAMUEL[3], SAMUEL[2], THOMAS[1])* was born 13 Apr 1763 in Granville, NS., and died Nov 1844 in Kings, NS. He married SARAH BEECH 05 Oct 1797 in Granville, NS., daughter of ISAAC BEECH and EUNICE BLISS. She was born 06 Sep 1782 in Granville, NS., and died 28 Jun 1834.

Children of JOSEPH SPINNEY and SARAH BEECH are:
98.   i.   ABRAHAM[5] SPINNEY, b. 19 Sep 1798, Greenwood, NS.; d. 21 Jan 1867.
99.   ii.   CYRENA ANN SPINNEY, b. 04 Jul 1813, Annapolis, Nova Scotia, Canada; d. 14 Jul 1888, Tremont, Kings, Nova Scotia, Canada.
100.   iii. SAMUEL SPINNEY, b. 22 Nov 1802.
101.   iv.   BENIAH HOWE SPINNEY, b. 21 Jul 1805; d. 30 May 1893.

102.   v.   MARY SPINNEY, b. 07 May 1807, Aylesford, NS.; d. 15 Apr 1891.
103.   vi.   ELIJAH SPINNEY, b. 04 Sep 1809, Nova Scotia.
104.   vii. JAMES B SPINNEY, b. 04 Nov 1812; d. 30 Nov 1871.
        viii. WILLIAM SPINNEY, b. 09 Sep 1815, Nova Scotia; d. Aft. 1870, California.

        Notes for WILLIAM SPINNEY:
        Found in San Francisco in 1870

        ix.   CHARLOTTE SPINNEY, b. 09 Sep 1817; m. ISREAL WHITMAN.
105.   x.   SARAH ELIZABETH SPINNEY, b. 26 Aug 1819.
        xi.   JOHN SPINNEY, b. 03 Feb 1822.

45. DAVID[4] SPINNEY *(SAMUEL[3], SAMUEL[2], THOMAS[1])* was born 23 Oct 1767 in Granville, NS. He married SARAH POTTER.

Children of DAVID SPINNEY and SARAH POTTER are:
        i.   ELIZABETH[5] SPINNEY.
        ii.   HENRY SPINNEY, b. Abt. 1800, Marlborough, MA.
106.   iii. JANE SPINNEY, b. Abt. 1800.
        iv.   SARAH SPINNEY, b. Abt. 1800.

46. MARY[4] SPINNEY *(SAMUEL[3], SAMUEL[2], THOMAS[1])* was born Abt. 1770 in Cronwallis, NS.. She married GRIFFIN WEAVER 26 Jan 1796 in St John's Anglican Church Cornwallis Nova Scotia, son of SILAS WEAVER and SUSANNAH GREEN.

Children of MARY SPINNEY and GRIFFIN WEAVER are:
        i.   JOHN[5] WEAVER.
        ii.   DAVID WEAVER.
107.   iii. PETER CRANDALL WEAVER.
        iv.   JABEZ WEAVER.
        v.   HANNAH WEAVER.
        vi.   ELIZABETH WEAVER, b. 05 Feb 1805.
        vii. JOSEPH WEAVER, b. 05 Feb 1805.
        viii. SUSANNA WEAVER, b. 22 Feb 1808.

47. SAMUEL MCCLURE[4] SPINNEY *(SAMUEL[3], SAMUEL[2], THOMAS[1])* was born 11 Nov 1771 in Granville, NS., and died 24 Apr 1832 in Aylesford NS.. He married ELIZABETH BEECH 30 Dec 1795 in Aylesford, NS., daughter of ISAAC BEECH and ELIZABETH BERRY. She was born 03 Jun 1779 in Greenwood, NS., and died 08 Jul 1852.

Children of SAMUEL SPINNEY and ELIZABETH BEECH are:
108.   i.   ISAAC BEACH[5] SPINNEY, b. 04 Aug 1797, Greenwood, NS.; d. 27 Feb 1867, Greenwood, NS..
109.   ii.   JACOB BEACH SPINNEY, b. 15 Oct 1799, Aylesford, NS.; d. 05 Jun 1879, Aylesford, NS..
        iii. SARAH SPINNEY, b. 1801; d. 13 Dec 1869, Greenwood, Annapolis, Nova Scotia.
110.   iv.   ELIZABETH (ELIZA) SPINNEY, b. 01 Aug 1804, Granville Twp, NS.; d. 27 Aug 1885, Greenwood, NS..
111.   v.   EUNICE SPINNEY, b. 08 Jan 1807, Greenwood, NS.; d. 13 Feb 1876.
112.   vi.   JANE SPINNEY, b. 08 Nov 1809, Greenwood Sq NS.
        vii. ELISHA SPINNEY, b. 24 Sep 1811, Greenwood Sq NS; d. 11 Jun 1901.
113.   viii. INGERSON H SPINNEY, b. 18 Oct 1813, Greenwood Sq NS; d. 1896.
        ix.   CAROLINE SPINNEY, b. 17 Apr 1816, Greenwood Sq NS; m. THOMAS NIXON.
114.   x.   HENRY SPINNEY, b. 05 May 1819, Greenwood Sq NS; d. 1902.
115.   xi.   CATHERINE INGLIS SPINNEY, b. 24 May 1822, Greenwood Sq NS; d. 1907.
116.   xii. AMORET SPINNEY, b. 05 Jun 1825, Greenwood, NS.; d. 29 Dec 1859, Greenwood, NS..

48. BENIAH[4] SPINNEY *(SAMUEL[3], SAMUEL[2], THOMAS[1])* was born 1774 in Granville, NS., and died in Greenwood, NS.. He married CHARLOTTE DAVES 08 Dec 1812.

Children of BENIAH SPINNEY and CHARLOTTE DAVES are:
        i.   WILLIAM[5] SPINNEY, b. 1813, Nova Scotia.
117.   ii.   JOHN DAVIS SPINNEY, b. 21 Mar 1817; d. Aft. 1900.
        iii. NANCY SPINNEY, b. 1823.

	iv.	LETETIA SPINNEY, b. 1828; d. 1888; m. MARTIN CAVANAUGH.
118.	v.	MARY SPINNEY, b. Abt. 1830.
119.	vi.	THOMAS LEONARD SPINNEY, b. 1831, Gaspereau, Kings Co, N.S.
120.	vii.	DAVID GRIFFEN SPINNEY, b. 1833; d. 13 Dec 1886, Kings County, NS..
121.	viii.	GEORGE CRAFT SPINNEY, b. 12 May 1837, Gaspereaux, NS.; d. 1916, Bethel, ME.
122.	ix.	LINDEN SPINNEY, b. 1839, Nova Scotia; d. 19 Sep 1882.

49. JOHN[4] SPINNEY *(THOMAS[3], THOMAS[2], THOMAS[1])* was born 1733 in Kittery, ME, and died 1805 in Londonderry, NH. He married MARY STACY in Eliot, ME. She was born in Eliot, ME, and died 07 Oct 1812.

Notes for JOHN SPINNEY:
Moved to Londondery New Hampshire about 1790

Children of JOHN SPINNEY and MARY STACY are:

123.	i.	JOSEPH[5] SPINNEY, b. 1759; d. 1852.
124.	ii.	THOMAS SPINNEY, b. 12 Sep 1767, Portsmouth, NH; d. 22 Aug 1848.
125.	iii.	ALEXANDER SPINNEY, b. 1784, Portsmouth, NH; d. 26 Aug 1847, Londonderry, NH.
	iv.	MARY SPINNEY, b. 1770.

50. DOROTHY[4] SPINNEY *(THOMAS[3], THOMAS[2], THOMAS[1])* was born 1751. She married JOHN ROGERS 25 Nov 1773.

Children of DOROTHY SPINNEY and JOHN ROGERS are:

	i.	SAMUEL[5] ROGERS.
	ii.	CYRUS ROGERS, b. Abt. 1775, Eliot, ME; m. ELIZA GARDNER SPINNEY, 07 May 1815, New Hampshire; b. 25 May 1793; d. 26 Oct 1843.

51. JOHN[4] SPINNEY *(JOHN[3], JOHN[2], THOMAS[1])* was born 1733 in Kittery, York, Maine, USA, and died 08 Apr 1793 in Argle, Yarmouth, Nova Scotia, Canada. He married (1) EUNICE PETTEGREW 11 Mar 1758 in Kittery, ME, daughter of THOMAS PETTEGREW and MARY HUTCHINS. She was born 15 Aug 1735 in Kittery, ME. He married (2) JOANNA ROBERTS 19 Nov 1759. She was born 1744 in Kittery, York, Maine, USA, and died 16 Feb 1824.

Children of JOHN SPINNEY and EUNICE PETTEGREW are:

	i.	EUNICE[5] SPINNEY, b. 16 Sep 1759.
126.	ii.	GEORGE PETTEGREW SPINNEY, b. 12 Aug 1760, Kittery, ME; d. 13 Jul 1849.
127.	iii.	MARY SPINNEY, b. 12 Aug 1760, Kittery, ME; d. 28 Feb 1868.
128.	iv.	JOHN SPINNEY, b. 10 Aug 1761, Kittery, ME; d. 04 Jul 1832.
129.	v.	EUNICE SPINNEY, b. 29 Aug 1764, Kittery, ME; d. 1829.
	vi.	GEORGE SPINNEY, b. 1766.

Notes for GEORGE SPINNEY:
Died young

130.	vii.	BENJAMIN SPINNEY, b. 01 Nov 1767; d. 1840.
	viii.	WILLIAM SPINNEY, b. 09 Jul 1778; m. MARY PAUL, 13 Apr 1796, Kittery Maine.

Notes for WILLIAM SPINNEY:
Skipper of Chebacco boat.

131.	ix.	DAVID SPINNEY, b. 22 Aug 1778, Kittery, ME; d. 24 Nov 1862.
132.	x.	JEREMIAH SPINNEY, b. 10 Sep 1780, Kittery, ME; d. Bef. 1840.

Children of JOHN SPINNEY and JOANNA ROBERTS are:

133.	xi.	ISAAC[5] SPINNEY, b. 31 May 1761, Argyle, NS.; d. 24 Mar 1840.
134.	xii.	ANNIE SPINNEY, b. 15 Aug 1763, Argle, Yarmouth, Nova Scotia, Canada; d. 21 Oct 1784, Annapolis Royal, Nova Scotia, Canada.
135.	xiii.	JACOB SPINNEY, b. 30 Nov 1765, Argle, NS.; d. 16 Nov 1845, Argle, NS..
136.	xiv.	AARON SPINNEY, b. 06 Jan 1768, Argle, NS.; d. 21 Jan 1836, Argle, NS..
137.	xv.	ANDREW SPINNEY, b. 29 Mar 1770, Argle, NS.; d. 26 Jun 1837, Argle, NS..

xvi.	JOHN SPINNEY, b. 15 Jul 1772; d. 19 Feb 1793, Argyle Noa Scotia.
138.	xvii.	BENJAMIN SPINNEY, b. 22 Dec 1774, Argyle, NS.; d. 22 Jul 1847, Argyle, NS..
139.	xviii.	WILLIAM SPINNEY, b. 05 May 1777, Nova Scotia.
140.	xix.	DANIEL SPINNEY, b. 29 Jan 1780; d. 24 Mar 1840.
141.	xx.	JOANNAH SPINNEY, b. 30 Jul 1784; d. 04 Mar 1826, Argyle Nova Scotia.
	xxi.	EZRA SPINNEY, b. 1792.

52. TIMOTHY[4] SPINNEY *(JOHN[3], JOHN[2], THOMAS[1])* was born Abt. 1736, and died 1810. He married (1) HANNAH DAVIS. She was born 1754, and died 27 Oct 1842. He married (2) ABIGAIL PAUL 31 Oct 1765 in Newington, NH.

Children of TIMOTHY SPINNEY and HANNAH DAVIS are:
	i.	ANN[5] SPINNEY, b. Abt. 1760.
142.	ii.	STEPHEN L SPINNEY, b. Bet. 1765 - 1784; d. Bef. 1850.

53. MARY[4] TETHERLY *(MERCY[3] SPINNEY, JOHN[2], THOMAS[1])* was born 1712. She married JOHN DENNETT.

Child of MARY TETHERLY and JOHN DENNETT is:
143.	i.	WILLIAM[5] DENNETT, b. 01 Feb 1738/39, Kittery, York, Maine, USA; d. 25 Oct 1803.

54. SUSANNA[4] TETHERLY *(MERCY[3] SPINNEY, JOHN[2], THOMAS[1])* was born 1725. She married PETER STAPLE.

Children of SUSANNA TETHERLY and PETER STAPLE are:
	i.	MERCY[5] STAPLE.
	ii.	RICHARD STAPLE.
	iii.	JOHN STAPLE.
	iv.	SUSANNA STAPLE.
	v.	RUTH STAPLE.
	vi.	PETER STAPLE.
	vii.	GEORGE STAPLE.

55. WILLIAM[4] TETHERLY *(MERCY[3] SPINNEY, JOHN[2], THOMAS[1])* was born 28 Dec 1729. He married ANNE TETHERLY 28 Nov 1749.

Children of WILLIAM TETHERLY and ANNE TETHERLY are:
144.	i.	SAMUEL[5] TETHERLY, b. 25 Dec 1757, Eliot, ME; d. Abt. 1827, Eliot, ME.
	ii.	THOMAS TETHERLY, b. Abt. 1760; d. Abt. 1760.
	iii.	MARY TETHERLY, b. Abt. 1761.
	iv.	DANIEL TETHERLY, b. Abt. 1770.
	v.	DIAMOND TETHERLY, b. Abt. 1774.
	vi.	BETTY TETHERLY, b. Abt. 1775.

56. SAMUEL[4] TOBEY *(MARY[3] SPINNEY, JOHN[2], THOMAS[1])* was born Aug 1734, and died 05 Mar 1807. He married MARY PAUL. She was born 1738, and died 20 Nov 1801.

Children of SAMUEL TOBEY and MARY PAUL are:
	i.	JAMES[5] TOBEY, b. 1769; m. HANNAH SHAPLEIGH.
	ii.	ABIGAIL TOBEY, b. 1770; m. DAVID LIBBEY.
	iii.	STEPHEN TOBEY, b. 1770; m. SALLY SHAPLEIGH.
	iv.	SAMUEL TOBEY, b. 1772.
	v.	WILLIAM TOBEY, b. 1774.
	vi.	MARY TOBEY, b. 1776.
	vii.	SARAH TOBEY, b. 1776.
	viii.	JOHN TOBEY, b. 1780.
	ix.	WILLIAM TOBEY, b. 1782.
	x.	SAMUEL TOBEY, b. 1785; m. LUCY PAUL.

57. WILLIAM[4] SPINNEY *(ANDREW[3], JOHN[2], THOMAS[1])* was born 25 Mar 1729. He married MARY LIBBEY 1763, daughter of EPHRAIM LIBBEY and MARY AMBLER. She was born 1739 in Kittery, York, Maine, USA.

Children of WILLIAM SPINNEY and MARY LIBBEY are:

	i.	SARAH PAUL⁵ SPINNEY, b. Abt. 1760; m. TIMOTHY PAUL, 1788.
	ii.	MARY COTTLE SPINNEY, b. 08 Jul 1764, Kittery, ME.
	iii.	ELIZABETH SPINNEY, b. Abt. 1765, Kittery, ME; d. 1836.
	iv.	LOIS SPINNEY, b. 1767, Kittery, ME; d. 1831.
145.	v.	ANDREW SPINNEY, b. 1775, Kittery, ME; d. Bet. 1840 - 1850.
146.	vi.	ISAAC SPINNEY, b. 22 Mar 1778, Kittery, ME; d. 12 Sep 1853, Kittery, ME.
147.	vii.	TIMOTHY SPINNEY, b. 1781; d. 05 Jan 1839, Kittery, ME.
	viii.	WILLIAM SPINNEY, b. 1782, Kittery, ME; d. Aft. 1807.
	ix.	EPHRAIM SPINNEY, b. 1784, Kittery, ME; d. 1807; m. DEBORAH.

58. ABIGAIL⁴ SPINNEY *(ANDREW³, JOHN², THOMAS¹)* was born 13 Mar 1730/31 in Kittery, ME. She married WEYMOUTH LYDSTON 20 Sep 1750, son of JOHN LYDSTON and ABIGAIL PAUL.

Children of ABIGAIL SPINNEY and WEYMOUTH LYDSTON are:

148.	i.	WEYMOUTH⁵ LYDSTON, b. 04 Jun 1764, Kittery, ME; d. 1832.
	ii.	JOHN LYDSTON.
	iii.	ANDREW LYDSTON.
	iv.	SARAH LYDSTON.
	v.	ABIGAIL LYDSTON.
149.	vi.	ROBY LYDSTON, b. Jun 1760.
	vii.	MARY LYDSTON.
	viii.	ANN LYDSTON.

59. EDMUND⁴ SPINNEY *(ANDREW³, JOHN², THOMAS¹)* was born 18 Apr 1733 in Kittery, ME, and died 05 Jul 1811 in Kittery, ME. He married SUSANNA ROGERS 02 Mar 1775.

Children of EDMUND SPINNEY and SUSANNA ROGERS are:

	i.	REUBEN⁵ SPINNEY, b. 16 Nov 1779.
150.	ii.	STEPHEN R SPINNEY, b. 14 Jun 1780; d. Bef. 1850.

60. JOHN⁴ SPINNEY *(ANDREW³, JOHN², THOMAS¹)* was born 10 Sep 1737 in Kittery, ME, and died 1776 in Long Island, ME. He married JOANNA PETTEGREW 25 Nov 1750 in Somersworth, NH, daughter of THOMAS PETTEGREW and MARY HUTCHINS. She was born 29 Oct 1732 in Somersworth, NH, and died 06 Sep 1807 in Georgetown, ME.

Children of JOHN SPINNEY and JOANNA PETTEGREW are:

151.	i.	JOHN⁵ SPINNEY, b. 07 Mar 1750/51, Kittery, ME; d. 11 Feb 1825, Georgetown, ME.
	ii.	ELIZABETH SPINNEY, b. 25 Aug 1755; m. NICHOLAS OLIVER, 03 Jan 1775, Georgetown, ME; b. 04 Nov 1750, Georgetown, ME.
152.	iii.	JANE SPINNEY, b. 1757, Georgetown, ME; d. 18 Aug 1846, Starks, ME.
	iv.	ANNE SPINNEY, b. 10 Jan 1758, Georgetown, ME; m. JONATHAN SANBORN, 13 Sep 1797, Georgetown, ME.
153.	v.	JEREMIAH SPINNEY, b. 02 Sep 1759, Georgetown, ME; d. 20 Jun 1850.
	vi.	MARY SPINNEY, b. 24 Aug 1762.
154.	vii.	JOANNA SPINNEY, b. 07 Jun 1764, Georgetown, ME; d. 11 Apr 1849.
155.	viii.	RICHARD SPINNEY, b. 27 May 1766, Georgetown, ME; d. 19 Jul 1805, Georgetown, ME.
156.	ix.	EUNICE SPINNEY, b. 23 Aug 1768.
	x.	GEORGE B SPINNEY, b. 1790; m. ABIGAIL; b. 1796; d. 02 Oct 1849.

61. ANNE⁴ SPINNEY *(ANDREW³, JOHN², THOMAS¹)* was born Abt. 1740 in Kittery, ME, and died 16 Mar 1818. She married EPHRAIM LIBBEY 22 May 1762 in Kitery, ME, son of EPHRAIM LIBBEY and MARY AMBLER. He was born 22 Mar 1731/32, and died 11 Apr 1783.

Children of ANNE SPINNEY and EPHRAIM LIBBEY are:

	i.	OLIVER⁵ LIBBEY.
	ii.	ELIZABETH LIBBEY.

        iii.   ELIMOR LIBBEY.
        iv.   JOHN LIBBEY, b. 1762.
        v.   DAVID LIBBEY, b. 1764.
        vi.   ABEL LIBBEY, b. 1767.
        vii.   CLEMENT LIBBEY, b. 04 Sep 1768, Kittery, ME; d. 31 Jul 1848; m. PHOEBE TIBBETS, 24 Nov 1791; b. 1769; d. 1849.
        viii.   EZRA LIBBEY, b. 1770.
        ix.   SARAH LIBBEY, b. 1774.
157.   x.   NANCY ANN LIBBEY, b. 1776, Kittery, York, Maine, USA.

62. DORCAS⁴ HAMMOND *(LYDIA³ SPINNEY, JOHN², THOMAS¹)* was born 12 Jan 1722/23, and died 1807. She married MICHAEL KENNARD 11 Jun 1742. He died 26 Sep 1797.

Children of DORCAS HAMMOND and MICHAEL KENNARD are:
        i.   JOHN⁵ KENNARD, b. 07 Jun 1743; m. MERCY.
        ii.   WILLIAM KENNARD, b. 06 Nov 1745; m. HANNAH SARGENT, 25 Apr 1773.
        iii.   LYDIA KENNARD, b. 09 Mar 1749/50; m. JAMES NASON, 01 Nov 1770.
        iv.   DIAMOND KENNARD, b. 11 Jul 1753; m. ELIZABETH CHANDLER.
        v.   TIMOTHY KENNARD, b. 19 Feb 1756; m. ABIGAIL STEPHENS.

Generation No. 5

63. ANN⁵ FERNALD *(NATHANIEL⁴, NATHANIEL³, HANNAH² SPINNEY, THOMAS¹)* was born 1759. She married SAMUEL REMICK.

Child of ANN FERNALD and SAMUEL REMICK is:
158.   i.   JANE⁶ REMICK, b. 1784; d. 14 Dec 1870.

64. TIMOTHY⁵ FERNALD *(NATHANIEL⁴, NATHANIEL³, HANNAH² SPINNEY, THOMAS¹)* was born 18 Sep 1738. He married ELEANOR ADAMS.

Child of TIMOTHY FERNALD and ELEANOR ADAMS is:
159.   i.   NATHANIEL⁶ FERNALD.

65. MOSES⁵ WORCESTER *(ANNE⁴ SPINNEY, JOHN³, SAMUEL², THOMAS¹)* was born 10 Nov 1743, and died 02 Jul 1836. He married SUSANNA KNOWLES.

Children of MOSES WORCESTER and SUSANNA KNOWLES are:
160.   i.   MOSES⁶ WORCESTER, JR., b. 1762, Columbia, ME; d. 13 Oct 1855, Columbia, ME.
161.   ii.   ISAAC WORCESTER, b. 1784, Columbia, Me.

66. REBECCA⁵ SPINNEY *(JOHN⁴, THOMAS³, SAMUEL², THOMAS¹)* was born 03 Aug 1746 in Marblehead, MA, and died 25 Nov 1834 in Maugerville, NB.. She married SAMUEL UPTON 01 Apr 1765 in Salem, MA, son of SAMUEL UPTON and RUTH WHIPPLE. He was born 04 May 1744 in Salem, MA, and died 05 Oct 1832 in Maugerville, NB..

Children of REBECCA SPINNEY and SAMUEL UPTON are:
        i.   MARY⁶ UPTON, m. ISAAC SIMMONS.
        ii.   RUTH UPTON, d. Bef. 15 Sep 1831.
162.   iii.   JOHN UPTON, b. 16 May 1767, Maugerville, NB.; d. 1831.
163.   iv.   SAMUEL UPTON, b. 08 Dec 1770, Maugerville, NB.; d. 14 Aug 1834, Sheffield, NB..
        v.   REBECCA UPTON, b. 29 Nov 1772, Maugerville, NB.; d. Jul 1853; m. (1) ELIPHET OLMSTEAD, 23 Jan 1788, Sheffiled, NB.; m. (2) JOEL WATTERS, 1831.
        vi.   ASA UPTON, b. 07 May 1783; d. 19 Jun 1875, Florenceville, Carleton, NB; m. (1) SARAH PERLEY; m. (2) MARGERY LANGAN, 21 Jul 1802, Burton Parish, Sunbury, NB; m. (3) MARGARET NAPIER, 16 Jan 1819.

67. JOHN S⁵ SPINNEY *(JOHN⁴, THOMAS³, SAMUEL², THOMAS¹)* was born 19 Oct 1766 in Marblehead, MA. He married SARAH HENLEY 31 Jan 1790 in Marblehead, MA.

Children of JOHN SPINNEY and SARAH HENLEY are:
- i. JOHN[6] SPINNEY, b. 11 Dec 1791, Marblehead, MA.
- ii. SALLY SPINNEY, b. 22 Dec 1793, Marblehead, MA.

68. ROBERT[5] SPINNEY *(JOHN[4], THOMAS[3], SAMUEL[2], THOMAS[1])* was born 23 Oct 1768 in Marblehead, MA, and died 1811 in Lynnfield, MA. He married JANE NEWHALL 1797 in Lynnfield Mass.

Children of ROBERT SPINNEY and JANE NEWHALL are:
164.	i.	HARRIOT[6] SPINNEY, b. 26 Nov 1797; d. Aft. 1870.
165.	ii.	CHARLES SPINNEY, b. 13 Mar 1800, Keene NH; d. Aft. 1855.
166.	iii.	MARY SPINNEY, b. 01 Mar 1802, Keene NH; d. Bet. 1860 - 1870, Lynnfield, MA.
167.	iv.	ELIOT SPINNEY, b. 12 Jun 1804, Keene NH; d. 16 May 1848.
168.	v.	FRANCIS SPINNEY, b. 19 Jul 1806, Cheshire, NH; d. 29 Mar 1869, Lynnfield.
	vi.	GEORGE SPINNEY, b. 25 Mar 1809, Lynnfield, MA; d. Aft. 1860; m. ELIZABETH JANE HEWES, 27 Dec 1838, Saugus, MA; b. 27 Feb 1815, Lynnfield, MA; d. 1864.

Notes for ELIZABETH JANE HEWES:
1 ELIZA JANE, born 27 Feb., 1815; died in Lynnfield 7 Jan.,
      1864 (g. s.). She married at Saugus 27 Dec., 1838,
      (int. 29 Nov., 1838) GEORGE SPINNEY, who became insane.
      Mrs. Spinney was for some years a resident of
      Cincinnati, and joined the Roman Catholic church.

69. BENJAMIN[5] SPINNEY *(JOHN[4], THOMAS[3], SAMUEL[2], THOMAS[1])* was born 15 Sep 1771 in Marblehead, MA, and died 06 Dec 1842 in Taunton, MA. He married MARTHA NEWHALL 17 May 1795 in Lynn, MA, daughter of WILLIAM NEWHALL and MARTHA MANSFIELD. She was born 1778, and died 1864.

Children of BENJAMIN SPINNEY and MARTHA NEWHALL are:
	i.	MARTHA[6] SPINNEY, b. 05 Jun 1796, Lynn, MA; m. NATHANIEL LEONARD, 13 Oct 1816, Taunton, MA.
169.	ii.	JOHN SPINNEY, b. 07 May 1798; d. 1877.
170.	iii.	SUSAN SPINNEY, b. 20 Mar 1800, Taunton, MA.
171.	iv.	WILLIAM NEWHALL SPINNEY, b. 25 Sep 1802, Taunton, MA; d. 07 Feb 1885, Taunton MA.
172.	v.	BENJAMIN SPINNEY, b. 30 Mar 1805, Taunton, MA; d. 23 Oct 1888.
	vi.	FRANCIS SPINNEY, b. 29 Jul 1807, Taunton, Bristol, MA; d. 14 Aug 1807, Taunton, Mass.
	vii.	SARAH SPINNEY, b. 14 Jul 1810, Taunton, MA.
173.	viii.	CHARLES EDWIN SPINNEY, b. 07 Sep 1818, Taunton, MA; d. 1868, Lynn, MA.
174.	ix.	ELIZABETH GRACE SPINNEY, b. 1820; d. 1903.

70. THOMAS[5] SPINNEY *(JOHN[4], THOMAS[3], SAMUEL[2], THOMAS[1])* was born 02 Oct 1778 in Marblehead, MA, and died 22 May 1860. He married SARAH THOMPSON 21 Aug 1798 in Lynn, MA.

Children of THOMAS SPINNEY and SARAH THOMPSON are:
	i.	POLICY[6] SPINNEY, b. 09 Nov 1798, Lynn, MA.
175.	ii.	MARY M SPINNEY, b. 1799; d. 1875, Lynn, Ma.
	iii.	SALLY SPINNEY, b. 21 Jul 1800, Lynn, MA.
	iv.	JOHN SPINNEY, b. 30 Apr 1802, Lynn, Ma; d. 22 Feb 1888, Lynn, Ma.
176.	v.	GRACE SPINNEY, b. 27 Sep 1805, Lynn, MA; d. Alabama.
	vi.	LYDIA SPINNEY, b. 02 Mar 1807.
177.	vii.	THOMAS SPINNEY, b. 01 Sep 1808, Lynn, MA; d. Bet. 1870 - 1880.
178.	viii.	HANNAH SPINNEY, b. 16 Jun 1803, Lynn, MA; d. 1863, Lynn, MA.
	ix.	NANCY SPINNEY, b. 06 Jul 1812, Lynn, MA; d. 18 Feb 1843; m. ROBERT SISSON, 31 Jul 1831.

71. SAMUEL[5] SPINNEY *(JOHN[4], THOMAS[3], SAMUEL[2], THOMAS[1])* was born 02 Oct 1785 in Marblehead, MA. He married BETSEY HANSON 26 May 1801 in Lynn, MA.

Children of SAMUEL SPINNEY and BETSEY HANSON are:
| 179. | i. | JOHN WARREN[6] SPINNEY, b. 06 Apr 1803, Taunton, MA; d. 1888, Lynn, MA. |
| | ii. | SON SPINNEY, b. Bet. 1801 - 1804. |

iii.   DAUGHTER SPINNEY, b. Bet. 1802 - 1804.

72. FRANCIS[5] SPINNEY *(JOHN[4], THOMAS[3], SAMUEL[2], THOMAS[1])* was born 02 Oct 1785 in Marblehead, MA. He married SUSAN B NEWHALL 23 Dec 1821 in Lynn, MA, daughter of JAMES NEWHALL. She died 13 Jul 1830.

Child of FRANCIS SPINNEY and SUSAN NEWHALL is:
180.   i.   JOHN FRANCIS[6] SPINNEY, b. 02 May 1825, Lynn, MA; d. 1898, Clinton, Ma.

73. NICHOLAS[5] SPINNEY *(NICHOLAS[4], JAMES[3], SAMUEL[2], THOMAS[1])* was born 30 Jan 1745/46.

Children of NICHOLAS SPINNEY are:
         i.   SON[6] SPINNEY.
        ii.   SON SPINNEY.
       iii.   SON SPINNEY.
        iv.   DAUGHTER SPINNEY.

74. EUNICE[5] SPINNEY *(NICHOLAS[4], JAMES[3], SAMUEL[2], THOMAS[1])* was born 26 Dec 1750 in Kittery, ME. She married JOHN RICE. He died Bef. 1799.

Children of EUNICE SPINNEY and JOHN RICE are:
         i.   JOHN[6] RICE.
        ii.   ALEXANDER RICE.

75. CALEB[5] SPINNEY *(NICHOLAS[4], JAMES[3], SAMUEL[2], THOMAS[1])* was born 30 Apr 1755 in Kittery, ME, and died Aft. 1834 in Kittery, ME. He married (1) MARGERY MENDON 31 Oct 1780 in Kittery, ME, daughter of JONATHAN MENSUM and MARY FERNALD. She was born Abt. 1760 in Kittery, ME. He married (2) MARGERY MANSON 20 Mar 1784 in Kittery, ME. She was born in Kittery ME. He married (3) ABIGAIL COLE SPINNEY 29 Nov 1786, daughter of EBENEZER SPINNEY and PHEBE COLE. She was born 1765, and died 1834.

Children of CALEB SPINNEY and MARGERY MENDON are:
181.   i.   CALEB[6] SPINNEY, b. 1782, Kittery, ME; d. 22 Oct 1827.
182.   ii.   MARGERY SPINNEY, b. 13 Apr 1784; d. 02 May 1868.
        iii.   CHARLES SPINNEY, b. Abt. 1786, Kittery, ME; d. 1846.

Children of CALEB SPINNEY and ABIGAIL SPINNEY are:
183.   iv.   NICHOLAS[6] SPINNEY, b. 1788, Kittery, ME; d. 1866.
184.   v.   JOSIAH SPINNEY, b. 1790; d. 11 Aug 1843, Kittery Maine.
        vi.   MARY SPINNEY, b. 1792, Kittery, ME.

76. JOHN[5] SPINNEY *(NICHOLAS[4], JAMES[3], SAMUEL[2], THOMAS[1])* was born 07 Oct 1757. He married EUNICE DEARING. She was born 1757.

Children of JOHN SPINNEY and EUNICE DEARING are:
         i.   THOMAS[6] SPINNEY, b. Abt. 1790.
185.   ii.   NATHAN SPINNEY, b. 1792, Kittery, ME; d. 23 Apr 1881, Kittery, ME.

77. JOHN JAMES[5] DEARING *(EUNICE[4] SPINNEY, JAMES[3], SAMUEL[2], THOMAS[1])* He married MARY JAMESON 24 Jul 1784, daughter of WILLIAM JAMESON.

Children of JOHN DEARING and MARY JAMESON are:
         i.   JOHN[6] DEARING.
        ii.   WILLIAM DEARING.
       iii.   MARK DEARING.
        iv.   ALEXANDER DEARING.

78. MARY GUILFORD⁵ DEARING *(EUNICE⁴ SPINNEY, JAMES³, SAMUEL², THOMAS¹)* She married (1) AMOS ANDREWS.   She married (2) SAMUEL L EDGECOMB 07 Dec 1763. He was born 29 Aug 1739.

Children of MARY DEARING and SAMUEL EDGECOMB are:
- i. SAMUEL⁶ EDGECOMB.
- ii. ROBERT EDGECOMB.
- iii. JOHN EDGECOMB.
- iv. ELIAS EDGECOMB.
- v. NOAH EDGECOMB.
- vi. SARAH EDGECOMB.
- vii. EUNICE EDGECOMB.
- viii. THOMAS EDGECOMB, m. LUCRETIA DEARING.
- ix. MARK EDGECOMB.
- x. MARY EDGECOMB.
- xi. HANNAH EDGECOMB.

79. JOSEPH JOHN⁵ DEARING *(EUNICE⁴ SPINNEY, JAMES³, SAMUEL², THOMAS¹)* was born 06 Oct 1753, and died 25 Sep 1834 in Saco, ME. He married HANNAH JAMESON Mar 1779, daughter of WILLIAM JAMESON. She died 20 May 1841 in Saco, ME.

Children of JOSEPH DEARING and HANNAH JAMESON are:
- i. ESTER⁶ DEERING.
- ii. MARTIN DEARING.
- iii. NOAH DEARING.
- iv. ENOCH DEARING.
- v. JAMES DEARING.
- vi. ELIZABETH DEARING.
- vii. JANE DEARING, b. 12 Feb 1780.
- viii. EUNICE DEARING, b. 16 May 1782.
- ix. JOSEPH DEARING, b. 19 May 1785.
- x. SAMUEL DEARING, b. 15 Sep 1787.
- xi. WILLIAM DEERING, b. 20 Nov 1789.

80. JOHN⁵ MARR *(RUTH⁴ SPINNEY, JEREMIAH³, SAMUEL², THOMAS¹)* was born 1760, and died 1829 in Georgetown, ME. He married MARY CORNISH 11 Dec 1777 in Marr's Island, ME. She was born 11 Jul 1745, and died 1845.

Children of JOHN MARR and MARY CORNISH are:
	i.	WILLIAM⁶ MARR, b. 02 May 1779; d. 26 Jan 1801; m. HANNAH SPINNEY, 08 Jan 1801, Georgetown Maine; b. 10 Jun 1782.
	ii.	JOHN MARR.
186.	iii.	ISIAIH MARR, b. 02 Jun 1782.
187.	iv.	DENNIS MARR, b. 03 May 1786, Georgetown, ME; d. 05 Apr 1849.
	v.	JAMES MARR.
188.	vi.	ALEXANDER MARR, b. 11 May 1794.
189.	vii.	RICHARD MARR, b. 1792; d. 1852.
190.	viii.	THOMAS MARR, b. 01 Apr 1784, Marr's Island, ME; d. 17 Dec 1866.

81. OLIVE⁵ MARR *(RUTH⁴ SPINNEY, JEREMIAH³, SAMUEL², THOMAS¹)* was born 1751. She married SAMUEL BEAL.

Children of OLIVE MARR and SAMUEL BEAL are:
- i. JEREMIAH⁶ BEAL.
- ii. MARY BEAL.
- iii. RUTH BEAL.
- iv. ELIZABETH BEAL.
- v. JAMES BEAL.
- vi. HENRY BEAL.
- vii. OLIVE BEAL.

82. SARAH⁵ SPINNEY *(JEREMIAH⁴, JEREMIAH³, SAMUEL², THOMAS¹)* was born 22 Feb 1760 in Georgetown, ME, and died 1838. She married (1) THOMAS OLIVER, son of JOHN OLIVER and MARY SHORTWELL. He was born 22 Apr 1753 in Georgetown, ME. She married (2) ANDREW MC FADDEN 14 Feb 1801, son of JAMES MC FADDEN and REBECCA PIERCE. He was born 03 Jan 1742/43 in Georgetown, ME.

Child of SARAH SPINNEY and ANDREW MC FADDEN is:
191.   i.   ANDREW⁶ MC FADDEN, b. 1805.

83. MARY⁵ SPINNEY *(JEREMIAH⁴, JEREMIAH³, SAMUEL², THOMAS¹)* was born 19 Jan 1762, and died 07 Sep 1832 in Phippsburg Maine. She married JOHN OLIVER 11 Oct 1782 in Georgetown Maine, son of JOHN OLIVER and MARY SHORTWELL. He was born 15 Jan 1756 in Georgetown, ME, and died 06 May 1806.

Children of MARY SPINNEY and JOHN OLIVER are:
         i.   HENRY⁶ OLIVER, b. 06 Jan 1783.
192.   ii.   JACOB OLIVER, b. 30 Jan 1785, Phippsburg, ME; d. 23 Jan 1870, Phippsburg, ME.
193.   iii.   JOHN OLIVER, b. 10 Nov 1787; d. 05 Feb 1863.
194.   iv.   THOMAS OLIVER, b. 16 Dec 1789; d. 19 Jan 1867.
        v.   JANE OLIVER, b. 25 Feb 1792; d. 27 Feb 1830.
195.   vi.   SARAH OLIVER, b. 08 Nov 1795.
       vii.   WILLIAM OLIVER, b. 16 Apr 1798; d. 07 Jun 1818.
     viii.   MARY OLIVER, b. 18 May 1800.
       ix.   EZEKIEL OLIVER, b. 18 Oct 1802; d. 14 Oct 1820, New York.
196.   x.   JAMES OLIVER, b. 16 Jan 1805.

84. ANNA⁵ SPINNEY *(JEREMIAH⁴, JEREMIAH³, SAMUEL², THOMAS¹)* was born 14 Jan 1765, and died 1814. She married EPHRIAN OLIVER Bef. 1778. He was born 19 Dec 1752, and died 1828.

Children of ANNA SPINNEY and EPHRIAN OLIVER are:
         i.   ELIZABETH⁶ OLIVER, b. 18 May 1778, Georgetown, ME; d. Aft. 1850.
197.   ii.   JOANNA OLIVER, b. 30 May 1780; d. 15 Feb 1843.
       iii.   ABIGAIL OLIVER, b. 1782; d. 1849; m. EDMUND HINKLEY, 28 Dec 1805.
       iv.   WILLIAM OLIVER, b. 1784.
198.   v.   RICHARD OLIVER, b. 1786; d. 1860.
       vi.   EUNICE OLIVER, b. 1791; d. 1826.
      vii.   JANE OLIVER, b. 14 Jun 1794, Georgetown, ME; d. 1868; m. BENJAMIN O SPINNEY, 02 Jan 1845, Georgetown, ME; b. 16 Oct 1809, Georgetown, ME; d. 1869.
199.   viii.   EPHRAIM OLIVER, b. 1797; d. 14 Dec 1890.
       ix.   JOHN OLIVER, b. 1797.
200.   x.   JEREMIAH OLIVER, b. 1800; d. 1836.

85. ABIGAIL COLE⁵ SPINNEY *(EBENEZER⁴, JONATHAN³, SAMUEL², THOMAS¹)* was born 1765, and died 1834. She married CALEB SPINNEY 29 Nov 1786, son of NICHOLAS SPINNEY and ALICE GODSOE. He was born 30 Apr 1755 in Kittery, ME, and died Aft. 1834 in Kittery, ME.

Children are listed above under (75) Caleb Spinney.

86. HANNAH⁵ SPINNEY *(EBENEZER⁴, JONATHAN³, SAMUEL², THOMAS¹)* was born 05 Apr 1767, and died 13 Jan 1835. She married NATHANIEL FERNALD 29 Oct 1791 in Kittery Maine, son of TIMOTHY FERNALD and ELEANOR ADAMS.

Children of HANNAH SPINNEY and NATHANIEL FERNALD are:
         i.   OLIVE⁶ FERNALD, m. JOSEPH DAME.
        ii.   MARY FERNALD, m. WILLAM MARDEN.
       iii.   PATIENCE FERNALD.
201.   iv.   WILLIAM DENNETT FERNALD, b. 04 Jan 1807, Portsmouth, NH; d. 05 Dec 1893.

87. DAVID⁵ SPINNEY *(EBENEZER⁴, JONATHAN³, SAMUEL², THOMAS¹)* was born 14 Sep 1768 in Kittery, ME, and died 19 Jul 1848 in Wakefield, NH. He married (1) LYDIA PAUL 22 Nov 1792, daughter of STEPHEN PAUL and BARTHSAHBA WEARE. She was born 02 Jan 1774, and died 07 Aug 1842 in Wakefiled, NH. He married (2) SALLY CHAMBERLAIN 08 Dec 1842 in Wakefield, Nh, daughter of MOSES CHAMBERLAIN and MARY NASON.

She was born 21 Jul 1785, and died 26 Oct 1873 in Wakefield NH.

Notes for DAVID SPINNEY:
Capt. David Spinney, was born in Kittery, ME 14 Sep 1768, on what is known as "Commodore Hill" The house formerly stood near the road, it was burned a number of years ago, ut is yet makedy by the cellar hole, I am told it was know as the "Cole " house, proberly the home of Robert Cole, the father of Pheobe mother of David, who was called "Commodore Cole. Directly back of the house near the water is the monument erected to Nicholas Spinney, who married a Cole.

On the north west side of the house, on the slope of the hill, beside the road and in the corner of the lot, is evidently the family burial spot, where probably Commodore Robert Cole with his four wives are at rest. and very likely the body of Pheobe (Cole) Spinney, mother of Capt. David lies here also. Field stones mark the resting places, but without inscritions.

David was a Mariner, a master of may vessels-trading with the West Indies and South America, following the sea from the early age of twelve years, beginning soon after the death of father Ebenezer (who was lost at sea in 1779) and continueing until about 1823.

Tiring of the sea and his home in Kittery, in March of 1808, sold his farm there for $2500. and with a man names Andrew Libby, moved away from the coast to Wakefield, NH where he purchased a new home for $2400.

He lived there until his death July 19, 1848, except the time spent on his voyages. The writer has in his poscession the "Brace" of Flint-lock Pistols carried by Capt. David on these voyages

David was a very devout man, active in church affair both in Kittery and Wakefield, in the latter place there is a church now standing, called the "Spinney Meeting house, built through his efforts where his son Elder Joseph Spinney Preached for a period of Fifty years

{Records of Eugene Nathaniel Spinney}

Children of DAVID SPINNEY and LYDIA PAUL are:
	i.	STEPHEN[6] SPINNEY, b. 21 Jul 1793, Kittery, ME; d. Stillborn.
202.	ii.	BARTHSEHBA WEARE SPINNEY, b. 31 May 1794, Kittery, ME; d. 04 May 1878, Milton, NH.
	iii.	EBENEZER SPINNEY, b. 25 Sep 1794; d. 25 Sep 1794.
	iv.	PARKER SPINNEY, b. 23 Jul 1796.

        Notes for PARKER SPINNEY:
        Stillborn

	v.	LYDIA SPINNEY, b. 06 Aug 1797, Kittery, ME.
	vi.	HANNAH SPINNEY, b. 30 Sep 1798, Kittery, ME.
	vii.	PHEBE SPINNEY, b. 08 Aug 1799, Kittery, ME; d. 31 May 1866.
	viii.	DAVID SPINNEY, b. 22 Jun 1801, Kittery, ME; d. 1823, lost at sea; m. ELIZA LEAVITT, 1823; b. Milton, NH.
203.	ix.	PARKER FOSTER SPINNEY, b. 16 Aug 1803, Kittery, ME; d. 01 Aug 1874, Milton, NH.
	x.	PAULINE SPINNEY, b. 16 Aug 1803, Kittery, ME.
	xi.	LYDIA SPINNEY, b. 29 Aug 1805, Kittery, ME.
	xii.	LYDIA SPINNEY, b. 29 May 1808, Kittery, ME; d. 15 May 1817.
	xiii.	PAUL SPINNEY, b. 04 Jun 1809, Wakefield, NH; d. 18 Oct 1825.
204.	xiv.	ALVAH SPINNEY, b. 17 Aug 1810, Wakefield, NH; d. 03 Jul 1840, Tampico Mexico.
205.	xv.	JOSEPH SPINNEY, b. 11 Mar 1812, Wakefield, NH; d. 21 Dec 1899, Wakefield, NH.
206.	xvi.	ROWENA A SPINNEY, b. 06 Mar 1817, Wakefield, NH; d. 1863.

88. CHARLES[5] SPINNEY *(EBENEZER[4], JONATHAN[3], SAMUEL[2], THOMAS[1])* was born 1773, and died 07 Apr 1862 in Milton NH. He married (1) LUCY S STAPLES.   He married (2) ALICE RICE 29 May 1798 in Kittery Maine. She was born 29 May 1778, and died 1816.

Children of CHARLES SPINNEY and ALICE RICE are:
	i.	DAUGHTER[6] SPINNEY, b. 1799.
207.	ii.	CHARLES P SPINNEY, b. 1807; d. Aft. 1880, Lost at Sea.
208.	iii.	ELIZABETH SPINNEY, b. 08 Mar 1811; d. 30 Oct 1898.

89. PARKER[5] SPINNEY *(EBENEZER[4], JONATHAN[3], SAMUEL[2], THOMAS[1])* was born Abt. 1775, and died Bet. 1800 - 1810. He married ELIZABETH MENDUM 25 Jan 1795.

Child of PARKER SPINNEY and ELIZABETH MENDUM is:
209.　　i.　MARK[6] SPINNEY, b. 1797, Kittery, ME; d. 20 Nov 1874.

90. MARY GOWELL[5] SPINNEY *(EBENEZER[4], JONATHAN[3], SAMUEL[2], THOMAS[1])* was born 19 Apr 1775, and died 01 Mar 1867. She married STEPHEN PAUL 21 Sep 1794, son of STEPHEN PAUL and BARTHSAHBA WEARE. He was born 15 Mar 1769.

Children of MARY SPINNEY and STEPHEN PAUL are:
　　　　i.　STEPHEN[6] PAUL, b. 1802.
210.　　ii.　STEPHEN PAUL, b. 1808.

91. JOSIAH[5] SPINNEY *(EBENEZER[4], JONATHAN[3], SAMUEL[2], THOMAS[1])* was born Abt. 1776. He married SARAH JAMES 19 Jul 1799.

Children of JOSIAH SPINNEY and SARAH JAMES are:
　　　　i.　SON[6] SPINNEY, b. Bet. 1790 - 1800.
211.　　ii.　ABIGAIL SPINNEY, b. Abt. 1800.

92. EBENEZER[5] SPINNEY *(EBENEZER[4], JONATHAN[3], SAMUEL[2], THOMAS[1])* was born 22 Dec 1779, and died 12 Feb 1832. He married ALICE (ELSY) PAUL 10 Oct 1799, daughter of JAMES PAUL and MARY DIXON. She was born 12 Dec 1780 in Eliot, Me, and died 11 Aug 1856 in Boston.

Children of EBENEZER SPINNEY and ALICE PAUL are:
212.　　i.　EBENEZER[6] SPINNEY, b. 06 Sep 1800, Kittery, ME; d. Bet. 1870 - 1880, Deer Isle, ME.
213.　　ii.　NARCISSA SPRING SPINNEY, b. 09 Sep 1801; d. 1850, Boston, MA.
　　　　iii.　MARY SPINNEY, b. 07 Mar 1803; m. SAMUEL KINNISON.
　　　　iv.　JOSEPH SPINNEY, b. 22 Mar 1804; d. 11 Oct 1805.
214.　　v.　PHOEBE ANN CATHERINE SPINNEY, b. 19 Oct 1806; d. 20 Oct 1830.
　　　　vi.　LEONARD SPINNEY, b. 01 Sep 1807; d. 27 Mar 1826.
215.　　vii.　ELSEY SPINNEY, b. 04 Apr 1809; d. 07 Nov 1829.
　　　　viii.　JAMES PAUL SPINNEY, b. 08 Apr 1810; d. 12 Apr 1831.
216.　　ix.　LYMAN P SPINNEY, b. 05 Oct 1812; d. 05 Apr 1892.
　　　　x.　JOSEPH SPINNEY, b. 19 Mar 1814; d. 13 May 1826.
　　　　xi.　SARAH ANN SPINNEY, b. 24 Jan 1817; d. 07 Sep 1834; m. GEORGE FLETCHER.
　　　　xii.　OLIVE SPINNEY, b. 03 Oct 1819, Gosham, NH.; m. ALVAH AYERS, 03 Jun 1836.
　　　　xiii.　FRANCES JANE SPINNEY, b. 13 Dec 1822; m. JOHN BELL.
217.　　xiv.　LYDIA AUGUSTA SPINNEY, b. 20 Jan 1824.
　　　　xv.　DAUGHTER SPINNEY, b. Abt. 1800.

93. SALLY[5] FERNALD *(HANNAH (BETSY)[4] SPINNEY, JONATHAN[3], SAMUEL[2], THOMAS[1])* was born 1777 in Columbia, Maine. She married ICHABOD WILLEY 10 Jan 1793, son of ICHABOD WILLEY and ELIZABETH BUMFORD. He was born Sep 1770 in Cherryfield, ME.

Children of SALLY FERNALD and ICHABOD WILLEY are:
　　　　i.　ABRAHAM[6] WILLEY, b. 1795.
　　　　ii.　JOHN WILLEY, b. 1796.
　　　　iii.　SABIN WILLEY, b. 1798.
218.　　iv.　ABIGAIL WILLEY, b. 1812; d. 1882.
　　　　v.　LYDIA WILLEY, b. 1805.
　　　　vi.　SALLY WILLEY, b. 1807.

94. JONATHAN[5] SPINNEY *(NATHANIEL[4], JONATHAN[3], SAMUEL[2], THOMAS[1])* was born 1777 in Kennebunk, ME, and died 26 Feb 1867 in St. Stevens NB.. He married (1) MARY CATHERINE TROKE, daughter of JOHN TROKE. She was born in Canada, and died Aft. 1825. He married (2) ELIZABETH (HARVEY) HATT 13 May 1828 in St George

New Brunswick. She was born 1798 in New Brunswick, and died 03 Mar 1863 in St George New Brunswick.

Notes for JONATHAN SPINNEY:
From St Croix courier
MARCH 1, 1867
DIED :
SPINNEY - In St. Stephen on Tuesday February 26th, Jonathan Spinney aged 90 years.

Excerpts from the Material compiled by John Oliver Spinney

To get a starting point. Lets go to a spot near the old puplic whaf in Upper L'Etang River narrows and the tide rushes through, both flood and ebb, from the wide bays - both above and below. This spot is called PULL-AND-BE-DAM. Nearby is an old cellar, built of field rocks and stones. The ground, in the immediate area, when plowed in my young days, showed great depth of calm shell, indicating that at some date long past, Indians of some eastern tribe lived there. My information is that the cellar was under a house inhabited by one Jonathan Spinney, in the late 1700 and early 1800's

Note: Now at this time, I feel that we must go back and connect with the ancestore of the First THOMAS SPINNEY, as detailed in story # 116 (Maine and Nova Scotia) because when a certain JOHN SPINNEY came from New England to Nova Scotia, about the turn of the 17th to 18th century, they settled at Argyle and Yarmouth (some still are). They prospered, bred and spread like rabbits: and in a generation or two, a lad named Jonathan got across the bay of Fundy and located at PULL-AND-BE-DAM.

If I am correct Jonathan sired my grandfather James along with others that I shall mention later on. If so be was my great grandfather and whatever land owned, or claimed was devided. One of the sons (my grandfather, James homesteaded the 100 acred lot onth of PULL-AND-BE-DAM. This is the place where afterwards my uncle Tobias lived and the house still stands. I was a very small boy when my grandfather James fied and I can only just remember him.

I believe that old Jonathan had several other sons besides my grandfather James, because about the year 1866, my father James V acquired by some means, a lot of 100 acres, running due west of PULL-AND-BE-DAM and next to his father, James. Part of this block was known as NEd's Field and lay next to John Grey's line south. It is reasoned therefore, that Ned was another of Jonathan's and therefore was my father's uncle. The Public road to L'Etang wharf split this property along the side of the Ned's Field,

A little further along the L'Etang Road was a corner, and a road ran south to connect Upper L'Etang. This was known in my time as Thorp Road, because about half-way through, lived one of the oldest settlers, named Henry Thorp. The corner was then known as Nat's corner, which means that Nathaniel being another son of Jonathan was given acreage there. Finally my father must have acquired his 100 acres somehow from his Uncle Ned and Nathaniel about the year 1866 - when he was 20 years old

---

When Edward (Ned) was a boy, after his mother died, his father brough home a new wife and said to the boys who were wroking in the yard " I have brought you a new mother_ It is said that James put down his hoe, walked away and never come home again per family stories of daughters of Edward Spinney, also told by the family of James

---

According to Death Records of Jonathan's children, Jonathan was born in Kennebunk Maine not in Nova Scotia

Children of JONATHAN SPINNEY and MARY TROKE are:
219.   i.   STEPHEN[6] SPINNEY, b. 28 Oct 1801, Eastport, ME; d. Abt. 1846, St George, NB..
        ii.   CALEB SPINNEY, b. 15 Mar 1804, Eastport, ME; d. 27 Jun 1881, Eastport ME.
220.   iii. JOSEPH SPINNEY, b. 1806, New Brunswick; d. 11 Oct 1874, Norton, Ma.
221.   iv.   JAMES S SPINNEY, b. 1807, New Brunswick; d. 25 Jan 1896, St George, NB..
222.   v.   LOUISA ANN SPINNEY, b. 1811, New Brunswick; d. Aft. 1860.

223. vi. NATHANIEL SPINNEY, b. Mar 1814, New Brunswick; d. 05 Jan 1892, Calais, Maine.
224. vii. DOROTHY SPINNEY, b. 1816, New Brunswick; d. Aft. 1880.
225. viii. SARAH E SPINNEY, b. 1819, New Brunswick; d. Aft. 1881.
226. ix. CHARLES EDWARD SPINNEY, b. 1822, L'Etang, NB.; d. 06 Jul 1884, Calais, ME buried blk 9 Lot4.
     x. GEORGE SPINNEY, b. Feb 1825, St George, NB.; d. 03 Sep 1901, Calais, ME; m. SULTANY HALL, 09 Mar 1882; b. 1828; d. 15 Jan 1894, Calais, ME.

Children of JONATHAN SPINNEY and ELIZABETH HATT are:
227. xi. MARY ANN[6] SPINNEY, b. Dec 1828; d. 06 Nov 1906, Attleboro, MA.
     xii. JOSEPH SPINNEY, b. 1829; d. 1859, Calais Maine.
228. xiii. EBENEZER SPINNEY, b. Feb 1832, St George, NB.; d. 04 Feb 1905, Lowell, MA.
229. xiv. ARCHIBALD BARNEY SPINNEY, b. 1833, St George, NB.; d. 12 Oct 1895, Gand Lake Stream, ME.
230. xv. JONATHAN SPINNEY, b. 1835, St. George, N.B.; d. 14 Apr 1914, Calais, ME.
231. xvi. JOHN SPINNEY, b. Abt. 1846; d. Bet. 1890 - 1900.

95. HANNAH[5] SPINNEY *(NATHANIEL[4], JONATHAN[3], SAMUEL[2], THOMAS[1])* was born 1780, and died Bef. 1881. She married JAMES LEE. He was born 1791, and died Aft. 1881.

Children of HANNAH SPINNEY and JAMES LEE are:
     i. SARAH[6] LEE, b. 1811.
232. ii. PAUL OLIVER LEE, b. 1814.

96. LOUISA[5] SPINNEY *(NATHANIEL[4], JONATHAN[3], SAMUEL[2], THOMAS[1])* was born Abt. 1787, and died 02 Dec 1846 in Portsmouth, NH. She married (1) JOHN D CHASE 13 Mar 1807 in Eastport, ME, son of BENJAMIN CHASE and PHOEBE BUCK. He was born 21 Apr 1785 in Haverhill, MA, and died 1809 in Eastport, ME. She married (2) TIMOTHY LADD JONES Aft. 1810, son of EVAN JONES and REBECCA. He was born 23 Jun 1771 in Rockingham Co, NH, and died Aft. 1850.

Children of LOUISA SPINNEY and JOHN CHASE are:
233. i. JAMES[6] CHASE.
234. ii. JOHN CHASE, b. 12 Sep 1807, Eastport, ME; d. 25 Aug 1869, Portsmouth, NH.

Child of LOUISA SPINNEY and TIMOTHY JONES is:
     iii. ELIZABETH[6] JONES, b. 1827, Portsmouth, NH; d. 14 Feb 1847, Charlestown, MA; m. SAMUEL PIERSON HARTLEY WHITE, 30 Oct 1846, Portsmouth, NH; b. 28 Aug 1825, Biddeford, ME; d. 30 Jul 1915, Biddeford, ME.

     Notes for ELIZABETH JONES:
     10-30-1846 Sam P.H.White of Biddeford & Eliza Jones of Portsmouth, NH have this day entered their intentins of marriage with ME, town clerk. P94

     Notes for SAMUEL PIERSON HARTLEY WHITE:
     Entered at Thornton Academy 1833 Age 7
     Bidderford Daily Journal 7-31-1915 Page 8 Obit
     Oldest Masoon & Odd Fellow in Two Cities
     Samuel P H Whites Dies at home on Middle Street Friday
     "Samuel P.H. White, Better known as "Uncle Sam" the oldest Mason & Odd Fellow in the Two cities, died at his home on Middle St., Friday evening at 9:20 O'Clock, following a long illness. Death was due to imfirmities incident to his great age. For a number of months he had been unable to get out of doors by himself, owing to an ever increasing weakness an for some years his ability to walk had been restricted from this same cause. Then end seemed to come as a result of the gradual wearing away of the vital forces which had stood him in a so good stead through the many years of his long life. He was 89 years, 11 months and 2 days old.

     In the death of Mr. White, the city loses an interesting and lovable character and those who knew him best will learn of his passing with sincere sorrow. Dating back, as his life did, to the early days of Biddeford, he could tell with surprising exactness of the early history of Biddeford and many of its important residents of a day and generation now long since passed away. Particularly interesting were the

accounts of the adventures of his father who was a captain and followed the seas
during the turbulent times of the war of 1812. These included tales of
blackade-running and other thrilling adventures of that exciting period. M. White
could also tell much of interest in regard to the early history of the city, as he say
it grow from a mere hamlet and remembered many of the old-time customs and
conditions

Uncle Sam came from on the old and aristrocratic families of the city, his
grandfather, Deacon Samuel Pierson, being one of the influential men of his day, for
whom Piersons Land was named. Interesting it was inded to hear Mr. Whie when in
reminiscent mood, as he told of this old-timne gentleman who lived in such style, in
what is now known as the Maxwell House, on High Street. In those day this section
was the aristocratic part of the city, with fine residences surronded with
spacious lawn reaching away toward the river and interspersed tihe shade trees.
Just as now in those days boys were boys, and it was very funny to hear how, as a
boy, he with some juvenile friends, stole the Deacon's One-Horse Chaise and,
attaching thereto the veneralbe horse with which he wont to preambulate about
the country, whet for a drive, which ended so disastoradsly that the chaise was
overturned and neatly broken beyond repair.

UncleSam was a member of the famous club known as the boys of 1825. The club was
composed of the late Benj. F. Day, Danl. F. Meeds, Saml. W. Hackett, S.P.H. White all of
Biddeford, and Capt. Abithar W. Leavitt of Saco, the only srviving member. Up yo
witing a few years, the club met each year at the home of some member to celebrate
the year of their birth. Owing to the infirmitites of age this custom was given up of
late years.

Mr. White enjoyed the best of health, although unale to go about as much as he
would have liked. Yet he enjoyed life, as he sat by his own open fire and read, or
dreamed of the past. Callers were ever welcome and his old-time hospility would
manifest itself in the ever welcome mug of cider and dish of apples. And then,
quietly seated in his easy chair, he would tell those quaintly interesting tales of
the past while ever and anon he sipped from his glass, as if drawing inspiration from
its amber depths.

Mr. White was initiated a member of Laconia Lodge of Odd Fellows July 18, 1848, and
became Past Grand, July 1, 1852. He became a member of the Saco Lodge of Mason in
1849 or 50

Mr. White as born in this city August 28, 1825, a son of Captain Sam White and Sarah
Pierson. He is survived by a daugher, Miss Sarah P White of this city, who has
faithfully cared for her father during the years of his infirmity. A brother, John
White, of Dorchester, Mass., also survives.

Mr. White was a Machinist and worked for many years on the Perrerell.

Funeral dervices will be conducted in the Chapel at Laurel Hill in Saco, Monday
Afternoon at 2 O'Clock.

His picture is in the Biddeford Daily Journal Saturday, July 31, 1915
at Bidderford, ME Library

97. EBENEZER[5] SPINNEY *(NATHANIEL[4], JONATHAN[3], SAMUEL[2], THOMAS[1])* was born Abt. 1788 in Portsmouth, NH,
and died 05 Oct 1865 in St George, NB.. He married MEHITABLE FERNALD 05 Aug 1806 in Portsmouth, NH,
daughter of BENJAMIN FERNALD and SARAH BEAVER. She was born 1784 in Kittery, ME, and died 11 Aug 1858
in St George, NB..

Children of EBENEZER SPINNEY and MEHITABLE FERNALD are:
235.   i.   EBENEZER[6] SPINNEY, b. 1808, Portsmouth, NH; d. 17 Mar 1888, Grant Park, IL.
236.   ii.   OLIVER W SPINNEY, b. 1810, Portsmouth, NH; d. May 1908.
237.   iii. NATHANIEL SPINNEY, b. Jan 1813, Jonesport, ME; d. 28 Apr 1902, Eastport, ME.
238.   iv.   JAMES PARKER SPINNEY, b. 1814, Maine; d. 16 Dec 1884, Eastport, ME.
239.   v.   ARTHUR JONES SPINNEY, b. 13 Jun 1817, Portsmouth, NH; d. 21 Mar 1900, Goodland, IN.

240.   vi.   CATHERINE SPINNEY, b. 1820, St George, NB..
241.   vii. SIMON F SPINNEY, b. 1822, St George, NB.; d. Aft. 1881.

98. ABRAHAM[5] SPINNEY *(JOSEPH[4], SAMUEL[3], SAMUEL[2], THOMAS[1])* was born 19 Sep 1798 in Greenwood, NS., and died 21 Jan 1867. He married JANE PATTERSON PIERCE 10 Jan 1820 in Aylesford, Kings, NS, daughter of WILLIAM PEARCE and JANE PATTERSON. She was born 16 Sep 1798 in Nova Scotia, and died 01 Feb 1869 in Aylesford, NS..

Children of ABRAHAM SPINNEY and JANE PIERCE are:
         i.   SARAH JANE[6] SPINNEY.
242.   ii. JOSEPH SPINNEY, b. 09 Oct 1820; d. 14 Feb 1893.
         iii. MARY ANN SPINNEY, b. 1826; d. 1874; m. ISAAC BISHOP.
243.   iv. ELIZABETH SPINNEY, b. 20 Jun 1826; d. 06 May 1892, Kings, NS..
244.   v.   SUSANAH SPINNEY, b. 1831; d. 1912.
245.   vi. CHARLES SPINNEY, b. Nov 1831; d. 23 Mar 1869, Aylesford NS.

99. CYRENA ANN[5] SPINNEY *(JOSEPH[4], SAMUEL[3], SAMUEL[2], THOMAS[1])* was born 04 Jul 1813 in Annapolis, Nova Scotia, Canada, and died 14 Jul 1888 in Tremont, Kings, Nova Scotia, Canada. She married JOHN SAUNDERS BANKS 1836, son of TIMOTHY BANKS and MARGARET BASS. He was born 14 Sep 1811 in Aylesford, Annapolis, Nova Scotia, Canada, and died 09 Apr 1896.

Children of CYRENA SPINNEY and JOHN BANKS are:
246.   i.   CHARLOTTE E[6] BANKS, b. 22 Apr 1849, Nova Scotia, Canada; d. 27 Dec 1894.
247.   ii.   CHARLES ARCHIBALD BANKS, b. 26 Jul 1851, Nova Scotia, Canada; d. 1919.
248.   iii. JOSEPH ENGLES BANKS, b. 23 Jul 1836, Nova Scotia, Canada.
249.   iv.   CHARLES ARCHIBALD BANKS, b. 26 Jul 1851, Nova Scotia, Canada; d. 1919.
         v.   ELMIRA BANKS.
250.   vi.   MARY LAVANIA BANKS, b. 07 Feb 1841, Nova Scotia, Canada; d. 28 Feb 1929.
251.   vii. SARAH ANN BANKS, b. 21 Nov 1834, Annapolis, Nova Scotia, Canada; d. 30 May 1893, Torbrook, Annapolis, Nova Scotia, Canada.
252.   viii. JOSEPH ENGLES BANKS, b. 23 Jul 1836, Nova Scotia, Canada.
253.   ix.   TIMOTHY EDWARD BANKS, b. 04 Nov 1853, Nova Scotia, Canada; d. 17 Apr 1919.

100. SAMUEL[5] SPINNEY *(JOSEPH[4], SAMUEL[3], SAMUEL[2], THOMAS[1])* was born 22 Nov 1802. He married MARY RHODES 1822 in Aylesford Nova Scotia.

Children of SAMUEL SPINNEY and MARY RHODES are:
254.   i.   ISABEL[6] SPINNEY, b. 22 May 1826, Aylesford NS; d. Charlestown Ma.
255.   ii.   WILLIAM A SPINNEY, b. 1847, Aylesford, NS.

101. BENIAH HOWE[5] SPINNEY *(JOSEPH[4], SAMUEL[3], SAMUEL[2], THOMAS[1])* was born 21 Jul 1805, and died 30 May 1893. He married (1) MARY BANKS 1835, daughter of TIMOTHY BANKS and MARGARET BASS. She was born 30 Jun 1813, and died 01 Oct 1852. He married (2) ABIGAIL LOCKE 08 Feb 1852 in Lockport NS. She was born 1820, and died 15 Aug 1910.

Notes for BENIAH HOWE SPINNEY:
Per the Genealogy of Captain John Locke they did not have any children

Children of BENIAH SPINNEY and MARY BANKS are:
         i.   HARTLEY[6] SPINNEY, b. 1835; d. 31 Aug 1855.
256.   ii.   AMANDA SPINNEY, b. 1838; d. 1919.
         iii. MELINDA SPINNEY, b. 1841; d. 11 Aug 1861.
257.   iv.   PRYOR M SPINNEY, b. 1843, Nova Scotia; d. 25 Nov 1920, Annapolis Nova Scotia.
258.   v.   NORMAN B SPINNEY, b. Abt. 1847; d. 1889.
259.   vi.   MARGARET SPINNEY, b. 1849; d. 1901.

102. MARY[5] SPINNEY *(JOSEPH[4], SAMUEL[3], SAMUEL[2], THOMAS[1])* was born 07 May 1807 in Aylesford, NS., and died 15 Apr 1891. She married (1) DANIEL DUKESHIRE 1823 in Clements, NS..   She married (2) ERIC WELTON

1827.

Children of MARY SPINNEY and DANIEL DUKESHIRE are:
- i. LETORA[6] DUKESHIRE, m. KENNEDY.
- ii. LEONA DUKESHIRE, b. Abt. 1824, Clements, NS.; d. 1905, Queens County, NS.; m. JOHN JACOB RAWDING, 02 May 1845, Queens County, NS..
- iii. ESTER DUKESHIRE, b. Abt. 1828; d. 31 Oct 1884; m. AUSTIN C RAWDING, Abt. 1848.
- iv. WILLIAM FREEMAN TWYING DUKESHIRE, b. 14 Jun 1830, Kempt, NS.; d. 17 May 1915, Northfield, NS.; m. SUSAN KEMPTON, 27 Jul 1858, Free Baptist at Harmony, NS..
- v. ABRAM DUKESHIRE, b. 06 Oct 1833; d. 31 Jan 1895, Harmony, Queens Nova Scotia; m. MARY KEMPTON, 12 May 1857.
- vi. ISAAC DUKESHIRE, b. 1834, Clements, NS.; d. 06 Dec 1873, Lake May, NS.; m. ELIZA JANE LEADBETTER, 01 Jan 1860, Lake May, NS..
- vii. SUSAN DUKESHIRE, b. 1835, Annapolis, NS; m. ALVAH B RAWDING.
- viii. ISREAL POTTER DUKESHIRE, b. 1837; d. 1910; m. REBECCA MILNER TURPIN, 02 Feb 1856, Clements Annapolis Nova Scotia.
- ix. ABIGAIL DUKESHIRE, b. Abt. 1840; m. ANTHONY DIMOCK RINGER, 13 Nov 1859.
- x. EUNICE DUKESHIRE, b. 17 Sep 1843, Kempt, NS.; m. JOSPEH D KEMPTON, 25 Jun 1863.

103. ELIJAH[5] SPINNEY *(JOSEPH[4], SAMUEL[3], SAMUEL[2], THOMAS[1])* was born 04 Sep 1809 in Nova Scotia. He married MARGERY RHODES.

Children of ELIJAH SPINNEY and MARGERY RHODES are:
- i. CELIA[6] SPINNEY, d. 04 Sep 1856.
- 260. ii. GERTRUDE A SPINNEY, b. 1837, Nova Scotia, Canada; d. 1890, Winthrop, MA.
- iii. AGNES M SPINNEY, b. 1856, Nova Scotia, Canada.

104. JAMES B[5] SPINNEY *(JOSEPH[4], SAMUEL[3], SAMUEL[2], THOMAS[1])* was born 04 Nov 1812, and died 30 Nov 1871. He married LETICIA WHEELOCK 1834. She was born 15 Jul 1816, and died Aft. 1880.

Children of JAMES SPINNEY and LETICIA WHEELOCK are:
- i. JOSEPH W[6] SPINNEY, b. 17 Jan 1835.
- 261. ii. SARAH W SPINNEY, b. 06 Jan 1836.
- 262. iii. MATILDA SALOME SPINNEY, b. 29 May 1838; d. 1911.
- 263. iv. JAMES PELEG SPINNEY, b. 06 Apr 1840, Annapolis, NS.; d. 02 Dec 1911, Alberta Canada.
- 264. v. WILLIAM J SPINNEY, b. 18 May 1842; d. 1927.
- 265. vi. JOSEPH W SPINNEY, b. May 1844; d. 1909, Leominster, Ma.
- vii. ALEXANDER M SPINNEY, b. 19 Apr 1846.
- 266. viii. ISAAC B SPINNEY, b. 25 Jul 1847; d. 22 Jun 1901, Lowell, MA.
- ix. MARY JANE MAY SPINNEY, b. 22 Jun 1849; d. 1930; m. (1) VAN BUSKIRK; m. (2) JOHN DOLPH.
- 267. x. ARTHUR MILLEDGE SPINNEY, b. 16 Aug 1851; d. 1925.
- xi. CHARLES BIDLEY SPINNEY, b. 11 Sep 1853.
- xii. EDWARD LATIMER SPINNEY, b. Sep 1854; d. 30 Apr 1859.
- xiii. ABBY ANN J SPINNEY, b. Jan 1856; d. 10 Apr 1859.

105. SARAH ELIZABETH[5] SPINNEY *(JOSEPH[4], SAMUEL[3], SAMUEL[2], THOMAS[1])* was born 26 Aug 1819. She married GEORGE NEILY, son of JOHN NEILY and ELIZABETH DRULAND. He was born 1815, and died 10 Sep 1880.

Child of SARAH SPINNEY and GEORGE NEILY is:
- 268. i. ERNEST H.[6] NEILY, b. 1867.

106. JANE[5] SPINNEY *(DAVID[4], SAMUEL[3], SAMUEL[2], THOMAS[1])* was born Abt. 1800. She married JOSEPH BROWN.

Child of JANE SPINNEY and JOSEPH BROWN is:
- 269. i. AMORET[6] BROWN, b. 31 Dec 1833; d. 1921.

107. PETER CRANDALL[5] WEAVER *(MARY[4] SPINNEY, SAMUEL[3], SAMUEL[2], THOMAS[1])* He married MATILDA ANN PINEO.

Child of PETER WEAVER and MATILDA PINEO is:
270.   i.   MARY ELIZA CRANDALL[6] WEAVER.

108. ISAAC BEACH[5] SPINNEY *(SAMUEL MCCLURE[4], SAMUEL[3], SAMUEL[2], THOMAS[1])* was born 04 Aug 1797 in Greenwood, NS., and died 27 Feb 1867 in Greenwood, NS.. He married THAMER BAKER, daughter of HENRY BAKER. She was born 1800.

Children of ISAAC SPINNEY and THAMER BAKER are:
      i.   MARY JANE[6] SPINNEY, b. Greenwood Sq NS; d. 05 Jun 1869; m. GEORGE HARRIS.
      ii.   FRANCES SPINNEY, d. 1859; m. CHARLES CAREY.
      iii. ELIZABETH SPINNEY, b. 1819; d. 02 Sep 1846.
      iv.   SUSAN SPINNEY, b. Abt. 1820, Greenwood Sq NS; m. LENIHAN.
271.   v.   SAMUEL SPINNEY, b. 1821, Greenwood, NS.; d. 27 Apr 1912.
272.   vi.   JOHN SPINNEY, b. 1829; d. 15 Nov 1898.
      vii. ISAAC B SPINNEY, b. 1833; d. 19 Nov 1863.
273.   viii. SARAH SPINNEY, b. 1837, Greenwood Sq NS.

109. JACOB BEACH[5] SPINNEY *(SAMUEL MCCLURE[4], SAMUEL[3], SAMUEL[2], THOMAS[1])* was born 15 Oct 1799 in Aylesford, NS., and died 05 Jun 1879 in Aylesford, NS.. He married ANN G CROCKER 1826, daughter of PAUL CROCKER and THANKFUL GATES. She was born 1803 in Greenwood, NS., and died 1890.

Children of JACOB SPINNEY and ANN CROCKER are:
274.   i.   AUSTIN WELTON[6] SPINNEY, b. 14 Sep 1827, Aylesford, NS.; d. 18 Jan 1891.
275.   ii.   JACOB BEACH SPINNEY, b. 13 Nov 1828, Aylesford NS; d. 1907.
      iii. SARAH SPINNEY, b. Abt. 1830.
276.   iv.   HARDING THEODORE SPINNEY, b. 09 Sep 1831, Aylesford NS; d. 1877, Greenwood Sq NS.
      v.   JACOB BEACH SPINNEY, b. 09 Sep 1831, Greenwood, NS.; d. 1907, Greenwood, NS..
277.   vi.   CALEB SPINNEY, b. 17 Dec 1832, Aylesford, NS.; d. 1906.
      vii. HARRIET ANN SPINNEY, b. 22 Dec 1835, Aylesford NS; d. 14 Dec 1865; m. STEPHEN C BANKS.
278.   viii. BENIAH B SPINNEY, b. 22 Mar 1838, Aylesford NS; d. 1923.
279.   ix.   ENOCH SPINNEY, b. 18 Feb 1840, Greenwood, NS.; d. 03 Jun 1907, Harmony, NS..
      x.   MARIA ELIZABETH SPINNEY, b. 1843; d. 1847.
280.   xi.   CLARK THOMAS SPINNEY, b. 21 Jun 1846; d. 20 Jun 1926.

110. ELIZABETH (ELIZA)[5] SPINNEY *(SAMUEL MCCLURE[4], SAMUEL[3], SAMUEL[2], THOMAS[1])* was born 01 Aug 1804 in Granville Twp, NS., and died 27 Aug 1885 in Greenwood, NS.. She married JONATHAN MORSE.

Children of ELIZABETH SPINNEY and JONATHAN MORSE are:
      i.   JOSEPH[6] MORSE.
      ii.   HARRIETTA MORSE.
      iii. ELISHA MORSE, b. 1829.
281.   iv.   ELIZABETH JANE MORSE, b. 02 Dec 1829, Harmony, NS.; d. 12 Nov 1904, Harmony, NS..
282.   v.   HELEN AMORET MORSE, b. 11 Sep 1830, Harmony, NS.; d. 12 Mar 1883, Harmony, NS..
283.   vi.   SAMUEL CHURCH MORSE, b. 27 Feb 1832, Harmony, NS.; d. 27 Feb 1863, Harmony, NS..
284.   vii. EUNICE HARRIET MORSE, b. 12 Feb 1834, Harmony, NS.; d. 15 Apr 1862, Greenwood, NS..
285.   viii. CAROLINE AMELIA MORSE, b. 19 Jan 1838, Harmony, NS.; d. 18 Nov 1913, Tremont, NS..
286.   ix.   ELISHA SPINNEY MORSE, b. 08 Dec 1839, Harmony, NS.; d. 24 Jan 1914, Millville, NS.
287.   x.   ABNER PARKER MORSE, b. 17 Jan 1842, Harmony, NS.; d. 29 Aug 1906, Harmony, NS..
      xi.   BENAIAH MORSE, b. 1844.
288.   xii. JONATHAN CHURCH MORSE, b. 27 Dec 1844, Harmony, NS.; d. 1890, Harmony, NS..
289.   xiii. BENAIAH HOWE "JOE" MORSE, b. 21 Jul 1846, Harmony, NS.; d. 20 Jul 1919, Harmony, NS..
      xiv. AUSTIN W. MORSE, b. 16 Jul 1849, Harmony, NS.; d. 20 Dec 1872.

111. EUNICE[5] SPINNEY *(SAMUEL MCCLURE[4], SAMUEL[3], SAMUEL[2], THOMAS[1])* was born 08 Jan 1807 in Greenwood, NS., and died 13 Feb 1876. She married TIMOTHY SAUNDERS, son of TIMOTHY SAUNDERS and MARTHA NEILY. He was born 1787.

Children of EUNICE SPINNEY and TIMOTHY SAUNDERS are:
      i.   TIMOTHY[6] SAUNDERS, b. 1825; d. 1890; m. LUCY PIENO.
      ii.   CALEB SAUNDERS, b. 1827.

290.	iii.	SAMUEL SAUNDERS, b. 1828; d. 1912.
291.	iv.	ALFRED PARKER SAUNDERS, b. 08 Feb 1831, Greenwood, Kings, Nova Scotia, Canada; d. 09 Aug 1918, Harmon, Kings, Nova Scotia, Canada.
292.	v.	CATHERINE SAUNDERS, b. 11 May 1833; d. 1902.
	vi.	CAROLINE SAUNDERS, b. 1834; d. 1902.
	vii.	GUILFORD D SAUNDERS, b. 1835.
293.	viii.	MARTHA SAUNDERS, b. 1836; d. 05 Oct 1872.
	ix.	HENRY SAUNDERS, b. 1837; d. 1912.
	x.	SARAH SAUNDERS, b. 1838; d. 13 Dec 1869; m. CHARLES WELTON.

112. JANE[5] SPINNEY *(SAMUEL MCCLURE[4], SAMUEL[3], SAMUEL[2], THOMAS[1])* was born 08 Nov 1809 in Greenwood Sq NS. She married JAMES CROCKER. He was born 1806.

Children of JANE SPINNEY and JAMES CROCKER are:
    i. CALVIN[6] CROCKER.
    ii. JOHN CROCKER.

113. INGERSON H[5] SPINNEY *(SAMUEL MCCLURE[4], SAMUEL[3], SAMUEL[2], THOMAS[1])* was born 18 Oct 1813 in Greenwood Sq NS, and died 1896. He married (1) HANNAH PARKER ROACH. She was born 1817, and died 1869. He married (2) SARAH ANN NEWCOMB 1870. She was born 1838.

Children of INGERSON SPINNEY and HANNAH ROACH are:
	i.	ZEBINA[6] SPINNEY, b. 1850.
294.	ii.	JOHN NEILY SPINNEY, b. 1858.
	iii.	ZABINA SPINNEY.
	iv.	MARY JANE SPINNEY, b. Abt. 1830, Greenwood Sq, NS.; m. MOORE.
	v.	ADA SPINNEY, b. 1850; d. 1893; m. ALONZO D. BENT, Abt. 1870; b. 1850.
	vi.	SPURGEON SPINNEY, b. 20 Oct 1857; d. 1920.
	vii.	ROBERT E SPINNEY, b. 1853; d. Aft. 1920, California; m. LUELLA STARRETT.
295.	viii.	E FREEMAN SPINNEY, b. 1841, South, Aylesford, Kings, Nova Scotia.
	ix.	FRANCES SPINNEY, b. 1842, Nova Scotia; m. ALBERT EMERY.

Children of INGERSON SPINNEY and SARAH NEWCOMB are:
296.	x.	CHIPMAN L[6] SPINNEY, b. 1872; d. 1938.
	xi.	BESSIE SPINNEY, b. 1874; d. 22 May 1884.
	xii.	EUGENIA SPINNEY, b. 1875; d. 1956; m. SMALLWOOD MORSE.

114. HENRY[5] SPINNEY *(SAMUEL MCCLURE[4], SAMUEL[3], SAMUEL[2], THOMAS[1])* was born 05 May 1819 in Greenwood Sq NS, and died 1902. He married MARGARET WALKER. She was born 1827, and died Bet. 1900 - 1910.

Notes for MARGARET WALKER:
5 children alive in 1900

Children of HENRY SPINNEY and MARGARET WALKER are:
297.	i.	JESSIE[6] SPINNEY, b. 04 Apr 1855; d. Aft. 1901.
	ii.	LUCRETIA SPINNEY.
	iii.	ELIZABETH SPINNEY, b. 1855.
	iv.	JAMES MILLAGE SPINNEY, b. 1859; m. ADA V STEDMAN, 1882, Boston, MA; b. 1851, Nova Scotia; d. 1895, Boston, MA.
	v.	CAROLINE SPINNEY, b. 1860.
	vi.	JUDSON SPINNEY, b. 1863.
	vii.	HELEN SPINNEY, b. 1867; m. ALBERT WEBBER.
298.	viii.	HIRAM R SPINNEY, b. 16 Sep 1873; d. Aft. 1930, Cambridge, MA.

115. CATHERINE INGLIS[5] SPINNEY *(SAMUEL MCCLURE[4], SAMUEL[3], SAMUEL[2], THOMAS[1])* was born 24 May 1822 in Greenwood Sq NS, and died 1907. She married (1) OSCAR P. GRIFFIN. She married (2) STEPHEN GRIFFIN 1847. He was born 1822, and died 1905.

Children of CATHERINE SPINNEY and OSCAR GRIFFIN are:
- i. STEPHEN[6] GRIFFIN, b. 1874.
- ii. WILLIAM R. GRIFFIN, b. 1877; d. 1878.
- 299. iii. RUBY ARDELLISS GRIFFIN, b. 1885; d. 1961.

Children of CATHERINE SPINNEY and STEPHEN GRIFFIN are:
- iv. OSCAR[6] GRIFFIN.
- v. ROSE GRIFFIN.
- vi. DELLIS GRIFFIN.
- vii. SARAH ELIZA GRIFFIN.
- viii. HANNAH H. GRIFFIN, b. 1850; d. 1857.
- ix. RUBY E. GRIFFIN, b. 01 May 1853; d. 05 May 1857.
- x. NINA CATHERINE GRIFFIN, b. 1855; d. 1939.
- xi. ROSALIND CAROLINE GRIFFIN, b. 1857; d. 1926.
- xii. MARY ARDELLIS GRIFFIN, b. 1860; d. 1879.
- 300. xiii. JAMES E. GRIFFIN, b. 1864; d. 1948.

116. AMORET[5] SPINNEY *(SAMUEL MCCLURE[4], SAMUEL[3], SAMUEL[2], THOMAS[1])* was born 05 Jun 1825 in Greenwood, NS., and died 29 Dec 1859 in Greenwood, NS.. She married JOHN FOSTER PIERCE, son of JAMES PIERCE and ELIZABETH FOSTER. He was born 1821 in Greenwood, NS., and died 05 Nov 1869.

Children of AMORET SPINNEY and JOHN PIERCE are:
- i. ALLAN[6] PIERCE.
- ii. GEORGE PIERCE.

     Notes for GEORGE PIERCE:

     Drowned in Lake Erie

- 301. iii. CHARLES A. PIERCE, b. 10 May 1846; d. 23 Aug 1913, Greenwood, Kings Co Ns.
- iv. EZEKIEL E PIERCE, b. 1848; d. 29 Nov 1868.
- v. ELIZABETH PIERCE, b. 1849, Aylesford, NS.; m. WILLIAM WINGARD, 29 Apr 1877.
- 302. vi. SARAH J PIERCE, b. Oct 1850; d. 06 Feb 1872, Kingston Nova Scotia.
- vii. ELISHA PIERCE, b. 1852; d. 19 Sep 1859.
- 303. viii. CAROLINE PIERCE, b. 1857.
- 304. ix. SHERMAN PIERCE, b. 1859.

117. JOHN DAVIS[5] SPINNEY *(BENIAH[4], SAMUEL[3], SAMUEL[2], THOMAS[1])* was born 21 Mar 1817, and died Aft. 1900. He married DORCAS REDLON. She was born Jan 1825, and died Aft. 1900.

Children of JOHN SPINNEY and DORCAS REDLON are:
- i. JOHN M[6] SPINNEY, b. 1854; d. 1892.
- ii. CHARLOTTE SPINNEY, b. 1856; d. Bef. 1900.
- iii. GEORGE REUBEN SPINNEY, b. Jun 1858; d. 1929.
- iv. WILLIAM SPINNEY, b. 1860; d. Bef. 1900.

118. MARY[5] SPINNEY *(BENIAH[4], SAMUEL[3], SAMUEL[2], THOMAS[1])* was born Abt. 1830. She married DANIEL EAGLES.

Children of MARY SPINNEY and DANIEL EAGLES are:
- 305. i. FRANK[6] SPINNEY, b. 11 Nov 1852; d. Nov 1945.
- 306. ii. JAMES HARRY SPINNEY, b. 1873.

119. THOMAS LEONARD[5] SPINNEY *(BENIAH[4], SAMUEL[3], SAMUEL[2], THOMAS[1])* was born 1831 in Gaspereau, Kings Co, N.S. He married BRIDGET MCLACHLIN 20 Jul 1854. She was born 1833 in Amherst, NS.

Children of THOMAS SPINNEY and BRIDGET MCLACHLIN are:
- i. DANIEL[6] SPINNEY, b. 1855, Nova Scotia.

307. ii. JOHN ALEXANDER SPINNEY, b. Nov 1857, Cumb, NS.; d. Bet. 1900 - 1920.
308. iii. WILLIAM LUKE SPINNEY, b. 1853, Nova Scotia.
iv. ANNIE ELIZABETH SPINNEY, b. 31 May 1866, Mill Village, NS..
309. v. THOMAS LEONARD SPINNEY, b. 1869.

120. DAVID GRIFFEN⁵ SPINNEY *(BENIAH⁴, SAMUEL³, SAMUEL², THOMAS¹)* was born 1833, and died 13 Dec 1886 in Kings County, NS.. He married EMELINE FIELDING 18 Dec 1860.

Children of DAVID SPINNEY and EMELINE FIELDING are:
310. i. BRENTON ARTHUR⁶ SPINNEY, b. 15 Jan 1861.
ii. SARAH LINDON SPINNEY, b. 21 Feb 1863; m. HENRY THOMAS MITCHELL, 03 Oct 1897.
iii. ELIZABETH JANE SPINNEY, b. 02 Sep 1865.
311. iv. THOMAS LEONARD SPINNEY, b. 17 Sep 1867; d. 11 Jan 1937.
v. NANCY MORIAH SPINNEY, b. 05 Apr 1870; d. 1947.
312. vi. GEORGE EMERSON SPINNEY, b. 07 Mar 1874; d. 23 Oct 1946.
313. vii. WILLIAM HENRY SPINNEY, b. 23 Oct 1875; d. 21 May 1968.
314. viii. GRIFFEN MINOR SPINNEY, b. 02 Feb 1878.
315. ix. JAMES O SPINNEY, b. 05 Dec 1879, Nova Scotia; d. 16 Jan 1960, Nova Scotia.
316. x. CLARENCE ALLISON SPINNEY, b. 18 Jul 1882; d. 30 Jun 1960.

121. GEORGE CRAFT⁵ SPINNEY *(BENIAH⁴, SAMUEL³, SAMUEL², THOMAS¹)* was born 12 May 1837 in Gaspereaux, NS., and died 1916 in Bethel, ME. He married ELIZABETH LONG 14 Jan 1863 in New Brunswick. She was born Nov 1840, and died Aft. 1900 in Maine.

Children of GEORGE SPINNEY and ELIZABETH LONG are:
i. SARAH AMANDA⁶ SPINNEY, b. 25 Nov 1857; m. HERBERT KENDALL.
ii. CARRY BLANCHE SPINNEY, m. ALMON ROY GROVER.
317. iii. LEWIS LEONARD SPINNEY, b. 28 Aug 1863, Gaspereau, NS.; d. 1938, Maine.
iv. ANSON SPINNEY, b. Abt. 1870.
v. MARGARET SPINNEY, b. Abt. 1870, Kings CO. NS.; d. 1896.
318. vi. JAMES J SPINNEY, b. 30 Sep 1870, Nova Scotia; d. Aft. 1930, Maine.
vii. WILLIAM SPINNEY, b. 07 May 1872; m. MARY.
319. viii. BERTHA MARIE SPINNEY, b. 07 May 1874, King Co, NS.; d. Aft. 1930.
ix. JOSEPH LONG SPINNEY, b. 1877.

122. LINDEN⁵ SPINNEY *(BENIAH⁴, SAMUEL³, SAMUEL², THOMAS¹)* was born 1839 in Nova Scotia, and died 19 Sep 1882. She married LEWIS HARVIE 22 Feb 1860.

Notes for LEWIS HARVIE:
Lewis HARVIE (James , Archibald , Archibald , James ,) was born about 1832 in Newport, Hants Co., Nova Scotia. He died 8 Apr 1921 in , Hants Co., Nova Scotia and was buried in Elmsdale, Hants Co., Nova Scotia Lewis married Linden SPINNEY, daughter of Benaiah SPINNEY and DAVIES, on 23 Feb 1860 in Horton, Kings Co., Nova Scotia. Linden was born about 1839 in Horton, Kings Co., Nova Scotia. She died 19 Sep 1882 in Wolfville, Kings Co., Nova Scotia and was buried in Willowbank Cem., Wolfville, Nova Scotia.

Children of LINDEN SPINNEY and LEWIS HARVIE are:
i. CLARA EVELENA⁶ HARVIE, b. 25 Nov 1867, Newport NS; m. GEORGE KENTY, 03 Sep 1886, Grand Lake Halifax NS.
ii. GEORGE ARTHUR HARVIE, b. 15 Apr 1871, Newport NS.

123. JOSEPH⁵ SPINNEY *(JOHN⁴, THOMAS³, THOMAS², THOMAS¹)* was born 1759, and died 1852. He married ELIZABETH GERDNER.

Children of JOSEPH SPINNEY and ELIZABETH GERDNER are:
i. ANN⁶ SPINNEY, b. Abt. 1780.
ii. ADELINE SPINNEY, b. Abt. 1790.
iii. CAROLINE SPINNEY.
iv. MEHITABLE SPINNEY.

        v.   ELIZA SPINNEY.

       vi.   SALLY SPINNEY, b. Abt. 1780.

      vii.   SUSAN SPINNEY, b. Abt. 1800.

320.   viii.   JOSEPH S SPINNEY, b. 1805, New Hampsire; d. Aft. 1880, New York.

124. THOMAS[5] SPINNEY *(JOHN[4], THOMAS[3], THOMAS[2], THOMAS[1])* was born 12 Sep 1767 in Portsmouth, NH, and died 22 Aug 1848. He married MARY HUNTRESS 1790. She was born 1771 in Portsmouth, NH, and died 19 Feb 1846.

Children of THOMAS SPINNEY and MARY HUNTRESS are:

        i.   MARY W[6] SPINNEY, b. 03 Nov 1792, Portsmouth, NH; d. 22 Oct 1812, Portsmouth, NH.

       ii.   SAMUEL SPINNEY, b. 1793, Portsmouth, NH.

321.   iii.   THOMAS SPINNEY, b. 09 May 1795, Portsmouth, NH; d. 16 Apr 1872, Portsmouth, NH.

      iv.   ROBERT H SPINNEY, b. 25 Aug 1797; d. 02 Dec 1824, Boston, MA.

           Notes for ROBERT H SPINNEY:
           Robert Died unmarried

       v.   PHEBE HAM SPINNEY, b. 05 Oct 1799, Portsmouth, NH; d. 28 Aug 1823.

           Notes for PHEBE HAM SPINNEY:
           Phebe died unmarried

322.   vi.   JOHN ROGERS SPINNEY, b. 23 Jan 1802, Portsmouth, NH; d. 20 Dec 1879.

      vii.   WILLIAM CUTTER SPINNEY, b. 20 Dec 1804, Portsmouth, NH; d. 18 Aug 1829, Rio Janerio Brazil.

           Notes for WILLIAM CUTTER SPINNEY:
           William Died unmarried

     viii.   DANIEL HENTRESS SPINNEY, b. 1805, 1812.

323.   ix.   SAMUEL SPINNEY, b. 02 Nov 1807, Portsmouth, NH; d. 02 Jun 1890, Portsmouth, NH.

       x.   IZETTE SHAW SPINNEY, b. 10 Nov 1810, Portsmouth, NH.; d. 30 Mar 1893, Portsmouth, NH..

           Notes for IZETTE SHAW SPINNEY:
           Izette died unmarried

324.   xi.   DANIEL HUNTRESS SPINNEY, b. 01 Nov 1812, Portsmouth, NH; d. 14 Aug 1884, North Berwick, ME.

325.   xii.   JOSEPH SPINNEY, b. 25 Mar 1815; d. 07 Feb 1893.

125. ALEXANDER[5] SPINNEY *(JOHN[4], THOMAS[3], THOMAS[2], THOMAS[1])* was born 1784 in Portsmouth, NH, and died 26 Aug 1847 in Londonderry, NH. He married ZELAH M DOW 1806. She died 08 Jan 1849.

Children of ALEXANDER SPINNEY and ZELAH DOW are:

326.   i.   MARY A[6] SPINNEY, b. 1809.

       ii.   GEORGE F SPINNEY, b. 1811; d. 09 Jan 1892, Londonderry New Hampshire.

327.   iii.   JANE P SPINNEY, b. 16 Mar 1814; d. 17 Oct 1866, Londonderry NH.

328.   iv.   JOHN DICKEY SPINNEY, b. 07 Dec 1816; d. 28 Oct 1890.

329.   v.   EMILY SPINNEY, b. 1819, Londonderry, NH; d. 26 Jun 1906.

      vi.   HUGH BARTLY SPINNEY, b. 09 Oct 1822, Massachusetts; d. 27 Jun 1862; m. OLIVE ANN ROWELL, 1852, Londonderry, NH.

           Notes for HUGH BARTLY SPINNEY:
           Hugh B Spinney
           Claimed Residence in Derry
            Worked as a Farmer
            Enlist Date   20 February 1862
            Enlist Place
            Enlist Rank   Priv
            Enlist Age   38

           Served Massachusetts Enlisted L Co. 1st HA Reg. MA disch disability at Fort Albany, VA on 16 June 1862
                Source: Massachusetts Soldiers, Sailors and Marines in the Civil War
                   Abbreviation: MASSCW

330.   vii.   NANCY SPINNEY, b. 09 Jan 1824, Hillboro, NH; d. 29 Jul 1903.

126. GEORGE PETTEGREW[5] SPINNEY *(JOHN[4], JOHN[3], JOHN[2], THOMAS[1])* was born 12 Aug 1760 in Kittery, ME, and died 13 Jul 1849. He married ANN LIBBEY 06 Aug 1788 in Kittery, Maine, daughter of AZARIAH LIBBEY and ELIZABETH PAUL. She was born 1765, and died 10 Mar 1842.

Children of GEORGE SPINNEY and ANN LIBBEY are:
      i.   SON[6] SPINNEY, b. Bet. 1784 - 1790.
331.   ii.   ALEXANDER SPINNEY, b. 1788; d. 10 Dec 1837.
332.   iii.   OLIVE A SPINNEY, b. 1790; d. 12 May 1852.
      iv.   JOSEPH SPINNEY, b. 1791; d. 17 Feb 1869; m. ESTHER STONE; b. Abt. 1790; d. 07 Mar 1880.
333.   v.   JAMES SPINNEY, b. 1793; d. Aft. 1850.
334.   vi.   SIMON SPINNEY, b. 1798; d. Bet. 1850 - 1860.
335.   vii.   FRANCIS SPINNEY, b. Bet. 1800 - 1810; d. 22 Oct 1849.
336.   viii.   WILLIAM SPINNEY, b. Bet. 1800 - 1810; d. Bef. 1850.
337.   ix.   REBECCA P SPINNEY, b. 03 Mar 1801; d. 24 Sep 1895.
338.   x.   MIRIAM L SPINNEY, b. 09 Jun 1796; d. 07 Jan 1873.

127. MARY[5] SPINNEY *(JOHN[4], JOHN[3], JOHN[2], THOMAS[1])* was born 12 Aug 1760 in Kittery, ME, and died 28 Feb 1868. She married DANIEL BROOKS 31 Dec 1792, son of SAMUEL BROOKS and OLIVE KNIGHT. He was born Abt. 1760, and died 28 Apr 1841.

Children of MARY SPINNEY and DANIEL BROOKS are:
      i.   ELIZABETH[6] BROOKS, m. WILLIAM REMICK.
339.   ii.   JEREMIAH BROOKS, b. 1798; d. 15 Nov 1880.
340.   iii.   DANIEL BROOKS, b. 1795.
341.   iv.   ABRAHAM BROOKS, b. 1809; d. 04 Jan 1890.
      v.   OLIVE H BROOKS, m. MARTIN REMICK.
      vi.   JOHN BROOKS.

128. JOHN[5] SPINNEY *(JOHN[4], JOHN[3], JOHN[2], THOMAS[1])* was born 10 Aug 1761 in Kittery, ME, and died 04 Jul 1832. He married HANNAH PETTEGREW 16 Nov 1782, daughter of JOSEPH PETTEGREW and MARY WALKER. She was born 12 Mar 1763.

Notes for JOHN SPINNEY:
From Rambles about Portsmouth

    We all knew Cap Spinney many years, and time and again witnessed fis arrival and departures from the spring market. He was portly in person, upright in posture, of dark skin, long beard and was invariable clad in petticoat trwoers and a pea jacket so covered with patched of every color that it was a ;matter of dought what was the original - a blue knit cap was drawn close to his head, and red edging and ear pieces turned up around. His attention to this cap gave him the above designated name. He was a man of system and independence, and his routine for business was strictly adhered to. He would leave his home at Eliot at any hour between midnight and day-light, that the tide served, and alone in his canoe proceed to the mouth of the river. When the tide required him to leave before he had done up his sleep, on reaching the fishing gound he would bait his hooks, giving one ture of his line abound the tholepins and then another turn aroun his wrist, compose himself to sleep. When the fish bit, the check at the thole-pin would secure it, and the slight pull at the wrist would notify him to take it in. He would then rebait, redrink, and continue his nap, and in due time he might he seen coming up the river and rowing into the Market Landing To the calls "Have you any fish" the reply would be made. As soon as his painter was fastened, he would rise his cuddy cover, take out his coconut shell, visit a patriculat shop near the maket, get it filled with "O-be-joy-ful" them return to his boat, take his seat, raise his coconut to his mouth and take two or three swigs, resting between each with a smack of his lips - then depositing it safely in the cuddy, he uncovered his fish and give snotive "Now gentlemen, I am ready for business" By the time his fish were sold, his shell would ned replenishing, and then with another swig he would push off into the stream, and his boat preceed almost intuitively to his home, Thus year after year through the smae routine, until 1832, on the 4th day of July - a day which he regarded as worth a particular observance in is way, his boat struck against Portsmouth bridge, and at the age of 73 he closed his life in the river in which he had almost lived for three score and ten year. He left about fifteen hunded dollars as a results of his labor, and the reputation of a freindly disposition to men and beast, as wel as to his coconut shell. His like we have never since looked upon.

Children of JOHN SPINNEY and HANNAH PETTEGREW are:

342.   i.   EUNICE[6] SPINNEY, b. Kittery, ME; d. 1836.
        ii.   MARY SPINNEY, b. Abt. 1790; d. 1874; m. JOSHUA STACKPOLE, 22 May 1836; b. 1785, Somersworth, NH.; d. 1854.

129. EUNICE[5] SPINNEY *(JOHN[4], JOHN[3], JOHN[2], THOMAS[1])* was born 29 Aug 1764 in Kittery, ME, and died 1829. She married WEYMOUTH LYDSTON 1787 in Kittery Maine, son of WEYMOUTH LYDSTON and ABIGAIL SPINNEY. He was born 04 Jun 1764 in Kittery, ME, and died 1832.

Children of EUNICE SPINNEY and WEYMOUTH LYDSTON are:

        i.   MARY ANN[6] LYDSTON.
        ii.   EUNICE LYDSTON, d. 25 Dec 1814.
       iii.   NANCY LYDSTON, m. JOHN PEARSON; b. Newburyport, MA.
       iv.   ABIGAIL LYDSTON, m. EZEKIEL FRY.
       v.   BETSY LYDSTON, m. GEORGE JOHNSON; b. Nahant, MA.
343.   vi.   WILLIAM LYDSTON, b. Abt. 1790, Kittery, ME; d. 26 May 1850, Newburyport, MA.
      vii.   LIBBY LYDSTON, b. 1807.
     viii.   CLARA CLARK LYDSTON, b. 1808; d. 03 Nov 1881; m. JOSHUA JOHNSON MESSER, 10 Nov 1828.

130. BENJAMIN[5] SPINNEY *(JOHN[4], JOHN[3], JOHN[2], THOMAS[1])* was born 01 Nov 1767, and died 1840. He married MARY PETTEGREW 17 Apr 1822 in Eliot, ME, daughter of SAMUEL PETEIGREW and OLIVE WELCH. She was born 1808.

Children of BENJAMIN SPINNEY and MARY PETTEGREW are:

        i.   ALBERT[6] SPINNEY, b. 1825; d. 1861, Portsmouth NH.
        ii.   GEORGE A SPINNEY, b. 1838; d. 17 Jun 1863, Aldie, VA.

          Notes for GEORGE A SPINNEY:
          George A Spinney
          Claimed Residence in South Boston
          Worked as a Carpenter
          Enlist Date   21 September 1861
          Enlist Place
          Enlist Rank   Priv
          Enlist Age 23

          Served Massachusetts Enlisted D Co. 1st Cav Reg. MA Killed at Aldie, VA on 17 June 1863
               Source: Massachusetts Soldiers, Sailors and Marines in the Civil War
                     Abbreviation: MASSCW
              Published by Adjutant General on 1931-37

344.   iii.   LUCY ANN SPINNEY, b. 24 Jul 1823; d. 30 May 1885.

131. DAVID[5] SPINNEY *(JOHN[4], JOHN[3], JOHN[2], THOMAS[1])* was born 22 Aug 1778 in Kittery, ME, and died 24 Nov 1862. He married MOLLY MARINER 11 Oct 1790. She was born Abt. 1779, and died 07 May 1821 in Kittery, Me.

Notes for DAVID SPINNEY:
A step over the Rive r -- The Celebrities of Kittery in former days --The Spinney Family.

DAVID SPINNEY died in Eliot Nov. 24th, 1862 , at the age of 92 years. He was the last of six brothers, who all lived and died old men, after spending years of their lives in canoes, and much of the time three or four miles outside of Fort Constitution, fishing. Mr. David Spinney was probably the last survivor of the workmen on the U. S. Frigate Congress, built here on Badger's Island, 1799. The pay roll for the month of August of that year we have before us. Mr. Spinney's pay was 58 1/3 cents. He was then 28 years old. The highest pay on the roll of eighty-nine men is two dollars per day, and but two master-workmen received that sum. The average pay of the whole was about 83 cents.

A remarkable incident marked his old age. Mr. Spinney's hair, after he became advanced in life, for many years had been very white. Within the last few years it all came off, and a new growth of fine silken black hair grew out, covering his head (except a part which had been previously bald) and so continuing until his death. His wife was Mary Mariner, sister of that well-known market woman, Hannah Mariner.

There were six of these brothers, nearly all of whom lived in the same neighborhood in Eliot, a mile or two above Portsmouth Bridge. There was Samuel Spinney, who died about half a century since. His business was to catch lobsters and plaice, and he was ever punctual to his post in the market.

Jeremiah and George were also fishermen. William Spinney, however, was not content to be confined to his canoe, and was a skipper of a Chebacco boat. Then there was John Spinney, or as more generally known from the perpetual knit covering of his head, Cap Spinney, an account of whom is given in Ramble 132.

The first of the Spinney family who came to America was born in the interior of England, near Manchester. He went to Wapping Stairs, near London, and shipped to go Cod Hauling, (as fishing was then called,) to the Bay of Chaleur, on the northern coast of America. From the fishing ground he was carried to the Piscataway by a Capt. Fernald, and about the year 1630 he settled in Kittery, Me. He was the first schoolmaster of the place, and the ancestor of all the Spinneys on the American continent, so far as known. [Original Editor's Note: The first one of the name came from Normandy to England with William the Conqueror. The name, according to English Heraldry, was three times knighted -- first "DeSpiny," second "Spiny" and third "Spinney" as it is now spelt.]

There is a legend in the family that after Thomas, the first settler, came over, a brother who had not seen him from childhood, emigrated, having no knowledge that his brother was living. The new comer landed at Kittery Point. Taking his gun one day he struck up through the woods on the shore of the river in pursuit of game. He came to a small house and asked for refreshments. They were provided, and it was not until after some general conversation, in which the stranger said he came from the same town in England in which the host was born, that the name was given and they discovered themselves to be brothers.

As Thomas Spinney had a grant of 200 acres of land and lived on Eliot Neck, in 1657, it is probable that he was a son of the first settler; and as the residence of the family is still on the same spot, it has probably never been alienated from the name.

About the year 1690 there appears to have been James, Samuel and John Spinney living in Kittery. They were probably sons of Thomas.

Samuel had eight children, Samuel, James, John, Thomas, Nathan, David,

Jeremiah, and Jonathan. His son John married Mary Waterhouse in 1727, and their son John was the father of the family of hardy fishermen, the death of the last of whom is mentioned at the beginning of this Ramble.

Thomas Spinney, who died in 1850, at the age of 83, and Joseph Spinney, who died in 1852, at the age of 83, were the sons of Thomas Spinney, and grandsons of (probably) John Spinney of 1690. We cannot make out the line distinctly from the records.

The location of the small cottages of the Piscataqua tribe of Zebulon was at Eliot Neck, near the site of the old Salt-works. Their cottages which, a few years since made a small village, are now either enlarged and modernized or torn down, so that the appearance of former days, like the inhabitants, has passed away.

Text scanned courtesy of The Brewster Family Network
Copy of Rambles courtesy Peter E. Randall
History Hypertext project by SeacoastNH.com
Design © 2002 SeacoastNH.com

Children of DAVID SPINNEY and MOLLY MARINER are:
  i.   SALLY[6] SPINNEY, b. 1800.
  ii. DAVID SPINNEY.

132. JEREMIAH[5] SPINNEY *(JOHN[4], JOHN[3], JOHN[2], THOMAS[1])* was born 10 Sep 1780 in Kittery, ME, and died Bef. 1840. He married FANNY REMICK 21 Aug 1802 in Kittery, ME, daughter of JACOB REMICK and MARY GROVER. She was born 1782, and died Aft. 1850.

Children of JEREMIAH SPINNEY and FANNY REMICK are:
  i.   RANDALL[6] SPINNEY.
345. ii.   FANNIE SPINNEY, b. 1804, Eliot, ME.
346. iii. JACOB REMICK SPINNEY, b. 1806, Eliot, ME; d. 25 Dec 1873.
      iv.   DANIEL SPINNEY, b. 1808, Kittery, ME.
      v.   ABRAHAM SPINNEY, b. 1810, Eliot, ME.
347. vi.   SARAH JANE SPINNEY, b. 19 Nov 1813; d. 18 Dec 1896, Iowa.
348. vii. JANE "ANN" SPINNEY, b. 1816, Eliot, ME.
      viii. HENRY D SPINNEY, b. 1836; d. 18 Nov 1889, Kittery.

133. ISAAC[5] SPINNEY *(JOHN[4], JOHN[3], JOHN[2], THOMAS[1])* was born 31 May 1761 in Argyle, NS., and died 24 Mar 1840. He married EUNICE FROST 17 Oct 1784 in Argyle, NS., daughter of JOHN FROST and LYDIA. She was born 1750 in Argyle, NS., and died 01 Mar 1820.

Children of ISAAC SPINNEY and EUNICE FROST are:
       i.   ISAAC[6] SPINNEY, b. 05 Apr 1786, Argyle, NS.; d. 28 Nov 1807, Argyle, NS..
349.   ii.   DAVID SPINNEY, b. 12 Sep 1787, Argyle, NS.; d. 06 Jul 1836.
350.   iii. ANNE SPINNEY, b. 21 Mar 1789, Argyle, NS..
351.   iv.   EUNICE SPINNEY, b. 12 Jul 1790, Argyle, NS.; d. Argyle, NS..
352.   v.   LYDIA SPINNEY, b. 24 Aug 1793, Argyle, NS..
353.   vi.   DANIEL SPINNEY, b. 03 Nov 1796, Argyle, NS.; d. Aft. 1880.
354.   vii. REBEKAH SPINNEY, b. 09 Dec 1797, Argyle, NS..
355.   viii. REUBEN SPINNEY, b. 24 Mar 1799, Argyle, NS.; d. 03 Oct 1851.
       ix.   NELSON SPINNEY, b. 31 May 1803, Argyle, NS.; d. 28 Jul 1807, Argyle, NS..
356.   x.   HANNAH SPINNEY, b. 18 Mar 1795, Argyle, NS..

134. ANNIE[5] SPINNEY *(JOHN[4], JOHN[3], JOHN[2], THOMAS[1])* was born 15 Aug 1763 in Argle, Yarmouth, Nova Scotia, Canada, and died 21 Oct 1784 in Annapolis Royal, Nova Scotia, Canada. She married JACOB WHITMAN 1784 in Annapolis, Nova Scotia, Canada. He was born 14 Oct 1757 in Stow, Middlesex, Massachusetts, USA, and died Sep 1837 in Rosette, Annapolis, Nova Scotia, Canada.

Children of ANNIE SPINNEY and JACOB WHITMAN are:
357.   i.   MARY[6] WHITMAN, b. 1785, Rosette, Annapolis, Nova Scotia, Canada; d. 1847, Round Hill, Nova Scotia, Canada.
358.   ii.   DAVID WHITMAN, b. 1786.
       iii. DAVID WHITMAN, b. 1786, Rosette, Annapolis, Nova Scotia, Canada; d. 08 Jul 1826, Paradise, Annapolis, Nova Scotia, Canada.
359.   iv.   JACOB WHITMAN, b. 11 Jun 1786, Rosette, Annapolis, Nova Scotia, Canada; d. 13 Aug 1834, Milton, Nova, Nova Scotia, Canada.
360.   v.   ANN WHITMAN, b. 1791, Rosette, Annapolis, Nova Scotia, Canada.
       vi.   ELIZABETH WHITMAN, b. 1798, Nova Scotia, Canada; m. GEORGE HARRIS.
361.   vii. SPINNEY WHITMAN, b. 1798, Nova Scotia, Canada; d. 11 Dec 1878, Canso, Nova, Nova Scotia, Canada.
362.   viii. WHITEFIELD WHITMAN, b. 02 Feb 1802; d. 19 Feb 1863, Illinois.
363.   ix.   JOANNA WHITMAN, b. 1808, Rosette, Annapolis, Nova Scotia, Canada; d. 1831, Horton, Kings, Nova Scotia, Canada.

135. JACOB[5] SPINNEY *(JOHN[4], JOHN[3], JOHN[2], THOMAS[1])* was born 30 Nov 1765 in Argyle, NS., and died 16 Nov 1845 in Argyle, NS.. He married SUSANNA ATWOOD 02 Dec 1790. She was born 1773, and died 1810.

Children of JACOB SPINNEY and SUSANNA ATWOOD are:

	i.	DEBORAH[6] SPINNEY, b. 31 Aug 1791; d. 09 Jul 1812; m. THOMAS ROBERTS, 1805; b. 11 Nov 1785, Argyle, NS..
	ii.	MARY SPINNEY, b. 24 Jan 1793; m. MORRIS HUBB; b. 24 Feb 1786.
364.	iii.	JACOB SPINNEY, b. 26 Apr 1795; d. 1883.
365.	iv.	JOSEPH SPINNEY, b. 11 Jun 1797, Argyle, NS..
366.	v.	FREEMAN SPINNEY, b. 10 Oct 1801.
	vi.	ELIZABETH SPINNEY, b. 10 Jun 1804; d. 02 Feb 1812.
367.	vii.	EBENEZER SPINNEY, b. 28 Dec 1807, Nova Scotia; d. 1850.
368.	viii.	JEREMIAH SPINNEY, b. 24 Jun 1810; d. 05 Mar 1839.
	ix.	REBECCA SPINNEY, b. 22 Sep 1811; d. 29 Oct 1826; m. ROBERTS.
	x.	DEBORAH SPINNEY, b. 02 Dec 1813.
369.	xi.	THOMAS W SPINNEY, b. 20 Mar 1817, Argyle, NS.; d. Aft. 1881, New Brunswick.
370.	xii.	JAMES SPINNEY, b. 28 Sep 1799, Argyle, NS.; d. 24 Jun 1890.

136. AARON[5] SPINNEY *(JOHN[4], JOHN[3], JOHN[2], THOMAS[1])* was born 06 Jan 1768 in Argyle, NS., and died 21 Jan 1836 in Argyle, NS.. He married MARY KENNEY 21 Mar 1792 in Barrington, NS., daughter of HEMAN KENNEY and MERCY NICKERSON. She was born 14 Aug 1775, and died 15 Apr 1869 in Argyle, NS..

Children of AARON SPINNEY and MARY KENNEY are:

	i.	AARON[6] SPINNEY, b. 02 Jul 1798, Argyle, NS.; d. 05 Mar 1827, Argyle, NS..
	ii.	JOANNA SPINNEY, b. 09 Aug 1800; m. DAVID JEFFREY, 21 Jan 1823.
371.	iii.	SIMEON SPINNEY, b. 09 Aug 1802, Argyle, NS.; d. 20 Feb 1864, Argyle, NS..
	iv.	ELIZABETH SPINNEY, b. 27 Nov 1804, Argyle, NS.; m. JOHN RYDER, 02 Jan 1827, Argyle, NS.; b. 24 Jul 1805, Argyle, NS..
	v.	NELSON SPINNEY, b. 16 Oct 1807.
	vi.	POLLY SPINNEY, b. 26 Dec 1810; m. JONATHAN SANNSY.
372.	vii.	EZARA SPINNEY, b. 16 Jun 1813; d. Aft. 1880.
	viii.	MARY SPINNEY, b. 1816, Argyle, NS.; d. 1890; m. JOSHUA GOODWIN.
373.	ix.	HARVEY SPINNEY, b. 27 Jul 1817, Argyle, NS.; d. Aft. 1880.
374.	x.	SUSANAH SPINNEY, b. 26 May 1796; d. 06 Nov 1883.
375.	xi.	JOHN SPINNEY, b. 29 Jun 1794, Argyle, NS..

137. ANDREW[5] SPINNEY *(JOHN[4], JOHN[3], JOHN[2], THOMAS[1])* was born 29 Mar 1770 in Argyle, NS., and died 26 Jun 1837 in Argyle, NS.. He married EXPERIENCE CROWELL. She died 14 Apr 1835 in Argyle, NS..

Children of ANDREW SPINNEY and EXPERIENCE CROWELL are:

376.	i.	MERCY[6] SPINNEY, b. 07 Nov 1794.
	ii.	WILLIAM SPINNEY, b. 11 Feb 1797.
	iii.	RHODE SPINNEY, b. 07 Sep 1799.
	iv.	SARAH SPINNEY, b. 23 Oct 1803, Argyle, NS.; d. 30 Jan 1822, Argyle, NS..
	v.	ANNA SPINNEY, b. 24 Sep 1807; d. 21 Mar 1831, Argyle Nova Scotia.
377.	vi.	ANDREW SPINNEY, b. 26 May 1810, Nova Scotia, Canada.
	vii.	EUNICE SPINNEY, b. 03 Feb 1813.
	viii.	LYDIA SPINNEY, b. 27 Dec 1815.
	ix.	EXPEARENCE SPINNEY, b. 07 Sep 1819; d. 26 Feb 1835, Argyle Nova Scotia.

138. BENJAMIN[5] SPINNEY *(JOHN[4], JOHN[3], JOHN[2], THOMAS[1])* was born 22 Dec 1774 in Argyle, NS., and died 22 Jul 1847 in Argyle, NS.. He married DEBORAH CROWELL 12 Dec 1796 in Argyle, NS., daughter of CROWELL. She died 30 Jun 1849.

Children of BENJAMIN SPINNEY and DEBORAH CROWELL are:

378.	i.	BENJAMIN[6] SPINNEY, b. 03 May 1798.
379.	ii.	LETITIA SPINNEY, b. 17 Oct 1800, Argyle, NS..
	iii.	JONATHAN SPINNEY, b. 21 Feb 1803.
380.	iv.	WHITMAN SPINNEY, b. 01 Sep 1805; d. 06 Jun 1891.
381.	v.	SOLOMAN ROBERT SPINNEY, b. 02 Aug 1808.
382.	vi.	RHONDA SPINNEY, b. 26 Apr 1811; d. 04 Apr 1888.
	vii.	GEORGE SPINNEY, b. 07 Dec 1813.
	viii.	DAVID SPINNEY, b. 10 Nov 1818.
383.	ix.	NORMAN SPINNEY, b. 21 Feb 1821.
	x.	DEBORAH SPINNEY, b. 26 Aug 1816; d. 1874; m. EZARA SPINNEY; b. 16 Jun 1813; d. Aft. 1880.

139. WILLIAM⁵ SPINNEY *(JOHN⁴, JOHN³, JOHN², THOMAS¹)* was born 05 May 1777 in Nova Scotia. He married EUNICE ROBERTS 24 Nov 1801 in Argyle Nova Scotia, daughter of BENJAMIN ROBERTS and DIADMEMIA HOBBS.

Children of WILLIAM SPINNEY and EUNICE ROBERTS are:
	i.	DIADAMA⁶ SPINNEY, b. 17 Apr 1805, Argyle, NS.; m. JACOB NORTEN, 13 Nov 1818, Argyle, NS..
	ii.	ISAAC SPINNEY, b. 24 Dec 1807, Argyle, NS..
	iii.	WILLIAM SPINNEY, b. 25 Jan 1810, Argyle, NS..
	iv.	JANE SPINNEY, b. 21 Sep 1813, Argyle, NS..
	v.	MARY ANN SPINNEY, b. 11 Aug 1815, Argyle, NS..
	vi.	ELIJAH G SPINNEY, b. 11 Apr 1818, Argyle, NS.; d. 1883, Beverly, Ma; m. LUCY D OAKES, 17 Dec 1851, Gloucester, MA; b. 1837, Gloucester, Massachusetts; d. Aft. 1880.
384.	vii.	LEMUEL SPINNEY, b. 03 Feb 1822, Argyle, NS..
385.	viii.	MINOR SPINNEY, b. 18 Nov 1802, Argyle, NS.; d. May 1884.

140. DANIEL⁵ SPINNEY *(JOHN⁴, JOHN³, JOHN², THOMAS¹)* was born 29 Jan 1780, and died 24 Mar 1840. He married DESIRE CROWELL 29 Dec 1801 in Argyle, NS., daughter of CROWELL. She was born 11 Feb 1784, and died 19 Jan 1858 in Argyle, NS..

Children of DANIEL SPINNEY and DESIRE CROWELL are:
	i.	RUTH⁶ SPINNEY, b. 30 Nov 1802, Argyle, NS.; m. EBENEZER HOBBS, 26 Jan 1828.
386.	ii.	DANIEL SPINNEY, b. 13 Jun 1805, Argyle, NS.; d. 14 Nov 1873.
	iii.	SOPHINE SPINNEY, b. 27 Oct 1807, Argyle, NS.; d. 03 Dec 1807, Argyle, NS..
387.	iv.	DESIAH SPINNEY, b. 17 Oct 1808; d. 07 Jun 1884.
388.	v.	PRINCE SPINNEY, b. 30 Jun 1811, Argyle, NS.; d. 19 Feb 1883, Nova Scotia.
389.	vi.	MARY ELENER SPINNEY, b. 21 May 1814, Argyle, NS..
	vii.	CROWELL SPINNEY, b. 02 Apr 1817, Argyle, NS..
	viii.	JOANNA SPINNEY, b. 14 Mar 1819, Argyle, NS..
	ix.	SOPHIA SPINNEY, b. 17 Oct 1823, Argyle, NS.; d. 07 Jul 1906; m. HENRY RYDER.
	x.	ELIZABETH SPINNEY, b. 17 Sep 1825, Argyle, NS.; m. EPHRIAM ROBERTS.
390.	xi.	EDWARD SPINNEY, b. 23 Feb 1830; d. Aft. 1880.

141. JOANNAH⁵ SPINNEY *(JOHN⁴, JOHN³, JOHN², THOMAS¹)* was born 30 Jul 1784, and died 04 Mar 1826 in Argyle Nova Scotia. She married SOLOMAN RYDER 21 Dec 1803 in Argyle Nova Scotia, son of SOLMON RYDER and SARAH YOUNY. He was born 1778, and died 01 Feb 1821 in Argyle Nova Scotia.

Children of JOANNAH SPINNEY and SOLOMAN RYDER are:
	i.	JOHN⁶ RYDER, b. 24 Jul 1805, Argyle, NS.; m. ELIZEBETH SPINNEY, 02 Jan 1827, Argyle, NS.; b. 27 Nov 1804, Argyle, NS..
	ii.	SARAH RYDER, b. 29 Sep 1807, Argyle, NS..
391.	iii.	ASENATH RYDER, b. 11 Nov 1809.
	iv.	ELIZA ANN RYDER, b. 19 Oct 1812.
392.	v.	LUCY RYDER, b. 01 Dec 1817; d. 03 Dec 1848.
393.	vi.	JOANNA RYDER, b. 10 Feb 1814; d. 1859.

142. STEPHEN L⁵ SPINNEY *(TIMOTHY⁴, JOHN³, JOHN², THOMAS¹)* was born Bet. 1765 - 1784, and died Bef. 1850. He married SARAH ADAMS 18 Jan 1795. She was born 1775, and died Aft. 1850.

Children of STEPHEN SPINNEY and SARAH ADAMS are:
394.	i.	JOSEPH A⁶ SPINNEY, b. Abt. 1800; d. 03 Aug 1848.
	ii.	SON SPINNEY, b. Bet. 1800 - 1810.
	iii.	DAUGHTER SPINNEY, b. Bet. 1800 - 1810.
	iv.	DAUGHTER SPINNEY, b. Bet. 1800 - 1810.

143. WILLIAM⁵ DENNETT *(MARY⁴ TETHERLY, MERCY³ SPINNEY, JOHN², THOMAS¹)* was born 01 Feb 1738/39 in Kittery, York, Maine, USA, and died 25 Oct 1803. He married MARY ADAMS. She was born 17 May 1752 in Kittery, York, Maine, USA, and died 06 Mar 1843 in Maine, USA.

Child of WILLIAM DENNETT and MARY ADAMS is:

395.   i.   JOSEPH⁶ DENNETT, b. 24 Nov 1774, Kittery, York, Maine, USA; d. 10 Jan 1808.

144. SAMUEL⁵ TETHERLY *(WILLIAM⁴, MERCY³ SPINNEY, JOHN², THOMAS¹)* was born 25 Dec 1757 in Eliot, ME, and died Abt. 1827 in Eliot, ME. He married ELIZABETH KENNARD.

Children of SAMUEL TETHERLY and ELIZABETH KENNARD are:

         i.   ROBERT⁶ TETHERLY, b. 1787; d. Eastport Maine.
396.   ii.   CHARLES TETHERLY, b. 14 Dec 1787; d. 07 Aug 1845.
        iii.   DIAMOND TETHERLY, b. 1785.
        iv.   OLIVER TETHERLY, b. 1791.
397.   v.   SAMUEL TETHERLY, b. 1790; d. 06 Mar 1828.
        vi.   ANDREW TETHERLY, b. 1793.
        vii.   POLLY TETHERLY, b. 1795.
        viii. SALLY TETHERLY, b. 1797.
        ix.   NANCY TETHERLY, b. 1799.
        x.   BETSY TETHERLY, b. 1801.

145. ANDREW⁵ SPINNEY *(WILLIAM⁴, ANDREW³, JOHN², THOMAS¹)* was born 1775 in Kittery, ME, and died Bet. 1840 - 1850. He married NANCY ANN LIBBEY 03 Jan 1805, daughter of EPHRAIM LIBBEY and ANNE SPINNEY. She was born 1776 in Kittery, York, Maine, USA.

Child of ANDREW SPINNEY and NANCY LIBBEY is:

         i.   WILLIAM⁶ SPINNEY, b. Aft. 1805.

146. ISAAC⁵ SPINNEY *(WILLIAM⁴, ANDREW³, JOHN², THOMAS¹)* was born 22 Mar 1778 in Kittery, ME, and died 12 Sep 1853 in Kittery, ME. He married MARY TOBEY 16 Aug 1807 in Kittery, Me. She was born 22 May 1785 in Elliott, Maine, and died Aug 1869 in Charlestown, MA.

Children of ISAAC SPINNEY and MARY TOBEY are:

398.   i.   LEONARD⁶ SPINNEY, b. 31 Oct 1807, Eliot, ME; d. 1874, Charlestown, Ma.
        ii.   JAMES M SPINNEY, b. 28 Oct 1809, Kittery, ME; d. 1887, Sandwich, Massachusetts; m. ALICE SWANSEY; b. 1804, Ireland; d. 1886, Sandwich. Ma.
399.   iii.   DANIEL SPINNEY, b. 20 May 1812, Kittery, Me; d. Mar 1891.
        iv.   OLIVER SPINNEY, b. 22 Apr 1815; d. 20 Apr 1839, Pensicola Florida.
400.   v.   ISAAC SPINNEY, b. 13 Apr 1818, Eliot, ME; d. 19 Jul 1859.
        vi.   MARY E SPINNEY, b. 25 May 1821, Eliot, ME; d. 1867; m. EDWARD K PAUL, 16 Jan 1853.
401.   vii.   WALDRON S SPINNEY, b. 12 Jan 1824, Eliot, ME; d. 17 Feb 1911, California.
        viii. ELIZABETH SPINNEY, b. 27 Jul 1827, Eliot, ME; d. Dec 1844.

147. TIMOTHY⁵ SPINNEY *(WILLIAM⁴, ANDREW³, JOHN², THOMAS¹)* was born 1781, and died 05 Jan 1839 in Kittery, ME. He married (1) HANNAH LITTTLEFIELD HAMMOND 30 Dec 1805, daughter of JOSEPH HAMMOND and MARY FERNALD. She was born 1785. He married (2) SARAH HAMMOND 04 Nov 1813. She was born 1792, and died 29 Apr 1866.

Children of TIMOTHY SPINNEY and HANNAH HAMMOND are:

         i.   PERSIS L⁶ SPINNEY, b. 1806; d. Aft. 1850.

               Notes for PERSIS L SPINNEY:
               In the 1850 Censue Persis was listed with her sister Mary and Brother in law Geroge Rogers and their family

        ii.   HANNAH S SPINNEY, b. 1809, Kittery, ME.
402.   iii.   MARY E SPINNEY, b. 1811; d. 14 Apr 1876, Kittery, ME.

Children of TIMOTHY SPINNEY and SARAH HAMMOND are:

        iv.   HANNAH S⁶ SPINNEY.
        v.   ELLEN SPINNEY, b. 1817, Kittery, ME.
        vi.   IRENE SPINNEY, b. 1819, Kittery, ME.

	vii.	SARAH SPINNEY, b. Abt. 1820.
	viii.	ANN EMILY SPINNEY, b. 1821, Kittery, ME; d. Aft. 1900; m. ARCHELAUS WELCH.
	ix.	MARTHA G SPINNEY, b. 1825, Kittery, ME.
403.	x.	ALBION P SPINNEY, b. Jul 1825, Kittery, ME; d. Bet. 1900 - 1910, Pennsylvania.
	xi.	HOSEA B SPINNEY, b. 1827, Kittery, ME.

148. WEYMOUTH[5] LYDSTON *(ABIGAIL[4] SPINNEY, ANDREW[3], JOHN[2], THOMAS[1])* was born 04 Jun 1764 in Kittery, ME, and died 1832. He married EUNICE SPINNEY 1787 in Kittery Maine, daughter of JOHN SPINNEY and EUNICE PETTEGREW. She was born 29 Aug 1764 in Kittery, ME, and died 1829.

Children are listed above under (129) Eunice Spinney.

149. ROBY[5] LYDSTON *(ABIGAIL[4] SPINNEY, ANDREW[3], JOHN[2], THOMAS[1])* was born Jun 1760. He married OLIVE SCRIGGINS 01 Mar 1785, daughter of JOHN SCRIGGINS and KEZIAH WILLEY. She was born 1769.

Child of ROBY LYDSTON and OLIVE SCRIGGINS is:
404.	i.	SALLY[6] LYDSTON, b. 06 Aug 1789.

150. STEPHEN R[5] SPINNEY *(EDMUND[4], ANDREW[3], JOHN[2], THOMAS[1])* was born 14 Jun 1780, and died Bef. 1850. He married ANNA REMICK 26 Nov 1801 in Kittery Maine. She was born 1785, and died Aft. 1860.

Children of STEPHEN SPINNEY and ANNA REMICK are:
	i.	ANN MARIA[6] SPINNEY.
	ii.	CLARISSA SPINNEY.
	iii.	ELEANOR SPINNEY.
	iv.	LYDIA SPINNEY.
	v.	CHARLES SPINNEY, b. Abt. 1800.
	vi.	OLIVER SPINNEY, b. 1806.
405.	vii.	WILLIAM H SPINNEY, b. 1827, Raymond, NH; d. Bef. 1900.
	viii.	WARREN SPINNEY, b. 1830; d. Aft. 1880.

151. JOHN[5] SPINNEY *(JOHN[4], ANDREW[3], JOHN[2], THOMAS[1])* was born 07 Mar 1750/51 in Kittery, ME, and died 11 Feb 1825 in Georgetown, ME. He married (1) EUNICE PORTERFIELD HUTCHINS. She was born 1758 in Porterfield, Oxford, Maine, USA, and died 19 Feb 1848 in Georgetown, Lincoln, Maine, USA. He married (2) EUNICE POTTERFIELD HUTCHINGS Abt. 1775 in Georgetown, ME, daughter of JOHN HUTCHINS and SARAH PORTERFIELD. She was born 1758 in Porterfield, Oxford, Maine, USA, and died 19 Feb 1848 in Georgetown, Lincoln, Maine, USA.

Child of JOHN SPINNEY and EUNICE HUTCHINS is:
406.	i.	EUNICE[6] SPINNEY, b. 18 Apr 1784, Boothbay, Lincoln, Maine, USA; d. 1810.

Children of JOHN SPINNEY and EUNICE HUTCHINGS are:
407.	ii.	JOHN[6] SPINNEY, b. 26 May 1776, Georgetown, ME; d. 20 Feb 1819, Georgetown, ME.
408.	iii.	NICHOLAS SPINNEY, b. 28 Jan 1778, Georgetown, ME; d. 1856.
	iv.	MARY SPINNEY, b. 26 May 1780, Georgetown, Lincoln, Maine, USA; d. 17 Sep 1840, Georgetown, Maine, USA.
409.	v.	HANNAH SPINNEY, b. 10 Jun 1782.
	vi.	EUNICE SPINNEY, b. 18 Apr 1784, Boothbay, Lincoln, Maine, USA; d. 01 Aug 1810.
410.	vii.	RICHARD SPINNEY, b. 04 Sep 1786, Georgetown, ME; d. Bet. 1860 - 1870.
411.	viii.	JEREMIAH SPINNEY, b. 02 Oct 1788, Georgetown, ME; d. Bef. 1840.
412.	ix.	CALEB SPINNEY, b. 20 Apr 1791, Phippsburg, Lincoln, Maine, USA; d. Aft. 1870.
413.	x.	DAVID SPINNEY, b. 17 Mar 1793, Georgetown, ME; d. Aft. 1860.
414.	xi.	EPHRAIM SPINNEY, b. 01 Nov 1794; d. 18 Jun 1886.
415.	xii.	JANE SPINNEY, b. 30 Nov 1795, Phippsburg, ME; d. 1884.
	xiii.	TIMOTHY SPINNEY, b. 26 Oct 1798, Phippsburg, ME; d. 27 Feb 1820.
	xiv.	SUSANNA SPINNEY, b. 30 Apr 1801, Phippsburg, ME; d. Aft. 1850.

152. JANE[5] SPINNEY *(JOHN[4], ANDREW[3], JOHN[2], THOMAS[1])* was born 1757 in Georgetown, ME, and died 18 Aug

1846 in Starks, ME. She married JAMES BEALE OLIVER 12 Jan 1789 in Maine. He was born 02 Apr 1757 in Phippsburg, ME, and died 20 Apr 1846 in Starks, ME.

Notes for JAMES BEALE OLIVER:
The National Society of the Daughters of the American Revolution Volume 110
page 251

Mrs. Sarah R. Oliver Merry.
DAR ID Number: 109809
Born in New Sharon, Me.
Wife of Charles E. Merry.
Descendant of James B. Oliver, as follows:
1. Eli Noyse Oliver (1836-1912) m. 1856 Diantha H. Nichols (1832-1913).
2. John C. Oliver (1796-1870) m. Huldah Robinson (1804-65).
3. James B. Oliver m. Jane Spinney (1769-1846).
James B. Oliver (1757-1846) served as private in Capt. Jordan Parker's company, Col. Samuel Parker's Massachusetts regiment. He was born in Georgetown; died in Starks, Me.

Children of JANE SPINNEY and JAMES OLIVER are:
416.   i.   ANNA⁶ OLIVER, b. 1789; d. Aft. 1850.
417.   ii.   JOHN C OLIVER, b. 1796; d. 1870.
418.   iii.   RACHEL OLIVER, b. 05 Oct 1802, Georgetown, ME; d. 30 May 1854, Industry, ME.

153. JEREMIAH⁵ SPINNEY *(JOHN⁴, ANDREW³, JOHN², THOMAS¹)* was born 02 Sep 1759 in Georgetown, ME, and died 20 Jun 1850. He married ABIGAIL BARSTOW 01 Nov 1787 in Sagadahoc Maine. She was born Abt. 1764, and died 20 Dec 1840.

Notes for JEREMIAH SPINNEY:
Massachusetts Soldiers and Sailors in the War of the Revolution, 17 Vols.

Volume 14
page 730
Spinney, Jeremiah. Marine, sloop "Defence," commanded by Capt. James Nivens; engaged Aug. 2, 1781; discharged Sept. 26, 1781; service, 1 mo. 24 days. Roll dated Boston.

Children of JEREMIAH SPINNEY and ABIGAIL BARSTOW are:
            i.   ELIZA⁶ SPINNEY, b. 01 Nov 1787; d. Aft. 1850.
419.   ii.   GEORGE B SPINNEY, b. 18 May 1789, Georgetown, ME; d. 09 Oct 1874, Phippsburg, ME.
420.   iii.   SOPHIA SPINNEY, b. 26 Aug 1791, Georgetown, ME; d. 1860.
421.   iv.   MOSES B SPINNEY, b. 10 Feb 1793, Georgetown, ME; d. Aft. 1880, Georgetown, ME.
422.   v.   JERUSHA SPINNEY, b. 23 Sep 1797, Georgetown, ME; d. 01 May 1879.
423.   vi.   MARY SPINNEY, b. 28 Feb 1800; d. 25 Jun 1870, Georgetown, ME.
424.   vii.   JOHN SPINNEY, b. 17 Sep 1802; d. Aft. 1860.
            viii.   DANIEL H SPINNEY, b. 04 Feb 1804, Georgetown, ME; d. 03 Nov 1829, At Sea.
            ix.   BENJAMIN O SPINNEY, b. 16 Oct 1809, Georgetown, ME; d. 1869; m. JANE OLIVER, 02 Jan 1845, Georgetown, ME; b. 14 Jun 1794, Georgetown, ME; d. 1868.
425.   x.   JEREMIAH SPINNEY, b. 25 Feb 1814, Georgetown, ME; d. Aft. 1880, Penn.

154. JOANNA⁵ SPINNEY *(JOHN⁴, ANDREW³, JOHN², THOMAS¹)* was born 07 Jun 1764 in Georgetown, ME, and died 11 Apr 1849. She married JOTHAM TRAFTON 1784, son of BENJAMIN TRAFTON and EUNICE FISHER. He was born 28 Aug 1760, and died 20 Jan 1857.

Children of JOANNA SPINNEY and JOTHAM TRAFTON are:
426.   i.   LYDIA⁶ TRAFTON, b. 09 Mar 1786.
427.   ii.   KEZIAH TRAFTON, b. 02 Apr 1794.
428.   iii.   JOTHAM TRAFTON, b. 18 May 1801; d. Aft. 1850.
429.   iv.   THOMAS TRAFTON.

155. RICHARD[5] SPINNEY *(JOHN[4], ANDREW[3], JOHN[2], THOMAS[1])* was born 27 May 1766 in Georgetown, ME, and died 19 Jul 1805 in Georgetown, ME. He married MARY BURGESS 29 Jul 1794. She was born Abt. 1790 in Maine, and died Bef. 1850 in Ohio.

Child of RICHARD SPINNEY and MARY BURGESS is:
430.   i.   RICHARD[6] SPINNEY, b. 1798; d. Aft. 1830, Ohio.

156. EUNICE[5] SPINNEY *(JOHN[4], ANDREW[3], JOHN[2], THOMAS[1])* was born 23 Aug 1768. She married EZEKIEL HINCKLEY. He was born 14 Jun 1770.

Children of EUNICE SPINNEY and EZEKIEL HINCKLEY are:
           i.   JOHN[6] HINCKLEY, b. 02 May 1794.
          ii.   HANNAH HINCKLEY, b. 10 May 1796; m. (1) BENJAMIN ATHEARN; m. (2) JOEL MACKINNEY.
431.   iii.   SARAH HINCKLEY, b. 1799.

157. NANCY ANN[5] LIBBEY *(ANNE[4] SPINNEY, ANDREW[3], JOHN[2], THOMAS[1])* was born 1776 in Kittery, York, Maine, USA. She married ANDREW SPINNEY 03 Jan 1805, son of WILLIAM SPINNEY and MARY LIBBEY. He was born 1775 in Kittery, ME, and died Bet. 1840 - 1850.

Child is listed above under (145) Andrew Spinney.

Generation No. 6

158. JANE[6] REMICK *(ANN[5] FERNALD, NATHANIEL[4], NATHANIEL[3], HANNAH[2] SPINNEY, THOMAS[1])* was born 1784, and died 14 Dec 1870. She married SAMUEL SHAPLEIGH 1806, son of SAMUEL SHAPLEIGH and ELIZABETH YEATON. He was born 1784, and died 26 Jun 1858.

Children of JANE REMICK and SAMUEL SHAPLEIGH are:
432.   i.   ALEXANDER[7] SHAPLEIGH, b. 10 Apr 1807.
          ii.   JANE SHAPLEIGH, b. 01 May 1809; d. 10 Sep 1835.

159. NATHANIEL[6] FERNALD *(TIMOTHY[5], NATHANIEL[4], NATHANIEL[3], HANNAH[2] SPINNEY, THOMAS[1])* He married HANNAH SPINNEY 29 Oct 1791 in Kittery Maine, daughter of EBENEZER SPINNEY and PHEBE COLE. She was born 05 Apr 1767, and died 13 Jan 1835.

Children are listed above under (86) Hannah Spinney.

160. MOSES[6] WORCESTER, JR. *(MOSES[5], ANNE[4] SPINNEY, JOHN[3], SAMUEL[2], THOMAS[1])* was born 1762 in Columbia, ME, and died 13 Oct 1855 in Columbia, ME. He married HANNAH LEIGHTON 1791.

Child of MOSES WORCESTER and HANNAH LEIGHTON is:
433.   i.   MOSES[7] WORCESTER III, b. 11 Aug 1810; d. 10 Feb 1879, Columbia, Me..

161. ISAAC[6] WORCESTER *(MOSES[5], ANNE[4] SPINNEY, JOHN[3], SAMUEL[2], THOMAS[1])* was born 1784 in Columbia, Me. He married LYDIA TUCKER, daughter of SAMUAL TUCKER and ESTHER.

Child of ISAAC WORCESTER and LYDIA TUCKER is:
434.   i.   MARK[7] WORCESTER, b. 17 Mar 1816, Columbia, ME; d. 26 Oct 1902, Springfield, ME.

162. JOHN[6] UPTON *(REBECCA[5] SPINNEY, JOHN[4], THOMAS[3], SAMUEL[2], THOMAS[1])* was born 16 May 1767 in Maugerville, NB., and died 1831. He married REBECCA SMITH Abt. 1790.

Children of JOHN UPTON and REBECCA SMITH are:
           i.   CHILD[7] UPTON.
          ii.   CHILD UPTON.

iii. CHILD UPTON.

163. SAMUEL[6] UPTON *(REBECCA[5] SPINNEY, JOHN[4], THOMAS[3], SAMUEL[2], THOMAS[1])* was born 08 Dec 1770 in Maugerville, NB., and died 14 Aug 1834 in Sheffield, NB.. He married BETSY BRAWN ESTEY 07 Oct 1790 in Gagetown, NB.. She was born 11 Nov 1772 in Maugerville, NB..

Children of SAMUEL UPTON and BETSY ESTEY are:

         i. SAMUEL[7] UPTON, b. 1792; d. 19 Feb 1885, Lakeville Corner, New Brunswick.

435.   ii. ASA UPTON, b. 1797, Canning Parish, Newcastle, NB.; d. Dec 1870, Newcastle Bridge, NB..

        iii. MARY S. UPTON, b. 1804.

        iv. RUTH UPTON, b. 1809.

164. HARRIOT[6] SPINNEY *(ROBERT[5], JOHN[4], THOMAS[3], SAMUEL[2], THOMAS[1])* was born 26 Nov 1797, and died Aft. 1870. She married JAMES D ABORN 21 Nov 1829 in Lynnfield, MA.

Child of HARRIOT SPINNEY and JAMES ABORN is:

        i. JOHN[7] ABORN, b. 1829.

165. CHARLES[6] SPINNEY *(ROBERT[5], JOHN[4], THOMAS[3], SAMUEL[2], THOMAS[1])* was born 13 Mar 1800 in Keene NH, and died Aft. 1855. He married ELIZA NEWHALL. She was born 1811, and died Aft. 1855.

Children of CHARLES SPINNEY and ELIZA NEWHALL are:

        i. MARY JANE[7] SPINNEY, b. 11 Jan 1833, Lynnfield, MA; d. 11 Sep 1835, Lynnfield, MA.

        ii. CHARLES HENRY SPINNEY, b. 25 Aug 1836; d. 08 Apr 1860, Lynnfield, MA.

        iii. EDWARD HORACE SPINNEY, b. 18 May 1842, Lynnfield, MA; d. 04 Nov 1929, Lynnfield, MA; m. LOUISE MANSFIELD, 1879; b. Jul 1835.

166. MARY[6] SPINNEY *(ROBERT[5], JOHN[4], THOMAS[3], SAMUEL[2], THOMAS[1])* was born 01 Mar 1802 in Keene NH, and died Bet. 1860 - 1870 in Lynnfield, MA. She married EBENEZER ABORN 19 Dec 1821 in Lynnfield, MA. He was born 1789, and died Aft. 1870 in Lynnfield, MA.

Children of MARY SPINNEY and EBENEZER ABORN are:

        i. MARY SILVER[7] ABORN, b. 14 Sep 1827; m. JOSEPH MOULTON.

        ii. JOSEPH HENRY ABORN, b. 07 May 1825, Lynnfield, MA; d. 21 May 1825, Lynnfield, MA.

        iii. JANE ELIZABETH ABORN, b. 14 Oct 1822, Lynnfield, MA.

167. ELIOT[6] SPINNEY *(ROBERT[5], JOHN[4], THOMAS[3], SAMUEL[2], THOMAS[1])* was born 12 Jun 1804 in Keene NH, and died 16 May 1848. He married SALLY B TWISS 01 Oct 1829, daughter of EBENEZER TWISS and ELIZABETH DUNKLE. She was born Abt. 1805.

Children of ELIOT SPINNEY and SALLY TWISS are:

436.   i. ELIOT F[7] SPINNEY, b. 27 Feb 1829.

        ii. JANE NEWHALL SPINNEY, b. 03 May 1837; d. 1878, Lynn, MA.

168. FRANCIS[6] SPINNEY *(ROBERT[5], JOHN[4], THOMAS[3], SAMUEL[2], THOMAS[1])* was born 19 Jul 1806 in Cheshire, NH, and died 29 Mar 1869 in Lynnfield. He married MARY PAGE 24 Sep 1838 in Lynnfield, MA. She was born 1813, and died Aft. 1870.

Children of FRANCIS SPINNEY and MARY PAGE are:

        i. HARRIET W[7] SPINNEY, b. 1840; d. Aft. 1870.

        ii. MARY F SPINNEY, b. 1842; m. ELBRIDGE MANSFIELD, 1862.

169. JOHN[6] SPINNEY *(BENJAMIN[5], JOHN[4], THOMAS[3], SAMUEL[2], THOMAS[1])* was born 07 May 1798, and died 1877. He married (1) BETSEY WILBOUR 04 Sep 1819 in Taunton. She was born 1798, and died 24 Oct 1848 in Lynn, MA. He married (2) ANTONIETTE WITT 17 Jan 1849, daughter of THOMAS WITT and ELIZABETH. She was born

1809, and died 1866 in Lynn, MA. He married (3) SALLY B TWISS 29 Apr 1869 in Lynnfield, Ma, daughter of EBENEZER TWISS and ELIZABETH DUNKLE. She was born Abt. 1805.

Children of JOHN SPINNEY and BETSEY WILBOUR are:
-     i. JOHN B[7] SPINNEY, b. 1825, Lynn, MA; d. 1893, Lynn, MA; m. SUSAN P FRYE, 05 Sep 1847; b. 1822; d. 1885, Woburn, MA.
- 437. ii. GEORGE SPINNEY, b. 1827, Lynn, MA; d. 1906, Lynn, MA.
-    iii. ELIZABETH SPINNEY, b. 1829, Lynn, MA; d. 20 Feb 1849, Lynn, MA.
-    iv. FRANCES A SPINNEY, b. 1829, Lynn, MA; d. Aft. 1870.
- 438. v. CHARLES EDWIN SPINNEY, b. 21 May 1831, Lynn, MA; d. Bef. 1900, Milwaukee, WI.
-    vi. JAMES A SPINNEY, b. 1834, Lynn, MA; d. Aft. 1860, Ohio.
- 439. vii. MARY SPINNEY, b. 1840, Lynn, MA; d. 1891, Lynn, MA.
-   viii. HENRY WILLIAM SPINNEY, b. 13 Jan 1842, Lynn, MA; d. 23 Aug 1844, Lynn, MA.

170. SUSAN[6] SPINNEY (*BENJAMIN[5], JOHN[4], THOMAS[3], SAMUEL[2], THOMAS[1]*) was born 20 Mar 1800 in Taunton, MA. She married SYLVESTER BURT 17 Mar 1825 in Taunton, Ma. He was born 30 Nov 1794 in Taunton, MA, and died 30 Nov 1794 in Taunton, MA.

Child of SUSAN SPINNEY and SYLVESTER BURT is:
-     i. ISAAC ERASTUS[7] BURT, b. 27 Jul 1843.

171. WILLIAM NEWHALL[6] SPINNEY (*BENJAMIN[5], JOHN[4], THOMAS[3], SAMUEL[2], THOMAS[1]*) was born 25 Sep 1802 in Taunton, MA, and died 07 Feb 1885 in Taunton MA. He married (1) ADELINE WILLIAMS 23 Apr 1827 in Wrentham, MA. She was born 1804 in Briston MA, and died 24 May 1838 in Taunton, ME. He married (2) CHARLOTTE MELINDA HACK 15 Sep 1839 in Taunton, MA, daughter of NATHAN HACK and OLIVE CROSSMAN.

Children of WILLIAM SPINNEY and ADELINE WILLIAMS are:
- 440. i. WILLIAM FRANCIS[7] SPINNEY, b. 08 Mar 1828, Lynn, Ma; d. Aft. 1910, Reading, MA.
-    ii. ADELINE W. SPINNEY, b. 1831, Lynn, MA; m. OREN SIKES, 1857, Lynn, Ma.
- 441. iii. GUSTAVUS NEWHALL SPINNEY, b. 13 Jun 1833, Lynn, MA; d. 10 Feb 1913, Indianapolis, IN.
-    iv. JULIA DODD SPINNEY, b. 1838, Lynn, MA; d. 23 Mar 1888; m. JOHN HOWARD RAND, 19 Apr 1866.

Children of WILLIAM SPINNEY and CHARLOTTE HACK are:
- 442. v. ZEPHADIAH HACK[7] SPINNEY, b. 21 May 1842, Lynn, MA; d. 1908, Lynn, MA.
-    vi. ELLERY CHANNING SPINNEY, b. 11 Jul 1844, Lynn MA; d. 1848, Lynn MA.
-    vii. CHARLOTTE OLIVE SPINNEY, b. 26 Jul 1847, Lynn, MA.
- 443. viii. ELLERY CHANNING SPINNEY, b. 06 Feb 1850, Lynn, MA; d. 19 Jul 1894, Chicago, IL.
-    ix. CAROLINE HACK SPINNEY, b. 31 Jan 1852, Lynn, MA.

172. BENJAMIN[6] SPINNEY (*BENJAMIN[5], JOHN[4], THOMAS[3], SAMUEL[2], THOMAS[1]*) was born 30 Mar 1805 in Taunton, MA, and died 23 Oct 1888. He married MARY BEEBE SEAVER 26 Sep 1829 in Taunton, MA, daughter of MARY. She was born 1806.

Children of BENJAMIN SPINNEY and MARY SEAVER are:
-     i. BENJAMIN F[7] SPINNEY, b. Nov 1830; d. 06 Oct 1831.
- 444. ii. BENJAMIN FRANKLIN SPINNEY, b. 01 Sep 1832, Taunton, MA; d. 21 Jun 1928, Lynn, MA.
-    iii. LEONARD N SPINNEY, b. 18 Nov 1836, Taunton MA; d. 03 Sep 1837, Taunton MA.

173. CHARLES EDWIN[6] SPINNEY (*BENJAMIN[5], JOHN[4], THOMAS[3], SAMUEL[2], THOMAS[1]*) was born 07 Sep 1818 in Taunton, MA, and died 1868 in Lynn, MA. He married REBECCA BURILL 17 Apr 1845. She was born 1824, and died Aft. 1880.

Children of CHARLES SPINNEY and REBECCA BURILL are:
-     i. EDWIN M[7] SPINNEY, b. 1846; d. 26 May 1849, Lynn, MA.
- 445. ii. BRADFORD HENRY SPINNEY, b. 12 Apr 1849, Lynn, Ma; d. 1885.
- 446. iii. FRED L SPINNEY, b. 1852, Lynn, MA; d. Aft. 1880.
-    iv. ISABELLA M SPINNEY, b. 1855.
- 447. v. MARY BURILL SPINNEY, b. 1855.

      vi.   MARTHA L SPINNEY, b. 1859.
     vii.   EMMA MARIA SPINNEY, b. 1861, Lynn, Ma; d. 1863, Lynn, Ma.
    viii.   ANN ELIZA SPINNEY, b. 1862; d. 1862.

174. ELIZABETH GRACE⁶ SPINNEY *(BENJAMIN⁵, JOHN⁴, THOMAS³, SAMUEL², THOMAS¹)* was born 1820, and died 1903. She married DAVID S THRASHER 20 Jan 1841 in Taunton, MA. He was born 31 Jul 1819 in Lynn, MA, and died Aft. 1880 in Lynn, MA.

Children of ELIZABETH SPINNEY and DAVID THRASHER are:
       i.   ELIZABETH⁷ THRASHER, b. 22 Dec 1842.
      ii.   ELLA F THRASHER, b. 17 Mar 1845.
     iii.   HELEN THRASHER, b. 1848.
     iv.   ANNA THRASHER, b. 1857.
      v.   KATIE MARY THRASHER, b. 1859.

175. MARY M⁶ SPINNEY *(THOMAS⁵, JOHN⁴, THOMAS³, SAMUEL², THOMAS¹)* was born 1799, and died 1875 in Lynn, Ma. She married WILLIAM SENTER 05 May 1827 in Salem, MA, son of EDWARD SENTER and RUTH REED. He was born 1795 in New Hampshire, and died 05 Feb 1875 in Lynn, Ma.

Children of MARY SPINNEY and WILLIAM SENTER are:
       i.   EMELINE⁷ SENTER, b. 1833.
      ii.   JOSEPH SENTER, b. 1837.
     iii.   WILLIAM CORNEILOUS SENTER, b. 20 May 1838, Lynn, Ma; d. 1895.
448.   iv.   GEORGE LEONARD SENTER, b. 22 Apr 1839, Lynn, Ma; d. Aft. 1880, Penn.
      v.   WILLIAM E SENTER, b. 1853.
     vi.   NELLIE SENTER, b. 1855.
     vii.   CHARLES W SENTER, b. 1857.
    viii.   LIZZIE SENTER, b. 1858.

176. GRACE⁶ SPINNEY *(THOMAS⁵, JOHN⁴, THOMAS³, SAMUEL², THOMAS¹)* was born 27 Sep 1805 in Lynn, MA, and died in Alabama. She married WILLIAM HENRY BANCROFT. He was born 1804, and died Aft. 1850 in Alabama.

Children of GRACE SPINNEY and WILLIAM BANCROFT are:
       i.   ELVIRA⁷ BANCROFT.
      ii.   WILLIAM BANCROFT.
449.   iii.   SARAH ELIZABETH BANCROFT, b. 27 Jun 1826.
     iv.   MATILDA BANCROFT, b. 1841.

177. THOMAS⁶ SPINNEY *(THOMAS⁵, JOHN⁴, THOMAS³, SAMUEL², THOMAS¹)* was born 01 Sep 1808 in Lynn, MA, and died Bet. 1870 - 1880. He married SUSAN L NEWHALL 1832 in Lynn, MA, daughter of JOSEPH NEWHALL and POLLY SPINNEY. She was born 30 Nov 1804, and died Aft. 1880.

Children of THOMAS SPINNEY and SUSAN NEWHALL are:
450.   i.   GEORGE F⁷ SPINNEY, b. Feb 1834, Maine; d. Aft. 1900, Swampscott, MA.
451.   ii.   EDWARD HERBERT SPINNEY, b. 1838; d. Aft. 1880.

178. HANNAH⁶ SPINNEY *(THOMAS⁵, JOHN⁴, THOMAS³, SAMUEL², THOMAS¹)* was born 16 Jun 1803 in Lynn, MA, and died 1863 in Lynn, MA. She married BENJAMIN COATES 11 Apr 1833 in Lynn, MA. He died Bef. 1850.

Children of HANNAH SPINNEY and BENJAMIN COATES are:
       i.   BENJAMIN⁷ COATES, b. 1835.
452.   ii.   PHILLIP COATES, b. 1845.

179. JOHN WARREN⁶ SPINNEY *(SAMUEL⁵, JOHN⁴, THOMAS³, SAMUEL², THOMAS¹)* was born 06 Apr 1803 in Taunton, MA, and died 1888 in Lynn, MA. He married LYDIA ANNIS 17 Dec 1826 in Lynn Mass. She was born 1807.

Children of JOHN SPINNEY and LYDIA ANNIS are:
453.   i.   SAMUEL[7] SPINNEY, b. 21 Oct 1827, Lynn, MA; d. 08 Apr 1881.
454.   ii.   JOHN WARREN SPINNEY, b. 20 Mar 1830, Lynn, MA; d. Aft. 1910, Medford, Ma.
455.   iii.   WILLIAM HENRY SPINNEY, b. 31 Dec 1831, Lynn, MA; d. 04 Apr 1911, Lynn, Ma.
456.   iv.   CHARLES HERBERT SPINNEY, b. 26 Feb 1834, Lynn, MA; d. 11 Jun 1912, Lynn, MA.
      v.   JOSEPH S SPINNEY, b. Abt. 1835, Lynn, MA; d. Bef. 1850.
457.   vi.   LYDIA MARIA SPINNEY, b. 21 Sep 1836, Lynn, MA; d. 07 Jan 1912.
458.   vii.   MARY E SPINNEY, b. 1841, Lynn, MA; d. 31 Jul 1905, Lynn, MA.

180. JOHN FRANCIS[6] SPINNEY *(FRANCIS[5], JOHN[4], THOMAS[3], SAMUEL[2], THOMAS[1])* was born 02 May 1825 in Lynn, MA, and died 1898 in Clinton, Ma. He married ELIZABETH MARIA BEAMAN 02 May 1853 in Lunenburg, MA, daughter of WORTHY BEAMAN and BETSEY. She was born 1832.

Children of JOHN SPINNEY and ELIZABETH BEAMAN are:
      i.   MARY SUSAN[7] SPINNEY, b. 1855, Lunenburg, Ma.
      ii.   WILLIE FRANCIS SPINNEY, b. Jun 1859, Shirley, MA; d. 16 Jul 1859.
      iii.   SARAH REBECCA SPINNEY, b. 1863; m. PATRICK MCGRAIL, 1890, Clinton, MA.
      iv.   NELLIE F SPINNEY, b. 1864.
      v.   FREDERICK N SPINNEY, b. 1868; d. Aft. 1920.
      vi.   LEONA E SPINNEY, b. 1870; d. 1870.
      vii.   DAZIE SPINNEY, b. Oct 1874.
459.   viii.   PAUL ARTHUR SPINNEY, b. 1881, Shirley, MA.

181. CALEB[6] SPINNEY *(CALEB[5], NICHOLAS[4], JAMES[3], SAMUEL[2], THOMAS[1])* was born 1782 in Kittery, ME, and died 22 Oct 1827. He married SALLY SCRIGGINS 19 Feb 1806 in Kittery Maine. She was born Abt. 1785, and died Aft. 1860.

Children of CALEB SPINNEY and SALLY SCRIGGINS are:
      i.   ELIZABETH[7] SPINNEY, b. 1807; d. 05 Aug 1852; m. WILLIAM JOHNSON; b. 1799, Kittery, ME.
      ii.   DAUGHTER SPINNEY, b. Bet. 1800 - 1830; m. DWYER.
      iii.   SON SPINNEY, b. 1815.
460.   iv.   SALLY ANN SPINNEY, b. 1807; d. 18 Jun 1892.
461.   v.   MARY JANE SPINNEY, b. 1804, Kittery, ME; d. Bet. 1860 - 1870, Portsmouth, NH.

182. MARGERY[6] SPINNEY *(CALEB[5], NICHOLAS[4], JAMES[3], SAMUEL[2], THOMAS[1])* was born 13 Apr 1784, and died 02 May 1868. She married JOHN JAMES. He was born 04 Feb 1773.

Children of MARGERY SPINNEY and JOHN JAMES are:
      i.   MARGERY[7] JAMES.
      ii.   ELIZABETH JAMES.
462.   iii.   CIDNEY JAMES, b. 1811; d. 1895.
      iv.   ABBY JAMES, m. LINDSEY.

183. NICHOLAS[6] SPINNEY *(CALEB[5], NICHOLAS[4], JAMES[3], SAMUEL[2], THOMAS[1])* was born 1788 in Kittery, ME, and died 1866. He married PATIENCE COLE 22 Feb 1815, daughter of JOHN COLE. She was born 1788, and died 1871.

Children of NICHOLAS SPINNEY and PATIENCE COLE are:
463.   i.   CALEB S[7] SPINNEY, b. 19 Feb 1815, Kittery, ME; d. 16 Feb 1879.
464.   ii.   EMILY D SPINNEY, b. 29 Sep 1816, Kittery, ME.
      iii.   ABIGAIL M SPINNEY, b. 1820, Kittery, ME; m. WILLIAM W DAME, 20 Jul 1845, Kittery Maine; b. 11 Feb 1815.
      iv.   EPHRAIM C SPINNEY, b. 14 Dec 1821; d. 07 Jul 1898; m. MARY PAUL, 13 Jun 1872, Kittery Maine; b. 26 Apr 1835; d. 02 May 1903.
      v.   ELLEN C SPINNEY, b. 1823; d. 1841.
      vi.   GEORGE SPINNEY, b. 1823, Kittery, ME.
465.   vii.   ROWENA R SPINNEY, b. 14 Jul 1828, Berwick, ME.
      viii.   ALICE P SPINNEY, b. Mar 1831, Kittery, ME; d. 1905.

184. JOSIAH[6] SPINNEY *(CALEB[5], NICHOLAS[4], JAMES[3], SAMUEL[2], THOMAS[1])* was born 1790, and died 11 Aug 1843 in Kittery Maine. He married CLARISSA KNIGHT 13 Jun 1826. She was born 1802, and died 11 Aug 1839 in Kittery Maine.

Children of JOSIAH SPINNEY and CLARISSA KNIGHT are:
| 466. | i. | DANIEL PARKER[7] SPINNEY, b. 21 Jan 1827, Kittery, ME; d. 04 Oct 1905, Kittery, ME. |
| | ii. | ROWENA SPINNEY, b. 1828; d. 14 Jan 1832, Kittery Maine. |

185. NATHAN[6] SPINNEY *(JOHN[5], NICHOLAS[4], JAMES[3], SAMUEL[2], THOMAS[1])* was born 1792 in Kittery, ME, and died 23 Apr 1881 in Kittery, ME. He married NANCY K SPINNEY 06 Dec 1821. She was born 1802, and died 03 Sep 1883.

Children of NATHAN SPINNEY and NANCY SPINNEY are:
467.	i.	ROBERT[7] SPINNEY, b. Oct 1823, Eliot, ME; d. 05 Apr 1904.
	ii.	TOBIAS SPINNEY, b. 1828.
468.	iii.	NATHAN SPINNEY, b. 1830; d. Aft. 1880.
	iv.	BENJAMIN SPINNEY, b. 1834; d. 05 Aug 1857, Kittery.
469.	v.	JOHN P SPINNEY, b. May 1835, Maine; d. Aft. 1920, Raynham, MA.
	vi.	JULIA F SPINNEY, b. 1836; d. 19 Jun 1858, Kittery.
470.	vii.	EMILY ANN SPINNEY, b. 15 May 1839; d. 20 Mar 1894.
471.	viii.	ALMIRA SPINNEY, b. 18 Aug 1841; d. 17 Sep 1920.
	ix.	ALVIN H SPINNEY, b. Feb 1844; d. 09 Apr 1844, Kittery.
472.	x.	ANNETTE H SPINNEY, b. 18 Nov 1845.

186. ISIAIH[6] MARR *(JOHN[5], RUTH[4] SPINNEY, JEREMIAH[3], SAMUEL[2], THOMAS[1])* was born 02 Jun 1782. He married (1) HANNAH SPINNEY 23 Jun 1803, daughter of JOHN SPINNEY and EUNICE HUTCHINGS. She was born 10 Jun 1782. He married (2) MARY MERCY OLIVER 16 May 1808. She was born 11 Feb 1787, and died 02 Jan 1850.

Child of ISIAIH MARR and HANNAH SPINNEY is:
| | i. | ISAIAH[7] MARR, b. 04 Jul 1804. |

Children of ISIAIH MARR and MARY OLIVER are:
	ii.	HANNAH[7] MARR.
	iii.	MARY MARR.
	iv.	PARKER MARR.
	v.	ELIZABETH ANN MARR.
	vi.	ELSIE MARR.
	vii.	IRENE MARR.

187. DENNIS[6] MARR *(JOHN[5], RUTH[4] SPINNEY, JEREMIAH[3], SAMUEL[2], THOMAS[1])* was born 03 May 1786 in Georgetown, ME, and died 05 Apr 1849. He married (1) REBECCA OLIVER 24 Dec 1807. She died 20 Sep 1808. He married (2) LUCY ALEXANDER 18 Jan 1811. She died 22 Dec 1836.

Children of DENNIS MARR and LUCY ALEXANDER are:
	i.	NANCY[7] MARR.
	ii.	HIRAM MARR.
	iii.	REBECCA MARR.
	iv.	CHARLES MARR.
	v.	CATHERINE MARR.
	vi.	CATHERINE MARR.

188. ALEXANDER[6] MARR *(JOHN[5], RUTH[4] SPINNEY, JEREMIAH[3], SAMUEL[2], THOMAS[1])* was born 11 May 1794. He married KEZIAH TRAFTON 08 Jul 1815, daughter of JOTHAM TRAFTON and JOANNA SPINNEY. She was born 02 Apr 1794.

Children of ALEXANDER MARR and KEZIAH TRAFTON are:
| | i. | ZACHEUS TRAFTON[7] MARR. |
| | ii. | JOSIAH MARR. |

     iii.   MARY ANN MARR.
     iv.   BAXTER MARR.
     v.   EVELINE MARR.
     vi.   KEZIAH MARR.

189. RICHARD[6] MARR *(JOHN[5], RUTH[4] SPINNEY, JEREMIAH[3], SAMUEL[2], THOMAS[1])* was born 1792, and died 1852. He married SOPHIA SPINNEY 01 Nov 1818 in Georgetown Maine, daughter of JEREMIAH SPINNEY and ABIGAIL BARSTOW. She was born 26 Aug 1791 in Georgetown, ME, and died 1860.

Children of RICHARD MARR and SOPHIA SPINNEY are:
     i.   DEIDAMA[7] MARR, b. 14 Apr 1819.
     ii.   JESHUA MARR, b. 27 Sep 1820.
     iii.   HARRIETT MARR, b. 23 Jan 1822.
     iv.   ABIGAIL S MARR, b. 25 Jun 1824.
     v.   NANCY MARR, b. 10 Oct 1829.

190. THOMAS[6] MARR *(JOHN[5], RUTH[4] SPINNEY, JEREMIAH[3], SAMUEL[2], THOMAS[1])* was born 01 Apr 1784 in Marr's Island, ME, and died 17 Dec 1866. He married (1) EUNICE SPINNEY 1806, daughter of JOHN SPINNEY and EUNICE HUTCHINS. She was born 18 Apr 1784 in Boothbay, Lincoln, Maine, USA, and died 1810. He married (2) LYDIA TRAFTON 1811, daughter of JOTHAM TRAFTON and JOANNA SPINNEY. She was born 09 Mar 1786.

Children of THOMAS MARR and EUNICE SPINNEY are:
473.   i.   EUNICE[7] MARR, b. 16 Jun 1809, Boothbay, Lincoln, Maine, USA; d. Apr 1855.
     ii.   JOHN MARR, b. 1804; d. 1890.

Children of THOMAS MARR and LYDIA TRAFTON are:
     iii.   IRETTA[7] MARR.
     iv.   LYDIA MARR.
     v.   THOMAS MARR, b. 09 Jun 1827; d. 29 Sep 1870.
     vi.   MARY MARR.
     vii.   JOTHAM TRAFTON MARR.
     viii.   JERUEL MARR.
     ix.   LEMUEL MARR.
474.   x.   MIRANDA A MARR, b. 1835.

191. ANDREW[6] MC FADDEN *(SARAH[5] SPINNEY, JEREMIAH[4], JEREMIAH[3], SAMUEL[2], THOMAS[1])* was born 1805. He married ELIZABETH.

Children of ANDREW MC FADDEN and ELIZABETH are:
     i.   ELIZABETH[7] MC FADDEN.
     ii.   CAROLINE MC FADDEN.
     iii.   HARRIETT MC FADDEN.
     iv.   ABBA MC FADDEN.
     v.   AMELIA MC FADDEN.

192. JACOB[6] OLIVER *(MARY[5] SPINNEY, JEREMIAH[4], JEREMIAH[3], SAMUEL[2], THOMAS[1])* was born 30 Jan 1785 in Phippsburg, ME, and died 23 Jan 1870 in Phippsburg, ME. He married NAOMI GREENLAW 22 Jan 1808 in Phippsburg, ME.

Children of JACOB OLIVER and NAOMI GREENLAW are:
     i.   DORCAS[7] OLIVER.
     ii.   HENRY OLIVER.
     iii.   MARY JANE OLIVER.
     iv.   REBECCA OLIVER.
     v.   SARAH OLIVER.
     vi.   THOMAS OLIVER, b. 1810; d. 1868.
475.   vii.   EZEKIEL OLIVER, b. 1822; d. 1892.

193. JOHN[6] OLIVER *(MARY[5] SPINNEY, JEREMIAH[4], JEREMIAH[3], SAMUEL[2], THOMAS[1])* was born 10 Nov 1787, and died 05 Feb 1863. He married CATHERINE OLIVER 06 Jun 1811. She was born 01 Oct 1793, and died 01 Oct 1859.

Children of JOHN OLIVER and CATHERINE OLIVER are:
- i. CATHERINE[7] OLIVER, m. TIMOTHY WRIGHT, 15 Jul 1842.
- ii. LUCINDA OLIVER.
- iii. MARY A. OLIVER.
- iv. RACHEL OLIVER.
- v. OCTAVIA OLIVER.
- 476. vi. JOHN OLIVER, b. 04 Apr 1820, Phippsburg, ME; d. 02 Dec 1903, Bath, ME.
- vii. LORING C. OLIVER, b. 1827; m. MARIA; b. 1830.
- viii. FRANCIS OLIVER, b. 1838; d. 09 Aug 1862; m. EMMA HOWARD, 10 Apr 1860.

194. THOMAS[6] OLIVER *(MARY[5] SPINNEY, JEREMIAH[4], JEREMIAH[3], SAMUEL[2], THOMAS[1])* was born 16 Dec 1789, and died 19 Jan 1867. He married (1) ALICE. She was born in Boothbay, ME. He married (2) NANCY ROGERS 01 Jan 1818. She was born 09 Jan 1794 in Phippsburg, ME, and died 29 Oct 1847.

Child of THOMAS OLIVER and ALICE is:
- 477. i. JAMES H.[7] OLIVER, b. 1830; d. 17 Mar 1888, Phippsburg, ME.

Child of THOMAS OLIVER and NANCY ROGERS is:
- ii. CHARLES THOMAS[7] OLIVER, b. 23 Dec 1818.

195. SARAH[6] OLIVER *(MARY[5] SPINNEY, JEREMIAH[4], JEREMIAH[3], SAMUEL[2], THOMAS[1])* was born 08 Nov 1795. She married CHARLES OLIVER 01 Apr 1820. He was born 20 Sep 1800.

Children of SARAH OLIVER and CHARLES OLIVER are:
- i. CHARLES[7] OLIVER, b. 1823; d. 1827.
- ii. CAROLINE OLIVER, b. 1831; d. 1836.

196. JAMES[6] OLIVER *(MARY[5] SPINNEY, JEREMIAH[4], JEREMIAH[3], SAMUEL[2], THOMAS[1])* was born 16 Jan 1805. He married BETSY MCINTYRE.

Children of JAMES OLIVER and BETSY MCINTYRE are:
- 478. i. WILLIAM RAIRDEN[7] OLIVER, b. 06 Mar 1825, Phippsburg, ME; d. 01 Apr 1868, Bath, ME.
- ii. REBECCA PERRY OLIVER, b. 15 Nov 1826.
- iii. JAMES FRANCIS OLIVER, b. 24 Feb 1829.
- iv. TIMOTHY BATCHELDER OLIVER, b. 06 Mar 1831.
- v. GEORGE MCINTYRE OLIVER, b. 13 Apr 1833; d. 1834.
- vi. MARIA MEREEN OLIVER, b. 06 Aug 1835.
- vii. RACHEL SPRAGUE OLIVER, b. 21 Dec 1837.
- 479. viii. HARRISON PRIEST OLIVER, b. 31 May 1840, Phippsburg, ME; d. 25 Nov 1907, Portsmouth, ME.
- 480. ix. JOSIAH PERRY OLIVER, b. 02 Sep 1842, Phippsburg, ME; d. 20 Dec 1927, Bath, ME.
- x. LUCY A. OLIVER, b. 1847.

197. JOANNA[6] OLIVER *(ANNA[5] SPINNEY, JEREMIAH[4], JEREMIAH[3], SAMUEL[2], THOMAS[1])* was born 30 May 1780, and died 15 Feb 1843. She married JAMES WILLIAMS 12 Dec 1830.

Children of JOANNA OLIVER and JAMES WILLIAMS are:
- i. SARAH BUTLER[7] WILLIAMS, b. 02 Nov 1833.
- ii. NANCY WILLIAMS, b. 07 Dec 1836.
- iii. OLIVER WILLIAMS, b. 07 Dec 1836.
- iv. RUEL WILLIAMS, b. 28 Nov 1840.

198. RICHARD[6] OLIVER *(ANNA[5] SPINNEY, JEREMIAH[4], JEREMIAH[3], SAMUEL[2], THOMAS[1])* was born 1786, and died

1860. He married MARY OLIVER 07 Jul 1810. She was born 1793, and died 1874.

Child of RICHARD OLIVER and MARY OLIVER is:
481.   i.   JEREMIAH⁷ OLIVER, b. Oct 1810; d. 1869.

199. EPHRAIM⁶ OLIVER *(ANNA⁵ SPINNEY, JEREMIAH⁴, JEREMIAH³, SAMUEL², THOMAS¹)* was born 1797, and died 14 Dec 1890. He married JERUSHA SPINNEY 30 May 1822 in Georgetown, ME, daughter of JEREMIAH SPINNEY and ABIGAIL BARSTOW. She was born 23 Sep 1797 in Georgetown, ME, and died 01 May 1879.

Children of EPHRAIM OLIVER and JERUSHA SPINNEY are:
482.   i.   MARIA⁷ OLIVER, b. 28 Jan 1822.
       ii.   LORING OLIVER, b. 1823.
483.   iii. MATTHEW OLIVER, b. 05 May 1825, Georgetown, ME; d. 26 Mar 1898, Bath, ME.
      iv. TEMPERANCE OLIVER, b. 1827.
484.   v.   BENJAMIN S. OLIVER, b. 06 Oct 1829, Georgetown, ME; d. 15 Jan 1894, Bath, ME.
485.   vi. LEVI S. OLIVER, b. 1831.
     vii. HARRIETT OLIVER, b. 1834.
   viii. ABIGAIL OLIVER, b. 1836.
     ix. LOUISA OLIVER, b. 1838.
      x. ALVIN OLIVER, b. 1840.

200. JEREMIAH⁶ OLIVER *(ANNA⁵ SPINNEY, JEREMIAH⁴, JEREMIAH³, SAMUEL², THOMAS¹)* was born 1800, and died 1836. He married MARY SPINNEY. She was born 1800, and died 1859.

Children of JEREMIAH OLIVER and MARY SPINNEY are:
       i.   WARREN⁷ OLIVER, b. 14 Aug 1825.
      ii.   EUNICE OLIVER, b. 16 Feb 1827.
     iii. ISABELLA OLIVER, b. 08 May 1829.
     iv. MARY ELIZABETH. OLIVER, b. 02 Feb 1831.
      v. DANIEL WATERMAN OLIVER, b. 29 Sep 1833; m. MARY A. OLIVER, 08 Dec 1865; b. 1836; d. 1914.
486.   vi. JOHN OLIVER, b. 23 Apr 1835; d. 1908.

201. WILLIAM DENNETT⁶ FERNALD *(NATHANIEL⁶, TIMOTHY⁵, NATHANIEL⁴, NATHANIEL³, HANNAH² SPINNEY, THOMAS¹)* was born 04 Jan 1807 in Portsmouth, NH, and died 05 Dec 1893. He married MEHITABLE ORDOINE 18 Jan 1828. She was born 1807.

Notes for WILLIAM DENNETT FERNALD:
was born on 4 Jan 1807. He died on 5 Dec 1893 in of Portsmouth, Rockingham, New Hampshire. Was a spar maker (mast or boom of ships) at Portsmouth, NH. Had 7 children.

Children of WILLIAM FERNALD and MEHITABLE ORDOINE are:
       i.   GEORGE W⁷ FERNALD, b. 1828.
      ii.   ALBERT FERNALD, b. 1830.
     iii. NATHANIEL FERNALD, b. 1833.
     iv. WILLIAM H FERNALD, b. 1835.
      v. CHARLES W FERNALD, b. 1840.
     vi. FRANKLIN FERNALD, b. 1843.
    vii. ANN FERNALD, b. 1845.

202. BARTHSEHBA WEARE⁶ SPINNEY *(DAVID⁵, EBENEZER⁴, JONATHAN³, SAMUEL², THOMAS¹)* was born 31 May 1794 in Kittery, ME, and died 04 May 1878 in Milton, NH. She married JEREMIAH GOODWIN 11 Sep 1811. He was born 28 Nov 1784 in Kittery, ME, and died 21 Nov 1853 in Milton, NH.

Children of BARTHSEHBA SPINNEY and JEREMIAH GOODWIN are:
487.   i.   LYDIA PAUL⁷ GOODWIN, b. 30 Aug 1813; d. 17 Mar 1863.
      ii.   MARY GOODWIN, b. 27 Jun 1816; d. 09 Jul 1915; m. FRANKLIN GARLAND, 25 Nov 1841.
488.   iii. BATHASHEBA GOODWIN, b. 13 Sep 1820; d. 30 Nov 1889.
     iv. DAVID GOODWIN, b. 21 Apr 1823; d. 26 Jan 1899.
489.   v. PHOEBE GOODWIN, b. 26 Oct 1824, Milton, NH; d. 17 Feb 1902, Portsmouth, NH.

203. PARKER FOSTER[6] SPINNEY *(DAVID[5], EBENEZER[4], JONATHAN[3], SAMUEL[2], THOMAS[1])* was born 16 Aug 1803 in Kittery, ME, and died 01 Aug 1874 in Milton, NH. He married MARY DEARBORN 13 Oct 1825, daughter of NATHANIEL DEARBORN and MARY WHIDDEN. She was born 29 Jan 1805 in Milton. NH, and died 10 Feb 1856 in Kittery, ME.

Children of PARKER SPINNEY and MARY DEARBORN are:

490.	i.	ABIGAIL PAUL[7] SPINNEY, b. 03 Nov 1826, Wakefield, NH; d. 10 Apr 1913, Milton, NH.
491.	ii.	PAUL SPINNEY, b. 27 Jun 1828, Wakefield, NH; d. 1901, Ipswich, Ma.
	iii.	MARY E SPINNEY, b. 1829; d. Aft. 1850.
	iv.	MARY ELIZABETH SPINNEY, b. 23 Sep 1832; d. 08 Sep 1852, Somersworth Maine.
492.	v.	PARKER SPINNEY, b. 08 Mar 1833; d. 14 Dec 1920.
	vi.	MACK SPINNEY, b. 1835; d. 20 Nov 1874, Kittery Maine.
493.	vii.	NATHANIAL DEARBORN SPINNEY, b. 26 Jan 1835, Wakefield, NH; d. 07 Apr 1900.
494.	viii.	JOSEPH FRANKLIN SPINNEY, b. 13 Aug 1839, Rorchester, NH; d. 15 Nov 1902.
	ix.	LYDIA ELLEN SPINNEY, b. 15 Sep 1841; d. 28 Apr 1919; m. GEORGE W FELLOWS, 12 Dec 1867.

Notes for LYDIA ELLEN SPINNEY:

In the 1900 Census Lydia was living with her brother Joseph in Milton New Hampshire

| 495. | x. | WILLIAM RICE SPINNEY, b. 21 Aug 1851; d. 23 Sep 1919. |

204. ALVAH[6] SPINNEY *(DAVID[5], EBENEZER[4], JONATHAN[3], SAMUEL[2], THOMAS[1])* was born 17 Aug 1810 in Wakefield, NH, and died 03 Jul 1840 in Tampico Mexico. He married JOANNA TROMBLY 27 Oct 1823, daughter of TOBIAS TROMBLY and LOIS WENTWORTH. She was born 17 Jan 1811, and died 05 Feb 1895 in Wakefield, NH.

Child of ALVAH SPINNEY and JOANNA TROMBLY is:

| 496. | i. | JAMES T[7] SPINNEY, b. 10 Aug 1834, Somersworth, NH.; d. 14 Mar 1894. |

205. JOSEPH[6] SPINNEY *(DAVID[5], EBENEZER[4], JONATHAN[3], SAMUEL[2], THOMAS[1])* was born 11 Mar 1812 in Wakefield, NH, and died 21 Dec 1899 in Wakefield, NH. He married ELIZABETH SPINNEY 10 May 1840, daughter of CHARLES SPINNEY and ALICE RICE. She was born 08 Mar 1811, and died 30 Oct 1898.

Children of JOSEPH SPINNEY and ELIZABETH SPINNEY are:

	i.	MARY ELIZABETH[7] SPINNEY, b. 03 Aug 1844; d. 11 Feb 1850.
	ii.	ELIZA ANN SPINNEY, b. 11 May 1846; d. 29 Jan 1852.
	iii.	MARTHA ABBA SPINNEY, b. 17 Oct 1847; d. 22 Jan 1850.

206. ROWENA A[6] SPINNEY *(DAVID[5], EBENEZER[4], JONATHAN[3], SAMUEL[2], THOMAS[1])* was born 06 Mar 1817 in Wakefield, NH, and died 1863. She married JOSIAH GARLAND 26 Jan 1842, son of JOHN GARLAND and SALLY KIMBALL. He was born 21 Oct 1819, and died 12 Apr 1880.

Children of ROWENA SPINNEY and JOSIAH GARLAND are:

	i.	JERIMIAH[7] GARLAND, b. 20 Nov 1842; d. 05 Feb 1850.
	ii.	JOSEPH PAUL GARLAND, b. 29 Jan 1845; d. 15 Mar 1860.
	iii.	MARY ELLEN GARLAND, b. 25 Sep 1846; d. 10 Jul 1867.
497.	iv.	ALVAH SPINNEY GARLAND, b. 08 Jun 1849.

207. CHARLES P[6] SPINNEY *(CHARLES[5], EBENEZER[4], JONATHAN[3], SAMUEL[2], THOMAS[1])* was born 1807, and died Aft. 1880 in Lost at Sea. He married (1) HANNAH. She was born Feb 1820, and died Aft. 1900. He married (2) ANN RICE REMICK 09 Apr 1822 in Kittery, ME, daughter of WILLIAM REMICK and LUCY HAMMOND. She was born 29 Jun 1799, and died 23 Jul 1868.

Children of CHARLES SPINNEY and HANNAH are:

| 498. | i. | CHARLES H[7] SPINNEY, b. 1841, Eliot, ME; d. 1923. |
| | ii. | SAMUEL L SPINNEY, b. Mar 1843; d. Aft. 1900; m. MARY E STAPLES, Aug 1891; b. Jun 1867; d. Aft. 1900. |

      iii.   GEORGE SPINNEY, b. 1848.
      iv.   HANNAH SPINNEY, b. 1855.
      v.   RUFUS M SPINNEY, b. 1858; m. MARY BLANCHARD.
      vi.   SARAH SPINNEY, b. 1858.
      vii.   LEVI SPINNEY, b. Oct 1859; d. Aft. 1920; m. HATTIE TWOMBLY, 03 Jun 1891, Portsmouth NH; b. 1858, Portsmouth, NH.
      viii.   EMMA SPINNEY, b. 1866.

Children of CHARLES SPINNEY and ANN REMICK are:
      ix.   SUSAN R⁷ SPINNEY, b. 01 Dec 1823.
      x.   CHARLES EDWARD SPINNEY, b. Abt. 1825; m. ANN SARAH DIXON; b. Abt. 1825.
499.   xi.   JAMES W SPINNEY, b. 06 Mar 1826.
500.   xii.   AUGUSTUS RICE SPINNEY, b. 14 Mar 1828; d. 22 Dec 1906, Chelsea, MA.
501.   xiii.   ELBRIDGE HERBERT SPINNEY, b. 1836; d. 1863, Haverhill, MA.

208. ELIZABETH⁶ SPINNEY *(CHARLES⁵, EBENEZER⁴, JONATHAN³, SAMUEL², THOMAS¹)* was born 08 Mar 1811, and died 30 Oct 1898. She married JOSEPH SPINNEY 10 May 1840, son of DAVID SPINNEY and LYDIA PAUL. He was born 11 Mar 1812 in Wakefield, NH, and died 21 Dec 1899 in Wakefield, NH.

Children are listed above under (205) Joseph Spinney.

209. MARK⁶ SPINNEY *(PARKER⁵, EBENEZER⁴, JONATHAN³, SAMUEL², THOMAS¹)* was born 1797 in Kittery, ME, and died 20 Nov 1874. He married (1) LUCY EMERY 03 May 1825, daughter of SIMON EMERY and ELIZABETH MENDUM. She was born 1797, and died 12 Nov 1833 in Eliot Maine. He married (2) SOPHIA EMERY Aft. 1833, daughter of SIMON EMERY and ELIZABETH MENDUM. She was born 1794, and died 06 Mar 1853. He married (3) MARY E GREENOUGH 11 May 1854. She was born 1816, and died Aft. 1870.

Notes for MARK SPINNEY:
Was living sith son Horace in 1850

Children of MARK SPINNEY and LUCY EMERY are:
      i.   HENRIETTA⁷ SPINNEY, b. 1823; d. 18 Aug 1826.
502.   ii.   MARK SPINNEY, b. Abt. 1825.
      iii.   DAUGHTER SPINNEY, b. Bet. 1825 - 1830.
      iv.   HORACE P SPINNEY, b. 1826; d. 06 Jun 1826, Eliot Maine.
503.   v.   HORACE P SPINNEY, b. 1828, Kittery, ME; d. Aft. 1850.

Child of MARK SPINNEY and SOPHIA EMERY is:
      vi.   LUCY⁷ SPINNEY, b. 1835.

Children of MARK SPINNEY and MARY GREENOUGH are:
504.   vii.   HENRY CHAPIN⁷ SPINNEY, b. 1855, Maine; d. Aft. 1920.
505.   viii.   GEORGE F SPINNEY, b. 1858; d. Aft. 1900, Haverhill, MA.

210. STEPHEN⁶ PAUL *(MARY GOWELL⁵ SPINNEY, EBENEZER⁴, JONATHAN³, SAMUEL², THOMAS¹)* was born 1808. He married MARY. She was born 1811.

Children of STEPHEN PAUL and MARY are:
      i.   MARY⁷ PAUL, b. 26 Apr 1835; d. 02 May 1903; m. EPHRAIM C SPINNEY, 13 Jun 1872, Kittery Maine; b. 14 Dec 1821; d. 07 Jul 1898.
      ii.   ANNIE PAUL, b. Mar 1845.
506.   iii.   DANIEL P PAUL, b. Aug 1841.

211. ABIGAIL⁶ SPINNEY *(JOSIAH⁵, EBENEZER⁴, JONATHAN³, SAMUEL², THOMAS¹)* was born Abt. 1800. She married (1) JAMES W DWYER Abt. 1820. She married (2) WILLIAM JOHNSON 29 Apr 1828 in Kittery Maine.

Children of ABIGAIL SPINNEY and JAMES DWYER are:

        i.   MARTHA[7] DWYER, b. Abt. 1820.
        ii. MARY DWYER, b. Abt. 1820.

212. EBENEZER[6] SPINNEY *(EBENEZER[5], EBENEZER[4], JONATHAN[3], SAMUEL[2], THOMAS[1])* was born 06 Sep 1800 in Kittery, ME, and died Bet. 1870 - 1880 in Deer Isle, ME. He married (1) MARY ANN FLETCHER 25 Aug 1822. She was born in Charlestown, MA. He married (2) LUCY HUTCHINGSON 03 Sep 1837 in Deer Island, ME. She was born 1800, and died Bet. 1870 - 1880.

Children of EBENEZER SPINNEY and MARY FLETCHER are:
507.   i.   MARY ANN[7] SPINNEY, b. 1824; d. Bet. 1870 - 1880, North Bridgewater, MA.
        ii. FRANCIS SPINNEY, b. 1826, Deer Isle, ME.
        iii. DAUGHTER SPINNEY.

Children of EBENEZER SPINNEY and LUCY HUTCHINGSON are:
508.   iv. JOSEPH WILLIAM[7] SPINNEY, b. 10 Aug 1838, Deer Island, ME; d. Aft. 1880.
        v.   EBENEZER SPINNEY, b. 28 Sep 1839, Deer Isle, ME.
        vi. WILLIAM A SPINNEY, b. 05 Apr 1841, Deer Isle, ME; d. Bef. 1850.
        vii. SUSAN LUCY SPINNEY, b. 15 Jan 1843, Deer Isle, ME.
        viii. NANCY SPINNEY, b. 1844, Deer Isle, ME.
        ix. JANE SPINNEY, b. 1846, Deer Island, ME.
        x.   JONATHAN SPINNEY, b. 05 Aug 1848, Deer Island, ME; d. Bef. 1860.
509.   xi. WILLIAM P SPINNEY, b. 25 Aug 1850, Deer Isle, ME.

213. NARCISSA SPRING[6] SPINNEY *(EBENEZER[5], EBENEZER[4], JONATHAN[3], SAMUEL[2], THOMAS[1])* was born 09 Sep 1801, and died 1850 in Boston, MA. She married GEORGE WILDER DWELLEY 03 Apr 1822, son of MELZAR DWELLEY and SALLY SMITH. He was born in Marshfield, MA, and died Aft. 1870 in Stockbridge, WI.

Children of NARCISSA SPINNEY and GEORGE DWELLEY are:
        i.   LOUISA GODDARD[7] DWELLEY.
        ii. ABBIE ANN DWELLEY.
        iii. GEORGE FREDERICK AUGUSTUS DWELLEY.
        iv. SARAH DWELLEY.
510.   v.   HARRIET VESTA DWELLEY, b. 29 May 1824, Boston, MA.
511.   vi. OSCAR DWELLEY, b. 17 Aug 1826.
512.   vii. ALICE CATHERINE DWELLEY, b. 01 Mar 1829, Portsmouth, NH or VT; d. 11 Mar 1911, Silk Creek, OR.
        viii. FRANKLIN DWELLEY, b. 01 Sep 1831.
513.   ix. JOSEPH FRANKLIN DWELLEY, b. 11 Apr 1839; d. 06 Dec 1933.

214. PHOEBE ANN CATHERINE[6] SPINNEY *(EBENEZER[5], EBENEZER[4], JONATHAN[3], SAMUEL[2], THOMAS[1])* was born 19 Oct 1806, and died 20 Oct 1830. She married SILAS MCINTIRE 03 Jan 1826. He was born in Dover, NH.

Children of PHOEBE SPINNEY and SILAS MCINTIRE are:
        i.   OREIN[7] MCINTIRE.
        ii. KATHERINE MCINTIRE.

215. ELSEY[6] SPINNEY *(EBENEZER[5], EBENEZER[4], JONATHAN[3], SAMUEL[2], THOMAS[1])* was born 04 Apr 1809, and died 07 Nov 1829. She married BENJAMIN WELCH.

Child of ELSEY SPINNEY and BENJAMIN WELCH is:
        i.   ARCHELAUS[7] WELCH, m. ANN EMILY SPINNEY; b. 1821, Kittery, ME; d. Aft. 1900.

216. LYMAN P[6] SPINNEY *(EBENEZER[5], EBENEZER[4], JONATHAN[3], SAMUEL[2], THOMAS[1])* was born 05 Oct 1812, and died 05 Apr 1892. He married LYDIA STAPLES 19 Jul 1835. She was born 07 Jan 1817, and died 07 Aug 1878.

Children of LYMAN SPINNEY and LYDIA STAPLES are:
        i.   WILLIAM[7] SPINNEY, b. 1837.
514.   ii. HORACE STACEY SPINNEY, b. 29 Oct 1838; d. 08 Jan 1882, Portsmouth New Hampshire.

515.   iii.   LYMAN P SPINNEY, b. 03 Jan 1842; d. 1899.

          iv.   JAMES A SPINNEY, b. 1843.

          v.   ALPHONSE SPINNEY, b. 1846; d. 14 Aug 1862, Beaufort, North Carolina.

          vi.   CALVIN A SPINNEY, b. 1856, New Hampshire; d. Bef. 1870.

          vii.   EBENEZER SPINNEY, b. 26 Aug 1859; d. Aft. 1900; m. ELLA ISABELLE FOLLETT, 20 Dec 1886; b. Jul 1859.

217. LYDIA AUGUSTA[6] SPINNEY *(EBENEZER[5], EBENEZER[4], JONATHAN[3], SAMUEL[2], THOMAS[1])* was born 20 Jan 1824. She married ROBERT S BENNETT. He was born 1815.

Children of LYDIA SPINNEY and ROBERT BENNETT are:

          i.   GEORGE[7] BENNETT.

          ii.   FRANK BENNETT.

          iii.   ELIZABETH BENNETT.

          iv.   ELLEN BENNETT.

          v.   OSCOR BENNETT.

          vi.   CHARLES BENNETT.

          vii.   ARTHUR BENNETT.

          viii.   MARY BENNETT.

          ix.   MAUD BENNETT.

218. ABIGAIL[6] WILLEY *(SALLY[5] FERNALD, HANNAH (BETSY)[4] SPINNEY, JONATHAN[3], SAMUEL[2], THOMAS[1])* was born 1812, and died 1882. She married ORRIN OTIS HALL. He was born 1805.

Children of ABIGAIL WILLEY and ORRIN HALL are:

516.   i.   ABRAHAM[7] HALL, b. 1831; d. 1915.

          ii.   ABIGAIL HALL, b. 1837; d. 1914; m. JERRY RANDALL.

          iii.   WARREN L HALL, b. 1843; d. 1864.

          iv.   HARRIET HALL, b. 1845; d. 1867.

517.   v.   NATHANIEL PULSIFER HALL, b. 30 May 1847; d. 1923.

          vi.   SOPHRONA HALL, b. 1849; m. (1) WILLIAM WELCH; b. 1849; m. (2) WILLIAM FRYE; b. 1849.

          vii.   IRENE HALL, b. 1862.

518.   viii.   JOHN L HALL, b. 1855; d. 1922.

          ix.   ZEMRO HALL, b. 1834; d. 1910.

219. STEPHEN[6] SPINNEY *(JONATHAN[5], NATHANIEL[4], JONATHAN[3], SAMUEL[2], THOMAS[1])* was born 28 Oct 1801 in Eastport, ME, and died Abt. 1846 in St George, NB.. He married ELEANOR ELLEN) HURLEY 01 Nov 1824 in St George, NB., daughter of WILLIAM HURLEY and NANCY HURLEY. She was born 1803 in Pennfield, NB., and died 30 Dec 1869 in St George, NB..

Children of STEPHEN SPINNEY and ELEANOR HURLEY are:

519.   i.   JAMES ALEXANDER[7] SPINNEY, b. 29 Aug 1825, Pennfiled, NB; d. 27 Mar 1908, Pennfield, NB.

520.   ii.   ALFRED HURLEY SPINNEY, b. 28 Aug 1830, St George, NB.; d. 11 Oct 1910, St George, NB..

521.   iii.   HORATIO NELSON SPINNEY, b. 27 Aug 1839, Calais, ME; d. 29 Aug 1929, Musquash, NB..

220. JOSEPH[6] SPINNEY *(JONATHAN[5], NATHANIEL[4], JONATHAN[3], SAMUEL[2], THOMAS[1])* was born 1806 in New Brunswick, and died 11 Oct 1874 in Norton, Ma. He married JANE HASTE BARSTOW 16 Oct 1849, daughter of GIDEON BARSTOW and ANNIE MCCOY. She was born 1822 in Maine, and died 1898 in Norton, MA.

Children of JOSEPH SPINNEY and JANE BARSTOW are:

          i.   CATHERINE[7] SPINNEY, b. Jun 1846; d. 1923; m. LYMAN FRANKLIN, 22 Sep 1877, Norton, MA; b. Jul 1850.

          ii.   JONATHAN SPINNEY, b. Abt. 1848; d. 18 Sep 1850, Calais Maine.

          iii.   MARY ANN SPINNEY, b. 1850; d. Aft. 1860.

          iv.   EMILY H SPINNEY, b. 1852; d. 24 Mar 1853, Calais Maine.

          v.   EMILY J SPINNEY, b. 1854; d. Aft. 1920; m. (1) ISREAL THOMPSON, 1875; m. (2) EDWARD C FRANKLIN, 1876; b. 1850, Attleboro, MA; d. Aft. 1920.

          vi.   GEORGE SPINNEY, b. Mar 1864; d. 10 Jun 1864.

          vii.   SARAH A SPINNEY, b. 1866; d. Aft. 1900, Calais Maine.

221. JAMES S[6] SPINNEY *(JONATHAN[5], NATHANIEL[4], JONATHAN[3], SAMUEL[2], THOMAS[1])* was born 1807 in New Brunswick, and died 25 Jan 1896 in St George, NB.. He married MARTHA "ANNE" LOWE 01 Dec 1829. She was born 1808, and died 13 Jul 1889 in St George, NB..

Children of JAMES SPINNEY and MARTHA LOWE are:

522.	i.	KATHERINE M[7] SPINNEY, b. 1830, St George, NB.; d. 05 Apr 1857.
523.	ii.	JOSEPH L SPINNEY, b. 1832, St George, NB.; d. 23 Apr 1928, Eureka, California.
	iii.	MARY ANN SPINNEY, b. Mar 1834; d. Bef. 1851.
	iv.	MARTHA SPINNEY, b. 1835; d. Aft. 1881.
	v.	EMILY SPINNEY, b. 1841; d. 13 Sep 1858, St George New Brunswick.
	vi.	GEORGE WASHINGTON SPINNEY, b. Apr 1844; d. 13 Jun 1861, St George New Brunswick.
524.	vii.	MARY JANE SPINNEY, b. 07 Jun 1844; d. 01 Apr 1919, Pleasant Ridge, NB..
525.	viii.	JAMES VAN BUREN SPINNEY, b. 07 May 1846, Pull and BE Dam, Letang St, NB.; d. 20 Dec 1913, St George, NB..
526.	ix.	SARAH ELLEN SPINNEY, b. 1848; d. 04 Dec 1884, Pennfield, NB..
	x.	ALICE ADELADE SPINNEY, b. 1852, St George, NB.; d. 31 Oct 1878, L'Etang New Brunswick.

Notes for ALICE ADELADE SPINNEY:

"The Saint Croix Courier Journey Through Time
A Collection of Amusing and Informative News and Opinions from Past Issues
Written with permission of Saint Croix Courier
Courtesy of Joan Christie

OCTOBER 31, 1878
DIED :
SPINNEY - At Le'Tang, St. George, on the 16th inst., Alice A. Spinney, fifth daughter of James and Ann Spinney, aged 25
years.

	xi.	TOBIAS G SPINNEY, b. 06 Jun 1854; d. 12 Nov 1926, L'Etang New Brunswick; m. MARY LOUISA CARMAN, 30 Sep 1891, Pennfield New Brunswick Canada.

Notes for TOBIAS G SPINNEY:
Married but no family buried s/e coner lot, Rural Cemetery- has monument. According to " A history of Abandoned settlements in Charlotte Co. Tobias was a farmer who also played the fiddle giving the neighborhood many evenings of toe-tapping music

527.	xii.	HORATIO NELSON SPINNEY, b. 20 Jan 1860, St George, NB.; d. 14 Oct 1885, Upper L'Etang New Brunswick.

222. LOUISA ANN[6] SPINNEY *(JONATHAN[5], NATHANIEL[4], JONATHAN[3], SAMUEL[2], THOMAS[1])* was born 1811 in New Brunswick, and died Aft. 1860. She married SAMUEL HUSON 22 Apr 1832 in St George, NB.. He was born 1802, and died Aft. 1860.

Children of LOUISA SPINNEY and SAMUEL HUSON are:

528.	i.	CHARLOTTE ELIZABETH[7] HUSON, b. 1834; d. Bef. 1901.
	ii.	SARAH A HUSON, b. 1836; m. JAMES PHELAN, 07 Oct 1854, Calais, ME.
	iii.	PHEBE HUSON, b. 1839; d. 23 Aug 1845, Calais, ME.
	iv.	JAMES A HUSON, b. 1841; d. Aft. 1917; m. SARAH A STEWART.
529.	v.	GEORGE H HUSON, b. 16 Jul 1844, Calais, ME; d. 28 Apr 1934, Calais, ME.
530.	vi.	THOMAS ALBERT HUSON, b. 19 Nov 1847, Calais, ME; d. 1918.
	vii.	CHARLES CRAWFORD HUSON, b. 1850, Calais, Maine.
531.	viii.	MELVINA HUSON, b. 1849, Calais, ME; d. Bef. 1860.
	ix.	PHEBE ELLIS HUSON, b. Abt. 1854, Calais, ME.

223. NATHANIEL[6] SPINNEY *(JONATHAN[5], NATHANIEL[4], JONATHAN[3], SAMUEL[2], THOMAS[1])* was born Mar 1814 in New Brunswick, and died 05 Jan 1892 in Calais, Maine. He married MARY LOWE 01 Dec 1834 in St George New Brunswick. She was born 1819, and died 14 Mar 1879 in Calais, Maine.

Children of NATHANIEL SPINNEY and MARY LOWE are:

| 532. | i. | WILLIAM L[7] SPINNEY, b. Mar 1835, St George, NB.; d. 10 Oct 1915, Calais, ME. |

532. i. WILLIAM L[7] SPINNEY, b. Mar 1835, St George, NB.; d. 10 Oct 1915, Calais, ME.
533. ii. NANCY (SARAH) ANN SPINNEY, b. 13 Apr 1838, St George, NB.; d. 26 Jul 1934, Calais, ME.
534. iii. STEPHEN ALEXANDER SPINNEY, b. Sep 1842, St George, NB.; d. 08 Dec 1914, Calais, ME.
       iv. ZEBADIAH SPINNEY, b. 10 Jan 1845, Calais, ME; d. Aft. 1870.
        v. SARAH JANE SPINNEY, b. 10 May 1845, Calais, ME; d. 28 Nov 1895, Calais ME; m. THOMAS ROGERS, 07 Nov 1867, Calais Maine; d. Bef. 1881.
535. vi. ZEBALON D SPINNEY, b. 10 Jan 1848, Calais, ME; d. 08 Sep 1893, Calais, ME.
536. vii. SHUBAL T SPINNEY, b. 1849, Calais, ME; d. 24 Mar 1889, Calais, ME.
      viii. CATHERINE SPINNEY, b. Abt. 1851.
       ix. GEORGE A SPINNEY, b. 15 Mar 1853, St George, NB.; d. 19 May 1854, Calais Maine.
        x. MARY E SPINNEY, b. 1855; d. 19 Mar 1863, Calais Maine.
       xi. GEORGE F SPINNEY, b. 1857; d. 21 Mar 1863, Calais Maine.
      xii. LEBERTON SPINNEY, b. 1859, Calais, ME; d. 25 Mar 1863, Calais, ME.
537. xiii. NELLIE SPINNEY, b. Jun 1861, Maine; d. 12 Mar 1936, Haverhill, MA.

224. DOROTHY[6] SPINNEY *(JONATHAN[5], NATHANIEL[4], JONATHAN[3], SAMUEL[2], THOMAS[1])* was born 1816 in New Brunswick, and died Aft. 1880. She married JOHN HATT. He was born 1817, and died Bef. 1870.

Children of DOROTHY SPINNEY and JOHN HATT are:
538. i. MARGARET[7] HATT, b. Feb 1842.
       ii. WILLIAM H HATT, b. 1844.
      iii. MARY ANN HATT, b. 1846.
       iv. DORCAS HATT, b. 1848; m. JEFFERSON WHEELER, 04 Jun 1866.
        v. SARAH HATT, b. 1850.
       vi. JAMES HATT, b. 1851.

225. SARAH E[6] SPINNEY *(JONATHAN[5], NATHANIEL[4], JONATHAN[3], SAMUEL[2], THOMAS[1])* was born 1819 in New Brunswick, and died Aft. 1881. She married ZEBEDIAH SHATTUCK HOLT, son of BARACHIAS HOLT and ELIZABETH SHATTUCK. He was born 11 May 1797 in NH, and died 13 Aug 1874 in St. Stephen, N.B.

Children of SARAH SPINNEY and ZEBEDIAH HOLT are:
       i. EMILY[7] HOLT, b. 1834.
539. ii. CHARLES MELVILLE HOLT, b. 15 Jan 1844, Calais, ME; d. 01 Apr 1875.
      iii. ADALINE D HOLT, b. 01 Feb 1847; m. JOHN CALWALLADER, 23 May 1871, St Stephens New Brunswick.
       iv. ZEBEDIAH HOLT, b. 1849; d. Aft. 1871.
        v. FRANK P HOLT, b. 1854.
       vi. GEORGE HOLT, b. 1856; d. 16 Jun 1862.

226. CHARLES EDWARD[6] SPINNEY *(JONATHAN[5], NATHANIEL[4], JONATHAN[3], SAMUEL[2], THOMAS[1])* was born 1822 in L'Etang, NB., and died 06 Jul 1884 in Calais, ME buried blk 9 Lot4. He married (1) HANNAH HOLT 18 Oct 1846 in Calais, Maine. She was born 1822, and died 29 Dec 1852. He married (2) JANE L GOLDEN 13 Aug 1853 in St Stephen, NB., daughter of PETER GOLDEN and LUCY PARKS. She was born 1834 in Dublin, Ireland, and died 06 Jan 1912 in Calais, ME.

Children of CHARLES SPINNEY and HANNAH HOLT are:
       i. ELIZA DUNBAR[7] SPINNEY, b. 11 Aug 1847, Calais, ME; d. 15 Aug 1850, Calais, Me.
       ii. AMBROSE A SPINNEY, b. 1850, Calais, ME; d. 11 May 1876, Calais, ME.
      iii. INFANT SPINNEY, b. 29 Dec 1852, Calais, ME; d. 02 Feb 1853, Calais, ME.

           Notes for INFANT SPINNEY:
           Hannah Holt Spinney died in childbirth with this child and the child at the same time died in her arms

Children of CHARLES SPINNEY and JANE GOLDEN are:
       iv. JASON ALBERT (BUB)[7] SPINNEY, b. 15 Aug 1854, Merseyside, ME; d. 13 Jul 1930, Kings Park Long Island, NY.

           Notes for JASON ALBERT (BUB) SPINNEY:
           Albert Jason Spinney, born August 15, 1854, Calais, Maine; died July 13, 1930
           Kings Park, Long Island, N.Y. Buried in Hospital Cemetery. He was an inmate
           of the institution (The Sailors' Snug Harbor) for four years, nine months and

29 days.

v. CHARLES EDWARD SPINNEY, b. 1859, Calais, ME; d. 21 May 1865, Calais, Me.

Notes for CHARLES EDWARD SPINNEY:
Little Eddie as he was called was hit by a train and killed as a young child

540.	vi.	HANNAH ELIZA SPINNEY, b. 26 Nov 1859, Calais, ME; d. 18 Aug 1934, Montreal Canada.
541.	vii.	JESSIE SPINNEY, b. Jun 1861; d. Aft. 1910.
542.	viii.	NELLIE M SPINNEY, b. 13 Sep 1865, Calais, ME; d. 13 Oct 1927, Calais ME.
543.	ix.	GEORGE FREDERICK SPINNEY, b. 18 Nov 1868, Calais, ME; d. 15 Jan 1946, Milltown.
544.	x.	FRANKLIN P SPINNEY, b. 20 Feb 1875, Calais, ME; d. 18 Aug 1948.
545.	xi.	LOUISE PARKS SPINNEY, b. 14 Nov 1876, Calais, ME; d. 28 Nov 1957, Malden, MA.
546.	xii.	CAROLYN B (CARRIE) SPINNEY, b. 14 Apr 1879, Calais, ME; d. 24 Feb 1961, Newton, MA.
547.	xiii.	EDWARD CHARLES SPINNEY, b. Aug 1880, Calais, ME; d. 16 Dec 1939, Portland, ME.

227. MARY ANN[6] SPINNEY *(JONATHAN[5], NATHANIEL[4], JONATHAN[3], SAMUEL[2], THOMAS[1])* was born Dec 1828, and died 06 Nov 1906 in Attleboro, MA. She married JOSEPH GREEN 04 Dec 1853 in St Andrews NB, son of SARAH. He was born Jun 1831, and died Aft. 1900.

Children of MARY SPINNEY and JOSEPH GREEN are:

	i.	ELIZABETH[7] GREEN, b. 01 Sep 1854, Calais, Me.
	ii.	MARY LOUISA GREEN, b. 26 Nov 1856, Calais, ME.
	iii.	THOMAS GREEN, b. 23 Mar 1859, Calais, ME; d. 16 Apr 1859, Calais, ME.
	iv.	JOSEPH GREEN, b. 13 Dec 1860, Calais, ME.
	v.	SARAH E GREEN, b. 31 May 1862, Calais, ME.
548.	vi.	LAURA DEXTER GREEN, b. 28 Dec 1866.

228. EBENEZER[6] SPINNEY *(JONATHAN[5], NATHANIEL[4], JONATHAN[3], SAMUEL[2], THOMAS[1])* was born Feb 1832 in St George, NB., and died 04 Feb 1905 in Lowell, MA. He married ANNA GREEN ISLES 27 Dec 1853 in St George, NB., daughter of JOSEPH GREEN and SARAH MARKS. She was born Sep 1840, and died 13 Feb 1907 in Lowell, MA.

Children of EBENEZER SPINNEY and ANNA ISLES are:

549.	i.	SARAH ELIZABETH[7] SPINNEY, b. 02 Jul 1854, Calais, ME; d. Bet. 1910 - 1920, Massachusetts.
	ii.	THOMAS STILLMAN SPINNEY, b. 1857; d. Bef. 1905.
550.	iii.	WILLARD SPINNEY, b. 1859; d. 22 May 1899, Lowell, MA.
	iv.	HEZEKIAH SPINNEY, b. 1861; d. Bef. 1905.
	v.	JESSIE SPINNEY, b. 1864; d. Bef. 1905.
	vi.	MARY SPINNEY, b. 1866.
	vii.	CELIA SPINNEY, b. Sep 1871.
	viii.	LULA SPINNEY, b. Sep 1871.
	ix.	GEORGIA A SPINNEY, b. Jan 1874; d. Aft. 1900.
	x.	IRA B SPINNEY, b. May 1877; d. Aft. 1910.

229. ARCHIBALD BARNEY[6] SPINNEY *(JONATHAN[5], NATHANIEL[4], JONATHAN[3], SAMUEL[2], THOMAS[1])* was born 1833 in St George, NB., and died 12 Oct 1895 in Gand Lake Stream, ME. He married (1) SARAH J BAKER 21 Aug 1854 in Calais, ME. She was born 1832 in Nova Scotia, and died 24 Jan 1863 in Bangor, Me. He married (2) LOUISA C FICKETT 15 Nov 1864 in Princeton, Washington County, Maine, daughter of BENJAMIN FICKETT and REBECCA HAMILTON. She was born 03 Dec 1847 in Princeton, ME.

Children of ARCHIBALD SPINNEY and SARAH BAKER are:

551.	i.	ABBIE[7] SPINNEY, b. 22 Apr 1859, Calais, ME; d. 30 Dec 1917, Oakland, Ca.
552.	ii.	HERBERT HARRISON FICKETT SPINNEY, b. 15 Dec 1862, Princeton, ME; d. 09 Nov 1943, Washington, DC.
553.	iii.	BENJAMIN FRANK SPINNEY, b. 26 Mar 1863, Princeton, ME; d. Apr 1939, Bangor, ME.

230. JONATHAN[6] SPINNEY *(JONATHAN[5], NATHANIEL[4], JONATHAN[3], SAMUEL[2], THOMAS[1])* was born 1835 in St. George, N.B., and died 14 Apr 1914 in Calais, ME. He married SARAH JANE STEEN 30 Sep 1860, daughter of JAMES STEEN and ELLEN. She was born 1835 in St George, NB., and died Bet. 1870 - 1880.

Children of JONATHAN SPINNEY and SARAH STEEN are:
    i.   RACHEL[7] SPINNEY, b. 10 Oct 1860; d. Aft. 1880.
   ii.   JAMES HENRY SPINNEY, b. 10 Jan 1861; d. Aft. 1880.

        Notes for JAMES HENRY SPINNEY:
        Was listed living with grandfather Steen in 1871

   iii.   RICHARD SPINNEY, b. Abt. 1862; d. Bef. 1870.
   iv.   LIZZIE SPINNEY, b. 1864; d. 09 Nov 1870.
    v.   MINNIE B SPINNEY, b. 1867; d. Aft. 1920; m. WILLIAM C ROBINSON, 05 Apr 1890, Calais, Maine; b. 1847; d. Bef. 1900.

        Notes for MINNIE B SPINNEY:
        Was listed living with Grandfather Steen in 1871

   vi.   JOSEPH E SPINNEY, b. 1869; d. Bef. 1881.

231. JOHN[6] SPINNEY *(JONATHAN[5], NATHANIEL[4], JONATHAN[3], SAMUEL[2], THOMAS[1])* was born Abt. 1846, and died Bet. 1890 - 1900. He married SUSAN MARIAH KIMBALL 05 Nov 1892, daughter of SAMUEL KIMBALL and ANNIE MCGREGOR. She was born Feb 1850 in Liverpool, N.S, and died 26 Jan 1929 in Lynn Ma.

Child of JOHN SPINNEY and SUSAN KIMBALL is:
554.   i.   EDWARD P[7] SPINNEY, b. Sep 1884; d. Aft. 1930.

232. PAUL OLIVER[6] LEE *(HANNAH[5] SPINNEY, NATHANIEL[4], JONATHAN[3], SAMUEL[2], THOMAS[1])* was born 1814. He married MARY ANN. She was born 1824.

Children of PAUL LEE and MARY ANN are:
    i.   HANNAH COX[7] LEE, b. 1836.
   ii.   JAMES LEE, b. 1840.
   iii.   OLIVER LEE, b. 1845.
   iv.   ANN LEE, b. 1847.
    v.   THOMAS LEE, b. 1852.
   vi.   GEORGE LEE, b. 1856.
   vii.   STEWART LEE, b. 1858.
   viii.   DUGLES LEE, b. 1861.

233. JAMES[6] CHASE *(LOUISA[5] SPINNEY, NATHANIEL[4], JONATHAN[3], SAMUEL[2], THOMAS[1])* He married MARY.

Children of JAMES CHASE and MARY are:
    i.   JOHN[7] CHASE, b. 1839, New Brunswick; m. PHEBE A BROWN, 07 Nov 1859, Calais Maine.
   ii.   LOUISA CHASE, b. 1842, Maine; m. THOMAS STINSON, 28 Jan 1860.
   iii.   ISAAC CHASE, b. 1843, Maine.
   iv.   ROBERT CHASE, b. 1849, Maine.

234. JOHN[6] CHASE *(LOUISA[5] SPINNEY, NATHANIEL[4], JONATHAN[3], SAMUEL[2], THOMAS[1])* was born 12 Sep 1807 in Eastport, ME, and died 25 Aug 1869 in Portsmouth, NH. He married CAROLINE E SIMES 07 Oct 1833 in Portsmouth, NH, daughter of HANNAH SIMES. She was born 08 Mar 1813 in Portsmouth, NH, and died 22 Nov 1890 in Portsmouth, NH.

Children of JOHN CHASE and CAROLINE SIMES are:
    i.   WILLIAM S[7] CHASE, b. 25 Jul 1834; d. 27 Jul 1865, Portsmouth, NH.
555.   ii.   JOHN E CHASE, b. 1837, Portsmouth, NH; d. 25 Oct 1886, Brooklyn, NY.
556.   iii.   ALBERT P CHASE, b. 13 Jul 1839; d. 25 Feb 1907, Portsmouth, NH.

235. EBENEZER[6] SPINNEY *(EBENEZER[5], NATHANIEL[4], JONATHAN[3], SAMUEL[2], THOMAS[1])* was born 1808 in Portsmouth, NH, and died 17 Mar 1888 in Grant Park, IL. He married (1) MARY JANE WILSON 09 Dec 1844, daughter of WILLIAM WILSON and JANE. She was born 1821 in Pennfield, NB., and died 07 Nov 1853 in St Stephens New Brunswick block 60. He married (2) MARY CROUSE 16 Oct 1858 in Calais Maine. She was born Abt. 1813.

Children of EBENEZER SPINNEY and MARY WILSON are:

557.	i.	WILLIAM L[7] SPINNEY, b. 03 Oct 1835, St George, NB.; d. Aft. 1870.
	ii.	LUCY SPINNEY, b. 1848.
	iii.	HORACE SPINNEY, b. 1850.
	iv.	ANNIE SPINNEY, b. 1851.
	v.	HENRY SPINNEY, b. 1853.

236. OLIVER W[6] SPINNEY *(EBENEZER[5], NATHANIEL[4], JONATHAN[3], SAMUEL[2], THOMAS[1])* was born 1810 in Portsmouth, NH, and died May 1908. He married JANE PRATT. She was born 1818, and died 1909.

Children of OLIVER SPINNEY and JANE PRATT are:

558.	i.	ARTHUR JONES[7] SPINNEY, b. 1839, New Brunswick; d. Aft. 1880.
	ii.	BENJAMIN SPINNEY, b. 1841.
	iii.	OLIVER K SPINNEY, b. 1843, Calais, ME; d. 04 May 1908; m. (1) MELISSA JANE BARNES, 29 Sep 1866, Eastport, Me; b. St George, NB.; m. (2) CAROLINE MARCHALL, 26 Aug 1874, Calais, ME; b. 09 Dec 1841, Calais, ME; d. 05 May 1933, Lewiston, ME.

Notes for OLIVER K SPINNEY:
Lived in St Stephen in 1881

	iv.	DAVID GETCHELL SPINNEY, b. 1845; d. 25 May 1868.
	v.	PRICILLA SPINNEY, b. 1846.
559.	vi.	CHARLES M SPINNEY, b. 1848, Calais, ME; d. Aft. 1900, Bancroft Me.
560.	vii.	GEORGE H SPINNEY, b. 23 Dec 1852; d. 1913, Nova Scotia.
	viii.	MARY JANE SPINNEY, b. 1855.
561.	ix.	EMILY E SPINNEY, b. 1859.
	x.	SIDNEY H SPINNEY, b. 1866.

237. NATHANIEL[6] SPINNEY *(EBENEZER[5], NATHANIEL[4], JONATHAN[3], SAMUEL[2], THOMAS[1])* was born Jan 1813 in Jonesport, ME, and died 28 Apr 1902 in Eastport, ME. He married MARGARET R QUIGLEY 04 Nov 1843 in St George, NB., daughter of DAVID QUIGLEY and MARTHA MOORE. She was born 1823 in Grand Manan, ME, and died Bef. 1871.

Children of NATHANIEL SPINNEY and MARGARET QUIGLEY are:

	i.	ABIEL[7] SPINNEY, b. Aug 1844; d. Bef. 1851.
562.	ii.	WILLIAM L SPINNEY, b. 15 Nov 1846, Calais, ME; d. 29 Jun 1904, Eastport, ME.
	iii.	HIRAM FRANKLIN SPINNEY, b. 21 Feb 1850; d. Aft. 1861.
	iv.	SARAH ADELINE SPINNEY, b. 1852; d. 23 Jan 1929, Calais Maine.
563.	v.	LYDIA "ANNIE" SPINNEY, b. 1854; d. 22 Jan 1936.
564.	vi.	MARGARET JANE SPINNEY, b. Apr 1857; d. Aft. 1900.
	vii.	ANTHONY SPINNEY, b. 17 Dec 1863; d. Aft. 1881.
565.	viii.	MARTHA JANE SPINNEY, b. 25 Feb 1865, Eastport, ME; d. 23 Jul 1948, St George, NB..

238. JAMES PARKER[6] SPINNEY *(EBENEZER[5], NATHANIEL[4], JONATHAN[3], SAMUEL[2], THOMAS[1])* was born 1814 in Maine, and died 16 Dec 1884 in Eastport, ME. He married (1) MARGARET. He married (2) SARAH MOSS 19 Aug 1845 in St George, NB.. She was born 1821, and died Aft. 1871.

Children of JAMES SPINNEY and MARGARET are:

566.	i.	WILLIAM[7] SPINNEY, b. 1839; d. Aft. 1900.
567.	ii.	MARTHA A SPINNEY, b. 1843, St Andrews, NB.; d. Aft. 1880.

Children of JAMES SPINNEY and SARAH MOSS are:

	iii.	MEHITABLE[7] SPINNEY, b. 02 Mar 1846; d. 27 Apr 1849, St GeorgeNew Brunswick.
	iv.	CATHERINE SPINNEY, b. 27 Aug 1848, St George, NB.; d. 18 Mar 1868, St George, NB.; m. JOSEPH BULLOCK, 05 Jul 1865.

        v.   JOHN PARKER SPINNEY, b. 1851; d. 28 Jun 1862, St George New Brunswick.
568.   vi.   SUSAN SPINNEY, b. 1854.
569.   vii.   MARY E SPINNEY, b. 1857; d. 1935.

239. ARTHUR JONES[6] SPINNEY *(EBENEZER[5], NATHANIEL[4], JONATHAN[3], SAMUEL[2], THOMAS[1])* was born 13 Jun 1817 in Portsmouth, NH, and died 21 Mar 1900 in Goodland, IN. He married SUSANNA BOYD 23 Dec 1841 in St. George St Patricks Parish, N.B., daughter of JOHN BOYD and ISABELLA. She was born Bet. 1820 - 1830.

Children of ARTHUR SPINNEY and SUSANNA BOYD are:
570.   i.   SARAH[7] SPINNEY, b. 22 Oct 1842, St George, NB.; d. 07 Aug 1933, Wenatchee, WA.
        ii.   ALBERT SPINNEY, b. 20 Jun 1846, St Stephens, NB.; d. 12 Mar 1854, St Stephens, NB..
        iii.   THOMAS SPINNEY, b. 10 Jul 1850, St Stephens, NB.; d. 17 Mar 1872, Goodland, IN.
571.   iv.   SUSANNA SPINNEY, b. 07 Oct 1853, St Stephens, NB.; d. 08 Oct 1893, Goodland, IN.
        v.   DAVID SPINNEY, b. 14 Jul 1859, Manesteque, MI; d. 18 Oct 1860, Cedar River, MI.
572.   vi.   ARTHUR JONES SPINNEY, b. 30 Jul 1861, Summer, IL; d. 1932, Goodland, IN.
573.   vii.   AURELIA ISABELLE SPINNEY, b. 04 Dec 1864, Grant Park, Il; d. 20 Mar 1942, Fort Wayne, IN.
574.   viii.   CHARLES WILLIAM SPINNEY, b. 01 Oct 1867, Summer, IL; d. 1907.
        ix.   ELIZABETH SPINNEY, b. 1872.

240. CATHERINE[6] SPINNEY *(EBENEZER[5], NATHANIEL[4], JONATHAN[3], SAMUEL[2], THOMAS[1])* was born 1820 in St George, NB.. She married DAVID GETCHELL 11 Apr 1844 in St Andrews, NB., son of BENJAMIN GETCHELL and MEHITABLE MESERVE. He was born Abt. 1791 in St. Stephen, , NB, and died Bef. 1851 in Miramichi, , NB.

Children of CATHERINE SPINNEY and DAVID GETCHELL are:
        i.   ANN MARIA[7] GETCHELL, b. 1846.
        ii.   FRANCES GETCHELL, b. 1848.
        iii.   JAMES GETCHELL, b. 1855.

241. SIMON F[6] SPINNEY *(EBENEZER[5], NATHANIEL[4], JONATHAN[3], SAMUEL[2], THOMAS[1])* was born 1822 in St George, NB., and died Aft. 1881. He married PRUDENCE L WILSON 01 Oct 1846 in St George, NB., daughter of WILLIAM WILSON and JANE. She was born 1825, and died Aft. 1891.

Children of SIMON SPINNEY and PRUDENCE WILSON are:
575.   i.   LOUISA JONES[7] SPINNEY, b. 29 Aug 1848, St George, NB.; d. 15 Jun 1931, St George NB..
        ii.   HELEN SPINNEY, b. 1849; d. Aft. 1871.
        iii.   FRANCES (GETCHEL) SPINNEY, b. 1853.
        iv.   GINEY V SPINNEY, b. 1853; d. 01 Apr 1872, St George New Brunswick.
576.   v.   ISAAC HOPKINS SPINNEY, b. 1856; d. Aft. 1891.
        vi.   PRUDENCE SPINNEY, b. 1859.
        vii.   EVAGELINE SPINNEY, b. 1862.
577.   viii.   SAMUEL JAMES SPINNEY, b. 1869, St George, NB.; d. 1905.

242. JOSEPH[6] SPINNEY *(ABRAHAM[5], JOSEPH[4], SAMUEL[3], SAMUEL[2], THOMAS[1])* was born 09 Oct 1820, and died 14 Feb 1893. He married LOUISA DODGE. She was born 12 Jun 1819, and died Aug 1880 in Greenwood, NS..

Children of JOSEPH SPINNEY and LOUISA DODGE are:
578.   i.   ABRAHAM[7] SPINNEY, b. 19 Jan 1847; d. 1919, Greenwood Nova Scotia.
579.   ii.   OWEN SPINNEY, b. 08 Jan 1850; d. 03 Jun 1933.

243. ELIZABETH[6] SPINNEY *(ABRAHAM[5], JOSEPH[4], SAMUEL[3], SAMUEL[2], THOMAS[1])* was born 20 Jun 1826, and died 06 May 1892 in Kings, NS.. She married GILBERT WELLESLY WOODBURY. He was born Bef. Jul 1824, and died 18 Jul 1900 in Annapolis, NS..

Children of ELIZABETH SPINNEY and GILBERT WOODBURY are:
        i.   STANLEY[7] WOODBURY, b. 1852; d. 1927.
580.   ii.   ALEPH WOODBURY, b. 11 Jun 1855, Kingston, NS.; d. 22 Jan 1938, Lexington, MA.
        iii.   AMANDA HERITAGE WOODBURY, b. 1856; d. 16 Jan 1943.
        iv.   LOUISA WOODBURY, b. 1858; d. 10 Jan 1882, Greenwood, Kings, Nova Scotia.

   v.   ABRAM WOODBURY.
   vi.   JONATHAN WOODBURY.
   vii.   FAIRFIELD WOODBURY.

244. SUSANAH[6] SPINNEY *(ABRAHAM[5], JOSEPH[4], SAMUEL[3], SAMUEL[2], THOMAS[1])* was born 1831, and died 1912. She married SAMUEL SAUNDERS Abt. 1860, son of TIMOTHY SAUNDERS and EUNICE SPINNEY. He was born 1828, and died 1912.

Children of SUSANAH SPINNEY and SAMUEL SAUNDERS are:
581.   i.   EDITH[7] SAUNDERS.
      ii.   FRANK SAMUEL SAUNDERS, b. 1870; d. Mar 1950.
     iii.   EMMA E. SAUNDERS, b. 1873; d. 1948.

245. CHARLES[6] SPINNEY *(ABRAHAM[5], JOSEPH[4], SAMUEL[3], SAMUEL[2], THOMAS[1])* was born Nov 1831, and died 23 Mar 1869 in Aylesford NS. He married MARTHA SAUNDERS, daughter of TIMOTHY SAUNDERS and EUNICE SPINNEY. She was born 1836, and died 05 Oct 1872.

Children of CHARLES SPINNEY and MARTHA SAUNDERS are:
      i.   JOSEPH HOWE[7] SPINNEY, b. 1858; d. 05 Mar 1936, Aylesford Nova Scotia; m. DOLLIE.
      ii.   MARTHA J. SPINNEY, b. 23 Mar 1869; d. 05 Jun 1870, Greenwood Nova Scotia.

246. CHARLOTTE E[6] BANKS *(CYRENA ANN[5] SPINNEY, JOSEPH[4], SAMUEL[3], SAMUEL[2], THOMAS[1])* was born 22 Apr 1849 in Nova Scotia, Canada, and died 27 Dec 1894. She married JOHN E BANKS, son of WILLIAM BANKS and RACHEL ELLIOT.

Child of CHARLOTTE BANKS and JOHN BANKS is:
      i.   HARDY[7] BANKS.

247. CHARLES ARCHIBALD[6] BANKS *(CYRENA ANN[5] SPINNEY, JOSEPH[4], SAMUEL[3], SAMUEL[2], THOMAS[1])* was born 26 Jul 1851 in Nova Scotia, Canada, and died 1919. He married EDITH SAUNDERS, daughter of SAMUEL SAUNDERS and SUSANAH SPINNEY.

Children of CHARLES BANKS and EDITH SAUNDERS are:
      i.   BRITA[7] BANKS.
      ii.   LEAH BANKS.
     iii.   FOREST BANKS.
     iv.   WILLIAM BANKS.
     v.   GUILFORD BANKS.

248. JOSEPH ENGLES[6] BANKS *(CYRENA ANN[5] SPINNEY, JOSEPH[4], SAMUEL[3], SAMUEL[2], THOMAS[1])* was born 23 Jul 1836 in Nova Scotia, Canada. He married (1) ESTHER KATE HODGE PATTENDEN. She was born 1894 in Horsmonden, Ken. He married (2) BARBARA ANN MAPPLEBECK 1879. She was born 1841. He married (3) RACHEL S MARSHALL 1859. She was born 1839, and died 02 Dec 1927.

Children of JOSEPH BANKS and RACHEL MARSHALL are:
      i.   GEORGE INGLES[7] BANKS, b. 25 Aug 1879; d. 22 Jun 1963, E Margretsville, Annapolis, Nova Scotia, Canada.
      ii.   ERNEST GARFIELD BANKS, b. 12 Dec 1883.
     iii.   SPURGEON JOSEPH BANKS, b. 25 Jun 1881.
     iv.   MILLEDGE W BANKS, b. 07 Dec 1866.
     v.   ELDRIDGE BANKS.
     vi.   IOLA MAE BANKS.

249. CHARLES ARCHIBALD[6] BANKS *(CYRENA ANN[5] SPINNEY, JOSEPH[4], SAMUEL[3], SAMUEL[2], THOMAS[1])* was born 26 Jul 1851 in Nova Scotia, Canada, and died 1919. He married EDITH SAUNDERS 24 Nov 1873 in Kingston, Kings, Nova Scotia, Canada. She was born 18 Oct 1854, and died 27 Feb 1926.

Children of CHARLES BANKS and EDITH SAUNDERS are:
  i.   FORREST ERIE[7] BANKS, b. 25 May 1874, Canada.
  ii. GUILDFORD ARCHIBALD BANKS, b. 20 Jun 1884, Nova Scotia, Canada.
  iii. IDA MAY BANKS, b. 09 Nov 1876.
  iv. BRITTA BEATRICE BANKS, b. 23 Jun 1896.
  v.   LILA VAUGHN BANKS, b. 12 May 1894.
  vi. WINSLOW HOWE BANKS, b. 15 Aug 1886.
  vii. CHARLOTTE BANKS, b. 15 Nov 1889.
  viii. WILLIAM HOWARD BANKS, b. 24 Jan 1879, Canada.
  ix. LOTTIE BANKS.

250. MARY LAVANIA[6] BANKS (*CYRENA ANN[5] SPINNEY, JOSEPH[4], SAMUEL[3], SAMUEL[2], THOMAS[1]*) was born 07 Feb 1841 in Nova Scotia, Canada, and died 28 Feb 1929. She married SIMEON CROCKER 01 Dec 1859. He was born 14 Feb 1837, and died 03 Jan 1899.

Children of MARY BANKS and SIMEON CROCKER are:
  i.   SARAH[7] CROCKER, b. 11 Dec 1865; d. 1942, Tremont, Kings, Nova Scotia, Canada.
  ii. ELWOOD CROCKER, b. 1870; d. 1955.
  iii. CLARA CROCKER, b. 1861; d. 1942.
  iv. WALLACE CROCKER, b. 1881; d. 1899.
  v.   HARTLEY CROCKER, b. 1876; d. 1880.
  vi. WALLACE CROCKER, b. 1881.
  vii. HARRY E CROCKER, b. 28 May 1870.

251. SARAH ANN[6] BANKS (*CYRENA ANN[5] SPINNEY, JOSEPH[4], SAMUEL[3], SAMUEL[2], THOMAS[1]*) was born 21 Nov 1834 in Annapolis, Nova Scotia, Canada, and died 30 May 1893 in Torbrook, Annapolis, Nova Scotia, Canada. She married SAMUEL W BARTEAUX 22 Feb 1859. He was born 05 Jul 1834 in Torbrook, Annapolis, Nova Scotia, Canada, and died 1901 in Meadowvale, Annapolis, Nova Scotia, Canada.

Children of SARAH BANKS and SAMUEL BARTEAUX are:
  i.   JAMES E[7] BARTEAUX, b. Jan 1861.
  ii. MARGARET IRENE BARTEAUX.
  iii. MARY ANN BARTEAUX.
  iv. JOHN BARTEAUX.
  v.   MARGARET MAGGIE BARTEAUX.

252. JOSEPH ENGLES[6] BANKS (*CYRENA ANN[5] SPINNEY, JOSEPH[4], SAMUEL[3], SAMUEL[2], THOMAS[1]*) was born 23 Jul 1836 in Nova Scotia, Canada. He married (1) ESTHER KATE HODGE PATTENDEN. She was born 1894 in Horsmonden, Ken. He married (2) BARBARA ANN MAPPLEBECK 1879. She was born 1841. He married (3) RACHEL S MARSHALL 1859. She was born 1839, and died 02 Dec 1927.

Children of JOSEPH BANKS and RACHEL MARSHALL are:
  i.   GEORGE INGLES[7] BANKS, b. 25 Aug 1879; d. 22 Jun 1963, E Margretsville, Annapolis, Nova Scotia, Canada.
  ii. ERNEST GARFIELD BANKS, b. 12 Dec 1883.
  iii. SPURGEON JOSEPH BANKS, b. 25 Jun 1881.
  iv. MILLEDGE W BANKS, b. 07 Dec 1866.
  v.   ELDRIDGE BANKS.
  vi. IOLA MAE BANKS.

253. TIMOTHY EDWARD[6] BANKS (*CYRENA ANN[5] SPINNEY, JOSEPH[4], SAMUEL[3], SAMUEL[2], THOMAS[1]*) was born 04 Nov 1853 in Nova Scotia, Canada, and died 17 Apr 1919. He married (1) MITTIE WHEELOCK PARKER. She was born 31 Dec 1864. He married (2) MITTIE WHEELOCK PARKER 1874. She was born 06 Oct 1853, and died 10 May 1926.

Children of TIMOTHY BANKS and MITTIE PARKER are:
  i.   BURPEE ROY[7] BANKS, b. 04 Aug 1886, Torbrook, Annapolis, Nova Scotia, Canada; d. 21 Dec 1972, Middleton, Nova Scotia, Canada.

    ii.   OWEN PARKER BANKS, b. 16 Mar 1879, Torbrook, Annapolis, Nova Scotia, Canada; d. 10 Sep 1912.

    iii. ENON H. ROY, b. Aug 1882, Torbrook, Annapolis, Nova Scotia, Canada; d. Jun 1996, Torbrook, Annapolis, Nova Scotia, Canada.

    iv. NORRIS LESLIE BANKS, b. 04 May 1877; d. 09 Mar 1963.

254. ISABEL[6] SPINNEY *(SAMUEL[5], JOSEPH[4], SAMUEL[3], SAMUEL[2], THOMAS[1])* was born 22 May 1826 in Aylesford NS, and died in Charlestown Ma. She married JAMES SAMPSON MORSE. He was born 11 Feb 1826.

Child of ISABEL SPINNEY and JAMES MORSE is:

    i.   CAROLINE "CARRIE" ISABEL[7] MORSE, b. 19 Feb 1864, Charlestown, MA; d. 19 Apr 1877, Charlestown, MA.

255. WILLIAM A[6] SPINNEY *(SAMUEL[5], JOSEPH[4], SAMUEL[3], SAMUEL[2], THOMAS[1])* was born 1847 in Aylesford, NS. He married (1) CAROLINE STARBUCK. She died 1895. He married (2) MARY P SYLVESTER 1895.

Child of WILLIAM SPINNEY and CAROLINE STARBUCK is:

    i.   EDMUND STARBUCK[7] SPINNEY, b. 1883.

256. AMANDA[6] SPINNEY *(BENIAH HOWE[5], JOSEPH[4], SAMUEL[3], SAMUEL[2], THOMAS[1])* was born 1838, and died 1919. She married CHARLES JACQUES.

Children of AMANDA SPINNEY and CHARLES JACQUES are:

582.   i.   HARTLEY SPINNEY[7] JACQUES, b. 1860; d. 1912, Annapolis Nova Scotia.

583.   ii. COLIN LOCKE JACQUES, b. 1864; d. 1894.

    iii. STELLA MARGARET JACQUES, b. 1873; m. HARRY L BUSTIN.

257. PRYOR M[6] SPINNEY *(BENIAH HOWE[5], JOSEPH[4], SAMUEL[3], SAMUEL[2], THOMAS[1])* was born 1843 in Nova Scotia, and died 25 Nov 1920 in Annapolis Nova Scotia. He married (1) SARAH J PIERCE 1870, daughter of JOHN PIERCE and AMORET SPINNEY. She was born Oct 1850, and died 06 Feb 1872 in Kingston Nova Scotia. He married (2) MARIA WARREN 1872. She was born in PEI.

Children of PRYOR SPINNEY and SARAH PIERCE are:

    i.   ABBY[7] SPINNEY, b. Abt. 1870; m. CAMPBELL.

    ii. MARY SPINNEY, b. 1872.

Child of PRYOR SPINNEY and MARIA WARREN is:

    iii. LILLIE[7] SPINNEY, b. 1875.

258. NORMAN B[6] SPINNEY *(BENIAH HOWE[5], JOSEPH[4], SAMUEL[3], SAMUEL[2], THOMAS[1])* was born Abt. 1847, and died 1889. He married MINA L. She was born 1847, and died 10 Sep 1886.

Children of NORMAN SPINNEY and MINA L are:

    i.   CHARLES[7] SPINNEY, b. Abt. 1880.

584.   ii. FRED SPINNEY, b. 15 Dec 1873.

    iii. CLIFFORD SPINNEY.

    iv. EVERIND B SPINNEY, b. 1882; d. 1951; m. LILLIAN M; b. 1894; d. 1962.

259. MARGARET[6] SPINNEY *(BENIAH HOWE[5], JOSEPH[4], SAMUEL[3], SAMUEL[2], THOMAS[1])* was born 1849, and died 1901. She married HENRY MUNRO.

Children of MARGARET SPINNEY and HENRY MUNRO are:

    i.   FEDERICK M[7] MUNRO.

    ii. MARY ELIZA MUNRO.

    iii. GEORGE MUNRO.

    iv. HIBBERT MUNRO.

    v. JAMES MUNRO.

260. GERTRUDE A[6] SPINNEY *(ELIJAH[5], JOSEPH[4], SAMUEL[3], SAMUEL[2], THOMAS[1])* was born 1837 in Nova Scotia, Canada, and died 1890 in Winthrop, MA. She married CHARLES L REED 1869 in Charlestown, MA. He was born 1836, and died Aft. 1900.

Child of GERTRUDE SPINNEY and CHARLES REED is:
    i.   HERBURT[7] REED, b. 1875; d. Aft. 1900.

261. SARAH W[6] SPINNEY *(JAMES B[5], JOSEPH[4], SAMUEL[3], SAMUEL[2], THOMAS[1])* was born 06 Jan 1836. She married ISAAC JAMES WHITMAN.

Child of SARAH SPINNEY and ISAAC WHITMAN is:
    i.   BENAIAH LONGLEY[7] WHITMAN, m. MARY SCOTT, 06 Dec 1888.

        Notes for BENAIAH LONGLEY WHITMAN:
        WHITMAN, Benaiah Longley, educator, was born in Totbrook, Nova Scotia, Nov. 21, 1862; son of Isaac James and Sarah (Spinney) Whitman; grandson of James and Margeret (Longley) Whitman, and of James and Lettie (Wheelock) Spinney; and a descendant of John Whitman of Weymouth, Mass. He removed with his parents to Marlboro, Mass., in 1879; attended the Worcester academy, 1880-83, and was graduated from Brown university, A. B., 1887, A.M., 1890, and from the Newton Theological institution in 1890. He was ordained to the Baptist ministry, Sept. 13, 1887, at Newton Upper Falls, Mass., where he remained as pastor, 1887-88. He was married, Dec. 6, 1888, to Mary, daughter of Charles and Phebe (Lovejoy) Scott of Newton, Mass. He was pastor at North Grafton, Mass., 1888-89, and of the Free Street church, Portland, Maine, 1890-92; president of Colby university, 1892-95, and of Columbian university, Washington, D.C., 1895-1900, and in 1900 accepted a call to the fifth Baptist church, Philadelphia, Pa. The honorary degree of D.D. was conferred on him by Bowdoin college in 1894 and that of LL.D. by Harvard university in 1899. In 1903 he was president of the American Baptist Historical society, a trustee of Newton Theological institution, and of Crozer Theological seminary, and lecturer at Bucknell university, Lewisburg, Pa.. and Temple college, Philadelphia.

262. MATILDA SALOME[6] SPINNEY *(JAMES B[5], JOSEPH[4], SAMUEL[3], SAMUEL[2], THOMAS[1])* was born 29 May 1838, and died 1911. She married MILLEDGE CHIPMAN ARMSTRONG 03 May 1855 in Annapolis, NS., son of WALTER ARMSTRONG and ELIZA BISHOP. He was born 10 Nov 1833 in Bloomington, NS., and died 17 Jan 1921 in Bridgeton, NS..

Children of MATILDA SPINNEY and MILLEDGE ARMSTRONG are:
    i.   WILLIAM BURTON[7] ARMSTRONG, b. 27 Feb 1857, Wilnot, NS.; d. 12 Apr 1935, Everett, MA; m. EVA MARIE C HOFFMAN, 24 Mar 1880, Annapolis, NS..
    ii.   WHEELOCK ABEL ARMSTRONG, b. 08 May 1857, Annapolis, NS.; d. 10 May 1859, Nictaux Annapolis, NS..
    iii.   WHEELOCK ARMSTRONG, b. 20 Apr 1860, Annapolis, NS.; d. 25 Mar 1877, Annapolis, NS..
    iv.   ABIGAIL ANN JUDSON ARMSTRONG, b. 20 Sep 1861, Annapolis, NS.; d. 30 Jun 1862, Annapolis, NS..
    v.   LETITIA MARIA ARMSTRONG, b. 15 Jul 1864, Annapolis, NS.; d. 07 Aug 1866, Nictaux Annapolis, NS..
    vi.   ARBELLE ARMSTRONG, b. 1865.
    vii.   MARGARET ELIZABETH ARMSTRONG, b. 04 Mar 1866, Annapolis, NS.; d. 10 May 1867, Nictaux Annapolis, NS..
    viii.   SARAH MAUD ARMSTRONG, b. 25 Nov 1867, Annapolis, NS.; d. 10 Jun 1872, Annapolis, NS..
    ix.   WINFRED MAY ARMSTRONG, b. 25 Nov 1867, Annapolis, NS.; d. 06 Nov 1897, Nictaux, NS.; m. REIRDEN.
    x.   MILLEDGE C ARMSTRONG, b. 1869; d. 1935.
    xi.   MINNIE M ARMSTRONG, b. 22 Jul 1879, Annapolis, NS.; d. 09 Dec 1964, Troobrook Mines, NS.; m. EDGERT HENSHAW.

263. JAMES PELEG[6] SPINNEY *(JAMES B[5], JOSEPH[4], SAMUEL[3], SAMUEL[2], THOMAS[1])* was born 06 Apr 1840 in Annapolis, NS., and died 02 Dec 1911 in Alberta Canada. He married MARY ELIZABETH ARMSTRONG 26 Apr 1862 in Annapolis, NS., daughter of WALTER ARMSTRONG and ELIZA BISHOP. She was born 26 Oct 1840 in Bloomington, NS., and died 1927.

Notes for JAMES PELEG SPINNEY:

MUSICAL ACTIVITIES

The first singing school in Lawrencetown was directed by Mr. Norman Franks in 1865. He began his career as "Singing School Master" and his only transportation was horseback. He travelled to many
surrounding communities to teach interested people to read and sing music. He possessed a bass voice
which he used to enhance the Lawrencetown Methodist Choir. Mr. Franks died in 1925. Some other musicians of this time that taught in Lawrencetown were Mr. Judson Morse of Nictaux, who taught piano lessons; Mr. Peleg Spinney of Margaretville; Mr. Oscar Neilly of Brooklyn and Mr. Norman Phinney of Lawrencetown.

Children of JAMES SPINNEY and MARY ARMSTRONG are:
  i. WINNIFRED[7] SPINNEY.
  ii. LAURA SPINNEY, b. Abt. 1870.
  iii. JAMES WALKER SPINNEY, b. 13 Aug 1871.
  iv. BRIGNOLIA SPINNEY, b. 13 Jul 1881, Annapolis, NS..

264. WILLIAM J[6] SPINNEY *(JAMES B[5], JOSEPH[4], SAMUEL[3], SAMUEL[2], THOMAS[1])* was born 18 May 1842, and died 1927. He married (1) SARAH. She was born 17 Sep 1848. He married (2) MARY L. She was born 1847.

Children of WILLIAM SPINNEY and SARAH are:
  i. MADIE[7] SPINNEY.
  ii. MAUD SPINNEY, b. 1874; m. THOMAS PZANT.
585. iii. ELMORE W SPINNEY, b. 1877; d. 1963, Toorbrook Nova Scotia.
  iv. MARY SPINNEY, b. 1873.

265. JOSEPH W[6] SPINNEY *(JAMES B[5], JOSEPH[4], SAMUEL[3], SAMUEL[2], THOMAS[1])* was born May 1844, and died 1909 in Leominster, Ma. He married ADA NORTHRUP. She was born Jul 1846, and died Aft. 1910.

Children of JOSEPH SPINNEY and ADA NORTHRUP are:
  i. MILLEDGE[7] SPINNEY.
586. ii. JAMES BERT SPINNEY, b. 1872; d. Aft. 1900.
587. iii. LIZZIE LUTICIA SPINNEY, b. 1879; d. Aft. 1910.
  iv. LATINES SPINNEY, b. 1881.
  v. EDWARD SPINNEY, b. May 1882; d. Aft. 1900.
  vi. WILLIAM J SPINNEY, b. Oct 1883; d. Aft. 1900.

266. ISAAC B[6] SPINNEY *(JAMES B[5], JOSEPH[4], SAMUEL[3], SAMUEL[2], THOMAS[1])* was born 25 Jul 1847, and died 22 Jun 1901 in Lowell, MA. He married ELLEN M COPELAND 1872. She was born Aug 1853, and died 1905 in Lowell, MA.

Children of ISAAC SPINNEY and ELLEN COPELAND are:
588. i. DEXTER L[7] SPINNEY, b. 24 May 1876, Nova Scotia; d. Aft. 1910.
  ii. ELLEN M SPINNEY, b. 1878.
  iii. ISAAC F SPINNEY, b. 1879.
  iv. CHRISTY D SPINNEY, b. 1880.
589. v. FLORA V SPINNEY, b. Feb 1881; d. 09 May 1901, Lowell, MA.
590. vi. GAYLON M SPINNEY, b. 1886; d. Aft. 1900.
591. vii. FORREST R SPINNEY, b. 28 May 1889; d. Apr 1965, Houston, Harris, TX.

267. ARTHUR MILLEDGE[6] SPINNEY *(JAMES B[5], JOSEPH[4], SAMUEL[3], SAMUEL[2], THOMAS[1])* was born 16 Aug 1851, and died 1925. He married (1) SUSAN SYBRONTE WHEELOCK. She was born 08 Mar 1857, and died 1954. He married (2) HETTIE. She was born 1851, and died 24 Mar 1883.

Children of ARTHUR SPINNEY and SUSAN WHEELOCK are:
  i. HATTIE SWAYNE[7] SPINNEY, b. 10 Apr 1885; d. 1922; m. REGINALD BANNING STEVENS.
  ii. ARTHUR LAMERT SPINNEY, b. 20 Oct 1888.
  iii. MINNIE W SPINNEY, b. 16 Feb 1890.
  iv. MABEL ROBERTS SPINNEY, b. 10 Jun 1887, Kerrobert , Saskatchewan; d. 20 Aug 1945; m. FREDERICK
   NORMAND BURKE, 09 Dec 1914, Kerrobert, Saskatchewan; b. 07 Jun 1886, Carievale, Saskatchewan; d. 03
   Feb 1985.

Children of ARTHUR SPINNEY and HETTIE are:
- v. GEORGE V[7] SPINNEY, b. 1875; d. 1959.
- vi. LAMBERT L SPINNEY, b. 1882; d. 20 Dec 1883, Toorbrook Nova Scotia.

268. ERNEST H.[6] NEILY *(SARAH ELIZABETH[5] SPINNEY, JOSEPH[4], SAMUEL[3], SAMUEL[2], THOMAS[1])* was born 1867. He married HARRIET I. SPINNEY, daughter of JACOB SPINNEY and JANE DUNCANSON. She was born 1866, and died 1955.

Children of ERNEST NEILY and HARRIET SPINNEY are:
- i. GRANT[7] NEILY, b. 1902.
- ii. JENNIE NEILY, b. 1906.

269. AMORET[6] BROWN *(JANE[5] SPINNEY, DAVID[4], SAMUEL[3], SAMUEL[2], THOMAS[1])* was born 31 Dec 1833, and died 1921. She married JOHN BROWN LUTZ, son of WILLIAM LUTZ and MARYANN BROWN. He was born 01 Jan 1825.

Child of AMORET BROWN and JOHN LUTZ is:
- i. NELSON[7] LUTZ, b. 1874; m. BLANCH.

270. MARY ELIZA CRANDALL[6] WEAVER *(PETER CRANDALL[5], MARY[4] SPINNEY, SAMUEL[3], SAMUEL[2], THOMAS[1])* She married JAMES BENJAMIN ALLEN, son of JAMES ALLEN and MARY SALTER.

Child of MARY WEAVER and JAMES ALLEN is:
- 592. i. CHARLES WESLEY[7] ALLEN.

271. SAMUEL[6] SPINNEY *(ISAAC BEACH[5], SAMUEL MCCLURE[4], SAMUEL[3], SAMUEL[2], THOMAS[1])* was born 1821 in Greenwood, NS., and died 27 Apr 1912. He married SARAH ANN ROACH 27 Feb 1850, daughter of ZEBINA ROACH and FRANCES NEILY. She was born 1829, and died 1919.

Children of SAMUEL SPINNEY and SARAH ROACH are:
- 593. i. JULIA IDA[7] SPINNEY, b. 11 Jan 1850, Burlington, NS..
- 594. ii. FANNY (FRANCIS) ANN SPINNEY, b. 09 May 1853; d. 20 Nov 1911.
- 595. iii. SARAH J. SPINNEY, b. 24 Mar 1856; d. 1942.
- iv. WILLIAM LEANDER SPINNEY, b. 08 Dec 1857.
- v. HIBBERT SPINNEY, b. 15 Aug 1859.
- vi. ELLA M. SPINNEY, b. 1861; d. 1947; m. NEIL WARNER.
- 596. vii. AZUBALE MAUDE SPINNEY, b. 27 Jun 1862; d. 1928.
- viii. BENIAH SPINNEY, b. Bet. 1863 - 1865; d. Bet. 1863 - 1865.
- ix. MILDRED JOSEPHINE SPINNEY, b. 11 Dec 1866; m. (1) OUTHIT LIGHTIZER; b. 1865; m. (2) OUTHIT LIGHTIZER.

     Notes for MILDRED JOSEPHINE SPINNEY:

     Around the Square indicates only that Mildred "died young".

- 597. x. ISAAC CALVIN SPINNEY, b. 27 Jun 1871, Nova Scotia; d. 1949, Petersham, MA.

272. JOHN[6] SPINNEY *(ISAAC BEACH[5], SAMUEL MCCLURE[4], SAMUEL[3], SAMUEL[2], THOMAS[1])* was born 1829, and died 15 Nov 1898. He married IRENE WILSON Abt. 1860. She was born 1833, and died 10 May 1901.

Child of JOHN SPINNEY and IRENE WILSON is:
- i. GEORGIANNA[7] SPINNEY, b. 1863.

273. SARAH[6] SPINNEY *(ISAAC BEACH[5], SAMUEL MCCLURE[4], SAMUEL[3], SAMUEL[2], THOMAS[1])* was born 1837 in

Greenwood Sq NS. She married (1) JOSEPH LIGHTIZER.   She married (2) JOHN LIGHTIZER.

Children of SARAH SPINNEY and JOSEPH LIGHTIZER are:
- i.   HARRY[7] LIGHTIZER, b. 1861.
- ii. ANNA LIGHTIZER, b. 1862.
- iii. OUTHIT LIGHTIZER, b. 1865; m. MILDRED JOSEPHINE SPINNEY; b. 11 Dec 1866.

Notes for MILDRED JOSEPHINE SPINNEY:

Around the Square indicates only that Mildred "died young".

- iv. HARRIET LIGHTIZER, b. 1867.
- v.   ELIZABETH LIGHTIZER, b. 1871.

Child of SARAH SPINNEY and JOHN LIGHTIZER is:
- vi. OUTHIT[7] LIGHTIZER, b. 1865.

274. AUSTIN WELTON[6] SPINNEY *(JACOB BEACH[5], SAMUEL MCCLURE[4], SAMUEL[3], SAMUEL[2], THOMAS[1])* was born 14 Sep 1827 in Aylesford, NS., and died 18 Jan 1891. He married ELIZABETH JANE MORSE, daughter of JONATHAN MORSE and ELIZABETH SPINNEY. She was born 02 Dec 1829 in Harmony, NS., and died 12 Nov 1904 in Harmony, NS..

Children of AUSTIN SPINNEY and ELIZABETH MORSE are:
598.	i.	ELIZABETH MARIA[7] SPINNEY, b. 17 Apr 1847, Harmony, NS.; d. 17 Sep 1886, Harmony, NS..
599.	ii.	ANN MELISSA SPINNEY, b. 1848, Harmony, NS; d. 1928.
	iii.	JACOB CHURCH SPINNEY, b. 18 Mar 1850, Harmony, NS.; d. 04 Apr 1857, Harmony, NS..
	iv.	CHARLOTTE LAVINIA SPINNEY, b. 25 Jun 1851, Harmony, NS.; d. 19 Feb 1853, Harmony, NS..
	v.	ZILPHA SOPHIA SPINNEY, b. 12 Jun 1853, Harmony, NS.; d. 24 Oct 1925; m. WILLIAM ASAPH FANCY, 08 Apr 1891.
600.	vi.	JONATHAN RIED MORSE SPINNEY, b. 01 Jun 1856.
601.	vii.	MINNIE SALOME SPINNEY, b. 1857.
602.	viii.	AUSTIN SPURR SPINNEY, b. Oct 1858, Nova Scotia; d. Aft. 1920, Massachusetts.
	ix.	EUNICE HARRIET SPINNEY, b. 17 Mar 1862, Harmony, NS.; d. 13 Oct 1865, Harmony, NS..
603.	x.	CALEB SNOW SPINNEY, b. 15 Jul 1865, Harmony, NS.; d. 1931.
	xi.	JOSHUA NOBLE SPINNEY, b. 09 May 1867, Harmony, NS.; d. 09 Dec 1878, Harmony, NS..
	xii.	IDA ODESSA SPINNEY, b. 02 Feb 1871, Harmony, NS.; d. 22 Dec 1877, Harmony, NS..

275. JACOB BEACH[6] SPINNEY *(JACOB BEACH[5], SAMUEL MCCLURE[4], SAMUEL[3], SAMUEL[2], THOMAS[1])* was born 13 Nov 1828 in Aylesford NS, and died 1907. He married JANE R. DUNCANSON. She was born 1831.

Children of JACOB SPINNEY and JANE DUNCANSON are:
	i.	JACOB C.[7] SPINNEY, b. 1850; d. 1857.
604.	ii.	WILLIAM G. SPINNEY, b. 1854; d. 1935.
605.	iii.	ANNA IRENE SPINNEY, b. 04 Jun 1858, Greenwood, NS.; d. 25 Nov 1935.
	iv.	ELIZA J. SPINNEY, b. 1860; d. 1861.
606.	v.	HARRIET I. SPINNEY, b. 1866; d. 1955.

276. HARDING THEODORE[6] SPINNEY *(JACOB BEACH[5], SAMUEL MCCLURE[4], SAMUEL[3], SAMUEL[2], THOMAS[1])* was born 09 Sep 1831 in Aylesford NS, and died 1877 in Greenwood Sq NS. He married HELEN F. BERTEAUX 09 Oct 1856, daughter of JAMES BARTEAUX and PARNEY WEELOCK. She was born 1833, and died Aft. 1901.

Notes for HARDING THEODORE SPINNEY:
Twin of Jacob B. Jr. ???

Children of HARDING SPINNEY and HELEN BERTEAUX are:
607.	i.	RUBY LAVINA[7] SPINNEY, b. 1857.
608.	ii.	JAMES BARTEAUX SPINNEY, b. 1860, Greenwood, N.S.; d. 1921, Greenwood, N.S..
	iii.	INGRAM JUDSON SPINNEY, b. 1862; d. 1866.

    iv.   ANNA ELIZABETH SPINNEY, b. 1863; m. ISIAH BRUCE.
     v.   PARNIE SAMANTHA SPINNEY, b. 1865; m. CHARLES B WILLIAMS.
    vi.   ROWENA SALOME SPINNEY, b. 1870; d. 1905; m. NOBLE LYONS.

277. CALEB[6] SPINNEY *(JACOB BEACH[5], SAMUEL MCCLURE[4], SAMUEL[3], SAMUEL[2], THOMAS[1])* was born 17 Dec 1832 in Aylesford, NS., and died 1906. He married PARNEY BARTEAUX 27 Jan 1858, daughter of JAMES BARTEAUX and PARNEY WEELOCK. She was born 1834.

Children of CALEB SPINNEY and PARNEY BARTEAUX are:
609.   i.   MARY EMMA[7] SPINNEY, b. 25 Feb 1851; d. 16 Aug 1888.
610.   ii.   FLORA BELLE SPINNEY, b. 05 Jun 1861; d. 1934.
611.   iii.   BERTHA MAUDE SPINNEY, b. 09 Dec 1863; d. 1939.
      iv.   ULYSSES GRANT SPINNEY, b. 06 Jan 1865; d. 1865.
612.   v.   EDWARD MANNING SPINNEY, b. 14 Mar 1867; d. 1961.
      vi.   MARY JANE SPINNEY, b. 06 Jan 1870; m. HERBERT BURKE.
     vii.   JULIA ETTA SPINNEY, b. 25 Apr 1872.
    viii.   HELENA AMANDA SPINNEY, b. 20 Aug 1874.
      ix.   SADIE ANN SPINNEY, b. 01 Mar 1894.
      x.   CHESTER BARTEAUX SPINNEY, b. 01 Dec 1896; d. 02 Feb 1919.
     xi.   CARLTON T. SPINNEY, b. 01 Sep 1898; d. 16 Oct 1936.
    xii.   ORA LOUISE SPINNEY, b. 10 Jan 1902.

278. BENIAH B[6] SPINNEY *(JACOB BEACH[5], SAMUEL MCCLURE[4], SAMUEL[3], SAMUEL[2], THOMAS[1])* was born 22 Mar 1838 in Aylesford NS, and died 1923. He married (1) MARY JANE WHITMAN. She was born 1844. He married (2) MARGARET MCKENNA. She was born 1840.

Children of BENIAH SPINNEY and MARY WHITMAN are:
613.   i.   MELBURNE E.[7] SPINNEY, b. 1864; d. 1928.
      ii.   AMELIA SPINNEY, b. Jan 1866; d. Feb 1866.
    iii.   ANNIS W. SPINNEY, b. 11 May 1868; d. 09 Jan 1869.
     iv.   EMMA MAUDE SPINNEY, b. 1878; m. ARTHUR PATTERSON; b. 1874.

279. ENOCH[6] SPINNEY *(JACOB BEACH[5], SAMUEL MCCLURE[4], SAMUEL[3], SAMUEL[2], THOMAS[1])* was born 18 Feb 1840 in Greenwood, NS., and died 03 Jun 1907 in Harmony, NS.. He married PHEBE BOWLBY. She was born 1845.

Children of ENOCH SPINNEY and PHEBE BOWLBY are:
      i.   LILY BLANCHE[7] SPINNEY, b. 1863, Harmony, N.S.; d. 27 Sep 1865, Harmony, N.S..
614.   ii.   BLANCHE LILY SPINNEY, b. 10 Dec 1865, Harmony, N.S.; d. 22 Sep 1908, New Germany, N.S..
615.   iii.   EVERETT LAMONT SPINNEY, b. 29 Dec 1866, Harmony, N.S.; d. 24 Apr 1930, W. Acton, MA.
616.   iv.   GEORGE ELBURN SPINNEY, b. 06 Apr 1870, Harmony, N.S.; d. May 1924.
617.   v.   HARRY ATWOOD SPINNEY, b. 1874, Harmony, N.S.; d. 10 Aug 1901.
618.   vi.   LELAND TEASDALE SPINNEY, b. 05 Oct 1875, Harmony, NS.; d. 21 Jun 1950, Harmony, NS..

280. CLARK THOMAS[6] SPINNEY *(JACOB BEACH[5], SAMUEL MCCLURE[4], SAMUEL[3], SAMUEL[2], THOMAS[1])* was born 21 Jun 1846, and died 20 Jun 1926. He married ORINDA SLOCUM 06 Jan 1873. She was born 1855, and died 1944.

Notes for CLARK THOMAS SPINNEY:
Clark's son Burpee Spinney lived in Barre, Massachusetts

Children of CLARK SPINNEY and ORINDA SLOCUM are:
      i.   ALTHEA LAURA[7] SPINNEY, b. 1873; m. EVERETT SMITH.
      ii.   ANNA W. SPINNEY, b. 1874; d. 15 Aug 1894.
619.   iii.   BURPEE ALBINA SPINNEY, b. 1883; d. 1969, Barre, MA.
620.   iv.   GEORGIA E. SPINNEY, b. 24 Jul 1887; d. 1936.

281. ELIZABETH JANE[6] MORSE *(ELIZABETH (ELIZA)[5] SPINNEY, SAMUEL MCCLURE[4], SAMUEL[3], SAMUEL[2], THOMAS[1])* was born 02 Dec 1829 in Harmony, NS., and died 12 Nov 1904 in Harmony, NS.. She married AUSTIN WELTON

SPINNEY, son of JACOB SPINNEY and ANN CROCKER. He was born 14 Sep 1827 in Aylesford, NS., and died 18 Jan 1891.

Children are listed above under (274) Austin Welton Spinney.

282. HELEN AMORET[6] MORSE *(ELIZABETH (ELIZA)[5] SPINNEY, SAMUEL MCCLURE[4], SAMUEL[3], SAMUEL[2], THOMAS[1])* was born 11 Sep 1830 in Harmony, NS., and died 12 Mar 1883 in Harmony, NS.. She married ALEXANDER BANKS 11 Mar 1852 in Harmony, NS.. He was born 18 Jun 1812.

Children of HELEN MORSE and ALEXANDER BANKS are:
- i.   ABIGAIL "ABBIE" LAVINIA[7] BANKS.
- ii.   HARRIET MARIA BANKS.
- iii. BURPEE URIAH BANKS.
- iv.   RICHARD CLARK BANKS, b. 24 Mar 1854, Harmony, NS.; d. 26 Mar 1860, Harmony, NS..
- v.   CAROLINE ELIZA BANKS, b. 12 Feb 1856, Harmony, NS.; d. 1936, Auburn, NS.; m. LEWIS BEALS.
- vi.   JOHNATHAN REID BANKS, b. 22 Dec 1861, Harmony, NS.; d. 1924, Halls Harbour, NS.; m. BEATRICE DUNHAM.
- vii. BANKS, b. Abt. 1862.
- viii. ELIZABETH MAY BANKS, b. 30 Nov 1866, Harmony, NS.; d. 19 Nov 1878, Harmony, NS..
- ix.   MYRTLE MAZETTA BANKS, b. 09 Jun 1873, Harmony, NS.; d. 29 Jul 1887, Harmony, NS..

283. SAMUEL CHURCH[6] MORSE *(ELIZABETH (ELIZA)[5] SPINNEY, SAMUEL MCCLURE[4], SAMUEL[3], SAMUEL[2], THOMAS[1])* was born 27 Feb 1832 in Harmony, NS., and died 27 Feb 1863 in Harmony, NS.. He married CHARLOTTE LIGHTIZER 14 May 1857 in Aylesford Twp NS.. She was born 1837.

Children of SAMUEL MORSE and CHARLOTTE LIGHTIZER are:
- i.   ELIZABETH"LIZZIE" ALTHEA[7] MORSE.
- ii.   ELIZABETH MORSE, b. 1858; d. 1930; m. EBER POTTER.
- iii. ALTHEA MORSE, b. 1860; d. 1860.
- iv.   ALTHEA"ALLIE"SOPHRONIA MORSE, b. 10 Feb 1860, Harmony, NS.; d. 25 Dec 1860, Harmony, NS..

284. EUNICE HARRIET[6] MORSE *(ELIZABETH (ELIZA)[5] SPINNEY, SAMUEL MCCLURE[4], SAMUEL[3], SAMUEL[2], THOMAS[1])* was born 12 Feb 1834 in Harmony, NS., and died 15 Apr 1862 in Greenwood, NS.. She married WILLIAM SAUNDERS WILSON Abt. 1858. He was born 1825.

Children of EUNICE MORSE and WILLIAM WILSON are:
- i.   MARY ELIZABETH "LIBBIE"[7] WILSON, b. 14 Jun 1859, Harmony, NS.; d. 19 Sep 1942, Lynn, MA; m. LEVI FOSTER HOLDEN, 1904, Lynn, MA.
- ii.   LAVENIA WILSON, b. Abt. 1861, Harmony, NS.; d. Abt. 1861, Greenwood Sq, NS..

285. CAROLINE AMELIA[6] MORSE *(ELIZABETH (ELIZA)[5] SPINNEY, SAMUEL MCCLURE[4], SAMUEL[3], SAMUEL[2], THOMAS[1])* was born 19 Jan 1838 in Harmony, NS., and died 18 Nov 1913 in Tremont, NS.. She married G. F. PARKER WARD 12 Oct 1855 in Harmony, NS.. He was born 29 Jul 1832.

Children of CAROLINE MORSE and G. WARD are:
- i.   SILAS HARDY[7] WARD.
- ii.   SAMUEL "CHURCH" WARD.
- iii. ELIZABETH "LIZZIE" WARD, b. 05 Jun 1882, Tremont, NS.; d. 14 Sep 1885, Tremont, NS..

286. ELISHA SPINNEY[6] MORSE *(ELIZABETH (ELIZA)[5] SPINNEY, SAMUEL MCCLURE[4], SAMUEL[3], SAMUEL[2], THOMAS[1])* was born 08 Dec 1839 in Harmony, NS., and died 24 Jan 1914 in Millville, NS. He married ALALIA ADELIA GRAVES 25 Jan 1871 in Harmony, Kings Co Ns. She was born 02 Oct 1856.

Children of ELISHA MORSE and ALALIA GRAVES are:
- i.   WILLIAM HARRIS[7] MORSE.
- 621. ii.   JESSIE F. MORSE.
- iii. LILLIAN BLANCHE MORSE.
- iv.   SILAS PARKER MORSE, b. 18 Mar 1887, Harmony, NS.; d. 1944, Florida; m. KATE CASSIE.

287. ABNER PARKER[6] MORSE *(ELIZABETH (ELIZA)[5] SPINNEY, SAMUEL MCCLURE[4], SAMUEL[3], SAMUEL[2], THOMAS[1])* was born 17 Jan 1842 in Harmony, NS., and died 29 Aug 1906 in Harmony, NS.. He married LOIS MELISSA BANKS 31 Dec 1868. She was born 12 Jul 1845.

Children of ABNER MORSE and LOIS BANKS are:
    i.   HARDY PARKER[7] MORSE.
    ii. HARRIET"HATTIE" ELIZABET MORSE.
    iii. REUBEN TALFORD MORSE.
    iv. MINNIE ETHEL MORSE.
    v.   GRANT LEANDER MORSE.
    vi. ALMIRA "MYRA" AMELIA MORSE.
    vii. CHURCH ABNER MORSE.
   viii. AUBREY DEVERE MORSE.
    ix. PAULINE MORSE, b. 1870.
    x.   PAUL MORSE, b. 1870.

288. JONATHAN CHURCH[6] MORSE *(ELIZABETH (ELIZA)[5] SPINNEY, SAMUEL MCCLURE[4], SAMUEL[3], SAMUEL[2], THOMAS[1])* was born 27 Dec 1844 in Harmony, NS., and died 1890 in Harmony, NS.. He married ANGELINA ELIZABETH BANKS 04 Oct 1865. She was born 10 Aug 1839.

Children of JONATHAN MORSE and ANGELINA BANKS are:
    i.   CORA E.[7] MORSE.
    ii. ALICE M. MORSE.
    iii. LENA MAUDE MORSE.
    iv. ELIZABETH EDNA MORSE.
    v.   ERNEST SNOW MORSE, b. 14 Mar 1866, Harmony, NS.; d. 11 Dec 1927, Acton, MA; m. ESTELLA BEACH.
    vi. GEORGIANNA MORSE, b. 05 May 1874, Harmony, NS.; d. 1889, Harmony, NS..
   vii. PAULINE A. MORSE, b. 03 Oct 1881, Harmony, NS.; d. 06 Oct 1886, Harmony, NS..

289. BENAIAH HOWE "JOE"[6] MORSE *(ELIZABETH (ELIZA)[5] SPINNEY, SAMUEL MCCLURE[4], SAMUEL[3], SAMUEL[2], THOMAS[1])* was born 21 Jul 1846 in Harmony, NS., and died 20 Jul 1919 in Harmony, NS.. He married HANNAH MEHITABLE BANKS 30 Dec 1868. She was born 27 Aug 1847.

Children of BENAIAH MORSE and HANNAH BANKS are:
    i.   ALDEN BANKS[7] MORSE.
    ii. HOWE BENAIAH MORSE.
    iii. SERAPHINA MORSE.
    iv. MARIAM "MAMIE" BERTAH MORSE.
622.   v.   VERNON LLOYD MORSE.
    vi. HARLAN CHURCH MORSE, b. 13 Feb 1875, Harmony, NS.; d. 24 Jun 1966, Waterville, NS..

290. SAMUEL[6] SAUNDERS *(EUNICE[5] SPINNEY, SAMUEL MCCLURE[4], SAMUEL[3], SAMUEL[2], THOMAS[1])* was born 1828, and died 1912. He married SUSANAH SPINNEY Abt. 1860, daughter of ABRAHAM SPINNEY and JANE PIERCE. She was born 1831, and died 1912.

Children are listed above under (244) Susanah Spinney.

291. ALFRED PARKER[6] SAUNDERS *(EUNICE[5] SPINNEY, SAMUEL MCCLURE[4], SAMUEL[3], SAMUEL[2], THOMAS[1])* was born 08 Feb 1831 in Greenwood, Kings, Nova Scotia, Canada, and died 09 Aug 1918 in Harmon, Kings, Nova Scotia, Canada. He married ANN MELISSA SPINNEY, daughter of AUSTIN SPINNEY and ELIZABETH MORSE. She was born 1848 in Harmony, NS, and died 1928.

Children of ALFRED SAUNDERS and ANN SPINNEY are:
    i.   MARY ELIZABETH[7] SAUNDERS, b. 1874; d. 1881.
    ii. ARTHUR CHURCH SAUNDERS, b. 1876.
    iii. ALFRED NOBLE SAUNDERS, b. 1879.

292. CATHERINE[6] SAUNDERS *(EUNICE[5] SPINNEY, SAMUEL MCCLURE[4], SAMUEL[3], SAMUEL[2], THOMAS[1])* was born 11 May 1833, and died 1902. She married CALVIN CROCKER. He was born 1829, and died 24 Nov 1899.

Children of CATHERINE SAUNDERS and CALVIN CROCKER are:
- 623.   i.   ABIGAIL A[7] CROCKER, b. 08 Dec 1852; d. 19 Jan 1916.
-           ii. SUSAN A CROCKER, b. 1857; d. 10 Aug 1875.
- 624.   iii. JAMES H. CROCKER, b. 27 Jan 1859.
- 625.   iv.   WILLIAM E. CROCKER, b. 1862.
- 626.   v.   ELLA M CROCKER, b. 30 Sep 1863; d. 1938.
-           vi. MARTHA OLIVE CROCKER, b. 17 Feb 1872; m. ALBERT LUTZ; b. 1878.

293. MARTHA[6] SAUNDERS *(EUNICE[5] SPINNEY, SAMUEL MCCLURE[4], SAMUEL[3], SAMUEL[2], THOMAS[1])* was born 1836, and died 05 Oct 1872. She married CHARLES SPINNEY, son of ABRAHAM SPINNEY and JANE PIERCE. He was born Nov 1831, and died 23 Mar 1869 in Aylesford NS.

Children are listed above under (245) Charles Spinney.

294. JOHN NEILY[6] SPINNEY *(INGERSON H[5], SAMUEL MCCLURE[4], SAMUEL[3], SAMUEL[2], THOMAS[1])* was born 1858. He married EVA ST CLAIR CLARK 1885.

Child of JOHN SPINNEY and EVA CLARK is:
-           i.   EDGAR WALDO[7] SPINNEY, b. 25 May 1891, Massachusetts; d. 14 May 1982, California.

295. E FREEMAN[6] SPINNEY *(INGERSON H[5], SAMUEL MCCLURE[4], SAMUEL[3], SAMUEL[2], THOMAS[1])* was born 1841 in South, Aylesford, Kings, Nova Scotia. He married ANNA ISABELLA NEILY. She was born 1849.

Children of E SPINNEY and ANNA NEILY are:
-           i.   ALICE SAMANTHA[7] SPINNEY, b. 1874, South, Aylesford, Kings, Nova Scotia.
-           ii. DORA HASTINGSSPINNEY, b. 1879, South, Aylesford, Kings, Nova Scotia; m. GEORGE WILLIAM BALCOM.

296. CHIPMAN L[6] SPINNEY *(INGERSON H[5], SAMUEL MCCLURE[4], SAMUEL[3], SAMUEL[2], THOMAS[1])* was born 1872, and died 1938. He married MARTHA ODESSA NICHOLS 02 Dec 1896 in Nicholsville, N.S.. She was born 1876.

Children of CHIPMAN SPINNEY and MARTHA NICHOLS are:
-           i.   BESSIE[7] SPINNEY, b. 1897; d. 1965.
-           ii. ERDENA SPINNEY, b. 1900; d. 1959.
-           iii. MURIEL SPINNEY, b. 1907; m. (1) WILFRED WHITE; m. (2) PAUL BISHOP.
- 627.   iv.   CLINTON SPINNEY, b. 1907.

297. JESSIE[6] SPINNEY *(HENRY[5], SAMUEL MCCLURE[4], SAMUEL[3], SAMUEL[2], THOMAS[1])* was born 04 Apr 1855, and died Aft. 1901. She married CHARLES I VAN-BUSKIRK. He was born 19 Jan 1841, and died Aft. 1901.

Children of JESSIE SPINNEY and CHARLES VAN-BUSKIRK are:
-           i.   FRED[7] VAN-BUSKIRK.
-           ii. GEORGIE VAN-BUSKIRK.

298. HIRAM R[6] SPINNEY *(HENRY[5], SAMUEL MCCLURE[4], SAMUEL[3], SAMUEL[2], THOMAS[1])* was born 16 Sep 1873, and died Aft. 1930 in Cambridge, MA. He married CATHERINE FARR. She was born 1877 in Vermont, and died Aft. 1930 in Cambridge, MA.

Children of HIRAM SPINNEY and CATHERINE FARR are:
-           i.   MABEL M[7] SPINNEY, b. 1897, Vermont; d. Aft. 1910.
-           ii. CHARLES L SPINNEY, b. 1898, Vermont; d. Aft. 1920.
-           iii. CLARENCE SPINNEY, b. 1900, Vermont; d. Aft. 1920.
-           iv. GRACE SPINNEY, b. 1902; d. Aft. 1920.
-           v.   LILLIAN SPINNEY, b. 1904; d. Aft. 1920.
-           vi. IRENE B SPINNEY, b. 1905; d. 1905.

    vii.   FRANK L SPINNEY, b. 1908; d. Aft. 1920.
   viii.   WILLIAM EDSON SPINNEY, b. 1910; d. Bef. 1920.
    ix.   IRVING SPINNEY, b. 1911; d. Aft. 1930.
     x.   DOROTHY SPINNEY, b. 1916; d. Aft. 1930.

299. RUBY ARDELLISS[6] GRIFFIN *(CATHERINE INGLIS[5] SPINNEY, SAMUEL McCLURE[4], SAMUEL[3], SAMUEL[2], THOMAS[1])* was born 1885, and died 1961. She married HOWARD E. ARMSTRONG. He was born 01 Jul 1870.

Children of RUBY GRIFFIN and HOWARD ARMSTRONG are:
628.   i.   ELLESWORTH[7] ARMSTRONG.
       ii.   VERA ARMSTRONG, m. WATTSON WHITMAN.
629.   iii.   MARION ARMSTRONG.

300. JAMES E.[6] GRIFFIN *(CATHERINE INGLIS[5] SPINNEY, SAMUEL McCLURE[4], SAMUEL[3], SAMUEL[2], THOMAS[1])* was born 1864, and died 1948. He married SOPHIA NEILY. She was born 1860.

Child of JAMES GRIFFIN and SOPHIA NEILY is:
      i.   RUTH[7] GRIFFIN.

301. CHARLES A.[6] PIERCE *(AMORET[5] SPINNEY, SAMUEL McCLURE[4], SAMUEL[3], SAMUEL[2], THOMAS[1])* was born 10 May 1846, and died 23 Aug 1913 in Greenwood, Kings Co Ns. He married (1) EDITH LUCILLA McKENNA 1870. She was born 1848, and died 1892. He married (2) LAVINIA CLARISSA MORSE 1895. She was born 02 Oct 1848.

Notes for CHARLES A. PIERCE:
It is said that the Pierces first lived in Aylesford on the Pierce Road. Charles Pierce came to Greenwood to take care of his uncle Elisah Spinney, who lived on Spinney Road.

Children of CHARLES PIERCE and EDITH McKENNA are:
630.   i.   HOWARD ELIZA[7] PIERCE, b. 1873; d. 30 Nov 1909.
631.   ii.   FRANK LOVETT PIERCE, b. 1887; d. 1956.
     iii.   JOHN PIERCE, b. 1892; d. 1914.
     iv.   OWEN PIERCE.

302. SARAH J[6] PIERCE *(AMORET[5] SPINNEY, SAMUEL McCLURE[4], SAMUEL[3], SAMUEL[2], THOMAS[1])* was born Oct 1850, and died 06 Feb 1872 in Kingston Nova Scotia. She married PRYOR M SPINNEY 1870, son of BENIAH SPINNEY and MARY BANKS. He was born 1843 in Nova Scotia, and died 25 Nov 1920 in Annapolis Nova Scotia.

Children are listed above under (257) Pryor M Spinney.

303. CAROLINE[6] PIERCE *(AMORET[5] SPINNEY, SAMUEL McCLURE[4], SAMUEL[3], SAMUEL[2], THOMAS[1])* was born 1857. She married LERSON STEVENSON. He was born 1848.

Children of CAROLINE PIERCE and LERSON STEVENSON are:
      i.   GRACE[7] STEVENSON.
     ii.   ARTHUR STEVENSON, b. 1875.

304. SHERMAN[6] PIERCE *(AMORET[5] SPINNEY, SAMUEL McCLURE[4], SAMUEL[3], SAMUEL[2], THOMAS[1])* was born 1859. He married MARY KEAVIL.

Children of SHERMAN PIERCE and MARY KEAVIL are:
      i.   CARRIE[7] PIERCE.
     ii.   IVAN PIERCE.
    iii.   MARY PIERCE.

305. FRANK[6] SPINNEY *(MARY[5], BENIAH[4], SAMUEL[3], SAMUEL[2], THOMAS[1])* was born 11 Nov 1852, and died Nov 1945. He married ADELIA JANE ATWELL 07 Jan 1873, daughter of CYRUS ATWELL and MARIA. She was born 09

Jul 1850, and died 14 Aug 1918.

Children of FRANK SPINNEY and ADELIA ATWELL are:

632.	i.	MARY ELIZABETH[7] SPINNEY, b. 25 May 1872; d. 1911.
633.	ii.	AUGUSTA SPINNEY, b. 16 Aug 1876; d. 1910.
	iii.	MARIA SPINNEY, b. 03 Nov 1878.
	iv.	GEORGE OTIS SPINNEY, b. 03 Jul 1880, Black River, NS..
	v.	ENOS SPINNEY, b. 09 Apr 1883.
	vi.	LINDEN ESTELLA SPINNEY, b. 28 Oct 1886.
634.	vii.	EMERY CLARENCE SPINNEY, b. 13 Feb 1891, Black River, NS.; d. 02 Apr 1958.

306. JAMES HARRY[6] SPINNEY *(MARY[5], BENIAH[4], SAMUEL[3], SAMUEL[2], THOMAS[1])* was born 1873. He married (1) JESSIE EYE. He married (2) INEZ MABEL ROBARTS 23 Oct 1902.

Children of JAMES SPINNEY and JESSIE EYE are:
- i. EVA[7] SPINNEY, b. 1896.
- ii. GEORGE SPINNEY, b. 1897.

307. JOHN ALEXANDER[6] SPINNEY *(THOMAS LEONARD[5], BENIAH[4], SAMUEL[3], SAMUEL[2], THOMAS[1])* was born Nov 1857 in Cumb, NS., and died Bet. 1900 - 1920. He married SARAH CHAMBERS 12 Dec 1882 in Richmond Maine. She was born May 1858 in New Brunswick, Canada, and died Aft. 1920.

Child of JOHN SPINNEY and SARAH CHAMBERS is:

| 635. | i. | ANNIE L[7] SPINNEY, b. 03 Dec 1887, Richmond, ME. |

308. WILLIAM LUKE[6] SPINNEY *(THOMAS LEONARD[5], BENIAH[4], SAMUEL[3], SAMUEL[2], THOMAS[1])* was born 1853 in Nova Scotia. He married FANNY E PATE 05 May 1875 in St. Louis, Missouri. She was born 1855.

Children of WILLIAM SPINNEY and FANNY PATE are:
- i. WILLIAM[7] SPINNEY, b. 1876, Missouri.
- ii. LILY SPINNEY, b. 1876, Missouri.

309. THOMAS LEONARD[6] SPINNEY *(THOMAS LEONARD[5], BENIAH[4], SAMUEL[3], SAMUEL[2], THOMAS[1])* was born 1869. He married MARY T GALLIVAN.

Child of THOMAS SPINNEY and MARY GALLIVAN is:
- i. JAMES WILLIAM[7] SPINNEY, b. 1898.

310. BRENTON ARTHUR[6] SPINNEY *(DAVID GRIFFEN[5], BENIAH[4], SAMUEL[3], SAMUEL[2], THOMAS[1])* was born 15 Jan 1861. He married MILDRED BLANCHE BLOIS, daughter of WILLIAM BLOIS and IDA CORKUM. She was born 18 Mar 1889 in Canning Kings NS.

Children of BRENTON SPINNEY and MILDRED BLOIS are:
- i. GORDON FIELDING[7] SPINNEY, b. Abt. 1910.
- ii. LEONARD ALLISON SPINNEY, b. Abt. 1910.
- iii. MYRTLE BLANCHE SPINNEY, b. 25 Mar 1912, Canning, NS.; m. ALBERT STEWART EDDY, 20 Oct 1932, Kentville, NS..

311. THOMAS LEONARD[6] SPINNEY *(DAVID GRIFFEN[5], BENIAH[4], SAMUEL[3], SAMUEL[2], THOMAS[1])* was born 17 Sep 1867, and died 11 Jan 1937. He married WINNIFRED JANE SCHOFIELD 28 Mar 1892, daughter of JAMES SCHOFIELD and DEBORAH WOODWORTH. She was born 07 Oct 1870 in Canning, NS., and died 03 Nov 1952 in Wakefield, MA.

Children of THOMAS SPINNEY and WINNIFRED SCHOFIELD are:
- i. HARRY GRIFFIN[7] SPINNEY, b. Jan 1894, North Quincy, MA; m. MARION GREENE.
- ii. JAMES EMERSON SPINNEY, b. 1896, North Quincy, MA; d. 1960; m. ALBERTA MELLOR; b. 1900.

iii. GORDON SPINNEY, b. 13 Apr 1899, North Quincy, MA; d. 20 Nov 1971, Stoneham, MA; m. HAZEL B LEECO.
iv. PERCY A. SPINNEY, b. 28 Jul 1901, Quincy, MA; d. Abt. 1980; m. CATHERINE GERTRUDE THOMPSON.

312. GEORGE EMERSON[6] SPINNEY *(DAVID GRIFFEN[5], BENIAH[4], SAMUEL[3], SAMUEL[2], THOMAS[1])* was born 07 Mar 1874, and died 23 Oct 1946. He married MARGARET PERCY 14 Nov 1899 in Truro, NS., daughter of PETER PERCY and SARAH JANE. She was born Abt. 1862 in Truro, NS., and died Abt. 1940.

Child of GEORGE SPINNEY and MARGARET PERCY is:
i. HARRIETT[7] SPINNEY, b. 1907, Truro, NS.; d. 1952.

313. WILLIAM HENRY[6] SPINNEY *(DAVID GRIFFEN[5], BENIAH[4], SAMUEL[3], SAMUEL[2], THOMAS[1])* was born 23 Oct 1875, and died 21 May 1968. He married ALICE MAUDE KEATING 02 Dec 1914 in Upper Canard, NS.. She was born 31 Jan 1883 in Sheffield Mills, NS., and died 30 Jun 1966.

Child of WILLIAM SPINNEY and ALICE KEATING is:
i. HARRY EATON[7] SPINNEY, b. 1915, Canning, NS.; d. Abt. 1980.

314. GRIFFEN MINOR[6] SPINNEY *(DAVID GRIFFEN[5], BENIAH[4], SAMUEL[3], SAMUEL[2], THOMAS[1])* was born 02 Feb 1878. He married IDA JANE LUTHER.

Child of GRIFFEN SPINNEY and IDA LUTHER is:
i. GEORGE W[7] SPINNEY, b. 1913, Canning, NS.

315. JAMES O[6] SPINNEY *(DAVID GRIFFEN[5], BENIAH[4], SAMUEL[3], SAMUEL[2], THOMAS[1])* was born 05 Dec 1879 in Nova Scotia, and died 16 Jan 1960 in Nova Scotia. He married JANE KANE 24 Jan 1905. She was born 01 Apr 1888, and died 11 Jan 1972.

Children of JAMES SPINNEY and JANE KANE are:
i. MILLER BRENTON[7] SPINNEY, b. 22 Oct 1905.
ii. ARTHUR WILLIAM SPINNEY, b. 20 Apr 1908; d. 09 Jul 1972; m. DORIS TURNER.
iii. GILBERT LEANDER SPINNEY, b. 04 Feb 1910; m. ETHEL MARY HALES.

Notes for ETHEL MARY HALES:
SPINNEY, Ethel Mary
SPINNEY, Ethel Mary - 89, Coldbrook, Kings Co., formerly of Canning, Kings Co., passed away Sunday, June 1, 2003, in the Valley Regional Hospital, Kentville. Born in Birmingham, England, she was a daughter of the late Harry and Minnie (Inchley) Hales. She spent her early childhood in Birmingham, England, and was honoured by the Birmingham and surrounding schools by being named the "May Queen". She immigrated to Canada in 1926 and settled in Canning, where she met and married Gilbert Spinney, they were married for 60 years at the time of his passing. She was a long-time member of the Canning Baptist Church, where she was active in the music program. Together with her husband, they owned and operated Spinney's Canteen, Hillaton, Kings Co., and Spinney's Grocery, Nictaux Falls, Annapolis Co. She had a great love for music, playing, singing and teaching. She was a loving mother, grandmother, great-grandmother, great great-grandmother and friend. She is survived by daughters, Joyce (Kenneth) Carey, Hamilton, Ont.; Reverend Ardythe Ashe, Black Point, Halifax Co.; Marguerite (Keith) Rogers, Bridgewater, Lunenburg Co.; Rita (Kenneth) Jess and Joanne (Michael) Johnston, both of Coldbrook, Kings Co.; sons, Donald, North Alton, Kings Co.; Eugene (Sheila), Coldbrook; Frank (Donna), Aylesford, Kings Co.; Greg (Dorothy), Coldbrook; sister, Minnie Lynk, Kentville; 20 grandchildren; 23 great-grandchildren; three great great-grandchildren; many nieces, nephews and cousins throughout Canada, England and Australia. She was predeceased by her husband, Gilbert Leander Spinney; son, James Gilbert Spinney; sister, Elsie; brothers, Harry, Stanley, Frederick, and Joseph; daughter-in-law, Sheila (Rogers) Spinney; son-in-law, James Ashe. Visitation will be held from 2-4, 7-9 p.m. Tuesday, June 3, in W.C. Hiltz/White Family Funeral Home, Kentville. Funeral service will be held 2 p.m., Wednesday, June 4, in Canning Baptist Church, Canning, Rev. Philip Locke, Rev. Ardythe Ashe and Rev. Dr. Mark Parent officiating. Burial will take place in the Hillaton Cemetery, Hillaton. Family flowers only by request. Donations in memory may be made to the Canadian Diabetes Association or Canning Baptist Church. Funeral arrangements have been entrusted to the W.C. Hiltz/White Family Funeral Home, Kentville.

    iv.   FRANK HAROLD SPINNEY, b. 22 May 1912.
    v.   MARGARET HATTIE SPINNEY, b. 04 Jun 1918.
   vi.   HOWARD WILSON SPINNEY, b. 08 Jun 1920.

316. CLARENCE ALLISON[6] SPINNEY *(DAVID GRIFFEN[5], BENIAH[4], SAMUEL[3], SAMUEL[2], THOMAS[1])* was born 18 Jul 1882, and died 30 Jun 1960. He married INEZ REBECCA PORTER 17 Nov 1904 in Nova Scotia. She was born 09 May 1884.

Children of CLARENCE SPINNEY and INEZ PORTER are:
636.   i.   HOLLIS RUPERT[7] SPINNEY, b. 17 Jul 1905; d. 29 Aug 1994.
       ii.   HAZEL SPINNEY, b. 23 Jun 1908; d. 09 Nov 1915.

317. LEWIS LEONARD[6] SPINNEY *(GEORGE CRAFT[5], BENIAH[4], SAMUEL[3], SAMUEL[2], THOMAS[1])* was born 28 Aug 1863 in Gaspereau, NS., and died 1938 in Maine. He married ANNIE L WARD 26 Sep 1888 in Kentville, NS., daughter of EBENEZER WARD and ELIZABETH ENGLISH. She was born 06 Mar 1865 in North Alton, NS., and died Aft. 1900 in Maine.

Children of LEWIS SPINNEY and ANNIE WARD are:
637.   i.   GEORGE E.[7] SPINNEY, b. Feb 1889, Kentville, NS..
       ii.   WILLIAM R SPINNEY, b. Feb 1892, Bethel, ME; m. NETTIE THOMPSON, 31 Dec 1921, Bethel, ME.
     iii.   FRANK WALTER SPINNEY, b. 1902, Bethel, ME; d. 04 Aug 1996, San Diego, Ca.
     iv.   HAROLD J SPINNEY, b. Jun 1894, Bethel, ME.
638.   v.   GLADYS A SPINNEY, b. Aug 1898, Bethel, ME; d. Before 1929.
     vi.   ELSIE SPINNEY, b. Abt. 1899, Bethel, ME; m. COLON FULLER, 1940.
    vii.   MOLLY SPINNEY, b. Abt. 1901, Bethel, ME.
   viii.   JOHN L SPINNEY, b. 19 May 1904, Bethel, ME; m. OLIVE WARDELL, 10 Oct 1942.
     ix.   MILDRED SPINNEY, b. 1912; m. GUY PHILLIPS, 1930, Bethel, Me.

318. JAMES J[6] SPINNEY *(GEORGE CRAFT[5], BENIAH[4], SAMUEL[3], SAMUEL[2], THOMAS[1])* was born 30 Sep 1870 in Nova Scotia, and died Aft. 1930 in Maine. He married MARION ANNIE RAMSEY. She was born Mar 1871.

Children of JAMES SPINNEY and MARION RAMSEY are:
639.   i.   JAMES A[7] SPINNEY, b. Jul 1890.
       ii.   BESSIE SPINNEY, b. May 1892.
     iii.   EDITH SPINNEY, b. Mar 1897.

319. BERTHA MARIE[6] SPINNEY *(GEORGE CRAFT[5], BENIAH[4], SAMUEL[3], SAMUEL[2], THOMAS[1])* was born 07 May 1874 in King Co, NS., and died Aft. 1930. She married FREDERICK AUGUST THEODORE MUNDT 05 Jun 1895 in Errol, NH., son of AUGUST MUNDT and LISETTE MUNDT. He was born 25 Jan 1866 in Wismar, Germany.

Children of BERTHA SPINNEY and FREDERICK MUNDT are:
       i.   JAMES FRED[7] MUNDT, b. 1903; d. 1951.
       ii.   GEORGE AUGUST MUNDT, b. 1903; d. 1919, France.
     iii.   MARGARET LUZZETTA MUNDT, b. 1904; d. 1904.
     iv.   ALICE LOUISE MUNDT, b. 07 Feb 1905, Bethel, ME; d. 1992, Worcester, MA.

         Notes for ALICE LOUISE MUNDT:
         Headline: Alice L. Mundt, 86; art museum curator
         Publication Date: February 04, 1992
         Source: Telegram & Gazette Worcester, MA
         Page: C6
         Subjects:
         Region: Massachusetts
         Obituary: Alice L. Mundt, 86, of 32 Boynton St. died Sunday in Worcester County Hospital, Boylston, after an illness.
         She leaves a brother, Ernest Mundt of Bethel, Maine; a nephew; and two nieces. She was born in Bethel, Maine, daughter of Fred A. and Bertha (Spinney) Mundt. She graduated from Gould Academy in Bethel. Miss Mundt retired in 1979 as head librarian and special curator of prints and drawings at Worcester Art Museum, where she worked for 51 years.

She earned a bachelor's degree in library science from Simmons College in Boston. After a year traveling in Europe, she joined the museum staff in 1928, and started her career as assistant librarian. In 1937, Miss Mundt became head librarian and the first to receive the Frances A. Kinnicutt Travel Fund Award to study collections in Europe. She received the award again in 1957. Miss Mundt was the museum's curator of prints and drawings from 1950 to 1976, when she became curator of Japanese prints, a position she held until she retired in 1979.

In the 1970s she focused on her special love, ukiyo-e prints, which depict Japanese life in the 18th and 19th centuries, and mounted a series of exhibitions drawn from the museum's John Chandler Bancroft collection of Japanese prints. A recognized authority on prints, Miss Mundt arranged several major exhibitions, including "The Floating World" (Japanese prints) in 1959, "Parade of Prints"in 1964, "The World of Goya" in 1967, "'The World of the Japanese Print" in 1970 and "The graphic Work of Toulouse-Lautrec" in 1971, along with many smaller exhibitions. She also prepared the 1948 museum handbook "Art Through Fifty Centuries." She also researched works of art being considered by the museum trustees for acquisition.

Miss Mundt was named a "Living Worcester Art Museum Treasure" at the reopening of the Asiatic galleries in 1986. In 1938 she was elected to the Special Libraries Association.

Memorial services will be at 11 a.m. tomorrow in Caswell-King Funeral Home, 474 Grove St. Burial will be in Mason, Maine. There are no calling hours. The family requests that flowers be omitted. Memorial contributions may be made instead to the Worcester Art Museum, 55 Salisbury St., Worcester, 01609.

-- ------

640.	v.	ERNEST ARTHUR MUNDT, b. 15 Dec 1905.
641.	vi.	BERTHA MARION MUNDT, b. 06 Feb 1910; d. 04 Oct 1964.
642.	vii.	MALCOLM CRAFT MUNDT, b. 27 Apr 1916.

320. JOSEPH S[6] SPINNEY (JOSEPH[5], JOHN[4], THOMAS[3], THOMAS[2], THOMAS[1]) was born 1805 in New Hampsire, and died Aft. 1880 in New York. He married MARYANN PRAY 24 Jan 1828. She was born 1809 in New York, and died Aft. 1880 in New York.

Children of JOSEPH SPINNEY and MARYANN PRAY are:

    i. JOSEPH S[7] SPINNEY, b. 1829; d. Aft. 1880; m. (1) EMILY LODER; b. 1842; m. (2) SARAH FRANCES BUNKER, 31 Jul 1855; m. (3) ANN AUGUSTA HART, 1863, Brooklyn, NY; b. 1842.

    Notes for ANN AUGUSTA HART:
    New York Obituaries - 1864 - Ann Augusta (Hart) Spinney

    In Brooklyn, on Thursday, Dec 29, Ann Augusta, wife of Joseph S. Spinney, and daughter of James Hart, esq., aged 22 years and 6 months.

    Relatives and friends of the family are invited to attend her funeral from the Washington st. M. E. Church, on Sunday, Jan 1, at 2 o'clock P. M.

    Source: NY Times, Saturday, Dec 31, 1864

| 643. | ii. | MARY SPINNEY, b. 1837. |

321. THOMAS[6] SPINNEY (THOMAS[5], JOHN[4], THOMAS[3], THOMAS[2], THOMAS[1]) was born 09 May 1795 in Portsmouth, NH, and died 16 Apr 1872 in Portsmouth, NH. He married (1) ABIGAIL T SAVORY, daughter of THOMAS SAVERY and ABIGAIL EVERSON. She was born Aug 1796 in Plymouth, MA, and died 07 Nov 1839. He married (2) ANN L SPINNEY 02 Apr 1840, daughter of JOSEPH SPINNEY and TREFETHEN. She was born 1808, and died 1893 in Boston, MA.

Notes for THOMAS SPINNEY:
* M. April 8,1840; S. Boston, MA
* Both were formerly from Portsmouth, NH

Children of THOMAS SPINNEY and ABIGAIL SAVORY are:

644.	i.	SAMUEL ROGERS[7] SPINNEY, b. Abt. 1822; d. Bef. 1900.
	ii.	AUGUSTA TREFALON SPINNEY, b. 1824.
	iii.	ELIZABETH R SPINNEY, b. 1827.

645.   iv.   THOMAS M SPINNEY, b. Aug 1829, Boston, MA; d. Aft. 1900.
646.   v.   EDWIN BUCKINGHAM SPINNEY, b. 26 Jun 1831, Portsmouth, NH; d. 19 Sep 1902.

Children of THOMAS SPINNEY and ANN SPINNEY are:
         vi.   ELIZABETH R[7] SPINNEY, b. 1843; d. Aft. 1880.
         vii. FRANKLIN B SPINNEY, b. 1846; d. Aft. 1910.
647.   viii. MARY FRANCIS SPINNEY, b. 26 Jun 1851, Boston, MA; d. Aft. 1910.

322. JOHN ROGERS[6] SPINNEY *(THOMAS[5], JOHN[4], THOMAS[3], THOMAS[2], THOMAS[1])* was born 23 Jan 1802 in Portsmouth, NH, and died 20 Dec 1879. He married SOPHIA SAVERY, daughter of THOMAS SAVERY and JOANNA BURBANK. She was born 24 Dec 1807 in Plymouth, MA.

Children of JOHN SPINNEY and SOPHIA SAVERY are:
         i.   JOHN D[7] SPINNEY, b. 1824, Portsmouth, NH; d. 24 Sep 1852; m. SUSAN FLANDERS, 1850, Charlestown, MA; b. 1815.
         ii.   SOPHIA SPINNEY, b. 1829; m. ROCKWELL VARNEY, 1851, Charlestown, MA.
648.   iii. SAMUEL A SPINNEY, b. 1830.
         iv.   WILLIAM SPINNEY, b. 1833.
649.   v.   DANIEL JACKSON SPINNEY, b. 02 Dec 1838, Plymouth, MA; d. Aft. 1870.
         vi.   LONETTE SPINNEY, b. 1842.
650.   vii. SAMUEL HOUSTON SPINNEY, b. Mar 1847, Portsmouth, NH; d. Bet. 1900 - 1910.

323. SAMUEL[6] SPINNEY *(THOMAS[5], JOHN[4], THOMAS[3], THOMAS[2], THOMAS[1])* was born 02 Nov 1807 in Portsmouth, NH, and died 02 Jun 1890 in Portsmouth, NH. He married SYBIL "LYDIA" BUNKER 30 Oct 1828, daughter of VALENTINE BUNKER and HANNAH PHILLIPS. She was born 25 Nov 1807 in Kittery, ME, and died 08 Apr 1895 in Medford, MA.

Children of SAMUEL SPINNEY and SYBIL BUNKER are:
651.   i.   THOMAS JEFFERSON[7] SPINNEY, b. 30 Jan 1830, Portsmouth, NH; d. 06 Mar 1878.
         ii.   DANIEL T H SPINNEY, b. 1832; d. 20 Jan 1836.
         iii. ELLEN M SPINNEY, b. 1833; d. Aft. 1900.

               Notes for ELLEN M SPINNEY:
               Ellen was listed as being a servant living in Ohio in the 1900 Census

         iv.   DANIEL H SPINNEY, b. 1835; d. 18 Oct 1860, Portsmouth New Hampshire; m. MARY; b. 1838.
652.   v.   HARRIET SPINNEY, b. 1837.
653.   vi.   ROBERT MORRISON SPINNEY, b. 29 Jun 1839, Portsmouth, NH; d. 22 May 1913, Medford, MA.
         vii. SARAH SPINNEY, b. 1841.
654.   viii. CHESLEY SPINNEY, b. 1843, Portsmouth, NH.
         ix.   VIRGINIA S SPINNEY, b. 1845; d. 1868.
         x.   GRACE SPINNEY, b. 1848.
         xi.   DELIA SPINNEY, b. 1851.
         xii. FRANK THORNTON SPINNEY, b. 1853, Portsmouth, NH; d. Aft. 1880, Medford, MA; m. JOSEPHINE ROBERTS, 1872, Charlestown, MA; b. 1850.

324. DANIEL HUNTRESS[6] SPINNEY *(THOMAS[5], JOHN[4], THOMAS[3], THOMAS[2], THOMAS[1])* was born 01 Nov 1812 in Portsmouth, NH, and died 14 Aug 1884 in North Berwick, ME. He married (1) SARAH A WENTWORTH 01 Nov 1843, daughter of JOHN WENTWORTH and SARAH. She was born 1825, and died 28 Mar 1858 in Portsmouth, NH. He married (2) RUTH QUIMBY HALL 07 Feb 1860. She was born 26 Jan 1841, and died 24 Jun 1921 in Portsmouth New Hampshire.

Notes for SARAH A WENTWORTH:
from
AS I PLEASE
By J Dennis Robinson

A Murderous History of Portsmouth

Then there are Portsmouth's domestic horrors, too numerous to catalog here. Notable is the day Nelson Downing killed Sarah Anne Spinney on her doorstep in 1858. Plenty of people saw him heading through town drunk with that shotgun intending to shoot Sarah's husband Daniel. Daniel was winged in the arm and Sarah was hit in the head as her children stood by. They named a road after her.

Children of DANIEL SPINNEY and SARAH WENTWORTH are:

    i. STARK[7] SPINNEY, b. 1844, Portsmouth, NH; d. 07 Dec 1902.
    ii. SELIM SPINNEY, b. 1846, Portsmouth, NH; d. 1847, Portsmouth, NH.
    iii. DELTA SPINNEY, b. 1848; m. WILLIAM ASH, 27 Jul 1872.
    iv. DELHI SPINNEY, b. 1852; d. 1853, Portsmouth New Hampshire.
    v. AVA SPINNEY, b. 1854; d. 1876, Portsmouth New Hampshire.
    vi. HARRIET SPINNEY, b. 1858; d. 04 Jun 1860, Portsmouth New Hampshire.

Children of DANIEL SPINNEY and RUTH HALL are:

    vii. AVA[7] SPINNEY, b. 15 Sep 1861; m. LUDD.
    viii. DELHI SPINNEY, b. 25 Sep 1861; d. 14 Apr 1934, Portsmouth New Hampshire; m. CLARA M LADD.
    ix. CEYLON SPINNEY, b. 06 Jun 1867, Portsmouth, NH; d. 26 Jan 1939, Portsmouth New Hampshire.

        Notes for CEYLON SPINNEY:
        Surname: SPINNEY
        Source: History of Rockingham County, New Hampshire and Representative Citizens
            by Charles A. Hazlett, Richmond-Arnold Publishing Co., Chicago, Ill., 1915

        Page 812

        CEYLON SPINNEY, sheriff of Rockingham County, N. H., and one of the county's most prominent citizens, was born in Portsmouth, N. H., June 6, 1867, being one of the three children of Daniel H. and Ruth Hall Spinney. The father, a native of Portsmouth also, followed the vocation of a wood dealer until he retired from active business life. His death occurred August 13, 1884. The mother of our subject is spending her declining years with her son in comfort and ease.

        Ceylon Spinney obtained his elementary education in the public schools of his native town and graduated from the high school in the class of 1884. Immediately thereafter, being ambitious, he gave his services, in the capacity of clerk, to the Boston & Maine Railroad, remaining thus occupied for two years. He next located on the farm, where he continued until 1901, having been elected in 1900 as county commissioner and qualifying for the same in 1901. He remained in that office for four terms and until he was elected sheriff of Rockingham County in 1908, qualifying for the office in 1909. He was re-elected sheriff of Rockingham County in 1911 and again in 1913.

        Sheriff Spinney belongs to the Red Men, Lodge No. 16; also to the B. P. 0. Elks, the St. John's Lodge of Masons, the Royal Arch Chapter, De Witt Clinton Commandery, and Davenport Council No. 5. Politically he is a staunch Republican and takes an active part in the politics of Rockingham County. He has under his supervision thirteen deputies, they being scattered over the county. He is also interested extensively with his partner, W. L. Conlon, in the insurance business.

    x. CLYDE SPINNEY, b. 07 Jan 1870; d. 19 May 1937, Portsmouth New Hampshire.

325. JOSEPH[6] SPINNEY *(THOMAS[5], JOHN[4], THOMAS[3], THOMAS[2], THOMAS[1])* was born 25 Mar 1815, and died 07 Feb 1893. He married LYDIA WARNER. She was born 1823 in Conn, and died Aft. 1850.

Notes for JOSEPH SPINNEY:
Joseph was a Mariner in Philadelphia Pennsylvania

Children of JOSEPH SPINNEY and LYDIA WARNER are:
    i. ELLEN[7] SPINNEY, b. 1843; m. GEORGE BROWN.

ii.   MIRIAM W SPINNEY, b. 21 Mar 1846, Penn; m. DANIEL WEBSTER ADAMS, 16 Mar 1869, Portsmouth; b. 27 May 1845.

Notes for DANIEL WEBSTER ADAMS:
VIII. DANIEL WEBSTER ADAMS8 was the eighth child of V. Charles Adams7 and II. Sarah
   Noyes. He married Mariam W. Spinney, of Portsmouth, N. H., in 1869. He took a notion to go to
   sea at an early age and went on his first voyage in the ship Crown Point, bound to Bombay. He
went other voyages for a while, bu after he married he left off going to sea. He now (1895) lives in
Portsmouth, N. H., at No. 11 Penhallow street, and has been employed some of the time in the   navy
yard at Kittery, and some of the time in the carpenter business. They have no children living.

655.   iii.   JOSEPH F SPINNEY, b. Dec 1849, Penn; d. Aft. 1900.
       iv.   IDA V SPINNEY, b. 1851; m. GEORGE H ABBOTT, 28 Nov 1872, Portsmouth, NH.
       v.   ANNA M SPINNEY, b. 1859.

326. MARY A⁶ SPINNEY *(ALEXANDER⁵, JOHN⁴, THOMAS³, THOMAS², THOMAS¹)* was born 1809. She married SAMUEL KIDDER. He was born in Manchester NH.

Child of MARY SPINNEY and SAMUEL KIDDER is:
       i.   MARY A⁷ KIDDER, m. GEORGE V REYNOLDS.

Notes for MARY A KIDDER:
The National Society of the Daughters of the American Revolution Volume 91
page 109
Mrs. Grace Reynolds Olcott.
DAR ID Number: 90336
Born in Collinsville, Conn.
Wife of Ralph T. Olcott.
Descendant of Maj.-Gen. John Stark, as follows:
1. George V. Reynolds (1833-1901) m. 1855 Mary A. Kidder (1838-86).
2. Samuel B. Kidder (1806-85) m. 1828 Mary A. Spinney (1809-93).
3. Samuel P. Kidder (1768-1822) m. 1818 Betsey Stark (1788-1865).
4. John Stark, Jr. (1763-1844), m. 1782 Mary (Polly) Huse (1765-1838).
5. John Stark m. 1758 Elizabeth Page (1737-1814).
John Stark (1728-1822), who fought in the early wars, rose from colonel to major-general in the Revolution.
His great victory at Bennington was a master stroke, and he recived the thanks of Congress. He was born in
Londonderry; died in Manchester, N. H.
Also Nos. 38344, 84414.

327. JANE P⁶ SPINNEY *(ALEXANDER⁵, JOHN⁴, THOMAS³, THOMAS², THOMAS¹)* was born 16 Mar 1814, and died 17 Oct 1866 in Londonderry NH. She married JOHN ROWELL 11 Dec 1839 in Londonderry NH. He was born 1809, and died Aft. 1854.

Children of JANE SPINNEY and JOHN ROWELL are:
       i.   CLARA JANE⁷ ROWELL, b. 17 Apr 1846.
656.   ii.   IRVING JOHN ROWELL, b. 23 Nov 1850.
       iii.   LAURA Z ROWELL, b. 12 Feb 1854.

328. JOHN DICKEY⁶ SPINNEY *(ALEXANDER⁵, JOHN⁴, THOMAS³, THOMAS², THOMAS¹)* was born 07 Dec 1816, and died 28 Oct 1890. He married ZILLAH MILLS TAYLOR 07 Dec 1841. She was born 1819 in Londonderry, NH., and died 10 Apr 1893.

Children of JOHN SPINNEY and ZILLAH TAYLOR are:
       i.   GEORGIA F⁷ SPINNEY, b. 28 Jun 1844; m. CHARLES E CONANT.
657.   ii.   JULIA M SPINNEY, b. 31 Dec 1846; d. Aft. 1880.
658.   iii.   ELLEN AUGUSTA SPINNEY, b. 17 May 1852; d. 10 Dec 1944.
659.   iv.   EUGENE LAROY SPINNEY, b. 19 May 1852, Londonderry, NH.
       v.   EMMA K SPINNEY, b. 06 Sep 1856; m. LEONARD A FREEMAN, 16 Nov 1878, Londonderry New Hampshire.

329. EMILY[6] SPINNEY *(ALEXANDER[5], JOHN[4], THOMAS[3], THOMAS[2], THOMAS[1])* was born 1819 in Londonderry, NH, and died 26 Jun 1906. She married (1) CHARLES FRANKLIN BRICKETT 16 Sep 1844 in Londonderry New Hampshire. He was born 10 Apr 1825, and died 28 Nov 1855. She married (2) ORRIVILLE PEABODY 17 Dec 1873. He was born 1825.

Children of EMILY SPINNEY and CHARLES BRICKETT are:
     i. CHARLES HENRY[7] BRICKETT, b. 08 Aug 1846.
    ii. GEORGE W BRICKETT, b. 31 Dec 1848.
   iii. FRANK H BRICKETT, b. 18 Feb 1850.

330. NANCY[6] SPINNEY *(ALEXANDER[5], JOHN[4], THOMAS[3], THOMAS[2], THOMAS[1])* was born 09 Jan 1824 in Hillboro, NH, and died 29 Jul 1903. She married BENJAMIN F GARVIN 20 Jan 1841 in Londonderry, NH.

Children of NANCY SPINNEY and BENJAMIN GARVIN are:
     i. GEORGE S[7] GARVIN, d. 25 Oct 1907.
    ii. CLARENCE GARVIN.

        Notes for CLARENCE GARVIN:
        Source: History of Rockingham County, New Hampshire and Representative Citizens
            by Charles A. Hazlett, Richmond-Arnold Publishing Co., Chicago, Ill., 1915

        Page 1164

        CLARENCE N. GARVIN, who has been postmaster of Derry, N. H., since 1903, is one of the leading and progressive men of the community. As the executive of the affairs of his office he has been most capable, which, together with his courteous treatment of all the patrons, has made him a very satisfactory public official. Mr. Garvin was born in Londonderry, N. H., and is a son of Benjamin F. and Nancy M. (Spinney) Garvin. The father was born in Litchfield, N. H., and for twenty or more years was station agent at Londonderry. The mother was born in Manchester, N. H., but was reared in Londonderry .
        After leaving school, C. N. Garvin was for a number of years a bookkeeper in Manchester, N. H. He then came to Derry and was with the Pillsburys in shoe manufacturing until 1903, when he received appointment on February 1St as postmaster of West Derry. The name of the village was changed in July, 1907, to Derry and Mr. Garvin received a vacation appointment as postmaster, serving under that commission until Congress convened in December of that year, when he was honored with reappointment. Mr. Garvin was joined in marriage with Miss Abbie D. Wilson, a daughter of John Pinkerton Wilson, who was descended from the old and well known Wilson family of Londonderry, his mother being a Pinkerton. Mrs. Garvin died in 1910, and besides her husband is survived by three children, namely: Fred E. of Newark, New Jersey, Lillie B. and Chester A., who is

331. ALEXANDER[6] SPINNEY *(GEORGE PETTEGREW[5], JOHN[4], JOHN[3], JOHN[2], THOMAS[1])* was born 1788, and died 10 Dec 1837. He married DOROTHY SCRIGGINS 1821. She was born Abt. 1790, and died Aft. 1840.

Notes for ALEXANDER SPINNEY:
1820 Census Durham New Hampshire

2 males 5 to 10
1 Male 30 to 40
1 Female 30 to 40

Notes for DOROTHY SCRIGGINS:
1840 Census

Child of ALEXANDER SPINNEY and DOROTHY SCRIGGINS is:
660.   i. WILLIAM[7] SPINNEY, b. 06 Jan 1821, New Market, NH; d. 31 May 1894, Providence, RI.

332. OLIVE A⁶ SPINNEY *(GEORGE PETTEGREW⁵, JOHN⁴, JOHN³, JOHN², THOMAS¹)* was born 1790, and died 12 May 1852. She married SAMUEL TETHERLY 30 Sep 1811, son of SAMUEL TETHERLY and ELIZABETH KENNARD. He was born 1790, and died 06 Mar 1828.

Children of OLIVE SPINNEY and SAMUEL TETHERLY are:
	i.	SAMUEL⁷ TETHERLY, b. 1827; d. 07 Oct 1846.
	ii.	SON TETHERLY.
	iii.	DAUGHTER TETHERLY.
661.	iv.	SERENA TETHERLY, b. 30 Dec 1822; d. 10 Jul 1907.

333. JAMES⁶ SPINNEY *(GEORGE PETTEGREW⁵, JOHN⁴, JOHN³, JOHN², THOMAS¹)* was born 1793, and died Aft. 1850. He married NANCY LIBBEY Nov 1813, daughter of AZARIAH LIBBEY and JANE STAPLE. She was born 1796, and died Aft. 1850.

Children of JAMES SPINNEY and NANCY LIBBEY are:
662.	i.	CAROLINE⁷ SPINNEY, b. 1818; d. Aft. 1850.
663.	ii.	OLIVER P SPINNEY, b. Abt. 1820, Eliot, ME; d. Bef. 1850.
664.	iii.	BENJAMIN SPINNEY, b. 1824, Eliot, Maine; d. 1870, Winchenton, Ma.
665.	iv.	JOSEPH SPINNEY, b. 1821; d. 20 Oct 1870.
	v.	SARAH SPINNEY, b. 1824.
666.	vi.	JAMES H SPINNEY, b. 1825; d. 10 Oct 1894.
	vii.	NANCY A SPINNEY, b. 1832; d. 1890, Eliot, ME; m. JOHN KNIGHT, 18 Oct 1859; b. 1830; d. 1909.
	viii.	CAROLINE SPINNEY, b. 1832.
667.	ix.	HENRY PARKER SPINNEY, b. 06 Jan 1836; d. 28 Aug 1917.

334. SIMON⁶ SPINNEY *(GEORGE PETTEGREW⁵, JOHN⁴, JOHN³, JOHN², THOMAS¹)* was born 1798, and died Bet. 1850 - 1860. He married OLIVE GROVER 1827. She was born 1813, and died Aft. 1860.

Children of SIMON SPINNEY and OLIVE GROVER are:
668.	i.	AUGUSTUS W⁷ SPINNEY, b. 08 Aug 1827, Eliot, ME; d. 06 Oct 1892, Eliot, ME.
	ii.	DAUGHTER SPINNEY, b. Bet. 1828 - 1830.
669.	iii.	MOSES J SPINNEY, b. Apr 1832, Portsmouth, NH; d. 1900.
	iv.	SUSAN F SPINNEY, b. Abt. 1835.
670.	v.	SIMON FREDERICK SPINNEY, b. 1835, Portsmouth, NH; d. 13 Dec 1893, Eliot, ME.
671.	vi.	MARY OLIVE SPINNEY, b. 1838; d. 1910, Medford, Ma.

335. FRANCIS⁶ SPINNEY *(GEORGE PETTEGREW⁵, JOHN⁴, JOHN³, JOHN², THOMAS¹)* was born Bet. 1800 - 1810, and died 22 Oct 1849. He married MARY ROGERS PAUL 04 Apr 1824 in Kittery Maine. She was born 1805, and died 12 Nov 1878.

Children of FRANCIS SPINNEY and MARY PAUL are:
672.	i.	HAMMOND⁷ SPINNEY, b. 10 Nov 1824, Kittery, ME; d. 05 Aug 1900.
673.	ii.	HAMILTON SPINNEY, b. 06 Nov 1826, Kittery, ME; d. 09 Sep 1907, Newburyport, Ma.
674.	iii.	SYLVESTER SPINNEY, b. 18 Dec 1828; d. 14 Jun 1892, Kittery Maine.
	iv.	LYDIA FRANCES SPINNEY, b. 08 Jun 1831.
675.	v.	ANN MARY SPINNEY, b. 28 Oct 1833, Kittery, ME; d. 05 Aug 1921.
	vi.	LEONA SPINNEY, b. 28 Apr 1836.
	vii.	MARSHA ELLEN SPINNEY, b. 11 May 1838; d. 03 Oct 1849, Kittery Maine.
676.	viii.	FRANCIS LEMUEL SPINNEY, b. 01 Oct 1840; d. Aft. 1930.
677.	ix.	HENRY HOWARD SPINNEY, b. 23 Jun 1844; d. 1916.
	x.	MELINDA SPINNEY, b. 16 Feb 1847; d. 09 Oct 1849, Kittery Maine.

336. WILLIAM⁶ SPINNEY *(GEORGE PETTEGREW⁵, JOHN⁴, JOHN³, JOHN², THOMAS¹)* was born Bet. 1800 - 1810, and died Bef. 1850. He married SUSAN PETTEGREW 08 Dec 1824, daughter of SAMUEL PETEIGREW and OLIVE WELCH. She was born Abt. 1800, and died Bef. 1850.

Children of WILLIAM SPINNEY and SUSAN PETTEGREW are:

     i.   JOSEPH W⁷ SPINNEY, b. 1829; d. 30 Jun 1834, Kittery Maine.
    ii.   WILLIAM H SPINNEY, b. 1830; d. 04 Mar 1831, Kittery Maine.
   iii. SARAH OLIVE SPINNEY, b. 1835; d. 05 Jan 1836, Kittery Maine.
   iv. SON SPINNEY.

337. REBECCA P⁶ SPINNEY *(GEORGE PETTEGREW⁵, JOHN⁴, JOHN³, JOHN², THOMAS¹)* was born 03 Mar 1801, and died 24 Sep 1895. She married CHARLES TETHERLY 14 Oct 1819 in Eliot, Me, son of SAMUEL TETHERLY and ELIZABETH KENNARD. He was born 14 Dec 1787, and died 07 Aug 1845.

Children of REBECCA SPINNEY and CHARLES TETHERLY are:

678.	i.	MARY R⁷ TETHERLY, b. 18 Feb 1820; d. 1892.
679.	ii.	SARAH TETHERLY, b. 10 Oct 1822; d. 1901.
	iii.	REBECCA TETHERLY, b. 1830; m. BENJAMIN GREEN, Aft. 1850.
680.	iv.	BETSY DOWNS TETHERLY, b. 1832; d. 10 Mar 1899, Kittery Maine.
681.	v.	CHARLES WILLIAM TETHERLY, b. 1833.
682.	vi.	LYDIA N. TETHERLY, b. 15 Nov 1825; d. 1902.
	vii.	CONSTANTINE TETHERLY, b. 1842; d. 19 May 1909, Kittery Maine; m. GEORGE A TOBEY; b. 13 Nov 1838; d. 11 Jun 1923, Kittery Maine.

338. MIRIAM L⁶ SPINNEY *(GEORGE PETTEGREW⁵, JOHN⁴, JOHN³, JOHN², THOMAS¹)* was born 09 Jun 1796, and died 07 Jan 1873. She married OLIVER HANSCOM 07 Jan 1819, son of STEPHEN HANSCOM and HANNAH REMICK. He was born 1798, and died 1854.

Children of MIRIAM SPINNEY and OLIVER HANSCOM are:

	i.	COMFORT⁷ HANSCOM.
	ii.	GEORGE HANSCOM.
	iii.	HANNAH HANSCOM.
	iv.	NANCY HANSCOM.
	v.	ANN HANSCOM.
	vi.	CHARLES HANSCOM.
	vii.	MARY ELLEN HANSCOM.
683.	viii.	MIRIUM HANSCOM.

339. JEREMIAH⁶ BROOKS *(MARY⁵ SPINNEY, JOHN⁴, JOHN³, JOHN², THOMAS¹)* was born 1798, and died 15 Nov 1880. He married LUCY SCRIGGINS 17 May 1823 in Eliot, Maine. She was born 1797, and died 06 Sep 1878.

Children of JEREMIAH BROOKS and LUCY SCRIGGINS are:

     i.   FRANCIS⁷ BROOKS, b. 1833.
    ii.   GEORGE BROOKS, b. 1835.
   iii. HORACE BROOKS, b. 1837.
   iv. BENJAMIN BROOKS, b. 1853.
    v. WILLIAM BROOKS, b. 1861.

340. DANIEL⁶ BROOKS *(MARY⁵ SPINNEY, JOHN⁴, JOHN³, JOHN², THOMAS¹)* was born 1795. He married ELIZABETH REMICK 1815.

Children of DANIEL BROOKS and ELIZABETH REMICK are:

684.	i.	DANIEL LANGDON⁷ BROOKS, b. 06 May 1819, Eliot, ME; d. 31 May 1904, Eliot, ME.
	ii.	MARY ANN BROOKS, b. 1816.
	iii.	ISAAC REMICK BROOKS, b. 1821.
	iv.	CHARLES HENRY BROOKS, b. 1822.
	v.	JOHN L BROOKS, b. 1825.
	vi.	ELIZABETH JANE BROOKS, b. 1835.
	vii.	WALTER J BROOKS, b. 1835.

341. ABRAHAM⁶ BROOKS *(MARY⁵ SPINNEY, JOHN⁴, JOHN³, JOHN², THOMAS¹)* was born 1809, and died 04 Jan 1890. He married (1) MARY G BROOKS, daughter of WILLIAM BROOKS and PRUDENCE. She was born 12 Jan 1841. He married (2) HATTIE. He married (3) ELIZABETH J CARD. She was born 1819, and died 20 Jul 1879.

Child of ABRAHAM BROOKS and ELIZABETH CARD is:
      i. ELBRIDGE[7] BROOKS, b. 1859; m. IDA M FERNALD.

342. EUNICE[6] SPINNEY *(JOHN[5], JOHN[4], JOHN[3], JOHN[2], THOMAS[1])* was born in Kittery, ME, and died 1836. She married JOSHUA STACKPOLE 30 Apr 1806. He was born 1785 in Somersworth, NH., and died 1854.

Child of EUNICE SPINNEY and JOSHUA STACKPOLE is:
685.   i. HANNAH[7] STACKPOLE, b. 1810, Kittery, ME; d. 22 Feb 1896.

343. WILLIAM[6] LYDSTON *(WEYMOUTH[5], ABIGAIL[4] SPINNEY, ANDREW[3], JOHN[2], THOMAS[1])* was born Abt. 1790 in Kittery, ME, and died 26 May 1850 in Newburyport, MA. He married (1) MARY COLLINS 11 Jun 1812 in Newburyport, Ma, daughter of JOSEPH COLLINS and MARY. He married (2) MARY JOHNSON Abt. 1830 in Newburyport MA.

Children of WILLIAM LYDSTON and MARY COLLINS are:
      i. MARY ELIZABETH[7] LYDSTON, b. Abt. 1815, Kittery, ME; d. 17 Sep 1820, Newburyport, MA.
      ii. WEYMOUTH LYDSTON, b. Abt. 1816, Kittery, ME; m. EMILY W BAKER, 25 Oct 1846.
686.   iii. FRANCIS ARTHUR LYDSTON, b. 24 Oct 1819, Newburyport, MA.
      iv. MARY ANN LYDSTON, b. 30 Dec 1821, Newburypor, MA; m. JOSEPH STICKLEY, 11 Jun 1842, Newburyport, MA.
      v. JOHN LYDSTON, b. 12 Mar 1824, Newburyport MA.
      vi. JOSEPH COLLINS LYDSTON, b. 07 Mar 1826, Newburyport MA.
      vii. SARAH ELIZABETH LYDSTON, b. 30 Apr 1828, Newburyport MA.

Children of WILLIAM LYDSTON and MARY JOHNSON are:
      viii. HARRIET[7] LYDSTON.
      ix. CHAROLTTE FRANCES LYDSTON, b. Abt. 1840.
      x. CLAIRE LYDSTON, b. 1840.

344. LUCY ANN[6] SPINNEY *(BENJAMIN[5], JOHN[4], JOHN[3], JOHN[2], THOMAS[1])* was born 24 Jul 1823, and died 30 May 1885. She married JEREMIAH NOBLE 05 May 1844.

Children of LUCY SPINNEY and JEREMIAH NOBLE are:
      i. VICTORIA[7] NOBLE, b. 10 Jun 1845; d. 28 Aug 1847.
      ii. SARAH AUSTIN NOBLE, b. 28 Dec 1846; d. 31 Aug 1847.
      iii. ROBERT VALENTINE NOBLE, b. 14 Feb 1848.
      iv. JEREMIAH CONSTANTINE NOBLE, b. 28 Sep 1849.
      v. ANN NOBLE, b. 28 Jul 1851.
      vi. CHARLES BORROUGH NOBLE, b. 27 Apr 1853.
      vii. MARK NOBLE, b. 28 Dec 1854.
      viii. ELLA OSTELENA NOBLE, b. 05 Jan 1859.

345. FANNIE[6] SPINNEY *(JEREMIAH[5], JOHN[4], JOHN[3], JOHN[2], THOMAS[1])* was born 1804 in Eliot, ME. She married (1) JOHN BORROUGHS. She married (2) HENRY T DIXON 20 Mar 1823, son of JOSEPH DIXON and ELIZABETH LIBBEY.

Child of FANNIE SPINNEY and HENRY DIXON is:
      i. JOHN H[7] DIXON.

346. JACOB REMICK[6] SPINNEY *(JEREMIAH[5], JOHN[4], JOHN[3], JOHN[2], THOMAS[1])* was born 1806 in Eliot, ME, and died 25 Dec 1873. He married LUCINDA L DIXON, daughter of JOSEPH DIXON and ELIZABETH LIBBEY. She was born Jan 1810, and died 10 Oct 1891 in Kittery, ME.

Children of JACOB SPINNEY and LUCINDA DIXON are:
      i. ALEXANDER[7] SPINNEY, b. Abt. 1830.
687.   ii. ELIZABETH F SPINNEY, b. 29 Aug 1832, Eliot, ME; d. Aft. 1880.

        iii.   EMILY SPINNEY, b. 1843.
688.   iv.   HENRY DAME SPINNEY, b. 1837, Eliot, ME; d. 18 Nov 1889.

347. SARAH JANE⁶ SPINNEY *(JEREMIAH⁵, JOHN⁴, JOHN³, JOHN², THOMAS¹)* was born 19 Nov 1813, and died 18 Dec 1896 in Iowa. She married ABNER KIMBALL 11 Apr 1838 in Springfield Mass.

Children of SARAH SPINNEY and ABNER KIMBALL are:
        i.   SARAH JANE⁷ KIMBALL.
        ii.   ABNER MERRILL KIMBALL.
        iii. JOHN MASEY KIMBALL.
        iv.   ANN MARY KIMBALL, m. JOHN CONLY.
        v.   MARSHALL KIMBALL.
689.   vi.   ELLEN KIMBALL.

348. JANE "ANN"⁶ SPINNEY *(JEREMIAH⁵, JOHN⁴, JOHN³, JOHN², THOMAS¹)* was born 1816 in Eliot, ME. She married DANIEL CARD. He was born 1807.

Children of JANE SPINNEY and DANIEL CARD are:
        i.   DANIEL⁷ CARD, b. 1834.
        ii.   SYLVESTER CARD, b. 1836.
        iii. ANDREW CARD, b. 1838.
        iv.   SARAH CARD, b. 1844.

349. DAVID⁶ SPINNEY *(ISAAC⁵, JOHN⁴, JOHN³, JOHN², THOMAS¹)* was born 12 Sep 1787 in Argyle, NS., and died 06 Jul 1836. He married RHONDA ROBERTS 09 Jan 1811.

Children of DAVID SPINNEY and RHONDA ROBERTS are:
        i.   DAVID⁷ SPINNEY, b. 18 Dec 1811.
690.   ii.   ZILPHA SPINNEY, b. 28 Feb 1814; d. 1905, Somerville, Ma.
        iii. NELSON SPINNEY, b. 20 Jul 1816.
        iv.   EUNICE SPINNEY, b. 09 Aug 1820.
        v.   RHONDA ANN SPINNEY, b. 26 Jan 1823.
691.   vi.   HIRAM SPINNEY, b. 10 Jan 1827; d. 10 Jul 1936.
        vii. LYDIA SPINNEY, b. 10 Jun 1827.
692.   viii. SOPHRONIA L SPINNEY, b. 04 Oct 1829, Argyle, NS.

350. ANNE⁶ SPINNEY *(ISAAC⁵, JOHN⁴, JOHN³, JOHN², THOMAS¹)* was born 21 Mar 1789 in Argyle, NS.. She married THOMAS GAYTON 05 Jan 1814. He was born 1792 in Tipperary, Ireland.

Children of ANNE SPINNEY and THOMAS GAYTON are:
        i.   LYDIA⁷ GAYTON.
        ii.   DANIEL GAYTON.
        iii. JERIMIAH GAYTON.
        iv.   JOHN GAYTON, b. 03 Oct 1815, Argyle, NS..

            Notes for JOHN GAYTON:
            Gayton
            John Gayton (s/o Thomas Gayton - b. oct 3rd,1815 in Argyle, Yarmouth, Nova Scotia
            Married (m. Feb. 1843) Abigail Smith d/o Thomas K Smith of Barrington, Nova Scotia. Then followed with
            their family, Rev Knowles to a new settlement (Knowlesville) and settled there. They died there, John (d.1858
            - 67), Abigail (May 3rd, 1855 - 65) and their remains are still in the church graveyard.
            The children were:
            Anne Elizabeth Gayton:(b. 10-24-1844) no issue,
             + Jonathan Cornell Jones s/o Walter Jones (m. 1-31-1866)(d. 5-3-1897)
            Emily Jane Gayton:(b. 09-28-1846)(m. 5-24-1886)
             + Henry Alexander Morehouse s/o William Henry Morehouse of Knowlesville.
                Children
                Franklin Burns Morehouse:
                Annie Letitia Morehouse:
                Leslie Orin Morehouse:

Grace Adella Morehouse:
John Avard Gayton Morehouse:
Edna Montez Morehouse:
Harry Crowell Morehouse:
John Avard Gayton:(b. 09-20-1850)(m. 12-30-1897)
  + Lavinia Nixon of Washington, D. C.
      Children:
          Anna Lavinia Gayton
Ebenezer Crowell Smith Gayton:(b. 11-22-1852)(m. 12-18-1883)
  + Letitia Adelaide Henderson d/o John Henderson of Winsor, NB
      Children:
          Carol Genevieve Gayton (b. 09-22-1884)
          Claude Victor Gayton (b. 1886)
          Martha Abigail Gayton (d. In infancy)
          John Avard Gayton (b. 1893)
          Dolald McLeod Vince Gayton (b. 1898)
Joseph Henry Gayton:(b. 02-17-1855)(m. 03-19-1882)
  + Delphin Roper Whitehouse, d/o Joseph Whitehouse of Knowlesville NB (b.
6-15-
      1857)(d. 11-09-1911
      Children:
          Albert Raymond Gayton
          Agnes Pearl Gayton (b. 03-27-1888)
          Frank Leon Gayton (b. 4-1-1892)
          Grace Gayton (b. 10-04-1895)
  +Bertha Dean of Watkins of New York (m. 04-30-1913)
Nahamiah Spinney Gayton: (b. 01-26-1857)(m. 1884)(d. 1918)
  + Myra Carl (B. 01-07-1857)of Knowlesville NB (d. Nov 1912)
      Children
          Glen Fremont Gayton
          Edna Violet Gayton
          Harold Carl Gayton
          Mildred Irene Gayton
          Ralph Stanley Gayton
Samuel Raymond Gayton:(b. 09-30-1859)(m . 04-15-1891)
  + Joanna Wilbraham, d/o Thomas Wilbraham of Philadelphia
      Children
          Florence Linda Gayton
          John Raymond Gayton
  + Olevia F. Price d/o David A Price of Wilmington, Kent County, Maryland,
her Grandfather was the first Gov. of Maryland Charles Horace Stanley Gayton: (b. 09-05-1861)(m. 09-08-
1889)
  + Armina Whitehouse, d/o Jacob Whitehouse of Knowlesville NB
      Children
          Arleigh Raymond Gayton
          Avard Wendall Gayton
          Charles Arnold Gayton
          Reba Cathleen Gayton
          Joseph L. Gayton
          Warren W. Gayton

693.   v.   EUNICE GAYTON, b. 03 May 1818, Argyle, NS.; d. Aft. 1881, New Brunswick.
          vi. THOMAS GAYTON, b. 02 Dec 1819, Argyle, NS..
694.   vii. JAMES GAYTON, b. 09 Jan 1820, Argyle, NS.; d. Aft. 1881.
          viii. ELONOR GAYTON, b. 08 Sep 1822, Argyle, NS..

351. EUNICE[6] SPINNEY *(ISAAC[5], JOHN[4], JOHN[3], JOHN[2], THOMAS[1])* was born 12 Jul 1790 in Argyle, NS., and died in Argyle, NS.. She married JEREMIAH FROST 09 Jan 1811 in Argyle, NS.. He was born 1787.

Children of EUNICE SPINNEY and JEREMIAH FROST are:
          i.   LYDIA[7] FROST, b. 12 Oct 1811, Argyle, NS..
          ii. ISAAC FROST, b. 11 Feb 1813, Argyle, NS..
          iii. ANDREW FROST, b. 17 May 1815, Argyle, NS..

        iv.   LUCY FROST, b. 13 Jun 1817, Argyle, NS..
         v.   JEREMIAH FROST, b. 28 Jul 1820.
        vi.   MARY FROST, b. 28 Sep 1823, Argyle, NS..
695.   vii.   GEORGE FROST, b. 11 Feb 1826, Argyle, NS..
       viii.   JAMES G FROST, b. 29 Nov 1828, Argyle, NS..
        ix.   SARAH FROST, b. 07 Jan 1830, Argyle, NS..

352. LYDIA[6] SPINNEY *(ISAAC[5], JOHN[4], JOHN[3], JOHN[2], THOMAS[1])* was born 24 Aug 1793 in Argyle, NS.. She married JOHN RIDER 02 Jan 1817 in Argyle Nova Scotia. He was born Abt. 1790.

Children of LYDIA SPINNEY and JOHN RIDER are:
         i.   HENERY[7] RIDER, b. 15 Nov 1817, Argyle, NS..
        ii.   SOLOMON RIDER, b. 14 Jun 1819, Argyle, NS..
       iii.   EBENZAR RYDER, b. 12 Nov 1821, Argyle, NS..

353. DANIEL[6] SPINNEY *(ISAAC[5], JOHN[4], JOHN[3], JOHN[2], THOMAS[1])* was born 03 Nov 1796 in Argyle, NS., and died Aft. 1880. He married LYDIA NICKERSON 18 Jan 1820 in Argyle, NS.. She died 21 Jan 1863 in Argyle, NS..

Children of DANIEL SPINNEY and LYDIA NICKERSON are:
         i.   ELIZABETH[7] SPINNEY, m. EPHRIAM ROBERTS; b. 09 Feb 1823.
        ii.   HEMAN SPINNEY, b. 25 Dec 1821, Argyle, NS.; d. 1843, Lost at Sea.
       iii.   ISAAC SPINNEY, b. 31 Aug 1825, Argyle, NS.; d. 1867; m. MARY SPINNEY, 1853, Boston, MA.
        iv.   AZUBA SPINNEY, b. 15 Feb 1829, Argyle, NS.; d. 18 Nov 1839, Argyle, NS..
         v.   LUCY SPINNEY, b. 10 May 1830, Argyle, NS..
696.   vi.   LYDIA ANN SPINNEY, b. 15 Jun 1832, Argyle, NS..
697.   vii.   WHITFIELD SPINNEY, b. 13 Oct 1834, Argyle, NS.; d. Aft. 1881, Argyle Nova Scotia.
       viii.   EMELY SPINNEY, b. 10 Jun 1836, Argyle, NS.; d. 22 Apr 1850, Argyle, NS..
        ix.   WENTWORTH SPINNEY, b. 28 Feb 1842, Argyle, NS.; m. LIZZIE STUBERT, 03 Oct 1870.

354. REBEKAH[6] SPINNEY *(ISAAC[5], JOHN[4], JOHN[3], JOHN[2], THOMAS[1])* was born 09 Dec 1797 in Argyle, NS.. She married BENJAMIN SPINNEY 22 Dec 1819 in Argyle, NS., son of BENJAMIN SPINNEY and DEBORAH CROWELL. He was born 03 May 1798.

Children of REBEKAH SPINNEY and BENJAMIN SPINNEY are:
698.   i.   LYMAN[7] SPINNEY, b. 15 Jan 1820, Argyle, NS.; d. Aft. 1901.
699.   ii.   HANNAH SPINNEY, b. 12 Jan 1822, Argyle, NS..
700.   iii.   SIMEON SPINNEY, b. 14 Jan 1824, Argyle, NS.; d. 1925, Argyle, NS..
701.   iv.   SAMUEL R SPINNEY, b. 01 Jan 1826; d. 1860.
702.   v.   JONATHAN SPINNEY, b. 05 Apr 1829, Argyle, NS.; d. 25 Nov 1889, Gloucester, MA.
        vi.   REBECCA SPINNEY, b. 22 Oct 1830, Argyle, NS..
703.   vii.   HARRIS"CAPT" HARDING SPINNEY, b. 08 Nov 1832; d. 1876, Weymouth, MA.
       viii.   ENOS "CAPT" SPINNEY, b. 08 Nov 1835.
704.   ix.   HENRY SPINNEY, b. 19 Feb 1837, Argyle, NS.; d. 27 Sep 1873.
         x.   ROSE ANN SPINNEY, b. 19 Oct 1841.

355. REUBEN[6] SPINNEY *(ISAAC[5], JOHN[4], JOHN[3], JOHN[2], THOMAS[1])* was born 24 Mar 1799 in Argyle, NS., and died 03 Oct 1851. He married MARTHA NICKERSON 27 Jan 1829 in Argyle Nova Scotia. She was born 1808, and died 26 May 1881.

Children of REUBEN SPINNEY and MARTHA NICKERSON are:
         i.   MARTHA[7] SPINNEY, b. 15 Nov 1829.
        ii.   CHARLES SPINNEY, b. Nov 1831, Argyle, NS..
       iii.   EZEKIEL SPINNEY, b. 05 Aug 1833; d. Mar 1856.
705.   iv.   REUBEN HAWES SPINNEY, b. 05 Sep 1840, Argyle, NS.; d. 21 Dec 1920, Sanford, ME.
         v.   AZUBA SPINNEY, b. 01 Jul 1842; d. 18 Feb 1929.
706.   vi.   JAMES EMERY SPINNEY, b. 24 Sep 1844; d. Jul 1917.
       vii.   DORCAS SPINNEY, b. 04 May 1849; d. 1915; m. ABNER VAN NORDEN.
707.   viii.   ADALINE SPINNEY, b. 05 Dec 1836, Argyle, NS..

356. HANNAH[6] SPINNEY *(ISAAC[5], JOHN[4], JOHN[3], JOHN[2], THOMAS[1])* was born 18 Mar 1795 in Argyle, NS.. She married JOHN SPINNEY 17 Apr 1817, son of AARON SPINNEY and MARY KENNEY. He was born 29 Jun 1794 in Argyle, NS..

Children of HANNAH SPINNEY and JOHN SPINNEY are:
708.	i.	ELIZABETH[7] SPINNEY, b. 1839, Arglye, Nova Scotia; d. 1916; Stepchild.
709.	ii.	CALVIN CANN SPINNEY, b. Abt. 1820.
	iii.	ABIGAIL SPINNEY, b. Abt. 1820; m. HILL.
710.	iv.	JAMES HARVEY SPINNEY, b. 1839, Arglye, Nova Scotia; d. Bef. 1910.
711.	v.	JOSEPH WILSON SPINNEY, b. 1844, Nova Scotia; d. Aft. 1900.
712.	vi.	AMIEL SPINNEY, b. 1843, Yarmouth Nova Scotia.

357. MARY[6] WHITMAN *(ANNIE[5] SPINNEY, JOHN[4], JOHN[3], JOHN[2], THOMAS[1])* was born 1785 in Rosette, Annapolis, Nova Scotia, Canada, and died 1847 in Round Hill, Nova Scotia, Canada. She married EDWARD BERTEAUX 05 Dec 1810.

Children of MARY WHITMAN and EDWARD BERTEAUX are:
- i. FREEMAN[7] BERTEAUX, b. 27 Aug 1811; m. LUCY ANN RICE.
- ii. EDWARD JAMES BERTEAUX, b. 03 Jul 1813.
- iii. BENJAMIN SPINNEY BERTEAUX, b. 1815; m. ANNE BAKER.
- iv. ANN WHITMAN BERTEAUX, b. 1818; m. WILLIAM POTTER.
- v. LOUISA BERTEAUX, b. 15 Apr 1820; m. JOSIAH SPURR POTTER.
- vi. ELIZA JANE BERTEAUX, b. 1822.
- vii. DAVID BERTEAUX, b. 1824.

358. DAVID[6] WHITMAN *(ANNIE[5] SPINNEY, JOHN[4], JOHN[3], JOHN[2], THOMAS[1])* was born 1786. He married SARAH STARRATT 1806.

Children of DAVID WHITMAN and SARAH STARRATT are:
- i. SAMUEL[7] WHITMAN.
- ii. ANNE MARIA WHITMAN.
- iii. WILLIAM WHITMAN, b. 1809.
- iv. AMOS WHITMAN, b. 1810.
- v. MERCY WHITMAN, b. 1812; d. 1900.
- vi. LEONA WHITMAN, b. 1819; m. HENRY SAUNDERS.
- vii. ROBERT WHITMAN, b. 1822; m. LYDIA TUPPER WATERMAN.

359. JACOB[6] WHITMAN *(ANNIE[5] SPINNEY, JOHN[4], JOHN[3], JOHN[2], THOMAS[1])* was born 11 Jun 1786 in Rosette, Annapolis, Nova Scotia, Canada, and died 13 Aug 1834 in Milton, Nova, Nova Scotia, Canada. He married LYDIA TUPPER.

Children of JACOB WHITMAN and LYDIA TUPPER are:
- i. AUGUSTUS FREDERICK[7] WHITMAN, b. 1812.
- ii. JACOB WHITMAN, b. 26 May 1813.
- iii. NATHAN TUPPER WHITMAN, b. 1815.
- iv. CHARLOTTE WHITMAN, b. 1819, Eldridge Burnaby.
- v. LOUISA WHITMAN, b. 1821; m. ALEXANDER WATERMAN.
- vi. CHARLES HENRY WHITMAN, b. 1823; m. ELIZA BACKER MACK.

360. ANN[6] WHITMAN *(ANNIE[5] SPINNEY, JOHN[4], JOHN[3], JOHN[2], THOMAS[1])* was born 1791 in Rosette, Annapolis, Nova Scotia, Canada. She married EDWARD DUNN.

Child of ANN WHITMAN and EDWARD DUNN is:
- i. ANNA[7] DUNN, b. 1812; m. GEORGE WILLETT.

361. SPINNEY[6] WHITMAN *(ANNIE[5] SPINNEY, JOHN[4], JOHN[3], JOHN[2], THOMAS[1])* was born 1798 in Nova Scotia, Canada, and died 11 Dec 1878 in Canso, Nova, Nova Scotia, Canada. He married (1) CAROLINE NELSON HARRIS, daughter of JOHN HARRIS and ABIGAIL SPURR. She was born 20 Apr 1800, and died Abt. 1820. He married (2) MARTHA HART 1829. She died 1878 in Amherst, N.S..

Notes for SPINNEY WHITMAN:
Spinney Whitman first came to Canso as a young man, encouraged by his uncle Abraham, who assisted Spinney in his business as a tanner and shoemaker. However, hides were difficult to come by and he gave up the business. His first wife Caroline died of tuberculosis after four years of marriage at age 20. Spinney was reportedly "a most upright man and honest", and was highly respected in the community. A hill in Canso is named "Spinney's Hill" in his memory.

Child of SPINNEY WHITMAN and CAROLINE HARRIS is:
713.   i.   JACOB⁷ WHITMAN, b. Abt. 1820; d. 1886.

Children of SPINNEY WHITMAN and MARTHA HART are:
      ii.   CAROLINE⁷ WHITMAN, b. 1835; d. 1853.
     iii. SARAH WHITMAN, b. 1839.

362. WHITEFIELD⁶ WHITMAN (*ANNIE⁵ SPINNEY, JOHN⁴, JOHN³, JOHN², THOMAS¹*) was born 02 Feb 1802, and died 19 Feb 1863 in Illinois. He married ELIZABETH SINNER MARTIN 07 Dec 1834.

Children of WHITEFIELD WHITMAN and ELIZABETH MARTIN are:
      i.   ELIZABETH⁷ WHITMAN.
      ii.   JACOB WHITMAN.
     iii. ELIJAH WHITMAN.
     iv. MARY WHITMAN.
      v. WHITFIELD WHITMAN.

363. JOANNA⁶ WHITMAN (*ANNIE⁵ SPINNEY, JOHN⁴, JOHN³, JOHN², THOMAS¹*) was born 1808 in Rosette, Annapolis, Nova Scotia, Canada, and died 1831 in Horton, Kings, Nova Scotia, Canada. She married WILLIAM BENT.

Children of JOANNA WHITMAN and WILLIAM BENT are:
      i.   WILLIAM HENRY⁷ BENT, b. 1829; d. 1849.
      ii.   ELIZA BENT, b. 1830; m. DANIEL COLLINS.

364. JACOB⁶ SPINNEY (*JACOB⁵, JOHN⁴, JOHN³, JOHN², THOMAS¹*) was born 26 Apr 1795, and died 1883. He married SUSANAH SPINNEY 17 Apr 1817 in Argyle Nova Scotia, daughter of AARON SPINNEY and MARY KENNEY. She was born 26 May 1796, and died 06 Nov 1883.

Notes for JACOB SPINNEY:
JACOB AND HIS BROTHER JOSEPH moved to Tatamagoushe about 1833 along with Henry Roberts and Daniel Goodwin. Judge Patterson in his history states that "one of the Spinney brothers was the first to visit Tatamagouche, and he returned to tell the others of a place so peculiarly suited to fishing and ship building". Jacob settled his family on a farm described by Patterson as "being along the slopes at the head of Tatamagouche Harbor" He and his wife Susannah had arrived in 1817 and had eight children, including a son Morris whose grandson John Havelock Spinney was still living on the old homestead in 1978. Most of this written information has come from his great granddaughter Mrs. Nellie Semple who was at that time still a resident of Tatamagouche. Joseph Spinney, brother of Jacob, settled on a farm near his brother in the area called Bayhead. Joseph had married Annie R. Goodwin the daughter of William Goodwin and their children were: Joanna 1823-1923
Joseph 1827-1912
Sarah 1830-1912
Mary Jane
Susan
Stillman According to my information, Joanna was born October 2, 1823 at Argyle and married to Griffin Smith. She died at m Pugwash August 23, 1912. Joseph died at Tatamagouche March 13, 1912. He married Flora Ross the daughter of Rev. Hugh Ross, a graduate of the first class of Presbyterian ministers from the Rev. Thomas McCullocks

Change Date: 17 JAN 2003 at 10:35:11

Children of JACOB SPINNEY and SUSANAH SPINNEY are:
| | i. | ELIZABETH[7] SPINNEY, b. 06 Oct 1817. |

       i.   ELIZABETH[7] SPINNEY, b. 06 Oct 1817.
714.   ii. MORRIS SPINNEY, b. 04 Dec 1820.
715.   iii. SARAH SPINNEY, b. 16 Jun 1822.
716.   iv. AARON SPINNEY, b. 19 Nov 1824, Nova Scotia; d. 16 Nov 1911, York, ME.
717.   v. JOANNNA SPINNEY, b. 1836.
718.   vi. JAMES SPINNEY, b. 16 Apr 1839, Nova Scotia; d. Aft. 1901.

365. JOSEPH[6] SPINNEY *(JACOB[5], JOHN[4], JOHN[3], JOHN[2], THOMAS[1])* was born 11 Jun 1797 in Argyle, NS.. He married ANNIE R GOODWIN 19 Jan 1823 in Argyle, NS..

Children of JOSEPH SPINNEY and ANNIE GOODWIN are:
       i.   MARY JANE[7] SPINNEY, m. CROWELL.
       ii. JOANNA SPINNEY, b. 02 Oct 1823; d. 23 Aug 1912, Pugwash Nova Scotia; m. GRIFFIN SMITH.
719.   iii. JOSEPH SPINNEY, b. Aug 1827; d. 1912.
       iv. SUSAN SPINNEY, b. Abt. 1830; m. WOODBURY.
720.   v. SARAH SPINNEY, b. 29 Aug 1830, Argyle, NS.; d. 1912.
721.   vi. STILLMAN SPINNEY, b. 1834; d. 1888.

366. FREEMAN[6] SPINNEY *(JACOB[5], JOHN[4], JOHN[3], JOHN[2], THOMAS[1])* was born 10 Oct 1801. He married RUTH ATWOOD 22 Dec 1825 in Argyle, NS..

Children of FREEMAN SPINNEY and RUTH ATWOOD are:
722.   i.   RUTH[7] SPINNEY, b. 1833, Argyle, NS..
       ii. MARY L SPINNEY, b. 1834; m. HENRY WALCOTT.
       iii. ALFRED K SPINNEY, b. 22 Apr 1842, Argyle, NS.; d. Bef. 1910; m. HORTENCE HILL, 09 Jun 1894, Maine; b. Jul 1863, Vermont; d. Aft. 1910.
       iv. SUSAN SPINNEY, b. Abt. 1840.
       v. LAVINIA SPINNEY, b. 1847; m. ROBERT MAXWELL.

367. EBENEZER[6] SPINNEY *(JACOB[5], JOHN[4], JOHN[3], JOHN[2], THOMAS[1])* was born 28 Dec 1807 in Nova Scotia, and died 1850. He married RHONDA SPINNEY 15 Jan 1833, daughter of BENJAMIN SPINNEY and DEBORAH CROWELL. She was born 26 Apr 1811, and died 04 Apr 1888.

Children of EBENEZER SPINNEY and RHONDA SPINNEY are:
723.   i.   JEREMIAH[7] SPINNEY, b. 10 Apr 1839, Nova Scotia; d. Aft. 1901, Argyle, Yarmouth, Nova Scotia.
724.   ii. DAVID MCLARREN SPINNEY, b. 20 Sep 1844, Argyle, Yarmouth, Ns; d. Aft. 1930, Malden, MA.
725.   iii. BENJAMIN F SPINNEY, b. 25 Apr 1847, Argyle, Nova Scotia; d. 1898.
       iv. LETITIA SPINNEY, b. 1853, Argyle, NS.; m. NICHOLAS GOODWIN, 10 Jan 1871, Argyle, NS.; b. 1855.

368. JEREMIAH[6] SPINNEY *(JACOB[5], JOHN[4], JOHN[3], JOHN[2], THOMAS[1])* was born 24 Jun 1810, and died 05 Mar 1839. He married MATILDA MCLARREN 12 Jan 1836, daughter of CHARLES MCCLARREN and JESUHA HAMILTON. She was born 11 Oct 1808, and died 10 Jul 1898.

Children of JEREMIAH SPINNEY and MATILDA MCLARREN are:
726.   i.   LOUISA BURNS[7] SPINNEY, b. 19 Jun 1837.
       ii. ESTHER JEREMIAH SPINNEY, b. 12 Jan 1839.

369. THOMAS W[6] SPINNEY *(JACOB[5], JOHN[4], JOHN[3], JOHN[2], THOMAS[1])* was born 20 Mar 1817 in Argyle, NS., and died Aft. 1881 in New Brunswick. He married EUNICE GAYTON 16 May 1839, daughter of THOMAS GAYTON and ANNE SPINNEY. She was born 03 May 1818 in Argyle, NS., and died Aft. 1881 in New Brunswick.

Children of THOMAS SPINNEY and EUNICE GAYTON are:
727.   i.   ELLEN GAYTON[7] SPINNEY, b. 07 Jun 1841.
       ii. ESTER SPINNEY.

      iii.   MAURICE FORBES SPINNEY, b. 1850.
728.   iv.   JACOB SPINNEY, b. 1845, Nova Scotia; d. Aft. 1881.
729.   v.   MATILDA SPINNEY, b. 1852.

370. JAMES[6] SPINNEY *(JACOB[5], JOHN[4], JOHN[3], JOHN[2], THOMAS[1])* was born 28 Sep 1799 in Argyle, NS., and died 24 Jun 1890. He married DEBORAH HAMILTON. She was born 1809, and died 1875.

Children of JAMES SPINNEY and DEBORAH HAMILTON are:
730.   i.   JAMES[7] SPINNEY, b. 1830, Argyle, NS..
731.   ii.   CALEB SPINNEY, b. 1837; d. 1932.
732.   iii.   CALVIN SPINNEY, b. 1831, Argyle, NS.; d. 10 Oct 1871.
733.   iv.   WHITFIELD SPINNEY, b. 10 Dec 1823, Argyle, Nova Scotia; d. Dec 1868, Lost At Sea.

371. SIMEON[6] SPINNEY *(AARON[5], JOHN[4], JOHN[3], JOHN[2], THOMAS[1])* was born 09 Aug 1802 in Argyle, NS., and died 20 Feb 1864 in Argyle, NS.. He married LETITIA SPINNEY 15 Jan 1829, daughter of BENJAMIN SPINNEY and DEBORAH CROWELL. She was born 17 Oct 1800 in Argyle, NS..

Children of SIMEON SPINNEY and LETITIA SPINNEY are:
      i.   LETTICIA[7] SPINNEY, b. 16 Nov 1829, Argyle, NS.; d. Apr 1849.
      ii.   MORIAH SPINNEY, b. 27 Sep 1831, Argyle, NS..

372. EZARA[6] SPINNEY *(AARON[5], JOHN[4], JOHN[3], JOHN[2], THOMAS[1])* was born 16 Jun 1813, and died Aft. 1880. He married (1) DEBORAH SPINNEY, daughter of BENJAMIN SPINNEY and DEBORAH CROWELL. She was born 26 Aug 1816, and died 1874. He married (2) LUCY RYDER 20 Feb 1840, daughter of SOLOMAN RYDER and JOANNAH SPINNEY. She was born 01 Dec 1817, and died 03 Dec 1848.

Children of EZARA SPINNEY and LUCY RYDER are:
734.   i.   AARON[7] SPINNEY, b. 22 Dec 1840, Yarmouth, Nova Scotia; d. 1923.
      ii.   ALVA SPINNEY, b. 1856.
735.   iii.   DENNIS H SPINNEY, b. 21 May 1843, Arglye, Nova Scotia; d. 29 Jul 1924, Arglye, Nova Scotia.
736.   iv.   AGNES, b. 1844; d. Aft. 1910.

373. HARVEY[6] SPINNEY *(AARON[5], JOHN[4], JOHN[3], JOHN[2], THOMAS[1])* was born 27 Jul 1817 in Argyle, NS., and died Aft. 1880. He married (1) JOANNA RYDER, daughter of SOLOMAN RYDER and JOANNAH SPINNEY. She was born 10 Feb 1814, and died 1859. He married (2) MARGARET ARCHIBALD Nov 1860, daughter of JAMES ARCHIBALD and AMY HARVEY. She was born 06 May 1836 in Colchester, NS..

Children of HARVEY SPINNEY and JOANNA RYDER are:
737.   i.   EDGAR KEITH[7] SPINNEY, b. 1851, Nova Scotia; d. Aft. 1880.
738.   ii.   MARY SPINNEY, b. 1844, Yarmouth, NS.; d. 1920.

Children of HARVEY SPINNEY and MARGARET ARCHIBALD are:
      iii.   AMY JOANNA[7] SPINNEY, b. 1862, 21 Jan 1862.
      iv.   LIZZIE SPINNEY, b. 1864.
      v.   MARIA SPINNEY, b. 1867.
739.   vi.   HEMAN SPINNEY, b. 1869.
      vii.   HERBERT SPINNEY, b. 1872.

374. SUSANAH[6] SPINNEY *(AARON[5], JOHN[4], JOHN[3], JOHN[2], THOMAS[1])* was born 26 May 1796, and died 06 Nov 1883. She married JACOB SPINNEY 17 Apr 1817 in Argyle Nova Scotia, son of JACOB SPINNEY and SUSANNA ATWOOD. He was born 26 Apr 1795, and died 1883.

Notes for JACOB SPINNEY:
JACOB AND HIS BROTHER JOSEPH moved to Tatamagoushe about 1833 along with Henry Roberts and Daniel Goodwin. Judge Patterson in his history states that "one of the Spinney brothers was the first to visit Tatamagouche, and he returned to tell the others of a place so peculiarly suited to fishing and ship building".

Jacob settled his family on a farm described by Patterson as "being along the slopes at the head of Tatamagouche Harbor" He and his wife Susannah had arrived in 1817 and had eight children, including a son Morris whose grandson John Havelock Spinney was still living on the old homestead in 1978. Most of this written information has come from his great granddaughter Mrs. Nellie Semple who was at that time still a resident of Tatamagouche. Joseph Spinney, brother of Jacob, settled on a farm near his brother in the area called Bayhead. Joseph had married Annie R. Goodwin the daughter of William Goodwin and their children were: Joanna 1823-1923
Joseph 1827-1912
Sarah 1830-1912
Mary Jane
Susan
Stillman According to my information, Joanna was born October 2, 1823 at Argyle and married to Griffin Smith. She died at m Pugwash August 23, 1912. Joseph died at Tatamagouche March 13, 1912. He married Flora Ross the daughter of Rev. Hugh Ross, a graduate of the first class of Presbyterian ministers from the Rev. Thomas McCullocks
Change Date: 17 JAN 2003 at 10:35:11

Children are listed above under (364) Jacob Spinney.

375. JOHN[6] SPINNEY *(AARON[5], JOHN[4], JOHN[3], JOHN[2], THOMAS[1])* was born 29 Jun 1794 in Argyle, NS.. He married HANNAH SPINNEY 17 Apr 1817, daughter of ISAAC SPINNEY and EUNICE FROST. She was born 18 Mar 1795 in Argyle, NS..

Children are listed above under (356) Hannah Spinney.

376. MERCY[6] SPINNEY *(ANDREW[5], JOHN[4], JOHN[3], JOHN[2], THOMAS[1])* was born 07 Nov 1794. She married STEPHEN SNIDER.

Children of MERCY SPINNEY and STEPHEN SNIDER are:
- i. STEPHEN[7] SNIDER, b. 10 May 1827, Argyle, NS..
- ii. SARAH SNIDER, b. 11 Aug 1829, Argyle, NS..
- iii. ANN SNIDER, b. 21 Jan 1833, Argyle, NS..
- iv. ANDREW SNIDER, b. 04 Aug 1838, Argyle, NS..

377. ANDREW[6] SPINNEY *(ANDREW[5], JOHN[4], JOHN[3], JOHN[2], THOMAS[1])* was born 26 May 1810 in Nova Scotia, Canada. He married HANNAH SPINNEY 21 Jan 1841, daughter of BENJAMIN SPINNEY and REBEKAH SPINNEY. She was born 12 Jan 1822 in Argyle, NS..

Children of ANDREW SPINNEY and HANNAH SPINNEY are:
- i. NELSON J[7] SPINNEY, b. 29 Oct 1841, Brockton, Ma; d. 12 May 1907, Rhode Island; m. BERTHA GOODWIN, 20 Nov 1867; b. Mar 1846, Maine.
- ii. SARAH SPINNEY, b. 19 Jan 1844.
- iii. CHAPMAN SPINNEY, b. 07 Nov 1845.
- iv. BENJAMIN SPINNEY, b. 04 Nov 1847; m. AGATHA.
- v. TRUSTMEN SPINNEY, b. 05 Apr 1850.
- vi. FRANCES EVELYN SPINNEY, b. 19 Nov 1852.
- vii. HANNAH L SPINNEY, b. 23 Jul 1855.
- viii. DELINA F SPINNEY, b. 19 Jul 1858; m. HERBERT HINES.

378. BENJAMIN[6] SPINNEY *(BENJAMIN[5], JOHN[4], JOHN[3], JOHN[2], THOMAS[1])* was born 03 May 1798. He married REBEKAH SPINNEY 22 Dec 1819 in Argyle, NS., daughter of ISAAC SPINNEY and EUNICE FROST. She was born 09 Dec 1797 in Argyle, NS..

Children are listed above under (354) Rebekah Spinney.

379. LETITIA[6] SPINNEY *(BENJAMIN[5], JOHN[4], JOHN[3], JOHN[2], THOMAS[1])* was born 17 Oct 1800 in Argyle, NS.. She married SIMEON SPINNEY 15 Jan 1829, son of AARON SPINNEY and MARY KENNEY. He was born 09 Aug 1802 in Argyle, NS., and died 20 Feb 1864 in Argyle, NS..

Children are listed above under (371) Simeon Spinney.

380. WHITMAN⁶ SPINNEY *(BENJAMIN⁵, JOHN⁴, JOHN³, JOHN², THOMAS¹)* was born 01 Sep 1805, and died 06 Jun 1891. He married DESIAH SPINNEY 09 Jan 1840 in Argyle Nova Scotia, daughter of DANIEL SPINNEY and DESIRE CROWELL. She was born 17 Oct 1808, and died 07 Jun 1884.

Children of WHITMAN SPINNEY and DESIAH SPINNEY are:
- i. JUDSON RAYMOND⁷ SPINNEY, b. 21 Oct 1840; d. 07 Dec 1863.
- ii. JOSEPH NORMAN SPINNEY, b. 26 Aug 1842; d. 1863.

  Notes for JOSEPH NORMAN SPINNEY:
  Lost from Shipboard, off Mabou 6 October 1863

- iii. LORAN HOMER SPINNEY, b. 25 Sep 1844; d. 20 Jun 1875.
- iv. DEBORAH SPINNEY, b. 05 Oct 1847; m. WILLIAM KENNEY, 05 Nov 1877.

381. SOLOMAN ROBERT⁶ SPINNEY *(BENJAMIN⁵, JOHN⁴, JOHN³, JOHN², THOMAS¹)* was born 02 Aug 1808. He married MARY ANN SNOW. She was born 1812.

Children of SOLOMAN SPINNEY and MARY SNOW are:
- i. LOUISA⁷ SPINNEY, m. BENJAMIN SMITH.
- 740. ii. ROBERT M SPINNEY, b. Sep 1854; d. 13 Jun 1912, New York.
- 741. iii. JOSIAH SPINNEY, b. 13 Apr 1855; d. Aft. 1901.
- 742. iv. GEORGE NELSON SPINNEY, b. Oct 1848, Port Latour, Shelburn, Nova Scotia, Canada; d. 01 Feb 1907, Yarmouth Nova Scotia.

382. RHONDA⁶ SPINNEY *(BENJAMIN⁵, JOHN⁴, JOHN³, JOHN², THOMAS¹)* was born 26 Apr 1811, and died 04 Apr 1888. She married EBENEZER SPINNEY 15 Jan 1833, son of JACOB SPINNEY and SUSANNA ATWOOD. He was born 28 Dec 1807 in Nova Scotia, and died 1850.

Children are listed above under (367) Ebenezer Spinney.

383. NORMAN⁶ SPINNEY *(BENJAMIN⁵, JOHN⁴, JOHN³, JOHN², THOMAS¹)* was born 21 Feb 1821. He married ISABELLA. She was born 1830.

Children of NORMAN SPINNEY and ISABELLA are:
- i. LUCY⁷ SPINNEY, b. 1854.
- ii. MELVINA G SPINNEY, b. 1856; d. Aft. 1920; m. CHARLES HABER.
- 743. iii. SOLOMAN R SPINNEY, b. 1858; d. Aft. 1901.
- 744. iv. AUSTIN SPINNEY, b. 02 Nov 1860.
- v. JONATHAN SPINNEY, b. 1861.
- vi. GEORGIA SPINNEY, b. 1868.
- vii. CHARLES SPINNEY, b. 1870.
- viii. CLARA SPINNEY, b. 1876.
- ix. WILSON SPINNEY, b. 1877; d. Aft. 1901.
- x. ROBERT E SPINNEY, b. 1868; d. 1868.

384. LEMUEL⁶ SPINNEY *(WILLIAM⁵, JOHN⁴, JOHN³, JOHN², THOMAS¹)* was born 03 Feb 1822 in Argyle, NS.. He married LYDIA NICHOLSON.

Children of LEMUEL SPINNEY and LYDIA NICHOLSON are:
- 745. i. EMMA MARIA⁷ SPINNEY, b. 1855, Nova Scotia, Canada.
- 746. ii. ADALIZA C SPINNEY, b. 1861, Nova Scotia, Canada.

385. MINOR⁶ SPINNEY *(WILLIAM⁵, JOHN⁴, JOHN³, JOHN², THOMAS¹)* was born 18 Nov 1802 in Argyle, NS., and died May 1884. He married MARIA MC CLASEN.

Children of MINOR SPINNEY and MARIA MC CLASEN are:
- 747. i. MINOR H⁷ SPINNEY, b. 1837; d. 1922, Sandford, ME.

748.   ii.   ADELIA JANE SPINNEY, b. 14 Nov 1841, Argyle, NS.; d. 04 Mar 1923.
749.   iii.   CHARLES W SPINNEY, b. Jun 1835, Greenwood Nova Scotia; d. 1907, Fitchburg, MA.

386. DANIEL[6] SPINNEY *(DANIEL[5], JOHN[4], JOHN[3], JOHN[2], THOMAS[1])* was born 13 Jun 1805 in Argyle, NS., and died 14 Nov 1873. He married ELIZABETH HOPKINS. She died 24 Apr 1892.

Children of DANIEL SPINNEY and ELIZABETH HOPKINS are:
        i.   SARAH[7] SPINNEY, b. 1841; m. CHARLES CARLTON; b. 1833.
        ii.   ELSINORA SPINNEY, b. 1846.

387. DESIAH[6] SPINNEY *(DANIEL[5], JOHN[4], JOHN[3], JOHN[2], THOMAS[1])* was born 17 Oct 1808, and died 07 Jun 1884. She married WHITMAN SPINNEY 09 Jan 1840 in Argyle Nova Scotia, son of BENJAMIN SPINNEY and DEBORAH CROWELL. He was born 01 Sep 1805, and died 06 Jun 1891.

Children are listed above under (380) Whitman Spinney.

388. PRINCE[6] SPINNEY *(DANIEL[5], JOHN[4], JOHN[3], JOHN[2], THOMAS[1])* was born 30 Jun 1811 in Argyle, NS., and died 19 Feb 1883 in Nova Scotia. He married ELIZA ANN RYDER. She was born 1812, and died 20 Jan 1900 in Nova Scotia.

Children of PRINCE SPINNEY and ELIZA RYDER are:
        i.   LEONARD[7] SPINNEY, b. 1851; d. Aft. 1901; m. MARTHA; b. 1853; d. Aft. 1901.
        ii.   EMELINE SPINNEY, b. 1843; d. Aft. 1901.
750.   iii.   HOWARD SPINNEY, b. 1846; d. 1919.

389. MARY ELENER[6] SPINNEY *(DANIEL[5], JOHN[4], JOHN[3], JOHN[2], THOMAS[1])* was born 21 May 1814 in Argyle, NS.. She married WILLIAM SPINNEY. He was born Abt. 1800.

Child of MARY SPINNEY and WILLIAM SPINNEY is:
751.   i.   ANGELINE[7] SPINNEY, b. 1848.

390. EDWARD[6] SPINNEY *(DANIEL[5], JOHN[4], JOHN[3], JOHN[2], THOMAS[1])* was born 23 Feb 1830, and died Aft. 1880. He married LYDIA SYMONDS 27 Jan 1852.

Children of EDWARD SPINNEY and LYDIA SYMONDS are:
752.   i.   ASENATH[7] SPINNEY, b. 27 Sep 1852, Nova Scotia; d. Beverly, Ma.
        ii.   RUFAS SYMONDS SPINNEY, b. 19 Aug 1854; d. 1874.
        iii.   EMILY SPINNEY, b. 27 Sep 1856; m. GEORGE W MOORE.
        iv.   LOUISA H SPINNEY, b. 27 Dec 1859; m. AUGUSTUS STEVENS.
753.   v.   LAURA ETTA SPINNEY, b. 06 Apr 1861; d. 04 Feb 1942.
754.   vi.   LYDIA MATHILDA SPINNEY, b. 24 Aug 1863.
755.   vii.   ANGUS HARVEY SPINNEY, b. 25 Oct 1865; d. 29 Jan 1913.
        viii. BESSIE LEE SPINNEY, b. 12 Feb 1867.
756.   ix.   BOWMAN E SPINNEY, b. 13 Oct 1869, Yarmouth, NS; d. 15 Oct 1907, Boston, Ma.
        x.   LALIA GERTRUDE SPINNEY, b. 19 Sep 1871.
        xi.   MINERVA BERNICE SPINNEY, b. 14 Oct 1875; m. CHARLES E LYONS.

391. ASENATH[6] RYDER *(JOANNAH[5] SPINNEY, JOHN[4], JOHN[3], JOHN[2], THOMAS[1])* was born 11 Nov 1809. She married DANIEL SPINNEY.

Child of ASENATH RYDER and DANIEL SPINNEY is:
757.   i.   ALBERT[7] SPINNEY, b. 1841, Argyle, Nova Scotia; d. 1898, Lynn, MA.

392. LUCY[6] RYDER *(JOANNAH[5] SPINNEY, JOHN[4], JOHN[3], JOHN[2], THOMAS[1])* was born 01 Dec 1817, and died 03 Dec 1848. She married EZARA SPINNEY 20 Feb 1840, son of AARON SPINNEY and MARY KENNEY. He was born 16 Jun 1813, and died Aft. 1880.

Children are listed above under (372) Ezara Spinney.

393. JOANNA[6] RYDER *(JOANNAH[5] SPINNEY, JOHN[4], JOHN[3], JOHN[2], THOMAS[1])* was born 10 Feb 1814, and died 1859. She married HARVEY SPINNEY, son of AARON SPINNEY and MARY KENNEY. He was born 27 Jul 1817 in Argyle, NS., and died Aft. 1880.

Children are listed above under (373) Harvey Spinney.

394. JOSEPH A[6] SPINNEY *(STEPHEN L[5], TIMOTHY[4], JOHN[3], JOHN[2], THOMAS[1])* was born Abt. 1800, and died 03 Aug 1848. He married PAMELA JENKINS 11 Mar 1827. She was born 1799, and died Aft. 1850.

Children of JOSEPH SPINNEY and PAMELA JENKINS are:
      i.   ADELINE SARAH[7] SPINNEY, b. 1830; m. WATSON.
      ii. ROBERT J SPINNEY, b. 1831; d. Aft. 1850.
758.   iii. PAMELIA A SPINNEY, b. 1832; d. Bet. 1870 - 1880.
      iv. STEPHEN SAMUEL SPINNEY, b. 23 Aug 1834; d. 17 Aug 1891, York County Maine; m. HELEN M CURRIER, 20 Jan 1873, Portsmouth, NH; b. 20 Aug 1838; d. 10 Jul 1922.
      v.   ELIZABETH COLE SPINNEY, b. Abt. 1835.
      vi. MARY AUGUSTA SPINNEY, b. Feb 1837.
      vii. MESHACH SPINNEY, b. Dec 1838; d. 31 Oct 1896.

395. JOSEPH[6] DENNETT *(WILLIAM[5], MARY[4] TETHERLY, MERCY[3] SPINNEY, JOHN[2], THOMAS[1])* was born 24 Nov 1774 in Kittery, York, Maine, USA, and died 10 Jan 1808. He married ABIGAIL SPINNEY 10 Apr 1796 in Kittery Maine. She was born Abt. 1776.

Children of JOSEPH DENNETT and ABIGAIL SPINNEY are:
      i.   JOSEPH[7] DENNETT, b. 07 Jul 1796; d. 30 Jun 1839.
      ii. WILLIAM DENNETT, b. 07 Jul 1798; d. 16 Mar 1812.
      iii. SARAH DENNETT, b. 25 Jul 1802; d. 15 Oct 1818.

396. CHARLES[6] TETHERLY *(SAMUEL[5], WILLIAM[4], MERCY[3] SPINNEY, JOHN[2], THOMAS[1])* was born 14 Dec 1787, and died 07 Aug 1845. He married REBECCA P SPINNEY 14 Oct 1819 in Eliot, Me, daughter of GEORGE SPINNEY and ANN LIBBEY. She was born 03 Mar 1801, and died 24 Sep 1895.

Children are listed above under (337) Rebecca P Spinney.

397. SAMUEL[6] TETHERLY *(SAMUEL[5], WILLIAM[4], MERCY[3] SPINNEY, JOHN[2], THOMAS[1])* was born 1790, and died 06 Mar 1828. He married OLIVE A SPINNEY 30 Sep 1811, daughter of GEORGE SPINNEY and ANN LIBBEY. She was born 1790, and died 12 May 1852.

Children are listed above under (332) Olive A Spinney.

398. LEONARD[6] SPINNEY *(ISAAC[5], WILLIAM[4], ANDREW[3], JOHN[2], THOMAS[1])* was born 31 Oct 1807 in Eliot, ME, and died 1874 in Charlestown, Ma. He married MARTHA ESTES HILL 13 Oct 1840 in Eliot, Me. She was born 05 Dec 1816.

Children of LEONARD SPINNEY and MARTHA HILL are:
      i.   LAURA ANAH[7] SPINNEY, b. 23 Jul 1840, Kittery, ME; d. 14 Dec 1891.
759.   ii. MARY ADA SPINNEY, b. 06 Jan 1843, Kittery, ME.
      iii. LEONARD CHAPIN SPINNEY, b. 30 Oct 1845, Kittery, ME; d. 05 May 1847.
760.   iv. LEONARD CHAUNCEY SPINNEY, b. 02 Nov 1849, Kittery, ME; d. Aft. 1930.

399. DANIEL[6] SPINNEY *(ISAAC[5], WILLIAM[4], ANDREW[3], JOHN[2], THOMAS[1])* was born 20 May 1812 in Kittery, Me, and died Mar 1891. He married ANNIS WARD 29 Jan 1840 in East Eddington, Me, daughter of PETER WARD and TAMISON TUCKER. She was born 15 Oct 1818, and died 27 Feb 1865.

Children of DANIEL SPINNEY and ANNIS WARD are:

          i.   OLIVER WALDRON[7] SPINNEY, b. 13 May 1846, East Eddington, ME; d. 21 Feb 1859.
        ii.   LEONARD LAMARTINE SPINNEY, b. 14 May 1848, East Eddington, ME; d. 01 May 1878.
      iii.   E CHAPIN SPINNEY, b. 09 Apr 1850, East Eddington, ME; d. 08 Sep 1863.
761.   iv.   NELLIE ESTELLE "ELEANOR" SPINNEY, b. 26 Nov 1856, East Eddington, ME; d. Aft. 1935.

400. ISAAC[6] SPINNEY *(ISAAC[5], WILLIAM[4], ANDREW[3], JOHN[2], THOMAS[1])* was born 13 Apr 1818 in Eliot, ME, and died 19 Jul 1859. He married MARY N GREEN. She was born 1822.

Child of ISAAC SPINNEY and MARY GREEN is:
762.   i.   MARY HELENA[7] SPINNEY, b. 31 Aug 1849, Eliot , ME.

401. WALDRON S[6] SPINNEY *(ISAAC[5], WILLIAM[4], ANDREW[3], JOHN[2], THOMAS[1])* was born 12 Jan 1824 in Eliot, ME, and died 17 Feb 1911 in California. He married LUCETTA ATWOOD MORRILL 10 Jan 1856, daughter of THOMAS MORRILL. She was born 12 May 1828, and died 27 Nov 1910.

Children of WALDRON SPINNEY and LUCETTA MORRILL are:
          i.   EMMA[7] SPINNEY, b. 21 Feb 1861; m. VOLMER A. H. HOFFMEYER, 03 Jul 1897; b. Denmark.
        ii.   HATTIE SPINNEY, b. 02 Apr 1863; d. Aft. 1900; m. CHARLES J ROBERTSON, 28 Feb 1888; d. Bef. 1900.

402. MARY E[6] SPINNEY *(TIMOTHY[5], WILLIAM[4], ANDREW[3], JOHN[2], THOMAS[1])* was born 1811, and died 14 Apr 1876 in Kittery, ME. She married GEORGE ROGERS. He was born 1805 in Palmyra, ME, and died 08 May 1877.

Children of MARY SPINNEY and GEORGE ROGERS are:
          i.   HENRY[7] ROGERS, b. 1836.
        ii.   WILLIAM ROGERS, b. 1838.
      iii.   MARY E ROGERS, b. 1842.
      iv.   ANNA ROGERS, b. 1843.
       v.   EMMA ROGERS, b. 1847.
      vi.   FRANKY ROGERS, b. 23 Jul 1854; d. 02 Oct 1858, Kittery.

403. ALBION P[6] SPINNEY *(TIMOTHY[5], WILLIAM[4], ANDREW[3], JOHN[2], THOMAS[1])* was born Jul 1825 in Kittery, ME, and died Bet. 1900 - 1910 in Pennsylvania. He married MARY M BAHN. She was born 1825, and died Bet. 1900 - 1910.

Children of ALBION SPINNEY and MARY BAHN are:
          i.   MARY[7] SPINNEY, b. 1848.
        ii.   ANNA SPINNEY, b. 1850; d. Aft. 1910.
      iii.   MATILDA SPINNEY, b. 1852.
      iv.   EMILY IRENE SPINNEY, b. 1863, Pennsylvania; d. Aft. 1900; m. GEORGE EVERETT HAMMOND, 06 Nov 1901, Elliott, Maine.
       v.   ELEANOR M SPINNEY, b. 1865; d. Aft. 1910.
      vi.   KATE G SPINNEY, b. 1866; d. Aft. 1880.
     vii.   THOMAS R SPINNEY, b. 1868; d. Aft. 1900.

404. SALLY[6] LYDSTON *(ROBY[5], ABIGAIL[4] SPINNEY, ANDREW[3], JOHN[2], THOMAS[1])* was born 06 Aug 1789. She married JOHN NORTON.

Child of SALLY LYDSTON and JOHN NORTON is:
          i.   CAROLINE[7] NORTON.

405. WILLIAM H[6] SPINNEY *(STEPHEN R[5], EDMUND[4], ANDREW[3], JOHN[2], THOMAS[1])* was born 1827 in Raymond, NH, and died Bef. 1900. He married (1) SARAH J AIKEN. She was born 1851 in Dover, NH, and died Aft. 1900. He married (2) MEHITABLE MEEDER 28 Aug 1844 in Lowell, MA. She died Aft. 1860.

Children of WILLIAM SPINNEY and SARAH AIKEN are:
763.   i.   IDA MAY[7] SPINNEY, b. 1879.
764.   ii.   CLARENCE A SPINNEY, b. 20 Aug 1882, Raymond, NH.

     iii.   BERTHA SPINNEY, b. Nov 1885.

     iv.   GEORGE HERBERT SPINNEY, b. 25 Mar 1892.

Children of WILLIAM SPINNEY and MEHITABLE MEEDER are:

     v.   JAMES[7] SPINNEY, b. Jul 1845; d. 23 May 1846, Canton, MA.

     vi.   ALMIRA SPINNEY, b. 1846; d. Aft. 1880; m. ELIJAH MORRISON; b. 1835, Sandwich, New Hampshire; d. Aft. 1880.

     vii.   CHARLES E SPINNEY, b. 1848; d. Aft. 1860.

406. EUNICE[6] SPINNEY *(JOHN[5], JOHN[4], ANDREW[3], JOHN[2], THOMAS[1])* was born 18 Apr 1784 in Boothbay, Lincoln, Maine, USA, and died 1810. She married THOMAS MARR 1806, son of JOHN MARR and MARY CORNISH. He was born 01 Apr 1784 in Marr's Island, ME, and died 17 Dec 1866.

Children are listed above under (190) Thomas Marr.

407. JOHN[6] SPINNEY *(JOHN[5], JOHN[4], ANDREW[3], JOHN[2], THOMAS[1])* was born 26 May 1776 in Georgetown, ME, and died 20 Feb 1819 in Georgetown, ME. He married MIRIAM OLIVER 20 Jun 1800 in Georgetown Maine. She was born Abt. 1780, and died 19 Jul 1838 in Cook Head, Lincoln Maine.

Children of JOHN SPINNEY and MIRIAM OLIVER are:

765.   i.   PATIENCE[7] SPINNEY, b. 02 Dec 1801, Georgetown, ME; d. Bef. 1880.

766.   ii.   THOMAS SPINNEY, b. 07 Nov 1803, Georgetown, ME; d. 05 Nov 1894, Georgetown, ME.

767.   iii.   MIRIAM SPINNEY, b. 23 Jul 1806; d. Aft. 1860.

768.   iv.   LOUISA SPINNEY, b. 23 Mar 1809, Georgetown, ME; d. 13 Dec 1857, Monticello, ME.

     v.   HEZEKIAH SPINNEY, b. 19 Feb 1811; m. LAVINIA PARSONS, 19 Sep 1833, Massachusetts.

     vi.   ALTHEA SPINNEY, b. 26 Feb 1813, Georgetown, ME; m. CHARLES BANKS.

     vii.   REUBEN SPINNEY, b. 14 Dec 1814, Georgetown, ME; d. 19 Jul 1815, Georgetown, ME.

     viii.   CAROLINE S SPINNEY, b. 19 Aug 1816, Phippsburg, ME; m. JOHN L COOK, 13 Jun 1837.

408. NICHOLAS[6] SPINNEY *(JOHN[5], JOHN[4], ANDREW[3], JOHN[2], THOMAS[1])* was born 28 Jan 1778 in Georgetown, ME, and died 1856. He married SUSANNA BURGESS 12 Dec 1799. She was born 1780 in CT, and died 1854.

Children of NICHOLAS SPINNEY and SUSANNA BURGESS are:

769.   i.   ROXANNA BURGESS[7] SPINNEY, b. 22 Mar 1801, Georgetown, ME; d. 12 Aug 1879, Bath, Me.

770.   ii.   WILLIAM M SPINNEY, b. 02 Oct 1802, Georgetown, ME; d. 23 Jan 1857, Freedom, ME.

771.   iii.   NICHOLAS J SPINNEY, b. 19 Aug 1804, Georgetown, ME; d. 09 Jan 1861, Georgetown, ME.

     iv.   EUNICE SPINNEY, b. 21 Jan 1807, Georgetown, ME.

     v.   ROBERT SPINNEY, b. 09 Jul 1809, Georgetown, ME.

772.   vi.   ROBERT CURTIS SPINNEY, b. 02 Sep 1811, Georgetown, ME; d. 27 Jan 1873.

     vii.   JOAN SPINNEY, b. 22 Jun 1813, Georgetown, ME.

     viii.   MARY ANN SPINNEY, b. 20 Nov 1815, Georgetown, ME.

     ix.   REUBEN SPINNEY, b. 14 Sep 1818, Georgetown, ME.

409. HANNAH[6] SPINNEY *(JOHN[5], JOHN[4], ANDREW[3], JOHN[2], THOMAS[1])* was born 10 Jun 1782. She married (1) WILLIAM MARR 08 Jan 1801 in Georgetown Maine, son of JOHN MARR and MARY CORNISH. He was born 02 May 1779, and died 26 Jan 1801. She married (2) ISIAIH MARR 23 Jun 1803, son of JOHN MARR and MARY CORNISH. He was born 02 Jun 1782.

Child is listed above under (186) Isiaih Marr.

410. RICHARD[6] SPINNEY *(JOHN[5], JOHN[4], ANDREW[3], JOHN[2], THOMAS[1])* was born 04 Sep 1786 in Georgetown, ME, and died Bet. 1860 - 1870. He married ELIZABETH (BETSY) SPINNEY 03 Jun 1813 in Georgetown Maine. She was born 1786, and died Aft. 1870.

Children of RICHARD SPINNEY and ELIZABETH SPINNEY are:

773.   i.   EZRA[7] SPINNEY, b. 28 Mar 1815, Georgetown, ME; d. Aft. 1870.

     ii.   TIMOTHY SPINNEY, b. 03 Jun 1816, Georgetown, ME.

     iii.   MOSES SPINNEY, b. 25 Mar 1818; d. Bef. 1850.

     iv.   EPHRIAM SPINNEY, b. 26 Jul 1819, Georgetown, ME.

   v. JEREMIAH SPINNEY, b. 16 Jan 1821, Georgetown, ME; d. Bef. 1860.
   vi. MAILINDA SPINNEY, b. 1822.
774. vii. RHONDA SPINNEY, b. 03 Oct 1822, Georgetown, ME.
775. viii. WILLIAM STACEY SPINNEY, b. 27 Jun 1824; d. Abt. 1850.
   ix. JEREMIAH SPINNEY, b. 07 Jun 1826, Georgetown, ME; d. Bef. 1860.
776. x. THOMAS J SPINNEY, b. 14 Mar 1828, Georgetown, ME.

411. JEREMIAH[6] SPINNEY (*JOHN[5], JOHN[4], ANDREW[3], JOHN[2], THOMAS[1]*) was born 02 Oct 1788 in Georgetown, ME, and died Bef. 1840. He married ANNA OLIVER 15 Nov 1810 in Georgetown Maine, daughter of JAMES OLIVER and JANE SPINNEY. She was born 1789, and died Aft. 1850.

Children of JEREMIAH SPINNEY and ANNA OLIVER are:
   i. MARY JANE[7] SPINNEY, b. 01 Sep 1811.
777. ii. JAMES M SPINNEY, b. 21 Sep 1815; d. Aft. 1850.
778. iii. JOHN SPINNEY, b. 21 Jan 1817; d. Aft. 1880.
779. iv. RACHEL ANN SPINNEY, b. 20 Mar 1819, Georgetown, ME.
   v. RUTH K SPINNEY, b. 11 Feb 1823, Georgetown, ME.
   vi. HANNAH E SPINNEY, b. 16 Jun 1825, Georgetown, ME; d. Aft. 1850.
   vii. NANCY SPINNEY, b. 18 May 1827, Georgetown, ME.
   viii. ZINA SPINNEY, b. 17 May 1831; d. Bef. 1880.

412. CALEB[6] SPINNEY (*JOHN[5], JOHN[4], ANDREW[3], JOHN[2], THOMAS[1]*) was born 20 Apr 1791 in Phippsburg, Lincoln, Maine, USA, and died Aft. 1870. He married (1) MIRIAM OLIVER 23 Sep 1819 in Georgetown Maine. She was born Abt. 1780, and died 19 Jul 1838 in Cook Head, Lincoln Maine. He married (2) ELIZA PERCY 14 Nov 1839 in Phippsburg, ME.

Children of CALEB SPINNEY and MIRIAM OLIVER are:
780. i. CHARLES OLIVER[7] SPINNEY, b. 20 Jan 1820, Phippsburg, ME; d. 08 Jan 1911.
781. ii. OLIVER R SPINNEY, b. 22 Jan 1822; d. Aft. 1880.
   iii. SUSAN SPINNEY, b. 18 Mar 1825, Georgetown, ME.
782. iv. NANCY R SPINNEY, b. 1828; d. 1905.

413. DAVID[6] SPINNEY (*JOHN[5], JOHN[4], ANDREW[3], JOHN[2], THOMAS[1]*) was born 17 Mar 1793 in Georgetown, ME, and died Aft. 1860. He married MARY OLIVER 24 Dec 1812 in Georgetown, ME. She was born 1785 in Georgetown, ME, and died Aft. 1850.

Children of DAVID SPINNEY and MARY OLIVER are:
783. i. ZINA H[7] SPINNEY, b. 24 May 1814, Georgetown, ME; d. Aft. 1880, Somerville, MA.
   ii. DAUGHTER SPINNEY, b. Bet. 1815 - 1820.
784. iii. LUCRETIA SPINNEY, b. 25 Dec 1818; d. Aft. 1850.
   iv. MARTIN SPINNEY, b. 1828.
   v. SARAH S SPINNEY, b. 07 Mar 1830, Georgetown, ME.
   vi. WINFIELD S SPINNEY, b. 1849.

414. EPHRAIM[6] SPINNEY (*JOHN[5], JOHN[4], ANDREW[3], JOHN[2], THOMAS[1]*) was born 01 Nov 1794, and died 18 Jun 1886. He married MARY SPINNEY 01 Jan 1822 in Georgetown Maine, daughter of JEREMIAH SPINNEY and ABIGAIL BARSTOW. She was born 28 Feb 1800, and died 25 Jun 1870 in Georgetown, ME.

Children of EPHRAIM SPINNEY and MARY SPINNEY are:
   i. CATHERINE[7] SPINNEY, b. 1824.
   ii. RACHEL SPINNEY, b. 1831.
785. iii. ZINA H SPINNEY, b. 1833; d. Aft. 1880.

415. JANE[6] SPINNEY (*JOHN[5], JOHN[4], ANDREW[3], JOHN[2], THOMAS[1]*) was born 30 Nov 1795 in Phippsburg, ME, and died 1884. She married EBENEZER MCKINNEY 05 Nov 1814 in Georgetown, ME. He was born 1786, and died 1884.

Child of JANE SPINNEY and EBENEZER MCKINNEY is:

786.   i.   SUSAN⁷ MCKINNEY, b. 09 Apr 1820; d. Aft. 1880.

416. ANNA⁶ OLIVER *(JANE⁵ SPINNEY, JOHN⁴, ANDREW³, JOHN², THOMAS¹)* was born 1789, and died Aft. 1850. She married JEREMIAH SPINNEY 15 Nov 1810 in Georgetown Maine, son of JOHN SPINNEY and EUNICE HUTCHINGS. He was born 02 Oct 1788 in Georgetown, ME, and died Bef. 1840.

Children are listed above under (411) Jeremiah Spinney.

417. JOHN C⁶ OLIVER *(JANE⁵ SPINNEY, JOHN⁴, ANDREW³, JOHN², THOMAS¹)* was born 1796, and died 1870. He married HULDAH ROBINSON, daughter of BRYANT ROBINSON and PATIENCE OLIVER. She was born 16 Dec 1804, and died 1865.

Child of JOHN OLIVER and HULDAH ROBINSON is:
          i.   ELI NOYSE⁷ OLIVER, b. 1836; d. 1912; m. DIANTHA H NICHOLS; b. 1832; d. 1913.

418. RACHEL⁶ OLIVER *(JANE⁵ SPINNEY, JOHN⁴, ANDREW³, JOHN², THOMAS¹)* was born 05 Oct 1802 in Georgetown, ME, and died 30 May 1854 in Industry, ME. She married SILAS BEARSE Abt. 1827 in Maine. He was born 25 Jan 1806 in Starks, ME, and died 08 Sep 1880 in Eau Claire, WI.

Children of RACHEL OLIVER and SILAS BEARSE are:
          i.   LYDIA MARGARET⁷ BURCE, b. 24 Jun 1828, West Mills, ME; d. 02 May 1870, Eau Claire, WI; m.
               BENJAMIN GENNINGS MCINTOSH, 11 Nov 1852, Willing, NY.
787.   ii. RUFUS LOREN BURCE, b. 26 Jun 1830, Somerset Co., ME; d. 23 Aug 1892, Seattle, WA.
          iii. DORCAS BURCE, b. Abt. 1832.
788.   iv. JOHN CALVIN BURCE, b. 14 Jun 1834, Starks, ME; d. 23 Oct 1864, PA.
          v.   STACY O. BURCE, b. Abt. 1835, Industry, ME; d. 19 Apr 1836, Industry, ME.
          vi. MARY JANE BURCE, b. Abt. 1838, Eau Claire, WI; d. 1920, Eau Claire, WI.
          vii. AMELIA (PERMELIA) BURCE, b. 1839, Industry, ME; d. Abt. 1870, Eau Claire, WI; m. LAVINCES HERD,
               Abt. 1860, Wisconsin.
          viii. LEANDER BURCE, b. 1842, Industry, ME; d. 27 Dec 1851, Industry, ME.
          ix. CHARLES E. BURCE, b. 30 Apr 1844, Industry, ME; d. 07 May 1916, Eau Claire, WI.
          x.   JAMES OLIVER BURCE, b. 19 Apr 1846, Industry, ME; d. 27 Feb 1911, Bemidji, MN.
          xi. WILLIAM STACY BURCE, b. 09 Feb 1849, Industry, ME; d. 07 Jan 1935, Janesville, MN.

419. GEORGE B⁶ SPINNEY *(JEREMIAH⁵, JOHN⁴, ANDREW³, JOHN², THOMAS¹)* was born 18 May 1789 in Georgetown, ME, and died 09 Oct 1874 in Phippsburg, ME. He married ABIGAIL BAKER 19 Jun 1814 in Phippsburg, ME. She was born Abt. 1794, and died 02 Oct 1849 in Phippsburg, ME.

Children of GEORGE SPINNEY and ABIGAIL BAKER are:
          i.   BENJAMIN B⁷ SPINNEY, b. 1815.
789.   ii. ROLLAND SPINNEY, b. 23 Apr 1815; d. Bef. 1880.
          iii. EMILY SPINNEY, b. 17 Nov 1816.
790.   iv. RHONDA J SPINNEY, b. 1824.
791.   v.   GEORGE A SPINNEY, b. 1825; d. Aft. 1900.
          vi. PHILEMA SPINNEY, b. 1826.

420. SOPHIA⁶ SPINNEY *(JEREMIAH⁵, JOHN⁴, ANDREW³, JOHN², THOMAS¹)* was born 26 Aug 1791 in Georgetown, ME, and died 1860. She married RICHARD MARR 01 Nov 1818 in Georgetown Maine, son of JOHN MARR and MARY CORNISH. He was born 1792, and died 1852.

Children are listed above under (189) Richard Marr.

421. MOSES B⁶ SPINNEY *(JEREMIAH⁵, JOHN⁴, ANDREW³, JOHN², THOMAS¹)* was born 10 Feb 1793 in Georgetown, ME, and died Aft. 1880 in Georgetown, ME. He married PATIENCE SPINNEY 19 Nov 1819 in Georgetown, ME, daughter of JOHN SPINNEY and MIRIAM OLIVER. She was born 02 Dec 1801 in Georgetown, ME, and died Bef. 1880.

Children of MOSES SPINNEY and PATIENCE SPINNEY are:

	i.	LYDIA[7] SPINNEY.
792.	ii.	ALVAH SPINNEY, b. Abt. 1820, Phippsburg, ME.
793.	iii.	MILENDIA SPINNEY, b. 01 Nov 1820, Georgetown, ME; d. Bef. 1860.
	iv.	ELIZABETH SPINNEY, b. 1822.
794.	v.	FRANKLIN SPINNEY, b. 29 Jan 1822, Georgetown, ME; d. Aft. 1881.
	vi.	EMILY SPINNEY, b. 1824.
795.	vii.	JULIA A SPINNEY, b. 03 Jan 1824, Georgetown, ME; d. Aft. 1870, Industry, ME.
	viii.	SUSAN SPINNEY, b. 17 Oct 1825, Georgetown, ME; d. Aft. 1860.
	ix.	EVELYN SPINNEY, b. 1826.
	x.	JAMES SPINNEY, b. 30 Oct 1827; d. Aft. 1850.
	xi.	GEORGE B SPINNEY, b. 1828.
	xii.	PAMELIA CHURCHILL SPINNEY, b. 30 Jul 1830, Georgetown, ME.
	xiii.	ROLAND SPINNEY, b. 1832.
	xiv.	CAROLINE SPINNEY, b. 05 Apr 1833, Georgetown, ME.
	xv.	TIMOTHY SPINNEY, b. 01 Mar 1835, Georgetown, ME; d. Aft. 1900; m. AMANDA, 1866; b. Jun 1835; d. Aft. 1900.

Notes for TIMOTHY SPINNEY:
The 1900 census shows Timothy married to Amanda and that they did not have any children

	xvi.	LAVINIA SPINNEY, b. 06 Feb 1837, Georgetown, ME; d. Aft. 1881.
796.	xvi.	LAVINIA SPINNEY, b. 06 Feb 1837, Georgetown, ME; d. Aft. 1881.
	xvii.	HEZEKIAH SPINNEY, b. 20 Apr 1839; d. Aft. 1860.
	xviii.	EDWIN SPINNEY, b. 10 Mar 1842, Georgetown, ME.
	xix.	EDWIN SPINNEY, b. 11 Jan 1844.
	xx.	IVORY E SPINNEY, b. 16 May 1845, Georgetown, ME; d. Bef. 1850.
797.	xxi.	ANDREW JACKSON SPINNEY, b. 10 Nov 1846, Georgetown, ME; d. Aft. 1900, ME..

422. JERUSHA[6] SPINNEY *(JEREMIAH[5], JOHN[4], ANDREW[3], JOHN[2], THOMAS[1])* was born 23 Sep 1797 in Georgetown, ME, and died 01 May 1879. She married EPHRAIM OLIVER 30 May 1822 in Georgetown, ME, son of EPHRIAN OLIVER and ANNA SPINNEY. He was born 1797, and died 14 Dec 1890.

Children are listed above under (199) Ephraim Oliver.

423. MARY[6] SPINNEY *(JEREMIAH[5], JOHN[4], ANDREW[3], JOHN[2], THOMAS[1])* was born 28 Feb 1800, and died 25 Jun 1870 in Georgetown, ME. She married EPHRAIM SPINNEY 01 Jan 1822 in Georgetown Maine, son of JOHN SPINNEY and EUNICE HUTCHINGS. He was born 01 Nov 1794, and died 18 Jun 1886.

Children are listed above under (414) Ephraim Spinney.

424. JOHN[6] SPINNEY *(JEREMIAH[5], JOHN[4], ANDREW[3], JOHN[2], THOMAS[1])* was born 17 Sep 1802, and died Aft. 1860. He married MIRIAM SPINNEY Bet. 1820 - 1828, daughter of JOHN SPINNEY and MIRIAM OLIVER. She was born 23 Jul 1806, and died Aft. 1860.

Children of JOHN SPINNEY and MIRIAM SPINNEY are:

	i.	LOUISA J[7] SPINNEY, b. 1828; d. Aft. 1881.
798.	i.	LOUISA J[7] SPINNEY, b. 1828; d. Aft. 1881.
799.	ii.	SILAS CURTIS SPINNEY, b. 23 Sep 1829, Georgetown, ME; d. Aft. 1880.
	iii.	FRANCES SPINNEY, b. 14 Aug 1831.
800.	iv.	DANIEL WILLIAM SPINNEY, b. 16 Jan 1834, Georgetown, ME; d. Aft. 1920.
801.	v.	PATIENCE R SPINNEY, b. 14 Aug 1835, Georgetown, ME; d. 31 Aug 1897.
	vi.	HANNAH B SPINNEY, b. 04 Apr 1837, Georgetown, ME.
	vii.	EZRA SPINNEY, b. 19 May 1839, Georgetown, ME; d. Bef. 1850.
	viii.	LEMUEL BRADFORD SPINNEY, b. 07 Apr 1841; d. 15 Sep 1864, Bath, ME.

Notes for LEMUEL BRADFORD SPINNEY:
Danville National Cemetery
Danville, Virginia

Service Record:
  Enlisted as a Sergeant on 16 April 1864 at the age of 21
Enlisted in Company G, 32nd Infantry Regiment Maine on 16 April 1864.
POW on 30 July 1864 at Petersburg, VA
Died as a prisoner Company G, 32nd Infantry Regiment Maine on 15 September 1864

ix.   SAMUEL B SPINNEY, b. 1842; d. Bef. 1850.

425. JEREMIAH[6] SPINNEY *(JEREMIAH[5], JOHN[4], ANDREW[3], JOHN[2], THOMAS[1])* was born 25 Feb 1814 in Georgetown, ME, and died Aft. 1880 in Penn. He married (1) JANE HUTCHINGS. She was born 1815, and died Aft. 1850. He married (2) MARY. She was born 1830 in Penn, and died Aft. 1900.

Notes for JEREMIAH SPINNEY:
Listed in the 1850 Census Industry Maine

Children of JEREMIAH SPINNEY and JANE HUTCHINGS are:
	i.	PHILENA[7] SPINNEY, b. 1837.
802.	ii.	IRA SPINNEY, b. Jan 1838; d. 1927.
803.	iii.	GUSTAVUS W SPINNEY, b. 01 Dec 1839, Georgetown, ME.
	iv.	REUBEN F SPINNEY, b. 1842; d. 30 Mar 1863.
	v.	DORCAS SPINNEY, b. 1849.
804.	vi.	JAMES J SPINNEY, b. Jun 1849; d. Aft. 1880.

426. LYDIA[6] TRAFTON *(JOANNA[5] SPINNEY, JOHN[4], ANDREW[3], JOHN[2], THOMAS[1])* was born 09 Mar 1786. She married THOMAS MARR 1811, son of JOHN MARR and MARY CORNISH. He was born 01 Apr 1784 in Marr's Island, ME, and died 17 Dec 1866.

Children are listed above under (190) Thomas Marr.

427. KEZIAH[6] TRAFTON *(JOANNA[5] SPINNEY, JOHN[4], ANDREW[3], JOHN[2], THOMAS[1])* was born 02 Apr 1794. She married ALEXANDER MARR 08 Jul 1815, son of JOHN MARR and MARY CORNISH. He was born 11 May 1794.

Children are listed above under (188) Alexander Marr.

428. JOTHAM[6] TRAFTON *(JOANNA[5] SPINNEY, JOHN[4], ANDREW[3], JOHN[2], THOMAS[1])* was born 18 May 1801, and died Aft. 1850. He married (1) BERTHA. He married (2) RESETTA ADAMS 30 Apr 1826.

Children of JOTHAM TRAFTON and BERTHA are:
	i.	SILAS[7] TRAFTON.
	ii.	MARTIN TRAFTON.
	iii.	WOODBURY TRAFTON.
	iv.	MARY TRAFTON.
	v.	EDWIN TRAFTON.
	vi.	STEPHEN TRAFTON.
	vii.	ANN TRAFTON.

429. THOMAS[6] TRAFTON *(JOANNA[5] SPINNEY, JOHN[4], ANDREW[3], JOHN[2], THOMAS[1])* He married JESHUA OLIVER 04 Feb 1819.

Child of THOMAS TRAFTON and JESHUA OLIVER is:
805.   i.   CLARK[7] TRAFTON.

430. RICHARD[6] SPINNEY *(RICHARD[5], JOHN[4], ANDREW[3], JOHN[2], THOMAS[1])* was born 1798, and died Aft. 1830 in Ohio. He married RHONDA DUTTON, daughter of ASA DUTTON and EUNICE TOWNSEND. She was born 05 Nov 1806 in Belgrade, Kennebec, Maine, USA, and died Aft. 1830 in Ohio.

Children of RICHARD SPINNEY and RHONDA DUTTON are:
806.	i.	ASA D[7] SPINNEY, b. 1829, Ohio.
807.	ii.	EUNICE E. SPINNEY, b. May 1835, Ohio; d. 09 Jul 1904, Bath, ME.
	iii.	SON SPINNEY, b. Bet. 1825 - 1830.
	iv.	SON SPINNEY, b. Bet. 1825 - 1830.
	v.	SON SPINNEY, b. Bet. 1820 - 1830.

431. SARAH[6] HINCKLEY *(EUNICE[5] SPINNEY, JOHN[4], ANDREW[3], JOHN[2], THOMAS[1])* was born 1799. She married OLIVER HINCKLEY 1815, son of MILLER HINCKLEY and RACHEL WHITNEY. He was born 1805.

Children of SARAH HINCKLEY and OLIVER HINCKLEY are:
808.   i.   SAMANTHA[7] HINCKLEY, b. 05 Feb 1829; d. 10 Sep 1896.
        ii.   JULIAN AMELIA HINCKLEY, b. 22 Dec 1831.
       iii.   JOSIAH HINCKLEY, b. 1834.
       iv.   JULIETTE HINCKLEY, b. 1835.
        v.   ENOCH HINCKLEY, b. 1838; m. ELIZABETH; b. 1841.

Generation No. 7

432. ALEXANDER[7] SHAPLEIGH *(JANE[6] REMICK, ANN[5] FERNALD, NATHANIEL[4], NATHANIEL[3], HANNAH[2] SPINNEY, THOMAS[1])* was born 10 Apr 1807. He married ELIZABETH JANE HILL.

Children of ALEXANDER SHAPLEIGH and ELIZABETH HILL are:
        i.   SAMANTHA[8] SHAPLEIGH, b. 1832.
       ii.   GEORGE OWEN SHAPLEIGH, m. LIZZIE KENNARD.
      iii.   MARTHA JANE SHAPLEIGH, m. JOHN MOULTON.

433. MOSES[7] WORCESTER III *(MOSES[6], MOSES[5], ANNE[4] SPINNEY, JOHN[3], SAMUEL[2], THOMAS[1])* was born 11 Aug 1810, and died 10 Feb 1879 in Columbia, Me.. He married DIADEMA BOOTH SMITH 31 Oct 1838.

Child of MOSES WORCESTER and DIADEMA SMITH is:
809.   i.   ALGENAID[8] WORCESTER, b. 14 Dec 1841, Columbia, ME; d. 30 May 1883, Jonesport, ME.

434. MARK[7] WORCESTER *(ISAAC[6], MOSES[5], ANNE[4] SPINNEY, JOHN[3], SAMUEL[2], THOMAS[1])* was born 17 Mar 1816 in Columbia, ME, and died 26 Oct 1902 in Springfield, ME. He married SUSAN LEIGHTON 14 Nov 1837 in Springrield, ME, daughter of JOSEPH LEIGHTON and BETSEY DOWNES. She was born in Springfield, ME.

Children of MARK WORCESTER and SUSAN LEIGHTON are:
        i.   EMMA[8] WORCESTER.
       ii.   ROXIE WORCESTER.
      iii.   ROBERT WORCESTER, b. 1848.
810.   iv.   MARGARET WORCESTER, b. 12 Feb 1857, Webster Plantation, ME; d. 10 May 1904, Caribou, ME.

435. ASA[7] UPTON *(SAMUEL[6], REBECCA[5] SPINNEY, JOHN[4], THOMAS[3], SAMUEL[2], THOMAS[1])* was born 1797 in Canning Parish, Newcastle, NB., and died Dec 1870 in Newcastle Bridge, NB.. He married OLIVE PORTER 13 Jan 1823 in Sheffield, NB.. She was born 1803, and died 1885.

Children of ASA UPTON and OLIVE PORTER are:
        i.   SAMUEL[8] UPTON.
       ii.   THOMAS PORTER UPTON, b. Abt. 1826; d. 15 Oct 1905.
      iii.   ASA UPTON, b. 1828.
      iv.   CHARLES HENRY UPTON, b. 1833.
811.   v.   ROBERT UPTON, b. Abt. 1836, New Brunswick; d. 31 Jan 1910, Lakeville Corner, New Brunswick.
      vi.   GEORGE UPTON, b. Abt. 1838.
    vii.   WILLIAM UPTON, b. 17 Feb 1839; d. 03 Jun 1905, Philadelphia, Pennsylvannia.
   viii.   JAMES FENWICK UPTON, b. 1843; d. Chipman, New Brunswick.

436. ELIOT F[7] SPINNEY *(ELIOT[6], ROBERT[5], JOHN[4], THOMAS[3], SAMUEL[2], THOMAS[1])* was born 27 Feb 1829. He married SALLY BARR. She was born 1813.

Child of ELIOT SPINNEY and SALLY BARR is:
812.   i.   ELIOT FRANKLIN[8] SPINNEY, b. 01 Feb 1845, Lynnfield, MA; d. Aft. 1880.

437. GEORGE[7] SPINNEY *(JOHN[6], BENJAMIN[5], JOHN[4], THOMAS[3], SAMUEL[2], THOMAS[1])* was born 1827 in Lynn, MA, and died 1906 in Lynn, MA. He married MARY JANE PARROTT 1854 in Lynn, MA, daughter of OTIS PARROTT. She was born 1833, and died 1905 in Lynn, MA.

Notes for GEORGE SPINNEY:
1850 was living with parents in Lynn

Child of GEORGE SPINNEY and MARY PARROTT is:
813.　　i.　LYDIA ALICE[8] SPINNEY, b. 1855, Lynn, MA; d. 1908, Lynn, MA.

438. CHARLES EDWIN[7] SPINNEY *(JOHN[6], BENJAMIN[5], JOHN[4], THOMAS[3], SAMUEL[2], THOMAS[1])* was born 21 May 1831 in Lynn, MA, and died Bef. 1900 in Milwaukee, WI. He married HANNAH ELIZABETH HALL 05 Jan 1861 in Brookfield, WI, daughter of JAMES HALL and MARY. She was born Aug 1840 in England, and died Aft. 1910 in Milwaukee, WI.

Notes for CHARLES EDWIN SPINNEY:
From Amherst College Records
Spinney, Charles Edwin. S. of John and Betsey (Wilbur), b. Taunton, May 24, 1831. Phi Beta Kappa; Psi
  Upsilon.

  Prepared Lynn H. S.; A. C., 1852-55; B. S. Taught Lynn H. S., 1855-56; commercial college, Milwaukee, Wis.,
  1856-61; prin. public schools Oconomowoc, Wis., 1861-62; taught public schools Milwaukee, Wis., 1863-86.
D.
  Milwaukee, Wis., F. 28, 1886.

  Married Jan. 5, 1861, Elsie H., da. of Rev. James Hall, Brookfield, Wis. 5 ch.

Children of CHARLES SPINNEY and HANNAH HALL are:
　　i.　BESSIE[8] SPINNEY, b. 1862.
　　ii.　ALICE SPINNEY, b. Aug 1864, Milwaukee, WI.
　　iii.　JAMES SPINNEY, b. 1869.
814.　　iv.　JAMES WILBUR SPINNEY, b. Jun 1875, Milwaukee, WI.

439. MARY[7] SPINNEY *(JOHN[6], BENJAMIN[5], JOHN[4], THOMAS[3], SAMUEL[2], THOMAS[1])* was born 1840 in Lynn, MA, and died 1891 in Lynn, MA. She married SUMNER RICHARDSON 1866 in Lynn, MA. He was born 1842.

Children of MARY SPINNEY and SUMNER RICHARDSON are:
　　i.　LIZZIE[8] RICHARDSON, d. Aft. 1880.
　　ii.　ALICE RICHARDSON, d. Aft. 1880.
　　iii.　GEORGE RICHARDSON, d. Aft. 1880.

440. WILLIAM FRANCIS[7] SPINNEY *(WILLIAM NEWHALL[6], BENJAMIN[5], JOHN[4], THOMAS[3], SAMUEL[2], THOMAS[1])* was born 08 Mar 1828 in Lynn, Ma, and died Aft. 1910 in Reading, MA. He married (1) AUGUSTA WINSLOW DREW 19 Oct 1853 in Plymouth Ma, daughter of WINSLOW DREW and ABBY. She was born 1833, and died 22 Nov 1864. He married (2) JULIANNA BARKER 1869 in Lynn, MA. She died 1887 in Reading, MA.

Notes for WILLIAM FRANCIS SPINNEY:
Plymouth Church Records, Vol. I and II, 1620-1859
[271] 1853 Continued

Oct. 19 Mr Wm F. Spinney of Lynn2 & Miss Augusta W. Drew of Plymouth By Mr Myrick Junior Pastor

Children of WILLIAM SPINNEY and AUGUSTA DREW are:
　　i.　ABBY MARIA[8] SPINNEY, b. 1858; d. Aft. 1930, Reading, MA.
　　ii.　HELEN AUGUSTA SPINNEY, b. 1860; d. Aft. 1930.

iii. JULIA FRANCES SPINNEY, b. 1864; d. Aft. 1930.

441. GUSTAVUS NEWHALL[7] SPINNEY *(WILLIAM NEWHALL[6], BENJAMIN[5], JOHN[4], THOMAS[3], SAMUEL[2], THOMAS[1])* was born 13 Jun 1833 in Lynn, MA, and died 10 Feb 1913 in Indianapolis, IN. He married (1) ABBIE GEORGE. She was born 1835 in Haverhill, MA, and died Jun 1862. He married (2) MAY ROBINSON KINNEY 1871 in Lynn, MA. She was born 22 May 1851 in East Wareham, MA, and died 09 Nov 1929.

Child of GUSTAVUS SPINNEY and ABBIE GEORGE is:
815.   i. HENRY HOWARD[8] SPINNEY, b. 20 Apr 1860, Lynn, MA; d. 01 Apr 1951.

Child of GUSTAVUS SPINNEY and MAY KINNEY is:
        ii. LUCY WYMAN[8] SPINNEY, b. 23 Jul 1876, Lynn, MA; d. 06 Dec 1976, San Diego, CA.

442. ZEPHADIAH HACK[7] SPINNEY *(WILLIAM NEWHALL[6], BENJAMIN[5], JOHN[4], THOMAS[3], SAMUEL[2], THOMAS[1])* was born 21 May 1842 in Lynn, MA, and died 1908 in Lynn, MA. He married ALICE 1867. She was born Dec 1840.

Child of ZEPHADIAH SPINNEY and ALICE is:
        i. EDNA ALICE[8] SPINNEY, b. Apr 1881.

443. ELLERY CHANNING[7] SPINNEY *(WILLIAM NEWHALL[6], BENJAMIN[5], JOHN[4], THOMAS[3], SAMUEL[2], THOMAS[1])* was born 06 Feb 1850 in Lynn, MA, and died 19 Jul 1894 in Chicago, IL. He married ELIZA KNIGHT COX Abt. 1874 in Lynn, MA, daughter of SAMUEL COX and ELIZABETH PHILLIPS. She was born Aug 1850.

Notes for ELLERY CHANNING SPINNEY:
Sometime after their marriage in 1874 and before the birth of their first child Ellery and Eliza moved to Chicago. They settled in the Hyde Park area. The family was very prosperous.. had a bank on 39th and Cottage Grove, worked at the Chicago Board of Trade, was the first of four generation of Spinney's to do so. The family lost everyting when Ellery built several apartment buildings on 63rd Street just before and during the World's Fair. His son Harry said they even had a nursemaid in their home. Their home was on Drexel Blvd and about 40th St.. It became very run down...Harry said that a rat bit his ear one night

There was a depression that started in 1892. Even though there was great prosperity in the year 1892, upheavals were in the making. Strikes broke out in steel mills in Pennsylvania and before the year was oover there were some 1300 additiona striked.. Wheat and corn prices were at or below the cost to produce them. The depression tightened its grip in the opening monthe of 1893. The year 1894 say things go from bad to worse to disastrous. There were two to three million unemployed, mor than 12,00 businesses failures and almost a fifth of the nation's railroad mileage in receivership. This also was a year of strikes, the biggest was the Pullman strike in Chicago. t was properour, and hard working. However, they lost most of their money in the mid 1890's when Ellery built several apartment buildings on 63rd Street before/during the World's Fair

Ellery committed suicide after losing all of his money. However, Eliza was always able to return to Lynn in the summer time to visit with various relatives

But after Ellery killed himself... the family home becare rather run down. Their home was on Drexel Blvd and about 40th Street. Lter they moved to an apartment at abut 40th and Lake Streets. Maud and Harry were married in the apartment

Notes from Judie Deliane

Children of ELLERY SPINNEY and ELIZA COX are:
816.   i. CHARLOTTE HACK[8] SPINNEY, b. 07 Sep 1878, Chicago, IL; d. 02 May 1948, Chicago, IL.
817.   ii. LOUISE C. SPINNEY, b. 21 Jun 1880, Chicago, IL; d. 03 Nov 1971, Chicago, IL.
818.   iii. HAROLD ELLERY SPINNEY, b. 04 Mar 1883, Chicago, IL; d. 10 Jun 1972, Wilmette, IL.
       iv. ROBERT H. SPINNEY, b. 27 Sep 1885, Chicago, Cook, IL; d. 1886, Chicago, Cook, IL.
       v. WILLIAM E. SPINNEY, b. 12 Jan 1889, Chicago, Cook, IL; d. 1890, Chicago, Cook, IL.
      vi. FREDERICK CHANNING SPINNEY, b. Dec 1892, Chicago, IL; d. 06 Mar 1945, Wilmette, IL; m. MARGARET SCOTT.

444. BENJAMIN FRANKLIN[7] SPINNEY *(BENJAMIN[6], BENJAMIN[5], JOHN[4], THOMAS[3], SAMUEL[2], THOMAS[1])* was born 01 Sep 1832 in Taunton, MA, and died 21 Jun 1928 in Lynn, MA. He married SARAH STETSON CASWELL 04 Nov 1858 in Taunton, MA. She was born 12 May 1835 in Lynn, MA, and died Aft. 1900.

Children of BENJAMIN SPINNEY and SARAH CASWELL are:
819.   i.   FRANK (BENJAMIN) CASWELL[8] SPINNEY, b. 14 Dec 1864, Lynn, MA; d. 1949.
        ii.   LOUIS SEAVER SPINNEY, b. 15 Apr 1870; d. 21 Mar 1889.
        iii. CELIA M SPINNEY, b. 03 Apr 1891, Lynn, MA; d. 10 May 1892.
        iv. STILLBORN SPINNEY, b. 1863.

445. BRADFORD HENRY[7] SPINNEY *(CHARLES EDWIN[6], BENJAMIN[5], JOHN[4], THOMAS[3], SAMUEL[2], THOMAS[1])* was born 12 Apr 1849 in Lynn, Ma, and died 1885. He married CLARA E MORTON, daughter of RANSOM MORTON and OLIVE.

Children of BRADFORD SPINNEY and CLARA MORTON are:
        i.   CHARLES EDWIN[8] SPINNEY, b. 1874, Lynn, MA; d. 1879, Lynn, MA.
        ii.   ADA MARTIN SPINNEY, b. 1876, Lynn, MA; m. HARRISON MORTON, 1898, Lynn, Ma.
        iii. HOWARD SPINNEY, b. 1878; d. 1878.

446. FRED L[7] SPINNEY *(CHARLES EDWIN[6], BENJAMIN[5], JOHN[4], THOMAS[3], SAMUEL[2], THOMAS[1])* was born 1852 in Lynn, MA, and died Aft. 1880. He married HANNAH A COX 1874. She was born 1851, and died Aft. 1880.

Children of FRED SPINNEY and HANNAH COX are:
        i.   EDITH L[8] SPINNEY.
        ii.   CHARLES E SPINNEY, b. Abt. 1875.
        iii. ELIZABETH COOLIDGE SPINNEY, b. 22 Apr 1876.

447. MARY BURILL[7] SPINNEY *(CHARLES EDWIN[6], BENJAMIN[5], JOHN[4], THOMAS[3], SAMUEL[2], THOMAS[1])* was born 1855. She married JOHN BERRY ALLEY 1882. He was born 1856, and died in After 1900.

Children of MARY SPINNEY and JOHN ALLEY are:
        i.   MARY[8] ALLEY.
        ii.   JESSIE ALLEY.

448. GEORGE LEONARD[7] SENTER *(MARY M[6] SPINNEY, THOMAS[5], JOHN[4], THOMAS[3], SAMUEL[2], THOMAS[1])* was born 22 Apr 1839 in Lynn, Ma, and died Aft. 1880 in Penn. He married KATIE. She was born 1849.

Children of GEORGE SENTER and KATIE are:
        i.   KATIE[8] SENTER, b. 1867, PA.
        ii.   ALMIRA SENTER, b. 1870, PA.

449. SARAH ELIZABETH[7] BANCROFT *(GRACE[6] SPINNEY, THOMAS[5], JOHN[4], THOMAS[3], SAMUEL[2], THOMAS[1])* was born 27 Jun 1826. She married JOHN JULIUS DELCHAMPS.

Children of SARAH BANCROFT and JOHN DELCHAMPS are:
        i.   JULIUS A[8] DELCHAMPS, b. 1845.
        ii.   JOSPEH W DELCHAMPS, b. 1846.
        iii. EDWIN DELCHAMPS, b. 1849.

450. GEORGE F[7] SPINNEY *(THOMAS[6], THOMAS[5], JOHN[4], THOMAS[3], SAMUEL[2], THOMAS[1])* was born Feb 1834 in Maine, and died Aft. 1900 in Swampscott, MA. He married ANGELINE ELIZABETH FLYE 1865, daughter of ISAAC FLYE and PRUDENT EMERSON. She was born Jan 1838 in Boothbay, Maine, and died 29 Jan 1907 in Swampscott, MA.

Children of GEORGE SPINNEY and ANGELINE FLYE are:
- i. NELLIE EMERSON[8] SPINNEY, b. 1866.
- 820. ii. JOSEPH D SPINNEY, b. Sep 1867; d. Aft. 1900.
- iii. FREDDIE SPINNEY, b. 1875.

451. EDWARD HERBERT[7] SPINNEY *(THOMAS[6], THOMAS[5], JOHN[4], THOMAS[3], SAMUEL[2], THOMAS[1])* was born 1838, and died Aft. 1880. He married EMMA.

Children of EDWARD SPINNEY and EMMA are:
- i. MARY SUSAN[8] SPINNEY, b. 1861.
- 821. ii. HERBERT AHLBORN SPINNEY, b. May 1864.
- iii. MILDRED ELLA SPINNEY, b. 1869.
- iv. ROBERT SPINNEY, b. 1864.

452. PHILLIP[7] COATES *(HANNAH[6] SPINNEY, THOMAS[5], JOHN[4], THOMAS[3], SAMUEL[2], THOMAS[1])* was born 1845. He married BRIDGET.

Children of PHILLIP COATES and BRIDGET are:
- i. JAMES[8] COATES.
- ii. MARY COATES.
- iii. EDWARD COATES.
- iv. ANNA COATES.

453. SAMUEL[7] SPINNEY *(JOHN WARREN[6], SAMUEL[5], JOHN[4], THOMAS[3], SAMUEL[2], THOMAS[1])* was born 21 Oct 1827 in Lynn, MA, and died 08 Apr 1881. He married PERSIS G PERRY 28 Apr 1852 in Lynn, MA, daughter of ISAAC PERRY. She was born 1828, and died 1905 in Saugus, Ma.

Children of SAMUEL SPINNEY and PERSIS PERRY are:
- 822. i. CARRIE LOUISE[8] SPINNEY, b. 1855; d. 1894, Lynn, MA.
- ii. FRANK HERBERT SPINNEY, b. 1860.
- iii. FRED PERRY SPINNEY, b. 1866.

454. JOHN WARREN[7] SPINNEY *(JOHN WARREN[6], SAMUEL[5], JOHN[4], THOMAS[3], SAMUEL[2], THOMAS[1])* was born 20 Mar 1830 in Lynn, MA, and died Aft. 1910 in Medford, Ma. He married (1) MARY AVERY 15 Jan 1848 in Boston Mass. She was born Apr 1837. He married (2) MARY BAILEY 1871.

Children of JOHN SPINNEY and MARY AVERY are:
- i. EZRA W[8] SPINNEY, b. 22 Apr 1859, Lynn, Ma; d. 01 Apr 1919, Lynn, Ma.
- ii. THOMAS SPINNEY, b. 1862.
- 823. iii. GEORGE R SPINNEY, b. Mar 1863, Massachusetts; d. Aft. 1930, Tulsa. OK.
- iv. JOHN ARTHUR SPINNEY, b. 31 May 1864, Placer, CA; d. 30 Apr 1941, California.
- v. HENRY C SPINNEY, b. 1867; d. Aft. 1930; m. MINNIE NEAL; d. 1899.
- vi. CHARLES HERBERT SPINNEY, b. 1861.

455. WILLIAM HENRY[7] SPINNEY *(JOHN WARREN[6], SAMUEL[5], JOHN[4], THOMAS[3], SAMUEL[2], THOMAS[1])* was born 31 Dec 1831 in Lynn, MA, and died 04 Apr 1911 in Lynn, Ma. He married MARIA A AMBLER. She was born 03 May 1845, and died 25 Jun 1887 in Lynn, MA.

Children of WILLIAM SPINNEY and MARIA AMBLER are:
- i. CHARLOTTE AUGUSTA[8] SPINNEY, b. 24 Mar 1869, Lynn, MA; d. 30 Mar 1871, Lynn, MA.
- ii. SAMUEL A. SPINNEY, b. 25 Apr 1871, Lynn, MA; d. 05 Mar 1883, Lynn, MA.
- iii. MARTHA AMBLER. SPINNEY, b. 24 Oct 1875, Lynn, MA; d. 04 Aug 1876, Lynn, MA.
- iv. ROLAND SPINNEY, b. 25 Dec 1881; d. 21 Dec 1899.
- v. JULIA CARLTON SPINNEY.

456. CHARLES HERBERT[7] SPINNEY *(JOHN WARREN[6], SAMUEL[5], JOHN[4], THOMAS[3], SAMUEL[2], THOMAS[1])* was born 26 Feb 1834 in Lynn, MA, and died 11 Jun 1912 in Lynn, MA. He married HARRIET DOW 1863 in Lynn, MA, daughter of WILLIAM DOW and ISABELLA. She was born 1846, and died Bef. 1900.

Children of CHARLES SPINNEY and HARRIET DOW are:
      i.   ARTHUR H[8] SPINNEY, b. 1864.
      ii.   CHARLES C SPINNEY, b. 1865; d. 1869.
824.   iii. INEZ MAUDE SPINNEY, b. Jun 1867; d. Aft. 1900.
      iv. RALPH WALDO SPINNEY, b. 1870; d. 1873, Lynn, Ma.
      v.   ANNIE SPINNEY, b. 1872; d. 1872.
825.   vi. ERNEST EDWARD SPINNEY, b. 28 Nov 1873, Chelsea, MA; d. 22 Feb 1916, Lynn, MA.
      vii. ZELINDA JOSEPHINE SPINNEY, b. 1876; d. died in California; m. ABBOTT.
826.   viii. HARRIETT SPINNEY, b. May 1883.
      ix. HARRIETT ADA SPINNEY, b. 1879, Lynn, MA; d. 1879, Lynn, MA.

457. LYDIA MARIA[7] SPINNEY *(JOHN WARREN[6], SAMUEL[5], JOHN[4], THOMAS[3], SAMUEL[2], THOMAS[1])* was born 21 Sep 1836 in Lynn, MA, and died 07 Jan 1912. She married DUDLEY B. FISKE 1863. He was born 21 Dec 1836, and died 25 Jun 1908.

Children of LYDIA SPINNEY and DUDLEY FISKE are:
      i.   INFANT CHILD[8] FISKE, b. Nov 1864, Lynn, Essex, MA; d. 25 Nov 1864, Lynn, Essex, MA.
      ii.   FLORENCE G. FISKE, b. 19 Mar 1867, Lynn, Essex, MA; d. 15 Oct 1867, Lynn, Essex, MA.

458. MARY E[7] SPINNEY *(JOHN WARREN[6], SAMUEL[5], JOHN[4], THOMAS[3], SAMUEL[2], THOMAS[1])* was born 1841 in Lynn, MA, and died 31 Jul 1905 in Lynn, MA. She married (1) WILLIAM R BADGER. She married (2) WILLIAM R. BADGER 1866. He was born 02 Feb 1844 in Lynn, MA, and died 28 Dec 1908 in Lynn, MA.

Child of MARY SPINNEY and WILLIAM BADGER is:
      i.   GEORGE[8] BADGER, b. Sep 1870, Lynn, MA; d. 21 Sep 1872, Lynn, MA.

459. PAUL ARTHUR[7] SPINNEY *(JOHN FRANCIS[6], FRANCIS[5], JOHN[4], THOMAS[3], SAMUEL[2], THOMAS[1])* was born 1881 in Shirley, MA. He married WINIFRED CLIFFORD.

Children of PAUL SPINNEY and WINIFRED CLIFFORD are:
      i.   ARTHUR[8] SPINNEY, b. 1905, Boston, MA.
      ii.   DOROTHEA SPINNEY.

460. SALLY ANN[7] SPINNEY *(CALEB[6], CALEB[5], NICHOLAS[4], JAMES[3], SAMUEL[2], THOMAS[1])* was born 1807, and died 18 Jun 1892. She married WILLIAM ADAMS 01 Apr 1824, son of NATHAN ADAMS and ELIZABETH COLE. He was born 14 Mar 1807 in Newington, NH, and died 1850 in Boston, Ma.

Children of SALLY SPINNEY and WILLIAM ADAMS are:
827.   i.   CAROLINE FRANCES[8] ADAMS, b. 03 Dec 1824.
      ii.   ELIZABETH SARAH ADAMS, b. 07 Apr 1826; m. JOHN DANFORTH.
828.   iii. JAMES NATHAN ADAMS, b. 05 Jun 1828, Portsmouth, NH; d. 27 May 1888, Ellsworth, Wisconsin.
829.   iv. JULIA ANN ADAMS, b. 13 May 1830, Portsmouth, NH.
      v.   MARY ABBY ADAMS, b. 11 Sep 1834, Portsmouth, NH; d. 1850, Portsmouth, NH.

461. MARY JANE[7] SPINNEY *(CALEB[6], CALEB[5], NICHOLAS[4], JAMES[3], SAMUEL[2], THOMAS[1])* was born 1804 in Kittery, ME, and died Bet. 1860 - 1870 in Portsmouth, NH. She married JONAS FLINT. He was born in Portsmouth NH, and died Bef. 1860.

Children of MARY SPINNEY and JONAS FLINT are:
      i.   CAROLINE[8] FLINT, b. 1833.
      ii.   SARAH FLINT, b. 1838.
      iii. JOHN FLINT, b. 1842.

462. CIDNEY[7] JAMES *(MARGERY[6] SPINNEY, CALEB[5], NICHOLAS[4], JAMES[3], SAMUEL[2], THOMAS[1])* was born 1811, and died 1895. She married THEODORE KEEN. He was born 1812, and died 1881.

Children of CIDNEY JAMES and THEODORE KEEN are:
  i. SAMUEL[8] KEEN, b. 1838.
  ii. SARAH KEEN, b. 1841.

463. CALEB S[7] SPINNEY *(NICHOLAS[6], CALEB[5], NICHOLAS[4], JAMES[3], SAMUEL[2], THOMAS[1])* was born 19 Feb 1815 in Kittery, ME, and died 16 Feb 1879. He married LUCY ANN HALEY 13 Feb 1845 in Kittery, ME, daughter of THOMAS HALEY. She was born 09 Jun 1821, and died 29 Jun 1877.

Children of CALEB SPINNEY and LUCY HALEY are:
  i. LUCY E[8] SPINNEY, b. 26 Feb 1846; d. 02 Sep 1867.
  ii. MARILLA SPINNEY, b. 04 Apr 1847; d. 20 Dec 1884.
  iii. ABIGAIL E SPINNEY, b. 1848, Kittery, ME; d. Aft. 1880.
  iv. GRANVILLE B SPINNEY, b. 1853; d. 1930.
  v. HENRIETTE SPINNEY, b. 1853; d. 1932.
  vi. MELVILLE F SPINNEY, b. 1856; d. 1910.
  vii. ANNAH H SPINNEY, b. 1860, Kittery, ME.
  viii. BELL A SPINNEY, b. 09 Apr 1861; d. 04 Dec 1876.

464. EMILY D[7] SPINNEY *(NICHOLAS[6], CALEB[5], NICHOLAS[4], JAMES[3], SAMUEL[2], THOMAS[1])* was born 29 Sep 1816 in Kittery, ME. She married WILLIAM W DAME 25 May 1837 in Kittery, ME. He was born 11 Feb 1815.

Children of EMILY SPINNEY and WILLIAM DAME are:
  i. WILLIAM HENRY[8] DAME, b. 17 Dec 1838; d. Oct 1841.
  ii. NICHOLAS HARTWELL DAME, b. 15 Oct 1839; d. 09 Feb 1841.
  iii. WILLIAM F DAME, b. 15 Sep 1841; d. 17 Nov 1908.
  iv. EMILY ELIZ DAME, b. May 1846; d. 1847.

465. ROWENA R[7] SPINNEY *(NICHOLAS[6], CALEB[5], NICHOLAS[4], JAMES[3], SAMUEL[2], THOMAS[1])* was born 14 Jul 1828 in Berwick, ME. She married LEONARD C COOK 06 Mar 1856 in Berwick, ME. He was born in Kitttery, ME.

Children of ROWENA SPINNEY and LEONARD COOK are:
  i. CLARA A[8] COOK, b. Abt. 1870.
  ii. ROWENA M COOK, b. 09 Apr 1864, York, ME; d. 03 Aug 1934, Eliot, ME.
  iii. DANIEL B COOK, b. 17 Oct 1856, Kittery, ME; d. 08 Mar 1915, Kittery, ME; m. FLORENCE MUDGE; b. 1863; d. 1915.
  iv. EPHRAIM A COOK, b. 07 Jan 1858, Kittery, ME; d. 23 Nov 1923, Kittery, ME; m. ANNIE M ELKINS, 28 Aug 1884, Kittery, ME.
830. v. LEONARD FRANK COOK, b. 25 Apr 1860, York, ME; d. 13 Jan 1910, Portsmouth, NH.
  vi. ALICE L COOK, b. 02 Sep 1860, York, ME; d. 10 Aug 1863, York, ME.
  vii. JEFFERSON DAVIS COOK, b. 27 Jul 1865; m. HENRIETTA HOLMAN.
  viii. GEORGE F COOK, b. 22 Nov 1868, York, ME; d. 19 Dec 1869, York, ME.
  ix. NICHOLAS COOK, b. 05 Sep 1870, York, ME; d. 14 Oct 1928, Portsmouth, NH.

466. DANIEL PARKER[7] SPINNEY *(JOSIAH[6], CALEB[5], NICHOLAS[4], JAMES[3], SAMUEL[2], THOMAS[1])* was born 21 Jan 1827 in Kittery, ME, and died 04 Oct 1905 in Kittery, ME. He married ANN MARY SPINNEY 1854, daughter of FRANCIS SPINNEY and MARY PAUL. She was born 28 Oct 1833 in Kittery, ME, and died 05 Aug 1921.

Children of DANIEL SPINNEY and ANN SPINNEY are:
  i. MARILLA MELLISSA[8] SPINNEY, b. 15 Aug 1854; d. 04 Aug 1873.
831. ii. FRANK HERBERT SPINNEY, b. 26 Jan 1856; d. 25 Jul 1891, Eliot, ME.
  iii. EDWIN WILBUR SPINNEY, b. 08 Mar 1858; d. 21 Jun 1878.
  iv. EVERETT ELMER SPINNEY, b. 05 Sep 1863; d. 21 May 1865.
  v. MARY ELIZABETH SPINNEY, b. 18 May 1866; d. Aug 1928.

467. ROBERT[7] SPINNEY *(NATHAN[6], JOHN[5], NICHOLAS[4], JAMES[3], SAMUEL[2], THOMAS[1])* was born Oct 1823 in Eliot, ME, and died 05 Apr 1904. He married MARTHA J COLE 12 Nov 1846. She was born Jan 1825, and died 05 Jul 1911.

Children of ROBERT SPINNEY and MARTHA COLE are:
      i.   CLARA ELLEN[8] SPINNEY, b. 1847; m. T FRANK STAPLES.
      ii. MARIA SPINNEY, b. 1849.
      iii. ISABELLE SPINNEY, b. 1856.
832.   iv. GRACE GREENWOOD SPINNEY, b. 26 Sep 1860; d. 1921.
      v. ROBERT W SPINNEY, b. 1863; d. 1943; m. SARAH A, Aft. 1880; b. 1863; d. 1933.
833.   vi. FRED L SPINNEY, b. Jun 1865, Maine; d. 1946.
834.   vii. BERTHA P SPINNEY, b. 1870; d. 1929.

468. NATHAN[7] SPINNEY *(NATHAN[6], JOHN[5], NICHOLAS[4], JAMES[3], SAMUEL[2], THOMAS[1])* was born 1830, and died Aft. 1880. He married MARTHA JANE SPINNEY 10 Mar 1853, daughter of MARK SPINNEY and ELIZABETH SPINNEY. She was born 1828, and died 16 Feb 1898.

Children of NATHAN SPINNEY and MARTHA SPINNEY are:
      i.   ALWILDDA[8] SPINNEY, b. 1854.
      ii. ADDA SPINNEY, b. 1856.
835.   iii. NATHAN G SPINNEY, b. Sep 1857; d. 1935.
836.   iv. WILBRA H SPINNEY, b. Jul 1864, Eliot, ME; d. Feb 1948.

469. JOHN P[7] SPINNEY *(NATHAN[6], JOHN[5], NICHOLAS[4], JAMES[3], SAMUEL[2], THOMAS[1])* was born May 1835 in Maine, and died Aft. 1920 in Raynham, MA. He married ANNIE S MERRILL 24 Jan 1867. She was born Feb 1846 in South Berwick, ME, and died Aft. 1910.

Children of JOHN SPINNEY and ANNIE MERRILL are:
      i.   JOHN C[8] SPINNEY, b. Aug 1869; d. Aft. 1910.
837.   ii. CHARLES WARD SPINNEY, b. 1864; d. Aft. 1910.
      iii. GEORGE R SPINNEY, b. 1873; d. 1877, Taunton.
      iv. ANNA MAY SPINNEY, b. 1875, Taunton; d. Bef. 1910; m. JOHN FESTING; b. 1861, New York; d. Aft. 1920.

470. EMILY ANN[7] SPINNEY *(NATHAN[6], JOHN[5], NICHOLAS[4], JAMES[3], SAMUEL[2], THOMAS[1])* was born 15 May 1839, and died 20 Mar 1894. She married APCHELUS WELCH 13 May 1857.

Children of EMILY SPINNEY and APCHELUS WELCH are:
      i.   ALICE ANETTE[8] WELCH, b. 05 Dec 1857; m. ANDREW BROOKS.
      ii. ANNIE LEMOYNE WELCH, b. 30 Jul 1860; m. EDGAR REMICK.
      iii. FRANK MORRIS WELCH, b. 08 Apr 1865; m. MILDRED CHILDS.
      iv. ALFRED WELCH, b. 26 Feb 1874; m. MABEL GAMMON.
      v. AMY L WELCH, b. 20 Nov 1880; m. BOYDE YORK, 02 Apr 1902.

471. ALMIRA[7] SPINNEY *(NATHAN[6], JOHN[5], NICHOLAS[4], JAMES[3], SAMUEL[2], THOMAS[1])* was born 18 Aug 1841, and died 17 Sep 1920. She married THEODORE FERNALD, son of WILLIAM FERNALD and MIRIAM SPINNEY. He was born 1839, and died 1921.

Children of ALMIRA SPINNEY and THEODORE FERNALD are:
      i.   EDWIN[8] FERNALD, b. 1867; d. 1937; m. NELLIE; b. 1872; d. 1965.
      ii. FRANK FERNALD, b. 1875; d. 1919.
      iii. HAROLD FERNALD, b. 1902; d. 1960.

472. ANNETTE H[7] SPINNEY *(NATHAN[6], JOHN[5], NICHOLAS[4], JAMES[3], SAMUEL[2], THOMAS[1])* was born 18 Nov 1845. She married JAMES WESLEY PAUL, son of OLIVER PAUL and MARY TOBEY.

Child of ANNETTE SPINNEY and JAMES PAUL is:
      i.   WESLEY[8] PAUL, m. GERTRUDE DELAILT.

473. EUNICE[7] MARR *(THOMAS[6], JOHN[5], RUTH[4] SPINNEY, JEREMIAH[3], SAMUEL[2], THOMAS[1])* was born 16 Jun 1809 in Boothbay, Lincoln, Maine, USA, and died Apr 1855. She married JOHN PERKINS 30 Aug 1827. He was born

1806.

Children of EUNICE MARR and JOHN PERKINS are:
  i.   THOMAS MARR[8] PERKINS, b. 1828.
  ii.   BENJAMIN PERKINS, b. 1830.
  iii. LOUISA PERKINS, b. 1833.
  iv.   JOHN PERKINS, b. 1835.
  v.   LYDIA M PERKINS, b. 1837.
  vi.   HENRY PERKINS, b. 1840.
  vii. MARTHA PERKINS, b. 1844.
  viii. ALONZO PERKINS, b. 1847.
  ix.   ARTHUR PERKINS, b. 1849.

474. MIRANDA A[7] MARR *(THOMAS[6], JOHN[5], RUTH[4] SPINNEY, JEREMIAH[3], SAMUEL[2], THOMAS[1])* was born 1835. She married LEVI S. OLIVER, son of EPHRAIM OLIVER and JERUSHA SPINNEY. He was born 1831.

Children of MIRANDA MARR and LEVI OLIVER are:
  i.   NELLIA E.[8] OLIVER.
  ii.   LILLIE OLIVER.
  iii. LEVI OLIVER.

475. EZEKIEL[7] OLIVER *(JACOB[6], MARY[5] SPINNEY, JEREMIAH[4], JEREMIAH[3], SAMUEL[2], THOMAS[1])* was born 1822, and died 1892. He married (1) BEULAH BLAISDELL 18 Jul 1847. She was born 1832, and died 1856. He married (2) PAULINE EMERY 27 Mar 1857. She was born 1839, and died 1905.

Children of EZEKIEL OLIVER and BEULAH BLAISDELL are:
  i.   ANGELA[8] OLIVER.
  ii.   BEULAH OLIVER.
  iii. CHARLES OLIVER, b. 1850.
  iv.   SUSIE C. OLIVER, b. 1852.

Children of EZEKIEL OLIVER and PAULINE EMERY are:
  v.   ANGIE F.[8] OLIVER.
  vi.   FRANKLIN OLIVER.
  vii. GRACIE OLIVER.
  viii. HERMAN OLIVER.
  ix.   LILLIAN R. OLIVER.
  x.   PAULINE OLIVER.
  xi.   VINCENT OLIVER.
  xii. ABBIE J. OLIVER, b. 1858.

476. JOHN[7] OLIVER *(JOHN[6], MARY[5] SPINNEY, JEREMIAH[4], JEREMIAH[3], SAMUEL[2], THOMAS[1])* was born 04 Apr 1820 in Phippsburg, ME, and died 02 Dec 1903 in Bath, ME. He married ELSIE MARR 25 Jun 1843 in Phippsburg, ME. She was born Jun 1823, and died 08 Apr 1902 in Bath, ME.

Children of JOHN OLIVER and ELSIE MARR are:
          i.   CAMELIA[8] OLIVER.
  838.   ii.   LUCRETIA ANN OLIVER, b. 25 Mar 1844, Phippsburg, ME; d. 30 Jul 1904, Bath, ME.
  839.   iii. CLEAVELAND MANSON OLIVER, b. 18 Feb 1846, Phippsburg, ME; d. 16 Sep 1920, Bath, ME.
  840.   iv.   CHARLES WARREN OLIVER, b. 05 Dec 1850, Phippsburg, ME; d. 04 Sep 1927, Bath, ME.
  841.   v.   CHESTER MARR OLIVER, b. 04 Oct 1852, Phippsburg, ME; d. 08 May 1920, Bath, ME.
          vi.   GEORGE L. OLIVER, b. 1853.
          vii. CATHELINA OLIVER, b. 02 Mar 1855, Phippsburg, ME.
          viii. EMMA ELIZABETH OLIVER, b. 18 Mar 1857, Phippsburg, ME; d. 05 Sep 1945, Bath, ME.
  842.   ix.   WILBER CARTER OLIVER, b. 26 Feb 1860, Phippsburg, ME; d. 31 Jan 1943, Bath, ME.

477. JAMES H.[7] OLIVER *(THOMAS[6], MARY[5] SPINNEY, JEREMIAH[4], JEREMIAH[3], SAMUEL[2], THOMAS[1])* was born 1830, and died 17 Mar 1888 in Phippsburg, ME. He married PATIENCE R SPINNEY 26 Jul 1855 in Bath, Sagadahoc,

ME, daughter of JOHN SPINNEY and MIRIAM SPINNEY. She was born 14 Aug 1835 in Georgetown, ME, and died 31 Aug 1897.

Children of JAMES OLIVER and PATIENCE SPINNEY are:
- i. CHARLES LESLEY[8] OLIVER, b. 04 Sep 1856, Phippsburg, ME; d. 20 Dec 1922, Bath, ME; m. SARAH E. AVERILL; b. 1865; d. 30 Mar 1939, Bath, ME.
- ii. WILLIAM BANKS OLIVER, b. 29 Dec 1857, Phippsburg, ME.
- iii. LIZZIE FRANCES OLIVER, b. 29 Nov 1865, Phippsburg, ME; d. 25 Mar 1927, Bath, ME; m. FERNALD D. CROOKER.
- 843. iv. LEMUEL BRADFORD OLIVER, b. 02 Jan 1867, Phippsburg, ME; d. 30 Oct 1926, Bath, ME.
- v. ANN MARIA OLIVER, b. 24 Dec 1869, Phippsburg, ME; m. CHARLES JONES.
- vi. JOHN THOMAS OLIVER, b. 20 Sep 1872, Phippsburg, ME.
- 844. vii. HARRY FREEMAN OLIVER, b. 15 Sep 1874, Phippsburg, ME; d. 11 May 1948, Tampa, FL.

478. WILLIAM RAIRDEN[7] OLIVER *(JAMES[6], MARY[5] SPINNEY, JEREMIAH[4], JEREMIAH[3], SAMUEL[2], THOMAS[1])* was born 06 Mar 1825 in Phippsburg, ME, and died 01 Apr 1868 in Bath, ME. He married NANCY R SPINNEY 05 Oct 1848 in Phippsburg, ME, daughter of CALEB SPINNEY and MIRIAM OLIVER. She was born 1828, and died 1905.

Children of WILLIAM OLIVER and NANCY SPINNEY are:
- i. DIMANENS[8] OLIVER, b. 1849.
- ii. LAFAYETTE OLIVER, b. 1850.
- iii. GEORGE OLIVER, b. 1852.
- 845. iv. WILLIAM SMITH OLIVER, b. Dec 1855; d. 14 Feb 1937, Bath, ME.
- v. MARY E. OLIVER, b. 1859; m. EVERETT JEWELL.
- 846. vi. BAXTER M. OLIVER, b. May 1864; d. Aft. 1900.
- vii. WINSLOW R OLIVER, b. 1868; d. 11 Jun 1945, Boston, Suffolk, MA; m. EFFIE.

479. HARRISON PRIEST[7] OLIVER *(JAMES[6], MARY[5] SPINNEY, JEREMIAH[4], JEREMIAH[3], SAMUEL[2], THOMAS[1])* was born 31 May 1840 in Phippsburg, ME, and died 25 Nov 1907 in Portsmouth, ME. He married (1) NANCY RANDALL 26 Feb 1866 in Bath, ME. She was born 1836, and died 23 Jul 1876 in Bath, ME. He married (2) MARY BURNHAM 03 Dec 1877.

Child of HARRISON OLIVER and NANCY RANDALL is:
- i. LUCY A.[8] OLIVER, b. 1867; d. 1882, Bath, Sagadahoc, ME.

480. JOSIAH PERRY[7] OLIVER *(JAMES[6], MARY[5] SPINNEY, JEREMIAH[4], JEREMIAH[3], SAMUEL[2], THOMAS[1])* was born 02 Sep 1842 in Phippsburg, ME, and died 20 Dec 1927 in Bath, ME. He married GEORGIANNA ALLEN 03 Jul 1866 in Bath, ME. She was born Sep 1844, and died 21 Jul 1940 in Jamaica, NY.

Children of JOSIAH OLIVER and GEORGIANNA ALLEN are:
- 847. i. HERBERT A.[8] OLIVER, b. 30 Mar 1867, Bath, ME; d. 16 Feb 1925, Bath, ME.
- ii. LILLA M. OLIVER, b. Nov 1871; m. GEORGE PEMBROKE.

481. JEREMIAH[7] OLIVER *(RICHARD[6], ANNA[5] SPINNEY, JEREMIAH[4], JEREMIAH[3], SAMUEL[2], THOMAS[1])* was born Oct 1810, and died 1869. He married ELIZA HINKLEY 26 May 1839. She was born 1811, and died 1900.

Children of JEREMIAH OLIVER and ELIZA HINKLEY are:
- i. ANNA A.[8] OLIVER, b. 1840; d. 1881.
- ii. WILLIAM STACEY OLIVER, b. 1841; d. 1928.
- iii. HARRIET F. OLIVER, b. 1842.
- iv. THOMAS P. OLIVER, b. 1845; d. 1897.
- v. WARREN PAGE OLIVER, b. 1851.

482. MARIA[7] OLIVER *(EPHRAIM[6], ANNA[5] SPINNEY, JEREMIAH[4], JEREMIAH[3], SAMUEL[2], THOMAS[1])* was born 28 Jan 1822. She married EPHRAIM OLIVER HINCKLEY.

Children of MARIA OLIVER and EPHRAIM HINCKLEY are:
- i. WILLIAM LORING[8] HINCKLEY, b. 31 Aug 1846.

ii. GEORGIANA HINCKLEY, b. 25 Jan 1848; d. Bef. 1850.

Notes for GEORGIANA HINCKLEY:
Presumably died young

iii. GEORGIANA HINCKLEY, b. 14 Feb 1850; m. ELIPHALET HARFORD.
iv. SARA ELIZABETH HINCKLEY, b. 08 Mar 1852; m. HORACE A MCKENNEY, 08 Dec 1877.
v. FREDERICK JAMES HINCKLEY, b. 25 Nov 1854.
vi. ABBY ELLEN HINCKLEY, b. 17 Nov 1856; m. ABRAM W KELLEY, 10 Jun 1882.
vii. EDWARD CLARENCE HINCKLEY, b. 09 Jan 1858; d. Aft. 1891; m. (1) RACHEL E MCKENNEY; m. (2) EDNA AMSBURY.
viii. MARY M HINCKLEY, b. 16 Aug 1860.

483. MATTHEW[7] OLIVER *(EPHRAIM[6], ANNA[5] SPINNEY, JEREMIAH[4], JEREMIAH[3], SAMUEL[2], THOMAS[1])* was born 05 May 1825 in Georgetown, ME, and died 26 Mar 1898 in Bath, ME. He married SALOME OLIVER 14 Oct 1850 in Georgetown, ME. She was born 17 Apr 1835 in Phippsburg, ME, and died 24 May 1883 in Bath, ME.

Children of MATTHEW OLIVER and SALOME OLIVER are:
i. JULIETTE M.[8] OLIVER, b. 1852; d. 13 Nov 1913, Boston, Suffolk, MA; m. (1) LORENZO CRAFTS; m. (2) FRED E. WILSON, 26 Apr 1878, Boston, Suffolk, MA.
ii. JOSEPHINE H. OLIVER, b. 1854; d. 04 Aug 1898, Bath, Sagadahoc, ME; m. WILLARD A. HODGKINS, 24 Dec 1870, Bath, Sagadahoc, ME.
848. iii. CHARLES H. OLIVER, b. 24 Jul 1855, Arrowsic, ME; d. 11 Jan 1930, Bath, ME.
iv. CLEMENT P. OLIVER, b. 1858.
849. v. WALTER J. OLIVER, b. 1863; d. 11 Aug 1911, Newton, MA.
vi. ANNIE M. OLIVER, b. 1869.
vii. WILLARD A. OLIVER, b. 22 Oct 1870; d. 29 Oct 1940, Bath, Sagadahoc, ME; m. HARRIET E. PLANT, 07 Nov 1893, Bath, Sagadahoc, ME; b. 1870; d. 10 Sep 1930, Portland, Cumberland, ME.
viii. EVA L. OLIVER, b. 1873; d. 14 Jul 1958; m. BRENTON DODGE BISHOP; d. 08 Jan 1915.

484. BENJAMIN S.[7] OLIVER *(EPHRAIM[6], ANNA[5] SPINNEY, JEREMIAH[4], JEREMIAH[3], SAMUEL[2], THOMAS[1])* was born 06 Oct 1829 in Georgetown, ME, and died 15 Jan 1894 in Bath, ME. He married EUNICE E. SPINNEY 22 Aug 1852 in Georgetown, ME, daughter of RICHARD SPINNEY and RHONDA DUTTON. She was born May 1835 in Ohio, and died 09 Jul 1904 in Bath, ME.

Children of BENJAMIN OLIVER and EUNICE SPINNEY are:
i. ANNIE MAHALA[8] OLIVER, b. 1855; d. 17 Sep 1910; m. FREDRICK SPENCER; d. 17 Jan 1927, Brunswick, ME.
ii. ASA DUTTON OLIVER, b. Aug 1857; d. 21 Jan 1939, Bath, ME; m. MARY P. MCIVER, 17 Sep 1889, Bath, ME; b. 08 May 1865, Inverness, NS.; d. 16 Feb 1953, Bath, ME.
850. iii. HANNAH ELIZABETH OLIVER, b. 18 Feb 1862, Bath, ME; d. 22 Apr 1919, Bath, ME.
iv. RHODA ELLEN OLIVER, b. 13 Jan 1865, Bath, ME; d. 05 Feb 1917, Bath, ME; m. JAMES F. ROBINSON; b. Bet. 1863 - 1866; d. 13 Aug 1913.
v. HARRIET E. OLIVER, b. 1867; m. JOHN W. PASSMORE, 18 Oct 1885, Bath, Sagadahoc, ME.
vi. JERUSHA MABEL OLIVER, b. Oct 1868; d. 08 Nov 1939, Bath, Sagadahoc, ME; m. WILLIAM H. HARRINGTON, 25 Jul 1891, Bath, Sagadahoc, ME; d. 02 Jun 1914, Bath, Sagadahoc, ME.

485. LEVI S.[7] OLIVER *(EPHRAIM[6], ANNA[5] SPINNEY, JEREMIAH[4], JEREMIAH[3], SAMUEL[2], THOMAS[1])* was born 1831. He married MIRANDA A MARR, daughter of THOMAS MARR and LYDIA TRAFTON. She was born 1835.

Children are listed above under (474) Miranda A Marr.

486. JOHN[7] OLIVER *(JEREMIAH[6], ANNA[5] SPINNEY, JEREMIAH[4], JEREMIAH[3], SAMUEL[2], THOMAS[1])* was born 23 Apr 1835, and died 1908. He married ELIZABETH J. JEWELL. She was born 1844, and died 1920.

Child of JOHN OLIVER and ELIZABETH JEWELL is:
i. EDWIN N.[8] OLIVER, b. 1868, Phippsburg, ME.

487. LYDIA PAUL[7] GOODWIN *(BARTHSEHBA WEARE[6] SPINNEY, DAVID[5], EBENEZER[4], JONATHAN[3], SAMUEL[2],*

Thomas¹) was born 30 Aug 1813, and died 17 Mar 1863. She married JONATHAN HODSDON 02 Jul 1838.

Children of LYDIA GOODWIN and JONATHAN HODSDON are:
- i.   OLIVE⁸ HODSDON, b. 22 Jan 1839; d. 17 Apr 1915; m. WILLIAM WALCH.
- ii. LYDIA HODSDON, b. 22 Dec 1840; d. 03 Sep 1865.
- iii. JEREMIAH HODSDON, b. 25 Dec 1842; d. 22 Dec 1864.
- iv. JOSEPH HODSDON, b. 03 Mar 1845.
- v.   GEORGE HODSDON, b. Mar 1846; d. 12 Jul 1866.
- vi. MARY ABBIE HODSDON, b. Aug 1850; d. 05 Sep 1865; m. WILLIAM WALCH.
- vii. ELLEN HODSDON, b. Aug 1850; d. 01 Oct 1850.

488. BATHASHEBA⁷ GOODWIN *(BARTHSEHBA WEARE⁶ SPINNEY, DAVID⁵, EBENEZER⁴, JONATHAN³, SAMUEL², THOMAS¹)* was born 13 Sep 1820, and died 30 Nov 1889. She married EDWARD HUSSEY 12 Dec 1857.

Child of BATHASHEBA GOODWIN and EDWARD HUSSEY is:
- i.   EDWARD F⁸ HUSSEY, b. 13 Sep 1858; m. MITTLE LEACITT, Dec 1878.

489. PHOEBE⁷ GOODWIN *(BARTHSEHBA WEARE⁶ SPINNEY, DAVID⁵, EBENEZER⁴, JONATHAN³, SAMUEL², THOMAS¹)* was born 26 Oct 1824 in Milton, NH, and died 17 Feb 1902 in Portsmouth, NH. She married JOSIAH W HUSSEY 28 Dec 1842. He was born 15 Jan 1815 in Milton, NH.

Children of PHOEBE GOODWIN and JOSIAH HUSSEY are:
- i.   LIZZIE A⁸ HUSSEY, b. 08 Dec 1843; m. JACOB W CRAM, 07 Nov 1867.
- 851. ii. LYDIA HUSSEY, b. 15 May 1846.
- iii. JOHN ADAMS HUSSEY, b. 03 Jan 1850; m. EMMA F HILL, 23 Nov 1870.
- iv. ELIZA WIGGIN HUSSEY, b. 12 May 1855; m. JAMES W HOYT, 28 Sep 1884.

490. ABIGAIL PAUL⁷ SPINNEY *(PARKER FOSTER⁶, DAVID⁵, EBENEZER⁴, JONATHAN³, SAMUEL², THOMAS¹)* was born 03 Nov 1826 in Wakefield, NH, and died 10 Apr 1913 in Milton, NH. She married CHARLES CHESLEY HAYES 26 Nov 1851 in Somersworth, NH. He was born 01 Sep 1822, and died 10 Feb 1893.

Children of ABIGAIL SPINNEY and CHARLES HAYES are:
- i.   SON⁸ HAYES, b. 20 May 1853; d. infancy.
- ii. EUGENE AUGUSTUS HAYES, b. 24 Nov 1854; d. 19 Jan 1856.
- iii. ABIGAIL LOUISE HAYES, b. 05 Sep 1857.
- iv. MARY ELIZABETH HAYES, b. 05 May 1859; d. 03 Mar 1904.

491. PAUL⁷ SPINNEY *(PARKER FOSTER⁶, DAVID⁵, EBENEZER⁴, JONATHAN³, SAMUEL², THOMAS¹)* was born 27 Jun 1828 in Wakefield, NH, and died 1901 in Ipswich, Ma. He married MARY ELIZABETH EMERY 20 Dec 1849.

Children of PAUL SPINNEY and MARY EMERY are:
- 852. i.   GEORGE FRANKLIN⁸ SPINNEY, b. 09 Jul 1852, Great Falls, NH; d. Aft. 1900.
- ii. ISABELLA F SPINNEY, b. 30 Jul 1853, Somersworth, NH; d. Aft. 1910.

492. PARKER⁷ SPINNEY *(PARKER FOSTER⁶, DAVID⁵, EBENEZER⁴, JONATHAN³, SAMUEL², THOMAS¹)* was born 08 Mar 1833, and died 14 Dec 1920. He married ABBIE HANSON 08 Nov 1866. She was born 1845, and died 1883 in Boston, MA.

Children of PARKER SPINNEY and ABBIE HANSON are:
- i.   ALICE ELLEN⁸ SPINNEY, b. 28 Jan 1868; m. D FLANDERS WILDER.
- ii. MARY A SPINNEY, b. 1870.
- iii. MAUD SPINNEY, b. 1874.

493. NATHANIAL DEARBORN⁷ SPINNEY *(PARKER FOSTER⁶, DAVID⁵, EBENEZER⁴, JONATHAN³, SAMUEL², THOMAS¹)* was born 26 Jan 1835 in Wakefield, NH, and died 07 Apr 1900. He married LUCY ELLIOTT 23 Feb 1870. She was born 1847, and died Aft. 1880.

Child of Nathanial Spinney and Lucy Elliott is:
      i.   RUSSELL[8] SPINNEY, b. 1871.

494. JOSEPH FRANKLIN[7] SPINNEY *(PARKER FOSTER[6], DAVID[5], EBENEZER[4], JONATHAN[3], SAMUEL[2], THOMAS[1])* was born 13 Aug 1839 in Rorchester, NH, and died 15 Nov 1902. He married HELEN AUGUSTA WENTWORTH 09 Feb 1863, daughter of LEWIS WENTWORTH and PARMELIA HAYES. She was born 12 Feb 1845 in Rochester, NH, and died 31 Oct 1897 in Milton, NH.

Notes for JOSEPH FRANKLIN SPINNEY:
Joseph received his education in the "Little Red School House" in Wakefield, Located near the so called "Spinney MEtting House".

Leaving home at an early age he learned the trade of makin shoes, at a time when nealy all shoes were made hand. He went "West" when he was about twenty years old, was there only a short time when the war broke out, so he entered the ranks there, enlistin at Peoria, IL, as a private in CO. E 17th Illinois Infanry, 25 may 1861 for three years.

He was in several engagements including Fort Donaldson and in the Battle fo Shiloh were he was severely wounded 5 April 1862. He was taken the hospital and from there to the private residence of a man names James Tarlton, whose home was on Clarke St in St Louis, where he received the kindest treatment, being cared for by Mr Tarlton's two daughters Jennie and Lillie. The writer has in his possession the A Dageorreotype containg the likeness of these two girls.

He was Discharged from the army as a invalid 2 aug 1862, at Boliver TN and returned to Rorchester, then after all the tender nursing maried the "Girl he left behind him" Helen A Wentworth 9 Feb 1863

Children of JOSEPH SPINNEY and HELEN WENTWORTH are:
      i.   STILLBORN[8] SPINNEY, b. 1864, Stilborn.
853.   ii. EUGENE NATHANIAL SPINNEY, b. 06 Apr 1866, Rorchester NH; d. 19 Jan 1936, Milton NH.
      iii. WILLIAM ROSCOE SPINNEY, b. 03 Nov 1872; d. Aft. 1930.

495. WILLIAM RICE[7] SPINNEY *(PARKER FOSTER[6], DAVID[5], EBENEZER[4], JONATHAN[3], SAMUEL[2], THOMAS[1])* was born 21 Aug 1851, and died 23 Sep 1919. He married HATTIE BUCK 14 Jun 1883. She was born Aug 1852, and died Aft. 1900.

Notes for WILLIAM RICE SPINNEY:
William and his family at some point moved to New York where they can be found in the 1900 census

Child of WILLIAM SPINNEY and HATTIE BUCK is:
854.   i.   CROSBY BUCK[8] SPINNEY, b. 11 Aug 1884; d. Nov 1967, Monclair NJ.

496. JAMES T[7] SPINNEY *(ALVAH[6], DAVID[5], EBENEZER[4], JONATHAN[3], SAMUEL[2], THOMAS[1])* was born 10 Aug 1834 in Somersworth, NH., and died 14 Mar 1894. He married MARY A FARNUM 01 Nov 1863. She was born 1841, and died Aft. 1870.

Children of JAMES SPINNEY and MARY FARNUM are:
      i.   WILLIE[8] SPINNEY, b. 1865.
      ii. GEORGE W SPINNEY, b. 1870.

497. ALVAH SPINNEY[7] GARLAND *(ROWENA A[6] SPINNEY, DAVID[5], EBENEZER[4], JONATHAN[3], SAMUEL[2], THOMAS[1])* was born 08 Jun 1849. He married PRISCILLA L. LATHROP 17 Nov 1873. She was born 1849.

Children of ALVAH GARLAND and PRISCILLA LATHROP are:
      i.   GEORGE LATHROP[8] GARLAND, b. 24 May 1874.
      ii. JOSEPH PAUL GARLAND, b. 16 Mar 1876; d. 05 Oct 1877.
      iii. RUTH BUTLER GARLAND, b. 23 Aug 1881.

iv.   JOSEPH SPINNEY GARLAND, b. 20 Aug 1883.

498. CHARLES H[7] SPINNEY *(CHARLES P[6], CHARLES[5], EBENEZER[4], JONATHAN[3], SAMUEL[2], THOMAS[1])* was born 1841 in Eliot, ME, and died 1923. He married SARAH J NOWELL, daughter of JOEL NOWELL and MERCY. She was born 1841, and died 1919.

Children of CHARLES SPINNEY and SARAH NOWELL are:
      i.   ERVIN[8] SPINNEY, b. 1869, Maine; d. 1901, Maine.
855. ii.   ATTA SPINNEY, b. Jul 1873.
      iii.   CARRIE SPINNEY, b. 1879.

499. JAMES W[7] SPINNEY *(CHARLES P[6], CHARLES[5], EBENEZER[4], JONATHAN[3], SAMUEL[2], THOMAS[1])* was born 06 Mar 1826. He married MATILDA GOULDING. She was born 1832, and died 1879 in Sherborn, MA.

Children of JAMES SPINNEY and MATILDA GOULDING are:
      i.   FLORENCE[8] SPINNEY, b. 1853.
      ii.   MARTHA SPINNEY, b. 1856.

500. AUGUSTUS RICE[7] SPINNEY *(CHARLES P[6], CHARLES[5], EBENEZER[4], JONATHAN[3], SAMUEL[2], THOMAS[1])* was born 14 Mar 1828, and died 22 Dec 1906 in Chelsea, MA. He married FRANCES ANGELINA PIERCE 25 May 1851 in East Weare, NH. She was born 05 Jun 1835 in Springfield, VT, and died 1902 in Chelsea, Ma.

Children of AUGUSTUS SPINNEY and FRANCES PIERCE are:
      i.   EDWIN A[8] SPINNEY, b. 03 Jul 1852; m. ELLEN LOW.
      ii.   HATTIE A SPINNEY, b. 31 Dec 1854; d. Aft. 1900.
      iii.   CHARLES F SPINNEY, b. 09 Oct 1856, Weare, NH.
856. iv.   IDA F SPINNEY, b. 21 Nov 1858.

501. ELBRIDGE HERBERT[7] SPINNEY *(CHARLES P[6], CHARLES[5], EBENEZER[4], JONATHAN[3], SAMUEL[2], THOMAS[1])* was born 1836, and died 1863 in Haverhill, MA. He married LYDIA ANN STICKNEY 04 Jul 1858, daughter of ERASTUS STICKNEY and LUCY JAMERSON. She was born 1833 in Groveland, MA.

Child of ELBRIDGE SPINNEY and LYDIA STICKNEY is:
      i.   HERBERT[8] SPINNEY, b. 1859.

502. MARK[7] SPINNEY *(MARK[6], PARKER[5], EBENEZER[4], JONATHAN[3], SAMUEL[2], THOMAS[1])* was born Abt. 1825. He married WHITEHOUSE.

Children of MARK SPINNEY and WHITEHOUSE are:
      i.   HORACE[8] SPINNEY, b. Abt. 1850.
      ii.   AUGUSTA SPINNEY.
      iii.   MARK SPINNEY, b. Abt. 1850.

503. HORACE P[7] SPINNEY *(MARK[6], PARKER[5], EBENEZER[4], JONATHAN[3], SAMUEL[2], THOMAS[1])* was born 1828 in Kittery, ME, and died Aft. 1850. He married ANNA M BRADBURY 1850 in Boston, MA. She was born 1830 in Boston.

Children of HORACE SPINNEY and ANNA BRADBURY are:
      i.   CHILD[8] SPINNEY, b. Aft. 1860.
      ii.   HORACE L SPINNEY, b. 12 Dec 1860, Portsmouth, NH.
      iii.   CHARLES F SPINNEY, b. 22 May 1867.
857. iv.   HANNAH L SPINNEY, b. 18 Jan 1875, Portsmouth, NH.
      v.   GEORGE T SPINNEY, b. 08 Sep 1854; d. 18 Sep 1854, Boston, Ma.
      vi.   HORACE CHAPIN SPINNEY, b. 1852; d. 1855.

504. HENRY CHAPIN[7] SPINNEY *(MARK[6], PARKER[5], EBENEZER[4], JONATHAN[3], SAMUEL[2], THOMAS[1])* was born 1855 in

Maine, and died Aft. 1920. He married (1) CARRIE B HUSSEY 1874. She was born 1861, and died Bef. 1900. He married (2) ANNIE E MCENTEE 1902, daughter of OWEN MCENTEE and MARY GREENE. She was born 1838 in Maine, and died 06 Mar 1908 in Lynn, Ma.

Children of HENRY SPINNEY and CARRIE HUSSEY are:
858.	i.	ARTHUR F^8 SPINNEY, b. 18 Jul 1877, Portsmouth, NH.
	ii.	CLARENCE C SPINNEY, b. 1884, Portsmouth, NH.
	iii.	EDITH SPINNEY, b. 1800.
859.	iv.	HARRY HENRY SPINNEY, b. 1876.

505. GEORGE F^7 SPINNEY *(MARK^6, PARKER^5, EBENEZER^4, JONATHAN^3, SAMUEL^2, THOMAS^1)* was born 1858, and died Aft. 1900 in Haverhill, MA. He married ISABELLA F HOLMES, daughter of ABBY. She was born 1857, and died 1889.

Children of GEORGE SPINNEY and ISABELLA HOLMES are:
| 860. | i. | FRANCIS WARREN^8 SPINNEY, b. 28 May 1878; d. 04 Jul 1958, Bradford, MA. |
| | ii. | ISABELL F SPINNEY. |

506. DANIEL P^7 PAUL *(STEPHEN^6, MARY GOWELL^5 SPINNEY, EBENEZER^4, JONATHAN^3, SAMUEL^2, THOMAS^1)* was born Aug 1841. He married SARAH. She was born Apr 1847.

Children of DANIEL PAUL and SARAH are:
	i.	DRUCILLA^8 PAUL, b. 1872.
	ii.	MARY G PAUL, b. Nov 1876.
	iii.	DANIEL P PAUL, b. Jul 1889.

507. MARY ANN^7 SPINNEY *(EBENEZER^6, EBENEZER^5, EBENEZER^4, JONATHAN^3, SAMUEL^2, THOMAS^1)* was born 1824, and died Bet. 1870 - 1880 in North Bridgewater, MA. She married LUTHER AMES 22 Oct 1849 in Brockton, MA, son of JOEL AMES and RELIENCE EDSON. He was born 02 Mar 1828 in Bridgewater, MA, and died Aft. 1880 in Richmond, NH.

Children of MARY SPINNEY and LUTHER AMES are:
	i.	RELIANCE FULLER^8 AMES, b. 29 Sep 1850, Brockton, MA; d. 15 Apr 1882.
	ii.	MARTHA FLETCHER AMES, b. 26 Dec 1851, Brockton, MA.
	iii.	ALBERT AMES, b. 01 Sep 1852, Brockton, MA; d. 01 Sep 1897, Santa Barbara, CA.
	iv.	BETSEY ANN AMES, b. 26 Mar 1855, Brockton, MA; d. 26 Aug 1951, Ashfield, MA.
	v.	FRANCES HUNT AMES, b. 27 Jun 1858, Brockton MA; d. 26 Aug 1886, San Jacinto, CA.
	vi.	FRANK VERNON AMES, b. 16 Nov 1860, Brockton, MA; d. 11 Nov 1944; m. NELLIE JOSEPHINE SMITH; b. 16 Dec 1866.
	vii.	ARTHUR MONTROSE AMES, b. 01 Oct 1863, Brockton, MA.
	viii.	EDITH HALL AMES, b. 16 Oct 1865, Brockton, MA; m. THOMAS H SENTELL, 01 Jan 1897, Santa Barbara, CA.

508. JOSEPH WILLIAM^7 SPINNEY *(EBENEZER^6, EBENEZER^5, EBENEZER^4, JONATHAN^3, SAMUEL^2, THOMAS^1)* was born 10 Aug 1838 in Deer Island, ME, and died Aft. 1880. He married ELIZABETH. She was born 1838, and died Aft. 1880.

Children of JOSEPH SPINNEY and ELIZABETH are:
861.	i.	CLARA S^8 SPINNEY, b. 15 Jan 1859; d. Deer Island Maine.
	ii.	PATIENCE F SPINNEY, b. 1861.
	iii.	SOPHIA SPINNEY, b. 1863.
	iv.	JOSEPHINE SPINNEY, b. 1869.

509. WILLIAM P^7 SPINNEY *(EBENEZER^6, EBENEZER^5, EBENEZER^4, JONATHAN^3, SAMUEL^2, THOMAS^1)* was born 25 Aug 1850 in Deer Isle, ME. He married ADELIA. She was born 1858.

Children of WILLIAM SPINNEY and ADELIA are:
| | i. | SUSIE^8 SPINNEY, b. 1876; m. FRANK STROUT, 25 Oct 1893. |

862. ii. NANCY J SPINNEY, b. 1879.

510. HARRIET VESTA[7] DWELLEY *(NARCISSA SPRING[6] SPINNEY, EBENEZER[5], EBENEZER[4], JONATHAN[3], SAMUEL[2], THOMAS[1])* was born 29 May 1824 in Boston, MA. She married WILLIAM PARSONS.

Children of HARRIET DWELLEY and WILLIAM PARSONS are:
- i. BURLEY[8] PARSONS.
- ii. ELLEN PARSONS.
- iii. CLARA PARSONS.
- iv. BILLY PARSONS.
- v. CHARLES PARSONS.
- vi. CORA PARSONS.
- vii. FLORA PARSONS.

511. OSCAR[7] DWELLEY *(NARCISSA SPRING[6] SPINNEY, EBENEZER[5], EBENEZER[4], JONATHAN[3], SAMUEL[2], THOMAS[1])* was born 17 Aug 1826. He married CATHERINE C PHILLIPS.

Children of OSCAR DWELLEY and CATHERINE PHILLIPS are:
- i. JOHN F[8] DWELLEY.
- ii. L GERTRUDE DWELLEY.
- iii. CORA N DWELLEY.
- iv. MARY A DWELLEY.
- v. GEORGE DWELLEY.

512. ALICE CATHERINE[7] DWELLEY *(NARCISSA SPRING[6] SPINNEY, EBENEZER[5], EBENEZER[4], JONATHAN[3], SAMUEL[2], THOMAS[1])* was born 01 Mar 1829 in Portsmouth, NH or VT, and died 11 Mar 1911 in Silk Creek, OR. She married SAMUEL F. WHEELER 13 May 1847, son of FRANKLIN WHEELER and MEHITEBELL LUFKIN. He was born 26 Dec 1825 in Charleston, NH, and died 27 Jan 1911 in Silk Creek, OR.

Children of ALICE DWELLEY and SAMUEL WHEELER are:
- i. OSCAR DWELLEY[8] WHEELER, b. 26 May 1848.
- ii. ALMON LUFKIN WHEELER, b. 10 Oct 1851.
- iii. AUGUSTUS DWELLEY WHEELER, b. 07 Sep 1853.
- iv. WALTER NAHUM WHEELER, b. 11 Jan 1857.
- v. ELBRIDGE ALBERT WHEELER, b. 11 Dec 1859.
- vi. JOSEPH FRANKLIN WHEELER, b. 20 Jul 1862.
- vii. MARY LOUISE WHEELER, b. 11 Jan 1865.
- 863. viii. ELLA GERTRUDE WHEELER, b. 03 Jun 1867, Wisconsin; d. 1912, St Helena CA.
- ix. HATTIE CAROLINE WHEELER, b. 18 Jul 1870.

513. JOSEPH FRANKLIN[7] DWELLEY *(NARCISSA SPRING[6] SPINNEY, EBENEZER[5], EBENEZER[4], JONATHAN[3], SAMUEL[2], THOMAS[1])* was born 11 Apr 1839, and died 06 Dec 1933. He married ANGELINE ELIZABETH WELLS.

Child of JOSEPH DWELLEY and ANGELINE WELLS is:
864. i. ALICE CATHERINE[8] DWELLEY.

514. HORACE STACEY[7] SPINNEY *(LYMAN P[6], EBENEZER[5], EBENEZER[4], JONATHAN[3], SAMUEL[2], THOMAS[1])* was born 29 Oct 1838, and died 08 Jan 1882 in Portsmouth New Hampshire. He married MERRY ODIORNE 03 Jul 1859, daughter of BENJAMIN ODIORNE. She was born 14 Feb 1843.

Children of HORACE SPINNEY and MERRY ODIORNE are:
- i. HORACE STACY[8] SPINNEY, b. 13 Dec 1860; d. 11 Jul 1935; m. ADDIE M, 1885; b. 1860; d. 1935.
- 865. ii. NELLIE ANNE SPINNEY, b. 12 Dec 1862; d. 10 Apr 1908.
- 866. iii. ALPHONSO BENJAMIN SPINNEY, b. 31 Mar 1866; d. 04 Mar 1940.
- iv. CHARLES FRANKLIN SPINNEY, b. 21 May 1867; d. 16 Jul 1867.
- v. GEORGIANNA ANN SPINNEY, b. 12 Jun 1868; d. 24 Apr 1929; m. OREN DOWNS.
- vi. LUCIAN A SPINNEY, b. 02 Jun 1871; d. 21 Aug 1871.
- vii. CHARLES A SPINNEY, b. Jul 1871; d. 21 Aug 1871, Portsmouth New Hampshire.

     viii. JOSEPHINE E SPINNEY, b. 21 Jul 1872; d. 06 Aug 1939.
      ix. JOHN E SPINNEY, b. 03 Sep 1873, Portsmouth, NH; d. 1874.
       x. HANNAH L SPINNEY, b. 17 Jan 1875; d. 09 Apr 1936; m. TAEFETHEN.
      xi. SUSAN SPINNEY, b. 05 Feb 1876.
     xii. LYDIA AUGUSTA SPINNEY, b. 25 Jul 1877; d. 21 Jan 1948.
    xiii. HOWARD E SPINNEY, b. 24 Feb 1879; d. 25 Jan 1925; m. NELLIE F; b. 10 May 1877; d. 27 Oct 1921.

515. LYMAN P⁷ SPINNEY *(LYMAN P⁶, EBENEZER⁵, EBENEZER⁴, JONATHAN³, SAMUEL², THOMAS¹)* was born 03 Jan 1842, and died 1899. He married ELIZABETH STACKPOLE 25 Dec 1864. She was born 1846, and died 1917.

Children of LYMAN SPINNEY and ELIZABETH STACKPOLE are:
       i. ELIZABETH F⁸ SPINNEY, b. 1868, Charlestown, MA.
      ii. LYDIA AUGUSTA SPINNEY, b. 16 Apr 1870, Woburn Mass.
867.   iii. CHARLES L SPINNEY, b. 06 Jul 1872, Woburn, MA.
868.   iv. BESSIE MILDRED SPINNEY, b. 1874, Woburn, MA.
       v. JENNIE SPINNEY, b. 1877.
      vi. GERTRUDE SPINNEY, b. Aug 1880.
     vii. EPHRAIM C SPINNEY, b. 1882; d. 1909; m. EVA M ALBEE, 28 Nov 1907, Whitefield, ME.
    viii. GRACE SPINNEY, b. Aug 1887.

516. ABRAHAM⁷ HALL *(ABIGAIL⁶ WILLEY, SALLY⁵ FERNALD, HANNAH (BETSY)⁴ SPINNEY, JONATHAN³, SAMUEL², THOMAS¹)* was born 1831, and died 1915. He married LUCY P.

Children of ABRAHAM HALL and LUCY P are:
       i. CHARLES⁸ HALL.
      ii. ALFRED HALL.
     iii. SUSIE HALL.

517. NATHANIEL PULSIFIER⁷ HALL *(ABIGAIL⁶ WILLEY, SALLY⁵ FERNALD, HANNAH (BETSY)⁴ SPINNEY, JONATHAN³, SAMUEL², THOMAS¹)* was born 30 May 1847, and died 1923. He married (1) MARY ELLA STROUT.   He married (2) DELIA LOWE. She was born 1846.

Children of NATHANIEL HALL and DELIA LOWE are:
       i. LILLIAN⁸ HALL.
      ii. PULSIFIER HALL.
     iii. NORA HALL.
     iv. LUCY HALL.
869.   v. SIMEON HALL, b. 1812.

518. JOHN L⁷ HALL *(ABIGAIL⁶ WILLEY, SALLY⁵ FERNALD, HANNAH (BETSY)⁴ SPINNEY, JONATHAN³, SAMUEL², THOMAS¹)* was born 1855, and died 1922. He married HATTIE.

Child of JOHN HALL and HATTIE is:
       i. FREDDIE⁸ HALL, b. 1879.

519. JAMES ALEXANDER⁷ SPINNEY *(STEPHEN⁶, JONATHAN⁵, NATHANIEL⁴, JONATHAN³, SAMUEL², THOMAS¹)* was born 29 Aug 1825 in Pennfiled, NB, and died 27 Mar 1908 in Pennfield, NB. He married MARY BORTHWICK 01 Apr 1853 in Calais, ME. She was born 07 Jul 1826, and died 15 Nov 1905 in Pennfield, NB.

Children of JAMES SPINNEY and MARY BORTHWICK are:
       i. THOMAS ALBERT⁸ SPINNEY, b. 14 Sep 1856, Pennfield, NB.; d. 24 Feb 1907; m. LYDIA ELLEN JUSTASON, 22 Feb 1897; b. 27 Dec 1866, Pennfield, NB.; d. 12 Nov 1961, North Lubuc, ME.
870.   ii. DOUGLAS SPINNEY, b. 09 Jan 1858, Pennfield, NB.; d. 09 Jan 1954.

520. ALFRED HURLEY⁷ SPINNEY *(STEPHEN⁶, JONATHAN⁵, NATHANIEL⁴, JONATHAN³, SAMUEL², THOMAS¹)* was born 28 Aug 1830 in St George, NB., and died 11 Oct 1910 in St George, NB.. He married CATHERINE ANNE MCPIKE 05 Oct 1857 in St George, NB..

Children of ALFRED SPINNEY and CATHERINE MCPIKE are:

871.   i.   CHARLES MCPIKE[8] SPINNEY, b. 16 Sep 1858, Pennfield, NB.; d. 30 Apr 1923, Musquash, NB..

872.   ii.   MARY ELLEN SPINNEY, b. 26 Dec 1861, Pennfield, NB.; d. 02 Sep 1936, Pennfield, NB..

873.   iii.   EDWARD HENRY SPINNEY, b. 03 Aug 1864, St George, NB.; d. Bradford, PA.

874.   iv.   ALFRED HURLEY SPINNEY, b. Nov 1866, Pennfield, NB.; d. 31 May 1900, St George, NB..

875.   v.   JAMES THOMAS SPINNEY, b. 20 Jun 1868, Pennfield, NB; d. 14 Oct 1941, Runford, ME.

876.   vi.   CLARENCE JOHN SPINNEY, b. Mar 1870, Pennfield, NB.; d. 1901.

        vii.   MARY GRACE SPINNEY, b. Jun 1872, Pennfield, NB.; d. Bef. 1881.

877.   viii.   CATHERINE "ALICE" SPINNEY, b. 01 Jan 1876, Pennfield, NB.; d. May 1957, Ypsilanti, MI.

521. HORATIO NELSON[7] SPINNEY *(STEPHEN[6], JONATHAN[5], NATHANIEL[4], JONATHAN[3], SAMUEL[2], THOMAS[1])* was born 27 Aug 1839 in Calais, ME, and died 29 Aug 1929 in Musquash, NB.. He married (1) WINIFRED THOMPSON. He married (2) ELLEN STEEN 03 Jun 1863 in Calais, ME, daughter of JAMES STEEN and JANE MITCHELL. She was born 10 May 1847 in Calais, ME.

Children of HORATIO SPINNEY and ELLEN STEEN are:

878.   i.   FREDERICK[8] SPINNEY, b. 01 Feb 1864, St George, NB.; d. 06 Mar 1932, Saint John, NB..

        ii.   JAMES CHANDLER SPINNEY, b. Feb 1866; d. 23 Apr 1869.

        iii.   MINNIE R SPINNEY, b. 1867; d. Bef. 1871.

879.   iv.   HORATIO NELSON SPINNEY, b. 06 May 1868, Musquash, NB.; d. 1948, Prince of Wales, NB..

        v.   JAMES "GEORGE" SPINNEY, b. 08 Dec 1870, Musquash, NB.; d. 16 Dec 1924, Musquash, NB.; m. LOLA REED.

880.   vi.   DOUGLAS SPINNEY, b. 01 May 1874, Musquash, NB.; d. 1943, Musquash, NB..

        vii.   SILAS SPINNEY, b. 08 Mar 1876, Musquash, NB.; d. 1912.

522. KATHERINE M[7] SPINNEY *(JAMES S[6], JONATHAN[5], NATHANIEL[4], JONATHAN[3], SAMUEL[2], THOMAS[1])* was born 1830 in St George, NB., and died 05 Apr 1857. She married EDWARD HUNTER 05 Apr 1857. He was born in St Andrews, NB..

Children of KATHERINE SPINNEY and EDWARD HUNTER are:

        i.   SARAH[8] HUNTER.

881.   ii.   JAMES HUNTER.

        iii.   KATHERINE HUNTER.

        iv.   MARTHA HUNTER.

523. JOSEPH L[7] SPINNEY *(JAMES S[6], JONATHAN[5], NATHANIEL[4], JONATHAN[3], SAMUEL[2], THOMAS[1])* was born 1832 in St George, NB., and died 23 Apr 1928 in Eureka, California. He married ANN JANE STEEN 15 Nov 1853 in St George, NB., daughter of JOHN STEEN and JANE. She was born 1835 in St George, NB., and died 13 Mar 1907.

Notes for JOSEPH L SPINNEY:

Joseph being older and marrying young. His father deeded part of his farm to him, on which he built a house and barn on it. Later it was sold to a John Spires who lived there and then his sons Michael, Charles, and Pat. Some years later, Tobias who lived on his fathers farm purchased it back, so as to keep the estate intact. It remained in the Spinney Family. It was Vacant after the Rist War.

Joe owned several teams of heavy draft horses and his job was to haul lumber form the fresh water landing in St George, over the hill to the public wharf on salt waher, where it was loaded in ships for export to the UK and USA. The lumber was a sawn in three-inch deal on the Magaguadic River and its tributaries, where there were several mills. It was wafted down to the landing, where it was loaded on carts (two-wheelere) to go across town - hence the name Portage Street

When Joe's two oldest sons grew up they headed for California and started in the lumber business (Redwood and Mahonany) at Eureka, in Humbold County. Before long, they sent for their father, mother and family. One or more of the youngest was born there

Children of JOSEPH SPINNEY and ANN STEEN are:

        i.   CHILD[8] SPINNEY, b. 1852; d. 29 Mar 1853, Calais Maine.

        ii.   JOHN CROZIER SPINNEY, b. 04 Apr 1854, St George, NB.; d. 10 Dec 1911.

           iii.   ROBERT SPINNEY, b. 14 Jun 1856, St George, NB.; d. 15 Jul 1878, Humbolt, CA.

882.   iv.   GIDEON WEBSTER SPINNEY, b. 12 Mar 1859, St George, NB.; d. 21 Oct 1919, California.

           v.   JANE SPINNEY, b. 03 Jan 1861; d. 19 Dec 1869, St George, NB..

           vi.   MARY ELLEN SPINNEY, b. 01 May 1863, St George, NB.; d. 1940; m. ANGUS MCDONALD.

883.   vii.   ANNIE LOUISA SPINNEY, b. 09 Aug 1865; d. 16 Aug 1896.

           viii.   GEORGE SPINNEY, b. 09 Nov 1867; d. 16 Dec 1869, St George New Brunswick.

884.   ix.   JOSEPH WALTER SPINNEY, b. 22 Feb 1870, St George, NB.; d. 15 Dec 1948, Humbult, CA.

           x.   JAMES SPINNEY, b. Dec 1871; d. 13 Jan 1872.

885.   xi.   MAGGIE JANE SPINNEY, b. 18 Aug 1873; d. 20 Dec 1939.

           xii.   FRED SPINNEY, b. 18 Mar 1876; d. 19 Oct 1877.

           xiii.   MELVIN LESTER SPINNEY, b. 14 Oct 1879.

           xiv.   CHESTER SPINNEY, b. 1881.

524. MARY JANE[7] SPINNEY *(JAMES S[6], JONATHAN[5], NATHANIEL[4], JONATHAN[3], SAMUEL[2], THOMAS[1])* was born 07 Jun 1844, and died 01 Apr 1919 in Pleasant Ridge, NB.. She married WILLIAM STEWART 10 Oct 1858 in St George New Brunswick. He was born 07 Sep 1835 in Pleasant Ridge, NB., and died 12 Jul 1894 in Pleasant Ridge, NB..

Children of MARY SPINNEY and WILLIAM STEWART are:

           i.   WASHINGTON[8] STEWART.

           ii.   TOBIAS STEWART.

           iii.   EMMA STEWART.

           iv.   CHARLES STEWART.

           v.   MAMIE ORR STEWART.

           vi.   JOHN STEWART.

           vii.   WILLIAM STEWART.

886.   viii.   GEORGE GILMAN STEWART, b. 1860; d. 1937.

887.   ix.   JAMES ALFRED STEWART, b. 10 May 1863, Pleasant Ridge, NB.; d. 09 Nov 1922, Pleasant Ridge, NB..

525. JAMES VAN BUREN[7] SPINNEY *(JAMES S[6], JONATHAN[5], NATHANIEL[4], JONATHAN[3], SAMUEL[2], THOMAS[1])* was born 07 May 1846 in Pull and BE Dam, Letang St, NB., and died 20 Dec 1913 in St George, NB.. He married REBECCA CARVER 27 Nov 1873 in St George, NB., daughter of WILLIAM CARVER and SUSAN COX. She was born 26 May 1852 in Utopia, NB., and died 14 Jan 1945 in St Stephens, NB..

Children of JAMES SPINNEY and REBECCA CARVER are:

888.   i.   ANNIE[8] SPINNEY, b. 20 Aug 1874, St George, NB.; d. 14 Jan 1957, Calais, ME.

889.   ii.   SUSAN JANE SPINNEY, b. 22 Jan 1877, Upper Letang, NB.; d. 22 Jul 1957, St George, NB..

890.   iii.   LETITIA SPINNEY, b. 05 Apr 1879, Upper L'Etang, NG; d. 10 Dec 1954, St Stephen, NB.

891.   iv.   CATHERINE SPINNEY, b. 22 May 1881, Upper L'Etang, NB..

892.   v.   GEORGE ROSS SPINNEY, b. 25 Oct 1883, Upper L'Etang, NB.; d. 01 Sep 1960, St John, NB..

           vi.   JOSEPH H SPINNEY, b. 25 Feb 1885, Upper L'Etang, NB.; d. 1887, Upper L'Etang, NB..

893.   vii.   JAMES RENFORTH SPINNEY, b. 13 Jul 1886, Upper L'Etang, NB.; d. 26 Sep 1956, St George, NB..

           viii.   ELLEN LOWE SPINNEY, b. 01 Mar 1891; d. 01 May 1965.

894.   ix.   JOHN OLIVER SPINNEY, b. 08 Feb 1895, St George, NB.; d. 10 Mar 1975, St John, NB..

           x.   HAROLD EDWARD SPINNEY, b. 07 Apr 1897, Upper L'Etang, NB.; d. Jun 1960, Upper L'Etang, NB..

526. SARAH ELLEN[7] SPINNEY *(JAMES S[6], JONATHAN[5], NATHANIEL[4], JONATHAN[3], SAMUEL[2], THOMAS[1])* was born 1848, and died 04 Dec 1884 in Pennfield, NB.. She married JAMES HUNTER, son of EDWARD HUNTER and KATHERINE SPINNEY.

Children of SARAH SPINNEY and JAMES HUNTER are:

           i.   JOHN[8] HUNTER, b. 1873.

           ii.   JANE VIOLA HUNTER, b. 1881; m. SELLERS, Aft. 1901.

           iii.   SARAH HUNTER, b. 1881.

           iv.   MINNIE HUNTER, b. 1879.

527. HORATIO NELSON[7] SPINNEY *(JAMES S[6], JONATHAN[5], NATHANIEL[4], JONATHAN[3], SAMUEL[2], THOMAS[1])* was born 20 Jan 1860 in St George, NB., and died 14 Oct 1885 in Upper L'Etang New Brunswick. He married WINIFRED D THOMAS 20 Nov 1882 in Eastport Maine, daughter of JOHN THOMAS and SARAH DUSTIN. She was born 1858, and died Aft. 1930.

Child of HORATIO SPINNEY and WINIFRED THOMAS is:

895.   i.   NELSON PEABODY[8] SPINNEY, b. 01 Oct 1884; d. Aft. 1930.

528. CHARLOTTE ELIZABETH[7] HUSON *(LOUISA ANN[6] SPINNEY, JONATHAN[5], NATHANIEL[4], JONATHAN[3], SAMUEL[2], THOMAS[1])* was born 1834, and died Bef. 1901. She married AMOS COGSWELL 17 Jul 1852 in Calais, ME. He was born 10 Oct 1826, and died Aft. 1901.

Children of CHARLOTTE HUSON and AMOS COGSWELL are:
      i.   ANNA[8] COGSWELL, b. 1854.
      ii.   JOSEPH COGSWELL, b. 1858; d. Bef. 1880.
      iii.   CHARLES EARL COGSWELL, b. 1861; d. 1883; m. (1) MARY J CALDWELL, 04 Feb 1879; m. (2) DAISY IRENE RAND, 20 May 1909.
      iv.   GEORGE A COGSWELL, b. 1862.
      v.   MINNIE COGSWELL, b. 1870.
      vi.   WILLIAM F COGSWELL, b. 1867.
      vii.   LELONS COGSWELL, b. 1869.
      viii.   NELLIE COGSWELL, b. 1875.
      ix.   EMILY COGSWELL, b. 1877.
      x.   MARY OLIVE COGSWELL, b. 1856; d. 1916; m. JOHN IRVING, 1876.
      xi.   JANE COGSWELL, b. 1860.

529. GEORGE H[7] HUSON *(LOUISA ANN[6] SPINNEY, JONATHAN[5], NATHANIEL[4], JONATHAN[3], SAMUEL[2], THOMAS[1])* was born 16 Jul 1844 in Calais, ME, and died 28 Apr 1934 in Calais, ME. He married SARAH M. She was born 1847, and died 1917.

Children of GEORGE HUSON and SARAH M are:
      i.   GEORGE W[8] HUSON, b. 1873; d. 1881.
      ii.   CLARENCE S HUSON, b. 1876; d. 1879.
896.   iii.   JAME A HUSON, b. 1878; d. 1961.
      iv.   GRACE HUSON, b. Jan 1890.

530. THOMAS ALBERT[7] HUSON *(LOUISA ANN[6] SPINNEY, JONATHAN[5], NATHANIEL[4], JONATHAN[3], SAMUEL[2], THOMAS[1])* was born 19 Nov 1847 in Calais, ME, and died 1918. He married VICTORIA ELIZABETH KEEN 12 Nov 1867 in Princeton, Me. She was born 1844, and died 1911.

Children of THOMAS HUSON and VICTORIA KEEN are:
      i.   EDGAR[8] HUSON, b. 1866.
      ii.   EFFA HUSON, b. 1869.
      iii.   PHOEBE HUSON, b. 1872; d. 1880.
      iv.   FRED HUSON, b. 1873; d. 1876.
      v.   MARY HUSON, b. 1875.
      vi.   CHARLES HUSON, b. 1878.
      vii.   GRACE HUSON, b. 1880; d. 1951.
      viii.   FRANK HUSON, b. 1881.
      ix.   THOMAS HUSON, b. 1885.

531. MELVINA[7] HUSON *(LOUISA ANN[6] SPINNEY, JONATHAN[5], NATHANIEL[4], JONATHAN[3], SAMUEL[2], THOMAS[1])* was born 1849 in Calais, ME, and died Bef. 1860. She married HENRY CAIN.

Children of MELVINA HUSON and HENRY CAIN are:
      i.   HENRY[8] CAIN.
      ii.   BESSIE CAIN.
      iii.   ANNIE CAIN.

532. WILLIAM L[7] SPINNEY *(NATHANIEL[6], JONATHAN[5], NATHANIEL[4], JONATHAN[3], SAMUEL[2], THOMAS[1])* was born Mar 1835 in St George, NB., and died 10 Oct 1915 in Calais, ME. He married SARAH A CONNORS 07 Jun 1860 in Calais, ME, daughter of PATRICK CONNORS and JANE MCCLUSKEE. She was born 30 Nov 1836, and died 28

Oct 1896 in Calais, ME.

Children of WILLIAM SPINNEY and SARAH CONNORS are:
    i.   LIZZIE[8] SPINNEY.
    ii. ADDIE SPINNEY.
    iii. CHARLES F SPINNEY, b. 24 Apr 1862, Calais, ME; d. 1913; m. JENNIE M BERRY, 16 Oct 1883, Calais, ME; b. St Stephens, NB..
    iv. WILLIE SPINNEY, b. 1863; d. 1867.
897.   v. GEORGE A SPINNEY, b. 25 Dec 1863, Calais, ME.
    vi. MARY E SPINNEY, b. 1867; d. 1886.
    vii. CARRIE A SPINNEY, b. 1871.

533. NANCY (SARAH) ANN[7] SPINNEY *(NATHANIEL[6], JONATHAN[5], NATHANIEL[4], JONATHAN[3], SAMUEL[2], THOMAS[1])* was born 13 Apr 1838 in St George, NB., and died 26 Jul 1934 in Calais, ME. She married HUGH CONNERS 03 May 1863 in Calais, ME. He was born 1836 in St Stephens, NB., and died 1874 in Calais, ME.

Children of NANCY SPINNEY and HUGH CONNERS are:
    i. MARY E[8] CONNERS, b. Jan 1867, Calais, ME; d. Sep 1867, Calais, ME.
    ii. CHARLOTTE CONNERS, b. 1868, Calais, ME; d. 01 Aug 1945, Salisbury, MA; m. GEORGE W OAKES.

534. STEPHEN ALEXANDER[7] SPINNEY *(NATHANIEL[6], JONATHAN[5], NATHANIEL[4], JONATHAN[3], SAMUEL[2], THOMAS[1])* was born Sep 1842 in St George, NB., and died 08 Dec 1914 in Calais, ME. He married EMMA JANE "ADDIE" HARRIS 24 Aug 1865 in Calais, ME. She was born 1844, and died 04 Jun 1929 in Lynn, MA.

Children of STEPHEN SPINNEY and EMMA HARRIS are:
898.   i. FRANK HERBERT[8] SPINNEY, b. 04 Jun 1866, Calais, ME; d. 28 Jul 1934, Calais, ME.
    ii. MARY A SPINNEY, b. 1868.
899.   iii. ALICE SPINNEY, b. Abt. 1870, Calais, ME.
    iv. MABLE C SPINNEY, b. 1876, Calais, ME; d. 01 Oct 1927, Lynn, MA; m. GILBERT BALLARD.
    v. GERTRUDE SPINNEY, b. 24 Feb 1883.

535. ZEBALON D[7] SPINNEY *(NATHANIEL[6], JONATHAN[5], NATHANIEL[4], JONATHAN[3], SAMUEL[2], THOMAS[1])* was born 10 Jan 1848 in Calais, ME, and died 08 Sep 1893 in Calais, ME. He married ANNIE M READON 15 Aug 1873 in Calais, ME, daughter of JOHN READON. She was born 20 Jan 1856 in Calais, ME, and died 26 Oct 1933 in Waltham, Ma.

Child of ZEBALON SPINNEY and ANNIE READON is:
    i. WALTER N[8] SPINNEY, b. 10 Apr 1875, Calais, ME; d. 18 Mar 1942, Waltham, MA; m. (1) ELLA J HOLDER; m. (2) KATIE "EFFIE" BLAKE, 30 Jul 1895, Calais Maine.

536. SHUBAL T[7] SPINNEY *(NATHANIEL[6], JONATHAN[5], NATHANIEL[4], JONATHAN[3], SAMUEL[2], THOMAS[1])* was born 1849 in Calais, ME, and died 24 Mar 1889 in Calais, ME. He married EMELINE COX 09 Apr 1873 in Calais, ME. She was born 1855 in Calais, ME, and died Aft. 1880.

Child of SHUBAL SPINNEY and EMELINE COX is:
    i. MARY E[8] SPINNEY, b. 1873; d. 18 Jul 1874, Calais, ME.

537. NELLIE[7] SPINNEY *(NATHANIEL[6], JONATHAN[5], NATHANIEL[4], JONATHAN[3], SAMUEL[2], THOMAS[1])* was born Jun 1861 in Maine, and died 12 Mar 1936 in Haverhill, MA. She married GEORGE JOHNSON. He was born Sep 1860 in Canada, and died Bef. 1930.

Children of NELLIE SPINNEY and GEORGE JOHNSON are:
    i. SARAH[8] JOHNSON, b. May 1884.
    ii. EARNEST JOHNSON, b. Dec 1885.
    iii. LLOYD JOHNSON, b. Dec 1886.

538. MARGARET[7] HATT *(DOROTHY[6] SPINNEY, JONATHAN[5], NATHANIEL[4], JONATHAN[3], SAMUEL[2], THOMAS[1])* was born Feb 1842. She married DAVID MARRS 1880, son of ANDREW MARRS and BETSY. He was born 1854.

Children of MARGARET HATT and DAVID MARRS are:
  i.   JOSIE[8] MARRS, b. Dec 1880.
  ii. BRYCE MARRS, b. 1883.

539. CHARLES MELVILLE[7] HOLT *(SARAH E[6] SPINNEY, JONATHAN[5], NATHANIEL[4], JONATHAN[3], SAMUEL[2], THOMAS[1])* was born 15 Jan 1844 in Calais, ME, and died 01 Apr 1875. He married MARGARET J MCCARTHY 01 Oct 1866 in St Stephens, NB.. She was born 1839, and died Aft. 1881.

Children of CHARLES HOLT and MARGARET MCCARTHY are:
  i.   GEORGIE[8] HOLT, b. 1868.
  ii.   FRANK HOLT, b. 1870.
  iii. MARY HOLT, b. 1871.
  iv.   HARRY HOLT, b. 1873.
  v.   FREDERICK HOLT, b. 1874.

540. HANNAH ELIZA[7] SPINNEY *(CHARLES EDWARD[6], JONATHAN[5], NATHANIEL[4], JONATHAN[3], SAMUEL[2], THOMAS[1])* was born 26 Nov 1859 in Calais, ME, and died 18 Aug 1934 in Montreal Canada. She married ROBERT THOMPSON STUART 19 Feb 1885 in St Stephen, NB., son of JOSEPH STUART and MARGARET WILSON. He was born 18 Jun 1850 in St Stephen Parish, Charlotte, New Brunswick, Canada, and died 29 Apr 1925.

Children of HANNAH SPINNEY and ROBERT STUART are:
  i.   ROY MILLIDGE[8] STUART, b. 1890, St Stephen, Charlotte, New Brunswick, Canada; m. ALMA DUMAS.
900. ii.   JENNIE LOUISA STUART, b. 1895.
  iii.   JESSIE STUART, b. 1886, St Stephen Parish, Charlotte, New Brunswick, Canada; d. 1983; m. (1) LANCELOT GIBSON; b. 1850, Salem, MA; m. (2) WILLIAM REID; b. Rhode Island.
901. iv.   MARGARET ELLEN (NELLIE) STUART, b. 1900, St Stephen Parish, Charlotte, New Brunswick, Canada.
  v.   BLAINA HAMLIN STUART, b. 1891, St Stephen, Charlotte, New Brunswick, Canada; m. HARRY GORTON MANNING; d. Nov 1999.
902. vi.   GRACE INA STUART, b. 1888.
903. vii.   MARION BEATRICE STUART, b. 1892, St Stephen, Charlotte, New Brunswick, Canada.
  viii. RALPH BYRNE STUART, b. 1894; d. 1916.

541. JESSIE[7] SPINNEY *(CHARLES EDWARD[6], JONATHAN[5], NATHANIEL[4], JONATHAN[3], SAMUEL[2], THOMAS[1])* was born Jun 1861, and died Aft. 1910. She married FRED B APT, son of DANIEL APT and SARAH. He was born Feb 1860, and died Aft. 1900.

Children of JESSIE SPINNEY and FRED APT are:
  i.   CARRIE[8] APT, b. Sep 1881; m. LINGLEY.
  ii.   FREDERICK P APT, b. May 1885; m. ELEANOR S TROTT, 25 Feb 1904.
  iii.   HORACE E APT, b. Apr 1887; m. JULIA M DUNN, 01 Dec 1911.
  iv.   ALMA APT, b. Sep 1888; m. JOSEPH F SPEAR, 06 Apr 1910.
  v.   GEORGE APT, b. Abt. 1890; m. DOROTHY HEYWOOD.
  vi.   ALICE L APT, b. Aug 1891; m. ARTHUR B COLCORD, 28 Dec 1912.
  vii.   GLADYS APT, b. Apr 1894; m. CHARLES BALTZER, 07 May 1911.
  viii. SADIE APT, b. Feb 1896; m. ANGUS MCLEAN, 09 Nov 1920.
  ix.   JOHN APT, b. 01 Nov 1898.
  x.   WALTER APT, b. 13 Oct 1904.
  xi.   CHESTER O APT, b. Dec 1907; m. HARRIET GRINDLE.

542. NELLIE M[7] SPINNEY *(CHARLES EDWARD[6], JONATHAN[5], NATHANIEL[4], JONATHAN[3], SAMUEL[2], THOMAS[1])* was born 13 Sep 1865 in Calais, ME, and died 13 Oct 1927 in Calais ME. She married WILLIAM THOMPSON 14 Sep 1895 in Baptist Church Calais, ME, son of JOSEPH THOMPSON and ANN STAPLES. He was born 1864 in Calais, ME.

Children of NELLIE SPINNEY and WILLIAM THOMPSON are:
  i.   RUTH A[8] THOMPSON, b. 1896; d. 10 Sep 1896, Calais Maine.

ii. ALBERT THOMPSON, b. 1898.

iii. WILLIAM THOMPSON, b. 1900.

543. GEORGE FREDERICK[7] SPINNEY *(CHARLES EDWARD[6], JONATHAN[5], NATHANIEL[4], JONATHAN[3], SAMUEL[2], THOMAS[1])* was born 18 Nov 1868 in Calais, ME, and died 15 Jan 1946 in Milltown. He married (1) ELLEN (NELLIE) SCULLIN, daughter of WILLIAM SCULLIN and ANN MCSHANE. She was born 1867 in Rollingdam N.B, and died 13 Dec 1909 in Calais, ME. He married (2) SARAH EDITH JOYE 01 Dec 1920, daughter of ROBERT JOYE and HARRIETT JOHNSON. She was born 16 Nov 1884 in Baker Settlement, N.B., and died 1970 in St Stephen.

Children of GEORGE SPINNEY and ELLEN SCULLIN are:

904.   i.   JANE GOLDEN[8] SPINNEY, b. 1899, New York.

           ii.   SARAH SPINNEY, b. Abt. 1890; d. Melrose Ma.

544. FRANKLIN P[7] SPINNEY *(CHARLES EDWARD[6], JONATHAN[5], NATHANIEL[4], JONATHAN[3], SAMUEL[2], THOMAS[1])* was born 20 Feb 1875 in Calais, ME, and died 18 Aug 1948. He married CASSIE F GARNETT 27 Jul 1895 in Calias, ME. She was born Jun 1875 in Pembroke, ME, and died Aft. 1910.

Children of FRANKLIN SPINNEY and CASSIE GARNETT are:

905.   i.   FRANCES M[8] SPINNEY, b. 09 Nov 1895; d. 04 Apr 1981, Hartford, Connecticut.

           ii.   FRANKLIN SPINNEY, b. 16 Aug 1897; d. Bef. 1900.

           iii.   REGINALD SPINNEY, b. 29 Jul 1898; d. Bef. 1900.

           iv.   GLADYS J SPINNEY, b. 31 Jan 1900; d. Aft. 1910; m. ARCHIE KATZ.

545. LOUISE PARKS[7] SPINNEY *(CHARLES EDWARD[6], JONATHAN[5], NATHANIEL[4], JONATHAN[3], SAMUEL[2], THOMAS[1])* was born 14 Nov 1876 in Calais, ME, and died 28 Nov 1957 in Malden, MA. She married ALEXANDER BARRY MILLS 20 Aug 1894 in St. Stevens N.B, son of JAMES MILLS and MARYANN CAMPBELL. He was born 02 Oct 1872 in Boston, MA, and died 24 Aug 1947 in Malden, MA.

Children of LOUISE SPINNEY and ALEXANDER MILLS are:

906.   i.   GORDON VICTOR[8] MILLS, b. 16 May 1896, Calais, ME; d. 20 Sep 1965, Waltham, MA.

           ii.   ELIZABETH MILLS, b. 25 Dec 1897; d. May 1980; m. HANS HAUGAARD; b. 22 Mar 1889, Denmark; d. Jul 1971, Belmont, MA.

907.   iii.   EDWARD L MILLS, b. May 1899, Mass.

546. CAROLYN B (CARRIE)[7] SPINNEY *(CHARLES EDWARD[6], JONATHAN[5], NATHANIEL[4], JONATHAN[3], SAMUEL[2], THOMAS[1])* was born 14 Apr 1879 in Calais, ME, and died 24 Feb 1961 in Newton, MA. She married FRANK H BARCLAY 17 May 1913 in Calais Maine.

Child of CAROLYN SPINNEY and FRANK BARCLAY is:

908.   i.   DOROTHY ELAINE[8] BARCLAY, b. 1914.

547. EDWARD CHARLES[7] SPINNEY *(CHARLES EDWARD[6], JONATHAN[5], NATHANIEL[4], JONATHAN[3], SAMUEL[2], THOMAS[1])* was born Aug 1880 in Calais, ME, and died 16 Dec 1939 in Portland, ME. He married ANNIE MUSTARD 23 Jun 1906 in Calias, ME, daughter of ROBERT MUSTARD and JANE FURGERSON. She was born 03 Jan 1879 in Dundee, Scotland, and died 11 May 1931 in Portland, Me.

Children of EDWARD SPINNEY and ANNIE MUSTARD are:

           i.   BERT[8] SPINNEY, b. 09 Sep 1903, Calais, ME; d. 20 Jul 1924, Calais, ME.

909.   ii.   RUTH GOLDEN SPINNEY, b. 30 Nov 1906, Calais, ME; d. 23 Feb 1985, Calais, ME.

           iii.   ANNA SPINNEY, b. 1911, Calais, ME; d. 1911, Calais, ME.

548. LAURA DEXTER[7] GREEN *(MARY ANN[6] SPINNEY, JONATHAN[5], NATHANIEL[4], JONATHAN[3], SAMUEL[2], THOMAS[1])* was born 28 Dec 1866. She married BENJAMIN FRANK BARSTOW 1881 in Norton, MA.

Child of LAURA GREEN and BENJAMIN BARSTOW is:

910.   i.   ANNIE MAUDE[8] BARSTOW, b. 31 Mar 1882.

549. SARAH ELIZABETH[7] SPINNEY *(EBENEZER[6], JONATHAN[5], NATHANIEL[4], JONATHAN[3], SAMUEL[2], THOMAS[1])* was born 02 Jul 1854 in Calais, ME, and died Bet. 1910 - 1920 in Massachusetts. She married THOMAS HADDOCK 1880. He was born May 1851, and died Bet. 1910 - 1920 in Boston, MA.

Children of SARAH SPINNEY and THOMAS HADDOCK are:
  i.   HARRY[8] HADDOCK, b. Dec 1880.
  ii.   MARY HADDOCK, b. Feb 1882, Maine.
  iii. THOMAS E HADDOCK, b. Jan 1884, Maine; d. Aft. 1920; m. HELEN.
  iv.   FRED W HADDOCK, b. Nov 1885, Maine.
  v.   ROY HADDOCK, b. May 1888.
  vi.   LILLIAN HADDOCK, b. Dec 1889.
  vii. HAVEN HADDOCK, b. Feb 1892.
  viii. ANNE HADDOCK, b. May 1894, Maine.

550. WILLARD[7] SPINNEY *(EBENEZER[6], JONATHAN[5], NATHANIEL[4], JONATHAN[3], SAMUEL[2], THOMAS[1])* was born 1859, and died 22 May 1899 in Lowell, MA.

Children of WILLARD SPINNEY are:
  i.   OLIVER[8] SPINNEY, b. Abt. 1880; m. AUNT CAD.
  ii.   CARRIE SPINNEY.

551. ABBIE[7] SPINNEY *(ARCHIBALD BARNEY[6], JONATHAN[5], NATHANIEL[4], JONATHAN[3], SAMUEL[2], THOMAS[1])* was born 22 Apr 1859 in Calais, ME, and died 30 Dec 1917 in Oakland, Ca. She married (1) CHARLES HOLT. He died in Before 1900. She married (2) HENRY JACKSON WELLS DAM 1884 in California, son of ALPHONSO DAM and LUCY DECKER. He was born 27 Apr 1856 in San Francisco, California, USA, and died 26 Apr 1906 in Havana, Cuba.

Child of ABBIE SPINNEY and CHARLES HOLT is:
  i.   CHARLES HENRY[8] HOLT, b. 23 Jun 1885, Almeda, California; d. 12 Apr 1955, Santa Clara, California; m. MARGARET PRENTISS, 1919.

       Notes for CHARLES HENRY HOLT:
       CHARLES HENRY HOLT. Few men in San Francisco have had a greater experience or success in the handling of land subdivisions than Mr. C. H. Holt, a native son and regarded as a genius in everything concerned with getting the land to the people and the people to the land. His business operations cover an extensive territory around San Francisco. Mr. Holt was born at Alameda, California, June 23, 1885, son of Charles H. and Abbie (Spinney) Holt. He was only six months old when his father died. Charles H. Holt, Sr., was a newspaper man. He was of Scotch-English descent and of Revolutionary stock. His wife, Abbie Spinney, who also died when her son Charles was a small boy, was born in Maine of English descent. Charles H. Holt was reared by a foster father, Mr. Cleveland Darn, a pioneer of Alameda County, and one of the ablest and most forceful citizens of that community, greatly loved by all with whom he came in contact. To him Charles Henry Holt owes a lasting debt of gratitude and affection. Educated in the public schools of Oakland, graduating from high school in 1902, Charles H. Holt soon afterward entered the service of the Anglo-London Paris Bank. He was with that institution ten years, being exchange teller when he resigned in 1913. He gave up a banking career to engage in the real estate business, and he conducted his operations alone under the name of C. H. Holt Realty Company until February, 1922. At that date he formed a partnership with George L. Leonard, under the firm name of Leonard & Holt. Leonard & Holt is one of the two firms that operate on a large scale in the construction business as well as handling the land itself. In some of their enterprises they have had as high as a hundred houses under construction at one time. They subdivided and sold Ingleside Terraces in San Francisco, and at the present time buildings to the value of about $2,000,000 stand on this property. Their present program is the subdividing of property at Redwood City, Burlingame, Tamalpais Valley and the Cascades at Fairfax, all of these being large properties. Mr. Holt is a member of the San Francisco Realty Board, the Chamber of Commerce, the Down Town Association and the California Real Estate Association. His offices are at 39 Montgomery Street. Mr. Holt is a member of Mill Valley Lodge, Free and Accepted Masons, San Francisco Commandery of the Knights Templar and Islam Temple of the Mystic Shrine. He also belongs to San Rafael Lodge, Benevolent and Protective Order of Elks, the Crystal Spring Country Club, the Emerald Lake Country Club, and is a republican voter. In August, 1919, at Auburn, California, Mr. Holt married Miss Madge Prentiss. She was born in San Francisco, daughter of John Prentiss. She is a member of the Woman's Civic Club, is organist for her chapter of the Eastern Star, and attends the

Episcopal Church. Mr. and Mrs. Holt have three children, Cleveland Loring, Jean and Sally.

552. HERBERT HARRISON FICKETT[7] SPINNEY *(ARCHIBALD BARNEY[6], JONATHAN[5], NATHANIEL[4], JONATHAN[3], SAMUEL[2], THOMAS[1])* was born 15 Dec 1862 in Princeton, ME, and died 09 Nov 1943 in Washington, DC. He married BESSIE HELENE MITCHELL 20 May 1882 in Grand Lake Stream, ME.

Children of HERBERT SPINNEY and BESSIE MITCHELL are:
911.   i.   ERNEST LINWOOD[8] SPINNEY, b. 26 Nov 1884, Castle Hill, ME; d. 15 Mar 1938, Boston, Me.
       ii.   GERTRUDE FLINT SPINNEY, b. 13 Nov 1885, Princeton, ME; d. 08 Feb 1965; m. FRANK MCINTYRE.
      iii.   MYLES ARBO SPINNEY, b. 11 Aug 1888; d. 1965; m. JANE WILCOX.
      iv.   GRACE VERA SPINNEY, b. 21 Oct 1890, Princeton, ME; d. 13 Jun 1951.
       v.   ABBIE MAY SPINNEY, b. 03 May 1894, Princeton, ME; d. 1934; m. LOUIS BROWN.
      vi.   SARA SPINNEY, b. 1900; d. 08 Feb 1951; m. JACK ADAMS.
     vii.   ARCHIBALD SPINNEY, b. 28 Jan 1901, Mapleton, ME; d. 14 Aug 1983, Silver Springs, MD; m. IRENE MURL WALLS.

          Notes for IRENE MURL WALLS:
          SPINNEY, Irene M.
          On October 21, 2000, IRENE MURL SPINNEY (nee Walls), beloved wifeof the late Archie Spinney, dear aunt of Bernice Robinson and her husband Harry, loving great-aunt of Carole Robinson and Gail Goss. Friends may call at the Mitchell-Wiedefeld Funeral Home, Inc., 6500 York Road (at Overbrook) on Thursday from 9 to 10 A.M. at which time a Funeral Service will be held. Interment Dulaney Valley Memorial Gardens.

     viii.   HERBERT FICKETT SPINNEY, b. 07 Aug 1903, Presque Isle, ME.

553. BENJAMIN FRANK[7] SPINNEY *(ARCHIBALD BARNEY[6], JONATHAN[5], NATHANIEL[4], JONATHAN[3], SAMUEL[2], THOMAS[1])* was born 26 Mar 1863 in Princeton, ME, and died Apr 1939 in Bangor, ME. He married ANNIE L ELLSMORE 28 Feb 1880 in Grand Lakes Stream, ME. She was born 1867, and died 30 May 1933.

Children of BENJAMIN SPINNEY and ANNIE ELLSMORE are:
       i.   SARA JANE[8] SPINNEY, b. Oct 1880.
912.   ii.   FRANKLIN PIERCE SPINNEY, b. Sep 1884; d. Aft. 1930.
      iii.   BENJAMIN SPINNEY, b. Sep 1887.
      iv.   BEULAH SPINNEY, b. 1891; d. 1899, Calais, Maine.
       v.   CLARA L SPINNEY, b. 1894; d. 17 May 1895, Calais Maine.
      vi.   RALPH L SPINNEY, b. 02 Apr 1896; d. 09 Aug 1897.
     vii.   IDA G SPINNEY, b. 13 Apr 1901, Eastport, ME; m. ROBERT DURANT.
    viii.   AUGUSTA G SPINNEY, m. CHARLES PADGETT, 10 Oct 1936, Bangor, Me.

554. EDWARD P[7] SPINNEY *(JOHN[6], JONATHAN[5], NATHANIEL[4], JONATHAN[3], SAMUEL[2], THOMAS[1])* was born Sep 1884, and died Aft. 1930. He married AGNES ELIZABETH FARRELL 11 Nov 1903 in Tewksbury, MA, daughter of PATRICK FARRELL and MARGARET FINN. She was born 19 May 1885.

Notes for AGNES ELIZABETH FARRELL:
OBIT: DAILY EVENING ITEM
Mrs. Agnes E. (FARRELL) MILLER, 93, fomerly of 330 Essex St., died Monday in a local nursing home after a lengthy illness. She was the widow of John
MILLER.
A native of Lynn, she was the daughter of the late Patrick J. and
Margaret (FINN) FARRELL and graduated from St. Mary's schools.
She was employed for many years by the former Daley Golden Shoe Co. until
her retirement.
She was a member of Our Lady's Sodality of St. Joseph's Church.
Mrs. MILLER leaves a sister, Mrs. Ellen CONNORS of Lynn and several nieces
and nephews including Joseph CONNORS, David LOMASNEY, Edward LOMASNEY, Mrs.
Doris KANE and Mrs. Mary HERSEY all of Lynn.
She was also the aunt of the late Margaret McELROY of Lynn.
The funeral will be held Thursday at 8 a.m. from the Cuffe-McGinn Funeral

Home, 157 Maple St., followed by a Mass at 9 at St. Pius V Church and burial in St. Mary's Cemetery

Child of EDWARD SPINNEY and AGNES FARRELL is:
913.   i.   MABEL[8] SPINNEY, b. 24 Feb 1904, Lynn, MA.

555. JOHN E[7] CHASE *(JOHN[6], LOUISA[5] SPINNEY, NATHANIEL[4], JONATHAN[3], SAMUEL[2], THOMAS[1])* was born 1837 in Portsmouth, NH, and died 25 Oct 1886 in Brooklyn, NY. He married (1) PHEBE J HEWLETT, daughter of JACOB HEWLETT and ELIZABETH JONES. He married (2) HELEN STEWART 17 Sep 1873, daughter of CHARLES P STEWART.

Children of JOHN CHASE and HELEN STEWART are:
          i.   CAROLINE[8] CHASE, b. 17 Jul 1875.
          ii.   JOHN CHASE, b. 27 Mar 1878.

556. ALBERT P[7] CHASE *(JOHN[6], LOUISA[5] SPINNEY, NATHANIEL[4], JONATHAN[3], SAMUEL[2], THOMAS[1])* was born 13 Jul 1839, and died 25 Feb 1907 in Portsmouth, NH. He married GERTIE. She was born 1854.

Child of ALBERT CHASE and GERTIE is:
          i.   LOUISA[8] CHASE, b. 1876.

557. WILLIAM L[7] SPINNEY *(EBENEZER[6], EBENEZER[5], NATHANIEL[4], JONATHAN[3], SAMUEL[2], THOMAS[1])* was born 03 Oct 1835 in St George, NB., and died Aft. 1870. He married SARAH LEE 03 Jun 1865 in Eastport Maine. She was born 1837, and died Aft. 1870.

Notes for WILLIAM L SPINNEY:
LEE, SPINNEY; Sarah LEE; Marriages: In Eastport, 3 Jun 1865, by J.E.C. Sawyer, William L. SPINNEY of St. George to Sarah LEE of Eastport. Vital Records from the Eastport Sentinal of Eastport, Maine 1818-1900.

Children of WILLIAM SPINNEY and SARAH LEE are:
914.   i.   CLARA E[8] SPINNEY, b. 21 Jan 1867, Onarga, IL; d. 04 Apr 1930.
          ii.   MARY A SPINNEY, b. 20 Apr 1869; d. 27 Aug 1881.
915.   iii. EBENEZER SPINNEY, b. 20 Sep 1871, Onarga, IL; d. 17 Oct 1939, Lansing, MI.
          iv.   LUCY A SPINNEY, b. 23 Aug 1872; d. 10 Oct 1943; m. STEPHEN SAPPINGTON, 23 Jan 1889, Vermilion, IL.
          v.   WILLIAM JOHN SPINNEY, b. 27 Aug 1876.
          vi.   SAMUEL H SPINNEY, b. 06 Dec 1878.
          vii. DAVID J SPINNEY, b. 10 Aug 1880, Illinois; d. 26 Dec 1881.
          viii. MYRTLE M SPINNEY, b. 22 Feb 1882.

558. ARTHUR JONES[7] SPINNEY *(OLIVER W[6], EBENEZER[5], NATHANIEL[4], JONATHAN[3], SAMUEL[2], THOMAS[1])* was born 1839 in New Brunswick, and died Aft. 1880. He married MARY G. She was born 1841 in England, and died Aft. 1880.

Children of ARTHUR SPINNEY and MARY G are:
          i.   EUDAH[8] SPINNEY, b. 1868.
          ii.   MARY E SPINNEY, b. 1870.
          iii. GRACE J SPINNEY, b. 1876.
          iv.   CHARLES A SPINNEY, b. 1879.

559. CHARLES M[7] SPINNEY *(OLIVER W[6], EBENEZER[5], NATHANIEL[4], JONATHAN[3], SAMUEL[2], THOMAS[1])* was born 1848 in Calais, ME, and died Aft. 1900 in Bancroft Me. He married ELIZABETH J THOMPSON 14 Jul 1868 in Calais, Me. She was born in Calias, ME.

Children of CHARLES SPINNEY and ELIZABETH THOMPSON are:
          i.   WILLIAM D[8] SPINNEY, b. 1869.
          ii.   HANNAH E SPINNEY, b. 1871; d. Aft. 1880.
          iii. HERBERT M SPINNEY, b. Nov 1874; d. Aft. 1900.

    iv.   ROBERT W SPINNEY, b. Aug 1876; d. Aft. 1900.
    v.   CHARLES F SPINNEY, b. 1878.
    vi.   MAGGIE MAY SPINNEY, b. May 1879; d. Aft. 1900.
    vii.   CARRIE SPINNEY, b. Feb 1882; d. Aft. 1900.
    viii.   HOWARD SPINNEY, b. Feb 1882; d. Aft. 1900.

560. GEORGE H[7] SPINNEY *(OLIVER W[6], EBENEZER[5], NATHANIEL[4], JONATHAN[3], SAMUEL[2], THOMAS[1])* was born 23 Dec 1852, and died 1913 in Nova Scotia. He married DEBORAH G O'BRIEN, daughter of SARAH. She was born 1861 in Calais, ME, and died 09 Sep 1914 in Baring, ME.

Notes for GEORGE H SPINNEY:
lived in St Stephen in 1881

Child of GEORGE SPINNEY and DEBORAH O'BRIEN is:
    i.   MILLIE E[8] SPINNEY, b. 1880.

561. EMILY E[7] SPINNEY *(OLIVER W[6], EBENEZER[5], NATHANIEL[4], JONATHAN[3], SAMUEL[2], THOMAS[1])* was born 1859. She married CHARLES E NODDIN Sep 1873 in Calais, ME. He was born 1848.

Children of EMILY SPINNEY and CHARLES NODDIN are:
    i.   CHARLES FURNAL[8] NODDIN, b. 1886; m. LAVANIA HASTY.
    ii.   CHESTER ERNEST NODDIN, b. 1890.
    iii.   GEORGE NODDIN, b. 1885.

562. WILLIAM L[7] SPINNEY *(NATHANIEL[6], EBENEZER[5], NATHANIEL[4], JONATHAN[3], SAMUEL[2], THOMAS[1])* was born 15 Nov 1846 in Calais, ME, and died 29 Jun 1904 in Eastport, ME. He married HELEN AUGUSTA GRAY 02 Sep 1867 in Grand Manan, ME, daughter of BENJAMIN GRAY and MARY LOVEJOY. She was born Jun 1849 in Eastport, ME, and died Aft. 1900 in Eastport, ME.

Children of WILLIAM SPINNEY and HELEN GRAY are:
916.	i.	MILLAGE[8] SPINNEY, b. Abt. 1870; d. Bef. 1871.
917.	ii.	ADDIE ESTELLA SPINNEY, b. Mar 1871; d. Aft. 1900.
	iii.	MARGARET SPINNEY, b. 02 Feb 1871; d. Aft. 1880.
	iv.	LYDIA SPINNEY, b. 1873; d. Aft. 1880.
918.	v.	JOHN W SPINNEY, b. Jun 1875, New Brunswick, Canada; d. Aft. 1930, Eastport, Me.
	vi.	WILLIAM SPINNEY, b. 1877; d. Aft. 1880.
919.	vii.	ALVAH C SPINNEY, b. Jul 1878; d. 28 Jul 1906, Eastport, Me.
	viii.	FLORENCE SPINNEY, b. Aug 1882; d. Aft. 1900.
	ix.	FRED SPINNEY, b. Oct 1884; d. Aft. 1900.
	x.	CORA B SPINNEY, b. Jun 1890; d. 07 Dec 1906.
920.	xi.	ALFRED WINFIELD SPINNEY, b. 30 Oct 1893, Canada; d. 18 Jan 1959, Costra Conta, CA.

563. LYDIA "ANNIE"[7] SPINNEY *(NATHANIEL[6], EBENEZER[5], NATHANIEL[4], JONATHAN[3], SAMUEL[2], THOMAS[1])* was born 1854, and died 22 Jan 1936. She married CHARLES HARKINS. He was born 1845, and died 13 Aug 1930.

Children of LYDIA SPINNEY and CHARLES HARKINS are:
	i.	CHARLES[8] HARKINS, b. 1879.
921.	ii.	WILLIAM JAMES HARKINS, b. 20 Jan 1882.
	iii.	ANNIE HARKINS, b. 25 Apr 1887.
	iv.	JOHN BURTON HARKINS, b. 03 May 1890.
	v.	DANIEL HARKINS.
	vi.	JAMES HARKINS.

564. MARGARET JANE[7] SPINNEY *(NATHANIEL[6], EBENEZER[5], NATHANIEL[4], JONATHAN[3], SAMUEL[2], THOMAS[1])* was born Apr 1857, and died Aft. 1900. She married JAMES WENTHORTHY QUIGLEY 1877, son of WILLIAM QUIGLEY and EMILY KENNEY. He was born Oct 1854.

Children of MARGARET SPINNEY and JAMES QUIGLEY are:

922.   i.   JAMES[8] QUIGLEY, b. 1879; d. Aft. 1930.
        ii.   DAVID QUIGLEY, b. 1880.
        iii.   ELSON QUIGLEY, b. Jun 1887; d. Aft. 1900.
        iv.   ARTHUR QUIGLEY, b. 25 Dec 1891; d. Aft. 1900.
        v.   CHILD QUIGLEY.
        vi.   CHILD QUIGLEY.
        vii.   CHILD QUIGLEY.

565. MARTHA JANE[7] SPINNEY *(NATHANIEL[6], EBENEZER[5], NATHANIEL[4], JONATHAN[3], SAMUEL[2], THOMAS[1])* was born 25 Feb 1865 in Eastport, ME, and died 23 Jul 1948 in St George, NB.. She married JOHN HENRY BROWN 23 Jul 1880 in St George, NB.. He was born 01 Apr 1852, and died 1942.

Children of MARTHA SPINNEY and JOHN BROWN are:
    i.   GEORGE EDWARD[8] BROWN, b. 31 May 1882, St George. N.B.; d. 01 May 1952, St George. N.B.; m. JENNIE BEATRICE MCGEE, 25 Sep 1906, St George, N.B..
    ii.   ARTHUR GUY BROWN, b. 19 Mar 1887, Lancaster, NH; d. 22 Aug 1915; m. JENNIE MCGEE, 02 Sep 1908.
    iii.   HARRY WATSON BROWN, b. 16 Apr 1889.
    iv.   ANNIE LOUISA BROWN, b. 25 Jun 1890.
    v.   LAURA ISABEL BROWN, b. 27 Feb 1893.
    vi.   JAMES ARNOLD BROWN, b. 15 Mar 1895.
    vii.   ISABELA BROWN, b. 28 Jan 1897.
    viii.   MAGGIE BROWN, b. 28 Jan 1897.
    ix.   EDNA ESTEAAL BROWN, b. 11 Apr 1898.
    x.   HERBERT CLARENCE BROWN, b. 30 Jul 1899.

566. WILLIAM[7] SPINNEY *(JAMES PARKER[6], EBENEZER[5], NATHANIEL[4], JONATHAN[3], SAMUEL[2], THOMAS[1])* was born 1839, and died Aft. 1900. He married SARAH A. She was born 1840, and died Bef. 1900.

Children of WILLIAM SPINNEY and SARAH A are:
    i.   CHARLES S[8] SPINNEY, b. May 1861.
    ii.   CARRIE SPINNEY, b. Jul 1870.

567. MARTHA A[7] SPINNEY *(JAMES PARKER[6], EBENEZER[5], NATHANIEL[4], JONATHAN[3], SAMUEL[2], THOMAS[1])* was born 1843 in St Andrews, NB., and died Aft. 1880. She married CHARLES BULLOCK. He was born 1840 in St George, NB., and died Aft. 1880.

Children of MARTHA SPINNEY and CHARLES BULLOCK are:
    i.   ANN[8] BULLOCK, b. 1864.
    ii.   EDWARD BULLOCK, b. 1866.
    iii.   ISAAC BULLOCK, b. 14 Feb 1868, St Stephens, NB.; d. 22 Nov 1936, Wales, ME.
    iv.   JAMES BULLOCK, b. 1871.
    v.   ANNEI BULLOCK, b. 1880.

568. SUSAN[7] SPINNEY *(JAMES PARKER[6], EBENEZER[5], NATHANIEL[4], JONATHAN[3], SAMUEL[2], THOMAS[1])* was born 1854. She married ELDERADO G LEE 14 Mar 1873 in Eastport Maine, son of RICHARD LEE and MARGARET. He was born 1849 in New Brunswick.

Child of SUSAN SPINNEY and ELDERADO LEE is:
    i.   JAMES PARKER[8] LEE, b. 1874; m. FLORENCE JOHNSON.

569. MARY E[7] SPINNEY *(JAMES PARKER[6], EBENEZER[5], NATHANIEL[4], JONATHAN[3], SAMUEL[2], THOMAS[1])* was born 1857, and died 1935. She married GEORGE S MORRISON. He was born 1857.

Children of MARY SPINNEY and GEORGE MORRISON are:
    i.   ARTHUR LEO[8] MORRISON, b. 1882.
    ii.   SYLVANUS MORRISON, b. 1888; m. STELLA BROCHER.

570. SARAH[7] SPINNEY *(ARTHUR JONES[6], EBENEZER[5], NATHANIEL[4], JONATHAN[3], SAMUEL[2], THOMAS[1])* was born 22 Oct 1842 in St George, NB., and died 07 Aug 1933 in Wenatchee, WA. She married WILLIAM MILLS 11 Dec 1862 in Summer, IL, son of THOMAS MILLS and CAROLINE HEWITT. He was born 18 May 1834 in New Castle, Ontario, and died 02 Mar 1910 in Wenatchee, WA.

Children of SARAH SPINNEY and WILLIAM MILLS are:

923.	i.	ARTHUR JONES[8] MILLS, b. 04 Jan 1864, Summer, IL; d. 26 Oct 1931, Cashmere, WA.
924.	ii.	CAROLINE LEVINA MILLS, b. 14 Apr 1865, Crediton, Ontario Canada; d. 22 Jan 1947, Spokane, WA.
925.	iii.	SUSANNA JANE "JEN" MILLS, b. 22 Feb 1867; d. 14 Dec 1940, Wenatchee Washington.
926.	iv.	ANGELINE ELIZABETH MILLS, b. 19 Mar 1869, Goodland Indiana; d. 29 Apr 1925, Alberta Canada.
927.	v.	WILLIAM HENRY MILLS, b. 06 May 1871, Goodland, IN; d. 05 Dec 1926, Los Angeles, CA.

571. SUSANNA[7] SPINNEY *(ARTHUR JONES[6], EBENEZER[5], NATHANIEL[4], JONATHAN[3], SAMUEL[2], THOMAS[1])* was born 07 Oct 1853 in St Stephens, NB., and died 08 Oct 1893 in Goodland, IN. She married JOSEPH W CONES 02 Apr 1872 in Goodland, IN. He was born 1848, and died Aft. 1900.

Children of SUSANNA SPINNEY and JOSEPH CONES are:

928.	i.	JENNIE OPAL[8] CONES, b. 1873.
	ii.	LENA CONES, m. JOSEPH TREFNY.
	iii.	ARTHUR J CONES, b. 22 Aug 1874; m. IDA FIESET.

> Notes for ARTHUR J CONES:
> Name: Arthur Joseph Cones
> Sex: M
> Birth: AUG 1874 in Illinois 1
> Death: 6 DEC 1908 in St. Paul, Ramsey County, Minnesota 2 3 of Typhoid Fever 3
> Burial: 12 DEC 1908 Chicago, Cook County, Indiana
> Event: Grave Photographed 25 SEP 2004 I.O.O.F. Cemetery, Rochester, Fulton County, Indiana 4
> Residence: 13 JUN 1900 Minneapolis, Hennepin County, Minnesota 1
> Event: Burial # 3 20 NOV 1912 Removed from Mausoleum and burried in same lot behind Mausoleum. Mausoleum Sealed due to frequent breakins
> Event: Burial # 2 I.O.O.F. Cemetery, Rochester, Fulton County, Indiana (Section 9)
> Reference Number: 16415
> Note:
> Minnesota Land Records
> Ancestry.com
>
> Name: ARTHUR J CONES (Bureau of Land Management Record reveals middle name Joseph)
> Land Office: CROOKSTON
>
> Document Number: 2177
> Total Acres: 160
> Signature: Yes
> Canceled Document: No
> Issue Date: February 05, 1906
> Mineral Rights Reserved: No
> Metes and Bounds: No
> Statutory Reference: 3 Stat. 566
> Multiple Warantee Names: No
> Act or Treaty: April 24, 1820
> Multiple Patentee Names: No
> Entry Classification: Sale Cash Entries
> Land Description: 1 SE 5TH PM No 161 N 35 W 16
>
> Source Information:
> United States. Bureau of Land Management. Minnesota Land Records. [database on line] Provo, UT: Ancestry.com, 1997 . Original electronic data from: United States. Bureau of Land Management. Minnesota Pre 1908 Homestead and Cash Entry Patents, General Land Office Automated Records Project, 1995.
>
> ---
>
> 1900 Census
> Minneapolis, Hennepin County, Minnesota
> Sheet 18 A
> Ennumeration District 60

June 13 & 14, 1900

1610 Adams St
Dwelling 395, Family 428

Cones, Arthur J, August 1874, 25 Years, Boarder, Married 2 Years,
born Illinois, Father born Indiana, Mother born Maine, occupation Traveller
Ida V, Jan 1877, 23 Years, Boarder, Married 2 Years, Mother of 0 children, Born Indiana, Father born
Canada, Mother born Indiana

_____

Saturday, Dec 12, 1908
Rochester Sentinel
Fulton County, Indiana
A. J. Cones

Rochester relatives and friends received the news Sunday that A. J. Cones, of Warroads, Minnesota, died
Sunday morning of Typhoid Fever in a hospital at St. Paul.

Mr. Cones, who conducted a general store at Warroads, wason his way to Chicago to purchase goods, when
he took ill of typhoid fever and was removed to a hospital in St. Paul. he grew repidly worse and Sunday
morning about 5 o'clock passed away.

Mr. Cones was well known here, having married Miss Ida Fieser, of this city, who with a young son, survive
to mourn their loss.

Burial was made in Chicago today. Mrs. J.B. Fieser and son, Ed (Fieser) of this city, went to that city, Sunday
evening to attend the funera

_____

Monday, May 10, 1909
Rochester Sentinel
Fulton County, Indiana

Mrs. A. Cones, of this city, is having a fine mausleum of Bedford stone built in the Odd Fellows cemetery.
When completed the body of her late husand Arthur Cones will be brought to this city from Chicago.

_____

Monday, October 4, 1909
Rochester Evening Sentinel
Fulton County, Indiana

The remains of Arthur Joseph Cones, who died December 13, 1908, in St. Paul, Minn., were brought here
Saturday afternoon an laid away in the private mausoleum prepared for same. The body was accompanied by
his wife and little son and father and mother.

_____

I.O.O.F. Cemetery Records
Rochester, Fulton County, Indiana

Death July 13, 1908 St. Paul Minnesota
Body Returned to Rochester on Saturday .... accompanied by Widow, Son and Deceased's Mother.
Original Burial in Small Private Mausoleum
Due to frequent breakin's at Mausoleum, Body was reburied in the ground at north end of his lot November
20, 1912 and Mausoleum sealed

Suggested Next Step:
Search OneWorldTree for:
Cones, Arthur Joseph

Included with this search:

View multiple generations
Change tree views to get the look you want
View supporting source, i.e., census images
View alternate information
Anonymously contact submitters of tree data

Marriage 1 Ida Viola Fieser b: JAN 1877 in Rochester, Indiana, Fulton County
Married: 28 FEB 1898 in Chicago, Cook County, Illinois 5
Children
 Arthur Cones b: ABT 1902 in Minnesota

Sources:
Title: 1900 United States Federal Census
Repository:
Note: www.ancestry.com
Call Number:
Media: Ancestry.com
Title: cemetery Records
Repository:
Call Number:
Media: Book
Text: I.O.O.F. Cemetery, Rochester Fulton County, Indiana
Title: Obituary
Repository:
Call Number:
Media: Newspaper
Text: Saturday, Dec 12, 1908
Rochester Sentinel
Fulton County, Indiana
A. J. Cones
Title: Roberta Wunder email roberta@robertawunder.com
Note: Contact me for copies of Photographs and Documents referred to in this database
Repository:
Call Number:
Media: Book
Title: IGI Ancestral File www.familysearch.org
Repository:
Call Number:
Media: Book

----

    iv.   CHARLES W CONES, b. 1876; d. Aft. 1900.
     v.   CHILD CONES.
    vi.   CHILD CONES.

572. ARTHUR JONES[7] SPINNEY *(ARTHUR JONES[6], EBENEZER[5], NATHANIEL[4], JONATHAN[3], SAMUEL[2], THOMAS[1])* was born 30 Jul 1861 in Summer, IL, and died 1932 in Goodland, IN. He married ALICE MAUD TEDFORD 21 Jun 1893 in Newton County, In. She was born 1873, and died 27 Dec 1934 in Goodland, In.

Children of ARTHUR SPINNEY and ALICE TEDFORD are:
     i.   RUTH I[8] SPINNEY, b. 1894; m. HARVEY G DICKSON, 02 Sep 1915, Newton County Indiana.
    ii.   LOUISE SPINNEY, b. 1896.
   iii.   CHARLEY SPINNEY, b. Abt. 1900.

573. AURELIA ISABELLE[7] SPINNEY *(ARTHUR JONES[6], EBENEZER[5], NATHANIEL[4], JONATHAN[3], SAMUEL[2], THOMAS[1])* was born 04 Dec 1864 in Grant Park, Il, and died 20 Mar 1942 in Fort Wayne, IN. She married WILLIAM BANES

13 Nov 1879 in Goodland, IN, son of WILLIAM BANES and BETSY MILLS. He was born 27 Jun 1853 in Ontario, Canada, and died 20 Dec 1926.

Children of AURELIA SPINNEY and WILLIAM BANES are:
929.　　i.　MYRTLE ISABELLE[8] BANES, b. 20 Jan 1881, Goodland, IN; d. Jul 1942, Knox, IN.
930.　　ii.　REXFORD BANES, b. 1883, Goodland, IN.
931.　　iii.　LELA BANES, b. 1885, Goodland, IN.
932.　　iv.　BETHEL BANES, b. 1887, Goodland, IN.

574. CHARLES WILLIAM[7] SPINNEY *(ARTHUR JONES[6], EBENEZER[5], NATHANIEL[4], JONATHAN[3], SAMUEL[2], THOMAS[1])* was born 01 Oct 1867 in Summer, IL, and died 1907. He married DORA M GREEN 12 Feb 1890 in Goodland, IN. She was born 1871, and died 1957.

Children of CHARLES SPINNEY and DORA GREEN are:
　　i.　VERA[8] SPINNEY, b. May 1891; m. HARLAN HOWARD.
　　ii.　HELEN L SPINNEY, b. 1901; d. 1919.

575. LOUISA JONES[7] SPINNEY *(SIMON F[6], EBENEZER[5], NATHANIEL[4], JONATHAN[3], SAMUEL[2], THOMAS[1])* was born 29 Aug 1848 in St George, NB., and died 15 Jun 1931 in St George NB.. She married SAMUEL HAMILTON 1872, son of JAMES HAMILTON and CATHERINE. He was born 11 Aug 1842 in St George, NB., and died 05 Mar 1934.

Children of LOUISA SPINNEY and SAMUEL HAMILTON are:
　　i.　JAMES WESLEY[8] HAMILTON, b. 12 Aug 1873, St George, NB..
　　ii.　ALBERT FULTON HAMILTON, b. 07 Jun 1875, St George, NB..
　　iii.　SAMUEL BURTON HAMILTON, b. 05 Jul 1877, St George, NB..
　　iv.　ISAAC EDWARD HAMILTON, b. 07 Dec 1879, St George, NB..
　　v.　EDITH MYRTLE HAMILTON, b. 29 Nov 1881, St George, NB..
　　vi.　UPTON JOHN HAMILTON, b. 05 Mar 1884, St George, NB..
　　vii.　GEORGE PRESTON HAMILTON, b. 16 Jan 1887, Topsfield, ME.
　　viii.　LENA PRUDENCE HAMILTON, b. 06 Apr 1893, Topsfield, ME.

576. ISAAC HOPKINS[7] SPINNEY *(SIMON F[6], EBENEZER[5], NATHANIEL[4], JONATHAN[3], SAMUEL[2], THOMAS[1])* was born 1856, and died Aft. 1891. He married ELIZABETH GRAY. She was born 1857, and died Aft. 1891.

Children of ISAAC SPINNEY and ELIZABETH GRAY are:
　　i.　GEORGE E[8] SPINNEY, b. 1886.
　　ii.　ELMER SPINNEY, b. 1889.
　　iii.　EVA SPINNEY.
　　iv.　WILLIE P SPINNEY, b. 1888; d. 04 Nov 1888.
　　v.　LAURA SPINNEY, b. Abt. 1890.
　　vi.　EARL WINFIELD SPINNEY, b. 24 Feb 1891, St George, NB..
　　vii.　ANNIE PRUDENCE SPINNEY, b. 26 Aug 1896.
　　viii.　FRANK KITCHENER SPINNEY, b. 06 Sep 1898, St George, NB.; d. 04 Sep 1952; m. THELMA GOODEILL, 15 Nov 1921.

577. SAMUEL JAMES[7] SPINNEY *(SIMON F[6], EBENEZER[5], NATHANIEL[4], JONATHAN[3], SAMUEL[2], THOMAS[1])* was born 1869 in St George, NB., and died 1905. He married ANNIE PERRY 10 Dec 1901 in St George, NB.. She was born Abt. 1880 in Beaver Harbour, NB..

Children of SAMUEL SPINNEY and ANNIE PERRY are:
　　i.　GUY E[8] SPINNEY, b. Dec 1902, St George, NB.; d. 24 Apr 1903, St George, NB..
　　ii.　ISAAC HENRY SPINNEY, b. 04 Mar 1904, New Brunswick; d. Oct 1977, Waltham, MA.
　　iii.　ANNIE EULALIA SPINNEY, b. 13 May 1905.

578. ABRAHAM[7] SPINNEY *(JOSEPH[6], ABRAHAM[5], JOSEPH[4], SAMUEL[3], SAMUEL[2], THOMAS[1])* was born 19 Jan 1847, and died 1919 in Greenwood Nova Scotia. He married SOPHIA LEONARD. She was born 02 Nov 1855.

Children of ABRAHAM SPINNEY and SOPHIA LEONARD are:

        i.   LUCY[8] SPINNEY, b. 1872.
933.   ii.   INEZ LINWOOD SPINNEY, b. 1873; d. 1955.
       iii. GRACIE SPINNEY, b. 14 Feb 1880.
       iv. PEARL SPINNEY, b. 02 Mar 1990.

579. OWEN[7] SPINNEY *(JOSEPH[6], ABRAHAM[5], JOSEPH[4], SAMUEL[3], SAMUEL[2], THOMAS[1])* was born 08 Jan 1850, and died 03 Jun 1933. He married LALIA BERTHA SNELL. She was born 06 Oct 1849.

Child of OWEN SPINNEY and LALIA SNELL is:
934.   i.   GEORGE LAMERT[8] SPINNEY, b. 02 Apr 1881.

580. ALEPH[7] WOODBURY *(ELIZABETH[6] SPINNEY, ABRAHAM[5], JOSEPH[4], SAMUEL[3], SAMUEL[2], THOMAS[1])* was born 11 Jun 1855 in Kingston, NS., and died 22 Jan 1938 in Lexington, MA. She married CHARLES FRANKLIN FRIEND BERTWELL 21 May 1879 in West Somerville, MA. He was born 07 Oct 1855 in Bedford, MA, and died 14 Nov 1930 in Lexington, MA.

Children of ALEPH WOODBURY and CHARLES BERTWELL are:
       i.   CHARLES FAIRFIELD[8] BERTWELL, b. 28 Feb 1880, Somerville, MA; d. 09 Oct 1881, Somerville, MA.
       ii.   WILLIAM EDWARD BERTWELL, b. 10 Aug 1881, Somerville, MA; d. 28 Aug 1881, Somerville, MA.
       iii. ALEPH WOODBURY BERTWELL, b. 24 Oct 1885, Somerville, MA; d. 20 Jun 1965, Bedford, MA; m. HALLETT R. ROBBINS, 23 Aug 1913; d. Tuscon, AZ.
935.   iv. CORA MAUDE BERTWELL, b. 10 Oct 1888, Somerville, MA; d. 07 Feb 1916, Utica, NY.

581. EDITH[7] SAUNDERS *(SAMUEL[6], EUNICE[5] SPINNEY, SAMUEL MCCLURE[4], SAMUEL[3], SAMUEL[2], THOMAS[1])* She married CHARLES ARCHIBALD BANKS, son of JOHN BANKS and CYRENA SPINNEY. He was born 26 Jul 1851 in Nova Scotia, Canada, and died 1919.

Children are listed above under (247) Charles Archibald Banks.

582. HARTLEY SPINNEY[7] JACQUES *(AMANDA[6] SPINNEY, BENIAH HOWE[5], JOSEPH[4], SAMUEL[3], SAMUEL[2], THOMAS[1])* was born 1860, and died 1912 in Annapolis Nova Scotia. He married MARGARET LOCKE 24 Feb 1897 in Halifax, N.S.

Children of HARTLEY JACQUES and MARGARET LOCKE are:
       i.   ABAGAL AMANDA[8] JACQUES, m. FRED LANE.

           Notes for ABAGAL AMANDA JACQUES:
           The Abbie Lane Hospital, in Halfax, Halifax County, Nova Scotia, was named in her honour.

       ii.   STELLA MARGARET JACQUES, b. 1901; d. 1903.

583. COLIN LOCKE[7] JACQUES *(AMANDA[6] SPINNEY, BENIAH HOWE[5], JOSEPH[4], SAMUEL[3], SAMUEL[2], THOMAS[1])* was born 1864, and died 1894. He married JERUSHA S MIDDLEMAS.

Children of COLIN JACQUES and JERUSHA MIDDLEMAS are:
       i.   EDWIN MILLS[8] JACQUES.
       ii.   CHARLES MIDDLEMAS JACQUES.

584. FRED[7] SPINNEY *(NORMAN B[6], BENIAH HOWE[5], JOSEPH[4], SAMUEL[3], SAMUEL[2], THOMAS[1])* was born 15 Dec 1873. He married ANNIE.

Child of FRED SPINNEY and ANNIE is:
       i.   NORMAN E[8] SPINNEY, b. 1900.

585. ELMORE W[7] SPINNEY *(WILLIAM J[6], JAMES B[5], JOSEPH[4], SAMUEL[3], SAMUEL[2], THOMAS[1])* was born 1877, and died 1963 in Toorbrook Nova Scotia.

Child of ELMORE W SPINNEY is:
    i.   AGNES[8] SPINNEY, b. 1914; d. 1944.

586. JAMES BERT[7] SPINNEY *(JOSEPH W[6], JAMES B[5], JOSEPH[4], SAMUEL[3], SAMUEL[2], THOMAS[1])* was born 1872, and died Aft. 1900. He married (1) MARYANN BENNETT 1895 in Fitchburg, MA, daughter of JOHN BENNETT. She was born 1874 in England, and died in 1898. He married (2) FLORA AMANDA GALBRAITH 1901 in Leominster, Ma.

Child of JAMES SPINNEY and MARYANN BENNETT is:
    i.   RONALD T[8] SPINNEY, b. 25 Dec 1896.

587. LIZZIE LUTICIA[7] SPINNEY *(JOSEPH W[6], JAMES B[5], JOSEPH[4], SAMUEL[3], SAMUEL[2], THOMAS[1])* was born 1879, and died Aft. 1910. She married JOHN WILLIAM DAWSON 1897 in Fitchburg, MA. He was born 1867.

Child of LIZZIE SPINNEY and JOHN DAWSON is:
    i.   ADA MARY[8] DAWSON, b. 1898.

588. DEXTER L[7] SPINNEY *(ISAAC B[6], JAMES B[5], JOSEPH[4], SAMUEL[3], SAMUEL[2], THOMAS[1])* was born 24 May 1876 in Nova Scotia, and died Aft. 1910. He married MARGARET FRAZIER.

Child of DEXTER SPINNEY and MARGARET FRAZIER is:
    i.   MARION[8] SPINNEY.

589. FLORA V[7] SPINNEY *(ISAAC B[6], JAMES B[5], JOSEPH[4], SAMUEL[3], SAMUEL[2], THOMAS[1])* was born Feb 1881, and died 09 May 1901 in Lowell, MA.

Child of FLORA V SPINNEY is:
    i.   EDNA[8] SPINNEY, b. 1901, Stoughton, Ma; d. 10 Dec 1900, Lowell, MA.

590. GAYLON M[7] SPINNEY *(ISAAC B[6], JAMES B[5], JOSEPH[4], SAMUEL[3], SAMUEL[2], THOMAS[1])* was born 1886, and died Aft. 1900. He married MATILDA B WHALEN. She was born 1888.

Children of GAYLON SPINNEY and MATILDA WHALEN are:
    i.   ELLEN[8] SPINNEY.
    ii. FORREST R SPINNEY.
    iii. HERBERT B SPINNEY.
    iv. AGNES SPINNEY, b. 1905; d. 14 May 1906, Lowell, MA.
    v.   GAYLON N SPINNEY, b. 18 Dec 1909; d. 08 Nov 1974.
    vi. ARTHUR MILLEDGE SPINNEY, b. 24 Dec 1921, Massachusetts; d. 13 Aug 2004, Tampa, Fl; m. DORIS MELANSON.

        Notes for ARTHUR MILLEDGE SPINNEY:
        Arthur Spinney

        Arthur Milledge Anthony Spinney, 82, formerly of Annapolis, died Aug. 13 at his home in Tampa, Fla., after a long struggle with Alzheimer's disease.

        He had spent a wonderful day with his daughter, Denise Anderson, and her family who cared for him during his illness, his family said.

        Born Dec. 24, 1921, he grew up near the Upham's Corner section of Dorchester in Boston, Mass. He was the last survivor and the youngest of three brothers and one sister.

        After graduating from the Boston Latin School in 1936, he apprenticed as a boilermaker at the Chelsea, Mass., Navy Yard. He joined the Army in 1941 and served in the South Pacific during World War II, earning the Bronze Star medal at Guadalcanal.

In 1945, Mr. Spinney returned to Boston and married Doris Melanson.

Fifteen years and four children later, the family moved to Annapolis, where he headed the maintenance department at the Naval Academy and had two more children.

He concluded his career in the federal service as director of maintenance at the Subic Bay Naval Base in the Philippines, and retired to Tampa.

He began his second government career as director of maintenance for the Pinellas County School Board in Florida, retiring after 10 years.

He was an avid golfer and was active in the Veterans of Foreign Wars.

Mrs. Spinney died in 1997. Mr. Spinney is survived by his six children and seven grandchildren.

Private services are planned. Condolences may be mailed to the Spinney Family, 14327 Diplomat Drive, Tampa, FL 33613. In lieu of flowers, contributions may be made to USF Suncoast Gerontology Center, 12901 Bruce B. Downs Blvd., MDC 50, Tampa, FL 33612-4799.

591. FORREST R[7] SPINNEY *(ISAAC B[6], JAMES B[5], JOSEPH[4], SAMUEL[3], SAMUEL[2], THOMAS[1])* was born 28 May 1889, and died Apr 1965 in Houston, Harris, TX. He married EVA BACKMAN, daughter of BACKMAN and EVA. She was born 1886.

Children of FORREST SPINNEY and EVA BACKMAN are:
    i.   CAROLINE[8] SPINNEY.
    ii.   HELEN SPINNEY.

592. CHARLES WESLEY[7] ALLEN *(MARY ELIZA CRANDALL[6] WEAVER, PETER CRANDALL[5], MARY[4] SPINNEY, SAMUEL[3], SAMUEL[2], THOMAS[1])* He married MALINDA BURTON.

Child of CHARLES ALLEN and MALINDA BURTON is:
936.   i.   GLADYS BURTON[8] ALLEN.

593. JULIA IDA[7] SPINNEY *(SAMUEL[6], ISAAC BEACH[5], SAMUEL MCCLURE[4], SAMUEL[3], SAMUEL[2], THOMAS[1])* was born 11 Jan 1850 in Burlington, NS.. She married WILLIAM H. CLEM.

Notes for WILLIAM H. CLEM:
Berwick Register 19 April 1922.

Obituary - Wm. H. CLEM
  Athol (Mass.) Transcript: - William Henry Clem, for 33 years a resident of
Petersham, died Thursday, March 22nd, at his home on North Main Street,
of pneumonia, aged 74 years, eight months and 10 days.
He was born in Harbourville, N.S., son of Allen and Mary A. (Gould) Clem.
He leaves, besides his wife, Mary Etta (Sanderson) Clem, three daughters,
Mrs. Otto C. Stroeble of Springfield, Mrs. Herbert Ward of Worcester and
Mrs. Melbourne Palmer of Auburn, N.S., and three brothers, George W. of
Republbi, (--).; Charles of Ludlow, and John W. of Seattle, Wash.
  Funeral services were held at the North Congregational church, Saturday at
2
pm. Burial, in charge of the Higgins Undertaking Co., of Athol, was in the
Eastside cemetery.

Children of JULIA SPINNEY and WILLIAM CLEM are:

937.   i.   ELIZABETH[8] CLEM.
        ii.   ANNA CLEM, m. OTTO STROBELE.
938.   iii.   NELLIE CLEM, b. 22 Aug 1874, Burlington, NS..

594. FANNY (FRANCIS) ANN[7] SPINNEY *(SAMUEL[6], ISAAC BEACH[5], SAMUEL MCCLURE[4], SAMUEL[3], SAMUEL[2], THOMAS[1])* was born 09 May 1853, and died 20 Nov 1911. She married HERMAN PATTERSON. He was born 1851, and died 1915.

Notes for FANNY (FRANCIS) ANN SPINNEY:
Berwick Register: publ. 30 Nov 1911:
Greenwood:
   Mrs. H. PATTERSON

On Monday, 20th, Fanny, beloved wife of Mr. Herman Patterson, was stricken with cerebral hemorrage and only lived an hour. She was in her usual health when her husband left home to go to Auburn on business. When he arrived there, he received a telephone message that she was dead. She leaves to mourn her loss a husband and three children, Mrs. Bessie Gray, of Penobscot, Me., Arthur of Petersham, Mass., and Mrs. Eva Shepherd, of Marlboro, Mass., who was with her mother when she died. An aged father and mother, Mr. & Mrs. Samuel Spinney, also mourn the loss of a loved and loving daughter.

   The funeral which took place on Thursday morning at Greenwood Church was conducted by her pastor, the Rev, Norman A. Whitman, and the Methodist pastor, Rev. H. L. Eisenhaur. The Oddfellows and Rebekahs attended in a body.

   Mrs. Patterson was a typical Rebekah, always to be found where she could do the most good. She will be greatly missed from the church and choir of which she was a member.

   Among the floral offerings was a beautiful wreath from Evangeline Rebekah Lodge. The sympathy of the community is with Mr. Patterson and family in their sad and sudden bereavement.

Notes for HERMAN PATTERSON:
Berwick Register, 30 June 1915:

   Obituary for   H. PATTERSON
   Deacon Herman Patterson passed away very suddenly at his residence on the Poor Farm Road, Auburn, on the evening of June 21st. He was alone at the time, as his wife was called away that afternoon to attend her father, Mr. Isreal Banks, who had been taken suddenly ill. Mr. Patterson was as well as usual when she left him. When she returned, about eight o'clock, she found him dead of heart disease.

   Mr. Patterson was an honorable Christian gentleman and will be very much missed in the community in which he lived as he was always at the head of every good work. He was a deacon in the Greenwood Baptist Church; a Justice of the Peace; a member of the Kingston Lodge of Oddfellows and a member of the Rebekahs, also an Orangeman. It will be a long time before his place will be filled in the community.

   He was twice married, his first wife was Miss Fanny Spinney, who died very suddenly four years ago last fall. He married Miss Mabel Banks, of Greenwood, about two years ago.

   He had three children by his first wife, Arthur, of Petersham, Mass.; Bessie Grey of Penobscot, Me., and Mrs. Eva Shepherd, of Everett, Mass., all of

whom were home to the funeral. He was buried last Thursday in Greenwood
Cemetery by the Oddfellows. The funeral sermon was preached by his pastor,
Rev. Geo. Hudson, Revs. E. H. Howe and H. Tucker were also present.
In spite of the inclement weather a large member of friends gathered to pay
their last respects to their friend and Brother. The floral offerings were
beautiful.

Among them were wreaths from the I.O.O.F. Lodge and the Rebekahs.
Also three links of pansies from Mr. C. Neily.

Children of FANNY SPINNEY and HERMAN PATTERSON are:
     i.   ARTHUR[8] PATTERSON, b. 1874; m. EMMA MAUDE SPINNEY; b. 1878.
    ii.   BESSIE PATTERSON, b. 1876; m. WILLIAM GRAY; b. 1863.
   iii.   EVA PATTERSON, m. SHEPHERD.

595. SARAH J.[7] SPINNEY *(SAMUEL[6], ISAAC BEACH[5], SAMUEL MCCLURE[4], SAMUEL[3], SAMUEL[2], THOMAS[1])* was born
24 Mar 1856, and died 1942. She married (1) W. WATSON NEILY. He was born 1861. She married (2) WATSON
NEILYWATSON.

Children of SARAH SPINNEY and W. NEILY are:
     i.   ALMINA J.[8] NEILY, b. 1885; d. 1945.
    ii.   MAUD NEILY, b. 1887; d. 1964; m. JOSEPH GORDON.

596. AZUBALE MAUDE[7] SPINNEY *(SAMUEL[6], ISAAC BEACH[5], SAMUEL MCCLURE[4], SAMUEL[3], SAMUEL[2], THOMAS[1])*
was born 27 Jun 1862, and died 1928. She married (1) JOHN GORDON.   She married (2) ELLARD CUNNINGHAM.

Children of AZUBALE SPINNEY and JOHN GORDON are:
     i.   AGGIE[8] GORDON.
    ii.   PRIMROSE GORDON.

597. ISAAC CALVIN[7] SPINNEY *(SAMUEL[6], ISAAC BEACH[5], SAMUEL MCCLURE[4], SAMUEL[3], SAMUEL[2], THOMAS[1])* was
born 27 Jun 1871 in Nova Scotia, and died 1949 in Petersham, MA. He married SUSAN STONE WARD. She was
born Aug 1875, and died 1926.

Notes for SUSAN STONE WARD:
Susan's mother was married twice, her second husband was _____ CLEM.
Susan was called Susie by her husband, Isaac.
They moved to Petersham, Massachusetts abt 1903 and are both burried in the East Cemetery in Petersham.

Children of ISAAC SPINNEY and SUSAN WARD are:
939.   i.   GLADYS MAY[8] SPINNEY, b. 28 Oct 1896, Greenwood, NS.; d. North Reading, MA.
940.   ii.   CHESTER LEVERETT SPINNEY, b. 07 Nov 1897, Greenwood, NS.; d. Jan 1981.
941.   iii.   VIOLA SPINNEY, b. 1904.

598. ELIZABETH MARIA[7] SPINNEY *(AUSTIN WELTON[6], JACOB BEACH[5], SAMUEL MCCLURE[4], SAMUEL[3], SAMUEL[2],
THOMAS[1])* was born 17 Apr 1847 in Harmony, NS., and died 17 Sep 1886 in Harmony, NS.. She married
THOMAS CORNELIUS STEELE. He was born 04 Jul 1839.

Children of ELIZABETH SPINNEY and THOMAS STEELE are:
     i.   ELMIRA AMELIA[8] STEELE, b. 1864; d. 1879.
    ii.   CHURCH MORSE STEELE, b. 1866.
   iii.   BURPEE CLARKE STEELE, b. 1867.
   iv.   ANNIS SOPHIA STEELE, b. 1871; d. 1879.
    v.   HARRIS ATWOOD STEELE, b. 1875.
   vi.   HARRY FRANKLIN STEELE, b. 1875.

599. ANN MELISSA⁷ SPINNEY *(AUSTIN WELTON⁶, JACOB BEACH⁵, SAMUEL McCLURE⁴, SAMUEL³, SAMUEL², THOMAS¹)* was born 1848 in Harmony, NS, and died 1928. She married ALFRED PARKER SAUNDERS, son of TIMOTHY SAUNDERS and EUNICE SPINNEY. He was born 08 Feb 1831 in Greenwood, Kings, Nova Scotia, Canada, and died 09 Aug 1918 in Harmon, Kings, Nova Scotia, Canada.

Children are listed above under (291) Alfred Parker Saunders.

600. JONATHAN RIED MORSE⁷ SPINNEY *(AUSTIN WELTON⁶, JACOB BEACH⁵, SAMUEL McCLURE⁴, SAMUEL³, SAMUEL², THOMAS¹)* was born 01 Jun 1856. He married ALMIRA E. BOWLBY. She was born 1859.

Children of JONATHAN SPINNEY and ALMIRA BOWLBY are:
      i.   HAZEL M⁸ SPINNEY.
942.   ii.   ELIZABETH SPINNEY, b. 27 Nov 1901; d. 1991.

601. MINNIE SALOME⁷ SPINNEY *(AUSTIN WELTON⁶, JACOB BEACH⁵, SAMUEL McCLURE⁴, SAMUEL³, SAMUEL², THOMAS¹)* was born 1857. She married JAMES WILLIAM JEFFERSON. He was born 1853.

Children of MINNIE SPINNEY and JAMES JEFFERSON are:
      i.   ARTHUR SPURGEON⁸ JEFFERSON, b. 1880.
     ii.   BURPEE SEYMOUR JEFFERSON, b. 1882; d. 1886.

602. AUSTIN SPURR⁷ SPINNEY *(AUSTIN WELTON⁶, JACOB BEACH⁵, SAMUEL McCLURE⁴, SAMUEL³, SAMUEL², THOMAS¹)* was born Oct 1858 in Nova Scotia, and died Aft. 1920 in Massachusetts. He married LIZZIE S TENNY 28 Apr 1887 in Leominster, MA. She was born 1862 in Leominster, Ma, and died Aft. 1900.

Children of AUSTIN SPINNEY and LIZZIE TENNY are:
      i.   BERTHA ELIZABETH⁸ SPINNEY, b. 26 Jun 1889.
     ii.   CARLTON AUSTIN SPINNEY, b. 13 May 1896.

           Notes for CARLTON AUSTIN SPINNEY:
           Leominster records says Carlton was still born

603. CALEB SNOW⁷ SPINNEY *(AUSTIN WELTON⁶, JACOB BEACH⁵, SAMUEL McCLURE⁴, SAMUEL³, SAMUEL², THOMAS¹)* was born 15 Jul 1865 in Harmony, NS., and died 1931. He married MARGARET IRENE BARTEAUX, daughter of SAMUEL BARTEAUX and SARAH BANKS. She was born 1867, and died 06 Jan 1944.

Children of CALEB SPINNEY and MARGARET BARTEAUX are:
       i.   ORA⁸ SPINNEY, m. ROY CREIGHTON.
943.   ii.   AUSTIN WHEELOCK SPINNEY, b. 06 Jul 1890.
     iii. LESTER RALEIGH SPINNEY, b. 14 Apr 1892; d. 29 Jul 1950; m. ETHEL WHARTON.
     iv. SARAH SPINNEY, b. 01 Apr 1894; m. JAMES LEROY COLLINS, 23 Dec 1914, Harmony N.S.
      v. CHARLES SPINNEY, b. 20 Jan 1895.
     vi. CARLTON SPINNEY, b. 05 Oct 1897.
944. vii. SEAWARD SPINNEY, b. 31 Jan 1904, Harmony, NS.; d. 12 Feb 1991, Berlin, MA.
   viii. FERNA SPINNEY, b. 25 Dec 1906; d. 03 Apr 1990, Tyngsboro, MA; m. KEITH ILLSLEY.

           Notes for FERNA SPINNEY:
           The Register, Berwick, N.S. 1990

           FERNA M. ILLSELY

           Mrs. Ferna M. (Spinney) Illsley, 198 Middlesex Road, Tyngsboro, died April 3
           at Lowell General Hospital.

           She was married to H. Keith Illsley with whom she celebrated their 60th
           wedding anniversary on Nov. 12, 19889.

           Born in Harmony, Kings County, on Dec 25, 1906, the daughter of the late Caleb
           S. and Margaret (Barteaux) Spinney, she graduated from Acadia Seminary in
           Wolfville.

She and her husband were one of the founders of the Westford Baptist Church known as the Nashoba Valley Baptist Church.

For the past 45 years she and her husband had lived in Dracut, Harvard, Westford, Littleton and Tyngsboro.

Besides her husband, she is survived by three daughters, Mrs. John (Jane E.) Vernarelli of Baltimore, Md., Mrs. Stephen (Janet L.) Salisbury of So. Berwick, Me., and Mrs. Richard (Judith A.) Ciarrocca of South Hope, Me.; two sons Austin R. and his wife Lillian (Gillett) Illsley of South Carolina, and H. Dale, and his wife Vivian (Kling) of Tyngsboro; a brother, Seward Spinney of Berlin, Mass.; also 16 grandchildren, nine great grandchildren, several nieces and nephews.

---

    ix.   LANA MAE SPINNEY, b. 1925, Harmony N.S; d. 03 Dec 1929, Harmony N.S.

604. WILLIAM G.[7] SPINNEY (*JACOB BEACH[6], JACOB BEACH[5], SAMUEL MCCLURE[4], SAMUEL[3], SAMUEL[2], THOMAS[1]*) was born 1854, and died 1935. He married FLORA BELLE HUTCHINSON. She was born 1861.

Children of WILLIAM SPINNEY and FLORA HUTCHINSON are:
945.   i.   EVA[8] SPINNEY, b. 1889; d. 1976.
946.   ii.   MILTON SPINNEY, b. 1904; d. 1976.

605. ANNA IRENE[7] SPINNEY (*JACOB BEACH[6], JACOB BEACH[5], SAMUEL MCCLURE[4], SAMUEL[3], SAMUEL[2], THOMAS[1]*) was born 04 Jun 1858 in Greenwood, NS., and died 25 Nov 1935. She married AVARD ERNEST POTTER 22 Sep 1886. He was born 16 Jan 1863 in Nova Scotia, and died 21 Dec 1921.

Notes for AVARD ERNEST POTTER:
Avard Ernest Potter Aaron, Aaron, Mary Rice, John; born 16 January 1863 at Nova Scotia; married Anna Irene Spinney, daughter of Jacob B Spinney and Jane Duncanson, 22 September 1886 at Greenwood, Annapolis Co, Nova Scotia;
died 21 December 1921.

He lived in 1881 at Hessian Line District, Annapolis Co, Nova Scotia; with his parents. He and Anna Irene Spinney lived
between 1891 and 1901 at Clementsvale District, Annapolis Co, Nova Scotia. He was a farmer between 1891 and 1901.

Anna Irene Spinney was also known as Anna I Potter. She was born on 4 June 1858 at Nova Scotia. She died on 25
November 1935.

Known children of Avard Ernest Potter and Anna Irene Spinney were as follows:

   i. Manning Roderick Potter; born 7 September 1890 at Nova Scotia; married Mary Elizabeth Potter, daughter of
   Edward Manoah Potter and Seraphina Berry, 26 September 1917 at Clementsvale, Annapolis Co, Nova Scotia; died
    18 February 1973.

   ii. Noble Aaron Potter; born 8 September 1896 at Clementsvale, Annapolis Co, Nova Scotia; married Maude Vera
   Lightziger 2 November 1923; died 1950; died 2 November 1950 at Upper Clements, Annapolis Co, Nova Scotia.

Children of ANNA SPINNEY and AVARD POTTER are:
    i.   MANNING RODERICK[8] POTTER, b. 07 Sep 1890; d. 18 Feb 1973; m. MARY ELIZABETH POTTER, 26 Sep

1917.
ii.   NOBLE AARON POTTER, b. 08 Sep 1896; d. 02 Nov 1950; m. MAUDE VERA LIGHTZIGER, 02 Nov 1923.

606. HARRIET I.[7] SPINNEY *(JACOB BEACH[6], JACOB BEACH[5], SAMUEL MCCLURE[4], SAMUEL[3], SAMUEL[2], THOMAS[1])* was born 1866, and died 1955. She married ERNEST H. NEILY, son of GEORGE NEILY and SARAH SPINNEY. He was born 1867.

Children are listed above under (268) Ernest H. Neily.

607. RUBY LAVINA[7] SPINNEY *(HARDING THEODORE[6], JACOB BEACH[5], SAMUEL MCCLURE[4], SAMUEL[3], SAMUEL[2], THOMAS[1])* was born 1857. She married ALBERT BENSON.

Notes for RUBY LAVINA SPINNEY:
Albert Benson, the son of Isaac Henry and Elizabeth (Winchester) Benson, was born during the year 1855, and he died on March 2, 1933, at Bear River, Nova Scotia - his home. He married Ruby Spinney on November 20, 1879.

Albert and Ruby (Spinney) Benson had the following children:

1.Harding Benson, born September 25, 1880; married Edith Ray. She was deceased by the year 1936. They lived at Bear River, Nova Scotia.

   Issue: Edith Benson, born around the year 1906, married Vernon Harris.

2.Edith Benson, born October 27, 1886; died at the age of 13 years.

Bear River, Nova Scotia, January 4, 1938. There passed away at her home here Saturday evening, Mrs. Ruby (Spinney) Benson 80, widow of Albert Benson, after a short illness. Mrs. Benson was born at Greenwood, Annapolis County, a daughter of the late Mr. And Mrs. Harding Spinney. She married, when young, and came as a bride to this town where she has since resided. She was a member of the United Baptist Church, and is survived by one son, Harding Benson , and one grand-daughter, Mrs. Vernon Harris, both living at Bear River. The funeral was held from her late home Monday afternoon, conducted by Rev. G.D. Brydon, assisted by Rev. C.P. Henderson. Interment was in Mount Hope.

Children of RUBY SPINNEY and ALBERT BENSON are:
   i.   HARDING[8] BENSON.
   ii.   EDITH BENSON.

608. JAMES BARTEAUX[7] SPINNEY *(HARDING THEODORE[6], JACOB BEACH[5], SAMUEL MCCLURE[4], SAMUEL[3], SAMUEL[2], THOMAS[1])* was born 1860 in Greenwood, N.S., and died 1921 in Greenwood, N.S.. He married MARY ELIZABETH FITCH 1889. She was born 1865.

Children of JAMES SPINNEY and MARY FITCH are:
          i.   LEROY HOWARD[8] SPINNEY, b. 1890, Greenwood, N.S.; d. 1894, Greenwood, N.S..
947.   ii.   HELEN LUCY SPINNEY, b. 1895; d. 1981.
948.   iii. ANNIE MIRA SPINNEY, b. 1902; d. 1967.
949.   iv.   LAURA BLANCHE SPINNEY, b. 1897; d. 1977.

609. MARY EMMA[7] SPINNEY *(CALEB[6], JACOB BEACH[5], SAMUEL MCCLURE[4], SAMUEL[3], SAMUEL[2], THOMAS[1])* was born 25 Feb 1851, and died 16 Aug 1888. She married ALEXANDER BANKS, son of ALDEN BANKS and HANNAH COGSWELL. He was born 31 May 1851.

Children of MARY SPINNEY and ALEXANDER BANKS are:
   i.   ZENA M[8] BANKS, b. 1886; d. 1913; m. GEORGE LAMERT SPINNEY; b. 02 Apr 1881.
   ii.   ULYSSES GRANT BANKS, b. 01 Apr 1883, Kingston Station, Kings, NS.
   iii. LESLIE W BANKS.

610. FLORA BELLE[7] SPINNEY *(CALEB[6], JACOB BEACH[5], SAMUEL MCCLURE[4], SAMUEL[3], SAMUEL[2], THOMAS[1])* was born 05 Jun 1861, and died 1934.

Child of FLORA BELLE SPINNEY is:
    i.   ZINA[8] SPINNEY, b. 21 Sep 1886.

611. BERTHA MAUDE[7] SPINNEY (*CALEB[6], JACOB BEACH[5], SAMUEL MCCLURE[4], SAMUEL[3], SAMUEL[2], THOMAS[1]*) was born 09 Dec 1863, and died 1939. She married AVERY BANKS. He was born 26 Feb 1867.

Children of BERTHA SPINNEY and AVERY BANKS are:
    i.   GLADYS[8] BANKS, b. 16 Mar 1891.
    ii. MARY BANKS, b. 21 Jul 1895.
    iii. ARLEIGH BANKS.

612. EDWARD MANNING[7] SPINNEY (*CALEB[6], JACOB BEACH[5], SAMUEL MCCLURE[4], SAMUEL[3], SAMUEL[2], THOMAS[1]*) was born 14 Mar 1867, and died 1961. He married BESSIE A. WEBBER 1895. She was born 1868.

Children of EDWARD SPINNEY and BESSIE WEBBER are:
950.   i.   CALEB MAYNARD[8] SPINNEY, b. 1897; d. 1980.
951.   ii. LESLIE MANNING SPINNEY, b. 1898; d. 1982.
952.   iii. ZELDA HOPE SPINNEY, b. 1904.
953.   iv. ALBERT WEBBER SPINNEY, b. 1908, Greenwood, NS.; d. 06 Oct 1994, Middleton, NS..

613. MELBURNE E.[7] SPINNEY (*BENIAH B[6], JACOB BEACH[5], SAMUEL MCCLURE[4], SAMUEL[3], SAMUEL[2], THOMAS[1]*) was born 1864, and died 1928. He married HARRIET E. SMALL. She was born 1862.

Children of MELBURNE SPINNEY and HARRIET SMALL are:
954.   i.   HORACE LESTER[8] SPINNEY, b. 1851; d. 1951.
955.   ii. EDITH ADELAIDE SPINNEY, b. 1889; d. 1975.
956.   iii. LORING VICTOR SPINNEY, b. 1890, Greenwood, N.S.; d. 13 Feb 1957, Greenwood, N.S..
        iv. RALPH WHITMAN SPINNEY, b. 1892; d. 1967.
957.   v. HOWE BELL SPINNEY, b. 1894; d. 1965.
958.   vi. BEATRICE MAE SPINNEY, b. 1899, Greenwood, NS.; d. 30 Aug 2000.

614. BLANCHE LILY[7] SPINNEY (*ENOCH[6], JACOB BEACH[5], SAMUEL MCCLURE[4], SAMUEL[3], SAMUEL[2], THOMAS[1]*) was born 10 Dec 1865 in Harmony, N.S., and died 22 Sep 1908 in New Germany, N.S.. She married BERTRUM JEFFERSON.

Children of BLANCHE SPINNEY and BERTRUM JEFFERSON are:
    i.   FREDERICK[8] JEFFERSON.
    ii. HAROLD JEFFERSON.
    iii. GEORGE JEFFERSON.

615. EVERETT LAMONT[7] SPINNEY (*ENOCH[6], JACOB BEACH[5], SAMUEL MCCLURE[4], SAMUEL[3], SAMUEL[2], THOMAS[1]*) was born 29 Dec 1866 in Harmony, N.S., and died 24 Apr 1930 in W. Acton, MA. He married LILLIAN MAY WOLFE 1891 in Boxborough. She was born 25 Aug 1871 in Waterville, N.S, and died 02 Sep 1951.

Children of EVERETT SPINNEY and LILLIAN WOLFE are:
959.   i.   EVELYN BEATRICE[8] SPINNEY, b. 23 Jul 1893, Darthmouth, N.S; d. 1956.
960.   ii. EVERETT RHEE SPINNEY, b. 13 Aug 1895, Acton, MA; d. 1937.
961.   iii. LILLIAN BICKNELL SPINNEY, b. 1898.
        iv. ETHEL WOLFE SPINNEY, b. 1899; m. GRAY TOZIER.
962.   v. ORLAND ELWOOD SPINNEY, b. 15 Jun 1901, Acton, MA; d. Oct 1979.

616. GEORGE ELBURN[7] SPINNEY (*ENOCH[6], JACOB BEACH[5], SAMUEL MCCLURE[4], SAMUEL[3], SAMUEL[2], THOMAS[1]*) was born 06 Apr 1870 in Harmony, N.S., and died May 1924. He married MARTHA JANE SAUNDERS 24 Mar 1897. She was born 09 Feb 1873 in Harmony, Kings, Nova Scotia, Canada, and died 08 Apr 1952.

Children of GEORGE SPINNEY and MARTHA SAUNDERS are:
963.   i.   ALFRED[8] SPINNEY, b. Abt. 1890.
964.   ii.   WILEY SPINNEY.
965.   iii.   ROBIE SPINNEY.
966.   iv.   KENNETH EARLE SPINNEY, b. 1906.

617. HARRY ATWOOD[7] SPINNEY *(ENOCH[6], JACOB BEACH[5], SAMUEL MCCLURE[4], SAMUEL[3], SAMUEL[2], THOMAS[1])* was born 1874 in Harmony, N.S., and died 10 Aug 1901. He married BERTHA DOWNIE.

Notes for HARRY ATWOOD SPINNEY:
Harry Atwood SPINNEY was born in 1874 in Harmony, Kings Co.N.S.. He died on 10 Aug 1901. He has reference number FTJ#137. Drowned while gathering water-lilies for his wife, who was pregnant with son Harry at the time. There is a reference to a Harry
Spinney, employed in the building of the Margaretsville wharf, which
is probably this same Harry. "Over the Mountain and Down to the Bay"
(Compiled by The Margaretsville Ladies Institute)

Child of HARRY SPINNEY and BERTHA DOWNIE is:
   i.   HARRY[8] SPINNEY, b. 1902.

618. LELAND TEASDALE[7] SPINNEY *(ENOCH[6], JACOB BEACH[5], SAMUEL MCCLURE[4], SAMUEL[3], SAMUEL[2], THOMAS[1])* was born 05 Oct 1875 in Harmony, NS., and died 21 Jun 1950 in Harmony, NS.. He married AGNES GEORGINA HARRIS 19 Oct 1898 in Southboro, MA. She was born 25 Jun 1877, and died 1952.

Children of LELAND SPINNEY and AGNES HARRIS are:
967.   i.   WINTHROP HARRIS[8] SPINNEY, b. 27 Sep 1900, Harmony, NS.; d. 22 Mar 1974, Westboro, MA.
968.   ii.   KINGSLEY SELLAR SPINNEY, b. 23 Jul 1902, Harmony, N.S.; d. 22 Mar 1973, Nicholsville, N.S..
969.   iii.   VERA BELLE SPINNEY, b. 26 Mar 1904, Harmony, N.S.; d. 27 Apr 1951, Nicholsville, N.S..
970.   iv.   EARLE WINFRED SPINNEY, b. 12 Jan 1914, Harmony, N.S.; d. 28 Apr 1980, Greenwood, N.S..
971.   v.   FRANCIS LELAND SPINNEY, b. 15 Aug 1915, Harmony, N.S.; d. 28 Aug 1979, Harmony, N.S..
   vi.   MARGARET LOUISE SPINNEY, b. 12 Sep 1919, Harmony, N.S.; d. 25 Mar 1992, Greenwood, N.S..

619. BURPEE ALBINA[7] SPINNEY *(CLARK THOMAS[6], JACOB BEACH[5], SAMUEL MCCLURE[4], SAMUEL[3], SAMUEL[2], THOMAS[1])* was born 1883, and died 1969 in Barre, MA. He married MARIA LEONA STEELE 19 Sep 1911. She was born 13 May 1891.

Children of BURPEE SPINNEY and MARIA STEELE are:
972.   i.   BURPEE CLYDE[8] SPINNEY, b. 18 Aug 1912, Greenwood, N.S..
   ii.   MARJORIE LEOTA SPINNEY, b. 06 Mar 1915, Greenwood, N.S.; m. KENNETH GUERTIN.
   iii.   LLOYD HERBERT SPINNEY, b. 01 Mar 1917, Greenwood, N.S.; m. BERNICE COTE, 21 Jun 1941.
   iv.   ELLA LEONA SPINNEY, b. 06 Mar 1921, Greenwood, N.S.; m. JAMES WALCH, 21 Oct 1940.
   v.   LEROY CLARK SPINNEY, b. 08 Mar 1923, Greenwood, N.S.; m. ELIZABETH TROY, 22 Jan 1944.
   vi.   LEWIS ARTHUR SPINNEY, b. 02 Aug 1930, Barre, MA; m. NORMA KYES, 22 Oct 1949.

620. GEORGIA E.[7] SPINNEY *(CLARK THOMAS[6], JACOB BEACH[5], SAMUEL MCCLURE[4], SAMUEL[3], SAMUEL[2], THOMAS[1])* was born 24 Jul 1887, and died 1936. She married WILLIAM SMALL 1911. He was born 1884.

Children of GEORGIA SPINNEY and WILLIAM SMALL are:
   i.   LEMERT[8] SMALL.
   ii.   ETHEL SMALL.

621. JESSIE F.[7] MORSE *(ELISHA SPINNEY[6], ELIZABETH (ELIZA)[5] SPINNEY, SAMUEL MCCLURE[4], SAMUEL[3], SAMUEL[2], THOMAS[1])*

Child of JESSIE F. MORSE is:
   i.   JONATHAN CHURCH[8] MORSE.

622. VERNON LLOYD[7] MORSE *(BENAIAH HOWE "JOE"[6], ELIZABETH (ELIZA)[5] SPINNEY, SAMUEL MCCLURE[4], SAMUEL[3], SAMUEL[2], THOMAS[1])* He married ETHEL BERNICE MCGEE 1919. She was born 1894.

Children of VERNON MORSE and ETHEL MCGEE are:
- i. ALVAH SARGEANT[8] MORSE, b. 1921.
- ii. HOLMES MCGEE MORSE, b. 1922.
- iii. CHARLES VERNON MORSE, b. 1924.
- iv. DONALD OSGOOD MORSE, b. 1926.

623. ABIGAIL A[7] CROCKER *(CATHERINE[6] SAUNDERS, EUNICE[5] SPINNEY, SAMUEL MCCLURE[4], SAMUEL[3], SAMUEL[2], THOMAS[1])* was born 08 Dec 1852, and died 19 Jan 1916. She married ISAAAC DAY. He was born 01 Nov 1845.

Children of ABIGAIL CROCKER and ISAAAC DAY are:
- i. SUSIE T[8] DAY, b. 1876; m. JOHN CLARK HARRIS, 21 Sep 1899; b. Abt. 1860.
- ii. ANNIE DAY, b. 26 Oct 1879.
- iii. BESSIE DAY, b. 03 Jan 1880.

624. JAMES H.[7] CROCKER *(CATHERINE[6] SAUNDERS, EUNICE[5] SPINNEY, SAMUEL MCCLURE[4], SAMUEL[3], SAMUEL[2], THOMAS[1])* was born 27 Jan 1859. He married CORA D JODREY 20 Jan 1894.

Child of JAMES CROCKER and CORA JODREY is:
- i. KENNETH[8] CROCKER, b. Abt. 1894.

625. WILLIAM E.[7] CROCKER *(CATHERINE[6] SAUNDERS, EUNICE[5] SPINNEY, SAMUEL MCCLURE[4], SAMUEL[3], SAMUEL[2], THOMAS[1])* was born 1862. He married ELIZABETH TUPPER 05 Jan 1887.

Children of WILLIAM CROCKER and ELIZABETH TUPPER are:
- i. MAUD[8] CROCKER, b. 21 Jul 1888; d. 1983; m. RUPERT L VEINOTT; b. 1886; d. 1953.
- 973. ii. NORA CROCKER, b. 11 Jul 1889; d. 1910.
- iii. MARTHA CROCKER, b. 14 Mar 1892.
- iv. MABEL CROCKER, b. 06 Jul 1894.
- v. WILFORD CROCKER, b. 24 Aug 1896; d. 1930; m. DAISY; b. 1892; d. 1931.
- vi. MABEL CROCKER, b. 18 Jul 1899.

626. ELLA M[7] CROCKER *(CATHERINE[6] SAUNDERS, EUNICE[5] SPINNEY, SAMUEL MCCLURE[4], SAMUEL[3], SAMUEL[2], THOMAS[1])* was born 30 Sep 1863, and died 1938. She married WILLIAM LUTZ. He was born 22 Mar 1857.

Children of ELLA CROCKER and WILLIAM LUTZ are:
- i. LAURA[8] LUTZ, b. 13 Jun 1882.
- ii. GEORGE LUTZ, b. 07 Aug 1888.
- iii. ETHEL LUTZ, b. 06 Sep 1891.
- iv. LLOYD LUTZ, b. 23 Feb 1893.
- v. ROY STANLEY LUTZ, b. 01 May 1894.
- vi. NORMA LUTZ, b. 24 Dec 1900.

627. CLINTON[7] SPINNEY *(CHIPMAN L[6], INGERSON H[5], SAMUEL MCCLURE[4], SAMUEL[3], SAMUEL[2], THOMAS[1])* was born 1907. He married ELLEN LYNCH 1945.

Children of CLINTON SPINNEY and ELLEN LYNCH are:
- i. SHIRLEY[8] SPINNEY, b. 1945; d. 1970.
- ii. BETTY JEAN SPINNEY, b. 1949.

628. ELLESWORTH[7] ARMSTRONG *(RUBY ARDELLISS[6] GRIFFIN, CATHERINE INGLIS[5] SPINNEY, SAMUEL MCCLURE[4], SAMUEL[3], SAMUEL[2], THOMAS[1])* He married CLARA LANGILLE.

Children of ELLESWORTH ARMSTRONG and CLARA LANGILLE are:

   i. VERA[8] ARMSTRONG.
974. ii. JOANNE ARMSTRONG.
   iii. WATTSON ARMSTRONG.
   iv. WARREN ARMSTRONG.

629. MARION[7] ARMSTRONG *(RUBY ARDELLISS[6] GRIFFIN, CATHERINE INGLIS[5] SPINNEY, SAMUEL MCCLURE[4], SAMUEL[3], SAMUEL[2], THOMAS[1])* She married AMOS FREEMAN.

Children of MARION ARMSTRONG and AMOS FREEMAN are:
   i. ROSIE[8] FREEMAN, m. DENNIS DUBOIS.
   ii. VIRGINIA FREEMAN, m. (?) NAUGLER.

630. HOWARD ELIZA[7] PIERCE *(CHARLES A.[6], AMORET[5] SPINNEY, SAMUEL MCCLURE[4], SAMUEL[3], SAMUEL[2], THOMAS[1])* was born 1873, and died 30 Nov 1909. He married KIZBORO FOREST POTTER.

Children of HOWARD PIERCE and KIZBORO POTTER are:
   i. EDITH[8] PIERCE.
   ii. FREDERICK WILLIAM PIERCE.
975. iii. CLAYTON ABNER PIERCE, b. 13 Jan 1897; d. Aug 1969.
976. iv. RALPH ALMER PIERCE, b. 01 Sep 1899, Clementport, NS.; d. 18 Feb 1983, Digby, NS..

631. FRANK LOVETT[7] PIERCE *(CHARLES A.[6], AMORET[5] SPINNEY, SAMUEL MCCLURE[4], SAMUEL[3], SAMUEL[2], THOMAS[1])* was born 1887, and died 1956. He married ANNIE WOODWORTH 1908. She was born 1886, and died 1968.

Children of FRANK PIERCE and ANNIE WOODWORTH are:
   i. SHERMAN F[8] PIERCE.
977. ii. EDITH PIERCE, b. 1909; d. 1981.
978. iii. RUTH HANNAH ELIZABETH PIERCE, b. 12 Nov 1912; d. 11 Apr 1987.
979. iv. PAUL ELLIOT PIERCE, b. 31 Mar 1914; d. 23 Nov 1992.
980. v. LUCILLE PIERCE, b. 25 May 1917.
981. vi. CATHERINE PEARL PIERCE, b. 15 Sep 1919.

632. MARY ELIZABETH[7] SPINNEY *(FRANK[6], MARY[5], BENIAH[4], SAMUEL[3], SAMUEL[2], THOMAS[1])* was born 25 May 1872, and died 1911. She married AINSLEY REID 26 Dec 1894 in Gaspereaux, NS.. He was born 1872, and died 1904.

Children of MARY SPINNEY and AINSLEY REID are:
   i. VERA ZENA[8] REID, b. 1895; m. CHARLES NOWLIN.
   ii. FRANK REID, b. 30 Jul 1897; m. LILL LEYMAN.
   iii. ROY REID, b. 1899.
   iv. EMMA REID, b. Abt. 1901.

633. AUGUSTA[7] SPINNEY *(FRANK[6], MARY[5], BENIAH[4], SAMUEL[3], SAMUEL[2], THOMAS[1])* was born 16 Aug 1876, and died 1910. She married (1) FRED NOWLAN. She married (2) DOUGALD BEMISTER 1903 in Chelsea, MA. He was born 1876 in Newfoundland.

Children of AUGUSTA SPINNEY and FRED NOWLAN are:
   i. ETHEL[8] NOWLAN.
   ii. NELLIE NOWLAN.

Children of AUGUSTA SPINNEY and DOUGALD BEMISTER are:
   iii. EDWARD F[8] BEMISTER, b. 1903.
   iv. BLANCHE H BEMISTER, b. 1906.
   v. FRANK SPINNEY BEMISTER, b. 1908.

634. EMERY CLARENCE[7] SPINNEY *(FRANK[6], MARY[5], BENIAH[4], SAMUEL[3], SAMUEL[2], THOMAS[1])* was born 13 Feb 1891 in Black River, NS., and died 02 Apr 1958. He married BESSIE SCHOFIELD.

Children of EMERY SPINNEY and BESSIE SCHOFIELD are:
982. i. GERALD[8] SPINNEY, b. 1920.
 ii. FLORENCE GERTRUDE SPINNEY.

> Notes for FLORENCE GERTRUDE SPINNEY:
> Halifax Chronicle Herald, Jul 11, 1984
>
> HANTSPORT - Florence Gertrude Benjamin, 65, of Hantsport, died Tuesday at Hants Community Hospital, Windsor.
> Born in Black River, she was a daughter of the late Emery Spinney and Bessie (Schofield) Spinney.
> She is survived by her common-law husband, Tom Wilson; five daughters, Maxine (Mrs. Floyd Swinamer), Three Mile Plains; Marie (Mrs. Fred Patterson), Woodville, Kings County; Pat (Mrs. Hubert Gannon), Medford; Helen (Mrs. Roy Cousins), White Rock; Gladys Miller, Dartmouth; three sons, Clarence and Ray, both of Bishopville, and Wayne, New Minas; three sisters, Mrs. Rena Keaton, Wolfville; Ann (Mrs. Dean Schofield), White Rock; Sandra (Mrs. Bernard Forsythe), Wolfville Ridge; six brothers, Leo and Blake, both of Black River; Franzel, Harlan and Frank, all of White Rock; and Eldon, Dundas, Ont.; 24 grandchildren; and eight great-grandchildren.
> She was predeceased by a brother, Gerald, and a sister, Velda.
> The body is in Lohnes Funeral Home, Windsor. Funeral will be Thursday at 2 p.m. in St. Andrew's Anglican Church, Hantsport, Rev. Michael Boyd officiating, with burial in Maple Wood Cemetery, Windsor.
> Donations may be made to the Nova Scotia Heart Fund.

635. ANNIE L[7] SPINNEY *(JOHN ALEXANDER[6], THOMAS LEONARD[5], BENIAH[4], SAMUEL[3], SAMUEL[2], THOMAS[1])* was born 03 Dec 1887 in Richmond, ME. She married HERBERT PEASE 24 Jul 1905.

Children of ANNIE SPINNEY and HERBERT PEASE are:
 i. GEORGE W[8] PEASE, b. 1908.
 ii. FRED L PEASE, b. 1912; d. 25 May 1986.

636. HOLLIS RUPERT[7] SPINNEY *(CLARENCE ALLISON[6], DAVID GRIFFEN[5], BENIAH[4], SAMUEL[3], SAMUEL[2], THOMAS[1])* was born 17 Jul 1905, and died 29 Aug 1994. He married FLORENCE HAZEL COCHRANE.

Child of HOLLIS SPINNEY and FLORENCE COCHRANE is:
 i. DOROTHY ELIZABETH[8] SPINNEY.

637. GEORGE E.[7] SPINNEY *(LEWIS LEONARD[6], GEORGE CRAFT[5], BENIAH[4], SAMUEL[3], SAMUEL[2], THOMAS[1])* was born Feb 1889 in Kentville, NS.. He married MARY O. She was born 1889.

Children of GEORGE SPINNEY and MARY O are:
 i. LOUIS C[8] SPINNEY, b. 01 May 1915; d. 21 May 1998, Warren, PA.
 ii. MARY V SPINNEY, b. 1920.
 iii. GEORGIE STEPHEN SPINNEY, b. 1925.

638. GLADYS A[7] SPINNEY *(LEWIS LEONARD[6], GEORGE CRAFT[5], BENIAH[4], SAMUEL[3], SAMUEL[2], THOMAS[1])* was born Aug 1898 in Bethel, ME, and died in Before 1929. She married FRANK P CHAPMAN 1915 in Bethel, Me. He was born 1892, and died 1969.

Children of GLADYS SPINNEY and FRANK CHAPMAN are:
 i. ROBERT B[8] CHAPMAN, b. 1916.
 ii. ANNIE CHAPMAN, b. 1919.
 iii. ERNEST CHAPMAN, b. 1920.

    iv.   HAROLD CHAPMAN, b. 1924.
    v.   GWENDOLYN CHAPMAN, b. 1925.
    vi. RAYMOND CHAPMAN, b. 1928.

639. JAMES A[7] SPINNEY *(JAMES J[6], GEORGE CRAFT[5], BENIAH[4], SAMUEL[3], SAMUEL[2], THOMAS[1])* was born Jul 1890. He married (1) EDITH INGALLS 08 Jul 1913. She was born 1896. He married (2) MARGARETTA YOUNG 31 Dec 1921 in Bethel, ME.

Child of JAMES SPINNEY and EDITH INGALLS is:
    i.   MARION G[8] SPINNEY, b. 1915.

        Notes for MARION G SPINNEY:
        WATERVILLE — Marion Spinney Soule, 84, of North Palermo Road, Palermo, died Tuesday, Feb. 9, at the Willows Nursing Care Center.

        Born in Portland on May 19, 1914, she was the daughter of James and Edith (Ingalls) Spinney. She attended Portland schools. She was married to Charles Henry Bachelor Soule on March 25, 1939.

        She worked as a telephone operator in the town of Palermo. She was also a cook at Palermo Consolidated School and worked as a telephone operator at the Togus Veterans Hospital until her retirement in 1974. Mrs. Soule enjoyed playing cards and traveling with her family and friends. Over the years, she belonged to many clubs and organizations in town.

        She will be sadly missed by her close friends, Gary Dyer (loved as a son) and wife Vicki of Palermo.

        Surviving are her sister, Leah Deegan, formerly of Bethel, who had lived with and cared for Marion for the past two years during her illness; her half-sister, Mary Jane Gaudreau and husband Harold of Bethel; a devoted niece, Kathryn Lessard, and husband Hank and their children Dan and Marie, all of Palermo; her nephew, Henry Deegan of Cape Elizabeth; her nieces, Sally Smith of Locke Mills and Joan Kimball of Albany; and many other nieces, nephews, and all of their families.

        She was predeceased by her husband, Feb. 19, 1975; and her only son, Alan Lee, Feb. 9, 1974; her parents; and her stepfather, Lester Rankin.

Child of JAMES SPINNEY and MARGARETTA YOUNG is:
    ii. LEAH[8] SPINNEY, b. 1929.

640. ERNEST ARTHUR[7] MUNDT *(BERTHA MARIE[6] SPINNEY, GEORGE CRAFT[5], BENIAH[4], SAMUEL[3], SAMUEL[2], THOMAS[1])* was born 15 Dec 1905. He married INA POTTER.

Child of ERNEST MUNDT and INA POTTER is:
    i.   NEVA[8] MUNDT.

641. BERTHA MARION[7] MUNDT *(BERTHA MARIE[6] SPINNEY, GEORGE CRAFT[5], BENIAH[4], SAMUEL[3], SAMUEL[2], THOMAS[1])* was born 06 Feb 1910, and died 04 Oct 1964. She married CLAYTON MILLS, son of ZENAS MILLS and MARY BARKER. He was born 05 Jun 1904, and died 18 Sep 1995.

Children of BERTHA MUNDT and CLAYTON MILLS are:
    i.   MARIE LOUISE[8] MILLS.
    ii. ARTHUR CLAYTON MILLS.
    iii. ELINORALICE MILLS.
    iv. ANN RUTH MILLS.
    v.   BURTON RAYMOND MILLS, m. ELIZABETH MAABRE.

642. MALCOLM CRAFT[7] MUNDT *(BERTHA MARIE[6] SPINNEY, GEORGE CRAFT[5], BENIAH[4], SAMUEL[3], SAMUEL[2], THOMAS[1])* was born 27 Apr 1916. He married (1) VIRGINIA CRAGIN. He married (2) EDITH RICE.

Children of MALCOLM MUNDT and VIRGINIA CRAGIN are:

  i. BARBARA ZANE[8] MUNDT.
  ii. MARGARET MUNDT.
  iii. DEBORAH MUNDT.

643. MARY[7] SPINNEY *(JOSEPH S[6], JOSEPH[5], JOHN[4], THOMAS[3], THOMAS[2], THOMAS[1])* was born 1837. She married SAMUAL BURNETT.

Children of MARY SPINNEY and SAMUAL BURNETT are:
  i. DOUGLAS[8] BURNETT.
  ii. HAROLD BURNETT.

644. SAMUEL ROGERS[7] SPINNEY *(THOMAS[6], THOMAS[5], JOHN[4], THOMAS[3], THOMAS[2], THOMAS[1])* was born Abt. 1822, and died Bef. 1900. He married MARTHA WILSON. She was born Jan 1825, and died Aft. 1900.

Children of SAMUEL SPINNEY and MARTHA WILSON are:
  i. MARTHA ABIGAIL[8] SPINNEY, b. 1849.

   Notes for MARTHA ABIGAIL SPINNEY:
   The National Society of the Daughters of the American Revolution Volume 31
   page 114
   Miss Martha Abigail Spinney.
   DAR ID Number: 30332
   Born in Suffolk county, Massachusetts.
   Descendant of Samuel Wilson, of Massachusetts.
   Daughter of Samuel Rogers Spinney and Martha Dana Wilson, his wife.
   Granddaughter of Jabez Wilson (1775-1836) and Elizabeth Prentiss, his wife.
   Gr.-granddaughter of Samuel Wilson.
   Samuel Wilson served, 1775, as a private from Woburn where in 1745 he was born

983. ii. SAMUEL ROGERS SPINNEY, b. 01 Jan 1853; d. 09 Jan 1884.
  iii. ALFRED B SPINNEY, b. Nova Scotia, Canada; d. 1855, Boston, Ma.

645. THOMAS M[7] SPINNEY *(THOMAS[6], THOMAS[5], JOHN[4], THOMAS[3], THOMAS[2], THOMAS[1])* was born Aug 1829 in Boston, MA, and died Aft. 1900. He married MARTHA ELEANOR ANDREWS 17 Nov 1853. She was born Oct 1834 in Boston, MA, and died Aft. 1900.

Children of THOMAS SPINNEY and MARTHA ANDREWS are:
984. i. EMMA AUGUSTA[8] SPINNEY, b. 02 Jan 1856, Boston, MA; d. 18 Oct 1936.
  ii. EDWIN ROGERS SPINNEY, b. 21 Dec 1857.

646. EDWIN BUCKINGHAM[7] SPINNEY *(THOMAS[6], THOMAS[5], JOHN[4], THOMAS[3], THOMAS[2], THOMAS[1])* was born 26 Jun 1831 in Portsmouth, NH, and died 19 Sep 1902. He married (1) SARAH AMANDA SOUTHER 09 Nov 1858 in Boston, MA. She was born 1835, and died 24 Mar 1871 in Boston, MA. He married (2) MARY AGNES REID 14 Oct 1874.

Children of EDWIN SPINNEY and MARY REID are:
  i. EDWIN BUCKINGHAM[8] SPINNEY, b. 18 Aug 1875; d. 08 Apr 1900.
  ii. THOMAS SHERWIN SPINNEY, b. 19 May 1881.

   Notes for THOMAS SHERWIN SPINNEY:
   1913 Harvard University Alumni Directory

647. MARY FRANCIS[7] SPINNEY *(THOMAS[6], THOMAS[5], JOHN[4], THOMAS[3], THOMAS[2], THOMAS[1])* was born 26 Jun 1851 in Boston, MA, and died Aft. 1910. She married SUMNER W HAMMOND 15 Apr 1880. He was born 15 Sep 1856.

Child of MARY SPINNEY and SUMNER HAMMOND is:
    i.   ANNIE S[8] HAMMOND, b. Jun 1882.

648. SAMUEL A[7] SPINNEY *(JOHN ROGERS[6], THOMAS[5], JOHN[4], THOMAS[3], THOMAS[2], THOMAS[1])* was born 1830. He married MARY E WALDRON 07 Nov 1852.

Child of SAMUEL SPINNEY and MARY WALDRON is:
    i.   CLARA[8] SPINNEY, b. 1855.

649. DANIEL JACKSON[7] SPINNEY *(JOHN ROGERS[6], THOMAS[5], JOHN[4], THOMAS[3], THOMAS[2], THOMAS[1])* was born 02 Dec 1838 in Plymouth, MA, and died Aft. 1870. He married LYDIA A. She was born 1840.

Children of DANIEL SPINNEY and LYDIA A are:
    i.   HANNAH[8] SPINNEY, b. Aug 1866.
    ii.   MARTHA SPINNEY, b. Aug 1866.
    iii.   FRED G SPINNEY, b. 03 May 1873, Portsmouth, NH; m. ELIZABETH P.

        Notes for FRED G SPINNEY:
        Fred was a stilborn

    iv.   HENRY B SPINNEY, b. 03 Sep 1879.
    v.   MABEL F SPINNEY, b. 01 Feb 1882.

650. SAMUEL HOUSTON[7] SPINNEY *(JOHN ROGERS[6], THOMAS[5], JOHN[4], THOMAS[3], THOMAS[2], THOMAS[1])* was born Mar 1847 in Portsmouth, NH, and died Bet. 1900 - 1910. He married IDA F STILES 07 Sep 1884. She was born Dec 1866 in Portsmouth, NH.

Children of SAMUEL SPINNEY and IDA STILES are:
    i.   IDA MAY[8] SPINNEY, b. 01 Jul 1885.
    ii.   ETTA FLORENCE SPINNEY, b. 27 Apr 1888; m. ELLIOTT.
    iii.   ELIZABETH M SPINNEY, b. Aug 1892.
    iv.   MARION GLADYS SPINNEY, b. 05 Oct 1894.
    v.   GEORGE DEWEY SPINNEY, b. 05 Aug 1898, Portsmouth, NH.
    vi.   CHARLES W SPINNEY, b. 1900.
    vii.   MABEL SPINNEY.
985.   viii.   ARTHUR C SPINNEY, b. 1891, New Hampsire; d. 1968, Eliot, ME.

651. THOMAS JEFFERSON[7] SPINNEY *(SAMUEL[6], THOMAS[5], JOHN[4], THOMAS[3], THOMAS[2], THOMAS[1])* was born 30 Jan 1830 in Portsmouth, NH, and died 06 Mar 1878. He married (1) SARAH WITHAM. She was born 1836, and died 1913. He married (2) SARAH ELIZABETH ADAMS 07 Nov 1853, daughter of CHARLES ADAMS and SARAH NOYES. She was born 16 Feb 1832, and died 04 Jun 1860.

Children of THOMAS SPINNEY and SARAH WITHAM are:
    i.   ARTHUR H[8] SPINNEY, b. 13 Aug 1866, Portsmouth, NH; d. Aft. 1920.
    ii.   BERTHA A SPINNEY, b. 1870.
    iii.   THOMAS D SPINNEY, b. 05 Jul 1872; d. 1910.
    iv.   PEARL E SPINNEY, b. 18 Dec 1876.

Children of THOMAS SPINNEY and SARAH ADAMS are:
    v.   EMMA STONE[8] SPINNEY, b. 05 Sep 1854; d. 15 May 1863.
986.   vi.   CHARLES EDWIN SPINNEY, b. 14 Oct 1857, Portsmouth, NH; d. 23 Feb 1890, Bridgewater, Ma.
    vii.   SARAH ELIZABETH SPINNEY, b. 25 May 1860; m. BERMIS.

652. HARRIET[7] SPINNEY *(SAMUEL[6], THOMAS[5], JOHN[4], THOMAS[3], THOMAS[2], THOMAS[1])* was born 1837. She married ANDREWS.

Child of HARRIET SPINNEY and ANDREWS is:

i. FLORA[8] ANDREWS, b. 1860.

653. ROBERT MORRISON[7] SPINNEY (*SAMUEL[6], THOMAS[5], JOHN[4], THOMAS[3], THOMAS[2], THOMAS[1]*) was born 29 Jun 1839 in Portsmouth, NH, and died 22 May 1913 in Medford, MA. He married SUSAN MARIA CARLTON, daughter of ALBERT CARLETON.

Notes for ROBERT MORRISON SPINNEY:
Enlisted in the Cical War 19 April 1961
Promoted to Full Corpl
Promoted to Full Sergt on 14 February 1863
Promoted to Full 2nd Lieut on 10 March 1864 (As of Co. D 7th UC Inf)
Promoted to Brevet Capt on 13 March 1865
Promoted to Full 1st Lieut on 30 May 1865 (As of Co. B)
Served Massachusetts Enlisted D Co. 7th Inf Reg. UC Mustered Out on 13 October 1866
Died on 22 May 1913

Children of ROBERT SPINNEY and SUSAN CARLTON are:
    i. CARLETON F[8] SPINNEY, b. 04 Mar 1868, Charlestown, MA; m. BLANCH CANNON, 1892; b. Mar 1872, Pennsylvania.
    ii. SYBIIL C SPINNEY, b. 1871; d. 1875, Boston, MA.
    iii. ALICE VIRGINIA SPINNEY, b. 08 Jun 1871, Charlestown, MA.
987.   iv. PAUL REVERE SPINNEY, b. Mar 1879.
    v. ROBERT M SPINNEY, b. Jan 1885.

654. CHESLEY[7] SPINNEY (*SAMUEL[6], THOMAS[5], JOHN[4], THOMAS[3], THOMAS[2], THOMAS[1]*) was born 1843 in Portsmouth, NH. He married MARY F WHITEHOUSE 29 Dec 1869. She was born in Great Falls, NH.

Child of CHESLEY SPINNEY and MARY WHITEHOUSE is:
    i. HENRY C[8] SPINNEY, b. 11 Jul 1878, Great Falls, NH.

655. JOSEPH F[7] SPINNEY (*JOSEPH[6], THOMAS[5], JOHN[4], THOMAS[3], THOMAS[2], THOMAS[1]*) was born Dec 1849 in Penn, and died Aft. 1900. He married SARAH A CONNERY 1868 in Boston, MA, daughter of DAVID CONNERY and ELLEN. She was born Nov 1848, and died Aft. 1920.

Children of JOSEPH SPINNEY and SARAH CONNERY are:
    i. MINNIE I[8] SPINNEY, b. 1872; d. 1872.
    ii. WALTER FIFIELD SPINNEY, b. 27 Nov 1873, Boston, MA; d. Aft. 1900; m. LOUISE ADAMS, 1899, Boston, MA; b. 1881.
    iii. DAVID FREDERICK SPINNEY, b. Sep 1875, Boston, MA; d. Aft. 1920.
    iv. JOSEPH SPINNEY, b. 1878; d. 1879.
    v. ELLA FRANCES SPINNEY, b. Nov 1880; d. Aft. 1920.

656. IRVING JOHN[7] ROWELL (*JANE P[6] SPINNEY, ALEXANDER[5], JOHN[4], THOMAS[3], THOMAS[2], THOMAS[1]*) was born 23 Nov 1850. He married (1) SARAH E CROSBY, daughter of WALTER CROSBY and ELIZABETH. She was born 1869, and died Bet. 1880 - 1890. He married (2) EMMA G DOW 24 May 1892, daughter of THOMAS DOW and GEORGIANNA ROLLINS. She was born 14 Jan 1865.

Child of IRVING ROWELL and SARAH CROSBY is:
    i. BERTHA[8] ROWELL, b. Jul 1878.

657. JULIA M[7] SPINNEY (*JOHN DICKEY[6], ALEXANDER[5], JOHN[4], THOMAS[3], THOMAS[2], THOMAS[1]*) was born 31 Dec 1846, and died Aft. 1880. She married JAMES N MOULTON Sep 1868. He was born 1841, and died Aft. 1880.

Child of JULIA SPINNEY and JAMES MOULTON is:
    i. WILBUR V[8] MOULTON, b. 1864.

658. ELLEN AUGUSTA[7] SPINNEY *(JOHN DICKEY[6], ALEXANDER[5], JOHN[4], THOMAS[3], THOMAS[2], THOMAS[1])* was born 17 May 1852, and died 10 Dec 1944. She married WALTER FRANK GREGG May 1874 in Londonderry, NH.

Children of ELLEN SPINNEY and WALTER GREGG are:
988.   i.   MAUDE AUGUSTA[8] GREGG, b. 1875.
          ii.   HUBERT GREGG, b. 1878.

659. EUGENE LAROY[7] SPINNEY *(JOHN DICKEY[6], ALEXANDER[5], JOHN[4], THOMAS[3], THOMAS[2], THOMAS[1])* was born 19 May 1852 in Londonderry, NH. He married LAURA A MERRILL 01 Jan 1879 in Londonderry, NH.

Children of EUGENE SPINNEY and LAURA MERRILL are:
          i.   ETHEL[8] SPINNEY, b. 1880, Haverhill, MA.
          ii.   ALICE SPINNEY, b. 1883.
          iii.   GRACE M SPINNEY, b. 1888.
          iv.   LAURA SPINNEY, b. 1886.
          v.   GLADYS SPINNEY, b. 1892.
          vi.   DORIS SPINNEY, b. 1892.

660. WILLIAM[7] SPINNEY *(ALEXANDER[6], GEORGE PETTEGREW[5], JOHN[4], JOHN[3], JOHN[2], THOMAS[1])* was born 06 Jan 1821 in New Market, NH, and died 31 May 1894 in Providence, RI. He married ABIGAIL M BICKFORD 04 May 1845 in Dover, NH, daughter of WILLIAM BICKFORD and MARY NELSON. She was born 1824 in Maine, and died 1901 in Attleboro, Ma.

Children of WILLIAM SPINNEY and ABIGAIL BICKFORD are:
          i.   GEORGIANNA[8] SPINNEY, b. 1847, Rhode Island; m. CHARLES PAINE.
          ii.   EDWARD R SPINNEY, b. 1849, Rhode Island; d. 1919, Rhode Island; m. ALICE J CLARK, 05 Apr 1888, Rhode Island; b. 1845; d. 1937, Rhode Island.
989.   iii.   JAMES A SPINNEY, b. 1854; d. 22 Dec 1897, Rhode Island.
          iv.   IDA J SPINNEY, b. 1855; m. ADELBERT L HEATH, 1881, Attleboro; b. 1849.
          v.   FREDERIC SPINNEY, b. 1858; d. 1865.
990.   vi.   CHARLES J SPINNEY, b. 1862.
          vii.   EMMA A SPINNEY, b. 19 Jul 1870, Rhode Island.

661. SERENA[7] TETHERLY *(SAMUEL[6], SAMUEL[5], WILLIAM[4], MERCY[3] SPINNEY, JOHN[2], THOMAS[1])* was born 30 Dec 1822, and died 10 Jul 1907. She married DANIEL LANGDON BROOKS 28 Oct 1841 in Eliot, ME, son of DANIEL BROOKS and ELIZABETH REMICK. He was born 06 May 1819 in Eliot, ME, and died 31 May 1904 in Eliot, ME.

Children of SERENA TETHERLY and DANIEL BROOKS are:
991.   i.   ALFRED LANGDON[8] BROOKS, b. 22 May 1842, Eliot, ME; d. 07 Dec 1903, Kittery, ME.
992.   ii.   EMILY ANN BROOKS, b. 05 Dec 1847; d. 12 Sep 1913.
993.   iii.   CLARA FRANCES BROOKS, b. 14 Dec 1847; d. 16 Mar 1913.
994.   iv.   MARY OLIVIA BROOKS, b. 14 Oct 1850; d. 1935.
995.   v.   FRANK PIERCE BROOKS, b. 08 Jul 1852; d. 08 Oct 1913.
          vi.   FLORA SYRENA BROOKS, b. 17 Apr 1858; d. 12 Dec 1910; m. (1) JOHN HUTCHINS; m. (2) RICHARD REMICK.

662. CAROLINE[7] SPINNEY *(JAMES[6], GEORGE PETTEGREW[5], JOHN[4], JOHN[3], JOHN[2], THOMAS[1])* was born 1818, and died Aft. 1850. She married NATHAN MCKENNEY 11 Feb 1838. He died Bef. 1850.

Children of CAROLINE SPINNEY and NATHAN MCKENNEY are:
          i.   MARY ELIZA[8] MCKENNEY, b. 1839.
          ii.   ANNA MCKENNEY, b. 1843.
          iii.   JULIA MCKENNEY, b. 1843.
          iv.   NATHAN MCKENNEY, b. 1845; m. (1) ROSE POWELL; m. (2) MARY BURKE.

          Notes for NATHAN MCKENNEY:
          History of Rockingham County, New Hampshire and Representative Citizens
             by Charles A. Hazlett, Richmond-Arnold Publishing Co., Chicago, Ill., 1915

NATHAN A. McKENNEY, after many years of business activity at Portsmouth, New Hampshire, is now living in practical retirement, giving his attention only to personal realty investments. He engaged extensively in carpentering and contracting for many years, and also for a few years was in the lumber business in association with Mr. E. J. F. Littlefield. He is a man of ability and substance and has always occupied a position high in the regard of his fellow men.

Mr. McKenney was born in Eliot, Maine, August 4, 1845, and is a son of Nathan and Caroline (Spinney) McKenney, both natives of Maine, Mrs. McKenney having been born in Eliot. Both are deceased. The father was lost at sea when Nathan was but six months old. The other children of the family are Mary Elizabeth, Anna and Julia A., the two last named being twins.

Nathan A. McKenney received but meager schooling in the public schools, as it was necessary for him to start work at the early age of ten years. He learned the carpenter's trade with B. F. Webster with whom he continued four years. He followed his trade in the navy yard, and for a period of twenty-five years was in business for himself, engaged in carpentering and contracting. In September, 1910, with E. J. F. Littlefield as a partner, he purchased the Thomas Call and Son Lumber Company. In 1913 he sold out his interest in this company, retiring from active business life. His operations have been extensive, and he well merits the success which has been his.

In 1867, Mr. McKenney was joined in marriage with Rose Powell, who died in 1882, leaving the following daughters: Anna Gertrude, Esther Maude, Bertha Emma, and Susan Lillian. In March, 1885, he was married to Mary Ellen Burke, who was born in Portsmouth, and is a daughter of David and Hannah (Orne) Burke, her father being a native of Nova Scotia and her mother of Durham, N. H. Religiously, they attend the Hanover Street Advent Church.

663. OLIVER P[7] SPINNEY *(JAMES[6], GEORGE PETTEGREW[5], JOHN[4], JOHN[3], JOHN[2], THOMAS[1])* was born Abt. 1820 in Eliot, ME, and died Bef. 1850. He married NANCY WHITEHOUSE 23 Nov 1837 in Dover, New Hampshire, daughter of SAMUEL WHITEHOUSE. She was born in South Berwick, ME, and died 14 Oct 1877 in Portsmouth, NH.

Child of OLIVER SPINNEY and NANCY WHITEHOUSE is:
996.   i.   AZARIAH L[8] SPINNEY, b. 1840; d. 10 Dec 1898.

664. BENJAMIN[7] SPINNEY *(JAMES[6], GEORGE PETTEGREW[5], JOHN[4], JOHN[3], JOHN[2], THOMAS[1])* was born 1824 in Eliot, Maine, and died 1870 in Winchenton, Ma. He married MARY ANN HALL. She was born 1829 in New Hampshire.

Children of BENJAMIN SPINNEY and MARY HALL are:
          i.   JAMES FREEMAN[8] SPINNEY, b. 17 May 1855, Reading, Massachusetts; d. 1872, Stoneham, Ma.
         ii.   FLORA SPINNEY, b. 24 Mar 1857, Reading, Ma.

665. JOSEPH[7] SPINNEY *(JAMES[6], GEORGE PETTEGREW[5], JOHN[4], JOHN[3], JOHN[2], THOMAS[1])* was born 1821, and died 20 Oct 1870. He married (1) ELIZABETH P DIXON 16 Mar 1848, daughter of JOSEPH DIXON and ELIZABETH LIBBEY. She was born 1816, and died 11 Dec 1848. He married (2) ELIZABETH J BROOKS 09 Jan 1857. She was born Jul 1832, and died Aft. 1880.

Children of JOSEPH SPINNEY and ELIZABETH BROOKS are:
          i.   ADRIANNA[8] SPINNEY, b. 1858.
         ii.   JOSEPH EVERETT SPINNEY, b. 1860; d. 02 Oct 1860.
        iii.   HERMAN C SPINNEY, b. 1862; d. 15 Jun 1884.
997.   iv.   JOSEPH ELMOR SPINNEY, b. 1868; d. Bef. 1900.

666. JAMES H[7] SPINNEY *(JAMES[6], GEORGE PETTEGREW[5], JOHN[4], JOHN[3], JOHN[2], THOMAS[1])* was born 1825, and died 10 Oct 1894. He married OLIVE G ASPINWALL 1860 in Rollinsford New Hampshire. She was born 1831, and died 07 Aug 1869.

Children of JAMES SPINNEY and OLIVE ASPINWALL are:
      i.   ALEXANDER HAVEN[8] SPINNEY, b. 1859; d. 12 Jan 1905, Lynn, Ma.
      ii.   JAMES W SPINNEY, b. 1869; d. 31 Mar 1870.

667. HENRY PARKER[7] SPINNEY *(JAMES[6], GEORGE PETTEGREW[5], JOHN[4], JOHN[3], JOHN[2], THOMAS[1])* was born 06 Jan 1836, and died 28 Aug 1917. He married OLIVE NEWBEGIN. She was born 1838, and died 21 Apr 1872.

Children of HENRY SPINNEY and OLIVE NEWBEGIN are:
998.   i.   EUGENE H[8] SPINNEY, b. Apr 1861, Maine; d. Aft. 1900.
        ii.   ADDIE SPINNEY, b. 1863; m. TETHERLY.
999.   iii. HENRY C SPINNEY, b. 1865.
1000.   iv. HARRIS E SPINNEY, b. 26 Mar 1868, Eliot, Maine; d. 22 Mar 1951, Eliot, Maine.

668. AUGUSTUS W[7] SPINNEY *(SIMON[6], GEORGE PETTEGREW[5], JOHN[4], JOHN[3], JOHN[2], THOMAS[1])* was born 08 Aug 1827 in Eliot, ME, and died 06 Oct 1892 in Eliot, ME. He married SARAH SHAPLEIGH, daughter of IVORY SHAPLEIGH and SARAH CHICK. She was born 12 Oct 1828 in Eliot, ME, and died Aft. 1910.

Children of AUGUSTUS SPINNEY and SARAH SHAPLEIGH are:
       i.   SARAH[8] SPINNEY, b. 1851; d. 10 Jun 1868, Eliot Maine.
1001.   ii.   AUGUSTA SPINNEY, b. 1854; d. 14 Sep 1918, Malden, MA.
1002.   iii. ALMON SPINNEY, b. Feb 1857; d. 24 Dec 1923.
       iv. HELEN AUGUSTA SPINNEY, b. 1860.
       v.   HERMAN SPINNEY, b. 1861, Eliot, ME; d. 24 Feb 1867, Eliot, ME.
1003.   vi. LEANDER E SPINNEY, b. 1863, Kittery, ME.

669. MOSES J[7] SPINNEY *(SIMON[6], GEORGE PETTEGREW[5], JOHN[4], JOHN[3], JOHN[2], THOMAS[1])* was born Apr 1832 in Portsmouth, NH, and died 1900. He married JESSIE. She was born 1831, and died 1897.

Children of MOSES SPINNEY and JESSIE are:
1004.   i.   CALVIN A[8] SPINNEY, b. 1854, New Hampshire; d. Aft. 1910.
1005.   ii.   CAROLINE A SPINNEY, b. 1854; d. Aft. 1900.
       iii. ADELINE A SPINNEY, b. 1856; d. Aft. 1880.
       iv. IDA MAY SPINNEY, b. 04 May 1858; d. Aft. 1870.

670. SIMON FREDERICK[7] SPINNEY *(SIMON[6], GEORGE PETTEGREW[5], JOHN[4], JOHN[3], JOHN[2], THOMAS[1])* was born 1835 in Portsmouth, NH, and died 13 Dec 1893 in Eliot, ME. He married MARGARET A. She was born Jun 1837, and died 26 Jan 1906.

Children of SIMON SPINNEY and MARGARET A are:
1006.   i.   IDA M[8] SPINNEY, b. 1858.
       ii.   WILLIE DAVIS SPINNEY, b. 1872.

671. MARY OLIVE[7] SPINNEY *(SIMON[6], GEORGE PETTEGREW[5], JOHN[4], JOHN[3], JOHN[2], THOMAS[1])* was born 1838, and died 1910 in Medford, Ma. She married CHARLES W. BREWSTER. He was born 1829, and died 1886.

Children of MARY SPINNEY and CHARLES BREWSTER are:
      i.   ADA[8] BREWSTER.
      ii.   HERBERT BREWSTER.
      iii. JOSHUA BREWSTER.
      iv. WILLIE BREWSTER.
      v.   EMMA BREWSTER.
      vi. WALTER BREWSTER.
      vii. ARTHUR BREWSTER.

672. HAMMOND[7] SPINNEY *(FRANCIS[6], GEORGE PETTEGREW[5], JOHN[4], JOHN[3], JOHN[2], THOMAS[1])* was born 10 Nov 1824 in Kittery, ME, and died 05 Aug 1900. He married LIZZIE URCH, daughter of EPHRAIM URCH and MARIA SHERMAN. She was born Jul 1837, and died 21 Sep 1924.

Children of HAMMOND SPINNEY and LIZZIE URCH are:
1007.	i.	WILMONT E[8] SPINNEY, b. 1865; d. 1949.
1008.	ii.	HENRY B SPINNEY, b. 1866; d. 1945.
1009.	iii.	ALBERT S SPINNEY, b. Jun 1870; d. 1959.
	iv.	CARRIE SPINNEY, b. 1871; d. 05 Apr 1872.
	v.	ANNIE M SPINNEY, b. 1873; d. 01 Nov 1884.
	vi.	WALTER SPINNEY, b. 1876, Kittery, ME; d. 20 Dec 1878.

673. HAMILTON[7] SPINNEY *(FRANCIS[6], GEORGE PETTEGREW[5], JOHN[4], JOHN[3], JOHN[2], THOMAS[1])* was born 06 Nov 1826 in Kittery, ME, and died 09 Sep 1907 in Newburyport, Ma. He married BETSY DOWNS TETHERLY Aft. 1850, daughter of CHARLES TETHERLY and REBECCA SPINNEY. She was born 1832, and died 10 Mar 1899 in Kittery Maine.

Children of HAMILTON SPINNEY and BETSY TETHERLY are:
	i.	REBECCA[8] SPINNEY, b. 1851.
	ii.	LAURA SPINNEY, b. 1853.
1010.	iii.	WILLIAM HERBERT SPINNEY, b. Jun 1855, Eliot, ME; d. Aft. 1920.
1011.	iv.	CHARLES HAMILTON SPINNEY, b. 02 Nov 1859, Kittery, ME; d. 05 Apr 1936, Dover, NH.
	v.	MARY E SPINNEY, b. 1860.
1012.	vi.	MARCIA MELINDA SPINNEY, b. 01 Sep 1861, Eliot, ME; d. 1937.
1013.	vii.	FLORENCE OLIVIA SPINNEY, b. Oct 1869; d. Aft. 1900.
	viii.	HENRY A SPINNEY, b. 1873.
1014.	ix.	SADIE R SPINNEY, b. 21 Apr 1864; d. 12 Feb 1931.

674. SYLVESTER[7] SPINNEY *(FRANCIS[6], GEORGE PETTEGREW[5], JOHN[4], JOHN[3], JOHN[2], THOMAS[1])* was born 18 Dec 1828, and died 14 Jun 1892 in Kittery Maine. He married MARY A URCH, daughter of EPHRAIM URCH and MARIA SHERMAN. She was born 25 May 1834, and died 20 Jun 1916 in Kittery Maine.

Children of SYLVESTER SPINNEY and MARY URCH are:
1015.	i.	VIENNA[8] SPINNEY, b. 1854; d. Chelsea, MA.
1016.	ii.	ALFRED SPINNEY, b. 04 Oct 1855; d. 12 Jan 1939.
1017.	iii.	FRANK A SPINNEY, b. 1856; d. 1936, Kittery Maine.
1018.	iv.	MELVILLE SYLVESTER SPINNEY, b. 1858; d. 1930.
1019.	v.	GEORGE E SPINNEY, b. Jul 1863; d. 1933.
	vi.	ERNEST CHESTER SPINNEY, b. Apr 1873; d. 1952; m. BERNICE M SHAPLEIGH, 14 Oct 1896; b. Oct 1878; d. 1950.
1020.	vii.	ALBERT LESTER SPINNEY, b. 06 May 1875; d. 19 Apr 1969.

675. ANN MARY[7] SPINNEY *(FRANCIS[6], GEORGE PETTEGREW[5], JOHN[4], JOHN[3], JOHN[2], THOMAS[1])* was born 28 Oct 1833 in Kittery, ME, and died 05 Aug 1921. She married DANIEL PARKER SPINNEY 1854, son of JOSIAH SPINNEY and CLARISSA KNIGHT. He was born 21 Jan 1827 in Kittery, ME, and died 04 Oct 1905 in Kittery, ME.

Children are listed above under (466) Daniel Parker Spinney.

676. FRANCIS LEMUEL[7] SPINNEY *(FRANCIS[6], GEORGE PETTEGREW[5], JOHN[4], JOHN[3], JOHN[2], THOMAS[1])* was born 01 Oct 1840, and died Aft. 1930. He married (1) ELIZABETH FREEMAN Aft. 1860. She died Bef. 1880. He married (2) CLESSIE PLACE 30 Oct 1906. She was born 1890.

Children of FRANCIS SPINNEY and ELIZABETH FREEMAN are:
	i.	HATTIE[8] SPINNEY.
	ii.	MELINDA SPINNEY, b. 1866.
	iii.	FRANCIS E SPINNEY, b. 14 Aug 1866.
1021.	iv.	AMMI ADVILLE SPINNEY, b. 1868; d. 1932.
	v.	GEORGE P SPINNEY, b. Abt. 1870.
	vi.	ARTHUR O SPINNEY, b. 1873.

1022.   vii.   LEONORA SPINNEY, b. 1875.
1023.   viii.   PEARL SPINNEY, b. 05 Aug 1875; d. 1943.
          ix.   MABEL SPINNEY, b. 15 Mar 1876; m. GEORGE DIXON; b. Abt. 1870.

Children of FRANCIS SPINNEY and CLESSIE PLACE are:
          x.   BERTHA[8] SPINNEY, b. 1905.
          xi.   MILDRED SPINNEY, b. 1907.

677. HENRY HOWARD[7] SPINNEY *(FRANCIS[6], GEORGE PETTEGREW[5], JOHN[4], JOHN[3], JOHN[2], THOMAS[1])* was born 23 Jun 1844, and died 1916. He married FRANCES. She was born 1845, and died 1913.

Children of HENRY SPINNEY and FRANCES are:
1024.   i.   MYRON E[8] SPINNEY, b. 1869; d. 1924.
          ii.   ADA A SPINNEY, b. 1863; m. GEORGE L WILLETT.

678. MARY R[7] TETHERLY *(CHARLES[6], SAMUEL[5], WILLIAM[4], MERCY[3] SPINNEY, JOHN[2], THOMAS[1])* was born 18 Feb 1820, and died 1892. She married ICHABOD COLE 25 Nov 1841 in Kittery Maine, son of ICABOD COLE and ANN VARNEY. He was born 12 Jul 1818, and died 1904.

Children of MARY TETHERLY and ICHABOD COLE are:
          i.   GEORGE C[8] COLE, b. 12 Sep 1842.
          ii.   ICHABOD COLE, b. 18 Jul 1844.
          iii.   FRANK COLE, b. 10 Nov 1846.
          iv.   HANNIBAL COLE.
          v.   JOHN COLE.
          vi.   FLORENCE COLE.

679. SARAH[7] TETHERLY *(CHARLES[6], SAMUEL[5], WILLIAM[4], MERCY[3] SPINNEY, JOHN[2], THOMAS[1])* was born 10 Oct 1822, and died 1901. She married SAMUEL COLE 30 Oct 1842 in Kittery Maine, son of ICABOD COLE and ANN VARNEY. He was born 06 Jun 1820, and died Nov 1900.

Children of SARAH TETHERLY and SAMUEL COLE are:
1025.   i.   ANNIE R[8] COLE, b. 1845; d. 1877.
1026.   ii.   HENRY C COLE, b. 1847.
          iii.   CAROLINE COLE, b. 1849.
1027.   iv.   SAMUEL E COLE, b. 1852.
          v.   SARA COLE, b. 1854.
1028.   vi.   AURELLA COLE, b. 02 Sep 1856; d. 24 May 1939.
1029.   vii.   ARBELLA COLE, b. 1858; d. 1930.

680. BETSY DOWNS[7] TETHERLY *(CHARLES[6], SAMUEL[5], WILLIAM[4], MERCY[3] SPINNEY, JOHN[2], THOMAS[1])* was born 1832, and died 10 Mar 1899 in Kittery Maine. She married HAMILTON SPINNEY Aft. 1850, son of FRANCIS SPINNEY and MARY PAUL. He was born 06 Nov 1826 in Kittery, ME, and died 09 Sep 1907 in Newburyport, Ma.

Children are listed above under (673) Hamilton Spinney.

681. CHARLES WILLIAM[7] TETHERLY *(CHARLES[6], SAMUEL[5], WILLIAM[4], MERCY[3] SPINNEY, JOHN[2], THOMAS[1])* was born 1833. He married MARY.

Children of CHARLES TETHERLY and MARY are:
          i.   ABBIE[8] TETHERLY.
          ii.   CHARLES TETHERLY.
          iii.   AUGUSTA TETHERLY.
          iv.   MARY TETHERLY.

682. LYDIA N.[7] TETHERLY *(CHARLES[6], SAMUEL[5], WILLIAM[4], MERCY[3] SPINNEY, JOHN[2], THOMAS[1])* was born 15 Nov

1825, and died 1902. She married DANIEL S. DIXON 28 Dec 1843. He was born 14 Sep 1822 in Eliot, ME, and died 07 Apr 1891 in Eliot, ME.

Children of LYDIA TETHERLY and DANIEL DIXON are:
-     i.   ARABELLA⁸ DIXON, b. 25 Oct 1844; d. 08 Apr 1850.
- 1030.   ii.   CHARLES H. DIXON, b. 06 Dec 1846; d. 1894.
-     iii.   LYDIA O DIXON, b. 06 Nov 1848; d. 12 Apr 1850.
- 1031.   iv.   ADRIANNA A. DIXON, b. 14 Oct 1850.
-     v.   DANIEL W. DIXON, b. 15 Sep 1852; m. ARBELLA.
-     vi.   ABBIE A. DIXON, b. 21 Oct 1854.
- 1032.   vii.   MARY EVA DIXON, b. 06 Dec 1856, South Eliot, ME; d. 19 May 1932, South Eliot, ME.
-     viii.   INFANT DIXON, b. 12 Nov 1860, died young.

683. MIRIUM⁷ HANSCOM (*MIRIAM L⁶ SPINNEY, GEORGE PETTEGREW⁵, JOHN⁴, JOHN³, JOHN², THOMAS¹*) She married WILLIAM ADAMS.

Child of MIRIUM HANSCOM and WILLIAM ADAMS is:
-     i.   LAURA⁸ ADAMS.

684. DANIEL LANGDON⁷ BROOKS (*DANIEL⁶, MARY⁵ SPINNEY, JOHN⁴, JOHN³, JOHN², THOMAS¹*) was born 06 May 1819 in Eliot, ME, and died 31 May 1904 in Eliot, ME. He married SERENA TETHERLY 28 Oct 1841 in Eliot, ME, daughter of SAMUEL TETHERLY and OLIVE SPINNEY. She was born 30 Dec 1822, and died 10 Jul 1907.

Children are listed above under (661) Serena Tetherly.

685. HANNAH⁷ STACKPOLE (*EUNICE⁶ SPINNEY, JOHN⁵, JOHN⁴, JOHN³, JOHN², THOMAS¹*) was born 1810 in Kittery, ME, and died 22 Feb 1896. She married (1) JOHN W HARMON. He was born 1805 in York, ME, and died Bef. 1850. She married (2) JOHN DEVINE 29 Oct 1856.

Children of HANNAH STACKPOLE and JOHN HARMON are:
-     i.   JOHN W⁸ HARMON, b. 1834.
-     ii.   WILLIAM M HARMON, b. 21 Jul 1836, Kittery, ME; d. 02 Mar 1890, Barnstead, NH; m. SOPHRONA L SMITH, 15 Nov 1863, Portsmouth, NH.
-     iii.   CHARLES HENRY HARMON, b. 1840, Portsmouth, NH; m. MARY ELIZABETH BLY, 21 Oct 1871.
-     iv.   LUTHER HARMON, b. 1843.
-     v.   FRANLIN HARMON, b. 1845; m. ELIZABETH G DOWNING.
-     vi.   JEFFERSON HARMON, b. 1847.

686. FRANCIS ARTHUR⁷ LYDSTON (*WILLIAM⁶, WEYMOUTH⁵, ABIGAIL⁴ SPINNEY, ANDREW³, JOHN², THOMAS¹*) was born 24 Oct 1819 in Newburyport, MA. He married (1) CHARLOTTE MCDOUGALL 1841 in Boston MA, daughter of JOHN MCDOUGALL and MARY ANN. He married (2) SUSAN PETTENGILL 14 Nov 1853. She was born in Springfield, MA.

Children of FRANCIS LYDSTON and CHARLOTTE MCDOUGALL are:
- 1033.   i.   ARTHUR FRANCIS⁸ LYDSTON, b. Abt. 1844, Newburyport MA; d. 1892, San Jose, CA.
-     ii.   CLARENCE WILLIAM LYDSTON, b. Abt. 1849.

Children of FRANCIS LYDSTON and SUSAN PETTENGILL are:
-     iii.   WALTER⁸ LYDSTON, b. Abt. 1855.
-     iv.   CHARLOTTE LYDSTON, b. 01 Apr 1858.

687. ELIZABETH F⁷ SPINNEY (*JACOB REMICK⁶, JEREMIAH⁵, JOHN⁴, JOHN³, JOHN², THOMAS¹*) was born 29 Aug 1832 in Eliot, ME, and died Aft. 1880. She married TIMOTHY DAME 07 Feb 1853 in Newburyport, Ma, son of TIMOTHY DAME and SALLY. He was born 1832 in Newington, NH, and died Aft. 1880.

Children of ELIZABETH SPINNEY and TIMOTHY DAME are:
-     i.   LIZZIE MAY⁸ DAME.

         ii.   ELLA A DAME.
        iii.   ANGIE A DAME.
         iv.   LAURA V DAME.
          v.   LILLIAN A DAME.

688. HENRY DAME[7] SPINNEY *(JACOB REMICK[6], JEREMIAH[5], JOHN[4], JOHN[3], JOHN[2], THOMAS[1])* was born 1837 in Eliot, ME, and died 18 Nov 1889. He married FLORIA ROSELLA DIXON in Eliot Maine, daughter of CHARLES DIXON and MARY STAPLES. She was born 03 Dec 1852 in Eliot, ME, and died 12 Jun 1946 in Camdem, ME.

Children of HENRY SPINNEY and FLORIA DIXON are:
1034.   i.   IVAH WELLINGTON[8] SPINNEY, b. 07 Jun 1879, Eliot, ME; d. 1963, Rockhingham C0 NH.
         ii.   EDWIN H SPINNEY, b. 23 Jul 1875; d. 23 Feb 1948.
        iii.   MELINDA MAY SPINNEY, b. 1879; m. LOUIS SHERMAN.

689. ELLEN[7] KIMBALL *(SARAH JANE[6] SPINNEY, JEREMIAH[5], JOHN[4], JOHN[3], JOHN[2], THOMAS[1])* She married C E BRUNTLETT.

Child of ELLEN KIMBALL and C BRUNTLETT is:
          i.   ELSIE[8] BRUNTLETT.

690. ZILPHA[7] SPINNEY *(DAVID[6], ISAAC[5], JOHN[4], JOHN[3], JOHN[2], THOMAS[1])* was born 28 Feb 1814, and died 1905 in Somerville, Ma. She married GEORGE NICKERSON.

Children of ZILPHA SPINNEY and GEORGE NICKERSON are:
1035.   i.   GEORGIANNA[8] NICKERSON, b. 1844.
         ii.   ALEXANDER NICKERSON, b. 1846.
        iii.   MARY NICKERSON, b. 1843.

691. HIRAM[7] SPINNEY *(DAVID[6], ISAAC[5], JOHN[4], JOHN[3], JOHN[2], THOMAS[1])* was born 10 Jan 1827, and died 10 Jul 1936. He married EDITH A NICKERSON 1851 in Boston, MA, daughter of ALEXANDER NICKERSON. She was born 10 Aug 1828.

Children of HIRAM SPINNEY and EDITH NICKERSON are:
          i.   OSCAR D[8] SPINNEY, b. 29 Aug 1852.
1036.   ii.   ALLISON FAIRBANKS SPINNEY, b. 03 Nov 1853; d. Aft. 1930.
        iii.   GENEVA A SPINNEY, b. 27 Aug 1855.
1037.   iv.   ESTELLA BERTILLA SPINNEY, b. 23 Jul 1857, Argyle, NS..
1038.   v.   ERVIN H SPINNEY, b. 20 Jul 1860.
         vi.   CLARA E SPINNEY, b. 28 Nov 1861.
        vii.   MELZERT T SPINNEY, b. 28 Jul 1863.
1039. viii.   GEORGE N SPINNEY, b. 28 Sep 1865, Nova Scotia; d. Aft. 1900, Malden, MA.
         ix.   EDMUND SPINNEY, b. 1866.
          x.   CHARLES E SPINNEY, b. 25 Nov 1866.
         xi.   HERBERT D SPINNEY, b. 23 Aug 1868.
1040.   xii.   LEROY B SPINNEY, b. Abt. 1870, Central Argyle, NS..
       xiii.   ALONZO L SPINNEY, b. 28 Sep 1872; d. 11 Aug 1909, At Sea.
        xiv.   EVA L SPINNEY, b. 27 Feb 1878.

692. SOPHRONIA L[7] SPINNEY *(DAVID[6], ISAAC[5], JOHN[4], JOHN[3], JOHN[2], THOMAS[1])* was born 04 Oct 1829 in Argyle, NS. She married GEORGE W NEVENS 04 May 1853 in Boston, MA, son of JONTHAN NEVENS and LYDIA LANE. He was born 1820 in Calais, ME.

Children of SOPHRONIA SPINNEY and GEORGE NEVENS are:
1041.   i.   ARDELLA S[8] NEVENS, b. 1854, Boston, Ma.
         ii.   GEORGE NEVENS.

693. EUNICE[7] GAYTON *(ANNE[6] SPINNEY, ISAAC[5], JOHN[4], JOHN[3], JOHN[2], THOMAS[1])* was born 03 May 1818 in

Argyle, NS., and died Aft. 1881 in New Brunswick. She married THOMAS W SPINNEY 16 May 1839, son of JACOB SPINNEY and SUSANNA ATWOOD. He was born 20 Mar 1817 in Argyle, NS., and died Aft. 1881 in New Brunswick.

Children are listed above under (369) Thomas W Spinney.

694. JAMES[7] GAYTON *(ANNE[6] SPINNEY, ISAAC[5], JOHN[4], JOHN[3], JOHN[2], THOMAS[1])* was born 09 Jan 1820 in Argyle, NS., and died Aft. 1881. He married MYRA. She was born 1819, and died Aft. 1881.

Children of JAMES GAYTON and MYRA are:
  i. EUNICE[8] GAYTON, b. 1856.
  ii. LESLIE GAYTON, b. 1859.
  iii. ANNIE GAYTON, b. 1862.
  iv. SARAH E GAYTON, b. 1868.

695. GEORGE[7] FROST *(EUNICE[6] SPINNEY, ISAAC[5], JOHN[4], JOHN[3], JOHN[2], THOMAS[1])* was born 11 Feb 1826 in Argyle, NS.. He married (1) TAMZIN HOLSER in 22 aug 1855. He married (2) HANNAH BRIDGEO 01 Jun 1848.

Child of GEORGE FROST and HANNAH BRIDGEO is:
  i. ALBERT WALLACE[8] FROST, b. 30 Sep 1849, Argyle, NS..

696. LYDIA ANN[7] SPINNEY *(DANIEL[6], ISAAC[5], JOHN[4], JOHN[3], JOHN[2], THOMAS[1])* was born 15 Jun 1832 in Argyle, NS.. She married JOSEPH ROBERTS, son of JOSEPH ROBERTS and MERCY CHANDLER. He was born 1821.

Child of LYDIA SPINNEY and JOSEPH ROBERTS is:
  i. DELANCY[8] ROBERTS, b. 1858.

697. WHITFIELD[7] SPINNEY *(DANIEL[6], ISAAC[5], JOHN[4], JOHN[3], JOHN[2], THOMAS[1])* was born 13 Oct 1834 in Argyle, NS., and died Aft. 1881 in Argyle Nova Scotia. He married MARY. She was born 1838, and died Aft. 1881.

Children of WHITFIELD SPINNEY and MARY are:
  i. FREDERIC[8] SPINNEY, b. 1861.
  ii. WINEFORD SPINNEY, b. 1869.
  iii. FRANK SPINNEY, b. 1880.

698. LYMAN[7] SPINNEY *(BENJAMIN[6], BENJAMIN[5], JOHN[4], JOHN[3], JOHN[2], THOMAS[1])* was born 15 Jan 1820 in Argyle, NS., and died Aft. 1901. He married (1) RUTH. She was born 1828, and died Aft. 1881. He married (2) PATIENCE HAMILTON. She died 1873.

Child of LYMAN SPINNEY and PATIENCE HAMILTON is:
1042.   i. LYDIA[8] SPINNEY, b. 09 Dec 1855; d. 1926, Barrington, Shelburne, Nova Scotia, Canada.

699. HANNAH[7] SPINNEY *(BENJAMIN[6], BENJAMIN[5], JOHN[4], JOHN[3], JOHN[2], THOMAS[1])* was born 12 Jan 1822 in Argyle, NS.. She married ANDREW SPINNEY 21 Jan 1841, son of ANDREW SPINNEY and EXPERIENCE CROWELL. He was born 26 May 1810 in Nova Scotia, Canada.

Children are listed above under (377) Andrew Spinney.

700. SIMEON[7] SPINNEY *(BENJAMIN[6], BENJAMIN[5], JOHN[4], JOHN[3], JOHN[2], THOMAS[1])* was born 14 Jan 1824 in Argyle, NS., and died 1925 in Argyle, NS.. He married ABIGAIL. She was born 1831.

Children of SIMEON SPINNEY and ABIGAIL are:
  i. TINA[8] SPINNEY, b. 1858.
  ii. AGNES SPINNEY, b. 1860.
  iii. MATILDA SPINNEY, b. 1865.
  iv. THEORA SPINNEY, b. 1869.
1043.   v. ENOS SPINNEY, b. 1857, Canada; d. Aft. 1930, Massachusetts.

1044.	vi.	EMERSON E SPINNEY, b. 1863; d. 01 Dec 1942, Skagit, WA.

701.	SAMUEL R[7] SPINNEY *(BENJAMIN[6], BENJAMIN[5], JOHN[4], JOHN[3], JOHN[2], THOMAS[1])* was born 01 Jan 1826, and died 1860. He married MARIE ALLEN 1851 in Gloucester, MA. She was born 1833.

Children of SAMUEL SPINNEY and MARIE ALLEN are:
- i.	FRANCITIA[8] SPINNEY, b. 1855.
- ii.	INIS SPINNEY, b. 1857.
- iii.	HERMON SPINNEY, b. 1858.

702.	JONATHAN[7] SPINNEY *(BENJAMIN[6], BENJAMIN[5], JOHN[4], JOHN[3], JOHN[2], THOMAS[1])* was born 05 Apr 1829 in Argyle, NS., and died 25 Nov 1889 in Gloucester, MA. He married ALICE SAUNDERS 22 Jul 1854 in Mass, daughter of SAMUEL SAUNDERS and MARY ANN. She was born Oct 1830, and died Jun 1920 in Gloucester, MA.

Children of JONATHAN SPINNEY and ALICE SAUNDERS are:
	i.	EMMA H[8] SPINNEY, b. 20 Jul 1856, Gloucester, MA.
1045.	ii.	BENJAMIN H SPINNEY, b. 31 Dec 1858; d. Mar 1930.
	iii.	WILLIAM E SPINNEY, b. 1862; d. 1863.
	iv.	NELLIE C SPINNEY, b. 1867.
1046.	v.	ALICE ESTELLE SPINNEY, b. Apr 1872; d. 1944.
1047.	vi.	WALLACE CLIFFORD SPINNEY, b. 19 Dec 1874.

703.	HARRIS"CAPT" HARDING[7] SPINNEY *(BENJAMIN[6], BENJAMIN[5], JOHN[4], JOHN[3], JOHN[2], THOMAS[1])* was born 08 Nov 1832, and died 1876 in Weymouth, MA. He married MARY LOVELL CUSHING 1855 in Weymouth, Ma. She was born 30 Oct 1834 in Weymouth, Ma, and died 1876 in Weymouth, Ma.

Children of HARRIS"CAPT" SPINNEY and MARY CUSHING are:
1048.	i.	ALBERT L[8] SPINNEY, b. 1858, Massachusetts; d. Bet. 1910 - 1930.
	ii.	ISABELLA REBECCA WILDE SPINNEY, b. 1870.
	iii.	MARY H SPINNEY, b. 1859; d. 18 Aug 1859, Weymouth.

704.	HENRY[7] SPINNEY *(BENJAMIN[6], BENJAMIN[5], JOHN[4], JOHN[3], JOHN[2], THOMAS[1])* was born 19 Feb 1837 in Argyle, NS., and died 27 Sep 1873. He married SOPHIA GOODWIN 12 Dec 1860 in Argyle, NS., daughter of WARREN GOODWIN and FLORA KENNEY. She was born 06 Oct 1842 in Argyle, Yarmouth, Nova Scotia, Canada, and died 1937 in Argyle, Yarmouth, Nova Scotia, Canada.

Notes for HENRY SPINNEY:
The house of Mr. Henry Spinney, Argyle, was burned to the ground on Saturday evening, February 17th, and his five children perished in the flames. Mr. Spinney and his wife went to a neighbor's house about 7 o'clock that evening and remained until 9. The five children slept in one room upstairs, in two beds, and Mr. Spinney's mother (who was old and insane) in a room below. When the fire was discovered, Mr. Spinney being the first to arrive, the building was all ablaze. He carried a heavy ladder and placed it at an upper window, which he broke and made several attempts to enter the room and rescue the children, but in vain, as the smoke was so stifling and the flames so fierce that he failed to effect an entrance. He thought he heard two of the children cry out. The old woman was found in her bed asleep, and was carried out by some men uninjured. The fire was accidental, caused by the stovepipe igniting the woodwork around it. The names and ages of the children were as follows: Herman E., aged 10 years and 5 months; Rebecca L., 9 years; Ella J., 7 years and 4 months; Delphenia B., 4 years; and Eudora E., 1 year and 6 months. Two of the children had evidently arisen from their beds and tried to escape, as their remains were found some distance from the bedroom. This sad event cast a deep gloom over the locality and County, and a profound sympathy for Mr. and Mrs. Spinney was evinced in their sweeping and distressing bereavement. There was no insurance on the property.

Children of HENRY SPINNEY and SOPHIA GOODWIN are:
- i.	NORMAN E[8] SPINNEY, b. Sep 1861, Argyle, NS.; d. 17 Feb 1872, Argyle, NS..
- ii.	REBECCA L SPINNEY, b. 1863, Argyle, NS.; d. 17 Feb 1872, Argyle, NS..
- iii.	ELLEN H MERRICK (ELLA) SPINNEY, b. 03 Nov 1864, Argyle, NS.; d. 17 Feb 1872, Argyle, NS..
- iv.	WARREN G SPINNEY, b. 27 May 1867, Argyle, NS.; d. 17 Feb 1872.
- v.	DELPHENIA B SPINNEY, b. 1868, Argyle, NS.; d. 17 Feb 1872, Argyle, NS..

vi.   ANDORA E SPINNEY, b. 27 Aug 1872, Argyle, NS.; d. 17 Feb 1872, Argyle, NS..

705. REUBEN HAWES[7] SPINNEY *(REUBEN[6], ISAAC[5], JOHN[4], JOHN[3], JOHN[2], THOMAS[1])* was born 05 Sep 1840 in Argyle, NS., and died 21 Dec 1920 in Sanford, ME. He married ADELIA JANE SPINNEY 23 Jan 1862, daughter of MINOR SPINNEY and MARIA MC CLASEN. She was born 14 Nov 1841 in Argyle, NS., and died 04 Mar 1923.

Children of REUBEN SPINNEY and ADELIA SPINNEY are:
- i.   HELEN REED[8] SPINNEY, b. Sep 1862, Sanford, ME; d. 11 Nov 1928; m. ARTHUR HORTON GREENWOOD; b. Jan 1854, England.
- ii.   FRED WILFRED SPINNEY, b. 29 Jan 1864; d. Ventura, CA; m. (1) MINNIE MOULTON; b. 1864; m. (2) MAUD STUART.
- iii.   ALBERTA SPINNEY, b. 01 Nov 1866; d. 20 Oct 1881; m. MILLARD FILLMORE TEBBETTS, 11 Jun 1881; b. 22 Dec 1848; d. 31 Dec 1927.
- iv.   EDNA M SPINNEY, b. 30 Aug 1868; d. 23 Apr 1938, Bridgeton Maine; m. (1) EBEN COOLBROTH; m. (2) GEORGE KILBORN.
- 1049.   v.   SIDNEY H SPINNEY, b. 04 Apr 1870; d. 1925.
- 1050.   vi.   ALICE A SPINNEY, b. 25 Jul 1872, Argyle, NS.; d. 31 Jul 1899.
- vii.   HENRIETTA SPINNEY, b. 04 Sep 1875; d. 07 Jan 1876.
- viii.   HARRY REGINALD SPINNEY, b. 05 Aug 1877, Sanford, ME; d. 20 Jul 1934, Rhode Island; m. ETTA BIGELOW; b. 1873; d. 1941, Rhode Island.
- 1051.   ix.   CHARLES EMERY SPINNEY, b. 13 Dec 1880, Sanford, ME; d. Feb 1951.
- x.   JESSIE ADELIA SPINNEY, b. 14 Aug 1885, Sanford, ME; m. LEROY JONATHAN ABBOTT, 18 Apr 1906, Sandford Maine; b. 10 Feb 1882, North Paris, ME; d. 20 Mar 1963, North Paris, ME.

706. JAMES EMERY[7] SPINNEY *(REUBEN[6], ISAAC[5], JOHN[4], JOHN[3], JOHN[2], THOMAS[1])* was born 24 Sep 1844, and died Jul 1917. He married LIZZIE. She was born 1855.

Child of JAMES SPINNEY and LIZZIE is:
- 1052.   i.   NELLIE SOPHIA[8] SPINNEY, b. 17 Sep 1884, Nova Scotia, Canada; d. 1957.

707. ADALINE[7] SPINNEY *(REUBEN[6], ISAAC[5], JOHN[4], JOHN[3], JOHN[2], THOMAS[1])* was born 05 Dec 1836 in Argyle, NS.. She married ALBERT HENRY HOBART 15 Mar 1857 in Plymouth MA. He was born Dec 1834 in Hingham, MA, and died 05 Apr 1887 in Chelsea, MA.

Children of ADALINE SPINNEY and ALBERT HOBART are:
- i.   HARRY MARTIN[8] HOBART, b. 20 Aug 1858, Hingham, MA.
- ii.   CHARLES WHITON HOBART, b. 27 Aug 1860, Boston, MA; m. LINNIE AUGUSTA PARMENTER, Dec 1885.
- iii.   ALBERTINA FRANCES HOBART, b. 08 Oct 1862, Chelsea, MA.
- iv.   SUSAN WHITEN HOBART, b. 17 Sep 1865, Chelsea, MA.
- v.   WALTER LEON HOBART, b. 01 Oct 1868, Chelsea, MA.
- vi.   ALBERT EDWARD HOBART, b. 18 Jul 1874, Chelsea, MA.
- vii.   FRANK WILLIS HOBART, b. 30 Oct 1876, Chelsea, MA.
- viii.   FLORENCE ISABELLA HOBART, b. 28 Mar 1880, Chelsea, MA; d. Nov 1881, Chelsea, MA.

708. ELIZABETH[7] SPINNEY *(JOHN[6], AARON[5], JOHN[4], JOHN[3], JOHN[2], THOMAS[1])* was born 1839 in Arglye, Nova Scotia, and died 1916. She married MINOR H SPINNEY 1865, son of MINOR SPINNEY and MARIA MC CLASEN. He was born 1837, and died 1922 in Sandford, ME.

Children of ELIZABETH SPINNEY and MINOR SPINNEY are:
- i.   BERNICE[8] SPINNEY, b. 1881, Canada.
- ii.   JOSEPHINE SPINNEY, b. 1864.
- 1053.   iii.   NEHEMIAH SPINNEY, b. 19 Aug 1866; d. 1927.
- iv.   EFFIE SPINNEY, b. 1867.
- v.   MAUD SPINNEY, b. 1873.
- vi.   ALVENIA SPINNEY, b. 1879.

709. CALVIN CANN[7] SPINNEY *(JOHN[6], AARON[5], JOHN[4], JOHN[3], JOHN[2], THOMAS[1])* was born Abt. 1820. He married GEORGIANNA JANE CAMPBELL 1872.

Children of CALVIN SPINNEY and GEORGIANNA CAMPBELL are:
1054.   i.   ORETHA F[8] SPINNEY, b. 1875, Yarmouth, NS.; d. 1945, Gloucester, MA.
       ii.   CLAYTON DONALD SPINNEY, b. 1880; d. 1940; m. AGATHA GOODWIN, 1900.
      iii.   DORA SPINNEY, b. 1884.
      iv.   GILBERT SPINNEY, b. 1885.
      v.   MATTIE SPINNEY, b. 1886.
      vi.   ROBERT OZERO SPINNEY, b. 1883; d. 1950.

710. JAMES HARVEY[7] SPINNEY (*JOHN[6], AARON[5], JOHN[4], JOHN[3], JOHN[2], THOMAS[1]*) was born 1839 in Arglye, Nova Scotia, and died Bef. 1910. He married SARAH MCCLARREN 1866. She was born 1847, and died Aft. 1910 in Andover, Ma.

Children of JAMES SPINNEY and SARAH MCCLARREN are:
      i.   GERTRUDE[8] SPINNEY, b. 1869; d. Aft. 1910.
      ii.   EDWIN SPINNEY, b. 1871.
      iii.   JULIA M SPINNEY, b. 1873; d. Aft. 1910.
      iv.   ADA SPINNEY, b. 1874.
      v.   CORA SPINNEY, b. 1876.
      vi.   VIOLA SPINNEY, b. 1879.
1055.   vii.   CHARLES HARVEY SPINNEY, b. 02 Feb 1884; d. Oct 1969.
     viii.   ELIZABETH A SPINNEY, b. 1891; d. 21 Jan 1910, Andover, MA.

711. JOSEPH WILSON[7] SPINNEY (*JOHN[6], AARON[5], JOHN[4], JOHN[3], JOHN[2], THOMAS[1]*) was born 1844 in Nova Scotia, and died Aft. 1900. He married AGNES 1865, daughter of EZARA SPINNEY and LUCY RYDER. She was born 1844, and died Aft. 1910.

Children of JOSEPH SPINNEY and AGNES are:
      i.   LUCY ALICE[8] SPINNEY, b. 1867, Nova Scotia; m. ANDREW MCKAY; b. 1865.
      ii.   JOHN MELVIN SPINNEY, b. 1868; d. 1868.
1056.   iii.   LESLIE ATHERTON SPINNEY, b. Oct 1869, Nova Scotia; d. 1912, Provincetown, MA.
      iv.   ARTHUR ERNEST SPINNEY, b. 1874, Massachusetts; d. 1874.
1057.   v.   LAURA ELLA SPINNEY, b. 1875, Boston, Massachusetts; d. Aft. 1930.
      vi.   LILLAN HANNAH SPINNEY, b. 1877, Massachusetts; m. REGINALD GAYTON; b. 1872, Canada.

712. AMIEL[7] SPINNEY (*JOHN[6], AARON[5], JOHN[4], JOHN[3], JOHN[2], THOMAS[1]*) was born 1843 in Yarmouth Nova Scotia. He married ABIGAIL GILLISON. She was born 1846.

Children of AMIEL SPINNEY and ABIGAIL GILLISON are:
      i.   FRANK[8] SPINNEY, b. 1868.
      ii.   NELLIE SPINNEY, b. 1869.
      iii.   CARRIE SPINNEY, b. 1872.
      iv.   GRACIE SPINNEY, b. 1875.

713. JACOB[7] WHITMAN (*SPINNEY[6], ANNIE[5] SPINNEY, JOHN[4], JOHN[3], JOHN[2], THOMAS[1]*) was born Abt. 1820, and died 1886. He married CHARLOTTE WILT.

Children of JACOB WHITMAN and CHARLOTTE WILT are:
      i.   LEVI[8] WHITMAN.
1058.   ii.   CLEMENT WHITMAN.
      iii.   CHARLOTTE WHITMAN.

714. MORRIS[7] SPINNEY (*JACOB[6], JACOB[5], JOHN[4], JOHN[3], JOHN[2], THOMAS[1]*) was born 04 Dec 1820. He married MARGARET.

Children of MORRIS SPINNEY and MARGARET are:
1059.   i.   HAVELOCK[8] SPINNEY, b. 18 Feb 1858; d. Aft. 1901.
      ii.   ELIZA SPINNEY, b. 1851.

   iii.   STILLMAN SPINNEY, b. 1858; m. ELIZABETH (LIZZIE) LEONARD, 1883, Boston, MA; b. 1859; d. 1889.
   iv.   MATILDA SPINNEY, b. 1861.
   v.   EUNICE SPINNEY, b. 1864; m. ABRAM HENDERSON.
   vi.   MARY SPINNEY, b. 1856; m. NATHAN MACPHEE.

715. SARAH[7] SPINNEY *(JACOB[6], JACOB[5], JOHN[4], JOHN[3], JOHN[2], THOMAS[1])* was born 16 Jun 1822. She married BAILEY PALMER. He was born 1823 in PEI, and died in Cumberland Nova Scotia.

Children of SARAH SPINNEY and BAILEY PALMER are:
1060.   i.   SARAH[8] PALMER, b. 1848, Nova Scotia; d. 02 Apr 1929, Roxbury, MA, USA.
        ii.   SUSAN PALMER.
        iii.   JACOB PALMER.
        iv.   JAMES PALMER.
        v.   AMELIA PALMER.

716. AARON[7] SPINNEY *(JACOB[6], JACOB[5], JOHN[4], JOHN[3], JOHN[2], THOMAS[1])* was born 19 Nov 1824 in Nova Scotia, and died 16 Nov 1911 in York, ME. He married EUNICE E GOWEN 1852 in Boston Mass. She was born 1831 in Maine, and died 1900 in Maine.

Children of AARON SPINNEY and EUNICE GOWEN are:
    i.   ELIZABETH E[8] SPINNEY, b. 1852; d. 1939, Maine; m. GEORGE H NOWELL; b. 1851; d. 1921, Maine.
    ii.   ALBERT A SPINNEY, b. 17 Feb 1855, Charlestown, MA; m. (1) SUZIE TEBBITS, 04 Nov 1882, Rorchester New Hampsire; b. 1863; m. (2) SADIE J MILLS, 02 Dec 1899, Rochester New Hampsire; b. 1858.

717. JOANNNA[7] SPINNEY *(JACOB[6], JACOB[5], JOHN[4], JOHN[3], JOHN[2], THOMAS[1])* was born 1836. She married ED LOCKWOOD.

Children of JOANNNA SPINNEY and ED LOCKWOOD are:
    i.   WILLOUGHY[8] LOCKWOOD, b. 1854.
    ii.   BENJAMIN LOCKWOOD, b. 1866.
    iii.   LAWRENCE LOCKWOOD, b. 1877.

718. JAMES[7] SPINNEY *(JACOB[6], JACOB[5], JOHN[4], JOHN[3], JOHN[2], THOMAS[1])* was born 16 Apr 1839 in Nova Scotia, and died Aft. 1901. He married ISABELLA DOBSON 21 Aug 1871. She was born 16 Jun 1841, and died Aft. 1901.

Children of JAMES SPINNEY and ISABELLA DOBSON are:
    i.   EMMA[8] SPINNEY, b. 1872.
    ii.   JEANNIE SPINNEY, b. 1874.
    iii.   JACOB SPINNEY, b. 1879.
    iv.   ROY SPINNEY, b. 24 Nov 1882.
    v.   WILLIE SPINNEY, b. 24 Mar 1885.

719. JOSEPH[7] SPINNEY *(JOSEPH[6], JACOB[5], JOHN[4], JOHN[3], JOHN[2], THOMAS[1])* was born Aug 1827, and died 1912. He married FLORA ROSS. She was born 30 Sep 1834.

Children of JOSEPH SPINNEY and FLORA ROSS are:
    i.   ANNA BELLE[8] SPINNEY, b. 15 Mar 1860; d. 1954.
    ii.   WILLIAM MCGREGOR SPINNEY, b. 06 Sep 1862; d. 1947.
    iii.   CAROLINE SPINNEY, b. 30 Dec 1864; d. 1944.
    iv.   ELLISE SPINNEY, b. 07 Oct 1866; d. 1952.
    v.   GEORGIE SPINNEY, b. 07 Oct 1870; d. 1964.

720. SARAH[7] SPINNEY *(JOSEPH[6], JACOB[5], JOHN[4], JOHN[3], JOHN[2], THOMAS[1])* was born 29 Aug 1830 in Argyle, NS., and died 1912. She married DAVID MCDONALD 29 Jun 1854, son of JAMES MCDONALD. He was born 1830, and died Bef. 1901.

Children of SARAH SPINNEY and DAVID MCDONALD are:

      i. HIRMAN⁸ MCDONALD, b. 1865; d. 1940; m. MARGARET INGRAM, 1891.

      ii. SARAH ANN MCDONALD, b. 1855; d. 1947; m. JIM THOMPSON.

      iii. STILLMAN JOSEPH MCDONALD, b. 1857; d. 1951; m. (1) JESSIE FITZGERALD, 1885; m. (2) SADIE CASSIE, 1892.

      iv. MARGARET MATILDA MCDONALD, b. 1859; d. 1951; m. PETER CALDWELL, 1877.

      v. JAMES WM MCDONALD, b. 1862; d. 1924; m. EMMA.

      vi. DAVID ROSS MCDONALD, b. 1867; d. 1924.

721. STILLMAN⁷ SPINNEY *(JOSEPH⁶, JACOB⁵, JOHN⁴, JOHN³, JOHN², THOMAS¹)* was born 1834, and died 1888. He married EMELINE WOODBURY 05 Nov 1866 in Argyle Nova Scotia. She died 1883.

Children of STILLMAN SPINNEY and EMELINE WOODBURY are:

1061.   i. FREEMAN⁸ SPINNEY, b. 02 Dec 1867, Argyle, N.S; d. 04 Mar 1934.

1062.   ii. EMMA JANE SPINNEY, b. 1870; d. 1964.

1063.   iii. AGNES GERTRUDE SPINNEY, b. 17 Mar 1874; d. 15 Mar 1966.

      iv. JOSEPH SPINNEY, b. 1877.

1064.   v. LAURA MAE SPINNEY, b. 03 Apr 1880, Nova Scotia; d. 14 May 1956, Massachusetts.

722. RUTH⁷ SPINNEY *(FREEMAN⁶, JACOB⁵, JOHN⁴, JOHN³, JOHN², THOMAS¹)* was born 1833 in Argyle, NS.. She married WILLIAM V HUTT 11 Nov 1850 in Gloucester, MA, son of ADAM HUTT and ANN. He was born in Nova Scotia.

Child of RUTH SPINNEY and WILLIAM HUTT is:

      i. FRANK W⁸ HUTT, b. 1870.

723. JEREMIAH⁷ SPINNEY *(EBENEZER⁶, JACOB⁵, JOHN⁴, JOHN³, JOHN², THOMAS¹)* was born 10 Apr 1839 in Nova Scotia, and died Aft. 1901 in Argyle, Yarmouth, Nova Scotia. He married (1) MARTHA GOODWIN 1858, daughter of WARREN GOODWIN and MARTHA. She was born 1841. He married (2) ANN FROST 1888. She was born 30 Oct 1836.

Child of JEREMIAH SPINNEY and MARTHA GOODWIN is:

1065.   i. ALICE⁸ SPINNEY, b. 07 Sep 1859.

724. DAVID MCLARREN⁷ SPINNEY *(EBENEZER⁶, JACOB⁵, JOHN⁴, JOHN³, JOHN², THOMAS¹)* was born 20 Sep 1844 in Argyle, Yarmouth, Ns, and died Aft. 1930 in Malden, MA. He married DORCAS ANN GOODWIN 11 Jan 1872, daughter of WILLOUGHBY GOODWIN and ELEANOR GAYTON. She was born 1853, and died Aft. 1930 in Malden, MA.

Children of DAVID SPINNEY and DORCAS GOODWIN are:

      i. GRANVILLE⁸ SPINNEY, b. 21 Jan 1873.

      ii. DAVID DOW SPINNEY, b. 15 Feb 1875, Argyle, NS..

      iii. BRANTON E SPINNEY, b. 07 Sep 1876.

      iv. GRACE N SPINNEY, b. 1879.

      v. HARRY M SPINNEY, b. 1881.

725. BENJAMIN F⁷ SPINNEY *(EBENEZER⁶, JACOB⁵, JOHN⁴, JOHN³, JOHN², THOMAS¹)* was born 25 Apr 1847 in Argyle, Nova Scotia, and died 1898. He married (1) EUGINA HINES. She was born 02 Aug 1863. He married (2) EMMALINE SMITH 02 Nov 1870. She was born 1836 in Nova Scotia, and died 1895.

Children of BENJAMIN SPINNEY and EMMALINE SMITH are:

1066.   i. THELSTON D⁸ SPINNEY, b. 25 Oct 1875, Nova Scotia; d. 13 Jun 1957.

1067.   ii. ORESSA MARIA SPINNEY, b. 05 Sep 1877; d. 30 Jan 1965.

1068.   iii. EMERSON SPINNEY, b. 22 Aug 1883, Nova Scotia; d. May 1968, Everett, MA.

726. LOUISA BURNS⁷ SPINNEY *(JEREMIAH⁶, JACOB⁵, JOHN⁴, JOHN³, JOHN², THOMAS¹)* was born 19 Jun 1837. She married JOHN M SMITH 20 Aug 1863.

Children of LOUISA SPINNEY and JOHN SMITH are:
     i.   ELLA ESTHER⁸ SMITH, b. 05 Mar 1865; m. JOHN F MCLARREN.
     ii. WILLIAM R SMITH, b. 08 Jun 1867; d. 01 Jul 1867.
     iii. WILLIAM LEONARD SMITH, b. 30 Aug 1868.
     iv. CHARLES EDWARD SMITH, b. 10 Feb 1871.

727. ELLEN GAYTON⁷ SPINNEY *(THOMAS W⁶, JACOB⁵, JOHN⁴, JOHN³, JOHN², THOMAS¹)* was born 07 Jun 1841. She married FREDRICK WEBSTER SIMMS.

Children of ELLEN SPINNEY and FREDRICK SIMMS are:
          i. ROBERT⁸ SIMMS, b. 02 Mar 1884.
1069.   ii. GEORGE WHITFIELD SIMMS, b. 24 Mar 1876.

728. JACOB⁷ SPINNEY *(THOMAS W⁶, JACOB⁵, JOHN⁴, JOHN³, JOHN², THOMAS¹)* was born 1845 in Nova Scotia, and died Aft. 1881. He married MARY WHITEHOUSE 1866 in New Brunswick. She was born 1847, and died Aft. 1881.

Notes for JACOB SPINNEY:
Was listed in the 1871 Carlton County New Burnswick Census

Children of JACOB SPINNEY and MARY WHITEHOUSE are:
          i.   ELLA⁸ SPINNEY, b. 1867; d. 13 Oct 1890.
1070.   ii.   WILLIAM EDMUND SPINNEY, b. 09 Jun 1868, Knolesville, NB..
          iii. ADA SPINNEY, b. 10 Jan 1870, Knolesville, NB.; m. EDMUND A ROBINSON, 1892, Knolesville, NB..
          iv. EVA ALBERTA SPINNEY, b. 05 Nov 1872; d. 1966; m. HENRY LANDON; b. 10 May 1866; d. 12 May 1925.
          v.   OPRA SPINNEY, b. 1874.
          vi. LAURA SPINNEY, b. 1877; m. OSMOND FRAZIER.
          vii. ADDISON DELMAR SPINNEY, b. 1880; d. 26 Oct 1962; m. (1) IDA HMPHILL, 1902; m. (2) LOIS FROST, 1914.
          viii. AGNES SPINNEY, b. 1882; m. FREDRICK HEMPHILL, 1903, Knolesville, NB.

729. MATILDA⁷ SPINNEY *(THOMAS W⁶, JACOB⁵, JOHN⁴, JOHN³, JOHN², THOMAS¹)* was born 1852. She married ROBERT HENDERSON.

Children of MATILDA SPINNEY and ROBERT HENDERSON are:
1071.   i.   ARMOND⁸ HENDERSON.
          ii. EUNICE HENDERSON.
          iii. CORA HENDERSON.

730. JAMES⁷ SPINNEY *(JAMES⁶, JACOB⁵, JOHN⁴, JOHN³, JOHN², THOMAS¹)* was born 1830 in Argyle, NS.. He married JANE GOODWIN. She was born 1837 in Argyle, NS..

Children of JAMES SPINNEY and JANE GOODWIN are:
1072.   i.   LAURA MAE⁸ SPINNEY, b. 1856; d. Aft. 1920.
1073.   ii. WESLEY F SPINNEY, b. 30 Sep 1857.
          iii. EUGINA SPINNEY, b. 1862.
          iv. ELDRIGE H SPINNEY, b. 1864; d. 27 Dec 1903; m. GEORGIANNA WILSON; d. 1897, Gloucester, Ma.

              Notes for ELDRIGE H SPINNEY:
              January 14, 1903
              Swept Away By Big Sea
              Capt. Eldred H. Spinney Washed from Vessel's Deck
              A Bright Career Closed
              Was One of Our Smartest All Around Skippers

              The sad news of the loss of Capt. Eldred H. Spinney of this port was received here this morning, when a telegram from one of the crew of his vessel, sch. Harvester, was received by the owners, M. Walen & Sons, stating that the vessel had just arrived at Shelburne, N. S., and that Capt. Spinney was washed overboard yesterday.

The sorrowful tale quickly spread, and turned the chief topic of conversation this morning, wherever vessel owners and fishermen met, and on every hand were heard expressions of genuine sorrow and regret at his sudden taking off.

The Harvester was engaged in the winter haddock fishery, and after taking out a trip, sailed from Boston Saturday night. The vessel probably encountered on Tuesday, the heavy gale which prevailed here Monday morning, and it is supposed that it was during this time that Capt. Spinney was washed overboard.

Capt. Spinney was about 38 years of age, a native of Argyle, N. S., and leaves a widow and three children, residing at 15 Harvard place in this city. He also leaves a brother and married sister in Argyle, and several relatives in this city, among them Capts. Lemuel and Wilson Spinney, who were his cousins.

He came to Gloucester many years ago and has always followed fishing from this port, having commanded vessels from the firm of M. Walen & Son for the past eight or ten years. He was a good type of the successful master mariner, and had made for himself an enviable record. He was one of the few who seemed capable of applying themselves with success to any branch of the fisheries and was one of the best all around skippers sailing from this port. He combined ability and judgment with rare modesty and quiet demeanor, and his sterling worth won for the respect and confidence, not only of the firm for whom he sailed and the fishermen generally, but the fishing firms of this port and Boston to whom he sold his fares. His sad end removes from the ranks of the master mariners a shining light. To the widow and children are extended the sympathy of the community.

1074.	v.	LINDA SPINNEY, b. 1866, Argyle, NS..
	vi.	GEORGE SPINNEY, b. 1873.
1075.	vii.	INA SPINNEY, b. 1877, Argyle, NS.; d. 1958.

731. CALEB[7] SPINNEY *(JAMES[6], JACOB[5], JOHN[4], JOHN[3], JOHN[2], THOMAS[1])* was born 1837, and died 1932. He married HANNAH SMITH 1869. She was born 1845, and died Aft. 1881.

Children of CALEB SPINNEY and HANNAH SMITH are:
1076.	i.	LEMUEL E[8] SPINNEY, b. 1865, Argyle, NS.; d. Aft. 1930, Gloucester, Ma.
	ii.	ELLA SPINNEY, b. 1868.
	iii.	JEANETTE SPINNEY, b. 1870.
	iv.	WILSON C SPINNEY, b. 1876; d. 1908, Gloucester, Ma.
1077.	v.	FOREMAN SPINNEY, b. 15 Sep 1879, Argyle, NS.; d. 23 Sep 1938, Gloucester, MA; Stepchild.
	vi.	DORA SPINNEY, b. Sep 1884.

732. CALVIN[7] SPINNEY *(JAMES[6], JACOB[5], JOHN[4], JOHN[3], JOHN[2], THOMAS[1])* was born 1831 in Argyle, NS., and died 10 Oct 1871. He married ELIABETH ELLEN GOODWIN 10 Oct 1871 in Yarmouth Nova Scotia.

Children of CALVIN SPINNEY and ELIABETH GOODWIN are:
	i.	CASSIA LASELLA[8] SPINNEY, b. 02 Sep 1872.
	ii.	JOSEPH HATFIELD SPINNEY, b. 10 Nov 1873.
1078.	iii.	JAMES CALVIN SPINNEY, b. 28 Nov 1875; d. 1943.
	iv.	LYDIA SPINNEY, b. 22 Sep 1883.

733. WHITFIELD[7] SPINNEY *(JAMES[6], JACOB[5], JOHN[4], JOHN[3], JOHN[2], THOMAS[1])* was born 10 Dec 1823 in Argyle, Nova Scotia, and died Dec 1868 in Lost At Sea. He married AMERLIA JANE CRITTENDEN, daughter of SAMUEL CRITTENDEN and EMELINE.

Notes for WHITFIELD SPINNEY:
NAMES OF FISHERMEN FROM NOVA SCOTIA LOST AT SEA
APPEARING ON THE GLOUCESTER FISHERMEN'S MEMORIAL CENTOTAPH
GLOUCESTER,MASSACHUSETTS,USA.

Whitfield Spinney, married, Argyle; entire crew lost with vessel James S. Ayer on Dec, 1868.

December 18, 1868 Missing Vessel Fears are apprehended for the safety of schooner James S. Ayer of this port, which sailed for the Grand Banks on the 24th of October, and has now been absent nearly eight weeks - three weeks longer than the time usually occupied in making a trip. She was spoken on the Banks, Nov. 2d, by schs. Mary G. Dennis and Everett Steele, since which time there have been no tidings of her. There is a bare possibility that she may have been disabled and may yet reach port, but we must confess the prospect is not very encouraging. The James S. Ayer was a first class vessel of 68.68 tons built in Alna, Me. in 1866 and owned by Messrs. Dennis & Ayer. She was valued at $8000, on which there was an insurance of $6900, and $300 on the outfits, in the Gloucester Mutual Fishing Insurance Office. Her crew list comprised twelve men, all belonging to this town. By this sad disaster, seven widows are left to mourn the loss of husbands, and twenty-one children are made fatherless. The crew list is as follows: John R. McDonald, master, single Colin McDonald, brother of captain, leaves a widow and three children Murdock McDonald, leaves a widow and three children Stephen McDonald, leaves a widow and three children Philip Riley, leaves a widow and two children, WHITFIELD SPINNEY, leaves a widow and four children, John W. Brown, leaves a widow and six children Daniel Kennedy, single Michael McCormick, single Angus McPhee, single Daniel McIntire, single J. E. Osier, single The James S. Ayer is the third vessel that has been lost in the Bank fishery the present year. Total loss of life in the three vessels, thirty. There are other vessels of the fleet which have been out a little over time, but we hope they will yet arrive in safety.

Children of WHITFIELD SPINNEY and AMERLIA CRITTENDEN are:
      i.   DEBORAH EVA[8] SPINNEY, b. 1861.
1079.   ii.   SAMUEL DANIEL SPINNEY, b. Feb 1863.
     iii.   EFFIE STEPHEN SPINNEY, b. 1866; m. GEORGE H ALLEN.
1080.   iv.   ADEN CLAYTON SPINNEY, b. Oct 1867; d. 16 Sep 1903.

734. AARON[7] SPINNEY *(EZARA[6], AARON[5], JOHN[4], JOHN[3], JOHN[2], THOMAS[1])* was born 22 Dec 1840 in Yarmouth, Nova Scotia, and died 1923. He married PENIAH SPINNEY 11 Oct 1865. She was born 03 Feb 1839, and died Aft. 1901.

Children of AARON SPINNEY and PENIAH SPINNEY are:
      i.   JOSIAH F[8] SPINNEY, b. 1867; d. 1897, Boston, Ma; m. FLORENCE E JOHNSON, 1891, Boston, MA.
     ii.   WALLACE D SPINNEY, b. 1870; d. Aft. 1880.
    iii.   DORA EVA SPINNEY, b. 20 Dec 1872; d. 1945, Yarmouth, Nova Scotia.

735. DENNIS H[7] SPINNEY *(EZARA[6], AARON[5], JOHN[4], JOHN[3], JOHN[2], THOMAS[1])* was born 21 May 1843 in Arglye, Nova Scotia, and died 29 Jul 1924 in Arglye, Nova Scotia. He married CAROLINE LARKIN SPINNEY 31 Jul 1876 in Yarmouth, NS., daughter of DAVID SPINNEY and JOANNA. She was born 06 Aug 1845 in Arglye, Nova Scotia, and died 19 Oct 1938 in Arglye, Nova Scotia.

Children of DENNIS SPINNEY and CAROLINE SPINNEY are:
      i.   ARTHUR WHITE EAKINS[8] SPINNEY, b. 09 Nov 1876, Nova Scotia; d. Aft. 1930, California; m. ALBERTA ATWOOD; b. 1868, Iowa; d. Aft. 1930.
     ii.   BESSIE SPINNEY, b. 27 Nov 1877.
    iii.   EVA J SPINNEY, b. 1880.
    iv.   ELMER SPINNEY.

736. AGNES[7] *(EZARA[6] SPINNEY, AARON[5], JOHN[4], JOHN[3], JOHN[2], THOMAS[1])* was born 1844, and died Aft. 1910. She married JOSEPH WILSON SPINNEY 1865, son of JOHN SPINNEY and HANNAH SPINNEY. He was born 1844 in Nova Scotia, and died Aft. 1900.

Children are listed above under (711) Joseph Wilson Spinney.

737. EDGAR KEITH[7] SPINNEY *(HARVEY[6], AARON[5], JOHN[4], JOHN[3], JOHN[2], THOMAS[1])* was born 1851 in Nova Scotia, and died Aft. 1880. He married EMMA ANDERSON. She was born 1849 in Nova Scotia.

Children of EDGAR SPINNEY and EMMA ANDERSON are:
      i.   ERIC H[8] SPINNEY, b. 1887, Nova Scotia.

    ii.   WILLIAM SPINNEY, b. 1875, Nova Scotia.
   iii.   EDWIN SPINNEY, b. 1875.
   iv.   ARTHUR SPINNEY, b. 1878.
    v.   KEITH SPINNEY, b. 1880.
   vi.   CATHERINE SPINNEY, b. 1884, Nova Scotia.

738. MARY[7] SPINNEY (*HARVEY[6], AARON[5], JOHN[4], JOHN[3], JOHN[2], THOMAS[1]*) was born 1844 in Yarmouth, NS., and died 1920. She married EBENEZER ERSKINE ARCHIBALD 03 May 1864 in Yarmouth, NS., son of JAMES ARCHIBALD and AMY HARVEY. He was born 16 Feb 1843 in Upper Stewiacke, NS., and died 1897.

Children of MARY SPINNEY and EBENEZER ARCHIBALD are:
    i.   JOANNA[8] ARCHIBALD, b. 30 Mar 1865, Yarmouth, NS..
   ii.   AMY ARCHIBALD, b. 28 Feb 1867, Yarmouth, NS.; d. 23 Jun 1951, Washington, DC.
  iii.   JAMES D ARCHIBALD, b. 10 Sep 1871, Yarmouth, NS..
   iv.   ALVIRA ARCHIBALD, b. 10 Sep 1871, Wolfville, NS..
    v.   MAGGIE ARCHIBALD, b. 1873.
   vi.   MARY ARCHIBALD, b. 1876.
  vii.   HOWARD ARCHIBALD, b. 1878.
 viii.   EMMA ARCHIBALD, b. 1879.
   ix.   EDGER ARCHIBALD, b. 1885.

739. HEMAN[7] SPINNEY (*HARVEY[6], AARON[5], JOHN[4], JOHN[3], JOHN[2], THOMAS[1]*) was born 1869. He married HARRIET WALSH.

Child of HEMAN SPINNEY and HARRIET WALSH is:
1081.   i.   CHARLES[8] SPINNEY.

740. ROBERT M[7] SPINNEY (*SOLOMAN ROBERT[6], BENJAMIN[5], JOHN[4], JOHN[3], JOHN[2], THOMAS[1]*) was born Sep 1854, and died 13 Jun 1912 in New York. He married ANNIE. She was born Sep 1855 in Sweden.

Notes for ROBERT M SPINNEY:
Robert M Spinney at some point moved to New York where he married Annie and can be found in the 1900 census

Brooklyn Daily Standard Union
July 28, 1912
Wills Filed

Robert M. SPINNEY died June 13 and by will of Jan 2?, 1901, left
jewelry to sons George W., Robert A., and Randolph A. SPINNEY; $25 each
to daughters Lillie F. and Jennie L. SPINNEY, and the residue of $1,500
estate to the widow, Annie SPINNEY, of 253 Fifty-fifth street.

Children of ROBERT SPINNEY and ANNIE are:
    i.   JEANNIE L[8] SPINNEY, b. Oct 1883.
   ii.   LILLIE SPINNEY, b. Oct 1884.
  iii.   ROBERT A SPINNEY, b. Apr 1887.
   iv.   GEORGE W SPINNEY, b. Sep 1891.
    v.   RANDOLPH A SPINNEY, b. Nov 1893; d. Jun 1978, New York.

741. JOSIAH[7] SPINNEY (*SOLOMAN ROBERT[6], BENJAMIN[5], JOHN[4], JOHN[3], JOHN[2], THOMAS[1]*) was born 13 Apr 1855, and died Aft. 1901. He married CORDELIA SNOW Abt. 1880. She was born 25 Nov 1858, and died Aft. 1901.

Children of JOSIAH SPINNEY and CORDELIA SNOW are:
1082.   i.   CONSTANCE[8] SPINNEY, b. 1884, Port Latour NS; d. 1960, Boston Mass.
   ii.   AMY SPINNEY, b. 1888.
  iii.   MABEL L SPINNEY, b. 1890.

742. GEORGE NELSON⁷ SPINNEY *(SOLOMAN ROBERT⁶, BENJAMIN⁵, JOHN⁴, JOHN³, JOHN², THOMAS¹)* was born Oct 1848 in Port Latour, Shelburn, Nova Scotia, Canada, and died 01 Feb 1907 in Yarmouth Nova Scotia. He married JOSEPHINE DOTY 15 Mar 1871. She was born Feb 1852, and died 14 Jun 1915.

Children of GEORGE SPINNEY and JOSEPHINE DOTY are:
1083.	i.	ALBERTA LOUISE⁸ SPINNEY, b. 1871.
1084.	ii.	HAROLD FARNHAM SPINNEY, b. 28 Dec 1878, Yarmouth, Nova Scotia, Canada; d. 22 Feb 1921.
	iii.	ETHEL B SPINNEY, b. 1881; m. STANLEY CAIN.
	iv.	MARY EMILY SPINNEY, b. 1887.
1085.	v.	GEORGE W SPINNEY, b. 03 Apr 1889, Yarmouth, Nova Scotia, Canada; d. 01 Feb 1948, Montreal, Quebec, Canada.

743. SOLOMAN R⁷ SPINNEY *(NORMAN⁶, BENJAMIN⁵, JOHN⁴, JOHN³, JOHN², THOMAS¹)* was born 1858, and died Aft. 1901. He married EMMA L KENNEY 09 Dec 1886 in Glenwood, Aroostook, ME, daughter of JAMES KENNEY and ELIZA FROST. She was born 29 Apr 1863, and died Aft. 1901.

Children of SOLOMAN SPINNEY and EMMA KENNEY are:
i.	LAWRENCE S⁸ SPINNEY, b. 1891, Canada.
ii.	MARION G SPINNEY, b. 1889.

744. AUSTIN⁷ SPINNEY *(NORMAN⁶, BENJAMIN⁵, JOHN⁴, JOHN³, JOHN², THOMAS¹)* was born 02 Nov 1860. He married ELLA. She was born 26 Aug 1864.

Children of AUSTIN SPINNEY and ELLA are:
i.	CLARA⁸ SPINNEY, b. 01 Sep 1894.
ii.	FRANK A SPINNEY, b. 24 Aug 1896.
iii.	CHARLES T SPINNEY, b. 1903.

745. EMMA MARIA⁷ SPINNEY *(LEMUEL⁶, WILLIAM⁵, JOHN⁴, JOHN³, JOHN², THOMAS¹)* was born 1855 in Nova Scotia, Canada. She married WESLEY B ATKINSON 1875 in Ipswich, MA. He was born 1854.

Child of EMMA SPINNEY and WESLEY ATKINSON is:
i.	BESSIE G⁸ ATKINSON, b. 1883, Ipswich, Ma.

746. ADALIZA C⁷ SPINNEY *(LEMUEL⁶, WILLIAM⁵, JOHN⁴, JOHN³, JOHN², THOMAS¹)* was born 1861 in Nova Scotia, Canada. She married GEORGE ROBERTS 1890 in Ipswich. He was born 1851.

Child of ADALIZA SPINNEY and GEORGE ROBERTS is:
i.	GEORGE⁸ ROBERTS, b. 1902, Hamilton, Ma; d. 1902, Hamilton, Ma.

747. MINOR H⁷ SPINNEY *(MINOR⁶, WILLIAM⁵, JOHN⁴, JOHN³, JOHN², THOMAS¹)* was born 1837, and died 1922 in Sandford, ME. He married ELIZABETH SPINNEY 1865, daughter of JOHN SPINNEY and HANNAH SPINNEY. She was born 1839 in Arglye, Nova Scotia, and died 1916.

Children are listed above under (708) Elizabeth Spinney.

748. ADELIA JANE⁷ SPINNEY *(MINOR⁶, WILLIAM⁵, JOHN⁴, JOHN³, JOHN², THOMAS¹)* was born 14 Nov 1841 in Argyle, NS., and died 04 Mar 1923. She married REUBEN HAWES SPINNEY 23 Jan 1862, son of REUBEN SPINNEY and MARTHA NICKERSON. He was born 05 Sep 1840 in Argyle, NS., and died 21 Dec 1920 in Sanford, ME.

Children are listed above under (705) Reuben Hawes Spinney.

749. CHARLES W⁷ SPINNEY *(MINOR⁶, WILLIAM⁵, JOHN⁴, JOHN³, JOHN², THOMAS¹)* was born Jun 1835 in Greenwood Nova Scotia, and died 1907 in Fitchburg, MA. He married HANNAH M GARDNER 1861 in Gloucester, MA, daughter of WILLIAM GARDNER and MARY. She was born May 1841 in Massachusetts, and died

Aft. 1910.

Child of CHARLES SPINNEY and HANNAH GARDNER is:
    i.   CHARLES WILLIAM[8] SPINNEY, b. Mar 1863, Gloucester, MA; m. ANNIE G TRIPP.

750. HOWARD[7] SPINNEY *(PRINCE[6], DANIEL[5], JOHN[4], JOHN[3], JOHN[2], THOMAS[1])* was born 1846, and died 1919. He married MELINDA LARKIN 1873.

Child of HOWARD SPINNEY and MELINDA LARKIN is:
1086.   i.   ADOLPHUS LARKIN[8] SPINNEY, b. 08 Sep 1874, Nova Scota; d. Aft. 1936.

751. ANGELINE[7] SPINNEY *(MARY ELENER[6], DANIEL[5], JOHN[4], JOHN[3], JOHN[2], THOMAS[1])* was born 1848. She married MARK F BURNHAN.

Children of ANGELINE SPINNEY and MARK BURNHAN are:
    i.   MARY[8] BURNHAN.
    ii. CHARLES BURNHAN.
    iii. GEORGE BURNHAN.
    iv. ABBY BURNHAN.

752. ASENATH[7] SPINNEY *(EDWARD[6], DANIEL[5], JOHN[4], JOHN[3], JOHN[2], THOMAS[1])* was born 27 Sep 1852 in Nova Scotia, and died in Beverly, Ma. She married CHARLES B HANSON 1873. He was born 1851.

Children of ASENATH SPINNEY and CHARLES HANSON are:
    i.   GRACE[8] HANSON, b. 1874.
    ii. CHARLES E HANSON, b. 1877.
    iii. RUFAS HANSON, b. 1879.

753. LAURA ETTA[7] SPINNEY *(EDWARD[6], DANIEL[5], JOHN[4], JOHN[3], JOHN[2], THOMAS[1])* was born 06 Apr 1861, and died 04 Feb 1942. She married CHARLES HIRAM FORBES 12 Nov 1881 in Yarmouth Nova Scotia. He was born 1860, and died 13 Feb 1927.

Children of LAURA SPINNEY and CHARLES FORBES are:
    i.   ENOLA VAUGHAN[8] FORBES, b. 29 Aug 1886.
    ii. HOWARD C FORBES, b. 20 Nov 1892.
    iii. KENNETH FORBES.
    iv. OTTO L FORBES, b. 01 Oct 1888.
    v. PERCY D FORBES, b. 06 Sep 1891.
    vi. ASHTON FORBES.
    vii. CHARLES BENJAMIN FORBES, b. 12 Sep 1887.
    viii. BEULAH FORBES.
    ix. ARTHUR H FORBES, b. 06 Jul 1894; d. Bef. 1901.

754. LYDIA MATHILDA[7] SPINNEY *(EDWARD[6], DANIEL[5], JOHN[4], JOHN[3], JOHN[2], THOMAS[1])* was born 24 Aug 1863. She married STANLEY HINES. He was born 16 Aug 1862.

Children of LYDIA SPINNEY and STANLEY HINES are:
    i.   WILLETTA[8] HINES.
    ii. CLAYTON HINES.
    iii. ASHTON HINES.
    iv. MILDRED HINES.
    v. MYRA HINES, d. 1923.
    vi. BEULAH HINES.

755. ANGUS HARVEY[7] SPINNEY *(EDWARD[6], DANIEL[5], JOHN[4], JOHN[3], JOHN[2], THOMAS[1])* was born 25 Oct 1865, and died 29 Jan 1913. He married KADY BROWNELL LYONS. She was born 1870, and died 1948.

Children of ANGUS SPINNEY and KADY LYONS are:
- i. EDNA[8] SPINNEY, b. 1896, Nova Scotia, Canada; d. 1940; m. JOHN L CANN.
- ii. HERMAN SPINNEY, b. 1899, Nova Scotia, Canada.
- iii. JENNIE SPINNEY, b. 1900, Nova Scotia, Canada.
- iv. EDWARD SPINNEY, b. 1903, Nova Scotia, Canada.

756. BOWMAN E[7] SPINNEY (*EDWARD[6], DANIEL[5], JOHN[4], JOHN[3], JOHN[2], THOMAS[1]*) was born 13 Oct 1869 in Yarmouth, NS, and died 15 Oct 1907 in Boston, Ma. He married MABEL SOLLOWS. She was born 08 Oct 1875, and died 10 Sep 1946.

Children of BOWMAN SPINNEY and MABEL SOLLOWS are:
1087.	i.	NINA MAE[8] SPINNEY, b. 09 Feb 1895; d. 04 Jun 1951.
1088.	ii.	WILLIAM RUFAS SPINNEY, b. 12 Mar 1897; d. 21 Apr 1937.
	iii.	ALTHEA ELIZABETH SPINNEY, b. 09 Sep 1900; d. 04 Aug 1957; m. JOSEPH JOHN PEIRRE.
1089.	iv.	BOWMAN EDWARD SPINNEY, b. 05 Nov 1905; d. 07 Feb 1945.
1090.	v.	LYMAN EUGENE SPINNEY, b. 13 Feb 1907, Nova Scotia; d. Jul 1967, Massachusetts.

757. ALBERT[7] SPINNEY (*ASENATH[6] RYDER, JOANNAH[5] SPINNEY, JOHN[4], JOHN[3], JOHN[2], THOMAS[1]*) was born 1841 in Argyle, Nova Scotia, and died 1898 in Lynn, MA. He married MARY LOUISE CAMPBELL. She was born Nov 1842, and died 1902 in Lynn, MA.

Children of ALBERT SPINNEY and MARY CAMPBELL are:
	i.	AUGUSTA[8] SPINNEY, b. 1863.
	ii.	ARDELLA SPINNEY, b. 1865.
	iii.	JAMES E SPINNEY, b. 1867; d. feb 2 1910; m. NORA HAMMOND, 1896, Lynn, Ma; b. 1872.
	iv.	ORPHA LAVINIA SPINNEY, b. 08 Sep 1868.
1091.	v.	GRACE SPINNEY, b. Dec 1870.
	vi.	IRONA SPINNEY, b. 1871.
	vii.	LUCENEY SPINNEY, b. 1875.
1092.	viii.	ROSCOE RUTHERFORD SPINNEY, b. 12 Mar 1877.
	ix.	HORACE A SPINNEY, b. 1883, Nova Scotia Canada; m. ANNA; b. 1882.
1093.	x.	CLEVELAND N SPINNEY, b. 1885, Maine; d. 26 Jul 1935.

758. PAMELIA A[7] SPINNEY (*JOSEPH A[6], STEPHEN L[5], TIMOTHY[4], JOHN[3], JOHN[2], THOMAS[1]*) was born 1832, and died Bet. 1870 - 1880. She married MAFFET BOWDEN Bet. 1851 - 1858, son of GEORGE BOWDEN and RACHEL. He was born 1830, and died Bet. 1870 - 1880.

Children of PAMELIA SPINNEY and MAFFET BOWDEN are:
1094.	i.	MEOURA[8] BOWDEN, b. 1859.
	ii.	HATTIE BOWDEN, b. 1867.
	iii.	GEORGIA BOWDEN, b. 1870; m. GEORGE TERRY, 1911.

759. MARY ADA[7] SPINNEY (*LEONARD[6], ISAAC[5], WILLIAM[4], ANDREW[3], JOHN[2], THOMAS[1]*) was born 06 Jan 1843 in Kittery, ME. She married HARVEY WOODWARD. 18 Oct 1870 in Kittery Maine.

Children of MARY SPINNEY and HARVEY WOODWARD. are:
- i. MABEL ADELAIDE[8] WOODWARD., b. 16 Oct 1872.
- ii. LEONARD WOODWARD., b. 24 Oct 1876.
- iii. ERNEST WOODWARD., b. 05 Jun 1878.

760. LEONARD CHAUNCEY[7] SPINNEY (*LEONARD[6], ISAAC[5], WILLIAM[4], ANDREW[3], JOHN[2], THOMAS[1]*) was born 02 Nov 1849 in Kittery, ME, and died Aft. 1930. He married ELIZABETH DANA HARDING 18 Sep 1884.

Child of LEONARD SPINNEY and ELIZABETH HARDING is:
- i. HELEN ELIZABETH[8] SPINNEY, b. 03 Jul 1888.

761. NELLIE ESTELLE "ELEANOR"[7] SPINNEY (*DANIEL[6], ISAAC[5], WILLIAM[4], ANDREW[3], JOHN[2], THOMAS[1]*) was born

26 Nov 1856 in East Eddington, ME, and died Aft. 1935. She married CLARENCE JOHNSON 25 Dec 1875. He was born in East Eddington.

Children of NELLIE SPINNEY and CLARENCE JOHNSON are:
  i.   CHAPIN OLIVER[8] JOHNSON, b. 16 Jun 1877; d. 08 Apr 1878.
  ii.   MOTA ANNIS JOHNSON, b. 28 Aug 1879.
  iii. HELEN LOUIS JOHNSON, b. 16 May 1888.
  iv.   FRANCES CHRISTINE JOHNSON, b. 25 Dec 1890.

762. MARY HELENA[7] SPINNEY *(ISAAC[6], ISAAC[5], WILLIAM[4], ANDREW[3], JOHN[2], THOMAS[1])* was born 31 Aug 1849 in Eliot , ME. She married EDWIN UNDERHILL. He was born in Sep 1829.

Children of MARY SPINNEY and EDWIN UNDERHILL are:
  i.   FRED CHASE[8] UNDERHILL, b. Jun 1875; m. ELIZABETH MARIE.
  ii.   ALMA UNDERHILL, b. Dec 1882.
  iii. ETHEL UNDERHILL, b. Jan 1886.

763. IDA MAY[7] SPINNEY *(WILLIAM H[6], STEPHEN R[5], EDMUND[4], ANDREW[3], JOHN[2], THOMAS[1])* was born 1879. She married HILLARD.

Child of IDA SPINNEY and HILLARD is:
  i.   LINLEY[8] HILLARD, b. Feb 1893.

764. CLARENCE A[7] SPINNEY *(WILLIAM H[6], STEPHEN R[5], EDMUND[4], ANDREW[3], JOHN[2], THOMAS[1])* was born 20 Aug 1882 in Raymond, NH. He married NELLIE.

Children of CLARENCE SPINNEY and NELLIE are:
  i.   GLADYS E[8] SPINNEY, b. 1906.
  ii.   EARL SPINNEY, b. 1909.

765. PATIENCE[7] SPINNEY *(JOHN[6], JOHN[5], JOHN[4], ANDREW[3], JOHN[2], THOMAS[1])* was born 02 Dec 1801 in Georgetown, ME, and died Bef. 1880. She married MOSES B SPINNEY 19 Nov 1819 in Georgetown, ME, son of JEREMIAH SPINNEY and ABIGAIL BARSTOW. He was born 10 Feb 1793 in Georgetown, ME, and died Aft. 1880 in Georgetown, ME.

Children are listed above under (421) Moses B Spinney.

766. THOMAS[7] SPINNEY *(JOHN[6], JOHN[5], JOHN[4], ANDREW[3], JOHN[2], THOMAS[1])* was born 07 Nov 1803 in Georgetown, ME, and died 05 Nov 1894 in Georgetown, ME. He married SUSAN GROVER 23 Jul 1829 in Georgetown ME. She was born May 1812, and died Aft. 1900.

Notes for SUSAN GROVER:
Letter written by Susan Grover Spinney

Pond Island L.S.
May 6, 1861

Dear Brother & Sister,

Thinking that perhaps you would like to hear from us by letter I now take a short leisure to write you and I am sure it would seem the next best thing if I cannot have a visit from you to have a good long letter which suggestion I suppose will make you a little nervous, you are always so busy, but I shall expect one nevertheless.

You will perceive by date we are yet on Pond Island but we do not know how soon we may be removed. Mean time my husband says he shall go west in August for certain, and we expect to move west next fall if nothing happens to prevent it. It seems a great undertaking but we think it best for the boys.

And now a few words about politics or rather no politics - is not our country in a dreadful state. Surely Abraham is Father and I hope we are children of his but are we not like Ishmaelites [?] rather it is every man's hand against the other. There is a company of volunteers here in Phippsburg ready for duty. Boys have not volunteered nor shall any of them if I can help it. They are busy now. Melville is building hedges and the rest of them go a fishing in their vessel.

Everything with regard to our nation is in such a state of uncertainty that it is impossible to foresee what will be next but one of two things seems certain - that is if this warfare of the States is not settled on peaceful terms there will be a war as I dare not think of. But I trust in the Sovereign of Him who said to the raging elements peace be still may now be heard controlling the yet fiercer elements of the passions of man.

I received a letter from Caroline this week she writes they are all well but she is much troubled about the war - she says several of their neighbor's boys have enlisted & Warren wants to. Catherine is at Bath yet to school but I expect her home soon. Nancy & her family are well -- I want you to come up and see us this summer and make us a good visit. Write on receipt of this & let us know of your welfare.

I believe Susan McKown has promised us a visit remind her we shall expect her to come. We should like very much from all your children my love & regards to them all. Milton received a letter from Little Master Nathan & he was highly pleased he wrote an answer but we had no postage stamps on the island then & I do not know if he sent it but if he did not he will write him soon. Milton goes a fishing with the boys. When you write please write about Woodbury and how himself & family like out where they live. I must close now. By.

Subscribing myself
Your affectionate sister
Susan Spinney

Children of THOMAS SPINNEY and SUSAN GROVER are:
	i.	MARY ALICE[8] SPINNEY, b. Feb 1830, Phippsburg, ME.
1095.	ii.	LORENZO DOW SPINNEY, b. 25 Jul 1832, Georgetown, ME; d. 16 Sep 1871.
1096.	iii.	MELVILLE B SPINNEY, b. 30 Dec 1834, Georgetown, ME.
1097.	iv.	NANCY JANE SPINNEY, b. 28 Oct 1837; d. 05 Mar 1909, Georgetown, ME.
	v.	CATHERINE WAITSTILL SPINNEY, b. 20 Jan 1841, Georgetown, ME; d. Aft. 1900.
	vi.	DAVID M SPINNEY, b. 1846.
	vii.	MILTON A SPINNEY, b. 28 Oct 1846; m. ABBIE JEWELL, 19 Aug 1878; b. 1847.

Notes for MILTON A SPINNEY:
A description of the storm of November 1849 and the wreck of the Hanover, written by Milton Spinney, son of the keeper of Pond Island Light. Quoted in Edward Rowe Snow's The Romance of Casco Bay.

The Hanover had sailed away in spring for a Russian port on the Black Sea where she had discharged her cargo, from there she sailed to Cadiz where she loaded salt for Bath, and was on her way home.

Without anything unusual happening to her she would be due at the mouth of the Kennebec about the first of November. As the time drew near for her to appear off the coast many pairs of eyes scanned the sea for a sight of the ship. It had been blowing a number of days with the wind east-north-east and it had created a heavy sea on the coast.

I was ashore with one of our neighbor boys and it was so rough that I could not get back to the island. I think it was on the fourth day of the blow that in the morning we saw Captain Rogers in the Hanover lying to the eastward of Seguin, which lies three miles off Pond Island.

There are two entrances to the Kennebec, one to the eastward and one to the westward of Seguin. Captain Rogers was considered a good pilot and fisherman and pilots on the shore wondered why he did not run into the river which he could easily have done with almost a fair wind by coming in the western way.

When it was seen by the men on shore what Captain Rogers intended to do they ran for a little hill that overlooked the beach and farther out the breaking on a bar. Behind them came the women and children, myself with the rest.

The ship, when she headed up, although close hauled by the wind, would have weathered the bar and Pond

Island if the tide had been running in, but just after she got by the point of the treacherous sand spit she met the tide coming out which caught her on the weather bow making impossible the ship's passing the island on that tack.

Taking the western way was one of the many unexplainable things connected with this tragedy. After lying all the forenoon in a position where he could easily have entered the river, Captain Rogers was seen to square away his yard, run down to leeward of Seguin and try to get in the western way.

Then we saw from our lookout that the Captain was going to put his ship about. Slowly the vessel came up to wind, but a short distance from the seething foam of the bar and dead to windward of it.

When in the wind's eye she refused to go farther and with all her sails aback she slowly forged astern. Back, back, until every watcher's heart was ready to burst with suspense, back to that fearful maelstrom. Back, to the octopus whose arms were extended to receive the doomed ship and her crew. Back, till in the hollow of a huge wave her stempost struck the sand beneath and the story is told.

The ship, when she struck, fell off broadside to the sea and the next comber rolled her down on her broadside, then every man on board, twenty-four all told, were seen on her side. The next waves rolled her bottom-up, breaking her spars off. As she rolled over the crew clambered up over the bilge and strung themselves out, holding on to the keel.

The third and fourth seas broke the ship in pieces and left the crew to battle for their lives till death should end their troubles. We knew that no man could come through alive.

As the wreckage came floating ashore the men went on the beach, and as the bodies came ashore they were reverently carried up on the high ground and laid down. Before the end of the day the bodies had been secured and now lie buried in a little cemetery within sound of the roaring waves which beat them to death.

	viii.	EUGENE H SPINNEY, b. 11 Mar 1856; d. Aft. 1900; m. MARGARET E WILLIAMS; b. 03 Sep 1877; d. Bef. 1900.
1098.	ix.	CHARLES SPINNEY, b. 24 Oct 1844, Maine; d. Bef. 1881.

767. MIRIAM[7] SPINNEY *(JOHN[6], JOHN[5], JOHN[4], ANDREW[3], JOHN[2], THOMAS[1])* was born 23 Jul 1806, and died Aft. 1860. She married JOHN SPINNEY Bet. 1820 - 1828, son of JEREMIAH SPINNEY and ABIGAIL BARSTOW. He was born 17 Sep 1802, and died Aft. 1860.

Children are listed above under (424) John Spinney.

768. LOUISA[7] SPINNEY *(JOHN[6], JOHN[5], JOHN[4], ANDREW[3], JOHN[2], THOMAS[1])* was born 23 Mar 1809 in Georgetown, ME, and died 13 Dec 1857 in Monticello, ME. She married HENRY LUCE 13 Dec 1829 in Industry, ME. He was born Abt. 1808, and died 04 May 1856.

Children of LOUISA SPINNEY and HENRY LUCE are:

1099.	i.	CHARLES SPINNEY[8] LUCE.
1100.	ii.	CELIA ANN LUCE.
1101.	iii.	ELIZABETH LUCE.
	iv.	HEZEKIAH SPINNEY LUCE, m. MARY ELIZABETH RANKIN.
	v.	GEORGE P LUCE.

769. ROXANNA BURGESS[7] SPINNEY *(NICHOLAS[6], JOHN[5], JOHN[4], ANDREW[3], JOHN[2], THOMAS[1])* was born 22 Mar 1801 in Georgetown, ME, and died 12 Aug 1879 in Bath, Me. She married JOSEPH OAKMAN HUNT 27 Jan 1820 in Maine. He was born 22 Dec 1797 in Georgetown, ME, and died 12 Oct 1861 in Harpswell, ME..

Children of ROXANNA SPINNEY and JOSEPH HUNT are:

1102.	i.	REUBEN[8] HUNT, b. 12 Jan 1821.
1103.	ii.	JOSEPH OAKMAN HUNT, b. 19 Mar 1823; d. Bef. 1880.
	iii.	JAMES L HUNT, b. 01 Feb 1826; m. WINNIFRED JACKSON HUNT.
	iv.	ROBERT M HUNT, b. Abt. 1830.
1104.	v.	WILLIAM SPINNEY HUNT, b. 11 Aug 1834, Bath, ME; d. 05 May 1907, Bath, ME.
	vi.	MARGARET A HUNT, b. 15 Jul 1838.

770. WILLIAM M[7] SPINNEY *(NICHOLAS[6], JOHN[5], JOHN[4], ANDREW[3], JOHN[2], THOMAS[1])* was born 02 Oct 1802 in Georgetown, ME, and died 23 Jan 1857 in Freedom, ME. He married (1) MARGERY E OLIVER 25 Jan 1827 in Georgetown Maine, daughter of BENJAMIN OLIVER and HANNAH. She was born 27 Oct 1806, and died 04 Feb 1842 in Fredom, ME. He married (2) ROZELLA G PURKINS 05 Jan 1843. She was born 1820, and died Bet. 1860 - 1870.

Children of WILLIAM SPINNEY and MARGERY OLIVER are:

1105.	i.	OREN WILLIAM[8] SPINNEY, b. 09 Nov 1827, Georgetown, ME; d. 29 Jan 1869, Salem, Ma.
1106.	ii.	MARGERY ELIZABETH SPINNEY, b. 13 Nov 1829, Georgetown, ME; d. Bef. 1861.
1107.	iii.	ANSON B SPINNEY, b. 05 Jul 1832, Georgetown, ME; d. 20 Jun 1900, Park City, Colorado.
1108.	iv.	BENJAMIN F SPINNEY, b. Jul 1835, Maine; d. Aft. 1870, Colorado.
1109.	v.	JOSEPH OAKMAN SPINNEY, b. 07 Nov 1837, Maine; d. 16 Aug 1916, Iowa.
1110.	vi.	NICHOLAS S SPINNEY, b. 1841, Maine; d. 04 Aug 1925, Oregon.

Children of WILLIAM SPINNEY and ROZELLA PURKINS are:

	vii.	ROSE VANDALIA[8] SPINNEY, b. 1844.
1111.	viii.	ALMSHA VIOLA SPINNEY, b. 1846, Maine; d. Aft. 1880, Colorado.
	ix.	MARY ADELIA SPINNEY, b. 1848; d. 10 May 1874, Unity, Maine; m. THOMAS H B HUSSEY; b. 1843.
	x.	ROBERT R SPINNEY, b. 1851.

771. NICHOLAS J[7] SPINNEY *(NICHOLAS[6], JOHN[5], JOHN[4], ANDREW[3], JOHN[2], THOMAS[1])* was born 19 Aug 1804 in Georgetown, ME, and died 09 Jan 1861 in Georgetown, ME. He married ALMIRA TODD 28 May 1827. She was born 1813 in Georgetown, Lincoln, Maine, USA.

Children of NICHOLAS SPINNEY and ALMIRA TODD are:

	i.	H. H.[8] SPINNEY, b. 1828, Georgetown, ME; d. 16 Nov 1843, Lost at sea.
	ii.	ALMIRA JANE SPINNEY, b. 03 Mar 1828, Arrowsic, ME; m. EDWARD K HADLEY, 19 Dec 1854; b. 11 Nov 1821, Eden, Hancock CO, ME; d. 06 Aug 1901.
1112.	iii.	ELIZABETH S SPINNEY, b. 02 Dec 1829, Arrowsic, ME; d. Aft. 1900.
	iv.	PHILENA SPINNEY, b. 1831; d. Aft. 1900; m. ELLWELL P TODD, 17 Oct 1857; b. 1829; d. Aft. 1900.
1113.	v.	HARRIETT HINKLEY SPINNEY, b. 17 Jul 1834, Arrowsic, ME; d. 1886, Boston, Ma.
	vi.	MARGARET HUNT SPINNEY, b. 03 Apr 1836, Arrowsic, ME; d. Aft. 1880; m. JOHN R CLIFFORD; b. 1834, Maine; d. Aft. 1880.
1114.	vii.	ANN MARIA SPINNEY, b. 02 Nov 1839, Arrowsic, ME; d. 12 Jul 1897.
	viii.	WILLIAM H SPINNEY, b. 1841; m. MARTHA M, Bet. 1870 - 1880; b. 1835.
1115.	ix.	JAMES L SPINNEY, b. Oct 1843; d. Aft. 1910.
	x.	JULIETTA SPINNEY, b. 31 Jan 1846, Arrowsic, ME; m. MATTHEW MCKENNEY; b. 1848, Maine.
	xi.	LAVINIA TODD SPINNEY, b. 27 Oct 1848, Arrowsic, ME; d. Aft. 1880; m. SILAS SNIPE; b. 1835; d. Bef. 1880.
	xii.	GEORGE P SPINNEY, b. Apr 1851; d. Aft. 1900, Maine; m. LOUISA SHEA; d. Aft. 1900.

772. ROBERT CURTIS[7] SPINNEY *(NICHOLAS[6], JOHN[5], JOHN[4], ANDREW[3], JOHN[2], THOMAS[1])* was born 02 Sep 1811 in Georgetown, ME, and died 27 Jan 1873. He married MARGARET KENNISTON 1832, daughter of DAVID KENNISTON and SARAH BEATH. She was born 03 Apr 1804 in Boothbay, ME, and died 02 Aug 1870 in Boothbay, ME.

Children of ROBERT SPINNEY and MARGARET KENNISTON are:

	i.	JOSEPH[8] SPINNEY, b. Abt. 1833, Boothbay, ME; m. ELIZABETH F JOHNSTON, 21 Sep 1873.
1116.	ii.	MARGARET JANE SPINNEY, b. 18 Mar 1833; d. 1895.
1117.	iii.	ELIZABETH SUSAN SPINNEY, b. 10 Sep 1834, Boothbay, ME; d. 1871.
	iv.	ROBERT CURTIS SPINNEY, b. 13 Oct 1835, Boothbay, ME; d. Jan 1905.
	v.	ROXANNE JULY SPINNEY, b. 17 Feb 1837, Boothbay, ME; m. LEVI WILLEY, 1864.
1118.	vi.	WILLIAM QUINMAN SPINNEY, b. 13 Oct 1838, Boothbay, ME; d. Aft. 1900.
1119.	vii.	MARY ANGELINA SPINNEY, b. 17 May 1840.
1120.	viii.	CAROLINE MCCLINTOCK SPINNEY, b. 13 Oct 1841.
	ix.	JOHN GILMAN SPINNEY, b. 22 Dec 1842; d. 20 Jul 1843.
1121.	x.	JOHN GILMAN SPINNEY, b. 02 Feb 1845, Boothbay, ME; d. Aft. 1880.
	xi.	STEPHEN STINSON SPINNEY, b. 21 Jul 1846, Boothbay, ME; d. 15 Aug 1846.
	xii.	CLARA P. SPINNEY, b. 30 Oct 1847; d. Bef. 1850.
	xiii.	MARTHA MARILLA. SPINNEY, b. 30 Oct 1847.

773. EZRA[7] SPINNEY *(RICHARD[6], JOHN[5], JOHN[4], ANDREW[3], JOHN[2], THOMAS[1])* was born 28 Mar 1815 in Georgetown, ME, and died Aft. 1870. He married MILENDIA SPINNEY 26 Dec 1844 in Georgetown, ME, daughter of MOSES SPINNEY and PATIENCE SPINNEY. She was born 01 Nov 1820 in Georgetown, ME, and died Bef. 1860.

Child of EZRA SPINNEY and MILENDIA SPINNEY is:
  i.   E[8] SPINNEY, b. 26 Dec 1845.

774. RHONDA[7] SPINNEY *(RICHARD[6], JOHN[5], JOHN[4], ANDREW[3], JOHN[2], THOMAS[1])* was born 03 Oct 1822 in Georgetown, ME. She married ROLLAND SPINNEY 17 Nov 1849, son of GEORGE SPINNEY and ABIGAIL BAKER. He was born 23 Apr 1815, and died Bef. 1880.

Children of RHONDA SPINNEY and ROLLAND SPINNEY are:
1122.   i.   HENRIETTA[8] SPINNEY, b. 1852.
1123.   ii. ABBIE E SPINNEY, b. 1854; d. Aft. 1900.
        iii. FRANCES J SPINNEY, b. 1855.
        iv. LEONARD W SPINNEY, b. 1863.

775. WILLIAM STACEY[7] SPINNEY *(RICHARD[6], JOHN[5], JOHN[4], ANDREW[3], JOHN[2], THOMAS[1])* was born 27 Jun 1824, and died Abt. 1850. He married JULIA A SPINNEY 18 Nov 1847, daughter of MOSES SPINNEY and PATIENCE SPINNEY. She was born 03 Jan 1824 in Georgetown, ME, and died Aft. 1870 in Industry, ME.

Child of WILLIAM SPINNEY and JULIA SPINNEY is:
  i.   AMASA[8] SPINNEY, b. 1849.

776. THOMAS J[7] SPINNEY *(RICHARD[6], JOHN[5], JOHN[4], ANDREW[3], JOHN[2], THOMAS[1])* was born 14 Mar 1828 in Georgetown, ME. He married RHONDA J SPINNEY 19 Nov 1853 in Georgetpwm, ME, daughter of GEORGE SPINNEY and ABIGAIL BAKER. She was born 1824.

Children of THOMAS SPINNEY and RHONDA SPINNEY are:
  i.   MARY E[8] SPINNEY, b. 1856.
  ii. LEVI D SPINNEY, b. May 1864; m. (1) CLARA H MALLETT, 20 Jan 1900; m. (2) MARY A O'BRIEN, 20 Jan 1902.

777. JAMES M[7] SPINNEY *(JEREMIAH[6], JOHN[5], JOHN[4], ANDREW[3], JOHN[2], THOMAS[1])* was born 21 Sep 1815, and died Aft. 1850. He married LUCRETIA SPINNEY 11 Jan 1840, daughter of DAVID SPINNEY and MARY OLIVER. She was born 25 Dec 1818, and died Aft. 1850.

Children of JAMES SPINNEY and LUCRETIA SPINNEY are:
1124.   i.   ANGELINE[8] SPINNEY, b. 23 Sep 1841.
        ii. ANDREW J SPINNEY, b. 1843.
        iii. GEORGIANNA SPINNEY, b. 1845.
        iv. RHONDA SPINNEY, b. 1847.

778. JOHN[7] SPINNEY *(JEREMIAH[6], JOHN[5], JOHN[4], ANDREW[3], JOHN[2], THOMAS[1])* was born 21 Jan 1817, and died Aft. 1880. He married PATIENCE S OLIVER 30 Jun 1841 in Starks, Somerset, ME, USA, daughter of JOHN OLIVER and HULDAH ROBINSON. She was born 06 Feb 1819, and died 07 Jul 1896 in Stark Maine.

Children of JOHN SPINNEY and PATIENCE OLIVER are:
1125.   i.   ABRAHAM[8] SPINNEY, b. 1821, New Hampshire; d. 1868, Charlestrown, MA.
1126.   ii. HULDAH OLIVER SPINNEY, b. 24 Apr 1842, Stark, ME; d. 1910, Stark, ME.
        iii. OLIVER SPINNEY, b. 12 Oct 1843, Starks, Somerset, ME, USA; d. 30 Dec 1848, Starks, Somerset, ME, USA.
1127.   iv. JOHN COLBY SPINNEY, b. 24 Oct 1844, Stark, ME; d. 11 Mar 1919, Stark, Me.
        v.   ANDREW J SPINNEY, b. 16 Jan 1846, Stark, ME; d. 19 Nov 1864, Barrancas,FL.
1128.   vi. ANNIE SPINNEY, b. 22 Dec 1847, Industry, ME; d. 23 Dec 1919.

vii.   MARY O SPINNEY, b. 10 Jun 1849; d. 14 Sep 1858.

viii.   ALMON SPINNEY, b. 29 Jul 1851, Stark, ME; d. 25 Oct 1852, Stark, ME.

ix.   JULIETTE E SPINNEY, b. 17 Mar 1853; d. 29 Apr 1917, Starks, Somerset, ME, USA; m. ALONZO SAWTELLE, 31 Oct 1874.

x.   GEORGE R SPINNEY, b. 21 Apr 1855; d. 14 Feb 1861.

1129.   xi.   ALMON ROBINSON SPINNEY, b. 12 Apr 1860; d. 26 Mar 1933, Industry Maine.

1130.   xii.   ROBERT R SPINNEY, b. 08 Mar 1861; d. 27 Dec 1901, Unity, ME.

779. RACHEL ANN[7] SPINNEY *(JEREMIAH[6], JOHN[5], JOHN[4], ANDREW[3], JOHN[2], THOMAS[1])* was born 20 Mar 1819 in Georgetown, ME. She married ZACCHEUIS MARR.

Child of RACHEL SPINNEY and ZACCHEUIS MARR is:

i.   ESMERELDA[8] MARR, b. 22 Feb 1853, Gardnier, ME.

780. CHARLES OLIVER[7] SPINNEY *(CALEB[6], JOHN[5], JOHN[4], ANDREW[3], JOHN[2], THOMAS[1])* was born 20 Jan 1820 in Phippsburg, ME, and died 08 Jan 1911. He married MARY HOPESTILL PERCY 21 Nov 1844 in Georgetown, ME. She was born 1823 in Phippsburg, ME, and died Aft. 1900.

Children of CHARLES SPINNEY and MARY PERCY are:

1131.   i.   CORDELIA ANN[8] SPINNEY, b. 13 Apr 1846, Phippsburg, ME.

ii.   ELIZA J SPINNEY, b. 05 Jul 1852.

781. OLIVER R[7] SPINNEY *(CALEB[6], JOHN[5], JOHN[4], ANDREW[3], JOHN[2], THOMAS[1])* was born 22 Jan 1822, and died Aft. 1880. He married RUTH J MALCOLM 27 Nov 1847 in Parker Head Maine. She was born Mar 1821 in Phippsburg, ME, and died Bef. 1880.

Children of OLIVER SPINNEY and RUTH MALCOLM are:

i.   CELIA MARIE[8] SPINNEY, b. 04 Nov 1848; m. JOHN TERRELL, 1873.

ii.   MARY ALATHEA SPINNEY, b. 24 May 1851; m. ALVIN GETCHELL.

iii.   ELLA M SPINNEY, b. May 1853; d. 05 Apr 1857.

iv.   RUTH E SPINNEY, b. Feb 1855; d. 20 Aug 1855.

1132.   v.   OLIVE ANN SPINNEY, b. 05 Jan 1859.

vi.   LORANA J SPINNEY, b. Sep 1861.

1133.   vii.   CARRIE EMMA SPINNEY, b. 01 Nov 1864.

viii.   NELLIE M SPINNEY, b. Mar 1868.

1134.   ix.   OLIVER FREEMAN SPINNEY, b. 1869, Bath, ME; d. 26 Nov 1912, Boston, Ma.

782. NANCY R[7] SPINNEY *(CALEB[6], JOHN[5], JOHN[4], ANDREW[3], JOHN[2], THOMAS[1])* was born 1828, and died 1905. She married (1) JAMES HUTCHINGS. He was born 1823. She married (2) WILLIAM RAIRDEN OLIVER 05 Oct 1848 in Phippsburg, ME, son of JAMES OLIVER and BETSY MCINTYRE. He was born 06 Mar 1825 in Phippsburg, ME, and died 01 Apr 1868 in Bath, ME.

Children are listed above under (478) William Rairden Oliver.

783. ZINA H[7] SPINNEY *(DAVID[6], JOHN[5], JOHN[4], ANDREW[3], JOHN[2], THOMAS[1])* was born 24 May 1814 in Georgetown, ME, and died Aft. 1880 in Somerville, MA. He married RACHEL OLIVER 19 Nov 1835 in Georgetown, ME. She was born 1815.

Children of ZINA SPINNEY and RACHEL OLIVER are:

i.   ALFRED O[8] SPINNEY, b. 1853; m. (1) CAROLINE UNDERWOOD, 1879, Boston, MA; d. 1889, Boston, Ma; m. (2) MARY GOLDING, 1900, Boston, MA.

ii.   MARY ELIZABETH SPINNEY, b. 09 Sep 1836, Georgetown, ME; d. Aft. 1850.

1135.   iii.   PALMER O SPINNEY, b. 18 Mar 1839, Georgetown, ME; d. 07 Aug 1920, Brunswick, ME.

1136.   iv.   CHARLES S SPINNEY, b. Aug 1857; d. Aft. 1930.

v.   DAVID SPINNEY, b. 30 Mar 1842.

1137.   vi.   DAVID S SPINNEY, b. 03 Apr 1843; d. Bet. 1920 - 1930.

vii.   WILLIAM OLIVER SPINNEY, b. 03 Apr 1843, Georgetown, ME.

viii.   PHILENA A SPINNEY, b. 1847; d. Aft. 1860.

784. LUCRETIA[7] SPINNEY *(DAVID[6], JOHN[5], JOHN[4], ANDREW[3], JOHN[2], THOMAS[1])* was born 25 Dec 1818, and died Aft. 1850. She married JAMES M SPINNEY 11 Jan 1840, son of JEREMIAH SPINNEY and ANNA OLIVER. He was born 21 Sep 1815, and died Aft. 1850.

Children are listed above under (777) James M Spinney.

785. ZINA H[7] SPINNEY *(EPHRAIM[6], JOHN[5], JOHN[4], ANDREW[3], JOHN[2], THOMAS[1])* was born 1833, and died Aft. 1880. He married RACHEL DOUGLAS 11 Jun 1851. She was born Jun 1831, and died Aft. 1881.

Children of ZINA SPINNEY and RACHEL DOUGLAS are:

1138.	i.	ELIJAH M[8] SPINNEY, b. 11 Oct 1852, Georgetown, ME; d. Aft. 1910, Georgetown, ME.
1139.	ii.	WILLIAM P SPINNEY, b. 1855; d. Aft. 1910.
	iii.	CARRIE IDA SPINNEY, b. 1857, Georgetown, ME.
1140.	iv.	JAMES M SPINNEY, b. 23 Oct 1857, Georgetown, ME.
	v.	ZINA W SPINNEY, b. 22 Sep 1861; m. CARRIE HIGGINS, 30 Apr 1881.
	vi.	FREDERIC H SPINNEY, b. 31 Aug 1867.

786. SUSAN[7] MCKINNEY *(JANE[6] SPINNEY, JOHN[5], JOHN[4], ANDREW[3], JOHN[2], THOMAS[1])* was born 09 Apr 1820, and died Aft. 1880. She married JOSEPH OAKMAN HUNT, son of JOSEPH HUNT and ROXANNA SPINNEY. He was born 19 Mar 1823, and died Bef. 1880.

Children of SUSAN MCKINNEY and JOSEPH HUNT are:

	i.	WINFIELD S[8] HUNT.
	ii.	IDA A HUNT, b. 1850.

787. RUFUS LOREN[7] BURCE *(RACHEL[6] OLIVER, JANE[5] SPINNEY, JOHN[4], ANDREW[3], JOHN[2], THOMAS[1])* was born 26 Jun 1830 in Somerset Co., ME, and died 23 Aug 1892 in Seattle, WA. He married (1) ACHSAH ANN STEBBINS 1857 in Maine. She was born WFT Est. 1819-1841, and died 1865 in Wisconsin. He married (2) ADA HURD ANDREWS 19 Jul 1867 in Eau Claire, WA. She was born 20 Jun 1839 in South Anson, ME, and died 29 Jun 1923 in Seattle, WA.

Children of RUFUS BURCE and ADA ANDREWS are:

1141.	i.	LYDIA M. "KITTY"[8] BURCE, b. 06 Aug 1871, Hannibal, MO; d. 06 Jul 1952, Snohomish, Snohomish Co., WA.
	ii.	CLARA A. BURCE, b. 15 Aug 1874, Hannibal, MO; d. 30 Aug 1874, Hannibal, MO.
1142.	iii.	DAISY MAY BURCE, b. 15 Nov 1876, Hannibal, MO; d. 04 Oct 1949, Snohomish, Snohomish Co., WA.

788. JOHN CALVIN[7] BURCE *(RACHEL[6] OLIVER, JANE[5] SPINNEY, JOHN[4], ANDREW[3], JOHN[2], THOMAS[1])* was born 14 Jun 1834 in Starks, ME, and died 23 Oct 1864 in PA. He married ADA HURD ANDREWS 04 Mar 1864 in Industry, ME. She was born 20 Jun 1839 in South Anson, ME, and died 29 Jun 1923 in Seattle, WA.

Child of JOHN BURCE and ADA ANDREWS is:

1143.	i.	SUSAN AUGUSTA RUBY[8] BURCE, b. 06 Dec 1864, Industry, ME; d. 25 Jan 1919, Granite Falls, WA.

789. ROLLAND[7] SPINNEY *(GEORGE B[6], JEREMIAH[5], JOHN[4], ANDREW[3], JOHN[2], THOMAS[1])* was born 23 Apr 1815, and died Bef. 1880. He married RHONDA SPINNEY 17 Nov 1849, daughter of RICHARD SPINNEY and ELIZABETH SPINNEY. She was born 03 Oct 1822 in Georgetown, ME.

Children are listed above under (774) Rhonda Spinney.

790. RHONDA J[7] SPINNEY *(GEORGE B[6], JEREMIAH[5], JOHN[4], ANDREW[3], JOHN[2], THOMAS[1])* was born 1824. She married THOMAS J SPINNEY 19 Nov 1853 in Georgetpwm, ME, son of RICHARD SPINNEY and ELIZABETH SPINNEY. He was born 14 Mar 1828 in Georgetown, ME.

Children are listed above under (776) Thomas J Spinney.

791. GEORGE A[7] SPINNEY (*GEORGE B[6], JEREMIAH[5], JOHN[4], ANDREW[3], JOHN[2], THOMAS[1]*) was born 1825, and died Aft. 1900. He married (1) PHILENA BUTLER. She was born 1826, and died Aft. 1860. He married (2) HARRIET F LOMBARD Feb 1864, daughter of JOSEPH LOMBARD and FRANCES PRESCOTT. She was born 1838, and died Aft. 1900.

Child of GEORGE SPINNEY and PHILENA BUTLER is:
  i. GEORGE E[8] SPINNEY, b. 1851; m. IDA; b. 1858.

Children of GEORGE SPINNEY and HARRIET LOMBARD are:
  ii. LENA[8] SPINNEY, b. 1865; d. Aft. 1900.
  iii. HELEN P SPINNEY, b. 1867; d. Aft. 1900.
1144. iv. ARLETTA LINDSEY SPINNEY, b. 09 Dec 1868; d. 1925.
  v. MARY A SPINNEY, b. Apr 1871.

792. ALVAH[7] SPINNEY (*MOSES B[6], JEREMIAH[5], JOHN[4], ANDREW[3], JOHN[2], THOMAS[1]*) was born Abt. 1820 in Phippsburg, ME. He married PHILENA (HATTIE) FRANCIS.

Children of ALVAH SPINNEY and PHILENA FRANCIS are:
  i. PHILENA FRANCIS[8] SPINNEY, b. 22 Nov 1864, Phippsburg, ME.
1145. ii. GEORGE EDWIN SPINNEY, b. 02 Nov 1851, Maine; d. Bef. 1930, California.

793. MILENDIA[7] SPINNEY (*MOSES B[6], JEREMIAH[5], JOHN[4], ANDREW[3], JOHN[2], THOMAS[1]*) was born 01 Nov 1820 in Georgetown, ME, and died Bef. 1860. She married EZRA SPINNEY 26 Dec 1844 in Georgetown, ME, son of RICHARD SPINNEY and ELIZABETH SPINNEY. He was born 28 Mar 1815 in Georgetown, ME, and died Aft. 1870.

Child is listed above under (773) Ezra Spinney.

794. FRANKLIN[7] SPINNEY (*MOSES B[6], JEREMIAH[5], JOHN[4], ANDREW[3], JOHN[2], THOMAS[1]*) was born 29 Jan 1822 in Georgetown, ME, and died Aft. 1881. He married LOUISA J SPINNEY 16 Dec 1850 in Georgetown, ME, daughter of JOHN SPINNEY and MIRIAM SPINNEY. She was born 1828, and died Aft. 1881.

Children of FRANKLIN SPINNEY and LOUISA SPINNEY are:
  i. EDWARD M[8] SPINNEY, b. Feb 1853; d. Aft. 1880.
  ii. LEONORA SPINNEY, b. 1854; d. Aft. 1880.
1146. iii. MELVINA F SPINNEY, b. 1858; d. Aft. 1880.
  iv. SARAH A SPINNEY, b. 1863; d. Aft. 1870.
  v. FRANK L SPINNEY, b. 1865; d. Aft. 1880; m. ELSIE ROGERS.
  vi. WILLIAM B SPINNEY, b. 1868; d. Aft. 1880.
1147. vii. GEORGE A SPINNEY, b. 1874; d. Aft. 1930.

795. JULIA A[7] SPINNEY (*MOSES B[6], JEREMIAH[5], JOHN[4], ANDREW[3], JOHN[2], THOMAS[1]*) was born 03 Jan 1824 in Georgetown, ME, and died Aft. 1870 in Industry, ME. She married (1) WILLIAM STACEY SPINNEY 18 Nov 1847, son of RICHARD SPINNEY and ELIZABETH SPINNEY. He was born 27 Jun 1824, and died Abt. 1850. She married (2) ALEXANDER OLIVER 10 Dec 1855 in Georgetown, ME. He died in Industry, ME.

Child is listed above under (775) William Stacey Spinney.

Children of JULIA SPINNEY and ALEXANDER OLIVER are:
  i. HENRY I[8] OLIVER, b. 1850; d. 02 Oct 1856.
  ii. WILLIAM H OLIVER, b. Sep 1856; d. 19 Dec 1856.

796. LAVINIA[7] SPINNEY (*MOSES B[6], JEREMIAH[5], JOHN[4], ANDREW[3], JOHN[2], THOMAS[1]*) was born 06 Feb 1837 in Georgetown, ME, and died Aft. 1881. She married WILLIAM C HATCH.

Children of LAVINIA SPINNEY and WILLIAM HATCH are:
  i. HATTIE[8] HATCH, b. 1877.
  ii. JOHN G HATCH, b. 1879.

797. ANDREW JACKSON[7] SPINNEY *(MOSES B[6], JEREMIAH[5], JOHN[4], ANDREW[3], JOHN[2], THOMAS[1])* was born 10 Nov 1846 in Georgetown, ME, and died Aft. 1900 in ME.. He married MARY H OLIVER 1869, daughter of JOHN OLIVER and JANE. She was born Sep 1839, and died Aft. 1900.

Children of ANDREW SPINNEY and MARY OLIVER are:
1148.	i.	HERBERT E[8] SPINNEY, b. 18 Jan 1870, Maine; d. Denver, Colorado.
	ii.	HATTIE L SPINNEY, b. 08 Aug 1871.
1149.	iii.	WILLIAM JAMES SPINNEY, b. 1876, Maine; d. 21 Feb 1939.
	iv.	CORA B SPINNEY, b. 29 Nov 1876; m. ANDREW GORDEN SPINNEY, 21 Aug 1899; b. Jul 1873; d. 21 Nov 1951.

798. LOUISA J[7] SPINNEY *(JOHN[6], JEREMIAH[5], JOHN[4], ANDREW[3], JOHN[2], THOMAS[1])* was born 1828, and died Aft. 1881. She married FRANKLIN SPINNEY 16 Dec 1850 in Georgetown, ME, son of MOSES SPINNEY and PATIENCE SPINNEY. He was born 29 Jan 1822 in Georgetown, ME, and died Aft. 1881.

Children are listed above under (794) Franklin Spinney.

799. SILAS CURTIS[7] SPINNEY *(JOHN[6], JEREMIAH[5], JOHN[4], ANDREW[3], JOHN[2], THOMAS[1])* was born 23 Sep 1829 in Georgetown, ME, and died Aft. 1880. He married MARTHA F. She was born 1841, and died Aft. 1880.

Children of SILAS SPINNEY and MARTHA F are:
	i.	FRED[8] SPINNEY, b. 1859.
	ii.	CHARLES C SPINNEY, b. 1872.
1150.	iii.	MILAN H SPINNEY, b. May 1874; d. Aft. 1910.

800. DANIEL WILLIAM[7] SPINNEY *(JOHN[6], JEREMIAH[5], JOHN[4], ANDREW[3], JOHN[2], THOMAS[1])* was born 16 Jan 1834 in Georgetown, ME, and died Aft. 1920. He married FRANCES MARY LOWELL 27 Jan 1858 in Maine. She was born 04 Apr 1840, and died Aft. 1900.

Children of DANIEL SPINNEY and FRANCES LOWELL are:
	i.	ELLA F[8] SPINNEY, b. 02 Dec 1859; d. Aft. 1920; m. HERYLCK.
1151.	ii.	ELMER ELLSWORTH SPINNEY, b. 07 Feb 1861; d. Aft. 1900.
1152.	iii.	LAURA GERTRUDE SPINNEY, b. 22 Apr 1863.
	iv.	FLORA SPINNEY, b. 1866.
	v.	MARION SPINNEY, b. 1870; d. Bef. 1900.
	vi.	FRED H SPINNEY, b. 06 Mar 1873; m. FLORENCE WELLS, 26 Dec 1900.
1153.	vii.	HARRY GARFIELD SPINNEY, b. 06 Jun 1877, Bath, ME.
	viii.	EDNA SPINNEY, b. Oct 1885.

801. PATIENCE R[7] SPINNEY *(JOHN[6], JEREMIAH[5], JOHN[4], ANDREW[3], JOHN[2], THOMAS[1])* was born 14 Aug 1835 in Georgetown, ME, and died 31 Aug 1897. She married JAMES H. OLIVER 26 Jul 1855 in Bath, Sagadahoc, ME, son of THOMAS OLIVER and ALICE. He was born 1830, and died 17 Mar 1888 in Phippsburg, ME.

Children are listed above under (477) James H. Oliver.

802. IRA[7] SPINNEY *(JEREMIAH[6], JEREMIAH[5], JOHN[4], ANDREW[3], JOHN[2], THOMAS[1])* was born Jan 1838, and died 1927. He married LAVANIA FREDERIC 11 Sep 1861. She was born Apr 1844.

Children of IRA SPINNEY and LAVANIA FREDERIC are:
	i.	JEANNIE[8] SPINNEY, b. 1862.
	ii.	FREDERICK L SPINNEY, b. 1875.
1154.	iii.	ALICE SPINNEY, b. 22 Jan 1878, Starks, ME; d. 03 Mar 1970.
	iv.	GLADYS V SPINNEY, b. Jan 1883.
1155.	v.	ELLSWORTH R SPINNEY, b. 1864, Maine; d. Aft. 1930, Lynn, MA.

803. GUSTAVUS W[7] SPINNEY *(JEREMIAH[6], JEREMIAH[5], JOHN[4], ANDREW[3], JOHN[2], THOMAS[1])* was born 01 Dec 1839 in Georgetown, ME. He married ANGELINE OLIVER.

Children of GUSTAVUS SPINNEY and ANGELINE OLIVER are:
      i.   CHARLES A[8] SPINNEY, b. 1859.
      ii.   LENA SPINNEY, b. 1871.
      iii.   ANN ELIZABETH SPINNEY, b. 25 Jul 1873; d. 11 Apr 1891, Phippsburg,ME; m. DESPER WEST OLIVER, 14 Feb 1891.
      iv.   JOSIE LOUISE SPINNEY.

804. JAMES J[7] SPINNEY *(JEREMIAH[6], JEREMIAH[5], JOHN[4], ANDREW[3], JOHN[2], THOMAS[1])* was born Jun 1849, and died Aft. 1880. He married ESTELLE OLIVER 03 Jan 1871. She was born Oct 1848, and died Aft. 1880.

Child of JAMES SPINNEY and ESTELLE OLIVER is:
      i.   MARIE[8] SPINNEY, b. Oct 1876.

805. CLARK[7] TRAFTON *(THOMAS[6], JOANNA[5] SPINNEY, JOHN[4], ANDREW[3], JOHN[2], THOMAS[1])* He married AMELIA FISHER 15 May 1841.

Child of CLARK TRAFTON and AMELIA FISHER is:
      i.   GEORGE[8] TRAFTON, m. MARTHA GREEN, 31 Aug 1875, Newton, IA.

806. ASA D[7] SPINNEY *(RICHARD[6], RICHARD[5], JOHN[4], ANDREW[3], JOHN[2], THOMAS[1])* was born 1829 in Ohio. He married ISABEL. She was born 1830.

Child of ASA SPINNEY and ISABEL is:
1156.   i.   SYLVESTER VESS[8] SPINNEY, b. 14 Jan 1851, Ohio; d. 1933.

807. EUNICE E.[7] SPINNEY *(RICHARD[6], RICHARD[5], JOHN[4], ANDREW[3], JOHN[2], THOMAS[1])* was born May 1835 in Ohio, and died 09 Jul 1904 in Bath, ME. She married BENJAMIN S. OLIVER 22 Aug 1852 in Georgetown, ME, son of EPHRAIM OLIVER and JERUSHA SPINNEY. He was born 06 Oct 1829 in Georgetown, ME, and died 15 Jan 1894 in Bath, ME.

Children are listed above under (484) Benjamin S. Oliver.

808. SAMANTHA[7] HINCKLEY *(SARAH[6], EUNICE[5] SPINNEY, JOHN[4], ANDREW[3], JOHN[2], THOMAS[1])* was born 05 Feb 1829, and died 10 Sep 1896. She married JAMES BRACKETT HOAR Bef. 1860, son of JOHN HOAR and LOIS BRACKETT. He was born 12 Oct 1832, and died 1906.

Children of SAMANTHA HINCKLEY and JAMES HOAR are:
      i.   DOLLY[8] NILE, b. 1851; d. Bet. 1860 - 1880.
      ii.   JAMES B NILE, b. 1855; d. Bet. 1870 - 1880.
      iii.   ANNA A NILE, b. 1857; d. Aft. 1870.
      iv.   CELIA NILE, b. 1860; d. Aft. 1870.
1157.   v.   CHARLES E NILE, b. 1863; d. Aft. 1900.
1158.   vi.   BENJAMNI F NILE, b. 1866; d. Aft. 1900.
      vii.   DANIEL L NILE, b. 1868; d. Aft. 1900.
      viii.   ZELAH NILE, b. 1869; d. Bef. 1880.
      ix.   CALVIN D (HOAR) NILE, b. 1872; d. Aft. 1900; m. (1) EDITH HALEY; m. (2) EDITH HALEY, 24 Apr 1902.

Generation No. 8

809. ALGENAID[8] WORCESTER *(MOSES[7], MOSES[6], MOSES[5], ANNE[4] SPINNEY, JOHN[3], SAMUEL[2], THOMAS[1])* was born 14 Dec 1841 in Columbia, ME, and died 30 May 1883 in Jonesport, ME. She married SAMUEL BOWDOIN CUMMINGS. He was born 12 Dec 1844, and died Bet. 1876 - 1935.

Child of ALGENAID WORCESTER and SAMUEL CUMMINGS is:
1159.   i.   HARRY[9] CUMMINGS, b. 15 Dec 1872, Jonesport, ME; d. 02 Feb 1939, Jonesport, ME.

810. MARGARET[8] WORCESTER *(MARK[7], ISAAC[6], MOSES[5], ANNE[4] SPINNEY, JOHN[3], SAMUEL[2], THOMAS[1])* was born 12 Feb 1857 in Webster Plantation, ME, and died 10 May 1904 in Caribou, ME. She married ISAAC BULMER 1877 in Prentis, ME, son of EPHRAIM BULMER and LUCY FRONT.

Children of MARGARET WORCESTER and ISAAC BULMER are:
       i.   BEN[9] BULMER.
      ii.   DAISEY BULMER, m. GURVIN GRANT.
1160.   iii.   MAMIE BULMER.
1161.   iv.   EPHRAIM TROTT BULMER, b. 01 Nov 1877, Webster Plantation, ME; d. 1970, Kingston Ontatio Canada.

811. ROBERT[8] UPTON *(ASA[7], SAMUEL[6], REBECCA[5] SPINNEY, JOHN[4], THOMAS[3], SAMUEL[2], THOMAS[1])* was born Abt. 1836 in New Brunswick, and died 31 Jan 1910 in Lakeville Corner, New Brunswick.

Children of ROBERT UPTON are:
       i.   MAUD[9] UPTON, b. 03 Jun 1879, Lakeville Corner, NB.; d. 03 Nov 1964, Ottawa, ON..
      ii.   CARRIE UPTON, b. 07 Apr 1881, Lakeville Corner, NB.; d. 29 Jul 1978, Chipman, NB..
     iii.   HAROLD UPTON, b. 04 Aug 1883, Lakeville Corner, NB.; d. 1964, Chipman, NB..
     iv.   CLARENCE S. UPTON, b. 09 Jan 1894; d. 25 Jan 1984, Lynn, Massachusetts.

812. ELIOT FRANKLIN[8] SPINNEY *(ELIOT F[7], ELIOT[6], ROBERT[5], JOHN[4], THOMAS[3], SAMUEL[2], THOMAS[1])* was born 01 Feb 1845 in Lynnfield, MA, and died Aft. 1880. He married SARAH ABBOTT 1868. She was born 1849.

Child of ELIOT SPINNEY and SARAH ABBOTT is:
1162.   i.   CHARLES FREDERICK[9] SPINNEY, b. 1869; d. Aft. 1930.

813. LYDIA ALICE[8] SPINNEY *(GEORGE[7], JOHN[6], BENJAMIN[5], JOHN[4], THOMAS[3], SAMUEL[2], THOMAS[1])* was born 1855 in Lynn, MA, and died 1908 in Lynn, MA. She married GEORGE F BURGESS 1875 in Lynn, MA.

Children of LYDIA SPINNEY and GEORGE BURGESS are:
       i.   GEORGE S[9] BURGESS.
      ii.   WALTER BURGESS.

814. JAMES WILBUR[8] SPINNEY *(CHARLES EDWIN[7], JOHN[6], BENJAMIN[5], JOHN[4], THOMAS[3], SAMUEL[2], THOMAS[1])* was born Jun 1875 in Milwaukee, WI. He married DOLLIE PETERSON 1902, daughter of DORA PETERSON. She was born 1875.

Children of JAMES SPINNEY and DOLLIE PETERSON are:
       i.   CHARLES E[9] SPINNEY, b. 11 Apr 1906.
      ii.   HELEN SPINNEY, b. 01 Apr 1904.

815. HENRY HOWARD[8] SPINNEY *(GUSTAVUS NEWHALL[7], WILLIAM NEWHALL[6], BENJAMIN[5], JOHN[4], THOMAS[3], SAMUEL[2], THOMAS[1])* was born 20 Apr 1860 in Lynn, MA, and died 01 Apr 1951. He married LILLIAN LOLA NEAL. She was born 12 Jan 1870 in Methuen, MA, and died 1960.

Children of HENRY SPINNEY and LILLIAN NEAL are:
1163.   i.   ABBIE LOLA[9] SPINNEY, b. 26 Jan 1888; d. Aft. 1930.
      ii.   MARGUERITE LILLIAN SPINNEY, b. 05 Mar 1890; d. 1981; m. KENNITH WOOD; b. 18 Jul 1894, Lynn, Essex, MA.; d. 1945.
1164.   iii.   LUCILLE HARRIET SPINNEY, b. 21 Feb 1898, Cliftondale, MA; d. 1989.
1165.   iv.   DOROTHY HOWARD SPINNEY, b. 06 Jun 1901, Lynn, MA; d. 1970, Danvers, MA.
1166.   v.   HAROLD NEAL SPINNEY, b. 07 Jul 1908, Lynn, MA; d. 07 Jul 1976.

816. CHARLOTTE HACK[8] SPINNEY *(ELLERY CHANNING[7], WILLIAM NEWHALL[6], BENJAMIN[5], JOHN[4], THOMAS[3], SAMUEL[2], THOMAS[1])* was born 07 Sep 1878 in Chicago, IL, and died 02 May 1948 in Chicago, IL. She married

(1) LORNE CAMPBELL. He was born Mar 1877. She married (2) ROBERT H STEWART 22 Jul 1926. He was born 19 Jan 1865, and died 27 Mar 1949.

Child of CHARLOTTE SPINNEY and LORNE CAMPBELL is:
1167.   i.   DOROTHY[9] CAMPBELL, b. 10 Aug 1899, Chicago, IL; d. 24 Apr 1972, Oak Park IL.

817. LOUISE C.[8] SPINNEY *(ELLERY CHANNING[7], WILLIAM NEWHALL[6], BENJAMIN[5], JOHN[4], THOMAS[3], SAMUEL[2], THOMAS[1])* was born 21 Jun 1880 in Chicago, IL, and died 03 Nov 1971 in Chicago, IL. She married GUY KNICKERBOCKER.

Children of LOUISE SPINNEY and GUY KNICKERBOCKER are:
    i.   KENNETH[9] KNICKERBOCKER.
    ii.   CHARLES KNICKERBOCKER.

818. HAROLD ELLERY[8] SPINNEY *(ELLERY CHANNING[7], WILLIAM NEWHALL[6], BENJAMIN[5], JOHN[4], THOMAS[3], SAMUEL[2], THOMAS[1])* was born 04 Mar 1883 in Chicago, IL, and died 10 Jun 1972 in Wilmette, IL. He married MAUD BATES 28 Jul 1907 in Chicago, IL, daughter of FREDRIC BATES and EVA WOODS. She was born 29 Sep 1882 in Omaho, NE, and died 17 Jun 1988 in Northfield, IL.

Children of HAROLD SPINNEY and MAUD BATES are:
1168.   i.   HAROLD ELLERY[9] SPINNEY, b. Private.
1169.   ii.   JANE LOUISE SPINNEY, b. Private.

819. FRANK (BENJAMIN) CASWELL[8] SPINNEY *(BENJAMIN FRANKLIN[7], BENJAMIN[6], BENJAMIN[5], JOHN[4], THOMAS[3], SAMUEL[2], THOMAS[1])* was born 14 Dec 1864 in Lynn, MA, and died 1949. He married JOSEPHINE CADY 21 Feb 1889.

Child of FRANK SPINNEY and JOSEPHINE CADY is:
    i.   CHILD[9].

820. JOSEPH D[8] SPINNEY *(GEORGE F[7], THOMAS[6], THOMAS[5], JOHN[4], THOMAS[3], SAMUEL[2], THOMAS[1])* was born Sep 1867, and died Aft. 1900. He married HATTIE F MCFARLAND. She was born Feb 1868.

Children of JOSEPH SPINNEY and HATTIE MCFARLAND are:
    i.   HAROLD D[9] SPINNEY, b. Oct 1893.
    ii.   CLARENCE E SPINNEY, b. Jan 1896.
    iii.   ALICE DOROTHY SPINNEY, b. Apr 1899.
1170.   iv.   ANGIE BELL SPINNEY, b. 1901; d. 1948.
    v.   GEORGE F SPINNEY, b. 1902; d. 13 Sep 1902.
    vi.   JOSEPHINE H SPINNEY, b. 1907.

821. HERBERT AHLBORN[8] SPINNEY *(EDWARD HERBERT[7], THOMAS[6], THOMAS[5], JOHN[4], THOMAS[3], SAMUEL[2], THOMAS[1])* was born May 1864. He married MARY JANE MELIA 1886. She was born Jun 1867.

Children of HERBERT SPINNEY and MARY MELIA are:
    i.   CLARA[9] SPINNEY, b. 1889.
    ii.   FRED SPINNEY, b. Dec 1891.
    iii.   ALBERT L SPINNEY, b. 1890; d. 1890.

822. CARRIE LOUISE[8] SPINNEY *(SAMUEL[7], JOHN WARREN[6], SAMUEL[5], JOHN[4], THOMAS[3], SAMUEL[2], THOMAS[1])* was born 1855, and died 1894 in Lynn, MA. She married HENRY A MARKS 14 Apr 1873 in Lynn, MA, son of JOHN MARKS and REBECCA. He was born 18 Jul 1851 in Salem, MA, and died Aft. 1910 in Florida.

Notes for HENRY A MARKS:
Henry A. Marks(1888), merchant, of Lynn, Mass., son of John Brooks and Rebecca Hawthorne (Perkins) Marks, was born in Salem, Mass., July 18, 1851. He married, (1) April 14, 1873, Carrie Louise Spinney, and, (2) June

21, 1899, Annette M. Sheldon. He spent his boyhood in Lynn, where he attended the public schools, and, later, Miss Boynton's Academy. He then entered mercantile life, in which he has since been engaged. He was a trustee of the Lynn Public Library twelve years, from 1880 to 1893; a member of the board of aldermen of Lynn in 1891, and has held numerous minor offices in that city. His military experience is confined to his membership in the Ancient and Honorable Artillery Company

Child of CARRIE SPINNEY and HENRY MARKS is:
1171. i. IRVING SPINNEY[9] MARKS, b. 1883, Lynn, MA; d. Jul 1957.

823. GEORGE R[8] SPINNEY *(JOHN WARREN[7], JOHN WARREN[6], SAMUEL[5], JOHN[4], THOMAS[3], SAMUEL[2], THOMAS[1])* was born Mar 1863 in Massachusetts, and died Aft. 1930 in Tulsa. OK. He married DELLA. She was born May 1864 in Massachusetts.

Children of GEORGE SPINNEY and DELLA are:
       i. JENNY[9] SPINNEY, b. Jul 1887, Massachusetts; m. GREGORY.
1172. ii. WARREN A SPINNEY, b. Apr 1890, Ohio.

824. INEZ MAUDE[8] SPINNEY *(CHARLES HERBERT[7], JOHN WARREN[6], SAMUEL[5], JOHN[4], THOMAS[3], SAMUEL[2], THOMAS[1])* was born Jun 1867, and died Aft. 1900. She married GEORGE BATCHELLER. He was born Sep 1857, and died Aft. 1900.

Children of INEZ SPINNEY and GEORGE BATCHELLER are:
       i. MILTON[9] BATCHELLER, b. Jul 1880.
       ii. RAYNOLD BATCHELLER, b. Dec 1893.
       iii. RUTH BATCHELLER, b. 1915; m. EARL BRADSHAW.

825. ERNEST EDWARD[8] SPINNEY *(CHARLES HERBERT[7], JOHN WARREN[6], SAMUEL[5], JOHN[4], THOMAS[3], SAMUEL[2], THOMAS[1])* was born 28 Nov 1873 in Chelsea, MA, and died 22 Feb 1916 in Lynn, MA. He married SARAH MATILDA HILLER 09 May 1897 in Saugus, MA, daughter of BENJAMIN HILLER and ALMIRA MILLS. She was born 18 Oct 1876 in Saugus, MA, and died 10 Aug 1911 in Saugus, MA.

Children of ERNEST SPINNEY and SARAH HILLER are:
1173. i. ARTHUR FRANKLIN[9] SPINNEY, b. 06 Apr 1898, Saugus, MA.
1174. ii. EVERETT EDWARD SPINNEY, b. 09 Jan 1900, Saugus, MA; d. 05 May 1966.
       iii. ELMER SPINNEY, b. 14 Jan 1902, Saugus, Essex, MA.; m. MARY RIDDLE, 26 Jun 1931, NY; b. 25 Jan 1906.
1175. iv. RALPH ERNEST SPINNEY, b. 14 Feb 1904, Saugus, MA; d. 26 Apr 1971, Attleboro, MA.
1176. v. BERTHA MAY SPINNEY, b. 09 Apr 1907, Saugus, Essex, MA; d. 27 Apr 1988, Lynn, Essex, MA..
1177. vi. MURIEL GERTRUDE SPINNEY, b. 25 Aug 1909, Saugus, MA; d. 24 Mar 1986.
       vii. SARAH MATHILDA SPINNEY, b. 10 Aug 1911, Saugus, MA; d. 10 Aug 1911, Saugus, MA.

826. HARRIETT[8] SPINNEY *(CHARLES HERBERT[7], JOHN WARREN[6], SAMUEL[5], JOHN[4], THOMAS[3], SAMUEL[2], THOMAS[1])* was born May 1883. She married UNKNOWN ABBOTT.

Child of HARRIETT SPINNEY and UNKNOWN ABBOTT is:
1178. i. WESLEY STARLING[9] ABBOTT, b. 15 Nov 1903, Massachusetts.

827. CAROLINE FRANCES[8] ADAMS *(SALLY ANN[7] SPINNEY, CALEB[6], CALEB[5], NICHOLAS[4], JAMES[3], SAMUEL[2], THOMAS[1])* was born 03 Dec 1824. She married ISAAC N HURD. He was born 1825.

Children of CAROLINE ADAMS and ISAAC HURD are:
       i. CHARLES[9] HURD.
       ii. ISAAC HURD.
       iii. LINCOLN HURD.

828. JAMES NATHAN[8] ADAMS *(SALLY ANN[7] SPINNEY, CALEB[6], CALEB[5], NICHOLAS[4], JAMES[3], SAMUEL[2], THOMAS[1])* was born 05 Jun 1828 in Portsmouth, NH, and died 27 May 1888 in Ellsworth, Wisconsin. He married LUCY

KNOLTON.

Child of JAMES ADAMS and LUCY KNOLTON is:
    i.   MARY⁹ ADAMS, m. HARTRAUFT.

        Notes for MARY ADAMS:
        The National Society of the Daughters of the American Revolution Volume 39
        page 279

        Mrs. Mary Adams Hartrauft.
        DAR ID Number: 38754
        Descendant of Deacon Benjamin Adams, of New Hampshire.
        Daughter of James N. Adams and Lucy Knowlton, his wife.
        Granddaughter of William Adams and Sally Spinney, his wife.
        Gr.-granddaughter of Nathan Webb Adams and Elizabeth Cole, his wife.
        Gr.-gr.-granddaughter of Benjamin Adams and Abigail Pickering, his wife.
        Benjamin Adams, (1728-1803), gave civil and military service from Newington, where he was born and died.
        Also Nos. 2687, 3080, 11520, 14145, 33948, 36359.

829. JULIA ANN⁸ ADAMS *(SALLY ANN⁷ SPINNEY, CALEB⁶, CALEB⁵, NICHOLAS⁴, JAMES³, SAMUEL², THOMAS¹)* was born 13 May 1830 in Portsmouth, NH. She married ASA G HAM. He was born 1829.

Children of JULIA ADAMS and ASA HAM are:
    i.   WILLIAM⁹ HAM.
    ii. JOHN HAM.
    iii. SARAH HAM.

830. LEONARD FRANK⁸ COOK *(ROWENA R⁷ SPINNEY, NICHOLAS⁶, CALEB⁵, NICHOLAS⁴, JAMES³, SAMUEL², THOMAS¹)* was born 25 Apr 1860 in York, ME, and died 13 Jan 1910 in Portsmouth, NH. He married EMMA M DALE 09 Apr 1887 in Lynn, MA.

Child of LEONARD COOK and EMMA DALE is:
1179.   i.   ARTHUR FRANK⁹ COOK, b. 21 Oct 1887, Lynn, MA; d. 28 Jul 1967, Kittery, ME.

831. FRANK HERBERT⁸ SPINNEY *(DANIEL PARKER⁷, JOSIAH⁶, CALEB⁵, NICHOLAS⁴, JAMES³, SAMUEL², THOMAS¹)* was born 26 Jan 1856, and died 25 Jul 1891 in Eliot, ME. He married ALICE BLANC WHERREN. She was born Dec 1858, and died 1946.

Child of FRANK SPINNEY and ALICE WHERREN is:
    i.   RALPH HERBERT⁹ SPINNEY, b. 07 May 1879; d. 1965.

832. GRACE GREENWOOD⁸ SPINNEY *(ROBERT⁷, NATHAN⁶, JOHN⁵, NICHOLAS⁴, JAMES³, SAMUEL², THOMAS¹)* was born 26 Sep 1860, and died 1921. She married GEORGE ALBERT FERNALD.

Child of GRACE SPINNEY and GEORGE FERNALD is:
1180.   i.   GILES WILLIS⁹ FERNALD.

833. FRED L⁸ SPINNEY *(ROBERT⁷, NATHAN⁶, JOHN⁵, NICHOLAS⁴, JAMES³, SAMUEL², THOMAS¹)* was born Jun 1865 in Maine, and died 1946. He married EMMA H. She was born Feb 1871, and died 1954.

Children of FRED SPINNEY and EMMA H are:
    i.   EDNA M⁹ SPINNEY, b. Oct 1889; d. 1919, Eliot, ME; m. ARTHUR C SPINNEY; b. 1891, New Hampsire; d. 1968, Eliot, ME.
1181.   ii. SIDNEY A SPINNEY, b. 16 Dec 1896, Eliot, ME.

834. BERTHA P⁸ SPINNEY *(ROBERT⁷, NATHAN⁶, JOHN⁵, NICHOLAS⁴, JAMES³, SAMUEL², THOMAS¹)* was born 1870, and died 1929. She married MYRON E SPINNEY 14 Oct 1892, son of HENRY SPINNEY and FRANCES. He was born 1869, and died 1924.

Children of BERTHA SPINNEY and MYRON SPINNEY are:
- i. FLORENCE[9] SPINNEY, b. 1893; m. RAYMOND ZILLHART; b. 1895; d. 1948.
- ii. CLYDE D SPINNEY, b. 1897; d. 1934, Eliot, Me.
- iii. HARVEY E SPINNEY, b. 1901.
- iv. EMERSON SPINNEY, b. 1905.
- v. ADA SPINNEY, b. 1910; d. 1933; m. CURTIS PORTER, 01 Jan 1931.

835. NATHAN G[8] SPINNEY (*NATHAN[7], NATHAN[6], JOHN[5], NICHOLAS[4], JAMES[3], SAMUEL[2], THOMAS[1]*) was born Sep 1857, and died 1935. He married LUCY E LEACH 1880. She was born Apr 1857, and died 1925.

Children of NATHAN SPINNEY and LUCY LEACH are:
1182.	i.	FORREST E[9] SPINNEY, b. Sep 1880, Maine; d. 1934, Maine.
	ii.	INEZ SPINNEY, b. Jan 1887; d. 1934; m. JOHN P BRENNAN.
	iii.	NELLIE M SPINNEY, b. Apr 1890.
1183.	iv.	LLOYD T SPINNEY, b. Dec 1892; d. 1945.
1184.	v.	ERNEST HARLOW SPINNEY, b. 15 Mar 1897; d. 08 Dec 1961.
	vi.	DORIS M SPINNEY, b. Aug 1899.

836. WILBRA H[8] SPINNEY (*NATHAN[7], NATHAN[6], JOHN[5], NICHOLAS[4], JAMES[3], SAMUEL[2], THOMAS[1]*) was born Jul 1864 in Eliot, ME, and died Feb 1948. He married AFFA FISBEE 1882. She was born Jun 1867, and died 1946.

Children of WILBRA SPINNEY and AFFA FISBEE are:
- i. EVA[9] SPINNEY, b. 1883.
- ii. PERCY SPINNEY, b. 1887; d. 1941.
- iii. ORA SPINNEY, b. 1889.
- iv. WILLIE RAY SPINNEY, b. 1892; m. LILLIAN M DIXON, 1910, Eliot, ME.
- v. WARREN SPINNEY, b. 1894.
- vi. GERTIE SPINNEY, b. 1898.
- vii. THERESA SPINNEY, b. 1901; d. 1943; m. KARL HODGDON, 1924, Eliot, ME.
- viii. OWEN TREADWELL SPINNEY, b. 1907; d. 26 Aug 1994, Eliot, ME; m. HELEN HODGDON, 11 Feb 1928, Eliot, ME.

837. CHARLES WARD[8] SPINNEY (*JOHN P[7], NATHAN[6], JOHN[5], NICHOLAS[4], JAMES[3], SAMUEL[2], THOMAS[1]*) was born 1864, and died Aft. 1910. He married NELLIE CASE 1889 in Raynham.

Children of CHARLES SPINNEY and NELLIE CASE are:
- i. LOUISE[9] SPINNEY, b. 1891.
- ii. HAZEL SPINNEY, b. 1896, Brockton, Ma.
- iii. ANNIE MERRILL SPINNEY, b. 1904, Brockton, Ma.

838. LUCRETIA ANN[8] OLIVER (*JOHN[7], JOHN[6], MARY[5] SPINNEY, JEREMIAH[4], JEREMIAH[3], SAMUEL[2], THOMAS[1]*) was born 25 Mar 1844 in Phippsburg, ME, and died 30 Jul 1904 in Bath, ME. She married (1) GEORGE E. REED 24 Dec 1863 in Phippsburg, ME. She married (2) RANDALL B. ROGERS 30 Sep 1865 in Phippsburg, Sagadahoc, ME. He died 12 Mar 1912 in Bath, Sagadahoc, ME.

Child of LUCRETIA OLIVER and RANDALL ROGERS is:
- i. JENNIE B.[9] ROGERS, b. 26 May 1882.

839. CLEAVELAND MANSON[8] OLIVER (*JOHN[7], JOHN[6], MARY[5] SPINNEY, JEREMIAH[4], JEREMIAH[3], SAMUEL[2], THOMAS[1]*) was born 18 Feb 1846 in Phippsburg, ME, and died 16 Sep 1920 in Bath, ME. He married SUSAN EMMA TERRELL 26 May 1867 in Phippsburg, ME. She was born Apr 1845 in Brunswick, ME, and died 23 Jun 1910 in Bath, ME.

Children of CLEAVELAND OLIVER and SUSAN TERRELL are:
- i. EUGENE L.[9] OLIVER, b. 1868; d. 01 Jan 1944.

1185.	ii.	MELISSA E. OLIVER, b. 28 Dec 1879.

840. CHESTER WARREN[8] OLIVER *(JOHN[7], JOHN[6], MARY[5] SPINNEY, JEREMIAH[4], JEREMIAH[3], SAMUEL[2], THOMAS[1])* was born 05 Dec 1850 in Phippsburg, ME, and died 04 Sep 1927 in Bath, ME. He married (1) FANNIE THOMPSON 17 Aug 1872 in Phippsburg, ME.   He married (2) ALICE A. DECKER 17 Jul 1880 in Bath, Sagadahoc, ME. She was born Dec 1854, and died 08 May 1913 in Bath, Sagadahoc, ME.

Children of CHARLES OLIVER and FANNIE THOMPSON are:
i.	MINNIE E.[9] OLIVER, b. 27 Feb 1874, Bath, ME.
1186.	ii.	FREDRICK E. OLIVER, b. 17 May 1877, Bath, ME; d. 10 Sep 1932, Bath, ME.

Children of CHARLES OLIVER and ALICE DECKER are:
iii.	JOHN L.[9] OLIVER, b. Aug 1882; d. 03 Dec 1905, Providence, Providence, RI.
iv.	JAMES OLIVER, b. Feb 1888; d. 01 Oct 1918, Lynn, Essex, MA.

841. CHESTER MARR[8] OLIVER *(JOHN[7], JOHN[6], MARY[5] SPINNEY, JEREMIAH[4], JEREMIAH[3], SAMUEL[2], THOMAS[1])* was born 04 Oct 1852 in Phippsburg, ME, and died 08 May 1920 in Bath, ME. He married (1) JENNIE HARDY 21 Nov 1875 in Bath, Sagadahoc, ME. She was born 1856, and died 15 Aug 1882 in Bath, Sagadahoc, ME. He married (2) ELLEN M. MURPHY 03 Dec 1887 in Bath, ME. She was born Dec 1851 in Nova Scotia. He married (3) MARY J. PRATT 28 Mar 1903 in Bath, Sagadahoc, ME. She was born 1854, and died 04 Mar 1937 in Portland, Cumberland, ME.

Child of CHESTER OLIVER and JENNIE HARDY is:
i.	HARRY H.[9] OLIVER, b. 14 Jun 1878, Bath, ME; d. 14 Dec 1939, Portland, ME.

Children of CHESTER OLIVER and ELLEN MURPHY are:
1187.	ii.	HERSHON BIRT[9] OLIVER, b. 27 Sep 1888, Bath, ME; d. 01 Jun 1975, Bath, ME.
iii.	EVA L. OLIVER, b. Feb 1890; d. 22 Jun 1941, Portland, ME; m. GEORGE GOODWIN, 15 Aug 1916, Bath, ME; b. Worcester, MA.
iv.	GEORGE L. OLIVER, b. 04 Apr 1891, Bath, ME; d. 04 Jun 1912, Bath, ME.
v.	ETHEL MAY OLIVER, b. Jun 1892; d. 20 Oct 1947, Dresden, Lincoln, ME; m. THOMAS LEASK, 10 Jun 1911, Bath, ME; b. Newport News, VA.

842. WILBER CARTER[8] OLIVER *(JOHN[7], JOHN[6], MARY[5] SPINNEY, JEREMIAH[4], JEREMIAH[3], SAMUEL[2], THOMAS[1])* was born 26 Feb 1860 in Phippsburg, ME, and died 31 Jan 1943 in Bath, ME. He married ESTHER GIBBS 09 Nov 1881 in Bath, ME. She was born 30 Sep 1859 in Chatham, NB., and died 15 Aug 1951 in Bath, ME.

Child of WILBER OLIVER and ESTHER GIBBS is:
1188.	i.	ARTHUR GIBBS[9] OLIVER, b. 02 May 1882, Bath, ME; d. 25 May 1946, Portland, ME.

843. LEMUEL BRADFORD[8] OLIVER *(JAMES H.[7], THOMAS[6], MARY[5] SPINNEY, JEREMIAH[4], JEREMIAH[3], SAMUEL[2], THOMAS[1])* was born 02 Jan 1867 in Phippsburg, ME, and died 30 Oct 1926 in Bath, ME. He married ANNIE P. WILDES 01 Feb 1893 in Bath, ME. She was born 18 Sep 1866 in Bath, ME, and died 04 Mar 1925 in Portland, ME.

Child of LEMUEL OLIVER and ANNIE WILDES is:
i.	BERNICE W.[9] OLIVER, b. 1897; d. 1973; m. GEORGE H. LOUGEE.

844. HARRY FREEMAN[8] OLIVER *(JAMES H.[7], THOMAS[6], MARY[5] SPINNEY, JEREMIAH[4], JEREMIAH[3], SAMUEL[2], THOMAS[1])* was born 15 Sep 1874 in Phippsburg, ME, and died 11 May 1948 in Tampa, FL. He married CLARA H. WILLIAMS 20 May 1913 in Bath, ME. She was born 1893, and died 17 Aug 1965 in Bath, ME.

Child of HARRY OLIVER and CLARA WILLIAMS is:
i.	CAROLINE AVIS[9] OLIVER, b. 1913; d. 1982; m. STEWART DAY, Private; b. Private.

845. WILLIAM SMITH[8] OLIVER *(WILLIAM RAIRDEN[7], JAMES[6], MARY[5] SPINNEY, JEREMIAH[4], JEREMIAH[3], SAMUEL[2], THOMAS[1])* was born Dec 1855, and died 14 Feb 1937 in Bath, ME. He married (1) NANCY H. OLIVER 08 Apr 1873 in Phippsburg, ME. She was born 15 Jun 1848 in Phippsburg, ME, and died 06 Jan 1875 in Georgetown, ME. He married (2) JENNIE M. JACK 11 Sep 1878 in Phippsburg, ME. She was born 1861 in Bowdoinham, ME, and died 23 Aug 1927 in Bath, ME.

Children of WILLIAM OLIVER and NANCY OLIVER are:
  i.   MINA[9] OLIVER, m. FRASER.
  ii. ALBERT E. OLIVER.

Children of WILLIAM OLIVER and JENNIE JACK are:
1189. iii. FRED ALBION[9] OLIVER, b. 22 May 1879, Phippsburg, ME; d. 19 Nov 1957, Bath, ME.
1190. iv.   SILAS MANSON OLIVER, b. 21 Nov 1881, Phippsburg, ME; d. 10 Aug 1951, Bath, ME.

846. BAXTER M.[8] OLIVER *(WILLIAM RAIRDEN[7], JAMES[6], MARY[5] SPINNEY, JEREMIAH[4], JEREMIAH[3], SAMUEL[2], THOMAS[1])* was born May 1864, and died Aft. 1900. He married ROSA JOSSLYN 24 Dec 1895. She was born Dec 1866.

Child of BAXTER OLIVER and ROSA JOSSLYN is:
  i.   MELBA[9] OLIVER, b. Jul 1897.

847. HERBERT A.[8] OLIVER *(JOSIAH PERRY[7], JAMES[6], MARY[5] SPINNEY, JEREMIAH[4], JEREMIAH[3], SAMUEL[2], THOMAS[1])* was born 30 Mar 1867 in Bath, ME, and died 16 Feb 1925 in Bath, ME. He married (1) ARABINE K. ROWE 01 Feb 1887 in Georgetown, ME. She was born 19 Dec 1868 in Georgetown, ME. He married (2) ANNIE C. WHITNEY 1905. She was born 1860, and died 10 Oct 1923 in Bath, Sagadahoc, ME.

Child of HERBERT OLIVER and ARABINE ROWE is:
1191. i.   HIRAM PERRY[9] OLIVER, b. 17 Jul 1887, Bath, ME.

848. CHARLES H.[8] OLIVER *(MATTHEW[7], EPHRAIM[6], ANNA[5] SPINNEY, JEREMIAH[4], JEREMIAH[3], SAMUEL[2], THOMAS[1])* was born 24 Jul 1855 in Arrowsic, ME, and died 11 Jan 1930 in Bath, ME. He married MARTHA D. BROWN 03 Jun 1882 in Bath, ME. She was born Oct 1858, and died 01 Oct 1936 in Bath, ME.

Child of CHARLES OLIVER and MARTHA BROWN is:
  i.   IRENE M.[9] OLIVER, b. Private; m. HOWARD M. RICE, Private.

849. WALTER J.[8] OLIVER *(MATTHEW[7], EPHRAIM[6], ANNA[5] SPINNEY, JEREMIAH[4], JEREMIAH[3], SAMUEL[2], THOMAS[1])* was born 1863, and died 11 Aug 1911 in Newton, MA. He married (1) SUSAN F. She was born 1875, and died 05 Nov 1961 in Braintree, MA. He married (2) ABBY M. HAGGETT 12 Aug 1883 in Bath, Sagadahoc, ME. She was born 1865, and died 01 Jun 1890.

Children of WALTER OLIVER and ABBY HAGGETT are:
  i.   MATTHEW[9] OLIVER.
  ii. VIRGINIA OLIVER.
  iii. FRED M. OLIVER, b. 1900; d. 09 Sep 1932, Taunton, Bristol, MA.

850. HANNAH ELIZABETH[8] OLIVER *(BENJAMIN S.[7], EPHRAIM[6], ANNA[5] SPINNEY, JEREMIAH[4], JEREMIAH[3], SAMUEL[2], THOMAS[1])* was born 18 Feb 1862 in Bath, ME, and died 22 Apr 1919 in Bath, ME. She married JOHN C. WAKEFIELD 17 May 1879 in Bath, ME. He died 08 Jul 1923 in Bath, ME.

Children of HANNAH OLIVER and JOHN WAKEFIELD are:
  i.   SAMUEL[9] WAKEFIELD.
  ii. FRANCES WAKEFIELD.

851. LYDIA[8] HUSSEY *(PHOEBE[7] GOODWIN, BARTHSEHBA WEARE[6] SPINNEY, DAVID[5], EBENEZER[4], JONATHAN[3], SAMUEL[2], THOMAS[1])* was born 15 May 1846. She married DANIEL L LOVELL 30 Oct 1870.

Children of LYDIA HUSSEY and DANIEL LOVELL are:
1192.   i.   MABEL[9] LOVELL, b. 13 Jul 1871.
        ii. JOSIAH H LOVELL, b. 01 Nov 1872; m. JEANNIE LESTER.
       iii. ANNIE LOVELL, b. 12 Feb 1876; m. WILLIAM STARR.
       iv. JOHN W LOVELL, b. 27 Feb 1880; m. SARAH LEVEE.
        v. HERBERT S LOVELL, b. 06 Oct 1881; m. ANNIE MCDONALD.
       vi. GERTRUDE E LOVELL, b. 30 Sep 1883.
      vii. MARION F LOVELL, b. 05 Mar 1889.

852. GEORGE FRANKLIN[8] SPINNEY *(PAUL[7], PARKER FOSTER[6], DAVID[5], EBENEZER[4], JONATHAN[3], SAMUEL[2], THOMAS[1])* was born 09 Jul 1852 in Great Falls, NH, and died Aft. 1900. He married OLIVE S. WITHINGTON 19 Sep 1877 in Ipswich, MA. She was born 01 Mar 1853 in Portland , ME, and died Aft. 1900.

Notes for GEORGE FRANKLIN SPINNEY:
George F Spinney moved to Brooklyn New York at some point before 1900 where he can be found in the census

Children of GEORGE SPINNEY and OLIVE WITHINGTON are:
        i.   PAULINE[9] SPINNEY, b. Sep 1878.
        ii. MABEL SPINNEY, b. 1879.
       iii. HELEN SPINNEY, b. 1888.

853. EUGENE NATHANIAL[8] SPINNEY *(JOSEPH FRANKLIN[7], PARKER FOSTER[6], DAVID[5], EBENEZER[4], JONATHAN[3], SAMUEL[2], THOMAS[1])* was born 06 Apr 1866 in Rorchester NH, and died 19 Jan 1936 in Milton NH. He married IZA THAYER STONE 27 Sep 1893 in Ipswich, Ma, daughter of LORENZO STONE and ETTA FALL. She was born 08 Oct 1870.

Children of EUGENE SPINNEY and IZA STONE are:
1193.   i.   PARKER THAYER[9] SPINNEY, b. 11 Sep 1894, Ipswich, MA; d. Oct 1965.
1194.   ii. HELEN AUGUSTA SPINNEY, b. 26 Oct 1902, Shelbourne, MA.

854. CROSBY BUCK[8] SPINNEY *(WILLIAM RICE[7], PARKER FOSTER[6], DAVID[5], EBENEZER[4], JONATHAN[3], SAMUEL[2], THOMAS[1])* was born 11 Aug 1884, and died Nov 1967 in Monclair NJ. He married FANNY DAVENPORT OAKMAN 31 Dec 1907. She was born 31 Oct 1882 in Massachusetts, and died 20 Sep 1958 in Los Angeles, California.

Children of CROSBY SPINNEY and FANNY OAKMAN are:
        i.   FRANK OAKMAN[9] SPINNEY, b. 14 Jan 1909; d. 2002.

           Notes for FRANK OAKMAN SPINNEY:
           From the New York Times, 23 June 2002:
           Frank Spinney, Museum Innovator, Dies at 93
           By ERIC PACE
           Frank O. Spinney, who played a principal role in the formation of Old
           Sturbridge Village, the outdoor historical museum in Massachusetts, died
           on June 4 in a Medford, N.J., retirement community. He was 93.
           Mr. Spinney, a leader in professionalizing the field of outdoor
           history-museum work in the United States, was professor of museum studies
           at Oneonta College in Oneonta, N.Y., for some years.
           From 1954 to 1962, Mr. Spinney was chief executive of Old Sturbridge Village, in
           southern Massachussetts. It was founded in 1946 to show visitors what
           life was like in a small town in New England in the early 19th
           century. Jack Larkin, Old Sturbridge's director of research, collections and library,
           said that Mr. Spinney, as its chief executive, emphasized careful
           research and historical accuracy, a course that the institution has
           followed ever since.
           While Mr. Spinney was in charge, Old Sturbridge Village made many of its most
           important acquisitions of old buildings, which now total 40 structures
           that were moved to its site. They are viewed by 400,000 visitors a year.

Mr. Spinney also improved the organization of the village's professional staff and began to expand its educational programs.

In the 1950's and 60's Mr. Spinney was a major figure in the teaching of museum professionals. He taught in an innovative graduate program that he devised for museum directors and curators at Oneonta College, which is part of the State University system.

He also had a deep interest in Augustus Saint-Gaudens, the American neoclassical sculptor whose works include the statue of Gen. William Tecumseh Sherman at the corner of 59th Street and Fifth Avenue in Manhattan. Mr. Spinney had a substantial role in the federal government's acquisition, in 1964, of the site in Cornish, N.H., where Saint-Gaudens lived and worked from 1885 until his death in 1907. The site was transferred to the National Park Service and is now the Saint-Gaudens National Historical Site. Mr. Spinney was instrumental in arranging for a Dartmouth College library to acquire a collection of more than two dozen boxes containing Saint-Gaudens's correspondence and other personal documents. Frank Oakman Spinney was born in Springfield, Mass., and grew up in Upper Montclair, N.J. He graduated from Phillips Academy in Andover, Mass., and received bachelor's and master's degrees from Yale.

He was in the field artillery in World War II. He is survived by his second wife, Alice, whom he married in 1935; a daughter, Jane Huber of Fly Creek, N.Y.; four grandchildren; and three great-grandchildren.

    ii.   BEATRICE SPINNEY, b. 08 Dec 1912.

855. ATTA[8] SPINNEY *(CHARLES H[7], CHARLES P[6], CHARLES[5], EBENEZER[4], JONATHAN[3], SAMUEL[2], THOMAS[1])* was born Jul 1873. She married HARRY L MITCHELL. He was born 1870, and died 1944.

Children of ATTA SPINNEY and HARRY MITCHELL are:
    i.   HARLON[9] MITCHELL, b. 1892; d. 1956.
    ii.   MINA MITCHELL, b. Nov 1895; d. 1957; m. JOHN LEROY WILLARD; b. 1884; d. 1966.

856. IDA F[8] SPINNEY *(AUGUSTUS RICE[7], CHARLES P[6], CHARLES[5], EBENEZER[4], JONATHAN[3], SAMUEL[2], THOMAS[1])* was born 21 Nov 1858. She married CHARLES GOODWIN.

Child of IDA SPINNEY and CHARLES GOODWIN is:
    i.   NETTIE[9] GOODWIN, b. 1877.

857. HANNAH L[8] SPINNEY *(HORACE P[7], MARK[6], PARKER[5], EBENEZER[4], JONATHAN[3], SAMUEL[2], THOMAS[1])* was born 18 Jan 1875 in Portsmouth, NH. She married BERTWOOD H TREFETHEN 16 Apr 1891 in Portsmouth NH, son of ABRAM TREFETHEN and FRANCES DAVIDSON. He was born 06 Sep 1869 in New Castle, NH.

Notes for BERTWOOD H TREFETHEN:
* B. New Castle, NH
* Boat builder/Boat keeper/Blacksmith
* M. 4/16/1891 in Ports. or New Castle, NH. Both res. Portsmouth. He was 23 & she 18. He b. New Castle s/o Abram & Frances E. (both dec.d); she was 18, d/o Horace & Annie.
* Had 'Boats to Let' in 1899 at 27 Mechanic St. [S36: 1899 PORTSMOUTH, NH DIRECTORY]
* Wife b. Portsmouth, NH; 1/?/1874
* 1900 Census has b. 1866
* Res. 10 Hunking, Portsmouth, NH in 1900 [Census].

(

Children of HANNAH SPINNEY and BERTWOOD TREFETHEN are:
    i.   FREDERICK[9] TREFETHEN, b. 21 Apr 1892, Portsmouth, NH.
    ii.   HAROLD TREFETHEN, b. 01 Aug 1893, Portsmouth, NH; d. 1893.

858. ARTHUR F[8] SPINNEY *(HENRY CHAPIN[7], MARK[6], PARKER[5], EBENEZER[4], JONATHAN[3], SAMUEL[2], THOMAS[1])* was born 18 Jul 1877 in Portsmouth, NH. He married (1) MARY AGENES MORRISSEY 1901. She was born May 1877. He married (2) EMMA CHAPMAN 1901.

Child of ARTHUR SPINNEY and MARY MORRISSEY is:
    i.   FLORENCE E[9] SPINNEY, b. Nov 1900; m. FRANK DOWNEY.

859. HARRY HENRY[8] SPINNEY *(HENRY CHAPIN[7], MARK[6], PARKER[5], EBENEZER[4], JONATHAN[3], SAMUEL[2], THOMAS[1])* was born 1876. He married (1) MAY AGNES MORRISSEY 1901 in Lynn, MA. She was born 1877. He married (2) EMMA CHAPMAN 1904.

Child of HARRY SPINNEY and MAY MORRISSEY is:
    i.   ARTHUR FRANCIS[9] SPINNEY, b. 1902, Lynn, Ma.

860. FRANCIS WARREN[8] SPINNEY *(GEORGE F[7], MARK[6], PARKER[5], EBENEZER[4], JONATHAN[3], SAMUEL[2], THOMAS[1])* was born 28 May 1878, and died 04 Jul 1958 in Bradford, MA. He married HELEN (ELLEN) MOOERS 1906 in Haverhill, MA. She was born 1879.

Children of FRANCIS SPINNEY and HELEN MOOERS are:
    i.   EARL FRANCIS[9] SPINNEY, b. 06 Oct 1916, Bradford, MA.
    ii. EDWARD DUDLEY SPINNEY, b. 06 Dec 1919, Bradford, MA.
1195.   iii. HAROLD WARREN SPINNEY, b. 31 Jan 1918, Bradford, MA; d. 04 Dec 1999, Groveland, MA.

861. CLARA S[8] SPINNEY *(JOSEPH WILLIAM[7], EBENEZER[6], EBENEZER[5], EBENEZER[4], JONATHAN[3], SAMUEL[2], THOMAS[1])* was born 15 Jan 1859, and died in Deer Island Maine. She married JOHN H BENNETT 04 Mar 1884 in Deer Island Maine. He was born Nov 1854.

Children of CLARA SPINNEY and JOHN BENNETT are:
    i.   GUY[9] BENNETT, b. Jan 1885.
    ii. HARRY BENNETT, b. Sep 1886.
    iii. FRED BENNETT, b. Jul 1888.

862. NANCY J[8] SPINNEY *(WILLIAM P[7], EBENEZER[6], EBENEZER[5], EBENEZER[4], JONATHAN[3], SAMUEL[2], THOMAS[1])* was born 1879. She married (1) THOMAS M HARRIS 06 Apr 1896. She married (2) HENRY BILLINGS 24 Oct 1905.

Children of NANCY SPINNEY and HENRY BILLINGS are:
    i.   RUTH L[9] BILLINGS.
    ii. ROSEBUD BILLINGS.

863. ELLA GERTRUDE[8] WHEELER *(ALICE CATHERINE[7] DWELLEY, NARCISSA SPRING[6] SPINNEY, EBENEZER[5], EBENEZER[4], JONATHAN[3], SAMUEL[2], THOMAS[1])* was born 03 Jun 1867 in Wisconsin, and died 1912 in St Helena CA. She married AMOS DOW OWENS, son of ISAAC OWENS and LUCY ESTES. He was born 16 Jan 1864 in Sycamore, IL, and died 1937 in Vancouver, WA.

Children of ELLA WHEELER and AMOS OWENS are:
    i.   ALMOND[9] OWENS.
    ii. ROSCOE OWENS.
    iii. ROLAND OWENS.
    iv. FRANKLIN OWENS.
    v. AMY OWENS.
1196.   vi. LLOYD MAXWELL OWENS, b. 26 Dec 1890, Cottage Grove OR; d. 31 Aug 1971, Meadow Glade WA.

864. ALICE CATHERINE[8] DWELLEY *(JOSEPH FRANKLIN[7], NARCISSA SPRING[6] SPINNEY, EBENEZER[5], EBENEZER[4], JONATHAN[3], SAMUEL[2], THOMAS[1])* She married PATRICK HENRY MALOY.

Children of ALICE DWELLEY and PATRICK MALOY are:
1197. i.   HELEN LOUISE[9] MALOY.
       ii. GEORGE LYMAN MALOY.
       iii. JOSEPH FRANKLIN MALOY.

865. NELLIE ANNE[8] SPINNEY *(HORACE STACEY[7], LYMAN P[6], EBENEZER[5], EBENEZER[4], JONATHAN[3], SAMUEL[2], THOMAS[1])* was born 12 Dec 1862, and died 10 Apr 1908. She married CHARLES STOVER 1881.

Child of NELLIE SPINNEY and CHARLES STOVER is:
       i.   FLORENCE[9] STOVER, m. EDWIN DINSMORE.

866. ALPHONSO BENJAMIN[8] SPINNEY *(HORACE STACEY[7], LYMAN P[6], EBENEZER[5], EBENEZER[4], JONATHAN[3], SAMUEL[2], THOMAS[1])* was born 31 Mar 1866, and died 04 Mar 1940. He married LENA C MORSE 21 Feb 1885 in Portsmouth. She was born Apr 1867.

Children of ALPHONSO SPINNEY and LENA MORSE are:
       i.   MABEL ISABEL[9] SPINNEY, b. 13 Jan 1886; m. GEORGE ARTHUR WESTOVER.
       ii. HATTIE I SPINNEY, b. 20 Apr 1888.
       iii. CLARA A SPINNEY, b. 09 Apr 1891, Portsmouth, NH; d. 1976.

867. CHARLES L[8] SPINNEY *(LYMAN P[7], LYMAN P[6], EBENEZER[5], EBENEZER[4], JONATHAN[3], SAMUEL[2], THOMAS[1])* was born 06 Jul 1872 in Woburn, MA. He married LILLIE U HUSSEY 14 May 1892 in Kittery, ME, daughter of DORPHUS HUSSEY and ELIZA KIMBALL.

Children of CHARLES SPINNEY and LILLIE HUSSEY are:
       i.   CHARLES R[9] SPINNEY, b. 15 Jan 1894.
       ii. JOSEPH P SPINNEY, b. Jul 1895.

868. BESSIE MILDRED[8] SPINNEY *(LYMAN P[7], LYMAN P[6], EBENEZER[5], EBENEZER[4], JONATHAN[3], SAMUEL[2], THOMAS[1])* was born 1874 in Woburn, MA. She married EDWARD L WOODMAN.

Child of BESSIE SPINNEY and EDWARD WOODMAN is:
       i.   RAYMOND[9] WOODMAN.

869. SIMEON[8] HALL *(NATHANIEL PULSIFIER[7], ABIGAIL[6] WILLEY, SALLY[5] FERNALD, HANNAH (BETSY)[4] SPINNEY, JONATHAN[3], SAMUEL[2], THOMAS[1])* was born 1812. He married LUCY WESCOTT DORR. She was born 1825.

Child of SIMEON HALL and LUCY DORR is:
       i.   EDWIN J[9] HALL, b. 1854.

870. DOUGLAS[8] SPINNEY *(JAMES ALEXANDER[7], STEPHEN[6], JONATHAN[5], NATHANIEL[4], JONATHAN[3], SAMUEL[2], THOMAS[1])* was born 09 Jan 1858 in Pennfield, NB., and died 09 Jan 1954. He married MARGARET TRYNOR 24 Sep 1890 in Pennfield, NB.. She was born 08 Feb 1867, and died 06 Nov 1942 in Utopia, NB.

Children of DOUGLAS SPINNEY and MARGARET TRYNOR are:
       i.   JAMES RANALD[9] SPINNEY, b. 26 May 1892, Utopia, NB; d. 24 Aug 1910, Pennfield, NB.
1198. ii. LLEWELLEN SPINNEY, b. 31 Oct 1894, Utopia, NB.; d. 01 Aug 1972, St George, NB..
       iii. VERNON KNIGHT SPINNEY, b. 10 Aug 1898, Utopia, NB.; d. 08 Feb 1983, Black's Harbour, NB.; m. MARY GRACE COOK, 23 Sep 1961.

       Notes for MARY GRACE COOK:
       SPINNEY - At the Charlotte County Hospital, St. Stephen, on December 14, 1992, Mrs. Mary G. (Cook) Spinney of St. George, wife of the late Vernon Spinney; survived by one cousin, Paul Erskine of St. Stephen, one niece, Anita, Mrs. Gerald Grearson of St. George and a sister-in-law, Mrs. Bessie Spinney of St. George. Rested at the St. George Funeral Home, 26 Portage Street, St. George. The funeral was held Thursday at 2 p.m. at the Presbyterian Kirk in St. George.

iv. FRANK DOUGLAS SPINNEY, b. 06 Jan 1904, Utopia, NB.; d. 23 Apr 1985, St George, NB.; m. BESSIE A SOUTHARD, 27 Jun 1927, St George, NB..

871. CHARLES MCPIKE[8] SPINNEY *(ALFRED HURLEY[7], STEPHEN[6], JONATHAN[5], NATHANIEL[4], JONATHAN[3], SAMUEL[2], THOMAS[1])* was born 16 Sep 1858 in Pennfield, NB., and died 30 Apr 1923 in Musquash, NB.. He married SUSANNAH LENNOX 1881. She was born 1851, and died Aft. 1901.

Children of CHARLES SPINNEY and SUSANNAH LENNOX are:
1199.   i. JOHN CHARLES THOMAS "JACK"[9] SPINNEY, b. 05 Apr 1882, Musquash, NB.; d. 1955, Berlin, NH..
       ii. CLARENCE EDWARD "CLARY" SPINNEY, b. 17 Dec 1883, Musquash, NB.; d. 10 Dec 1948, Musquash, NB.; m. ALICE "MAUD" GRAHAM, Feb 1925, St George, NB..
     iii. ANNIE AUGUSTA "GUSSIE" SPINNEY, b. 21 Sep 1887, Musquash, NB.; d. 05 Nov 1967, Lepreau, NB.; m. WALTER KILBY MCPHERSON, 1908; b. 1882, MUSQUASH, SAINT JOHN COUNTY,NB; d. 1968.
     iv. CORA MAY SPINNEY, b. 17 Mar 1890, Musquash, NB.; d. Bef. 1901.
      v. ELLEN MAY SPINNEY, b. 30 Nov 1900.

872. MARY ELLEN[8] SPINNEY *(ALFRED HURLEY[7], STEPHEN[6], JONATHAN[5], NATHANIEL[4], JONATHAN[3], SAMUEL[2], THOMAS[1])* was born 26 Dec 1861 in Pennfield, NB., and died 02 Sep 1936 in Pennfield, NB.. She married HUGH MCHUGH 20 Jun 1876 in St George, NB., son of DANEIL MCHUGH and NANCY MCKEEVER. He was born 31 Oct 1854 in Saint John, NB., and died 17 Jun 1914 in Pennfield, NB..

Children of MARY SPINNEY and HUGH MCHUGH are:
       i. JAMES DANIEL (MCHUGH)[9] MCCUE, b. 15 Apr 1878, Pennfield, NB.; d. 22 Aug 1940, Worcester, MA; m. HANNAH THERESE REYNOLDS, 1905, Worcester MA.
      ii. JOSEPH MCHUGH, b. 25 Dec 1879, Pennfield, NB.; d. 23 Sep 1936, St George, NB; m. MARGARET ELIZABETH MCLAUGHLIN, 16 Jul 1918, St George, NB..
     iii. CHARLES HUGH (MCHUGH) MCCUE, b. 07 Jan 1882, Pennfield, NB.; d. 09 Jul 1971, Worcester, MA; m. (1) ELIZABETH ANN BARRY; m. (2) MARY ANN (TRAVERSE) TRAVERS, 21 Oct 1920, Leicester, MA.
     iv. MARY ELLEN (MCHUGH) MCCUE, b. 15 Nov 1883, Pennfield, NB.; d. 03 Feb 1971, Cherry Valley, MA; m. JOHN FRANCIS "JACK" CONNOR, 23 Aug 1926.
      v. GEORGE RICHARD MCHUGH, b. 10 Nov 1885, Pennfield, NB.; d. 17 Dec 1935, St Stephen, NB.; m. ELLA GEORGIANNA TURNER, 23 Apr 1907, St George, NB..
     vi. FRANCIS EDWARD "NED" (MCHUGH) MCCUE, b. 23 May 1887, Pennfield, NB.; d. 23 Jun 1964, Worcester, Ma; m. NORA E HEAGHNEY, 30 Jun 1914, Worcester MA.
    vii. ANNIE "BERTHA" MCHUGH, b. 29 Dec 1889, Pennfield, NB.; d. 19 Oct 1920, Worcester, Ma; m. HARRY CLIFFORD TRAYNOR, 26 Sep 1910, Worcester MA.
   viii. ALICE CATHERINE MCHUGH, b. 21 Mar 1892, Pennfield, NB.; d. 14 Mar 1961, Saint John, NB.; m. OTIS ARMSTRONG, 13 Sep 1916, St George, NB..
     ix. JOHN ALFRED "RAYMOND" MCHUGH, b. 31 Aug 1894, Pennfield, NB.; d. 26 May 1923, Pennfield, NB..
      x. THOMAS LEO MCHUGH, b. 07 Feb 1897, Pennfield, NB.; d. 10 Mar 1897, Pennfield, NB..
     xi. ELIZABETH " IRENE" MCHUGH, b. 20 Jun 1898, Pennfield, NB.; d. 26 Jul 1972, Worcester, MA; m. ARTHUR C HILYARD, 17 Sep 1930.
    xii. CLARENCE BERNARD MCHUGH, b. 04 Jan 1901, Pennfield, NB.; d. 24 Nov 1982, Saint John, NB.; m. PEARLE ISOBEL HATT, 21 Apr 1930, St George, NB..
   xiii. MARGARET ALMA MCHUGH, b. 21 Mar 1904, Pennfield, NB.; d. 19 Feb 1987, Black's Harbour, NB.; m. WILLIAM HAINES MITCHELL, 03 May 1926, St George, NB..
   xiv. SARAH MCHUGH, b. 05 Jan 1906, Pennfield, NB.; d. 05 Jan 1906, Pennfield, NB..
    xv. CONRAD MCHUGH, b. 05 Jan 1906, Pennfield, NB.; d. 05 Jan 1906, Pennfield, NB..

873. EDWARD HENRY[8] SPINNEY *(ALFRED HURLEY[7], STEPHEN[6], JONATHAN[5], NATHANIEL[4], JONATHAN[3], SAMUEL[2], THOMAS[1])* was born 03 Aug 1864 in St George, NB., and died in Bradford, PA. He married FLORA FELLOWS. She was born in New York.

Children of EDWARD SPINNEY and FLORA FELLOWS are:
       i. EDWARD[9] SPINNEY, b. Abt. 1885.
      ii. ELLA SPINNEY, b. 1892; m. DANIEL STINSON.
     iii. ALICE SPINNEY, b. 1902; m. EDWARD FLAHERTY.

874. ALFRED HURLEY[8] SPINNEY *(ALFRED HURLEY[7], STEPHEN[6], JONATHAN[5], NATHANIEL[4], JONATHAN[3], SAMUEL[2], THOMAS[1])* was born Nov 1866 in Pennfield, NB., and died 31 May 1900 in St George, NB.. He married ALICE MAUD SUMMERTON 29 Oct 1889 in St Andrews, NB.. She was born 1868 in St George, NB., and died Aft. 1938.

Children of ALFRED SPINNEY and ALICE SUMMERTON are:

	i.	HOGES FREDERICK "FRED"[9] SPINNEY, b. 09 Aug 1890, St George, NB.; d. 31 Mar 1963, Calais, ME; m. LILLIAN B SPINNEY, 02 May 1938, Calais, ME; b. 1900, Augusta, ME; d. 23 Mar 1990, Calais, ME.
	ii.	HAROLD EDWARD "HARRY" SPINNEY, b. 24 Dec 1891.
1200.	iii.	JAMES H SPINNEY, b. 27 Jan 1893; d. 12 Oct 1951, Eastport, ME.
	iv.	JOHN HARVEY SPINNEY, b. 27 Jan 1894, Berlin, NH.
	v.	ALFRED H SPINNEY, b. 19 Feb 1896, St George, NB.; d. 1978, Waterville, ME; m. EDITH V LYON, 30 Aug 1919, Eastport, Me.
	vi.	ETHEL MAE SPINNEY, b. 10 Oct 1898, St George, NB.; d. 1966; m. JACOB MILTON FOWLER, 02 Jan 1926, Eastport, ME.
	vii.	LOUIS SYLVESTER SPINNEY, b. 10 Oct 1898; d. Aft. 1949.

875. JAMES THOMAS[8] SPINNEY *(ALFRED HURLEY[7], STEPHEN[6], JONATHAN[5], NATHANIEL[4], JONATHAN[3], SAMUEL[2], THOMAS[1])* was born 20 Jun 1868 in Pennfield, NB, and died 14 Oct 1941 in Runford, ME. He married (1) MYRTIE HIGHT 01 Jun 1901 in Greenvale, Maine. She was born 1880, and died 1901 in Rangeley Maine. He married (2) ALMENA TWOMBLY 16 Sep 1905 in Rangeley, ME, daughter of WALTER TWOMBLY and ANNIE COLLINS. She was born 1888, and died 1954 in Rangeley, ME.

Children of JAMES SPINNEY and ALMENA TWOMBLY are:

i.	JAMES A[9] SPINNEY, b. 1905; d. 1905, Rangeley Maine.
ii.	FLORENCE G SPINNEY, b. 1907; d. 1907, Rangeley Maine.
iii.	CHARLOTTE ARLENE "LOTTIE" SPINNEY, b. 1908; d. 1978; m. WILLIAM A SINCLAIR.
iv.	FRANK C SPINNEY, b. 1910; d. 1913, Rangeley Maine.
v.	ELIZABETH KATE "BETTY" SPINNEY, b. 25 Jun 1912; d. 20 Nov 1984; m. KENNETY F "SAM" CAMPBELL.
vi.	CLOUGH ROGERS "BUD" SPINNEY, b. 05 Aug 1917, Rangeley, ME; m. (1) LILLIAN CARRIE WING, 07 Jul 1940; m. (2) BARBARA IONA HOUGHTON, 06 Jun 1942.

876. CLARENCE JOHN[8] SPINNEY *(ALFRED HURLEY[7], STEPHEN[6], JONATHAN[5], NATHANIEL[4], JONATHAN[3], SAMUEL[2], THOMAS[1])* was born Mar 1870 in Pennfield, NB., and died 1901. He married ESSIE CURRIER 19 Oct 1893 in Bangor, ME, daughter of JAMES CURRIER and ABBIE WITHAM. She was born 1877 in Bangor, ME.

Children of CLARENCE SPINNEY and ESSIE CURRIER are:

1201.	i.	ALBERT J[9] SPINNEY, b. 26 Mar 1894, Maine; d. Nov 1979, Springfield, MA.
1202.	ii.	ALFRED J SPINNEY, b. 26 Mar 1894, Maine; d. Jun 1971, New Britain, Hartford, CT.
	iii.	RALPH EDWARD SPINNEY, b. 02 Nov 1897, Maine; d. Aft. 1930; m. MARIAN COLE, 19 May 1917, Bangor, ME.
	iv.	LILLIAN B SPINNEY, b. 1900, Augusta, ME; d. 23 Mar 1990, Calais, ME; m. (1) FRED J SUMMERTON, 30 Jun 1919, Augusta Maine; b. 1884; m. (2) HOGES FREDERICK "FRED" SPINNEY, 02 May 1938, Calais, ME; b. 09 Aug 1890, St George, NB.; d. 31 Mar 1963, Calais, ME.

877. CATHERINE "ALICE"[8] SPINNEY *(ALFRED HURLEY[7], STEPHEN[6], JONATHAN[5], NATHANIEL[4], JONATHAN[3], SAMUEL[2], THOMAS[1])* was born 01 Jan 1876 in Pennfield, NB., and died May 1957 in Ypsilanti, MI. She married GEORGE TARNEY" MCCORMICK 05 Nov 1902 in St George New Brunswick, son of JOSEPH MCCORMICK and MATILDA DAVIS. He was born 10 May 1870 in St George, NB., and died 12 Oct 1954 in Ypsilanti, MI.

Children of CATHERINE SPINNEY and GEORGE MCCORMICK are:

i.	LOUIS SYLVESTER[9] MCCORMICK, b. 02 Apr 1895, St George, NB.; d. Sep 1968, Flint, Genesie, MI.
ii.	MATILDA DAVIS MCCORMICK, b. 05 Aug 1903, St George, NB.; d. 20 Mar 1988, Ypsilanti, MI; m. (1) DELOS CUMMINGS; m. (2) CHAUNCEY F STUHLMANN, 01 Oct 1937, Ypsilanti, MI.

878. FREDERICK[8] SPINNEY *(HORATIO NELSON[7], STEPHEN[6], JONATHAN[5], NATHANIEL[4], JONATHAN[3], SAMUEL[2], THOMAS[1])* was born 01 Feb 1864 in St George, NB., and died 06 Mar 1932 in Saint John, NB.. He married ELIZA JANE LENNOX 14 Apr 1885 in Saint John, NB.. She was born 1865, and died Aft. 1901.

Children of FREDERICK SPINNEY and ELIZA LENNOX are:
- i. FLORENCE[9] SPINNEY, b. 12 Feb 1886, Musquash, NB.; d. 1906.
1203. ii. ALICE "MAUD" SPINNEY, b. 07 Nov 1888, Musquash, NB.; d. May 1939, Grand Bay, NB..
- iii. FREDERICK EVERETT SPINNEY, b. 30 Jul 1891, Musquash, NB.; d. 1906, Musquash, NB>.
1204. iv. STEPHEN PERCY SPINNEY, b. 24 Sep 1895, Musquash, NB.; d. 09 Feb 1984, Saint John, NB..
1205. v. STANLEY DOULGAS SPINNEY, b. 19 May 1898, Musquash, NB.; d. 09 Aug 1973, Musquash, NB..
- vi. GREGORY SPINNEY, b. 1904, Musquash, NB.; d. 1923.

879. HORATIO NELSON[8] SPINNEY *(HORATIO NELSON[7], STEPHEN[6], JONATHAN[5], NATHANIEL[4], JONATHAN[3], SAMUEL[2], THOMAS[1])* was born 06 May 1868 in Musquash, NB., and died 1948 in Prince of Wales, NB.. He married ISABELLA CATHERWOOD, daughter of ANDREW CATHERWOOD and JANE. She was born 06 Jul 1870 in Ghost Lake, NB., and died 25 Nov 1917 in St John, NB..

Children of HORATIO SPINNEY and ISABELLA CATHERWOOD are:
- i. HAZEL ISABELLA[9] SPINNEY, b. 10 Nov 1897, Cambridge, NB.; d. 1912.
- ii. JAMES SPINNEY, b. 1899; m. GEORGIE; b. 1901.
- iii. ELDON CATHERWOOD SPINNEY, b. 11 May 1899, St John, NB.; d. 1989, Niagra Falls, Ontario; m. WINNIFRED ROSETTA MABEL PATTERSON, 1936, Niagra Falls, Ontario.
- iv. MARY SPINNEY, b. 1901, St John, NB.; d. 1952, St John, NB..
- v. VICTOR PAUL SPINNEY, b. 1904, St John, NB.; d. 10 Mar 1967, Toronto, Ontario Canada; m. NELLIE WARD, 1929, Toronto, Ontario Canada.

880. DOUGLAS[8] SPINNEY *(HORATIO NELSON[7], STEPHEN[6], JONATHAN[5], NATHANIEL[4], JONATHAN[3], SAMUEL[2], THOMAS[1])* was born 01 May 1874 in Musquash, NB., and died 1943 in Musquash, NB.. He married NANCY LENNOX, daughter of THOMAS LENNOX and SUSANNAH CAIRNS. She was born 23 Oct 1867 in Musquash, NB., and died 1907 in Musquash, NB..

Children of DOUGLAS SPINNEY and NANCY LENNOX are:
- i. ELIZABETH M "BESSIE"[9] SPINNEY, b. 01 Apr 1898, St John, NB.; d. 1975, St John, NB..
- ii. GRACE SPINNEY, b. 22 Mar 1901; d. 1970; m. (1) CHESTER BROWN; m. (2) JULIUS NEUENHAUS.
- iii. RUBY SPINNEY, b. 1902, St John, NB.; d. 1981, Vancouver, BC.; m. CECIL SELLMAN.

881. JAMES[8] HUNTER *(KATHERINE M[7] SPINNEY, JAMES S[6], JONATHAN[5], NATHANIEL[4], JONATHAN[3], SAMUEL[2], THOMAS[1])* He married SARAH ELLEN SPINNEY, daughter of JAMES SPINNEY and MARTHA LOWE. She was born 1848, and died 04 Dec 1884 in Pennfield, NB..

Children are listed above under (526) Sarah Ellen Spinney.

882. GIDEON WEBSTER[8] SPINNEY *(JOSEPH L[7], JAMES S[6], JONATHAN[5], NATHANIEL[4], JONATHAN[3], SAMUEL[2], THOMAS[1])* was born 12 Mar 1859 in St George, NB., and died 21 Oct 1919 in California. He married (1) MARTHA CUTLER. He married (2) MAGGIE LITTLEFIELD. She was born 1879 in California.

Child of GIDEON SPINNEY and MARTHA CUTLER is:
- i. MARY[9] SPINNEY, b. 1890.

Children of GIDEON SPINNEY and MAGGIE LITTLEFIELD are:
- ii. ELENE[9] SPINNEY, b. 1892.
- iii. ALFRED SPINNEY, b. 1899.
- iv. GRACE F SPINNEY, b. 1902, California.

883. ANNIE LOUISA[8] SPINNEY *(JOSEPH L[7], JAMES S[6], JONATHAN[5], NATHANIEL[4], JONATHAN[3], SAMUEL[2], THOMAS[1])* was born 09 Aug 1865, and died 16 Aug 1896. She married EDWARD ALBEE.

Children of ANNIE SPINNEY and EDWARD ALBEE are:
- i. EDGAR HARRIS[9] ALBEE.
- ii. HORACE ARNOLD ALBEE.
- iii. MAURICE MELVIN ALBEE, b. 09 Oct 1893; d. 28 Oct 1957.

iv. ELMER ELDRIDGE ALBEE.
v. CLARENCE WILLARD ALBEE.
vi. CHESTER LEWIS ALBEE.
vii. HAROLD EDGAR ALBEE.
viii. MILDRED LOUISE ALBEE.
ix. WALTER SPINNEY ALBEE, b. 07 Apr 1894; d. 29 Apr 1955.
x. MABEL ELEANOR ALBEE, b. 04 Sep 1895; d. 21 May 1954.
xi. MILTON ELLSWORTH ALBEE.

884. JOSEPH WALTER[8] SPINNEY *(JOSEPH L[7], JAMES S[6], JONATHAN[5], NATHANIEL[4], JONATHAN[3], SAMUEL[2], THOMAS[1])* was born 22 Feb 1870 in St George, NB., and died 15 Dec 1948 in Humbult, CA. He married SARAH EVELYN WILSON 12 Jun 1904. She was born 04 Jul 1883 in Eureka, CA, and died 27 Nov 1939.

Children of JOSEPH SPINNEY and SARAH WILSON are:
i. LESTER[9] SPINNEY, b. 1906.
ii. MABEL SPINNEY, b. 1908.

885. MAGGIE JANE[8] SPINNEY *(JOSEPH L[7], JAMES S[6], JONATHAN[5], NATHANIEL[4], JONATHAN[3], SAMUEL[2], THOMAS[1])* was born 18 Aug 1873, and died 20 Dec 1939. She married FRED TAYLOR.

Children of MAGGIE SPINNEY and FRED TAYLOR are:
i. BLANCHE[9] TAYLOR.
ii. VERNON TAYLOR.

886. GEORGE GILMAN[8] STEWART *(MARY JANE[7] SPINNEY, JAMES S[6], JONATHAN[5], NATHANIEL[4], JONATHAN[3], SAMUEL[2], THOMAS[1])* was born 1860, and died 1937. He married GERTRUDE DAVIS CORNING 22 Oct 1894. She was born 15 Jan 1873, and died Aug 1957.

Child of GEORGE STEWART and GERTRUDE CORNING is:
i. FREDERICK[9] STEWART, b. 1896; d. 1965.

887. JAMES ALFRED[8] STEWART *(MARY JANE[7] SPINNEY, JAMES S[6], JONATHAN[5], NATHANIEL[4], JONATHAN[3], SAMUEL[2], THOMAS[1])* was born 10 May 1863 in Pleasant Ridge, NB., and died 09 Nov 1922 in Pleasant Ridge, NB.. He married EMILY ROSS 13 May 1900.

Children of JAMES STEWART and EMILY ROSS are:
i. LAWRENCE[9] STEWART.
ii. ALFRED ROSS STEWART.
iii. HENRY BERTON STEWART, b. 26 Aug 1903; d. 11 Jun 1976; m. BERLA LAURA NORDIN, Oct 1930; b. 06 Dec 1908.

888. ANNIE[8] SPINNEY *(JAMES VAN BUREN[7], JAMES S[6], JONATHAN[5], NATHANIEL[4], JONATHAN[3], SAMUEL[2], THOMAS[1])* was born 20 Aug 1874 in St George, NB., and died 14 Jan 1957 in Calais, ME. She married JAMES MERRIL BECKETT. He was born in Calais, ME, and died 22 May 1930.

Children of ANNIE SPINNEY and JAMES BECKETT are:
i. BETH[9] BECKETT, b. St George, NB.; d. Calais, ME.
ii. GEORGE BECKETT.
iii. DOROTHY BECKETT.
iv. LOUIS M BECKETT, b. 22 Oct 1910, St George, NB.; d. Jun 1964, Calais, ME.

889. SUSAN JANE[8] SPINNEY *(JAMES VAN BUREN[7], JAMES S[6], JONATHAN[5], NATHANIEL[4], JONATHAN[3], SAMUEL[2], THOMAS[1])* was born 22 Jan 1877 in Upper Letang, NB., and died 22 Jul 1957 in St George, NB.. She married EMERSON GRANT 26 Sep 1900 in St Stephen, NB.. He was born 09 Aug 1871 in Oak Bay, NB., and died in St George, NB..

Children of SUSAN SPINNEY and EMERSON GRANT are:
     i.   HATTIE[9] GRANT.
     ii. MARY GRANT.
     iii. HENRY GRANT.
     iv. JAMES GRANT.
     v.   ANGUS GRANT.
     vi. LESTER WHITMORE GRANT, b. 02 Nov 1901.
     vii. GLADYS P GRANT, b. 10 Nov 1904; d. 21 Jul 1974, Calais Maine; m. SIDNEY S DINSMORE.

890. LETITIA[8] SPINNEY *(JAMES VAN BUREN[7], JAMES S[6], JONATHAN[5], NATHANIEL[4], JONATHAN[3], SAMUEL[2], THOMAS[1])* was born 05 Apr 1879 in Upper L'Etang, NG, and died 10 Dec 1954 in St Stephen, NB. She married WILLIAM E STEWART 10 Feb 1899 in Gorham, NH.

Children of LETITIA SPINNEY and WILLIAM STEWART are:
     i.   NORMAN[9] STEWART, b. Gorham, NH.
     ii. IVA STEWART, m. RUSSELL MCCUMBER.
     iii. ANNIE MAY STEWART, d. 31 Dec 1929.
     iv. ADA STEWART, m. HAROLD MCCUMBER.
     v.   OLIVE STEWART.

891. CATHERINE[8] SPINNEY *(JAMES VAN BUREN[7], JAMES S[6], JONATHAN[5], NATHANIEL[4], JONATHAN[3], SAMUEL[2], THOMAS[1])* was born 22 May 1881 in Upper L'Etang, NB.. She married WILLIAM J GAGE 13 Oct 1915 in Calais Maine. He was born 1863 in Canada.

Child of CATHERINE SPINNEY and WILLIAM GAGE is:
1206.   i.   MARION E[9] GAGE, b. 1918.

892. GEORGE ROSS[8] SPINNEY *(JAMES VAN BUREN[7], JAMES S[6], JONATHAN[5], NATHANIEL[4], JONATHAN[3], SAMUEL[2], THOMAS[1])* was born 25 Oct 1883 in Upper L'Etang, NB., and died 01 Sep 1960 in St John, NB.. He married STELLA IRENE SMITH 24 Dec 1914 in St John, NB..

Children of GEORGE SPINNEY and STELLA SMITH are:
     i.   DOUGLAS[9] SPINNEY, b. Abt. 1900.
     ii. BEULAH SPINNEY, b. Abt. 1900; m. GEORGE DEWAR.
1207.   iii. ALICE SPINNEY, b. Abt. 1900.

893. JAMES RENFORTH[8] SPINNEY *(JAMES VAN BUREN[7], JAMES S[6], JONATHAN[5], NATHANIEL[4], JONATHAN[3], SAMUEL[2], THOMAS[1])* was born 13 Jul 1886 in Upper L'Etang, NB., and died 26 Sep 1956 in St George, NB.. He married GRACE ELIZABETH PARLEE 07 Nov 1930 in St John, NB., daughter of JOHN PARLEE and CHARLOTTE BREWER. She was born 24 May 1896 in St John, NB..

Children of JAMES SPINNEY and GRACE PARLEE are:
     i.   ESTER ELIZABETH[9] SPINNEY, m. CLIFTON SEYMORE BOYD, Jul 1957.
1208.   ii. ARTHUR GILMORE SPINNEY, b. Abt. 1930.

894. JOHN OLIVER[8] SPINNEY *(JAMES VAN BUREN[7], JAMES S[6], JONATHAN[5], NATHANIEL[4], JONATHAN[3], SAMUEL[2], THOMAS[1])* was born 08 Feb 1895 in St George, NB., and died 10 Mar 1975 in St John, NB.. He married (1) FLORENCE MARION STEWART. He married (2) BETTIE C ROBERTSON 11 Jun 1919 in Carlisle England, daughter of WILLIAM ROBERTSON and ELIAZBETH. She was born 15 Aug 1896 in Dunfries Scotland, and died 29 Oct 1965 in St George, NB..

Children of JOHN SPINNEY and BETTIE ROBERTSON are:
     i.   MILDRED AUDREY "MILLIE"[9] SPINNEY, b. 31 May 1920; m. RAY IRWIN.
     ii. BARBARA "JEANNE" SPINNEY, m. JAMES HERBERT DUNLAP, 12 Jul 1947, Military Camp Utopia, Charlotte, New Brunswick.
     iii. JOHN E SPINNEY, b. Abt. 1915.
1209.   iv. DOROTHEA "DOSSIE" SPINNEY, b. 22 Apr 1922, St George, NB..
     v.   BETTIE-ANNE SPINNEY, b. 08 Sep 1926; m. FRANK "LESLIE" BOUTLER, 11 Jul 1959, St George New

Brunswick.
vi.   JAMES ALEXANDER SPINNEY, b. 15 May 1928, St George, NB.; m. ELEANOR GAYE IRWIN, 24 Oct 1953, Ottawa Ontario Canada.

895. NELSON PEABODY[8] SPINNEY *(HORATIO NELSON[7], JAMES S[6], JONATHAN[5], NATHANIEL[4], JONATHAN[3], SAMUEL[2], THOMAS[1])* was born 01 Oct 1884, and died Aft. 1930. He married MARIA FRANCES STETSON, daughter of THOMAS STETSON and FRANCES RANDALL. She was born 1881, and died Aft. 1930.

Child of NELSON SPINNEY and MARIA STETSON is:
i.   HORATIO H[9] SPINNEY, b. 1905.

896. JAME A[8] HUSON *(GEORGE H[7], LOUISA ANN[6] SPINNEY, JONATHAN[5], NATHANIEL[4], JONATHAN[3], SAMUEL[2], THOMAS[1])* was born 1878, and died 1961. He married GERTRUDE S YOUNG 11 Oct 1905 in Calais, ME.

Child of JAME HUSON and GERTRUDE YOUNG is:
i.   RUTH[9] HUSON, b. 1906; d. 1987; m. LLOYD H GOODWIN, 01 Aug 1963.

897. GEORGE A[8] SPINNEY *(WILLIAM L[7], NATHANIEL[6], JONATHAN[5], NATHANIEL[4], JONATHAN[3], SAMUEL[2], THOMAS[1])* was born 25 Dec 1863 in Calais, ME. He married MARY E JOHNSON 08 Dec 1885 in Calais, ME, daughter of ARCHIE JOHNSON and MAGGIE ANDERSON. She was born Oct 1868 in Calais, ME, and died 11 Aug 1901 in Calais, ME.

Children of GEORGE SPINNEY and MARY JOHNSON are:
i.   GRACE[9] SPINNEY, b. May 1890.
ii.   MOLLY B SPINNEY, b. Nov 1893; d. 07 Apr 1915, Lynn, Ma.

898. FRANK HERBERT[8] SPINNEY *(STEPHEN ALEXANDER[7], NATHANIEL[6], JONATHAN[5], NATHANIEL[4], JONATHAN[3], SAMUEL[2], THOMAS[1])* was born 04 Jun 1866 in Calais, ME, and died 28 Jul 1934 in Calais, ME. He married (1) JEAN CAMPBELL. She was born 1886. He married (2) ELLA MORRIS 31 Dec 1885 in Calais, Maine. She was born Mar 1867 in Calais, ME, and died Bef. 1920.

Child of FRANK SPINNEY and JEAN CAMPBELL is:
i.   STEPHEN[9] SPINNEY, b. 1918.

899. ALICE[8] SPINNEY *(STEPHEN ALEXANDER[7], NATHANIEL[6], JONATHAN[5], NATHANIEL[4], JONATHAN[3], SAMUEL[2], THOMAS[1])* was born Abt. 1870 in Calais, ME. She married JEREMIAH JOHNSON 15 Apr 1886 in Calais, ME. He was born in St James, NB..

Children of ALICE SPINNEY and JEREMIAH JOHNSON are:
i.   FRANK[9] JOHNSON.
ii.   VERA JOHNSON.
iii.   STEPHEN JOHNSON.

900. JENNIE LOUISA[8] STUART *(HANNAH ELIZA[7] SPINNEY, CHARLES EDWARD[6], JONATHAN[5], NATHANIEL[4], JONATHAN[3], SAMUEL[2], THOMAS[1])* was born 1895. She married JOHN RONALD CARSON. He was born 1898 in Salem MA.

Children of JENNIE STUART and JOHN CARSON are:
i.   CLAUDIA[9] CARSON, b. 1927, Salem, Ma.
ii.   JERMONE CARSON, b. 1928, Salem, Ma.

901. MARGARET ELLEN (NELLIE)[8] STUART *(HANNAH ELIZA[7] SPINNEY, CHARLES EDWARD[6], JONATHAN[5], NATHANIEL[4], JONATHAN[3], SAMUEL[2], THOMAS[1])* was born 1900 in St Stephen Parish, Charlotte, New Brunswick, Canada. She married PAUL HAROLD INGERSOLL 17 Nov 1920, son of HARLEY INGERSOLL and LENA SMALL. He was born 03 Feb 1900, and died 1989.

Child of MARGARET STUART and PAUL INGERSOLL is:
      i.   PAUL[9] INGERSOLL, b. 1921; d. 19 Apr 1925.

902. GRACE INA[8] STUART *(HANNAH ELIZA[7] SPINNEY, CHARLES EDWARD[6], JONATHAN[5], NATHANIEL[4], JONATHAN[3], SAMUEL[2], THOMAS[1])* was born 1888. She married (1) JOSEPH REID. She married (2) ANDREW F TIBBETTS 11 Dec 1920 in Portland, ME.

Child of GRACE STUART and JOSEPH REID is:
      i.   DONALD STUART[9] REID, m. WINNEFRED PEARL WILLIAMS, 03 Sep 1923, St Stephen, New Brunswick.

903. MARION BEATRICE[8] STUART *(HANNAH ELIZA[7] SPINNEY, CHARLES EDWARD[6], JONATHAN[5], NATHANIEL[4], JONATHAN[3], SAMUEL[2], THOMAS[1])* was born 1892 in St Stephen, Charlotte, New Brunswick, Canada. She married SAMUEL A CAMPBELL 28 Apr 1918 in Salem, Ma, son of WILLIAM CAMPBELL and HANNAH CROMPTON. He was born Jul 1889 in Salem, MA.

Children of MARION STUART and SAMUEL CAMPBELL are:
      i.   FLORENCE[9] CAMPBELL, b. 1921, Salem, Ma.
1210.   ii. WALLACE STUART CAMPBELL, b. 13 Jan 1922, Salem, MA.

904. JANE GOLDEN[8] SPINNEY *(GEORGE FREDERICK[7], CHARLES EDWARD[6], JONATHAN[5], NATHANIEL[4], JONATHAN[3], SAMUEL[2], THOMAS[1])* was born 1899 in New York. She married JOSEPH O'KEEFE in Salem MA.

Children of JANE SPINNEY and JOSEPH O'KEEFE are:
      i.   EDWARD[9] O'KEEFE, b. Peabody, MA.
      ii. JOSEPH O'KEEFE.

905. FRANCES M[8] SPINNEY *(FRANKLIN P[7], CHARLES EDWARD[6], JONATHAN[5], NATHANIEL[4], JONATHAN[3], SAMUEL[2], THOMAS[1])* was born 09 Nov 1895, and died 04 Apr 1981 in Hartford, Connecticut. She married FRANC WOOD.

Child of FRANCES SPINNEY and FRANC WOOD is:
      i.   GLORIA[9] WOOD, b. 1925, Conn.

906. GORDON VICTOR[8] MILLS *(LOUISE PARKS[7] SPINNEY, CHARLES EDWARD[6], JONATHAN[5], NATHANIEL[4], JONATHAN[3], SAMUEL[2], THOMAS[1])* was born 16 May 1896 in Calais, ME, and died 20 Sep 1965 in Waltham, MA. He married SUZANNA GOSSE 18 Feb 1922 in West Somerville, MA, daughter of JOHN GOSSE and ANNA BAKER. She was born 04 Feb 1905 in Boston, MA, and died 17 May 1989 in Waltham, MA.

Children of GORDON MILLS and SUZANNA GOSSE are:
1211.   i.   RALPH EDWARD[9] MILLS, b. 26 Jun 1925, Brooklyn, NY.; d. 04 Jan 2005, Methuen, MA.
1212.   ii. GORDON MILLS, b. 14 Apr 1928.

907. EDWARD L[8] MILLS *(LOUISE PARKS[7] SPINNEY, CHARLES EDWARD[6], JONATHAN[5], NATHANIEL[4], JONATHAN[3], SAMUEL[2], THOMAS[1])* was born May 1899 in Mass. He married KATHRYN T SULLIVAN 17 May 1919 in Maine. She was born 1898.

Children of EDWARD MILLS and KATHRYN SULLIVAN are:
1213.   i.   KENNETH[9] MILLS.
1214.   ii. NORMAN MILLS, b. 1927.

908. DOROTHY ELAINE[8] BARCLAY *(CAROLYN B (CARRIE)[7] SPINNEY, CHARLES EDWARD[6], JONATHAN[5], NATHANIEL[4], JONATHAN[3], SAMUEL[2], THOMAS[1])* was born 1914. She married JAMES H CROSBY 21 Feb 1932 in Calais, ME. He was born 1915 in Newton, MA.

Children of DOROTHY BARCLAY and JAMES CROSBY are:

1215.   i.   VIRGINIA GAIL[9] CROSBY, d. 1975.
          ii. HAROLD CROSBY, b. St Stephens, NB..

909. RUTH GOLDEN[8] SPINNEY *(EDWARD CHARLES[7], CHARLES EDWARD[6], JONATHAN[5], NATHANIEL[4], JONATHAN[3], SAMUEL[2], THOMAS[1])* was born 30 Nov 1906 in Calais, ME, and died 23 Feb 1985 in Calais, ME. She married EDWIN HUGHES 05 Nov 1930. He was born in Portland, ME.

Child of RUTH SPINNEY and EDWIN HUGHES is:
          i.   JOYCE[9] HUGHES, b. Abt. 1930; m. BURDETT.

910. ANNIE MAUDE[8] BARSTOW *(LAURA DEXTER[7] GREEN, MARY ANN[6] SPINNEY, JONATHAN[5], NATHANIEL[4], JONATHAN[3], SAMUEL[2], THOMAS[1])* was born 31 Mar 1882. She married FRANK HOWARD DAVIS, son of STEPHEN DAVIS. He was born 1867.

Children of ANNIE BARSTOW and FRANK DAVIS are:
1216.   i.   LILLIAN MAE[9] DAVIS, b. 20 Oct 1906.
          ii.   HOWARD A DAVIS, b. 1904.
          iii. HAROLD BLISS DAVIS, b. 1902.
          iv.   MAYNARD WHEATON DAVIS, b. 1904.
          v.   CLIFFFORD MASON DAVIS, b. 1909.
          vi.   HAZEL DAVIS, b. 1915.
          vii. EMILY DAVIS, b. 1920.

911. ERNEST LINWOOD[8] SPINNEY *(HERBERT HARRISON FICKETT[7], ARCHIBALD BARNEY[6], JONATHAN[5], NATHANIEL[4], JONATHAN[3], SAMUEL[2], THOMAS[1])* was born 26 Nov 1884 in Castle Hill, ME, and died 15 Mar 1938 in Boston, Me. He married GLADYS EVELYN PENDEXTER 17 Jun 1905 in Chapman, ME.

Children of ERNEST SPINNEY and GLADYS PENDEXTER are:
1217.   i.   EVELYN MARION[9] SPINNEY, b. 04 Jun 1906, Mapleton, ME; d. 25 Mar 1954, Waterville, ME.
          ii. DOROTHY ERNESTINE SPINNEY, b. 24 Mar 1909, Mapleton, ME; d. 24 May 1984, Somerset, ME.

912. FRANKLIN PIERCE[8] SPINNEY *(BENJAMIN FRANK[7], ARCHIBALD BARNEY[6], JONATHAN[5], NATHANIEL[4], JONATHAN[3], SAMUEL[2], THOMAS[1])* was born Sep 1884, and died Aft. 1930. He married (1) CELIA MAY JAMES 17 Apr 1907 in Princeton, ME, daughter of JOSIAH JAMES and MARY GLIDDEN. She was born 28 Dec 1884 in Princeton, ME, and died 04 May 1914 in Princeton, ME. He married (2) LILLIAN GROVER 30 Aug 1922.

Children of FRANKLIN SPINNEY and CELIA JAMES are:
          i.   STILLBORN[9] SPINNEY, b. 07 Nov 1907, Princeton, ME.
          ii.   SADIE SPINNEY, b. 1908.
          iii. RUTH E SPINNEY, b. 30 May 1909, Hermon, ME.
          iv.   HANNAH ELIZABETH SPINNEY, b. 28 Nov 1911, Hermon, ME; m. KENNETH R GUNN, 19 Jul 1936, Portland, ME; b. 1910; d. 29 Jun 1969, Portland, ME.
1218.   v.   FRANK J SPINNEY, b. 27 Oct 1912, Hermon, ME; d. 02 Jan 1991.

913. MABEL[8] SPINNEY *(EDWARD P[7], JOHN[6], JONATHAN[5], NATHANIEL[4], JONATHAN[3], SAMUEL[2], THOMAS[1])* was born 24 Feb 1904 in Lynn, MA. She married CHARLES AUGUSTE BOULAY.

Notes for MABEL SPINNEY:
Mable was brought up in a convent in Three Rivers, Canada. Written on the back of one of the photos she had sent to her mother was the name of The Convent of St. Rose.
Family history says that her parents separated not too long after being married, when another woman showed up on their doorstep pregnant. Apparently it was too much for Aunt Aggie to raise Mabel after what her husband had done.

Children of MABEL SPINNEY and CHARLES BOULAY are:
          i.   PHILIP[9] BOULAY.

ii.   EDWARD BOULAY.

914. CLARA E⁸ SPINNEY *(WILLIAM L⁷, EBENEZER⁶, EBENEZER⁵, NATHANIEL⁴, JONATHAN³, SAMUEL², THOMAS¹)* was born 21 Jan 1867 in Onarga, IL, and died 04 Apr 1930. She married FRANCES COKE POWLEY 14 Oct 1882.

Children of CLARA SPINNEY and FRANCES POWLEY are:
    i.   JESSIE⁹ POWLEY, b. 1886.
    ii.   SARAH ELIZABETH POWLEY, b. 28 Jan 1886.
    iii.   CLARENCE A POWLEY, b. 17 Dec 1898; m. VESTA ELMORE, 30 Nov 1920.

915. EBENEZER⁸ SPINNEY *(WILLIAM L⁷, EBENEZER⁶, EBENEZER⁵, NATHANIEL⁴, JONATHAN³, SAMUEL², THOMAS¹)* was born 20 Sep 1871 in Onarga, IL, and died 17 Oct 1939 in Lansing, MI. He married (1) NETTIE PHILLIPS 10 Oct 1890.   He married (2) CARILEAN URSULA SMITH 18 May 1902 in Michigan.

Children of EBENEZER SPINNEY and CARILEAN SMITH are:
1219.   i.   OTIS LEVI⁹ SPINNEY, b. 15 Aug 1903, Onarga, IL; d. 09 Dec 1966, Lansing, MI.
         ii.   JOHN SPINNEY, b. 02 Feb 1905.
         iii.   MAUDIE L SPINNEY, b. 19 Jun 1906, Onarga, IL; d. 27 Mar 1907, Onarga, IL.
1220.   iv.   LUCY ALBION SPINNEY, b. 27 Apr 1908; d. 22 Jan 1988, Costa Mesa, CA.
         v.   WILLIAM J. B. SPINNEY, b. 27 Mar 1910, Onarga, IL; d. 16 Jan 1988, Costa Mesa, CA.
         vi.   CHARLES EBENEZER SPINNEY, b. 13 Nov 1914, Onarga, IL; d. 21 Oct 1975, Lansing, MI; m. MARIE HOWSE, 02 Sep 1939, Lansing, MI.
         vii.   CHESTER LEROY SPINNEY, b. 28 Aug 1917, Onarga, IL; d. 01 Jan 1975, Lansing, MI; m. EDNA CHURCH, 11 Jan 1957, Lansing, MI.
1221.   viii.   FRANCIS JOSEPH SPINNEY, b. 16 Sep 1923.
         ix.   KATHERYN SPINNEY, b. 13 Sep 1911.
         x.   MARIE SPINNEY.
         xi.   CORRINE SPINNEY.
1222.   xii.   MYRTLE MAY SPINNEY.

916. MILLAGE⁸ SPINNEY *(WILLIAM L⁷, NATHANIEL⁶, EBENEZER⁵, NATHANIEL⁴, JONATHAN³, SAMUEL², THOMAS¹)* was born Abt. 1870, and died Bef. 1871.

Child of MILLAGE SPINNEY is:
    i.   GEORGE⁹ SPINNEY, b. Abt. 1900, New Hampshire.

917. ADDIE ESTELLA⁸ SPINNEY *(WILLIAM L⁷, NATHANIEL⁶, EBENEZER⁵, NATHANIEL⁴, JONATHAN³, SAMUEL², THOMAS¹)* was born Mar 1871, and died Aft. 1900. She married GEORGE H LEEMAN 13 Oct 1889 in Eastport Maine. He was born Dec 1866 in Canada, and died Aft. 1900.

Children of ADDIE SPINNEY and GEORGE LEEMAN are:
    i.   MILLAGE⁹ LEEMAN, b. Jan 1890.
    ii.   GEORGE W LEEMAN, b. Sep 1894.
    iii.   REGINALD LEEMAN, b. Sep 1898.

918. JOHN W⁸ SPINNEY *(WILLIAM L⁷, NATHANIEL⁶, EBENEZER⁵, NATHANIEL⁴, JONATHAN³, SAMUEL², THOMAS¹)* was born Jun 1875 in New Brunswick, Canada, and died Aft. 1930 in Eastport, Me. He married (1) MARY THERESA JOHNSON 26 Nov 1900 in St George New Brunswick, daughter of JOHN JOHNSON and CAROLINE COOK. She was born 1873, and died 1907. He married (2) MELISSA BLANCH RICE 30 Jul 1911 in Eastport, ME.

Children of JOHN SPINNEY and MARY JOHNSON are:
1223.   i.   CHESTER ALVAH⁹ SPINNEY, b. 27 Jun 1901, New Brunswick; d. 05 Apr 1992, Ayer, MA.
         ii.   EDWIN SPINNEY, b. 1905.

919. ALVAH C⁸ SPINNEY *(WILLIAM L⁷, NATHANIEL⁶, EBENEZER⁵, NATHANIEL⁴, JONATHAN³, SAMUEL², THOMAS¹)* was born Jul 1878, and died 28 Jul 1906 in Eastport, Me. He married MABEL WOOD 27 Nov 1902, daughter of JEREMIAH WOOD and MARGARET.

Children of ALVAH SPINNEY and MABEL WOOD are:
    i.   BEATRICE[9] SPINNEY, b. 1904.
    ii. MARGARET SPINNEY, b. 1906.

920. ALFRED WINFIELD[8] SPINNEY *(WILLIAM L[7], NATHANIEL[6], EBENEZER[5], NATHANIEL[4], JONATHAN[3], SAMUEL[2], THOMAS[1])* was born 30 Oct 1893 in Canada, and died 18 Jan 1959 in Costra Conta, CA. He married WINIFRED MCDERMOTT 17 Jun 1908 in Lawrence Mass. She was born 1889 in Ireland.

Children of ALFRED SPINNEY and WINIFRED MCDERMOTT are:
        i.   NORMAN[9] SPINNEY, b. Mass.
        ii. DONALD SPINNEY, b. 07 Mar 1909, Lawrence, ME; d. 07 Mar 1909, Lawrence, ME.
1224.   iii. RAYMOND AUGUSTINE SPINNEY, b. 07 Mar 1909, Lawrence, MA.
1225.   iv. ALFRED WINFIELD SPINNEY, b. 18 Dec 1910, Lebanon. ME.
        v. DOROTHY W SPINNEY, b. Abt. 1912, Mass.
1226.   vi. EDITH E SPINNEY, b. Abt. 1915, Mass.

921. WILLIAM JAMES[8] HARKINS *(LYDIA "ANNIE"[7] SPINNEY, NATHANIEL[6], EBENEZER[5], NATHANIEL[4], JONATHAN[3], SAMUEL[2], THOMAS[1])* was born 20 Jan 1882. He married ETHEL CATHERINE KELLY 1939.

Child of WILLIAM HARKINS and ETHEL KELLY is:
    i.   WILLIAM[9] HARKINS.

922. JAMES[8] QUIGLEY *(MARGARET JANE[7] SPINNEY, NATHANIEL[6], EBENEZER[5], NATHANIEL[4], JONATHAN[3], SAMUEL[2], THOMAS[1])* was born 1879, and died Aft. 1930. He married PHOEBE ALLEY 1913 in Eastport, ME.

Child of JAMES QUIGLEY and PHOEBE ALLEY is:
    i.   JAMES MERRILL[9] QUIGLEY, b. 1914; d. 1994, Eastport, ME.

923. ARTHUR JONES[8] MILLS *(SARAH[7] SPINNEY, ARTHUR JONES[6], EBENEZER[5], NATHANIEL[4], JONATHAN[3], SAMUEL[2], THOMAS[1])* was born 04 Jan 1864 in Summer, IL, and died 26 Oct 1931 in Cashmere, WA. He married HATTIE BELLE BOYD 28 Oct 1885 in Andover South Dakota, daughter of DAVID BOYD and BRIDGET CARL. She was born 06 Sep 1866.

Children of ARTHUR MILLS and HATTIE BOYD are:
1227.   i.   CLAUDE EDWIN[9] MILLS, b. 04 Aug 1886, Andover, SD.
1228.   ii. PEARL EUDORA MILLS, b. 12 May 1890, Andover, SD; d. 13 Oct 1913.
1229.   iii. ARTHUR BOYD MILLS, b. 26 Jun 1892, Andover, SD.

924. CAROLINE LEVINA[8] MILLS *(SARAH[7] SPINNEY, ARTHUR JONES[6], EBENEZER[5], NATHANIEL[4], JONATHAN[3], SAMUEL[2], THOMAS[1])* was born 14 Apr 1865 in Crediton, Ontario Canada, and died 22 Jan 1947 in Spokane, WA. She married (1) ARTHUR SLUSSER 16 Apr 1884 in Andover South Dakota. She married (2) OSCAR FREDERICK STEWART 02 Mar 1886 in Andover South Dakota, son of DAVIS STEWART and ELIZABETH CHAMBERLAIN.

Child of CAROLINE MILLS and ARTHUR SLUSSER is:
    i.   ALBERT ELROY[9] SLUSSER, b. 05 Mar 1885, Andover, SD.

Children of CAROLINE MILLS and OSCAR STEWART are:
        ii. SHERMAN[9] STEWART, b. 05 Mar 1889, Andover, SD; d. 29 Jan 1895, Andover, SD.
1230.   iii. ARTHUR JONES STEWART, b. 31 Dec 1890, Day County, SD; d. 21 Jun 1956, Phoenix, AZ.
1231.   iv. CLIFFORD MILLS STEWART, b. 17 Jan 1896.
        v. SARAH ELIZABETH STEWART, b. Nov 1903, Wenatchee, WA; d. Dec 1903.

925. SUSANNA JANE "JEN"[8] MILLS *(SARAH[7] SPINNEY, ARTHUR JONES[6], EBENEZER[5], NATHANIEL[4], JONATHAN[3], SAMUEL[2], THOMAS[1])* was born 22 Feb 1867, and died 14 Dec 1940 in Wenatchee Washington. She married

ALBERT EDWARD SWAN. He was born 05 Sep 1863 in Ontario Canada.

Child of SUSANNA MILLS and ALBERT SWAN is:
1232.   i.   VERA TERESA[9] SWAN, b. 10 Jan 1897, Aberdeen, SD; d. 24 Jun 1995, Parkdale, BC..

926. ANGELINE ELIZABETH[8] MILLS *(SARAH[7] SPINNEY, ARTHUR JONES[6], EBENEZER[5], NATHANIEL[4], JONATHAN[3], SAMUEL[2], THOMAS[1])* was born 19 Mar 1869 in Goodland Indiana, and died 29 Apr 1925 in Alberta Canada. She married JAMES F COLLINS, son of PATRICK COLLINS and MARY MCMAHON. He was born 1863.

Children of ANGELINE MILLS and JAMES COLLINS are:
1233.   i.   WILLIAM HENRY[9] COLLINS, b. 14 Feb 1889, Goodland, IN; d. 1947.
        ii.   SADIE LILLIAN COLLINS, b. 29 Mar 1891; m. COEN.
1234.   iii.   LEOLA "LOLA" EILEEN COLLINS, b. 12 Sep 1893.
        iv.   JENNIE F COLLINS, b. 08 Aug 1896; m. CECIL MCKINLEY.

927. WILLIAM HENRY[8] MILLS *(SARAH[7] SPINNEY, ARTHUR JONES[6], EBENEZER[5], NATHANIEL[4], JONATHAN[3], SAMUEL[2], THOMAS[1])* was born 06 May 1871 in Goodland, IN, and died 05 Dec 1926 in Los Angeles, CA. He married MAUDE DAVIS 28 Aug 1895.

Child of WILLIAM MILLS and MAUDE DAVIS is:
        i.   HAROLD DAVIS[9] MILLS, b. 17 Apr 1898, Andover, SD; d. Apr 1928, Los Angeles, CA; m. GOLDA CEASE, 1920, Cashmere, WA.

928. JENNIE OPAL[8] CONES *(SUSANNA[7] SPINNEY, ARTHUR JONES[6], EBENEZER[5], NATHANIEL[4], JONATHAN[3], SAMUEL[2], THOMAS[1])* was born 1873. She married GUY HORACE POWELL 1898, son of RUBIN POWELL and ELVIRA. He was born 1867.

Children of JENNIE CONES and GUY POWELL are:
        i.   MADELINE[9] POWELL, b. 1895.
        ii.   DORIS POWELL, b. 1895.

929. MYRTLE ISABELLE[8] BANES *(AURELIA ISABELLE[7] SPINNEY, ARTHUR JONES[6], EBENEZER[5], NATHANIEL[4], JONATHAN[3], SAMUEL[2], THOMAS[1])* was born 20 Jan 1881 in Goodland, IN, and died Jul 1942 in Knox, IN. She married (1) ALBERT HENRY THOMPSON 28 Oct 1903 in Goodland, IN. He was born 02 Dec 1878 in Kentland, IN, and died 26 Feb 1923 in Fort Wayne, IN. She married (2) JOHN L. MOORMAN 10 Nov 1932 in Elkhart, Indiana. He was born 17 Mar 1869, and died 19 May 1942 in Knox, Indiana.

Children of MYRTLE BANES and ALBERT THOMPSON are:
1235.   i.   KATHRYN ISABELLE[9] THOMPSON, b. Francesville, IN; d. Birmingham, MI.
        ii.   MILDRED LEIGH THOMPSON, b. Private.
1236.   iii.   VIRGINIA ANNE THOMPSON, b. Private.

930. REXFORD[8] BANES *(AURELIA ISABELLE[7] SPINNEY, ARTHUR JONES[6], EBENEZER[5], NATHANIEL[4], JONATHAN[3], SAMUEL[2], THOMAS[1])* was born 1883 in Goodland, IN. He married LELA KESSLER.

Children of REXFORD BANES and LELA KESSLER are:
        i.   ESTELLE[9] BANES, b. Private.
1237.   ii.   ISABELLE BANES, b. Private.

931. LELA[8] BANES *(AURELIA ISABELLE[7] SPINNEY, ARTHUR JONES[6], EBENEZER[5], NATHANIEL[4], JONATHAN[3], SAMUEL[2], THOMAS[1])* was born 1885 in Goodland, IN. She married RALPH MCCONNELL.

Children of LELA BANES and RALPH MCCONNELL are:
1238.   i.   MARGARET[9] MCCONNELL, b. Private.
1239.   ii.   JOSEPH MCCONNELL, b. Private.

932. BETHEL[8] BANES *(AURELIA ISABELLE[7] SPINNEY, ARTHUR JONES[6], EBENEZER[5], NATHANIEL[4], JONATHAN[3], SAMUEL[2], THOMAS[1])* was born 1887 in Goodland, IN. She married CHARLES BOGAN.

Children of BETHEL BANES and CHARLES BOGAN are:
1240.   i.   DAVID[9] BOGAN, b. Private.
        ii.   ROBERT BOGAN, b. Private.
       iii.   THOMAS BOGAN, b. Private; m. AUDREY, Private; b. Private.

933. INEZ LINWOOD[8] SPINNEY *(ABRAHAM[7], JOSEPH[6], ABRAHAM[5], JOSEPH[4], SAMUEL[3], SAMUEL[2], THOMAS[1])* was born 1873, and died 1955. She married EVERETT B NEILY 1898, son of WILLIAM NEILY and MARY JACQUES. He was born 1871, and died 1954.

Children of INEZ SPINNEY and EVERETT NEILY are:
1241.   i.   IDA MAY[9] NEILY.
        ii.   FRANK NEILY.
       iii.   ARTHUR NEILY.
       iv.   EARL NEILY, b. 1900; d. 1974.
1242.   v.   WILLIAM LLOYD NEILY, b. 1907.

934. GEORGE LAMERT[8] SPINNEY *(OWEN[7], JOSEPH[6], ABRAHAM[5], JOSEPH[4], SAMUEL[3], SAMUEL[2], THOMAS[1])* was born 02 Apr 1881. He married (1) ZENA M BANKS, daughter of ALEXANDER BANKS and MARY SPINNEY. She was born 1886, and died 1913. He married (2) LAURA LOUISE BAILEY.

Child of GEORGE SPINNEY and LAURA BAILEY is:
1243.   i.   PAUL NATHANIEL[9] SPINNEY, b. 20 Feb 1917.

935. CORA MAUDE[8] BERTWELL *(ALEPH[7] WOODBURY, ELIZABETH[6] SPINNEY, ABRAHAM[5], JOSEPH[4], SAMUEL[3], SAMUEL[2], THOMAS[1])* was born 10 Oct 1888 in Somerville, MA, and died 07 Feb 1916 in Utica, NY. She married CHARLES WILLIAM BAILEY 18 Jan 1908 in Waltham, MA. He was born 28 Sep 1884 in Peabody, MA, and died 1971 in Hollywood, FL.

Children of CORA BERTWELL and CHARLES BAILEY are:
        i.   CLAYTON BERTWELL[9] BAILEY, b. 07 Jun 1908, Waltham, MA; m. THELMA ELSIE KENNEDY, 27 Jun 1932, Nashua, NH; b. 17 Jan 1908, Halifax, NS.; d. 09 Aug 1987, Brewster, MA.
1244.   ii.   RUSSELL FRANKLIN BAILEY, b. 08 Oct 1911, Providence, RI; d. 21 Jan 1996, Hernando, FL.

936. GLADYS BURTON[8] ALLEN *(CHARLES WESLEY[7], MARY ELIZA CRANDALL[6] WEAVER, PETER CRANDALL[5], MARY[4] SPINNEY, SAMUEL[3], SAMUEL[2], THOMAS[1])* She married JUDSON STEWART MACGREGOR.

Child of GLADYS ALLEN and JUDSON MACGREGOR is:
        i.   ROSAMOND JEAN[9] MACGREGOR, m. JACK EDWARD SIMON.

937. ELIZABETH[8] CLEM *(JULIA IDA[7] SPINNEY, SAMUEL[6], ISAAC BEACH[5], SAMUEL MCCLURE[4], SAMUEL[3], SAMUEL[2], THOMAS[1])* She married MELBOURNE PALMER.

Children of ELIZABETH CLEM and MELBOURNE PALMER are:
        i.   RUTH (DOUCETT)[9] PALMER.
        ii.   STELLA PALMER.
       iii.   JULIA (SMALL) PALMER, m. FRED SMALL.
       iv.   GRACE (CHAPMAN) PALMER.
       v.   OLIVE (DAYLEY) PALMER.

938. NELLIE[8] CLEM *(JULIA IDA[7] SPINNEY, SAMUEL[6], ISAAC BEACH[5], SAMUEL MCCLURE[4], SAMUEL[3], SAMUEL[2], THOMAS[1])* was born 22 Aug 1874 in Burlington, NS.. She married HERBERT WILLIAM WARD 22 Aug 1892 in Petershan, MA.

Notes for NELLIE CLEM:
[Spinney.FTW]

1949ish-moved to Petersham, MA. Bruce SPINNEY Sr. built their home near where COOLIDGE's lived

Child of NELLIE CLEM and HERBERT WARD is:
     i. J PEARL[9] WARD.

939. GLADYS MAY[8] SPINNEY *(ISAAC CALVIN[7], SAMUEL[6], ISAAC BEACH[5], SAMUEL McCLURE[4], SAMUEL[3], SAMUEL[2], THOMAS[1])* was born 28 Oct 1896 in Greenwood, NS., and died in North Reading, MA. She married EARL MILLS. He died 1974 in North Reading, MA.

Notes for GLADYS MAY SPINNEY:
[Spinney.FTW]

Buried in Riverside Cemetery in North Reading, Massachusetts.

Child of GLADYS SPINNEY and EARL MILLS is:
     i. GORDON[9] MILLS, b. 1924.

940. CHESTER LEVERETT[8] SPINNEY *(ISAAC CALVIN[7], SAMUEL[6], ISAAC BEACH[5], SAMUEL McCLURE[4], SAMUEL[3], SAMUEL[2], THOMAS[1])* was born 07 Nov 1897 in Greenwood, NS., and died Jan 1981. He married LAURA LARSON in Dana, MA, daughter of JOHAN LARSON and BERTHA ALMQUIST. She was born 07 Jan 1898 in New York, NY, and died 31 Mar 1992 in Wolfeboro, NH.

Children of CHESTER SPINNEY and LAURA LARSON are:
1245.	i.	BRUCE WARREN[9] SPINNEY, b. 22 Dec 1920, Barre, MA.
1246.	ii.	GLENN FRANCIS SPINNEY, b. 14 Oct 1922, Barre, MA; d. 12 Feb 1973.
1247.	iii.	CHESTER LEVERETT JR. SPINNEY, b. 12 Feb 1927.

941. VIOLA[8] SPINNEY *(ISAAC CALVIN[7], SAMUEL[6], ISAAC BEACH[5], SAMUEL McCLURE[4], SAMUEL[3], SAMUEL[2], THOMAS[1])* was born 1904. She married ELGIN BELCHER.

Children of VIOLA SPINNEY and ELGIN BELCHER are:
     i. ANDREA[9] BELCHER, m. SAMUEL GOODWIN.
     ii. LUCILLE BELCHER, m. LAWRENCE BEGIN.

942. ELIZABETH[8] SPINNEY *(JONATHAN RIED MORSE[7], AUSTIN WELTON[6], JACOB BEACH[5], SAMUEL McCLURE[4], SAMUEL[3], SAMUEL[2], THOMAS[1])* was born 27 Nov 1901, and died 1991. She married GEORGE EARL PAYSON, son of STEPHEN PAYSON and LOUISA MOORE. He was born 01 Sep 1889.

Notes for ELIZABETH SPINNEY:
Elizabeth (Betty to her friends) Worked for Eatons in Moose Jaw in the wool dept. I believe that just about all of the grand children received a beautiful Indian Sweater for Christmas. It wasn't long before she was demonstrating knitting and yarns for Maxwell Wool Company. She travelled alot in this position. When her son George was stationed in Soest Germany (1955-1957) she flew over to visit and travel with the family. The first night we made camp in Europe George showed his sons how to put up the tents. Two army pup tents! Two people could barely get into one. I can still hear her say "GEORGE, YOU DON'T THINK THAT I'M TO SLEEP IN THAT!" But she did and made the best of the trip.
From there she met her daughter Ruby in England

Notes for GEORGE EARL PAYSON:
George Earl came to Saskatchewan in about 1911 and obtained a homestead of 1/2 section near Central Butte. In about 1913, he hired on C.P.Railroad as a brakeman, working part time. In 1915 he returned to Nova Scotia and joined the army as a gunner in the war of 1914-1918. After the war he came back to Moose Jaw, worked on CPR and rented his land. As he couldn't work full time on CPR, came back to Nova Scotia. Met and married Elizabeth

Rebecca Spinney, Sept. 7, 1921. Came back to Moose Jaw in May 1927- Purchase the home at 422 Main St South. Retired from CPR in 1950. Died April 8 1964.

George Earl served in WWI as a gunner and had been gassed by the Germans at one time. George Spinney contributed this act as a cause of his dads' loss of memory. George said that when his dad was dying it appeared that he suddenly became alert and asked for a old friend that he hadn't seen for some time. Geo. Earl could not understand why he was in the hospital and talked to his friend about things they did in the past for some time in the night.

Children of ELIZABETH SPINNEY and GEORGE PAYSON are:
      i.   RUBY LOUISE[9] PAYSON.
     ii.   ELWOOD BRYON PAYSON.
   iii.   MARY ELEANOR PAYSON.
   iv.   GEORGE SPINNEY PAYSON, b. 08 Sep 1922.

943. AUSTIN WHEELOCK[8] SPINNEY *(CALEB SNOW[7], AUSTIN WELTON[6], JACOB BEACH[5], SAMUEL MCCLURE[4], SAMUEL[3], SAMUEL[2], THOMAS[1])* was born 06 Jul 1890. He married BERTHA ELVIRA ANDERSON. She was born 1890, and died 1956.

Child of AUSTIN SPINNEY and BERTHA ANDERSON is:
1248.   i.   ULMER WILLIAM[9] SPINNEY, b. Dec 1923, Austin, Tx; d. Dec 1979.

944. SEAWARD[8] SPINNEY *(CALEB SNOW[7], AUSTIN WELTON[6], JACOB BEACH[5], SAMUEL MCCLURE[4], SAMUEL[3], SAMUEL[2], THOMAS[1])* was born 31 Jan 1904 in Harmony, NS., and died 12 Feb 1991 in Berlin, MA. He married MARY A LAWRENCE.

Notes for SEAWARD SPINNEY:
Headline: Seaward S. Spinney, 87; ex-maintenance chief
      Publication Date: February 12, 1991
      Source: Telegram & Gazette Worcester, MA
      Page: C6
      Region: Massachusetts Obituary:

BERLIN - Seaward S. Spinney, 87, of 135 Pleasant St.died Sunday night in Oakdale Nursing Home, Oakdale. He leaves his wife, Mary A. (Lawrence) Spinney; a son, Seaward S. Spinney Jr. of Berlin; three daughters, Rose M. Sawyer and Eunice Hoban, both of Berlin, and Rita L. Morris of Montreal, Quebec, Canada; eight grandchildren; six great-grandchildren; nephews and nieces. Mr. and Mrs. Spinney observed their 57th wedding anniversary recently. He was born in Harmony, Nova Scotia, Canada, son of Caleb and Margaret (Bartow) Spinney, and later lived in Holden. He lived here 40 years.

Mr. Spinney was head of maintenance at Anna Maria College in Paxton, where he worked for 19 years, retiring in 1980. He began working in a grocery store in Acton. He was then a carpenter and home builder for his brother in Winter Park, Fla. He then became a caretaker for a mill owner in Acton. After that, he worked for 19 years in a machine shop in Ashland. At this point, he told the Sunday Telegram in 1979, the urge to get outside took over. He was a caretaker of an estate in Connecticut.

"I really liked that job," he recalled. " It was a big estate, always something to do."
He went to work at AnnaMaria College in 1961 Mr. Spinney was a former member of the Berlin Grange, the Berlin Board of Trade and Hudson Lodge of Odd Fellows.

His work was his hobby for years, he told the Sunday Telegram in 1979. "UNWAVERING FIDELITY Sister Irene Socquet, S.S.A., former president and later business manager of the college, said, "Mr. Spinney has shown Anna Maria unwavering fidelity, and has worked for the college in a way a man would work for himself in his own business. He must have an invisible fireman's pole, day and night. When things go wrong he shows up in an instant."

Another college insider said Mr. Spinney was "a real Yankee craftsman, blessed with an adaptability to all needs and purposes." Funeral services will be held at 11 a.m. tomorrow in Robert J. McNally Funeral Home, 304 Church St., Clinton. The Rev. Robert A. Grattaroti will officiate. Burial will be in South Cemetery. Calling hours at the funeral home are 2 to 4 and 7 to 9 p.m. today. The family requests that flowers be omitted. Memorial contributions may be made instead to the Berlin Rescue Squad, care of Andrew Munter, 11 South St. Berlin, 01503.

Notes for MARY A LAWRENCE:

> Headline: Mary A. Spinney, 78
> Publication Date: February 18, 1991
> Source: Telegram & Gazette Worcester, MA
> Page: C4
> Subjects:
> Region: Massachusetts

Obituary: BERLIN - Mary A. (Lawrence) Spinney, 78, of 135 Pleasant St. died Saturday in Oakdale Nursing Home, Oakdale, after an illness.

Her husband, Seaward S. Spinney Sr., died Feb. 10. She leaves a son, Seaward S. Spinney Jr. of Berlin; three daughters, Rose M. Sawyer and Eunice Hoban, both of Berlin, and Rita Morris of Montreal, Quebec, Canada; eight grandchildren; six great-grandchildren; nephews and nieces.
She was born in West Acton, daughter of William and Lena (Dufour) Lawrence, and lived here 40 years. She worked for several years in the library at Anna Maria College in Paxton. Mrs. Spinney was a founding member of St. Joseph the Good Provider Church and was its organist for many years.

She was a member of its Women's Club, the Berlin Tuesday Club and the Berlin Grange.
The funeral will be held Saturday from Robert J. McNally Funeral Home, 304 Church St, Clinton, with a Mass at 10 a.m. in St. Joseph the Good Provider Church, 52 West St. Burial will be in South Cemetery

Calling hours at the funeral home are 2 to 4 and 7 to 9 p.m. Friday. The family requests that flowers be omitted. Memorial contributions may be made instead to the Berlin Rescue Squad, care of Andrew Munter, 11 South St., Berlin, 01503.

Children of SEAWARD SPINNEY and MARY LAWRENCE are:
  - i. SEAWARD[9] SPINNEY.
  - ii. ROSE SPINNEY.
  - iii. EUNICE SPINNEY.
  - iv. RITA SPINNEY.

945. EVA[8] SPINNEY *(WILLIAM G.[7], JACOB BEACH[6], JACOB BEACH[5], SAMUEL MCCLURE[4], SAMUEL[3], SAMUEL[2], THOMAS[1])* was born 1889, and died 1976. She married SAMUEL H. GRIFFIN 1914.

Children of EVA SPINNEY and SAMUEL GRIFFIN are:
1249. i. LLOYD[9] GRIFFIN.
  - ii. VIVIAN GRIFFIN.
  - iii. HAZEL GRIFFIN, m. PERCY CHUTE.

946. MILTON[8] SPINNEY *(WILLIAM G.[7], JACOB BEACH[6], JACOB BEACH[5], SAMUEL MCCLURE[4], SAMUEL[3], SAMUEL[2], THOMAS[1])* was born 1904, and died 1976. He married RUBY PEARL Abt. 1930. She was born Bet. 1900 - 1910.

Children of MILTON SPINNEY and RUBY PEARL are:
  - i. JOYCE[9] SPINNEY, b. 1932; d. 1932.
  - ii. ROY SPINNEY, b. 1933; d. 1934.

947. HELEN LUCY[8] SPINNEY *(JAMES BARTEAUX[7], HARDING THEODORE[6], JACOB BEACH[5], SAMUEL MCCLURE[4], SAMUEL[3], SAMUEL[2], THOMAS[1])* was born 1895, and died 1981. She married JOHN GRIFFIN 1924. He was born

1898.

Children of HELEN SPINNEY and JOHN GRIFFIN are:
1250.   i.   ELSIE MAY[9] GRIFFIN, b. 1928.
1251.   ii. CURTIS JAMES GRIFFIN, b. 1930.

948. ANNIE MIRA[8] SPINNEY *(JAMES BARTEAUX[7], HARDING THEODORE[6], JACOB BEACH[5], SAMUEL MCCLURE[4], SAMUEL[3], SAMUEL[2], THOMAS[1])* was born 1902, and died 1967. She married LORIMER WOODBURY.

Child of ANNIE SPINNEY and LORIMER WOODBURY is:
          i.   BEA[9] WOODBURY.

949. LAURA BLANCHE[8] SPINNEY *(JAMES BARTEAUX[7], HARDING THEODORE[6], JACOB BEACH[5], SAMUEL MCCLURE[4], SAMUEL[3], SAMUEL[2], THOMAS[1])* was born 1897, and died 1977. She married CALEB MAYNARD SPINNEY 1925, son of EDWARD SPINNEY and BESSIE WEBBER. He was born 1897, and died 1980.

Children of LAURA SPINNEY and CALEB SPINNEY are:
          i.   GERALD EDWARD[9] SPINNEY, b. 1928; m. ANN FORTIN.
          ii. MARINA BLANCHE SPINNEY, b. 1935; m. (1) JAMES CLARK; m. (2) DEL CHRISTIANSON.

950. CALEB MAYNARD[8] SPINNEY *(EDWARD MANNING[7], CALEB[6], JACOB BEACH[5], SAMUEL MCCLURE[4], SAMUEL[3], SAMUEL[2], THOMAS[1])* was born 1897, and died 1980. He married LAURA BLANCHE SPINNEY 1925, daughter of JAMES SPINNEY and MARY FITCH. She was born 1897, and died 1977.

Children are listed above under (949) Laura Blanche Spinney.

951. LESLIE MANNING[8] SPINNEY *(EDWARD MANNING[7], CALEB[6], JACOB BEACH[5], SAMUEL MCCLURE[4], SAMUEL[3], SAMUEL[2], THOMAS[1])* was born 1898, and died 1982. He married BEATRICE MAE SPINNEY 07 Apr 1925 in Greenwood, NS., daughter of MELBURNE SPINNEY and HARRIET SMALL. She was born 1899 in Greenwood, NS., and died 30 Aug 2000.

Notes for BEATRICE MAE SPINNEY:
SPINNEY, Beatrice Mae - 101, Berwick, formerly of Aylesford, died August 30, 2000, in Thomas Rest Home, Berwick. Born in Greenwood Square, she was a daughter of the late Melbourne and Harriett (Small) Spinney. She had been the organist at the Union Church, Greenwood Square for many years. She had been active in U.C.W. Auxiliary both in Aylesford and Greenwood. She was a former member of Canadian Cancer Society and Canadian Red Cross. She was the last surviving member of her immediate family. Surviving are daughters, Connie (Mrs. Robert McMahon), Berwick; Frances Hatt, Middleton; seven grandchildren; 12 great-grandchildren. She was predeceased by her husband, Leslie; son-in-law, Keith Hatt; sister, Edith; brothers, Horace, Loring, Ralph and Howe. Funeral service 2 p.m. today, in Warren T. Roop Funeral Home, Middleton, Rev. Dr. Byron Fenwick officiating. Burial in Aylesford Union Cemetery. Donations to Canadian Cancer Society, Aylesford United Church or Greenwood Square Union Church

Children of LESLIE SPINNEY and BEATRICE SPINNEY are:
          i.   FRANCES[9] SPINNEY, b. 1929; m. KEITH HATT; d. Bef. 2000.
          ii. CONSTANCE SPINNEY, b. 1936; m. ROBERT MCMAHON.

952. ZELDA HOPE[8] SPINNEY *(EDWARD MANNING[7], CALEB[6], JACOB BEACH[5], SAMUEL MCCLURE[4], SAMUEL[3], SAMUEL[2], THOMAS[1])* was born 1904. She married ARNOLD ETTER 1933.

Children of ZELDA SPINNEY and ARNOLD ETTER are:
          i.   JOHN M.[9] ETTER, b. 1935.
          ii. DAVID A. ETTER, b. 1941.

953. ALBERT WEBBER[8] SPINNEY *(EDWARD MANNING[7], CALEB[6], JACOB BEACH[5], SAMUEL MCCLURE[4], SAMUEL[3], SAMUEL[2], THOMAS[1])* was born 1908 in Greenwood, NS., and died 06 Oct 1994 in Middleton, NS.. He married

DAISIE MARSHALL 1939, daughter of A MARSHALL and PHOEBE PIERCE.

Notes for ALBERT WEBBER SPINNEY:
Albert was born at home. Throughout his life, he participated in many aspects of community affairs. He was an active choir member and deacon of the Greenwood Square Union Meeting House. He served as a school trustee of Greenwood Square School district 2 and fire commissioner of the Kingston Fire Department between 1978 and 1992. He was one of the founders of the Kingston Steer Barbeque. He was an active member and past master of the Masonic Lodge, Markland 99. A Kingston merchant for some years, he operated the Western King's Hardware, providing the area with heating, refrigeration, and electrical services. In 1964, he joined O.H. Armstrong Ltd. as an accounts clerk and refrigeration specialist, retiring in 1974. He was an avid gardener, taking great pride in his vegetable and flower gardens.

Notes for DAISIE MARSHALL:
Daisie was a graduate of the Yarmouth School of Nursing, Yarmouth, Nova Scotia, 1936.

She was a supervisor at the Soldiers memorial Hospital, 1967 - 1980. She is an entrepreneur,

a skilled seamstress and continues to be an active volunteer in her community.

Birth place given is as recorded on her birth certificate, issued 30 May 1960.

Daisie & Albert's marriage was the first marriage celebrated at the Kingston Baptist Church.

Children of ALBERT SPINNEY and DAISIE MARSHALL are:
1252.   i.   ENA GWEN[9] SPINNEY, b. 1945.
        ii.   BRENDA LORRAINE SPINNEY, b. 1952; m. (1) ELDON SURETTE; m. (2) ROLAND FORBES.

954. HORACE LESTER[8] SPINNEY *(MELBURNE E.[7], BENIAH B[6], JACOB BEACH[5], SAMUEL MCCLURE[4], SAMUEL[3], SAMUEL[2], THOMAS[1])* was born 1851, and died 1951. He married GLADYS KEDDY 1910.

Children of HORACE SPINNEY and GLADYS KEDDY are:
        i.   NEIL[9] SPINNEY, b. 1912; m. EVA WORTHINGTON.
        ii.   ALLSTON SPINNEY, b. 1914; d. 1977; m. MYRTLE CLATTENBURG.

955. EDITH ADELAIDE[8] SPINNEY *(MELBURNE E.[7], BENIAH B[6], JACOB BEACH[5], SAMUEL MCCLURE[4], SAMUEL[3], SAMUEL[2], THOMAS[1])* was born 1889, and died 1975. She married WILFRED GROSS 1913.

Children of EDITH SPINNEY and WILFRED GROSS are:
        i.   CLYDE[9] GROSS.
        ii.   NORMA GROSS.

956. LORING VICTOR[8] SPINNEY *(MELBURNE E.[7], BENIAH B[6], JACOB BEACH[5], SAMUEL MCCLURE[4], SAMUEL[3], SAMUEL[2], THOMAS[1])* was born 1890 in Greenwood, N.S., and died 13 Feb 1957 in Greenwood, N.S.. He married CORA JACQUES 1926.

Child of LORING SPINNEY and CORA JACQUES is:
        i.   JUNE ROSE[9] SPINNEY, b. 08 May 1929; d. 10 May 1929.

957. HOWE BELL[8] SPINNEY *(MELBURNE E.[7], BENIAH B[6], JACOB BEACH[5], SAMUEL MCCLURE[4], SAMUEL[3], SAMUEL[2], THOMAS[1])* was born 1894, and died 1965. He married BESSIE PARKER 1926. She was born 1893.

Children of HOWE SPINNEY and BESSIE PARKER are:
1253.   i.   ELLIS[9] SPINNEY, b. 1927.
        ii.   MARY ELLEN SPINNEY, b. 1929.
1254.   iii.   CLARE SPINNEY, b. 1932.

958. BEATRICE MAE[8] SPINNEY *(MELBURNE E.[7], BENIAH B[6], JACOB BEACH[5], SAMUEL McCLURE[4], SAMUEL[3], SAMUEL[2], THOMAS[1])* was born 1899 in Greenwood, NS., and died 30 Aug 2000. She married LESLIE MANNING SPINNEY 07 Apr 1925 in Greenwood, NS., son of EDWARD SPINNEY and BESSIE WEBBER. He was born 1898, and died 1982.

Notes for BEATRICE MAE SPINNEY:
SPINNEY, Beatrice Mae - 101, Berwick, formerly of Aylesford, died August 30, 2000, in Thomas Rest Home, Berwick. Born in Greenwood Square, she was a daughter of the late Melbourne and Harriett (Small) Spinney. She had been the organist at the Union Church, Greenwood Square for many years. She had been active in U.C.W. Auxiliary both in Aylesford and Greenwood. She was a former member of Canadian Cancer Society and Canadian Red Cross. She was the last surviving member of her immediate family. Surviving are daughters, Connie (Mrs. Robert McMahon), Berwick; Frances Hatt, Middleton; seven grandchildren; 12 great-grandchildren. She was predeceased by her husband, Leslie; son-in-law, Keith Hatt; sister, Edith; brothers, Horace, Loring, Ralph and Howe. Funeral service 2 p.m. today, in Warren T. Roop Funeral Home, Middleton, Rev. Dr. Byron Fenwick officiating. Burial in Aylesford Union Cemetery. Donations to Canadian Cancer Society, Aylesford United Church or Greenwood Square Union Church

Children are listed above under (951) Leslie Manning Spinney.

959. EVELYN BEATRICE[8] SPINNEY *(EVERETT LAMONT[7], ENOCH[6], JACOB BEACH[5], SAMUEL McCLURE[4], SAMUEL[3], SAMUEL[2], THOMAS[1])* was born 23 Jul 1893 in Darthmouth, N.S, and died 1956. She married EARLE RAYMOUND LITTLEFIELD.

Children of EVELYN SPINNEY and EARLE LITTLEFIELD are:
    i.   KENNETH[9] LITTLEFIELD.
    ii. PATRICIA LITTLEFIELD.

960. EVERETT RHEE[8] SPINNEY *(EVERETT LAMONT[7], ENOCH[6], JACOB BEACH[5], SAMUEL McCLURE[4], SAMUEL[3], SAMUEL[2], THOMAS[1])* was born 13 Aug 1895 in Acton, MA, and died 1937. He married DAISY ALWARD. She was born 1898.

Children of EVERETT SPINNEY and DAISY ALWARD are:
    i.   EARLE RHEE[9] SPINNEY, b. 1917.
    ii. EVELYN RUTH SPINNEY, b. 1918.
    iii. RALPH EDWARD SPINNEY, b. 1920.
    iv. JANET SPINNEY, b. 1921.
    v.   MARJORIE SPINNEY, b. 1924.

961. LILLIAN BICKNELL[8] SPINNEY *(EVERETT LAMONT[7], ENOCH[6], JACOB BEACH[5], SAMUEL McCLURE[4], SAMUEL[3], SAMUEL[2], THOMAS[1])* was born 1898. She married VERNON LEE HUNKINS.

Child of LILLIAN SPINNEY and VERNON HUNKINS is:
    i.   FRANCIS[9] HUNKINS.

962. ORLAND ELWOOD[8] SPINNEY *(EVERETT LAMONT[7], ENOCH[6], JACOB BEACH[5], SAMUEL McCLURE[4], SAMUEL[3], SAMUEL[2], THOMAS[1])* was born 15 Jun 1901 in Acton, MA, and died Oct 1979. He married CATHERINE THERESA DOWNES. She was born 08 May 1904, and died Nov 1967 in Groton, MA.

Child of ORLAND SPINNEY and CATHERINE DOWNES is:
    i.   EVELYN MARY[9] SPINNEY, b. 1928, Groton, MA.

963. ALFRED[8] SPINNEY *(GEORGE ELBURN[7], ENOCH[6], JACOB BEACH[5], SAMUEL McCLURE[4], SAMUEL[3], SAMUEL[2], THOMAS[1])* was born Abt. 1890. He married ELIZABETH SARSFIELD.

Children of ALFRED SPINNEY and ELIZABETH SARSFIELD are:
    i.   GORDAN HARRIS[9] SPINNEY.
    ii. ARTHUR SPINNEY.

    iii.   EUGENE SPINNEY.
    iv.   SHIRLEY SPINNEY.
    v.   LINDA SPINNEY.
    vi.   MARY SPINNEY.

964. WILEY[8] SPINNEY *(GEORGE ELBURN[7], ENOCH[6], JACOB BEACH[5], SAMUEL MCCLURE[4], SAMUEL[3], SAMUEL[2], THOMAS[1])* He married JEAN SANFORD.

Child of WILEY SPINNEY and JEAN SANFORD is:
    i.   MAXINE[9] SPINNEY.

965. ROBIE[8] SPINNEY *(GEORGE ELBURN[7], ENOCH[6], JACOB BEACH[5], SAMUEL MCCLURE[4], SAMUEL[3], SAMUEL[2], THOMAS[1])* He married EILEEN REDMOND.

Children of ROBIE SPINNEY and EILEEN REDMOND are:
    i.   FREDA[9] SPINNEY.
    ii.   GRAHAM SPINNEY.

966. KENNETH EARLE[8] SPINNEY *(GEORGE ELBURN[7], ENOCH[6], JACOB BEACH[5], SAMUEL MCCLURE[4], SAMUEL[3], SAMUEL[2], THOMAS[1])* was born 1906. He married MAYFRED DELILAH CROCKER, daughter of LAMERT CROCKER and AGNES WINOTT. She was born 1909, and died 17 Jan 2005.

Notes for KENNETH EARLE SPINNEY:
Headline: Kenneth E. Spinney, 86
Publication Date: May 31, 1992
Source: Sunday Telegram Worcester, MA
Page: B8
Subjects:
Region: Massachusetts
Obituary: OXFORD - Kenneth E. Spinney, 86, of West Street died Friday night in The Medical Center of Central Massachusetts - Memorial, Worcester, after a long illness.
He leaves his wife, Mayfred D. (Crocker) Spinney; a son, Philip Spinney of Oxford; a daughter, Geraldine Smith of Sutton; seven grandchildren; 10 great-grandchildren; nephews and nieces. Mr. and Mrs. Spinney were married April 4, 1931. He was born in Harmony, Nova Scotia, Canada, son of George E. and Martha (Saunders) Spinney, and lived in Worcester 61 years.
He was a resizer in the abrasives division of Norton Co. in Worcester for 27 years, retiring in 1969.
Mr. Spinney was 46-year member of First Congregational Church, where he was a longtime sexton and deacon. He was a member of Oxford Lodge of Masons.
Funeral services will be at 11 a.m. Tuesday in First Congregational Church, Main Street. Burial will be in North Cemetery. Calling hours at Lullmann-Paradis Funeral Home, 357 Main St., are 7 to 9 p.m. tomorrow. Members of the Oxford Lodge of Masons will meet there at 7:30 p.m. tomorrow to conduct a service. In lieu of flowers, memorial contributions may be made to First Congregational Church, Main Street, Oxford, 01540.

Children of KENNETH SPINNEY and MAYFRED CROCKER are:
1255.   i.   GERALDINE DELORES[9] SPINNEY, b. 1932.
1256.   ii.   PHILIP KENNETH SPINNEY, b. 1938.
    iii.   GERALDINE SPINNEY.

967. WINTHROP HARRIS[8] SPINNEY *(LELAND TEASDALE[7], ENOCH[6], JACOB BEACH[5], SAMUEL MCCLURE[4], SAMUEL[3], SAMUEL[2], THOMAS[1])* was born 27 Sep 1900 in Harmony, NS., and died 22 Mar 1974 in Westboro, MA. He married MARJORIE EUNICE WHITAKER 12 Jun 1928 in Worcester, MA.. She was born 03 Feb 1911.

Notes for MARJORIE EUNICE WHITAKER:
Marjorie E. Spinney
1999-04-08

Marjorie E. Spinney, 88, Westborough, Mass., died March 22 at Memorial Hospital, Worcester, Mass., after a brief illness. Born Feb. 3, 1911 in Worcester, Mass., she was the daughter of Warren E. and Mary L. Leach Whitaker. She was educated in Worcester and earned her GED at the age of 68. She was the wife of the late Winthrop H. Spinney, former Westborough Fire Chief, who died in 1974. Mrs. Spinney was a resident of Westborough since 1926. She was a homemaker dedicated to her home and family.

She had a Nemeth degree in Braille aand a Library of Congress Certification and Doctorate in Braille. She was volunteer Braillist of college and high school text books for many years. She was a member of the First Baptist Church of Westborough, a member of the Mizpah Ladies of the Church, a 70 year member of the Westborough Grange, and a long time member and Past Matron of the Bethany Chapter Order of Eastern Star.

She was a long time summer visitor to Pemaquid Beach. Mrs. Spinney leaves a daughter, Charlotte C. Spinney of Westborough; two sons, James L. Spinney and his wife Janis of Jacksonville, Fla., and Winthrop W. Spinney and his wife Patricia of Naples, Fla.; five grandchildren, Jane, Jean and James Spinney, and Jenifer and Cathryn Spinney, all of Florida; and one great- grandchild, Lori Loftin. She was predeceased by a grandson, Winthrop J. Spinney, in 1995.

A funeral was held March 25 in the First Baptist Church, with the Rev. Paul Munro, pastor, officiating. A private graveside service was held in Pine Grove Cemetery, Westborough. Arrangements were by Rand-Harper Westborough Funeral Home.

Donations in her memory may be made to the Organ Repair Fund, First Baptist Church, 46 West Main St., Westborough, Mass.

Children of WINTHROP SPINNEY and MARJORIE WHITAKER are:
-     i.   CHARLOTTE CYNTHIA[9] SPINNEY, b. 21 Apr 1936, Worcester, MA.
- 1257.   ii.   JAMES LELAND SPINNEY, b. 16 Jul 1940, Worcester, MA.
- 1258.   iii.   WINTHROP WARREN SPINNEY, b. 19 Mar 1945, Milford, MA.

968. KINGSLEY SELLAR[8] SPINNEY *(LELAND TEASDALE[7], ENOCH[6], JACOB BEACH[5], SAMUEL MCCLURE[4], SAMUEL[3], SAMUEL[2], THOMAS[1])* was born 23 Jul 1902 in Harmony, N.S., and died 22 Mar 1973 in Nicholsville, N.S.. He married EVELYN MELETTA PALMER. She was born 1907.

Child of KINGSLEY SPINNEY and EVELYN PALMER is:
- 1259.   i.   PHYLLIS MAE[9] SPINNEY, b. 15 Jun 1935.

969. VERA BELLE[8] SPINNEY *(LELAND TEASDALE[7], ENOCH[6], JACOB BEACH[5], SAMUEL MCCLURE[4], SAMUEL[3], SAMUEL[2], THOMAS[1])* was born 26 Mar 1904 in Harmony, N.S., and died 27 Apr 1951 in Nicholsville, N.S.. She married CECIL P. PALMER 16 Dec 1925 in Nicholsville, N.S.. He was born 16 Sep 1900.

Children of VERA SPINNEY and CECIL PALMER are:
- 1260.   i.   GERALD EUGENE[9] PALMER, b. 12 Oct 1931.
- 1261.   ii.   JOYCE AGNES PALMER, b. 05 May 1936.
- 1262.   iii.   ALFRETTA BLANCHE PALMER, b. 06 Nov 1937, Harmony, N.S..

970. EARLE WINFRED[8] SPINNEY *(LELAND TEASDALE[7], ENOCH[6], JACOB BEACH[5], SAMUEL MCCLURE[4], SAMUEL[3], SAMUEL[2], THOMAS[1])* was born 12 Jan 1914 in Harmony, N.S., and died 28 Apr 1980 in Greenwood, N.S.. He married FLORA MAE MORSE 01 Jan 1938 in Bloomington, N.S.. She was born 01 Feb 1915.

Children of EARLE SPINNEY and FLORA MORSE are:
- 1263.   i.   SANDRA LOUISE[9] SPINNEY, b. 03 Nov 1939, Middleton, N.S..
- 1264.   ii.   DELMA PEARL SPINNEY, b. 04 Dec 1942, Middleton, N.S..
-     iii.   CRYSTAL AGNES SPINNEY, b. 26 Oct 1947, Middleton; m. DOUGLAS IAN WELLS, 21 Aug 1971, Greenwood, N.S..
-     iv.   MONA PATRICIA SPINNEY, b. 17 Sep 1950, Middleton, N.S.; m. JOHN ROGER RYER; b. 19 Oct 1947.

971. FRANCIS LELAND[8] SPINNEY *(LELAND TEASDALE[7], ENOCH[6], JACOB BEACH[5], SAMUEL MCCLURE[4], SAMUEL[3], SAMUEL[2], THOMAS[1])* was born 15 Aug 1915 in Harmony, N.S., and died 28 Aug 1979 in Harmony, N.S.. He married LEONORE MURIEL BRYDON 20 Apr 1946 in Black Rock, N.S.. She was born 02 Aug 1925.

Children of FRANCIS SPINNEY and LEONORE BRYDON are:
1265.　i.　PHILIP VANCE[9] SPINNEY, b. 15 Nov 1946.
1266.　ii.　DORIS AGNES SPINNEY, b. 17 Jan 1948.
1267.　iii.　VERA ANNE SPINNEY, b. 06 Oct 1953.
　　　iv.　CATHERINE FRANCES SPINNEY, b. 09 Dec 1961.

972. BURPEE CLYDE[8] SPINNEY *(BURPEE ALBINA[7], CLARK THOMAS[6], JACOB BEACH[5], SAMUEL MCCLURE[4], SAMUEL[3], SAMUEL[2], THOMAS[1])* was born 18 Aug 1912 in Greenwood, N.S.. He married BERTHA MAUD CHAMBERS 30 Nov 1935. She was born 21 Feb 1911.

Children of BURPEE SPINNEY and BERTHA CHAMBERS are:
　　　i.　AULDEN CLARKE[9] SPINNEY.
　　　ii.　CAROL GRACE SPINNEY, b. Abt. 1930; m. WILLARD S. SPINNEY; b. Abt. 1930.

973. NORA[8] CROCKER *(WILLIAM E.[7], CATHERINE[6] SAUNDERS, EUNICE[5] SPINNEY, SAMUEL MCCLURE[4], SAMUEL[3], SAMUEL[2], THOMAS[1])* was born 11 Jul 1889, and died 1910. She married J. W. TUPPER. He was born 1883, and died 1966.

Child of NORA CROCKER and J. TUPPER is:
　　　i.　MARION[9] TUPPER, b. 1910; d. 1910.

974. JOANNE[8] ARMSTRONG *(ELLESWORTH[7], RUBY ARDELLISS[6] GRIFFIN, CATHERINE INGLIS[5] SPINNEY, SAMUEL MCCLURE[4], SAMUEL[3], SAMUEL[2], THOMAS[1])* She married HARVIE SOLOMON.

Children of JOANNE ARMSTRONG and HARVIE SOLOMON are:
　　　i.　SHEVA[9] SOLOMON.
　　　ii.　GABRIEL SOLOMON.
　　　iii.　RACHEAL REBECCA SOLOMON.

975. CLAYTON ABNER[8] PIERCE *(HOWARD ELIZA[7], CHARLES A.[6], AMORET[5] SPINNEY, SAMUEL MCCLURE[4], SAMUEL[3], SAMUEL[2], THOMAS[1])* was born 13 Jan 1897, and died Aug 1969. He married (1) GLORIA BUSH. She was born 18 Oct 1901, and died 29 Feb 1984. He married (2) OUIDA LUCINDA HARRIS 24 Oct 1916. She was born 05 Jun 1898.

Child of CLAYTON PIERCE and GLORIA BUSH is:
1268.　i.　MELBA[9] PIERCE.

Children of CLAYTON PIERCE and OUIDA HARRIS are:
1269.　ii.　HOWARD MAXWELL[9] PIERCE.
1270.　iii.　DOUGLAS ARDEN PIERCE.
1271.　iv.　ARCHIE ARDEN PIERCE.
1272.　v.　THELMA KIZBARO PIERCE.
　　　vi.　RUSSELL FOREST HARRIS PIERCE.
1273.　vii.　ARDIS PIERCE.
1274.　viii.　ETHEL BERNEICE PIERCE.
1275.　ix.　ELMA MARIE PIERCE, d. 1972.
1276.　x.　HAZEL ALTHIA PIERCE.
1277.　xi.　CARL AUBREY PIERCE.
1278.　xii.　JEANIE PIERCE.

976. RALPH ALMER[8] PIERCE *(HOWARD ELIZA[7], CHARLES A.[6], AMORET[5] SPINNEY, SAMUEL MCCLURE[4], SAMUEL[3], SAMUEL[2], THOMAS[1])* was born 01 Sep 1899 in Clementport, NS., and died 18 Feb 1983 in Digby, NS.. He married (1) HAZEL VIOLA SIMPSON 01 Sep 1921. She was born 18 Jan 1894, and died 14 Feb 1973 in Annapolis, NS.. He married (2) VIVIANNE DENTEN 1974. She was born 1916.

Children of RALPH PIERCE and HAZEL SIMPSON are:
1279.   i.   MARJORIE JEAN[9] PIERCE, b. 10 Jun 1922.
1280.   ii.   AUDREY EDITH PIERCE, b. 16 Mar 1924.
1281.   iii.   ALLAN LESLIE PIERCE, b. 10 Aug 1929.
1282.   iv.   JAMES MAXWELL PIERCE, b. 21 Apr 1932.
1283.   v.   HOWARD ALLISON PIERCE, b. 26 Oct 1935.

977. EDITH[8] PIERCE *(FRANK LOVETT[7], CHARLES A.[6], AMORET[5] SPINNEY, SAMUEL McCLURE[4], SAMUEL[3], SAMUEL[2], THOMAS[1])* was born 1909, and died 1981. She married MARK HENRY CHUTE 1939. He was born 07 Apr 1901, and died 1979.

Children of EDITH PIERCE and MARK CHUTE are:
        i.   RAY[9] CHUTE, m. DOREEN LUTZ.
        ii.   DEBBIE CHUTE, m. JOHN SEWEET.

978. RUTH HANNAH ELIZABETH[8] PIERCE *(FRANK LOVETT[7], CHARLES A.[6], AMORET[5] SPINNEY, SAMUEL McCLURE[4], SAMUEL[3], SAMUEL[2], THOMAS[1])* was born 12 Nov 1912, and died 11 Apr 1987. She married HERMAN ARTHUR AVERY.

Children of RUTH PIERCE and HERMAN AVERY are:
1284.   i.   LEON MCAVOY[9] AVERY, b. 02 Mar 1936.
1285.   ii.   JOAN EVANGELINE AVERY, b. 13 May 1939.
1286.   iii.   JANET NADINE AVERY, b. 13 Aug 1940.
1287.   iv.   ANNA JOY AVERY, b. 26 Feb 1942.
1288.   v.   CONNIE LINDA AVERY, b. 28 Feb 1944.
1289.   vi.   DEAN HERMAN AVERY, b. 1946.
1290.   vii.   GWEN INICE AVERY, b. 02 Jul 1947.
1291.   viii.   DIANE RUTH AVERY, b. 06 Nov 1948.
1292.   ix.   SHIRLEY GAIL AVERY, b. 09 Feb 1950.
1293.   x.   JUDY ADALINE AVERY, b. 29 Jul 1951.
1294.   xi.   GODON RAY AVERY, b. 02 Jan 1953.
1295.   xii.   PRISCILLA JUNE AVERY, b. 21 Jun 1954.

979. PAUL ELLIOT[8] PIERCE *(FRANK LOVETT[7], CHARLES A.[6], AMORET[5] SPINNEY, SAMUEL McCLURE[4], SAMUEL[3], SAMUEL[2], THOMAS[1])* was born 31 Mar 1914, and died 23 Nov 1992. He married DOROTHY VIDITO 1931.

Children of PAUL PIERCE and DOROTHY VIDITO are:
        i.   DONALD PIERCE[9] PIERCE.
        ii.   CORINE PIERCE.
        iii.   SHERMAN PIERCE.
        iv.   ALAN PIERCE, d. Bef. 1992.

980. LUCILLE[8] PIERCE *(FRANK LOVETT[7], CHARLES A.[6], AMORET[5] SPINNEY, SAMUEL McCLURE[4], SAMUEL[3], SAMUEL[2], THOMAS[1])* was born 25 May 1917. She married GUILFORD MORSE WARD 09 Sep 1937. He was born 13 Mar 1915.

Children of LUCILLE PIERCE and GUILFORD WARD are:
        i.   LEROY SCOTT[9] WARD.
        ii.   WAREN LOVETT WARD.
        iii.   CHARLENE AURELIA WARD.
        iv.   BRIAN EARLE WARD WARD.
        v.   BARBARA ANN JOSEPHINE WARD.
        vi.   BRENDA LUCILLE WARD.
        vii.   ELLA MAE WARD.
        viii.   MARILYN MARIE WARD.
        ix.   SHERRY LOUISE WARD.

    x.   CHARLES GUILFORD WARD, b. 02 Dec 1949; d. 1950.
   xi.   MARCELLA JOY WARD, b. 15 Dec 1960; d. 15 Dec 1960.

981. CATHERINE PEARL[8] PIERCE *(FRANK LOVETT[7], CHARLES A.[6], AMORET[5] SPINNEY, SAMUEL MCCLURE[4], SAMUEL[3], SAMUEL[2], THOMAS[1])* was born 15 Sep 1919. She married WILLIAM ALLEN FREEMAN 04 Sep 1941 in Rockland Nova Scotia. He was born 23 Nov 1910.

Notes for CATHERINE PEARL PIERCE:
Catherine was known as Kathleen for the first twenty years of her lide, until she obtained a birth certificate and found her Catherine. She immediatly adopted Catherine as her give name.

Catherine reported that their eleven children became efficient and helpfull citizens: five were teachers; on a laboratory technician and among the others wee counted carpenters, painters and seamstresses

Notes for WILLIAM ALLEN FREEMAN:
William was the first gradualte of the Kington Bible College. Upon graduation he became a Bible Teacher at the same school and continued to teach, in this capacity for fifty years. William was also ordained to the Independent Bap[ist Ministry.

William was a skilled caprneter and helped to build many of the building on the Bible College Campus and he held the position of Commissioner of the Internationa Christian Mission for twenty two years

Children of CATHERINE PIERCE and WILLIAM FREEMAN are:
     i.   GLORIA MAE[9] FREEMAN, b. 30 Aug 1943.
    ii.   ELIZABETH ROSE FREEMAN, b. 30 Nov 1944.
   iii.   PEARL LOUISE FREEMAN, b. 29 Jan 1946.
   iv.   WILLIAM LOVETT FREEMAN, b. 03 Jun 1947.
    v.   GRACE MARIE FREEMAN, b. 17 Apr 1950.
   vi.   RODNEY GORHAM FREEMAN, b. 12 Jul 1951.
  vii.   LOIS JEAN FREEMAN, b. 18 Nov 1952.
 viii.   WESLEY GORDAN FREEMAN, b. 29 Mar 1954.
   ix.   CYNTHIA MIRIAM FREEMAN, b. 21 Sep 1955.
    x.   CHARLES BOYD FREEMAN, b. 12 Oct 1957.
   xi.   DANIEL BLANCHARD FREEMAN, b. 10 Apr 1959.

982. GERALD[8] SPINNEY *(EMERY CLARENCE[7], FRANK[6], MARY[5], BENIAH[4], SAMUEL[3], SAMUEL[2], THOMAS[1])* was born 1920.

Child of GERALD SPINNEY is:
1296.   i.   ALLEN[9] SPINNEY, b. 1953.

983. SAMUEL ROGERS[8] SPINNEY *(SAMUEL ROGERS[7], THOMAS[6], THOMAS[5], JOHN[4], THOMAS[3], THOMAS[2], THOMAS[1])* was born 01 Jan 1853, and died 09 Jan 1884. He married ALTHEA FRANCES YOUNG. She was born Feb 1856, and died Aft. 1900.

Child of SAMUEL SPINNEY and ALTHEA YOUNG is:
     i.   SAMUEL[9] SPINNEY, b. 22 Mar 1884.

984. EMMA AUGUSTA[8] SPINNEY *(THOMAS M[7], THOMAS[6], THOMAS[5], JOHN[4], THOMAS[3], THOMAS[2], THOMAS[1])* was born 02 Jan 1856 in Boston, MA, and died 18 Oct 1936. She married JOHN BARNHILL MCNUTT 18 Dec 1879 in Boston, MA, son of ALEX MCNUTT and ESTER. He was born 24 Oct 1849 in Halifax, NS..

Children of EMMA SPINNEY and JOHN MCNUTT are:
     i.   GRACE EDNA[9] MCNUTT, b. 29 Sep 1882; d. 01 Jun 1940, South Boston Ma; m. THEODORE L KELLY; b. 1876.
1297.   ii.   ETHAL M MCNUTT, b. 07 Sep 1886, Boston, MA; d. 16 Mar 1952, Dorchester, MA.
   iii.   EDWARD M MCNUTT, b. 03 Apr 1888; d. 17 Jun 1888.

985. ARTHUR C[8] SPINNEY *(SAMUEL HOUSTON[7], JOHN ROGERS[6], THOMAS[5], JOHN[4], THOMAS[3], THOMAS[2], THOMAS[1])* was born 1891 in New Hampsire, and died 1968 in Eliot, ME. He married (1) EDNA M SPINNEY, daughter of FRED SPINNEY and EMMA H. She was born Oct 1889, and died 1919 in Eliot, ME. He married (2) GERTRUDE L TOBEY. She was born 09 Oct 1895 in Maine, and died 15 Feb 1974.

Child of ARTHUR SPINNEY and GERTRUDE TOBEY is:
     i.   WINSTON C[9] SPINNEY, b. 03 Dec 1923, New Hampshire; d. 19 Mar 2004, Pensacola Florida.

986. CHARLES EDWIN[8] SPINNEY *(THOMAS JEFFERSON[7], SAMUEL[6], THOMAS[5], JOHN[4], THOMAS[3], THOMAS[2], THOMAS[1])* was born 14 Oct 1857 in Portsmouth, NH, and died 23 Feb 1890 in Bridgewater, Ma. He married NELLIE M CHANDLER. She was born 14 Jul 1861, and died 16 Jul 1896.

Child of CHARLES SPINNEY and NELLIE CHANDLER is:
     i.   CHARLES ADAMS[9] SPINNEY, b. Abt. 1880.

987. PAUL REVERE[8] SPINNEY *(ROBERT MORRISON[7], SAMUEL[6], THOMAS[5], JOHN[4], THOMAS[3], THOMAS[2], THOMAS[1])* was born Mar 1879. He married ELIZABETH ZAVIER MITCHELL 1907 in Medford.

Children of PAUL SPINNEY and ELIZABETH MITCHELL are:
     i.   VIGINIA H[9] SPINNEY.
    ii.   MARJORIES F SPINNEY.
   iii.   MADELINE T SPINNEY.
   iv.   PAUL ROCKWELL SPINNEY.
    v.   CLAIRE ELIZABETH SPINNEY.
   vi.   EDMUND JOHN SPINNEY.
  vii.   ALBERT VINCENT SPINNEY.

988. MAUDE AUGUSTA[8] GREGG *(ELLEN AUGUSTA[7] SPINNEY, JOHN DICKEY[6], ALEXANDER[5], JOHN[4], THOMAS[3], THOMAS[2], THOMAS[1])* was born 1875. She married ERNEST CLARENCE PRESCOTT. He died 15 Jun 1934.

Child of MAUDE GREGG and ERNEST PRESCOTT is:
     i.   PAULINE ZILLAH[9] PRESCOTT.

989. JAMES A[8] SPINNEY *(WILLIAM[7], ALEXANDER[6], GEORGE PETTEGREW[5], JOHN[4], JOHN[3], JOHN[2], THOMAS[1])* was born 1854, and died 22 Dec 1897 in Rhode Island. He married ANNIE ATTERBURY 23 Apr 1890 in Rhode Island, daughter of GEORGE ATTERBURY. She was born Jun 1864.

Children of JAMES SPINNEY and ANNIE ATTERBURY are:
     i.   CORA L[9] SPINNEY, b. 06 Mar 1892, Rhode Island; d. 06 Jan 1907, Rhode Island.
    ii.   GRACE E SPINNEY, b. Nov 1890; m. JOSEPH H ARMSTRONG, 09 Jun 1915.
   iii.   HARRIET V SPINNEY, b. Feb 1894, Rhode Island; m. FRED S RATHBUN, 21 Feb 1918.

990. CHARLES J[8] SPINNEY *(WILLIAM[7], ALEXANDER[6], GEORGE PETTEGREW[5], JOHN[4], JOHN[3], JOHN[2], THOMAS[1])* was born 1862. He married HATTIE BARNEY.

Child of CHARLES SPINNEY and HATTIE BARNEY is:
     i.   CHARLES L[9] SPINNEY, b. 1885; d. 1976, Rhode Island; m. HOPE GREEN JOHNSON; b. 1894; d. 1967, Rhode Island.

991. ALFRED LANGDON[8] BROOKS *(DANIEL LANGDON[7], DANIEL[6], MARY[5] SPINNEY, JOHN[4], JOHN[3], JOHN[2], THOMAS[1])* was born 22 May 1842 in Eliot, ME, and died 07 Dec 1903 in Kittery, ME. He married ANNIE AUGUSTA LEWIS 1865. She was born 04 May 1847, and died 11 Feb 1912 in Newington, NH.

Children of ALFRED BROOKS and ANNIE LEWIS are:
     i.   WILMER L[9] BROOKS, b. 05 Jan 1866; d. 25 Jul 1926, Newington, NH; m. MARIA F; b. 1856; d. 1931.

1298.	ii.	ERVING ELSWORTH BROOKS, b. 09 Dec 1866; d. 01 Jan 1945, Newington NH Lot #68 W.Div. Newington C..
	iii.	ALFRED A BROOKS, b. 28 Nov 1868.
1299.	iv.	VICTOR E BROOKS, b. 01 Oct 1872; d. 06 Nov 1938.
1300.	v.	BERNICE MILDRED BROOKS, b. 24 Nov 1875, Eliot, ME; d. 11 Jun 1959, Ports. NH Lot #11 Newington Ceme..
1301.	vi.	ARTHUR L BROOKS, b. 28 Jul 1877; d. 06 Apr 1900.
1302.	vii.	ANNIE MAE BROOKS, b. 16 Nov 1880; d. 30 Jan 1961.
1303.	viii.	NELLIE FLORENCE BLANCHE BROOKS, b. 05 May 1882; d. 12 Nov 1968.
	ix.	RALPH BROOKS, b. 1885; d. 20 Oct 1889, Newington NH Lot #11 W.Div. Newington C..
1304.	x.	LEROY ULMONT BROOKS, b. 19 Oct 1887; d. 03 Aug 1970, Attleboro MA.
1305.	xi.	ESSIE ROSE BROOKS, b. 24 Sep 1891; d. 16 Jun 1979.

992. EMILY ANN[8] BROOKS *(DANIEL LANGDON[7], DANIEL[6], MARY[5] SPINNEY, JOHN[4], JOHN[3], JOHN[2], THOMAS[1])* was born 05 Dec 1847, and died 12 Sep 1913. She married SAMUEL ALBERT NELSON.

Children of EMILY BROOKS and SAMUEL NELSON are:
| | i. | ALBERTA BELLE[9] NELSON, b. 16 Dec 1867. |
| 1306. | ii. | SAMUEL HERBERT NELSON, b. 1872; d. 1956. |

993. CLARA FRANCES[8] BROOKS *(DANIEL LANGDON[7], DANIEL[6], MARY[5] SPINNEY, JOHN[4], JOHN[3], JOHN[2], THOMAS[1])* was born 14 Dec 1847, and died 16 Mar 1913. She married ELIJAH VARNEY.

Child of CLARA BROOKS and ELIJAH VARNEY is:
| 1307. | i. | ADA SYRENA[9] VARNEY, b. 23 Jul 1866; d. 05 Apr 1914. |

994. MARY OLIVIA[8] BROOKS *(DANIEL LANGDON[7], DANIEL[6], MARY[5] SPINNEY, JOHN[4], JOHN[3], JOHN[2], THOMAS[1])* was born 14 Oct 1850, and died 1935. She married HENRY HUTCHINS.

Children of MARY BROOKS and HENRY HUTCHINS are:
1308.	i.	EVERETT[9] HUTCHINS.
1309.	ii.	IDA HUTCHINS.
	iii.	CHARLIE HUTCHINS, b. 1872.
1310.	iv.	FRANK HUTCHINS, b. 1885.
	v.	LEE HUTCHINS, b. 08 Dec 1885; d. 21 Dec 1888.
	vi.	EDWARD HUTCHINS, b. 29 Oct 1890; d. 14 Mar 1978.

995. FRANK PIERCE[8] BROOKS *(DANIEL LANGDON[7], DANIEL[6], MARY[5] SPINNEY, JOHN[4], JOHN[3], JOHN[2], THOMAS[1])* was born 08 Jul 1852, and died 08 Oct 1913. He married EMMA O TILTON.

Children of FRANK BROOKS and EMMA TILTON are:
| | i. | FRANK PIERCE[9] BROOKS, JR.. |
| 1311. | ii. | INEZ BELL BROOKS, b. 1874; d. 1966. |

996. AZARIAH L[8] SPINNEY *(OLIVER P[7], JAMES[6], GEORGE PETTEGREW[5], JOHN[4], JOHN[3], JOHN[2], THOMAS[1])* was born 1840, and died 10 Dec 1898. He married MARY HILL. She was born 19 Nov 1845 in Portsmouth, NH, and died 1938.

Notes for AZARIAH L SPINNEY:
1850 Census shows Azariah living with Azariah Libby at the age of 10

Children of AZARIAH SPINNEY and MARY HILL are:
	i.	FLORA IDA[9] SPINNEY, b. 22 May 1867; m. BERT COTTLE.
1312.	ii.	ALICE MARY SPINNEY, b. Abt. 1870; d. Aft. 1930.
	iii.	MABEL SPINNEY, b. 1873; m. JOHN W WATSON, 22 Jan 1891, Portsmouth NH.
	iv.	ELIZABETH J SPINNEY, b. 1875; m. (1) THOMPSON; m. (2) FRANK POTTS; b. 1870.
	v.	NELLIE C SPINNEY, b. 1878; m. GEORGE GRINDLEY.
	vi.	ARTHUR A SPINNEY, b. 19 Mar 1882, Portsmouth, NH; m. MARY O'NEIL.

997. JOSEPH ELMOR[8] SPINNEY *(JOSEPH[7], JAMES[6], GEORGE PETTEGREW[5], JOHN[4], JOHN[3], JOHN[2], THOMAS[1])* was born 1868, and died Bef. 1900. He married ALICE MARY SPINNEY, daughter of AZARIAH SPINNEY and MARY HILL. She was born Abt. 1870, and died Aft. 1930.

Children of JOSEPH SPINNEY and ALICE SPINNEY are:
    i.   FLORENCE[9] SPINNEY, b. Abt. 1890; m. MARTIN SEAVEY.
    ii. EDITH SPINNEY, b. Abt. 1890.
    iii. CHESTER SPINNEY, b. Abt. 1890.

998. EUGENE H[8] SPINNEY *(HENRY PARKER[7], JAMES[6], GEORGE PETTEGREW[5], JOHN[4], JOHN[3], JOHN[2], THOMAS[1])* was born Apr 1861 in Maine, and died Aft. 1900. He married (1) ALMIRA HANSCOM 05 Dec 1881, daughter of IRA HANSCOM and MARTHA. He married (2) ADELINE S BERCE 1897. She was born 1871, and died Aft. 1930.

Children of EUGENE SPINNEY and ALMIRA HANSCOM are:
            i.   AUGUSTUS[9] SPINNEY, b. May 1892, New Hampshire.
1313.   ii. FRANK W SPINNEY, b. Jun 1894, New Hampshire.

999. HENRY C[8] SPINNEY *(HENRY PARKER[7], JAMES[6], GEORGE PETTEGREW[5], JOHN[4], JOHN[3], JOHN[2], THOMAS[1])* was born 1865. He married (1) ETHEL E WEAVER. He married (2) MINNIE NEAL 1891 in Lynn, Ma. She died 1898 in Lynn, Ma.

Child of HENRY SPINNEY and ETHEL WEAVER is:
    i.   BEATRICE LOUISE[9] SPINNEY, b. 1903.

1000. HARRIS E[8] SPINNEY *(HENRY PARKER[7], JAMES[6], GEORGE PETTEGREW[5], JOHN[4], JOHN[3], JOHN[2], THOMAS[1])* was born 26 Mar 1868 in Eliot, Maine, and died 22 Mar 1951 in Eliot, Maine. He married (1) SADIE R SPINNEY 1898, daughter of HAMILTON SPINNEY and BETSY TETHERLY. She was born 21 Apr 1864, and died 12 Feb 1931. He married (2) INA M MANSON 12 May 1932, daughter of CLINTON MANSON and MYRTIE MCKENNEY. She was born 1896.

Children of HARRIS SPINNEY and SADIE SPINNEY are:
    i.   RAYMOND H[9] SPINNEY, b. 27 Jan 1899, Eliot, Maine; d. 28 Dec 1990.

          Notes for RAYMOND H SPINNEY:
          Name: Raymond H. Spinney
          Serial Number: 4918130
          Birth Place: So. Eliot, Maine
          Birth Date: 27 Jan 1899
          Residence: So. Eliot
          Comment: Ind: Kennebunk, York Co. No. 2, Oct. 10/18. Private. Org: SATC Colby College Waterville Me to Dec. 12/18. Hon disch on demob: Dec. 12, 1918

1314.   ii. LILLIAN B SPINNEY, b. 11 Jun 1903, Eliot, Maine; d. 15 Dec 1996, South Berwick, Me.
        iii. HENRY H SPINNEY, b. 1906, Eliot, Maine; d. 05 Apr 1907, Eliot, Maine.

1001. AUGUSTA[8] SPINNEY *(AUGUSTUS W[7], SIMON[6], GEORGE PETTEGREW[5], JOHN[4], JOHN[3], JOHN[2], THOMAS[1])* was born 1854, and died 14 Sep 1918 in Malden, MA. She married GEORGE C HAMMOND, son of JOHN HAMMOND and L JANE. He was born 17 Mar 1854 in Kittery, ME, and died 28 Nov 1913 in Malden, MA.

Child of AUGUSTA SPINNEY and GEORGE HAMMOND is:
    i.   IDELLA[9] HAMMOND, b. Nov 1887; d. 1965; m. JUSTIN T PARSONS, 16 Feb 1908.

1002. ALMON[8] SPINNEY *(AUGUSTUS W[7], SIMON[6], GEORGE PETTEGREW[5], JOHN[4], JOHN[3], JOHN[2], THOMAS[1])* was born Feb 1857, and died 24 Dec 1923. He married GEORGIA BELLE MUCHEMORE. She was born Aug 1862, and died 1945.

Children of ALMON SPINNEY and GEORGIA MUCHEMORE are:

1315.   i.   MYRON ROGER[9] SPINNEY, b. Jun 1886; d. 1966, Malden, MA.
      ii.   MILTON C SPINNEY, b. 1889; d. 1940.
      iii.   GEORGE WASHINGTON MUCHEMORE SPINNEY, b. 27 Oct 1891; d. 1962; m. HELEN MOORE.
      iv.   NEWTON R SPINNEY, b. 27 Dec 1893; d. May 1950.
      v.   GLADYS C SPINNEY, b. Jan 1896, Kittery, ME; m. (1) CHARLES MCNALL; m. (2) CUSHMAN PHILLIPS, 08 Oct 1913.
      vi.   DAVID C SPINNEY, b. 1899; d. 1901.
      vii.   DORIS A SPINNEY, b. 1899; d. 1901.

1003. LEANDER E[8] SPINNEY (*AUGUSTUS W[7], SIMON[6], GEORGE PETTEGREW[5], JOHN[4], JOHN[3], JOHN[2], THOMAS[1]*) was born 1863 in Kittery, ME. He married (1) MINNIE S FELLOWS, daughter of GEORGE FELLOWS and FANNIE B. She was born 07 Nov 1861 in Nashua, NH, and died Aft. 1930. He married (2) MARTHA SCOTT, daughter of JAMES SCOTT.

Children of LEANDER SPINNEY and MINNIE FELLOWS are:
      i.   SON[9] SPINNEY, b. 23 Mar 1888; d. Bef. 1900.
      ii.   FORREST H SPINNEY, b. 03 May 1889, Nashua, NH; d. 15 Oct 1970, South Hamilton, Essex, MA.

1004. CALVIN A[8] SPINNEY (*MOSES J[7], SIMON[6], GEORGE PETTEGREW[5], JOHN[4], JOHN[3], JOHN[2], THOMAS[1]*) was born 1854 in New Hampshire, and died Aft. 1910. He married MARY T LANE 03 Mar 1880 in Boston, Massachusetts, daughter of CORNELIUS and CATHERINE. She was born Sep 1857 in Massachusetts.

Children of CALVIN SPINNEY and MARY LANE are:
      i.   GRACE MAY[9] SPINNEY, b. 1880, Boston, MA.
      ii.   MARY SPINNEY, b. 1889, Massachusetts.
      iii.   GRACE E SPINNEY, b. 1890.
      iv.   CLARA SPINNEY, b. 1891, Connecticut; d. Aft. 1930, Massachusetts.
1316.   v.   FRANK MOSES SPINNEY, b. 01 Mar 1894, Connecticut; d. Aft. 1930, Providence, RI.

1005. CAROLINE A[8] SPINNEY (*MOSES J[7], SIMON[6], GEORGE PETTEGREW[5], JOHN[4], JOHN[3], JOHN[2], THOMAS[1]*) was born 1854, and died Aft. 1900. She married SAMUEL GERRISH. He was born 1842 in Massachusetts.

Children of CAROLINE SPINNEY and SAMUEL GERRISH are:
      i.   NORA[9] GERRISH, b. 1871, New Hampshire.
      ii.   ALICE GERRISH, b. 1874, New Hampshire.
      iii.   SAMUEL J. GERRISH, b. 1879, New Hampshire.

1006. IDA M[8] SPINNEY (*SIMON FREDERICK[7], SIMON[6], GEORGE PETTEGREW[5], JOHN[4], JOHN[3], JOHN[2], THOMAS[1]*) was born 1858. She married JAMES H BREWSTER. He was born Nov 1854 in Massachusetts.

Children of IDA SPINNEY and JAMES BREWSTER are:
      i.   FRANK M[9] BREWSTER, b. Mar 1884.
      ii.   ETHEL M BREWSTER, b. Jan 1887.
      iii.   JAMES H BREWSTER, b. Sep 1890.
      iv.   EDNA F BREWSTER, b. May 1894.

1007. WILMONT E[8] SPINNEY (*HAMMOND[7], FRANCIS[6], GEORGE PETTEGREW[5], JOHN[4], JOHN[3], JOHN[2], THOMAS[1]*) was born 1865, and died 1949. He married VALERIA URCH. She was born 1862, and died 1952.

Children of WILMONT SPINNEY and VALERIA URCH are:
      i.   EVA[9] SPINNEY, b. Aug 1892.
      ii.   FRED C SPINNEY, b. 1895; d. 20 Jan 1901, Kittery Maine.
      iii.   MURIEL V SPINNEY, b. 1896, Eliot, ME; d. 07 Aug 1994, Holden, MA; m. RUDOLPH C NELSON.

         Notes for MURIEL V SPINNEY:
         Headline:

Muriel V. Nelson, 98
      Publication Date: August 08, 1994
      Source: Telegram & Gazette Worcester, MA
      Page: B5
      Subjects:
      Region: Massachusetts

Obituary: HOLDEN - Muriel V. (Spinney) Nelson, 98, of 317 Salisbury St., one of the six original nurses at the former Holden Hospital, died yesterday in Holden Nursing Home, 32 Mayo Drive, after an illness.

Her husband, Rudolph C. Nelson, died in 1980. She leaves a nephew, Kenneth Fritz of Rye, N.H.; a niece, Jacqueline E. Holihan of North Hampton, N.H.; grandnephews and grandnieces; great-grandnephews and great-grandnieces.

She was born in Eliot, Maine, daughter of Wilmont E. and Valeria (Urch) Spinney, and lived here many years. She graduated from Eliot High School and the Portsmouth (N.H.) Hospital School of Nursing.

Mrs. Nelson was one of the first six nurses at Holden Hospital, which was then a cottage on Pleasant Street, and worked 26 years in several nursing capacities there. She retired as assistant superintendent of the hospital, which had been renamed Holden District Hospital and had been moved to Boyden Road. She was a member of St. Francis Episcopal Church.

Funeral services will be held at 2 p.m. tomorrow in Miles Funeral Home, 1158 Main St. Burial will be in Worcester County Memorial Park, Paxton. There are no calling hours.

    iv.   LAUREL SPINNEY, b. May 1896.

1008. HENRY B[8] SPINNEY (*HAMMOND[7], FRANCIS[6], GEORGE PETTEGREW[5], JOHN[4], JOHN[3], JOHN[2], THOMAS[1]*) was born 1866, and died 1945. He married JEANNIE DAVIS 04 Oct 1892 in Eliot, Me. She was born 1871, and died 1943.

Child of HENRY SPINNEY and JEANNIE DAVIS is:
    i.   NORMAN D[9] SPINNEY, b. 1901.

1009. ALBERT S[8] SPINNEY (*HAMMOND[7], FRANCIS[6], GEORGE PETTEGREW[5], JOHN[4], JOHN[3], JOHN[2], THOMAS[1]*) was born Jun 1870, and died 1959. He married MABEL F HANSCOM 16 Apr 1896 in Eliot, ME.. She was born Jul 1871, and died 1956.

Children of ALBERT SPINNEY and MABEL HANSCOM are:
    i.   EMERSON D[9] SPINNEY, b. Feb 1898; d. May 1971.
    ii.   VESTA SPINNEY, b. 1905.
    iii.   ROGER SPINNEY, b. 1909.

1010. WILLIAM HERBERT[8] SPINNEY (*HAMILTON[7], FRANCIS[6], GEORGE PETTEGREW[5], JOHN[4], JOHN[3], JOHN[2], THOMAS[1]*) was born Jun 1855 in Eliot, ME, and died Aft. 1920. He married MARIA FULLER 1884. She was born Apr 1857 in Portsmouth, NH, and died Aft. 1920.

Children of WILLIAM SPINNEY and MARIA FULLER are:
    i.   EMMA LOUISE[9] SPINNEY, b. 23 Mar 1884.
    ii.   ALICE M SPINNEY, b. 23 Mar 1885, Portsmouth, NH.
    iii.   HARRIET M SPINNEY, b. 01 Jul 1888.

1011. CHARLES HAMILTON[8] SPINNEY (*HAMILTON[7], FRANCIS[6], GEORGE PETTEGREW[5], JOHN[4], JOHN[3], JOHN[2], THOMAS[1]*) was born 02 Nov 1859 in Kittery, ME, and died 05 Apr 1936 in Dover, NH. He married CLARA MARYA DARLING 02 Oct 1887. She was born 1864 in Marlone, NY, and died Aft. 1920.

Children of CHARLES SPINNEY and CLARA DARLING are:
    i.   CHARLES HERBERT[9] SPINNEY, b. Abt. 1890.

       ii.   ALTA ARAMINE SPINNEY, b. Abt. 1890.
      iii.   FANNIE MAY SPINNEY, b. 07 Mar 1890, Wakefield, NH.
      iv.   HAROLD HAMILTON SPINNEY, b. 12 Aug 1894, Wolfboro, NH; d. 05 Jul 1961, Tehama, CA; m. MARGARET ELEANORA LARSEN.
      v.   JAMES LESLIE SPINNEY, b. 07 Mar 1898, Wolfeboro, NH.

1012. MARCIA MELINDA[8] SPINNEY *(HAMILTON[7], FRANCIS[6], GEORGE PETTEGREW[5], JOHN[4], JOHN[3], JOHN[2], THOMAS[1])* was born 01 Sep 1861 in Eliot, ME, and died 1937. She married WILLIAM A SHAPLEIGH. He was born Jul 1859, and died 1932.

Children of MARCIA SPINNEY and WILLIAM SHAPLEIGH are:
        i.   ROSCOE A[9] SHAPLEIGH, b. Apr 1882.
        ii.   NELLIE M SHAPLEIGH, b. Sep 1884.
       iii.   LETTIE A SHAPLEIGH, b. Feb 1886.
1317.   iv.   BESSIE A SHAPLEIGH, b. Jan 1889.
       v.   FLORENCE M SHAPLEIGH, b. Aug 1891.
       vi.   HARRY H SHAPLEIGH, b. Mar 1894.
      vii.   HENRY W SHAPLEIGH, b. Dec 1895.
     viii.   MARTHA L SHAPLEIGH, b. Jan 1898; d. 04 Oct 1898.
       ix.   EARL A SHAPLEIGH, b. Oct 1899.

1013. FLORENCE OLIVIA[8] SPINNEY *(HAMILTON[7], FRANCIS[6], GEORGE PETTEGREW[5], JOHN[4], JOHN[3], JOHN[2], THOMAS[1])* was born Oct 1869, and died Aft. 1900. She married GEORGE W URCH, son of EPHRAIM URCH and MARIA SHERMAN. He was born Jul 1860, and died Aft. 1900.

Children of FLORENCE SPINNEY and GEORGE URCH are:
        i.   LELAND[9] URCH, b. 03 Sep 1892; d. Jul 1973.
        ii.   GEORGE URCH, b. Apr 1899.
       iii.   JOHN W URCH, b. 1903.

1014. SADIE R[8] SPINNEY *(HAMILTON[7], FRANCIS[6], GEORGE PETTEGREW[5], JOHN[4], JOHN[3], JOHN[2], THOMAS[1])* was born 21 Apr 1864, and died 12 Feb 1931. She married (1) MCKENNEY. She married (2) HARRIS E SPINNEY 1898, son of HENRY SPINNEY and OLIVE NEWBEGIN. He was born 26 Mar 1868 in Eliot, Maine, and died 22 Mar 1951 in Eliot, Maine.

Children of SADIE SPINNEY and MCKENNEY are:
1318.   i.   CHESTER ERNEST[9] MCKENNEY, b. 21 Sep 1885; d. Feb 1967.
       ii.   HARRISON LEROY MCKENNEY, b. 1888; d. Aft. 1910.

Children are listed above under (1000) Harris E Spinney.

1015. VIENNA[8] SPINNEY *(SYLVESTER[7], FRANCIS[6], GEORGE PETTEGREW[5], JOHN[4], JOHN[3], JOHN[2], THOMAS[1])* was born 1854, and died in Chelsea, MA. She married WALTER C ROGERS 03 Jul 1875, son of JOHN ROGERS and EMMA. He was born 1849, and died in Chelsea, MA.

Children of VIENNA SPINNEY and WALTER ROGERS are:
        i.   FRANK LEO[9] ROGERS, b. May 1880.
1319.   ii.   BURTON C ROGERS, b. Jan 1889.

1016. ALFRED[8] SPINNEY *(SYLVESTER[7], FRANCIS[6], GEORGE PETTEGREW[5], JOHN[4], JOHN[3], JOHN[2], THOMAS[1])* was born 04 Oct 1855, and died 12 Jan 1939. He married AURELLA COLE 1875, daughter of SAMUEL COLE and SARAH TETHERLY. She was born 02 Sep 1856, and died 24 May 1939.

Children of ALFRED SPINNEY and AURELLA COLE are:
1320.   i.   ARTHUR ROSCOE[9] SPINNEY, b. Dec 1875; d. 1951.
1321.   ii.   MILO SPINNEY, b. 07 Jan 1878; d. 06 Oct 1938.
       iii.   STELLA A SPINNEY, b. Feb 1892.
       iv.   SADIE M SPINNEY, b. Nov 1895.

1017. FRANK A[8] SPINNEY *(SYLVESTER[7], FRANCIS[6], GEORGE PETTEGREW[5], JOHN[4], JOHN[3], JOHN[2], THOMAS[1])* was born 1856, and died 1936 in Kittery Maine. He married ARBELLA COLE, daughter of SAMUEL COLE and SARAH TETHERLY. She was born 1858, and died 1930.

Notes for FRANK A SPINNEY:
FRANK A. SPINNEY, a mason contractor at Portsmouth, New Hampshire, enjoys a prosperous business in this city, where his entire business career thus far has been spent. He has been engaged in contracting some ten or twelve years, but has been working out of the same shop since 1875 when he began his apprenticeship. He employs from twelve to eighteen men, and the fact that he is always busy bespeaks the confidence of the people in his work and their regard for his ability.

Mr. Spinney was born in York County, Maine, in 1856 and was one of seven children born to Sylvester and Mary A. (Urch) Spinney. The father was born in Maine and was a cabinet maker by trade. The mother was a native of England. Mrs. Spinney is now deceased and is survived by her husband.

Frank A. Spinney attended the public schools first, and later Elliot Academy. He then learned the trade of a mason, which he has followed continuously since. He married Arabella F. Cole, who was born in Eliot and is a daughter of Samuel and Sarah (Tutherly) Cole. Her father was a fish merchant at Portsmouth although his residence was in Eliot, Me. Three children have blessed this union, Elroy, Annie M., and Alice B., who was the wife of Patrick Powers and died when twenty-two years of age. Annie M. is the wife of Arthur Lewis and they have a daughter, Mazie B. Mr. Spinney is a Republican in politics. Fraternally he is a member of the Odd Fellows and of the Pilgrim Fathers. The family attends the Advent Church.

Children of FRANK SPINNEY and ARBELLA COLE are:
        i.   ELROY S[9] SPINNEY, b. Nov 1880; d. 1941, Kittery Maine.
        ii. ALICE B SPINNEY, b. Aug 1883, Eliot, ME; d. 20 Aug 1905, Eliot, ME; m. PATRICK POWERS.
1322.   iii. ANNIE M SPINNEY, b. May 1881.

1018. MELVILLE SYLVESTER[8] SPINNEY *(SYLVESTER[7], FRANCIS[6], GEORGE PETTEGREW[5], JOHN[4], JOHN[3], JOHN[2], THOMAS[1])* was born 1858, and died 1930. He married GENIEVA A STAPLES. She was born 1860, and died 1915.

Children of MELVILLE SPINNEY and GENIEVA STAPLES are:
        i.   LESLIE MELVILLE[9] SPINNEY, b. 1883; d. 1911.
1323.   ii. GENIEVA EVANGELINE SPINNEY, b. 1896; d. Jan 1973, Winchester, MA.
        iii. ARCHER LEE SPINNEY, b. 1881.

1019. GEORGE E[8] SPINNEY *(SYLVESTER[7], FRANCIS[6], GEORGE PETTEGREW[5], JOHN[4], JOHN[3], JOHN[2], THOMAS[1])* was born Jul 1863, and died 1933. He married CORA DAVIS. She was born Aug 1867, and died 1940.

Children of GEORGE SPINNEY and CORA DAVIS are:
        i.   SHERMAN A[9] SPINNEY, b. Dec 1888.
        ii. LAWRENCE P SPINNEY, b. Mar 1889; m. ELLA M WILLEY, 19 May 1917, Maine.
        iii. JEANNIE SPINNEY, b. Jun 1891.
        iv. DORIS M SPINNEY, b. Apr 1897.

1020. ALBERT LESTER[8] SPINNEY *(SYLVESTER[7], FRANCIS[6], GEORGE PETTEGREW[5], JOHN[4], JOHN[3], JOHN[2], THOMAS[1])* was born 06 May 1875, and died 19 Apr 1969. He married SADIE BELL STAPLES 1898. She was born Jun 1879.

Children of ALBERT SPINNEY and SADIE STAPLES are:
1324.   i.   ARNOLD CLAYTON[9] SPINNEY, b. 22 Feb 1900; d. 31 Jan 2000, Manchester, NH.
        ii. MARJORIE SPINNEY, b. 05 Mar 1924, York Co, ME; d. 17 Mar 1924, York Co, ME.

iii.   ALBERT S SPINNEY, b. 1905.
iv.   GERTRUDE SPINNEY, b. 1902; m. FREDERICK A SHAPLEIGH; b. 1901, Eliot, ME.
v.   MILTON E SPINNEY, b. 1905.

1021. AMMI ADVILLE[8] SPINNEY *(FRANCIS LEMUEL[7], FRANCIS[6], GEORGE PETTEGREW[5], JOHN[4], JOHN[3], JOHN[2], THOMAS[1])* was born 1868, and died 1932. He married LIDA. She was born 1873, and died 1958.

Notes for AMMI ADVILLE SPINNEY:
When Advill and Elsie were first married they lived with his parents at 15 Main Street. They rented for a time and later purchased a home which is still standing as of 1991. The road, which was originally the driveway of the home, ran from Main Street through to Pleasant Street. This is now known as Cove Road. In later years they purchased a home at 9 Bolt Hill Road which also still stands as of 1991 although the original barns, hen houses and garage have been razed. When their fAmily was all grown they sold this large farm and rented until purchasing a house at 112 Main Street which is still owned by Elsie as of 1991.

Advill worked for the Portsmouth Naval Shipyard (now called Kittery Naval Shipyard). He hired in as an apprentice plumber and worked his way through the ranks to retire with the title of Master of Public Works. When Advill and Elsie lived in the house on what is now Cove Road, Elsie's father Ernest Wood moved in with them and the two men established a poultry business known as Riverside Poultry Farm. Besides working on the Navy Yard and helping run the poultry farm Advill kept cows and pigs and had gardens which supplied most of the fAmilies table foods.

Advill served as fire chief in the towns voluntary fire department for many years. He was one of the men who fought for, and saw built, the first Eliot High School gymnasium. He was active in the South Eliot Methodist Church and the Eliot Lions Club. In March 1954, at town meeting, Advill was given the Fabyan Drake Memorial Award for Outstanding Citizen. He was the first citizen to receive this award which is still presented yearly to a citizen of Eliot ME.

Children of AMMI SPINNEY and LIDA are:
       i.   WALLACE F[9] SPINNEY, b. 1900; d. 1900.
      ii.   HARRY S SPINNEY, b. 1901; d. 1915.
1325.   iii.   ADVILLE A SPINNEY, b. 1898.

1022. LEONORA[8] SPINNEY *(FRANCIS LEMUEL[7], FRANCIS[6], GEORGE PETTEGREW[5], JOHN[4], JOHN[3], JOHN[2], THOMAS[1])* was born 1875. She married JACOBSON.

Child of LEONORA SPINNEY and JACOBSON is:
       i.   ELEANOR[9] JACOBSON, b. 1916.

1023. PEARL[8] SPINNEY *(FRANCIS LEMUEL[7], FRANCIS[6], GEORGE PETTEGREW[5], JOHN[4], JOHN[3], JOHN[2], THOMAS[1])* was born 05 Aug 1875, and died 1943. He married HANNA MINA. She was born 1879, and died 1969.

Children of PEARL SPINNEY and HANNA MINA are:
       i.   TREOLA[9] SPINNEY, b. Apr 1896.
1326.   ii.   ARTHUR E SPINNEY, b. Oct 1897; d. 1968.
      iii.   LIZZIE E SPINNEY, b. Oct 1899; d. 1970; m. HAROLD CLARK; b. 1902; d. 1974.

1024. MYRON E[8] SPINNEY *(HENRY HOWARD[7], FRANCIS[6], GEORGE PETTEGREW[5], JOHN[4], JOHN[3], JOHN[2], THOMAS[1])* was born 1869, and died 1924. He married BERTHA P SPINNEY 14 Oct 1892, daughter of ROBERT SPINNEY and MARTHA COLE. She was born 1870, and died 1929.

Children are listed above under (834) Bertha P Spinney.

1025. ANNIE R[8] COLE *(SARAH[7] TETHERLY, CHARLES[6], SAMUEL[5], WILLIAM[4], MERCY[3] SPINNEY, JOHN[2], THOMAS[1])* was born 1845, and died 1877. She married SAMUEL A TOBEY. He was born 1841.

Children of ANNIE COLE and SAMUEL TOBEY are:
    i.   IDA[9] TOBEY.
    ii. WILLIE TOBEY.
    iii. SAMUEL O TOBEY.
    iv. RALPH TOBEY.

1026. HENRY C[8] COLE *(SARAH[7] TETHERLY, CHARLES[6], SAMUEL[5], WILLIAM[4], MERCY[3] SPINNEY, JOHN[2], THOMAS[1])* was born 1847. He married ELIZAABETH.

Children of HENRY COLE and ELIZAABETH are:
    i.   ERNEST[9] COLE.
    ii. ELIZABETH COLE.
    iii. CHARLES COLE.

1027. SAMUEL E[8] COLE *(SARAH[7] TETHERLY, CHARLES[6], SAMUEL[5], WILLIAM[4], MERCY[3] SPINNEY, JOHN[2], THOMAS[1])* was born 1852. He married ELLA.

Child of SAMUEL COLE and ELLA is:
    i.   CYRUS[9] COLE.

1028. AURELLA[8] COLE *(SARAH[7] TETHERLY, CHARLES[6], SAMUEL[5], WILLIAM[4], MERCY[3] SPINNEY, JOHN[2], THOMAS[1])* was born 02 Sep 1856, and died 24 May 1939. She married ALFRED SPINNEY 1875, son of SYLVESTER SPINNEY and MARY URCH. He was born 04 Oct 1855, and died 12 Jan 1939.

Children are listed above under (1016) Alfred Spinney.

1029. ARBELLA[8] COLE *(SARAH[7] TETHERLY, CHARLES[6], SAMUEL[5], WILLIAM[4], MERCY[3] SPINNEY, JOHN[2], THOMAS[1])* was born 1858, and died 1930. She married FRANK A SPINNEY, son of SYLVESTER SPINNEY and MARY URCH. He was born 1856, and died 1936 in Kittery Maine.

Notes for FRANK A SPINNEY:
FRANK A. SPINNEY, a mason contractor at Portsmouth, New Hampshire, enjoys a prosperous business in this city, where his entire business career thus far has been spent. He has been engaged in contracting some ten or twelve years, but has been working out of the same shop since 1875 when he began his apprenticeship. He employs from twelve to eighteen men, and the fact that he is always busy bespeaks the confidence of the people in his work and their regard for his ability.

  Mr. Spinney was born in York County, Maine, in 1856 and was one of seven children born to Sylvester and Mary A. (Urch) Spinney. The father was born in Maine and was a cabinet maker by trade. The mother was a native of England. Mrs. Spinney is now deceased and is survived by her husband.

 Frank A. Spinney attended the public schools first, and later Elliot Academy. He then learned the trade of a mason, which he has followed continuously since. He married Arabella F. Cole, who was born in Eliot and is a daughter of Samuel and Sarah (Tutherly) Cole. Her father was a fish merchant at Portsmouth although his residence was in Eliot, Me. Three children have blessed this union, Elroy, Annie M., and Alice B., who was the wife of Patrick Powers and died when twenty-two years of age. Annie M. is the wife of Arthur Lewis and they have a daughter, Mazie B. Mr. Spinney is a Republican in politics. Fraternally he is a member of the Odd Fellows and of the Pilgrim Fathers. The family attends the Advent Church.

Children are listed above under (1017) Frank A Spinney.

1030. CHARLES H.[8] DIXON *(LYDIA N.[7] TETHERLY, CHARLES[6], SAMUEL[5], WILLIAM[4], MERCY[3] SPINNEY, JOHN[2], THOMAS[1])* was born 06 Dec 1846, and died 1894. He married ANNIE.

Children of CHARLES DIXON and ANNIE are:
  i.   ANNIE[9] DIXON.
  ii. CARRIE DIXON.

1031. ADRIANNA A.[8] DIXON *(LYDIA N.[7] TETHERLY, CHARLES[6], SAMUEL[5], WILLIAM[4], MERCY[3] SPINNEY, JOHN[2], THOMAS[1])* was born 14 Oct 1850. She married CHARLES H COLE.

Children of ADRIANNA DIXON and CHARLES COLE are:
  i.   LULU[9] COLE, b. 1870.
  ii. MARY COLE, b. 1875.

1032. MARY EVA[8] DIXON *(LYDIA N.[7] TETHERLY, CHARLES[6], SAMUEL[5], WILLIAM[4], MERCY[3] SPINNEY, JOHN[2], THOMAS[1])* was born 06 Dec 1856 in South Eliot, ME, and died 19 May 1932 in South Eliot, ME. She married CHARLES E. HUNTRESS 21 Sep 1875 in Eliot, ME. He was born 09 Feb 1853 in Eliot, ME, and died 08 Dec 1916 in Eliot, ME.

Children of MARY DIXON and CHARLES HUNTRESS are:
  i.   FRED W.[9] HUNTRESS, b. 29 Feb 1876.
  ii.   EDWIN D. HUNTRESS, b. 29 Feb 1876.
1327. iii. ALTIE A. HUNTRESS, b. 31 Jul 1877.
1328. iv.   GRACE M. HUNTRESS, b. 25 Dec 1881.
1329. v.   FLORENCE WINIFRED HUNTRESS, b. 20 Dec 1884, Eliot, ME; d. 14 Nov 1972, Webster, MA.
       vi.   EVA L. HUNTRESS, b. 12 Sep 1887; d. 1918.
       vii. CHARLIE B. HUNTRESS, b. 05 Jul 1890; d. 20 Nov 1960.
       viii. HARLON E. HUNTRESS, b. 12 May 1895.

1033. ARTHUR FRANCIS[8] LYDSTON *(FRANCIS ARTHUR[7], WILLIAM[6], WEYMOUTH[5], ABIGAIL[4] SPINNEY, ANDREW[3], JOHN[2], THOMAS[1])* was born Abt. 1844 in Newburyport MA, and died 1892 in San Jose, CA. He married MARY ANN KNAPP 29 Nov 1865 in Racine Wisconsin, daughter of HORACE KNAPP and LUCRETIA DICKERSON.

Children of ARTHUR LYDSTON and MARY KNAPP are:
1330. i.   LILLIAN MAUD[9] LYDSTON, b. 28 Dec 1866, Racine, WI; d. 08 Jan 1950, Sacramento, CA.
       ii. CLARENCE LYDSTON, b. Abt. 1883.

1034. IVAH WELLINGTON[8] SPINNEY *(HENRY DAME[7], JACOB REMICK[6], JEREMIAH[5], JOHN[4], JOHN[3], JOHN[2], THOMAS[1])* was born 07 Jun 1879 in Eliot, ME, and died 1963 in Rockhingham C0 NH. He married BERTHA FRANCIS JOHNSON FERNALD, daughter of PETER JOHNSON and MARY JOHNSON. She was born 14 Aug 1883 in Rockhingham Co NH, and died 29 Jan 1966 in Rockhingham Co NH.

Children of IVAH SPINNEY and BERTHA FERNALD are:
       i.   IRVING W[9] SPINNEY.
       ii. ERNEST O SPINNEY, b. 1909.
1331. iii. AGNES SPINNEY, b. Abt. 1900.
1332. iv. JOHN EDWARD SPINNEY, b. 1913, Rockingham CO, NH; d. 20 Jun 2000.

1035. GEORGIANNA[8] NICKERSON *(ZILPHA[7] SPINNEY, DAVID[6], ISAAC[5], JOHN[4], JOHN[3], JOHN[2], THOMAS[1])* was born 1844. She married JAMES WELLNER. He was born 1839 in Nova Scotia.

Children of GEORGIANNA NICKERSON and JAMES WELLNER are:
  i.   GEO S[9] WELLNER, b. 1880, Nova Scotia.
  ii.   JOSEPH H WELLNER, b. 1882, Connecticut.
  iii. MOLLIE B WELLNER, b. 1884, Rhode Island.
  iv.   GEORGEIA C WELLNER, b. 1887, Massachusetts.

1036. ALLISON FAIRBANKS[8] SPINNEY *(HIRAM[7], DAVID[6], ISAAC[5], JOHN[4], JOHN[3], JOHN[2], THOMAS[1])* was born 03 Nov 1853, and died Aft. 1930. He married EFFIE GRACE CROWELL 21 Apr 1877. She was born 26 Oct 1860.

Children of ALLISON SPINNEY and EFFIE CROWELL are:
1333.	i.	AMY BELLE[9] SPINNEY, b. 06 Jul 1879.
	ii.	VESTA MAY SPINNEY, b. 18 Oct 1881.
1334.	iii.	ALMA EDITH SPINNEY, b. 14 Sep 1883.
	iv.	GEORGE ALLISON SPINNEY, b. 15 Aug 1887.
	v.	JENNIE ESTELLA SPINNEY, b. 07 Nov 1888.
1335.	vi.	LLOYD ELLSWORTH SPINNEY, b. 14 Nov 1889, Nova Scotia; d. 17 Dec 1949.
1336.	vii.	IVAN HAROLD SPINNEY, b. 22 Jun 1892.

1037. ESTELLA BERTILLA[8] SPINNEY *(HIRAM[7], DAVID[6], ISAAC[5], JOHN[4], JOHN[3], JOHN[2], THOMAS[1])* was born 23 Jul 1857 in Argyle, NS.. She married NATHAN GOODWIN 21 Dec 1880 in Argyle, NS., son of WILLOUGHBY GOODWIN and ELEANOR GAYTON. He was born 1857.

Children of ESTELLA SPINNEY and NATHAN GOODWIN are:
	i.	ERVIN[9] GOODWIN.
	ii.	LINFORD GOODWIN, m. KATHERINE CURLEY.
	iii.	VIVA GOODWIN.
	iv.	MARION G GOODWIN.
	v.	DAVID GOODWIN.

1038. ERVIN H[8] SPINNEY *(HIRAM[7], DAVID[6], ISAAC[5], JOHN[4], JOHN[3], JOHN[2], THOMAS[1])* was born 20 Jul 1860. He married DEBORAH. She was born 13 Dec 1860.

Children of ERVIN SPINNEY and DEBORAH are:
| | i. | CLARA[9] SPINNEY, b. 20 Oct 1894; m. MORTON LANGTHORN, 1914. |
| | ii. | LETHA SPINNEY, b. 1896. |

1039. GEORGE N[8] SPINNEY *(HIRAM[7], DAVID[6], ISAAC[5], JOHN[4], JOHN[3], JOHN[2], THOMAS[1])* was born 28 Sep 1865 in Nova Scotia, and died Aft. 1900 in Malden, MA. He married MINNIE THOMPSON 1885. She was born Jan 1863, and died Aft. 1900.

Children of GEORGE SPINNEY and MINNIE THOMPSON are:
	i.	OSCAR P[9] SPINNEY, b. Dec 1886.
	ii.	CHESTER E SPINNEY, b. Aug 1892.
	iii.	ALICE LOUISE SPINNEY, b. Oct 1898.
1337.	iv.	EDITH MABEL SPINNEY, b. 25 Jan 1905.
	v.	ARTHUR G SPINNEY, b. 1908, Malden, MA.

1040. LEROY B[8] SPINNEY *(HIRAM[7], DAVID[6], ISAAC[5], JOHN[4], JOHN[3], JOHN[2], THOMAS[1])* was born Abt. 1870 in Central Argyle, NS.. He married (1) JOSEPHINE GOODWIN 07 Mar 1892. He married (2) MARGARET B (MAGGIE) GOODWIN 28 Dec 1904 in Yarmouth, NS., daughter of THOMAS GOODWIN and MARY CROWELL. She was born 13 Jun 1882 in Argyle, NS..

Children of LEROY SPINNEY and MARGARET GOODWIN are:
	i.	DONALD[9] SPINNEY, b. Abt. 1898, Yarmouth, NS..
	ii.	STELLA SPINNEY, b. Abt. 1900, Yarmouth, NS..
1338.	iii.	EDYTH SPINNEY, b. 1906, Yarmouth, NS.; d. 31 Mar 1997, Worcester, MA.

1041. ARDELLA S[8] NEVENS *(SOPHRONIA L[7] SPINNEY, DAVID[6], ISAAC[5], JOHN[4], JOHN[3], JOHN[2], THOMAS[1])* was born 1854 in Boston, Ma. She married WINTHROP PERKINS. He was born 1837 in Calais, ME.

Children of ARDELLA NEVENS and WINTHROP PERKINS are:
| | i. | CHARLES[9] PERKINS. |

ii.   DAISEY PERKINS.

1042. LYDIA[8] SPINNEY *(LYMAN[7], BENJAMIN[6], BENJAMIN[5], JOHN[4], JOHN[3], JOHN[2], THOMAS[1])* was born 09 Dec 1855, and died 1926 in Barrington, Shelburne, Nova Scotia, Canada. She married GILBERT CROWELL 1874, son of NATHAN CROWELL and ANN CROWELL. He was born 1846 in Barrington, Shelburne, Nova Scotia, Canada, and died 1920 in Barrington, Shelburne, Nova Scotia, Canada.

Children of LYDIA SPINNEY and GILBERT CROWELL are:
  i.   ETHEL B[9] CROWELL, b. 01 Jun 1877; d. 1950, Barrington, Shelburne, Nova Scotia, Canada.
  ii.   CLARA CROWELL, b. 1879.
  iii. MARY CROWELL, b. 1880.
  iv.   WILLIAM R CROWELL, b. 19 Oct 1883.
  v.   BESSIE CROWELL, b. 23 Apr 1886.
  vi.   G SHIRLEY CROWELL, b. 10 Mar 1888, Barrington, Shelburne, Nova Scotia, Canada; d. 19 Mar 1978, Barrington, Shelburne, Nova Scotia, Canada.
  vii. MARION CROWELL, b. 28 Jun 1890.
  viii. STELLA B CROWELL, b. 1881, Barrington, Shelburne, Nova Scotia, Canada; d. 1959, Barrington, Shelburne, Nova Scotia, Canada.
  ix.   ELIZABETH CROWELL.

1043. ENOS[8] SPINNEY *(SIMEON[7], BENJAMIN[6], BENJAMIN[5], JOHN[4], JOHN[3], JOHN[2], THOMAS[1])* was born 1857 in Canada, and died Aft. 1930 in Massachusetts. He married PININA 1885. She was born 1862.

Children of ENOS SPINNEY and PININA are:
  i.   RALPH E[9] SPINNEY, b. 1888.
1339. ii.   EDWIN L SPINNEY, b. 07 Jul 1889, Boothbay Harbor, ME; d. 26 Sep 1976, Boothbay Harbor, ME.
  iii. HENRY E SPINNEY, b. 1891.
  iv.   BERTHA L SPINNEY, b. 1894.

1044. EMERSON E[8] SPINNEY *(SIMEON[7], BENJAMIN[6], BENJAMIN[5], JOHN[4], JOHN[3], JOHN[2], THOMAS[1])* was born 1863, and died 01 Dec 1942 in Skagit, WA. He married (1) RUTH FLYNN. She died Bef. 1920. He married (2) SYBIL. She was born 1881, and died 13 Sep 1942.

Children of EMERSON SPINNEY and RUTH FLYNN are:
  i.   JOHN E[9] SPINNEY, b. Oct 1888; m. ALMY.
  ii.   RUTH SPINNEY, b. Oct 1892.
  iii. HAZEL SPINNEY, b. 1894.
  iv.   MARION SPINNEY, b. Jun 1895.
  v.   GRACE SPINNEY, b. Jul 1897.

1045. BENJAMIN H[8] SPINNEY *(JONATHAN[7], BENJAMIN[6], BENJAMIN[5], JOHN[4], JOHN[3], JOHN[2], THOMAS[1])* was born 31 Dec 1858, and died Mar 1930. He married FOSTINA 1885. She was born 02 Sep 1857, and died Nov 1938.

Child of BENJAMIN SPINNEY and FOSTINA is:
  i.   LILLIAN V[9] SPINNEY, b. 27 Mar 1886; d. Mar 1971.

1046. ALICE ESTELLE[8] SPINNEY *(JONATHAN[7], BENJAMIN[6], BENJAMIN[5], JOHN[4], JOHN[3], JOHN[2], THOMAS[1])* was born Apr 1872, and died 1944. She married GEORGE PARSONS. He was born Feb 1865.

Children of ALICE SPINNEY and GEORGE PARSONS are:
  i.   ROY[9] PARSONS, b. Jun 1893.
  ii.   EVERETT PARSONS, b. May 1895.
  iii. WALLACE A PARSONS, b. 1901.

1047. WALLACE CLIFFORD[8] SPINNEY *(JONATHAN[7], BENJAMIN[6], BENJAMIN[5], JOHN[4], JOHN[3], JOHN[2], THOMAS[1])* was born 19 Dec 1874. He married JOSEPHINE HATFIELD WESTON 1902 in Brookfield.

Children of WALLACE SPINNEY and JOSEPHINE WESTON are:
- i. ELIZABETH[9] SPINNEY, b. Abt. 1900, Worcester, Ma.
- ii. ALICE SPINNEY, b. 1905, Worcester, MA.

1048. ALBERT L[8] SPINNEY *(HARRIS"CAPT" HARDING[7], BENJAMIN[6], BENJAMIN[5], JOHN[4], JOHN[3], JOHN[2], THOMAS[1])* was born 1858 in Massachusetts, and died Bet. 1910 - 1930. He married ELLA M BURGESS 1887 in Weymouth, Ma. She was born 1859, and died Aft. 1932.

Children of ALBERT SPINNEY and ELLA BURGESS are:

1340.	i.	BURGESS HARRIS[9] SPINNEY, b. 09 Feb 1889, Weymouth, MA; d. Jul 1971.
1341.	ii.	CECIL LAWRENCE SPINNEY, b. 23 Dec 1890, Hingham, Ma; d. Aft. 1930.

1049. SIDNEY H[8] SPINNEY *(REUBEN HAWES[7], REUBEN[6], ISAAC[5], JOHN[4], JOHN[3], JOHN[2], THOMAS[1])* was born 04 Apr 1870, and died 1925. He married ELIZABETH FUER. She was born 1868, and died 1957.

Child of SIDNEY SPINNEY and ELIZABETH FUER is:
- i. ANNIE[9] SPINNEY.

1050. ALICE A[8] SPINNEY *(REUBEN HAWES[7], REUBEN[6], ISAAC[5], JOHN[4], JOHN[3], JOHN[2], THOMAS[1])* was born 25 Jul 1872 in Argyle, NS., and died 31 Jul 1899. She married FRANK MILLER EMERY 02 Aug 1890 in Kittery Maine.

Child of ALICE SPINNEY and FRANK EMERY is:
- i. RALPH BENTON[9] EMERY, b. 18 Feb 1891, 19 Apr 1943; m. EDITH ADA STUBBS.

1051. CHARLES EMERY[8] SPINNEY *(REUBEN HAWES[7], REUBEN[6], ISAAC[5], JOHN[4], JOHN[3], JOHN[2], THOMAS[1])* was born 13 Dec 1880 in Sanford, ME, and died Feb 1951. He married PRUDENCE ASHWORTH. She was born 1880, and died 1959.

Child of CHARLES SPINNEY and PRUDENCE ASHWORTH is:
- i. ARLINE CHADWICK[9] SPINNEY, b. 1907; m. ARTHUR L THOMPSON; b. 1909.

1052. NELLIE SOPHIA[8] SPINNEY *(JAMES EMERY[7], REUBEN[6], ISAAC[5], JOHN[4], JOHN[3], JOHN[2], THOMAS[1])* was born 17 Sep 1884 in Nova Scotia, Canada, and died 1957. She married RUPERT VAN EMBURG, son of JAMES VAN AMBURG and ELIZA KENNEY.

Children of NELLIE SPINNEY and RUPERT VAN EMBURG are:
- i. RUSSELL[9] VAN EMBURG.
- ii. HELEN VAN EMBURG.
- iii. EVELYN VAN EMBURG.
- iv. KEITH VAN EMBURG.
- v. LENLY VAN EMBURG.
- vi. EDWIN VAN EMBURG.

1053. NEHEMIAH[8] SPINNEY *(MINOR H[7], MINOR[6], WILLIAM[5], JOHN[4], JOHN[3], JOHN[2], THOMAS[1])* was born 19 Aug 1866, and died 1927. He married MYRTIE ROWE 17 Dec 1890.

Notes for NEHEMIAH SPINNEY:
Fram Maine a History pg 438

Nehemiah Spinney - Haivng been connected with Catering and Allied pursuits for more thatn 35 years, the late Nehemiah Spinney was perhaps one of the most prominent figures in the department of Business in the State of Maine

Children of NEHEMIAH SPINNEY and MYRTIE ROWE are:
- i. CARRIE BERNICE[9] SPINNEY, b. 12 Nov 1891.
- ii. EVELYN SPINNEY, b. 03 Jan 1894.

iii.   LUCILLE SPINNEY, b. 25 May 1910.

1054. ORETHA F[8] SPINNEY *(CALVIN CANN[7], JOHN[6], AARON[5], JOHN[4], JOHN[3], JOHN[2], THOMAS[1])* was born 1875 in Yarmouth, NS., and died 1945 in Gloucester, MA. She married LEMUEL E SPINNEY 19 Oct 1893 in Yarmouth, NS., son of CALEB SPINNEY and HANNAH SMITH. He was born 1865 in Argyle, NS., and died Aft. 1930 in Gloucester, Ma.

Notes for LEMUEL E SPINNEY:

April 15, 1903
Witnesses by Three Halibuters on Peak of Quero
Capt. Spinney of Dictator Tells the Story
It Seemed as Though Fire Rained From Above
A weird, uncanny tale of the sea is that which Capt. Lemuel Spinney of the sch. Dictator tells. The vessel arrived yesterday with a fare of halibut and today Capt. Spinney is relating to his friends a story which, as he says himself, seems almost incredible. To use his own words in regard to it, "If I had been on deck alone and witnessed it, I would hardly have dared tell my crew for they would surely have thought that I was crazy or trying to fool them." As exaggeration is not in Capt. Spinney's dictionary it is safe to say that the tale he tells is free from embellishment and flights of fancy -- just the plain unvarnished truth of an occurrence awful and almost beyond comprehension.
When asked to tell his story for the benefit of the public, Capt. Spinney said "I will gladly tell you, but I couldn't blame anybody if they didn't believe it. I saw it and yet I can hardly realize it."
The story as told by Capt. Spinney is to the effect that his vessel, in company with the Arbitrator, commanded by his brother Wilson and the Monitor, Capt. McCuish, were fishing on March 29 on the southeast peak of Quero. The day promised fair, but turned out bad. The Arbitrator was to an anchor with her riding sail set, while the Monitor and Dictator were jogging, standing off and on around her.
Big black clouds began to roll upon the horizon and in a very short space of time the heavens were blackened and darkness almost of evening spread about. It looked just like a terrible thunder storm of mid-summer and such it proved to be -- the most terrible thunder storm ever heard of.
With the rising cloud the wind began to pick up and blew fitfully in little sharp gusts from every direction of the compass and steadily gaining in strength until at the climax of the storm, they were squalls, the like of which in spitefulness, fury and strength Capt. Spinney never before experienced.
The rain came and with it thunder and lightning. It rained hard, then it hailed hard - was no name for it. So fiercely did it hail that he particles did not have time to melt when they struck the water, but just se4emed at saturate through and formed on the surface, looking just like a field of slob ice or slush, such as is seen in winter time. The vessel was jogging all this time and Capt. Spinney says the sight of so much hail on the water looking like ice, can better be imagined than described.
Then the storm began to come nearer and nearer and still it rained and hailed. The thunder seemed only over head and came directly with the lightning. Capt. Spinney was on deck with three of his crew when there came an awful crash. It seemed as if everything was tumbling. With it came a flash, and such a flash! Capt. Spinney says it wasn't a flash, but a great livid sheet of flame almost blinding to the sight. It struck the water not 100 feet out ahead of the vessel and instantly the water there was white with foam and sparks of fire flew in all directions about the vessel. The air seemed full of sparks.
Capt. Spinney was speechless. He looked at his men and wondered if they saw what he did. Their faces showed plainly that they had. All went below and told the rest of the crew. Most of them were skeptical and laughed, but the quartet stuck to their story and finally all hands came on deck, as Capt. Spinney said "to watch for one of them things."
The thunder still roared and lightning played about. The squalls were coming more and more fierce and some sail was taken in. Suddenly, giving no warning, came another of those awful crashed and simultaneously another sheet of flame and sparks descended from above, and struck the water, acting about the same as did its terrible predecessor. Capt. Spinney says it was awful and beyond description. The crew, all hands, saw. They were convinced and farther than that, they all went below quickly. They had seen enough and didn't wish another such close acquaintance with descending fire.
After this came some severe squalls and all hands were needed on deck as care and quick action meant much should one hit the vessel fair. One big squall, blacker than all the rest and fiercer was seen coming and things looked serious. Capt. Spinney says it piled the water straight up in front of it at least three feet in the air and like a moving white wall rushed on threatening destruction to everything in its path. It crossed the bow of the Dictator, not 25 yards ahead and passed by, but those on the Dictator saw that it was headed in the direction of the

Arbitrator, at anchor near by, with her riding sail set. It struck the latter vessel fair and with full force. The sheets on the riding sail parted and are going yet, while the sail went over the side. The vessel heeled down till it seemed that she would surely be hove on her beam ends and then righted as the squall passed. Capt. Wilson Spinney said that if it had struck his vessel with bank sail on, it would have taken the spars out of her.

While the thunder storm lasted two more of those awful visitations of fire came with their terrible noise and crash. Capt. Spinney does not hesitate to say that he and his men were frightened. He says frankly that he never saw or heard anything like it and that to describe it as it actually was would be impossible. He says had it happened at night he didn't know but what he would have thought that the world was coming to an end.

During the whole storm there were but four of those awful indescribable sheets of flame seen, but the memory of those will life long in the minds of the men who witnessed the phenomena.

After the storm abated, as if by common consent the captains of the Arbitrator and Monitor came on board the Dictator. Each seemed inclined to almost doubt this own eyesight, but a careful comparison of notes showed that the same phenomena, the same sheets of fire had been observed by all three captains and their crews. Capt. McCuish of the Monitor said that when the first flash came, his crew were on deck and were shortening sail. The effect of the flash was felt all over the vessel and two of the crew were knocked insensible to the deck, having been struck or at least received a severe shock from the big flash. It was some time before they were brought around.

This is the tale as Capt. Spinney tells it and that is sufficient authority for its authenticity and non-exaggeration

Children of ORETHA SPINNEY and LEMUEL SPINNEY are:
  i. CLARA J⁹ SPINNEY, b. Aug 1897.
  ii. HESTER SPINNEY, b. 1901.
1342. iii. LEMUEL E SPINNEY, b. 15 May 1902; d. Feb 1975, Gloucester, MA.
  iv. RUSSELL SPINNEY, b. 1909.

1055. CHARLES HARVEY⁸ SPINNEY (*JAMES HARVEY⁷, JOHN⁶, AARON⁵, JOHN⁴, JOHN³, JOHN², THOMAS¹*) was born 02 Feb 1884, and died Oct 1969. He married MAUDE VERRILL Aft. 1910. She was born 1885.

Children of CHARLES SPINNEY and MAUDE VERRILL are:
  i. CHARLES H⁹ SPINNEY, b. 1916, Massachusetts.
  ii. EVELYN V SPINNEY, b. 1919, Massachusetts.
  iii. DONALD SPINNEY, b. 1920, Massachusetts.
  iv. GEORGE SPINNEY, b. 1924, Massachusetts.

1056. LESLIE ATHERTON⁸ SPINNEY (*JOSEPH WILSON⁷, JOHN⁶, AARON⁵, JOHN⁴, JOHN³, JOHN², THOMAS¹*) was born Oct 1869 in Nova Scotia, and died 1912 in Provincetown, MA. He married NELLIE FRELLICK 1895. She was born Jul 1876.

Children of LESLIE SPINNEY and NELLIE FRELLICK are:
  i. BESSIE⁹ SPINNEY, b. Aug 1896.
  ii. DOROTHY SPINNEY, b. Feb 1897.
  iii. JOSEPH H SPINNEY, b. Nov 1899.
  iv. NELLIE L SPINNEY.

1057. LAURA ELLA⁸ SPINNEY (*JOSEPH WILSON⁷, JOHN⁶, AARON⁵, JOHN⁴, JOHN³, JOHN², THOMAS¹*) was born 1875 in Boston, Massachusetts, and died Aft. 1930. She married FRED W WILSON 1895 in Boston, MA.

Children of LAURA SPINNEY and FRED WILSON are:
  i. VESTA⁹ WILSON.
  ii. GERTRUDE WILSON.
  iii. ROBERT WILSON.
  iv. AGNES WILSON.
  v. HAZEL WILSON.
  vi. RICHARD WILSON.
  vii. PHILIP WILSON.

1058. CLEMENT⁸ WHITMAN (*JACOB⁷, SPINNEY⁶, ANNIE⁵ SPINNEY, JOHN⁴, JOHN³, JOHN², THOMAS¹*) He married SOPHIA WORTH.

Children of CLEMENT WHITMAN and SOPHIA WORTH are:
- i.   AUBREY^9 WHITMAN.
- ii. CLARA WHITMAN.

1059. HAVELOCK^8 SPINNEY *(MORRIS^7, JACOB^6, JACOB^5, JOHN^4, JOHN^3, JOHN^2, THOMAS^1)* was born 18 Feb 1858, and died Aft. 1901. He married NELLIE MACDONALD. She was born 05 Oct 1876.

Children of HAVELOCK SPINNEY and NELLIE MACDONALD are:
- i.   WILEY M^9 SPINNEY, b. 27 Dec 1895.
- ii.   ROBERT W SPINNEY, b. 17 May 1897.
- 1343. iii. EARL B SPINNEY, b. 07 Jan 1899; d. 29 Sep 1993.
- iv.   TILLEY SPINNEY.
- v.   VERA SPINNEY.
- 1344. vi. LAURA SPINNEY.
- vii. NELLIE SPINNEY, b. Abt. 1900.
- viii. JOHN HAVELOCK SPINNEY, b. 1904; d. 1983.

1060. SARAH^8 PALMER *(SARAH^7 SPINNEY, JACOB^6, JACOB^5, JOHN^4, JOHN^3, JOHN^2, THOMAS^1)* was born 1848 in Nova Scotia, and died 02 Apr 1929 in Roxbury, MA, USA. She married IMBERT HATFIELD 1866 in Boston, MA, son of JAMES HATFIELD and CATHERINE ELLS. He was born 03 Oct 1844 in Brookville, Ns, and died 03 Feb 1881 in Brookville, Nova Scotia, Canada.

Children of SARAH PALMER and IMBERT HATFIELD are:
- i.   SUSAN^9 HATFIELD, b. 10 Oct 1873; d. 12 Sep 1925, Melrose, Massachusetts, USA; m. (1) DAVID ROBBINS; m. (2) FRANK ISBISTER; m. (3) FRED THOMFORTH.
- ii. ALICE MAUDE HATFIELD, b. 02 Oct 1867; m. THOMAS HADLEY.
- iii. CLARA HATFIELD, b. 02 Oct 1867.
- iv. JAMES HATFIELD, b. 13 Sep 1869, Brookville, Nova Scotia, Canada; d. 26 Feb 1910, Roxbury, Massachusetts, USA.
- v.   ALMIRA HATFIELD, b. 26 Sep 1871, Brookville, Nova Scotia, Canada.

1061. FREEMAN^8 SPINNEY *(STILLMAN^7, JOSEPH^6, JACOB^5, JOHN^4, JOHN^3, JOHN^2, THOMAS^1)* was born 02 Dec 1867 in Argyle, N.S, and died 04 Mar 1934. He married MARY JANE MCGUIRE. She was born 1865.

Children of FREEMAN SPINNEY and MARY MCGUIRE are:
- i.   GEORGE^9 SPINNEY, b. Abt. 1890.
- ii. WILLIAM J SPINNEY, b. Abt. 1890; m. CATHERINE.
- iii. ELIZABETH EMELINE SPINNEY, b. 1898; d. 14 Apr 1904.
- iv. MAY ETTA SPINNEY, b. 21 Dec 1899.
- v.   HOWARD T SPINNEY, b. 18 Jan 1906; d. Aft. 1930; m. EVELYN.

1062. EMMA JANE^8 SPINNEY *(STILLMAN^7, JOSEPH^6, JACOB^5, JOHN^4, JOHN^3, JOHN^2, THOMAS^1)* was born 1870, and died 1964. She married HENRY SCANELL.

Children of EMMA SPINNEY and HENRY SCANELL are:
- i.   HENRY^9 SCANNELL.
- ii. THERESA SCANNELL.
- iii. MARION SCANNELL.
- iv. ELIZABETH SCANNELL.
- v.   HELEN SCANNELL.
- vi. JOHN JAMES SCANNELL.

1063. AGNES GERTRUDE^8 SPINNEY *(STILLMAN^7, JOSEPH^6, JACOB^5, JOHN^4, JOHN^3, JOHN^2, THOMAS^1)* was born 17 Mar 1874, and died 15 Mar 1966. She married EDWIN CROSBY VICKERY 25 Oct 1892 in Argyle Nova Scotia.

Children of AGNES SPINNEY and EDWIN VICKERY are:
- i.   ALFRETA R^9 VICKERY.

ii.   MURIEL E VICKERY.
iii. LEO H.C.R VICKERY.
iv.   MILDRED VICKERY.
v.   DOROTHY VICKERY.
vi.   LOTTIE C VICKERY.
vii. ELSIE O VICKERY.
viii. GERTRUDE LOUISE VICKERY.
ix.   ALEXANDER J VICKERY, b. 23 Mar 1898; d. 20 Dec 1918, Overseas Canadian Army.
x.   MARTHA VICKERY, b. 09 Mar 1901.

1064. LAURA MAE[8] SPINNEY *(STILLMAN[7], JOSEPH[6], JACOB[5], JOHN[4], JOHN[3], JOHN[2], THOMAS[1])* was born 03 Apr 1880 in Nova Scotia, and died 14 May 1956 in Massachusetts. She married JAMES PATRICK FORD 1901 in Watertown Mass. He was born 04 Mar 1880 in Galloway, Ireland, and died 05 Jun 1931.

Children of LAURA SPINNEY and JAMES FORD are:
1345. i.   JAMES ELMER[9] FORD, b. 19 Aug 1902, Boston, MA; d. 05 Jul 1979.
       ii.   GRACE H. FORD, b. 16 Oct 1907; d. 30 Oct 1993; m. EDWARD; d. 16 Jul 1985.
       iii. EDWARD T. FORD, b. 22 Apr 1911; d. 02 Sep 1979.
       iv.   JOHN F. FORD, b. 30 Nov 1914; d. 23 Nov 1920.
       v.   ELEANOR M. FORD, b. 04 Aug 1917; d. 07 Sep 1976; m. FRANK; d. January 13, 1986.
       vi.   MARION A. FORD, b. Private.

1065. ALICE[8] SPINNEY *(JEREMIAH[7], EBENEZER[6], JACOB[5], JOHN[4], JOHN[3], JOHN[2], THOMAS[1])* was born 07 Sep 1859. She married NELSON RYDER. He was born 1841 in Canada, and died Bef. 1880.

Child of ALICE SPINNEY and NELSON RYDER is:
       i.   NELSON[9] RYDER, b. 1881, Nova Scotia.

1066. THELSTON D[8] SPINNEY *(BENJAMIN F[7], EBENEZER[6], JACOB[5], JOHN[4], JOHN[3], JOHN[2], THOMAS[1])* was born 25 Oct 1875 in Nova Scotia, and died 13 Jun 1957. He married ADA DAKIN 05 Jul 1899 in Gloucester Mass.

Children of THELSTON SPINNEY and ADA DAKIN are:
1346. i.   EMMALINE DORIS[9] SPINNEY, b. 24 Apr 1900; d. Oct 1978.
       ii.   RALPH SEYMOUR SPINNEY, b. 22 Apr 1901; d. 1974, LaPlata, Maryland.
1347. iii. ROBERT MARTIN SPINNEY, b. 1918.

1067. ORESSA MARIA[8] SPINNEY *(BENJAMIN F[7], EBENEZER[6], JACOB[5], JOHN[4], JOHN[3], JOHN[2], THOMAS[1])* was born 05 Sep 1877, and died 30 Jan 1965. She married CHARLES JEFFREY FROST 25 Dec 1912, son of GEORGE FROST and IDA WHITEHOUSE.

Children of ORESSA SPINNEY and CHARLES FROST are:
       i.   RAYMOND ST CLAIR[9] FROST, m. LAURA ELAINE PEARL SMITH.
       ii.   RONALD FROST.
       iii. CHARLES JEFFREY FROST, m. (1) THELMA LENA STEEN; m. (2) ANNA RUTH BROWN.
1348. iv.   DONALD GENE FROST.

1068. EMERSON[8] SPINNEY *(BENJAMIN F[7], EBENEZER[6], JACOB[5], JOHN[4], JOHN[3], JOHN[2], THOMAS[1])* was born 22 Aug 1883 in Nova Scotia, and died May 1968 in Everett, MA. He married MABEL LANE. She was born 1883 in Massachusetts, and died Aft. 1930.

Child of EMERSON SPINNEY and MABEL LANE is:
       i.   SHIRLEY[9] SPINNEY, b. 1929.

1069. GEORGE WHITFIELD[8] SIMMS *(ELLEN GAYTON[7] SPINNEY, THOMAS W[6], JACOB[5], JOHN[4], JOHN[3], JOHN[2], THOMAS[1])* was born 24 Mar 1876. He married GRACE ADELINE HEMPHILL. She was born 23 Jun 1881.

Children of GEORGE SIMMS and GRACE HEMPHILL are:

i.　ALMA FERN[9] SIMMS, b. 11 Mar 1901.
　　ii.　FRANK GRAHAM SIMMS, b. 10 Feb 1905.
　iii.　LORNE WETMORE SIMMS, b. 08 May 1903.
　iv.　MARION ELLEN SIMMS, b. 05 Jun 1899.

1070. WILLIAM EDMUND[8] SPINNEY (*JACOB[7], THOMAS W[6], JACOB[5], JOHN[4], JOHN[3], JOHN[2], THOMAS[1]*) was born 09 Jun 1868 in Knolesville, NB.. He married JEANNIE CURRIE.

Children of WILLIAM SPINNEY and JEANNIE CURRIE are:
　　i.　WILLIAM ABERDEEN[9] SPINNEY, b. 1894, Frederickton, NB..
　　ii.　STELLA FERN SPINNEY, b. 05 May 1896.
　iii.　WEBSTER SPINNEY, b. 1899; d. Jan 1986.
　iv.　VICTORIA SPINNEY, b. 27 Jun 1901.

1071. ARMOND[8] HENDERSON (*MATILDA[7] SPINNEY, THOMAS W[6], JACOB[5], JOHN[4], JOHN[3], JOHN[2], THOMAS[1]*) He married SUZAN RANDOLPH.

Children of ARMOND HENDERSON and SUZAN RANDOLPH are:
　　i.　RANDOLF[9] HENDERSON.
　　ii.　ARTHUR HENDERSON.
　iii.　CHARLOTTE HENDERSON.

1072. LAURA MAE[8] SPINNEY (*JAMES[7], JAMES[6], JACOB[5], JOHN[4], JOHN[3], JOHN[2], THOMAS[1]*) was born 1856, and died Aft. 1920. She married GEORGE GOODWIN 15 Sep 1873. He was born 1835.

Children of LAURA SPINNEY and GEORGE GOODWIN are:
　　i.　ASA[9] GOODWIN, b. 1874.
　　ii.　CAROLINE GOODWIN, b. 1876.
　iii.　ETHEL GOODWIN, b. 1879.

1073. WESLEY F[8] SPINNEY (*JAMES[7], JAMES[6], JACOB[5], JOHN[4], JOHN[3], JOHN[2], THOMAS[1]*) was born 30 Sep 1857. He married (1) CAROLINE DALEY, daughter of JOHN DALEY and CLARISSA NICKERSON. He married (2) ALMIRA FLETCHER.

Children of WESLEY SPINNEY and CAROLINE DALEY are:
　　　　i.　ARTHUR[9] SPINNEY.
1349.　　ii.　CLINTON SPINNEY, b. 02 Feb 1880; d. May 1948.
　　　iii.　NORA SPINNEY, b. 1883.
1350.　　iv.　FRANK WESLEY SPINNEY, b. 13 Aug 1885, Argyle, NS.; d. 30 May 1967, Gloucester, MA..
　　　　v.　TOM SPINNEY, b. 1888.

　　　　　　Notes for TOM SPINNEY:
　　　　　　Drowned while fishing when he was young

1351.　　vi.　LOVETT ELDRIDGE SPINNEY, b. 23 Sep 1892, Pubnico, N.S.; d. 18 Jul 1972, Gloucester, MA..
　　　vii.　RUBY SPINNEY, b. 1896.

1074. LINDA[8] SPINNEY (*JAMES[7], JAMES[6], JACOB[5], JOHN[4], JOHN[3], JOHN[2], THOMAS[1]*) was born 1866 in Argyle, NS.. She married JAMES A GOODWIN.

Child of LINDA SPINNEY and JAMES GOODWIN is:
　　i.　EFFIE[9] GOODWIN, b. Oct 1890.

1075. INA[8] SPINNEY (*JAMES[7], JAMES[6], JACOB[5], JOHN[4], JOHN[3], JOHN[2], THOMAS[1]*) was born 1877 in Argyle, NS., and died 1958. She married WILLIAM CROWELL GOODWIN 12 Dec 1894 in Pubnico, NS., son of JOSHUA GOODWIN and MAHALIA NICKERSON. He was born 11 Sep 1871 in West Pubnico, NS., and died 1954.

Children of INA SPINNEY and WILLIAM GOODWIN are:
  i.   DORIS H⁹ GOODWIN, b. 05 Oct 1897, Argyle, NS.; d. 02 Dec 1900, Argyle, NS..
  ii. M ROSS GOODWIN, b. 02 Apr 1900, Argyle, NS.; d. 05 Nov 1969.
  iii. WILLIAM A GOODWIN, b. 29 Mar 1917, Argyle, NS.; d. 31 Mar 1921, Argyle, NS..

1076. LEMUEL E⁸ SPINNEY *(CALEB⁷, JAMES⁶, JACOB⁵, JOHN⁴, JOHN³, JOHN², THOMAS¹)* was born 1865 in Argyle, NS., and died Aft. 1930 in Gloucester, Ma. He married ORETHA F SPINNEY 19 Oct 1893 in Yarmouth, NS., daughter of CALVIN SPINNEY and GEORGIANNA CAMPBELL. She was born 1875 in Yarmouth, NS., and died 1945 in Gloucester, MA.

Notes for LEMUEL E SPINNEY:

April 15, 1903
Witnesses by Three Halibuters on Peak of Quero
Capt. Spinney of Dictator Tells the Story
It Seemed as Though Fire Rained From Above
A weird, uncanny tale of the sea is that which Capt. Lemuel Spinney of the sch. Dictator tells. The vessel arrived yesterday with a fare of halibut and today Capt. Spinney is relating to his friends a story which, as he says himself, seems almost incredible. To use his own words in regard to it, "If I had been on deck alone and witnessed it, I would hardly have dared tell my crew for they would surely have thought that I was crazy or trying to fool them." As exaggeration is not in Capt. Spinney's dictionary it is safe to say that the tale he tells is free from embellishment and flights of fancy -- just the plain unvarnished truth of an occurrence awful and almost beyond comprehension.
When asked to tell his story for the benefit of the public, Capt. Spinney said "I will gladly tell you, but I couldn't blame anybody if they didn't believe it. I saw it and yet I can hardly realize it."
The story as told by Capt. Spinney is to the effect that his vessel, in company with the Arbitrator, commanded by his brother Wilson and the Monitor, Capt. McCuish, were fishing on March 29 on the southeast peak of Quero. The day promised fair, but turned out bad. The Arbitrator was to an anchor with her riding sail set, while the Monitor and Dictator were jogging, standing off and on around her.
Big black clouds began to roll upon the horizon and in a very short space of time the heavens were blackened and darkness almost of evening spread about. It looked just like a terrible thunder storm of mid-summer and such it proved to be -- the most terrible thunder storm ever heard of.
With the rising cloud the wind began to pick up and blew fitfully in little sharp gusts from every direction of the compass and steadily gaining in strength until at the climax of the storm, they were squalls, the like of which in spitefulness, fury and strength Capt. Spinney never before experienced.
The rain came and with it thunder and lightning. It rained hard, then it hailed hard - was no name for it. So fiercely did it hail that he particles did not have time to melt when they struck the water, but just se4emed at saturate through and formed on the surface, looking just like a field of slob ice or slush, such as is seen in winter time. The vessel was jogging all this time and Capt. Spinney says the sight of so much hail on the water looking like ice, can better be imagined than described.
Then the storm began to come nearer and nearer and still it rained and hailed. The thunder seemed only over head and came directly with the lightning. Capt. Spinney was on deck with three of his crew when there came an awful crash. It seemed as if everything was tumbling. With it came a flash, and such a flash! Capt. Spinney says it wasn't a flash, but a great livid sheet of flame almost blinding to the sight. It struck the water not 100 feet out ahead of the vessel and instantly the water there was white with foam and sparks of fire flew in all directions about the vessel. The air seemed full of sparks.
Capt. Spinney was speechless. He looked at his men and wondered if they saw what he did. Their faces showed plainly that they had. All went below and told the rest of the crew. Most of them were skeptical and laughed, but the quartet stuck to their story and finally all hands came on deck, as Capt. Spinney said "to watch for one of them things."
The thunder still roared and lightning played about. The squalls were coming more and more fierce and some sail was taken in. Suddenly, giving no warning, came another of those awful crashed and simultaneously another sheet of flame and sparks descended from above, and struck the water, acting about the same as did its terrible predecessor. Capt. Spinney says it was awful and beyond description. The crew, all hands, saw. They were convinced and farther than that, they all went below quickly. They had seen enough and didn't wish another such close acquaintance with descending fire.
After this came some severe squalls and all hands were needed on deck as care and quick action meant much should one hit the vessel fair. One big squall, blacker than all the rest and fiercer was seen coming and things looked serious. Capt. Spinney says it piled the water straight up in front of it at least three feet in the air and like a

moving white wall rushed on threatening destruction to everything in its path. It crossed the bow of the Dictator, not 25 yards ahead and passed by, but those on the Dictator saw that it was headed in the direction of the Arbitrator, at anchor near by, with her riding sail set. It struck the latter vessel fair and with full force. The sheets on the riding sail parted and are going yet, while the sail went over the side. The vessel heeled down till it seemed that she would surely be hove on her beam ends and then righted as the squall passed. Capt. Wilson Spinney said that if it had struck his vessel with bank sail on, it would have taken the spars out of her.

While the thunder storm lasted two more of those awful visitations of fire came with their terrible noise and crash. Capt. Spinney does not hesitate to say that he and his men were frightened. He says frankly that he never saw or heard anything like it and that to describe it as it actually was would be impossible. He says had it happened at night he didn't know but what he would have thought that the world was coming to an end.

During the whole storm there were but four of those awful indescribable sheets of flame seen, but the memory of those will life long in the minds of the men who witnessed the phenomena.

After the storm abated, as if by common consent the captains of the Arbitrator and Monitor came on board the Dictator. Each seemed inclined to almost doubt this own eyesight, but a careful comparison of notes showed that the same phenomena, the same sheets of fire had been observed by all three captains and their crews. Capt. McCuish of the Monitor said that when the first flash came, his crew were on deck and were shortening sail. The effect of the flash was felt all over the vessel and two of the crew were knocked insensible to the deck, having been struck or at least received a severe shock from the big flash. It was some time before they were brought around.

This is the tale as Capt. Spinney tells it and that is sufficient authority for its authenticity and non-exaggeration

Children are listed above under (1054) Oretha F Spinney.

1077. FOREMAN[8] SPINNEY *(CALEB[7], JAMES[6], JACOB[5], JOHN[4], JOHN[3], JOHN[2], THOMAS[1])* was born 15 Sep 1879 in Argyle, NS., and died 23 Sep 1938 in Gloucester, MA. He married NELLIE ELLIS 19 Sep 1905, daughter of COLIN ELLIS and CECELIA FREEMAN. She was born 02 Dec 1879 in Milton, Queens Co., Nova Scotia, and died 05 Sep 1979 in Gloucester, MA.

Notes for FOREMAN SPINNEY:
Capt. Forman Spinney

Capt. Forman Spinney, 59 years, passed away suddenly last Friday aboard the local dory trawler Edith C. Rose, Capt. Albert Hines, at sea. His remains were landed at Shelburne, Nova Scotia, shipped to his home in Malden, from where the funeral is to be held this afternoon, with burial at Fisherman's Rest, Beechbrook Cemetery, West Gloucester. He leaves a widow and eight children.

The late Capt. Spinney was born in Argyle, Yarmouth County, Nova Scotia, September 15, 1879, but came to this city in his early youth and followed the fisheries, along with his older brother, Capt. Lemuel R. Spinney, noted halibuting skipper. In more recent years he moved with his family to Malden. He was engineer aboard the Edith C. Rose , but among his former commands were such well known vessels as the sch. Senator, and the Oretha F. Spinney. He was considered an able ship-mate and highly esteemed as a mariner.

He is survived by his wife, Mrs. Nellie (Ellis) Spinney, six daughters, Marion, wife of Frank Spinney; Dorothy, wife of Steven Dodge; Laura Spinney; Ella, wife of Phillips Powell, and Misses Bertha and Alice Spinney; two sons, Carl and Wilson Spinney; and a brother, Capt. Lemuel R. Spinney, this city.

From lost at sea
Forman Spinney, age 59, married, Argyle; died Edith C. Rose on Sep 23, 1938; natural causes; buried at Fishermen's Rest, Beeckbrook, Gloucester.

Children of FOREMAN SPINNEY and NELLIE ELLIS are:
    i.   MARION[9] SPINNEY, b. 1906; m. FRANK SPINNEY.
   ii.   DOROTHY SPINNEY, m. STEPHEN DODGE; b. 02 Sep 1910; d. Jul 1982, Reading, Ma.
  iii.   LAURA SPINNEY.
  iv.   ELLA SPINNEY, b. 1908; m. PHILLIPS POWELL.
   v.   BERTHA SPINNEY.
  vi.   ALICE SPINNEY, b. Abt. 1900.
 vii.   CARL SPINNEY, b. 1905; m. MARIE E HEIDE, 01 Mar 1930.

viii.   WILSON C SPINNEY, b. 11 Mar 1912; d. 19 Feb 1992, Gloucester, MA.

1078. JAMES CALVIN[8] SPINNEY *(CALVIN[7], JAMES[6], JACOB[5], JOHN[4], JOHN[3], JOHN[2], THOMAS[1])* was born 28 Nov 1875, and died 1943. He married MARGARET THORBURN 19 Aug 1908 in East Jordan, Nova Scotia, Canada. She was born 1882, and died 1959.

Children of JAMES SPINNEY and MARGARET THORBURN are:
  i.   WOODBURY LEIGH[9] SPINNEY, b. 25 Aug 1909, Argyle Sound, Nova Scotia, Canada; d. 25 Aug 1909, Argyle Sound, Nova Scotia, Canada.
  ii.   JAMES ERIC SPINNEY.
  iii. HUGH THORBURN SPINNEY, b. 24 Jul 1915, Liverpool, Nova Scotia, Canada; d. 04 Sep 1941, Shubenacadie, Nova Scotia, Canada.
  iv.   SIDNEY ST CLAIR SPINNEY.
  v.   LOUIS SPINNEY.
  vi.   EDITH LYDIA SPINNEY, b. 15 Jun 1913, Liverpool, Nova Scotia, Canada.

1079. SAMUEL DANIEL[8] SPINNEY *(WHITFIELD[7], JAMES[6], JACOB[5], JOHN[4], JOHN[3], JOHN[2], THOMAS[1])* was born Feb 1863. He married MATILDA MAY 1896. She was born May 1867.

Notes for SAMUEL DANIEL SPINNEY:
He is listed in the 1900 census in Manhattan, New York at ED 1016 Image 9,Roll T_623-1126 Image 409.City of New York, Thirty-fifth Assembly District.; 18th Election District. (part of) Bounded by E. 167th, Fulton Ave., & Third Ave., E. 164th, Washington Ave., Blocks numbered. He was living at 111 Third Ave.in the Bronx Burrough. He entered the USA in 1867 at the age of four, which is the same year his brother Aden Clayton was born. He is listed as a Railroad Brakeman. He and Matilda were married for 8 years as of 1900 census. Matilda was born in Germany and immigrated to the USA in 1869. In the 1930 census of Gloucester his nephew, Clayton Whitfield Spinney, is listed as working for the Railroad.

He is in the 1910 census in Bronx New York 10th Precinct, 34th Assembly District
T624-1000 ED 1542 on Ancestry.com Image 25 Grandelin? Avenue.
Wife is now listed as Anna M. He is 46 yrs old.She is 43 yrs old. Daughters are:
Jennie M. 16 yrs old. Secretary for department store.
Cora A 13 yrs old.
Catherine A 9 yrs old.
He is a conductor for the Railroad.
Now Anna Matilda is listed as entering the USA in 1871 and Samuel 1869.
Note:
Gloucester, Massachusetts Directories 1888-91
Adin C. Spinney Fisherman Boards 10 Rockwood Place
Samuel D. Spinney Fisherman Boards 10 Rockwood Place
This is Aden and his brother.

In the 1880 census he is listed with William Younger and Jane (Crittendon/Spinney)Younger as a step-son with his sisters Effie and Eva, in Gloucester,Mass.

Children of SAMUEL SPINNEY and MATILDA MAY are:
  i.   JENNIE[9] SPINNEY, b. 1893.
  ii.   CORA A SPINNEY, b. 12 Jan 1897.
  iii. HENRIETTA SPINNEY, b. 1899.
  iv.   CATHERINE SPINNEY, b. 1901.

1080. ADEN CLAYTON[8] SPINNEY *(WHITFIELD[7], JAMES[6], JACOB[5], JOHN[4], JOHN[3], JOHN[2], THOMAS[1])* was born Oct 1867, and died 16 Sep 1903. He married ABBIE C MURRAY 1894. She was born 1869.

Children of ADEN SPINNEY and ABBIE MURRAY are:
1352.   i.   PRESCOTT YOUNGER[9] SPINNEY, b. 11 Apr 1895; d. Oct 1979, Texas.
         ii.   EDWIN M SPINNEY, b. Nov 1896.

iii. CLAYTON W SPINNEY, b. Oct 1899; m. ABBIE.

1081. CHARLES[8] SPINNEY *(HEMAN[7], HARVEY[6], AARON[5], JOHN[4], JOHN[3], JOHN[2], THOMAS[1])* He married ALICE FREDRICSION.

Child of CHARLES SPINNEY and ALICE FREDRICSION is:
    i. STEVE[9] SPINNEY.

1082. CONSTANCE[8] SPINNEY *(JOSIAH[7], SOLOMAN ROBERT[6], BENJAMIN[5], JOHN[4], JOHN[3], JOHN[2], THOMAS[1])* was born 1884 in Port Latour NS, and died 1960 in Boston Mass. She married FRED LEANDER GORDON SHOLDS, son of CHRISTOPHER SHOLDS and MARY SMITH. He was born 21 Dec 1883 in Port Latour NS, and died 16 Jan 1960 in Hyde Park Boston MA.

Child of CONSTANCE SPINNEY and FRED SHOLDS is:
1353.   i. FRED ALLISON[9] SHOLDS, b. 30 Dec 1920, Port Latour NS.

1083. ALBERTA LOUISE[8] SPINNEY *(GEORGE NELSON[7], SOLOMAN ROBERT[6], BENJAMIN[5], JOHN[4], JOHN[3], JOHN[2], THOMAS[1])* was born 1871. She married GEORGE BRADFORD ALLEN.

Children of ALBERTA SPINNEY and GEORGE ALLEN are:
    i. IVAN[9] ALLEN.
    ii. VICTOR ALLEN.
    iii. ERIC ALLEN.
    iv. RUTH ALLEN.
    v. FRANCIS ALLEN.

1084. HAROLD FARNHAM[8] SPINNEY *(GEORGE NELSON[7], SOLOMAN ROBERT[6], BENJAMIN[5], JOHN[4], JOHN[3], JOHN[2], THOMAS[1])* was born 28 Dec 1878 in Yarmouth, Nova Scotia, Canada, and died 22 Feb 1921. He married JOSEPHINE RICKER 14 Oct 1911. She was born 18 Oct 1888 in Chebogue, Nova Scotia, Canada, and died 17 Apr 1957 in Halifax, Nova Scotia, Canada.

Children of HAROLD SPINNEY and JOSEPHINE RICKER are:
1354.   i. HAROLD F[9] SPINNEY, b. 06 Feb 1916, Brooklyn, New York, USA; d. 1986, Narragansett, Rhode Island, USA.
    ii. MARY EMILY SPINNEY.

1085. GEORGE W[8] SPINNEY *(GEORGE NELSON[7], SOLOMAN ROBERT[6], BENJAMIN[5], JOHN[4], JOHN[3], JOHN[2], THOMAS[1])* was born 03 Apr 1889 in Yarmouth, Nova Scotia, Canada, and died 01 Feb 1948 in Montreal, Quebec, Canada. He married MARTHA MAUDE RAMSEY 02 Aug 1916. She was born 31 Jan 1889, and died 21 Jan 1974 in Montreal, Quebec, Canada.

Children of GEORGE SPINNEY and MARTHA RAMSEY are:
    i. WILBUR RAMSAY[9] SPINNEY, b. 27 Jun 1918, Montral, Quebec, Canada; d. 03 Jun 1945, Basingstoke, England.
    ii. RUTH SPINNEY.
    iii. MARTHA LOUISE SPINNEY, b. 1928, RV, Montreal, Quebec, Canada; d. 11 Jan 1982, Montreal, Quebec, Canada.

1086. ADOLPHUS LARKIN[8] SPINNEY *(HOWARD[7], PRINCE[6], DANIEL[5], JOHN[4], JOHN[3], JOHN[2], THOMAS[1])* was born 08 Sep 1874 in Nova Scota, and died Aft. 1936. He married EVA VAN EMBURG 1903, daughter of JAMES VAN AMBURG and ELIZA KENNEY. She was born 22 Aug 1886, and died 02 Jan 1968.

Children of ADOLPHUS SPINNEY and EVA VAN EMBURG are:
    i. RUTH[9] KENNEY.
    ii. BARBARA KENNEY.
    iii. ELIZABETH KENNEY.

iv.   HOWARD L KENNEY.

1087. NINA MAE[8] SPINNEY *(BOWMAN E[7], EDWARD[6], DANIEL[5], JOHN[4], JOHN[3], JOHN[2], THOMAS[1])* was born 09 Feb 1895, and died 04 Jun 1951. She married CHARLES ALEXANDER CRITHER. He was born 09 Aug 1891, and died 28 Sep 1935.

Children of NINA SPINNEY and CHARLES CRITHER are:
  i.   HAZEL[9] CRITHER, b. 30 Mar 1917; m. WILLIAM RANDOLPH CANN.
  ii. KEITH CAMERON CRITHER, b. 17 Feb 1914; d. 25 Nov 1971; m. MARY JANE PITMAN.
  iii. LILLIAN CRITHER, d. 1996; m. DOUGLAS NOGIE.
  iv. RONALD E CRITHER, m. LUELLA SANDERS.
  v.   RUBY ALICE CRITHER, b. 23 Dec 1926; d. 19 Sep 1970; m. WILBERT HAROLD PROUSE.
  vi. MARION CRITHER, m. CHESTER BENJAMIN LAWRENCE.
  vii. CHARLES SPINNEY CRITHER, b. 05 Mar 1931; d. 17 Apr 1931.

1088. WILLIAM RUFAS[8] SPINNEY *(BOWMAN E[7], EDWARD[6], DANIEL[5], JOHN[4], JOHN[3], JOHN[2], THOMAS[1])* was born 12 Mar 1897, and died 21 Apr 1937. He married ETHEL IRELAND. She was born Abt. 1900, and died 05 Mar 1934.

Children of WILLIAM SPINNEY and ETHEL IRELAND are:
  i.   JEAM ELIZABETH[9] SPINNEY, b. 23 Oct 1927.
  ii. ROBERT WILLIAM SPINNEY, b. 11 Feb 1930; d. 26 Aug 1944.

1089. BOWMAN EDWARD[8] SPINNEY *(BOWMAN E[7], EDWARD[6], DANIEL[5], JOHN[4], JOHN[3], JOHN[2], THOMAS[1])* was born 05 Nov 1905, and died 07 Feb 1945. He married FLORENCE AMELIA HOWARTH.

Children of BOWMAN SPINNEY and FLORENCE HOWARTH are:
1355.   i.   ALTHEA JEAN[9] SPINNEY, b. 03 Mar 1928.
1356.   ii. ELIZABETH FRANCES SPINNEY, b. 25 Sep 1929.

1090. LYMAN EUGENE[8] SPINNEY *(BOWMAN E[7], EDWARD[6], DANIEL[5], JOHN[4], JOHN[3], JOHN[2], THOMAS[1])* was born 13 Feb 1907 in Nova Scotia, and died Jul 1967 in Massachusetts. He married EVELYN MAY LARSON.

Children of LYMAN SPINNEY and EVELYN LARSON are:
1357.   i.   EUGENE ROBERT[9] SPINNEY, b. 07 Nov 1929; d. 02 Apr 1988, Hood County, TX.
1358.   ii. DONALD N SPINNEY, b. 07 Jul 1931; d. Apr 2003.
1359.   iii. JACK L SPINNEY, b. 16 Apr 1935; d. 30 Dec 1994.
1360.   iv. BRUCE SPINNEY, b. 14 Jul 1936.

1091. GRACE[8] SPINNEY *(ALBERT[7], ASENATH[6] RYDER, JOANNAH[5] SPINNEY, JOHN[4], JOHN[3], JOHN[2], THOMAS[1])* was born Dec 1870. She married LEONARD HANSON 1896 in Lynn, MA, son of WILLIAM HANSON and MARTHA. He was born 1875 in Massachusetts.

Children of GRACE SPINNEY and LEONARD HANSON are:
  i.   FRANK[9] HANSON, b. 1900.
  ii. MAUD HANSON.

1092. ROSCOE RUTHERFORD[8] SPINNEY *(ALBERT[7], ASENATH[6] RYDER, JOANNAH[5] SPINNEY, JOHN[4], JOHN[3], JOHN[2], THOMAS[1])* was born 12 Mar 1877. He married HELEN. She was born 1885.

Child of ROSCOE SPINNEY and HELEN is:
  i.   HELEN[9] SPINNEY, b. 1913.

1093. CLEVELAND N[8] SPINNEY *(ALBERT[7], ASENATH[6] RYDER, JOANNAH[5] SPINNEY, JOHN[4], JOHN[3], JOHN[2], THOMAS[1])* was born 1885 in Maine, and died 26 Jul 1935. He married (1) CLARA R CARDRAN. He married (2) SARAH A BEAR 21 Aug 1906. She was born 09 Jan 1903 in Pennsylvania, and died Apr 1987.

Child of CLEVELAND SPINNEY and CLARA CARDRAN is:
    i.   ALBERT CLEVELAND[9] SPINNEY, b. 1908, Lynn, Ma.

Child of CLEVELAND SPINNEY and SARAH BEAR is:
    ii. ELIZABETH[9] SPINNEY, b. 1924.

1094. MEOURA[8] BOWDEN *(PAMELIA A[7] SPINNEY, JOSEPH A[6], STEPHEN L[5], TIMOTHY[4], JOHN[3], JOHN[2], THOMAS[1])* was born 1859. She married FRANK TUTTLE. He was born 1852.

Child of MEOURA BOWDEN and FRANK TUTTLE is:
    i.   JOSEPHINE[9] TUTTLE, b. 1878.

1095. LORENZO DOW[8] SPINNEY *(THOMAS[7], JOHN[6], JOHN[5], JOHN[4], ANDREW[3], JOHN[2], THOMAS[1])* was born 25 Jul 1832 in Georgetown, ME, and died 16 Sep 1871. He married MARY E MARR 29 Nov 1859. She was born 1836.

Children of LORENZO SPINNEY and MARY MARR are:
1361.   i.   HERBERT LINDEN[9] SPINNEY, b. 25 Sep 1862.
1362.   ii. MILLARD SPINNEY, b. 28 May 1864; d. 1932.
1363.   iii. LORENZO DOW SPINNEY, b. 22 Aug 1865.

1096. MELVILLE B[8] SPINNEY *(THOMAS[7], JOHN[6], JOHN[5], JOHN[4], ANDREW[3], JOHN[2], THOMAS[1])* was born 30 Dec 1834 in Georgetown, ME. He married (1) MARY R GRANT 05 Oct 1861 in Kennebec Maine.   He married (2) ABBIE VESTA BARRON 02 Jul 1881 in Phippsburg, ME. She was born Abt. 1852 in Melrose, MA.

Child of MELVILLE SPINNEY and ABBIE BARRON is:
    i.   JOSEPH BODWELL[9] SPINNEY, b. 17 Dec 1884.

1097. NANCY JANE[8] SPINNEY *(THOMAS[7], JOHN[6], JOHN[5], JOHN[4], ANDREW[3], JOHN[2], THOMAS[1])* was born 28 Oct 1837, and died 05 Mar 1909 in Georgetown, ME. She married CHARLES A CLARK 01 Jan 1854 in Brunswick Maine. He was born 1823, and died Aft. 1900.

Children of NANCY SPINNEY and CHARLES CLARK are:
    i.   LILLA[9] CLARK, b. 30 Dec 1854.
    ii.   ANNIE CLARK, b. 09 Jan 1861; m. (1) ANSON OLIVER; m. (2) JOHN HUTCHINGS STACY.
    iii. CHARLES A CLARK, b. 09 Jan 1861.
    iv.   ALICE F CLARK, b. 26 Jul 1869.
1364.   v.   CHARLES M CLARK, b. 19 Oct 1872, Georgetown, ME; d. Massachusetts.

1098. CHARLES[8] SPINNEY *(THOMAS[7], JOHN[6], JOHN[5], JOHN[4], ANDREW[3], JOHN[2], THOMAS[1])* was born 24 Oct 1844 in Maine, and died Bef. 1881. He married SARAH MERRICK 27 Mar 1867 in London, Ontario, Canada 2nd Husb, daughter of LEVI MERRICK and ELIZABETH BOSTWICK. She was born 16 Apr 1830 in London, Ontario, Canada.

Children of CHARLES SPINNEY and SARAH MERRICK are:
    i.   MILTON[9] SPINNEY, b. 22 Sep 1867, London, Ontario, Canada; d. 07 Mar 1896.
    ii. CHARLES EUGENE SPINNEY, b. 02 Dec 1874, London, Ontario, Canada; d. 31 Aug 1877.

1099. CHARLES SPINNEY[8] LUCE *(LOUISA[7] SPINNEY, JOHN[6], JOHN[5], JOHN[4], ANDREW[3], JOHN[2], THOMAS[1])* He married REBECCA HIGGINS LOWELL.

Children of CHARLES LUCE and REBECCA LOWELL are:
    i.   FRANCES V[9] LUCE.
    ii. LAURA LAVENIA LUCE.
    iii. CLINTON CASIUS LUCE.
    iv. ISA MABEL LUCE.

v. SUSAN LOWELL LUCE.
vi. NELLIS MAY LUCE.

1100. CELIA ANN[8] LUCE *(LOUISA[7] SPINNEY, JOHN[6], JOHN[5], JOHN[4], ANDREW[3], JOHN[2], THOMAS[1])* She married HIRUM STACKPOLE.

Children of CELIA LUCE and HIRUM STACKPOLE are:
    i. HELEN[9] STACKPOLE.
    ii. FRANCES STACKPOLE.

1101. ELIZABETH[8] LUCE *(LOUISA[7] SPINNEY, JOHN[6], JOHN[5], JOHN[4], ANDREW[3], JOHN[2], THOMAS[1])* She married JOHN AUGUSTE.

Children of ELIZABETH LUCE and JOHN AUGUSTE are:
    i. HERBERT HENRY[9] AUGUSTE.
    ii. ALBERT FREMONT AUGUSTE.
    iii. JOHN SCOTT AUGUSTE.

1102. REUBEN[8] HUNT *(ROXANNA BURGESS[7] SPINNEY, NICHOLAS[6], JOHN[5], JOHN[4], ANDREW[3], JOHN[2], THOMAS[1])* was born 12 Jan 1821. He married SARAH ROBINSON, daughter of ALEXANDER ROBINSON and BETHIAH BROWN.

Children of REUBEN HUNT and SARAH ROBINSON are:
    i. EDWIN R[9] HUNT, b. 1844.
    ii. REUBEN TALLMAN HUNT, b. 1846.
1365. iii. SARAH A HUNT, b. 13 Oct 1848.
    iv. CHARLES A HUNT, b. 24 Mar 1850.

1103. JOSEPH OAKMAN[8] HUNT *(ROXANNA BURGESS[7] SPINNEY, NICHOLAS[6], JOHN[5], JOHN[4], ANDREW[3], JOHN[2], THOMAS[1])* was born 19 Mar 1823, and died Bef. 1880. He married SUSAN MCKINNEY, daughter of EBENEZER MCKINNEY and JANE SPINNEY. She was born 09 Apr 1820, and died Aft. 1880.

Children are listed above under (786) Susan McKinney.

1104. WILLIAM SPINNEY[8] HUNT *(ROXANNA BURGESS[7] SPINNEY, NICHOLAS[6], JOHN[5], JOHN[4], ANDREW[3], JOHN[2], THOMAS[1])* was born 11 Aug 1834 in Bath, ME, and died 05 May 1907 in Bath, ME. He married (1) FLORA S OLIVER. He married (2) AMANDA MALVINA NEWCOMB 18 Oct 1857 in Bath, ME. She was born 25 Jun 1832 in New Bedford, MA, and died 03 Aug 1881 in Bath, ME.

Children of WILLIAM HUNT and FLORA OLIVER are:
    i. ISAIAH WILDES[9] HUNT.
    ii. MADELINE HUNT.

Children of WILLIAM HUNT and AMANDA NEWCOMB are:
    iii. MYRA FRANCES[9] HUNT, b. 12 Jun 1858; m. NATHANIEL RICE, Oct 1877, Phippsburg, Maine.
    iv. SUMNER LINCOLN HUNT, b. 26 Jul 1859; d. 02 Jun 1881, Bath, ME.
1366. v. ALICE MARY HUNT, b. 07 Feb 1861, Bath, ME; d. 15 May 1945, Malden, MA (Buried: Forestdale Cemetery).
    vi. ERNEST HOWARD HUNT, b. 14 Jun 1863; d. 20 Aug 1873, Bath, Maine.
    vii. FRED EUGENE HUNT, b. 25 May 1866; d. 04 Jun 1944, Malden, Massachusetts; m. CAROLINE ADDY, 10 Dec 1890, Malden, Massachusetts.

1105. OREN WILLIAM[8] SPINNEY *(WILLIAM M[7], NICHOLAS[6], JOHN[5], JOHN[4], ANDREW[3], JOHN[2], THOMAS[1])* was born 09 Nov 1827 in Georgetown, ME, and died 29 Jan 1869 in Salem, Ma. He married MARY MARIE CHOATE 27 Apr 1852 in Salem, MA. She was born 1833.

Children of OREN SPINNEY and MARY CHOATE are:

      i.   WILLIAM F[9] SPINNEY, b. 1853.
     ii.   HATTIE SPINNEY, b. 1857.

1106. MARGERY ELIZABETH[8] SPINNEY *(WILLIAM M[7], NICHOLAS[6], JOHN[5], JOHN[4], ANDREW[3], JOHN[2], THOMAS[1])* was born 13 Nov 1829 in Georgetown, ME, and died Bef. 1861. She married HORATIO G SCRIBNER 13 Feb 1851, son of JOHN SCRIBNER and SUSANNA SPENCER. He was born 09 May 1822 in Belfast, ME, and died 1877 in Bradford, Il.

Notes for HORATIO G SCRIBNER:
Horatio and Elizabeth and family moved to Stark County, Illinois, during the 1850's. He was a farmer in Bradford, Osceola Township. Like most of the farmers in that area, he grew and harvested sorghum. His second wife, Hannah, was born in England, and naturalized an American citizen in 1858. Her first husband was James Scholes, who died in 1859.
In the 1865 State Census of Illinois (Roll 39, Page 8), Horatio is shown with 2 male children between the ages of 10 and 20, and 1 female child within the same age grouping. No further information about this family is known.

Children of MARGERY SPINNEY and HORATIO SCRIBNER are:
      i.   ARTEMUS[9] SCRIBNER, b. 1852, Maine; d. 24 Apr 1891, Colorado.
     ii.   CAROLINE SCRIBNER, b. 1853.

1107. ANSON B[8] SPINNEY *(WILLIAM M[7], NICHOLAS[6], JOHN[5], JOHN[4], ANDREW[3], JOHN[2], THOMAS[1])* was born 05 Jul 1832 in Georgetown, ME, and died 20 Jun 1900 in Park City, Colorado. He married (1) JANE. She was born 1833 in Massachusetts, and died Bet. 1860 - 1870. He married (2) HATTIE Aft. 1860. She was born 1844 in Wisonsin. He married (3) MARY EMMA COOKE 02 Apr 1879 in Mobile, AL. She was born 1862 in Alabama, and died 1880. He married (4) LOTTIE ROACH Jul 1890 in Kentucky.

Notes for ANSON B SPINNEY:
Anson is listed in Michigan in the 1900 census with no family

Children of ANSON SPINNEY and JANE are:
      i.   LOUISA J[9] SPINNEY, b. 1851, Maine.
1367.   ii.   ALICE L SPINNEY, b. 26 Jul 1858, Illinois.

Child of ANSON SPINNEY and MARY COOKE is:
1368.   iii.   EMMA PEARL[9] SPINNEY, b. Mar 1880, Alabama; d. Aft. 1930.

1108. BENJAMIN F[8] SPINNEY *(WILLIAM M[7], NICHOLAS[6], JOHN[5], JOHN[4], ANDREW[3], JOHN[2], THOMAS[1])* was born Jul 1835 in Maine, and died Aft. 1870 in Colorado. He married MARY A ROSE. She was born 1848 in Illinois, and died Aft. 1910.

Children of BENJAMIN SPINNEY and MARY ROSE are:
      i.   ANSON B[9] SPINNEY, b. May 1876; m. LENA OLIVER, 19 Jun 1916, Vancouver, Canada; b. 05 Oct 1881; d. 20 May 1969.
     ii.   IMOGENE V SPINNEY, b. 1878.
1369.   iii.   FAYETTE A SPINNEY, b. 1882, Colorado.

1109. JOSEPH OAKMAN[8] SPINNEY *(WILLIAM M[7], NICHOLAS[6], JOHN[5], JOHN[4], ANDREW[3], JOHN[2], THOMAS[1])* was born 07 Nov 1837 in Maine, and died 16 Aug 1916 in Iowa. He married JULIA H BEVIER 01 Jan 1866 in Stark, IL. She was born 1838 in New York, and died 1924 in Iowa.

Notes for JOSEPH OAKMAN SPINNEY:
1920 census list Joseph in Cass Iowa

Children of JOSEPH SPINNEY and JULIA BEVIER are:
      i.   ANSON BERTRUM[9] SPINNEY, b. 1868, Illinois; d. Aft. 1930.
1370.   ii.   LOUIS BEVIER SPINNEY, b. 1869, Illinois; d. 1951.

1371.   iii.   HOWARD C SPINNEY, b. 1874, Illinois; d. Aft. 1930.

1110. NICHOLAS S⁸ SPINNEY *(WILLIAM M⁷, NICHOLAS⁶, JOHN⁵, JOHN⁴, ANDREW³, JOHN², THOMAS¹)* was born 1841 in Maine, and died 04 Aug 1925 in Oregon. He married ELIZABETH OLIVER 14 Sep 1879. She was born 1845.

Child of NICHOLAS SPINNEY and ELIZABETH OLIVER is:
        i.   EARL⁹ SPINNEY, b. 11 Jun 1880, Portland, OR; d. 15 Jul 1968, Portland, OR.

1111. ALMSHA VIOLA⁸ SPINNEY *(WILLIAM M⁷, NICHOLAS⁶, JOHN⁵, JOHN⁴, ANDREW³, JOHN², THOMAS¹)* was born 1846 in Maine, and died Aft. 1880 in Colorado. She married JEROME E HARRINGTON 16 Jul 1873 in Colorado. He was born 1835 in New York, and died Aft. 1880 in Colorado.

Children of ALMSHA SPINNEY and JEROME HARRINGTON are:
        i.   JEROME E⁹ HARRINGTON, b. Jan 1875.
        ii.   ADELIA HARRINGTON, b. 1877.
        iii. EDITH HARRINGTON, b. Jun 1878.

1112. ELIZABETH S⁸ SPINNEY *(NICHOLAS J⁷, NICHOLAS⁶, JOHN⁵, JOHN⁴, ANDREW³, JOHN², THOMAS¹)* was born 02 Dec 1829 in Arrowsic, ME, and died Aft. 1900. She married GEORGE S DRUMMOND. He was born 1826, and died Bef. 1900.

Children of ELIZABETH SPINNEY and GEORGE DRUMMOND are:
        i.   STELLA E⁹ DRUMMOND, b. 1856; d. Aft. 1900.
        ii.   MYRA DRUMMOND, b. 1866.

1113. HARRIETT HINKLEY⁸ SPINNEY *(NICHOLAS J⁷, NICHOLAS⁶, JOHN⁵, JOHN⁴, ANDREW³, JOHN², THOMAS¹)* was born 17 Jul 1834 in Arrowsic, ME, and died 1886 in Boston, Ma. She married THOMAS F CROWELL 1861 in Mass. He was born 1831 in Maine.

Children of HARRIETT SPINNEY and THOMAS CROWELL are:
        i.   ALICE M⁹ CROWELL, b. 1863.
        ii.   HATTIE WOOD CROWELL, b. 1867.
        iii. FRED L CROWELL, b. 1871.

1114. ANN MARIA⁸ SPINNEY *(NICHOLAS J⁷, NICHOLAS⁶, JOHN⁵, JOHN⁴, ANDREW³, JOHN², THOMAS¹)* was born 02 Nov 1839 in Arrowsic, ME, and died 12 Jul 1897. She married SETH T SNIPE 1864. He was born 05 Feb 1839 in Arrowsic, Sagadahoc, Maine, USA, and died 20 Apr 1911 in Bath, Sagadahoc, Maine, USA.

Child of ANN SPINNEY and SETH SNIPE is:
1372.   i.   LANGDON TRUFANT⁹ SNIPE, b. 27 May 1867, Boston, Suffolk, Massachusetts, USA.

1115. JAMES L⁸ SPINNEY *(NICHOLAS J⁷, NICHOLAS⁶, JOHN⁵, JOHN⁴, ANDREW³, JOHN², THOMAS¹)* was born Oct 1843, and died Aft. 1910. He married MARY Bef. 1874. She was born Sep 1847, and died Aft. 1900.

Children of JAMES SPINNEY and MARY are:
        i.   FLORENCE L⁹ SPINNEY, b. Aug 1873; d. Aft. 1900; m. WALTER L JOHNSON, 1898, Bath, ME; b. 1876.
        ii.   J CLIFFORD SPINNEY, b. Dec 1880; d. Aft. 1910.
        iii. J ARTHUR SPINNEY, b. Jul 1884; d. Aft. 1900.
        iv.   M LEONARD SPINNEY, b. Nov 1885; d. Aft. 1900.

1116. MARGARET JANE⁸ SPINNEY *(ROBERT CURTIS⁷, NICHOLAS⁶, JOHN⁵, JOHN⁴, ANDREW³, JOHN², THOMAS¹)* was born 18 Mar 1833, and died 1895. She married ARAD DAY 30 Jan 1851. He was born 1822, and died 1879.

Children of MARGARET SPINNEY and ARAD DAY are:

i. ARAD[9] DAY, b. 1858.
ii. ROBERT DAY, b. 1856.

1117. ELIZABETH SUSAN[8] SPINNEY *(ROBERT CURTIS[7], NICHOLAS[6], JOHN[5], JOHN[4], ANDREW[3], JOHN[2], THOMAS[1])* was born 10 Sep 1834 in Boothbay, ME, and died 1871. She married FREDERICK REED. He was born 1825.

Child of ELIZABETH SPINNEY and FREDERICK REED is:
i. LILLA[9] REED, b. 1858.

1118. WILLIAM QUINMAN[8] SPINNEY *(ROBERT CURTIS[7], NICHOLAS[6], JOHN[5], JOHN[4], ANDREW[3], JOHN[2], THOMAS[1])* was born 13 Oct 1838 in Boothbay, ME, and died Aft. 1900. He married (1) CLARA BERRY. She was born 1839, and died Aft. 1900. He married (2) DAMENDA GILMAN RICHARDSON 19 Mar 1898.

Children of WILLIAM SPINNEY and CLARA BERRY are:
i. EFFIE[9] SPINNEY, b. 1859.
ii. NELLIE A SPINNEY, b. 1863.
1373. iii. JULIA A SPINNEY, b. 1866; d. WFT Est. 1894-1963.
iv. ELIZABETH SPINNEY, b. 1869; m. GEORGE ADAMS.
v. FRED G SPINNEY, b. 1871.
vi. BURTON W SPINNEY, b. 1873.
vii. LILLIAN SPINNEY, b. 1875.

1119. MARY ANGELINA[8] SPINNEY *(ROBERT CURTIS[7], NICHOLAS[6], JOHN[5], JOHN[4], ANDREW[3], JOHN[2], THOMAS[1])* was born 17 May 1840. She married RICHARD M WEBBER 1865 in Chelsea, MA. He was born 1834.

Children of MARY SPINNEY and RICHARD WEBBER are:
i. EDITH[9] WEBBER, b. 1869.
ii. GILMAN WEBBER, b. 1871.
iii. CHARLES WEBBER, b. 1879.

1120. CAROLINE MCCLINTOCK[8] SPINNEY *(ROBERT CURTIS[7], NICHOLAS[6], JOHN[5], JOHN[4], ANDREW[3], JOHN[2], THOMAS[1])* was born 13 Oct 1841. She married GILMAN PAGE HODGDON.

Children of CAROLINE SPINNEY and GILMAN HODGDON are:
i. CLARENCE[9] HODGDOM.
ii. GERTRUDE HODGDON.
iii. L MAUD HODGDON.
iv. LOUISE HODGDON.
v. MARGARET HODGDON.

1121. JOHN GILMAN[8] SPINNEY *(ROBERT CURTIS[7], NICHOLAS[6], JOHN[5], JOHN[4], ANDREW[3], JOHN[2], THOMAS[1])* was born 02 Feb 1845 in Boothbay, ME, and died Aft. 1880. He married JULIE E BERRY. She was born 1848, and died Aft. 1880.

Children of JOHN SPINNEY and JULIE BERRY are:
i. JOHN S[9] SPINNEY, b. 03 May 1869; d. 1931; m. ABIGAIL B ABBOTT; b. 04 Sep 1872.
ii. VIOLA SPINNEY, b. 14 Jun 1871, Boothbay, ME.
iii. C. H. RAYMOND SPINNEY, b. 11 Sep 1874; m. NELLIE HARRIS.
1374. iv. CLARA SPINNEY, b. 1877.

1122. HENRIETTA[8] SPINNEY *(ROLLAND[7], GEORGE B[6], JEREMIAH[5], JOHN[4], ANDREW[3], JOHN[2], THOMAS[1])* was born 1852. She married FERDINAND POTTLE.

Children of HENRIETTA SPINNEY and FERDINAND POTTLE are:
i. GEORGE R[9] POTTLE, b. 1876.
ii. HERBERT R POTTLE, b. 1879.
iii. SARAH F POTTLE, b. 1882; m. ARTHUR HUTCHINS, 26 Nov 1902.

1123. ABBIE E[8] SPINNEY *(ROLLAND[7], GEORGE B[6], JEREMIAH[5], JOHN[4], ANDREW[3], JOHN[2], THOMAS[1])* was born 1854, and died Aft. 1900. She married WILLIAM S VARNEY 04 Dec 1875 in Bath, Sagadahoc, Maine. He was born 1846, and died Bef. 1900.

Children of ABBIE SPINNEY and WILLIAM VARNEY are:
    i.   EDITH[9] VARNEY, b. Oct 1876.
    ii. FRANK A VARNEY, b. Apr 1878.
    iii. OSCAR W VARNEY, b. 1879.
    iv. HENREITTA VARNEY, b. Nov 1879.
    v. CHARLOTTE VARNEY, b. Oct 1881.

1124. ANGELINE[8] SPINNEY *(JAMES M[7], JEREMIAH[6], JOHN[5], JOHN[4], ANDREW[3], JOHN[2], THOMAS[1])* was born 23 Sep 1841. She married JAMES E COOMBS. He was born 1839.

Children of ANGELINE SPINNEY and JAMES COOMBS are:
    i.   IMOGENE[9] COOMBS, b. 1858.
    ii. JACOB L COOMBS, b. 1860.

1125. ABRAHAM[8] SPINNEY *(JOHN[7], JEREMIAH[6], JOHN[5], JOHN[4], ANDREW[3], JOHN[2], THOMAS[1])* was born 1821 in New Hampshire, and died 1868 in Charlestrown, MA. He married (1) MARY HUTCHINGSON 22 Jun 1847 in Charlestown, Mass. She was born 1830, and died 23 May 1848. He married (2) CATHERINE FAULKNER 25 Sep 1848 in Charlestown, Ma, daughter of JAMES FAULKNER and MARY. She was born 1823.

Children of ABRAHAM SPINNEY and CATHERINE FAULKNER are:
    i.   CHARLES W[9] SPINNEY, b. 04 Jan 1849; d. Aft. 1870.
    ii. AMELIA SPINNEY, b. 1851; d. Aft. 1870; m. LEVI C SANBORN, 1872, Lynn, Ma; b. 1845, New Hampshire; d. 1894.

1126. HULDAH OLIVER[8] SPINNEY *(JOHN[7], JEREMIAH[6], JOHN[5], JOHN[4], ANDREW[3], JOHN[2], THOMAS[1])* was born 24 Apr 1842 in Stark, ME, and died 1910 in Stark, ME. She married HOSEA WASHBURN EMERY.

Children of HULDAH SPINNEY and HOSEA EMERY are:
    i.   MARTHA-LOUISE[9] EMERY.
    ii. ANDREW SPINNEY EMERY.

1127. JOHN COLBY[8] SPINNEY *(JOHN[7], JEREMIAH[6], JOHN[5], JOHN[4], ANDREW[3], JOHN[2], THOMAS[1])* was born 24 Oct 1844 in Stark, ME, and died 11 Mar 1919 in Stark, Me. He married ROSE GORDON. She was born 1851, and died 24 Mar 1944 in Stark, ME.

Children of JOHN SPINNEY and ROSE GORDON are:
1375.   i.   ALMON I[9] SPINNEY, b. Apr 1871; d. 30 Aug 1965, Augusta,ME.
          ii. ANDREW GORDEN SPINNEY, b. Jul 1873; d. 21 Nov 1951; m. CORA B SPINNEY, 21 Aug 1899; b. 29 Nov 1876.
1376.   iii. JOHN DELBERT SPINNEY, b. 1881.

1128. ANNIE[8] SPINNEY *(JOHN[7], JEREMIAH[6], JOHN[5], JOHN[4], ANDREW[3], JOHN[2], THOMAS[1])* was born 22 Dec 1847 in Industry, ME, and died 23 Dec 1919. She married JOHN A SEAVEY 29 Jan 1870. He was born 1847, and died 1918.

Children of ANNIE SPINNEY and JOHN SEAVEY are:
    i.   OLIVE O[9] SEAVEY, b. 04 Aug 1870.
    ii. ALVIN SEAVEY, b. 22 Nov 1871.
    iii. ARTHUR F SEAVEY, b. 24 Aug 1873.
    iv. JOHN W SEAVEY, b. 23 Jul 1878.
    v. ANNIE M SEAVEY, b. 11 Sep 1885.

1129. ALMON ROBINSON[8] SPINNEY *(JOHN[7], JEREMIAH[6], JOHN[5], JOHN[4], ANDREW[3], JOHN[2], THOMAS[1])* was born 12 Apr 1860, and died 26 Mar 1933 in Industry Maine. He married ALICE D MOULTON 15 Nov 1882, daughter of JOHN MOULTON and MARY COPP. She was born 07 Aug 1858, and died 1947.

Children of ALMON SPINNEY and ALICE MOULTON are:
- i. GEORGE ALBERT[9] SPINNEY, b. 08 Jun 1883; d. May 1967; m. JESSIE JASQUITH, 1923.
- 1377. ii. CARRIE L SPINNEY, b. 03 Jul 1885.
- 1378. iii. RALPH 0 SPINNEY, b. 04 Feb 1887; d. 30 Jan 1979, South Portland, ME.
- iv. HAROLD H SPINNEY, b. 1891.
- v. FLORA SPINNEY, b. 1902; d. Aft. 1930.
- vi. FRANK JOHN SPINNEY, b. 03 Oct 1896, Industry, ME; d. Aft. 1930; m. (1) IDA E WITHEY; b. 1892, Maine; m. (2) HAZEL C MARTIN, 22 Nov 1919; b. 1897.

1130. ROBERT R[8] SPINNEY *(JOHN[7], JEREMIAH[6], JOHN[5], JOHN[4], ANDREW[3], JOHN[2], THOMAS[1])* was born 08 Mar 1861, and died 27 Dec 1901 in Unity, ME. He married CORA. She was born 06 Sep 1858, and died 16 Sep 1936 in Unity, ME.

Children of ROBERT SPINNEY and CORA are:
- 1379. i. WARREN N[9] SPINNEY, b. Nov 1881.
- ii. WILIAM RILEY SPINNEY, b. 05 Dec 1888; d. 04 Apr 1978, California.
- iii. FREDERICK SPINNEY, b. Jan 1893.

1131. CORDELIA ANN[8] SPINNEY *(CHARLES OLIVER[7], CALEB[6], JOHN[5], JOHN[4], ANDREW[3], JOHN[2], THOMAS[1])* was born 13 Apr 1846 in Phippsburg, ME. She married CHARLES T. HANNAFORD 10 Sep 1871.

Children of CORDELIA SPINNEY and CHARLES HANNAFORD are:
- i. FLORENCE[9] HANNAFORD.
- ii. LEON HANNAFORD.
- iii. CHARLES HANNAFORD.
- iv. BLANCHE HANNAFORD.

1132. OLIVE ANN[8] SPINNEY *(OLIVER R[7], CALEB[6], JOHN[5], JOHN[4], ANDREW[3], JOHN[2], THOMAS[1])* was born 05 Jan 1859. She married EDGAR H WILLICE.

Child of OLIVE SPINNEY and EDGAR WILLICE is:
- i. JOHN C[9] WILLICE, b. 1880.

1133. CARRIE EMMA[8] SPINNEY *(OLIVER R[7], CALEB[6], JOHN[5], JOHN[4], ANDREW[3], JOHN[2], THOMAS[1])* was born 01 Nov 1864. She married JAMES ALBERT WRIGHT.

Children of CARRIE SPINNEY and JAMES WRIGHT are:
- i. EDGAR[9] WRIGHT.
- ii. LELAND WRIGHT.
- iii. CELIA WRIGHT.
- iv. LAWRENCE WRIGHT, b. 1900.

1134. OLIVER FREEMAN[8] SPINNEY *(OLIVER R[7], CALEB[6], JOHN[5], JOHN[4], ANDREW[3], JOHN[2], THOMAS[1])* was born 1869 in Bath, ME, and died 26 Nov 1912 in Boston, Ma. He married ANN LOUISE PETERSON.

Child of OLIVER SPINNEY and ANN PETERSON is:
- i. GEORGE BOWKER[9] SPINNEY, b. 29 Nov 1909; m. MARY ELMIRA ROGERS.

1135. PALMER O[8] SPINNEY *(ZINA H[7], DAVID[6], JOHN[5], JOHN[4], ANDREW[3], JOHN[2], THOMAS[1])* was born 18 Mar 1839 in Georgetown, ME, and died 07 Aug 1920 in Brunswick, ME. He married MARY J TODD 21 Nov 1859. She died Aft. 1917.

Children of PALMER SPINNEY and MARY TODD are:
        i.   ALFRED[9] SPINNEY, b. Abt. 1860.
       ii. ANNIE L SPINNEY, b. 1863.
1380.   iii. ELVINGTON PALMER SPINNEY, b. 30 Jun 1868, Georgetown, ME.
       iv. LEVA LESTER SPINNEY, b. 1871.
       v.   INEZ P SPINNEY, b. 1872.

1136. CHARLES S[8] SPINNEY *(ZINA H[7], DAVID[6], JOHN[5], JOHN[4], ANDREW[3], JOHN[2], THOMAS[1])* was born Aug 1857, and died Aft. 1930. He married HARRIET M JONES. She was born Jan 1857, and died Aft. 1930.

Children of CHARLES SPINNEY and HARRIET JONES are:
1381.   i.   CHESTER RAYMOND[9] SPINNEY, b. Apr 1884.
       ii. LOWELL J SPINNEY, b. Jan 1890.

1137. DAVID S[8] SPINNEY *(ZINA H[7], DAVID[6], JOHN[5], JOHN[4], ANDREW[3], JOHN[2], THOMAS[1])* was born 03 Apr 1843, and died Bet. 1920 - 1930. He married LOTTIE ANDERSON 1873 in Charlestown, MA. She was born 1850 in Nova Scotia, and died 1907 in Malden, Ma.

Child of DAVID SPINNEY and LOTTIE ANDERSON is:
       i.   GRACE MABEL[9] SPINNEY, b. 1875.

1138. ELIJAH M[8] SPINNEY *(ZINA H[7], EPHRAIM[6], JOHN[5], JOHN[4], ANDREW[3], JOHN[2], THOMAS[1])* was born 11 Oct 1852 in Georgetown, ME, and died Aft. 1910 in Georgetown, ME. He married MARY ELIZABETH HIGGINS 30 Nov 1873 in Georgetown, ME. She was born Sep 1851, and died Aft. 1900.

Children of ELIJAH SPINNEY and MARY HIGGINS are:
       i.   CALVIN MAURICE[9] SPINNEY, b. 27 Oct 1874; d. Aft. 1930; m. ESTELLA SUSAN EVANS, 05 May 1897, Auburn, Maine; b. 1871.
       ii. GEORGE L SPINNEY, b. May 1878.
      iii. FRED H SPINNEY, b. Oct 1879; m. VESTA WOODIS, 23 Apr 1913.
      iv. HERMAN A SPINNEY, b. 1881; m. LILA CAMPBELL, 09 Jun 1906, Georgetown, ME.
1382.   v.   ERNEST L SPINNEY, b. Apr 1884.
1383.   vi. RALPH E SPINNEY, b. Apr 1884.
      vii. ETHEL H SPINNEY, b. 1892.
     viii. WILLIE F SPINNEY, b. Aug 1892.
      ix. JENNIE M SPINNEY, b. Apr 1894; m. ARTHUR L STROUT, 01 Jun 1902, Auburn, ME.

1139. WILLIAM P[8] SPINNEY *(ZINA H[7], EPHRAIM[6], JOHN[5], JOHN[4], ANDREW[3], JOHN[2], THOMAS[1])* was born 1855, and died Aft. 1910. He married CARRIE A PLUMMER 03 Jun 1878. She was born 1862, and died Aft. 1910.

Children of WILLIAM SPINNEY and CARRIE PLUMMER are:
       i.   ALBERT W[9] SPINNEY, b. 1878; d. Bef. 1910; m. ANNIE EDWARDS, 1905, Malden, MA.
       ii. RACHEL SPINNEY, b. 1886.

1140. JAMES M[8] SPINNEY *(ZINA H[7], EPHRAIM[6], JOHN[5], JOHN[4], ANDREW[3], JOHN[2], THOMAS[1])* was born 23 Oct 1857 in Georgetown, ME. He married (1) MARGARET EVELYN WARD. She died Abt. 1884. He married (2) EVELYN 1884. She was born Nov 1856.

Children of JAMES SPINNEY and MARGARET WARD are:
       i.   LOUISA L[9] SPINNEY, b. 22 Sep 1881.
1384.   ii. HOWARD APPLETON SPINNEY, b. 18 Jan 1884.
      iii. ELEANOR BLAIR SPINNEY, b. 1904, Marblehead, Ma; d. Marblehead, Ma.

Children of JAMES SPINNEY and EVELYN are:
1385.   iv. CLARENCE P[9] SPINNEY, b. Mar 1889.
      v.   CHRISTINE M SPINNEY, b. Oct 1892.

1141. LYDIA M. "KITTY"[8] BURCE *(RUFUS LOREN[7], RACHEL[6] OLIVER, JANE[5] SPINNEY, JOHN[4], ANDREW[3], JOHN[2], THOMAS[1])* was born 06 Aug 1871 in Hannibal, MO, and died 06 Jul 1952 in Snohomish, Snohomish Co., WA. She married CHARLES GOFF.

Child of LYDIA BURCE and CHARLES GOFF is:

    i.   MARGUERITE[9] GOFF, b. 10 Dec 1900, Snohomish, Snohomish Co., WA; d. Jan 1929, Snohomish, Snohomish Co., WA.

1142. DAISY MAY[8] BURCE *(RUFUS LOREN[7], RACHEL[6] OLIVER, JANE[5] SPINNEY, JOHN[4], ANDREW[3], JOHN[2], THOMAS[1])* was born 15 Nov 1876 in Hannibal, MO, and died 04 Oct 1949 in Snohomish, Snohomish Co., WA. She married JOHN J. STEPHENSON 15 Nov 1898 in Everett, Snohomish Co., WA.

Child of DAISY BURCE and JOHN STEPHENSON is:

1386.   i.   BEATRICE S.[9] STEPHENSON, b. 05 Feb 1902, Winters, CA; d. 05 Feb 1988, Milwaukie, OR.

1143. SUSAN AUGUSTA RUBY[8] BURCE *(JOHN CALVIN[7], RACHEL[6] OLIVER, JANE[5] SPINNEY, JOHN[4], ANDREW[3], JOHN[2], THOMAS[1])* was born 06 Dec 1864 in Industry, ME, and died 25 Jan 1919 in Granite Falls, WA. She married THOMAS NICHOLAS LOVERING RICHARDS 18 Dec 1880 in Seattle, WA. He was born 21 Dec 1847 in Ilfracombe, Devon, England, and died 02 Jun 1923 in Maltby, WA.

Children of SUSAN BURCE and THOMAS RICHARDS are:

1387.   i.   ADA ESTHER[9] RICHARDS, b. 25 Mar 1882, Coupeville, WA; d. 01 Jun 1970, Anacortes, WA.
    ii.   THOMAS WILLIAM LOVERING RICHARDS, b. 24 Apr 1883, Coupeville, WA.
    iii.   OTILDA RUBY RICHARDS, b. 19 Oct 1885, Coupeville, WA; d. 24 Mar 1937, CA.
    iv.   JOHN CALVIN RICHARDS, b. 02 Oct 1887, Coupeville, WA; d. 01 Sep 1949, Everett, WA; m. MABEL EVELYN THOMAS, 10 Oct 1908, Coupeville, WA.
    v.   MARGARET ELIZABETH RICHARDS, b. 13 Sep 1888, Seattle, WA; d. Apr 1933, Orange Co., CA.
    vi.   JAMES LOREN RICHARDS, b. 18 Jul 1890, Coupeville, WA; d. 28 Jan 1967, Everett, WA.
    vii.   GROVER NICHOLAS RICHARDS, b. 14 Jun 1892, Coupeville, WA; d. 28 Jun 1959, Tacoma, WA.
    viii.   ELSIE MAY RICHARDS, b. 21 May 1894, Coupeville, WA; d. 17 Mar 1940, Everett, WA.
    ix.   LAEL HANCOCK RICHARDS, b. 24 Nov 1895, Coupeville, WA; d. 07 Feb 1958, Redlands, CA.
    x.   EDMOND ARTHUR RICHARDS, b. 22 Oct 1897, Coupeville, WA; d. 18 Nov 1919.
    xi.   MARIAN GERTRUDE RICHARDS, b. 02 Dec 1898, Coupeville, WA; d. 04 Jan 1976, CA.
    xii.   HELEN ROWENA RICHARDS, b. 25 Sep 1900, Coupeville, WA; d. 06 Aug 1987, Sedro Wooley, WA; m. PETER LONG.
    xiii.   DONALD ALLEN RICHARDS, b. Nov 1901, Snohomish, WA; d. 09 Jun 1903, Snohomish, WA.
    xiv.   CHARLES HENRY RICHARDS, b. Feb 1903, Snohomish, WA; d. 05 Jul 1903, Snohomish, WA.
    xv.   ROBERT DOUGLAS RICHARDS, b. 25 Oct 1904, Snohomish Co., WA; d. 05 Mar 1960, Seattle, King Co., WA.
    xvi.   LAWRENCE PARKER RICHARDS, b. 16 Oct 1905, Snohomish Co., WA; d. Oct 1973, Seattle, King Co., WA.
    xvii.   EARL RICHARDS, b. 25 Oct 1906, Snohomish Co, WA; d. Oct 1906, Snohomish Co., WA.
    xviii.   CLIFFORD MONROE RICHARDS, b. 11 Nov 1907, Monroe, WA; d. 31 Aug 1962, Seattle, WA.
    xix.   IRVING BURCE RICHARDS, b. 26 Apr 1911, Snohomish Co., WA; d. 10 Jan 1929, San Pedro Harbor, L.A. County, CA.

1144. ARLETTA LINDSEY[8] SPINNEY *(GEORGE A[7], GEORGE B[6], JEREMIAH[5], JOHN[4], ANDREW[3], JOHN[2], THOMAS[1])* was born 09 Dec 1868, and died 1925. She married JOSEPH TORREY 1891. He was born 1870.

Children of ARLETTA SPINNEY and JOSEPH TORREY are:

    i.   KATHERINE[9] TORREY.
    ii.   MARGARET TORREY.
    iii.   BOWEN TORREY.
    iv.   JOSEPH HOWARD TORREY.

1145. GEORGE EDWIN[8] SPINNEY *(ALVAH[7], MOSES B[6], JEREMIAH[5], JOHN[4], ANDREW[3], JOHN[2], THOMAS[1])* was born 02 Nov 1851 in Maine, and died Bef. 1930 in California. He married FLORA H. She was born Jan 1868 in Washington, and died Aft. 1930.

Children of GEORGE SPINNEY and FLORA H are:
    i.   EDNA H^9 SPINNEY, b. Jun 1888, California; d. Aft. 1930.
    ii. ALVAH HARRY SPINNEY, b. 19 Jul 1893, California; d. 11 Sep 1978, California.
    iii. LAWRENCE HARLAND SPINNEY, b. 19 Aug 1901, California; d. 11 Jan 1973.

1146. MELVINA F^8 SPINNEY *(FRANKLIN^7, MOSES B^6, JEREMIAH^5, JOHN^4, ANDREW^3, JOHN^2, THOMAS^1)* was born 1858, and died Aft. 1880. She married ASA MELVILLE OLIVER.

Children of MELVINA SPINNEY and ASA OLIVER are:
    i.   CARRIE M^9 OLIVER.
    ii. JAMES W G OLIVER.

1147. GEORGE A^8 SPINNEY *(FRANKLIN^7, MOSES B^6, JEREMIAH^5, JOHN^4, ANDREW^3, JOHN^2, THOMAS^1)* was born 1874, and died Aft. 1930. He married EMMA VARNER 05 Oct 1898. She died Aft. 1930.

Children of GEORGE SPINNEY and EMMA VARNER are:
    i.   CLIFTON G^9 SPINNEY, b. 1901, Maine; d. Aft. 1930.
    ii. BYRON B SPINNEY, b. 1906; m. DORIS HAYES.
    iii. GLADYS M SPINNEY, b. 1912; d. Aft. 1930; m. WILLIAM T DONNELL.

1148. HERBERT E^8 SPINNEY *(ANDREW JACKSON^7, MOSES B^6, JEREMIAH^5, JOHN^4, ANDREW^3, JOHN^2, THOMAS^1)* was born 18 Jan 1870 in Maine, and died in Denver, Colorado. He married SARAH. She was born 1878.

Children of HERBERT SPINNEY and SARAH are:
    i.   MARION^9 SPINNEY, b. 1899.
    ii. RUTH SPINNEY, b. 1902.
    iii. EDWARD SPINNEY, b. 1909.

1149. WILLIAM JAMES^8 SPINNEY *(ANDREW JACKSON^7, MOSES B^6, JEREMIAH^5, JOHN^4, ANDREW^3, JOHN^2, THOMAS^1)* was born 1876 in Maine, and died 21 Feb 1939. He married SARAH LOUISE PRATT 20 Aug 1903.

Children of WILLIAM SPINNEY and SARAH PRATT are:
    i.   LEONA^9 SPINNEY.
    ii. ANDREW OLIVER SPINNEY, b. 1910, Medford, Ma.
    iii. PRICILLA SPINNEY.
    iv. LUCILE SPINNEY.
1388.   v. WILLIAM ABORN SPINNEY, b. 05 Jun 1904, Boston, MA; d. 01 Feb 1968, Mededith, NH.
    vi. PHILIP SPINNEY.

1150. MILAN H^8 SPINNEY *(SILAS CURTIS^7, JOHN^6, JEREMIAH^5, JOHN^4, ANDREW^3, JOHN^2, THOMAS^1)* was born May 1874, and died Aft. 1910. He married FLORA EDITH PREBLE 24 Jun 1893. She was born 1876, and died Aft. 1900.

Children of MILAN SPINNEY and FLORA PREBLE are:
1389.   i.   FLORA R^9 SPINNEY, b. 1897.
    ii. MARTHA A SPINNEY, b. 1899; m. FRANK V WEST, 1917, Auburn, Maine.
    iii. LESTER SPINNEY, b. 1903; m. LENA LAKIN, 02 Sep 1933.

1151. ELMER ELLSWORTH^8 SPINNEY *(DANIEL WILLIAM^7, JOHN^6, JEREMIAH^5, JOHN^4, ANDREW^3, JOHN^2, THOMAS^1)* was born 07 Feb 1861, and died Aft. 1900. He married ANNIE AUGUSTA FOLSOM 20 Sep 1883 in Portland Maine. She was born 24 Jun 1861 in Maine, and died 06 Oct 1952 in Los Angeles California.

Children of ELMER SPINNEY and ANNIE FOLSOM are:
    i.   PHILIP ELLSWORTH^9 SPINNEY, b. 10 Aug 1884, Portland, ME; d. 26 Dec 1884.
    ii. EDNA ISABELE SPINNEY, b. 28 Oct 1885, Portland, ME.
    iii. ETHEL MAY SPINNEY, b. 16 Jan 1887, Portland, ME; d. 30 Jan 1887.

iv. ELMER FREMONT SPINNEY, b. 10 Jul 1889, Bath, ME; d. 10 May 1890.

1152. LAURA GERTRUDE[8] SPINNEY *(DANIEL WILLIAM[7], JOHN[6], JEREMIAH[5], JOHN[4], ANDREW[3], JOHN[2], THOMAS[1])* was born 22 Apr 1863. She married FREDERICK W HAYES. He was born 1862.

Children of LAURA SPINNEY and FREDERICK HAYES are:
1390.   i. ARTHUR MILTON[9] HAYES, b. 1884.
      ii. MILDRED F HAYES, b. 1881.
     iii. ELMOR HAYES, b. 1894.

1153. HARRY GARFIELD[8] SPINNEY *(DANIEL WILLIAM[7], JOHN[6], JEREMIAH[5], JOHN[4], ANDREW[3], JOHN[2], THOMAS[1])* was born 06 Jun 1877 in Bath, ME. He married ALICE WRAMPE 17 Jan 1912.

Child of HARRY SPINNEY and ALICE WRAMPE is:
1391.   i. FREMONT EDWARD[9] SPINNEY, b. 21 Jul 1913.

1154. ALICE[8] SPINNEY *(IRA[7], JEREMIAH[6], JEREMIAH[5], JOHN[4], ANDREW[3], JOHN[2], THOMAS[1])* was born 22 Jan 1878 in Starks, ME, and died 03 Mar 1970. She married HARRY MOORE.

Children of ALICE SPINNEY and HARRY MOORE are:
1392.   i. MERLE[9] MOORE, b. 15 Aug 1901, Starks, ME.
1393.   ii. VERA M MOORE, b. 11 Aug 1915.

1155. ELLSWORTH R[8] SPINNEY *(IRA[7], JEREMIAH[6], JEREMIAH[5], JOHN[4], ANDREW[3], JOHN[2], THOMAS[1])* was born 1864 in Maine, and died Aft. 1930 in Lynn, MA. He married (1) HALLIE POWERS, daughter of TIMOTHY POWERS and ELECTRA BATCH. She was born 1864 in Vermont. He married (2) MARY E RICHARDS 1902 in Lynn, MA. He married (3) WILHELMINA GULLIVER 27 Aug 1923.

Children of ELLSWORTH SPINNEY and HALLIE POWERS are:
1394.   i. HERBERT ELLSWORTH[9] SPINNEY, b. 25 Mar 1887, Lynn, MA; d. May 1973.
      ii. GRACIE SPINNEY, b. 1885.

1156. SYLVESTER VESS[8] SPINNEY *(ASA D[7], RICHARD[6], RICHARD[5], JOHN[4], ANDREW[3], JOHN[2], THOMAS[1])* was born 14 Jan 1851 in Ohio, and died 1933. He married LUCINDA EVALINE WOODSIDE 18 Sep 1878, daughter of ROBERT WOODSIDE and MARTHA PETTIT. She was born 1856.

Children of SYLVESTER SPINNEY and LUCINDA WOODSIDE are:
1395.   i. LILLIE MAE[9] SPINNEY, b. 21 May 1879.
      ii. MARGARET ISABELLE SPINNEY, b. 17 Apr 1884.
1396.   iii. CLEVELAND GROVER SPINNEY, b. 12 Oct 1888; d. 29 May 1958, St Louis, MO, USA.
     iv. MARY AMANDA SPINNEY, b. 24 Mar 1891; m. WILLIAM MCCRARY.
1397.   v. WILLIAM JOHN SPINNEY, b. 01 Apr 1894, Randolph, Il; d. 22 Oct 1958, Randolph, Il.

1157. CHARLES E[8] NILE *(SAMANTHA[7] HINCKLEY, SARAH[6], EUNICE[5] SPINNEY, JOHN[4], ANDREW[3], JOHN[2], THOMAS[1])* was born 1863, and died Aft. 1900. He married FLORA.

Children of CHARLES NILE and FLORA are:
      i. LELAND[9] NILE.
      ii. JAMES NILE.
     iii. JOHN NILE.
     iv. ADDIE NILE.
      v. HATTIE NILE.

1158. BENJAMNI F[8] NILE *(SAMANTHA[7] HINCKLEY, SARAH[6], EUNICE[5] SPINNEY, JOHN[4], ANDREW[3], JOHN[2], THOMAS[1])* was born 1866, and died Aft. 1900. He married NELLIE.

Children of BENJAMNI NILE and NELLIE are:
    i.   ANNA[9] NILE.
    ii.   NAIOMA NILE.
    iii. MARY NILE.
    iv. DOLLIE NILE.
    v.   FRANK NILE.

Generation No. 9

1159. HARRY[9] CUMMINGS (*ALGENAID[8] WORCESTER, MOSES[7], MOSES[6], MOSES[5], ANNE[4] SPINNEY, JOHN[3], SAMUEL[2], THOMAS[1]*) was born 15 Dec 1872 in Jonesport, ME, and died 02 Feb 1939 in Jonesport, ME. He married ELLA NORTON. She was born 1876, and died Bet. 1908 - 1970.

Children of HARRY CUMMINGS and ELLA NORTON are:
    i.   ALGIE10TH[10] CUMMINGS, b. 01 Aug 1896, Jonesport, ME; d. Apr 1978, Gray, ME.
    ii.   HAZEL CUMMINGS, b. 07 Oct 1902; d. Bet. 1942 - 1996, Palm Bay, FL.
1398.   iii. ETHEL CUMMINGS, b. 03 Feb 1906, Jonesport, ME; d. 08 Oct 1990, Worchester, MA.

1160. MAMIE[9] BULMER (*MARGARET[8] WORCESTER, MARK[7], ISAAC[6], MOSES[5], ANNE[4] SPINNEY, JOHN[3], SAMUEL[2], THOMAS[1]*) She married HAROLD CALHOUN.

Child of MAMIE BULMER and HAROLD CALHOUN is:
    i.   HAROLD[10] CALHOUN.

1161. EPHRAIM TROTT[9] BULMER (*MARGARET[8] WORCESTER, MARK[7], ISAAC[6], MOSES[5], ANNE[4] SPINNEY, JOHN[3], SAMUEL[2], THOMAS[1]*) was born 01 Nov 1877 in Webster Plantation, ME, and died 1970 in Kingston Ontatio Canada. He married IVA BETSY STINSON 09 Mar 1898 in Caribou , ME, daughter of FRED STINSON and MARILLA GOULD.

Children of EPHRAIM BULMER and IVA STINSON are:
    i.   DOROTHY[10] BULMER.
1399.   ii.   DEAN BULMER.
1400.   iii. LELAND BRYANT BULMER, b. 14 Jun 1906, Houlton, ME; d. 03 Jan 1996, Smithfield, ME.

1162. CHARLES FREDERICK[9] SPINNEY (*ELIOT FRANKLIN[8], ELIOT F[7], ELIOT[6], ROBERT[5], JOHN[4], THOMAS[3], SAMUEL[2], THOMAS[1]*) was born 1869, and died Aft. 1930. He married (1) SUSAN CAROLINE ALBRO 1899 in Lynn, MA, daughter of WARREN ALBRO and VESTA TUCKER. She was born 1871. He married (2) HANNAH E Aft. 1910. She was born 1863.

Children of CHARLES SPINNEY and SUSAN ALBRO are:
    i.   ALBRO ELLIOTT[10] SPINNEY, b. 1902, Lynn, MA.
    ii.   ILAH EVELYN SPINNEY, b. 1905, Lynn, MA.

1163. ABBIE LOLA[9] SPINNEY (*HENRY HOWARD[8], GUSTAVUS NEWHALL[7], WILLIAM NEWHALL[6], BENJAMIN[5], JOHN[4], THOMAS[3], SAMUEL[2], THOMAS[1]*) was born 26 Jan 1888, and died Aft. 1930. She married RAYMOND EDWARD NICHOLS 1910 in Lynn, MA. He was born 07 Dec 1886, and died 29 Apr 1946.

Children of ABBIE SPINNEY and RAYMOND NICHOLS are:
    i.   CONSTANCE[10] NICHOLS.
    ii.   RAE NICHOLS.
    iii. MARILYN NICHOLS.

1164. LUCILLE HARRIET[9] SPINNEY (*HENRY HOWARD[8], GUSTAVUS NEWHALL[7], WILLIAM NEWHALL[6], BENJAMIN[5], JOHN[4], THOMAS[3], SAMUEL[2], THOMAS[1]*) was born 21 Feb 1898 in Cliftondale, MA, and died 1989. She married HARVEY LESTER COOK. He was born 01 Dec 1895 in Marion, SC., and died 28 Nov 1959.

Children of LUCILLE SPINNEY and HARVEY COOK are:

  i. HARVEY L. COOK[10] JR., b. 15 Jul 1921, Sanford, FL; m. (1) ROSE J. FULLERTON; b. 1910, Ireland; d. 05 Jan 1996; m. (2) VICTORIA A. NIELSON; b. 18 Dec 1938, West Hartford, CT.

  ii. MARJORIE R. COOK, b. 22 Nov 1924, Salem, MA; m. CLIFTON L. PRADY; b. 17 Apr 1921, Glouchester, MA.

  iii. EVELYN LOLA COOK, b. 04 Oct 1927, Salem, MA; m. STANLEY E. LEAMAN; b. 27 Jan 1924, Glouchester, MA.

  iv. GERALDINE P. COOK, b. 23 Aug 1938, Essex, Essex, MA; m. JONATHAN S. RADCLIFF; b. 20 Jun 1932.

1165. DOROTHY HOWARD[9] SPINNEY *(HENRY HOWARD[8], GUSTAVUS NEWHALL[7], WILLIAM NEWHALL[6], BENJAMIN[5], JOHN[4], THOMAS[3], SAMUEL[2], THOMAS[1])* was born 06 Jun 1901 in Lynn, MA, and died 1970 in Danvers, MA. She married (1) CHESTER WILLIAM KIRK. He was born Abt. 1899. She married (2) WILLIAM MEDDING DENNING. He was born Abt. 1900 in Nashville, TN., and died 28 Aug 1960.

Children of DOROTHY SPINNEY and CHESTER KIRK are:

  i. CHESTER WILLIAM KIRK[10] JR., b. 24 Sep 1922, Lynn, Essex, MA..

  ii. BARBARA KIRK, b. 08 Aug 1923, Lynn, MA.

Child of DOROTHY SPINNEY and WILLIAM DENNING is:

  iii. HENRY ROBERT[10] DENNING, b. 23 Jun 1927, Lynn, MA..

1166. HAROLD NEAL[9] SPINNEY *(HENRY HOWARD[8], GUSTAVUS NEWHALL[7], WILLIAM NEWHALL[6], BENJAMIN[5], JOHN[4], THOMAS[3], SAMUEL[2], THOMAS[1])* was born 07 Jul 1908 in Lynn, MA, and died 07 Jul 1976. He married BARBARA HOWE. She was born 12 Oct 1910, and died 1981.

Children of HAROLD SPINNEY and BARBARA HOWE are:

1401. i. JOAN LOUISE[10] SPINNEY, b. 13 Jul 1936, Newburyport, MA.

1402. ii. MARCIA SPINNEY, b. 29 May 1942, Ipswich, MA.

1403. iii. MADELYN[10TH] SPINNEY, b. 25 Apr 1944, Ipswich, MA.

1167. DOROTHY[9] CAMPBELL *(CHARLOTTE HACK[8] SPINNEY, ELLERY CHANNING[7], WILLIAM NEWHALL[6], BENJAMIN[5], JOHN[4], THOMAS[3], SAMUEL[2], THOMAS[1])* was born 10 Aug 1899 in Chicago, IL, and died 24 Apr 1972 in Oak Park IL. She married LESLIE PETER DEGROOT.

Children of DOROTHY CAMPBELL and LESLIE DEGROOT are:

  i. LESLIE PETER[10] DEGROOT, m. MARY LEE BRINKLEY.

  ii. GRETCHEN DEGROOT.

1168. HAROLD ELLERY[9] SPINNEY *(HAROLD ELLERY[8], ELLERY CHANNING[7], WILLIAM NEWHALL[6], BENJAMIN[5], JOHN[4], THOMAS[3], SAMUEL[2], THOMAS[1])* was born Private. He married VIRGINIA TISS Private.

Notes for HAROLD ELLERY SPINNEY:

Harold E. "Bud" Spinney Jr., 91, beloved husband of the late Virginia Tiss; devoted father of Bonnie S. (George) Cerveny, David A. (Jennifer) Spinney, Kim V.D. Spinney and Lynne S. (Dennis) Swieton; loving grandfather of Gretchen, Heidi, Lisa, Britain, John, Scott, Melissa and Stephen; dear great-grandfather of Croix; adoring brother of Jane S. (Peter) Allen. Bud was born in Chicago, IL and was a 1927 graduate of New Trier High School and graduated from Lafayette University in 1931. He began his career as a third generation Chicago Board of Trade member in 1931. In 1944 he was commissioned as a lieutenant in the Navy and served in the Pacific Theater during WWII. After the war he returned to the Chicago Board of Trade where he completed his 56 year career in 1986. He was the founding Scoutmaster of Boy Scout Troop 2 in Wilmette in 1931 and Troop 222 in Round Lake in 1950. Bud was a lifelong volunteer in the Boy Scouts of America and served on the Round Lake School Board in the 1960's. Funeral Service Saturday, Jan. 13, 2001 at 1 p.m. at Memorial Park Mausoleum, Main Chapel, 9900 Gross Point Rd., Skokie. In lieu of flowers, memorials may be made to Juvenile Diabetes Foundation, 120 Wall St., 19th floor, New York, NY 10005-4001. Info, Donnellan Family Funeral Services

Children of HAROLD SPINNEY and VIRGINIA TISS are:

        i.   BONNIE GAIL[10] SPINNEY, b. Private.
        ii.   DAVID SPINNEY, b. Private.
        iii. KIM SPINNEY, b. Private.
        iv.   LYNN SPINNEY, b. Private.

1169. JANE LOUISE[9] SPINNEY *(HAROLD ELLERY[8], ELLERY CHANNING[7], WILLIAM NEWHALL[6], BENJAMIN[5], JOHN[4], THOMAS[3], SAMUEL[2], THOMAS[1])* was born Private. She married UZERNE WHELLER ALLEN, son of UZERNE ALLEN and DOROTHY HARTMAN.

Children of JANE SPINNEY and UZERNE ALLEN are:
1404.   i.   JOHN SPINNEY[10] ALLEN.
1405.   ii.   JUDITH MAUD ALLEN.
1406.   iii. STEVEN SPINNEY ALLEN.

1170. ANGIE BELL[9] SPINNEY *(JOSEPH D[8], GEORGE F[7], THOMAS[6], THOMAS[5], JOHN[4], THOMAS[3], SAMUEL[2], THOMAS[1])* was born 1901, and died 1948. She married SAMUEL BARNES MOODY. He was born 1887, and died 1940.

Child of ANGIE SPINNEY and SAMUEL MOODY is:
        i.   VIRGINIA JEAN[10] MOODY.

1171. IRVING SPINNEY[9] MARKS *(CARRIE LOUISE[8] SPINNEY, SAMUEL[7], JOHN WARREN[6], SAMUEL[5], JOHN[4], THOMAS[3], SAMUEL[2], THOMAS[1])* was born 1883 in Lynn, MA, and died Jul 1957. He married HELEN. She was born 1888.

Children of IRVING MARKS and HELEN are:
        i.   PERSIS[10] MARKS, b. 1913.
        ii.   BARBARA MARKS, b. 1916.
        iii. GEORGE MARKS, b. 1917.
        iv.   CALEB MARKS, b. 1920.
        v.   ANN MARKS, b. 1922.
        vi.   RHONDA MARKS, b. 1924.
        vii. PHOEBE MARKS, b. 1925.

1172. WARREN A[9] SPINNEY *(GEORGE R[8], JOHN WARREN[7], JOHN WARREN[6], SAMUEL[5], JOHN[4], THOMAS[3], SAMUEL[2], THOMAS[1])* was born Apr 1890 in Ohio. He married GLADYS CLARK.

Children of WARREN SPINNEY and GLADYS CLARK are:
        i.   WARREN CLARK[10] SPINNEY, b. 25 May 1923, Oklahoma; d. 14 Mar 1983, California.
        ii.   BETTY SPINNEY.
        iii. MARGARET SPINNEY.

1173. ARTHUR FRANKLIN[9] SPINNEY *(ERNEST EDWARD[8], CHARLES HERBERT[7], JOHN WARREN[6], SAMUEL[5], JOHN[4], THOMAS[3], SAMUEL[2], THOMAS[1])* was born 06 Apr 1898 in Saugus, MA. He married NELLIE JENKINS. She was born in Saugus, MA.

Children of ARTHUR SPINNEY and NELLIE JENKINS are:
1407.   i.   MAGARET[10] SPINNEY, b. 25 Dec 1919.
1408.   ii.   MURIEL G. SPINNEY, b. 23 Aug 1921.
1409.   iii. ARTHUR FRANKLIN SPINNEY, b. 08 Nov 1927, Saugus, MA; d. 1995, Lynn. MA..
1410.   iv.   JEAN SPINNEY, b. 16 Sep 1933.
1411.   v.   EVELYN L. SPINNEY, b. 16 Apr 1938.

1174. EVERETT EDWARD[9] SPINNEY *(ERNEST EDWARD[8], CHARLES HERBERT[7], JOHN WARREN[6], SAMUEL[5], JOHN[4], THOMAS[3], SAMUEL[2], THOMAS[1])* was born 09 Jan 1900 in Saugus, MA, and died 05 May 1966. He married MILLE BASSETT 01 Aug 1928 in Rochester, NY. She was born 06 Sep 1912, and died 06 Sep 1985.

Child of EVERETT SPINNEY and MILLE BASSETT is:

1412.   i.   EVERETT EDWARD SPINNEY[10] JR., b. 01 Aug 1928.

1175. RALPH ERNEST[9] SPINNEY *(ERNEST EDWARD[8], CHARLES HERBERT[7], JOHN WARREN[6], SAMUEL[5], JOHN[4], THOMAS[3], SAMUEL[2], THOMAS[1])* was born 14 Feb 1904 in Saugus, MA, and died 26 Apr 1971 in Attleboro, MA. He married HAZEL EMMA SCOWN Feb 1929 in Attleboro, MA. She was born 06 Mar 1904 in Fall River, MA, and died 27 Apr 1977 in Attleboro, MA.

Children of RALPH SPINNEY and HAZEL SCOWN are:
        i.   RUTH EDA[10] SPINNEY, b. 08 Nov 1929, Attleboro, MA; d. 17 May 1994, Attleboro, MA.
1413.   ii.   RALPH ERNEST SPINNEY, b. 28 Feb 1936, Attleboro, MA.

1176. BERTHA MAY[9] SPINNEY *(ERNEST EDWARD[8], CHARLES HERBERT[7], JOHN WARREN[6], SAMUEL[5], JOHN[4], THOMAS[3], SAMUEL[2], THOMAS[1])* was born 09 Apr 1907 in Saugus, Essex, MA, and died 27 Apr 1988 in Lynn, Essex, MA.. She married HARRY FRANCIS SANDBERG 11 Feb 1927 in Newport, RI. He was born 31 Dec 1906 in Buffalo, NY, and died 01 Jan 1970 in Warren, MI.

Children of BERTHA SPINNEY and HARRY SANDBERG are:
1414.   i.   FRANCES RUTH[10] SANDBERG, b. 31 Dec 1927, Newport, RI..
1415.   ii.   ERNEST EDWARD SANDBERG, b. 20 Jan 1929, Lynn, MA.
1416.   iii.   MARJORIE ELLEN SANDBERG, b. 08 Dec 1930, Winthrop, MA.
        iv.   RICHARD ARNOLD SANDBERG, b. 29 Sep 1933, Winthrop, MA.
1417.   v.   BARBARA SANDBERG, b. 01 Jun 1935, Tewksbury, MA..

1177. MURIEL GERTRUDE[9] SPINNEY *(ERNEST EDWARD[8], CHARLES HERBERT[7], JOHN WARREN[6], SAMUEL[5], JOHN[4], THOMAS[3], SAMUEL[2], THOMAS[1])* was born 25 Aug 1909 in Saugus, MA, and died 24 Mar 1986. She married NATHAN ARRON NICHOLSON in Lynn, MA. He was born 25 Sep 1909, and died 09 Aug 1960.

Children of MURIEL SPINNEY and NATHAN NICHOLSON are:
1418.   i.   NANCY-ANN[10] NICHOLSON, b. 28 Sep 1935.
        ii.   RALPH LESTER NICHOLSON, b. 25 Aug 1942; m. HEATHER UNKNOWN.
        iii.   SUE ELLEN NICHOLSON, b. 22 Oct 1944; m. JOHN HEALEY.

1178. WESLEY STARLING[9] ABBOTT *(HARRIETT[8] SPINNEY, CHARLES HERBERT[7], JOHN WARREN[6], SAMUEL[5], JOHN[4], THOMAS[3], SAMUEL[2], THOMAS[1])* was born 15 Nov 1903 in Massachusetts. He married ESTELLE BATES, daughter of GEORGE W BATES.

Child of WESLEY ABBOTT and ESTELLE BATES is:
        i.   BARBARA[10] ABBOTT, b. 1930.

1179. ARTHUR FRANK[9] COOK *(LEONARD FRANK[8], ROWENA R[7] SPINNEY, NICHOLAS[6], CALEB[5], NICHOLAS[4], JAMES[3], SAMUEL[2], THOMAS[1])* was born 21 Oct 1887 in Lynn, MA, and died 28 Jul 1967 in Kittery, ME. He married ELLEN O LOON.

Children of ARTHUR COOK and ELLEN LOON are:
        i.   NORMAN ARTHUR[10] COOK.
        ii.   JEFFERSON ERNEST COOK.
        iii.   FRANCES ELLEN COOK.
        iv.   STERLING JAMES COOK.

1180. GILES WILLIS[9] FERNALD *(GRACE GREENWOOD[8] SPINNEY, ROBERT[7], NATHAN[6], JOHN[5], NICHOLAS[4], JAMES[3], SAMUEL[2], THOMAS[1])*

Child of GILES WILLIS FERNALD is:
        i.   LILLIAN FRANCES[10] FERNALD, m. EVERETT BRUSO.

1181. SIDNEY A^9 SPINNEY *(FRED L^8, ROBERT^7, NATHAN^6, JOHN^5, NICHOLAS^4, JAMES^3, SAMUEL^2, THOMAS^1)* was born 16 Dec 1896 in Eliot, ME. He married (1) MARION F TAYLOR 19 Nov 1921. She was born 1899, and died 1923. He married (2) ALMA LEAVITT 25 Nov 1925. She was born 23 Apr 1904.

Children of SIDNEY SPINNEY and ALMA LEAVITT are:
1419.	i.	ROBERT E^{10} SPINNEY, b. 1927.
	ii.	DENNIS SPINNEY.
	iii.	LOUISE SPINNEY.

1182. FORREST E^9 SPINNEY *(NATHAN G^8, NATHAN^7, NATHAN^6, JOHN^5, NICHOLAS^4, JAMES^3, SAMUEL^2, THOMAS^1)* was born Sep 1880 in Maine, and died 1934 in Maine. He married FLORENCE CHANDLER 01 Feb 1925. She was born 1892, and died 1964.

Children of FORREST SPINNEY and FLORENCE CHANDLER are:
	i.	MAE^{10} SPINNEY, d. Aft. Aug 1999; m. RELEA.
1420.	ii.	EARL W SPINNEY, b. 03 Aug 1925, Portsmouth, NH; d. 18 Aug 1999.

1183. LLOYD T^9 SPINNEY *(NATHAN G^8, NATHAN^7, NATHAN^6, JOHN^5, NICHOLAS^4, JAMES^3, SAMUEL^2, THOMAS^1)* was born Dec 1892, and died 1945. He married ANNIE OLIVE FROST 05 Dec 1911. She was born 16 Sep 1892 in Eliot, ME, and died 07 Feb 1938 in Eliot, ME.

Child of LLOYD SPINNEY and ANNIE FROST is:
        i.   LLOYD N^{10} SPINNEY, b. 1907; m. ANNIE REGAN, 10 Apr 1939.

1184. ERNEST HARLOW^9 SPINNEY *(NATHAN G^8, NATHAN^7, NATHAN^6, JOHN^5, NICHOLAS^4, JAMES^3, SAMUEL^2, THOMAS^1)* was born 15 Mar 1897, and died 08 Dec 1961. He married FLORENCE A WHEELER 16 Jun 1920.

Child of ERNEST SPINNEY and FLORENCE WHEELER is:
1421.	i.	HARLOW RODNEY^{10} SPINNEY, b. 1926.

1185. MELISSA E.^{9} OLIVER *(CLEAVELAND MANSON^8, JOHN^7, JOHN^6, MARY^5 SPINNEY, JEREMIAH^4, JEREMIAH^3, SAMUEL^2, THOMAS^1)* was born 28 Dec 1879. She married ARTHUR PRENEY.

Child of MELISSA OLIVER and ARTHUR PRENEY is:
        i.   ARNOLD C.^{10} PRENEY, b. 1898.

1186. FREDRICK E.^{9} OLIVER *(CHARLES WARREN^8, JOHN^7, JOHN^6, MARY^5 SPINNEY, JEREMIAH^4, JEREMIAH^3, SAMUEL^2, THOMAS^1)* was born 17 May 1877 in Bath, ME, and died 10 Sep 1932 in Bath, ME. He married JENNIE M. GALLAGHER 26 Dec 1896 in Bath, ME. She was born 10 Jun 1879 in Saint John, ME, and died 07 May 1967 in Bath, ME.

Children of FREDRICK OLIVER and JENNIE GALLAGHER are:
        i.   CLARENCE L.^{10} OLIVER, b. 18 Jul 1899, Bath, ME.
        ii.   ELSA MAY OLIVER, b. Private; m. JOHN F. SPELLMAN, Private.
        iii. PERCY W. OLIVER, b. Private.
        iv.   THELMA HAZEL OLIVER, b. Private; m. FRANK J. SNOW, Private; b. Private.
        v.   PEARL M. OLIVER, b. Private.

1187. HERSHON BIRT^9 OLIVER *(CHESTER MARR^8, JOHN^7, JOHN^6, MARY^5 SPINNEY, JEREMIAH^4, JEREMIAH^3, SAMUEL^2, THOMAS^1)* was born 27 Sep 1888 in Bath, ME, and died 01 Jun 1975 in Bath, ME. He married (1) ANNIE THURSTON 13 Dec 1909 in Bath, ME. He married (2) CHARLOTTE M. BARR 09 Nov 1929 in Bath, Sagadahoc, ME. She died 20 May 1961 in New York, NY.

Child of HERSHON OLIVER and CHARLOTTE BARR is:
        i.   ELLEN^{10} OLIVER, b. Private; m. ??? PERRY, Private; b. Private.

1188. ARTHUR GIBBS[9] OLIVER *(WILBER CARTER[8], JOHN[7], JOHN[6], MARY[5] SPINNEY, JEREMIAH[4], JEREMIAH[3], SAMUEL[2], THOMAS[1])* was born 02 May 1882 in Bath, ME, and died 25 May 1946 in Portland, ME. He married ELNORA DAIN 25 Nov 1903 in Bath, ME. She was born 1886, and died 12 Dec 1952 in Bath, ME.

Children of ARTHUR OLIVER and ELNORA DAIN are:
    i.   EVELYN[10] OLIVER, b. Private.
    ii. WARREN D. OLIVER, b. Private.
    iii. WILBUR C. OLIVER, b. Private.

1189. FRED ALBION[9] OLIVER *(WILLIAM SMITH[8], WILLIAM RAIRDEN[7], JAMES[6], MARY[5] SPINNEY, JEREMIAH[4], JEREMIAH[3], SAMUEL[2], THOMAS[1])* was born 22 May 1879 in Phippsburg, ME, and died 19 Nov 1957 in Bath, ME. He married ELIZABETH MAYERS UPTON. She was born 05 Jul 1875 in Phippsburg, ME, and died 15 Dec 1955 in Bath, ME.

Children of FRED OLIVER and ELIZABETH UPTON are:
    i.   EDWIN F.[10] OLIVER, b. Private.
    ii. LENA OLIVER, b. Private; m. LARRABEE, Private; b. Private.

1190. SILAS MANSON[9] OLIVER *(WILLIAM SMITH[8], WILLIAM RAIRDEN[7], JAMES[6], MARY[5] SPINNEY, JEREMIAH[4], JEREMIAH[3], SAMUEL[2], THOMAS[1])* was born 21 Nov 1881 in Phippsburg, ME, and died 10 Aug 1951 in Bath, ME. He married MARTHA JANE WILSON. She was born 24 Nov 1888 in Phippsburg, ME, and died 08 Oct 1962 in Bath, ME.

Children of SILAS OLIVER and MARTHA WILSON are:
    i.   GRACE[10] OLIVER, b. 02 Jan 1906; d. 06 Dec 1908.
    ii. WILLIAM W. OLIVER, b. Private.
    iii. ALICE G. OLIVER, b. Private; m. HENRY ROGERS, Private; b. Private.

1191. HIRAM PERRY[9] OLIVER *(HERBERT A.[8], JOSIAH PERRY[7], JAMES[6], MARY[5] SPINNEY, JEREMIAH[4], JEREMIAH[3], SAMUEL[2], THOMAS[1])* was born 17 Jul 1887 in Bath, ME. He married GRACE M. FLEMMING 1909.

Child of HIRAM OLIVER and GRACE FLEMMING is:
    i.   PHYLLIS MAY[10] OLIVER, b. Private.

1192. MABEL[9] LOVELL *(LYDIA[8] HUSSEY, PHOEBE[7] GOODWIN, BARTHSEHBA WEARE[6] SPINNEY, DAVID[5], EBENEZER[4], JONATHAN[3], SAMUEL[2], THOMAS[1])* was born 13 Jul 1871. She married GEORGE G DURRELL.

Child of MABEL LOVELL and GEORGE DURRELL is:
    i.   CHARLES[10] DURRELL, b. 28 May 1888.

1193. PARKER THAYER[9] SPINNEY *(EUGENE NATHANIAL[8], JOSEPH FRANKLIN[7], PARKER FOSTER[6], DAVID[5], EBENEZER[4], JONATHAN[3], SAMUEL[2], THOMAS[1])* was born 11 Sep 1894 in Ipswich, MA, and died Oct 1965. He married (1) MARY THORNLEY 28 Mar 1922 in Indianapolis, IN. She was born 07 Apr 1905. He married (2) DOROTHEA WILLIAMS 31 Oct 1928.

Children of PARKER SPINNEY and MARY THORNLEY are:
          i.   RUTH LENORE[10] SPINNEY, b. 02 Sep 1926.
1422.   ii. PARKER THAYER SPINNEY, b. Private; d. Feb 1986.

1194. HELEN AUGUSTA[9] SPINNEY *(EUGENE NATHANIAL[8], JOSEPH FRANKLIN[7], PARKER FOSTER[6], DAVID[5], EBENEZER[4], JONATHAN[3], SAMUEL[2], THOMAS[1])* was born 26 Oct 1902 in Shelbourne, MA. She married (1) VICTOR WHITNEY 30 Aug 1926. She married (2) ULMONT MARVIN CARLTON 19 Apr 1930 in Watertown, MA.

Child of HELEN SPINNEY and ULMONT CARLTON is:
    i.   HELEN A[10] CARLTON.

1195. HAROLD WARREN[9] SPINNEY *(FRANCIS WARREN[8], GEORGE F[7], MARK[6], PARKER[5], EBENEZER[4], JONATHAN[3], SAMUEL[2], THOMAS[1])* was born 31 Jan 1918 in Bradford, MA, and died 04 Dec 1999 in Groveland, MA. He married BEATRICE P JOHNSON 11 Jul 1943 in Bradford, MA. She died 30 May 2005 in Coral Springs, Fl.

Children of HAROLD SPINNEY and BEATRICE JOHNSON are:
| 1423. | i. | ROBERT WAYNE[10] SPINNEY, b. 20 Nov 1946. |
| 1424. | ii. | JEANNE LAURIE SPINNEY, b. 14 Mar 1956. |

1196. LLOYD MAXWELL[9] OWENS *(ELLA GERTRUDE[8] WHEELER, ALICE CATHERINE[7] DWELLEY, NARCISSA SPRING[6] SPINNEY, EBENEZER[5], EBENEZER[4], JONATHAN[3], SAMUEL[2], THOMAS[1])* was born 26 Dec 1890 in Cottage Grove OR, and died 31 Aug 1971 in Meadow Glade WA. He married ALTHA ELIZABETH GILDERSLEEVE 20 Dec 1911 in Cottage Grove OR, daughter of JOHN GILDERSLEEVE and HARRIET DUNHAM. She was born 24 Mar 1894 in Fruitland WA, and died Unknown in ?.

Children of LLOYD OWENS and ALTHA GILDERSLEEVE are:
	i.	MAXINE[10] OWENS.
	ii.	GRATTON OWENS.
	iii.	VERDELL OWENS.
	iv.	VIRGINIA OWENS.
1425.	v.	LAUREL MAE OWENS, b. 29 Aug 1915, Angwin , CA; d. 23 Nov 1966.

1197. HELEN LOUISE[9] MALOY *(ALICE CATHERINE[8] DWELLEY, JOSEPH FRANKLIN[7], NARCISSA SPRING[6] SPINNEY, EBENEZER[5], EBENEZER[4], JONATHAN[3], SAMUEL[2], THOMAS[1])* She married MELVIN JAY BECKLEY.

Child of HELEN MALOY and MELVIN BECKLEY is:
| 1426. | i. | MELINDA LOU[10] BECKLEY. |

1198. LLEWELLEN[9] SPINNEY *(DOUGLAS[8], JAMES ALEXANDER[7], STEPHEN[6], JONATHAN[5], NATHANIEL[4], JONATHAN[3], SAMUEL[2], THOMAS[1])* was born 31 Oct 1894 in Utopia, NB., and died 01 Aug 1972 in St George, NB.. He married ROYCE LAVONNE GOSS 16 Jan 1920 in St George, NB.. She was born 14 Jun 1894 in Bonny River, NB., and died 01 Aug 1972.

Child of LLEWELLEN SPINNEY and ROYCE GOSS is:
| 1427. | i. | ANITA[10] SPINNEY, b. 05 Oct 1926. |

1199. JOHN CHARLES THOMAS "JACK"[9] SPINNEY *(CHARLES MCPIKE[8], ALFRED HURLEY[7], STEPHEN[6], JONATHAN[5], NATHANIEL[4], JONATHAN[3], SAMUEL[2], THOMAS[1])* was born 05 Apr 1882 in Musquash, NB., and died 1955 in Berlin, NH.. He married EMILY ETHELIRE DALEY 21 Sep 1904.

Child of JOHN SPINNEY and EMILY DALEY is:
| | i. | VERNON LEMMOX[10] SPINNEY, b. 22 Aug 1909. |

1200. JAMES H[9] SPINNEY *(ALFRED HURLEY[8], ALFRED HURLEY[7], STEPHEN[6], JONATHAN[5], NATHANIEL[4], JONATHAN[3], SAMUEL[2], THOMAS[1])* was born 27 Jan 1893, and died 12 Oct 1951 in Eastport, ME. He married CHARLOTTE A WARD. She was born 1899.

Children of JAMES SPINNEY and CHARLOTTE WARD are:
| | i. | ELEANOR[10] SPINNEY, b. 1917. |
| | ii. | AGATHA SPINNEY, b. 1919. |

1201. ALBERT J[9] SPINNEY *(CLARENCE JOHN[8], ALFRED HURLEY[7], STEPHEN[6], JONATHAN[5], NATHANIEL[4], JONATHAN[3], SAMUEL[2], THOMAS[1])* was born 26 Mar 1894 in Maine, and died Nov 1979 in Springfield, MA. He married ANNIE M TRACEY 01 Sep 1917 in Bangor, ME. She was born 1895.

Child of ALBERT SPINNEY and ANNIE TRACEY is:
    i.   CAROL J[10] SPINNEY, b. 1929, Bangor, ME.

1202. ALFRED J[9] SPINNEY *(CLARENCE JOHN[8], ALFRED HURLEY[7], STEPHEN[6], JONATHAN[5], NATHANIEL[4], JONATHAN[3], SAMUEL[2], THOMAS[1])* was born 26 Mar 1894 in Maine, and died Jun 1971 in New Britain, Hartford, CT. He married MARY MCKERVEY 08 May 1916 in Bangor, ME. She was born 1894.

Children of ALFRED SPINNEY and MARY MCKERVEY are:
    i.   RUTH[10] SPINNEY, b. 1918.
    ii. CATHERINE SPINNEY, b. 1920.
    iii. MARGERIE SPINNEY, b. 1924.
    iv. MARY SPINNEY, b. 1928.

1203. ALICE "MAUD"[9] SPINNEY *(FREDERICK[8], HORATIO NELSON[7], STEPHEN[6], JONATHAN[5], NATHANIEL[4], JONATHAN[3], SAMUEL[2], THOMAS[1])* was born 07 Nov 1888 in Musquash, NB., and died May 1939 in Grand Bay, NB.. She married STEPHEN LEWIS MOORE 01 Jun 1910 in Musquash, NB., son of ANDREW MOORE and ISABELLA.

Children of ALICE SPINNEY and STEPHEN MOORE are:
    i.   STEPHEN LEWIS "LEW"[10] MOORE, b. 08 Oct 1911, Newcastle, NB.; d. 1981; m. GENE CARLETON PLUMMER, 08 Jun 1940, Saint John, NB..
    ii. HAROLD GREGORY MOORE, b. 16 Nov 1915, Newcastle, NB.; d. 01 Mar 1955, Fairvale, NB.; m. NORA ANGELA MCELWAINE, 26 Dec 1941.
    iii. JOYCE LENNOX MOORE, b. 14 Apr 1926, Grand Bay, NB.; m. GEORGE MILTON SMITH, 13 Oct 1951, Rothesay, NB..

1204. STEPHEN PERCY[9] SPINNEY *(FREDERICK[8], HORATIO NELSON[7], STEPHEN[6], JONATHAN[5], NATHANIEL[4], JONATHAN[3], SAMUEL[2], THOMAS[1])* was born 24 Sep 1895 in Musquash, NB., and died 09 Feb 1984 in Saint John, NB.. He married LILLA HAZEL ORCHARD 01 Sep 1915 in Saint John, NB., daughter of ABRAHAM ORCHARD and THEODOSIA BLACK. She was born 29 Jan 1891 in Cambridge, NB., and died 08 Oct 1982 in St John, NB..

Children of STEPHEN SPINNEY and LILLA ORCHARD are:
    i.   FLORENCE HAZEL[10] SPINNEY, b. 09 Oct 1916, St John, NB.; m. ALWARD PEER HARNED, May 1941, St John New Brunswick.
    ii. FAULDS PERCIVAL SPINNEY, b. 19 Feb 1919, St John, NB.; m. MARGARET DOREEN ROBERTSON, 01 Dec 1945, Saskatoon, Canada.
1428. iii. JACK BENTLEY SPINNEY, b. 31 Dec 1920, St John, NB.; d. 14 Mar 2002.
    iv. JESSIE "ROBERTA" SPINNEY, b. 01 Apr 1923, St John, NB.; d. 1993, Fory Meyers Florida; m. RONALD MAXWELL SMITH, 06 Aug 1949, St John, NB..

1205. STANLEY DOULGAS[9] SPINNEY *(FREDERICK[8], HORATIO NELSON[7], STEPHEN[6], JONATHAN[5], NATHANIEL[4], JONATHAN[3], SAMUEL[2], THOMAS[1])* was born 19 May 1898 in Musquash, NB., and died 09 Aug 1973 in Musquash, NB.. He married SIBYL ANIE UMNIATI RICHMOND 1921 in Saint John, NB., daughter of WILLIAM RICHMOND and ANIE HUGHES. She was born 15 Feb 1901 in Zimbabwe, South Africa, and died 09 Sep 1987 in St John, NB..

Children of STANLEY SPINNEY and SIBYL RICHMOND are:
    i.   STANLEY "HUBERT"[10] SPINNEY, b. 24 May 1922, St John, NB.; d. 22 Sep 2007; m. FELICIA MIGNAN "BUNTY" BROWN, 01 Jun 1943, St John, NB..

       Notes for STANLEY "HUBERT" SPINNEY:
       SPINNEY, Stanley Hubert "Hugh" - (Former member of the Orillia Wind Ensemble, Champlain Music Makers, Orillia Little Big Band, Jerry White Quartet and the Shriner Music Makers) - Passed away at the Orillia Soldiers' Memorial Hospital on Saturday, September 22, 2007; in his 86th year and has gone to be with the love of his life and best friend Felicia. Father of Bruce (Jill) and Shawne. Papa to Troy, Mary-lu (John), Duke (Heather) and Melissa. Pookie to Miranda and great papa to Quinn. Son of the late Stanley and Sybil Spinney. Brother to Melicent Macaulay, Shirley (Bruce, predeceased) Cobham and Patsy (Bill) Ryan. Visitation will be held at the Mundell Funeral Home, 79 West St. N., Orillia on Wednesday from 7-9 p.m. Funeral service will be held in the chapel on Thursday, September 27, 2007 at 11 o'clock. If desired,

memorial donations to the Shriner's Children's Hospital or the Alzheimers Society would be gratefully appreciated. Messages of condolence are welcomed at www.mundellfuneralhome.ca 10837879

    ii.   SIBYL "MELICENT" SPINNEY, b. 27 Jun 1926, St John, NB.; m. WALLACE DONALD MACAULEY, 10 Sep 1949, St John, NB..

    iii. SHIRLEY ELIZABETH SPINNEY, b. 22 Mar 1929, St John, NB.; m. ROBERT "BRUCE" WINSTON COBHAM, 14 Feb 1951, St John, NB..

    iv. PATRICIA JUNE SPINNEY, b. 12 Jun 1936, St John, NB.; m. WILLIAM FREDERICK RYAN, 07 Nov 1959, St John, NB..

1206. MARION E[9] GAGE *(CATHERINE[8] SPINNEY, JAMES VAN BUREN[7], JAMES S[6], JONATHAN[5], NATHANIEL[4], JONATHAN[3], SAMUEL[2], THOMAS[1])* was born 1918. She married HOWARD BRUMMITT 1951.

Child of MARION GAGE and HOWARD BRUMMITT is:

    i.   DOUGLAS[10] GAGE, b. Ottawa Canada.

1207. ALICE[9] SPINNEY *(GEORGE ROSS[8], JAMES VAN BUREN[7], JAMES S[6], JONATHAN[5], NATHANIEL[4], JONATHAN[3], SAMUEL[2], THOMAS[1])* was born Abt. 1900. She married ARTHUR PARKS Abt. 1920.

Notes for ALICE SPINNEY:
PARKS, ALICE LOIS - After a brief illness at the Saint John Regional Hospital on March 18, 2001 Mrs. Alice Lois (Spinney) Parks of St. George, NB wife of the late Arthur Herbert Parks. Born in Upper Letang, NB on June 24, 1917 she was the daughter of the late George and Stella (Smith) Spinney. A loving mother and grandmother she is survived by her son Byron (Anne) of Port Hawkesbury, NS; three daughters Inez Taylor of St. George, Marilyn Munn of Beaver Harbour and Lois McLanaghan (Eugene) of Pennfield; four grandchildren; Lisa Needle, Melissa Saunders, Ross Munn and Rodney Munn; one great grandson Zachary Needle; one brother Douglas Spinney (Heather) of Saint John; one sister Beulah Dewar of St. George; several nieces, nephews and cousins. Alice was a life member of the Ladies Auxiliary Royal Canadian Legion Branch #40 St. George as well as a member of the St. Mark's Anglican Church and St. Marks A.C.W. She enjoyed quilting and gardening especially flowers. Resting at the St. George Funeral Home, 26 Portage Street, St. George, NB (755-3533). Service will be held on Wednesday at 2 PM from St. Mark's Anglican Church, St. George, NB with Reverend Mary Anne Langmaid officiating. Interment in the St. George Rural Cemetery in the spring. Visiting hours at the funeral home on Tuesday from 2-4 and 7-9 PM. In her memory, remembrances to the St. Mark's Building Fund, The NB Heart and Stroke Foundation or to the charity of the donor's choice would be appreciated by the family. | Times Globe | Telegraph Journal |

Children of ALICE SPINNEY and ARTHUR PARKS are:

    i.   DOUGLAS[10] PARKS.

    ii. BYRON PARKS.

    iii. INEZ PARKS, m. TAYLOR.

1429.   iv. MARILYN PARKS.

    v.   LOIS PARKS, m. MCLANAHAN.

1208. ARTHUR GILMORE[9] SPINNEY *(JAMES RENFORTH[8], JAMES VAN BUREN[7], JAMES S[6], JONATHAN[5], NATHANIEL[4], JONATHAN[3], SAMUEL[2], THOMAS[1])* was born Abt. 1930. He married MARIE RACHAEL FRENNETTE Sep 1956 in Peti Rocher, NB..

Child of ARTHUR SPINNEY and MARIE FRENNETTE is:

    i.   ESTER[10] SPINNEY, m. CLIFFORD BOYD.

1209. DOROTHEA "DOSSIE"[9] SPINNEY *(JOHN OLIVER[8], JAMES VAN BUREN[7], JAMES S[6], JONATHAN[5], NATHANIEL[4], JONATHAN[3], SAMUEL[2], THOMAS[1])* was born 22 Apr 1922 in St George, NB.. She married DONALD MORTON "PETE" BALDWIN, son of MORTON BALDWIN and JESSIE ARMSTRONG.

Children of DOROTHEA SPINNEY and DONALD BALDWIN are:

    i.   MORTON EDGAR[10] BALDWIN.

ii.   JOHN MORTON BALDWIN, b. 16 Mar 1958, Fredericton, NB..

1210. WALLACE STUART[9] CAMPBELL *(MARION BEATRICE[8] STUART, HANNAH ELIZA[7] SPINNEY, CHARLES EDWARD[6], JONATHAN[5], NATHANIEL[4], JONATHAN[3], SAMUEL[2], THOMAS[1])* was born 13 Jan 1922 in Salem, MA. He married FLORENCE.

Child of WALLACE CAMPBELL and FLORENCE is:
       i.   ELLEN[10] CAMPBELL.

1211. RALPH EDWARD[9] MILLS *(GORDON VICTOR[8], LOUISE PARKS[7] SPINNEY, CHARLES EDWARD[6], JONATHAN[5], NATHANIEL[4], JONATHAN[3], SAMUEL[2], THOMAS[1])* was born 26 Jun 1925 in Brooklyn, NY., and died 04 Jan 2005 in Methuen, MA. He married (1) ALICE LORRAINE DAVIS, daughter of DANIEL DAVIS and MARY LYONS. She was born 01 Mar 1929 in Medford, MA. He married (2) DOROTHY MITCHELL.

Children of RALPH MILLS and ALICE DAVIS are:
1430.	i.	ELEANOR[10] MILLS, b. 06 Feb 1952, Medford, MA.
	ii.	JUDITH E MILLS, b. 12 Aug 1953, Medford, MA; m. (1) JOHN CALHOUN, 31 Aug 1974; b. 04 Aug 1951; m. (2) THOMAS PHILLIPS, 21 Dec 1996; b. 12 Aug 1950.
1431.	iii.	RALPH JR MILLS, b. 07 Sep 1954, Medford, MA; d. 29 Apr 2006, Woburn, Ma.
	iv.	BARRY MILLS, b. 15 Jul 1958, Winchester, MA; m. JANICE ROTTLER.
1432.	v.	PHILIP MILLS, b. 01 Oct 1959, Winchester, MA.
1433.	vi.	NANCY MARIE MILLS, b. 01 Mar 1964, Medford, MA.

Children of RALPH MILLS and DOROTHY MITCHELL are:
	vii.	BRIAN[10] MILLS, b. 27 Jan 1965; m. NANCY.
1434.	viii.	ROBERT MILLS, b. Apr 1966.
	ix.	MELISSA MILLS, b. 29 Sep 1975, Lowell, MA.

1212. GORDON[9] MILLS *(GORDON VICTOR[8], LOUISE PARKS[7] SPINNEY, CHARLES EDWARD[6], JONATHAN[5], NATHANIEL[4], JONATHAN[3], SAMUEL[2], THOMAS[1])* was born 14 Apr 1928. He married JOAN.

Children of GORDON MILLS and JOAN are:
| 1435. | i. | STEPHEN[10] MILLS, b. 1952. |
| 1436. | ii. | SUSAN MILLS, b. 1962. |

1213. KENNETH[9] MILLS *(EDWARD L[8], LOUISE PARKS[7] SPINNEY, CHARLES EDWARD[6], JONATHAN[5], NATHANIEL[4], JONATHAN[3], SAMUEL[2], THOMAS[1])* He married MARY FAY, daughter of ALBERT FAY and MARY SULLIVAN.

Children of KENNETH MILLS and MARY FAY are:
       i.   KEITH[10] MILLS.
      ii.   DEBBIE MILLS.
     iii.   MARY MILLS.

1214. NORMAN[9] MILLS *(EDWARD L[8], LOUISE PARKS[7] SPINNEY, CHARLES EDWARD[6], JONATHAN[5], NATHANIEL[4], JONATHAN[3], SAMUEL[2], THOMAS[1])* was born 1927. He married RUTH.

Children of NORMAN MILLS and RUTH are:
1437.	i.	NORMAN[10] MILLS.
1438.	ii.	BRIAN MILLS.
1439.	iii.	RICHARD MILLS.
	iv.	PAUL MILLS.
1440.	v.	PATRICIA MILLS.

1215. VIRGINIA GAIL[9] CROSBY *(DOROTHY ELAINE[8] BARCLAY, CAROLYN B (CARRIE)[7] SPINNEY, CHARLES EDWARD[6], JONATHAN[5], NATHANIEL[4], JONATHAN[3], SAMUEL[2], THOMAS[1])* died 1975. She married ALLAN KINGSLEY PARKER, son of ALLAN PARKER.

Children of VIRGINIA CROSBY and ALLAN PARKER are:
  i.   KRISTEN[10] PARKER.
  ii.   DAVID PARKER.
  iii. JONATHAN PARKER.
  iv.   ALLAN PARKER.

1216. LILLIAN MAE[9] DAVIS *(ANNIE MAUDE[8] BARSTOW, LAURA DEXTER[7] GREEN, MARY ANN[6] SPINNEY, JONATHAN[5], NATHANIEL[4], JONATHAN[3], SAMUEL[2], THOMAS[1])* was born 20 Oct 1906. She married EARL H WHITCOMB.

Children of LILLIAN DAVIS and EARL WHITCOMB are:
  i.   HAZEL[10] WHITCOMB, b. 03 Jul 1930; m. CARL HOLANDER, 28 Aug 1948.
  ii.   MILDRED WHITCOMB, b. 1929.

1217. EVELYN MARION[9] SPINNEY *(ERNEST LINWOOD[8], HERBERT HARRISON FICKETT[7], ARCHIBALD BARNEY[6], JONATHAN[5], NATHANIEL[4], JONATHAN[3], SAMUEL[2], THOMAS[1])* was born 04 Jun 1906 in Mapleton, ME, and died 25 Mar 1954 in Waterville, ME. She married STANLEY GUY GRENDELL 24 Jun 1925.

Child of EVELYN SPINNEY and STANLEY GRENDELL is:
  i.   LIN[10] GRENDELL, m. ELAINE.

1218. FRANK J[9] SPINNEY *(FRANKLIN PIERCE[8], BENJAMIN FRANK[7], ARCHIBALD BARNEY[6], JONATHAN[5], NATHANIEL[4], JONATHAN[3], SAMUEL[2], THOMAS[1])* was born 27 Oct 1912 in Hermon, ME, and died 02 Jan 1991. He married CHRISTINE ELENOR SCULLIN, daughter of CHARLES SCULLIN and MARY SHAIN. She was born 13 Aug 1913 in Rollingdam, New Brunswick, and died 31 Mar 2002 in Gray, ME.

Child of FRANK SPINNEY and CHRISTINE SCULLIN is:
1441. i.   CHARLES JAMES[10] SPINNEY.

1219. OTIS LEVI[9] SPINNEY *(EBENEZER[8], WILLIAM L[7], EBENEZER[6], EBENEZER[5], NATHANIEL[4], JONATHAN[3], SAMUEL[2], THOMAS[1])* was born 15 Aug 1903 in Onarga, IL, and died 09 Dec 1966 in Lansing, MI. He married KATHLEEN HICKS.

Children of OTIS SPINNEY and KATHLEEN HICKS are:
  i.   BRUCE ALLISON[10] SPINNEY.
  ii.   VIVIAN JEAN SPINNEY.
  iii. LAURA BELLE SPINNEY.
  iv.   MARJORIE SPINNEY.
  v.   ROY ARNOLD SPINNEY.
  vi.   FRED SPINNEY.

1220. LUCY ALBION[9] SPINNEY *(EBENEZER[8], WILLIAM L[7], EBENEZER[6], EBENEZER[5], NATHANIEL[4], JONATHAN[3], SAMUEL[2], THOMAS[1])* was born 27 Apr 1908, and died 22 Jan 1988 in Costa Mesa, CA. She married SELON SAMUEL STRUBLE 04 Apr 1925.

Children of LUCY SPINNEY and SELON STRUBLE are:
  i.   DOROTHY[10] STRUBLE.
  ii.   LILLIAN STRUBLE.
  iii. SELON SAMUEL STRUBLE.
  iv.   DARYL STRUBLE.
  v.   DARLENE STRUBLE.
  vi.   VIVIAN JOAN STRUBLE, b. 17 Jul 1927, Covert, MI; d. 1984, Costa Mesa, CA; m. DOANLD MOORE, 1948, Lansing, MI.
  vii. LEROY ALVIN/LEROY STRUBLE/STRUBLE, b. 17 Dec 1930, Covert, MI; d. 28 Jun 1977, Lansing, MI.

1221. FRANCIS JOSEPH[9] SPINNEY *(EBENEZER[8], WILLIAM L[7], EBENEZER[6], EBENEZER[5], NATHANIEL[4], JONATHAN[3], SAMUEL[2], THOMAS[1])* was born 16 Sep 1923. He married NORMA IRENE SMITH.

Notes for FRANCIS JOSEPH SPINNEY:
SPINNEY, Francis J., died April 29, 2000

SPINNEY, SMITH, KING

Sturgis; Francis Joseph SPINNEY, 76, of 69945 S. Nottawa St., Sturgis, Mich. died peacefully at his home on Saturday, April 29, 2000.

He was born Sept. 16, 1923 in Lansing, Mich., a son to Eben and Carilean (SMITH) SPINNEY.

Mr. SPINNEY had been a Sturgis resident for the past 10 years. For many years he lived in Arizona.

On June 10, 1944 he married Norma SMITH in Albion, Ind. He was a retired tool and die maker by trade and enjoyed fishing and hunting.

He is survived by his wife of 55 years, Norma SPINNEY; a daughter and her husband, Karon and Ronald KING of Sturgis; a son and his wife, Art and Marie SPINNEY of Ann Arbor; 5 grandchildren; 3 great-grandchildren; 2 sisters; and numerous nieces and nephews.

Preceding him in death were his parents and several brothers and sisters.

In accordance with his wishes, cremation has taken place and there will be no service.

The family suggests those wishing to make a memorial donation in Mr. SPINNEY'S memory consider a charity of one's own choice.

Arrangements were handled by the Hackman-Foglesong Funeral Home of Sturgis. (Additional information, www.legacy.com)

END

Children of FRANCIS SPINNEY and NORMA SMITH are:
      i. KARON[10] SPINNEY, m. RONALD KING.
1442. ii. ARTHUR SPINNEY.

1222. MYRTLE MAY[9] SPINNEY (*EBENEZER[8], WILLIAM L[7], EBENEZER[6], EBENEZER[5], NATHANIEL[4], JONATHAN[3], SAMUEL[2], THOMAS[1]*)

Child of MYRTLE MAY SPINNEY is:
      i. HARRIETTE[10] SPINNEY.

1223. CHESTER ALVAH[9] SPINNEY (*JOHN W[8], WILLIAM L[7], NATHANIEL[6], EBENEZER[5], NATHANIEL[4], JONATHAN[3], SAMUEL[2], THOMAS[1]*) was born 27 Jun 1901 in New Brunswick, and died 05 Apr 1992 in Ayer, MA. He married MARGARET ELLEN FAGEN, daughter of JAMES FAGEN. She was born 17 Dec 1902 in Bolton, England, and died 03 May 1992 in Ayer, MA.

Children of CHESTER SPINNEY and MARGARET FAGEN are:
      i. CAROLL[10] SPINNEY, b. 26 Dec 1933; m. DEBRA.
1443. ii. DONALD A SPINNEY.
     iii. DAVID SPINNEY, b. 1929.

1224. RAYMOND AUGUSTINE[9] SPINNEY (*ALFRED WINFIELD[8], WILLIAM L[7], NATHANIEL[6], EBENEZER[5], NATHANIEL[4],*

JONATHAN³, SAMUEL², THOMAS¹) was born 07 Mar 1909 in Lawrence, MA. He married ELSIE LOUISE BLACKBURN 12 Sep 1930 in New Hampshire. She died 21 Jan 2002.

Notes for ELSIE LOUISE BLACKBURN:
Elsie L. Donnelly
NEWBURYPORT -- Elsie L. (Blackburn) (Spinney) Donnelly, formerly of Methuen and Salem, N.H., passed away Monday, Jan. 21, 2002 at Port Nursing Home in Newburyport, where she had been a resident for several years.
Elsie was the widow of Raymond Spinney and later married Edward L. Donnelly, who died in 1996.

Elsie worked at the Ayer Mills in the drawing room for many years. Elsie was an artist who studied with Carl Pennisi. She was a member of several artist associations and exhibited her paintings throughout Massachusetts and New Hampshire.

She and her late husband Edward were avid sailing partners and were members of the Lake Massabesic Yacht Club, and competed in numerous races in New Hampshire and Florida.

Elsie is survived by daughters Virginia (Spinney) and her husband Harry J. McKenna of Seabrook Beach, N.H., and Tralee (Donnelly) and her husband John Chatalian of Marlboro; sister Florence Spinney of Wakefield, R.I.; granddaughter Erin L. (McKenna) Stroup of Seabrook Beach; grandsons Brian and Jeffrey Chatalian of Marlboro; and several nieces and nephews.

There will be no calling hours. A memorial Mass will be in the spring at Star of the Sea Church in Salisbury. Arrangements are by the Pollard Funeral Home, 233 Lawrence St., Methuen.

Children of RAYMOND SPINNEY and ELSIE BLACKBURN are:
  i. VIRGINA MARGARET¹⁰ SPINNEY.
  ii. TRALEE SPINNEY.

1225. ALFRED WINFIELD⁹ SPINNEY *(ALFRED WINFIELD⁸, WILLIAM L⁷, NATHANIEL⁶, EBENEZER⁵, NATHANIEL⁴, JONATHAN³, SAMUEL², THOMAS¹)* was born 18 Dec 1910 in Lebanon. ME. He married FLORENCE IRENE BLACKBURN 08 Sep 1940 in Methuen, MA.

Children of ALFRED SPINNEY and FLORENCE BLACKBURN are:
  i. ALFRED WINFIELD¹⁰ SPINNEY, b. Abt. 1945.
  ii. MARGARET WINIFRED SPINNEY, b. Abt. 1945; m. PRATT.
  iii. GAYLE RUTH SPINNEY, b. Abt. 1945.

1226. EDITH E⁹ SPINNEY *(ALFRED WINFIELD⁸, WILLIAM L⁷, NATHANIEL⁶, EBENEZER⁵, NATHANIEL⁴, JONATHAN³, SAMUEL², THOMAS¹)* was born Abt. 1915 in Mass.

Child of EDITH E SPINNEY is:
  i. CLAUDIA¹⁰ SPINNEY.

1227. CLAUDE EDWIN⁹ MILLS *(ARTHUR JONES⁸, SARAH⁷ SPINNEY, ARTHUR JONES⁶, EBENEZER⁵, NATHANIEL⁴, JONATHAN³, SAMUEL², THOMAS¹)* was born 04 Aug 1886 in Andover, SD. He married BESSIE LEONA MISEL 20 Oct 1909 in Alberta, Canada. She died 05 Dec 1988 in Tacoma, WA.

Children of CLAUDE MILLS and BESSIE MISEL are:
  i. IVAN ARTHUR¹⁰ MILLS, b. 08 Sep 1911; d. 04 Oct 1911, Irricana Alberta Canada.
  ii. BETHEL LEONA MILLS, b. 01 Oct 1913, Beiseker, Alberta Canada; m. RAY JACOBSON; b. 18 Feb 1910.
1444. iii. ARTHUR EDWIN MILLS, b. 02 Jul 1915; d. 21 Mar 1976, Grass Valley Califorina.
1445. iv. HAROLD GLEN MILLS, b. 01 Sep 1917, Andover, SD.
1446. v. PEARL LOUISE MILLS, b. 24 May 1924, Andover, SD.

1228. PEARL EUDORA⁹ MILLS *(ARTHUR JONES⁸, SARAH⁷ SPINNEY, ARTHUR JONES⁶, EBENEZER⁵, NATHANIEL⁴,*

JONATHAN³, SAMUEL², THOMAS¹) was born 12 May 1890 in Andover, SD, and died 13 Oct 1913. She married OLIVER BERMOND SIMPSON. He was born 18 Nov 1890 in Harvard, NE, and died 28 Feb 1957.

Children of PEARL MILLS and OLIVER SIMPSON are:
1447.   i.   ORWAN BERMOND¹⁰ SIMPSON, b. 01 Oct 1913, Cashmere, WA.
1448.   ii. ARTHUR MILLS SIMPSON, b. 01 Oct 1913, Cashmere. WA; d. 09 Nov 1995.

1229. ARTHUR BOYD⁹ MILLS *(ARTHUR JONES⁸, SARAH⁷ SPINNEY, ARTHUR JONES⁶, EBENEZER⁵, NATHANIEL⁴, JONATHAN³, SAMUEL², THOMAS¹)* was born 26 Jun 1892 in Andover, SD. He married LEONORA "NORA" PENDLETON 24 Feb 1917.

Child of ARTHUR MILLS and LEONORA PENDLETON is:
          i.   ARTHUR UHULE¹⁰ MILLS, b. 01 Oct 1918, Peshastin, WA; m. AILEEN HENDERSON, Jan 1943.

1230. ARTHUR JONES⁹ STEWART *(CAROLINE LEVINA⁸ MILLS, SARAH⁷ SPINNEY, ARTHUR JONES⁶, EBENEZER⁵, NATHANIEL⁴, JONATHAN³, SAMUEL², THOMAS¹)* was born 31 Dec 1890 in Day County, SD, and died 21 Jun 1956 in Phoenix, AZ. He married (1) IVA GERTRUDE WHISNAND. She was born 01 Nov 1893 in Hope, ND, and died 01 Jun 1943 in Newberg, OR. He married (2) ETHEL. He married (3) ELSIE KEEPLER. He married (4) CORA MCPHERSON.

Children of ARTHUR STEWART and IVA WHISNAND are:
1449.   i.   WREATHA ALMEDA¹⁰ STEWART, b. 29 Jan 1916, McMinnville, OR.
1450.   ii. ARTHUR JAY STEWART, b. 03 Sep 1919, McMinnville, OR.
1451.   iii. IVA MAY STEWART, b. 08 Oct 1921, McMinnville OR.

1231. CLIFFORD MILLS⁹ STEWART *(CAROLINE LEVINA⁸ MILLS, SARAH⁷ SPINNEY, ARTHUR JONES⁶, EBENEZER⁵, NATHANIEL⁴, JONATHAN³, SAMUEL², THOMAS¹)* was born 17 Jan 1896. He married FLORANCE HENRIETTA BARRIGAN.

Children of CLIFFORD STEWART and FLORANCE BARRIGAN are:
1452.   i.   CAROLINE MARGARET¹⁰ STEWART, b. 20 Oct 1917, Lougheed Alberta Canada.
        ii. HELEN FLORENCE STEWART, b. 28 Dec 1918, Red Deer Alberta Canada; m. RONALD SCOTT CLARK, 23 Nov 1938, Salem Oregon; b. 28 Apr 1916.
1453.   iii. CLIFFORD THOMAS STEWART, b. 30 Jun 1920, Edmonton Alberta Canada.

1232. VERA TERESA⁹ SWAN *(SUSANNA JANE "JEN"⁸ MILLS, SARAH⁷ SPINNEY, ARTHUR JONES⁶, EBENEZER⁵, NATHANIEL⁴, JONATHAN³, SAMUEL², THOMAS¹)* was born 10 Jan 1897 in Aberdeen, SD, and died 24 Jun 1995 in Parkdale, BC.. She married JOHN JACQUES BARRIGAN, son of THOAMS BARRIGAN and MARGARET JACQUES. He was born 28 Oct 1890 in Lancashire, England.

Children of VERA SWAN and JOHN BARRIGAN are:
1454.   i.   DONALD¹⁰ BARRIGAN, b. 24 Oct 1923, Omak, WA.
1455.   ii. JANE MARGARET BARRIGAN, b. 21 Nov 1928.

1233. WILLIAM HENRY⁹ COLLINS *(ANGELINE ELIZABETH⁸ MILLS, SARAH⁷ SPINNEY, ARTHUR JONES⁶, EBENEZER⁵, NATHANIEL⁴, JONATHAN³, SAMUEL², THOMAS¹)* was born 14 Feb 1889 in Goodland, IN, and died 1947. He married ELIZABETH PANNEBAKER 14 Aug 1912 in Mapleton, SD. She was born 1892, and died 1944.

Children of WILLIAM COLLINS and ELIZABETH PANNEBAKER are:
          i.   KATHLEEN HELEN "BILLIE"¹⁰ COLLINS, m. LORIMER OLSON, 08 May 1948.
1456.   ii. MARIAN FRANCES COLLINS, b. 30 Nov 1913.
          iii. MARJORIE ELIZABETH COLLINS, b. 1915, Mapleton, SD; m. EDWIN PEITSCH, 12 Mar 1934.
1457.   iv. LILA JEAN COLLINS, b. Mar 1921, Fargo, SD.

1234. LEOLA "LOLA" EILEEN⁹ COLLINS *(ANGELINE ELIZABETH⁸ MILLS, SARAH⁷ SPINNEY, ARTHUR JONES⁶, EBENEZER⁵, NATHANIEL⁴, JONATHAN³, SAMUEL², THOMAS¹)* was born 12 Sep 1893. She married HILES.

Child of LEOLA COLLINS and HILES is:
  i. EDNA[10] HILES, m. W SERIGHT.

1235. KATHRYN ISABELLE[9] THOMPSON *(MYRTLE ISABELLE[8] BANES, AURELIA ISABELLE[7] SPINNEY, ARTHUR JONES[6], EBENEZER[5], NATHANIEL[4], JONATHAN[3], SAMUEL[2], THOMAS[1])* was born in Francesville, IN, and died in Birmingham, MI. She married PETER BURR LOOMIS III in Elkhart, Indiana. He was born in Woodbury, NJ, and died in Ithaca, NY.

Children of KATHRYN THOMPSON and PETER LOOMIS are:
1458. i. MARCIA ANNE[10] LOOMIS, b. Private.
1459. ii. LINDA LOOMIS, b. Private.
1460. iii. PETER BURR LOOMIS IV, b. Private.

1236. VIRGINIA ANNE[9] THOMPSON *(MYRTLE ISABELLE[8] BANES, AURELIA ISABELLE[7] SPINNEY, ARTHUR JONES[6], EBENEZER[5], NATHANIEL[4], JONATHAN[3], SAMUEL[2], THOMAS[1])* was born Private. She married LEONARD KEITH RAFTREE Private. He was born Private.

Children of VIRGINIA THOMPSON and LEONARD RAFTREE are:
  i. WILLIAM MATHIAS[10] RAFTREE, b. Private.
  ii. ANNE LOUISE RAFTREE, b. Private.
1461. iii. LEONARD KEITH RAFTREE, JR., b. Private.
  iv. CAROL(E) JEAN RAFTREE, b. Private.

1237. ISABELLE[9] BANES *(REXFORD[8], AURELIA ISABELLE[7] SPINNEY, ARTHUR JONES[6], EBENEZER[5], NATHANIEL[4], JONATHAN[3], SAMUEL[2], THOMAS[1])* was born Private. She married WILLIAM FREEMAN Private. He was born Private.

Children of ISABELLE BANES and WILLIAM FREEMAN are:
  i. WILLIAM[10] FREEMAN, b. Private.
  ii. THOMAS FREEMAN, b. Private.

1238. MARGARET[9] MCCONNELL *(LELA[8] BANES, AURELIA ISABELLE[7] SPINNEY, ARTHUR JONES[6], EBENEZER[5], NATHANIEL[4], JONATHAN[3], SAMUEL[2], THOMAS[1])* was born Private. She married WILLIAM PEREIRA Private. He was born Private.

Children of MARGARET MCCONNELL and WILLIAM PEREIRA are:
  i. WILLIAM[10] PEREIRA, JR., b. Private.
  ii. MONICA PEREIRA, b. Private.

1239. JOSEPH[9] MCCONNELL *(LELA[8] BANES, AURELIA ISABELLE[7] SPINNEY, ARTHUR JONES[6], EBENEZER[5], NATHANIEL[4], JONATHAN[3], SAMUEL[2], THOMAS[1])* was born Private. He married JOSEPHINE Private. She was born Private.

Children of JOSEPH MCCONNELL and JOSEPHINE are:
  i. JOSEPH[10] MCCONNELL, b. Private.
  ii. JUDY MCCONNELL, b. Private.

1240. DAVID[9] BOGAN *(BETHEL[8] BANES, AURELIA ISABELLE[7] SPINNEY, ARTHUR JONES[6], EBENEZER[5], NATHANIEL[4], JONATHAN[3], SAMUEL[2], THOMAS[1])* was born Private.

Child of DAVID BOGAN is:
  i. DONNA[10] BOGAN, b. Private.

1241. IDA MAY[9] NEILY *(INEZ LINWOOD[8] SPINNEY, ABRAHAM[7], JOSEPH[6], ABRAHAM[5], JOSEPH[4], SAMUEL[3], SAMUEL[2],*

THOMAS[1]*)* She married FRED MIDDLETON GORDON.

Children of IDA NEILY and FRED GORDON are:
      i.   ELLIS[10] GORDON.
      ii. GERALD GORDON.
1462. iii. SHRIELY GORDON, b. 28 Oct 1939.

1242. WILLIAM LLOYD[9] NEILY *(INEZ LINWOOD*[8] *SPINNEY, ABRAHAM*[7]*, JOSEPH*[6]*, ABRAHAM*[5]*, JOSEPH*[4]*, SAMUEL*[3]*, SAMUEL*[2]*, THOMAS*[1]*)* was born 1907. He married LILIAM MIRIAM FLEMMING. She died 1969.

Children of WILLIAM NEILY and LILIAM FLEMMING are:
1463. i. CLIFFORD[10] NEILEY, b. 20 Aug 1934, Provost AB.
1464. ii. KENNETH ROGER NEILY, b. 12 Sep 1938.

1243. PAUL NATHANIEL[9] SPINNEY *(GEORGE LAMERT*[8]*, OWEN*[7]*, JOSEPH*[6]*, ABRAHAM*[5]*, JOSEPH*[4]*, SAMUEL*[3]*, SAMUEL*[2]*, THOMAS*[1]*)* was born 20 Feb 1917. He married DORIS HOLLOWAY 15 Sep 1945 in Portsmouth England. She was born 05 Dec 1915.

Children of PAUL SPINNEY and DORIS HOLLOWAY are:
1465. i. ALAN BLAIR[10] SPINNEY.
1466. ii. ELAINE MARY SPINNEY, b. 30 Nov 1948.

1244. RUSSELL FRANKLIN[9] BAILEY *(CORA MAUDE*[8] *BERTWELL, ALEPH*[7] *WOODBURY, ELIZABETH*[6] *SPINNEY, ABRAHAM*[5]*, JOSEPH*[4]*, SAMUEL*[3]*, SAMUEL*[2]*, THOMAS*[1]*)* was born 08 Oct 1911 in Providence, RI, and died 21 Jan 1996 in Hernando, FL. He married ELEANOR RODEN METZLER 06 Apr 1935 in Nashua, NH. She was born 14 Feb 1915 in Boston, MA, and died 20 Dec 1982 in Hyannis, MA.

Child of RUSSELL BAILEY and ELEANOR METZLER is:
1467. i. ROBERT BERTWELL[10] BAILEY, b. 18 Oct 1935, Arlington, MA.

1245. BRUCE WARREN[9] SPINNEY *(CHESTER LEVERETT*[8]*, ISAAC CALVIN*[7]*, SAMUEL*[6]*, ISAAC BEACH*[5]*, SAMUEL McCLURE*[4]*, SAMUEL*[3]*, SAMUEL*[2]*, THOMAS*[1]*)* was born 22 Dec 1920 in Barre, MA. He married CONSTANCE JOSEPHINE PRATT Jul 1946 in Barre, MA.

Children of BRUCE SPINNEY and CONSTANCE PRATT are:
1468. i. BRUCE WARREN[10] SPINNEY, b. 28 Jan 1948.
1469. ii. DAVID LYLE SPINNEY, b. 02 Oct 1950.
      iii. EILEEN JOY SPINNEY, b. 13 Oct 1960.
      iv. LAUREEN GAIL SPINNEY, b. 13 Oct 1960.

1246. GLENN FRANCIS[9] SPINNEY *(CHESTER LEVERETT*[8]*, ISAAC CALVIN*[7]*, SAMUEL*[6]*, ISAAC BEACH*[5]*, SAMUEL McCLURE*[4]*, SAMUEL*[3]*, SAMUEL*[2]*, THOMAS*[1]*)* was born 14 Oct 1922 in Barre, MA, and died 12 Feb 1973. He married RHODA MERRON.

Children of GLENN SPINNEY and RHODA MERRON are:
      i. LINDA[10] SPINNEY.
      ii. REBECCA SPINNEY.
      iii. MELISSA SPINNEY.

         Notes for MELISSA SPINNEY:
         [Spinney.FTW]

         Origin ??

1247. CHESTER LEVERETT JR.[9] SPINNEY *(CHESTER LEVERETT*[8]*, ISAAC CALVIN*[7]*, SAMUEL*[6]*, ISAAC BEACH*[5]*, SAMUEL McCLURE*[4]*, SAMUEL*[3]*, SAMUEL*[2]*, THOMAS*[1]*)* was born 12 Feb 1927. He married RUTH BEATRICE WATERMAN 23

Nov 1946 in Barre, MA, daughter of ERNEST WATERMAN and ELIZA BURGESS. She was born 06 Oct 1925.

Notes for RUTH BEATRICE WATERMAN:
[Spinney.FTW]

Ware Hospital

Children of CHESTER SPINNEY and RUTH WATERMAN are:
1470.   i.   CHESTER LEVERETT[10] SPINNEY, b. 05 Apr 1948, Worchester, MA.
1471.   ii.   PHILIP CRAIG SPINNEY, b. 29 Apr 1949, Holden, MA.
1472.   iii.   ROBIN LISA SPINNEY, b. 28 Mar 1954, Exeter, NH.
       iv.   DANA BARRE SPINNEY, b. 28 Jul 1958, Winchester, MA.

            Notes for DANA BARRE SPINNEY:
            [Spinney.FTW]

            Dana for Dana, Massachusettes now under the Quabbin Resevior and where our paternal great grandparents on the Spinney side lived.

            Barre for the town in central Massachusettes where our parents were raised.

            Family resided in North Reading, Massachusetts.

1248. ULMER WILLIAM[9] SPINNEY (*AUSTIN WHEELOCK*[8], *CALEB SNOW*[7], *AUSTIN WELTON*[6], *JACOB BEACH*[5], *SAMUEL McCLURE*[4], *SAMUEL*[3], *SAMUEL*[2], *THOMAS*[1]) was born Dec 1923 in Austin, Tx, and died Dec 1979. He married FRANCES HORGER.

Children of ULMER SPINNEY and FRANCES HORGER are:
    i.   BERTHA ANN[10] SPINNEY, b. 16 Sep 1951, Texas.
    ii.   WILLIAM BRYANT SPINNEY, b. 25 Oct 1964, Texas.
    iii.   DAVID SEAWARD SPINNEY, b. 31 May 1953, Texas.

1249. LLOYD[9] GRIFFIN (*EVA*[8] *SPINNEY*, *WILLIAM G.*[7], *JACOB BEACH*[6], *JACOB BEACH*[5], *SAMUEL McCLURE*[4], *SAMUEL*[3], *SAMUEL*[2], *THOMAS*[1]) He married ETHEL PIERCE.

Children of LLOYD GRIFFIN and ETHEL PIERCE are:
    i.   HAROLD[10] GRIFFIN, m. PAMELA MEISNER.
    ii.   ROY GRIFFIN, m. MURIAL HILTZ.
    iii.   VELORIA GRIFFIN, m. RICK GIBSON.

1250. ELSIE MAY[9] GRIFFIN (*HELEN LUCY*[8] *SPINNEY*, *JAMES BARTEAUX*[7], *HARDING THEODORE*[6], *JACOB BEACH*[5], *SAMUEL McCLURE*[4], *SAMUEL*[3], *SAMUEL*[2], *THOMAS*[1]) was born 1928. She married EARL FOSTER 1946.

Children of ELSIE GRIFFIN and EARL FOSTER are:
    i.   MARGUERITE ANNE[10] FOSTER, b. 1946; m. BILL RIUTTA.
    ii.   DAVID EARL FOSTER, b. 1951; m. SHELLY MONK.
    iii.   GEORGE VERNON FOSTER, b. 1957; m. JOCELYN GOULD.

1251. CURTIS JAMES[9] GRIFFIN (*HELEN LUCY*[8] *SPINNEY*, *JAMES BARTEAUX*[7], *HARDING THEODORE*[6], *JACOB BEACH*[5], *SAMUEL McCLURE*[4], *SAMUEL*[3], *SAMUEL*[2], *THOMAS*[1]) was born 1930. He married EVELYN CRAWFORD 1958.

Children of CURTIS GRIFFIN and EVELYN CRAWFORD are:
    i.   LINDA MARIE[10] GRIFFIN, b. 1959.
    ii.   ERIC JAMES GRIFFIN, b. 1961.
    iii.   SUSAN MARY GRIFFIN, b. 1963.

1252. ENA GWEN[9] SPINNEY (*ALBERT WEBBER*[8], *EDWARD MANNING*[7], *CALEB*[6], *JACOB BEACH*[5], *SAMUEL McCLURE*[4], *SAMUEL*[3], *SAMUEL*[2], *THOMAS*[1]) was born 1945. She married DAVID JONES.

Children of ENA SPINNEY and DAVID JONES are:
- i. LESLIE JELLA EMMA[10] JONES, b. 14 Sep 1972.
- ii. JAMES MARTIN ALBERT JONES, b. 01 Jun 1976.
- iii. DAVID EVAN JONES, b. 1977.
- iv. LEWELLAN STANLEY. DAVID JONES, b. 22 Aug 1977.

1253. ELLIS[9] SPINNEY *(HOWE BELL[8], MELBURNE E.[7], BENIAH B[6], JACOB BEACH[5], SAMUEL MCCLURE[4], SAMUEL[3], SAMUEL[2], THOMAS[1])* was born 1927. He married IRENE HERGET 1957.

Children of ELLIS SPINNEY and IRENE HERGET are:
- i. JANICE[10] SPINNEY, b. 1958.
- ii. ALAN SPINNEY, b. 1959.
- iii. GLENNA SPINNEY, b. 1963.
- iv. WYNNE SPINNEY, b. 1966.

1254. CLARE[9] SPINNEY *(HOWE BELL[8], MELBURNE E.[7], BENIAH B[6], JACOB BEACH[5], SAMUEL MCCLURE[4], SAMUEL[3], SAMUEL[2], THOMAS[1])* was born 1932. He married JACQUELINE FARNSWORTH 1952.

Child of CLARE SPINNEY and JACQUELINE FARNSWORTH is:
- i. THOMAS HOWE[10] SPINNEY, b. 1956.

1255. GERALDINE DELORES[9] SPINNEY *(KENNETH EARLE[8], GEORGE ELBURN[7], ENOCH[6], JACOB BEACH[5], SAMUEL MCCLURE[4], SAMUEL[3], SAMUEL[2], THOMAS[1])* was born 1932. She married DONALD F. SMITH.

Children of GERALDINE SPINNEY and DONALD SMITH are:
- i. SUSAN[10] SMITH.
- ii. DEBORAH JUNE SMITH, m. PHILIP ANTHONY TROPASSO.
- iii. PAMELA GAIL SMITH, m. MIKE PERRY.
- iv. CHRISTOPHER SMITH, m. PAULA THEODORE.
- v. DOUGLAS SMITH.

1256. PHILIP KENNETH[9] SPINNEY *(KENNETH EARLE[8], GEORGE ELBURN[7], ENOCH[6], JACOB BEACH[5], SAMUEL MCCLURE[4], SAMUEL[3], SAMUEL[2], THOMAS[1])* was born 1938. He married MARTHA HILL.

Children of PHILIP SPINNEY and MARTHA HILL are:
- i. KAREN[10] SPINNEY.
- ii. STEPHEN SPINNEY, b. Abt. 1958.

1257. JAMES LELAND[9] SPINNEY *(WINTHROP HARRIS[8], LELAND TEASDALE[7], ENOCH[6], JACOB BEACH[5], SAMUEL MCCLURE[4], SAMUEL[3], SAMUEL[2], THOMAS[1])* was born 16 Jul 1940 in Worcester, MA. He married JANIS ELIZABETH BROWN 12 Oct 1963 in Westboro, MA. She was born 17 Jan 1937.

Children of JAMES SPINNEY and JANIS BROWN are:
- i. JANE MARJORIE[10] SPINNEY, b. 31 Aug 1964, Miami, Fl.
- ii. JEAN ELIZABETH SPINNEY, b. 14 Jun 1966, Miami, Fl.
- iii. JAMES WINTHROP SPINNEY, b. 29 May 1968, Miami, Fl.

1258. WINTHROP WARREN[9] SPINNEY *(WINTHROP HARRIS[8], LELAND TEASDALE[7], ENOCH[6], JACOB BEACH[5], SAMUEL MCCLURE[4], SAMUEL[3], SAMUEL[2], THOMAS[1])* was born 19 Mar 1945 in Milford, MA. He married PATRICIA ANN COOPER 15 Apr 1967 in Marlboro, Ma. Usa.. She was born 06 Oct 1947.

Children of WINTHROP SPINNEY and PATRICIA COOPER are:
- i. WINTHROP JAMES[10] SPINNEY, b. 01 Jun 1970, Rantoul, IL.
- ii. JENIFER MARIE SPINNEY, b. 26 Apr 1973, Sumter, S.C.
- iii. CATHRYN JEAN SPINNEY, b. 27 Jan 1977, Tampa, Fl..

1259. PHYLLIS MAE⁹ SPINNEY *(KINGSLEY SELLAR⁸, LELAND TEASDALE⁷, ENOCH⁶, JACOB BEACH⁵, SAMUEL MCCLURE⁴, SAMUEL³, SAMUEL², THOMAS¹)* was born 15 Jun 1935. She married ERVIN CLIFFORD WARD 22 Sep 1954.

Children of PHYLLIS SPINNEY and ERVIN WARD are:
      i.   BARBARA LOUISE¹⁰ WARD, b. 13 Dec 1955; m. MICHAEL ROSS.
1473. ii. CAROLYN WARD, b. 06 Aug 1958.
     iii. KATHLEEN WARD, b. 27 Aug 1961; m. MICHEAL SCHMEISSER.

1260. GERALD EUGENE⁹ PALMER *(VERA BELLE⁸ SPINNEY, LELAND TEASDALE⁷, ENOCH⁶, JACOB BEACH⁵, SAMUEL MCCLURE⁴, SAMUEL³, SAMUEL², THOMAS¹)* was born 12 Oct 1931. He married JOAN CLARK Jun 1951 in Harmony, N.S..

Children of GERALD PALMER and JOAN CLARK are:
      i.   DEBORAH LYNN¹⁰ PALMER, b. 14 Jun 1952.
     ii. PATRICIA JOY PALMER, b. 23 Feb 1954.

1261. JOYCE AGNES⁹ PALMER *(VERA BELLE⁸ SPINNEY, LELAND TEASDALE⁷, ENOCH⁶, JACOB BEACH⁵, SAMUEL MCCLURE⁴, SAMUEL³, SAMUEL², THOMAS¹)* was born 05 May 1936. She married (1) HOWARD JOHNSON 19 Jun 1963. She married (2) LEONARD ALLEN MACINNIS 03 Jul 1965.

Children of JOYCE PALMER and HOWARD JOHNSON are:
      i.   GARY A.¹⁰ JOHNSON, b. 17 Mar 1954.
     ii. WAYNE JOHNSON, b. 28 Jun 1955.
     iii. KIM JOHNSON, b. 18 Jul 1956.

Children of JOYCE PALMER and LEONARD MACINNIS are:
     iv. PETER¹⁰ MACINNIS, b. 10 May 1968.
      v. DWIGHT MACINNIS, b. 01 May 1971.

1262. ALFRETTA BLANCHE⁹ PALMER *(VERA BELLE⁸ SPINNEY, LELAND TEASDALE⁷, ENOCH⁶, JACOB BEACH⁵, SAMUEL MCCLURE⁴, SAMUEL³, SAMUEL², THOMAS¹)* was born 06 Nov 1937 in Harmony, N.S.. She married ALMON LAWRENCE MORSE 20 Sep 1958 in Aylesford, N.S..

Children of ALFRETTA PALMER and ALMON MORSE are:
      i.   HEATHER¹⁰ MORSE, b. 15 May 1965.
     ii. SHEILA MORSE, b. 23 Jan 1968.
     iii. DIANNA MORSE, b. 27 Mar 1969.
     iv. ANTHONY MORSE, b. 13 Nov 1970.

1263. SANDRA LOUISE⁹ SPINNEY *(EARLE WINFRED⁸, LELAND TEASDALE⁷, ENOCH⁶, JACOB BEACH⁵, SAMUEL MCCLURE⁴, SAMUEL³, SAMUEL², THOMAS¹)* was born 03 Nov 1939 in Middleton, N.S.. She married JAMES THAIN 19 Dec 1959 in Greenwood, N.S.. He was born 12 Oct 1938.

Children of SANDRA SPINNEY and JAMES THAIN are:
1474. i.   KIMBERLY ANN¹⁰ THAIN, b. 05 Dec 1960, Middleton, N.S..
1475. ii. LISA CAROL THAIN, b. 30 Dec 1961, Middleton, N.S..
     iii. JAMES THAIN, b. 25 Jun 1963, Middleton, N.S..
1476. iv. SUSAN LOUISE THAIN, b. 10 Feb 1965, Middleton, N.S..
      v. STEVEN EARLE THAIN, b. 30 Sep 1968, Ottawa, Ont..
     vi. TASHIA MARIE THAIN, b. 23 Apr 1970, Ottawa, Ont.; m. LARRY GALLANT.

1264. DELMA PEARL⁹ SPINNEY *(EARLE WINFRED⁸, LELAND TEASDALE⁷, ENOCH⁶, JACOB BEACH⁵, SAMUEL MCCLURE⁴, SAMUEL³, SAMUEL², THOMAS¹)* was born 04 Dec 1942 in Middleton, N.S.. She married JEFFREY OLIVER NEWMAN 12 Mar 1960 in Greenwood, N.S.. He was born 08 Sep 1934.

Children of DELMA SPINNEY and JEFFREY NEWMAN are:

1477.   i.   DEBRA PEARL[10] NEWMAN, b. 10 Nov 1960, Middleton, N.S..
      ii.   JACQUELINE MARGARET NEWMAN, b. 19 Nov 1961, Middleton, N.S.; m. IVAN RAYMOND LOVELY, 03 Mar 1981, Mission, B.C.; b. 17 Nov 1944.
      iii.   JOHN THOMAS NEWMAN, b. 15 Oct 1963, Middleton, NS..
      iv.   PAMELA HELEN (TAMMI) NEWMAN, b. 15 Dec 1968, Edmonton, Alta.; m. MARK VICTOR LUSK, 26 Aug 1989, Mission, B.C..
      v.   RANDAL JEFFREY NEWMAN, b. 27 Mar 1971, Edmonton, Alta..

1265. PHILIP VANCE[9] SPINNEY *(FRANCIS LELAND[8], LELAND TEASDALE[7], ENOCH[6], JACOB BEACH[5], SAMUEL MCCLURE[4], SAMUEL[3], SAMUEL[2], THOMAS[1])* was born 15 Nov 1946. He married PHYLLIS DONNA PARSONS 11 Nov 1967.

Children of PHILIP SPINNEY and PHYLLIS PARSONS are:

      i.   STEPHANIE[10] SPINNEY.
      ii.   CANDACE NADINE SPINNEY, b. 29 Apr 1970.
      iii.   JENNIFER DAWN SPINNEY, b. 08 Nov 1971.
      iv.   JUSTIN PHILIP SPINNEY, b. 28 Jan 1979; d. 06 Feb 1979.

1266. DORIS AGNES[9] SPINNEY *(FRANCIS LELAND[8], LELAND TEASDALE[7], ENOCH[6], JACOB BEACH[5], SAMUEL MCCLURE[4], SAMUEL[3], SAMUEL[2], THOMAS[1])* was born 17 Jan 1948. She married MARSHALL HEDLEY SCHOFIELD 14 Oct 1967.

Children of DORIS SPINNEY and MARSHALL SCHOFIELD are:

      i.   DENISE JEANETTE[10] SCHOFIELD, b. 28 Jul 1972.
      ii.   DWAYNE MARSHALL SCHOFIELD, b. 23 Feb 1978.

1267. VERA ANNE[9] SPINNEY *(FRANCIS LELAND[8], LELAND TEASDALE[7], ENOCH[6], JACOB BEACH[5], SAMUEL MCCLURE[4], SAMUEL[3], SAMUEL[2], THOMAS[1])* was born 06 Oct 1953. She married JORDON YARN 25 Mar 1972.

Children of VERA SPINNEY and JORDON YARN are:

      i.   LUCINDA KELLEY[10] YARN, b. May 1978.
      ii.   PHILIP JORDON YARN, b. 06 Oct 1980.

1268. MELBA[9] PIERCE *(CLAYTON ABNER[8], HOWARD ELIZA[7], CHARLES A.[6], AMORET[5] SPINNEY, SAMUEL MCCLURE[4], SAMUEL[3], SAMUEL[2], THOMAS[1])* She married KENNETH ROGER NEILY 12 Jun 1963, son of WILLIAM NEILY and LILIAM FLEMMING. He was born 12 Sep 1938.

Children of MELBA PIERCE and KENNETH NEILY are:

      i.   KAREN LYNN[10] NEILY.
      ii.   ARDEN LEE NEILY.
      iii.   CHANTEL DELORIS NEILY.

1269. HOWARD MAXWELL[9] PIERCE *(CLAYTON ABNER[8], HOWARD ELIZA[7], CHARLES A.[6], AMORET[5] SPINNEY, SAMUEL MCCLURE[4], SAMUEL[3], SAMUEL[2], THOMAS[1])* He married MARGARET ALICE DAVIS in Woldinghorn England.

Children of HOWARD PIERCE and MARGARET DAVIS are:

      i.   JENNIFER PAULINE[10] PIERCE.
      ii.   MARGARET RODALIND PIERCE.
      iii.   HOWARD MALCOLM PIERCE, b. Prince Albert, NS.; m. WINONA FERN SANDS, 07 Jun 1970, Yarmouth, NS..
      iv.   ELEANOR BERNICE PIERCE, b. Middleton, NS.; m. DONALD LEWIS TREEL.
      v.   MARSHA LEE PIERCE, m. DONALD WAYNE WHITE, 29 Jul 1978.

1270. DOUGLAS ARDEN[9] PIERCE *(CLAYTON ABNER[8], HOWARD ELIZA[7], CHARLES A.[6], AMORET[5] SPINNEY, SAMUEL MCCLURE[4], SAMUEL[3], SAMUEL[2], THOMAS[1])* He married VIVIAN BANKS.

Child of DOUGLAS PIERCE and VIVIAN BANKS is:
    i.   MILDRED OUIDA[10] PIERCE.

1271. ARCHIE ARDEN[9] PIERCE *(CLAYTON ABNER[8], HOWARD ELIZA[7], CHARLES A.[6], AMORET[5] SPINNEY, SAMUEL McCLURE[4], SAMUEL[3], SAMUEL[2], THOMAS[1])* He married VERA NOREEN BLYES.

Children of ARCHIE PIERCE and VERA BLYES are:
    i.   CAROLYN FREDA[10] PIERCE.
    ii.   RUSSELL CLAYTON PIERCE.
    iii. ARDEN LESTER PIERCE.
    iv.   RAYMOND JAMES PIERCE.
    v.   KEITH ALAN PIERCE PIERCE.
    vi.   SCOTT GRAHAME PIERCE.
    vii. NOREEN THELMA PIERCE.
    viii. JOYCE BARBARA PIERCE, d. 1947.
    ix.   MELVYN GORDON PIERCE, d. Sep 1971.

          Notes for MELVYN GORDON PIERCE:
          Melvyn was killed in a tragic automobile accident, n Lawrencetown Nova Scotia. He was taking a Chef's course at the Middleton Vocation School at the time of his untimely death

    x.   MICHAEL FREDERICK PIERCE, m. AUDREY HILTZ.
    xi.   LINDA JOY PIERCE.

1272. THELMA KIZBARO[9] PIERCE *(CLAYTON ABNER[8], HOWARD ELIZA[7], CHARLES A.[6], AMORET[5] SPINNEY, SAMUEL McCLURE[4], SAMUEL[3], SAMUEL[2], THOMAS[1])* She married (1) MELVIN DESCHAMP.   She married (2) DON RADDON.

Children of THELMA PIERCE and MELVIN DESCHAMP are:
    i.   THERESA[10] DESCHAMP.
    ii. BONNIE DESCHAMP.
    iii. KENNETH DESCHAMP.
    iv. ROBERT DESCHAMP.

1273. ARDIS[9] PIERCE *(CLAYTON ABNER[8], HOWARD ELIZA[7], CHARLES A.[6], AMORET[5] SPINNEY, SAMUEL McCLURE[4], SAMUEL[3], SAMUEL[2], THOMAS[1])* She married REGINALD SCHOFIELD.

Children of ARDIS PIERCE and REGINALD SCHOFIELD are:
    i.   JOHN[10] SCHOFIELD.
    ii. DONNA SCHOFIELD.
    iii. CLYDE SCHOFIELD.
    iv. ELSIE SCHOFIELD.
    v.   CONRAD SCHOFIELD.

1274. ETHEL BERNEICE[9] PIERCE *(CLAYTON ABNER[8], HOWARD ELIZA[7], CHARLES A.[6], AMORET[5] SPINNEY, SAMUEL McCLURE[4], SAMUEL[3], SAMUEL[2], THOMAS[1])* She married WILLIAM LLOYD GRIFFIN.

Notes for ETHEL BERNEICE PIERCE:
Ethel and Lloyd raised Pauline Ann Thomkinson , daughter of Frank and Elma Marie Pierce Thomkinson (sister of Ethel) after the death of her parents.

Children of ETHEL PIERCE and WILLIAM GRIFFIN are:
    i.   ROY HARRIS[10] GRIFFIN.
    ii. VELORA BERNEICE GRIFFIN.

1275. ELMA MARIE[9] PIERCE *(CLAYTON ABNER[8], HOWARD ELIZA[7], CHARLES A.[6], AMORET[5] SPINNEY, SAMUEL*

McClure⁴, Samuel³, Samuel², Thomas¹) died 1972. She married FRANK THOMKINSON. He died 20 Dec 1973.

Children of ELMA PIERCE and FRANK THOMKINSON are:
  - i. NANCY ELLA¹⁰ THOMKINSON.
  - ii. PAULINE ANN.
  - iii. FRANCES MARIE THOMKINSON, b. 1949; d. 29 Jul 1952.

> Notes for FRANCES MARIE THOMKINSON:
> Frances was most tragially run over by her fathers own car. The car was on a ramp and the children, playing in the car released the emergency brake running over Frances who was playing behind the car

1276. HAZEL ALTHIA⁹ PIERCE *(CLAYTON ABNER⁸, HOWARD ELIZA⁷, CHARLES A.⁶, AMORET⁵ SPINNEY, SAMUEL McCLURE⁴, SAMUEL³, SAMUEL², THOMAS¹)* She married RALPH VERNON DOWNIE.

Children of HAZEL PIERCE and RALPH DOWNIE are:
  - i. ALTON ARTHUR¹⁰ DOWNIE.
  - ii. PHYLLIP RALPH DOWNIE.
  - iii. MURRAY EMERY REID DOWNIE.
  - iv. MARILYN FLORENCE DOWNIE.
  - v. FLOYD ARDEN DOWNIE.

1277. CARL AUBREY⁹ PIERCE *(CLAYTON ABNER⁸, HOWARD ELIZA⁷, CHARLES A.⁶, AMORET⁵ SPINNEY, SAMUEL McCLURE⁴, SAMUEL³, SAMUEL², THOMAS¹)* He married (1) JOAN ARKETT. He married (2) BARBARA BALL. He married (3) BERNICE KNOX.

Child of CARL PIERCE and JOAN ARKETT is:
  - i. BERNADETT¹⁰ PIERCE.

Children of CARL PIERCE and BARBARA BALL are:
  - ii. GLEN HOWARD¹⁰ PIERCE.
  - iii. RODNEY JAMES PIERCE.

Child of CARL PIERCE and BERNICE KNOX is:
  - iv. DARRYL LLOYD¹⁰ PIERCE.

1278. JEANIE⁹ PIERCE *(CLAYTON ABNER⁸, HOWARD ELIZA⁷, CHARLES A.⁶, AMORET⁵ SPINNEY, SAMUEL McCLURE⁴, SAMUEL³, SAMUEL², THOMAS¹)* She married GEORGE WESTLAKE.

Children of JEANIE PIERCE and GEORGE WESTLAKE are:
  - i. RAYMOND¹⁰ WESTLAKE.
  - ii. DAVID WESTLAKE.
  - iii. DARLENE WESTLAKE.

1279. MARJORIE JEAN⁹ PIERCE *(RALPH ALMER⁸, HOWARD ELIZA⁷, CHARLES A.⁶, AMORET⁵ SPINNEY, SAMUEL McCLURE⁴, SAMUEL³, SAMUEL², THOMAS¹)* was born 10 Jun 1922. She married RUSSEL ARTHUR DOWE.

Children of MARJORIE PIERCE and RUSSEL DOWE are:
  - i. CATHERINE JEAN¹⁰ DOWE.
  - ii. ELIZABETH DOWE.
  - iii. MARY JUDITH DOWE.

1280. AUDREY EDITH⁹ PIERCE *(RALPH ALMER⁸, HOWARD ELIZA⁷, CHARLES A.⁶, AMORET⁵ SPINNEY, SAMUEL McCLURE⁴, SAMUEL³, SAMUEL², THOMAS¹)* was born 16 Mar 1924. She married CALVIN GOULD.

Children of AUDREY PIERCE and CALVIN GOULD are:
  - i. ROBERT¹⁰ GOULD.

    ii.   DAVID GOULD.
    iii. MARILYN GOULD.

1281. ALLAN LESLIE⁹ PIERCE *(RALPH ALMER⁸, HOWARD ELIZA⁷, CHARLES A.⁶, AMORET⁵ SPINNEY, SAMUEL McCLURE⁴, SAMUEL³, SAMUEL², THOMAS¹)* was born 10 Aug 1929. He married ANNA MARIE COOPER.

Children of ALLAN PIERCE and ANNA COOPER are:
    i.   SHARON¹⁰ PIERCE, b. 1953; m. BRUCE HAYWARD.
    ii.   SANDRA PIERCE, b. 1955; m. COLDWELL.
    iii. STEPHEN COLLIN PIERCE, b. 1969.

1282. JAMES MAXWELL⁹ PIERCE *(RALPH ALMER⁸, HOWARD ELIZA⁷, CHARLES A.⁶, AMORET⁵ SPINNEY, SAMUEL McCLURE⁴, SAMUEL³, SAMUEL², THOMAS¹)* was born 21 Apr 1932. He married (1) BETH.   He married (2) MONA.

Children of JAMES PIERCE and BETH are:
    i.   JUDY¹⁰ PIERCE, m. DAVID FULLARD.
    ii.   KAREN PIERCE.

1283. HOWARD ALLISON⁹ PIERCE *(RALPH ALMER⁸, HOWARD ELIZA⁷, CHARLES A.⁶, AMORET⁵ SPINNEY, SAMUEL McCLURE⁴, SAMUEL³, SAMUEL², THOMAS¹)* was born 26 Oct 1935. He married JEANNE DOREEN SPURR. She was born 12 Jun 1935.

Children of HOWARD PIERCE and JEANNE SPURR are:
    i.   MICHAEL STEVEN¹⁰ PIERCE.
    ii.   PETER JOHN PIERCE.
    iii. JANET CARROL PIERCE, b. 30 Nov 1954.

1284. LEON McAVOY⁹ AVERY *(RUTH HANNAH ELIZABETH⁸ PIERCE, FRANK LOVETT⁷, CHARLES A.⁶, AMORET⁵ SPINNEY, SAMUEL McCLURE⁴, SAMUEL³, SAMUEL², THOMAS¹)* was born 02 Mar 1936. He married BARBARA HAMILTON.

Children of LEON AVERY and BARBARA HAMILTON are:
    i.   STEPHEN¹⁰ AVERY.
    ii.   LINDA AVERY.
    iii. KIRK AVERY.

1285. JOAN EVANGELINE⁹ AVERY *(RUTH HANNAH ELIZABETH⁸ PIERCE, FRANK LOVETT⁷, CHARLES A.⁶, AMORET⁵ SPINNEY, SAMUEL McCLURE⁴, SAMUEL³, SAMUEL², THOMAS¹)* was born 13 May 1939. She married LESTER RAFUSE.

Children of JOAN AVERY and LESTER RAFUSE are:
    i.   CINDY¹⁰ RAFUSE.
    ii.   CRAIG RAFUSE.
    iii. JOHN RAFUSE.

1286. JANET NADINE⁹ AVERY *(RUTH HANNAH ELIZABETH⁸ PIERCE, FRANK LOVETT⁷, CHARLES A.⁶, AMORET⁵ SPINNEY, SAMUEL McCLURE⁴, SAMUEL³, SAMUEL², THOMAS¹)* was born 13 Aug 1940. She married FREDERICK DUCKETT.

Children of JANET AVERY and FREDERICK DUCKETT are:
    i.   KAREN¹⁰ DUCKETT.
    ii.   CHARLES DUCKETT.
    iii. SUSAN DUCKETT.
    iv.   GLEN DUCKETT.

1287. ANNA JOY[9] AVERY *(RUTH HANNAH ELIZABETH[8] PIERCE, FRANK LOVETT[7], CHARLES A.[6], AMORET[5] SPINNEY, SAMUEL MCCLURE[4], SAMUEL[3], SAMUEL[2], THOMAS[1])* was born 26 Feb 1942. She married MITCHELL BOWER.

Children of ANNA AVERY and MITCHELL BOWER are:
    i.   DEBRA[10] BOWER.
    ii.   SCOTT BOWER.

1288. CONNIE LINDA[9] AVERY *(RUTH HANNAH ELIZABETH[8] PIERCE, FRANK LOVETT[7], CHARLES A.[6], AMORET[5] SPINNEY, SAMUEL MCCLURE[4], SAMUEL[3], SAMUEL[2], THOMAS[1])* was born 28 Feb 1944. She married HOWARD ANDREWS.

Children of CONNIE AVERY and HOWARD ANDREWS are:
    i.   SHELLEY[10] ANDREWS.
    ii.   HOWARD ANDREWS.
    iii. CHERYL ANDREWS.

1289. DEAN HERMAN[9] AVERY *(RUTH HANNAH ELIZABETH[8] PIERCE, FRANK LOVETT[7], CHARLES A.[6], AMORET[5] SPINNEY, SAMUEL MCCLURE[4], SAMUEL[3], SAMUEL[2], THOMAS[1])* was born 1946. He married MARYANN.

Children of DEAN AVERY and MARYANN are:
    i.   DARREN[10] AVERY.
    ii.   MIRANDA AVERY.

1290. GWEN INICE[9] AVERY *(RUTH HANNAH ELIZABETH[8] PIERCE, FRANK LOVETT[7], CHARLES A.[6], AMORET[5] SPINNEY, SAMUEL MCCLURE[4], SAMUEL[3], SAMUEL[2], THOMAS[1])* was born 02 Jul 1947. She married DREW EISNOR.

Children of GWEN AVERY and DREW EISNOR are:
    i.   PAUL[10] EISNOR.
    ii.   TREVOR EISNOR.

1291. DIANE RUTH[9] AVERY *(RUTH HANNAH ELIZABETH[8] PIERCE, FRANK LOVETT[7], CHARLES A.[6], AMORET[5] SPINNEY, SAMUEL MCCLURE[4], SAMUEL[3], SAMUEL[2], THOMAS[1])* was born 06 Nov 1948. She married RONALD COCHRANE.

Children of DIANE AVERY and RONALD COCHRANE are:
    i.   ROCHELLE[10] COCHRANE.
    ii.   JAMES COCHRANE.
    iii. ERIN COCHRANE.
    iv. JOSHUA COCHRANE.

1292. SHIRLEY GAIL[9] AVERY *(RUTH HANNAH ELIZABETH[8] PIERCE, FRANK LOVETT[7], CHARLES A.[6], AMORET[5] SPINNEY, SAMUEL MCCLURE[4], SAMUEL[3], SAMUEL[2], THOMAS[1])* was born 09 Feb 1950. She married DOUGLAS OICKLE.

Children of SHIRLEY AVERY and DOUGLAS OICKLE are:
    i.   KARLA[10] OICKLE.
    ii.   CRYSTAL OICKLE.

1293. JUDY ADALINE[9] AVERY *(RUTH HANNAH ELIZABETH[8] PIERCE, FRANK LOVETT[7], CHARLES A.[6], AMORET[5] SPINNEY, SAMUEL MCCLURE[4], SAMUEL[3], SAMUEL[2], THOMAS[1])* was born 29 Jul 1951. She married GARY JOLLIMORE.

Child of JUDY AVERY and GARY JOLLIMORE is:
    i.   JENNIFER[10] JOLLIMORE.

1294. GODON RAY[9] AVERY *(RUTH HANNAH ELIZABETH[8] PIERCE, FRANK LOVETT[7], CHARLES A.[6], AMORET[5] SPINNEY, SAMUEL MCCLURE[4], SAMUEL[3], SAMUEL[2], THOMAS[1])* was born 02 Jan 1953. He married HEATHER READING.

Children of GODON AVERY and HEATHER READING are:
    i.   LINDSAY[10] AVERY.
    ii. LAUREN AVERY.

1295. PRISCILLA JUNE[9] AVERY *(RUTH HANNAH ELIZABETH[8] PIERCE, FRANK LOVETT[7], CHARLES A.[6], AMORET[5] SPINNEY, SAMUEL MCCLURE[4], SAMUEL[3], SAMUEL[2], THOMAS[1])* was born 21 Jun 1954. She married SERGE NADEAU.

Children of PRISCILLA AVERY and SERGE NADEAU are:
    i.   SYLVIE[10] NADEAU.
    ii. SARA NADEAU.
    iii. CHANTEL NADEAU.

1296. ALLEN[9] SPINNEY *(GERALD[8], EMERY CLARENCE[7], FRANK[6], MARY[5], BENIAH[4], SAMUEL[3], SAMUEL[2], THOMAS[1])* was born 1953.

Children of ALLEN SPINNEY are:
    i.   STEPHEN[10] SPINNEY.
    ii. COLIN SPINNEY.

1297. ETHAL M[9] MCNUTT *(EMMA AUGUSTA[8] SPINNEY, THOMAS M[7], THOMAS[6], THOMAS[5], JOHN[4], THOMAS[3], THOMAS[2], THOMAS[1])* was born 07 Sep 1886 in Boston, MA, and died 16 Mar 1952 in Dorchester, MA. She married HENRY FRANCIS MCWHIRK, son of MCWHIRT and ANN HOWARD. He was born 13 Feb 1887 in Boston, MA, and died 16 Feb 1960 in Weymouth, MA.

Children of ETHAL MCNUTT and HENRY MCWHIRK are:
1478.   i.   RUTH ALMA[10] MCWHIRK.
1479.   ii. ETHEL MCWHIRK.
1480.   iii. ELENOR MCWHIRK.
1481.   iv. CAROL JEAN MCWHIRK.
          v. EVELYN MCWHIRK.
          vi. MARGARET MCWHIRK, b. 26 Sep 1908; d. 01 Oct 1918.
1482.   vii. EDNA MCWHIRK, b. 23 Aug 1910; d. 16 Apr 1987, Massachusetts.
1483.   viii. DOROTHY FRANCES MCWHIRK, b. 22 Mar 1913; d. 02 Jun 1994.
1484.   ix. OLIVE MCWHIRK, b. 01 Oct 1918.
          x. HENRY "BUDDY" FRANCIS MCWHIRK, b. 22 Nov 1928; d. 22 Mar 1930.

1298. ERVING ELSWORTH[9] BROOKS *(ALFRED LANGDON[8], DANIEL LANGDON[7], DANIEL[6], MARY[5] SPINNEY, JOHN[4], JOHN[3], JOHN[2], THOMAS[1])* was born 09 Dec 1866, and died 01 Jan 1945 in Newington NH Lot #68 W.Div. Newington C.. He married HARRIET PEARL GORDON 09 Aug 1890 in Newington NH by Rev. William Thompson. She was born Abt. 1876, and died 16 Jan 1965 in Barrington NH Lot #68 W.Div. Newington C..

Children of ERVING BROOKS and HARRIET GORDON are:
1485.   i.   GRACE E.[10] BROOKS, b. 27 Apr 1891.
1486.   ii. NELLIE E. BROOKS, b. 24 May 1893.
1487.   iii. HAZEL P. BROOKS, b. 20 Oct 1894; d. 05 Jun 1969.
          iv. HAROLD G. BROOKS, b. 22 Jan 1896; d. 25 Feb 1896.
1488.   v. ELMER IRWIN BROOKS, b. 22 Mar 1898; d. 15 May 1971.
1489.   vi. WILFRED ELSWORTH BROOKS, b. 21 Jun 1905, Dover NH; d. 01 Sep 1990, Exeter NH Lot #30 W.Div.Ext. Newington C..
1490.   vii. RALPH GORDON BROOKS, b. 05 Aug 1907; d. 27 Apr 1967, Spartonburg SC Lot #27 W.Div. Newington C.
1491.   viii. EVELYN A. BROOKS, b. 02 Dec 1909; d. 01 May 1949.
1492.   ix. KENNETH EARL BROOKS, b. 31 Jan 1911; d. 03 May 1978.
          x. CLARENCE E. BROOKS, b. 22 Apr 1913; d. 30 Jul 1913.
1493.   xi. MARJORIE R. BROOKS, b. Private.

xii.   DOROTHY M. BROOKS, b. Private; m. MOULTON JONES, Private; b. Private.

1299. VICTOR E[9] BROOKS *(ALFRED LANGDON[8], DANIEL LANGDON[7], DANIEL[6], MARY[5] SPINNEY, JOHN[4], JOHN[3], JOHN[2], THOMAS[1])* was born 01 Oct 1872, and died 06 Nov 1938. He married (1) ADDIE PARDOE.   He married (2) ADDIE PARDOE.

Children of VICTOR BROOKS and ADDIE PARDOE are:
1494.	i.	LEWIS SIDNEY[10] BROOKS, b. 03 Dec 1900; d. 12 Sep 1928.
1495.	ii.	CHESTER E BROOKS, b. 12 Apr 1903; d. 23 Jan 1958.
1496.	iii.	HOWARD R BROOKS, b. 30 Jul 1905; d. 07 May 1961.
	iv.	EDITH M BROOKS, b. Private; m. CHARLES DUNCAN, Private; b. Private.
1497.	v.	CARL F BROOKS, b. Private.
1498.	vi.	PAULENA T BROOKS, b. Private.
1499.	vii.	GEORGE L BROOKS, b. Private.

1300. BERNICE MILDRED[9] BROOKS *(ALFRED LANGDON[8], DANIEL LANGDON[7], DANIEL[6], MARY[5] SPINNEY, JOHN[4], JOHN[3], JOHN[2], THOMAS[1])* was born 24 Nov 1875 in Eliot, ME, and died 11 Jun 1959 in Ports. NH Lot #11 Newington Ceme.. She married ALFRED TERRIO. He was born Apr 1865 in New Brunswick, Canada, and died 06 Mar 1940 in Ports. NH Lot #11 Newington Ceme..

Children of BERNICE BROOKS and ALFRED TERRIO are:
1500.	i.	AUGUSTA MAY[10] TERRIO, b. 08 Dec 1896, Portsmouth NH; d. 12 Apr 1969, Portsmouth NH.
1501.	ii.	FLORENCE MILDRED TERRIO, b. 14 Jul 1899, Portsmouth, NH; d. 20 Oct 1982, Rome, NY.
1502.	iii.	ANNIE MAYBELLE TERRIO, b. 02 Aug 1902, Portsmouth, NH; d. 30 Oct 1980, Portsmouth, NH.
1503.	iv.	ALFRED LEE TERRIO, b. 15 May 1905, Portsmouth, NH; d. 18 Nov 1946, Ports. NH Lot #11 Newington Ceme..
	v.	ALBERT E. TERRIO, b. 15 May 1905, Portsmouth NH; d. Nov 1985, Portsmouth NH; m. VIOLA SMITH, Private; b. Private.
1504.	vi.	JOHN W. TERRIO, b. 1908, Portsmouth, NH; d. 19 Nov 1975, Ports. NH Lot #17 S.Div. Newington Ceme..
1505.	vii.	LEROY BROOKS TERRIO, SR., b. Private.

1301. ARTHUR L[9] BROOKS *(ALFRED LANGDON[8], DANIEL LANGDON[7], DANIEL[6], MARY[5] SPINNEY, JOHN[4], JOHN[3], JOHN[2], THOMAS[1])* was born 28 Jul 1877, and died 06 Apr 1900. He married ADDIE PARDOE.

Children of ARTHUR BROOKS and ADDIE PARDOE are:
	i.	RALPH[10] BROOKS, b. 03 Dec 1897.
1506.	ii.	MABEL LEONA BROOKS, b. Private.

1302. ANNIE MAE[9] BROOKS *(ALFRED LANGDON[8], DANIEL LANGDON[7], DANIEL[6], MARY[5] SPINNEY, JOHN[4], JOHN[3], JOHN[2], THOMAS[1])* was born 16 Nov 1880, and died 30 Jan 1961. She married (1) WILLIAM WARD.   She married (2) PERCY SMART.   She married (3) MIKE O'CONNELL COMPANION.

Children of ANNIE BROOKS and WILLIAM WARD are:
	i.	HAROLD WARD STEP[10] CHILD, b. Private; m. GLADYS HANDY, Private; b. Private.
	ii.	DOROTHY WARD STEP CHILD, b. Private; m. GEORGE FARRINGTON, Private; b. Private.
	iii.	EDITH WARD STEP CHILD, b. Private.

1303. NELLIE FLORENCE BLANCHE[9] BROOKS *(ALFRED LANGDON[8], DANIEL LANGDON[7], DANIEL[6], MARY[5] SPINNEY, JOHN[4], JOHN[3], JOHN[2], THOMAS[1])* was born 05 May 1882, and died 12 Nov 1968. She married JOSEPH PERRY.

Child of NELLIE BROOKS and JOSEPH PERRY is:
1507.	i.	JOSEPH[10] PERRY, JR., b. Private.

1304. LEROY ULMONT[9] BROOKS *(ALFRED LANGDON[8], DANIEL LANGDON[7], DANIEL[6], MARY[5] SPINNEY, JOHN[4], JOHN[3], JOHN[2], THOMAS[1])* was born 19 Oct 1887, and died 03 Aug 1970 in Attleboro MA. He married JULIA P GILLIS.

Child of LEROY BROOKS and JULIA GILLIS is:
1508.   i.   DORIS HEWITT[10] BROOKS, b. Private.

1305. ESSIE ROSE[9] BROOKS *(ALFRED LANGDON[8], DANIEL LANGDON[7], DANIEL[6], MARY[5] SPINNEY, JOHN[4], JOHN[3], JOHN[2], THOMAS[1])* was born 24 Sep 1891, and died 16 Jun 1979. She married (1) IRA ELLSWORTH CASWELL. She married (2) ALEXANDER JENNINGS Private. He was born Private. She married (3) HOWARD CHASE Private. He was born Private.

Children of ESSIE BROOKS and IRA CASWELL are:
1509.   i.   ETHEL BERNICE[10] CASWELL, b. 08 Aug 1917; d. 23 Feb 1969.
1510.   ii.   MARJORIE AUGUSTA CASWELL, b. Private.
1511.   iii. ANNIE HEWITT CASWELL, b. Private.

Child of ESSIE BROOKS and ALEXANDER JENNINGS is:
1512.   iv.   WILLIAM LANGDON[10] JENNINGS, b. Private.

1306. SAMUEL HERBERT[9] NELSON *(EMILY ANN[8] BROOKS, DANIEL LANGDON[7], DANIEL[6], MARY[5] SPINNEY, JOHN[4], JOHN[3], JOHN[2], THOMAS[1])* was born 1872, and died 1956. He married (1) ADDIE REMICK. He married (2) NELLIE PAYNE.

Child of SAMUEL NELSON and ADDIE REMICK is:
1513.   i.   SAMUEL MURRAY[10] NELSON, b. 20 May 1895; d. 01 Aug 1967.

1307. ADA SYRENA[9] VARNEY *(CLARA FRANCES[8] BROOKS, DANIEL LANGDON[7], DANIEL[6], MARY[5] SPINNEY, JOHN[4], JOHN[3], JOHN[2], THOMAS[1])* was born 23 Jul 1866, and died 05 Apr 1914. She married GEORGE EDWIN LEACH.

Children of ADA VARNEY and GEORGE LEACH are:
1514.   i.   CLARA BELLE[10] LEACH, b. 14 Jul 1890; d. 26 Jul 1967.
1515.   ii.   FRANK EDWIN LEACH, b. 02 Aug 1894; d. 03 Jan 1968.
1516.   iii. SADIE ADA LEACH, b. Private.

1308. EVERETT[9] HUTCHINS *(MARY OLIVIA[8] BROOKS, DANIEL LANGDON[7], DANIEL[6], MARY[5] SPINNEY, JOHN[4], JOHN[3], JOHN[2], THOMAS[1])* He married LIZZIE SHEAN.

Children of EVERETT HUTCHINS and LIZZIE SHEAN are:
         i.   MARGUERITE[10] HUTCHINS, b. Private.
         ii.   BERNARD HUTCHINS, b. Private.

1309. IDA[9] HUTCHINS *(MARY OLIVIA[8] BROOKS, DANIEL LANGDON[7], DANIEL[6], MARY[5] SPINNEY, JOHN[4], JOHN[3], JOHN[2], THOMAS[1])* She married (1) EVERETT BRAY. She married (2) GEORGE ALLEN.

Child of IDA HUTCHINS and EVERETT BRAY is:
         i.   GIRL BRAY[10] ADOPTED, b. Private.

1310. FRANK[9] HUTCHINS *(MARY OLIVIA[8] BROOKS, DANIEL LANGDON[7], DANIEL[6], MARY[5] SPINNEY, JOHN[4], JOHN[3], JOHN[2], THOMAS[1])* was born 1885. He married EDITH LUPIN.

Child of FRANK HUTCHINS and EDITH LUPIN is:
         i.   JACQUELINE[10] HUTCHINS, b. Private.

1311. INEZ BELL[9] BROOKS *(FRANK PIERCE[8], DANIEL LANGDON[7], DANIEL[6], MARY[5] SPINNEY, JOHN[4], JOHN[3], JOHN[2], THOMAS[1])* was born 1874, and died 1966. She married (1) WILLIAM KIEF. She married (2) CHARLES NOYES HOYT.

Child of INEZ BROOKS and WILLIAM KIEF is:
  i. HAROLD TILTON[10] KIEF, b. 27 Oct 1897.

1312. ALICE MARY[9] SPINNEY *(AZARIAH L[8], OLIVER P[7], JAMES[6], GEORGE PETTEGREW[5], JOHN[4], JOHN[3], JOHN[2], THOMAS[1])* was born Abt. 1870, and died Aft. 1930. She married (1) JOSEPH ELMOR SPINNEY, son of JOSEPH SPINNEY and ELIZABETH BROOKS. He was born 1868, and died Bef. 1900. She married (2) SPENCER HUTTON 12 Nov 1904 in Portsmouth, NH. He was born 1871 in Newington.

Children are listed above under (997) Joseph Elmor Spinney.

Child of ALICE SPINNEY and SPENCER HUTTON is:
  i. GERTRUDE A[10] HUTTON, b. 1906, New Hampshire, New Hampshire.

1313. FRANK W[9] SPINNEY *(EUGENE H[8], HENRY PARKER[7], JAMES[6], GEORGE PETTEGREW[5], JOHN[4], JOHN[3], JOHN[2], THOMAS[1])* was born Jun 1894 in New Hampshire. He married ALMENA HERSEY. She was born 02 Sep 1884 in New Hampshire.

Children of FRANK SPINNEY and ALMENA HERSEY are:
  i. MILDRED L[10] SPINNEY, b. 04 Apr 1924; d. 12 Nov 2002; m. PIZ.

      Notes for MILDRED L SPINNEY:
      Mildred L. "Ma" (Spinney) Pizz

      PORTSMOUTH - Mildred L. "Ma" (Spinney) Pizz, 78, of 1600 Islington St., died unexpectedly on Tuesday, Nov. 12, 2002, at the Portsmouth Regional Hospital, surrounded by all her loving family.

      She was born in Portsmouth on April 4, 1924, a daughter of Frank W. and A. Viola (Hersey) Spinney. She was a member of the North Congregational Church of Portsmouth and had belonged to the Blue Birds, Campfire Girls and Rogers Mission of the church. She was a graduate of Portsmouth High School, Class of 1942, and had worked at Woolworth's during high school. In 1946 she married Stanley Pizz; they were married for 40 years before his death in 1986.

      She was a loving, caring and devoted mother and grandmother. She enjoyed knitting sweaters and mittens for the church fair and always made sure her grandchildren had homemade sweaters and blankets. She also enjoyed reading and telling stories. She will be sadly missed by all who knew her.

      Survivors include her three sons, Richard Pizz and his wife, Linda, of Epping, Frank Pizz and his companion Patty of Portsmouth, and Kevin Pizz and his companion Samantha of Portsmouth; two daughters, Diane Pizz of Massachusetts and Janice Brown and her husband, Russ, of Portsmouth; 10 grandchildren; nine great-grandchildren; a sister, Beatrice Brightman and her husband, Russ, of Greenland and Florida; a brother, Francis Spinney and his wife, Dawn, of Portsmouth; several nieces and nephews; and her devoted friend for 60 years Helen Foley of Sanford, Maine.

      She was predeceased by a son, Paul Stephen Pizz, who died in 1979; and twin infant daughters, Janet and Janice.

  ii. BEATRICE SPINNEY, b. 1927; m. RUSSELL BRIGHTMAN.

      Notes for BEATRICE SPINNEY:
      Beatrice Viola (Spinney) Brightman

      PORTSMOUTH - Mrs. Beatrice Viola (Spinney) Brightman, 76, wife of T. Russell Brightman, of 143 Bluefish Blvd., died peacefully at her home after a brief illness on Tuesday, Sept. 30, 2003.

      She was a native of Portsmouth, born on Aug. 25, 1927, the daughter of the late Frank W. and A. Viola (Hersey) Spinney. She was a graduate of Portsmouth High School, Class of 1945.

      Mrs. Brightman was formerly employed as a teller for the Maine National Bank and First National Bank of Portsmouth.

She was a lifetime member of the North Congregational Church in Portsmouth, where she was a former deaconess, member of the North Church Women, and a proud volunteer of the Nearly New Shop.

Mrs. Brightman was a former Girl Scout Leader; Den Mother of Troop 164; former member of the Advisory Board of the Portsmouth Assembly No. 2, International Order of Rainbow for Girls; and a member of Rivermouth Chapter No. 54, Order of Eastern Star in Portsmouth.

Bea and Russ enjoyed 15 years of retirement at their home in Lady Lake, Fla. They summered in the Seacoast area. Bea enjoyed playing golf in the south with their many friends. Bea was a devoted wife, mother, grandmother, and great-grandmother. Her family bestowed upon her many affectionate names: Mom, Mum, Grammie and G.G. Bea enjoyed sewing, knitting, baking and spending time with her family, most recently her grandchildren and great-grandchildren.

Besides her husband of 55 years, survivors include a son, Thomas Brightman and his wife, Donna, of Bow; two daughters, Linda Kittredge and friend Russ Brackett of Barrington; Debra V. Brightman-Jones and her husband, Gene, of Greenland; five grandchildren, Laurie Lent and husband Tom of Portsmouth, Timothy Bean and wife Jennifer of Elizabethtown, Pa., Laura O'Neill Brightman of Bow, Sarah Eyre Jones and Nathan Russell Jones of Greenland; three great-grandchildren, Erin and Justin Lent of Portsmouth, and Gavin Bean of Elizabethtown, Pa.; her brother, Francis Spinney of Portsmouth; and several nieces and nephews.

Beatrice was predeceased by her sister, Mildred, and infant daughter, Carol.

  iii. FRANCIS SPINNEY, b. Abt. 1929.

1314. LILLIAN B[9] SPINNEY (*HARRIS E*[8], *HENRY PARKER*[7], *JAMES*[6], *GEORGE PETTEGREW*[5], *JOHN*[4], *JOHN*[3], *JOHN*[2], *THOMAS*[1]) was born 11 Jun 1903 in Eliot, Maine, and died 15 Dec 1996 in South Berwick, Me. She married MARURICE A RICHARDSON 23 Aug 1933 in Eliot, Maine. He was born 02 Jul 1910, and died 27 Apr 1997 in South Berwick, Me.

Child of LILLIAN SPINNEY and MARURICE RICHARDSON is:
  i. MAURICE WINSLOW[10] RICHARDSON, b. 15 Feb 1944, South Berwick, Me; d. 26 Oct 2004, Wells, Me; m. LINDA FRANZ.

      Notes for MAURICE WINSLOW RICHARDSON:
      WELLS - Maurice "Sonny" Richardson, 60, of Wells, passed away quietly Oct. 26, 2004 at his home surrounded by his family.

      He was born Feb. 15, 1944 in South Berwick, a son of Maurice and Lillian Richardson. He served his country proudly in the United States Army for three years.

      For 16 years, he had been a grinder at Pratt & Whitney Aircraft in North Berwick.

      He is survived by his wife of 11 years, Linda (Franz) Richardson; three step-daughters and their spouses, Deborah Fenderson and her husband Larry Fenderson of Wells, Catherine Sullivan and her husband Michael of Rochester, N.H.; and Kimberly Daggett of Wells; four grandsons, Andrew and Alex Sullivan, David Williams and Donald Fenderson.

      Funeral services were held Friday at the Johnson Funeral Home, 26 Market St., North Berwick. Interment at a later date in the Maine Veteran's Cemetery in Augusta. (York County Coast Star, Thursday 4 November 2004)

1315. MYRON ROGER[9] SPINNEY (*ALMON*[8], *AUGUSTUS W*[7], *SIMON*[6], *GEORGE PETTEGREW*[5], *JOHN*[4], *JOHN*[3], *JOHN*[2], *THOMAS*[1]) was born Jun 1886, and died 1966 in Malden, MA. He married HAZEL B CLARK 1910 in Malden, MA. She was born 1887.

Children of MYRON SPINNEY and HAZEL CLARK are:
  i. HELENA[10] SPINNEY, b. 1912.
  ii. GLADYS SPINNEY, b. 1914.

1316. FRANK MOSES[9] SPINNEY *(CALVIN A[8], MOSES J[7], SIMON[6], GEORGE PETTEGREW[5], JOHN[4], JOHN[3], JOHN[2], THOMAS[1])* was born 01 Mar 1894 in Connecticut, and died Aft. 1930 in Providence, RI. He married ANNIE WHITE.

Children of FRANK SPINNEY and ANNIE WHITE are:
- i. MAE[10] SPINNEY.
- ii. ROBERT SPINNEY.
- iii. NORMAN SPINNEY.
- iv. ANDREW SPINNEY.
- v. WALTER SPINNEY.

1317. BESSIE A[9] SHAPLEIGH *(MARCIA MELINDA[8] SPINNEY, HAMILTON[7], FRANCIS[6], GEORGE PETTEGREW[5], JOHN[4], JOHN[3], JOHN[2], THOMAS[1])* was born Jan 1889. She married EDSON JASPER SHAPLEIGH, son of JASPER SHAPLEIGH and HATTIE STAPLES.

Children of BESSIE SHAPLEIGH and EDSON SHAPLEIGH are:
- i. WALSRON EDSON[10] SHAPLEIGH.
- ii. ELOISE MAY SHAPLEIGH.
- iii. LEON CHESTER SHAPLEIGH.
- iv. FORREST KENNETH SHAPLEIGH.
- v. GERALDINE HARRIOT SHAPLEIGH.

1318. CHESTER ERNEST[9] MCKENNEY *(SADIE R[8] SPINNEY, HAMILTON[7], FRANCIS[6], GEORGE PETTEGREW[5], JOHN[4], JOHN[3], JOHN[2], THOMAS[1])* was born 21 Sep 1885, and died Feb 1967. He married GEORGIE PLACE.

Children of CHESTER MCKENNEY and GEORGIE PLACE are:
- i. ERNEST[10] MCKENNEY.
- ii. HARLON MCKENNEY.
- iii. SHIRLEY MCKENNEY.
- iv. PAULINE MCKENNEY.
- v. RAYMOND MCKENNEY.
- vi. AVIS MCKENNEY.
- vii. MARJORIE MCKENNEY.
- viii. RALPH MCKENNEY.

1319. BURTON C[9] ROGERS *(VIENNA[8] SPINNEY, SYLVESTER[7], FRANCIS[6], GEORGE PETTEGREW[5], JOHN[4], JOHN[3], JOHN[2], THOMAS[1])* was born Jan 1889. He married MARY.

Child of BURTON ROGERS and MARY is:
- i. HELEN[10] ROGERS.

1320. ARTHUR ROSCOE[9] SPINNEY *(ALFRED[8], SYLVESTER[7], FRANCIS[6], GEORGE PETTEGREW[5], JOHN[4], JOHN[3], JOHN[2], THOMAS[1])* was born Dec 1875, and died 1951. He married ANNIE M CHICK 20 Jan 1897. She was born Dec 1877, and died 1963.

Children of ARTHUR SPINNEY and ANNIE CHICK are:
- 1517.   i.   LILLIAN M[10] SPINNEY, b. Aug 1897.
-       ii.   IRMA CELIA SPINNEY, b. 03 Aug 1899, Eliot, ME; m. ROLAND A RAITT, 28 Oct 1925.
- 1518.   iii.   REGINALD I SPINNEY, b. 16 May 1903.

1321. MILO[9] SPINNEY *(ALFRED[8], SYLVESTER[7], FRANCIS[6], GEORGE PETTEGREW[5], JOHN[4], JOHN[3], JOHN[2], THOMAS[1])* was born 07 Jan 1878, and died 06 Oct 1938. He married MINA WILLIAMS 27 May 1899 in Kittery, ME. She was born 04 Dec 1875, and died 18 Mar 1938.

Children of MILO SPINNEY and MINA WILLIAMS are:
- 1519.   i.   NORMAN E[10] SPINNEY, b. Dec 1899; d. Aft. 1920.
-       ii.   EVELYN SPINNEY, b. 1904.

1520.   iii.   PHYLIS SPINNEY, b. 1907.

1322. ANNIE M[9] SPINNEY *(FRANK A[8], SYLVESTER[7], FRANCIS[6], GEORGE PETTEGREW[5], JOHN[4], JOHN[3], JOHN[2], THOMAS[1])* was born May 1881. She married ARTHUR LEWIS.

Child of ANNIE SPINNEY and ARTHUR LEWIS is:
     i.   MAZIE[10] LEWIS.

1323. GENIEVA EVANGELINE[9] SPINNEY *(MELVILLE SYLVESTER[8], SYLVESTER[7], FRANCIS[6], GEORGE PETTEGREW[5], JOHN[4], JOHN[3], JOHN[2], THOMAS[1])* was born 1896, and died Jan 1973 in Winchester, MA. She married RALPH MANNING.

Child of GENIEVA SPINNEY and RALPH MANNING is:
     i.   RALPH M[10] MANNING.

1324. ARNOLD CLAYTON[9] SPINNEY *(ALBERT LESTER[8], SYLVESTER[7], FRANCIS[6], GEORGE PETTEGREW[5], JOHN[4], JOHN[3], JOHN[2], THOMAS[1])* was born 22 Feb 1900, and died 31 Jan 2000 in Manchester, NH. He married MILDRED ORVILLE MOULTON 16 Aug 1918 in York, Me, daughter of LEON MOULTON and ORVILLE MOULTON. She was born 1898, and died 26 Mar 1993 in York, Maine.

Notes for ARNOLD CLAYTON SPINNEY:
Arnold C. Spinney

MANCHESTER - Arnold C. Spinney, 99, of 465 Medford St., formerly of Eliot, widower of Mildred L. (Moulton) Spinney, died Monday, Jan. 31, 2000, at his grandsons residence in Manchester.

Born Feb. 22, 1900, in Eliot, he was the son of Albert L. and Sadie (Staples) Spinney and attended local schools.

He worked for 25 years at the Portsmouth Naval Shipyard, retiring in 1949. He then worked locally as a painter for many years.

He was a member of the Eliot Baptist Church. He enjoyed hunting, fishing, boating, playing cards, watching boxing on television as well as the Red Sox.

He is survived by seven grandchildren, Arnold R. Dow of Raymond, Janice (Dow) Brown of Amesbury, Mass., Andrea (Dow) Rogers of Seabrook, Douglass Dow of Epping, Dennis Dow of Manchester, Denise (Dow) Spaulding of Byfield, Mass., William R. Dow Jr. of Byfield, Mass.; 19 great-grandchildren; six great great-grandchildren; a nephew, Frederick Shapleigh Jr. of Eliot; a niece, Julia Spinney Dufore of Kittery; and his son-in-law, William Dow Sr. of Epping.

Besides his wife, who died in 1993, he was predeceased by two daughters, Margaret Spinney, who died in 1924, and Marion L. Spinney Dow, who died in 1981. He was also predeceased by a grandson, Kenneth Dow in 1997.

Children of ARNOLD SPINNEY and MILDRED MOULTON are:
1521.   i.   MARION L[10] SPINNEY, b. 1919; d. 1981.
     ii.   MARGARET SPINNEY, d. 1924.

1325. ADVILLE A[9] SPINNEY *(AMMI ADVILLE[8], FRANCIS LEMUEL[7], FRANCIS[6], GEORGE PETTEGREW[5], JOHN[4], JOHN[3], JOHN[2], THOMAS[1])* was born 1898. He married ELSIE WOOD 08 Jul 1916 in Eliot, ME. She was born 1898.

Children of ADVILLE SPINNEY and ELSIE WOOD are:
1522.   i.   DOROTHY[10] SPINNEY, b. 1917.
     ii.   DAVID R SPINNEY, b. 19 Feb 1919; d. 04 Dec 1965.
     iii.   JEANETTE SPINNEY, b. 1923; m. FRANCIS D PAUL, 19 Oct 1941, Portsmouth, NH.
     iv.   PHYLLIS SPINNEY, b. 1927.
     v.   ELIZABETH SPINNEY, b. 1928.
     vi.   DOUGLAS SPINNEY, b. 1929.

1326. ARTHUR E[9] SPINNEY *(PEARL[8], FRANCIS LEMUEL[7], FRANCIS[6], GEORGE PETTEGREW[5], JOHN[4], JOHN[3], JOHN[2], THOMAS[1])* was born Oct 1897, and died 1968. He married MARGARETE.

Children of ARTHUR SPINNEY and MARGARETE are:
    i.   ARLENE[10] SPINNEY, b. 1926.
    ii.   FRANCES SPINNEY, b. 1920.

1327. ALTIE A.[9] HUNTRESS *(MARY EVA[8] DIXON, LYDIA N.[7] TETHERLY, CHARLES[6], SAMUEL[5], WILLIAM[4], MERCY[3] SPINNEY, JOHN[2], THOMAS[1])* was born 31 Jul 1877. She married REMICK.

Children of ALTIE HUNTRESS and REMICK are:
    i.   LAURIE[10] REMICK, b. Private.
    ii.   PHYLIS REMICK, b. Private.
    iii. ALBERTA REMICK, b. Private.

1328. GRACE M.[9] HUNTRESS *(MARY EVA[8] DIXON, LYDIA N.[7] TETHERLY, CHARLES[6], SAMUEL[5], WILLIAM[4], MERCY[3] SPINNEY, JOHN[2], THOMAS[1])* was born 25 Dec 1881. She married TITUS.

Children of GRACE HUNTRESS and TITUS are:
            i.   RALPH[10] TITUS, b. Private.
            ii.   ALICE TITUS, b. Private.
1523.   iii. FLORENCE TITUS, b. Private.

1329. FLORENCE WINIFRED[9] HUNTRESS *(MARY EVA[8] DIXON, LYDIA N.[7] TETHERLY, CHARLES[6], SAMUEL[5], WILLIAM[4], MERCY[3] SPINNEY, JOHN[2], THOMAS[1])* was born 20 Dec 1884 in Eliot, ME, and died 14 Nov 1972 in Webster, MA. She married HORACE DAVID WALKER 18 Nov 1908 in South Eliot, ME. He was born 27 Feb 1884 in Kittery, ME, and died 05 Apr 1961 in Whitinsville, MA.

Children of FLORENCE HUNTRESS and HORACE WALKER are:
1524.   i.   JOHN BERKLEY[10] WALKER, b. 30 Jun 1910, South Eliot. MA; d. 17 Jun 1985, Holyoke, MA.
1525.   ii.   IRENE WALKER, b. 21 Sep 1915, Uxbridge, MA; d. 02 Jan 1993, Oxford, MA.
1526.   iii. HORACE ALLAN WALKER, b. 11 Jul 1920, Springfield, MA; d. 25 Dec 1985, Springfield, MA.
1527.   iv. CHARLES EDWIN WALKER, b. 15 Jun 1922, Springfield, MA; d. 03 Apr 1984, Agawam, MA.
1528.   v.   KENNETH DAVID WALKER, b. Private.
         vi. VIRGINIA WALKER, b. Private; m. LESTER TAFT, Private; b. 12 Sep 1916; d. 19 Apr 1991, Uxbridge, Mass., Lung Cancer.

1330. LILLIAN MAUD[9] LYDSTON *(ARTHUR FRANCIS[8], FRANCIS ARTHUR[7], WILLIAM[6], WEYMOUTH[5], ABIGAIL[4] SPINNEY, ANDREW[3], JOHN[2], THOMAS[1])* was born 28 Dec 1866 in Racine, WI, and died 08 Jan 1950 in Sacramento, CA. She married JOHN FRANK CAHILL Abt. 1891, son of ? CAHILL and ? MILLS.

Children of LILLIAN LYDSTON and JOHN CAHILL are:
1529.   i.   VEDA VIVIAN[10] CAHILL, b. 30 May 1892, Indian Valley, Ca; d. Sep 1984, Sacramento, Ca.
         ii.   VERNON CLARE CAHILL, b. Abt. 1894.
         iii. GOLDIE CAHILL, b. Abt. 1897.

1331. AGNES[9] SPINNEY *(IVAH WELLINGTON[8], HENRY DAME[7], JACOB REMICK[6], JEREMIAH[5], JOHN[4], JOHN[3], JOHN[2], THOMAS[1])* was born Abt. 1900. She married WILLIAM EDWARD GROGAN.

Children of AGNES SPINNEY and WILLIAM GROGAN are:
    i.   HERMAN WESLEY[10] GROGAN.
    ii.   DAVID GROGAN.
    iii. ERNEST HAROLD GROGAN.
    iv. DONALD EDWARD GROGAN.

1332. JOHN EDWARD[9] SPINNEY *(IVAH WELLINGTON[8], HENRY DAME[7], JACOB REMICK[6], JEREMIAH[5], JOHN[4], JOHN[3], JOHN[2], THOMAS[1])* was born 1913 in Rockingham CO, NH, and died 20 Jun 2000. He married ARLENE RASMUSSAN 1940 in Rockingham CO, NH. She was born 1922, and died 03 Feb 1995.

Children of JOHN SPINNEY and ARLENE RASMUSSAN are:
 i. SUSAN JANE[10] SPINNEY, b. 1941; m. FREDRICK LACKIE; b. 1941.
 ii. CONSTANCE LINDA SPINNEY, b. 1942; m. JOHN V MCCOLLETT; b. 1943.
 iii. JANICE LUCILLE SPINNEY, b. 1946.
 iv. ARNOLD SPINNEY, b. 1949.
 v. OWEN BALLARD SPINNEY, b. 1960.

1333. AMY BELLE[9] SPINNEY *(ALLISON FAIRBANKS[8], HIRAM[7], DAVID[6], ISAAC[5], JOHN[4], JOHN[3], JOHN[2], THOMAS[1])* was born 06 Jul 1879. She married RALPH F STONE 15 Nov 1904 in Otisfield, ME.

Children of AMY SPINNEY and RALPH STONE are:
 i. MARION[10] STONE, b. 18 Oct 1906; m. HENRY A LITTLE, 28 May 1950.
 ii. ELLA STONE.
 iii. DAVID STONE.
 iv. WILLARD STONE.
 v. ESTELLE STONE.
 vi. ELEANOR STONE.

1334. ALMA EDITH[9] SPINNEY *(ALLISON FAIRBANKS[8], HIRAM[7], DAVID[6], ISAAC[5], JOHN[4], JOHN[3], JOHN[2], THOMAS[1])* was born 14 Sep 1883. She married GEORGE STALEY WELLNER. He was born 29 Feb 1880.

Children of ALMA SPINNEY and GEORGE WELLNER are:
 i. LLOYD ALLISON[10] WELLNER, b. 29 Jan 1905.
1530. ii. ALMA FRANCES WELLNER, b. 30 Dec 1906.
 iii. DONALD VAN NUYS WELLNER, b. 07 Aug 1909.
 iv. EDITH ELIZABETH WELLNER, b. 16 Dec 1914.

1335. LLOYD ELLSWORTH[9] SPINNEY *(ALLISON FAIRBANKS[8], HIRAM[7], DAVID[6], ISAAC[5], JOHN[4], JOHN[3], JOHN[2], THOMAS[1])* was born 14 Nov 1889 in Nova Scotia, and died 17 Dec 1949. He married BARBARA. She was born 1891 in Massachusetts.

Child of LLOYD SPINNEY and BARBARA is:
 i. WEYMOUTH[10] SPINNEY, b. 1912.

1336. IVAN HAROLD[9] SPINNEY *(ALLISON FAIRBANKS[8], HIRAM[7], DAVID[6], ISAAC[5], JOHN[4], JOHN[3], JOHN[2], THOMAS[1])* was born 22 Jun 1892. He married FRANCES. She was born 1899.

Children of IVAN SPINNEY and FRANCES are:
 i. IRENE[10] SPINNEY, b. 1920.
 ii. MALCOLM D SPINNEY, b. 1924.

1337. EDITH MABEL[9] SPINNEY *(GEORGE N[8], HIRAM[7], DAVID[6], ISAAC[5], JOHN[4], JOHN[3], JOHN[2], THOMAS[1])* was born 25 Jan 1905. She married GORDON E CRANDELL.

Notes for EDITH MABEL SPINNEY:
Edith Mabel (Spinney) Crandall, 96, a retired buyer for the former Jordan Marsh Department Store, where she had worked for 25 years, died suddenly Saturday evening, March 3, 2001 at her son's home in East Falmouth, MA. Mrs. Crandall was born and educated in Malden, MA She was a life long resident of Malden, later residing in East Falmouth for the last 3 years. Mrs. Crandall was a life member of the Malden Hospital Ladies Aid, member of the Malden Old & New, Melrose Order of the Eastern Star Chapter # 99, Women's Society of the First Baptist Church and long time member of the the First Baptist Church in Malden.

She was a buyer for the former Joslin Department Store and the former Jordan Marsh Department Store in

Malden, retiring in 1970.

She is survived by her son, Gordon E. Crandall Jr. and his wife Harriet M. of East Falmouth, MA. Her daughter, Lois M. Crandall of Harpswell, ME Grandmother of 8 grandchildren & 11 great-grandchildren.

She was preceded in death by her late husband Gordon E. Crandall Sr., her father George Spinney, and her mother Minnie Thompson.

She was born January 25, 1905 in Malden, MA

Visiting hours have been omitted.

Contributions in Edith's memory may be made to the First Baptist Church, Memorial Fund, 493 Main St., Malden, MA 02148.

Funeral services will be held Thursday, March 8, 2001 at 11:00 A.M. at Weir - Mac Cuish Golden Rule Funeral Home, 144 Salem St., Malden. The Rev. Martha A. Dominy of the First Baptist Church will be officiating. Burial will be in the Forest Dale Cemetery in Malden.

Children of EDITH SPINNEY and GORDON CRANDELL are:
   i.   GORDON E[10] CRANDELL.
   ii. LOIS M CRANDELL.

1338. EDYTH[9] SPINNEY (LEROY B[8], HIRAM[7], DAVID[6], ISAAC[5], JOHN[4], JOHN[3], JOHN[2], THOMAS[1]) was born 1906 in Yarmouth, NS., and died 31 Mar 1997 in Worcester, MA. She married RICHARD M BAILEY.

Notes for EDYTH SPINNEY:
Headline: Edythe M. Bailey, 91
       Publication Date: March 31, 1997
       Source: Telegram & Gazette Worcester, MA
       Page: B5
       Subjects:
       Region: Massachusetts
Obituary: WORCESTER - Edythe M. (Spinney) Bailey, 91, formerly of Canterbury Towers, a shoe stitcher for 42 years, died yesterday in University Commons Nursing Care center after an illness. Her husband, Richard M. Bailey, died in 1985. She leaves a son, David O. Bailey of Lagrangeville, N.Y.; seven grandchildren; and six great-grandchildren. A son, Bruce Bailey of Hopkinton, died in 1988. She was born in Yarmouth County, Nova Scotia, daughter of Leroy and Margaret (Goodwin) Spinney, and lived here 76 years. She graduated from David Hale Fanning Trade High School. Mrs. Bailey was a stitcher at Bickford, Sweet & Hammond Shoe Co. for 42 years before she retired. She was a member of the Aldersgate United Methodist Church.

       A funeral service will be held at noon tomorrow in Miles Funeral Home, 1158 Main St, Holden. Burial will be private in Hope Cemetery. Calling hours are 11 a.m. to noon tomorrow at the funeral home. In lieu of flowers, memorial contributions may be made to Aldersgate United Methodist Church, 1048 Main St., Worcester 01603.

Child of EDYTH SPINNEY and RICHARD BAILEY is:
   i.   DAVID O[10] BAILEY.

1339. EDWIN L[9] SPINNEY (ENOS[8], SIMEON[7], BENJAMIN[6], BENJAMIN[5], JOHN[4], JOHN[3], JOHN[2], THOMAS[1]) was born 07 Jul 1889 in Boothbay Harbor, ME, and died 26 Sep 1976 in Boothbay Harbor, ME. He married EVA TILTON 04 Aug 1907. She was born 1888, and died 28 Mar 1972.

Children of EDWIN SPINNEY and EVA TILTON are:

i. RUBY[10] SPINNEY, b. 1908.
ii. MURIEL J SPINNEY, b. 1921.
iii. RALPH L SPINNEY, b. 1929; m. MARILYN SHERMAN, 20 Jun 1947, Boothbay Harbour, ME.

1340. BURGESS HARRIS[9] SPINNEY *(ALBERT L[8], HARRIS"CAPT" HARDING[7], BENJAMIN[6], BENJAMIN[5], JOHN[4], JOHN[3], JOHN[2], THOMAS[1])* was born 09 Feb 1889 in Weymouth, MA, and died Jul 1971. He married ELEANOR. She was born 1892.

Children of BURGESS SPINNEY and ELEANOR are:
i. BURGESS H[10] SPINNEY, b. 07 May 1913; d. 04 Dec 1998.
ii. VIRGINIA T SPINNEY, b. 1915.

1341. CECIL LAWRENCE[9] SPINNEY *(ALBERT L[8], HARRIS"CAPT" HARDING[7], BENJAMIN[6], BENJAMIN[5], JOHN[4], JOHN[3], JOHN[2], THOMAS[1])* was born 23 Dec 1890 in Hingham, Ma, and died Aft. 1930. He married CASSIE GRIGG. She was born 28 Sep 1889, and died 14 Jun 1991.

Children of CECIL SPINNEY and CASSIE GRIGG are:
i. PAULINA[10] SPINNEY, b. 1918.
ii. LAWRENCE SPINNEY, b. 1921.

1342. LEMUEL E[9] SPINNEY *(LEMUEL E[8], CALEB[7], JAMES[6], JACOB[5], JOHN[4], JOHN[3], JOHN[2], THOMAS[1])* was born 15 May 1902, and died Feb 1975 in Gloucester, MA. He married MILDRED.

Children of LEMUEL SPINNEY and MILDRED are:
i. MARJORIE[10] SPINNEY, b. 1925.
ii. PRICILLA SPINNEY, b. 1927.

1343. EARL B[9] SPINNEY *(HAVELOCK[8], MORRIS[7], JACOB[6], JACOB[5], JOHN[4], JOHN[3], JOHN[2], THOMAS[1])* was born 07 Jan 1899, and died 29 Sep 1993. He married ROSEMOND. She was born 1904.

Child of EARL SPINNEY and ROSEMOND is:
i. BARBARA E[10] SPINNEY.

1344. LAURA[9] SPINNEY *(HAVELOCK[8], MORRIS[7], JACOB[6], JACOB[5], JOHN[4], JOHN[3], JOHN[2], THOMAS[1])* She married FOSTER.

Child of LAURA SPINNEY and FOSTER is:
i. ALVIN[10] FOSTER.

1345. JAMES ELMER[9] FORD *(LAURA MAE[8] SPINNEY, STILLMAN[7], JOSEPH[6], JACOB[5], JOHN[4], JOHN[3], JOHN[2], THOMAS[1])* was born 19 Aug 1902 in Boston, MA, and died 05 Jul 1979. He married ANNA MAE KINNEY 05 Sep 1927 in Sacred Heart Church, Watertown, MA. She was born 23 Jul 1904 in Watertown, MA, and died 16 Jun 1971 in St. Patrick's Cemetery, Watertown, MA.

Children of JAMES FORD and ANNA KINNEY are:
i. JAMES ELMER[10] FORD, b. Sep 1929, Watertown, MA; d. Dec 1930, St. Patrick's Cemetery, Watertown, MA.
ii. ANN MARIE FORD, b. Private; m. RAYMOND JOHN GOULET, Private; b. Private.
1531. iii. EILEEN MARTHA FORD, b. Private.
1532. iv. CLAIRE THERESA FORD, b. Private.
1533. v. ROBERT EDWARD FORD, b. Private.
1534. vi. PAULINE DOROTHY FORD, b. Private.
1535. vii. MARION ANGELA FORD, b. Private.
1536. viii. JOAN ELIZABETH FORD, b. Private.
1537. ix. JOHN TIMOTHY FORD, b. Private.
1538. x. ELEANOR MAE FORD, b. Private.
1539. xi. JANET MARGARET FORD, b. Private.

1346. EMMALINE DORIS⁹ SPINNEY *(THELSTON D⁸, BENJAMIN F⁷, EBENEZER⁶, JACOB⁵, JOHN⁴, JOHN³, JOHN², THOMAS¹)* was born 24 Apr 1900, and died Oct 1978. She married FRANK STEAD.

Children of EMMALINE SPINNEY and FRANK STEAD are:
     i.   ELOISE¹⁰ STEAD, b. 1925.
     ii. VIRGINIA STEAD, b. 1930.

1347. ROBERT MARTIN⁹ SPINNEY *(THELSTON D⁸, BENJAMIN F⁷, EBENEZER⁶, JACOB⁵, JOHN⁴, JOHN³, JOHN², THOMAS¹)* was born 1918. He married CATHERINE ROBERTSON.

Child of ROBERT SPINNEY and CATHERINE ROBERTSON is:
     i.   ROBERT¹⁰ SPINNEY.

1348. DONALD GENE⁹ FROST *(ORESSA MARIA⁸ SPINNEY, BENJAMIN F⁷, EBENEZER⁶, JACOB⁵, JOHN⁴, JOHN³, JOHN², THOMAS¹)* He married MYRTEL BERVIECE WOODARD.

Children of DONALD FROST and MYRTEL WOODARD are:
     i.   JEFFREY EDWARD¹⁰ FROST.
     ii. TIMOTHY ANDREW FROST.

1349. CLINTON⁹ SPINNEY *(WESLEY F⁸, JAMES⁷, JAMES⁶, JACOB⁵, JOHN⁴, JOHN³, JOHN², THOMAS¹)* was born 02 Feb 1880, and died May 1948. He married ALETHIA HAMILTON.

Children of CLINTON SPINNEY and ALETHIA HAMILTON are:
     i.   DORIS¹⁰ SPINNEY, b. Aug 1917; d. 25 Dec 2000.
     ii. VERA SPINNEY, b. 1919; m. DARELL ROBERTS.
     iii. SARA SPINNEY, b. 1921; m. ROBERT GOODWIN.
1540.   iv. ADDISON WESLEY SPINNEY, b. 1923.

1350. FRANK WESLEY⁹ SPINNEY *(WESLEY F⁸, JAMES⁷, JAMES⁶, JACOB⁵, JOHN⁴, JOHN³, JOHN², THOMAS¹)* was born 13 Aug 1885 in Argyle, NS., and died 30 May 1967 in Gloucester, MA.. He married RUTH CORKUM.

Children of FRANK SPINNEY and RUTH CORKUM are:
1541.   i.   BARBARA¹⁰ SPINNEY.
1542.   ii. JOYCE SPINNEY.

1351. LOVETT ELDRIDGE⁹ SPINNEY *(WESLEY F⁸, JAMES⁷, JAMES⁶, JACOB⁵, JOHN⁴, JOHN³, JOHN², THOMAS¹)* was born 23 Sep 1892 in Pubnico, N.S., and died 18 Jul 1972 in Gloucester, MA. He married BERTHA MAY CAHOON 27 Dec 1916 in Gloucester, MA. She was born 1898.

Children of LOVETT SPINNEY and BERTHA CAHOON are:
     i.   GENEVA¹⁰ SPINNEY, b. 13 Oct 1917; m. ROBERT POWERS.
1543.   ii. LOVETT E SPINNEY, b. 30 Sep 1919; d. 08 Sep 1994.
     iii. MILDRED SPINNEY, b. 28 Oct 1921; m. FREDERICK FRANKS.

1352. PRESCOTT YOUNGER⁹ SPINNEY *(ADEN CLAYTON⁸, WHITFIELD⁷, JAMES⁶, JACOB⁵, JOHN⁴, JOHN³, JOHN², THOMAS¹)* was born 11 Apr 1895, and died Oct 1979 in Texas. He married ISABEL.

Children of PRESCOTT SPINNEY and ISABEL are:
     i.   RODERICK M¹⁰ SPINNEY, b. 27 Jan 1924.
1544.   ii. PRESCOTT Y SPINNEY, b. 12 Mar 1925.
1545.   iii. WILLIAM H SPINNEY, b. Feb 1926.
     iv. GEORGE C SPINNEY, b. 09 Oct 1927.
     v. ERNEST C SPINNEY, b. Jan 1930.

1353. FRED ALLISON[9] SHOLDS *(CONSTANCE[8] SPINNEY, JOSIAH[7], SOLOMAN ROBERT[6], BENJAMIN[5], JOHN[4], JOHN[3], JOHN[2], THOMAS[1])* was born 30 Dec 1920 in Port Latour NS. He married MARY ELIZABETH WOOD 12 Nov 1944.

Child of FRED SHOLDS and MARY WOOD is:
1546.   i. FREDRICK[10] SHOLDS.

1354. HAROLD F[9] SPINNEY *(HAROLD FARNHAM[8], GEORGE NELSON[7], SOLOMAN ROBERT[6], BENJAMIN[5], JOHN[4], JOHN[3], JOHN[2], THOMAS[1])* was born 06 Feb 1916 in Brooklyn, New York, USA, and died 1986 in Narragansett, Rhode Island, USA. He married MARTHA HEILHAMMER ZECHNER.

Children of HAROLD SPINNEY and MARTHA ZECHNER are:
    i. MARY JANE[10] SPINNEY.
    ii. SARAH LEGH SPINNEY.
    iii. CYNTHIA ANN SPINNEY.

1355. ALTHEA JEAN[9] SPINNEY *(BOWMAN EDWARD[8], BOWMAN E[7], EDWARD[6], DANIEL[5], JOHN[4], JOHN[3], JOHN[2], THOMAS[1])* was born 03 Mar 1928. She married VINCENT MARINO.

Children of ALTHEA SPINNEY and VINCENT MARINO are:
    i. ROBERT EDWARD[10] FOSTER.
    ii. GEORGE WAYNE FOSTER.

1356. ELIZABETH FRANCES[9] SPINNEY *(BOWMAN EDWARD[8], BOWMAN E[7], EDWARD[6], DANIEL[5], JOHN[4], JOHN[3], JOHN[2], THOMAS[1])* was born 25 Sep 1929. She married (1) DAVID PELLEGRINO. She married (2) FRANCES O'NEILL.

Child of ELIZABETH SPINNEY and DAVID PELLEGRINO is:
    i. DAVID[10] PELLEGRINO.

Child of ELIZABETH SPINNEY and FRANCES O'NEILL is:
    ii. STEPHEN[10] O'NEILL.

1357. EUGENE ROBERT[9] SPINNEY *(LYMAN EUGENE[8], BOWMAN E[7], EDWARD[6], DANIEL[5], JOHN[4], JOHN[3], JOHN[2], THOMAS[1])* was born 07 Nov 1929, and died 02 Apr 1988 in Hood County, TX. He married RENE FRANCES RANDALL.

Children of EUGENE SPINNEY and RENE RANDALL are:
1547.   i. RHONDA RENE[10] SPINNEY.
1548.   ii. KEITH EUGENE SPINNEY.
1549.   iii. ROBERT GLEN SPINNEY.
1550.   iv. DANA KEVIN SPINNEY.

1358. DONALD N[9] SPINNEY *(LYMAN EUGENE[8], BOWMAN E[7], EDWARD[6], DANIEL[5], JOHN[4], JOHN[3], JOHN[2], THOMAS[1])* was born 07 Jul 1931, and died Apr 2003. He married FRANCES SARAH JANE PATTON 18 Mar 1955.

Notes for DONALD N SPINNEY:
Donald N. Spinney, lived in Lynn, 71, carpenter, veteran

Lynn
Wednesday, April 16, 2003

Donald N. Spinney of Lynn, a carpenter, died Saturday at his home after a lengthy illness. He was 71.

Born in Peabody, he graduated from Lynn Classical High School in 1949 and later attended the University of Tokyo, Japan, Clemson University and North Shore Community College. He had been a Lynn resident for most of his life.

Mr. Spinney served in the Air Force as a sergeant in charge of all teenage activity at Johnson Air Force Base in Japan during the Korean War. Later in life, he also served for 10 years in the U.S. Selective Service.

He worked as a carpenter for Cutler Associates Inc. in Worcester for 10 years, retiring in 1989. He had worked previously at Fulton & Sons in Marlehead for 25 years.

Mr. Spinney was a member of the First Church of Christ Congregational, where he had served as a deacon for 10 years and was superintendent of the Sunday school for 16 years.

He was an active member of the Boy Scouts of America from the age of 11, was an Eagle Scout with Bronze Palm of the Far East Council in Japan and served with Scout Troop 28 at St. Mary's Church in Lynn. While serving as a scout master in Japan, he received the Order of the Arrow and later earned the Silver Beaver Award and the George Martin Award. He was a member of the first Shu-Shu-Ga Course.

Mr. Spinney was a former member of the Norfolk Correctional Institute Fellowship, was a past president of the Cobbet Junior High School PTA and was a past commander of the Franco American Amvets Post 161 in Lynn.

He was an active member of the Masons Golden Fleece Lodge AF & AM, the Scottish Rite, Valley of Boston, the New England Genealogical Society, the Professional Musicians Club and AARP. He enjoyed listening to country music and tracing geneology.

Mr. Spinney is survived by his wife, Frances S.J. (Patton); two sons, Donald S. and Daniel N., both of Amesbury; two daughters, Susan R. Snow and Alyson M., both of Lynn; a brother, Bruce A. of Jupiter, Fla.; 10 grandchildren; seven great-grandchildren; and several nieces and nephews.

A funeral service will be held at 11 a.m. today at Church of Christ Congregational, Lynn.

Burial will be in Pine Grove Cemetery, Lynn.

Arrangements by the Cuffe-McGinn Funeral Home, Lynn.

Children of DONALD SPINNEY and FRANCES PATTON are:
1551.   i.   DONALD STEPHEN[10] SPINNEY, b. 26 Feb 1957.
1552.   ii.   SUSAN RUTH SPINNEY, b. 26 Sep 1958.
1553.   iii.   DANIEL NEIL SPINNEY, b. 18 Mar 1962.
1554.   iv.   ALYSON MAE SPINNEY, b. 02 Oct 1965.

1359. JACK L[9] SPINNEY (*LYMAN EUGENE*[8], *BOWMAN E*[7], *EDWARD*[6], *DANIEL*[5], *JOHN*[4], *JOHN*[3], *JOHN*[2], *THOMAS*[1]) was born 16 Apr 1935, and died 30 Dec 1994. He married (1) SALLY RAMSDELL. She was born Abt. 1935. He married (2) SUZANNE DOW.

Child of JACK SPINNEY and SALLY RAMSDELL is:
1555.   i.   TAMMY LEE[10] SPINNEY.

Children of JACK SPINNEY and SUZANNE DOW are:
        ii.   DENISE MARGUERITE[10] DOW.
        iii.   JANET LUCILLE ROUSSEIN.
        iv.   DIANE MARIE ROUSSIN.
        v.   MICHAEL STEPHEN ROUSSIN.
        vi.   LINDA JEAN ROUSSIN DOW.
        vii.   JOSEPH ALBERT ROUSSIN.
1556.   viii.   SUSAN ANN SPINNEY, b. Abt. 1960.
1557.   ix.   JACK LYMAN SPINNEY.

1360. BRUCE[9] SPINNEY *(LYMAN EUGENE[8], BOWMAN E[7], EDWARD[6], DANIEL[5], JOHN[4], JOHN[3], JOHN[2], THOMAS[1])* was born 14 Jul 1936. He married (1) DIANE MILLS. He married (2) SHIRLEY BORDANARO.

Children of BRUCE SPINNEY and DIANE MILLS are:
1558.	i.	DENISE[10] SPINNEY.
1559.	ii.	DOREEN SPINNEY.
1560.	iii.	LYNNE SPINNEY.
1561.	iv.	BRUCE ALLEN SPINNEY MCGILVERY.
	v.	JEFFREY SPINNEY.

Children of BRUCE SPINNEY and SHIRLEY BORDANARO are:
- vi. ALLEN[10] ANGELI.
- vii. THOMAS P ANGELI.
- viii. SHARON A ANGELI.

1361. HERBERT LINDEN[9] SPINNEY *(LORENZO DOW[8], THOMAS[7], JOHN[6], JOHN[5], JOHN[4], ANDREW[3], JOHN[2], THOMAS[1])* was born 25 Sep 1862. He married (1) ALBERTA MUNSEY 01 Aug 1883. She was born 25 Oct 1863. He married (2) INA M BURRELL 02 Sep 1908, daughter of SARAH BURELL. She was born 1876.

Child of HERBERT SPINNEY and ALBERTA MUNSEY is:
- i. GRACE MILDRED[10] SPINNEY, b. 23 Jun 1884; m. ROY WALLACE, 08 Sep 1913, Bath, ME.

Children of HERBERT SPINNEY and INA BURRELL are:
- ii. MURIEL A[10] SPINNEY, b. 1910.
- iii. MARION L SPINNEY, b. 1921.

1362. MILLARD[9] SPINNEY *(LORENZO DOW[8], THOMAS[7], JOHN[6], JOHN[5], JOHN[4], ANDREW[3], JOHN[2], THOMAS[1])* was born 28 May 1864, and died 1932. He married ANNIE LEIGHTON 1898. She was born Mar 1867.

Child of MILLARD SPINNEY and ANNIE LEIGHTON is:
- i. EVERARD[10] SPINNEY, b. Feb 1900, ME; d. 12 Dec 1975, Boothbay, ME.

1363. LORENZO DOW[9] SPINNEY *(LORENZO DOW[8], THOMAS[7], JOHN[6], JOHN[5], JOHN[4], ANDREW[3], JOHN[2], THOMAS[1])* was born 22 Aug 1865. He married MABEL AIKENS.

Child of LORENZO SPINNEY and MABEL AIKENS is:
- i. PAUL WORTHINGTON[10] SPINNEY, b. 14 Dec 1913, Newington, NH; d. 30 Apr 1997, New Jersey.

1364. CHARLES M[9] CLARK *(NANCY JANE[8] SPINNEY, THOMAS[7], JOHN[6], JOHN[5], JOHN[4], ANDREW[3], JOHN[2], THOMAS[1])* was born 19 Oct 1872 in Georgetown, ME, and died in Massachusetts. He married LAURA VIRGINA JONES.

Children of CHARLES CLARK and LAURA JONES are:
- i. DONALD[10] CLARK.
- ii. DOROTHY CLARK.
- iii. ALLEN CLARK.

1365. SARAH A[9] HUNT *(REUBEN[8], ROXANNA BURGESS[7] SPINNEY, NICHOLAS[6], JOHN[5], JOHN[4], ANDREW[3], JOHN[2], THOMAS[1])* was born 13 Oct 1848. She married JAMES PURIEYTON.

Child of SARAH HUNT and JAMES PURIEYTON is:
- i. ANNIE[10] PURIEYTON.

1366. ALICE MARY[9] HUNT *(WILLIAM SPINNEY[8], ROXANNA BURGESS[7] SPINNEY, NICHOLAS[6], JOHN[5], JOHN[4], ANDREW[3], JOHN[2], THOMAS[1])* was born 07 Feb 1861 in Bath, ME, and died 15 May 1945 in Malden, MA (Buried: Forestdale Cemetery). She married WALTER LEWIS FULLER 06 May 1891 in Bath, Maine. He was born 09 Dec 1868 in New Vineyard, ME, and died 19 Dec 1943 in Malden, ME (Buried: Forestdale Cemetery).

Children of ALICE HUNT and WALTER FULLER are:
    i.   MILDRED[10] FULLER, m. HALL.
1562.   ii.   MYRA FULLER, b. 05 May 1893, Malden, MA; d. Oct 1983, Melrose, MA.

1367. ALICE L[9] SPINNEY *(ANSON B[8], WILLIAM M[7], NICHOLAS[6], JOHN[5], JOHN[4], ANDREW[3], JOHN[2], THOMAS[1])* was born 26 Jul 1858 in Illinois. She married JOSEPH DEVINE.

Child of ALICE SPINNEY and JOSEPH DEVINE is:
    i.   ANSON B S[10] DEVINE, b. 05 Jan 1879; m. MARY PETERSON, 27 Oct 1902.

1368. EMMA PEARL[9] SPINNEY *(ANSON B[8], WILLIAM M[7], NICHOLAS[6], JOHN[5], JOHN[4], ANDREW[3], JOHN[2], THOMAS[1])* was born Mar 1880 in Alabama, and died Aft. 1930. She married CLYDE LAVERNE HERRING, son of JAMES HERRING and ESTELLA. He was born 03 May 1879 in Michigan, and died 15 Sep 1945.

Notes for CLYDE LAVERNE HERRING:
Herring, Clyde LaVerne (1879-1945) -- also known as Clyde L. Herring -- of Des Moines, Polk County, Iowa. Born in Jackson, Jackson County, Mich., May 3, 1879. Democrat. Served in the U.S. Army during the Spanish-American War; member of Democratic National Committee from Iowa, 1924-28; Governor of Iowa, 1933-37; defeated, 1920; U.S. Senator from Iowa, 1937-43; defeated, 1922, 1942; delegate to Democratic National Convention from Iowa, 1940. Congregationalist. Died in Washington, D.C., September 15, 1945. Interment at Glendale Cemetery, Des Moines, Iowa. See also: congressional biography.

Leave it to a couple of country-bumpkin Midwestern schools to play a football game for a pig. Thanks to a bet between Iowa Gov. Clyde Herring and Minnesota Gov. Floyd B. Olson in 1935, the legend of "Floyd of Rosedale" was spawned and the trophy has been given to the winner each year since. The original bet was for an actual live pig, a product of Rosedale Farms near Fort Dodge, Iowa, and named for the Minnesota governor. After the Gophers won the 1935 game 13-6, Herring and the pig made the trip to the state capital to present Olson with his trophy.

Clyde LaVerne Herring was born on May 3, 1879, in Jackson, Michigan. He was part of Company D, 3rd Michigan Regiment during the Spanish-American War. After trying his hand at ranching in Colorado and farming in Iowa, Herring entered the automobile business in Atlantic, Iowa in 1908, and in 1910, he moved his business to Des Moines. As a member of the Iowa National Guard Herring was stationed on the Mexican border during WWI. In the early 1920s, Herring was the Iowa Democratic Party's unsuccessful candidate for the offices of governor and senator. However, in 1932, he defeated the incumbent governor, Dan Turner. He won a second term, again defeating Turner. As governor through the worst of the Great Depression, Herring ordered a moratorium on foreclosures and signed a law to help banks that were in danger of closing. Iowa next elected Herring to the U.S. Senate where he began his term in 1937. Losing his bid for reelection in 1942, Herring worked as a senior administrator in the Office of Price Administration for most of 1943. Returning to his automobile business in Des Moines, Iowa, Clyde L. Herring died on September 15, 1945.

Children of EMMA SPINNEY and CLYDE HERRING are:
    i.   VICTORIA[10] HERRING.
    ii.   CLYDE EDSEL HERRING, b. 1915.

        Notes for CLYDE EDSEL HERRING:
        Clyde Edsel Herring (1915 -- 1976) was born in Des Moines, Iowa, the son of former Governor and U.S.
        Senator Clyde L. and Pearl S. Herring. He received his B.A. degree from the University of Iowa in 1937 and
        his law degree from Drake University in 1940. He was admitted to the Iowa Bar that same year. A reserve
        officer since 1937, he was accepted into active duty in 1941. He served as with the 168th Infantry, 34th
        Division in the European Theater of Operations during W.W.II. In 1943 he was taken as a prisoner in Tunisia
        and spent until May, 1945 in Prisoner of War camps in Europe.

Returning to Iowa after the war he entered into a private law practice in Des Moines. In 1947 he was appointed Assistant County Attorney for Polk County. He resigned this post in 1949 to become a district supervisor for the U.S. Bureau of the Census. In 1950, he was elected County Attorney for Polk County. In 1954, he was the unsuccessful Democratic candidate for Governor. He was a delegate to the 1956 Democratic National convention. Herring was appointed to the Interstate Commerce Commission in 1959, by President Eisenhower. He served on the Division of Operating Rights and the Division of Rates and Practices. He remained there until 1964 when he was succeeded by Virginia Mae Brown. After leaving government service, Mr. Herring opened his own law firm in Washington, D.C. Clyde E. Herring died of a heart attack at the age of sixty-one.

1369. FAYETTE A[9] SPINNEY *(BENJAMIN F[8], WILLIAM M[7], NICHOLAS[6], JOHN[5], JOHN[4], ANDREW[3], JOHN[2], THOMAS[1])* was born 1882 in Colorado. He married HAZEL. She was born 1891 in Colorado.

Child of FAYETTE SPINNEY and HAZEL is:
    i.   MARGARET[10] SPINNEY, b. 1909.

1370. LOUIS BEVIER[9] SPINNEY *(JOSEPH OAKMAN[8], WILLIAM M[7], NICHOLAS[6], JOHN[5], JOHN[4], ANDREW[3], JOHN[2], THOMAS[1])* was born 1869 in Illinois, and died 1951. He married BERYL ANNA HOYT, daughter of MONROE HOYT and SUSAN BOWMAN. She was born Jul 1876.

Notes for LOUIS BEVIER SPINNEY:
Spinney House was named for Louis Bevier Spinney (1869-1951) who graduated from Iowa   State College in 1892 with a B.S. in electrical engineering and later returned as an educator. He was elected head the Physics and Electrical Engineering Department in 1897. Between 1909 and 1942 he was head of the physics department. Spinney also spent time working at Cornell University, in
Berlin, and at Polytechnikum in Zurich. He published textbooks about physics andnumerous scientific articles, held the position of vice-president at Ames National Bank, and received many awards and honors.

The fourth addition of Friley Hall was finished in 1954, completing the link between Friley Hall and Hughes Hall. This addition allowed for 216 additional residents to join the Friley-Hughes community, which, at that time, was composed entirely of men. With a total occupancy of 1400, Friley-Hughes Hall divided into 24 houses, one of which was Spinney House. The current Spinney House Constitution was drafted on April 20, 1964 and has persisted with slight modifications from time to time. In 1975 Spinney House became co-ed by vote of the men residing here at the time.

Portraits of Iowa State Luminaries

LOUIS BEVIER SPINNEY (1869-1951); painted by Johnson in 1944.

Professor of Physics and alumnus. Louis Bevier Spinney was born in Bradford, Illinois in 1869, came to Cass County, Iowa with his family in 1876, and grew up on a farm there. He received degrees from Iowa Agricultural College in 1892 and 1893, then studied for a year in Berlin, six months in Zurich, and completed a year at Cornell University. He became Head of the Department of Physics and Electrical Engineering in 1897, and remained as Head of Physics when Electrical Engineering became a separate department in 1909. He helped plan quarters for the Electrical Engineering Department in Engineering Hall, and then drew plans for the present Physics Hall, considered one of the finest buildings of its kind when it was dedicated in 1922. His life masterpiece has been his classic Textbook of Physics, published in five editions and more than 100,000 copies between 1911 and 1937. He was regarded as a great teacher of physics, and believed that students needed to exercise their thinking powers, not merely watch somebody else think. Prof. Spinney also served the university in a number of appointments until his retirement in the 1940s. Always civic-conscious, he served on both the City Council and Park Board of Ames. This oil portrait was presented to the College in 1945 by alumni, staff and friends.

Children of LOUIS SPINNEY and BERYL HOYT are:
1563.   i.   LOUIS BEVIER[10] SPINNEY, b. 16 Mar 1905.

    ii.   BERYL M SPINNEY, b. 16 Mar 1905; d. Aft. 1930.

1371. HOWARD C[9] SPINNEY *(JOSEPH OAKMAN[8], WILLIAM M[7], NICHOLAS[6], JOHN[5], JOHN[4], ANDREW[3], JOHN[2], THOMAS[1])* was born 1874 in Illinois, and died Aft. 1930. He married DOROTHY.

Child of HOWARD SPINNEY and DOROTHY is:
    i.   DAUGHTER[10] SPINNEY, b. 1906.

1372. LANGDON TRUFANT[9] SNIPE *(ANN MARIA[8] SPINNEY, NICHOLAS J[7], NICHOLAS[6], JOHN[5], JOHN[4], ANDREW[3], JOHN[2], THOMAS[1])* was born 27 May 1867 in Boston, Suffolk, Massachusetts, USA. He married (1) CHRISTINE C SNIPE. She was born 1861. He married (2) JESSIE CHRISTINE CARTER 08 Jul 1896 in Bath, Sagadahoc, Maine, USA. She was born 27 Sep 1871 in Off Coast, Ireland, and died 24 Sep 1952 in Bath, Sagadahoc, Maine, USA.

Children of LANGDON SNIPE and JESSIE CARTER are:
    i.   SNIPE[10], b. 26 Jan 1899, Bath, Sagadahoc, Maine, USA.
    ii.   SNIPE, b. 13 Jul 1897, Bath, Sagadahoc, Maine, USA.

1373. JULIA A[9] SPINNEY *(WILLIAM QUINMAN[8], ROBERT CURTIS[7], NICHOLAS[6], JOHN[5], JOHN[4], ANDREW[3], JOHN[2], THOMAS[1])* was born 1866, and died WFT Est. 1894-1963. She married CHARLES BRADDOCK 24 Mar 1889 in Belfast, ME.

Children of JULIA SPINNEY and CHARLES BRADDOCK are:
1564.   i.   FLORENCE MAY[10] BRADDOCK, b. 21 Mar 1891, Brooks, ME; d. 23 Jan 1977, Belfast, ME.
    ii.   LILLIAN BRADDOCK, b. Private.

1374. CLARA[9] SPINNEY *(JOHN GILMAN[8], ROBERT CURTIS[7], NICHOLAS[6], JOHN[5], JOHN[4], ANDREW[3], JOHN[2], THOMAS[1])* was born 1877. She married RAYMOND SHERMAN 21 Oct 1895.

Child of CLARA SPINNEY and RAYMOND SHERMAN is:
    i.   JOHN R[10] SHERMAN, b. 1904.

1375. ALMON I[9] SPINNEY *(JOHN COLBY[8], JOHN[7], JEREMIAH[6], JOHN[5], JOHN[4], ANDREW[3], JOHN[2], THOMAS[1])* was born Apr 1871, and died 30 Aug 1965 in Augusta,ME. He married LOTTIE FEILDING 25 Dec 1895. She was born Apr 1874.

Children of ALMON SPINNEY and LOTTIE FEILDING are:
    i.   BERTHA[10] SPINNEY, b. Apr 1899.
    ii.   DORIS ROSESPINNEY.
    iii.   LAWRENCE FIELDING SPINNEY, b. 07 Jun 1905; d. 13 Jun 1991; m. LEORA WENTWORTH, 1929; b. 1910; d. 06 Feb 1974.
    iv.   BAURIMA SPINNEY.
    v.   MARGERY ELIZABETH SPINNEY.

1376. JOHN DELBERT[9] SPINNEY *(JOHN COLBY[8], JOHN[7], JEREMIAH[6], JOHN[5], JOHN[4], ANDREW[3], JOHN[2], THOMAS[1])* was born 1881. He married MARY A CULHANE 20 Jan 1904 in Portland, ME. She was born 1879.

Children of JOHN SPINNEY and MARY CULHANE are:
    i.   JOHN GORDON[10] SPINNEY, b. 1905.
    ii.   CHARLES C SPINNEY, b. 1908.
    iii.   KATHRYN M SPINNEY, b. 1911.
    iv.   PHILIP B SPINNEY, b. 1915.

1377. CARRIE L[9] SPINNEY *(ALMON ROBINSON[8], JOHN[7], JEREMIAH[6], JOHN[5], JOHN[4], ANDREW[3], JOHN[2], THOMAS[1])* was born 03 Jul 1885. She married FRED YORK 21 Jul 1906.

Children of CARRIE SPINNEY and FRED YORK are:

    i.   DORIS[10] YORK.
   ii.   JULIA YORK.
  iii.   MAUD YORK.

1378. RALPH O[9] SPINNEY *(ALMON ROBINSON[8], JOHN[7], JEREMIAH[6], JOHN[5], JOHN[4], ANDREW[3], JOHN[2], THOMAS[1])* was born 04 Feb 1887, and died 30 Jan 1979 in South Portland, ME. He married EFFIE PERKINS. She was born 1897.

Children of RALPH SPINNEY and EFFIE PERKINS are:

    i.   ETHELYN[10] SPINNEY, b. 1914.
   ii.   DORIS SPINNEY, b. 1917.
  iii.   ERNESTINE SPINNEY, b. 1918.
   iv.   RALPH A SPINNEY, b. 1920.

1379. WARREN N[9] SPINNEY *(ROBERT R[8], JOHN[7], JEREMIAH[6], JOHN[5], JOHN[4], ANDREW[3], JOHN[2], THOMAS[1])* was born Nov 1881. He married MADGE MCKINNEY 10 Nov 1913.

Child of WARREN SPINNEY and MADGE MCKINNEY is:

    i.   OLIVE W[10] SPINNEY, b. 1914; d. 1978, Unity, ME; m. LLOYD BARROWS.

1380. ELVINGTON PALMER[9] SPINNEY *(PALMER O[8], ZINA H[7], DAVID[6], JOHN[5], JOHN[4], ANDREW[3], JOHN[2], THOMAS[1])* was born 30 Jun 1868 in Georgetown, ME. He married GRACE EMMA BURBANK. She was born Dec 1872.

Notes for ELVINGTON PALMER SPINNEY:
Maine Biographies, Vol. I, Records, Page 153

    Honerable Elvington Palmer Spinney, of North Berwick Maine, was born in Georgetown Maine, June 30, 1868 son of Palmer Oliver Spinney and Mary Jane (Todd) Spinney. His parents were Sturdy New England Stock and natives of Georgetown. His father in early life was a sea captain; Later he engaged in trade in Lewiston, Maine, and in 1875 the family moved from Lewiston to Brunswick, Maine, where they made their home unilt their deaths, the father at the age of eighty-two years, the mother at the age of eighty-four years

    Most of the Spinney ancestors were sea-faring people. One, for his bravery on the high seas, in defense of his native land, during furing the War of the Roses, received knighthoold at the hands of an English Knight. The Spinney crest hangs in Westminster Abbey.

    Elington P Spinney received his early education in the public school of Lewiston and Brunswick. He graduated from Bowdoin College, with a Bachelor of Arts Degree, in the class of 1890. After leaving college he devoted his energies to teaching for three years;one year as science heacher in Hillside Seminary in Wisonsin; one year as principal of Paris Hill Academy , Paris Maine; and one year as principal of Alfred Academy, Alfed Maine. During his teaching he employed all his spare moments in studying law. He read law in the oddices of Barrett Potter of Brunswich ad with Samuel M Come of Alfre. He was admitted to the York County bar in 1895, and to the United States Courts in 1898. As soon as he was admitted to practice law in 1895, he opened an ofice in North Berwick, where he is still in active practice. His practice is widely extended, often to remote parts of the State of Maine, as well as in New Hamshire and in Massachsetts. Besides his general law practice, he is counsel for banks, Industrial corporations, four town adn two vilage corporations, From 1911 to 1919 two terms, e was judge of the Yorkshire Municipal Court.

    Judge Spinney is a member of the york County Bar Association, The Maine State Bar Association. and the Amerian Bar Association. He is a member of and Past Nobel Grand of Ealel Lodge, Independent Order of Odd Fellows, member of the Past Chief Patriarch of Columbian Encampment, an member of the Past Sachem of Negutaquit Lodge of Improved Order of Red Men, he is a member of the Canton, the Grange, the Rebekah Lodge, of the Pocahontus, his is a member of the Baneg Beg Country Club, of the Sanford Town Club, is a Congregationalist and chariman of the board of trustees of the Congregational Church. and a member of the Alpha Delta Phi Fraternty. During the World War he was a member of the Legal Advisor Board, the draft boar, and thre Four-Minute Men.

Being an Independent in Politics, he never sought public office, but he has served his town for sereral years as selectman, and has held other town offices. He is interested in all civic, educational and philanthropic movements in his home town.

On October 30, 1895, Judge Spinney married Grace E Burbankof Alfred, Maine. They have two children 1. Dorothy S Gillette of Los Angeles California; a graduate of Wellesley College in 1923. Married in 1923 Waso A Gillete a Graduate of Harvard in 1922. 2. A son Leon L Spinney of Berwick; a graguate of Bowdoin Bollege in 1926 and now is a student in Boston University Law School.

Children of ELVINGTON SPINNEY and GRACE BURBANK are:
    i. DOROTHY S[10] SPINNEY, b. Nov 1899; m. WALDO GILLETTE, 1923.
    ii. LEON L SPINNEY, b. Aft. 1900.

1381. CHESTER RAYMOND[9] SPINNEY (*CHARLES S[8], ZINA H[7], DAVID[6], JOHN[5], JOHN[4], ANDREW[3], JOHN[2], THOMAS[1]*) was born Apr 1884. He married JENNIE LILIAN DOGHERTY. She was born 1888.

Children of CHESTER SPINNEY and JENNIE DOGHERTY are:
          i. KENNETH[10] SPINNEY, b. 1911.
1565.   ii. ROSAMOND SPINNEY, b. 19 Apr 1912, Somerville, MA; d. Nov 1982.
         iii. CHESTER R SPINNEY, b. 1915.
         iv. GORDON SPINNEY, b. 1919.

1382. ERNEST L[9] SPINNEY (*ELIJAH M[8], ZINA H[7], EPHRAIM[6], JOHN[5], JOHN[4], ANDREW[3], JOHN[2], THOMAS[1]*) was born Apr 1884. He married ENIED HAYNES 15 Jan 1909 in Auburn, Maine, daughter of ALBERT HAYNES and OLIVE MARTIN.

Children of ERNEST SPINNEY and ENIED HAYNES are:
1566.   i. RENA MAE[10] SPINNEY, b. 16 Sep 1907; d. 13 Sep 1978, Wyoming.
         ii. OLLIE SPINNEY, b. 29 Apr 1916; d. 18 Feb 1967; m. HARRY B PUSHARD, 26 Sep 1942, Phippsburg, ME; b. 1905.
         iii. FRED H SPINNEY, b. 20 Feb 1920; d. 28 Nov 1979.

1383. RALPH E[9] SPINNEY (*ELIJAH M[8], ZINA H[7], EPHRAIM[6], JOHN[5], JOHN[4], ANDREW[3], JOHN[2], THOMAS[1]*) was born Apr 1884. He married EFFIE L PERKINS 26 Dec 1912 in Georgetown, ME.

Children of RALPH SPINNEY and EFFIE PERKINS are:
    i. ETHELYN[10] SPINNEY.
    ii. DORIS SPINNEY.
    iii. ERNESTINE SPINNEY.
    iv. RALPH A SPINNEY, b. 1919.

1384. HOWARD APPLETON[9] SPINNEY (*JAMES M[8], ZINA H[7], EPHRAIM[6], JOHN[5], JOHN[4], ANDREW[3], JOHN[2], THOMAS[1]*) was born 18 Jan 1884. He married SUSAN PERKINS 1908.

Child of HOWARD SPINNEY and SUSAN PERKINS is:
    i. JAMES ANDREW[10] SPINNEY, b. 12 Jan 1909, Maine; d. 18 Sep 1983, Sacramento, CA.

1385. CLARENCE P[9] SPINNEY (*JAMES M[8], ZINA H[7], EPHRAIM[6], JOHN[5], JOHN[4], ANDREW[3], JOHN[2], THOMAS[1]*) was born Mar 1889. He married ADA MALCOLM 13 Oct 1909.

Children of CLARENCE SPINNEY and ADA MALCOLM are:
    i. CLARENCE L[10] SPINNEY, m. ELSIE LIGHT.
    ii. ELIZABETH SPINNEY.
    iii. MARY SPINNEY.

1386. BEATRICE S.[9] STEPHENSON (*DAISY MAY[8] BURCE, RUFUS LOREN[7], RACHEL[6] OLIVER, JANE[5] SPINNEY, JOHN[4],*

ANDREW³, JOHN², THOMAS¹) was born 05 Feb 1902 in Winters, CA, and died 05 Feb 1988 in Milwaukie, OR. She married GEORGE W. FETZER 1922 in Everett, WA.

Child of BEATRICE STEPHENSON and GEORGE FETZER is:
      i.   PAUL¹⁰ FETZER, b. 11 Aug 1923; d. 27 Jan 1952.

1387. ADA ESTHER⁹ RICHARDS *(SUSAN AUGUSTA RUBY⁸ BURCE, JOHN CALVIN⁷, RACHEL⁶ OLIVER, JANE⁵ SPINNEY, JOHN⁴, ANDREW³, JOHN², THOMAS¹)* was born 25 Mar 1882 in Coupeville, WA, and died 01 Jun 1970 in Anacortes, WA. She married JOHN SIMS CARTER 11 Jun 1904 in Coupeville, WA. He was born 03 Jul 1875 in New Berlin, IL, and died 26 Mar 1940 in AnacortesWA.

Children of ADA RICHARDS and JOHN CARTER are:
1567.	i.	LIONEL LEONARD¹⁰ CARTER, b. 30 Dec 1905, Anacortes, WA; d. 22 Apr 1994, Marysville, WA.
1568.	ii.	MARGARET RUBY CARTER, b. 29 Dec 1907, Snohomish, WA; d. 03 Jan 1988, Everett, WA.
1569.	iii.	MILDRED ADA CARTER, b. 12 Jun 1909, Snohomish, WA; d. 15 Dec 1993, Anacortes, WA.
	iv.	DOROTHY EVELYN CARTER, b. 16 Oct 1910, Olympia, WA; d. 31 Oct 1928, Anacortes, WA.
	v.	MAVIS HELEN CARTER, b. 20 Dec 1915, Anacortes, WA; d. 11 Dec 1923, Anacortes, WA.
1570.	vi.	JOAN CARTER, b. Private.
1571.	vii.	JOHN "S" CARTER, b. Private.

1388. WILLIAM ABORN⁹ SPINNEY *(WILLIAM JAMES⁸, ANDREW JACKSON⁷, MOSES B⁶, JEREMIAH⁵, JOHN⁴, ANDREW³, JOHN², THOMAS¹)* was born 05 Jun 1904 in Boston, MA, and died 01 Feb 1968 in Mededith, NH. He married ROSAMOND SPINNEY 28 Sep 1936, daughter of CHESTER SPINNEY and JENNIE DOGHERTY. She was born 19 Apr 1912 in Somerville, MA, and died Nov 1982.

Children of WILLIAM SPINNEY and ROSAMOND SPINNEY are:
| | i. | PETER DOGHERTY¹⁰ SPINNEY, m. SALLY MINER. |
| 1572. | ii. | WILLIAM ABORN JR SPINNEY, b. 21 Jul 1937, Winchester, MA. |

1389. FLORA R⁹ SPINNEY *(MILAN H⁸, SILAS CURTIS⁷, JOHN⁶, JEREMIAH⁵, JOHN⁴, ANDREW³, JOHN², THOMAS¹)* was born 1897. She married EARL L SMITH 1917 in Auburn, Maine.

Children of FLORA SPINNEY and EARL SMITH are:
      i.   WESLEY¹⁰ SMITH.
     ii.   ARNOLD SMITH.
    iii.   GEORGE SMITH.

1390. ARTHUR MILTON⁹ HAYES *(LAURA GERTRUDE⁸ SPINNEY, DANIEL WILLIAM⁷, JOHN⁶, JEREMIAH⁵, JOHN⁴, ANDREW³, JOHN², THOMAS¹)* was born 1884. He married MARTHA TEBBITS.

Child of ARTHUR HAYES and MARTHA TEBBITS is:
      i.   JOHN¹⁰ HAYES, m. DORIS KELLY.

1391. FREMONT EDWARD⁹ SPINNEY *(HARRY GARFIELD⁸, DANIEL WILLIAM⁷, JOHN⁶, JEREMIAH⁵, JOHN⁴, ANDREW³, JOHN², THOMAS¹)* was born 21 Jul 1913. He married DOROTHY LUCILLE SHEPHERD.

Children of FREMONT SPINNEY and DOROTHY SHEPHERD are:
      i.   JUDITH ELLEN¹⁰ SPINNEY, m. ADAMS.
     ii.   ROBIN ELAINE SPINNEY, m. CLIFFORD.
    iii.   BONNIE ELLEN SPINNEY, b. 1942, Santa Monica, CA.

1392. MERLE⁹ MOORE *(ALICE⁸ SPINNEY, IRA⁷, JEREMIAH⁶, JEREMIAH⁵, JOHN⁴, ANDREW³, JOHN², THOMAS¹)* was born 15 Aug 1901 in Starks, ME. He married EMMA FRANCIS BROWN 17 Sep 1921 in Madison, ME.

Children of MERLE MOORE and EMMA BROWN are:
      i.   FRANK HARRY¹⁰ MOORE.

ii. DOROTHY E MOORE.

1393. VERA M[9] MOORE *(ALICE[8] SPINNEY, IRA[7], JEREMIAH[6], JEREMIAH[5], JOHN[4], ANDREW[3], JOHN[2], THOMAS[1])* was born 11 Aug 1915. She married ASA DULEY.

Children of VERA MOORE and ASA DULEY are:
i. ROBET TODD[10] DULEY.
ii. SYLVIA JEAN DULEY.
iii. ROBERTA ALICE DULEY.
iv. GLORIA FAYE DULEY.
v. RICHARD DALE DULEY.

1394. HERBERT ELLSWORTH[9] SPINNEY *(ELLSWORTH R[8], IRA[7], JEREMIAH[6], JEREMIAH[5], JOHN[4], ANDREW[3], JOHN[2], THOMAS[1])* was born 25 Mar 1887 in Lynn, MA, and died May 1973. He married ANNIE MILDRED Abt. 1910. She was born 1892.

Children of HERBERT SPINNEY and ANNIE MILDRED are:
i. ALFRED[10] SPINNEY, b. 1911.
ii. WILLIAM E SPINNEY, b. 1919.
iii. BYRON H SPINNEY, b. 1921.
iv. VERNON P SPINNEY, b. 1926.

Notes for VERNON P SPINNEY:

Vernon P. Spinney
Radiologist and World War II veteran died Aug. 23 at the age of 72.

Spinney, son of Herbert and A. Mildred Spinney, was born Jan. 2, 1926.

Spinney served in the U.S. Navy during the war and was honorably discharged in 1946. He married Lillian Bacon in his hometown of Lynn, Mass.

He and his wife were host to many foster children and co-founded the Massachusetts Foster Parents Association.

The couple of 50 years moved to Benson in 1972. Spinney studied radiology and worked at the Lynn Hospital School before working at Benson Hospital as an X-ray technician.

Spinney had been working at the hospital longer than any other employee when he retired in December 1996

He is survived by his wife; six children; Dianne Spinney, of Clarkdale, Ariz.; Cheryl Fleming, of Benson; Robin Keiser, of Atwater, Calif.; Patricia Jacques, of Sierra Vista; Lori Allen, of Tombstone; Edward Philip, of Pima County; brothers Alfred Spinney, of Newport Richey, Fla.; William Spinney, of Lowman, N.Y.

Services were Aug. 27 at the First Baptist church in Tombstone

1395. LILLIE MAE[9] SPINNEY *(SYLVESTER VESS[8], ASA D[7], RICHARD[6], RICHARD[5], JOHN[4], ANDREW[3], JOHN[2], THOMAS[1])* was born 21 May 1879. She married JOHN WHITNEY.

Child of LILLIE SPINNEY and JOHN WHITNEY is:
i. PEARL[10] WHITNEY, b. 1899; d. 1912.

1396. CLEVELAND GROVER[9] SPINNEY *(SYLVESTER VESS[8], ASA D[7], RICHARD[6], RICHARD[5], JOHN[4], ANDREW[3], JOHN[2], THOMAS[1])* was born 12 Oct 1888, and died 29 May 1958 in St Louis, MO, USA. He married MARY JOSEPHINE MEYERS 18 Jan 1911 in St Louis, MO, USA, daughter of MEYERS and ALICE. She was born 11 Jan 1897 in IL, USA, and died 27 May 1986 in St Louis, MO, USA.

Children of CLEVELAND SPINNEY and MARY MEYERS are:
i. MARY AMANDA[10] SPINNEY.

ii.   WILLIAM JOHN SPINNEY.

1397. WILLIAM JOHN[9] SPINNEY (*SYLVESTER VESS*[8], *ASA D*[7], *RICHARD*[6], *RICHARD*[5], *JOHN*[4], *ANDREW*[3], *JOHN*[2], *THOMAS*[1]) was born 01 Apr 1894 in Randolph, Il, and died 22 Oct 1958 in Randolph, Il. He married MARGARET MAY YOUNG 15 Mar 1920.

Notes for WILLIAM JOHN SPINNEY:
He was a Sgt. in Co. M, 319 Infantry in World War I. He was a coal miner most of his life. He was an accomplished musician, and had sung with an Army quartet in World War I, although he had no formal musical training. He also played a number of musical instruments including the fiddle, piano, guitar, and mandolin. With his brother, Grover Cleveland Spinney, his son, William Douglas, and some friends, he played old-time music for dances during the depression in the Randolph Co., IL area.

Children of WILLIAM SPINNEY and MARGARET YOUNG are:
1573.   i.   WILLIAM DOUGLAS[10] SPINNEY, b. 05 Oct 1921, Sparta, IL; d. 08 Dec 2004, Sparta, IL.
          ii.   MARGARET EVELYN SPINNEY.
         iii.   JANIE SPINNEY.
          iv.   DORA MAE SPINNEY.

Generation No. 10

1398. ETHEL[10] CUMMINGS (*HARRY*[9], *ALGENAID*[8] *WORCESTER*, *MOSES*[7], *MOSES*[6], *MOSES*[5], *ANNE*[4] *SPINNEY*, *JOHN*[3], *SAMUEL*[2], *THOMAS*[1]) was born 03 Feb 1906 in Jonesport, ME, and died 08 Oct 1990 in Worchester, MA. She married KENNITH FOSTER WOODBURY. He was born 21 Jun 1901 in Gloucester, ME, and died 06 Dec 1984 in Portland, ME.

Children of ETHEL CUMMINGS and KENNITH WOODBURY are:
1574.   i.   KYLE HARRY[11] WOODBURY.
1575.   ii.   PARTICIA ANN WOODBURY.

1399. DEAN[10] BULMER (*EPHRAIM TROTT*[9], *MARGARET*[8] *WORCESTER*, *MARK*[7], *ISAAC*[6], *MOSES*[5], *ANNE*[4] *SPINNEY*, *JOHN*[3], *SAMUEL*[2], *THOMAS*[1]) He married DELLA BROOKS.

Child of DEAN BULMER and DELLA BROOKS is:
           i.   BERNARD DEAN[11] BULMER, b. 24 Oct 1921.

1400. LELAND BRYANT[10] BULMER (*EPHRAIM TROTT*[9], *MARGARET*[8] *WORCESTER*, *MARK*[7], *ISAAC*[6], *MOSES*[5], *ANNE*[4] *SPINNEY*, *JOHN*[3], *SAMUEL*[2], *THOMAS*[1]) was born 14 Jun 1906 in Houlton, ME, and died 03 Jan 1996 in Smithfield, ME. He married AMY ALBERTA RICKER 10 Jun 1931 in Smithfield, ME.

Children of LELAND BULMER and AMY RICKER are:
           i.   JOANNE MARCIA[11] BULMER, b. 16 Apr 1932, Smithfield, ME.
          ii.   CHRISTINE BULMER, b. 14 Mar 1934, Skowhegan, ME.
         iii.   HALE FREDERICK BULMER, b. 31 Mar 1936.
          iv.   BRIAN LELAND BULMER, b. 13 Jul 1938.
           v.   CONSTANCE IVA BULMER, b. 23 Jun 1942.

1401. JOAN LOUISE[10] SPINNEY (*HAROLD NEAL*[9], *HENRY HOWARD*[8], *GUSTAVUS NEWHALL*[7], *WILLIAM NEWHALL*[6], *BENJAMIN*[5], *JOHN*[4], *THOMAS*[3], *SAMUEL*[2], *THOMAS*[1]) was born 13 Jul 1936 in Newburyport, MA. She married FRED PERKINS. He was born 28 Apr 1935 in Beverly, MA.

Children of JOAN SPINNEY and FRED PERKINS are:
           i.   FREDERICK11TH PERKINS[11] JR., b. 19 May 1958.
          ii.   LARRY NEAL PERKINS, b. 14 Oct 1961.
1576.   iii.   BRIAN GEORGE PERKINS, b. 04 Apr 1963, Beverly, MA.
1577.   iv.   BARBARA ANN PERKINS, b. 26 May 1965, Ipswich, MA.

1402. MARCIA[10] SPINNEY *(HAROLD NEAL[9], HENRY HOWARD[8], GUSTAVUS NEWHALL[7], WILLIAM NEWHALL[6], BENJAMIN[5], JOHN[4], THOMAS[3], SAMUEL[2], THOMAS[1])* was born 29 May 1942 in Ipswich, MA. She married RICHARD LAUDAROWICZ. He was born 26 Aug 1936 in Ipswich, MA.

Children of MARCIA SPINNEY and RICHARD LAUDAROWICZ are:
    i.   RICHARD11TH B.[11] LAUDAROWICZ, b. 16 Nov 1961, Beverly, MA.
    ii. MICHAEL11TH W. LAUDAROWICZ, b. 17 Sep 1963, Ipswich, MA.

1403. MADELYN10TH[10] SPINNEY *(HAROLD NEAL[9], HENRY HOWARD[8], GUSTAVUS NEWHALL[7], WILLIAM NEWHALL[6], BENJAMIN[5], JOHN[4], THOMAS[3], SAMUEL[2], THOMAS[1])* was born 25 Apr 1944 in Ipswich, MA. She married KENNITH MANUEL HAYES. He was born 08 May 1943 in Boston, MA.

Children of MADELYN10TH SPINNEY and KENNITH HAYES are:
    i.   KENNITH11TH M. HAYES[11] JR., b. 01 May 1965.
    ii. TIMMOTHY11TH WAYNE HAYES, b. 07 Jan 1967.
    iii. CHRISTIAN NEAL HAYES, b. 29 Sep 1975.

1404. JOHN SPINNEY[10] ALLEN *(JANE LOUISE[9] SPINNEY, HAROLD ELLERY[8], ELLERY CHANNING[7], WILLIAM NEWHALL[6], BENJAMIN[5], JOHN[4], THOMAS[3], SAMUEL[2], THOMAS[1])* He married GRACE LEATHERBY.

Children of JOHN ALLEN and GRACE LEATHERBY are:
    i.   SCOTT MACKENZIE[11] ALLEN.
    ii. AMANDA HALIDAY ALLEN.

1405. JUDITH MAUD[10] ALLEN *(JANE LOUISE[9] SPINNEY, HAROLD ELLERY[8], ELLERY CHANNING[7], WILLIAM NEWHALL[6], BENJAMIN[5], JOHN[4], THOMAS[3], SAMUEL[2], THOMAS[1])* She married DAVID WILLIAM DELAINE.

Children of JUDITH ALLEN and DAVID DELAINE are:
    i.   MICHELLE LOUISE[11] DELAINE.
1578. ii. BRIAN DAVID DELAINE.
    iii. MATTHEW ALLEN DELAINE, m. SHELLEY JO LINDQUIST.

1406. STEVEN SPINNEY[10] ALLEN *(JANE LOUISE[9] SPINNEY, HAROLD ELLERY[8], ELLERY CHANNING[7], WILLIAM NEWHALL[6], BENJAMIN[5], JOHN[4], THOMAS[3], SAMUEL[2], THOMAS[1])* He married MARGARET WILHELM.

Children of STEVEN ALLEN and MARGARET WILHELM are:
    i.   JOSHUA[11] ALLEN.
    ii. CORY ALLEN.
    iii. MELISSA ALLEN.

1407. MAGARET[10] SPINNEY *(ARTHUR FRANKLIN[9], ERNEST EDWARD[8], CHARLES HERBERT[7], JOHN WARREN[6], SAMUEL[5], JOHN[4], THOMAS[3], SAMUEL[2], THOMAS[1])* was born 25 Dec 1919. She married ARTHUR H. ELLISON 02 Dec 1950 in Lynn, Essex, MA.

Notes for MAGARET SPINNEY:
Bertha L. Jenkins

EXETER - Bertha L. Jenkins, 92, formerly of Hayes Park, died Thursday, May 2, 2002 at the Exeter Healthcare.

She was born Dec. 6, 1909 in Pittsfield, the daughter of the late Harry M. and Fannie F. (French) Pierce. She was a resident of Pittsfield for 34 years and resided the rest of her life in Exeter. Mrs. Jenkins was a graduate of Pittsfield High School, Class of 1927.

She worked for 14 years as a clerk at Woolworth's in Exeter

Mrs. Jenkins enjoyed knitting, crocheting, and sewing.

She is survived by two sons, Merton Jenkins Jr. of Exeter, and Richard E. Jenkins of Niceville, Fla.; one daughter, Fay Cail of Milton Mills; 10 grandchildren; 22 great-grandchildren; and seven great-great grandchildren.

She was the widow of Merton Jenkins Sr., and was also predeceased by a sister, Beatrice Pierce, of Pittsfield.

Graveside services will be held Tuesday, May 7, at 11 a.m. at the Floral Park Cemetery in Pittsfield. Pastor Oden Woodward will officiate.

In lieu of flowers, donations may be made in her memory to the American Heart Association, NH Affiliate, 20 Merrimack St., Suite 1, Manchester 03101-2244.

Arrangements are by the Brewitt Funeral Service, Exeter.

Margaret F. Ellison

EXETER - Margaret F. Ellison, 83, of 277 Water St., died Thursday, May 2, 2002, at the Exeter Hospital after a brief illness.

She was born Dec. 25, 1918 in Saugus, Mass., the daughter of the late Arthur F. and Nellie (Jenkins) Spinney. A former resident of Saugus and Lynn, Mass., she had resided in Exeter since 1991.

Mrs. Ellison was employed for many years at Davidson's Shoe in Lynn. She also worked for Sears Roebuck in Lynn.

In her spare time, she enjoyed baking.

She is survived by her daughter, Mrs. Michael E. (Kathy A.) Austin of Exeter; two sisters, Evelyn Bangs of Saugus, Mass., and Jean Bedrosian of Wenham, Mass.; two grandchildren; five great-grandchildren; and several nieces, nephews, great-nieces, and great-nephews.

She was the widow of the late Arthur H. Ellison, who died Dec. 13, 1996. She was also predeceased by a brother, Arthur F. Spinney Jr., of Saugus, Mass., and a sister, Muriel G. Locke of Lynn, Mass.

A graveside service will be held Saturday, May 11 at 9 a.m. at the Pine Grove Cemetery in Lynn, Mass.

In lieu of flowers, donations may be made in her memory to a charity of one's choice.

Arrangements are by the Brewitt Funeral Home, Exeter.

Child of MAGARET SPINNEY and ARTHUR ELLISON is:
    i.   KATHY[11] ELLISON, b. 16 Nov 1952.

1408. MURIEL G.[10] SPINNEY *(ARTHUR FRANKLIN[9], ERNEST EDWARD[8], CHARLES HERBERT[7], JOHN WARREN[6], SAMUEL[5], JOHN[4], THOMAS[3], SAMUEL[2], THOMAS[1])* was born 23 Aug 1921. She married ROBERT LOCKE 18 Apr 1943 in Lynn, Essex, MA.

Children of MURIEL SPINNEY and ROBERT LOCKE are:
    i.   DAUGHTER2[11] LOCKE.
   ii.   ROBERTA LOCKE LOCKE, b. 01 Dec 1943.

1409. ARTHUR FRANKLIN[10] SPINNEY *(ARTHUR FRANKLIN[9], ERNEST EDWARD[8], CHARLES HERBERT[7], JOHN WARREN[6], SAMUEL[5], JOHN[4], THOMAS[3], SAMUEL[2], THOMAS[1])* was born 08 Nov 1927 in Saugus, MA, and died 1995 in Lynn. MA.. He married MARY G. PAPAS 29 May 1955 in Saugus, Essex, MA..

Notes for ARTHUR FRANKLIN SPINNEY:

Headline: OBITUARY Ex-NFL lineman Arthur Spinney of Saugus, at 66
Publication Date: May 30, 1994
Source: Boston Herald
Page: 045
Subjects:
Region: Boston Metro, Massachusetts
Obituary: Arthur F. Spinney Jr. of Saugus, a member of the Boston College Hall of Fame who played with two NFL championship teams with the Baltimore Colts, died of a heart attack Friday at Union Hospital in Lynn. He was 66.
Mr. Spinney was a public relations official for the Massachusetts Port Authority from 1974 until his death.
Born in Saugus, he graduated from Saugus High School in 1945 and from Boston College in 1950.
Mr. Spinney, who played end for Boston College, switched to left guard with the Colts and played nine years in Baltimore through 1960. The Colts were NFL champions in 1958 and 1959.
He left the team to serve in the Army during the Korean War.
Following his playing career, Mr. Spinney was offensive line coach with the Boston Patriots for several years.
He was a member of the NFL Alumni Association and the Saugus High School Hall of Fame.
Mr. Spinney is survived by his widow, Mary G. (Pappas) Spinney; five sons, Stephen A. of Naperville, Ill., John D. of Newburyport, Craig L. of Norwalk, Conn., and Michael A. and Neal E., both of Saugus; a daughter, Laura E. Epperly of Mahwah, N.J.; three sisters, Margaret Ellison of New Hampshire, Jean Bedrosian of Wenham and Evelyn Bangs of Saugus; and 12 grandchildren.
A funeral service will be held Wednesday at 10 a.m. in Bisbee-Porcella Funeral Home, Saugus.
Burial will be in Riverdale Cemetery, Saugus.

Children of ARTHUR SPINNEY and MARY PAPAS are:
    i.   STEPHEN A.[11] SPINNEY, b. Aft. 1955.
   ii.   JOHN D. SPINNEY, b. Aft. 1955.
  iii.   CRAIG L. SPINNEY, b. Aft. 1955.
   iv.   MICHAEL A. SPINNEY, b. Aft. 1955.
   v.   NEAL E. SPINNEY, b. Aft. 1955.
   vi.   LAURA E. SPINNEY, b. Aft. 1955; m. EPPERLY.

1410. JEAN[10] SPINNEY *(ARTHUR FRANKLIN[9], ERNEST EDWARD[8], CHARLES HERBERT[7], JOHN WARREN[6], SAMUEL[5], JOHN[4], THOMAS[3], SAMUEL[2], THOMAS[1])* was born 16 Sep 1933. She married CHARLES M BEDROSIAN.

Children of JEAN SPINNEY and CHARLES BEDROSIAN are:

      i.   M.BEDROSIAN[11].
     ii.   M.BEDROSIAN.
   iii.   M.BEDROSIAN.
   iv.   M.BEDROSIAN.

1411. EVELYN L.[10] SPINNEY *(ARTHUR FRANKLIN[9], ERNEST EDWARD[8], CHARLES HERBERT[7], JOHN WARREN[6], SAMUEL[5], JOHN[4], THOMAS[3], SAMUEL[2], THOMAS[1])* was born 16 Apr 1938. She married BANGS 1960.

Children of EVELYN SPINNEY and BANGS are:
      i.   BANGS[11].
     ii.   BANGS.
   iii.   BANGS.

1412. EVERETT EDWARD SPINNEY[10] JR. *(EVERETT EDWARD[9] SPINNEY, ERNEST EDWARD[8], CHARLES HERBERT[7], JOHN WARREN[6], SAMUEL[5], JOHN[4], THOMAS[3], SAMUEL[2], THOMAS[1])* was born 01 Aug 1928. He married ELIZABETH V. ABEL 17 Jun 1950. She was born 16 Jun 1930.

Children of EVERETT JR. and ELIZABETH ABEL are:
1579.   i.   WENDY L.[11] SPINNEY, b. 23 Jun 1952.
1580.   ii.   RANDY L. SPINNEY, b. 29 Sep 1955.

1413. RALPH ERNEST[10] SPINNEY *(RALPH ERNEST[9], ERNEST EDWARD[8], CHARLES HERBERT[7], JOHN WARREN[6], SAMUEL[5], JOHN[4], THOMAS[3], SAMUEL[2], THOMAS[1])* was born 28 Feb 1936 in Attleboro, MA. He married ALMA JANE ANDERSON 27 Jul 1964 in Wareham, MA. She was born 25 Apr 1937 in Attleboro, MA.

Children of RALPH SPINNEY and ALMA ANDERSON are:
      i.   HEATHER-ANN11TH[11] SPINNEY, b. 20 Jan 1965.
     ii.   ALYCE GAIL SPINNEY, b. 08 Apr 1969.
   iii.   RANDI LEE SPINNEY, b. 06 Dec 1975.

1414. FRANCES RUTH[10] SANDBERG *(BERTHA MAY[9] SPINNEY, ERNEST EDWARD[8], CHARLES HERBERT[7], JOHN WARREN[6], SAMUEL[5], JOHN[4], THOMAS[3], SAMUEL[2], THOMAS[1])* was born 31 Dec 1927 in Newport, RI.. She married JOHN LEONARD CARBONE 02 Jul 1947 in Cliftondale, MA. He was born 06 Jan 1921 in Saugus, MA, and died 29 May 1973 in Saugus, MA.

Children of FRANCES SANDBERG and JOHN CARBONE are:
1581.   i.   JOHN LEONARD CARBONE[11] JR., b. 08 Nov 1954, Lynn, MA.
     ii.   MARK WILLIAM CARBONE, b. 21 Jun 1956, Lynn, MA.
1582.   iii.   MARY ELLEN CARBONE, b. 08 Dec 1963, Lynn, MA.
   iv.   SANDRA JEAN CARBONE, b. 13 Sep 1966, Lynn, MA; m. KEVIN E. WALTERS, 21 Sep 1997, Saint Anne, Salem, MA.; b. Unknown.

1415. ERNEST EDWARD[10] SANDBERG *(BERTHA MAY[9] SPINNEY, ERNEST EDWARD[8], CHARLES HERBERT[7], JOHN WARREN[6], SAMUEL[5], JOHN[4], THOMAS[3], SAMUEL[2], THOMAS[1])* was born 20 Jan 1929 in Lynn, MA. He married GLENNA CREAMER 18 May 1963. She was born in Reading, MA..

Children of ERNEST SANDBERG and GLENNA CREAMER are:
      i.   KAREN11TH[11] SANDBERG, b. 03 May 1964.
     ii.   KEITH11TH SANDBERG, b. 04 Aug 1973.

1416. MARJORIE ELLEN[10] SANDBERG *(BERTHA MAY[9] SPINNEY, ERNEST EDWARD[8], CHARLES HERBERT[7], JOHN WARREN[6], SAMUEL[5], JOHN[4], THOMAS[3], SAMUEL[2], THOMAS[1])* was born 08 Dec 1930 in Winthrop, MA. She married JOSEPH NELSON DULONG 17 May 1953 in ST. Mary's Church, Lynn, MA.. He was born 17 Jul 1932 in Wakefield, MA.

Children of MARJORIE SANDBERG and JOSEPH DULONG are:

1583.   i.   JOSEPH NELSON DULONG[11] JR., b. 19 Mar 1954, Lynn, MA..
1584.   ii. CHERYL MAY DULONG, b. 02 Dec 1956, Lynn, MA..

1417. BARBARA[10] SANDBERG *(BERTHA MAY[9] SPINNEY, ERNEST EDWARD[8], CHARLES HERBERT[7], JOHN WARREN[6], SAMUEL[5], JOHN[4], THOMAS[3], SAMUEL[2], THOMAS[1])* was born 01 Jun 1935 in Tewksbury, MA.. She married ARTHUR THOMAS DALTON, JR. 28 May 1954 in Saugus, Essex, MA. He was born 03 May 1934 in Lynn, Essex, MA.

Children of BARBARA SANDBERG and ARTHUR DALTON are:
1585.   i.   DEBORAH MAY[11] DALTON, b. 09 Oct 1956, Lynn, Essex, MA.
       ii. WILLIAM CLIFFORD DALTON, b. 30 Apr 1971, Woonsockett, RI..

1418. NANCY-ANN[10] NICHOLSON *(MURIEL GERTRUDE[9] SPINNEY, ERNEST EDWARD[8], CHARLES HERBERT[7], JOHN WARREN[6], SAMUEL[5], JOHN[4], THOMAS[3], SAMUEL[2], THOMAS[1])* was born 28 Sep 1935. She married WARREN HARRISON LATHE. He was born 12 Jan 1921.

Child of NANCY-ANN NICHOLSON and WARREN LATHE is:
       i.   TERRI-LYNN11TH AUDRA[11] LATHE, b. 05 Sep 1966.

1419. ROBERT E[10] SPINNEY *(SIDNEY A[9], FRED L[8], ROBERT[7], NATHAN[6], JOHN[5], NICHOLAS[4], JAMES[3], SAMUEL[2], THOMAS[1])* was born 1927. He married DOROTHY SMITH.

Notes for ROBERT E SPINNEY:
Robert E. Spinney, 73

ELIOT Robert E. Spinney, 73, of Dolt Hill Road, died Sept. 28, 2000, at Portsmouth Regional Hospital in New Hampshire.

He was born here, a son of Sidney and Alma Leavitt Spinney, and graduated from Eliot High School.

Mr. Spinney worked for Dow Oil Co. and then as a fire captain for the Portsmouth Naval Shipyard Fire Department. He retired in 1974 but worked as a backhoe operator for many years.

He was affiliated with Naval Masonic Lodge 174 of Kittery and was a volunteer firefighter with the Eliot Volunteer Fire Department.

His interests included fishing and hunting.

A son, Paul, died in 1998.

Surviving are his wife of over 54 years, Dorothy Smith Spinney; two daughters, Mrs. James (Joyce) Dove of Clermont Fla., and Mrs. Frank (Judith) Jewett of Oxford; a son, Dennis of Eliot; a sister, Louise Stukas of Kennebunk; nine grandchildren and five great-grandchildren

Children of ROBERT SPINNEY and DOROTHY SMITH are:
       i.   JOYCE[11] SPINNEY, m. JAMES DOVE.
       ii. JUDITH SPINNEY, m. FRANK JEWETT.

1420. EARL W[10] SPINNEY *(FORREST E[9], NATHAN G[8], NATHAN[7], NATHAN[6], JOHN[5], NICHOLAS[4], JAMES[3], SAMUEL[2], THOMAS[1])* was born 03 Aug 1925 in Portsmouth, NH, and died 18 Aug 1999. He married ELIZABETH SPERRY. She died May 1999.

Notes for EARL W SPINNEY:

Headline: EARL W. 'BUCKY' SPINNEY WORKED FOR SEVERAL DAIRIES
Publication Date: August 20, 1999
Source: Portland Press Herald
Page:

Subjects:

Region:

Obituary: Earl W. "Bucky" Spinney, 74, of Clark Road died Wednesday at the Maine Medical Center in Portland after a brief illness.

He was born in Portsmouth, N.H., a son of Forrest E. and Florence Chandler Spinney. After attending schools in both Portsmouth and Eliot, Mr. Spinney moved to Alfred where he spent the remainder of his life.

He was employed with various dairies in New Hampshire and Maine, including Badger Farms Creameries in Portsmouth, Emery's Dairy at Kittery Point, Chabot's Dairy in Somersworth, N.H., and Clover Leaf Farms in Haverhill, Mass. He also worked at the former Nasson College in Springvale and Cohen Egg Farm in Dayton.

Mr. Spinney was a member of the Alfred Congregational Church, where he was a former deacon and president of the Men's Club. He was also a member and past president of the Parent's Club of the Alfred Elementary School.

Mr. Spinney's wife, Elizabeth Sperry Spinney, died n May of 1999; he also was predeceased by three brothers.

Surviving are two daughters, Karen Currier of Ray- mond, N.H., and Sybil Howe of Kennebunk; two sisters; Charlotte Mortgridge of Eliot and Mae Relea of Florida; and four grandchildren.

Visiting hours will be 6 to 8 p.m. Saturday at Heald Funeral Home,

61 Main St. in Springvale. A memorial service will be held at 3:30 p.m. Sunday at the Alfred Congregational Church, with the Rev.

Katherine Fiske officiating. Private interment will take place at the convenience of the family. Arrangements handled through Heald Funeral Homes.

(Copyright 1999)

--- ------

Notes for ELIZABETH SPERRY:

Headline: ELIZABETH E. SPINNEY SCHOOLTEACHER, CHURCH ORGANIST

Publication Date: May 12, 1999

Source: Portland Press Herald

Page:

Subjects:

Region:

Obituary: Elizabeth E. Spinney, 75, died early Monday morning in Sanford.

She was a daughter of Ammon B. and Ruth Austine Sperry of Eliot and attended Eliot schools.

She graduated from high school in 1944 and from Nasson College with a degree in education.

On Sept. 17, 1949, she married Earl W. Spinney and they moved to Alfred.

Mrs. Spinney worked as a home economics and substitute teacher, as well as for the Waterboro school district.

She was an active member of the Alfred Congregational Church. For

15 years she played organ for the church and was invited to be a guest organist in many other area churches.

She held many church offices, volunteered for many activities and was junior choir director for many years.

One of her greatest loves was the involvement with the Alive gospel singers.

Mrs. Spinney also volunteered as a 4-H leader and a camp cook.

Surviving are her husband of nearly 50 years of Alfred; two daughters, Karen A. Currier of Raymond, N.H., and Sybil J. Howe of Kennebunk; and four grandchildren.

Visiting hours will be 7 to 9 p.m. Friday at Heald Funeral Home, Springvale. A memorial service will be held at 4 p.m. Saturday at Alfred Congregational Church with the Revs. Katherine Fisk and   Neil Iverson officiating. A private burial will be held at the convenience of the family.

(Copyright 1999)

Children of EARL SPINNEY and ELIZABETH SPERRY are:

    i.   KAREN[11] SPINNEY, m. CURRIER.

    ii.   SYBIL SPINNEY, m. HOWE.

1421. HARLOW RODNEY[10] SPINNEY (*ERNEST HARLOW*[9], *NATHAN G*[8], *NATHAN*[7], *NATHAN*[6], *JOHN*[5], *NICHOLAS*[4],

JAMES[3], SAMUEL[2], THOMAS[1]) was born 1926. He married ELIZABETH TEBO.

Child of HARLOW SPINNEY and ELIZABETH TEBO is:
    i.   VESTA JOY[11] SPINNEY, m. TIDD.

1422. PARKER THAYER[10] SPINNEY *(PARKER THAYER[9], EUGENE NATHANIAL[8], JOSEPH FRANKLIN[7], PARKER FOSTER[6], DAVID[5], EBENEZER[4], JONATHAN[3], SAMUEL[2], THOMAS[1])* was born Private, and died Feb 1986. He married UNKNOWN Private. She was born Private.

Children of PARKER SPINNEY and UNKNOWN are:
    i.   VICTORIA HELEN[11] SPINNEY, b. Private.
    ii.   PATRICA SPINNEY, b. Private.
    iii.   KATHRYN SPINNEY, b. Private.
    iv.   SUSAN SPINNEY, b. Private.

1423. ROBERT WAYNE[10] SPINNEY *(HAROLD WARREN[9], FRANCIS WARREN[8], GEORGE F[7], MARK[6], PARKER[5], EBENEZER[4], JONATHAN[3], SAMUEL[2], THOMAS[1])* was born 20 Nov 1946. He married ELLEN LOUISE GEORGE 31 May 1969.

Child of ROBERT SPINNEY and ELLEN GEORGE is:
    i.   GREGORY ALLAN[11] SPINNEY, b. 09 Dec 1969.

1424. JEANNE LAURIE[10] SPINNEY *(HAROLD WARREN[9], FRANCIS WARREN[8], GEORGE F[7], MARK[6], PARKER[5], EBENEZER[4], JONATHAN[3], SAMUEL[2], THOMAS[1])* was born 14 Mar 1956. She married MICHAEL EDWARD DEGARA 09 Oct 1971.

Children of JEANNE SPINNEY and MICHAEL DEGARA are:
    i.   CHRISTOPHER MICHAEL[11] DEGARA, b. 15 Dec 1974, Newburyport, MA; m. ELIZABETH TAYLOR, 11 Nov 2005, Coral Springs, Fl.
    ii.   RAQUEL JEANNE DEGARA, b. 04 Aug 1978, Coral Springs, Fl.
    iii.   DANIEL EDWARD DEGARA, b. 17 Aug 1987, Coral Springs, Fl.

1425. LAUREL MAE[10] OWENS *(LLOYD MAXWELL[9], ELLA GERTRUDE[8] WHEELER, ALICE CATHERINE[7] DWELLEY, NARCISSA SPRING[6] SPINNEY, EBENEZER[5], EBENEZER[4], JONATHAN[3], SAMUEL[2], THOMAS[1])* was born 29 Aug 1915 in Angwin , CA, and died 23 Nov 1966. She married WILLIAM FLOYD WEHTJE, son of OTTO WEHTJE and EDITH BRADFORD. He was born 23 May 1910 in Castle Rock, WA.

Children of LAUREL OWENS and WILLIAM WEHTJE are:
1586.   i.   MARILYN[11] WEHTJE.
1587.   ii.   MYRON FLOYD WEHTJE, b. 21 Oct 1938, Longview WA.

1426. MELINDA LOU[10] BECKLEY *(HELEN LOUISE[9] MALOY, ALICE CATHERINE[8] DWELLEY, JOSEPH FRANKLIN[7], NARCISSA SPRING[6] SPINNEY, EBENEZER[5], EBENEZER[4], JONATHAN[3], SAMUEL[2], THOMAS[1])* She married JAMES ROBERT MCDONALD.

Children of MELINDA BECKLEY and JAMES MCDONALD are:
    i.   RYAN ANGUS[11] MCDONALD.
    ii.   MARC NATHAN MCDONALD.

1427. ANITA[10] SPINNEY *(LLEWELLEN[9], DOUGLAS[8], JAMES ALEXANDER[7], STEPHEN[6], JONATHAN[5], NATHANIEL[4], JONATHAN[3], SAMUEL[2], THOMAS[1])* was born 05 Oct 1926. She married GERALD EDWARD GREARSON 12 Aug 1947 in St George, NB.. He was born 01 Dec 1924 in St John, NB., and died 2007.

Child of ANITA SPINNEY and GERALD GREARSON is:
1588.   i.   JUDITH ANN[11] GREARSON, b. 19 Jul 1949.

1428. JACK BENTLEY[10] SPINNEY *(STEPHEN PERCY[9], FREDERICK[8], HORATIO NELSON[7], STEPHEN[6], JONATHAN[5], NATHANIEL[4], JONATHAN[3], SAMUEL[2], THOMAS[1])* was born 31 Dec 1920 in St John, NB., and died 14 Mar 2002. He married JANEY MURDOCH 16 Sep 1949 in St John, NB..

Child of JACK SPINNEY and JANEY MURDOCH is:
1589.   i.   JOANNE[11] SPINNEY.

1429. MARILYN[10] PARKS *(ALICE[9] SPINNEY, GEORGE ROSS[8], JAMES VAN BUREN[7], JAMES S[6], JONATHAN[5], NATHANIEL[4], JONATHAN[3], SAMUEL[2], THOMAS[1])* She married MUNN.

Children of MARILYN PARKS and MUNN are:
    i.   ROSS[11] MUNN.
   ii.   RODNEY MUNN.

1430. ELEANOR[10] MILLS *(RALPH EDWARD[9], GORDON VICTOR[8], LOUISE PARKS[7] SPINNEY, CHARLES EDWARD[6], JONATHAN[5], NATHANIEL[4], JONATHAN[3], SAMUEL[2], THOMAS[1])* was born 06 Feb 1952 in Medford, MA. She married BERNIE ROUILLARD.

Child of ELEANOR MILLS and BERNIE ROUILLARD is:
    i.   MIRIELLE[11] ROUILLARD, b. 20 May 1988, Manchester, NH.

1431. RALPH JR[10] MILLS *(RALPH EDWARD[9], GORDON VICTOR[8], LOUISE PARKS[7] SPINNEY, CHARLES EDWARD[6], JONATHAN[5], NATHANIEL[4], JONATHAN[3], SAMUEL[2], THOMAS[1])* was born 07 Sep 1954 in Medford, MA, and died 29 Apr 2006 in Woburn, Ma. He married KAREN MCDONOUGH.

Children of RALPH MILLS and KAREN MCDONOUGH are:
    i.   JUSTIN[11] MILLS, b. 17 Jul 1982, Winchester, Ma.
   ii.   RACHAEL MILLS, b. 17 Jul 1982, Winchester, Ma.
  iii.   SAMANTHA MILLS, b. 18 Aug 1989, Winchester, Ma.

1432. PHILIP[10] MILLS *(RALPH EDWARD[9], GORDON VICTOR[8], LOUISE PARKS[7] SPINNEY, CHARLES EDWARD[6], JONATHAN[5], NATHANIEL[4], JONATHAN[3], SAMUEL[2], THOMAS[1])* was born 01 Oct 1959 in Winchester, MA. He married (1) THERESA SPINDLER. He married (2) DENISE MANN 03 Oct 1992.

Children of PHILIP MILLS and THERESA SPINDLER are:
    i.   SHERRIE[11] MILLS, b. 12 Apr 1984, Waltham, MA.
   ii.   LAUREN MILLS, b. 18 Dec 1985, Derry, NH.

1433. NANCY MARIE[10] MILLS *(RALPH EDWARD[9], GORDON VICTOR[8], LOUISE PARKS[7] SPINNEY, CHARLES EDWARD[6], JONATHAN[5], NATHANIEL[4], JONATHAN[3], SAMUEL[2], THOMAS[1])* was born 01 Mar 1964 in Medford, MA. She married MICHAEL BLACK 28 Aug 1992 in Woburn, MA, son of JOHN BLACK and CLAIR.

Children of NANCY MILLS and MICHAEL BLACK are:
    i.   JAKE PATRICK[11] BLACK, b. 01 Mar 1993.
   ii.   CARA BLACK, b. 28 Feb 1996, Winchester, MA.

1434. ROBERT[10] MILLS *(RALPH EDWARD[9], GORDON VICTOR[8], LOUISE PARKS[7] SPINNEY, CHARLES EDWARD[6], JONATHAN[5], NATHANIEL[4], JONATHAN[3], SAMUEL[2], THOMAS[1])* was born Apr 1966. He married KAREN.

Children of ROBERT MILLS and KAREN are:
    i.   ROBERT[11] MILLS.
   ii.   ALEXA MILLS.

1435. STEPHEN[10] MILLS *(GORDON[9], GORDON VICTOR[8], LOUISE PARKS[7] SPINNEY, CHARLES EDWARD[6], JONATHAN[5],*

NATHANIEL[4], *JONATHAN*[3], *SAMUEL*[2], *THOMAS*[1]*)* was born 1952. He married (1) MARY BETH. She was born 31 Oct 1952. He married (2) PEGI.

Children of STEPHEN MILLS and MARY BETH are:
  i. TIMOTHY[11] MILLS, b. 26 Apr 1979.
  ii. SARAH MILLS, b. 17 Jul 1980.
  iii. JEFFREY MILLS, b. 09 Aug 1982.
  iv. ELIZABETH ANN MILLS, b. 20 Apr 1984.

Child of STEPHEN MILLS and PEGI is:
  v. PATRICK[11] MILLS, b. 27 Apr 1995.

1436. SUSAN[10] MILLS *(GORDON*[9], *GORDON VICTOR*[8], *LOUISE PARKS*[7] *SPINNEY, CHARLES EDWARD*[6], *JONATHAN*[5], *NATHANIEL*[4], *JONATHAN*[3], *SAMUEL*[2], *THOMAS*[1]*)* was born 1962. She married GERADO INUMERABLE. He was born 16 Feb 1960.

Children of SUSAN MILLS and GERADO INUMERABLE are:
  i. ERIC[11] INUMERABLE, b. 21 Jan 1996.
  ii. JILLIAN INUMERABLE, b. 02 Apr 1998.

1437. NORMAN[10] MILLS *(NORMAN*[9], *EDWARD L*[8], *LOUISE PARKS*[7] *SPINNEY, CHARLES EDWARD*[6], *JONATHAN*[5], *NATHANIEL*[4], *JONATHAN*[3], *SAMUEL*[2], *THOMAS*[1]*)* He married JANE.

Children of NORMAN MILLS and JANE are:
1590. i. JOHN[11] MILLS.
1591. ii. JULIE MILLS.
  iii. MATTHEW MILLS.
  iv. KATIE MILLS.

1438. BRIAN[10] MILLS *(NORMAN*[9], *EDWARD L*[8], *LOUISE PARKS*[7] *SPINNEY, CHARLES EDWARD*[6], *JONATHAN*[5], *NATHANIEL*[4], *JONATHAN*[3], *SAMUEL*[2], *THOMAS*[1]*)*

Children of BRIAN MILLS are:
  i. SHANNON[11] MILLS.
  ii. BRIANNA MILLS.

1439. RICHARD[10] MILLS *(NORMAN*[9], *EDWARD L*[8], *LOUISE PARKS*[7] *SPINNEY, CHARLES EDWARD*[6], *JONATHAN*[5], *NATHANIEL*[4], *JONATHAN*[3], *SAMUEL*[2], *THOMAS*[1]*)* He married ANDREA.

Children of RICHARD MILLS and ANDREA are:
  i. ANDREA[11] MILLS.
  ii. KRISTEN MILLS.
  iii. DAVID MILLS.

1440. PATRICIA[10] MILLS *(NORMAN*[9], *EDWARD L*[8], *LOUISE PARKS*[7] *SPINNEY, CHARLES EDWARD*[6], *JONATHAN*[5], *NATHANIEL*[4], *JONATHAN*[3], *SAMUEL*[2], *THOMAS*[1]*)* She married THOMAS SEMETER.

Children of PATRICIA MILLS and THOMAS SEMETER are:
  i. PATRICK[11] SEMETER.
  ii. RYAN SEMETER.

1441. CHARLES JAMES[10] SPINNEY *(FRANK J*[9], *FRANKLIN PIERCE*[8], *BENJAMIN FRANK*[7], *ARCHIBALD BARNEY*[6], *JONATHAN*[5], *NATHANIEL*[4], *JONATHAN*[3], *SAMUEL*[2], *THOMAS*[1]*)*

Children of CHARLES JAMES SPINNEY are:

    i.   KELLEY ANNE[11] SPINNEY.

   ii.   JENNIFER JEAN SPINNEY, m. KEITH ALLEN SHIRLEY, 14 Feb 1996, Windham, ME.

1442. ARTHUR[10] SPINNEY *(FRANCIS JOSEPH[9], EBENEZER[8], WILLIAM L[7], EBENEZER[6], EBENEZER[5], NATHANIEL[4], JONATHAN[3], SAMUEL[2], THOMAS[1])* He married MARIE ELIZABETH WOLFE.

Children of ARTHUR SPINNEY and MARIE WOLFE are:

    i.   ELIZABETH MARIE[11] SPINNEY.

   ii.   BRIAN SPINNEY.

1443. DONALD A[10] SPINNEY *(CHESTER ALVAH[9], JOHN W[8], WILLIAM L[7], NATHANIEL[6], EBENEZER[5], NATHANIEL[4], JONATHAN[3], SAMUEL[2], THOMAS[1])* He married BARBARA WADSWOTHH.

Children of DONALD SPINNEY and BARBARA WADSWOTHH are:

    i.   KIMBERLY K[11] SPINNEY, b. Private.

   ii.   BRYAN A SPINNEY, b. Private.

  iii.   MICHELLE D SPINNEY, b. Private.

1444. ARTHUR EDWIN[10] MILLS *(CLAUDE EDWIN[9], ARTHUR JONES[8], SARAH[7] SPINNEY, ARTHUR JONES[6], EBENEZER[5], NATHANIEL[4], JONATHAN[3], SAMUEL[2], THOMAS[1])* was born 02 Jul 1915, and died 21 Mar 1976 in Grass Valley Califorina. He married VIVIAN HARPER 01 Sep 1939. She was born 01 Jul 1916.

Child of ARTHUR MILLS and VIVIAN HARPER is:

1592.   i.   KETHERINE IRENE[11] MILLS, b. 06 Feb 1941.

1445. HAROLD GLEN[10] MILLS *(CLAUDE EDWIN[9], ARTHUR JONES[8], SARAH[7] SPINNEY, ARTHUR JONES[6], EBENEZER[5], NATHANIEL[4], JONATHAN[3], SAMUEL[2], THOMAS[1])* was born 01 Sep 1917 in Andover, SD. He married DAPHNE ALICE NEWTON 12 Jun 1939. She was born 13 Dec 1916 in Marseilles, IL, and died 20 Mar 1999.

Children of HAROLD MILLS and DAPHNE NEWTON are:

1593.   i.   DAPHNE ANNE[11] MILLS, b. 20 Mar 1940.

    ii.   RICHARD GLEN MILLS, b. 07 Mar 1945.

1446. PEARL LOUISE[10] MILLS *(CLAUDE EDWIN[9], ARTHUR JONES[8], SARAH[7] SPINNEY, ARTHUR JONES[6], EBENEZER[5], NATHANIEL[4], JONATHAN[3], SAMUEL[2], THOMAS[1])* was born 24 May 1924 in Andover, SD. She married HAROLD COOPRIDER. He was born 27 Sep 1921, and died 14 Oct 1995.

Children of PEARL MILLS and HAROLD COOPRIDER are:

1594.   i.   LEE[11] COOPRIDER, b. 04 Feb 1947.

1595.   ii.   TED COOPRIDER, b. 13 Jun 1950.

1447. ORWAN BERMOND[10] SIMPSON *(PEARL EUDORA[9] MILLS, ARTHUR JONES[8], SARAH[7] SPINNEY, ARTHUR JONES[6], EBENEZER[5], NATHANIEL[4], JONATHAN[3], SAMUEL[2], THOMAS[1])* was born 01 Oct 1913 in Cashmere, WA. He married BARBARA ABBOTT 01 Jan 1935 in Chelan, WA.

Children of ORWAN SIMPSON and BARBARA ABBOTT are:

    i.   BRUCE[11] SIMPSON, b. 04 Aug 1937.

   ii.   SONDRA SIMPSON, b. 01 Oct 1939, Cashmere, WA.

1448. ARTHUR MILLS[10] SIMPSON *(PEARL EUDORA[9] MILLS, ARTHUR JONES[8], SARAH[7] SPINNEY, ARTHUR JONES[6], EBENEZER[5], NATHANIEL[4], JONATHAN[3], SAMUEL[2], THOMAS[1])* was born 01 Oct 1913 in Cashmere. WA, and died 09 Nov 1995. He married (1) GALDYS ST. DENNIS. He married (2) RUTH MARGARET BECKER 04 Aug 1937 in Cashmere, WA. She was born in Walla Walla, WA, and died 13 Jan 1983.

Children of ARTHUR SIMPSON and RUTH BECKER are:

1596.   i.   RUTHANN PEARL[11] SIMPSON, b. 27 Apr 1941, Wenatchee, WA.

        ii.   SUSAN LOUISE SIMPSON, b. 12 Mar 1946; m. (1) VICTOR DAY; m. (2) AL LEISHMAN.

1449. WREATHA ALMEDA[10] STEWART *(ARTHUR JONES[9], CAROLINE LEVINA[8] MILLS, SARAH[7] SPINNEY, ARTHUR JONES[6], EBENEZER[5], NATHANIEL[4], JONATHAN[3], SAMUEL[2], THOMAS[1])* was born 29 Jan 1916 in McMinnville, OR. She married (1) HENRY H ALBERT GAMMONS. He was born 07 Mar 1905 in Boston MA. She married (2) FLOYD ELMER DRICKSON YOUNG 14 Oct 1939. He was born 22 Dec 1916 in Denton, MT.

Children of WREATHA STEWART and FLOYD YOUNG are:

        i.   STEPHEN LEWIS YOUNG[11] GAMMONS, b. 24 Oct 1940; m. WILHELMINA CAHERIN DROS, 22 Dec 1961, Pensicola Florida.

        ii.   SUSAN JANE YOUNG GAMMONS, b. 04 Sep 1944; m. JOHN ELMER BEARD, 23 May 1963, Boston Mass.

1450. ARTHUR JAY[10] STEWART *(ARTHUR JONES[9], CAROLINE LEVINA[8] MILLS, SARAH[7] SPINNEY, ARTHUR JONES[6], EBENEZER[5], NATHANIEL[4], JONATHAN[3], SAMUEL[2], THOMAS[1])* was born 03 Sep 1919 in McMinnville, OR. He married (1) MARJORIE IRENE SHEPLEY 29 Mar 1945. She was born 04 May 1923, and died 30 Mar 1961. He married (2) LORETTA MAE ROWE 09 Jun 1962 in Portland, Oregon. She was born 15 Sep 1933.

Children of ARTHUR STEWART and MARJORIE SHEPLEY are:

        i.   JANICE IRENE[11] STEWART, b. 05 Aug 1950, Newberg, OR; m. GRANT DEAN BEAUCHAMP, 15 Mar 1969.

        ii.   VIRGIANA LEE STEWART, b. 31 Dec 1952, Newberg, OR; m. FRANK MILTON MUSGRAVE, 06 Jun 1974, Salem, Or.

1451. IVA MAY[10] STEWART *(ARTHUR JONES[9], CAROLINE LEVINA[8] MILLS, SARAH[7] SPINNEY, ARTHUR JONES[6], EBENEZER[5], NATHANIEL[4], JONATHAN[3], SAMUEL[2], THOMAS[1])* was born 08 Oct 1921 in McMinnville OR. She married (1) RALPH E PIERSON. She married (2) GEORGE MEEKER 09 Dec 1939 in Newberg, WA.

Children of IVA STEWART and GEORGE MEEKER are:

        i.   MERTON EARL[11] MEEKER, b. 15 Mar 1941, Portland, OR; m. NANCY PENNY.

        ii.   KATHLEEN ANN MEEKER, b. 04 Mar 1943; m. JOHN F WALKER, 26 Jan 1963, Portland, Oregon.

        iii.   NANCY SUE MEEKER, b. 02 Apr 1944, Forest Grove, OR.

        iv.   DONALD KENT MEEKER, b. 01 Jun 1956, Portland, OR.

1452. CAROLINE MARGARET[10] STEWART *(CLIFFORD MILLS[9], CAROLINE LEVINA[8] MILLS, SARAH[7] SPINNEY, ARTHUR JONES[6], EBENEZER[5], NATHANIEL[4], JONATHAN[3], SAMUEL[2], THOMAS[1])* was born 20 Oct 1917 in Lougheed Alberta Canada. She married JACK STRILING FULLERTON 15 Jan 1947 in Portland, OR. He was born 18 May 1920 in Tacoma, WA.

Children of CAROLINE STEWART and JACK FULLERTON are:

1597.   i.   JACK STRILING[11] FULLERTON, b. 16 Nov 1948, Port Angeles, WA.

1598.   ii.   MARGARET LYNNE FULLERTON, b. 25 Jun 1951, Salem, OR.

1453. CLIFFORD THOMAS[10] STEWART *(CLIFFORD MILLS[9], CAROLINE LEVINA[8] MILLS, SARAH[7] SPINNEY, ARTHUR JONES[6], EBENEZER[5], NATHANIEL[4], JONATHAN[3], SAMUEL[2], THOMAS[1])* was born 30 Jun 1920 in Edmonton Alberta Canada. He married (1) ELLA MAE ZELLER, daughter of RUDOLPH ZELLER and ELSIE BETTS. She was born 27 Sep 1924 in Portland, OR. He married (2) ESTHER NORMA GUNNESDAL 06 Jun 1942 in Miami, FL, daughter of ANDRES GUNNESDAL and IDA BRYNILDSEN. She was born 23 Jul 1920 in Portland, OR, and died 17 Jun 1951 in Portland, OR.

Children of CLIFFORD STEWART and ESTHER GUNNESDAL are:

1599.   i.   LINDA JEANNE[11] STEWART, b. 01 Sep 1945, Miami, FL.

        ii.   ROBERT BRUCE STEWART, b. 27 Sep 1949, Portland, Or; m. (1) RUTH ANN DARLINGTON MARSHALL; m. (2) WANDA REYNOLDS, 29 Sep 1980, Pennsylvania.

1454. DONALD[10] BARRIGAN *(VERA TERESA[9] SWAN, SUSANNA JANE "JEN"[8] MILLS, SARAH[7] SPINNEY, ARTHUR JONES[6], EBENEZER[5], NATHANIEL[4], JONATHAN[3], SAMUEL[2], THOMAS[1])* was born 24 Oct 1923 in Omak, WA. He married DONNA OLSON. She was born 28 Jun 1923.

Child of DONALD BARRIGAN and DONNA OLSON is:
      i.   JANE VICTORIA[11] BARRIGAN, b. 06 Jun 1959, Gardenea, CA; m. DAN K SIMCHUK, 31 May 1989, Portland, OR.

1455. JANE MARGARET[10] BARRIGAN *(VERA TERESA[9] SWAN, SUSANNA JANE "JEN"[8] MILLS, SARAH[7] SPINNEY, ARTHUR JONES[6], EBENEZER[5], NATHANIEL[4], JONATHAN[3], SAMUEL[2], THOMAS[1])* was born 21 Nov 1928. She married CAL HANSEN Dec 1952 in Vancouver, BC..

Children of JANE BARRIGAN and CAL HANSEN are:
      i.   JAMES BRADLEY[11] HANSEN.
     ii.   KENNETH HANSEN.
   iii.   JANET LYNN HANSEN.

1456. MARIAN FRANCES[10] COLLINS *(WILLIAM HENRY[9], ANGELINE ELIZABETH[8] MILLS, SARAH[7] SPINNEY, ARTHUR JONES[6], EBENEZER[5], NATHANIEL[4], JONATHAN[3], SAMUEL[2], THOMAS[1])* was born 30 Nov 1913. She married GEORGE CARTER 1941 in St Paul Minnesota.

Child of MARIAN COLLINS and GEORGE CARTER is:
      i.   COLLEEN ELIZABETH[11] CARTER.

1457. LILA JEAN[10] COLLINS *(WILLIAM HENRY[9], ANGELINE ELIZABETH[8] MILLS, SARAH[7] SPINNEY, ARTHUR JONES[6], EBENEZER[5], NATHANIEL[4], JONATHAN[3], SAMUEL[2], THOMAS[1])* was born Mar 1921 in Fargo, SD. She married JAMES LEAHY 20 Sep 1941.

Child of LILA COLLINS and JAMES LEAHY is:
      i.   JAY PATRICK[11] LEAHY, b. 1943.

1458. MARCIA ANNE[10] LOOMIS *(KATHRYN ISABELLE[9] THOMPSON, MYRTLE ISABELLE[8] BANES, AURELIA ISABELLE[7] SPINNEY, ARTHUR JONES[6], EBENEZER[5], NATHANIEL[4], JONATHAN[3], SAMUEL[2], THOMAS[1])* was born Private. She married JOHN NORMAN CALVIN Private. He was born Private.

Children of MARCIA LOOMIS and JOHN CALVIN are:
1600.   i.   LUCY VIRGINIA[11] CALVIN, b. Private.
         ii.   NATHANIEL GLENN CALVIN, b. Private.

1459. LINDA[10] LOOMIS *(KATHRYN ISABELLE[9] THOMPSON, MYRTLE ISABELLE[8] BANES, AURELIA ISABELLE[7] SPINNEY, ARTHUR JONES[6], EBENEZER[5], NATHANIEL[4], JONATHAN[3], SAMUEL[2], THOMAS[1])* was born Private. She married PATRICK CARL FISCHER Private. He was born Private.

Child of LINDA LOOMIS and PATRICK FISCHER is:
      i.   CARL PERRY[11] FISCHER, b. Private.

1460. PETER BURR[10] LOOMIS IV *(KATHRYN ISABELLE[9] THOMPSON, MYRTLE ISABELLE[8] BANES, AURELIA ISABELLE[7] SPINNEY, ARTHUR JONES[6], EBENEZER[5], NATHANIEL[4], JONATHAN[3], SAMUEL[2], THOMAS[1])* was born Private. He married ANN RIPTON Private. She was born Private.

Children of PETER LOOMIS and ANN RIPTON are:
      i.   GILBERT RIPTON[11] LOOMIS, b. Private.
     ii.   AUSTIN GEORGE LOOMIS, b. Private.

1461. LEONARD KEITH[10] RAFTREE, JR. *(VIRGINIA ANNE[9] THOMPSON, MYRTLE ISABELLE[8] BANES, AURELIA ISABELLE[7] SPINNEY, ARTHUR JONES[6], EBENEZER[5], NATHANIEL[4], JONATHAN[3], SAMUEL[2], THOMAS[1])* was born Private. He married DEBORAH Private. She was born Private.

Children of LEONARD RAFTREE and DEBORAH are:
    i.   MARIA[11] RAFTREE, b. Private.
    ii. LEONARD KEITH RAFTREE III, b. Private.

1462. SHRIELY[10] GORDON *(IDA MAY[9] NEILY, INEZ LINWOOD[8] SPINNEY, ABRAHAM[7], JOSEPH[6], ABRAHAM[5], JOSEPH[4], SAMUEL[3], SAMUEL[2], THOMAS[1])* was born 28 Oct 1939. She married JOHN STEWART DOLLIVER.

Children of SHRIELY GORDON and JOHN DOLLIVER are:
    i.   GORDON STEWART[11] DOLLIVER, b. 24 Dec 1963.
    ii. JOHN DOUGLAS DOLLIVER, b. 04 Jan 1968.

1463. CLIFFORD[10] NEILEY *(WILLIAM LLOYD[9] NEILY, INEZ LINWOOD[8] SPINNEY, ABRAHAM[7], JOSEPH[6], ABRAHAM[5], JOSEPH[4], SAMUEL[3], SAMUEL[2], THOMAS[1])* was born 20 Aug 1934 in Provost AB. He married ALICE MAE BANKS 09 Apr 1955 in Greenwood Nova Scotia.

Children of CLIFFORD NEILEY and ALICE BANKS are:
1601.   i.   BRIAN CLIFFORD[11] NEILEY.
         ii. RAY VANCE NEILEY.
         iii. GLEN STEWARD NEILEY.

1464. KENNETH ROGER[10] NEILY *(WILLIAM LLOYD[9], INEZ LINWOOD[8] SPINNEY, ABRAHAM[7], JOSEPH[6], ABRAHAM[5], JOSEPH[4], SAMUEL[3], SAMUEL[2], THOMAS[1])* was born 12 Sep 1938. He married (2) MELBA PIERCE 12 Jun 1963, daughter of CLAYTON PIERCE and GLORIA BUSH.

Children of KENNETH ROGER NEILY are:
    i.   PEARLANN ROSE[11] NEILY.
    ii. KENNETH CECIL NEILY, b. 01 Jun 1960.

Children are listed above under (1268) Melba Pierce.

1465. ALAN BLAIR[10] SPINNEY *(PAUL NATHANIEL[9], GEORGE LAMERT[8], OWEN[7], JOSEPH[6], ABRAHAM[5], JOSEPH[4], SAMUEL[3], SAMUEL[2], THOMAS[1])* He married ROSE AUCOINE 08 Jan 1977.

Children of ALAN SPINNEY and ROSE AUCOINE are:
    i.   ALAN GREGORY[11] SPINNEY, b. 22 Feb 1977, Cape Benton, NS..
    ii. WILLIAM SPINNEY, b. 22 Aug 1978, Cape Benton, NS..

1466. ELAINE MARY[10] SPINNEY *(PAUL NATHANIEL[9], GEORGE LAMERT[8], OWEN[7], JOSEPH[6], ABRAHAM[5], JOSEPH[4], SAMUEL[3], SAMUEL[2], THOMAS[1])* was born 30 Nov 1948. She married KEITH NORTHROP.

Children of ELAINE SPINNEY and KEITH NORTHROP are:
    i.   KIMBERLY DAWN[11] NORTHROP, b. 16 Dec 1968.
    ii. KEITH BRETT LEE NORTHROP, b. 22 Feb 1983.

1467. ROBERT BERTWELL[10] BAILEY *(RUSSELL FRANKLIN[9], CORA MAUDE[8] BERTWELL, ALEPH[7] WOODBURY, ELIZABETH[6] SPINNEY, ABRAHAM[5], JOSEPH[4], SAMUEL[3], SAMUEL[2], THOMAS[1])* was born 18 Oct 1935 in Arlington, MA. He married JOAN ETHYL MESSINGER 16 Sep 1961 in Lexington, MA. She was born 14 Apr 1939 in Cambridge, MA.

Children of ROBERT BAILEY and JOAN MESSINGER are:
    i.   DEBORAH JOAN[11] BAILEY, b. 02 Aug 1963, Cambridge, MA; m. (1) KENNETH BIRSE, 24 Oct 1987, Lexington, MA; m. (2) ANTHONY PHILLIP MAHRE, 12 Jun 1994, Salt Lake, UT.
1602.   ii. CYNTHIA ROBERTA BAILEY, b. 29 Jun 1965, Cambridge, MA.

1468. BRUCE WARREN[10] SPINNEY *(BRUCE WARREN[9], CHESTER LEVERETT[8], ISAAC CALVIN[7], SAMUEL[6], ISAAC BEACH[5], SAMUEL MCCLURE[4], SAMUEL[3], SAMUEL[2], THOMAS[1])* was born 28 Jan 1948. He married (1) CAROLYN FERNANDES. He married (2) DIANE ROBERTS.

Children of BRUCE SPINNEY and CAROLYN FERNANDES are:
  i. TRACIA LEE[11] SPINNEY, b. 04 Nov 1974.
  ii. BRUCE WARREN SPINNEY, b. 04 Jun 1976.

Child of BRUCE SPINNEY and DIANE ROBERTS is:
  iii. DAVID GLEN[11] SPINNEY, b. 28 Apr 1981.

1469. DAVID LYLE[10] SPINNEY *(BRUCE WARREN[9], CHESTER LEVERETT[8], ISAAC CALVIN[7], SAMUEL[6], ISAAC BEACH[5], SAMUEL MCCLURE[4], SAMUEL[3], SAMUEL[2], THOMAS[1])* was born 02 Oct 1950. He married MARGERY "MARGGIE" LEISERSON KOENIG.

Children of DAVID SPINNEY and MARGERY KOENIG are:
  i. "EMILY"LESLIE MARGERT KOENIG-[11] STOCKERT.
  ii. ERIN LEE SPINNEY, b. 23 Jul 1984.

1470. CHESTER LEVERETT[10] SPINNEY *(CHESTER LEVERETT JR.[9], CHESTER LEVERETT[8], ISAAC CALVIN[7], SAMUEL[6], ISAAC BEACH[5], SAMUEL MCCLURE[4], SAMUEL[3], SAMUEL[2], THOMAS[1])* was born 05 Apr 1948 in Worchester, MA. He married JANET BERNARD 06 Jun 1970 in North Reading, MA. She was born 20 Feb 1947 in Massachusetts.

Notes for CHESTER LEVERETT SPINNEY:
[Spinney.FTW]

born in Worchester City Hospital, Worchester, Massachusetts. Family resided in Barre, Massachusetts

Children of CHESTER SPINNEY and JANET BERNARD are:
  i. LAURA RAY[11] SPINNEY, b. 30 Apr 1973; m. MICHAEL PARROW, 1997, North Reading, Massachusetts.
1603. ii. APRIL LYN SPINNEY, b. 03 Oct 1975.
  iii. JAIME SPINNEY, b. 17 Feb 1977.
  iv. CHESTER LEVERETT SPINNEY, b. 17 Feb 1977.

1471. PHILIP CRAIG[10] SPINNEY *(CHESTER LEVERETT JR.[9], CHESTER LEVERETT[8], ISAAC CALVIN[7], SAMUEL[6], ISAAC BEACH[5], SAMUEL MCCLURE[4], SAMUEL[3], SAMUEL[2], THOMAS[1])* was born 29 Apr 1949 in Holden, MA. He married SUSAN MAC IVER 20 Jul 1974 in Ossipee, NH. She was born 05 Apr 1954.

Notes for PHILIP CRAIG SPINNEY:
Born in the Holden Hospital, Holden, Massachusetts.

Children of PHILIP SPINNEY and SUSAN MAC IVER are:
  i. ERIK[11] SPINNEY, b. 02 Apr 1978.
  ii. JOEL SPINNEY, b. 01 Nov 1979.
  iii. AMBER DAWN SPINNEY, b. 18 Jun 1980.

1472. ROBIN LISA[10] SPINNEY *(CHESTER LEVERETT JR.[9], CHESTER LEVERETT[8], ISAAC CALVIN[7], SAMUEL[6], ISAAC BEACH[5], SAMUEL MCCLURE[4], SAMUEL[3], SAMUEL[2], THOMAS[1])* was born 28 Mar 1954 in Exeter, NH. She married TIMOTHY JOHN LENSING 15 May 1976 in North Reading, MA. He was born 17 Jun 1950 in Grand Rapids, MI.

Notes for ROBIN LISA SPINNEY:
[Spinney.FTW]

Family resided in Newton, New Hampshire.

Children of ROBIN SPINNEY and TIMOTHY LENSING are:

i. MARIAH RUTH[11] LENSING, b. 10 Aug 1981, Hanover, NH.

Notes for MARIAH RUTH LENSING:
[Spinney.FTW]

Born at Dartmouth Hitchcock Medical Center.

ii. KENDELL VICTORIA LENSING, b. 16 Sep 1984, Hanover, NH.

Notes for KENDELL VICTORIA LENSING:
[Spinney.FTW]

Born at Dartmouth Hitchcock Medical Center.

1473. CAROLYN[10] WARD *(PHYLLIS MAE[9] SPINNEY, KINGSLEY SELLAR[8], LELAND TEASDALE[7], ENOCH[6], JACOB BEACH[5], SAMUEL MCCLURE[4], SAMUEL[3], SAMUEL[2], THOMAS[1])* was born 06 Aug 1958. She married ALLAN MACCRELLOUGH.

Children of CAROLYN WARD and ALLAN MACCRELLOUGH are:
i. MICHEAL[11] MACCRELLOUGH.
ii. BARBARA MACCRELLOUGH.
iii. RONALD WARD.

1474. KIMBERLY ANN[10] THAIN *(SANDRA LOUISE[9] SPINNEY, EARLE WINFRED[8], LELAND TEASDALE[7], ENOCH[6], JACOB BEACH[5], SAMUEL MCCLURE[4], SAMUEL[3], SAMUEL[2], THOMAS[1])* was born 05 Dec 1960 in Middleton, N.S.. She married BLAIR STERLING THOMPSON 05 Apr 1980 in Belmont, Lot 16, P.E.I.. He was born 22 Apr 1955.

Children of KIMBERLY THAIN and BLAIR THOMPSON are:
i. JUSTIN BLAIR[11] THOMPSON, b. 01 Nov 1981, Summerside, P.E.I..
ii. JARRETT JAMES THOMPSON, b. 19 Mar 1983, Summerside, P.E.I..
iii. JOEL STEVEN THOMPSON, b. 30 Aug 1985, Summerside, P.E.I..

1475. LISA CAROL[10] THAIN *(SANDRA LOUISE[9] SPINNEY, EARLE WINFRED[8], LELAND TEASDALE[7], ENOCH[6], JACOB BEACH[5], SAMUEL MCCLURE[4], SAMUEL[3], SAMUEL[2], THOMAS[1])* was born 30 Dec 1961 in Middleton, N.S.. She married JOHN RUSSEL PETERS 04 Aug 1989 in Summerside, P.E.I.. He was born 16 May 1955.

Children of LISA THAIN and JOHN PETERS are:
i. MITCHELL DENNIS[11] PETERS, b. 10 Jan 1990, Sackville, N.B..
ii. MIKHEL JOHN PETERS, b. 1991, Sackville, N.B..
iii. MARYA LYN PETERS, b. 24 Aug 1993, Sackville, N.B..

1476. SUSAN LOUISE[10] THAIN *(SANDRA LOUISE[9] SPINNEY, EARLE WINFRED[8], LELAND TEASDALE[7], ENOCH[6], JACOB BEACH[5], SAMUEL MCCLURE[4], SAMUEL[3], SAMUEL[2], THOMAS[1])* was born 10 Feb 1965 in Middleton, N.S.. She married EDWIN CAMERON TRAIL 26 Jun 1987 in Fredericton, N.B.. He was born 01 Aug 1964.

Children of SUSAN THAIN and EDWIN TRAIL are:
i. CHRISTOPHER CAMERON[11] TRAIL, b. 09 Dec 1987, Fredricton, NB..
ii. ALYSSHEA LOUISE TRAIL, b. 15 Feb 1990, Fredricton, NB..
iii. NATIYA MARIE TRAIL, b. 12 Feb 1994, Summerside, P.E.I..

1477. DEBRA PEARL[10] NEWMAN *(DELMA PEARL[9] SPINNEY, EARLE WINFRED[8], LELAND TEASDALE[7], ENOCH[6], JACOB BEACH[5], SAMUEL MCCLURE[4], SAMUEL[3], SAMUEL[2], THOMAS[1])* was born 10 Nov 1960 in Middleton, N.S.. She married (1) STEPHEN LLOYD O'HEARN. She married (2) RUSSEL JOHN BLINCH 03 Mar 1979 in Abbotsford, B.C.. He was born 15 Apr 1949.

Child of DEBRA NEWMAN and RUSSEL BLINCH is:
i. STEVEN RUSSELL[11] BLINCH, b. 20 Apr 1979, Abbotsford, B.C..

1478. RUTH ALMA[10] McWHIRK *(ETHAL M[9] McNUTT, EMMA AUGUSTA[8] SPINNEY, THOMAS M[7], THOMAS[6], THOMAS[5], JOHN[4], THOMAS[3], THOMAS[2], THOMAS[1])* She married MARINES "RENE" DEWITT. He was born 03 Jun 1919.

Children of RUTH McWHIRK and MARINES DEWITT are:
    i.   RUTH MARY[11] DEWITT.
    ii. MARINES "BUTCHIE" DEWITT.
    iii. THOMAS DEWITT.

1479. ETHEL[10] McWHIRK *(ETHAL M[9] McNUTT, EMMA AUGUSTA[8] SPINNEY, THOMAS M[7], THOMAS[6], THOMAS[5], JOHN[4], THOMAS[3], THOMAS[2], THOMAS[1])* She married ED SKELLET.

Child of ETHEL McWHIRK and ED SKELLET is:
    i.   DOROTHY[11] SKELLETT.

1480. ELENOR[10] McWHIRK *(ETHAL M[9] McNUTT, EMMA AUGUSTA[8] SPINNEY, THOMAS M[7], THOMAS[6], THOMAS[5], JOHN[4], THOMAS[3], THOMAS[2], THOMAS[1])* She married BANNEN.

Child of ELENOR McWHIRK and BANNEN is:
    i.   JOHN[11] BANNEN.

1481. CAROL JEAN[10] McWHIRK *(ETHAL M[9] McNUTT, EMMA AUGUSTA[8] SPINNEY, THOMAS M[7], THOMAS[6], THOMAS[5], JOHN[4], THOMAS[3], THOMAS[2], THOMAS[1])* She married WILLIAM VIGEANT.

Child of CAROL McWHIRK and WILLIAM VIGEANT is:
    i.   JEANNINE[11] VIGEANT.

1482. EDNA[10] McWHIRK *(ETHAL M[9] McNUTT, EMMA AUGUSTA[8] SPINNEY, THOMAS M[7], THOMAS[6], THOMAS[5], JOHN[4], THOMAS[3], THOMAS[2], THOMAS[1])* was born 23 Aug 1910, and died 16 Apr 1987 in Massachusetts. She married (1) CHARLES DURAN. She married (2) DEREK BALLAM. She married (3) GERALD BOODEN. He was born 10 Sep 1904.

Children of EDNA McWHIRK and CHARLES DURAN are:
    i.   RICHARD[11] DURAN.
    ii. CAROL RAE DURAN, b. 24 Dec 1934; d. 26 Jun 1988; m. EDWARD HUNT.

Child of EDNA McWHIRK and DEREK BALLAM is:
    iii. WILLIAM[11] BALLAM.

Child of EDNA McWHIRK and GERALD BOODEN is:
    iv. GERALD[11] BOODEN.

1483. DOROTHY FRANCES[10] McWHIRK *(ETHAL M[9] McNUTT, EMMA AUGUSTA[8] SPINNEY, THOMAS M[7], THOMAS[6], THOMAS[5], JOHN[4], THOMAS[3], THOMAS[2], THOMAS[1])* was born 22 Mar 1913, and died 02 Jun 1994. She married JOHN BARTON FENECH, son of JOHN FENECH and CONCETTA BRANDI. He was born 13 Apr 1906.

Children of DOROTHY McWHIRK and JOHN FENECH are:
1604.   i.   JOAN BEVERLY[11] FENECH, b. 30 Jul 1933.
1605.   ii. HENRY ROBERT FENECH, b. 02 Mar 1935; d. 08 Jun 2004, Maryland.
1606.   iii. DOROTHY ETHEL FENECH, b. 23 Jun 1937.
         iv. JOHN BARTON FENECH, b. 12 Oct 1939; m. MERIDITH FULLER.
1607.   v.   GWENDOLYN LOIS FENECH, b. 23 Oct 1939; d. 26 Jun 1989.
         vi. KATHLEEN MARIE FENECH, b. 29 Oct 1943; m. (1) PATRICK RIZZA; m. (2) DANIEL PELLIGRINI.

1484. OLIVE[10] MCWHIRK *(ETHAL M[9] MCNUTT, EMMA AUGUSTA[8] SPINNEY, THOMAS M[7], THOMAS[6], THOMAS[5], JOHN[4], THOMAS[3], THOMAS[2], THOMAS[1])* was born 01 Oct 1918. She married SUMNER "BUTCH" ARCHER. He was born 08 Jan 1896.

Children of OLIVE MCWHIRK and SUMNER ARCHER are:

       i. MARJORIE[11] ARCHER, m. O'KANE.

      ii. VIRGINIA ARCHER, m. NYE.

1608.   iii. PAUL ARCHER, d. 1995.

      iv. LORRAINE "LORRIE" ARCHER.

1485. GRACE E.[10] BROOKS *(ERVING ELSWORTH[9], ALFRED LANGDON[8], DANIEL LANGDON[7], DANIEL[6], MARY[5] SPINNEY, JOHN[4], JOHN[3], JOHN[2], THOMAS[1])* was born 27 Apr 1891. She married ERNEST PINKHAM Dec 1909.

Children of GRACE BROOKS and ERNEST PINKHAM are:

       i. HELEN[11] PINKHAM, b. Private; m. RALPH RUTTER, Private; b. Private.

      ii. LOUISE PINKHAM, b. Private; m. EDWARD DONAVAN, Private; b. Private.

     iii. BEATRICE PINKHAM, b. Private.

     iv. DOROTHY PINKHAM, b. Private; m. FRANK OSGOOD, Private; b. Private.

1609.   v. ERNEST PINKHAM, JR., b. Private.

     vi. HAROLD PINKHAM, b. Private; m. ELLEN, Private; b. Private.

    vii. ROBERT PINKHAM, b. Private; m. RHENDA JONCAS, Private; b. Private.

   viii. ELWIN PINKHAM, b. Private.

1486. NELLIE E.[10] BROOKS *(ERVING ELSWORTH[9], ALFRED LANGDON[8], DANIEL LANGDON[7], DANIEL[6], MARY[5] SPINNEY, JOHN[4], JOHN[3], JOHN[2], THOMAS[1])* was born 24 May 1893. She married WALTER PICKERING Private. He was born Private.

Children of NELLIE BROOKS and WALTER PICKERING are:

       i. MARION[11] PICKERING, b. 1919; d. 1919.

1610.   ii. LEON ARTHUR PICKERING, b. Private.

1611.   iii. WALTER HARRISON PICKERING, b. Private.

1612.   iv. KENNETH EARL PICKERING, b. Private.

1613.   v. MARJORIE LOUISE PICKERING, b. Private.

1487. HAZEL P.[10] BROOKS *(ERVING ELSWORTH[9], ALFRED LANGDON[8], DANIEL LANGDON[7], DANIEL[6], MARY[5] SPINNEY, JOHN[4], JOHN[3], JOHN[2], THOMAS[1])* was born 20 Oct 1894, and died 05 Jun 1969. She married SIMON ISAACSON.

Children of HAZEL BROOKS and SIMON ISAACSON are:

1614.   i. CLARENCE[11] ISAACSON, b. 31 Mar 1914; d. 01 Feb 1965.

1615.   ii. ELINOR ISAACSON, b. Private.

1616.   iii. DOROTHY ISAACSON, b. Private.

1488. ELMER IRWIN[10] BROOKS *(ERVING ELSWORTH[9], ALFRED LANGDON[8], DANIEL LANGDON[7], DANIEL[6], MARY[5] SPINNEY, JOHN[4], JOHN[3], JOHN[2], THOMAS[1])* was born 22 Mar 1898, and died 15 May 1971. He married AGNES SULLIVAN Private. She was born Private.

Children of ELMER BROOKS and AGNES SULLIVAN are:

1617.   i. ARTHUR RALPH[11] BROOKS, b. Private.

1618.   ii. DORIS EVELYN BROOKS, b. Private.

     iii. ELIZABETH BROOKS, b. Private.

1489. WILFRED ELSWORTH[10] BROOKS *(ERVING ELSWORTH[9], ALFRED LANGDON[8], DANIEL LANGDON[7], DANIEL[6], MARY[5] SPINNEY, JOHN[4], JOHN[3], JOHN[2], THOMAS[1])* was born 21 Jun 1905 in Dover NH, and died 01 Sep 1990 in Exeter NH Lot #30 W.Div.Ext. Newington C.. He married DOROTHY FURBER Private. She was born Private.

Children of WILFRED BROOKS and DOROTHY FURBER are:

1619. i. VIRGINIA RUTH[11] BROOKS, b. Private.
1620. ii. PHILLIP F BROOKS, b. Private.

1490. RALPH GORDON[10] BROOKS (*ERVING ELSWORTH[9], ALFRED LANGDON[8], DANIEL LANGDON[7], DANIEL[6], MARY[5] SPINNEY, JOHN[4], JOHN[3], JOHN[2], THOMAS[1]*) was born 05 Aug 1907, and died 27 Apr 1967 in Spartonburg SC Lot #27 W.Div. Newington C. He married IDELLA BATCHELDER Private. She was born Private.

Children of RALPH BROOKS and IDELLA BATCHELDER are:
1621. i. BEVERLY DELL[11] BROOKS, b. Private.
1622. ii. RALPH GORDON BROOKS, JR., b. Private.
1623. iii. CRAIG HEWITT BROOKS, b. Private.

1491. EVELYN A.[10] BROOKS (*ERVING ELSWORTH[9], ALFRED LANGDON[8], DANIEL LANGDON[7], DANIEL[6], MARY[5] SPINNEY, JOHN[4], JOHN[3], JOHN[2], THOMAS[1]*) was born 02 Dec 1909, and died 01 May 1949. She married CARL LUNDGREN Private. He was born Private.

Children of EVELYN BROOKS and CARL LUNDGREN are:
  i. BARBARA[11] LUNDGREN, b. Private; m. KENNETH PALFREY, Private; b. Private.
  ii. MARILYN LUNDGREN, b. Private; m. FRANK HALL, Private; b. Private.

1492. KENNETH EARL[10] BROOKS (*ERVING ELSWORTH[9], ALFRED LANGDON[8], DANIEL LANGDON[7], DANIEL[6], MARY[5] SPINNEY, JOHN[4], JOHN[3], JOHN[2], THOMAS[1]*) was born 31 Jan 1911, and died 03 May 1978. He married FLORENCE BOSTON Private. She was born Private.

Children of KENNETH BROOKS and FLORENCE BOSTON are:
  i. BONNIE LEE[11] BROOKS, b. 16 Nov 1944; d. 08 Mar 1947.
1624. ii. ROSALIE ANNE BROOKS, b. Private.
  iii. EILEEN FAY BROOKS, b. Private; m. MAYLON WILLIAMS, Private; b. Private.

1493. MARJORIE R.[10] BROOKS (*ERVING ELSWORTH[9], ALFRED LANGDON[8], DANIEL LANGDON[7], DANIEL[6], MARY[5] SPINNEY, JOHN[4], JOHN[3], JOHN[2], THOMAS[1]*) was born Private. She married ROBERT PAYNE Private. He was born Private.

Child of MARJORIE BROOKS and ROBERT PAYNE is:
1625. i. ANNA[11] PAYNE, b. Private.

1494. LEWIS SIDNEY[10] BROOKS (*VICTOR E[9], ALFRED LANGDON[8], DANIEL LANGDON[7], DANIEL[6], MARY[5] SPINNEY, JOHN[4], JOHN[3], JOHN[2], THOMAS[1]*) was born 03 Dec 1900, and died 12 Sep 1928. He married ETTIE SHARPLE Private. She was born Private.

Children of LEWIS BROOKS and ETTIE SHARPLE are:
  i. VIOLET[11] BROOKS, b. 21 Apr 1922; d. 08 Nov 1954.
  ii. DORREEN BROOKS, b. Private.
  iii. REGINA BROOKS, b. Private.

1495. CHESTER E[10] BROOKS (*VICTOR E[9], ALFRED LANGDON[8], DANIEL LANGDON[7], DANIEL[6], MARY[5] SPINNEY, JOHN[4], JOHN[3], JOHN[2], THOMAS[1]*) was born 12 Apr 1903, and died 23 Jan 1958. He married ELLEN ERKLAR Private. She was born Private.

Child of CHESTER BROOKS and ELLEN ERKLAR is:
1626. i. CHESTER E[11] BROOKS, JR., b. Private.

1496. HOWARD R[10] BROOKS (*VICTOR E[9], ALFRED LANGDON[8], DANIEL LANGDON[7], DANIEL[6], MARY[5] SPINNEY, JOHN[4], JOHN[3], JOHN[2], THOMAS[1]*) was born 30 Jul 1905, and died 07 May 1961. He married NELLIE DAVIS Private. She was born Private.

Children of HOWARD BROOKS and NELLIE DAVIS are:
        i.   CHESTER ARNOLD[11] BROOKS, b. Private.
1627.   ii.   PHYLLIS BROOKS, b. Private.

1497. CARL F[10] BROOKS *(VICTOR E[9], ALFRED LANGDON[8], DANIEL LANGDON[7], DANIEL[6], MARY[5] SPINNEY, JOHN[4], JOHN[3], JOHN[2], THOMAS[1])* was born Private. He married FRANCES Private. She was born Private.

Children of CARL BROOKS and FRANCES are:
        i.   JAMES[11] BROOKS, b. Private.
       ii.   CARL F BROOKS, JR., b. Private.

1498. PAULENA T[10] BROOKS *(VICTOR E[9], ALFRED LANGDON[8], DANIEL LANGDON[7], DANIEL[6], MARY[5] SPINNEY, JOHN[4], JOHN[3], JOHN[2], THOMAS[1])* was born Private. She married RALPH TORREY Private. He was born Private.

Children of PAULENA BROOKS and RALPH TORREY are:
1628.   i.   GERALD SIDNEY[11] TORREY, b. Private.
1629.   ii.   JOYCE TORREY, b. Private.
1630.   iii. MARGARET TORREY, b. Private.

1499. GEORGE L[10] BROOKS *(VICTOR E[9], ALFRED LANGDON[8], DANIEL LANGDON[7], DANIEL[6], MARY[5] SPINNEY, JOHN[4], JOHN[3], JOHN[2], THOMAS[1])* was born Private. He married MURIEL Private. She was born Private.

Child of GEORGE BROOKS and MURIEL is:
1631.   i.   PATRICIA[11] BROOKS, b. Private.

1500. AUGUSTA MAY[10] TERRIO *(BERNICE MILDRED[9] BROOKS, ALFRED LANGDON[8], DANIEL LANGDON[7], DANIEL[6], MARY[5] SPINNEY, JOHN[4], JOHN[3], JOHN[2], THOMAS[1])* was born 08 Dec 1896 in Portsmouth NH, and died 12 Apr 1969 in Portsmouth NH. She married REGINALD CLIFFORD JONES. He was born 23 Aug 1890, and died 07 Jun 1977 in Portsmouth NH.

Children of AUGUSTA TERRIO and REGINALD JONES are:
1632.   i.   BARBARA ANN[11] JONES, b. Private.
1633.   ii.   MARJORIE LOUISE JONES, b. Private.
1634.   iii. ROBERT LEWIS JONES, b. Private.

1501. FLORENCE MILDRED[10] TERRIO *(BERNICE MILDRED[9] BROOKS, ALFRED LANGDON[8], DANIEL LANGDON[7], DANIEL[6], MARY[5] SPINNEY, JOHN[4], JOHN[3], JOHN[2], THOMAS[1])* was born 14 Jul 1899 in Portsmouth, NH, and died 20 Oct 1982 in Rome, NY. She married ELMER RAYMOND DAVIDSON 01 Sep 1920 in Portsmouth, NH. He was born 18 Aug 1896 in Neoga, IL, and died 27 Nov 1944 in Rome, NY.

Children of FLORENCE TERRIO and ELMER DAVIDSON are:
1635.   i.   EUGENE RAYMOND[11] DAVIDSON, b. 15 Jun 1921, Tulsa, OK; d. 02 Oct 1982, Danvers, MA.
1636.   ii.   DONALD DEAN DAVIDSON, b. Private.
1637.   iii. BETTY JANE DAVIDSON, b. Private.
1638.   iv. ROBERT EDWARD DAVIDSON, b. Private.
       v.   JACK RODNEY DAVIDSON, b. Private; m. CAROLYN AHLES, Private; b. Private.
      vi. WILLIAM HARRY DAVIDSON, b. Private; m. GAYLE, Private; b. Private.
1639.   vii. EDWARD PHILIP DAVIDSON, b. Private.

1502. ANNIE MAYBELLE[10] TERRIO *(BERNICE MILDRED[9] BROOKS, ALFRED LANGDON[8], DANIEL LANGDON[7], DANIEL[6], MARY[5] SPINNEY, JOHN[4], JOHN[3], JOHN[2], THOMAS[1])* was born 02 Aug 1902 in Portsmouth, NH, and died 30 Oct 1980 in Portsmouth, NH. She married SAMUEL HENRY KINGSBURY. He was born 26 Jan 1895, and died 01 May 1973.

Children of ANNIE TERRIO and SAMUEL KINGSBURY are:

1640.	i.	SHIRLEY VIRGINIA[11] KINGSBURY, b. Private.
1641.	ii.	MARY-ANN KINGSBURY, b. Private.
1642.	iii.	SAMUEL HENRY KINGSBURY, JR., b. Private.
1643.	iv.	CHARLES DALE KINGSBURY, b. Private.

1503. ALFRED LEE[10] TERRIO *(BERNICE MILDRED[9] BROOKS, ALFRED LANGDON[8], DANIEL LANGDON[7], DANIEL[6], MARY[5] SPINNEY, JOHN[4], JOHN[3], JOHN[2], THOMAS[1])* was born 15 May 1905 in Portsmouth, NH, and died 18 Nov 1946 in Ports. NH Lot #11 Newington Ceme.. He married RUTH DOROTHY HENDERSON Private. She was born Private.

Children of ALFRED TERRIO and RUTH HENDERSON are:
1644.	i.	DOLORES RUTH[11] TERRIO, b. Private.
1645.	ii.	BERNICE ELEANOR TERRIO, b. Private.
1646.	iii.	JOAN CONSTANCE TERRIO, b. Private.
	iv.	NORMA JEAN TERRIO, b. Private; m. RICHARD P. SIMONDS, Private; b. Private.
1647.	v.	CORRINE GRACE TERRIO, b. Private.

1504. JOHN W.[10] TERRIO *(BERNICE MILDRED[9] BROOKS, ALFRED LANGDON[8], DANIEL LANGDON[7], DANIEL[6], MARY[5] SPINNEY, JOHN[4], JOHN[3], JOHN[2], THOMAS[1])* was born 1908 in Portsmouth, NH, and died 19 Nov 1975 in Ports. NH Lot #17 S.Div. Newington Ceme.. He married (1) ELIZABETH (BETTY) HOYT. She was born 1923, and died 09 Dec 1985 in Lot #17 S.Div. Newington Ceme.. He married (2) IDA PRIMMERMAN. She died 1960 in Eliot ME.

Children of JOHN TERRIO and ELIZABETH HOYT are:
	i.	JON MICHELE[11] TERRIO, b. Private; m. SCHWARTZMILLER, Private; b. Private.
	ii.	JACQUELINE TERRIO, b. Private.
	iii.	KATHLEEN HOYT, b. Private; m. ROGERS, Private; b. Private.
	iv.	MADELINE HOYT, b. Private; m. MILLS, Private; b. Private.

Child of JOHN TERRIO and IDA PRIMMERMAN is:
| | v. | EDNA ANNE[11] TERRIO, b. Private; m. LEON COLBY, Private; b. Private. |

1505. LEROY BROOKS[10] TERRIO, SR. *(BERNICE MILDRED[9] BROOKS, ALFRED LANGDON[8], DANIEL LANGDON[7], DANIEL[6], MARY[5] SPINNEY, JOHN[4], JOHN[3], JOHN[2], THOMAS[1])* was born Private. He married ALICE REGINA CURRAN Private. She was born 07 Sep 1915 in Portsmouth, NH, and died 16 Aug 1986 in Sanford, ME.

Children of LEROY TERRIO and ALICE CURRAN are:
1648.	i.	MARY-ELLEN[11] TERRIO, b. Private.
1649.	ii.	SHIRLEY-ANN TERRIO, b. Private.
1650.	iii.	LEROY BROOKS TERRIO, JR., b. Private.
1651.	iv.	BETTY-JANE TERRIO, b. Private.
1652.	v.	JEFFREY LYNN TERRIO, b. Private.

1506. MABEL LEONA[10] BROOKS *(ARTHUR L[9], ALFRED LANGDON[8], DANIEL LANGDON[7], DANIEL[6], MARY[5] SPINNEY, JOHN[4], JOHN[3], JOHN[2], THOMAS[1])* was born Private. She married ANDREW HARRISON DAVIS Private. He was born Private.

Children of MABEL BROOKS and ANDREW DAVIS are:
1653.	i.	CLAYTON E[11] DAVIS, b. 03 Nov 1918; d. Sep 1969.
1654.	ii.	RICHARD E DAVIS, b. 22 Aug 1929; d. 28 Feb 1979.
1655.	iii.	CONSTANCE ANNABELLE DAVIS, b. Private.
1656.	iv.	ELMER DAVIS, b. Private.
1657.	v.	RUTH EVELYN DAVIS, b. Private.
1658.	vi.	ROBERT H DAVIS, b. Private.
1659.	vii.	CHESTER DAVIS, b. Private.
1660.	viii.	CARL L DAVIS, b. Private.
1661.	ix.	WILMA FLORENCE DAVIS, b. Private.

1507. JOSEPH[10] PERRY, JR. *(NELLIE FLORENCE BLANCHE[9] BROOKS, ALFRED LANGDON[8], DANIEL LANGDON[7], DANIEL[6], MARY[5] SPINNEY, JOHN[4], JOHN[3], JOHN[2], THOMAS[1])* was born Private. He married SHIRLEY Private. She was born Private.

Children of JOSEPH PERRY and SHIRLEY are:
  i.   ROBERT[11] PERRY, b. Private.
  ii. BEVERLY PERRY, b. Private; m. PAUL LIZOTTE, Private; b. Private.
  iii. MARILYN PERRY, b. Private.

1508. DORIS HEWITT[10] BROOKS *(LEROY ULMONT[9], ALFRED LANGDON[8], DANIEL LANGDON[7], DANIEL[6], MARY[5] SPINNEY, JOHN[4], JOHN[3], JOHN[2], THOMAS[1])* was born Private. She married EINAR ANDREW ANDERSON Private. He was born Private.

Children of DORIS BROOKS and EINAR ANDERSON are:
1662. i.   GAIL JUDITH[11] ANDERSON, b. Private.
1663. ii. STEPHEN BROOKS ANDERSON, b. Private.
       iii. CHARLES ROY ANDERSON, b. Private.

1509. ETHEL BERNICE[10] CASWELL *(ESSIE ROSE[9] BROOKS, ALFRED LANGDON[8], DANIEL LANGDON[7], DANIEL[6], MARY[5] SPINNEY, JOHN[4], JOHN[3], JOHN[2], THOMAS[1])* was born 08 Aug 1917, and died 23 Feb 1969. She married WILLIAM ALISON BROADHURST Private. He was born Private.

Children of ETHEL CASWELL and WILLIAM BROADHURST are:
       i.   WILLIAM ALISON[11] BROADHURST, JR., b. Private.
       ii. RICHARD BROADHURST, b. Private.
1664. iii. CHRISTINA BROADHURST, b. Private.
1665. iv. MARJORIE BROADHURST, b. Private.
1666. v.   THOMAS JOSEPH BROADHURST, b. Private.

1510. MARJORIE AUGUSTA[10] CASWELL *(ESSIE ROSE[9] BROOKS, ALFRED LANGDON[8], DANIEL LANGDON[7], DANIEL[6], MARY[5] SPINNEY, JOHN[4], JOHN[3], JOHN[2], THOMAS[1])* was born Private. She married CHARLES WINSOR DUNLAP Private. He was born Private.

Children of MARJORIE CASWELL and CHARLES DUNLAP are:
1667. i.   BARBARA MAY[11] DUNLAP, b. Private.
1668. ii. ELEANOR JEAN DUNLAP, b. Private.
1669. iii. GERALD CHARLES DUNLAP, b. Private.

1511. ANNIE HEWITT[10] CASWELL *(ESSIE ROSE[9] BROOKS, ALFRED LANGDON[8], DANIEL LANGDON[7], DANIEL[6], MARY[5] SPINNEY, JOHN[4], JOHN[3], JOHN[2], THOMAS[1])* was born Private. She married HERBERT S CUMMINGS, JR. Private. He was born Private.

Child of ANNIE CASWELL and HERBERT CUMMINGS is:
1670. i.   NANCY BROOKS[11] CUMMINGS, b. Private.

1512. WILLIAM LANGDON[10] JENNINGS *(ESSIE ROSE[9] BROOKS, ALFRED LANGDON[8], DANIEL LANGDON[7], DANIEL[6], MARY[5] SPINNEY, JOHN[4], JOHN[3], JOHN[2], THOMAS[1])* was born Private. He married ANNA BERGHAMMER Private. She was born Private.

Children of WILLIAM JENNINGS and ANNA BERGHAMMER are:
       i.   BARBARA ANNE[11] JENNINGS, b. Private; m. JOHN HERBERT GOODWIN, Private; b. Private.
       ii. SHIRLEY LORRAINE JENNINGS, b. Private.

1513. SAMUEL MURRAY[10] NELSON *(SAMUEL HERBERT[9], EMILY ANN[8] BROOKS, DANIEL LANGDON[7], DANIEL[6], MARY[5] SPINNEY, JOHN[4], JOHN[3], JOHN[2], THOMAS[1])* was born 20 May 1895, and died 01 Aug 1967. He married MARY TOBEY Private. She was born Private.

Children of SAMUEL NELSON and MARY TOBEY are:
      i.   FRANCES[11] NELSON, b. Private.
1671.   ii.   MARY EARLENE NELSON, b. Private.
1672.   iii. EMILY ALBERTA NELSON, b. Private.
1673.   iv. BARBARA NELSON, b. Private.
1674.   v.   SAMUEL MURRAY NELSON, JR., b. Private.
1675.   vi. THEODORE MACMILLAIN NELSON, b. Private.

1514. CLARA BELLE[10] LEACH *(ADA SYRENA[9] VARNEY, CLARA FRANCES[8] BROOKS, DANIEL LANGDON[7], DANIEL[6], MARY[5] SPINNEY, JOHN[4], JOHN[3], JOHN[2], THOMAS[1])* was born 14 Jul 1890, and died 26 Jul 1967. She married J. MARK O'MALLEY.

Children of CLARA LEACH and J. O'MALLEY are:
1676.   i.   STANTON GILBERT[11] O'MALLEY, b. 17 Jan 1911; d. 28 Jul 1967.
1677.   ii.   SYLVIA MARGUERITE O'MALLEY, b. Private.
1678.   iii. FREDERICK VARNEY O'MALLEY, b. Private.

1515. FRANK EDWIN[10] LEACH *(ADA SYRENA[9] VARNEY, CLARA FRANCES[8] BROOKS, DANIEL LANGDON[7], DANIEL[6], MARY[5] SPINNEY, JOHN[4], JOHN[3], JOHN[2], THOMAS[1])* was born 02 Aug 1894, and died 03 Jan 1968. He married (1) EMMA SHEVENELLE 24 May 1916. He married (2) MARY DEMARES 09 Sep 1922. She was born Private. He married (3) INA M MANSON Aug 1963, daughter of CLINTON MANSON and MYRTIE McKENNEY. She was born 1896.

Children of FRANK LEACH and EMMA SHEVENELLE are:
      i.   ROBERT EDWIN[11] LEACH, b. 1918; d. 1918.
     ii.   DONALD GEORGE LEACH, b. Private.

Children of FRANK LEACH and MARY DEMARES are:
     iii. RALPH[11] LEACH, b. 1923; d. 1923.
1679.   iv. IDA LOUISE LEACH, b. Private.
1680.   v.   GEORGE EDWIN LEACH, b. Private.
1681.   vi. ELEANOR MAE LEACH, b. Private.

1516. SADIE ADA[10] LEACH *(ADA SYRENA[9] VARNEY, CLARA FRANCES[8] BROOKS, DANIEL LANGDON[7], DANIEL[6], MARY[5] SPINNEY, JOHN[4], JOHN[3], JOHN[2], THOMAS[1])* was born Private. She married (1) CLYDE HARVEY HILL Private. She married (2) PEARLIE STEVENS Private. She married (3) GEORGE L CHAPMAN Private.

Children of SADIE LEACH and CLYDE HILL are:
1682.   i.   MADELINE SADIE[11] HILL, b. Private.
     ii.   JULIA FRANCES HILL, b. Private.

1517. LILLIAN M[10] SPINNEY *(ARTHUR ROSCOE[9], ALFRED[8], SYLVESTER[7], FRANCIS[6], GEORGE PETTEGREW[5], JOHN[4], JOHN[3], JOHN[2], THOMAS[1])* was born Aug 1897. She married PAYNE.

Child of LILLIAN SPINNEY and PAYNE is:
1683.   i.   MARTHA[11] PAYNE.

1518. REGINALD I[10] SPINNEY *(ARTHUR ROSCOE[9], ALFRED[8], SYLVESTER[7], FRANCIS[6], GEORGE PETTEGREW[5], JOHN[4], JOHN[3], JOHN[2], THOMAS[1])* was born 16 May 1903. He married CAROLINE BALISDELL.

Notes for CAROLINE BALISDELL:
Caroline S. Spinney
ELIOT, Maine - Caroline S. Spinney, 92, of Main Street, died Saturday, June 16, 2001, at York Hospital.
Born in Kittery on Dec. 9, 1908, she was a daughter of Edwin and Ethel (Staples) Blaisdell. She attended Kittery schools for a time before moving to Eliot and attending schools there. She graduated from Eliot High School, and

then attended Portsmouth Normal School, where she received her teachers training.

She and her husband for more than 71 years, Reginald I. Spinney Sr., operated the Reginald I. Spinney Construction Co. in Eliot. She maintained the office aspect of the business, ensuring the books and other necessary paperwork were always in order.

She attended and was active in the South Eliot United Methodist Church, enjoying close friendships with many of the parishioners in the Ladies Circle and other groups within the church.

She was a member of the Ladies Forum in Eliot. She enjoyed playing the violin, sewing and cooking, and was accomplished in all of them.

In addition to her husband, survivors include her sons, Reginald I. Spinney Jr. and his wife Dorothy Sutton Spinney of Groton, Conn., and Brian Spinney and his wife Norma Jean Spinney of Eliot; grandchildren, Carolyn Simmonds, Kathryn Sullivan, Susan Drew, Elaine Devirgilio, Park S. Spinney, Donna L. Tice, Michael Spinney and Kevin N. Spinney; 10 great-grandchildren; and her daughter-in-law Irene Spinney.

She was predeceased by her son, Stephen M. Spinney, and her sister, Gertrude Blaisdell.

Children of REGINALD SPINNEY and CAROLINE BALISDELL are:
    i.   REGINALD[11] SPINNEY, m. DOROTHY SUTTON.

        Notes for DOROTHY SUTTON:
        Dorothy S. Spinney
        GROTON, Conn. - Dorothy S. Spinney, 69, of 41 Blueberry Hill Road, died Sunday, Jan. 27, 2002, at her residence.
        She was born in San Diego, Calif., on March 9, 1932, the daughter of Park and Doris Conrad Sutton. She married Reginald I. Spinney Jr., on June 28, 1953, in York, Maine.
        She dedicated her whole life to her family.
        Besides her husband, she is survived by five sons, a daughter, and 15 grandchildren.

    ii.   BRIAN SPINNEY.
    iii. STEPHEN M SPINNEY.

1519. NORMAN E[10] SPINNEY (*MILO[9], ALFRED[8], SYLVESTER[7], FRANCIS[6], GEORGE PETTEGREW[5], JOHN[4], JOHN[3], JOHN[2], THOMAS[1]*) was born Dec 1899, and died Aft. 1920. He married GRACE DIXON 15 Jul 1917, daughter of MELVIN DIXON and GRACE. She was born 1900, and died Aft. 1920.

Children of NORMAN SPINNEY and GRACE DIXON are:
        i.   ALETHA[11] SPINNEY, b. 1920; m. JAMES NORTON.
1684.   ii. NORMAN K SPINNEY, b. 09 Mar 1922; d. 19 Apr 2000, Exeter New Hampsire.
        iii. DONALD E SPINNEY, b. 1924.

1520. PHYLIS[10] SPINNEY (*MILO[9], ALFRED[8], SYLVESTER[7], FRANCIS[6], GEORGE PETTEGREW[5], JOHN[4], JOHN[3], JOHN[2], THOMAS[1]*) was born 1907. She married IRVING MITCHELL. He was born 1902.

Child of PHYLIS SPINNEY and IRVING MITCHELL is:
    i.   GLORIA[11] MITCHELL, b. 30 Jun 1930.

        Notes for GLORIA MITCHELL:
        Gloria J. Babkirk

        BIDDEFORD, Maine - Gloria J. Babkirk, 73, of Eliot, died on Tuesday, March 30, 2004, at Southern Maine Medical Center in Biddeford, after a long illness.

        Gloria was born in Portsmouth on June 30, 1930, the daughter of Irving and Phyllis (Spinney) Mitchell. She lived in the Seacoast her entire life.

        She was a member of the New England Pony Owners and Breeders Association and loved anything to do with horses.

        Gloria was predeceased by her husband, Cecil Babkirk.

She is survived by her son, Leonard Babkirk and wife Sue of Eliot; a daughter, Donna Babkirk of Hampton; three sisters, Gail English and husband William, Sandra Wirth and husband Herbert, and Glenda Perkins and husband Arthur (all of Eliot); five grandchildren; three great-grandchildren; and many nieces and nephews.

1521. MARION L[10] SPINNEY (*ARNOLD CLAYTON[9], ALBERT LESTER[8], SYLVESTER[7], FRANCIS[6], GEORGE PETTEGREW[5], JOHN[4], JOHN[3], JOHN[2], THOMAS[1]*) was born 1919, and died 1981. She married WILLIAM DOW.

Children of MARION SPINNEY and WILLIAM DOW are:
- i. KENNETH[11] DOW, d. 1997.
- ii. ARNOLD R DOW.
- iii. JANICE DOW, m. BROWN.
- iv. ANDREA DOW, m. ROGERS.
- v. DOUGLASS DOW.
- vi. DENNIS DOW.
- vii. DENISE DOW.
- viii. WILLIAM R DOW.

1522. DOROTHY[10] SPINNEY (*ADVILLE A[9], AMMI ADVILLE[8], FRANCIS LEMUEL[7], FRANCIS[6], GEORGE PETTEGREW[5], JOHN[4], JOHN[3], JOHN[2], THOMAS[1]*) was born 1917. She married DELWYN MANSON.

Child of DOROTHY SPINNEY and DELWYN MANSON is:
1685.   i. JUDITH IRENE[11] MANSON.

1523. FLORENCE[10] TITUS (*GRACE M.[9] HUNTRESS, MARY EVA[8] DIXON, LYDIA N.[7] TETHERLY, CHARLES[6], SAMUEL[5], WILLIAM[4], MERCY[3] SPINNEY, JOHN[2], THOMAS[1]*) was born Private. She married VERNON O. SEARLES Private. He was born Abt. 1905 in Cape Neddick, ME, and died 29 Mar 1995 in York Harbour, ME.

Children of FLORENCE TITUS and VERNON SEARLES are:
- i. VERNON T.[11] SEARLES, b. Private.
- ii. ERNEST O. SEARLES, b. Private.

1524. JOHN BERKLEY[10] WALKER (*FLORENCE WINIFRED[9] HUNTRESS, MARY EVA[8] DIXON, LYDIA N.[7] TETHERLY, CHARLES[6], SAMUEL[5], WILLIAM[4], MERCY[3] SPINNEY, JOHN[2], THOMAS[1]*) was born 30 Jun 1910 in South Eliot. MA, and died 17 Jun 1985 in Holyoke, MA. He married ESTHER AGNES HOAR 01 Nov 1929 in Enfield, Ct.. She was born 23 Feb 1912 in Holyoke, MA, and died 20 Jan 1969 in Holyoke, MA.

Children of JOHN WALKER and ESTHER HOAR are:
1686.   i. DAVID BERKLEY[11] WALKER, b. Private.
1687.   ii. JOHN COYLE WALKER, b. Private.
1688.   iii. BRUCE HUNTRESS WALKER, b. Private.
1689.   iv. DANIEL HEYWOOD WALKER, b. Private.
1690.   v. KATHERINE MARY WALKER, b. Private.

1525. IRENE[10] WALKER (*FLORENCE WINIFRED[9] HUNTRESS, MARY EVA[8] DIXON, LYDIA N.[7] TETHERLY, CHARLES[6], SAMUEL[5], WILLIAM[4], MERCY[3] SPINNEY, JOHN[2], THOMAS[1]*) was born 21 Sep 1915 in Uxbridge, MA, and died 02 Jan 1993 in Oxford, MA. She married ARMAND GROISE 15 Sep 1940 in Chicopee, Mass., 232 Chicopee Str. He died 18 Dec 1992 in Oxford, MA.

Child of IRENE WALKER and ARMAND GROISE is:
- i. CAROL[11] GROISE, b. Private.

1526. HORACE ALLAN[10] WALKER (*FLORENCE WINIFRED[9] HUNTRESS, MARY EVA[8] DIXON, LYDIA N.[7] TETHERLY, CHARLES[6], SAMUEL[5], WILLIAM[4], MERCY[3] SPINNEY, JOHN[2], THOMAS[1]*) was born 11 Jul 1920 in Springfield, MA, and died 25 Dec 1985 in Springfield, MA. He married (1) DOROTHY LAFOND Private. She was born Private. He married (2) RUTH PRITCHARD Private. She was born Private. He married (3) SHIRLEY RIETH Private. She was born Private.

Child of HORACE WALKER and DOROTHY LAFOND is:
    i.   DAVID[11] WALKER, b. Private.

Children of HORACE WALKER and RUTH PRITCHARD are:
    ii. MARK[11] WALKER, b. Private.
    iii. ALLAN WALKER, b. Private.

1527. CHARLES EDWIN[10] WALKER *(FLORENCE WINIFRED[9] HUNTRESS, MARY EVA[8] DIXON, LYDIA N.[7] TETHERLY, CHARLES[6], SAMUEL[5], WILLIAM[4], MERCY[3] SPINNEY, JOHN[2], THOMAS[1])* was born 15 Jun 1922 in Springfield, MA, and died 03 Apr 1984 in Agawam, MA. He married DOROTHY ROSNER Private. She was born Private.

Children of CHARLES WALKER and DOROTHY ROSNER are:
    i.   ROBERT[11] WALKER, b. Private.
    ii. KENNETH WALKER, b. Private.
    iii. RICHARD WALKER, b. Private.

1528. KENNETH DAVID[10] WALKER *(FLORENCE WINIFRED[9] HUNTRESS, MARY EVA[8] DIXON, LYDIA N.[7] TETHERLY, CHARLES[6], SAMUEL[5], WILLIAM[4], MERCY[3] SPINNEY, JOHN[2], THOMAS[1])* was born Private. He married DOROTHY DUBIE Private. She was born Private.

Children of KENNETH WALKER and DOROTHY DUBIE are:
1691.   i.   KENNETH DWIGHT[11] WALKER, b. Private.
1692.   ii. JUNE WALKER, b. Private.

1529. VEDA VIVIAN[10] CAHILL *(LILLIAN MAUD[9] LYDSTON, ARTHUR FRANCIS[8], FRANCIS ARTHUR[7], WILLIAM[6], WEYMOUTH[5], ABIGAIL[4] SPINNEY, ANDREW[3], JOHN[2], THOMAS[1])* was born 30 May 1892 in Indian Valley, Ca, and died Sep 1984 in Sacramento, Ca. She married JAMES EDWARD CLIFFORD 02 Jun 1909 in Maryville, Ca, son of CHRISTOPHER CLIFFORD and HARRIET JAMES.

Child of VEDA CAHILL and JAMES CLIFFORD is:
1693.   i.   DOROTHY LILLIAN[11] CLIFFORD, b. 26 Dec 1909, Sacramento, CA; d. 24 Dec 1936, Sacramento, CA.

1530. ALMA FRANCES[10] WELLNER *(ALMA EDITH[9] SPINNEY, ALLISON FAIRBANKS[8], HIRAM[7], DAVID[6], ISAAC[5], JOHN[4], JOHN[3], JOHN[2], THOMAS[1])* was born 30 Dec 1906. She married SETH CARLETON SPRAGUE.

Children of ALMA WELLNER and SETH SPRAGUE are:
    i.   EDITH LOUISE[11] SPRAGUE, b. 18 Aug 1925.
    ii. HERBERT ALLISON SPRAGUE, b. 18 Aug 1927.
    iii. BARBARA FRANCES SPRAGUE, b. 05 Oct 1929.
    iv. GEORGE CARLETON SPRAGUE, b. 20 Jun 1931.
1694.   v.   DAVID MYLES SPRAGUE, b. 16 Jul 1934.

1531. EILEEN MARTHA[10] FORD *(JAMES ELMER[9], LAURA MAE[8] SPINNEY, STILLMAN[7], JOSEPH[6], JACOB[5], JOHN[4], JOHN[3], JOHN[2], THOMAS[1])* was born Private. She married ADELARD ST. ONGE Private. He was born Private.

Children of EILEEN FORD and ADELARD ST. ONGE are:
    i.   JEAN ANN[11] ST. ONGE, b. Private.
1695.   ii. EILEEN MARY ST. ONGE, b. Private.
    iii. JOHN KENNEDY ST. ONGE, b. Private.
    iv. ROBERT ADELARD ST. ONGE, b. Private; m. AMY LUCILLE WELLSO, Private; b. Private.

1532. CLAIRE THERESA[10] FORD *(JAMES ELMER[9], LAURA MAE[8] SPINNEY, STILLMAN[7], JOSEPH[6], JACOB[5], JOHN[4],*

JOHN[3], *JOHN[2]*, *THOMAS[1]*) was born Private. She married RAYMOND EDGAR BUTLER Private. He was born 26 Dec 1933 in Newark, NJ, and died 07 Oct 1996 in Waltham, MA.

Children of CLAIRE FORD and RAYMOND BUTLER are:
1696.   i.   RAYMOND EDGAR[11] BUTLER, b. Private.
1697.   ii.   JOANNE MARIE BUTLER, b. Private.
        iii. JAMES EDWARD BUTLER, b. Private.

1533. ROBERT EDWARD[10] FORD (*JAMES ELMER[9]*, *LAURA MAE[8]* SPINNEY, *STILLMAN[7]*, *JOSEPH[6]*, *JACOB[5]*, *JOHN[4]*, *JOHN[3]*, *JOHN[2]*, *THOMAS[1]*) was born Private. He married HELEN NORINE COUTURE Private. She was born Private.

Children of ROBERT FORD and HELEN COUTURE are:
1698.   i.   BRENDA JEAN[11] FORD, b. Private.
        ii.   DENNIS JOHN FORD, b. Private.
1699.   iii. ROBERT EDWARD FORD, b. Private.

1534. PAULINE DOROTHY[10] FORD (*JAMES ELMER[9]*, *LAURA MAE[8]* SPINNEY, *STILLMAN[7]*, *JOSEPH[6]*, *JACOB[5]*, *JOHN[4]*, *JOHN[3]*, *JOHN[2]*, *THOMAS[1]*) was born Private. She married (1) CHARLES CLARK Private. He was born 31 Mar 1928 in Watertown, MA, and died 06 Apr 1996 in Florida. She married (2) JOHN FRANKLIN BALES Private. He was born Private.

Children of PAULINE FORD and CHARLES CLARK are:
        i.   DANA WINGATE[11] CLARK, b. Private.
1700.   ii.   CHERYL ANN CLARK, b. Private.
        iii. JEFFREY FORD CLARK, b. Private.

1535. MARION ANGELA[10] FORD (*JAMES ELMER[9]*, *LAURA MAE[8]* SPINNEY, *STILLMAN[7]*, *JOSEPH[6]*, *JACOB[5]*, *JOHN[4]*, *JOHN[3]*, *JOHN[2]*, *THOMAS[1]*) was born Private. She married (1) SCOTT CRAWFORD FULTON Private. He was born 05 May 1935 in Cambridge, MA, and died 30 Jan 1961 in Newton, MA. She married (2) JOHN RICHARD ASTE Private. He was born Private.

Children of MARION FORD and SCOTT FULTON are:
        i.   KIM PATRICIA[11] FULTON, b. Private; m. JAMES PATRICK MARCHAND, Private; b. Private.
        ii.   SCOTT CRAWFORD FULTON, b. Private.
1701.   iii. PAMELA JEAN FULTON, b. Private.

Children of MARION FORD and JOHN ASTE are:
1702.   iv. LINDA MARIE[11] ASTE, b. Private.
1703.   v.   BETHANY ANGELA ASTE, b. Private.

1536. JOAN ELIZABETH[10] FORD (*JAMES ELMER[9]*, *LAURA MAE[8]* SPINNEY, *STILLMAN[7]*, *JOSEPH[6]*, *JACOB[5]*, *JOHN[4]*, *JOHN[3]*, *JOHN[2]*, *THOMAS[1]*) was born Private. She married JOHN THOMAS CAPPELLUCCI Private. He was born Private.

Children of JOAN FORD and JOHN CAPPELLUCCI are:
        i.   SUSAN JOAN[11] CAPPELLUCCI, b. 24 Jun 1954, Brighton, MA; d. 27 Nov 1975, Erving, MA.
1704.   ii.   KATHLEEN ANNE CAPPELLUCCI, b. Private.
1705.   iii. MICHAEL JOHN CAPPELLUCCI, b. Private.
        iv. JOHN THOMAS CAPPELLUCCI, b. Private; m. BETH DEGEER, Private; b. Private.
1706.   v.   LAURA MAE CAPPELLUCCI, b. Private.
1707.   vi. PATRICIA MARIE CAPPELLUCCI, b. Private.
1708.   vii. JAMES EDWARD CAPPELLUCCI, b. Private.

1537. JOHN TIMOTHY[10] FORD (*JAMES ELMER[9]*, *LAURA MAE[8]* SPINNEY, *STILLMAN[7]*, *JOSEPH[6]*, *JACOB[5]*, *JOHN[4]*, *JOHN[3]*, *JOHN[2]*, *THOMAS[1]*) was born Private. He married FRANCES CANTONE Private. She was born Private.

Children of JOHN FORD and FRANCES CANTONE are:
      i.   KELLY JEAN[11] FORD, b. Private; m. STEPHEN JOHN MCHALE, Private; b. Private.
1709.   ii.   JOHN TIMOTHY FORD, b. Private.

1538. ELEANOR MAE[10] FORD *(JAMES ELMER[9], LAURA MAE[8] SPINNEY, STILLMAN[7], JOSEPH[6], JACOB[5], JOHN[4], JOHN[3], JOHN[2], THOMAS[1])* was born Private. She married WILLIAM JOHN ROONEY Private. He was born Private.

Children of ELEANOR FORD and WILLIAM ROONEY are:
1710.   i.   JAN MARIE[11] ROONEY, b. Private.
      ii.   SANDRA JEAN ROONEY, b. Private.
     iii.   WILLIAM JOHN ROONEY, b. Private.
     iv.   KAREN MAE ROONEY, b. Private.

1539. JANET MARGARET[10] FORD *(JAMES ELMER[9], LAURA MAE[8] SPINNEY, STILLMAN[7], JOSEPH[6], JACOB[5], JOHN[4], JOHN[3], JOHN[2], THOMAS[1])* was born Private. She married (1) THOMAS H. MARCH Private. He was born Private. She married (2) WILLIAM WARREN STUDLEY Private. He was born Private.

Child of JANET FORD and THOMAS MARCH is:
1711.   i.   CHRISTINE THERESA[11] MARCH, b. Private.

1540. ADDISON WESLEY[10] SPINNEY *(CLINTON[9], WESLEY F[8], JAMES[7], JAMES[6], JACOB[5], JOHN[4], JOHN[3], JOHN[2], THOMAS[1])* was born 1923. He married MARION HUBBARD.

Child of ADDISON SPINNEY and MARION HUBBARD is:
      i.   TERRANCE[11] SPINNEY, Adopted child.

1541. BARBARA[10] SPINNEY *(FRANK WESLEY[9], WESLEY F[8], JAMES[7], JAMES[6], JACOB[5], JOHN[4], JOHN[3], JOHN[2], THOMAS[1])* She married ROBERT COOK.

Children of BARBARA SPINNEY and ROBERT COOK are:
      i.   DAVID[11] COOK.
      ii.   DEAN COOK.
     iii.   DONALD COOK.

1542. JOYCE[10] SPINNEY *(FRANK WESLEY[9], WESLEY F[8], JAMES[7], JAMES[6], JACOB[5], JOHN[4], JOHN[3], JOHN[2], THOMAS[1])* She married RICHARD DEL MONICO.

Children of JOYCE SPINNEY and RICHARD DEL MONICO are:
      i.   ROBIN[11] DEL MONICO.
      ii.   LORI DEL MONICO.

1543. LOVETT E[10] SPINNEY *(LOVETT ELDRIDGE[9], WESLEY F[8], JAMES[7], JAMES[6], JACOB[5], JOHN[4], JOHN[3], JOHN[2], THOMAS[1])* was born 30 Sep 1919, and died 08 Sep 1994. He married (1) EMMA GRACE HICKS. He married (2) AGNES M DEBENEDICTIS.

Children of LOVETT SPINNEY and EMMA HICKS are:
      i.   PETER E[11] SPINNEY, b. 19 Jan 1943.
      ii.   SUSAN SPINNEY, b. 1945.
     iii.   SHARYN SPINNEY, b. 1945.

1544. PRESCOTT Y[10] SPINNEY *(PRESCOTT YOUNGER[9], ADEN CLAYTON[8], WHITFIELD[7], JAMES[6], JACOB[5], JOHN[4], JOHN[3], JOHN[2], THOMAS[1])* was born 12 Mar 1925. He married DORIS ELLEN MOREY.

Children of PRESCOTT SPINNEY and DORIS MOREY are:
      i.   PATRICIA ELLEN[11] SPINNEY, b. 15 Jul 1947.

ii.   DAVID RICHARD SPINNEY, b. 25 Aug 1948.

1545. WILLIAM H[10] SPINNEY *(PRESCOTT YOUNGER[9], ADEN CLAYTON[8], WHITFIELD[7], JAMES[6], JACOB[5], JOHN[4], JOHN[3], JOHN[2], THOMAS[1])* was born Feb 1926.

Child of WILLIAM H SPINNEY is:
    i.   CHERYL[11] SPINNEY.

1546. FREDRICK[10] SHOLDS *(FRED ALLISON[9], CONSTANCE[8] SPINNEY, JOSIAH[7], SOLOMAN ROBERT[6], BENJAMIN[5], JOHN[4], JOHN[3], JOHN[2], THOMAS[1])*

Child of FREDRICK SHOLDS is:
    i.   ALLYSON[11] SHOLDS, m. DAVID THAYER.

1547. RHONDA RENE[10] SPINNEY *(EUGENE ROBERT[9], LYMAN EUGENE[8], BOWMAN E[7], EDWARD[6], DANIEL[5], JOHN[4], JOHN[3], JOHN[2], THOMAS[1])* She married BRUCE KING.

Children of RHONDA SPINNEY and BRUCE KING are:
    i.   BRITTANY MICHEILLE[11] BUFKIN.
    ii.   KRISTINA RENE THOMPSON.

1548. KEITH EUGENE[10] SPINNEY *(EUGENE ROBERT[9], LYMAN EUGENE[8], BOWMAN E[7], EDWARD[6], DANIEL[5], JOHN[4], JOHN[3], JOHN[2], THOMAS[1])* He married PATSY JEAN GABLES.

Children of KEITH SPINNEY and PATSY GABLES are:
    i.   HOLLY RENE[11] SPINNEY.
    ii.   CHRISTOPHERHEATH SPINNEY.

1549. ROBERT GLEN[10] SPINNEY *(EUGENE ROBERT[9], LYMAN EUGENE[8], BOWMAN E[7], EDWARD[6], DANIEL[5], JOHN[4], JOHN[3], JOHN[2], THOMAS[1])* He married DEBRA.

Child of ROBERT SPINNEY and DEBRA is:
    i.   SARAH[11] SPINNEY.

1550. DANA KEVIN[10] SPINNEY *(EUGENE ROBERT[9], LYMAN EUGENE[8], BOWMAN E[7], EDWARD[6], DANIEL[5], JOHN[4], JOHN[3], JOHN[2], THOMAS[1])* He married CLAUDIA ELANA CASTILIO.

Child of DANA SPINNEY and CLAUDIA CASTILIO is:
    i.   KEVIN BENJAMIN[11] SPINNEY.

1551. DONALD STEPHEN[10] SPINNEY *(DONALD N[9], LYMAN EUGENE[8], BOWMAN E[7], EDWARD[6], DANIEL[5], JOHN[4], JOHN[3], JOHN[2], THOMAS[1])* was born 26 Feb 1957. He married SANDRA RICHARDSON LANDRY.

Children of DONALD SPINNEY and SANDRA LANDRY are:
1712.	i.	HEIDI JEAN[11] SPINNEY, b. 24 Oct 1975.
1713.	ii.	KATIE MAE SPINNEY.
	iii.	DONALD STEPHEN SPINNEY.
	iv.	BARRIE MICHAEL SPINNEY.
	v.	JAMES BRAVERMAN SPINNEY.
1714.	vi.	APRIL LEE LANDRY SPINNEY.
	vii.	ROBERT PAUL LANDRY SPINNEY.
	viii.	DAWN MARIE LANDRY SPINNEY.
	ix.	TABATHA DAISEY LANDRY SPINNEY.

1552. SUSAN RUTH[10] SPINNEY *(DONALD N[9], LYMAN EUGENE[8], BOWMAN E[7], EDWARD[6], DANIEL[5], JOHN[4], JOHN[3],*

JOHN[2], THOMAS[1]) was born 26 Sep 1958. She married JACOB THOMAS SNOW.

Children of SUSAN SPINNEY and JACOB SNOW are:
-     i.   ERIN LEE SPINNEY[11] SNOW.
1715.   ii.   JOCOB THOMAS SNOW.

1553. DANIEL NEIL[10] SPINNEY *(DONALD N[9], LYMAN EUGENE[8], BOWMAN E[7], EDWARD[6], DANIEL[5], JOHN[4], JOHN[3], JOHN[2], THOMAS[1])* was born 18 Mar 1962. He married DONNA MARIE EASON.

Children of DANIEL SPINNEY and DONNA EASON are:
-     i.   JASON NEIL[11] SPINNEY.
-    ii.   DEREK RYAN SPINNEY.

1554. ALYSON MAE[10] SPINNEY *(DONALD N[9], LYMAN EUGENE[8], BOWMAN E[7], EDWARD[6], DANIEL[5], JOHN[4], JOHN[3], JOHN[2], THOMAS[1])* was born 02 Oct 1965. She married MARK DOUGLAS MELCHER.

Children of ALYSON SPINNEY and MARK MELCHER are:
-     i.   TYLER DOUGLAS[11] MELCHER.
-    ii.   ASHLEY MARGARET MELCHER.

1555. TAMMY LEE[10] SPINNEY *(JACK L[9], LYMAN EUGENE[8], BOWMAN E[7], EDWARD[6], DANIEL[5], JOHN[4], JOHN[3], JOHN[2], THOMAS[1])* She married JAMES CHOULNARD.

Children of TAMMY SPINNEY and JAMES CHOULNARD are:
-     i.   DANNEILLE[11] RATTE.
-    ii.   DEVIN CHOULNARD.
-   iii.   SAMANTHA CHOULNARD.

1556. SUSAN ANN[10] SPINNEY *(JACK L[9], LYMAN EUGENE[8], BOWMAN E[7], EDWARD[6], DANIEL[5], JOHN[4], JOHN[3], JOHN[2], THOMAS[1])* was born Abt. 1960. She married MICHAEL JAMES ROCKWOOD.

Children of SUSAN SPINNEY and MICHAEL ROCKWOOD are:
-     i.   KRISTEN LEE SPINNEY[11] ROCKWOOD.
-    ii.   KELLY MICHELLE ROCKWOOD.
-   iii.   MICHAEL JAMES ROCKWOOD.
-   iv.   JOSHUS THOMAS ROCKWOOD.

1557. JACK LYMAN[10] SPINNEY *(JACK L[9], LYMAN EUGENE[8], BOWMAN E[7], EDWARD[6], DANIEL[5], JOHN[4], JOHN[3], JOHN[2], THOMAS[1])* He married STACY THOMPSON.

Child of JACK SPINNEY and STACY THOMPSON is:
-     i.   KYLIE BRIE[11] SPINNEY.

1558. DENISE[10] SPINNEY *(BRUCE[9], LYMAN EUGENE[8], BOWMAN E[7], EDWARD[6], DANIEL[5], JOHN[4], JOHN[3], JOHN[2], THOMAS[1])* She married DENIS DORGAN.

Children of DENISE SPINNEY and DENIS DORGAN are:
-     i.   CASEY ELIZABETH[11] DORGAN.
-    ii.   ALIX MARIE DORGAN.
-   iii.   DENIS JOHN DORGAN.
-   iv.   CHLOE LYNNE DORGAN.

1559. DOREEN[10] SPINNEY *(BRUCE[9], LYMAN EUGENE[8], BOWMAN E[7], EDWARD[6], DANIEL[5], JOHN[4], JOHN[3], JOHN[2], THOMAS[1])* She married JOHN JOSEPH MANOOGIN.

Children of DOREEN SPINNEY and JOHN MANOOGIN are:
  i.   JAMIE LYN[11] MANOOGIN.
  ii. SAMANTHA MARIE MANOOGIN.
  iii. KYLE ANNE MANOOGIN.

1560. LYNNE[10] SPINNEY *(BRUCE[9], LYMAN EUGENE[8], BOWMAN E[7], EDWARD[6], DANIEL[5], JOHN[4], JOHN[3], JOHN[2], THOMAS[1])* She married FRANK FELIZE.

Children of LYNNE SPINNEY and FRANK FELIZE are:
  i.   LYNDSEY[11] FELIZE.
  ii. RYAN FELIZE.

1561. BRUCE ALLEN SPINNEY[10] MCGILVERY *(BRUCE[9] SPINNEY, LYMAN EUGENE[8], BOWMAN E[7], EDWARD[6], DANIEL[5], JOHN[4], JOHN[3], JOHN[2], THOMAS[1])* He married BERNARDITA SIBONGA SEDANO.

Children of BRUCE MCGILVERY and BERNARDITA SEDANO are:
  i.   IRENE ANNE[11] MCGILVERY.
  ii. CHRISTOPHER ALEN MCGILVERY.
  iii. HEATHER MCGILVERY.

1562. MYRA[10] FULLER *(ALICE MARY[9] HUNT, WILLIAM SPINNEY[8], ROXANNA BURGESS[7] SPINNEY, NICHOLAS[6], JOHN[5], JOHN[4], ANDREW[3], JOHN[2], THOMAS[1])* was born 05 May 1893 in Malden, MA, and died Oct 1983 in Melrose, MA. She married NELSON LORD ALLEN 18 Oct 1916 in Malden, MA. He was born 27 Aug 1883 in Malden, MA, and died 12 Aug 1979 in Melrose, MA.

Children of MYRA FULLER and NELSON ALLEN are:
  i.   ROBERT LORD[11] ALLEN, b. 19 Nov 1921, Melrose, MA; d. 06 Feb 1922, Melrose, MA.
1716. ii. JOSEPH KIRKWOOD ALLEN, b. Private.
1717. iii. RICHARD FULLER ALLEN, b. Private.

1563. LOUIS BEVIER[10] SPINNEY *(LOUIS BEVIER[9], JOSEPH OAKMAN[8], WILLIAM M[7], NICHOLAS[6], JOHN[5], JOHN[4], ANDREW[3], JOHN[2], THOMAS[1])* was born 16 Mar 1905.

Child of LOUIS BEVIER SPINNEY is:
1718. i. BRUCE H[11] SPINNEY, b. 15 Nov 1941, Salt Lake City, UT.

1564. FLORENCE MAY[10] BRADDOCK *(JULIA A[9] SPINNEY, WILLIAM QUINMAN[8], ROBERT CURTIS[7], NICHOLAS[6], JOHN[5], JOHN[4], ANDREW[3], JOHN[2], THOMAS[1])* was born 21 Mar 1891 in Brooks, ME, and died 23 Jan 1977 in Belfast, ME. She married (1) CARL HANSEN. She married (2) LEWIS SEAVEY AUSPLAND 06 Jul 1908 in Belfast, ME. He was born 1888 in Searsport, ME, and died 1953 in Portland, ME.

Child of FLORENCE BRADDOCK and LEWIS AUSPLAND is:
1719. i. CLARENCE GORDON[11] AUSPLAND, b. 19 Mar 1910, Belfast, ME; d. 06 Aug 1984, Portland, ME.

1565. ROSAMOND[10] SPINNEY *(CHESTER RAYMOND[9], CHARLES S[8], ZINA H[7], DAVID[6], JOHN[5], JOHN[4], ANDREW[3], JOHN[2], THOMAS[1])* was born 19 Apr 1912 in Somerville, MA, and died Nov 1982. She married WILLIAM ABORN SPINNEY 28 Sep 1936, son of WILLIAM SPINNEY and SARAH PRATT. He was born 05 Jun 1904 in Boston, MA, and died 01 Feb 1968 in Mededith, NH.

Children are listed above under (1388) William Aborn Spinney.

1566. RENA MAE[10] SPINNEY *(ERNEST L[9], ELIJAH M[8], ZINA H[7], EPHRAIM[6], JOHN[5], JOHN[4], ANDREW[3], JOHN[2], THOMAS[1])* was born 16 Sep 1907, and died 13 Sep 1978 in Wyoming. She married HENRY WASINGTON BAIRD 1929.

Notes for RENA MAE SPINNEY:

Enid, or Rena Mae, as she was known most of her life, was adopted by her aunt and uncle at some point for no known reason. It is possible that it occurred due to being born out of wedlock, although her parents eventually married two years after her birth. It is evident that she was adopted before the marriage, or at least at a very young age, for she was not aware of the adoption until she was 46.

Children of RENA SPINNEY and HENRY BAIRD are:
     i.   RENA MARIE[11] BAIRD, b. 1934, Powell Wyoming; m. ART GUTHRIE.
    ii.   ESTELLA BAIRD, m. HOWARD.
   iii.   ROBERT BAIRD.

1567. LIONEL LEONARD[10] CARTER *(ADA ESTHER[9] RICHARDS, SUSAN AUGUSTA RUBY[8] BURCE, JOHN CALVIN[7], RACHEL[6] OLIVER, JANE[5] SPINNEY, JOHN[4], ANDREW[3], JOHN[2], THOMAS[1])* was born 30 Dec 1905 in Anacortes, WA, and died 22 Apr 1994 in Marysville, WA. He married (1) ORA KING 1932. She died 1988. He married (2) HAZEL LUCE Private. She was born Private.

Child of LIONEL CARTER and ORA KING is:
1720.   i.   GILBERT[11] CARTER, b. Private.

Child of LIONEL CARTER and HAZEL LUCE is:
1721.   ii.   DONNA JEAN[11] CARTER, b. Private.

1568. MARGARET RUBY[10] CARTER *(ADA ESTHER[9] RICHARDS, SUSAN AUGUSTA RUBY[8] BURCE, JOHN CALVIN[7], RACHEL[6] OLIVER, JANE[5] SPINNEY, JOHN[4], ANDREW[3], JOHN[2], THOMAS[1])* was born 29 Dec 1907 in Snohomish, WA, and died 03 Jan 1988 in Everett, WA. She married (1) MR. KEIP Private. He was born Private. She married (2) FRED CRUMRINE Private. He was born Private.

Children of MARGARET CARTER and FRED CRUMRINE are:
     i.   LOIS[11] CRUMRINE, b. Private.
    ii.   MARGARET CRUMRINE, b. Private.

1569. MILDRED ADA[10] CARTER *(ADA ESTHER[9] RICHARDS, SUSAN AUGUSTA RUBY[8] BURCE, JOHN CALVIN[7], RACHEL[6] OLIVER, JANE[5] SPINNEY, JOHN[4], ANDREW[3], JOHN[2], THOMAS[1])* was born 12 Jun 1909 in Snohomish, WA, and died 15 Dec 1993 in Anacortes, WA. She married CHARLES FLOYD TAYLOR 21 Oct 1933 in Anacortes, WA. He was born 31 Mar 1901 in Cle Elum, WA, and died 09 Nov 1984 in Anacortes, WA.

Children of MILDRED CARTER and CHARLES TAYLOR are:
1722.   i.   CHARLES FLOYD[11] TAYLOR, JR., b. Private.
1723.   ii.   GARY LAVERN TAYLOR, b. Private.
1724.   iii.   LYNN CARTER TAYLOR, b. Private.

1570. JOAN[10] CARTER *(ADA ESTHER[9] RICHARDS, SUSAN AUGUSTA RUBY[8] BURCE, JOHN CALVIN[7], RACHEL[6] OLIVER, JANE[5] SPINNEY, JOHN[4], ANDREW[3], JOHN[2], THOMAS[1])* was born Private. She married HAROLD MARION LONG Private. He was born 08 Oct 1915 in Denton, MT, and died 02 Feb 1976 in Bellingham, WA.

Children of JOAN CARTER and HAROLD LONG are:
1725.   i.   SUSAN JEANNE[11] LONG, b. Private.
1726.   ii.   NANCY JOAN LONG, b. Private.
1727.   iii.   SANDRA JANE LONG, b. Private.

1571. JOHN "S"[10] CARTER *(ADA ESTHER[9] RICHARDS, SUSAN AUGUSTA RUBY[8] BURCE, JOHN CALVIN[7], RACHEL[6] OLIVER, JANE[5] SPINNEY, JOHN[4], ANDREW[3], JOHN[2], THOMAS[1])* was born Private. He married BERNADINE BROWN Private. She died Nov 1988 in Oregon.

Children of JOHN CARTER and BERNADINE BROWN are:
1728.   i.   DALE[11] CARTER, b. Private.

1729.   ii.   JOHN MICHAEL CARTER, b. Private.

1572. WILLIAM ABORN JR[10] SPINNEY *(WILLIAM ABORN[9], WILLIAM JAMES[8], ANDREW JACKSON[7], MOSES B[6], JEREMIAH[5], JOHN[4], ANDREW[3], JOHN[2], THOMAS[1])* was born 21 Jul 1937 in Winchester, MA. He married LORRAINE HORN.

Children of WILLIAM SPINNEY and LORRAINE HORN are:
    i.   DEBORAH LORRAINE[11] SPINNEY.
    ii.   SCOTT RAYMOND SPINNEY.

1573. WILLIAM DOUGLAS[10] SPINNEY *(WILLIAM JOHN[9], SYLVESTER VESS[8], ASA D[7], RICHARD[6], RICHARD[5], JOHN[4], ANDREW[3], JOHN[2], THOMAS[1])* was born 05 Oct 1921 in Sparta, IL, and died 08 Dec 2004 in Sparta, IL. He married ANNE MARIE BAILEY.

Children of WILLIAM SPINNEY and ANNE BAILEY are:
    i.   KAREN[11] SPINNEY.
    ii.   MARGARET SPINNEY.
    iii. LINDA SPINNEY.
    iv.   MARY ANN SPINNEY.

Generation No. 11

1574. KYLE HARRY[11] WOODBURY *(ETHEL[10] CUMMINGS, HARRY[9], ALGENAID[8] WORCESTER, MOSES[7], MOSES[6], MOSES[5], ANNE[4] SPINNEY, JOHN[3], SAMUEL[2], THOMAS[1])* He married (1) MARYLOU CARR.   He married (2) DOROTHY ECKHARDT.

Child of KYLE WOODBURY and MARYLOU CARR is:
    i.   DAYNA RENE[12] WOODBURY.

Children of KYLE WOODBURY and DOROTHY ECKHARDT are:
1730.   ii.   KYLE12TH HARRY WOODBURY[12] JR..
    iii. KIMBERLY WOODBURY.

1575. PARTICIA ANN[11] WOODBURY *(ETHEL[10] CUMMINGS, HARRY[9], ALGENAID[8] WORCESTER, MOSES[7], MOSES[6], MOSES[5], ANNE[4] SPINNEY, JOHN[3], SAMUEL[2], THOMAS[1])* She married ALBERT JUSTIS ZELLEY.

Children of PARTICIA WOODBURY and ALBERT ZELLEY are:
    i.   ALISON[12] ZELLEY, m. PATRICK JOEL ROBINSON.
    ii.   KYLEALBERT ZELLEY.
    iii. JAMIE TODD ZELLEY.

1576. BRIAN GEORGE[11] PERKINS *(JOAN LOUISE[10] SPINNEY, HAROLD NEAL[9], HENRY HOWARD[8], GUSTAVUS NEWHALL[7], WILLIAM NEWHALL[6], BENJAMIN[5], JOHN[4], THOMAS[3], SAMUEL[2], THOMAS[1])* was born 04 Apr 1963 in Beverly, MA. He married UNKNOWN.

Children of BRIAN PERKINS and UNKNOWN are:
    i.   BRAD[12] PERKINS, b. 09 Jul 1992.
    ii.   CODY PERKINS, b. 01 Sep 1994.

1577. BARBARA ANN[11] PERKINS *(JOAN LOUISE[10] SPINNEY, HAROLD NEAL[9], HENRY HOWARD[8], GUSTAVUS NEWHALL[7], WILLIAM NEWHALL[6], BENJAMIN[5], JOHN[4], THOMAS[3], SAMUEL[2], THOMAS[1])* was born 26 May 1965 in Ipswich, MA. She married UNKNOWN.

Child of BARBARA PERKINS and UNKNOWN is:
    i.   SHANE12TH[12] LITTLE, b. 03 Oct 1991, Dothun, AL.

1578. BRIAN DAVID[11] DELAINE *(JUDITH MAUD[10] ALLEN, JANE LOUISE[9] SPINNEY, HAROLD ELLERY[8], ELLERY CHANNING[7], WILLIAM NEWHALL[6], BENJAMIN[5], JOHN[4], THOMAS[3], SAMUEL[2], THOMAS[1])* He married PAULA CHRISTINE YELICK.

Children of BRIAN DELAINE and PAULA YELICK are:
  i. CATHERINE JANE[12] DELAINE.
  ii. DONALD JACOB DELAINE.

1579. WENDY L.[11] SPINNEY *(EVERETT EDWARD SPINNEY[10] JR., EVERETT EDWARD[9] SPINNEY, ERNEST EDWARD[8], CHARLES HERBERT[7], JOHN WARREN[6], SAMUEL[5], JOHN[4], THOMAS[3], SAMUEL[2], THOMAS[1])* was born 23 Jun 1952. She married PHILLIP QUALDIERI. He was born 26 May 1950.

Child of WENDY SPINNEY and PHILLIP QUALDIERI is:
  i. SHAUN P.[12] QUALDIERI, b. 22 Jul 1978.

1580. RANDY L.[11] SPINNEY *(EVERETT EDWARD SPINNEY[10] JR., EVERETT EDWARD[9] SPINNEY, ERNEST EDWARD[8], CHARLES HERBERT[7], JOHN WARREN[6], SAMUEL[5], JOHN[4], THOMAS[3], SAMUEL[2], THOMAS[1])* was born 29 Sep 1955. He married UNKNOWN.

Child of RANDY SPINNEY and UNKNOWN is:
  i. MICHAEL EDWARD[12] SPINNEY, b. 02 Sep 1985.

1581. JOHN LEONARD CARBONE[11] JR. *(FRANCES RUTH[10] SANDBERG, BERTHA MAY[9] SPINNEY, ERNEST EDWARD[8], CHARLES HERBERT[7], JOHN WARREN[6], SAMUEL[5], JOHN[4], THOMAS[3], SAMUEL[2], THOMAS[1])* was born 08 Nov 1954 in Lynn, MA. He married SUZANNE LYNNE SPICER 26 May 1985 in Westford, MA. She was born 04 Feb 1963 in Lynn, MA.

Children of JOHN JR. and SUZANNE SPICER are:
  i. JOSHUA JOHN[12] CARBONE, b. 23 Jan 1988, Hollywood, FL.
  ii. KIERSTON LEIGH CARBONE, b. 15 Mar 1990, Winchester, MA.
  iii. CODY DEAN CARBONE, b. 28 Nov 1993, Winchester, MA.

1582. MARY ELLEN[11] CARBONE *(FRANCES RUTH[10] SANDBERG, BERTHA MAY[9] SPINNEY, ERNEST EDWARD[8], CHARLES HERBERT[7], JOHN WARREN[6], SAMUEL[5], JOHN[4], THOMAS[3], SAMUEL[2], THOMAS[1])* was born 08 Dec 1963 in Lynn, MA. She married TIMMOTHY MICHAEL MOORE 10 Oct 1988 in Lynn, MA. He was born 21 Aug 1962 in Lynn, MA.

Children of MARY CARBONE and TIMMOTHY MOORE are:
  i. ZACAHERY ALBERT[12] MOORE, b. 11 Aug 1989, Beverly, MA.
  ii. ABIGAIL ELIZABETH MOORE, b. 17 May 1991, Beverly, MA..
  iii. AMANDA MARIE MOORE, b. 21 Mar 1993, Beverly, MA.

1583. JOSEPH NELSON DULONG[11] JR. *(MARJORIE ELLEN[10] SANDBERG, BERTHA MAY[9] SPINNEY, ERNEST EDWARD[8], CHARLES HERBERT[7], JOHN WARREN[6], SAMUEL[5], JOHN[4], THOMAS[3], SAMUEL[2], THOMAS[1])* was born 19 Mar 1954 in Lynn, MA.. He married ROSANNE MARIE MURPHY 11 Dec 1980 in ST. JOSEPH'S . Wakefield, MA. She was born 21 Jun 1958 in Somerville, MA.

Children of JOSEPH JR. and ROSANNE MURPHY are:
  i. JENNIFER ELLEN[12] DULONG, b. 11 Dec 1981, Malden, MA.
  ii. JOHN FRANCIS DULONG, b. 27 Oct 1983, Malden, MA.
  iii. KAITLYN ROSE DULONG, b. 11 Dec 1985, Melrose, MA.
  iv. MARY ELIZABETH DULONG, b. 18 Jan 1987, Winchester, MA.

1584. CHERYL MAY[11] DULONG *(MARJORIE ELLEN[10] SANDBERG, BERTHA MAY[9] SPINNEY, ERNEST EDWARD[8],*

CHARLES HERBERT[7], JOHN WARREN[6], SAMUEL[5], JOHN[4], THOMAS[3], SAMUEL[2], THOMAS[1]) was born 02 Dec 1956 in Lynn, MA.. She married PETER ALAN DONOVAN 19 Aug 1978 in Wakefield, MA. He was born 22 Aug 1955 in Hartford, CT.

Children of CHERYL DULONG and PETER DONOVAN are:
    i.   LISA ANN[12] DONOVAN, b. 22 May 1981, Melrose, MA.
    ii. KIM ANNE DONAVON, b. 28 Jul 1987, Stoneham, MA.
    iii. LYNN ELLEN DONOVAN, b. 28 Jul 1987, Stoneham, MA.

1585. DEBORAH MAY[11] DALTON *(BARBARA[10] SANDBERG, BERTHA MAY[9] SPINNEY, ERNEST EDWARD[8], CHARLES HERBERT[7], JOHN WARREN[6], SAMUEL[5], JOHN[4], THOMAS[3], SAMUEL[2], THOMAS[1])* was born 09 Oct 1956 in Lynn, Essex, MA. She married PAUL SHERWOOD PORT JR. 28 May 1977 in Lynn, Essex.MA.. He was born 21 Sep 1951 in Easton, PA.

Children of DEBORAH DALTON and PAUL JR. are:
    i.   DAMON MICHAEL[12] PORT, b. 18 Oct 1978, Cheyenne, WY.
    ii. BRANDON JOHN PORT, b. 09 Oct 1981, Oxnard, CA.; d. 14 Oct 2001, Las Vegas, NV.

        Notes for BRANDON JOHN PORT:
        Brandon Port

        Brandon John Port, 20, died Saturday at a Las Vegas hospital.

        He was born Oct. 9, 1981, in Oxnard, Calif. A cabinet maker in construction, he was a 10-year resident of Pahrump.

        He is survived by his companion, Teresa Falcone; parents, Deborah and Paul Jr.; brother, Damon; and sister, Cassandra, all of Pahrump; and grandparents, Annie Calderwood of Las Vegas, Paul Sr. of Cheyenne, Wyo., and Art Dalton and Barbara Dalton, both of Sanford, Maine.

        Services are pending. Nevada Funeral Service-Nevada Cremation or Burial Society handled arrangements.

    iii. CASSANDRA LYNN PORT, b. 14 Jan 1987, New London, CT..

1586. MARILYN[11] WEHTJE *(LAUREL MAE[10] OWENS, LLOYD MAXWELL[9], ELLA GERTRUDE[8] WHEELER, ALICE CATHERINE[7] DWELLEY, NARCISSA SPRING[6] SPINNEY, EBENEZER[5], EBENEZER[4], JONATHAN[3], SAMUEL[2], THOMAS[1])* She married ALBERT DEININGER.

Children of MARILYN WEHTJE and ALBERT DEININGER are:
    i.   ROBERT[12] DEININGER.
    ii. RONALD DEININGER.
    iii. RACHEL DEININGER.

1587. MYRON FLOYD[11] WEHTJE *(LAUREL MAE[10] OWENS, LLOYD MAXWELL[9], ELLA GERTRUDE[8] WHEELER, ALICE CATHERINE[7] DWELLEY, NARCISSA SPRING[6] SPINNEY, EBENEZER[5], EBENEZER[4], JONATHAN[3], SAMUEL[2], THOMAS[1])* was born 21 Oct 1938 in Longview WA. He married RENATE EISELT 03 Jun 1962 in Berrien Springs MI, daughter of FRANZ EISELT and ANNA KANTOR. She was born 22 Nov 1940 in Radeburg, Germany.

Children of MYRON WEHTJE and RENATE EISELT are:
    i.   THOMAS JEFFERSON[12] WEHTJE.
    ii. JAMES MADISON WEHTJE.
1731.   iii. JACQUELYN DIANE (EISELT) WEHTJE, b. 04 Jan 1965, Lacombe, Alberta, Canada.

1588. JUDITH ANN[11] GREARSON *(ANITA[10] SPINNEY, LLEWELLEN[9], DOUGLAS[8], JAMES ALEXANDER[7], STEPHEN[6], JONATHAN[5], NATHANIEL[4], JONATHAN[3], SAMUEL[2], THOMAS[1])* was born 19 Jul 1949. She married (1) CHARLES PATRICK NEATHWAY Jun 1971 in St George New Brunswick. She married (2) JOSEPH DONALD BREAU 29 Dec

1979 in St George New Brunswick.

Child of JUDITH GREARSON and JOSEPH BREAU is:
      i.   GILBERT JASON[12] BREAU, b. 11 Sep 1980, St John, NB..

1589. JOANNE[11] SPINNEY *(JACK BENTLEY[10], STEPHEN PERCY[9], FREDERICK[8], HORATIO NELSON[7], STEPHEN[6], JONATHAN[5], NATHANIEL[4], JONATHAN[3], SAMUEL[2], THOMAS[1])* She married RAYMOND J MARTIN.

Children of JOANNE SPINNEY and RAYMOND MARTIN are:
      i.   JANET[12] MARTIN.
     ii.   BRADLEY MARTIN.

1590. JOHN[11] MILLS *(NORMAN[10], NORMAN[9], EDWARD L[8], LOUISE PARKS[7] SPINNEY, CHARLES EDWARD[6], JONATHAN[5], NATHANIEL[4], JONATHAN[3], SAMUEL[2], THOMAS[1])*

Child of JOHN MILLS is:
      i.   CHRISTOPHER[12] MILLS.

1591. JULIE[11] MILLS *(NORMAN[10], NORMAN[9], EDWARD L[8], LOUISE PARKS[7] SPINNEY, CHARLES EDWARD[6], JONATHAN[5], NATHANIEL[4], JONATHAN[3], SAMUEL[2], THOMAS[1])*

Children of JULIE MILLS are:
      i.   SARAH[12] MILLS.
     ii.   LAUREN MILLS.

1592. KETHERINE IRENE[11] MILLS *(ARTHUR EDWIN[10], CLAUDE EDWIN[9], ARTHUR JONES[8], SARAH[7] SPINNEY, ARTHUR JONES[6], EBENEZER[5], NATHANIEL[4], JONATHAN[3], SAMUEL[2], THOMAS[1])* was born 06 Feb 1941. She married DON BAUGH.

Children of KETHERINE MILLS and DON BAUGH are:
      i.   JOHN[12] BAUGH, b. 09 Aug 1965.
     ii.   JIM BAUGH, b. 02 Jun 1967.
    iii.   SERENA BAUGH, b. 18 May 1969.

1593. DAPHNE ANNE[11] MILLS *(HAROLD GLEN[10], CLAUDE EDWIN[9], ARTHUR JONES[8], SARAH[7] SPINNEY, ARTHUR JONES[6], EBENEZER[5], NATHANIEL[4], JONATHAN[3], SAMUEL[2], THOMAS[1])* was born 20 Mar 1940. She married WILLIAM R MCKNIGHT.

Children of DAPHNE MILLS and WILLIAM MCKNIGHT are:
1732.   i.   LISA RAE[12] MCKNIGHT, b. 15 Feb 1963, Korea.
     ii.   DAPHNE MCKNIGHT, b. 13 Jul 1964.
    iii.   SAMANTHA MCKNIGHT, b. 03 Apr 1967.
    iv.   AMANDA S MCKNIGHT, b. 03 Jul 1970.
     v.   ANDREA MCKNIGHT, b. 22 Nov 1973.

1594. LEE[11] COOPRIDER *(PEARL LOUISE[10] MILLS, CLAUDE EDWIN[9], ARTHUR JONES[8], SARAH[7] SPINNEY, ARTHUR JONES[6], EBENEZER[5], NATHANIEL[4], JONATHAN[3], SAMUEL[2], THOMAS[1])* was born 04 Feb 1947. He married REBECCA 03 Oct 1970. She was born 23 Sep 1946.

Child of LEE COOPRIDER and REBECCA is:
      i.   ZOE[12] COOPRIDER, b. 08 Jul 1976.

1595. TED[11] COOPRIDER *(PEARL LOUISE[10] MILLS, CLAUDE EDWIN[9], ARTHUR JONES[8], SARAH[7] SPINNEY, ARTHUR JONES[6], EBENEZER[5], NATHANIEL[4], JONATHAN[3], SAMUEL[2], THOMAS[1])* was born 13 Jun 1950. He married SANDRA. She was born 03 May 1950.

Children of TED COOPRIDER and SANDRA are:
  i.   JASON[12] COOPRIDER, b. 05 Sep 1974.
  ii. ERIC COOPRIDER, b. 04 Apr 1977.

1596. RUTHANN PEARL[11] SIMPSON *(ARTHUR MILLS[10], PEARL EUDORA[9] MILLS, ARTHUR JONES[8], SARAH[7] SPINNEY, ARTHUR JONES[6], EBENEZER[5], NATHANIEL[4], JONATHAN[3], SAMUEL[2], THOMAS[1])* was born 27 Apr 1941 in Wenatchee, WA. She married SAMUEL P LOCKWOOD 27 Dec 1964 in Cashmere, WA, son of SAMUEL LOCKWOOD and MARGARET SPENCER.

Children of RUTHANN SIMPSON and SAMUEL LOCKWOOD are:
  i.   SPENCER MILLS[12] LOCKWOOD, b. 28 May 1969, Tacoma, WA.
  ii. CHRISTOPHER GAMBLE LOCKWOOD, b. 24 Dec 1973, Tacoma, WA.

1597. JACK STRILING[11] FULLERTON *(CAROLINE MARGARET[10] STEWART, CLIFFORD MILLS[9], CAROLINE LEVINA[8] MILLS, SARAH[7] SPINNEY, ARTHUR JONES[6], EBENEZER[5], NATHANIEL[4], JONATHAN[3], SAMUEL[2], THOMAS[1])* was born 16 Nov 1948 in Port Angeles, WA. He married (1) JAN RUTH. He married (2) JOCELYN COPE. He married (3) MELODY.

Children of JACK FULLERTON and JAN RUTH are:
  i.   CHRISTIANA LYNN[12] FULLERTON, b. 24 Jan 1974, El Paso, TX.
  ii. JEFFREY SCOTT FULLERTON, b. 28 Jul 1975, Westchester, PA.

Children of JACK FULLERTON and JOCELYN COPE are:
  iii. STEPHANIE GAIL[12] FULLERTON, b. 18 Mar 1984, Port Pold, LA.
  iv. JACK STIRLING FULLERTON, b. 17 Oct 1986, Heidelberg Germany.

1598. MARGARET LYNNE[11] FULLERTON *(CAROLINE MARGARET[10] STEWART, CLIFFORD MILLS[9], CAROLINE LEVINA[8] MILLS, SARAH[7] SPINNEY, ARTHUR JONES[6], EBENEZER[5], NATHANIEL[4], JONATHAN[3], SAMUEL[2], THOMAS[1])* was born 25 Jun 1951 in Salem, OR. She married (1) PAUL NEVILLE. She married (2) JOHN BAHAM 18 May 1991.

Children of MARGARET FULLERTON and PAUL NEVILLE are:
  i.   JONATHAN SCOTT[12] NEVILLE, b. 28 Jan 1977.
  ii. BRIANNE ELIZABETH NEVILLE, b. 26 Oct 1979.

1599. LINDA JEANNE[11] STEWART *(CLIFFORD THOMAS[10], CLIFFORD MILLS[9], CAROLINE LEVINA[8] MILLS, SARAH[7] SPINNEY, ARTHUR JONES[6], EBENEZER[5], NATHANIEL[4], JONATHAN[3], SAMUEL[2], THOMAS[1])* was born 01 Sep 1945 in Miami, FL. She married GREGORY LEE NELSON 06 Sep 1969, son of LEE NELSON and CHARLOTTE RATTRAY. He was born 24 Sep 1942 in Bremerton, WA.

Children of LINDA STEWART and GREGORY NELSON are:
  i.   BARRINGTON WILLIAM[12] NELSON, b. 08 Jan 1977, Portland, OR.
  ii. DAVID GREOGE NELSON, b. 16 Jan 1980, Salem, OR.

1600. LUCY VIRGINIA[11] CALVIN *(MARCIA ANNE[10] LOOMIS, KATHRYN ISABELLE[9] THOMPSON, MYRTLE ISABELLE[8] BANES, AURELIA ISABELLE[7] SPINNEY, ARTHUR JONES[6], EBENEZER[5], NATHANIEL[4], JONATHAN[3], SAMUEL[2], THOMAS[1])* was born Private. She married MICHAEL JOHN SKELDON Private. He was born Private.

Child of LUCY CALVIN and MICHAEL SKELDON is:
  i.   KATHRYN CHALMERS[12] SKELDON, b. Private.

1601. BRIAN CLIFFORD[11] NEILEY *(CLIFFORD[10], WILLIAM LLOYD[9] NEILY, INEZ LINWOOD[8] SPINNEY, ABRAHAM[7], JOSEPH[6], ABRAHAM[5], JOSEPH[4], SAMUEL[3], SAMUEL[2], THOMAS[1])* He married FLORA ELLENE POWER.

Children of BRIAN NEILEY and FLORA POWER are:

i. ASHLEY KATHERINE[12] NEILEY, b. 22 Apr 1984, Halifax, NS..
ii. ALLYSON KIMBERLY NEILEY, b. 02 Mar 1987, Halifax, NS..

1602. CYNTHIA ROBERTA[11] BAILEY *(ROBERT BERTWELL[10], RUSSELL FRANKLIN[9], CORA MAUDE[8] BERTWELL, ALEPH[7] WOODBURY, ELIZABETH[6] SPINNEY, ABRAHAM[5], JOSEPH[4], SAMUEL[3], SAMUEL[2], THOMAS[1])* was born 29 Jun 1965 in Cambridge, MA. She married JOHN ALVIN EPENETER 24 Jun 1988 in Kensington, MD. He was born 21 Apr 1965 in Arlington, MA.

Child of CYNTHIA BAILEY and JOHN EPENETER is:
i. JACQUELINE MAE[12] EPENETER, b. 19 Apr 1994, Salt Lake, UT.

1603. APRIL LYN[11] SPINNEY *(CHESTER LEVERETT[10], CHESTER LEVERETT JR.[9], CHESTER LEVERETT[8], ISAAC CALVIN[7], SAMUEL[6], ISAAC BEACH[5], SAMUEL MCCLURE[4], SAMUEL[3], SAMUEL[2], THOMAS[1])* was born 03 Oct 1975. She married ROBERT V. TIGHE III Sep 1994 in North Reading, Massachusetts.

Child of APRIL SPINNEY and ROBERT TIGHE III is:
i. AMANDA LYN[12] TIGHE, b. Feb 1997.

1604. JOAN BEVERLY[11] FENECH *(DOROTHY FRANCES[10] MCWHIRK, ETHAL M[9] MCNUTT, EMMA AUGUSTA[8] SPINNEY, THOMAS M[7], THOMAS[6], THOMAS[5], JOHN[4], THOMAS[3], THOMAS[2], THOMAS[1])* was born 30 Jul 1933. She married CHARLES WOOD.

Notes for CHARLES WOOD:
Killed in Auto Accident

Children of JOAN FENECH and CHARLES WOOD are:
i. CHARLES[12] WOOD.
ii. CHRISTINA WOOD.
iii. JOHN WOOD.

1605. HENRY ROBERT[11] FENECH *(DOROTHY FRANCES[10] MCWHIRK, ETHAL M[9] MCNUTT, EMMA AUGUSTA[8] SPINNEY, THOMAS M[7], THOMAS[6], THOMAS[5], JOHN[4], THOMAS[3], THOMAS[2], THOMAS[1])* was born 02 Mar 1935, and died 08 Jun 2004 in Maryland. He married SHIRLEY STALLARD 04 Feb 1961 in Baltimore, MD. She was born 24 Mar 1935 in Erwin, TX, and died 20 Sep 1995.

Child of HENRY FENECH and SHIRLEY STALLARD is:
1733. i. DOROTHY FRANCES[12] FENECH, Adopted child.

1606. DOROTHY ETHEL[11] FENECH *(DOROTHY FRANCES[10] MCWHIRK, ETHAL M[9] MCNUTT, EMMA AUGUSTA[8] SPINNEY, THOMAS M[7], THOMAS[6], THOMAS[5], JOHN[4], THOMAS[3], THOMAS[2], THOMAS[1])* was born 23 Jun 1937. She married (1) WILLIAM ALLEN. She married (2) CHARLES DYKE.

Child of DOROTHY FENECH and CHARLES DYKE is:
i. LISA[12] DYKE, m. CUMMINGS.

1607. GWENDOLYN LOIS[11] FENECH *(DOROTHY FRANCES[10] MCWHIRK, ETHAL M[9] MCNUTT, EMMA AUGUSTA[8] SPINNEY, THOMAS M[7], THOMAS[6], THOMAS[5], JOHN[4], THOMAS[3], THOMAS[2], THOMAS[1])* was born 23 Oct 1939, and died 26 Jun 1989. She married FRANK ANDERSON.

Children of GWENDOLYN FENECH and FRANK ANDERSON are:
i. CHERRY LYNN[12] ANDERSON, m. PETERS.
ii. ADAM ANDERSON.

1608. PAUL[11] ARCHER *(OLIVE[10] MCWHIRK, ETHAL M[9] MCNUTT, EMMA AUGUSTA[8] SPINNEY, THOMAS M[7], THOMAS[6], THOMAS[5], JOHN[4], THOMAS[3], THOMAS[2], THOMAS[1])* died 1995. He married CATHERINE L PERRY.

Children of PAUL ARCHER and CATHERINE PERRY are:
  i.   PAUL[12] ARCHER.
  ii. KATIE ARCHER.

1609. ERNEST[11] PINKHAM, JR. *(GRACE E.[10] BROOKS, ERVING ELSWORTH[9], ALFRED LANGDON[8], DANIEL LANGDON[7], DANIEL[6], MARY[5] SPINNEY, JOHN[4], JOHN[3], JOHN[2], THOMAS[1])* was born Private. He married ARLENE Private. She was born Private.

Children of ERNEST PINKHAM and ARLENE are:
  i.   DONNA[12] PINKHAM, b. Private.
  ii.   RONALD PINKHAM, b. Private.
  iii. RICHARD PINKHAM, b. Private.
  iv.   TIMOTHY PINKHAM, b. Private.

1610. LEON ARTHUR[11] PICKERING *(NELLIE E.[10] BROOKS, ERVING ELSWORTH[9], ALFRED LANGDON[8], DANIEL LANGDON[7], DANIEL[6], MARY[5] SPINNEY, JOHN[4], JOHN[3], JOHN[2], THOMAS[1])* was born Private. He married PHYLLIS P GARLAND Private. She was born Private.

Child of LEON PICKERING and PHYLLIS GARLAND is:
  i.   RICHARD PAUL[12] PICKERING, b. Private.

1611. WALTER HARRISON[11] PICKERING *(NELLIE E.[10] BROOKS, ERVING ELSWORTH[9], ALFRED LANGDON[8], DANIEL LANGDON[7], DANIEL[6], MARY[5] SPINNEY, JOHN[4], JOHN[3], JOHN[2], THOMAS[1])* was born Private.

Children of WALTER HARRISON PICKERING are:
  i.   JAMES[12] PICKERING, b. Private.
  ii.   JOHN PICKERING, b. Private.
  iii. DEBORAH PICKERING, b. Private.

1612. KENNETH EARL[11] PICKERING *(NELLIE E.[10] BROOKS, ERVING ELSWORTH[9], ALFRED LANGDON[8], DANIEL LANGDON[7], DANIEL[6], MARY[5] SPINNEY, JOHN[4], JOHN[3], JOHN[2], THOMAS[1])* was born Private. He married BARBARA MORRILL Private. She was born Private.

Children of KENNETH PICKERING and BARBARA MORRILL are:
  i.   KENNETH EARL[12] PICKERING, JR., b. Private.
  ii.   ROGER EARL PICKERING, b. Private.
  iii. PAUL EARL PICKERING, b. Private.
  iv.   BARBARA PICKERING, b. Private.

1613. MARJORIE LOUISE[11] PICKERING *(NELLIE E.[10] BROOKS, ERVING ELSWORTH[9], ALFRED LANGDON[8], DANIEL LANGDON[7], DANIEL[6], MARY[5] SPINNEY, JOHN[4], JOHN[3], JOHN[2], THOMAS[1])* was born Private. She married MARVIN D. BUCKINGHAM Private. He was born Private.

Child of MARJORIE PICKERING and MARVIN BUCKINGHAM is:
  i.   RICKY SCOTT[12] BUCKINGHAM, b. Private.

1614. CLARENCE[11] ISAACSON *(HAZEL P.[10] BROOKS, ERVING ELSWORTH[9], ALFRED LANGDON[8], DANIEL LANGDON[7], DANIEL[6], MARY[5] SPINNEY, JOHN[4], JOHN[3], JOHN[2], THOMAS[1])* was born 31 Mar 1914, and died 01 Feb 1965. He married ANN C SHIPLEY Private. She was born Private.

Children of CLARENCE ISAACSON and ANN SHIPLEY are:
  i.   HENRY C.[12] ISAACSON, b. Private.
  ii. CAROLINE ISAACSON, b. Private.

1615. ELINOR[11] ISAACSON *(HAZEL P.[10] BROOKS, ERVING ELSWORTH[9], ALFRED LANGDON[8], DANIEL LANGDON[7], DANIEL[6], MARY[5] SPINNEY, JOHN[4], JOHN[3], JOHN[2], THOMAS[1])* was born Private. She married (1) HUBERT WILDER Private. He was born Private. She married (2) DANA CALLANAN Private. He was born Private.

Children of ELINOR ISAACSON and HUBERT WILDER are:
    i.   ROBERT[12] WILDER, b. Private.
    ii.   RICHARD WILDER, b. Private.
    iii.   GARY WILDER, b. Private.

1616. DOROTHY[11] ISAACSON *(HAZEL P.[10] BROOKS, ERVING ELSWORTH[9], ALFRED LANGDON[8], DANIEL LANGDON[7], DANIEL[6], MARY[5] SPINNEY, JOHN[4], JOHN[3], JOHN[2], THOMAS[1])* was born Private. She married EDWARD LARABEE Private. He was born Private.

Children of DOROTHY ISAACSON and EDWARD LARABEE are:
    i.   GAIL[12] LARABEE, b. Private.
    ii.   BRADLEY LARABEE, b. Private.

1617. ARTHUR RALPH[11] BROOKS *(ELMER IRWIN[10], ERVING ELSWORTH[9], ALFRED LANGDON[8], DANIEL LANGDON[7], DANIEL[6], MARY[5] SPINNEY, JOHN[4], JOHN[3], JOHN[2], THOMAS[1])* was born Private. He married (1) NANCY FRENCH Private. She was born Private. He married (2) RITA R. DIGERONIMO Private. She was born Private.

Children of ARTHUR BROOKS and NANCY FRENCH are:
1734.   i.   RALPH JUSTIN[12] BROOKS, b. Private.
    ii.   CHERYL ANN BROOKS, b. Private; m. RANDOLPH BECKER, Private; b. Private.

1618. DORIS EVELYN[11] BROOKS *(ELMER IRWIN[10], ERVING ELSWORTH[9], ALFRED LANGDON[8], DANIEL LANGDON[7], DANIEL[6], MARY[5] SPINNEY, JOHN[4], JOHN[3], JOHN[2], THOMAS[1])* was born Private. She married ROBERT DOLPH Private. He was born Private.

Child of DORIS BROOKS and ROBERT DOLPH is:
    i.   JAMES ERVING[12] DOLPH, b. Private.

1619. VIRGINIA RUTH[11] BROOKS *(WILFRED ELSWORTH[10], ERVING ELSWORTH[9], ALFRED LANGDON[8], DANIEL LANGDON[7], DANIEL[6], MARY[5] SPINNEY, JOHN[4], JOHN[3], JOHN[2], THOMAS[1])* was born Private. She married ROBERT SIMPSON Private. He was born Private.

Children of VIRGINIA BROOKS and ROBERT SIMPSON are:
    i.   STEPHEN ROBERT[12] SIMPSON, b. Private.
    ii.   RICHARD LLOYD SIMPSON, b. Private.

1620. PHILLIP F[11] BROOKS *(WILFRED ELSWORTH[10], ERVING ELSWORTH[9], ALFRED LANGDON[8], DANIEL LANGDON[7], DANIEL[6], MARY[5] SPINNEY, JOHN[4], JOHN[3], JOHN[2], THOMAS[1])* was born Private. He married CYNTHIA HILL Private. She was born Private.

Children of PHILLIP BROOKS and CYNTHIA HILL are:
    i.   WAYNE[12] BROOKS, b. Private.
    ii.   LINDA BROOKS, b. Private.

1621. BEVERLY DELL[11] BROOKS *(RALPH GORDON[10], ERVING ELSWORTH[9], ALFRED LANGDON[8], DANIEL LANGDON[7], DANIEL[6], MARY[5] SPINNEY, JOHN[4], JOHN[3], JOHN[2], THOMAS[1])* was born Private. She married (1) ARTHUR W. DURANT Private. He was born Private. She married (2) JUSTIN WITHAM Private. He was born Private. She married (3) DAVID LEGAN Private. He was born Private.

Child of BEVERLY BROOKS and JUSTIN WITHAM is:
    i.   RICHARD[12] WITHAM, b. Private.

Child of BEVERLY BROOKS and DAVID LEGAN is:
    ii.   JYNX[12] LEGAN, b. Private; m. STEPHEN NASON, Private; b. Private.

1622. RALPH GORDON[11] BROOKS, JR. *(RALPH GORDON[10], ERVING ELSWORTH[9], ALFRED LANGDON[8], DANIEL LANGDON[7], DANIEL[6], MARY[5] SPINNEY, JOHN[4], JOHN[3], JOHN[2], THOMAS[1])* was born Private. He married (1) EVELYN MASSEY Private. She was born Private. He married (2) PATRICIA SMITH Private. She was born Private.

Children of RALPH BROOKS and EVELYN MASSEY are:
    i.   TAMMY S[12] BROOKS, b. Private; m. DENNIS HESTER, Private; b. Private.
    ii.   CLAY BROOKS I, b. Private; m. JUDY, Private; b. Private.
    iii.   STEPHANIE L BROOKS, b. Private; m. STEVE ABBOTT, Private; b. Private.

Children of RALPH BROOKS and PATRICIA SMITH are:
    iv.   KENNETH J[12] BROOKS, b. Private.
    v.   GORDON P BROOKS, b. Private.

1623. CRAIG HEWITT[11] BROOKS *(RALPH GORDON[10], ERVING ELSWORTH[9], ALFRED LANGDON[8], DANIEL LANGDON[7], DANIEL[6], MARY[5] SPINNEY, JOHN[4], JOHN[3], JOHN[2], THOMAS[1])* was born Private. He married JOANNE LaBRANCHE Private. She was born Private.

Children of CRAIG BROOKS and JOANNE LaBRANCHE are:
    i.   PAULA[12] BROOKS, b. Private.
    ii.   LESLIE BROOKS, b. Private.
    iii.   DAVID BROOKS, b. Private.
    iv.   SHELLY BROOKS, b. Private.
    v.   KEVIN BROOKS, b. Private.

1624. ROSALIE ANNE[11] BROOKS *(KENNETH EARL[10], ERVING ELSWORTH[9], ALFRED LANGDON[8], DANIEL LANGDON[7], DANIEL[6], MARY[5] SPINNEY, JOHN[4], JOHN[3], JOHN[2], THOMAS[1])* was born Private. She married DENNIS SCHWAB Private. He was born Private.

Children of ROSALIE BROOKS and DENNIS SCHWAB are:
    i.   KRISTINE ANNE[12] SCHWAB, b. Private.
    ii.   DENNIS MICHAEL SCHWAB, b. Private.
    iii.   AMY FLORENCE SCHWAB, b. Private.

1625. ANNA[11] PAYNE *(MARJORIE R.[10] BROOKS, ERVING ELSWORTH[9], ALFRED LANGDON[8], DANIEL LANGDON[7], DANIEL[6], MARY[5] SPINNEY, JOHN[4], JOHN[3], JOHN[2], THOMAS[1])* was born Private. She married THOMAS CONNERS Private. He was born Private.

Children of ANNA PAYNE and THOMAS CONNERS are:
    i.   MICHAEL[12] CONNERS, b. Private.
    ii.   MARC CONNERS, b. Private.

1626. CHESTER E[11] BROOKS, JR. *(CHESTER E[10], VICTOR E[9], ALFRED LANGDON[8], DANIEL LANGDON[7], DANIEL[6], MARY[5] SPINNEY, JOHN[4], JOHN[3], JOHN[2], THOMAS[1])* was born Private. He married DEE Private. She was born Private.

Children of CHESTER BROOKS and DEE are:
    i.   KATHLEEN[12] BROOKS, b. Private.
    ii.   LAURIE BROOKS, b. Private.
    iii.   ALLISON BROOKS, b. Private.
    iv.   PETER BROOKS, b. Private.

1627. PHYLLIS[11] BROOKS *(HOWARD R[10], VICTOR E[9], ALFRED LANGDON[8], DANIEL LANGDON[7], DANIEL[6], MARY[5] SPINNEY, JOHN[4], JOHN[3], JOHN[2], THOMAS[1])* was born Private. She married JOHN HANSON Private. He was born Private.

Child of PHYLLIS BROOKS and JOHN HANSON is:
    i.   JOHN[12] HANSON, b. Private.

1628. GERALD SIDNEY[11] TORREY *(PAULENA T[10] BROOKS, VICTOR E[9], ALFRED LANGDON[8], DANIEL LANGDON[7], DANIEL[6], MARY[5] SPINNEY, JOHN[4], JOHN[3], JOHN[2], THOMAS[1])* was born Private. He married MILDRED UPHAM Private. She was born Private.

Children of GERALD TORREY and MILDRED UPHAM are:
    i.   CINDY LOU[12] TORREY, b. Private.
    ii. JAMES PETER TORREY, b. Private.
    iii. JOHN PAUL TORREY, b. Private.
    iv. GERALD SIDNEY TORREY, JR., b. Private.

1629. JOYCE[11] TORREY *(PAULENA T[10] BROOKS, VICTOR E[9], ALFRED LANGDON[8], DANIEL LANGDON[7], DANIEL[6], MARY[5] SPINNEY, JOHN[4], JOHN[3], JOHN[2], THOMAS[1])* was born Private. She married JOHN (JACK) MORAN Private. He was born Private.

Children of JOYCE TORREY and JOHN MORAN are:
    i.   ALLISON[12] MORAN, b. Private.
    ii. JOHN MORAN, b. Private.
    iii. LINDA MORAN, b. Private.

1630. MARGARET[11] TORREY *(PAULENA T[10] BROOKS, VICTOR E[9], ALFRED LANGDON[8], DANIEL LANGDON[7], DANIEL[6], MARY[5] SPINNEY, JOHN[4], JOHN[3], JOHN[2], THOMAS[1])* was born Private. She married GEORGE GIOSTRA Private. He was born Private.

Children of MARGARET TORREY and GEORGE GIOSTRA are:
    i.   HOLI[12] GIOSTRA, b. Private.
    ii. MARY GIOSTRA, b. Private.
    iii. CHARLES GIOSTRA, b. Private.

1631. PATRICIA[11] BROOKS *(GEORGE L[10], VICTOR E[9], ALFRED LANGDON[8], DANIEL LANGDON[7], DANIEL[6], MARY[5] SPINNEY, JOHN[4], JOHN[3], JOHN[2], THOMAS[1])* was born Private. She married RICHARD GROSS Private. He was born Private.

Children of PATRICIA BROOKS and RICHARD GROSS are:
    i.   ANDREA[12] GROSS, b. Private.
    ii. RICHARD GROSS, JR., b. Private.

1632. BARBARA ANN[11] JONES *(AUGUSTA MAY[10] TERRIO, BERNICE MILDRED[9] BROOKS, ALFRED LANGDON[8], DANIEL LANGDON[7], DANIEL[6], MARY[5] SPINNEY, JOHN[4], JOHN[3], JOHN[2], THOMAS[1])* was born Private. She married STEPHEN C. CROWLEY Private. He was born Private.

Children of BARBARA JONES and STEPHEN CROWLEY are:
    i.   TIMOTHY GORDON[12] CROWLEY, b. Private.
    ii. PATRICIA ANN CROWLEY, b. Private.

1633. MARJORIE LOUISE[11] JONES *(AUGUSTA MAY[10] TERRIO, BERNICE MILDRED[9] BROOKS, ALFRED LANGDON[8], DANIEL LANGDON[7], DANIEL[6], MARY[5] SPINNEY, JOHN[4], JOHN[3], JOHN[2], THOMAS[1])* was born Private. She married ARTHUR W. FERNALD Private, son of WALTER FERNALD and EDITH VERITY. He was born 15 Apr 1927, and died 22 Jan 2003 in Portsmouth, NH.

Children of MARJORIE JONES and ARTHUR FERNALD are:
   i.   DIANE ELAINE[12] FERNALD, b. Private; m. PAUL GERACI, Private; b. Private.
1735.   ii.   MARCIA LOUISE FERNALD, b. Private.

1634. ROBERT LEWIS[11] JONES *(AUGUSTA MAY[10] TERRIO, BERNICE MILDRED[9] BROOKS, ALFRED LANGDON[8], DANIEL LANGDON[7], DANIEL[6], MARY[5] SPINNEY, JOHN[4], JOHN[3], JOHN[2], THOMAS[1])* was born Private. He married RUTH DOMENICK Private. She was born Private.

Child of ROBERT JONES and RUTH DOMENICK is:
   i.   STEPHEN[12] JONES, b. Private.

1635. EUGENE RAYMOND[11] DAVIDSON *(FLORENCE MILDRED[10] TERRIO, BERNICE MILDRED[9] BROOKS, ALFRED LANGDON[8], DANIEL LANGDON[7], DANIEL[6], MARY[5] SPINNEY, JOHN[4], JOHN[3], JOHN[2], THOMAS[1])* was born 15 Jun 1921 in Tulsa, OK, and died 02 Oct 1982 in Danvers, MA. He married MARJORIE AHLES Private. She was born Private.

Children of EUGENE DAVIDSON and MARJORIE AHLES are:
   i.   MARK AHLES[12] DAVIDSON, b. Private.
   ii.   PAMELA (MCKAY) DAVIDSON, b. Private.

1636. DONALD DEAN[11] DAVIDSON *(FLORENCE MILDRED[10] TERRIO, BERNICE MILDRED[9] BROOKS, ALFRED LANGDON[8], DANIEL LANGDON[7], DANIEL[6], MARY[5] SPINNEY, JOHN[4], JOHN[3], JOHN[2], THOMAS[1])* was born Private. He married ELIZABETH ANNE BLACKBURN Private. She was born Private.

Children of DONALD DAVIDSON and ELIZABETH BLACKBURN are:
1736.   i.   DONALD RAYMOND[12] DAVIDSON, b. Private.
1737.   ii.   DIANE ELIZABETH DAVIDSON, b. Private.
1738.   iii.   DOUGLAS EDWARD DAVIDSON, b. Private.
1739.   iv.   DEBORAH JOAN DAVIDSON, b. Private.
1740.   v.   DENISE ANNE DAVIDSON, b. Private.
1741.   vi.   DAWN ELLEN DAVIDSON, b. Private.
1742.   vii.   DWIGHT ERIC DAVIDSON, b. Private.

1637. BETTY JANE[11] DAVIDSON *(FLORENCE MILDRED[10] TERRIO, BERNICE MILDRED[9] BROOKS, ALFRED LANGDON[8], DANIEL LANGDON[7], DANIEL[6], MARY[5] SPINNEY, JOHN[4], JOHN[3], JOHN[2], THOMAS[1])* was born Private. She married (1) CARL FREDERICK PROPSON, JR. Private. He was born Private. She married (2) ROY G. ANDERSON Private. He was born Private.

Children of BETTY DAVIDSON and CARL PROPSON are:
1743.   i.   CARL FREDERICK[12] PROPSON III, b. Private.
1744.   ii.   BARBARA ANN PROPSON, b. Private.
1745.   iii.   PHILIP EUGENE PROPSON, b. Private.
1746.   iv.   PENNY ELAINE PROPSON, b. Private.

1638. ROBERT EDWARD[11] DAVIDSON *(FLORENCE MILDRED[10] TERRIO, BERNICE MILDRED[9] BROOKS, ALFRED LANGDON[8], DANIEL LANGDON[7], DANIEL[6], MARY[5] SPINNEY, JOHN[4], JOHN[3], JOHN[2], THOMAS[1])* was born Private. He married (1) MARION LOUISE MEAD Private. She was born Private. He married (2) VIRGINIA PLUMLEY Private. She was born Private.

Children of ROBERT DAVIDSON and MARION MEAD are:
1747.   i.   SANDRA LOU (DAVIDSON)[12] HOFFMAN, b. 11 Nov 1948; d. Divorced December 1973.
1748.   ii.   ROBERT EDWARD (DAVIDSON) HOFFMAN, b. Private.
1749.   iii.   BONNIE LOUISE (DAVIDSON) HOFFMAN, b. Private.

Children of ROBERT DAVIDSON and VIRGINIA PLUMLEY are:
   iv.   ELMER "DAVY" RAYMOND[12] DAVIDSON, b. Private.

v. REBECCA EVONNE DAVIDSON, b. Private.

1639. EDWARD PHILIP[11] DAVIDSON *(FLORENCE MILDRED[10] TERRIO, BERNICE MILDRED[9] BROOKS, ALFRED LANGDON[8], DANIEL LANGDON[7], DANIEL[6], MARY[5] SPINNEY, JOHN[4], JOHN[3], JOHN[2], THOMAS[1])* was born Private. He married SARAH RUTH WEST Private. She was born Private.

Children of EDWARD DAVIDSON and SARAH WEST are:
1750.   i. BRIAN KIRK[12] DAVIDSON, b. Private.
1751.   ii. CHRISTOPHER ALAN DAVIDSON, b. Private.
       iii. JENNIFER LISA DAVIDSON, b. Private; m. ARTHUR ALAN BARAD, Private; b. Private.

1640. SHIRLEY VIRGINIA[11] KINGSBURY *(ANNIE MAYBELLE[10] TERRIO, BERNICE MILDRED[9] BROOKS, ALFRED LANGDON[8], DANIEL LANGDON[7], DANIEL[6], MARY[5] SPINNEY, JOHN[4], JOHN[3], JOHN[2], THOMAS[1])* was born Private. She married GREGORY WINN Private. He was born 17 Nov 1913 in Portsmouth, NH, and died Dec 1974 in Portsmouth, NH.

Child of SHIRLEY KINGSBURY and GREGORY WINN is:
1752.   i. GREGORY[12] WINN, b. Private.

1641. MARY-ANN[11] KINGSBURY *(ANNIE MAYBELLE[10] TERRIO, BERNICE MILDRED[9] BROOKS, ALFRED LANGDON[8], DANIEL LANGDON[7], DANIEL[6], MARY[5] SPINNEY, JOHN[4], JOHN[3], JOHN[2], THOMAS[1])* was born Private. She married (1) LARRY HUNTER Private. He was born Private. She married (2) STEPHEN DEKRONE Private. He was born Private. She married (3) WAYNE ALLEN Private. He was born Private.

Children of MARY-ANN KINGSBURY and STEPHEN DEKRONE are:
       i. LISA ANN[12] DEKRONE, b. Private; m. DAVID STUHLER, Private; b. Private.
       ii. RUSSELL DEKRONE, b. Private.

Children of MARY-ANN KINGSBURY and WAYNE ALLEN are:
       iii. PATTY[12] ALLEN, b. Private; m. ANDREW DAVID SALTZER, Private; b. Private.
       iv. DEBORAH ALLEN, b. Private.

1642. SAMUEL HENRY[11] KINGSBURY, JR. *(ANNIE MAYBELLE[10] TERRIO, BERNICE MILDRED[9] BROOKS, ALFRED LANGDON[8], DANIEL LANGDON[7], DANIEL[6], MARY[5] SPINNEY, JOHN[4], JOHN[3], JOHN[2], THOMAS[1])* was born Private. He married (1) MARY LOUISE WORVEY Private. She was born Private. He married (2) LAURA MICHELLE BAGLEY Private. She was born Private.

Children of SAMUEL KINGSBURY and MARY WORVEY are:
       i. ANGELA MICHELLE[12] KINGSBURY, b. Private.
       ii. SAMUEL HENRY KINGSBURY III, b. Private.

Child of SAMUEL KINGSBURY and LAURA BAGLEY is:
       iii. JENNIFER LARON[12] KINGSBURY, b. Private.

1643. CHARLES DALE[11] KINGSBURY *(ANNIE MAYBELLE[10] TERRIO, BERNICE MILDRED[9] BROOKS, ALFRED LANGDON[8], DANIEL LANGDON[7], DANIEL[6], MARY[5] SPINNEY, JOHN[4], JOHN[3], JOHN[2], THOMAS[1])* was born Private.

Child of CHARLES DALE KINGSBURY is:
       i. DALE[12] KINGSBURY, b. Private.

1644. DOLORES RUTH[11] TERRIO *(ALFRED LEE[10], BERNICE MILDRED[9] BROOKS, ALFRED LANGDON[8], DANIEL LANGDON[7], DANIEL[6], MARY[5] SPINNEY, JOHN[4], JOHN[3], JOHN[2], THOMAS[1])* was born Private. She married HAROLD ROBERT FINLEY Private. He was born Private.

Children of DOLORES TERRIO and HAROLD FINLEY are:
1753.   i.   JANICE[12] FINLEY, b. 23 Sep 1950; d. 18 Feb 1992.
1754.   ii.   WAYNE BRIAN FINLEY, b. Private.
         iii. SHANNON FINLEY, b. Private; m. (1) DOUGLAS A. LEBBON, Private; b. Private; m. (2) ERIC WILLIAM SJOQUIST, Private; b. Private; m. (3) LEONARD FREDERICK FRITSCHE, Private; b. Private.

1645. BERNICE ELEANOR[11] TERRIO *(ALFRED LEE[10], BERNICE MILDRED[9] BROOKS, ALFRED LANGDON[8], DANIEL LANGDON[7], DANIEL[6], MARY[5] SPINNEY, JOHN[4], JOHN[3], JOHN[2], THOMAS[1])* was born Private. She married PATRICK WILLIAM EGEL Private. He was born Private.

Children of BERNICE TERRIO and PATRICK EGEL are:
1755.   i.   CHRISTINE MARIE[12] EGEL, b. Private.
1756.   ii.   MICHELLE EGEL, b. Private.

1646. JOAN CONSTANCE[11] TERRIO *(ALFRED LEE[10], BERNICE MILDRED[9] BROOKS, ALFRED LANGDON[8], DANIEL LANGDON[7], DANIEL[6], MARY[5] SPINNEY, JOHN[4], JOHN[3], JOHN[2], THOMAS[1])* was born Private. She married (1) HAROLD F. EDGERLY Private. He was born Private. She married (2) FRANCIS XAVIER O'DONNELL Private. He was born Private. She married (3) WILLIAM SMELSTOR Private. He died 04 Mar 1992 in Peabody, MA (?).

Child of JOAN TERRIO and HAROLD EDGERLY is:
1757.   i.   ALAN BRUCE[12] EDGERLY, b. Private.

1647. CORRINE GRACE[11] TERRIO *(ALFRED LEE[10], BERNICE MILDRED[9] BROOKS, ALFRED LANGDON[8], DANIEL LANGDON[7], DANIEL[6], MARY[5] SPINNEY, JOHN[4], JOHN[3], JOHN[2], THOMAS[1])* was born Private. She married EDWARD MACKEY Private. He was born Private.

Children of CORRINE TERRIO and EDWARD MACKEY are:
         i.   DEBRA ANN[12] MACKEY, b. Private.
         ii.   THOMAS EDWARD UNKNOWN, b. Private.
         iii. STEVEN PAUL UNKNOWN, b. Private.
         iv.   KEVIN MICHAEL UNKNOWN, b. Private.

1648. MARY-ELLEN[11] TERRIO *(LEROY BROOKS[10], BERNICE MILDRED[9] BROOKS, ALFRED LANGDON[8], DANIEL LANGDON[7], DANIEL[6], MARY[5] SPINNEY, JOHN[4], JOHN[3], JOHN[2], THOMAS[1])* was born Private. She married CHARLES EDWARD SLONE Private. He was born Private.

Children of MARY-ELLEN TERRIO and CHARLES SLONE are:
         i.   CHARLES EDWARD[12] SLONE, JR., b. 27 Oct 1959, Turner AFB, Albany GA; d. 28 Oct 1959, Same.
1758.   ii.   DIRK HIRAM SLONE, b. Private.
1759.   iii. CRAIG EDWARD SLONE, b. Private.

1649. SHIRLEY-ANN[11] TERRIO *(LEROY BROOKS[10], BERNICE MILDRED[9] BROOKS, ALFRED LANGDON[8], DANIEL LANGDON[7], DANIEL[6], MARY[5] SPINNEY, JOHN[4], JOHN[3], JOHN[2], THOMAS[1])* was born Private. She married JEROME EARL ROBBINS Private. He was born Private.

Children of SHIRLEY-ANN TERRIO and JEROME ROBBINS are:
1760.   i.   KARYN ANN[12] ROBBINS, b. Private.
         ii.   KEVIN EARL ROBBINS, b. Private.
         iii. KELLY ANN ROBBINS, b. Private.
         iv.   KENNETH EARL ROBBINS, b. Private.

1650. LEROY BROOKS[11] TERRIO, JR. *(LEROY BROOKS[10], BERNICE MILDRED[9] BROOKS, ALFRED LANGDON[8], DANIEL LANGDON[7], DANIEL[6], MARY[5] SPINNEY, JOHN[4], JOHN[3], JOHN[2], THOMAS[1])* was born Private. He married (1) LOIS KRAMER Private. She was born Private. He married (2) JOYCE DESJARDINS Private. She was born Private.

Child of LEROY TERRIO and JOYCE DESJARDINS is:

i.   AARON DAVID[12] TERRIO, b. Private.

1651. BETTY-JANE[11] TERRIO *(LEROY BROOKS[10], BERNICE MILDRED[9] BROOKS, ALFRED LANGDON[8], DANIEL LANGDON[7], DANIEL[6], MARY[5] SPINNEY, JOHN[4], JOHN[3], JOHN[2], THOMAS[1])* was born Private. She married JOHN PIERCE DOLLARD, SR. Private. He was born Private.

Children of BETTY-JANE TERRIO and JOHN DOLLARD are:
1761.   i.   PAMELA JEAN[12] DOLLARD, b. Private.
1762.   ii.   JOHN PIERCE DOLLARD, JR., b. Private.

1652. JEFFREY LYNN[11] TERRIO *(LEROY BROOKS[10], BERNICE MILDRED[9] BROOKS, ALFRED LANGDON[8], DANIEL LANGDON[7], DANIEL[6], MARY[5] SPINNEY, JOHN[4], JOHN[3], JOHN[2], THOMAS[1])* was born Private. He married JANICE EMMA FLETCHER Private. She was born Private.

Children of JEFFREY TERRIO and JANICE FLETCHER are:
i.   JASON JEFFREY[12] TERRIO, b. Private.
ii.   JARED LEROY JAMES TERRIO, b. Private.

1653. CLAYTON E[11] DAVIS *(MABEL LEONA[10] BROOKS, ARTHUR L[9], ALFRED LANGDON[8], DANIEL LANGDON[7], DANIEL[6], MARY[5] SPINNEY, JOHN[4], JOHN[3], JOHN[2], THOMAS[1])* was born 03 Nov 1918, and died Sep 1969. He married JOSEPHINE ROBERTS HASKELL Private. She was born Private.

Child of CLAYTON DAVIS and JOSEPHINE HASKELL is:
i.   KATHLEEN[12] DAVIS, b. Private.

1654. RICHARD E[11] DAVIS *(MABEL LEONA[10] BROOKS, ARTHUR L[9], ALFRED LANGDON[8], DANIEL LANGDON[7], DANIEL[6], MARY[5] SPINNEY, JOHN[4], JOHN[3], JOHN[2], THOMAS[1])* was born 22 Aug 1929, and died 28 Feb 1979. He married (1) SHIRLEY CLUFF Private. She was born Private. He married (2) MURIEL RAMSDELL Private. She was born Private.

Children of RICHARD DAVIS and SHIRLEY CLUFF are:
i.   SHIRLEY ANNE[12] DAVIS, b. Private.
1763.   ii.   AUDREY DAVIS, b. Private.
iii.   RICHARD E DAVIS, JR., b. Private.
iv.   TODD M DAVIS, b. Private.

Children of RICHARD DAVIS and MURIEL RAMSDELL are:
v.   VIRGINIA[12] DAVIS, b. Private.
vi.   REBECCA DAVIS, b. Private.

1655. CONSTANCE ANNABELLE[11] DAVIS *(MABEL LEONA[10] BROOKS, ARTHUR L[9], ALFRED LANGDON[8], DANIEL LANGDON[7], DANIEL[6], MARY[5] SPINNEY, JOHN[4], JOHN[3], JOHN[2], THOMAS[1])* was born Private. She married HARRY GOLDTHWAITE Private. He was born Private.

Children of CONSTANCE DAVIS and HARRY GOLDTHWAITE are:
1764.   i.   CLARENCE EARL[12] GOLDTHWAITE, b. Private.
1765.   ii.   DIANE LEONA GOLDTHWAITE, b. Private.
1766.   iii.   ANNA JEAN GOLDTHWAITE, b. Private.
1767.   iv.   JOAN RUTH GOLDTHWAITE, b. Private.

1656. ELMER[11] DAVIS *(MABEL LEONA[10] BROOKS, ARTHUR L[9], ALFRED LANGDON[8], DANIEL LANGDON[7], DANIEL[6], MARY[5] SPINNEY, JOHN[4], JOHN[3], JOHN[2], THOMAS[1])* was born Private. He married DONNA L GILMORE Private. She was born Private.

Children of ELMER DAVIS and DONNA GILMORE are:

1768.	i.	BONNIE ANN[12] DAVIS, b. Private.
1769.	ii.	DAVID ANDREW DAVIS, b. Private.
1770.	iii.	LEROY EDWARD DAVIS, b. Private.
1771.	iv.	LINDA DAVIS, b. Private.
1772.	v.	DANNY DAVIS, b. Private.
1773.	vi.	HELEN DAVIS, b. Private.

1657. RUTH EVELYN[11] DAVIS *(MABEL LEONA[10] BROOKS, ARTHUR L[9], ALFRED LANGDON[8], DANIEL LANGDON[7], DANIEL[6], MARY[5] SPINNEY, JOHN[4], JOHN[3], JOHN[2], THOMAS[1])* was born Private. She married ROBERT HAVEL WILLIAMS Private. He was born Private.

Children of RUTH DAVIS and ROBERT WILLIAMS are:
	i.	JACQUELINE[12] WILLIAMS, b. Private.
1774.	ii.	JAMES RONALD WILLIAMS, b. Private.
1775.	iii.	PAMELA ROSE WILLIAMS, b. Private.

1658. ROBERT H[11] DAVIS *(MABEL LEONA[10] BROOKS, ARTHUR L[9], ALFRED LANGDON[8], DANIEL LANGDON[7], DANIEL[6], MARY[5] SPINNEY, JOHN[4], JOHN[3], JOHN[2], THOMAS[1])* was born Private. He married DORIS PALMER Private. She was born Private.

Children of ROBERT DAVIS and DORIS PALMER are:
	i.	JIMMY[12] DAVIS, b. 1950; d. 1950.
1776.	ii.	SANDRA DAVIS, b. Private.
	iii.	DOUGLAS DAVIS, b. Private.
	iv.	KATHY DAVIS, b. Private.
	v.	DEBBIE DAVIS, b. Private.
	vi.	JEFFREY DAVIS, b. Private.
	vii.	ANDREW DAVIS, b. Private.

1659. CHESTER[11] DAVIS *(MABEL LEONA[10] BROOKS, ARTHUR L[9], ALFRED LANGDON[8], DANIEL LANGDON[7], DANIEL[6], MARY[5] SPINNEY, JOHN[4], JOHN[3], JOHN[2], THOMAS[1])* was born Private. He married (1) JUNE BRENNAN Private. She was born Private. He married (2) CONSTANCE CHABORNE BROWN Private. She was born Private.

Children of CHESTER DAVIS and JUNE BRENNAN are:
| | i. | ROSE MARIE[12] DAVIS, b. 1952; d. 1952. |
| 1777. | ii. | RONNIE JOE DAVIS, b. Private. |

Children of CHESTER DAVIS and CONSTANCE BROWN are:
	iii.	JIMMY[12] CHABORNE, b. Private.
	iv.	JULIE DAVIS, b. Private.
	v.	JOANNE DAVIS, b. Private.
	vi.	CHESTER DAVIS, b. Private.
	vii.	CARL DAVIS, b. Private.

1660. CARL L[11] DAVIS *(MABEL LEONA[10] BROOKS, ARTHUR L[9], ALFRED LANGDON[8], DANIEL LANGDON[7], DANIEL[6], MARY[5] SPINNEY, JOHN[4], JOHN[3], JOHN[2], THOMAS[1])* was born Private.

Children of CARL L DAVIS are:
| 1778. | i. | SONIA[12] DAVIS, b. Private. |
| 1779. | ii. | DORREEN DAVIS, b. Private. |

1661. WILMA FLORENCE[11] DAVIS *(MABEL LEONA[10] BROOKS, ARTHUR L[9], ALFRED LANGDON[8], DANIEL LANGDON[7], DANIEL[6], MARY[5] SPINNEY, JOHN[4], JOHN[3], JOHN[2], THOMAS[1])* was born Private. She married RUSHFORTH WILLIAMS Private. He was born Private.

Children of WILMA DAVIS and RUSHFORTH WILLIAMS are:
| | i. | ROGER[12] WILLIAMS, b. 29 Sep 1954; d. 15 Nov 1954. |

1780.   ii.   JOHN ANDREW WILLIAMS, b. Private.
          iii.   RUSHFORTH WILLIAMS II, b. Private.
          iv.   MICHAEL PAUL WILLIAMS, b. Private.

1662. GAIL JUDITH[11] ANDERSON *(DORIS HEWITT[10] BROOKS, LEROY ULMONT[9], ALFRED LANGDON[8], DANIEL LANGDON[7], DANIEL[6], MARY[5] SPINNEY, JOHN[4], JOHN[3], JOHN[2], THOMAS[1])* was born Private. She married RICHARD FARRIS Private. He was born Private.

Children of GAIL ANDERSON and RICHARD FARRIS are:
    i.   SCOTT DAVID[12] FARRIS, b. Private.
    ii.   NANCY JEAN FARRIS, b. Private.

1663. STEPHEN BROOKS[11] ANDERSON *(DORIS HEWITT[10] BROOKS, LEROY ULMONT[9], ALFRED LANGDON[8], DANIEL LANGDON[7], DANIEL[6], MARY[5] SPINNEY, JOHN[4], JOHN[3], JOHN[2], THOMAS[1])* was born Private. He married JANICE FRANKLIN Private. She was born Private.

Children of STEPHEN ANDERSON and JANICE FRANKLIN are:
    i.   STEPHEN BROOKS[12] ANDERSON, JR., b. Private.
    ii.   JAMES WILLIAM ANDERSON, b. Private.
    iii.   CLARK DAVID ANDERSON, b. Private.
    iv.   JILL FRANKLIN ANDERSON, b. Private.

1664. CHRISTINA[11] BROADHURST *(ETHEL BERNICE[10] CASWELL, ESSIE ROSE[9] BROOKS, ALFRED LANGDON[8], DANIEL LANGDON[7], DANIEL[6], MARY[5] SPINNEY, JOHN[4], JOHN[3], JOHN[2], THOMAS[1])* was born Private. She married DANIEL METEVIER Private. He was born Private.

Children of CHRISTINA BROADHURST and DANIEL METEVIER are:
    i.   TAMMY[12] METEVIER, b. Private.
    ii.   DENISE METEVIER, b. Private.
    iii.   DANNY METEVIER, b. Private.
    iv.   MIKE METEVIER, b. Private.

1665. MARJORIE[11] BROADHURST *(ETHEL BERNICE[10] CASWELL, ESSIE ROSE[9] BROOKS, ALFRED LANGDON[8], DANIEL LANGDON[7], DANIEL[6], MARY[5] SPINNEY, JOHN[4], JOHN[3], JOHN[2], THOMAS[1])* was born Private. She married ARMOND PATCH Private. He was born Private.

Children of MARJORIE BROADHURST and ARMOND PATCH are:
    i.   MICHELE LYN[12] PATCH, b. Private.
    ii.   SHEILA MARIE PATCH, b. Private.

1666. THOMAS JOSEPH[11] BROADHURST *(ETHEL BERNICE[10] CASWELL, ESSIE ROSE[9] BROOKS, ALFRED LANGDON[8], DANIEL LANGDON[7], DANIEL[6], MARY[5] SPINNEY, JOHN[4], JOHN[3], JOHN[2], THOMAS[1])* was born Private. He married GAIL DIANE FERNALD Private. She was born Private.

Children of THOMAS BROADHURST and GAIL FERNALD are:
    i.   SHANNON STAR[12] BROADHURST, b. Private.
    ii.   NEHA BREE BROADHURST, b. Private.

1667. BARBARA MAY[11] DUNLAP *(MARJORIE AUGUSTA[10] CASWELL, ESSIE ROSE[9] BROOKS, ALFRED LANGDON[8], DANIEL LANGDON[7], DANIEL[6], MARY[5] SPINNEY, JOHN[4], JOHN[3], JOHN[2], THOMAS[1])* was born Private. She married ALBERT EDWARD DOW, JR. Private. He was born Private.

Children of BARBARA DUNLAP and ALBERT DOW are:
    i.   CHRISTOPHER GEORGE[12] DOW, b. Private.
    ii.   DAPHNE ELAINE DOW, b. Private.
    iii.   ERROL KIRK DOW, b. Private.

1668. ELEANOR JEAN[11] DUNLAP *(MARJORIE AUGUSTA[10] CASWELL, ESSIE ROSE[9] BROOKS, ALFRED LANGDON[8], DANIEL LANGDON[7], DANIEL[6], MARY[5] SPINNEY, JOHN[4], JOHN[3], JOHN[2], THOMAS[1])* was born Private. She married GORDON DOUGLAS CLAY Private. He was born Private.

Children of ELEANOR DUNLAP and GORDON CLAY are:
- i. DOUGLAS PAUL[12] CLAY, b. Private.
- ii. TIMOTHY GENE CLAY, b. Private.
- iii. ROBERT VALLIER CLAY, b. Private.
- iv. WILLIAM BASTON CLAY, b. Private.

1669. GERALD CHARLES[11] DUNLAP *(MARJORIE AUGUSTA[10] CASWELL, ESSIE ROSE[9] BROOKS, ALFRED LANGDON[8], DANIEL LANGDON[7], DANIEL[6], MARY[5] SPINNEY, JOHN[4], JOHN[3], JOHN[2], THOMAS[1])* was born Private. He married (1) SUSAN PRAYTOR Private. She was born Private. He married (2) NANCY ALICE LITTLEFIELD Private. She was born Private.

Children of GERALD DUNLAP and NANCY LITTLEFIELD are:
- i. STEPHANIE LYNN[12] DUNLAP, b. Private.
- ii. SEAN KIRK DUNLAP, b. Private.
- iii. GABRIEL NOAH DUNLAP, b. Private.

1670. NANCY BROOKS[11] CUMMINGS *(ANNIE HEWITT[10] CASWELL, ESSIE ROSE[9] BROOKS, ALFRED LANGDON[8], DANIEL LANGDON[7], DANIEL[6], MARY[5] SPINNEY, JOHN[4], JOHN[3], JOHN[2], THOMAS[1])* was born Private. She married (1) LETHER TAYLOR Private. He was born Private. She married (2) LEE PALMER KRAGH Private. He was born Private.

Child of NANCY CUMMINGS and LETHER TAYLOR is:
- i. LAUREL LEE[12] TAYLOR, b. Private.

1671. MARY EARLENE[11] NELSON *(SAMUEL MURRAY[10], SAMUEL HERBERT[9], EMILY ANN[8] BROOKS, DANIEL LANGDON[7], DANIEL[6], MARY[5] SPINNEY, JOHN[4], JOHN[3], JOHN[2], THOMAS[1])* was born Private. She married VANSANTVOORD Private. He was born Private.

Children of MARY NELSON and VANSANTVOORD are:
- i. RICHARD NELSON[12] VANSANTVOORD, b. Private.
- ii. PETER STAATS VANSANTVOORD, b. Private.

1672. EMILY ALBERTA[11] NELSON *(SAMUEL MURRAY[10], SAMUEL HERBERT[9], EMILY ANN[8] BROOKS, DANIEL LANGDON[7], DANIEL[6], MARY[5] SPINNEY, JOHN[4], JOHN[3], JOHN[2], THOMAS[1])* was born Private. She married BUSSEY Private. He was born Private.

Child of EMILY NELSON and BUSSEY is:
- i. BARBARA ANN[12] BUSSEY, b. Private.

1673. BARBARA[11] NELSON *(SAMUEL MURRAY[10], SAMUEL HERBERT[9], EMILY ANN[8] BROOKS, DANIEL LANGDON[7], DANIEL[6], MARY[5] SPINNEY, JOHN[4], JOHN[3], JOHN[2], THOMAS[1])* was born Private. She married MARKEL Private. He was born Private.

Children of BARBARA NELSON and MARKEL are:
- i. NANCY[12] MARKEL, b. Private.
- ii. VINCENT ANTHONY MARKEL, b. Private.
- iii. LINDA MARY MARKEL, b. Private.

1674. SAMUEL MURRAY[11] NELSON, JR. *(SAMUEL MURRAY[10], SAMUEL HERBERT[9], EMILY ANN[8] BROOKS, DANIEL LANGDON[7], DANIEL[6], MARY[5] SPINNEY, JOHN[4], JOHN[3], JOHN[2], THOMAS[1])* was born Private.

Children of SAMUEL MURRAY NELSON, JR. are:
- i. SUSAN MARIE[12] NELSON, b. Private.
- ii. KENNETH MURRAY NELSON, b. Private.
- iii. LAURA NELSON, b. Private.

1675. THEODORE MACMILLAIN[11] NELSON *(SAMUEL MURRAY[10], SAMUEL HERBERT[9], EMILY ANN[8] BROOKS, DANIEL LANGDON[7], DANIEL[6], MARY[5] SPINNEY, JOHN[4], JOHN[3], JOHN[2], THOMAS[1])* was born Private.

Children of THEODORE MACMILLAIN NELSON are:
- i. JUDY[12] NELSON, b. Private.
- ii. THEODORE MACMILLIAN NELSON, JR., b. Private.

1676. STANTON GILBERT[11] O'MALLEY *(CLARA BELLE[10] LEACH, ADA SYRENA[9] VARNEY, CLARA FRANCES[8] BROOKS, DANIEL LANGDON[7], DANIEL[6], MARY[5] SPINNEY, JOHN[4], JOHN[3], JOHN[2], THOMAS[1])* was born 17 Jan 1911, and died 28 Jul 1967. He married MARY MORIN Private. She was born Private.

Children of STANTON O'MALLEY and MARY MORIN are:
- i. JOHN STANTON[12] O'MALLEY, b. 08 Feb 1940; d. 09 Jul 1960.
- 1781. ii. CATHERINE FRANCES O'MALLEY, b. Private.
- 1782. iii. VIRGINIA MARIE O'MALLEY, b. Private.
- 1783. iv. THOMAS MANLEY O'MALLEY, b. Private.
- v. STEPHEN JOSEPH O'MALLEY, b. Private.

1677. SYLVIA MARGUERITE[11] O'MALLEY *(CLARA BELLE[10] LEACH, ADA SYRENA[9] VARNEY, CLARA FRANCES[8] BROOKS, DANIEL LANGDON[7], DANIEL[6], MARY[5] SPINNEY, JOHN[4], JOHN[3], JOHN[2], THOMAS[1])* was born Private. She married PAUL Y DOW Private. He was born Private.

Children of SYLVIA O'MALLEY and PAUL DOW are:
- 1784. i. JACQUELINE[12] DOW, b. Private.
- 1785. ii. CLAIRE EILEEN DOW, b. Private.

1678. FREDERICK VARNEY[11] O'MALLEY *(CLARA BELLE[10] LEACH, ADA SYRENA[9] VARNEY, CLARA FRANCES[8] BROOKS, DANIEL LANGDON[7], DANIEL[6], MARY[5] SPINNEY, JOHN[4], JOHN[3], JOHN[2], THOMAS[1])* was born Private. He married (1) NADINE KENNISTON JONES Private. She was born Private. He married (2) OLYMPIA DONINNI Private. She was born Private.

Child of FREDERICK O'MALLEY and NADINE JONES is:
- i. AMBER[12] O'MALLEY, b. Private.

Children of FREDERICK O'MALLEY and OLYMPIA DONINNI are:
- ii. PRISCILLA[12] O'MALLEY, b. 1949; d. 1949.
- iii. PEARL O'MALLEY, b. 1949; d. 1949.
- iv. MICHAEL MARK O'MALLEY, b. Private.

1679. IDA LOUISE[11] LEACH *(FRANK EDWIN[10], ADA SYRENA[9] VARNEY, CLARA FRANCES[8] BROOKS, DANIEL LANGDON[7], DANIEL[6], MARY[5] SPINNEY, JOHN[4], JOHN[3], JOHN[2], THOMAS[1])* was born Private. She married (1) JACK STOLLBERG Private. He was born Private. She married (2) JOE WILSON Private. He was born Private.

Children of IDA LEACH and JACK STOLLBERG are:
- 1786. i. THERESA[12] STOLLBERG, b. Private.
- ii. JACK STOLLBERG, b. Private.

Child of IDA LEACH and JOE WILSON is:
- iii. BETTY JO[12] WILSON, b. 22 Aug 1954; d. 31 Jan 1971.

1680. GEORGE EDWIN[11] LEACH *(FRANK EDWIN[10], ADA SYRENA[9] VARNEY, CLARA FRANCES[8] BROOKS, DANIEL LANGDON[7], DANIEL[6], MARY[5] SPINNEY, JOHN[4], JOHN[3], JOHN[2], THOMAS[1])* was born Private. He married HELEN MARCOUX Private. She was born Private.

Children of GEORGE LEACH and HELEN MARCOUX are:
1787. i. MARK THOMAS[12] LEACH, b. Private.
    ii. FRANK EDWIN LEACH, b. Private.
    iii. MARY IRENE LEACH, b. Private.
    iv. JOHN SCOTT LEACH, b. Private.
    v. LORI ANN LEACH, b. Private.
    vi. TODD PETER LEACH, b. Private.

1681. ELEANOR MAE[11] LEACH *(FRANK EDWIN[10], ADA SYRENA[9] VARNEY, CLARA FRANCES[8] BROOKS, DANIEL LANGDON[7], DANIEL[6], MARY[5] SPINNEY, JOHN[4], JOHN[3], JOHN[2], THOMAS[1])* was born Private. She married JOSEPH BOULANGER Private. He was born Private.

Children of ELEANOR LEACH and JOSEPH BOULANGER are:
    i. JOSEPH ROY[12] BOULANGER, b. Private.
    ii. PAT ROY BOULANGER, b. Private.
    iii. BETTY JEAN BOULANGER, b. Private.

1682. MADELINE SADIE[11] HILL *(SADIE ADA[10] LEACH, ADA SYRENA[9] VARNEY, CLARA FRANCES[8] BROOKS, DANIEL LANGDON[7], DANIEL[6], MARY[5] SPINNEY, JOHN[4], JOHN[3], JOHN[2], THOMAS[1])* was born Private. She married (1) CLAYTON DOWNING Private. He was born Private. She married (2) RICHARD CURTIS MARTEL Private. He was born Private.

Children of MADELINE HILL and CLAYTON DOWNING are:
    i. DENISE ELIZABETH[12] DOWNING, b. Private.
    ii. JUDITH EILEEN DOWNING, b. Private.

Child of MADELINE HILL and RICHARD MARTEL is:
1788. iii. SANDRA MADELINE[12] MARTEL, b. Private.

1683. MARTHA[11] PAYNE *(LILLIAN M[10] SPINNEY, ARTHUR ROSCOE[9], ALFRED[8], SYLVESTER[7], FRANCIS[6], GEORGE PETTEGREW[5], JOHN[4], JOHN[3], JOHN[2], THOMAS[1])* She married GREENE.

Children of MARTHA PAYNE and GREENE are:
    i. MARTHA[12] GREENE.
    ii. GEORGIA GREENE.
    iii. JULIE GREENE.
    iv. SARAH GREENE.
    v. LYDIA GREENE.

1684. NORMAN K[11] SPINNEY *(NORMAN E[10], MILO[9], ALFRED[8], SYLVESTER[7], FRANCIS[6], GEORGE PETTEGREW[5], JOHN[4], JOHN[3], JOHN[2], THOMAS[1])* was born 09 Mar 1922, and died 19 Apr 2000 in Exeter New Hampsire. He married VRGINIA NORTON 12 Apr 1941.

Children of NORMAN SPINNEY and VRGINIA NORTON are:
    i. DIANE[12] SPINNEY, m. DECOFF.
    ii. VIRGINIA SPINNEY, m. MUNZ.
    iii. ARLENE SPINNEY, m. SABIN.
    iv. MELBA SPINNEY, m. GUNNISON.

1685. JUDITH IRENE[11] MANSON *(DOROTHY[10] SPINNEY, ADVILLE A[9], AMMI ADVILLE[8], FRANCIS LEMUEL[7], FRANCIS[6], GEORGE PETTEGREW[5], JOHN[4], JOHN[3], JOHN[2], THOMAS[1])* She married JAMES STAFFORD QUINN.

Child of JUDITH MANSON and JAMES QUINN is:
1789.   i.   HEATHER DAWN[12] QUINN.

1686. DAVID BERKLEY[11] WALKER *(JOHN BERKLEY[10], FLORENCE WINIFRED[9] HUNTRESS, MARY EVA[8] DIXON, LYDIA N.[7] TETHERLY, CHARLES[6], SAMUEL[5], WILLIAM[4], MERCY[3] SPINNEY, JOHN[2], THOMAS[1])* was born Private. He married DOROTHY ELLEN GRIFFITH Private. She was born Private.

Children of DAVID WALKER and DOROTHY GRIFFITH are:
      i.   DAVID EUGENE[12] WALKER, b. 10 Sep 1953, Springfield, MA; d. 16 Sep 1996, Ware, MA.
1790.   ii.   CHRISTINE MAE WALKER, b. Private.
      iii.   BARRY FORD WALKER, b. Private.
1791.   iv.   JEANETTE GAIL WALKER, b. Private.
1792.   v.   CYNTHIA MARRIE WALKER, b. Private.
1793.   vi.   DONNA LYNN WALKER, b. Private.
      vii.   VIVIAN LEE WALKER, b. Private.
      viii.   DANA ALLEN WALKER, b. Private.
      ix.   ERIC TODD WALKER, b. Private.

1687. JOHN COYLE[11] WALKER *(JOHN BERKLEY[10], FLORENCE WINIFRED[9] HUNTRESS, MARY EVA[8] DIXON, LYDIA N.[7] TETHERLY, CHARLES[6], SAMUEL[5], WILLIAM[4], MERCY[3] SPINNEY, JOHN[2], THOMAS[1])* was born Private. He married BARBARA NOONAN Private. She was born Private.

Children of JOHN WALKER and BARBARA NOONAN are:
      i.   JAMES JOHN[12] WALKER, b. Private.
      ii.   CAROLE LYNNE WALKER, b. Private.
      iii.   ELIZABETH ANNE WALKER, b. Private.

1688. BRUCE HUNTRESS[11] WALKER *(JOHN BERKLEY[10], FLORENCE WINIFRED[9] HUNTRESS, MARY EVA[8] DIXON, LYDIA N.[7] TETHERLY, CHARLES[6], SAMUEL[5], WILLIAM[4], MERCY[3] SPINNEY, JOHN[2], THOMAS[1])* was born Private. He married VERNA MAE SCHNOP Private. She was born Private.

Children of BRUCE WALKER and VERNA SCHNOP are:
1794.   i.   STEVEN B.[12] WALKER, b. Private.
      ii.   MATHEW V. WALKER, b. Private.
      iii.   LAURIE A. WALKER, b. Private.
1795.   iv.   PATRICIA A. WALKER, b. Private.
1796.   v.   BRUCE HUNTRESS WALKER, b. Private.

1689. DANIEL HEYWOOD[11] WALKER *(JOHN BERKLEY[10], FLORENCE WINIFRED[9] HUNTRESS, MARY EVA[8] DIXON, LYDIA N.[7] TETHERLY, CHARLES[6], SAMUEL[5], WILLIAM[4], MERCY[3] SPINNEY, JOHN[2], THOMAS[1])* was born Private. He married KAREN SHEEHAN Private. She was born Private.

Children of DANIEL WALKER and KAREN SHEEHAN are:
      i.   KELLY JEANNE[12] WALKER, b. Private.
      ii.   MEREDITH WALKER, b. Private.

1690. KATHERINE MARY[11] WALKER *(JOHN BERKLEY[10], FLORENCE WINIFRED[9] HUNTRESS, MARY EVA[8] DIXON, LYDIA N.[7] TETHERLY, CHARLES[6], SAMUEL[5], WILLIAM[4], MERCY[3] SPINNEY, JOHN[2], THOMAS[1])* was born Private. She married WILLIAM LAPORTE Private. He was born Private.

Children of KATHERINE WALKER and WILLIAM LAPORTE are:
      i.   MELINDA ANNE[12] LAPORTE, b. Private.
      ii.   JESSICA WALKER LAPORTE, b. Private.

1691. KENNETH DWIGHT[11] WALKER *(KENNETH DAVID[10], FLORENCE WINIFRED[9] HUNTRESS, MARY EVA[8] DIXON, LYDIA N.[7] TETHERLY, CHARLES[6], SAMUEL[5], WILLIAM[4], MERCY[3] SPINNEY, JOHN[2], THOMAS[1])* was born Private. He married (1) CAROL EVERETT Private. She was born Private. He married (2) JEANNETTE CARIER Private. She was born Private.

Children of KENNETH WALKER and JEANNETTE CARIER are:
     i.   BRENDA JEAN[12] WALKER, b. Private.
    ii.   JOHN ALFRED WALKER, b. Private.
   iii.   THOMAS KENNETH WALKER, b. Private.

1692. JUNE[11] WALKER *(KENNETH DAVID[10], FLORENCE WINIFRED[9] HUNTRESS, MARY EVA[8] DIXON, LYDIA N.[7] TETHERLY, CHARLES[6], SAMUEL[5], WILLIAM[4], MERCY[3] SPINNEY, JOHN[2], THOMAS[1])* was born Private. She married (1) KENNETH KING Private. He was born Private. She married (2) EDWARD FRANCIS COTE Private. He was born Private.

Child of JUNE WALKER and KENNETH KING is:
     i.   JEANNIFER[12] COTE, b. Private.

Children of JUNE WALKER and EDWARD COTE are:
    ii.   RICHARD KENNETH[12] COTE, b. Private.
   iii.   CHERIE LEE COTE, b. Private.
1797.   iv.   DARLENE COTE, b. Private.
    v.   DAVID EDWARD COTE, b. Private; m. MARY, Private; b. Private.

1693. DOROTHY LILLIAN[11] CLIFFORD *(VEDA VIVIAN[10] CAHILL, LILLIAN MAUD[9] LYDSTON, ARTHUR FRANCIS[8], FRANCIS ARTHUR[7], WILLIAM[6], WEYMOUTH[5], ABIGAIL[4] SPINNEY, ANDREW[3], JOHN[2], THOMAS[1])* was born 26 Dec 1909 in Sacramento, CA, and died 24 Dec 1936 in Sacramento, CA. She married ORVILE PETER FELT 16 Jan 1932 in Fairfield, CA, son of FRANK FELT and MARYANN HADLEY.

Child of DOROTHY CLIFFORD and ORVILE FELT is:
1798.   i.   DICK[12] FELT.

1694. DAVID MYLES[11] SPRAGUE *(ALMA FRANCES[10] WELLNER, ALMA EDITH[9] SPINNEY, ALLISON FAIRBANKS[8], HIRAM[7], DAVID[6], ISAAC[5], JOHN[4], JOHN[3], JOHN[2], THOMAS[1])* was born 16 Jul 1934. He married CAROL FERN AVERY. She was born 17 Jul 1938.

Children of DAVID SPRAGUE and CAROL AVERY are:
     i.   DAVID MYLES[12] SPRAGUE, b. 20 Jan 1957.
    ii.   PETER KEVIN SPRAGUE, b. 25 Sep 1958.
   iii.   MARY ELEANOR SPRAGUE, b. 13 Apr 1963.
   iv.   TIMOTHY JAY SPRAGUE, b. 18 Dec 1967.

1695. EILEEN MARY[11] ST. ONGE *(EILEEN MARTHA[10] FORD, JAMES ELMER[9], LAURA MAE[8] SPINNEY, STILLMAN[7], JOSEPH[6], JACOB[5], JOHN[4], JOHN[3], JOHN[2], THOMAS[1])* was born Private. She married THOMAS FRANCIS ROCCA Private. He was born Private.

Children of EILEEN ST. ONGE and THOMAS ROCCA are:
     i.   CHRISTINA RENEE'[12] ROCCA, b. Private.
    ii.   RACHELLE MARIE ROCCA, b. Private.
   iii.   DAVID THOMAS ROCCA, b. Private.
   iv.   JOEL PAUL ROCCA, b. Private.

1696. RAYMOND EDGAR[11] BUTLER *(CLAIRE THERESA[10] FORD, JAMES ELMER[9], LAURA MAE[8] SPINNEY, STILLMAN[7], JOSEPH[6], JACOB[5], JOHN[4], JOHN[3], JOHN[2], THOMAS[1])* was born Private. He married (1) JEAN COWING Private. She was born Private. He married (2) DEBORAH MAILLOUX Private. She was born Private.

Children of RAYMOND BUTLER and DEBORAH MAILLOUX are:
     i.   CONOR ROBERT[12] BUTLER, b. Private.

ii. CHRISTINA CLAIRE BUTLER, b. Private.

1697. JOANNE MARIE[11] BUTLER *(CLAIRE THERESA[10] FORD, JAMES ELMER[9], LAURA MAE[8] SPINNEY, STILLMAN[7], JOSEPH[6], JACOB[5], JOHN[4], JOHN[3], JOHN[2], THOMAS[1])* was born Private. She married ONOFRIO MERULLO Private. He was born Private.

Child of JOANNE BUTLER and ONOFRIO MERULLO is:
i. JEFFREY MATTHEW[12] BUTLER, b. Private.

1698. BRENDA JEAN[11] FORD *(ROBERT EDWARD[10], JAMES ELMER[9], LAURA MAE[8] SPINNEY, STILLMAN[7], JOSEPH[6], JACOB[5], JOHN[4], JOHN[3], JOHN[2], THOMAS[1])* was born Private. She married KEVIN MICHAEL LYONS Private. He was born Private.

Children of BRENDA FORD and KEVIN LYONS are:
i. BRENDAN MICHAEL[12] LYONS, b. Private.
ii. PATRICK KENNETH LYONS, b. Private.

1699. ROBERT EDWARD[11] FORD *(ROBERT EDWARD[10], JAMES ELMER[9], LAURA MAE[8] SPINNEY, STILLMAN[7], JOSEPH[6], JACOB[5], JOHN[4], JOHN[3], JOHN[2], THOMAS[1])* was born Private. He married MELISSA ANN Private. She was born Private.

Child of ROBERT FORD and MELISSA ANN is:
i. CODY ROBERT[12] FORD, b. Private.

1700. CHERYL ANN[11] CLARK *(PAULINE DOROTHY[10] FORD, JAMES ELMER[9], LAURA MAE[8] SPINNEY, STILLMAN[7], JOSEPH[6], JACOB[5], JOHN[4], JOHN[3], JOHN[2], THOMAS[1])* was born Private.

Children of CHERYL ANN CLARK are:
i. JENNIFER[12] CLARK, b. Private.
ii. LAURA NICHOLE CLARK, b. Private.
iii. BRITTANY LEIGH CLARK, b. Private.

1701. PAMELA JEAN[11] FULTON *(MARION ANGELA[10] FORD, JAMES ELMER[9], LAURA MAE[8] SPINNEY, STILLMAN[7], JOSEPH[6], JACOB[5], JOHN[4], JOHN[3], JOHN[2], THOMAS[1])* was born Private. She married MATTHEW MORAD Private. He was born Private.

Children of PAMELA FULTON and MATTHEW MORAD are:
i. EMILY MAE[12] MORAD, b. Private.
ii. ZACHARY SCOTT MORAD, b. Private.
iii. JOSHUA MICHAEL MORAD, b. Private.

1702. LINDA MARIE[11] ASTE *(MARION ANGELA[10] FORD, JAMES ELMER[9], LAURA MAE[8] SPINNEY, STILLMAN[7], JOSEPH[6], JACOB[5], JOHN[4], JOHN[3], JOHN[2], THOMAS[1])* was born Private. She married GARY JOSEPH SURRO Private. He was born Private.

Child of LINDA ASTE and GARY SURRO is:
i. JEREMY JOSEPH[12] SURRO, b. Private.

1703. BETHANY ANGELA[11] ASTE *(MARION ANGELA[10] FORD, JAMES ELMER[9], LAURA MAE[8] SPINNEY, STILLMAN[7], JOSEPH[6], JACOB[5], JOHN[4], JOHN[3], JOHN[2], THOMAS[1])* was born Private.

Child of BETHANY ANGELA ASTE is:
i. JESSE JOHN[12] ASTE-POWELL, b. Private.

1704. KATHLEEN ANNE[11] CAPPELLUCCI *(JOAN ELIZABETH[10] FORD, JAMES ELMER[9], LAURA MAE[8] SPINNEY, STILLMAN[7], JOSEPH[6], JACOB[5], JOHN[4], JOHN[3], JOHN[2], THOMAS[1])* was born Private. She married DAVID PAUL BANKSTON Private. He was born Private.

Children of KATHLEEN CAPPELLUCCI and DAVID BANKSTON are:
    i.   SUSAN DWAYNE[12] BANKSTON, b. Private.
    ii. JESSICA ANNE BANKSTON, b. Private.
    iii. AMANDA LEIGH BANKSTON, b. Private.

1705. MICHAEL JOHN[11] CAPPELLUCCI *(JOAN ELIZABETH[10] FORD, JAMES ELMER[9], LAURA MAE[8] SPINNEY, STILLMAN[7], JOSEPH[6], JACOB[5], JOHN[4], JOHN[3], JOHN[2], THOMAS[1])* was born Private. He married JUDITH ANN MURPHY Private. She was born Private.

Children of MICHAEL CAPPELLUCCI and JUDITH MURPHY are:
    i.   MICHAEL ANTHONY[12] CAPPELLUCCI, b. Private.
    ii. ANGELA MAE CAPPELLUCCI, b. Private.

1706. LAURA MAE[11] CAPPELLUCCI *(JOAN ELIZABETH[10] FORD, JAMES ELMER[9], LAURA MAE[8] SPINNEY, STILLMAN[7], JOSEPH[6], JACOB[5], JOHN[4], JOHN[3], JOHN[2], THOMAS[1])* was born Private. She married DAVID BEDSUN Private. He was born Private.

Children of LAURA CAPPELLUCCI and DAVID BEDSUN are:
    i.   ANDREW ANTHONY[12] BEDSUN, b. Private.
    ii. PAIGE LEIGH BEDSUN, b. Private.
    iii. MATTHEW GARRETT BEDSUN, b. Private.

1707. PATRICIA MARIE[11] CAPPELLUCCI *(JOAN ELIZABETH[10] FORD, JAMES ELMER[9], LAURA MAE[8] SPINNEY, STILLMAN[7], JOSEPH[6], JACOB[5], JOHN[4], JOHN[3], JOHN[2], THOMAS[1])* was born Private. She married DANIEL MUSETTI Private. He was born Private.

Children of PATRICIA CAPPELLUCCI and DANIEL MUSETTI are:
    i.   LISA MARIE[12] CAPPELLUCCI, b. Private.
    ii. MARIA DANIELLE CAPPELLUCCI, b. Private.

1708. JAMES EDWARD[11] CAPPELLUCCI *(JOAN ELIZABETH[10] FORD, JAMES ELMER[9], LAURA MAE[8] SPINNEY, STILLMAN[7], JOSEPH[6], JACOB[5], JOHN[4], JOHN[3], JOHN[2], THOMAS[1])* was born Private. He married BRENDA MARIE LYDON Private. She was born Private.

Children of JAMES CAPPELLUCCI and BRENDA LYDON are:
    i.   ERIN MARIE[12] CAPPELLUCCI, b. Private.
    ii. TARA KATHLEEN CAPPELLUCCI, b. Private.

1709. JOHN TIMOTHY[11] FORD *(JOHN TIMOTHY[10], JAMES ELMER[9], LAURA MAE[8] SPINNEY, STILLMAN[7], JOSEPH[6], JACOB[5], JOHN[4], JOHN[3], JOHN[2], THOMAS[1])* was born Private. He married LORI CATHERINE CURTIS Private. She was born Private.

Children of JOHN FORD and LORI CURTIS are:
    i.   MICHELLE ELIZABETH[12] FORD, b. Private.
    ii. JOHN TIMOTHY FORD, b. Private.

1710. JAN MARIE[11] ROONEY *(ELEANOR MAE[10] FORD, JAMES ELMER[9], LAURA MAE[8] SPINNEY, STILLMAN[7], JOSEPH[6], JACOB[5], JOHN[4], JOHN[3], JOHN[2], THOMAS[1])* was born Private. She married JOHN DANIEL RHEIN Private. He was born Private.

Child of JAN ROONEY and JOHN RHEIN is:
    i.   EMILY MARIE[12] RHEIN, b. Private.

1711. CHRISTINE THERESA[11] MARCH *(JANET MARGARET[10] FORD, JAMES ELMER[9], LAURA MAE[8] SPINNEY, STILLMAN[7], JOSEPH[6], JACOB[5], JOHN[4], JOHN[3], JOHN[2], THOMAS[1])* was born Private.

Children of CHRISTINE THERESA MARCH are:
    i.   ERICA MAY[12] FERRO, b. Private.
    ii. WILLIAM DEAN MCKENNA, b. Private.
    iii. IAN THOMAS FERRO, b. Private.

1712. HEIDI JEAN[11] SPINNEY *(DONALD STEPHEN[10], DONALD N[9], LYMAN EUGENE[8], BOWMAN E[7], EDWARD[6], DANIEL[5], JOHN[4], JOHN[3], JOHN[2], THOMAS[1])* was born 24 Oct 1975. She married JEFFREY HAROLD MACISAAC.

Child of HEIDI SPINNEY and JEFFREY MACISAAC is:
    i.   JEFFREY HAROLD[12] MACISAAC.

1713. KATIE MAE[11] SPINNEY *(DONALD STEPHEN[10], DONALD N[9], LYMAN EUGENE[8], BOWMAN E[7], EDWARD[6], DANIEL[5], JOHN[4], JOHN[3], JOHN[2], THOMAS[1])* She married KEITH WALTER ARSENAULT.

Children of KATIE SPINNEY and KEITH ARSENAULT are:
    i.   SEAN JAMES[12] ST CYR.
    ii. EMYLIE ROSE ARSENAULT.
    iii. ZACKARY KEITH ARSENAULT.

1714. APRIL LEE LANDRY[11] SPINNEY *(DONALD STEPHEN[10], DONALD N[9], LYMAN EUGENE[8], BOWMAN E[7], EDWARD[6], DANIEL[5], JOHN[4], JOHN[3], JOHN[2], THOMAS[1])* She married NORMAN CORMIER.

Children of APRIL SPINNEY and NORMAN CORMIER are:
    i.   VICTORIA GRACE LANDRY[12] CORMIER.
    ii. NATHAN ANDREW CORMIER.

1715. JOCOB THOMAS[11] SNOW *(SUSAN RUTH[10] SPINNEY, DONALD N[9], LYMAN EUGENE[8], BOWMAN E[7], EDWARD[6], DANIEL[5], JOHN[4], JOHN[3], JOHN[2], THOMAS[1])* He married ANEL GUZMAN.

Child of JOCOB SNOW and ANEL GUZMAN is:
    i.   JARNELL THOMAS MIGUEL[12] SNOW.

1716. JOSEPH KIRKWOOD[11] ALLEN *(MYRA[10] FULLER, ALICE MARY[9] HUNT, WILLIAM SPINNEY[8], ROXANNA BURGESS[7] SPINNEY, NICHOLAS[6], JOHN[5], JOHN[4], ANDREW[3], JOHN[2], THOMAS[1])* was born Private. He married PHYLLIS HOLMES LEATHERBEE Private. She was born 12 Oct 1925 in Milton, MA, and died 04 Jul 1997.

Children of JOSEPH ALLEN and PHYLLIS LEATHERBEE are:
1799.   i.   BARBARA JEAN ALLEN[12], b. Private.
         ii. DAVID KIRKWOOD ALLEN, b. Private.

1717. RICHARD FULLER[11] ALLEN *(MYRA[10] FULLER, ALICE MARY[9] HUNT, WILLIAM SPINNEY[8], ROXANNA BURGESS[7] SPINNEY, NICHOLAS[6], JOHN[5], JOHN[4], ANDREW[3], JOHN[2], THOMAS[1])* was born Private. He married JOYCE CARTWRIGHT Private. She was born Private.

Children of RICHARD ALLEN and JOYCE CARTWRIGHT are:
    i.   MARK FULLER[12] ALLEN, b. Private.
    ii. MERIDETH ALLEN, b. Private.

1718. BRUCE H[11] SPINNEY *(LOUIS BEVIER[10], LOUIS BEVIER[9], JOSEPH OAKMAN[8], WILLIAM M[7], NICHOLAS[6], JOHN[5], JOHN[4], ANDREW[3], JOHN[2], THOMAS[1])* was born 15 Nov 1941 in Salt Lake City, UT. He married JUDY.

Child of BRUCE SPINNEY and JUDY is:
1800.   i.   RUSSELL BEVIER[12] SPINNEY, b. 06 Sep 1966, Bolder, Colorado.

1719. CLARENCE GORDON[11] AUSPLAND *(FLORENCE MAY[10] BRADDOCK, JULIA A[9] SPINNEY, WILLIAM QUINMAN[8], ROBERT CURTIS[7], NICHOLAS[6], JOHN[5], JOHN[4], ANDREW[3], JOHN[2], THOMAS[1])* was born 19 Mar 1910 in Belfast, ME, and died 06 Aug 1984 in Portland, ME. He married EDNA MARIE ROGERS 17 Jun 1939 in Boothbay Harbor, ME. She was born 27 Nov 1919 in Richmond, ME, and died 28 Apr 1991 in Portland, ME.

Children of CLARENCE AUSPLAND and EDNA ROGERS are:
            i.   BRUCE GORDON[12] AUSPLAND, b. 19 Jun 1945, Boothbay, ME; d. Jul 1946.
1801.   ii.   MARSHA ANN AUSPLAND, b. Private.
1802.   iii. PAMELA RUTH AUSPLAND, b. Private.
1803.   iv.   CAROL LEE AUSPLAND, b. Private.
1804.   v.   LEWIS ROGERS AUSPLAND, b. Private.
1805.   vi.   KAREN STEPHANIE AUSPLAND, b. Private.
1806.   vii. SYBIL ELLEN AUSPLAND, b. Private.
1807.   viii. MONICA MAE AUSPLAND, b. Private.
1808.   ix.   KEITH OWEN AUSPLAND, b. Private.
1809.   x.   DAVID SCOTT AUSPLAND, b. Private.

1720. GILBERT[11] CARTER *(LIONEL LEONARD[10], ADA ESTHER[9] RICHARDS, SUSAN AUGUSTA RUBY[8] BURCE, JOHN CALVIN[7], RACHEL[6] OLIVER, JANE[5] SPINNEY, JOHN[4], ANDREW[3], JOHN[2], THOMAS[1])* was born Private.

Child of GILBERT CARTER is:
1810.   i.   RACHELLE[12] CARTER, b. Private.

1721. DONNA JEAN[11] CARTER *(LIONEL LEONARD[10], ADA ESTHER[9] RICHARDS, SUSAN AUGUSTA RUBY[8] BURCE, JOHN CALVIN[7], RACHEL[6] OLIVER, JANE[5] SPINNEY, JOHN[4], ANDREW[3], JOHN[2], THOMAS[1])* was born Private. She married FLOYD MATHENY Private. He was born Private.

Children of DONNA CARTER and FLOYD MATHENY are:
1811.   i.   KAREN[12] MATHENY, b. Private.
         ii.   NIKKI MATHENY, b. Private.
         iii. LARRY MATHENY, b. Private.
         iv.   SONNY MATHENY, b. Private.

1722. CHARLES FLOYD[11] TAYLOR, JR. *(MILDRED ADA[10] CARTER, ADA ESTHER[9] RICHARDS, SUSAN AUGUSTA RUBY[8] BURCE, JOHN CALVIN[7], RACHEL[6] OLIVER, JANE[5] SPINNEY, JOHN[4], ANDREW[3], JOHN[2], THOMAS[1])* was born Private. He married SARAH MARCEILE CROSBY Private. She was born Private.

Children of CHARLES TAYLOR and SARAH CROSBY are:
            i.   NATHAN CHARLES[12] TAYLOR, b. Private.
            ii.   HEATHER CATHRYN TAYLOR, b. Private.
            iii. CYNTHIA MARCIA TAYLOR, b. Private.

1723. GARY LAVERN[11] TAYLOR *(MILDRED ADA[10] CARTER, ADA ESTHER[9] RICHARDS, SUSAN AUGUSTA RUBY[8] BURCE, JOHN CALVIN[7], RACHEL[6] OLIVER, JANE[5] SPINNEY, JOHN[4], ANDREW[3], JOHN[2], THOMAS[1])* was born Private. He married CLARANN MARIE ROCK Private. She was born Private.

Children of GARY TAYLOR and CLARANN ROCK are:
            i.   STEPHEN JON[12] TAYLOR, b. Private.
            ii.   KELLY MARIE TAYLOR, b. Private.

1724. LYNN CARTER[11] TAYLOR *(MILDRED ADA[10] CARTER, ADA ESTHER[9] RICHARDS, SUSAN AUGUSTA RUBY[8] BURCE, JOHN CALVIN[7], RACHEL[6] OLIVER, JANE[5] SPINNEY, JOHN[4], ANDREW[3], JOHN[2], THOMAS[1])* was born Private.

He married JENIFER ANN TUCK Private. She was born Private.

Children of LYNN TAYLOR and JENIFER TUCK are:
    i. KIMBERLY KAY[12] TAYLOR, b. Private.
    ii. GAILYN MARIE TAYLOR, b. Private.

1725. SUSAN JEANNE[11] LONG *(JOAN[10] CARTER, ADA ESTHER[9] RICHARDS, SUSAN AUGUSTA RUBY[8] BURCE, JOHN CALVIN[7], RACHEL[6] OLIVER, JANE[5] SPINNEY, JOHN[4], ANDREW[3], JOHN[2], THOMAS[1])* was born Private. She married (1) GUADAUPE DESIDERIO GAMA Private. He was born Private. She married (2) HERBERT A. MCNUTT Private. He was born Private.

Children of SUSAN LONG and HERBERT MCNUTT are:
1812.   i. STEVEN ARNOLD[12] MCNUTT, b. Private.
1813.   ii. CHERYL RENEE MCNUTT, b. Private.
1814.   iii. KELLI DYAN MCNUTT, b. Private.

1726. NANCY JOAN[11] LONG *(JOAN[10] CARTER, ADA ESTHER[9] RICHARDS, SUSAN AUGUSTA RUBY[8] BURCE, JOHN CALVIN[7], RACHEL[6] OLIVER, JANE[5] SPINNEY, JOHN[4], ANDREW[3], JOHN[2], THOMAS[1])* was born Private. She married THOMAS JAMES HOFF Private. He was born Private.

Children of NANCY LONG and THOMAS HOFF are:
    i. CARTER ERICK[12] HOFF, b. Private.
    ii. RACHEL MARY HOFF, b. Private.

1727. SANDRA JANE[11] LONG *(JOAN[10] CARTER, ADA ESTHER[9] RICHARDS, SUSAN AUGUSTA RUBY[8] BURCE, JOHN CALVIN[7], RACHEL[6] OLIVER, JANE[5] SPINNEY, JOHN[4], ANDREW[3], JOHN[2], THOMAS[1])* was born Private. She married ROD DOUGLAS STRAIN Private. He was born Private.

Children of SANDRA LONG and ROD STRAIN are:
    i. SARAH KATHRYN[12] STRAIN, b. Private.
    ii. JESSICA ELISABETH STRAIN, b. Private.
    iii. EMILY JOHANNA STRAIN, b. Private.

1728. DALE[11] CARTER *(JOHN "S"[10], ADA ESTHER[9] RICHARDS, SUSAN AUGUSTA RUBY[8] BURCE, JOHN CALVIN[7], RACHEL[6] OLIVER, JANE[5] SPINNEY, JOHN[4], ANDREW[3], JOHN[2], THOMAS[1])* was born Private. She married WARREN CARLSON Private. He was born Private.

Child of DALE CARTER and WARREN CARLSON is:
    i. CALEB[12] CARLSON, b. Private.

1729. JOHN MICHAEL[11] CARTER *(JOHN "S"[10], ADA ESTHER[9] RICHARDS, SUSAN AUGUSTA RUBY[8] BURCE, JOHN CALVIN[7], RACHEL[6] OLIVER, JANE[5] SPINNEY, JOHN[4], ANDREW[3], JOHN[2], THOMAS[1])* was born Private. He married KATHY Private. She was born Private.

Child of JOHN CARTER and KATHY is:
    i. DAVID[12] CARTER, b. Private.

Generation No. 12

1730. KYLE12TH HARRY WOODBURY[12] JR. *(KYLE HARRY[11] WOODBURY, ETHEL[10] CUMMINGS, HARRY[9], ALGENAID[8] WORCESTER, MOSES[7], MOSES[6], MOSES[5], ANNE[4] SPINNEY, JOHN[3], SAMUEL[2], THOMAS[1])* He married LYNN KOST.

Children of KYLE12TH JR. and LYNN KOST are:
    i. JONATHAN[13] WOODBURY.
    ii. ALEXANDRA KATHERINE WOODBURY.

1731. JACQUELYN DIANE (EISELT)[12] WEHTJE *(MYRON FLOYD[11], LAUREL MAE[10] OWENS, LLOYD MAXWELL[9], ELLA GERTRUDE[8] WHEELER, ALICE CATHERINE[7] DWELLEY, NARCISSA SPRING[6] SPINNEY, EBENEZER[5], EBENEZER[4], JONATHAN[3], SAMUEL[2], THOMAS[1])* was born 04 Jan 1965 in Lacombe, Alberta, Canada. She married REYNALD POISSON 29 Jan 1991 in Broward County, FL, son of NELSON POISSON and ROSE ST. FLEUR. He was born 04 Feb 1963 in Limbe, Haiti.

Child of JACQUELYN WEHTJE and REYNALD POISSON is:
    i.   TOUSSAINT[13] POISSON, b. 28 Nov 1993, Fitchburg, MA.

1732. LISA RAE[12] MCKNIGHT *(DAPHNE ANNE[11] MILLS, HAROLD GLEN[10], CLAUDE EDWIN[9], ARTHUR JONES[8], SARAH[7] SPINNEY, ARTHUR JONES[6], EBENEZER[5], NATHANIEL[4], JONATHAN[3], SAMUEL[2], THOMAS[1])* was born 15 Feb 1963 in Korea. She married JEFFREY ALLEN.

Children of LISA MCKNIGHT and JEFFREY ALLEN are:
    i.   EDWIN GELN[13] ALLEN, b. 21 Aug 1987.
   ii.   MITCHELL ROY ALLEN, b. 08 Feb 1994.

1733. DOROTHY FRANCES[12] FENECH *(HENRY ROBERT[11], DOROTHY FRANCES[10] MCWHIRK, ETHAL M[9] MCNUTT, EMMA AUGUSTA[8] SPINNEY, THOMAS M[7], THOMAS[6], THOMAS[5], JOHN[4], THOMAS[3], THOMAS[2], THOMAS[1])* She married GEORGE W MOHNASKY.

Children of DOROTHY FENECH and GEORGE MOHNASKY are:
    i.   JOHN ROBERT FENECH[13] MOHNASKY.
   ii.   KATHERINE ANN FENECH MOHNASKY.

1734. RALPH JUSTIN[12] BROOKS *(ARTHUR RALPH[11], ELMER IRWIN[10], ERVING ELSWORTH[9], ALFRED LANGDON[8], DANIEL LANGDON[7], DANIEL[6], MARY[5] SPINNEY, JOHN[4], JOHN[3], JOHN[2], THOMAS[1])* was born Private. He married DEBORAH PEASE Private. She was born Private.

Children of RALPH BROOKS and DEBORAH PEASE are:
    i.   KELLEY VIRGINIA[13] BROOKS, b. Private.
   ii.   JUSTIN ARTHUR BROOKS, b. Private.

1735. MARCIA LOUISE[12] FERNALD *(MARJORIE LOUISE[11] JONES, AUGUSTA MAY[10] TERRIO, BERNICE MILDRED[9] BROOKS, ALFRED LANGDON[8], DANIEL LANGDON[7], DANIEL[6], MARY[5] SPINNEY, JOHN[4], JOHN[3], JOHN[2], THOMAS[1])* was born Private. She married JAMES MARCHESE Private. He was born Private.

Children of MARCIA FERNALD and JAMES MARCHESE are:
    i.   GREGORY JAMES[13] MARCHESE, b. Private.
   ii.   GENNA LOUISE MARCHESE, b. Private.

1736. DONALD RAYMOND[12] DAVIDSON *(DONALD DEAN[11], FLORENCE MILDRED[10] TERRIO, BERNICE MILDRED[9] BROOKS, ALFRED LANGDON[8], DANIEL LANGDON[7], DANIEL[6], MARY[5] SPINNEY, JOHN[4], JOHN[3], JOHN[2], THOMAS[1])* was born Private. He married BARBARA JEAN HALVERSON Private. She was born Private.

Children of DONALD DAVIDSON and BARBARA HALVERSON are:
    i.   DONALD ERICK[13] DAVIDSON, b. Private.
   ii.   JON PETER DAVIDSON, b. Private.
  iii.   BRYAN MCCALEB DAVIDSON, b. Private.

1737. DIANE ELIZABETH[12] DAVIDSON *(DONALD DEAN[11], FLORENCE MILDRED[10] TERRIO, BERNICE MILDRED[9] BROOKS, ALFRED LANGDON[8], DANIEL LANGDON[7], DANIEL[6], MARY[5] SPINNEY, JOHN[4], JOHN[3], JOHN[2], THOMAS[1])* was born Private. She married NORMAN PICKETT Private. He was born Private.

Children of DIANE DAVIDSON and NORMAN PICKETT are:

      i.   KELLEY ELIZABETH[13] BAKER, b. Private.
     ii.   AMY BETH BAKER, b. Private.

1738. DOUGLAS EDWARD[12] DAVIDSON *(DONALD DEAN[11], FLORENCE MILDRED[10] TERRIO, BERNICE MILDRED[9] BROOKS, ALFRED LANGDON[8], DANIEL LANGDON[7], DANIEL[6], MARY[5] SPINNEY, JOHN[4], JOHN[3], JOHN[2], THOMAS[1])* was born Private. He married SUSAN FLANDERS Private. She was born Private.

Children of DOUGLAS DAVIDSON and SUSAN FLANDERS are:
      i.   KIMBERLEY ANN[13] DAVIDSON, b. Private.
     ii.   SCOTT KENNETH DAVIDSON, b. Private.

1739. DEBORAH JOAN[12] DAVIDSON *(DONALD DEAN[11], FLORENCE MILDRED[10] TERRIO, BERNICE MILDRED[9] BROOKS, ALFRED LANGDON[8], DANIEL LANGDON[7], DANIEL[6], MARY[5] SPINNEY, JOHN[4], JOHN[3], JOHN[2], THOMAS[1])* was born Private. She married JOHN A. VOIGT Private. He was born Private.

Children of DEBORAH DAVIDSON and JOHN VOIGT are:
      i.   JUSTIN TRAVIS[13] DAVIDSON, b. Private.
     ii.   KATELYN ELIZABETH DAVIDSON, b. Private.

1740. DENISE ANNE[12] DAVIDSON *(DONALD DEAN[11], FLORENCE MILDRED[10] TERRIO, BERNICE MILDRED[9] BROOKS, ALFRED LANGDON[8], DANIEL LANGDON[7], DANIEL[6], MARY[5] SPINNEY, JOHN[4], JOHN[3], JOHN[2], THOMAS[1])* was born Private. She married CHARLES R. GETTY Private. He was born Private.

Children of DENISE DAVIDSON and CHARLES GETTY are:
      i.   JESSICA ERIN[13] WRIGHT, b. Private.
     ii.   JARED MATHEW WRIGHT, b. Private.

1741. DAWN ELLEN[12] DAVIDSON *(DONALD DEAN[11], FLORENCE MILDRED[10] TERRIO, BERNICE MILDRED[9] BROOKS, ALFRED LANGDON[8], DANIEL LANGDON[7], DANIEL[6], MARY[5] SPINNEY, JOHN[4], JOHN[3], JOHN[2], THOMAS[1])* was born Private. She married WILLIAM DINGMAN Private. He was born Private.

Children of DAWN DAVIDSON and WILLIAM DINGMAN are:
      i.   WILLIAM SPENCER[13] DINGMAN, b. Private.
     ii.   KATHERINE TAYLOR DINGMAN, b. Private.

1742. DWIGHT ERIC[12] DAVIDSON *(DONALD DEAN[11], FLORENCE MILDRED[10] TERRIO, BERNICE MILDRED[9] BROOKS, ALFRED LANGDON[8], DANIEL LANGDON[7], DANIEL[6], MARY[5] SPINNEY, JOHN[4], JOHN[3], JOHN[2], THOMAS[1])* was born Private. He married BARBARA ENTELISAN Private. She was born Private.

Child of DWIGHT DAVIDSON and BARBARA ENTELISAN is:
      i.   SARA RAE[13] DAVIDSON, b. Private.

1743. CARL FREDERICK[12] PROPSON III *(BETTY JANE[11] DAVIDSON, FLORENCE MILDRED[10] TERRIO, BERNICE MILDRED[9] BROOKS, ALFRED LANGDON[8], DANIEL LANGDON[7], DANIEL[6], MARY[5] SPINNEY, JOHN[4], JOHN[3], JOHN[2], THOMAS[1])* was born Private. He married (1) LINDA Private. She was born Private. He married (2) TONI TEDESCO Private. She died Nov 1976.

Child of CARL PROPSON and LINDA is:
      i.   CHRISTOPHER MICHEL[13] PROPSON, b. Private.

Children of CARL PROPSON and TONI TEDESCO are:
     ii.   CARL FREDERICK[13] PROPSON IV, b. Private.
    iii.   JOEL PHILIP PROPSON, b. Private.
    iv.   MATTHEW PROPSON, b. Private.

1744. BARBARA ANN[12] PROPSON *(BETTY JANE[11] DAVIDSON, FLORENCE MILDRED[10] TERRIO, BERNICE MILDRED[9] BROOKS, ALFRED LANGDON[8], DANIEL LANGDON[7], DANIEL[6], MARY[5] SPINNEY, JOHN[4], JOHN[3], JOHN[2], THOMAS[1])* was born Private. She married CHARLES STOPP Private. He was born Private.

Children of BARBARA PROPSON and CHARLES STOPP are:
      i. DAVID MICHAEL[13] STOPP, b. Private.
      ii. PETER JOHN STOPP, b. Private.

1745. PHILIP EUGENE[12] PROPSON *(BETTY JANE[11] DAVIDSON, FLORENCE MILDRED[10] TERRIO, BERNICE MILDRED[9] BROOKS, ALFRED LANGDON[8], DANIEL LANGDON[7], DANIEL[6], MARY[5] SPINNEY, JOHN[4], JOHN[3], JOHN[2], THOMAS[1])* was born Private. He married JANE Private. She was born Private.

Children of PHILIP PROPSON and JANE are:
      i. ELIZABETH CHRISTINE[13] PROPSON, b. Private.
      ii. DANIEL CHRISTOPHER PROPSON, b. Private.
      iii. LAURA ROSE PROPSON, b. Private.

1746. PENNY ELAINE[12] PROPSON *(BETTY JANE[11] DAVIDSON, FLORENCE MILDRED[10] TERRIO, BERNICE MILDRED[9] BROOKS, ALFRED LANGDON[8], DANIEL LANGDON[7], DANIEL[6], MARY[5] SPINNEY, JOHN[4], JOHN[3], JOHN[2], THOMAS[1])* was born Private. She married DONNIE STEWARD Private. He was born Private.

Child of PENNY PROPSON and DONNIE STEWARD is:
      i. ALLISON CORTNEY[13] STEWARD, b. Private.

1747. SANDRA LOU (DAVIDSON)[12] HOFFMAN *(ROBERT EDWARD[11] DAVIDSON, FLORENCE MILDRED[10] TERRIO, BERNICE MILDRED[9] BROOKS, ALFRED LANGDON[8], DANIEL LANGDON[7], DANIEL[6], MARY[5] SPINNEY, JOHN[4], JOHN[3], JOHN[2], THOMAS[1])* was born 11 Nov 1948, and died in Divorced December 1973. She married (1) DOUGLAS F. JAMES Private. He was born Private. She married (2) NICHOLAS J. PASCUCCI Private. He was born Private.

Child of SANDRA HOFFMAN and DOUGLAS JAMES is:
      i. TRISTA SUZANNE (JAMES)[13] HOFFMAN, b. Private.

1748. ROBERT EDWARD (DAVIDSON)[12] HOFFMAN *(ROBERT EDWARD[11] DAVIDSON, FLORENCE MILDRED[10] TERRIO, BERNICE MILDRED[9] BROOKS, ALFRED LANGDON[8], DANIEL LANGDON[7], DANIEL[6], MARY[5] SPINNEY, JOHN[4], JOHN[3], JOHN[2], THOMAS[1])* was born Private. He married SHEILA B. HARTMAN Private. She was born Private.

Children of ROBERT HOFFMAN and SHEILA HARTMAN are:
      i. COLLEEN ELIZABETH[13] HOFFMAN, b. Private.
      ii. ANDREW BRUCE HOFFMAN, b. Private.

1749. BONNIE LOUISE (DAVIDSON)[12] HOFFMAN *(ROBERT EDWARD[11] DAVIDSON, FLORENCE MILDRED[10] TERRIO, BERNICE MILDRED[9] BROOKS, ALFRED LANGDON[8], DANIEL LANGDON[7], DANIEL[6], MARY[5] SPINNEY, JOHN[4], JOHN[3], JOHN[2], THOMAS[1])* was born Private. She married RIKARD LYKLING Private. He was born Private.

Children of BONNIE HOFFMAN and RIKARD LYKLING are:
      i. NICHOLAS RIKARD[13] LYKLING, b. Private.
      ii. AARON LEE LYKLING, b. Private.

1750. BRIAN KIRK[12] DAVIDSON *(EDWARD PHILIP[11], FLORENCE MILDRED[10] TERRIO, BERNICE MILDRED[9] BROOKS, ALFRED LANGDON[8], DANIEL LANGDON[7], DANIEL[6], MARY[5] SPINNEY, JOHN[4], JOHN[3], JOHN[2], THOMAS[1])* was born Private. He married (1) LISA DEMAY Private. She was born Private. He married (2) KAREN ALTER Private. She was born Private.

Child of BRIAN DAVIDSON and LISA DEMAY is:
      i. ADAM DREW[13] DAVIDSON, b. Private.

Child of BRIAN DAVIDSON and KAREN ALTER is:
    ii.   SARAH JENELLE[13] DAVIDSON, b. Private.

1751. CHRISTOPHER ALAN[12] DAVIDSON *(EDWARD PHILIP[11], FLORENCE MILDRED[10] TERRIO, BERNICE MILDRED[9] BROOKS, ALFRED LANGDON[8], DANIEL LANGDON[7], DANIEL[6], MARY[5] SPINNEY, JOHN[4], JOHN[3], JOHN[2], THOMAS[1])* was born Private. He married ANDREA DRISCOLL Private. She was born Private.

Children of CHRISTOPHER DAVIDSON and ANDREA DRISCOLL are:
    i.   JORDAN CHRISTOPHER[13] DAVIDSON, b. Private.
    ii.   JUSTIN TAYLOR DAVIDSON, b. Private.
    iii.   CALEB ALEXANDER DAVIDSON, b. Private.

1752. GREGORY[12] WINN *(SHIRLEY VIRGINIA[11] KINGSBURY, ANNIE MAYBELLE[10] TERRIO, BERNICE MILDRED[9] BROOKS, ALFRED LANGDON[8], DANIEL LANGDON[7], DANIEL[6], MARY[5] SPINNEY, JOHN[4], JOHN[3], JOHN[2], THOMAS[1])* was born Private. He married PATTI NELSON Private. She was born Private.

Children of GREGORY WINN and PATTI NELSON are:
1815.   i.   SEAN GREGORY[13] WINN, b. Private.
1816.   ii.   KISA JO WINN, b. Private.

1753. JANICE[12] FINLEY *(DOLORES RUTH[11] TERRIO, ALFRED LEE[10], BERNICE MILDRED[9] BROOKS, ALFRED LANGDON[8], DANIEL LANGDON[7], DANIEL[6], MARY[5] SPINNEY, JOHN[4], JOHN[3], JOHN[2], THOMAS[1])* was born 23 Sep 1950, and died 18 Feb 1992. She married (1) JOSEPH HETTINGER Private. He was born Private. She married (2) JOHN STUART HILTON Private. He was born Private.

Children of JANICE FINLEY and JOSEPH HETTINGER are:
    i.   JESSE ELLIOT[13] FINLEY, b. Private.
    ii.   JORDAN ALEXANDRA FINLEY, b. Private.

1754. WAYNE BRIAN[12] FINLEY *(DOLORES RUTH[11] TERRIO, ALFRED LEE[10], BERNICE MILDRED[9] BROOKS, ALFRED LANGDON[8], DANIEL LANGDON[7], DANIEL[6], MARY[5] SPINNEY, JOHN[4], JOHN[3], JOHN[2], THOMAS[1])* was born Private. He married (1) DONNA BETH KRIEGER Private. She was born Private. He married (2) DIAN URMELA MOORE Private. She was born Private.

Children of WAYNE FINLEY and DIAN MOORE are:
    i.   BRIAN WAYNE[13] FINLEY, b. Private.
    ii.   MELANIE JOY FINLEY, b. Private.
    iii.   KERRIE ANN FINLEY, b. Private.

1755. CHRISTINE MARIE[12] EGEL *(BERNICE ELEANOR[11] TERRIO, ALFRED LEE[10], BERNICE MILDRED[9] BROOKS, ALFRED LANGDON[8], DANIEL LANGDON[7], DANIEL[6], MARY[5] SPINNEY, JOHN[4], JOHN[3], JOHN[2], THOMAS[1])* was born Private. She married (1) PATRICK WILLIAMS Private. He was born Private. She married (2) RANDY HEISLEN Private. He was born Private.

Child of CHRISTINE EGEL and RANDY HEISLEN is:
    i.   MATTHEW JAMES[13] HEISLEN, b. Private.

1756. MICHELLE[12] EGEL *(BERNICE ELEANOR[11] TERRIO, ALFRED LEE[10], BERNICE MILDRED[9] BROOKS, ALFRED LANGDON[8], DANIEL LANGDON[7], DANIEL[6], MARY[5] SPINNEY, JOHN[4], JOHN[3], JOHN[2], THOMAS[1])* was born Private. She married RALPH ZAHNER Private. He was born Private.

Children of MICHELLE EGEL and RALPH ZAHNER are:
    i.   JENNIFER MARIE[13] ZAHNER, b. Private.
    ii.   ELIZABETH SUSAN ZAHNER, b. Private.

iii. MICHAEL RALPH ZAHNER, b. Private.

1757. ALAN BRUCE[12] EDGERLY *(JOAN CONSTANCE[11] TERRIO, ALFRED LEE[10], BERNICE MILDRED[9] BROOKS, ALFRED LANGDON[8], DANIEL LANGDON[7], DANIEL[6], MARY[5] SPINNEY, JOHN[4], JOHN[3], JOHN[2], THOMAS[1])* was born Private. He married ROBIN-LYNNE MARIA LOSCO Private. She was born Private.

Children of ALAN EDGERLY and ROBIN-LYNNE LOSCO are:
    i. HEATHER LYNNE[13] EDGERLY, b. Private.
    ii. ALONA MARIA EDGERLY, b. Private.

1758. DIRK HIRAM[12] SLONE *(MARY-ELLEN[11] TERRIO, LEROY BROOKS[10], BERNICE MILDRED[9] BROOKS, ALFRED LANGDON[8], DANIEL LANGDON[7], DANIEL[6], MARY[5] SPINNEY, JOHN[4], JOHN[3], JOHN[2], THOMAS[1])* was born Private. He married SHARON LEIGH MCNALLY Private. She was born Private.

Children of DIRK SLONE and SHARON MCNALLY are:
    i. KYLE-THOMAS HIRAM[13] SLONE, b. Private.
    ii. AHLIA KAITLYN SLONE, b. Private.

1759. CRAIG EDWARD[12] SLONE *(MARY-ELLEN[11] TERRIO, LEROY BROOKS[10], BERNICE MILDRED[9] BROOKS, ALFRED LANGDON[8], DANIEL LANGDON[7], DANIEL[6], MARY[5] SPINNEY, JOHN[4], JOHN[3], JOHN[2], THOMAS[1])* was born Private. He married LORRAINE PAULA COFFIN Private. She was born Private.

Child of CRAIG SLONE and LORRAINE COFFIN is:
    i. CONNOR EDWARD[13] SLONE, b. Private.

1760. KARYN ANN[12] ROBBINS *(SHIRLEY-ANN[11] TERRIO, LEROY BROOKS[10], BERNICE MILDRED[9] BROOKS, ALFRED LANGDON[8], DANIEL LANGDON[7], DANIEL[6], MARY[5] SPINNEY, JOHN[4], JOHN[3], JOHN[2], THOMAS[1])* was born Private. She married TIMOTHY WELLS Private. He was born Private.

Children of KARYN ROBBINS and TIMOTHY WELLS are:
    i. ASHLEY CAROL[13] WELLS, b. Private.
    ii. JASON JEROME WELLS, b. Private.

1761. PAMELA JEAN[12] DOLLARD *(BETTY-JANE[11] TERRIO, LEROY BROOKS[10], BERNICE MILDRED[9] BROOKS, ALFRED LANGDON[8], DANIEL LANGDON[7], DANIEL[6], MARY[5] SPINNEY, JOHN[4], JOHN[3], JOHN[2], THOMAS[1])* was born Private. She married JOSEPH ANTHONY WENCKUS, JR. Private. He was born Private.

Children of PAMELA DOLLARD and JOSEPH WENCKUS are:
    i. BROOKE ALYCIA[13] WENCKUS, b. Private.
    ii. JOSEPH ANTHONY WENCKUS III, b. Private.

1762. JOHN PIERCE[12] DOLLARD, JR. *(BETTY-JANE[11] TERRIO, LEROY BROOKS[10], BERNICE MILDRED[9] BROOKS, ALFRED LANGDON[8], DANIEL LANGDON[7], DANIEL[6], MARY[5] SPINNEY, JOHN[4], JOHN[3], JOHN[2], THOMAS[1])* was born Private. He married VICTORIA LEE BERNIER Private. She was born Private.

Child of JOHN DOLLARD and VICTORIA BERNIER is:
    i. ERIK THOMAS[13] DOLLARD, b. Private.

1763. AUDREY[12] DAVIS *(RICHARD E[11], MABEL LEONA[10] BROOKS, ARTHUR L[9], ALFRED LANGDON[8], DANIEL LANGDON[7], DANIEL[6], MARY[5] SPINNEY, JOHN[4], JOHN[3], JOHN[2], THOMAS[1])* was born Private. She married KEITH DEMERS Private. He was born Private.

Child of AUDREY DAVIS and KEITH DEMERS is:
    i. NATHAN[13] DEMERS, b. Private.

1764. CLARENCE EARL[12] GOLDTHWAITE *(CONSTANCE ANNABELLE[11] DAVIS, MABEL LEONA[10] BROOKS, ARTHUR L[9], ALFRED LANGDON[8], DANIEL LANGDON[7], DANIEL[6], MARY[5] SPINNEY, JOHN[4], JOHN[3], JOHN[2], THOMAS[1])* was born Private. He married (1) HELEN Private. She was born Private. He married (2) BERNICE DARLING Private. She was born Private.

Children of CLARENCE GOLDTHWAITE and HELEN are:
- i. CLAYTON[13] GOLDTHWAITE, b. Private.
- ii. RICHARD GOLDTHWAITE, b. Private.
- iii. LISA GOLDTHWAITE, b. Private.

Child of CLARENCE GOLDTHWAITE and BERNICE DARLING is:
- iv. STEVEN[13] GOLDTHWAITE, b. Private.

1765. DIANE LEONA[12] GOLDTHWAITE *(CONSTANCE ANNABELLE[11] DAVIS, MABEL LEONA[10] BROOKS, ARTHUR L[9], ALFRED LANGDON[8], DANIEL LANGDON[7], DANIEL[6], MARY[5] SPINNEY, JOHN[4], JOHN[3], JOHN[2], THOMAS[1])* was born Private. She married CARLTON PARSLOW Private. He was born Private.

Children of DIANE GOLDTHWAITE and CARLTON PARSLOW are:
- i. PENNY[13] PARSLOW, b. Private.
- ii. LINDA PARSLOW, b. Private.
- iii. WAYNE PARSLOW, b. Private.

1766. ANNA JEAN[12] GOLDTHWAITE *(CONSTANCE ANNABELLE[11] DAVIS, MABEL LEONA[10] BROOKS, ARTHUR L[9], ALFRED LANGDON[8], DANIEL LANGDON[7], DANIEL[6], MARY[5] SPINNEY, JOHN[4], JOHN[3], JOHN[2], THOMAS[1])* was born Private.

Child of ANNA JEAN GOLDTHWAITE is:
- i. TODD[13], b. Private.

1767. JOAN RUTH[12] GOLDTHWAITE *(CONSTANCE ANNABELLE[11] DAVIS, MABEL LEONA[10] BROOKS, ARTHUR L[9], ALFRED LANGDON[8], DANIEL LANGDON[7], DANIEL[6], MARY[5] SPINNEY, JOHN[4], JOHN[3], JOHN[2], THOMAS[1])* was born Private.

Children of JOAN RUTH GOLDTHWAITE are:
- i. DAVID[13], b. Private.
- ii. GLORIA, b. Private.

1768. BONNIE ANN[12] DAVIS *(ELMER[11], MABEL LEONA[10] BROOKS, ARTHUR L[9], ALFRED LANGDON[8], DANIEL LANGDON[7], DANIEL[6], MARY[5] SPINNEY, JOHN[4], JOHN[3], JOHN[2], THOMAS[1])* was born Private. She married (1) RICHARD MONROE Private. He was born Private. She married (2) JOHN EAGLESON Private. He was born Private.

Children of BONNIE DAVIS and RICHARD MONROE are:
- i. BRENDA SUE[13] MONROE, b. Private.
- ii. BOBBY MONROE, b. Private.

1769. DAVID ANDREW[12] DAVIS *(ELMER[11], MABEL LEONA[10] BROOKS, ARTHUR L[9], ALFRED LANGDON[8], DANIEL LANGDON[7], DANIEL[6], MARY[5] SPINNEY, JOHN[4], JOHN[3], JOHN[2], THOMAS[1])* was born Private. He married JUNE BROWN Private. She was born Private.

Children of DAVID DAVIS and JUNE BROWN are:
- i. DONNA CECILE[13] DAVIS, b. Private.
- ii. ANDREW ELIOTT DAVIS, b. Private.

1770. LEROY EDWARD[12] DAVIS (*ELMER*[11], *MABEL LEONA*[10] *BROOKS*, *ARTHUR L*[9], *ALFRED LANGDON*[8], *DANIEL LANGDON*[7], *DANIEL*[6], *MARY*[5] *SPINNEY*, *JOHN*[4], *JOHN*[3], *JOHN*[2], *THOMAS*[1]) was born Private. He married AMY STANLEY Private. She was born Private.

Child of LEROY DAVIS and AMY STANLEY is:
      i.   TAMMY[13] DAVIS, b. Private.

1771. LINDA[12] DAVIS (*ELMER*[11], *MABEL LEONA*[10] *BROOKS*, *ARTHUR L*[9], *ALFRED LANGDON*[8], *DANIEL LANGDON*[7], *DANIEL*[6], *MARY*[5] *SPINNEY*, *JOHN*[4], *JOHN*[3], *JOHN*[2], *THOMAS*[1]) was born Private. She married (1) RICHARD SHERMAN Private. He was born Private. She married (2) GEORGE COOPER Private. He was born Private.

Child of LINDA DAVIS and RICHARD SHERMAN is:
      i.   MELISSA[13] SHERMAN, b. Private.

Child of LINDA DAVIS and GEORGE COOPER is:
      ii.   FELICIA[13] COOPER, b. Private.

1772. DANNY[12] DAVIS (*ELMER*[11], *MABEL LEONA*[10] *BROOKS*, *ARTHUR L*[9], *ALFRED LANGDON*[8], *DANIEL LANGDON*[7], *DANIEL*[6], *MARY*[5] *SPINNEY*, *JOHN*[4], *JOHN*[3], *JOHN*[2], *THOMAS*[1]) was born Private. He married BRENDA TULLIS Private. She was born Private.

Child of DANNY DAVIS and BRENDA TULLIS is:
      i.   TINA[13] DAVIS, b. Private.

1773. HELEN[12] DAVIS (*ELMER*[11], *MABEL LEONA*[10] *BROOKS*, *ARTHUR L*[9], *ALFRED LANGDON*[8], *DANIEL LANGDON*[7], *DANIEL*[6], *MARY*[5] *SPINNEY*, *JOHN*[4], *JOHN*[3], *JOHN*[2], *THOMAS*[1]) was born Private. She married DAVID SMITH Private. He was born Private.

Child of HELEN DAVIS and DAVID SMITH is:
      i.   GREGORY[13] SMITH, b. Private.

1774. JAMES RONALD[12] WILLIAMS (*RUTH EVELYN*[11] *DAVIS*, *MABEL LEONA*[10] *BROOKS*, *ARTHUR L*[9], *ALFRED LANGDON*[8], *DANIEL LANGDON*[7], *DANIEL*[6], *MARY*[5] *SPINNEY*, *JOHN*[4], *JOHN*[3], *JOHN*[2], *THOMAS*[1]) was born Private. He married KAREN GOOCH Private. She was born Private.

Children of JAMES WILLIAMS and KAREN GOOCH are:
      i.   DAVID CARROLL[13] WILLIAMS, b. Private.
      ii.   ROBERT JAMES WILLIAMS, b. Private.

1775. PAMELA ROSE[12] WILLIAMS (*RUTH EVELYN*[11] *DAVIS*, *MABEL LEONA*[10] *BROOKS*, *ARTHUR L*[9], *ALFRED LANGDON*[8], *DANIEL LANGDON*[7], *DANIEL*[6], *MARY*[5] *SPINNEY*, *JOHN*[4], *JOHN*[3], *JOHN*[2], *THOMAS*[1]) was born Private. She married ELDEN BEAN Private. He was born Private.

Children of PAMELA WILLIAMS and ELDEN BEAN are:
      i.   JESSICA RUE[13] BEAN, b. Private.
      ii.   JASON ELDEN BEAN, b. Private.

1776. SANDRA[12] DAVIS (*ROBERT H*[11], *MABEL LEONA*[10] *BROOKS*, *ARTHUR L*[9], *ALFRED LANGDON*[8], *DANIEL LANGDON*[7], *DANIEL*[6], *MARY*[5] *SPINNEY*, *JOHN*[4], *JOHN*[3], *JOHN*[2], *THOMAS*[1]) was born Private. She married TOBEY BOUCHER Private. He was born Private.

Child of SANDRA DAVIS and TOBEY BOUCHER is:
      i.   DUSTIN[13] BOUCHER, b. Private.

1777. RONNIE JOE[12] DAVIS *(CHESTER[11], MABEL LEONA[10] BROOKS, ARTHUR L[9], ALFRED LANGDON[8], DANIEL LANGDON[7], DANIEL[6], MARY[5] SPINNEY, JOHN[4], JOHN[3], JOHN[2], THOMAS[1])* was born Private. He married LINDA MACDONALD Private. She was born Private.

Children of RONNIE DAVIS and LINDA MACDONALD are:
    i.   JULIE[13] DAVIS, b. Private.
    ii. BECKY LYNN DAVIS, b. Private.

1778. SONIA[12] DAVIS *(CARL L[11], MABEL LEONA[10] BROOKS, ARTHUR L[9], ALFRED LANGDON[8], DANIEL LANGDON[7], DANIEL[6], MARY[5] SPINNEY, JOHN[4], JOHN[3], JOHN[2], THOMAS[1])* was born Private.

Children of SONIA DAVIS are:
    i.   STEVEN[13], b. Private.
    ii. SCOTT, b. Private.
    iii. MISTY, b. Private.

1779. DORREEN[12] DAVIS *(CARL L[11], MABEL LEONA[10] BROOKS, ARTHUR L[9], ALFRED LANGDON[8], DANIEL LANGDON[7], DANIEL[6], MARY[5] SPINNEY, JOHN[4], JOHN[3], JOHN[2], THOMAS[1])* was born Private.

Child of DORREEN DAVIS is:
    i.   SHERRY[13], b. Private.

1780. JOHN ANDREW[12] WILLIAMS *(WILMA FLORENCE[11] DAVIS, MABEL LEONA[10] BROOKS, ARTHUR L[9], ALFRED LANGDON[8], DANIEL LANGDON[7], DANIEL[6], MARY[5] SPINNEY, JOHN[4], JOHN[3], JOHN[2], THOMAS[1])* was born Private. He married JANICE BEAULIEU Private. She was born Private.

Children of JOHN WILLIAMS and JANICE BEAULIEU are:
    i.   JOHN CLAYTON MEDLEY[13] WILLIAMS, b. Private.
    ii. KRISTY LEI WILLIAMS, b. Private.

1781. CATHERINE FRANCES[12] O'MALLEY *(STANTON GILBERT[11], CLARA BELLE[10] LEACH, ADA SYRENA[9] VARNEY, CLARA FRANCES[8] BROOKS, DANIEL LANGDON[7], DANIEL[6], MARY[5] SPINNEY, JOHN[4], JOHN[3], JOHN[2], THOMAS[1])* was born Private. She married KENNETH THOMAS Private. He was born Private.

Children of CATHERINE O'MALLEY and KENNETH THOMAS are:
1817.   i.   TIMOTHY KENNETH[13] THOMAS, b. Private.
       ii. TERRANCE FRANCIS THOMAS, b. Private.
       iii. SHEILA CATHERINE THOMAS, b. Private.
       iv. BRENDA MARY THOMAS, b. Private.

1782. VIRGINIA MARIE[12] O'MALLEY *(STANTON GILBERT[11], CLARA BELLE[10] LEACH, ADA SYRENA[9] VARNEY, CLARA FRANCES[8] BROOKS, DANIEL LANGDON[7], DANIEL[6], MARY[5] SPINNEY, JOHN[4], JOHN[3], JOHN[2], THOMAS[1])* was born Private. She married (1) RAPHAEL MORGAN Private. He was born Private. She married (2) RONALD RIPLEY Private. He was born Private.

Child of VIRGINIA O'MALLEY and RAPHAEL MORGAN is:
    i.   SHANE PATRICK[13] MORGAN, b. Private.

Children of VIRGINIA O'MALLEY and RONALD RIPLEY are:
    ii. DANIEL EDWARD[13] RIPLEY, b. Private.
    iii. JAMES MICHAEL RIPLEY, b. Private.
    iv. KATHLEEN ANNE RIPLEY, b. Private.

1783. THOMAS MANLEY[12] O'MALLEY *(STANTON GILBERT[11], CLARA BELLE[10] LEACH, ADA SYRENA[9] VARNEY, CLARA FRANCES[8] BROOKS, DANIEL LANGDON[7], DANIEL[6], MARY[5] SPINNEY, JOHN[4], JOHN[3], JOHN[2], THOMAS[1])* was born

Private. He married (1) REBECCA MCPHERSON Private. She was born Private. He married (2) KATHY STARR Private. She was born Private.

Child of THOMAS O'MALLEY and REBECCA MCPHERSON is:
        i.   KERRY LYNNE[13] O'MALLEY, b. Private.

1784. JACQUELINE[12] DOW *(SYLVIA MARGUERITE[11] O'MALLEY, CLARA BELLE[10] LEACH, ADA SYRENA[9] VARNEY, CLARA FRANCES[8] BROOKS, DANIEL LANGDON[7], DANIEL[6], MARY[5] SPINNEY, JOHN[4], JOHN[3], JOHN[2], THOMAS[1])* was born Private. She married EUGENE WEDDINGTON Private. He was born Private.

Children of JACQUELINE DOW and EUGENE WEDDINGTON are:
        i.   EUGENE MARK[13] WEDDINGTON, b. Private.
       ii.   PEGGY ELIZABETH WEDDINGTON, b. Private.

1785. CLAIRE EILEEN[12] DOW *(SYLVIA MARGUERITE[11] O'MALLEY, CLARA BELLE[10] LEACH, ADA SYRENA[9] VARNEY, CLARA FRANCES[8] BROOKS, DANIEL LANGDON[7], DANIEL[6], MARY[5] SPINNEY, JOHN[4], JOHN[3], JOHN[2], THOMAS[1])* was born Private. She married DANIEL MCLAUGHLIN Private. He was born Private.

Child of CLAIRE DOW and DANIEL MCLAUGHLIN is:
        i.   MICHELLE[13] DOW, b. Private.

1786. THERESA[12] STOLLBERG *(IDA LOUISE[11] LEACH, FRANK EDWIN[10], ADA SYRENA[9] VARNEY, CLARA FRANCES[8] BROOKS, DANIEL LANGDON[7], DANIEL[6], MARY[5] SPINNEY, JOHN[4], JOHN[3], JOHN[2], THOMAS[1])* was born Private. She married ROBLES Private. He was born Private.

Child of THERESA STOLLBERG and ROBLES is:
        i.   CHRISTOPHER A[13] ROBLES, b. Private.

1787. MARK THOMAS[12] LEACH *(GEORGE EDWIN[11], FRANK EDWIN[10], ADA SYRENA[9] VARNEY, CLARA FRANCES[8] BROOKS, DANIEL LANGDON[7], DANIEL[6], MARY[5] SPINNEY, JOHN[4], JOHN[3], JOHN[2], THOMAS[1])* was born Private. He married KIM MARIE BURNHAM Private. She was born Private.

Children of MARK LEACH and KIM BURNHAM are:
        i.   ADAM[13] LEACH, b. Private.
       ii.   DOUGLAS ALLEN LEACH, b. Private.

1788. SANDRA MADELINE[12] MARTEL *(MADELINE SADIE[11] HILL, SADIE ADA[10] LEACH, ADA SYRENA[9] VARNEY, CLARA FRANCES[8] BROOKS, DANIEL LANGDON[7], DANIEL[6], MARY[5] SPINNEY, JOHN[4], JOHN[3], JOHN[2], THOMAS[1])* was born Private. She married (1) JOHN EUGENE POWELL Private. He was born Private. She married (2) ROBERT SHUTE Private. He was born Private.

Children of SANDRA MARTEL and JOHN POWELL are:
        i.   JOHN EUGENE[13] POWELL, JR., b. Private.
       ii.   WILLIAM SETH POWELL, b. Private.
      iii.   KATHLEEN SANDRA POWELL, b. Private.

1789. HEATHER DAWN[12] QUINN *(JUDITH IRENE[11] MANSON, DOROTHY[10] SPINNEY, ADVILLE A[9], AMMI ADVILLE[8], FRANCIS LEMUEL[7], FRANCIS[6], GEORGE PETTEGREW[5], JOHN[4], JOHN[3], JOHN[2], THOMAS[1])* She married JOSEPH DAVID SANFACON.

Child of HEATHER QUINN and JOSEPH SANFACON is:
        i.   ALLYSON JANE[13] SANFACON.

1790. CHRISTINE MAE[12] WALKER *(DAVID BERKLEY[11], JOHN BERKLEY[10], FLORENCE WINIFRED[9] HUNTRESS, MARY EVA[8] DIXON, LYDIA N.[7] TETHERLY, CHARLES[6], SAMUEL[5], WILLIAM[4], MERCY[3] SPINNEY, JOHN[2], THOMAS[1])* was born

Private. She married (1) DONALD BELCHER Private. He was born Private. She married (2) THOMAS SAUNDERS Private. He was born Private. She married (3) BYRL RICHARD MCCARTNEY Private. He was born Private. She married (4) MICHAEL JOHN KORTE Private. He was born Private.

Child of CHRISTINE WALKER and MICHAEL KORTE is:
    i.   KAYLA JO-ELLEN[13] KORTE, b. Private.

1791. JEANETTE GAIL[12] WALKER *(DAVID BERKLEY[11], JOHN BERKLEY[10], FLORENCE WINIFRED[9] HUNTRESS, MARY EVA[8] DIXON, LYDIA N.[7] TETHERLY, CHARLES[6], SAMUEL[5], WILLIAM[4], MERCY[3] SPINNEY, JOHN[2], THOMAS[1])* was born Private. She married (1) JOHN WILSON Private. He was born Private. She married (2) MILTON ELDREDGE Private. He was born Private.

Child of JEANETTE WALKER and JOHN WILSON is:
1818.   i.   STACY LEE ANNE[13] WALKER, b. Private.

Children of JEANETTE WALKER and MILTON ELDREDGE are:
    ii.   RENEE ROBIN[13] ELDREDGE, b. Private.
    iii.   JASON RUSSELL ELDREDGE, b. Private.
    iv.   TERRI ANN ELDREDGE, b. Private.

1792. CYNTHIA MARRIE[12] WALKER *(DAVID BERKLEY[11], JOHN BERKLEY[10], FLORENCE WINIFRED[9] HUNTRESS, MARY EVA[8] DIXON, LYDIA N.[7] TETHERLY, CHARLES[6], SAMUEL[5], WILLIAM[4], MERCY[3] SPINNEY, JOHN[2], THOMAS[1])* was born Private. She married DAVID ANTHONY GRZYWNA Private. He was born Private.

Children of CYNTHIA WALKER and DAVID GRZYWNA are:
    i.   KIETH[13] GRZYWNA, b. Private.
    ii.   SHAUN GRZYWNA, b. Private.

1793. DONNA LYNN[12] WALKER *(DAVID BERKLEY[11], JOHN BERKLEY[10], FLORENCE WINIFRED[9] HUNTRESS, MARY EVA[8] DIXON, LYDIA N.[7] TETHERLY, CHARLES[6], SAMUEL[5], WILLIAM[4], MERCY[3] SPINNEY, JOHN[2], THOMAS[1])* was born Private. She married (1) ??? ??? Private. He was born Private. She married (2) JOHN GEROME Private. He was born Private.

Child of DONNA WALKER and ??? ??? is:
    i.   APRIL SUNSHINE[13] WALKER, b. Private.

Child of DONNA WALKER and JOHN GEROME is:
    ii.   ADAM[13] GEROME, b. Private.

1794. STEVEN B.[12] WALKER *(BRUCE HUNTRESS[11], JOHN BERKLEY[10], FLORENCE WINIFRED[9] HUNTRESS, MARY EVA[8] DIXON, LYDIA N.[7] TETHERLY, CHARLES[6], SAMUEL[5], WILLIAM[4], MERCY[3] SPINNEY, JOHN[2], THOMAS[1])* was born Private. He married (1) COLLETTE GRANBOIS Private. She was born Private. He married (2) LAURIE WOOD Private. She was born Private.

Child of STEVEN WALKER and COLLETTE GRANBOIS is:
    i.   RYAN BRUCE[13] WALKER, b. Private.

1795. PATRICIA A.[12] WALKER *(BRUCE HUNTRESS[11], JOHN BERKLEY[10], FLORENCE WINIFRED[9] HUNTRESS, MARY EVA[8] DIXON, LYDIA N.[7] TETHERLY, CHARLES[6], SAMUEL[5], WILLIAM[4], MERCY[3] SPINNEY, JOHN[2], THOMAS[1])* was born Private. She married ROBERT NICHOLSON Private. He was born Private.

Child of PATRICIA WALKER and ROBERT NICHOLSON is:
    i.   TAYLOR KATHLEEN[13] NICHOLSON, b. Private.

1796. BRUCE HUNTRESS[12] WALKER *(BRUCE HUNTRESS[11], JOHN BERKLEY[10], FLORENCE WINIFRED[9] HUNTRESS, MARY EVA[8] DIXON, LYDIA N.[7] TETHERLY, CHARLES[6], SAMUEL[5], WILLIAM[4], MERCY[3] SPINNEY, JOHN[2], THOMAS[1])* was born Private. He married MARY Private. She was born Private.

Child of BRUCE WALKER and MARY is:
    i.   LAUREN ASHLEY[13] WALKER, b. Private.

1797. DARLENE[12] COTE *(JUNE[11] WALKER, KENNETH DAVID[10], FLORENCE WINIFRED[9] HUNTRESS, MARY EVA[8] DIXON, LYDIA N.[7] TETHERLY, CHARLES[6], SAMUEL[5], WILLIAM[4], MERCY[3] SPINNEY, JOHN[2], THOMAS[1])* was born Private. She married KEVIN JOUBERT Private. He was born Private.

Child of DARLENE COTE and KEVIN JOUBERT is:
    i.   MICHELE[13] JOUBERT, b. Private.

1798. DICK[12] FELT *(DOROTHY LILLIAN[11] CLIFFORD, VEDA VIVIAN[10] CAHILL, LILLIAN MAUD[9] LYDSTON, ARTHUR FRANCIS[8], FRANCIS ARTHUR[7], WILLIAM[6], WEYMOUTH[5], ABIGAIL[4] SPINNEY, ANDREW[3], JOHN[2], THOMAS[1])* He married MARYANN DOLORES HAICKEL, daughter of FREDERICK HAICKEL and HELEN AMUNDS.

Children of DICK FELT and MARYANN HAICKEL are:
1819.   i.   JUDITH JOANE[13] FELT.
1820.   ii. JACQUELYN KAY FELT.
        iii. BOBBIE GAYLE FELT.
1821.   iv. RICHARD WILLIAM FELT.

1799. BARBARA JEAN ALLEN[12] *(JOSEPH KIRKWOOD[11] ALLEN, MYRA[10] FULLER, ALICE MARY[9] HUNT, WILLIAM SPINNEY[8], ROXANNA BURGESS[7] SPINNEY, NICHOLAS[6], JOHN[5], JOHN[4], ANDREW[3], JOHN[2], THOMAS[1])* was born Private. She married JOHN STEVEN HAWLEY Private. He was born Private.

Children of BARBARA and JOHN HAWLEY are:
    i.   CORINNE ALEXANDRA[13] HAWLEY, b. Private.
    ii. CASSANDRA WESTON HAWLEY, b. Private.

1800. RUSSELL BEVIER[12] SPINNEY *(BRUCE H[11], LOUIS BEVIER[10], LOUIS BEVIER[9], JOSEPH OAKMAN[8], WILLIAM M[7], NICHOLAS[6], JOHN[5], JOHN[4], ANDREW[3], JOHN[2], THOMAS[1])* was born 06 Sep 1966 in Bolder, Colorado.

Child of RUSSELL BEVIER SPINNEY is:
    i.   KEREK SULLIVAN[13] SPINNEY.

1801. MARSHA ANN[12] AUSPLAND *(CLARENCE GORDON[11], FLORENCE MAY[10] BRADDOCK, JULIA A[9] SPINNEY, WILLIAM QUINMAN[8], ROBERT CURTIS[7], NICHOLAS[6], JOHN[5], JOHN[4], ANDREW[3], JOHN[2], THOMAS[1])* was born Private. She married RAYMOND STANLEY HODGKINS Private. He was born Private.

Children of MARSHA AUSPLAND and RAYMOND HODGKINS are:
    i.   SARA DIANE[13] HODGKINS, b. Private; m. DAVID MORIN, Private; b. Private.
    ii. JONATHAN SCOTT HODGKINS, b. Private.

1802. PAMELA RUTH[12] AUSPLAND *(CLARENCE GORDON[11], FLORENCE MAY[10] BRADDOCK, JULIA A[9] SPINNEY, WILLIAM QUINMAN[8], ROBERT CURTIS[7], NICHOLAS[6], JOHN[5], JOHN[4], ANDREW[3], JOHN[2], THOMAS[1])* was born Private. She married PAUL LEWIS Private. He was born Private.

Children of PAMELA AUSPLAND and PAUL LEWIS are:
    i.   SCOTT AARON[13] LEWIS, b. Private.
1822.   ii. PETER ANTHONY LEWIS, b. Private.
1823.   iii. AUDREY ANN LEWIS, b. Private.
1824.   iv. KARL AUSPLAND LEWIS, b. Private.
        v.   CHRISTOPHER ANDREW LEWIS, b. Private; m. KIMBERLY, Private; b. Private.

1825.   vi.   ROGER ALAN LEWIS, b. Private.

1803. CAROL LEE[12] AUSPLAND *(CLARENCE GORDON[11], FLORENCE MAY[10] BRADDOCK, JULIA A[9] SPINNEY, WILLIAM QUINMAN[8], ROBERT CURTIS[7], NICHOLAS[6], JOHN[5], JOHN[4], ANDREW[3], JOHN[2], THOMAS[1])* was born Private. She married (1) ANTHONY STILKEY Private. He was born Private. She married (2) EDWARD HORNE Private. He was born Private. She married (3) ROBERT MOSLEY Private. He was born Private. She married (4) JEAN GAUDETT Private. He was born Private.

Children of CAROL AUSPLAND and ANTHONY STILKEY are:
        i.   CHARLES[13] STILKEY, b. Private.
       ii.   SARA STILKEY, b. Private.
      iii.   ANTHONY STILKEY, b. Private.

1804. LEWIS ROGERS[12] AUSPLAND *(CLARENCE GORDON[11], FLORENCE MAY[10] BRADDOCK, JULIA A[9] SPINNEY, WILLIAM QUINMAN[8], ROBERT CURTIS[7], NICHOLAS[6], JOHN[5], JOHN[4], ANDREW[3], JOHN[2], THOMAS[1])* was born Private. He married CAROL JEAN SITEMAN Private. She was born Private.

Child of LEWIS AUSPLAND and CAROL SITEMAN is:
        i.   SHANNON LEIGH[13] AUSPLAND, b. Private.

1805. KAREN STEPHANIE[12] AUSPLAND *(CLARENCE GORDON[11], FLORENCE MAY[10] BRADDOCK, JULIA A[9] SPINNEY, WILLIAM QUINMAN[8], ROBERT CURTIS[7], NICHOLAS[6], JOHN[5], JOHN[4], ANDREW[3], JOHN[2], THOMAS[1])* was born Private. She married (1) PHILLIP WAYNE JOHNSON Private. He was born Private. She married (2) RAY R. CURTIS Private. He was born Private.

Children of KAREN AUSPLAND and PHILLIP JOHNSON are:
        i.   STEPHANIE ANNE[13] JOHNSON, b. Private.
       ii.   ANGELA MARIE JOHNSON, b. Private.

1806. SYBIL ELLEN[12] AUSPLAND *(CLARENCE GORDON[11], FLORENCE MAY[10] BRADDOCK, JULIA A[9] SPINNEY, WILLIAM QUINMAN[8], ROBERT CURTIS[7], NICHOLAS[6], JOHN[5], JOHN[4], ANDREW[3], JOHN[2], THOMAS[1])* was born Private. She married (1) DAVID MACK Private. He was born Private. She married (2) DONALD FLOYD TRENT Private. He was born Private. She married (3) DAVID DEDOMINICIS Private. He was born Private. She married (4) JOE KOCH Private. He was born Private.

Child of SYBIL AUSPLAND and DAVID MACK is:
1826.   i.   THERESA IRENE[13] MACK, b. Private.

Child of SYBIL AUSPLAND and DONALD TRENT is:
       ii.   DONALD[13] TRENT III, b. Private.

Children of SYBIL AUSPLAND and DAVID DEDOMINICIS are:
      iii.   KRISTEN[13] DEDOMINICIS, b. Private.
       iv.   DINA DEDOMINICIS, b. Private.
        v.   KARLA DEDOMINICIS, b. Private.

1807. MONICA MAE[12] AUSPLAND *(CLARENCE GORDON[11], FLORENCE MAY[10] BRADDOCK, JULIA A[9] SPINNEY, WILLIAM QUINMAN[8], ROBERT CURTIS[7], NICHOLAS[6], JOHN[5], JOHN[4], ANDREW[3], JOHN[2], THOMAS[1])* was born Private. She married (1) SCOTT SLEEPER Private. He was born Private. She married (2) GERALD L NASON Private. He was born Private.

Children of MONICA AUSPLAND and SCOTT SLEEPER are:
        i.   TRISTAN SCOTT[13] SLEEPER, b. Private.
       ii.   KYLE OWEN SLEEPER, b. Private.

1808. KEITH OWEN[12] AUSPLAND *(CLARENCE GORDON[11], FLORENCE MAY[10] BRADDOCK, JULIA A[9] SPINNEY, WILLIAM QUINMAN[8], ROBERT CURTIS[7], NICHOLAS[6], JOHN[5], JOHN[4], ANDREW[3], JOHN[2], THOMAS[1])* was born Private. He married CORRINE FULTON Private. She was born Private.

Children of KEITH AUSPLAND and CORRINE FULTON are:
  - i. DUSTIN[13] AUSPLAND, b. Private.
  - ii. DEVON AUSPLAND, b. Private.
  - iii. DANILLE AUSPLAND, b. Private.

1809. DAVID SCOTT[12] AUSPLAND *(CLARENCE GORDON[11], FLORENCE MAY[10] BRADDOCK, JULIA A[9] SPINNEY, WILLIAM QUINMAN[8], ROBERT CURTIS[7], NICHOLAS[6], JOHN[5], JOHN[4], ANDREW[3], JOHN[2], THOMAS[1])* was born Private. He married JANNA BERRY Private. She was born Private.

Children of DAVID AUSPLAND and JANNA BERRY are:
  - i. BAILEY RAE[13] AUSPLAND, b. Private.
  - ii. CHRISTIAN SCOTT AUSPLAND, b. Private.

1810. RACHELLE[12] CARTER *(GILBERT[11], LIONEL LEONARD[10], ADA ESTHER[9] RICHARDS, SUSAN AUGUSTA RUBY[8] BURCE, JOHN CALVIN[7], RACHEL[6] OLIVER, JANE[5] SPINNEY, JOHN[4], ANDREW[3], JOHN[2], THOMAS[1])* was born Private. She married GREG BENNETT Private. He was born Private.

Child of RACHELLE CARTER and GREG BENNETT is:
  - i. AUSTIN[13] BENNETT, b. Private.

1811. KAREN[12] MATHENY *(DONNA JEAN[11] CARTER, LIONEL LEONARD[10], ADA ESTHER[9] RICHARDS, SUSAN AUGUSTA RUBY[8] BURCE, JOHN CALVIN[7], RACHEL[6] OLIVER, JANE[5] SPINNEY, JOHN[4], ANDREW[3], JOHN[2], THOMAS[1])* was born Private. She married STEVE DAVIDSON Private. He was born Private.

Child of KAREN MATHENY and STEVE DAVIDSON is:
  - i. IAN[13] DAVIDSON, b. Private.

1812. STEVEN ARNOLD[12] MCNUTT *(SUSAN JEANNE[11] LONG, JOAN[10] CARTER, ADA ESTHER[9] RICHARDS, SUSAN AUGUSTA RUBY[8] BURCE, JOHN CALVIN[7], RACHEL[6] OLIVER, JANE[5] SPINNEY, JOHN[4], ANDREW[3], JOHN[2], THOMAS[1])* was born Private. He married SUSAN BUTENSCHOEN Private. She was born Private.

Child of STEVEN MCNUTT and SUSAN BUTENSCHOEN is:
  - i. NICHOLAS STEVEN[13] MCNUTT, b. Private.

1813. CHERYL RENEE[12] MCNUTT *(SUSAN JEANNE[11] LONG, JOAN[10] CARTER, ADA ESTHER[9] RICHARDS, SUSAN AUGUSTA RUBY[8] BURCE, JOHN CALVIN[7], RACHEL[6] OLIVER, JANE[5] SPINNEY, JOHN[4], ANDREW[3], JOHN[2], THOMAS[1])* was born Private.

Child of CHERYL RENEE MCNUTT is:
  - i. ELIZABETH MARIE[13] MCNUTT, b. Private.

1814. KELLI DYAN[12] MCNUTT *(SUSAN JEANNE[11] LONG, JOAN[10] CARTER, ADA ESTHER[9] RICHARDS, SUSAN AUGUSTA RUBY[8] BURCE, JOHN CALVIN[7], RACHEL[6] OLIVER, JANE[5] SPINNEY, JOHN[4], ANDREW[3], JOHN[2], THOMAS[1])* was born Private. She married MICHAEL COWIN Private. He was born Private.

Child of KELLI MCNUTT and MICHAEL COWIN is:
  - i. HANNAH ELIZABETH[13] COWIN, b. Private.

Generation No. 13

1815. SEAN GREGORY[13] WINN *(GREGORY[12], SHIRLEY VIRGINIA[11] KINGSBURY, ANNIE MAYBELLE[10] TERRIO, BERNICE MILDRED[9] BROOKS, ALFRED LANGDON[8], DANIEL LANGDON[7], DANIEL[6], MARY[5] SPINNEY, JOHN[4], JOHN[3], JOHN[2], THOMAS[1])* was born Private. He married KELLI Private. She was born Private.

Child of SEAN WINN and KELLI is:
    i.   HAILEY NICOLE[14] WINN, b. Private.

1816. KISA JO[13] WINN *(GREGORY[12], SHIRLEY VIRGINIA[11] KINGSBURY, ANNIE MAYBELLE[10] TERRIO, BERNICE MILDRED[9] BROOKS, ALFRED LANGDON[8], DANIEL LANGDON[7], DANIEL[6], MARY[5] SPINNEY, JOHN[4], JOHN[3], JOHN[2], THOMAS[1])* was born Private. She married SCOTT PICKLE Private. He was born Private.

Child of KISA WINN and SCOTT PICKLE is:
    i.   LENNON JO[14] PICKLE, b. Private.

1817. TIMOTHY KENNETH[13] THOMAS *(CATHERINE FRANCES[12] O'MALLEY, STANTON GILBERT[11], CLARA BELLE[10] LEACH, ADA SYRENA[9] VARNEY, CLARA FRANCES[8] BROOKS, DANIEL LANGDON[7], DANIEL[6], MARY[5] SPINNEY, JOHN[4], JOHN[3], JOHN[2], THOMAS[1])* was born Private. He married VICKI LYNN FOURNIER Private. She was born Private.

Children of TIMOTHY THOMAS and VICKI FOURNIER are:
    i.   MELLISSA ANNE[14] THOMAS, b. Private.
    ii.   CORY JOSEPH THOMAS, b. Private.

1818. STACY LEE ANNE[13] WALKER *(JEANETTE GAIL[12], DAVID BERKLEY[11], JOHN BERKLEY[10], FLORENCE WINIFRED[9] HUNTRESS, MARY EVA[8] DIXON, LYDIA N.[7] TETHERLY, CHARLES[6], SAMUEL[5], WILLIAM[4], MERCY[3] SPINNEY, JOHN[2], THOMAS[1])* was born Private. She married (1) RICHARD DAVID YELL Private. He was born Private. She married (2) SCOTT MICHAEL PAGEAU Private. He was born Private.

Child of STACY WALKER and RICHARD YELL is:
    i.   MACKENZI[14] ZEVA, b. Private.

1819. JUDITH JOANE[13] FELT *(DICK[12], DOROTHY LILLIAN[11] CLIFFORD, VEDA VIVIAN[10] CAHILL, LILLIAN MAUD[9] LYDSTON, ARTHUR FRANCIS[8], FRANCIS ARTHUR[7], WILLIAM[6], WEYMOUTH[5], ABIGAIL[4] SPINNEY, ANDREW[3], JOHN[2], THOMAS[1])* She married JESUS DENNIS ROMO.

Child of JUDITH FELT and JESUS ROMO is:
1827.   i.   ANTOHNY BRYANT[14] ROMO.

1820. JACQUELYN KAY[13] FELT *(DICK[12], DOROTHY LILLIAN[11] CLIFFORD, VEDA VIVIAN[10] CAHILL, LILLIAN MAUD[9] LYDSTON, ARTHUR FRANCIS[8], FRANCIS ARTHUR[7], WILLIAM[6], WEYMOUTH[5], ABIGAIL[4] SPINNEY, ANDREW[3], JOHN[2], THOMAS[1])* She married JACK ROBERT (DRAKE) SACKRIDER.

Children of JACQUELYN FELT and JACK SACKRIDER are:
    i.   JESSICA RENE[14] SACKRIDER.
    ii.   JEREMY ROBERT SACKRIDER.

1821. RICHARD WILLIAM[13] FELT *(DICK[12], DOROTHY LILLIAN[11] CLIFFORD, VEDA VIVIAN[10] CAHILL, LILLIAN MAUD[9] LYDSTON, ARTHUR FRANCIS[8], FRANCIS ARTHUR[7], WILLIAM[6], WEYMOUTH[5], ABIGAIL[4] SPINNEY, ANDREW[3], JOHN[2], THOMAS[1])* He married SUSAN GARCIA.

Children of RICHARD FELT and SUSAN GARCIA are:
    i.   MAREN KATE[14] FELT.
    ii.   KYLE WILLIAM FELT.

1822. PETER ANTHONY[13] LEWIS *(PAMELA RUTH[12] AUSPLAND, CLARENCE GORDON[11], FLORENCE MAY[10]*

BRADDOCK, JULIA A[9] *SPINNEY, WILLIAM QUINMAN*[8]*, ROBERT CURTIS*[7]*, NICHOLAS*[6]*, JOHN*[5]*, JOHN*[4]*, ANDREW*[3]*, JOHN*[2]*, THOMAS*[1]*)* was born Private. He married MICHELLE CHRISTINE PAGE Private. She was born Private.

Child of PETER LEWIS and MICHELLE PAGE is:
    i.   JAMES ANTHONY[14] LEWIS, b. Private.

1823. AUDREY ANN[13] LEWIS *(PAMELA RUTH*[12] *AUSPLAND, CLARENCE GORDON*[11]*, FLORENCE MAY*[10] *BRADDOCK, JULIA A*[9] *SPINNEY, WILLIAM QUINMAN*[8]*, ROBERT CURTIS*[7]*, NICHOLAS*[6]*, JOHN*[5]*, JOHN*[4]*, ANDREW*[3]*, JOHN*[2]*, THOMAS*[1]*)* was born Private.

Child of AUDREY ANN LEWIS is:
    i.   ZANTE ARIA[14] LEWIS, b. Private.

1824. KARL AUSPLAND[13] LEWIS *(PAMELA RUTH*[12] *AUSPLAND, CLARENCE GORDON*[11]*, FLORENCE MAY*[10] *BRADDOCK, JULIA A*[9] *SPINNEY, WILLIAM QUINMAN*[8]*, ROBERT CURTIS*[7]*, NICHOLAS*[6]*, JOHN*[5]*, JOHN*[4]*, ANDREW*[3]*, JOHN*[2]*, THOMAS*[1]*)* was born Private. He married BEATRICE MAE LEVESQUE Private. She was born Private.

Children of KARL LEWIS and BEATRICE LEVESQUE are:
    i.   KARL JUSTIN[14] LEWIS, b. Private.
    ii. CAMERON JOSHUA LEWIS, b. Private.
    iii. KATRINA MAE LEWIS, b. Private.

1825. ROGER ALAN[13] LEWIS *(PAMELA RUTH*[12] *AUSPLAND, CLARENCE GORDON*[11]*, FLORENCE MAY*[10] *BRADDOCK, JULIA A*[9] *SPINNEY, WILLIAM QUINMAN*[8]*, ROBERT CURTIS*[7]*, NICHOLAS*[6]*, JOHN*[5]*, JOHN*[4]*, ANDREW*[3]*, JOHN*[2]*, THOMAS*[1]*)* was born Private. He married TATIA SUE TYLER Private. She was born Private.

Children of ROGER LEWIS and TATIA TYLER are:
    i.   CASSANDRA LOUISE[14] LEWIS, b. Private.
    ii. JENNIFER LYNN LEWIS, b. Private.
    iii. ALEXANDRIA NICOLE LEWIS, b. Private.
    iv. NATHANIAL ALAN LEWIS, b. Private.

1826. THERESA IRENE[13] MACK *(SYBIL ELLEN*[12] *AUSPLAND, CLARENCE GORDON*[11]*, FLORENCE MAY*[10] *BRADDOCK, JULIA A*[9] *SPINNEY, WILLIAM QUINMAN*[8]*, ROBERT CURTIS*[7]*, NICHOLAS*[6]*, JOHN*[5]*, JOHN*[4]*, ANDREW*[3]*, JOHN*[2]*, THOMAS*[1]*)* was born Private. She married UNKNOWN Private. He was born Private.

Child of THERESA MACK and UNKNOWN is:
    i.   JOSEPH NICHOLAS AARON[14] MACK, b. Private.

Generation No. 14

1827. ANTOHNY BRYANT[14] ROMO *(JUDITH JOANE*[13] *FELT, DICK*[12]*, DOROTHY LILLIAN*[11] *CLIFFORD, VEDA VIVIAN*[10] *CAHILL, LILLIAN MAUD*[9] *LYDSTON, ARTHUR FRANCIS*[8]*, FRANCIS ARTHUR*[7]*, WILLIAM*[6]*, WEYMOUTH*[5]*, ABIGAIL*[4] *SPINNEY, ANDREW*[3]*, JOHN*[2]*, THOMAS*[1]*)* He married JEANETTE FOWLER.

Child of ANTOHNY ROMO and JEANETTE FOWLER is:
    i.   CAMERON ROBERT[15] ROMO.

Descendants of John Spinney

Generation No. 1

1. JOHN[1] SPINNEY was born 1752, and died 1842 in Port LaTour NS. He married SUSAN SNOW Feb 1776, daughter of NATHAN SNOW and MARY POLLY. She was born 1763, and died 1814 in Port La Tour NS.

Children of JOHN SPINNEY and SUSAN SNOW are:

2.	i.	THOMAS[2] SPINNEY, b. 05 Jul 1776, Barrington, NS.; d. 1845, Port Latour, NS..
3.	ii.	SARAH SPINNEY, b. 04 Jul 1779, Barrington, NS.; d. 1819.
4.	iii.	JOHN SPINNEY, b. 27 Oct 1784, Barrington, NS.; d. 09 Mar 1879, Barrington, NS..
5.	iv.	MARY SPINNEY, b. 29 Mar 1786, Barrington, NS.; d. Mar 1813, Barrington, NS..
6.	v.	SUSAN SPINNEY, b. 04 Jan 1787, Port La Tour, NS.; d. 15 Jun 1828, Smithville, NS.
7.	vi.	ELIZABETH SPINNEY, b. 15 Dec 1789, Barrington, NS.; d. Jan 1829.
8.	vii.	DEBORAH SPINNEY, b. 04 Jan 1793, Barrington, NS.; d. 23 Sep 1857.
9.	viii.	WILLIAM DOUGHTY SPINNEY, b. 15 Sep 1799, Barrington, NS.; d. 08 Nov 1886, Port La Tour, NS..

Generation No. 2

2. THOMAS[2] SPINNEY *(JOHN[1])* was born 05 Jul 1776 in Barrington, NS., and died 1845 in Port Latour, NS.. He married (1) SARAH DEXTER 29 Dec 1803 in Barrington, NS.. She was born 1778, and died Apr 1812. He married (2) MARGARET COFFIN Jan 1814 in Barringotn Twp NS, daughter of PETER COFFIN and ESTER. She was born 15 Jun 1790 in Barrington, NS., and died 1863 in Salem, Ma.

Children of THOMAS SPINNEY and SARAH DEXTER are:

- i. LAVINIA[3] SPINNEY, b. 24 Jan 1805, Barington, NS..
- ii. SAMUEL SPINNEY, b. 05 Aug 1807, Barrington, NS..
- iii. MARIA DEXTER SPINNEY, b. 28 Jul 1809, Shelburne, NS.; m. JOSEPH HOLDEN, 26 Jan 1831.
- iv. POLLY SPINNEY, b. 02 Apr 1813, Barrington, NS..

Children of THOMAS SPINNEY and MARGARET COFFIN are:

- v. THOMAS[3] SPINNEY, b. 29 Aug 1816, Shelburne, NS..
- vi. SARAH SPINNEY, b. 02 Apr 1818, Shelburne, NS..
- vii. JOHN SPINNEY, b. 05 Apr 1820, Shelburne, NS..
- viii. FLAVILLA COFFIN SPINNEY, b. 12 May 1822, Shelburne, NS..
- ix. SUSANNA SPINNEY, b. Bef. 1832.
- x. HIRAM LORIN SPINNEY, b. 25 Jan 1833, Shelburne, NS.; d. Bef. 1905; m. ANN WILLETT; b. Nova Scotia, Canada.

3. SARAH[2] SPINNEY *(JOHN[1])* was born 04 Jul 1779 in Barrington, NS., and died 1819. She married (1) ISAAC HUSKINS 1794. He was born 1775 in Barrington, NS.. She married (2) JOHN LYLE 1805, son of GAVIN LYLE and ISABELLE CURRY. He was born 1759 in Hamilton Scotland, and died 04 Apr 1831 in Clyde River NS.

Children of SARAH SPINNEY and JOHN LYLE are:

10.	i.	MARGARET[3] LYLE.
	ii.	SARAH LYLE, b. Apr 1807.
11.	iii.	JOHN LYLE, b. 19 Nov 1808, Clyde Rive, NS.; d. 16 Aug 1859, Dixon, IL.
12.	iv.	ALEXANDER LYLE, b. 1813, Clyde River NS; d. 22 Feb 1904, Blanche Nova Scotia.
13.	v.	SETH SNOW LYLE, b. 11 Feb 1814, Port Clyde, NS; d. 14 Oct 1893, Marblehead, MA.
	vi.	THOMAS LYLE, b. 1815, Clyde River, NS.; m. DEBORAH SPINNEY; b. 17 Sep 1814, Barrington, NS..
14.	vii.	SUSAN LYLE, b. 29 Mar 1815, Shelburne, NS.; d. 1861.

4. JOHN[2] SPINNEY *(JOHN[1])* was born 27 Oct 1784 in Barrington, NS., and died 09 Mar 1879 in Barrington, NS.. He married MERCY ATWOOD 1805. She was born 29 Mar 1785 in Barrington, NS., and died 15 Oct 1863.

Children of JOHN SPINNEY and MERCY ATWOOD are:
15.   i.   SOPHIA[3] SPINNEY, b. 03 Sep 1806, Barrington, NS..
16.   ii.   CURTIS SPINNEY, b. 1807; d. 02 Oct 1887, Poirt LaTour, NS..
      iii.   DEBORAH SPINNEY, b. 17 Sep 1814, Barrington, NS.; m. (1) THOMAS LYLE; b. 1815, Clyde River, NS.; m. (2) NATHAN SALISBURY.
      iv.   PRISCILLA SPINNEY, b. 02 Apr 1820, Barrington, NS.; d. 26 Oct 1908.
17.   v.   JOHN W SPINNEY, b. 17 Apr 1823, Barrington, NS..

5. MARY[2] SPINNEY *(JOHN[1])* was born 29 Mar 1786 in Barrington, NS., and died Mar 1813 in Barrington, NS.. She married THEOPHILUS CROWELL 31 Dec 1807 in Barrington, NS.. He was born 22 Jun 1787 in Barrington, NS., and died 1812 in Barrington, NS..

Child of MARY SPINNEY and THEOPHILUS CROWELL is:
18.   i.   JAMES[3] CROWELL, b. May 1809, Barrington, NS..

6. SUSAN[2] SPINNEY *(JOHN[1])* was born 04 Jan 1787 in Port La Tour, NS., and died 15 Jun 1828 in Smithville, NS. She married NATHANIEL SMITH 04 Jun 1807 in Shelburne County NS, son of NATHANIEL SMITH and PATIENCE SWAINE. He was born 15 Aug 1782 in Barrington, NS., and died 11 Apr 1860 in Barrington, NS..

Children of SUSAN SPINNEY and NATHANIEL SMITH are:
19.   i.   NATHANIEL[3] SMITH, b. 17 Jan 1808, Shelburne, NS.; d. 11 Apr 1860, Smithville, NS..
20.   ii.   DAVID SMITH, b. 09 Dec 1810, Smithville, NS.; d. 18 Mar 1890, Shelburne, NS..
      iii.   BENJAMIN SMITH, b. 10 Sep 1812, Shelburne, NS.; m. NANCY SNOW, 17 Jan 1838, Barrington, NS; b. 14 Oct 1816; d. 24 Aug 1907.
21.   iv.   MARY CROWELL SMITH, b. 06 Dec 1816, Shelburne, NS.; d. 18 Oct 1873, Barrington, NS..
22.   v.   WILLIAM SMITH, b. 25 Sep 1820, Smithville, NS.; d. 14 Jun 1910, Baccaro, NS..
      vi.   SUSANNA SMITH, b. 07 Nov 1823, Shelburne, NS.; d. 05 Mar 1869, Shelburne, NS.; m. ARCHELAUS CROWELL; b. 20 May 1822, Shelburne, NS.; d. 02 Jan 1870, Shelburne, NS..

7. ELIZABETH[2] SPINNEY *(JOHN[1])* was born 15 Dec 1789 in Barrington, NS., and died Jan 1829. She married STEPHEN SMITH 24 Jul 1812 in Barrington, NS., son of HEZEKIAH SMITH and ABIGAIL DOANE. He was born 06 Oct 1786.

Children of ELIZABETH SPINNEY and STEPHEN SMITH are:
      i.   ABIGAIL[3] SMITH, b. 19 Sep 1813; m. WHITFIELD SPINNEY.
      ii.   RELIANCE SMITH, b. 02 Nov 1815.
      iii.   STEPHEN SMITH, b. 29 Dec 1817.
      iv.   ELIAS SMITH, b. 29 Mar 1819.
      v.   NATHANIEL SMITH, b. 07 Jul 1821.
      vi.   RACHEL SMITH, b. 14 Aug 1823.
      vii.   SUSANNA SMITH, b. 06 Apr 1827.
      viii.   OSBORN DOANE SMITH, b. 02 Jan 1829.

8. DEBORAH[2] SPINNEY *(JOHN[1])* was born 04 Jan 1793 in Barrington, NS., and died 23 Sep 1857. She married JOSEPH ATWOOD 04 Jan 1811 in Barrington, NS, son of JOSEPH ATWOOD and SUSANNA SMITH. He was born 23 Jun 1789 in Barrington, NS..

Children of DEBORAH SPINNEY and JOSEPH ATWOOD are:
23.   i.   WILLIAM[3] ATWOOD, b. 20 Dec 1811, Shelburne, NS..
      ii.   BERTHA ATWOOD, b. 26 Mar 1814, Barrington, NS.; d. 15 Jul 1820, Barrington, NS..
24.   iii.   SARAH ATWOOD, b. 16 Sep 1816.
      iv.   JOSEPH ATWOOD, b. 24 Jun 1821, Barrington, NS..
25.   v.   DEBORAH ATWOOD, b. 02 Jul 1825, Barrington, NS..
      vi.   ISAAC ATWOOD, b. 04 Dec 1828, Barrington, NS..

9. WILLIAM DOUGHTY[2] SPINNEY *(JOHN[1])* was born 15 Sep 1799 in Barrington, NS., and died 08 Nov 1886 in Port La Tour, NS.. He married (1) ELIZABETH ATWOOD. He married (2) MARY SNOW 16 Jan 1822, daughter of SETH SNOW and REBECCA SMITH. She was born 11 Jul 1798 in Barrington, NS., and died Bef. Dec 1881.

Notes for WILLIAM DOUGHTY SPINNEY:
WILLIAM DOTY SPINNEY:

This William is often confused with the William Spinney of Argyle who married an Olivia Snow in February of 1825. They are not the same persons.
Deed Book 7:443 shows a William Spinney bought land " with improvements" from John and Susan Spinney on 21 June 1822. It was probably this William Spinney as these are his parents. He paid 30 pounds for this property.

William's father John died intestate in 1842 and his oldest brother Thomas was the administrator of the estate (Probate file # A390, Shelburn Court house, Shelburn, NOVA SCOTIA.) , but it was not settled until 1845.
On 20 Oct 1842 William Spinney was one of the persons owed money by the estate. The amount due to him was L40.19.0 and is the largest sum on the list. There were no papers in the records to indicate what this was for or if William ever received the monies owed to him. The debt, and others, was still owing on 1 April 1843 in an account of the estate by brother Thomas.
On 22 March 1845, Thomas Spinney presented another accounting of the estate showing William had purchased land from the estate : " By 1 lott of land (Wm Spinney) L4.7.6... " . Winthrop Snow and Josiah Snow also bought lots. This apparently made up the deficit for the estate and it was finally settled.

William witnessed the will of Josiah Snow on 19 December 1857 and was one of the appraisers for the estate who inventoried it on 5 February 1865.

William died November 8, 1886 according to a letter dated 29 November 1886 written by Lewis C. Snow to the Probate Court asking that the will be probated. It reads as follows:

" To Josiah Coffin Esq. Judge of the Court of Probate for the Dist. of Barrington
The petition of Lewis C. Snow of Port La Tour in the County of Shelburne respectfully sheweth that William Doty Spinny departed this life on the 8th day of November inst. possessed of certain real and personal estate having first made his last will and testament disposing of same---- that your petitioner had been appointed executor and is desirous of having the will proved and letters testamentary granted
and your petitioner as in duty bound will ever pray "

"Barrington Nov 29/86 Lewis C. Snow
executor"

The appraisers of the estate were John Nickerson and Edwin Snow.

William's will is dated 16 December 1881 and reads :

" Know all men by these presents that I William Doty Spinney of Port La Tour in the county of Shelburne Province of Nova Scotia and Dominion of Canada Widower being in good health and of sound mind and memory do make and publish this last will and testament.

I give , devise and bequeath my estate and property both real and personal as follows-------- that is to say
First--- I give and devise to Lewis C. Snow of Port La Tour aforesaid and to his heirs all and the whole of my homestead lands lying and being on the west side of the harbor of Port La Tour aforesaid together with the dwelling house and all other buildings thereon and the one half of the wharf and landing with all the priviliges and appurtances thereunto belonging or in any wise appertances-- also all and the whole of that certain half lot of woodland situate lying and being at Port La Tour aforesaid and known as the south half of the " Governor's Lot " on the west side of the North West Creek so called.
Also all and the whole of that certain piece or parcel of meadowland situate lying and being on the West side of North West Creek at Port La Tour aforesaid and adjoining that certain island known as " Stephen's Island " ---
Also one half share of land on John's Island in Port La Tour aforesaid.---- I also give and bequeath to the said Lewis C Snow and to his heirs one share in the firm of David Smith and Company at Port La Tour aforesaid.----
Also all promissory notes of hand and securities of whatsoever kind or nature which may be found due and owing to me at the time of my decease with the interest due or accruing thereon.

Second---------- I give and devise to Cornelius Snow of Port La Tour aforesaid and to his heirs All the rest and

residue of my real estate which I may own or be possessed of at the time of my decease. (It seems that this was a meadow valued at 10.00 in the appraisal , the shares in the barrington Mill and some personal property pieces excepting the promissory notes of hand).
" Also one half of my wharf and landing with all the rights and privileges thereto belonging.

Third--- I give and bequeath to William Oliver Snow the son of the aforesaid Lewis C. Snow four shares in the mercantile firm of David Smith and Company of Port La Tour aforesaid.
Also all my stock of sheep with my stock mark as registered in the proprietors records of the township of Barrington in the county aforesaid

Fourth----- I give and bequeath to William Powell of Port La Tour aforesaid one share in the mercantile firm of David Smith and Company of Port La Tour aforesaid.

Fifth---- I give and bequeath to my daughter Wealthy Snow the wife of Joseph A. Snow of Port La Tour aforesaid the sum of Twenty dollars lawful money of Canada to be paid to her by my executor within three months from the time of my decease.

Lastly--------- I hereby constitute and appoint the aforenamed Lewis C. Snow of Port La Tour aforesaid to be the executor of this my last will and testament hereby revoking all other wills I hereby declare this to be my last will and testament.

In testimony whereof I the said William Doty Spinney have signed and sealed and published and declared this instrument as my last will and Testament at Port La Tour on the sixteenth day of December in the year of our Lord one thousand eight hundred and eighty one."

The signature " William D. Spinney" is in a different handwriting than is the body of the will. Apparently he dictated it and then signed the written document.

The end of the document has this statement of the witnesses:
"The said William Doty Spinney as said Port La Tour on the sixteenth day of December in the year of Our Lord one thousand eight hundred and eighty one signed and sealed this instrument and published and declared the same for his last will and terstament and we at his request and in his presence and in the presence of each other have hereunto written our names as subscribing witnesses, "

The first signature looks like either " I or J Snow ", probably either Isaac or Josiah Snow
and the second signature is " Edwin Snow"

The estate appraisal done by John Nickerson and Edwin Snow is not dated.
real estate holdings were listed as:

Homestead lands & buildings	300.00
One half Governor's Lot	40.00
One piece meadow (Stephen's Island)	8.00
one piece meadow	10.00
one half share John's Island	.50
1/2 wharf and landing	8.00

Total 366.50

Personal Property

6 shares in firm of David Smith (@ 50.00)	300.00
2 shares in Barrington Woolen Mill	8.00
9 sheep & stock mark	18.00
1 bedstead	1.50
1 bed & bedding	18.00
1/2 wooden bottom chairs (sic)(probably 1/2 dz)	1.50
1 rocking chair	.50

372

1 dory boat.. .50
promissory notes of land 250.00
Total 598.00

Total of the estate was noted as 964.50(Canadian money) as appraised by John Nickerson and Edwin Snow.

Probate expenses were noted as follows:

2 affidavit to prove will .... .40
certified copy of will 1.50
registry of will.. 1.00
letters testamentary (there were 2)...................... 7.50 7.50
warrent of appt. .... .50 .50
certified copy of will for registry of deeds & his fee....... 2.00
Total 800 -12-90

Cash paid judge... 8.00
cash paid registrar 11.00

The largest portion of William's estate was bequeathed to Lewis C. Snow with a small bequest was given to William Oliver, eldest son of Lewis. No wife is mentioned so clearly any wife was deceased before the will was written as were three of his four daughters who also are not mentioned in the will . William calls himself widower in the text of the will. It is noted by Norway Historical Society of Norway, Maine ,that he married a second time to a Mrs. Elizabeth Atwood, widow of Joseph, but I have not found any record of this marriage and do not know what her maiden surname might be. Joan Crise, a consultant on Shelburne Co for GANS says that there was a Joseph Atwood whose wife is not accounted for.

I have not found evidence of any direct relationship between William Spinney and Lewis C. Snow or with Lewis' wife , Louisa, thought to be a daughter of Isaac (Seth, Nathan) by a second wife . (Cf notes under Isaac.) Lewis was a son of William, son of John Snow. If William Spinney's wife , Mary, was a daughter of Seth as I have supposed from circumstantial evidence (see notes) then Lewis' wife Louisa would have been Mary's niece and thus a direct descendant of Mary's father Seth. The bequest to Lewis and his role as executor would then be due to this family connection with William's first wife, Mary Snow. However, Louisa was not William's closest relative. He had one surviving daughter , Wealthy Spinney Snow, married to Joseph Snow who was William's first cousin, son of his mother's brother, Howes Stuart Snow .

Cornelius Snow, (William, Benjamin, Nathan) the other major heir was widower of William's daughter, Mary. She is not mentioned in the will presumably because she was already deceased. Cornelius and Mary had no children (or they died young) as his surviving children were born after his second marriage. Therefore none of his children were William's grandchildren.

Daughter Wealthy had the only surviving grandchildren, 2 of whom were sons. They are not mentioned in the will. She is mentioned by name as the wife of Joseph Snow of Port La Tour. They had married in 1850 and had at least 2 sons by the time William died, so it seems odd that this daughter should, in effect, be passed over (a 100 dollar monetary bequest was made to her) and William's entire real and personal estate left to others with more distant kinship ties.

William's children are from first wife, Mary Snow, probably the daughter of Seth or Benjamin Snow. (Note that they had a daughter named Rebecca, the name of Seth Snow's wife.)

Another minor legatee was William Powell. Elizabeth Snow and John Powell, Jr. had a son of that name born 10 June 1830 in Port La Tour and died 26 August 1905 at Barrington. He is buried at Barrington in the Hillside Cemetery and was aged 73 years and 3 Months.(# 15 , SCGS Cemetery Record Vol 1). He married 3 times according to information received from William Long of MA (who is a descendant of Elizabeth Snow/John Powell) : 1) Clarissa Swain circa 1850; 2) Mary Elizabeth Purdy on 3 February 1869; and Hannah Allan on 14 Sept 1873. None of his wives are buried with him. If this is the William Powell mentioned in the will, he would be a cousin of William if his mother Elizabeth Snow was a granddaughter of Nathan.

A William Spinney is mentioned in the records of Salem Chapel (Port la Tour) as a delegate to Baptist Meetings: Quarterly April 1860 at Pubnico; July 1860 at Barrington, October 1860 (with William Snow) at Cape Sable Island (with Seth Snow); August 1864; August 1865; and August 1871;

Children of WILLIAM SPINNEY and MARY SNOW are:
- i. REBECCA[3] SPINNEY, b. 04 Oct 1822, Barrington, NS..
- 26. ii. WEALTHY SPINNEY, b. 30 Nov 1824, Barrington, NS.; d. 05 Apr 1906, Norway, ME.
- 27. iii. MARY SPINNEY, b. 14 Sep 1826, Barrington, NS..
- iv. OLIVE SPINNEY, b. 13 May 1830, Barrington, NS..

Generation No. 3

10. MARGARET[3] LYLE *(SARAH[2] SPINNEY, JOHN[1])* She married JAMES NICKERSON 21 Jan 1841 in BArringotn Twp NS.

Children of MARGARET LYLE and JAMES NICKERSON are:
- i. JOHN[4] NICKERSON, m. STELLA SNOW, 11 Sep 1890.
- 28. ii. SUSAN NICKERSON, b. 1844.

11. JOHN[3] LYLE *(SARAH[2] SPINNEY, JOHN[1])* was born 19 Nov 1808 in Clyde Rive, NS., and died 16 Aug 1859 in Dixon, IL. He married ELIZABETH SNOW 1831, daughter of HEZEKIAH SNOW and LYDIA COVEL. She was born 04 Feb 1813 in Barrington, NS..

Children of JOHN LYLE and ELIZABETH SNOW are:
- i. PARNEL[4] LYLE, b. 20 Aug 1832, Clyde River, NS.; m. ALEXANDER WEBBER; b. Wenham, MA.
- ii. SUSAN LYLE, b. 08 Sep 1836, Shelburne, NS.; m. TIMOTHY HALLARD.
- iii. THOMAS JAMES LYLE, b. 04 Jun 1839, Shelburne, NS..
- iv. JOHN HARVEY LYLE, b. 17 Feb 1844, Newburyport, MA.

12. ALEXANDER[3] LYLE *(SARAH[2] SPINNEY, JOHN[1])* was born 1813 in Clyde River NS, and died 22 Feb 1904 in Blanche Nova Scotia. He married EUNICE BLADES.

Children of ALEXANDER LYLE and EUNICE BLADES are:
- i. JAMES[4] LYLE.
- 29. ii. GEORGE LYLE, b. Blanche NS.
- iii. ISAAC LYLE, b. 1846, Cape Negro, NS.; d. 02 Sep 1923, Cape Negro, NS..

13. SETH SNOW[3] LYLE *(SARAH[2] SPINNEY, JOHN[1])* was born 11 Feb 1814 in Port Clyde, NS, and died 14 Oct 1893 in Marblehead, MA. He married SOPHIA SNOW, daughter of HOWE SNOW and ZERVIAH SMITH. She was born 05 Aug 1818 in Barrington, NS., and died 04 May 1880 in Marblehead, MA.

Children of SETH LYLE and SOPHIA SNOW are:
- i. FRED[4] LYLE.
- ii. CHARLES LYLE, b. 14 Apr 1843, Port La Tour NS; d. 02 Oct 1911, Cape Negro Nova Scotia.
- iii. SARAH DELINA LYLE, b. 05 Feb 1852, Port la Tour NS; d. 24 Feb 1919, Cape Negro Nova Scotia; m. JACOB MILLER CROPLEY, 21 May 1872, Cape Negro Nova Scotia.
- iv. ALEXANDER STILLMAN LYLE, b. 1866, Port La Tour NS; d. 29 Jun 1951, Cape Negro Nova Scotia; m. ANNIE GOODICK, Abt. 1895, Cape Negro Nova Scotia.
- v. WILLIAM LYLE, b. 29 Jan 1877, Cape Negro, NS.; d. 07 Jan 1930, Cape Negro, NS..

14. SUSAN[3] LYLE *(SARAH[2] SPINNEY, JOHN[1])* was born 29 Mar 1815 in Shelburne, NS., and died 1861. She married JOHN W SPINNEY 29 Jan 1846 in Barringotn, NS., son of JOHN SPINNEY and MERCY ATWOOD. He was born 17 Apr 1823 in Barrington, NS..

Children of SUSAN LYLE and JOHN SPINNEY are:
  i. ELIZABETH MCNUTT[4] SPINNEY, d. Bef. 1860.
30. ii. THOMAS LYLE SPINNEY, b. 1847, Nova Scotia, Canada; d. Aft. 1860.
  iii. EMMA S SPINNEY, b. 1859; d. 30 Jan 1861, Marblehead, Ma.

15. SOPHIA[3] SPINNEY *(JOHN[2], JOHN[1])* was born 03 Sep 1806 in Barrington, NS.. She married NATHANIEL SMITH 06 Jan 1831 in Shelburne, NS., son of NATHANIEL SMITH and SUSAN SPINNEY. He was born 17 Jan 1808 in Shelburne, NS., and died 11 Apr 1860 in Smithville, NS..

Children of SOPHIA SPINNEY and NATHANIEL SMITH are:
31. i. JOHN[4] SMITH.
32. ii. MERCY SMITH, b. 1833; d. 11 Dec 1914.
33. iii. SOPHRONIA SMITH, b. 1842.
  iv. JAMES LEANDER SMITH, b. 1847; d. 22 Sep 1916.

16. CURTIS[3] SPINNEY *(JOHN[2], JOHN[1])* was born 1807, and died 02 Oct 1887 in Poirt LaTour, NS.. He married PRICILLA HUNT.

Child of CURTIS SPINNEY and PRICILLA HUNT is:
  i. HANNAH[4] SPINNEY, b. 1849.

17. JOHN W[3] SPINNEY *(JOHN[2], JOHN[1])* was born 17 Apr 1823 in Barrington, NS.. He married (1) SUSAN LYLE 29 Jan 1846 in Barringotn, NS., daughter of JOHN LYLE and SARAH SPINNEY. She was born 29 Mar 1815 in Shelburne, NS., and died 1861. He married (2) MARY A ADAMS Oct 1861 in Marblehead, MA, daughter of THOMAS ADAMS and ELIZABETH. She died 1895 in Marblehead, MA.

Children are listed above under (14) Susan Lyle.

18. JAMES[3] CROWELL *(MARY[2] SPINNEY, JOHN[1])* was born May 1809 in Barrington, NS.. He married MATILDA SNOW 04 Jan 1830 in Barrington, NS, daughter of HOWE SNOW and ZERVIAH SMITH. She was born 08 Sep 1808 in Port La Tour, NS..

Child of JAMES CROWELL and MATILDA SNOW is:
34. i. JAMES[4] CROWELL, b. 1837; d. 1912, Barrington, NS..

19. NATHANIEL[3] SMITH *(SUSAN[2] SPINNEY, JOHN[1])* was born 17 Jan 1808 in Shelburne, NS., and died 11 Apr 1860 in Smithville, NS.. He married SOPHIA SPINNEY 06 Jan 1831 in Shelburne, NS., daughter of JOHN SPINNEY and MERCY ATWOOD. She was born 03 Sep 1806 in Barrington, NS..

Children are listed above under (15) Sophia Spinney.

20. DAVID[3] SMITH *(SUSAN[2] SPINNEY, JOHN[1])* was born 09 Dec 1810 in Smithville, NS., and died 18 Mar 1890 in Shelburne, NS.. He married (1) SARAH ATWOOD 28 Dec 1835 in Barrington, NS, daughter of JOSEPH ATWOOD and DEBORAH SPINNEY. She was born 16 Sep 1816. He married (2) OLIVIA CROWELL 18 Dec 1866. She was born 10 May 1835 in Barrington, NS., and died 05 Jan 1903.

Children of DAVID SMITH and SARAH ATWOOD are:
35. i. THOMAS DOANE[4] SMITH, b. 22 Jan 1837, Smithville, NS.; d. 26 Aug 1911, Smithville, NS..
  ii. DEACON JOSEPH SMITH, b. 14 Jun 1842, Smithville, NS.; d. 13 Apr 1924, Smithville, NS.; m. MERCY SMITH REYNOLDS, 01 Apr 1863; b. 03 Apr 1842; d. 24 Jul 1916.

21. MARY CROWELL[3] SMITH *(SUSAN[2] SPINNEY, JOHN[1])* was born 06 Dec 1816 in Shelburne, NS., and died 18 Oct 1873 in Barrington, NS.. She married DANIEL PENNEY CROWELL, son of ROBERT CROWELL and SARAH PENNEY. He was born 04 Oct 1808 in Shelburne, NS., and died 10 Oct 1873 in Barrington, NS..

Children of MARY SMITH and DANIEL CROWELL are:
36. i. BENJAMIN⁴ CROWELL.
37. ii. NATHANIEL S CROWELL, b. 1837; d. 17 Oct 1913.

22. WILLIAM³ SMITH *(SUSAN² SPINNEY, JOHN¹)* was born 25 Sep 1820 in Smithville, NS., and died 14 Jun 1910 in Baccaro, NS.. He married LYDIA ANN WORTHEN 1842, daughter of THOMAS WORTHEN and CHARITY ALLEN. She was born 27 Aug 1817 in Barrington, NS., and died 13 Nov 1904 in Smithville, NS..

Children of WILLIAM SMITH and LYDIA WORTHEN are:
38. i. GEORGE⁴ SMITH, b. 1844; d. 30 May 1915.
39. ii. DAVID SMITH, b. Jan 1846; d. 22 Oct 1913, Barrington, NS..
40. iii. NATHANIEL E SMITH, b. 14 Nov 1847; d. 08 Aug 1902, Smithville Shelburne County NS.
41. iv. REBECCA SMITH, b. 02 Jun 1849; d. 19 May 1919, Barrington, NS..
     v. ISACC SMITH, b. 02 Jun 1849; d. died in infncy.
42. vi. SARAH ELEANOR SMITH, b. 24 Oct 1853.
43. vii. MARY J SMITH, b. 1857; d. 30 Mar 1904.

23. WILLIAM³ ATWOOD *(DEBORAH² SPINNEY, JOHN¹)* was born 20 Dec 1811 in Shelburne, NS.. He married CHARLOTTE CROWELL 27 Dec 1832 in Barrington, NS., daughter of JOHN CROWELL and RUTH KENNEY. She was born 01 Mar 1811.

Children of WILLIAM ATWOOD and CHARLOTTE CROWELL are:
44. i. ISAAC⁴ ATWOOD.
     ii. CARLOINE ATWOOD, b. 21 Jan 1834, Barrington, NS.; m. JESSE SMITH; b. 16 Jan 1827.

24. SARAH³ ATWOOD *(DEBORAH² SPINNEY, JOHN¹)* was born 16 Sep 1816. She married DAVID SMITH 28 Dec 1835 in Barrington, NS, son of NATHANIEL SMITH and SUSAN SPINNEY. He was born 09 Dec 1810 in Smithville, NS., and died 18 Mar 1890 in Shelburne, NS..

Children are listed above under (20) David Smith.

25. DEBORAH³ ATWOOD *(DEBORAH² SPINNEY, JOHN¹)* was born 02 Jul 1825 in Barrington, NS.. She married SETH HOPKINS.

Child of DEBORAH ATWOOD and SETH HOPKINS is:
45. i. WILLIAM O⁴ HOPKINS, d. 1929.

26. WEALTHY³ SPINNEY *(WILLIAM DOUGHTY², JOHN¹)* was born 30 Nov 1824 in Barrington, NS., and died 05 Apr 1906 in Norway, ME. She married JOSEPH A SNOW 1850 in Port Latou, NS., son of HOWE SNOW and ZERVIAH SMITH. He was born 05 Apr 1823 in Barrington, NS., and died 28 Apr 1902 in Norway, ME.

Notes for WEALTHY SPINNEY:
Wealthy was one of four daughters born to her parents, William D. Spinney and Mary Snow, and the only one to survive both her parents. She and Joseph were 2nd cousins. She was a granddaughter of Susan Snow Spinney and he was the nephew of Susan being the son of her younger brother Hoews Snow.
She is mentioned with her husband and youngest child , Harvey, in the 1881 census for Port La Tour and was age 57 at that time. A child named Honnora Thompson age 8 years, of Scots descent, was also counted with the family. She may have been a grandchild, the child of their daughter, Ann Elizabeth and a man surnamed Thompson (Thomson). Since Honnora was living with Wealthy and her husband, it is presumed that both her parents were deceased, or she may have been an out of wedlock daughter living with her maternal grandparents. (Perhaps this accounts for Welthy's father leaving his estate to other more distant kin in his will of 1881. See below.) The child would have been born circa 1872/3. See notes under daughter of Welthy & Joseph's daughter, Elizabeth. No further information has been found for this child.
Wealthy is mentioned by name in her father's will dated 16 December 1881, in section 5 of the will which reads:
" Fifth__ I give and bequeath to my daughter Wealthy Snow --- the wife of Joseph A. Snow of Port La Tour aforesaid the sum of Twenty dollars lawful money of Canada to be paid to her by my executor within three

months from the time of my decease."

Despite the fact she was William's only surviving child, he left his entire remaining estate to more distant Snow relations, and nothing to Wealthy's children who were his only grandchildren. Her husband, Joseph, a first cousin to William is mentioned only as Wealthy's husband.

The bulk of her father's rather considerable estate went to Lewis C. Snow, the husband of her presumed first cousin , Louisa Snow and a niece of Wealthy's mother. The residue of the estate went to Cornelius Snow, widower of her sister, Mary, with whom he had no children. Minor bequests went to Lewis & Louisa's son, William Oliver and to William Powell, perhaps the one of that name who was a son of Elizabeth Snow & John Powell, another first cousin of William .

It is odd that William would leave his entire estate of land holdings, stocks, household and personal belongings toless clsoely connected Snow kin rather than to Wealthy, his natural daughter, or her sons or husband, Joseph Snow, who was his cousin. William's daughter Mary had died leaving no children and her widower Cornelius had remarried by the time William died. In such a circumstance, the bequest to him and nothing to son-in-law, Joseph Snow, who was the father of his only grandchildren, ismystifying. Though left a token inheritance (relative to the rest of the estate), it seems clear that Welthy, her husband and children were intentionally overlooked by William in the dispersal of his estate. It seems clear that there had been some "break" between father and daughter. If Wealthy's daughter Anne did have a child out of wedlock and they took in the child to raise, this may have been the source of a rupture between father and daughter. This has not been verified to date.

In 1890, Wealthy and her husband, Joseph Snow, emigrated to Norway , Maine to be with their sons and grandchildren. They resided with the eldest son , Prince, his wife Hannah and daughter, Beatrice.

They were faithful attendees and participants of the Norway Baptist Church. Though they never became members there, both she and Joseph was very involved in the Sunday School and weekly study and meetings.

The child, Hannora Thompson apparently did not go with them to Norway. Whether she had died or married is not known at this time.

The notation of Wealthy's death due to consumption was found in the 1906 Norway town report, but no death record, obituary or burial information whas been found for Welthy in town newspapers or town records of Norway.

Children of WEALTHY SPINNEY and JOSEPH SNOW are:

      i.   PRINCE[4] SNOW, b. 25 Dec 1850, Port Latour, NS.; d. 02 Nov 1918, Lewiston, ME; m. HANNAH SHOLDS.

     ii.   ANN ELIZABETH SNOW, b. Aft. 1851, Port Latour, NS.; d. Bef. 1881.

46.   iii.   HARVEY SNOW, b. 02 Jun 1862; d. 19 Apr 1902, Norway, ME.

27. MARY[3] SPINNEY *(WILLIAM DOUGHTY[2], JOHN[1])* was born 14 Sep 1826 in Barrington, NS.. She married CORNELIUS SNOW in Barrington, NS, son of WILLIAM SNOW and ABIGAIL RYER. He was born 01 Jul 1828 in Barrington, NS., and died 15 Feb 1906.

Children of MARY SPINNEY and CORNELIUS SNOW are:

      i.   HOMER[4] SNOW, d. WFT Est. 1880-1986; m. MARIA WORTHEN, Private; b. Private.

     ii.   HOWARD SNOW, d. WFT Est. 1880-1986; m. JANE WORTHEN, Private; b. Private.

    iii.   MARY E. SNOW, b. Private; m. CHARLES MCGUIRE, Private; b. WFT Est. 1851-1909; d. WFT Est. 1876-1983.

    iv.   JESSIE SNOW, b. Private; m. ROBERT SMITH, Private; b. WFT Est. 1851-1909; d. WFT Est. 1876-1983.

Generation No. 4

28. SUSAN[4] NICKERSON *(MARGARET[3] LYLE, SARAH[2] SPINNEY, JOHN[1])* was born 1844. She married THOMAS W CROWELL, son of JONATHAN CROWELL and ELIZABETH WEST. He was born 1845, and died 17 Nov 1914 in Barrington Township NS.

Children of SUSAN NICKERSON and THOMAS CROWELL are:

      i.   BEULAH[5] CROWELL.

47.   ii.   LEONARD CROWELL, d. 1915.

    iii.   DEBORAH ELLEN CHAMBERLAIN CROWELL, b. 03 Jan 1869, Cape Negro NS; d. 17 Apr 1891, Barrington Township NS; m. JAMES WILLIAM SMITH; b. 1859; d. 10 Oct 1947.

    iv.   EVA DAWSON CROWELL, b. 06 Apr 1871, Cape Negro NS; d. 1916.

    v.   THOMAS GOLDWIN CROWELL, b. 30 Oct 1872, Cape Negro NS.

29. GEORGE[4] LYLE *(ALEXANDER[3], SARAH[2] SPINNEY, JOHN[1])* was born in Blanche NS. He married RUTH SMITH.

Child of GEORGE LYLE and RUTH SMITH is:
- i. BERTHA[5] LYLE, b. 1864, Blanche NS; d. 1938, Cape Negro NS; m. (1) THOMAS ROSS JR; m. (2) SAMUEL PATTERSON, Aft. 1917, Cape Negro Ns; b. 1858; d. 25 May 1940, Cape Negro NS.

30. THOMAS LYLE[4] SPINNEY *(JOHN W[3], JOHN[2], JOHN[1])* was born 1847 in Nova Scotia, Canada, and died Aft. 1860. He married ARBELLA BLISS 27 Oct 1869 in Marblehead, MA. She died 1872 in Andover, MA.

Child of THOMAS SPINNEY and ARBELLA BLISS is:
- i. AGNES ARBELLA BLISS[5] SPINNEY, b. 15 Feb 1871, Marblehead, MA; m. WILLIAM ARTHUR PICKETT, 1907, Andover, MA.

31. JOHN[4] SMITH *(NATHANIEL[3], SUSAN[2] SPINNEY, JOHN[1])* He married SARAH CROWELL, daughter of ROBERT CROWELL and SARAH PENNEY.

Children of JOHN SMITH and SARAH CROWELL are:
- 48.   i. SUSAN SOPHIA[5] SMITH, d. 1905.
-     ii. NATANIEL EDGARSMITH, b. 10 May 1861; d. 13 Nov 1930.
-     iii. JOHN ARTHUR SMITH, b. 08 May 1863; d. 14 Apr 1943; m. MARGARET SNOW; b. 01 Sep 1860; d. 1937.
- 49.   iv. MERCY JANE SMITH, b. 1868; d. 1921.

32. MERCY[4] SMITH *(NATHANIEL[3], SUSAN[2] SPINNEY, JOHN[1])* was born 1833, and died 11 Dec 1914. She married DAVID KIRBY SMITH, son of JOHN SMITH and HANNAH SMITH. He was born 07 Oct 1830 in Shelburne, NS., and died 18 Dec 1915.

Children of MERCY SMITH and DAVID SMITH are:
-     i. SUSAN[5] SMITH, b. 26 Nov 1857; d. 16 May 1944; m. JOHN HOLDEN; b. 19 Aug 1860, Jordon Falls, NS.; d. 22 Feb 1933.
- 50.   ii. ANNIE SOPHIA SMITH, b. 1858; d. 13 May 1937.
- 51.   iii. ORA ETTA SMITH, b. 18 Sep 1871, Cape Negro, NS..

33. SOPHRONIA[4] SMITH *(NATHANIEL[3], SUSAN[2] SPINNEY, JOHN[1])* was born 1842. She married PRINCE WILLIAM STODDARD.

Children of SOPHRONIA SMITH and PRINCE STODDARD are:
- 52.   i. CHARLOTTE SOPHIA[5] STODDARD, d. 22 Apr 1924.
- 53.   ii. ELIZABETH STODDARD, b. 1875; d. Sep 1967.

34. JAMES[4] CROWELL *(JAMES[3], MARY[2] SPINNEY, JOHN[1])* was born 1837, and died 1912 in Barrington, NS.. He married MAHALA SNOW 1860 in Barrington Township NS, daughter of SETH SNOW and MERCY DOWLING. She died 18 Jul 1924.

Children of JAMES CROWELL and MAHALA SNOW are:
-     i. WILHELMINA[5] CROWELL, b. 1866; d. 1949.
- 54.   ii. SETH SNOW CROWELL, b. 18 Aug 1869; d. 10 Oct 1945.
-     iii. BERNARD CROWELL, b. 18 Sep 1880, Shelburne, NS.; d. 1942, Barrington, NS; m. ADDIE GENEVA NICKERSON, 24 Jan 1906, Barrington, NS.; b. 02 Aug 1876; d. 1950, Barrington, NS..

35. THOMAS DOANE[4] SMITH *(DAVID[3], SUSAN[2] SPINNEY, JOHN[1])* was born 22 Jan 1837 in Smithville, NS., and died 26 Aug 1911 in Smithville, NS.. He married MARGARET CROWELL, daughter of PELEG CROWELL and LETITIA SWIM. She was born 05 Apr 1839 in Cape Sable, NS., and died 21 Oct 1931.

Children of THOMAS SMITH and MARGARET CROWELL are:

55.   i.   DEBORAH A⁵ SMITH, b. 26 Apr 1861; d. 05 Mar 1929.
56.   ii.   JAMES ALBERT SMITH, b. 26 Aug 1863, Smithville, NS.; d. 25 Feb 1936.
57.   iii.   SARAH LETITIA SMITH, b. 06 Aug 1866.
    iv.   HENRIETTA H SMITH, b. 23 Jan 1869; d. 22 Jan 1924; m. (1) JAMES EDWIN SMITH; b. 1859; d. 13 Feb 1915; m. (2) HENRY KELLEY STODDARD; b. 22 Dec 1858, Bear Point NS; d. 28 Dec 1939.

36. BENJAMIN⁴ CROWELL *(MARY CROWELL³ SMITH, SUSAN² SPINNEY, JOHN¹)* He married MELINDA HUSKINS.

Children of BENJAMIN CROWELL and MELINDA HUSKINS are:
    i.   MORTON⁵ CROWELL.
    ii.   CASSIE CROWELL.
    iii.   DANIEL CROWELL, b. 1869; d. 1871.
58.   iv.   EMMA LEIAH CROWELL, b. 06 Aug 1873; d. 18 Jul 1967.
59.   v.   JAMES LEWIS CROWELL, b. 25 Mar 1876; d. 22 Dec 1962.
60.   vi.   WILLIAM THOMAS CROWELL, b. 1878; d. 1960.
61.   vii.   CLARANCE BURTON CROWELL, b. 22 Dec 1880; d. 09 Oct 1962.
62.   viii.   LIZZIE CROWELL, b. 21 Sep 1902.

37. NATHANIEL S⁴ CROWELL *(MARY CROWELL³ SMITH, SUSAN² SPINNEY, JOHN¹)* was born 1837, and died 17 Oct 1913. He married SARAH JANE JOHNSON.

Children of NATHANIEL CROWELL and SARAH JOHNSON are:
    i.   MARY⁵ CROWELL, b. 02 Mar 1861; d. 13 Dec 1943; m. JAMES HARTLEY TREFRY, Sep 1890; b. 04 Jan 1864; d. 11 Jun 1922.
63.   ii.   ARCHIBALD LESLIE CROWELL, b. 06 Dec 1862; d. 04 Aug 1954.

38. GEORGE⁴ SMITH *(WILLIAM³, SUSAN² SPINNEY, JOHN¹)* was born 1844, and died 30 May 1915. He married ALICE MCLEAN. She was born 1844, and died 19 Apr 1916.

Children of GEORGE SMITH and ALICE MCLEAN are:
64.   i.   CHARLES⁵ SMITH.
65.   ii.   FREELAND A SMITH.
    iii.   WILLIE SMITH, b. 1864; d. 1867.
    iv.   NANCY SMITH, b. 1865; d. 17 Mar 1949.
    v.   NETTIE SMITH, b. Sep 1871; d. 15 Jul 1882.
    vi.   LILLIE SMITH, b. 1873; d. 03 Jan 1882, Barrington Township NS.
66.   vii.   EDITH SMITH, b. 08 Mar 1876; d. 07 Feb 1951.
    viii.   GEORGIA SMITH, b. 1879; d. 02 Mar 1944.
    ix.   EVERETT SMITH, b. Jan 1880; d. 27 Jan 1882, Barrington Township NS.
67.   x.   THOMAS EVERETT SMITH, b. 20 Sep 1883; d. 19 Nov 1930.

39. DAVID⁴ SMITH *(WILLIAM³, SUSAN² SPINNEY, JOHN¹)* was born Jan 1846, and died 22 Oct 1913 in Barrington, NS.. He married MATILDA CROWELL, daughter of PELEG CROWELL and LETITIA SWIM. She was born 1841 in Shelburne, NS., and died 31 Dec 1908.

Children of DAVID SMITH and MATILDA CROWELL are:
68.   i.   WILLIAM ETHELBERT⁵ SMITH, b. 28 Oct 1867, Smithville, NS.; d. 18 Oct 1924, Barrington, NS..
69.   ii.   MAGGIE LUZETTE SMITH, b. 27 Feb 1873; d. 20 Feb 1944.
    iii.   AUGUSTA SMITH, b. 12 Sep 1876.

40. NATHANIEL E⁴ SMITH *(WILLIAM³, SUSAN² SPINNEY, JOHN¹)* was born 14 Nov 1847, and died 08 Aug 1902 in Smithville Shelburne County NS. He married MARY ELIZA SWAINE, daughter of JAMES SWAINE and MARY PATTERSON. She was born 10 Jan 1844 in Cape Negro NS, and died 05 Aug 1927 in Smithville Shelburne County NS.

Children of NATHANIEL SMITH and MARY SWAINE are:
70.   i.   MINNIE BETHILDA⁵ SMITH, b. 17 May 1870; d. 19 Sep 1946.
    ii.   ANNIE VIOLA SMITH, b. 21 Mar 1872; d. 29 Jan 1914.

       iii.   EMMA ARDELLA MORGEN SMITH, b. 01 Sep 1874; d. 16 Feb 1955.
71.   iv.   FOSTER FREEMAN SMITH, b. 13 Nov 1878; d. 10 Mar 1910.
72.   v.   COLLINS WILSON SMITH, b. 31 Dec 1881; d. 24 Jan 1911.
       vi.   ERNEST M SMITH, b. 26 Aug 1884; d. 05 Sep 1943.

41. REBECCA[4] SMITH *(WILLIAM[3], SUSAN[2] SPINNEY, JOHN[1])* was born 02 Jun 1849, and died 19 May 1919 in Barrington, NS.. She married SAMUEL S SMITH 07 May 1876, son of THEORDORE SMITH and REBECCA WORTHEN. He was born 29 Aug 1847, and died 20 Dec 1919 in Barrington, NS..

Children of REBECCA SMITH and SAMUEL SMITH are:
73.   i.   THEODORE LESLIE[5] SMITH, b. 06 Apr 1871, Barrington, NS.; d. 1948.
74.   ii.   ROBERT WALLACE SMITH, b. 03 Feb 1873; d. 03 Sep 1949.
75.   iii.   FLORENCE ETHEL MAY SMITH, b. 02 Dec 1879; d. 14 Jun 1931.

42. SARAH ELEANOR[4] SMITH *(WILLIAM[3], SUSAN[2] SPINNEY, JOHN[1])* was born 24 Oct 1853. She married CHARLES L NICKERSON.

Children of SARAH SMITH and CHARLES NICKERSON are:
76.   i.   JOHN HARVEY[5] NICKERSON, b. 1884; d. 30 Mar 1949.
77.   ii.   IRVAN ROY NICKERSON, b. 28 May 1885; d. 05 Aug 1939.
       iii.   ALBERT NICKERSON, b. 1898; d. 28 Feb 1924.

43. MARY J[4] SMITH *(WILLIAM[3], SUSAN[2] SPINNEY, JOHN[1])* was born 1857, and died 30 Mar 1904. She married CHRISTOPHER O SHOLDS 18 Jan 1878 in Barrington Township NS. He was born Jun 1848, and died 10 Oct 1934.

Child of MARY SMITH and CHRISTOPHER SHOLDS is:
78.   i.   FRED LEANDER GORDON[5] SHOLDS, b. 21 Dec 1883, Port Latour NS; d. 16 Jan 1960, Hyde Park Boston MA.

44. ISAAC[4] ATWOOD *(WILLIAM[3], DEBORAH[2] SPINNEY, JOHN[1])* He married ABIGAIL STODDARD.

Child of ISAAC ATWOOD and ABIGAIL STODDARD is:
       i.   CAROLINE[5] ATWOOD, b. 1871; d. 1915; m. LEONARD EUGENE NICKERSON.

45. WILLIAM O[4] HOPKINS *(DEBORAH[3] ATWOOD, DEBORAH[2] SPINNEY, JOHN[1])* died 1929. He married MERCY JANE SMITH, daughter of JOHN SMITH and SARAH CROWELL. She was born 1868, and died 1921.

Children of WILLIAM HOPKINS and MERCY SMITH are:
79.   i.   THOMAS[5] HOPKINS.
80.   ii.   GEORGE HOPKINS, b. 1884; d. Sep 1927.

46. HARVEY[4] SNOW *(WEALTHY[3] SPINNEY, WILLIAM DOUGHTY[2], JOHN[1])* was born 02 Jun 1862, and died 19 Apr 1902 in Norway, ME. He married AGNES DIANE SMITH 10 Jul 1884 in Norway Maine.

Child of HARVEY SNOW and AGNES SMITH is:
81.   i.   FREEMAN LEROY[5] SNOW, b. 19 Jun 1895.

Generation No. 5

47. LEONARD[5] CROWELL *(SUSAN[4] NICKERSON, MARGARET[3] LYLE, SARAH[2] SPINNEY, JOHN[1])* died 1915. He married MABEL GREENWOOD.

Children of LEONARD CROWELL and MABEL GREENWOOD are:
       i.   HAROLD[6] CROWELL.
       ii.   UNKNOWN CROWELL.

48. SUSAN SOPHIA[5] SMITH *(JOHN[4], NATHANIEL[3], SUSAN[2] SPINNEY, JOHN[1])* died 1905. She married WILLIAM HENRY ATWOOD.

Children of SUSAN SMITH and WILLIAM ATWOOD are:
  i.   GILBERT KENNETY[6] ATWOOD.
  ii. EVERETT LAWSON ATWOOD, b. 15 Dec 1878; d. 22 Dec 1957.
  iii. LILA HAZEL ATWOOD, b. 08 Feb 1896; d. 29 Jun 1980; m. ROBERT GORDON STODDARD, 09 Nov 1918; b. 13 Oct 1894; d. 31 Mar 1948.

49. MERCY JANE[5] SMITH *(JOHN[4], NATHANIEL[3], SUSAN[2] SPINNEY, JOHN[1])* was born 1868, and died 1921. She married WILLIAM O HOPKINS, son of SETH HOPKINS and DEBORAH ATWOOD. He died 1929.

Children are listed above under (45) William O Hopkins.

50. ANNIE SOPHIA[5] SMITH *(MERCY[4], NATHANIEL[3], SUSAN[2] SPINNEY, JOHN[1])* was born 1858, and died 13 May 1937. She married GEORGE HOWARD SMITH. He was born 20 Sep 1857, and died 15 Nov 1939.

Child of ANNIE SMITH and GEORGE SMITH is:
  i.   IVAN B[6] SMITH, d. 1896.

51. ORA ETTA[5] SMITH *(MERCY[4], NATHANIEL[3], SUSAN[2] SPINNEY, JOHN[1])* was born 18 Sep 1871 in Cape Negro, NS.. She married JAMES WILLIAM SMITH 17 May 1894, son of JAMES SMITH and ELIZA WORTHEN. He was born 1859, and died 10 Oct 1947.

Child of ORA SMITH and JAMES SMITH is:
  i.   HAZEL HILDRED[6] SMITH, b. 1896; d. 13 Jul 1982.

52. CHARLOTTE SOPHIA[5] STODDARD *(SOPHRONIA[4] SMITH, NATHANIEL[3], SUSAN[2] SPINNEY, JOHN[1])* died 22 Apr 1924. She married WILBUR TRACY KENNEY 12 Dec 1906. He died 05 Dec 1923.

Child of CHARLOTTE STODDARD and WILBUR KENNEY is:
  i.   EDITH[6] KENNEY, b. 1906; d. 1949.

53. ELIZABETH[5] STODDARD *(SOPHRONIA[4] SMITH, NATHANIEL[3], SUSAN[2] SPINNEY, JOHN[1])* was born 1875, and died Sep 1967. She married THEODORE NEWELL.

Children of ELIZABETH STODDARD and THEODORE NEWELL are:
  i.   LAVANCE T[6] NEWELL, m. (1) LOTTIE BEATRICE HOPKINS; b. 1911; d. 02 Feb 1956; m. (2) MATILDA NICKERSON, 14 Nov 1970.
  ii.   PRESTON NEWELL.
  iii. CATHERINE NEWELL.
  iv.   OLIVE ISABELLE NEWELL.
  v.   SYLVESTER NEWELL, m. MAE NICKERSON.
  vi.   MURIEL NEWELL.
  vii. BURTON NEWELL.
  viii. AVETA NEWELL, m. ROBIE W ATWOOD, 1935; b. 1911; d. 30 Oct 1990.
  ix.   ALBERT/ALBERT MURRAY NEWELL/NEWELL, b. 1896; d. 13 Jul 1991; m. ETHEL HICKEY, 1940; d. 1943.
  x.   LESLIE NEWELL, b. 1900; d. 12 May 1977.
  xi.   GENEVIEVE NELLLIE NEWELL, b. 1901; d. Jul 1982; m. DEWEY ALBERT NICKERSON, 12 Nov 1917; b. 22 Jun 1898; d. 25 Oct 1983.
  xii. CHARLOTTE NEWELL, b. 1903; d. 08 Oct 1982.

54. SETH SNOW[5] CROWELL *(JAMES[4], JAMES[3], MARY[2] SPINNEY, JOHN[1])* was born 18 Aug 1869, and died 10 Oct 1945. He married ANNIE IDA CROWELL 10 Nov 1892. She was born 15 Jul 1867.

Child of SETH CROWELL and ANNIE CROWELL is:
- i. KENNETH[6] CROWELL, b. 21 Sep 1902; d. Feb 1938; m. VERA SNOW, 07 Oct 1925; b. 23 Mar 1902; d. 24 Mar 1969.

55. DEBORAH A[5] SMITH *(THOMAS DOANE[4], DAVID[3], SUSAN[2] SPINNEY, JOHN[1])* was born 26 Apr 1861, and died 05 Mar 1929. She married WILLIAM DOWLING 19 Nov 1881. He was born 1859, and died 15 Feb 1940.

Child of DEBORAH SMITH and WILLIAM DOWLING is:
82. i. BLANCHE MABEL[6] DOWLING, b. 08 Apr 1884.

56. JAMES ALBERT[5] SMITH *(THOMAS DOANE[4], DAVID[3], SUSAN[2] SPINNEY, JOHN[1])* was born 26 Aug 1863 in Smithville, NS., and died 25 Feb 1936. He married (1) JENNIE SHAND 01 Feb 1887. She was born 16 Feb 1866, and died 20 Dec 1920. He married (2) LAURIE FLORETTA JOHNSON 19 Sep 1931. She was born 06 Apr 1876, and died 13 Jun 1962.

Children of JAMES SMITH and JENNIE SHAND are:
- i. GUILFORD IRVING[6] SMITH, b. 15 Mar 1888; d. 03 May 1947; m. LEONA DEBORAH SWAINE, 05 Jun 1919; b. 17 Sep 1889; d. 21 Jan 1975.
- ii. ALBERT "CLAUDE" SMITH, b. 14 Aug 1890, Smithville, NS.; d. 22 Dec 1972; m. DEBORAH INGLES SMITH, 18 Oct 1916; b. 21 Apr 1896, Doctors Cove, NS.; d. 25 Sep 1979.
- iii. FRED MULLEN SMITH, b. 09 Oct 1892, Smithville, NS.; d. 06 Nov 1966, Stratford, CT; m. ANNIE ESTELLA SNOW, 23 May 1917; b. 26 Sep 1887; d. 31 Dec 1982, Bridgeport, CT.
- iv. HERSEY SOUTHWORTH SMITH, b. 15 Oct 1895, Smithville, NS.; d. 10 Jun 1916, France.
- v. JAMES DOUGLAS SMITH, b. 04 Jul 1897, Smithville, NS.; d. 25 Nov 1976; m. MINNIE MAE THOMAS, 24 Jan 1920, Barrington, NS.; b. 18 May 1897, Smithville, NS.; d. 05 Apr 1976.
- vi. MAURICE DENSHAM SMITH, b. 04 May 1900, Smithville, NS.; d. 25 Aug 1965, Bayonne, NJ; m. (1) LILLIAN BEATRICE WILSON, 17 Oct 1927, Barrington, NS.; b. 30 Sep 1901, Barrington, NS.; d. 08 Aug 1938; m. (2) MAE HRIEZKA, 1948; b. 14 Jun 1906; d. 31 Mar 1982.
- vii. FRANK SMITH, b. 23 May 1903, Smithville, NS.; d. 11 Feb 1991, Florida; m. MARION HALL, 28 Oct 1936; b. 15 Aug 1916, Maine.
- viii. GEORGE THOMAS SMITH, b. 03 Aug 1907, Smithville, NS.; d. 22 Jan 1988, Bayonne, NJ; m. DOROTHY VIVIIAN SWAINE, 19 Nov 1935; b. 01 Feb 1914.

57. SARAH LETITIA[5] SMITH *(THOMAS DOANE[4], DAVID[3], SUSAN[2] SPINNEY, JOHN[1])* was born 06 Aug 1866. She married EDWIN SNOW 07 Jun 1886.

Child of SARAH SMITH and EDWIN SNOW is:
- i. ANNIE ESTELLA[6] SNOW, b. 26 Sep 1887; d. 31 Dec 1982, Bridgeport, CT; m. FRED MULLEN SMITH, 23 May 1917; b. 09 Oct 1892, Smithville, NS.; d. 06 Nov 1966, Stratford, CT.

58. EMMA LEIAH[5] CROWELL *(BENJAMIN[4], MARY CROWELL[3] SMITH, SUSAN[2] SPINNEY, JOHN[1])* was born 06 Aug 1873, and died 18 Jul 1967. She married LEVI THOMAS. He was born 14 Mar 1870, and died 13 Dec 1933.

Children of EMMA CROWELL and LEVI THOMAS are:
- i. EDGAR[6] THOMAS, d. Mar 1967; m. EVELYN NICKERSON, 09 May 1925.
- ii. MINNIE MAE THOMAS, b. 18 May 1897, Smithville, NS.; d. 05 Apr 1976; m. JAMES DOUGLAS SMITH, 24 Jan 1920, Barrington, NS.; b. 04 Jul 1897, Smithville, NS.; d. 25 Nov 1976.
- iii. LILAH ALBERTA THOMAS, b. 04 Jun 1899; d. 26 Sep 1986; m. ROBERT STEWART BURKE, 29 Jun 1957; b. 14 Aug 1886, Lockeport; d. 24 Sep 1978.

59. JAMES LEWIS[5] CROWELL *(BENJAMIN[4], MARY CROWELL[3] SMITH, SUSAN[2] SPINNEY, JOHN[1])* was born 25 Mar 1876, and died 22 Dec 1962. He married CORDELIA ELLA OBED 15 Nov 1898. She was born 05 Nov 1879, and died 09 May 1973.

Children of JAMES CROWELL and CORDELIA OBED are:
- i. AMY "VERA"[6] CROWELL, b. 28 Aug 1907; d. 24 Sep 1992; m. LIONELL K.T. CROWELL; b. 1898.
- ii. CARL CROWELL, b. 1915; d. 10 Feb 1916.
- iii. MARION MAE CROWELL, b. 06 Jun 1917; d. 19 Apr 1930.

60. WILLIAM THOMAS[5] CROWELL *(BENJAMIN[4], MARY CROWELL[3] SMITH, SUSAN[2] SPINNEY, JOHN[1])* was born 1878, and died 1960. He married MAUDE.

Children of WILLIAM CROWELL and MAUDE are:
- i. CHESTER[6] CROWELL, b. 24 Mar 1904; d. 17 Oct 1936.
- ii. BENJAMIN CROWELL, b. 30 Mar 1910; m. WILETTA GERELDINE MADDEN, 03 Jan 1931; b. 1909; d. 04 May 1989.
- iii. LEIGH ELMORE CROWELL, b. 08 Feb 1916.
- iv. OSCAR LEWIS CROWELL, b. 07 Aug 1917; m. BERYL CHETWYND, Sep 1941; b. 17 May 1919.

61. CLARANCE BURTON[5] CROWELL *(BENJAMIN[4], MARY CROWELL[3] SMITH, SUSAN[2] SPINNEY, JOHN[1])* was born 22 Dec 1880, and died 09 Oct 1962. He married (1) JOYCE MAE BETHANE. He married (2) BLANCHE THOMAS 28 Oct 1908. She was born 06 May 1889, and died Jun 1918.

Child of CLARANCE CROWELL and JOYCE BETHANE is:
- i. JOYCE[6] CROWELL.

62. LIZZIE[5] CROWELL *(BENJAMIN[4], MARY CROWELL[3] SMITH, SUSAN[2] SPINNEY, JOHN[1])* was born 21 Sep 1902. She married DOUGLAS WARNER.

Children of LIZZIE CROWELL and DOUGLAS WARNER are:
- i. KARL[6] WARNER, m. JEAN.
- ii. WALTON KENNEY WARNER, b. 24 Feb 1920; d. Aug 1970.

63. ARCHIBALD LESLIE[5] CROWELL *(NATHANIEL S[4], MARY CROWELL[3] SMITH, SUSAN[2] SPINNEY, JOHN[1])* was born 06 Dec 1862, and died 04 Aug 1954. He married (1) BERTIE SMITH 22 Dec 1886 in Port Latour NS. She was born 24 Sep 1867, and died 05 Jan 1908. He married (2) MAUD CROWELL 04 Jan 1908. She was born 08 May 1877 in Barrington, NS., and died 25 Oct 1977.

Children of ARCHIBALD CROWELL and MAUD CROWELL are:
- i. OLIVE[6] CROWELL, b. 16 Jul 1911; d. 13 Dec 1914.
- ii. JEAN ELIZABETH CROWELL, b. 25 Mar 1915, Smithville, NS.; m. CHURCHILL EVERETT BOWER, 20 Mar 1942; b. 11 Dec 1914.

64. CHARLES[5] SMITH *(GEORGE[4], WILLIAM[3], SUSAN[2] SPINNEY, JOHN[1])* He married SUSAN HOPKINS.

Child of CHARLES SMITH and SUSAN HOPKINS is:
- i. GLADYS[6] SMITH.

65. FREELAND A[5] SMITH *(GEORGE[4], WILLIAM[3], SUSAN[2] SPINNEY, JOHN[1])* He married ALMA SOUTHERN 20 Sep 1911. She died Jun 1962.

Child of FREELAND SMITH and ALMA SOUTHERN is:
- i. EVERETT[6] SMITH.

66. EDITH[5] SMITH *(GEORGE[4], WILLIAM[3], SUSAN[2] SPINNEY, JOHN[1])* was born 08 Mar 1876, and died 07 Feb 1951. She married WILLIAM LOGAN.

Children of EDITH SMITH and WILLIAM LOGAN are:
- i. DAISY[6] LOGAN.
- ii. PEARLE N LOGAN, b. 1898; d. 21 Aug 1984.

67. THOMAS EVERETT[5] SMITH *(GEORGE[4], WILLIAM[3], SUSAN[2] SPINNEY, JOHN[1])* was born 20 Sep 1883, and died 19

Nov 1930. He married MATILDA OBER ATKINSON 25 Jun 1919. She was born 17 Nov 1884 in Newellton, and died 06 Dec 1970.

Child of THOMAS SMITH and MATILDA ATKINSON is:
  i.   GERTRUDE[6] SMITH, b. Dec 1922.

68. WILLIAM ETHELBERT[5] SMITH *(DAVID[4], WILLIAM[3], SUSAN[2] SPINNEY, JOHN[1])* was born 28 Oct 1867 in Smithville, NS., and died 18 Oct 1924 in Barrington, NS.. He married ETHELINDA MESSENGER. She was born 04 Feb 1869, and died Feb 1947.

Children of WILLIAM SMITH and ETHELINDA MESSENGER are:
  i.   LETA[6] SMITH, b. 12 Mar 1899; m. LAWRENCE TOWNE; b. USA; d. Jul 1974.
  ii.   MURRAY ETHELBERT SMITH, b. 21 Sep 1903; d. 1967; m. EVELYN BIRDETTA THURBER, 30 Dec 1941; b. 15 Dec 1910.
  iii. DAVID ALLANMORE SMITH, b. 02 Nov 1905; d. Jul 1971; m. EITHEL ADELIA WESTERDAL, 05 Nov 1930; b. Michigan.
  iv.   MARY ADA SMITH, b. 03 Sep 1907.

69. MAGGIE LUZETTE[5] SMITH *(DAVID[4], WILLIAM[3], SUSAN[2] SPINNEY, JOHN[1])* was born 27 Feb 1873, and died 20 Feb 1944. She married JAMES MELVIN CROWELL 05 Nov 1898 in Barrington, NS. He was born 30 Jun 1873 in Shelburnne, NS.

Children of MAGGIE SMITH and JAMES CROWELL are:
  i.   ARCHIBALD GLENDON[6] CROWELL, b. 12 Sep 1899; d. 22 Jul 1933, Barrington, NS; m. JENNIE ROBERTA SMITH, 07 Apr 1926, Barrington, NS; b. 16 Apr 1903.
  ii.   CHARLES FRANKLYN CROWELL, b. 09 Aug 1903; d. 28 Aug 1981.
  iii. BASIL LINDHURST CROWELL, b. 08 Jul 1912; m. ELLEN ALTHEA BOWER, 30 Dec 1930, Barrington Township NS; b. 16 Mar 1912.

70. MINNIE BETHILDA[5] SMITH *(NATHANIEL E[4], WILLIAM[3], SUSAN[2] SPINNEY, JOHN[1])* was born 17 May 1870, and died 19 Sep 1946. She married MITCHEL BROKER SMITH 23 Dec 1892, son of JUDAH SMITH and DELINA NEWELL. He was born 21 Nov 1869 in Centreville, and died 01 Aug 1958 in Shelbourne County NS.

Children of MINNIE SMITH and MITCHEL SMITH are:
  i.   LINA MAE[6] SMITH, b. 04 Dec 1893; d. 29 Apr 1981.
  ii.   DEBORAH INGLES SMITH, b. 21 Apr 1896, Doctors Cove, NS.; d. 25 Sep 1979; m. ALBERT "CLAUDE" SMITH, 18 Oct 1916; b. 14 Aug 1890, Smithville, NS.; d. 22 Dec 1972.
  iii. HAROLD JEFFREY SMITH, b. 20 May 1898; d. Jan 1983; m. ISABELLA THOMASINE PEARSE, 19 Sep 1920; b. 23 Jun 1899; d. 01 Mar 1986.
  iv.   EARLE DOUGLAS SMITH, b. 21 Jan 1900; m. (1) EILEEN ALIDA MCARTHUR, 04 Nov 1921; b. 15 Feb 1906; d. 26 Jul 1954; m. (2) BERNICE HARPELL, 19 Apr 1954; b. 26 Apr 1906.
  v.   IRVAN MITCHELL SMITH, b. 24 Jul 1902; d. 12 Jul 1906.
  vi.   FRANK FOSTER SMITH, b. 08 Nov 1905; d. Aug 1984; m. EMMA AUGUSTA COLES, 02 Nov 1929; b. 28 Apr 1906.

71. FOSTER FREEMAN[5] SMITH *(NATHANIEL E[4], WILLIAM[3], SUSAN[2] SPINNEY, JOHN[1])* was born 13 Nov 1878, and died 10 Mar 1910. He married ELIZABETH MARGARET HOLLAND 10 Oct 1905. She was born 1881, and died 27 Feb 1912.

Child of FOSTER SMITH and ELIZABETH HOLLAND is:
  i.   DAISY FLORENCE[6] SMITH, b. 22 Aug 1906; d. 03 Jan 1919.

72. COLLINS WILSON[5] SMITH *(NATHANIEL E[4], WILLIAM[3], SUSAN[2] SPINNEY, JOHN[1])* was born 31 Dec 1881, and died 24 Jan 1911. He married ELIZABETH MAUDE MACKAY 20 Oct 1909. She died 23 Oct 1966.

Child of COLLINS SMITH and ELIZABETH MACKAY is:
  i.   JAMES NATHANIEL[6] SMITH, b. 08 May 1910; d. 19 May 1944, Cussino Italy; m. WINNIFRED MARY COURT, 08 May 1943; b. 07 Mar 1906.

73. THEODORE LESLIE[5] SMITH *(REBECCA[4], WILLIAM[3], SUSAN[2] SPINNEY, JOHN[1])* was born 06 Apr 1871 in Barrington, NS., and died 1948. He married ARDELLA SKIDMORE 26 Jan 1897. She was born 1874, and died 18 Feb 1934.

Children of THEODORE SMITH and ARDELLA SKIDMORE are:
    i.   CHARLES GILBERT[6] SMITH, b. 12 Nov 1897; d. 27 Feb 1980; m. EVELYN INEZ POWEL; d. Jun 1970.
    ii. ROY E SMITH, b. 19 May 1901; d. 24 Dec 1926.
    iii. FLORIS ELANA SMITH, b. 25 Oct 1908; d. 30 Nov 1989.

74. ROBERT WALLACE[5] SMITH *(REBECCA[4], WILLIAM[3], SUSAN[2] SPINNEY, JOHN[1])* was born 03 Feb 1873, and died 03 Sep 1949. He married JESSIE HELEN SNOW 26 Nov 1900 in Barrington, NS., daughter of CORNELIUS SNOW and MARGARET REYNOLDS. She was born 29 Dec 1869, and died Oct 1952.

Children of ROBERT SMITH and JESSIE SNOW are:
    i.   ELIZABETH MAY[6] SMITH, b. 03 Sep 1901; d. 15 Mar 1952.
    ii. JENNIE ROBERTA SMITH, b. 16 Apr 1903; m. (1) ARCHIBALD GLENDON CROWELL, 07 Apr 1926, Barrington, NS; b. 12 Sep 1899; d. 22 Jul 1933, Barrington, NS; m. (2) WILLIAM TURNER, 27 Dec 1940.
    iii. REBA SMITH, b. 02 Apr 1905; d. 13 May 1913.
    iv. WALLACE WILBUR BAKER SMITH, b. 23 Apr 1908; d. 29 Oct 1908.
    v. NELLIE ERNESTINE SMITH, b. 25 Apr 1910; m. GEORGE ROLLINS, 21 Dec 1933.
    vi. GORDON SMITH, b. 06 Jun 1913; d. 30 Jan 1933.

75. FLORENCE ETHEL MAY[5] SMITH *(REBECCA[4], WILLIAM[3], SUSAN[2] SPINNEY, JOHN[1])* was born 02 Dec 1879, and died 14 Jun 1931. She married OLIVER CLIFFORD REYNOLDS.

Child of FLORENCE SMITH and OLIVER REYNOLDS is:
    i.   OLIVER CHURCHILL[6] REYNOLDS, b. 21 Aug 1914; m. LILLIAN PURDY.

76. JOHN HARVEY[5] NICKERSON *(SARAH ELEANOR[4] SMITH, WILLIAM[3], SUSAN[2] SPINNEY, JOHN[1])* was born 1884, and died 30 Mar 1949. He married BLANCHE MABEL DOWLING 15 Mar 1904 in Barrington Township NS, daughter of WILLIAM DOWLING and DEBORAH SMITH. She was born 08 Apr 1884.

Children of JOHN NICKERSON and BLANCHE DOWLING are:
    i.   IVAN WENTWORTH[6] NICKERSON, b. Mar 1905; d. 07 Oct 1913, Barrington Township NS.
    ii. NETTA SEATTLE NICKERSON, b. 06 Dec 1911; m. THOMAS DELBERT LOWE, 11 Jun 1930; b. 17 Feb 1910.

77. IRVAN ROY[5] NICKERSON *(SARAH ELEANOR[4] SMITH, WILLIAM[3], SUSAN[2] SPINNEY, JOHN[1])* was born 28 May 1885, and died 05 Aug 1939. He married MINNIE PERRY 1907.

Children of IRVAN NICKERSON and MINNIE PERRY are:
    i.   ROY[6] NICKERSON.
    ii. HAROLD NICKERSON.
    iii. NELLIE MAE NICKERSON, b. 12 Oct 1917; m. WILLIAM ARTHUR MCLAUGHLIN, 03 May 1941.

78. FRED LEANDER GORDON[5] SHOLDS *(MARY J[4] SMITH, WILLIAM[3], SUSAN[2] SPINNEY, JOHN[1])* was born 21 Dec 1883 in Port Latour NS, and died 16 Jan 1960 in Hyde Park Boston MA. He married CONSTANCE SPINNEY, daughter of JOSIAH SPINNEY and CORDELIA SNOW. She was born 1884 in Port Latour NS, and died 1960 in Boston Mass.

Child of FRED SHOLDS and CONSTANCE SPINNEY is:
83.   i.   FRED ALLISON[6] SHOLDS, b. 30 Dec 1920, Port Latour NS.

79. THOMAS[5] HOPKINS *(WILLIAM O[4], DEBORAH[3] ATWOOD, DEBORAH[2] SPINNEY, JOHN[1])* He married ISCEMA O'CONNELL.

Children of THOMAS HOPKINS and ISCEMA O'CONNELL are:

    i.   GERTRUDE[6] HOPKINS.
    ii.   MAYNARD HOPKINS.
   iii. ISAAC HOPKINS.
   iv. LOTTIE BEATRICE HOPKINS, b. 1911; d. 02 Feb 1956; m. LAVANCE T NEWELL.
    v.   SARAH HOPKINS, b. 1915; d. 04 Dec 1935; m. GEORGE E ROCKWELL, 1932.

80. GEORGE[5] HOPKINS (*WILLIAM O[4], DEBORAH[3] ATWOOD, DEBORAH[2] SPINNEY, JOHN[1]*) was born 1884, and died Sep 1927. He married WILHEMINA O'CONNELL.

Children of GEORGE HOPKINS and WILHEMINA O'CONNELL are:

    i.   FLORENCE[6] HOPKINS, m. CLARENCE LOCKHART BANKS, 21 Mar 1934; b. 1912; d. 03 Jan 1988.
    ii.   HAVELOCK HOPKINS, m. ALTHEA NICKERSON, 1921.
   iii. MILDRED HOPKINS, m. AVERY SHAND, 22 Dec 1931; b. 1911, Shag Harbor.
   iv. BLAKE HOPKINS.
    v.   DONALD EDWIN HOPKINS, m. ROWENA CHARLOTTE SEARS, Apr 1952; b. 31 Aug 1928.
   vi. WILLIAM CORNELIUS HOPKINS, b. 1912; d. Jun 1968.
  vii. EVA NINETTA HOPKINS, b. 1915; d. 12 Jan 1989.
 viii. LILLIAN BERNICE HOPKINS, b. 06 Sep 1919; m. NELSON CROMWELL PERRY, 23 Jun 1934; b. 12 Apr 1912.

81. FREEMAN LEROY[5] SNOW (*HARVEY[4], WEALTHY[3] SPINNEY, WILLIAM DOUGHTY[2], JOHN[1]*) was born 19 Jun 1895. He married MABEL IRENE WISWALL ALLEN.

Child of FREEMAN SNOW and MABEL ALLEN is:

    i.   HELENE IRENE[6] SNOW, b. 29 Jan 1922, Norway, ME; m. (1) FRANK LYMAN MCDONALD; m. (2) FREDERICK EDMUND HALL.

Generation No. 6

82. BLANCHE MABEL[6] DOWLING (*DEBORAH A[5] SMITH, THOMAS DOANE[4], DAVID[3], SUSAN[2] SPINNEY, JOHN[1]*) was born 08 Apr 1884. She married JOHN HARVEY NICKERSON 15 Mar 1904 in Barrington Township NS, son of CHARLES NICKERSON and SARAH SMITH. He was born 1884, and died 30 Mar 1949.

Children are listed above under (76) John Harvey Nickerson.

83. FRED ALLISON[6] SHOLDS (*FRED LEANDER GORDON[5], MARY J[4] SMITH, WILLIAM[3], SUSAN[2] SPINNEY, JOHN[1]*) was born 30 Dec 1920 in Port Latour NS. He married MARY ELIZABETH WOOD 12 Nov 1944.

Child of FRED SHOLDS and MARY WOOD is:
84.   i.   FREDRICK[7] SHOLDS.

Generation No. 7

84. FREDRICK[7] SHOLDS (*FRED ALLISON[6], FRED LEANDER GORDON[5], MARY J[4] SMITH, WILLIAM[3], SUSAN[2] SPINNEY, JOHN[1]*)

Child of FREDRICK SHOLDS is:

    i.   ALLYSON[8] SHOLDS, m. DAVID THAYER.

Descendants of Abigail Spinney

Generation No. 1

1. ABIGAIL[1] SPINNEY[1] was born Abt. 1776. She married JOSEPH DENNETT[1] 10 Apr 1796 in Kittery Maine, son of WILLIAM DENNETT and MARY ADAMS. He was born 24 Nov 1774 in Kittery, York, Maine, USA[1], and died 10 Jan 1808.

Children of ABIGAIL SPINNEY and JOSEPH DENNETT are:
  i. JOSEPH[2] DENNETT, b. 07 Jul 1796; d. 30 Jun 1839.
  ii. WILLIAM DENNETT, b. 07 Jul 1798; d. 16 Mar 1812.
  iii. SARAH DENNETT, b. 25 Jul 1802; d. 15 Oct 1818.

Endnotes

1. Ancestry.com, One World Tree (sm), Provo, UT, USA: The Generations Network, Inc., n.d., Online publication - Ancestry.com. OneWorldTree [database on-line]. Provo, UT, USA: The Generations Network, Inc.

Descendants of Ann L Spinney

Generation No. 1

1. ANN L[1] SPINNEY She married ABRAHAM TREFETHEN Jun 1828 in Portsmouth, NH. He was born Bef. 1811, and died Aft. 1868.

Children of ANN SPINNEY and ABRAHAM TREFETHEN are:
- i. ANNA L[2] TREFETHEN, b. 26 May 1840; m. REUBEN M ADAMS.
- ii. HARRY BARTER TREFETHEN, b. 1868; m. ELIZABETH RHONDA RHODES.

Notes for HARRY BARTER TREFETHEN:
HARRY BAXTER TREFETHEN
(7/8/1868 - 7/14/1933)
M: Elizabeth Rhoda Rhodes
PARENTS: # 202. ABRAHAM "HARRY" BAXTER
* Elizabeth was born in Wisconsin in Sept. of 1876 and died in 1949 [S36:1900 Soundex].
* NOTE: S58 says he's the son of #51; and I think this error is a common one.
* He & Family are found in the 1910 MN Census as living on 'P' St., City of Alexandria, Douglas Co. He was a House Carpenter at the time [S36]. They were living there in MN as early as 1894 when their dtr. Rose was born. This source is also where all his children were originally found, excepting Rose (#673).
* Leitha Trefren [s36] writes:

Soc Sec death index gives us more info on Harry Baxter's children.
Ralph b 10 Mar 1905, d Jun 1983 in Duluth MN.

He had a son Melford Trefethren but this one is too late, prob a grson b 05 May 1935 d Sep 1982 in Fargo, Cass Co, ND. Soc Sec was issued in MN.

There is a Margaret Trefethren b 16 Jan 1915 d 23 Oct 1994 Mples MN who has to be related somehow.

There is a Eugene Trefethren b 09 Nov 1916 d Jan 1985 at Carlisle, Elko NV. We found him in the phone book on one of our trips to Las Vegas, called only to find that he'd died a year or so before. His widow knew nothing about the family, her husband didn't discuss them, apparently there were hard feelings. He even spelled his name TRE FETHREN. Unknown who his first wife was. There's a Leola that may be the second wife (I've forgotten after all this time) b 08 May 1913 d Feb 1989, no place of residence or place of issue.

Plus a very few more who died under the spelling Trefethren---11 total.

William Trefethren b 11 Apr 1940 d 12 Oct 199b in Wendover, Elko Co NV, card iss NV 1952-53. He's probably Eugene's son.

Descendants of Chandler Spinney

Generation No. 1

1. CHANDLER[1] SPINNEY[1] was born 1821 in Maine, and died 15 Mar 1879 in Exeter New Hampshire. He married ELIZABETH L DOW Aft. 1840, daughter of JOHN DOW and DEBORAH PAGE. She was born 1814 in New Hampshire, and died 1890.

Notes for CHANDLER SPINNEY:
Enlisted in the Civil War 11 August 1862 Company A 11 New Hampshire Inf.

More About CHANDLER SPINNEY:
Military: 11 Aug 1862, New Hampshire[1]
Residence: 1850, Epping, NH

Children of CHANDLER SPINNEY and ELIZABETH DOW are:
2.   i.   ELLEN G[2] SPINNEY, b. 1846.
        ii.   MARY SPINNEY, b. 1851.

Generation No. 2

2. ELLEN G[2] SPINNEY *(CHANDLER[1])* was born 1846. She married MADISON SLEEPER.

Children of ELLEN SPINNEY and MADISON SLEEPER are:
        i.   CHARLES T[3] SLEEPER, b. 1865.
        ii.   FRANK C SLEEPER, b. 1869.
        iii. MARY J SLEEPER, b. 1871.

Endnotes

1. Historical Data Systems, comp., Military Records of Individual Civil War Soldiers, Provo, UT, USA: The Generations Network, Inc., 1999, Online publication - Historical Data Systems, comp.. American Civil War Soldiers [database on-line]. Provo, UT, USA: The Generations Network, Inc., 1999.Original data - Data compiled by Historical Data Systems of Kingston, MA form the <a href="a href="/handler/domainrd.ashx?domain=AncestryDomain&url=/search/rectype/military/cwrd/db.htm">following list of works</a>. Copyright 1997-2000 Historical Data Systems, Inc. PO Box 35 Duxbury.

Descendants of Ebenezer Spinney

Generation No. 1

1. EBENEZER[1] SPINNEY was born 1797 in Maine, and died 30 Jun 1855 in Portsmouth New Hampshire. He married TEMPERANCE A HODGESON 08 Jul 1819, daughter of ALEXANDER HODGESON. She was born 1791 in Newington, NH, and died 23 Dec 1887 in Portsmouth New Hampshire.

Children of EBENEZER SPINNEY and TEMPERANCE HODGESON are:

2.	i.	PLUMMER[2] SPINNEY, b. May 1815, Portsmouth, NH; d. 14 Jan 1907.
3.	ii.	WILLIAM A SPINNEY, b. 01 Apr 1819; d. 01 Apr 1862, Portsmouth, NH.
4.	iii.	ANN E SPINNEY, b. 30 Mar 1826, Eliot, ME; d. 13 Apr 1884.
	iv.	SARAH A SPINNEY, b. 1830; d. Aft. 1880; m. JAMES SMITH.
5.	v.	CAROLINE M SPINNEY, b. May 1835.
	vi.	ELLEN MARIA SPINNEY, b. 1856.

Generation No. 2

2. PLUMMER[2] SPINNEY *(EBENEZER[1])* was born May 1815 in Portsmouth, NH, and died 14 Jan 1907. He married OLIVE ANN GROVER 25 Dec 1842. She was born 1825, and died Aft. 1881.

Children of PLUMMER SPINNEY and OLIVE GROVER are:

	i.	ANNIE LOUISE[3] SPINNEY, b. 1844, Portsmouth NH; m. (1) PROWITT BOYDSTON; m. (2) KIMBALL; m. (3) FOWLE, 14 Dec 1884.
	ii.	HENRY P SPINNEY, b. 1850.
6.	iii.	OLIVIA SPINNEY, b. 1853.
7.	iv.	FRANK A SPINNEY, b. 1857; d. Aft. 1900.
	v.	HARLENA SPINNEY, b. 1880.

3. WILLIAM A[2] SPINNEY *(EBENEZER[1])* was born 01 Apr 1819, and died 01 Apr 1862 in Portsmouth, NH. He married LYDIA A PETIGREW 12 Apr 1847. She was born 1826, and died 03 Jan 1902.

Children of WILLIAM SPINNEY and LYDIA PETIGREW are:

8.	i.	WILLIAM A[3] SPINNEY, b. 1847; d. Bef. 1880.
9.	ii.	AUGUSTUS SPINNEY, b. 1848; d. 1924.
	iii.	LYDIA E SPINNEY, b. 1851.
10.	iv.	CHARLES OLDREN SPINNEY, b. 1854; d. Hawaii.
	v.	ANNE MARY SPINNEY, b. 1855.
	vi.	SARAH SPINNEY, b. 1856.

4. ANN E[2] SPINNEY *(EBENEZER[1])* was born 30 Mar 1826 in Eliot, ME, and died 13 Apr 1884. She married JOHN HARMON. He was born 1824.

Children of ANN SPINNEY and JOHN HARMON are:

	i.	JOHN EDWARD[3] HARMON, b. 1850.
11.	ii.	ELIZA J HARMON, b. 1852.
	iii.	CHARLES H HARMON, b. 1854.
12.	iv.	CELIA HARMON, b. 1855.
	v.	LILLIAN HARMON, b. 1856.
	vi.	FRANK HARMON, b. 1857.
	vii.	SIMON P HARMON, b. 1860.
	viii.	MARY A HARMON, b. 1861.
	ix.	EDWARD L HARMON, b. 1863.
	x.	MARY A HARMON, b. 1864.
	xi.	WILLIAM HARMON, b. 1865.
	xii.	WALLACE HARMON, b. 1867.
	xiii.	FRANK HARMON, b. 1868.

5. CAROLINE M[2] SPINNEY *(EBENEZER[1])* was born May 1835. She married C HIRAM GOVE 01 Sep 1861. He was born 17 Oct 1841.

Children of CAROLINE SPINNEY and C GOVE are:

	i.	FRANK E[3] GOVE, b. 28 Mar 1862; d. 19 Jan 1866.
13.	ii.	ALBERT GOVE, b. 23 Mar 1863.
	iii.	CARRIE E GOVE, b. 01 Feb 1865; m. WILLIAM F HUDSON.
14.	iv.	CORA MAY GOVE, b. 16 Jul 1867; d. Bef. 1920.
15.	v.	HIRAM D GOVE, b. 17 Jul 1869.
	vi.	IDA F GOVE, b. 28 Jan 1874.

Generation No. 3

6. OLIVIA[3] SPINNEY *(PLUMMER[2], EBENEZER[1])* was born 1853. She married FURBER.

Children of OLIVIA SPINNEY and FURBER are:
- i. GRACE[4] FURBER, b. 1873.
- ii. HARRY FURBER, b. 1875.

7. FRANK A[3] SPINNEY *(PLUMMER[2], EBENEZER[1])* was born 1857, and died Aft. 1900. He married ETTA W. She was born 1860 in Kittery, ME, and died Aft. 1900.

Child of FRANK SPINNEY and ETTA W is:
- i. ERNEST[4] SPINNEY, b. Sep 1888.

8. WILLIAM A[3] SPINNEY *(WILLIAM A[2], EBENEZER[1])* was born 1847, and died Bef. 1880. He married ELLEN. She died Bef. 1880.

Children of WILLIAM SPINNEY and ELLEN are:
- i.   EVA E[4] SPINNEY, b. 1871; d. 1919; m. PROCTOR.
- ii. FANNIE SPINNEY, b. 1868.
- iii. WILLIAM H SPINNEY, b. 1876.

9. AUGUSTUS[3] SPINNEY *(WILLIAM A[2], EBENEZER[1])* was born 1848, and died 1924. He married (1) 1ST WIFE. He married (2) MARY F JOHNSON 22 Nov 1880 in Portsmouth NH. She was born 1843, and died 1919.

Child of AUGUSTUS SPINNEY and MARY JOHNSON is:
- i. GEORGE A[4] SPINNEY, b. 16 Apr 1881, Portsmouth, NH.

10. CHARLES OLDREN[3] SPINNEY *(WILLIAM A[2], EBENEZER[1])* was born 1854, and died in Hawaii. He married MARY PIMENTEL 04 Apr 1882 in Hawaii. She was born 1854.

More About CHARLES OLDREN SPINNEY:
Residence: 1890, Honolulu, HI[1]

Child of CHARLES SPINNEY and MARY PIMENTEL is:
- 16. i. CHARLES OLDREN[4] SPINNEY, b. 22 Feb 1883, Honolulu, H T; d. 23 Jul 1958, Yolo, California.

11. ELIZA J[3] HARMON *(ANN E[2] SPINNEY, EBENEZER[1])* was born 1852. She married LYDSTON.

Child of ELIZA HARMON and LYDSTON is:
- i. EVA B[4] LYDSTON, b. 1873.

12. CELIA[3] HARMON *(ANN E[2] SPINNEY, EBENEZER[1])* was born 1855. She married GADDIS.

Child of CELIA HARMON and GADDIS is:
> i.   ARTHUR[4] GADDIS, b. 1878.

13. ALBERT[3] GOVE *(CAROLINE M[2] SPINNEY, EBENEZER[1])* was born 23 Mar 1863. He married HELEN HILTZ.

Child of ALBERT GOVE and HELEN HILTZ is:
> i.   CARA[4] GOVE, b. 1897.

14. CORA MAY[3] GOVE *(CAROLINE M[2] SPINNEY, EBENEZER[1])* was born 16 Jul 1867, and died Bef. 1920. She married EDWIN CONEY.

Child of CORA GOVE and EDWIN CONEY is:
> i.   EVERETT[4] CONEY.

15. HIRAM D[3] GOVE *(CAROLINE M[2] SPINNEY, EBENEZER[1])* was born 17 Jul 1869. He married NETTIE FARNHAM.

Child of HIRAM GOVE and NETTIE FARNHAM is:
> i.   IDA MAY[4] GOVE.

Generation No. 4

16. CHARLES OLDREN[4] SPINNEY *(CHARLES OLDREN[3], WILLIAM A[2], EBENEZER[1])*[2] was born 22 Feb 1883 in Honolulu, H T[2], and died 23 Jul 1958 in Yolo, California[3]. He married GRACE LONG. She was born 1891.

More About CHARLES OLDREN SPINNEY:
Residence: 1920, Eureka Ward 4, Humboldt, California[4]

Children of CHARLES SPINNEY and GRACE LONG are:
> i.   LOUIS O[5] SPINNEY, b. 04 Dec 1914; d. 23 Jan 1960, Mendocino, CA.
> ii. SON SPINNEY, b. 1927.

Endnotes

1. Honolulu, Hawaii Directory, 1890, Ancestry.com. Honolulu, Hawaii Directory, 1890. [database online] Provo, UT: Ancestry.com, 2000. Original data: Honolulu, HI, 1890. Honolulu, HI: The Pacific Press Publishing Company, 1890.
2. Ancestry.com, U.S. World War II Draft Registration Cards, 1942, Provo, UT, USA: The Generations Network, Inc., 2006, Online publication - Ancestry.com. U.S. World War II Draft Registration Cards, 1942 [database on-line]. Provo, UT, USA: The Generations Network, Inc., 2006.Original data - United States, Selective Service System. Selective Service Registration Cards, World War II: Fourth Registration. National Archives and Records Administration Branch locations: National Archives and Records Administration Region Branches.
3. Ancestry.com, California Death Index, 1940-1997, Provo, UT, USA: The Generations Network, Inc., 2000, Ancestry.com. California Death Index, 1940-1997. [database online] Provo, UT: Ancestry.com, 2000. Original electronic data: State of California. California Death Index, 1940-1997. Sacramento, CA: State of California Department of Health Services, Center for Health Statistics, 19--.
4. Ancestry.com, 1920 United States Federal Census, Provo, UT, USA: The Generations Network, Inc., 2005, Ancestry.com. 1920 United States Federal Census [database on-line]. Provo, UT: Ancestry.com, 2005. Indexed by Ancestry.com from microfilmed schedules of the 1920 U.S. Federal Decennial Census. Data imaged from National Archives and Records Administration.1920 Federal Population Census. T625, 2,076 rolls. National Archives and Records Administration, Washington D.C. For details on the contents of the film numbers, visit the following NARA web page: <a href="http://www.archives.gov/publications/microfilm-catalogs/census/1920/part-07.html">NARA</a>. Note: Enumeration Districts 819-839 on roll 323 (Chicago City, Cook County, Illinois) are missing, even though the NARA catalog lists them as being there. The Family History Library catalog also lists them as missing. Eureka Ward 4, Humboldt, California, ED , roll , page , image 884.

Descendants of Harry Judson Spinney

Generation No. 1

1. HARRY JUDSON[1] SPINNEY was born 26 Mar 1865 in Boston, MA, and died 04 Feb 1944. He married KATIE HELEN TOMKINS 1892, daughter of CORNEILOUS TOMKINS and HELEN SMART. She was born 1873 in Michigan.

Children of HARRY SPINNEY and KATIE TOMKINS are:

2.	i.	LOUIS H[2] SPINNEY, b. 02 Apr 1895, Michigan; d. Sep 1968.
3.	ii.	WALTER C SPINNEY, b. 05 Mar 1897, Michigan; d. 12 May 1975.
	iii.	ALLEN SPINNEY, b. 16 Dec 1900, Michigan; d. 30 Sep 1987, Ogemaw, MI; m. NAOMI.
4.	iv.	LAWRENCE SPINNEY, b. 1903, Michigan.
	v.	LESLIE SPINNEY, b. 1905, Michigan; d. Aft. 1920.
	vi.	BERTRICE SPINNEY, b. 1908, Michigan; d. Aft. 1900.
5.	vii.	BERNICE SPINNEY, b. 1908, Michigan; d. Aft. 1920.
6.	viii.	FRANCES B SPINNEY, b. 1909, Michigan; d. Aft. 1920.

Generation No. 2

2. LOUIS H[2] SPINNEY *(HARRY JUDSON[1])* was born 02 Apr 1895 in Michigan, and died Sep 1968. He married HELEN.

Child of LOUIS SPINNEY and HELEN is:
7.   i. ARLENE[3] SPINNEY.

3. WALTER C[2] SPINNEY *(HARRY JUDSON[1])* was born 05 Mar 1897 in Michigan, and died 12 May 1975. He married LESTA T. She was born 1901.

Child of WALTER SPINNEY and LESTA T is:
    i. JACK E[3] SPINNEY, b. 1923.

4. LAWRENCE[2] SPINNEY *(HARRY JUDSON[1])* was born 1903 in Michigan. He married ELDERVINE. She was born 08 Aug 1900.

Children of LAWRENCE SPINNEY and ELDERVINE are:
    i. HOWARD[3] SPINNEY, b. 1925.
    ii. JEAN SPINNEY, b. 1927.

5. BERNICE[2] SPINNEY *(HARRY JUDSON[1])* was born 1908 in Michigan, and died Aft. 1920. She married JONES.

Child of BERNICE SPINNEY and JONES is:
    i. MADELYN[3] JONES.

6. FRANCES B[2] SPINNEY *(HARRY JUDSON[1])* was born 1909 in Michigan, and died Aft. 1920. She married PIERCE.

Child of FRANCES SPINNEY and PIERCE is:
8.   i. DAN[3] PIERCE.

Generation No. 3

7. ARLENE[3] SPINNEY *(LOUIS H[2], HARRY JUDSON[1])*

Child of ARLENE SPINNEY is:
      i.   PENNY[4] SPINNEY, m. HURST.

8. DAN[3] PIERCE *(FRANCES B[2] SPINNEY, HARRY JUDSON[1])* He married CYD.

Child of DAN PIERCE and CYD is:
      i.   DEBBIE[4] PIERCE.

Lyman Spinney

Lucy Wyman Spinney

Miss Lucille Wyman Spinney, Brockton, Mass., 1912.
Prior to moving to San Diego, California.

Gustavus Newhall Spinney

Herbert Linden Spinney

Capt. Herbert L. Spinney.
Keeper of Seguin Light,
Pres. of Maine O.S.

Sarah Jane Spinney

Lafayette Griffen Spinney

L. G. SPINNEY

Robert Moirrison Spinney

Samuel Spinney

Index of Individuals

www.ingramcontent.com/pod-product-compliance
Lightning Source LLC
Chambersburg PA
CBHW081426270326
41932CB00019B/3108